INTERMEDIATE ACCOUNTING

FIFTH CANADIAN EDITION

VOLUME ONE

INTERMEDIATE ACCOUNTING

FIFTH CANADIAN EDITION
VOLUME ONE

Donald E. Kieso PhD, CPA
KPMG Peat Marwick Professor of Accounting
Northern Illinois University
DeKalb, Illinois

Jerry J. Weygandt PhD, CPA
Arthur Anderson Alumni Professor of Accounting
University of Wisconsin
Madison, Wisconsin

Canadian Edition prepared by

V. Bruce Irvine PhD, CMA, FCMA
University of Saskatchewan
Saskatoon, Saskatchewan

W. Harold Silvester PhD, CPA, CA
University of Saskatchewan (Emeritus)
Saskatoon, Saskatchewan

Nicola M. Young MBA, FCA
St. Mary's University
Halifax, Nova Scotia

JOHN WILEY & SONS CANADA, LTD
Toronto • New York • Chichester • Weinheim • Brisbane • Singapore

Canadian Cataloguing in Publication Data

Kieso, Donald E.
    Intermediate accounting

5th Canadian ed./prepared by V. Bruce Irvine,
W. Harold Silvester, Nicola M. Young.
Includes bibliographical references and indexes.
ISBN 0-471-64183-9 (v. 1)
ISBN 0-471-64184-7 (v. 2)

1. Accounting. I. Irvine, V. Bruce.
II. Silvester, W. Harold. III. Weygandt
Jerry J. IV. Young, Nicola M. V. Title.

HF5635.I573 1997   657'.044   C97–931411–9

Production Credits

Acquisitions Editor: John Horne

Publishing Services Director: Karen Bryan

Developmental Editor: Karen Staudinger

Assistant Editor: Michael Schellenberg

Copy Editor: Leah Johnson

Proofreader: Claudia Kutchukian

Graphic Designer: Christine Rae, RGD

Cover Photo Credits: I. Barrett / First Light

Typesetting & Film: Compeer Typographic Services

Printing and Binding: Tri-Graphic Printing Limited

Printed and bound in Canada
10 9 8 7 6 5 4 3 2 1

<u>Dedicated To</u>

Marilyn	*Viola*	*John*
Lee-Ann	*Susan*	*Hilary*
Cameron	*Dianne*	*Tim*
Sandra	*Daniel*	*Megan*

ABOUT THE AUTHORS

CANADIAN EDITION

V. Bruce Irvine PhD, CMA, FCMA, is a professor of Accounting at the University of Saskatchewan. He received his PhD in accounting from the University of Minnesota. Among his publications are articles and reviews in such journals as *CMA: The Management Accounting Magazine, CA Magazine, Managerial Planning, and The Accounting Review.* Designated "Professor of the Year" several times, Dr. Irvine has extensive teaching experience in financial and managerial accounting and has been instrumental in establishing innovative pedagogical techniques and instructional materials at the University of Saskatchewan. He has had considerable involvement with practising accountants through serving on various local, provincial, national, and international committees and boards of the Society of Management Accountants. At the international level, Dr. Irvine has been a Canadian delegate to the board of the International Accounting Standards Committee and a technical advisor to the International Federation of Accountants. Additionally, Dr. Irvine has served in various executive committee positions of the Canadian Academic Accounting Association.

W. Harold Silvester PhD, CPA, CA, received his doctorate from the University of Missouri, Columbia, and is Professor Emeritus of Accounting at the University of Saskatchewan. In his teaching capacity, he played a key role in introducing pedagogical improvements at the University of Saskatchewan and in developing instructional materials for the Accounting program there. He was named "Professor of the Year" in recognition of his substantial contributions to the College of Commerce. An important contribution has been the development of materials to integrate computers with accounting instruction. Articles by Professor Silvester have appeared in *CA Magazine* and other academic and professional journals.

Nicola M. Young, MBA, FCA, is an associate professor of accounting in the Frank H. Sobey Faculty of Commerce at Saint Mary's University in Halifax, Nova Scotia where her teaching responsibilities vary from the non-accounting major introductory course to final year advanced financial courses to the survey course in the Executive MBA program. She is the recipient of the Commerce Professor of the Year and the university-wide alumni teaching medal, and contributes to the academic and administrative life of the university through membership on the Senate and Board of Governors. Professor Young has been involved with the Atlantic School of Chartered Accountancy for many years on a variety of levels from program and course development and design to teaching, and authored a report on examination and evaluation objectives and processes for this organization. In addition to contributions to the accounting profession at the provincial level, Professor Young has served on various national boards of the CICA dealing with licensure, education and standard setting.

U.S. EDITION

Donald E. Kieso PhD, CPA, received his bachelors degree from Aurora University and his doctorate in accounting from the University of Illinois. He has served as chairman of the Department of Accountancy at Northern Illinois University. He has done postdoctorate work as a Visiting Scholar at the University of California at Berkeley and is a recipient of NIU's Teaching Excellence Award and four Golden Apple Teaching Awards (1986, 1990, 1992, and 1994). He has served as a member of the Board of Directors of the CPA Society, the Board of Governors of the American Accounting Association's Administrators of Accounting Programs Group, the AACSB's Accounting Accreditation and Visitation Committees, the State of Illinois Comptroller's Commission, as Secretary-Treasurer of the Federation of Schools of Accountancy, and as Secretary-Treasurer of the American Accounting Association. From 1989 to 1993 he served as a charter member of the national Accounting Education Change Commission. In 1988 he received the Outstanding Accounting Educator Award from the Illinois CPA Society, and in 1992 he received the FSA's Joseph A. Silvoso Award of Merit and the NIU Foundation's Humanitarian Award for Service to Higher Education.

Jerry J. Weygandt, PhD, CPA, is Arthur Andersen Alumni Professor of Accounting of the University of Wisconsin-Madison and has also served as President of the American Accounting Association. He holds a PhD in accounting from the University of Illinois. Articles by Professor Weygandt have appeared in the *Accounting Review, Journal of Accounting Research, The Journal of Accountancy,* and other professional journals. These articles have examined such financial reporting issues as accounting for price-level adjustments, pensions, convertible securities, stock option contracts, and interim reports. He has served on numerous committees of the American Accounting Association and as a member of the editorial board of the Accounting Review. In addition, he has been involved with the American Institute of Certified Public Accountants and has been a member of the Accounting Standards Executive Committee (AcSEC) of that organization. Professor Weygandt has received the Chancellor's Award for Excellence in Teaching; he also has served as Secretary-Treasurer of the American Accounting Association. In 1991 he received the Wisconsin Institute of CPA's Outstanding Educator's Award.

PREFACE

Accounting is an exciting, dynamic field of study; its body of knowledge, theories, and practices, as well as the methodologies for teaching these concepts, are constantly evolving. In the writing of this fifth Canadian edition of *Intermediate Accounting*, we have thoroughly revised and updated the text to include the latest developments in the financial accounting profession.

Continuing to keep pace with the complexities of the modern business enterprise and professional accounting pronouncements, we have added new topics, deleted obsolete material, clarified existing coverage, added illustrations, and updated material where necessary. To provide the instructor with greater flexibility in choosing topics to cover or omit, we have continued the use of judiciously selected appendices. The appendices are concerned primarily with complex subjects, less commonly used methods, or specialized topics.

Benefitting from the comments and recommendations of the many adopters of our previous editions, we have made significant revisions. Explanations have been expanded where necessary, complicated discussions and illustrations have been simplified; realism has been integrated to heighten interest and relevance; and new topics and coverage have been added to maintain currency.

Accountants must act as well as think; therefore, we believe it is important for students to understand the how as well as the why. The study of concepts develops an understanding of the procedures, and the performance of procedures enriches the understanding of the concepts. Keeping this in mind, we have maintained the balance in our coverage so the conceptual discussion and procedural presentation are mutually reinforcing.

We believe that individuals learn to account for financial events and phenomena best if they fully understand the nature of the business transactions and comprehend the behavioural and economic consequences of the events for which firms account and report. The ability to critically evaluate accounting alternatives and their consequences is important. Throughout this edition, we have provided coverage to help students develop a real understanding of how accounting can be used to make effective financial decisions.

NEW FEATURES

Based on extensive reviews and interactions with other intermediate accounting instructors and students, we have developed a number of new pedagogical features designed both to help students learn more effectively and to answer the changing needs of the course.

Using Your Judgement: We have created a new section of end-of-chapter assignments that go beyond routine problem solving and calculations. "Using Your Judgement" sections, appearing at the end of every chapter, help students develop analytical and critical thinking skills in an accounting environment, and include:

> *Financial Reporting Problems,* often involving analysis and interpretation of Moore Corporation's financial statements (Appendix 5A).

> *Ethics Cases* that sensitize students to ethical considerations, situations, and dilemmas encountered by practising accountants.

Summary of Learning Objectives: Completely rewritten end-of-chapter summaries reinforce important ideas from each chapter and link them to the learning objectives introduced at the beginning and integrated throughout.

Key Terms: Key terms used in each chapter are listed in the margin next to the Summary of Learning Objectives. The numbers after each term refer to the page on which the term appears (in bold, blue type for easy reference) with its definition.

Topical Boxes: Many chapters now feature short vignettes that relate to material covered in the chapter and either contrast international practices or discuss an ethical consideration or emerging issue pertaining to this material.

ENHANCED FEATURES

Real-World Emphasis: To help make material relevant and readily understandable to students, numerous real-world examples, most of them new, have been used throughout the text. Excerpts from the annual reports of over 50 Canadian corporations have been reprinted exactly as they originally appeared.

Ethics: Ethics in the accounting environment is introduced as a topic in chapter 1 and is included in every chapter in at least one Ethics Case in the "Using Your Judgement" section. These cases help students learn to identify when ethical issues are involved and how to approach ethical decision making.

Currency and Accuracy: Accounting continually changes as its environment changes, making an up-to-date book a necessity. As with past editions we have striven to make this edition the most up-to-date and accurate text available. This is exemplified by our coverage of the *Exposure Drafts* on Cash Flows Statements and Employees' Future Benefits and the new *Handbook* Section 3465 concerning Corporate Income Tax.

Readability: Adopters of previous editions have praised the readability of our text. In this edition, we have carefully reviewed each line of the text to further improve clarity and directness of language, to take out unnecessary detail, and to simplify complex presentations. Our streamlining efforts have both improved user-friendliness and allowed us to add needed new material while still maintaining the overall length of the text.

Design: The design of any text is an integral part of its pedagogical framework. The design of the fifth edition was conceived with this in mind. It presents the material in an open and eye-catching manner and facilitates use of all of the elements of the text.

CHANGES IN CHAPTER ORDER

In response to suggestions, Chapter 18 on Investments: Temporary and Long-Term in the fourth edition has been moved to Chapter 10 to include it with the other chapters covering assets topics. Section 1 on Temporary Investments and Section 2 on Long-Term Investments can be taught as stand-alone material for instructors who prefer a different placement in their courses.

CONTENT CHANGES

The list below outlines major revisions and improvements of the fifth edition by chapter.

Volume 1

Chapter 1   Material included regarding business reporting as considered by the Jenkins Committee.
Section on Environmental Factors that Influence Financial Accounting restructured.
Ethics section is given more significance and is moved to an earlier position in the chapter.

Chapter 2   Material on new Exposure Draft on Going Concern added.
Examples illustrating trade-offs among qualitative characteristics expanded.
Definitions for "investment by owners" and "distributions to owners" added.

Chapter 3   Appendix 3A, section on End of Period Procedures for Inventory and Related Accounts and exhibits for Prepaid Expenses and Unearned Revenues all completely rewritten.

Chapter 4   Discussion of intraperiod tax allocation simplified.
Illustration of a foreign income statement added.

Chapter 5   Statement of Cash Flows introduced.
               Illustration of a foreign balance sheet added.

Chapter 6   Material on the Percentage-of-Completion Method rewritten.
               Complex entries regarding Continuing Fees, Bargain Purchases and
               Options deleted from Appendix 6B.

Chapter 7   Coverage of notes receivable reorganized and simplified.
               Appendix 7A deleted.

Chapter 8   Inventory Errors section expanded; examines impact of errors on ratios.
               Management incentives in choosing inventory methods are covered.
               Appendix 8B deleted.

Chapter 9   Ethics box added.

Chapter 10   Cash Surrender Value and Accounting for Funds given appendix status.
               References to *Handbook* Section 3860 and section on consolidations added.

Chapter 11   Definitions from *Handbook* Section 3060 and coverage of GST added.

Chapter 12   Compound Interest Method discussed.
               Basic issues and accounting for Future Removal and Site Restoration
               Costs added.
               Sum-of-Years-Digits Method deleted.

Chapter 13   Explanation of terminology of *Handbook* Section 3060 updated.
               New section on Impairment of Intangibles added.

Volume 2

Chapter 14   Discussion of GST added.

Chapter 15   Updated to reflect *Handbook* Section 3860, including an expanded section
               on Financial Instrument Complexities.
               Reporting Long-Term Debt, the illustration covering the reacquisition of
               debt and Notes Payable have all been expanded.

Chapter 16   Updated to reflect *Handbook* Section 3860.
               Sections on Instalment Receipts and Shares Issued Financed by Company
               Loans added.

Chapter 17   Exhibit on Contributed Surplus expanded.
               Discussion on Dividends reorganized.
               Disclosure Requirements moved to the end of the chapter.

Chapter 18   Discussion of Dilutive Securities revised to reflect *Handbook* Section 3860.

Chapter 19   Chapter completely revised to conform to new *Handbook* Section 3465.

Chapter 20   Chapter revised to reflect June 1997 *Exposure Draft* on Employees' Future Benefits.

Chapter 21   Examples of actual lease disclosures increased.
New appendix added featuring relevant flowcharts from the *Handbook*.

Chapter 22   Revised to incorporate current proposals.

Chapter 23   Chapter revised to reflect *Exposure Draft* on Cash Flow Statements.
Both Worksheet and T Account Methods now in an appendix as chapter emphasizes Balance Sheet Approach.

Chapter 24   New introduction of the Ratio Analysis section added.
Summary of Ratios chart substantially revised.
Emphasis on Cash Flow Ratios increases.

Chapter 25   New illustrations of segment reporting added.
Coverage of auditor's report upgraded.

EXERCISES, PROBLEMS, AND CASES

At the end of each chapter we have provided a comprehensive set of review and home-work material consisting of exercises, problems, and cases. For this edition many of the exercises and problems have been revised, and a new section, "Using Your Judgement," has been added. Typically, an exercise covers a specific topic and requires less time and effort to solve than a problem or case. The problems are designed to develop a profes-sional level of achievement and are more challenging and time consuming to solve than the exercises. The cases generally require an essay as opposed to quantitative solutions; they are intended to confront the student with situations calling for conceptual analysis and the exercise of judgement in identifying problems and evaluating alternatives. The "Using Your Judgement" assignments are designed to develop students' critical thinking and analytical skills.

In the fourth edition, all exercises, problems, and cases included a short description of the topic tested. These descriptions have been retained in the exercises, but removed from the problems and cases in the fifth edition so that students are required to deter-mine what the key issues are themselves.

Probably no more than one-fourth of the total exercise, problem, and case material must be used to adequately cover the subject matter; consequently, problem assignment may be varied from year to year.

ACKNOWLEDGEMENTS

We thank the many users of our fourth edition who contributed to this revision through their comments and instructive criticism. Special thanks are extended to the reviewers of and contributors to our fifth edition manuscript.

Primary Text Reviewers

Judy Cumby
> Memorial University of Newfoundland

Pauline Downer
> Memorial University of Newfoundland

Margaret Forbes
> Lakehead University

Leo Gallant
> St Francis-Xavier University

Louise Hayes
> York University

Ron Hill
> Southern Alberta Institute of Technology

James Hughes
> British Columbia Institute of Technology

Wayne Irvine
> Mount Royal College

Larry Knechtel
> Grant MacEwan Community College

Robin Hemmingsen
> Centennial College

Michael Lee
> Humber College

Bruce McConomy
> Carleton University

David McPeak, CGA

Patrick O'Neill
> Algonquin College

Morina Rennie
> University of Regina

Tom Shoniker
> Ryerson Polytechnic University

Barbara Trenholm
> University of New Brunswick

Marilyn Willie
> Northern Alberta Institute of Technology

Betty Wong
> Athabasca University

Walter Woronchak
> Sheridan College

Preliminary Reviewers of the Fourth Edition

Judy Cumby
> Memorial University of Newfoundland

Sandra Felton
> Brock University

Bruce Hazelton
> Sheridan College

James Hughes
> British Columbia Institute of Technology

Wayne Irvine
> Mount Royal College

Michael Lee
> Humber College

Valorie Leonard
> Laurentian University

Terry Litovitz
> University of Toronto

Bruce McConomy
> Carleton University

Alistair Murdoch
> University of Manitoba

Peter Nissen
> Northern Alberta Institute of Technology

Patrick O'Neill
> Algonquin College

Wendy Roscoe
> Concordia University

Michael Welker
> Queen's University

Betty Wong
> Athabasca University

Focus Groups

Before the commencement of our writing the fifth edition, John Wiley & Sons Canada, Ltd held focus groups with both instructors and students of Intermediate Accounting from the following schools: Sheridan College, Mohawk College, Humber College, McMaster University, University of Toronto, Sir Sandford Fleming College and Brock University. These discussions lead to some of the pedagogical enhancements in this edition and we thank everyone who participated for their input.

Appreciation is also extended to our colleagues at the University of Saskatchewan and Saint Mary's University who worked on and examined portions of this work and who made valuable suggestions. These include David Bateman, John Brennan, Gary Entwistle, Len Gerspacher, Daryl Lindsay, Jack Vicq, and Mardell Volls.

We are most grateful to the staff at John Wiley & Sons Canada, Ltd: Diane Wood, John Horne, Karen Staudinger, Karen Bryan, Carolyn Wells, Michael Schellenberg and all of the sales representatives. As well, we would like to acknowledge the editorial contributions of Leah Johnson and Claudia Kutchukian.

Sincere appreciation is also extended to the following who provided the authors with excellent word-processing services and suggestions: Jill Mierke, Valerie Fink, Bernie Rodier, Evadne Merz, Eilene Sabat, and Lyla Sheppard. We also thank Jim Wightman and Dan L'Abbé for providing excellent research and proofreading assistance.

We appreciate the cooperation of the Canadian Institute of Chartered Accountants in permitting us to quote from their materials. We thank the Moore Corporation Limited for permitting us to use its 1995 Annual Report for our specimen financial statements. We also wish to acknowledge the cooperation of many Canadian companies from whose financial statements we have drawn excerpts.

If this book helps teachers instill in their students an appreciation of the challenges, worth, and limitations of accounting, if it encourages students to evaluate critically and understand financial accounting theory and practice, and if it prepares students for advanced study, professional examinations, and the successful and ethical pursuit of their careers in accounting or business, then we will have attained out objective.

Suggestions and comments from users of this book will be appreciated. We have striven to produce an error-free text. However, should anything have slipped through the variety of checks undertaken, we would like to know so corrections can be made to subsequent printings.

V. Bruce Irvine	W. Harold Silvester	Nicola M. Young
Saskatoon, Saskatchewan	*Olds, Alberta*	*Halifax, Nova Scotia*

July 1997

BRIEF TABLE OF CONTENTS

TABLE OF CONTENTS

CHAPTER 13

APPENDIX

FINANCIAL ACCOUNTING FUNCTIONS AND BASIC THEORY

part 1

chapter 1

THE ENVIRONMENT OF FINANCIAL ACCOUNTING AND THE DEVELOPMENT OF ACCOUNTING STANDARDS

CHAPTER 1

The Environment of Financial Accounting and the Development of Accounting Standards

Learning Objectives

After studying this chapter, you should be able to:

1. Define accounting and describe its essential characteristics.

2. Identify the major financial statements and other means of financial reporting.

3. Describe the environment that influences financial accounting.

4. Recognize the importance of accounting information and how it can influence decisions.

5. Understand issues related to ethics and financial accounting.

6. Identify the objectives of financial statements and appreciate the importance of having objectives.

7. Know what Generally Accepted Accounting Principles (GAAP) are, what they consist of, and where they are found.

8. Identify the purpose of the conceptual framework for financial accounting.

9. Appreciate the importance of the *CICA Handbook*, its recommendations, and the issues faced by the AcSB in developing these recommendations.

10. Appreciate why sources of GAAP other than the *CICA Handbook* must be used, identify what these sources are, and recognize the importance of professional judgement.

11. Know the nature of organizations that influence financial accounting.

Following a dinner, an intense discussion took place between two friends—one studying philosophy, and the other studying business who intended to become an accountant. The debate focused on whether or not the discipline of accounting had contributed, or ever could contribute, to the benefit of humanity. The long discussion did not resolve the issue. One reason was that the business student, while having completed an introductory accounting course, had difficulty in identifying and presenting convincing arguments. This student knew what financial statements were and what they looked like, and had a fairly good idea of how debits and credits worked, but could provide only fuzzy or no answers to some fundamental questions: What is accounting? What is the purpose of accounting? Why is accounting important to the social, political, legal, and economic environment of Canada? Is there a fundamental rationale underlying what is done in accounting? If so, what is it? What are the strengths and weaknesses of what accountants do, and why? Is accounting simply a product of what governments and pressure groups say it should be? Do accountants ever really exercise judgement in making important decisions, or do they simply carry out procedures that are purely mechanical and will eventually be performed entirely by computers? Are there any ethical dimensions associated with accounting?

Chapters 1 and 2 do not to tell the reader how to do accounting. They make no reference to debits and credits. Their purpose is to build a framework for understanding financial accounting in Canada. From this knowledge base, a student of accounting will be in a better position to answer fundamental questions about accounting, such as those raised in the preceding paragraph. With this knowledge, the reader will be better able to develop reasonable and justifiable solutions to accounting problems that are encountered (i.e., know why a decision to adopt a particular accounting policy or measurement in a given situation is or is not appropriate).

WHAT IS ACCOUNTING?

OBJECTIVE 1
Define accounting and describe its essential characteristics.

Is accounting a service activity, a descriptive/analytical discipline, or an information system? It is all three.

As a **service activity,** accounting provides interested parties with quantitative and qualitative information that helps them make decisions about the deployment and use of resources in business as well as nonbusiness entities. As a **descriptive/analytical discipline,** it identifies a great mass of events and transactions that characterize economic activity. Through measurement, classification, and summarization, it reduces those data to relatively few, highly significant, and interrelated items. When appropriately assembled and reported, these items describe the financial condition, results of operations, and cash flows of a specific economic entity. As an **information system,** it collects and communicates economic information about an entity to various people whose decisions and actions are related to the entity.

Each of these descriptions of accounting—different though they may seem—contains the three essential characteristics of accounting: (1) *recognition, measurement, and disclosure (communication) of financial information about* (2) *economic entities to* (3) *interested persons*. These characteristics have described accounting for hundreds of years. Yet, in the last 60 years, economic entities have grown so much in size and complexity, and interested persons have increased so greatly in number and diversity, that the responsibility placed on the accounting profession is greater today than ever before.

THE NATURE OF FINANCIAL ACCOUNTING

FINANCIAL ACCOUNTING

For purposes of study and practice, the discipline of accounting is commonly divided into the following areas or subsets: financial accounting, management accounting, tax accounting, and not-for-profit (public sector) accounting. *This book concentrates on financial accounting*.

Financial accounting is "concerned with the classification, recording, analysis, and interpretation of the overall financial position and operating results of an organization and providing such information to owners, managers and third parties."[1] Financial accounting encompasses the processes and decisions that culminate in the preparation of financial statements relative to the enterprise as a whole for use by parties inside and

---

[1] *Terminology for Accountants* (Toronto: Canadian Institute of Chartered Accountants, 1992), p. 92. Financial accounting is generally associated with profit-oriented enterprises. Not-for-profit accounting applies to the provision of financial statements for organizations in which there is no transferable ownership interest and which do not carry on a business with a view to distributing profits. Tax accounting deals with the provision of financial information to tax authorities. In this book, we focus on financial accounting for profit-oriented enterprises and, as such, do not examine many of the unique aspects of accounting for not-for-profit organizations or tax accounting.

outside the enterprise. **Management accounting** is "concerned with providing information to assist management in internal decision making, as contrasted with accounting directed towards providing information to outsiders, such as shareholders and creditors."[2] Such internal decision making relates to planning, control, and evaluation within an organization.

Typically, an organization employs accountants who are responsible for providing accounting information for internal use by management and for preparing its financial statements. Auditors (public accountants) are responsible for providing an independent assessment of the financial statements in terms of their fairness and conformity with generally accepted accounting principles.

FINANCIAL STATEMENTS, FINANCIAL REPORTING, AND BUSINESS REPORTING

Financial statements are a principal means of communicating financial information to those outside an enterprise. **Financial statements** for profit-oriented enterprises normally include (1) a balance sheet; (2) an income statement; (3) a statement of cash flows; and (4) a statement of retained earnings. Notes to financial statements and supporting schedules cross-referenced to these statements are an integral part of such statements.[3]

Some financial information is better provided, or can be provided only, by means of **financial reporting** other than through the formal financial statements. Such information may be available because it is required by authoritative pronouncement, regulatory rule, or custom, or because management wishes to disclose it voluntarily. Examples include the president's letter or supplementary schedules in the corporate annual report, prospectuses, reports filed with government agencies, news releases, management's forecasts, and descriptions of an enterprise's social or environmental impact.[4]

In 1994, a special committee studying financial reporting in the United States issued an important report that indicated possible future directions for business reporting.[5] The committee researched the information needs of users and recommended (among other things) that **business reporting** in the future include:

1. **Financial and nonfinancial data.**
   - Financial statements and related disclosures.
   - High-level operating data and performance measurements that management uses to manage the business.

2. **Management's analysis.**
   - Reasons for changes in the financial, operating, and performance-related data, and the identity and past effects of key trends.

3. **Forward-looking information.**
   - Opportunities and risks, including those resulting from key trends.
   - Management's plans, including critical success factors.
   - Comparison of actual business performance to previously disclosed forward-looking information.

---

[2] *Ibid.*, p. 132.

[3] *CICA Handbook* (Toronto: CICA), Section 1000, par. .04.

[4] *Information to be Included in the Annual Report to Shareholders* (Toronto: CICA, 1991). This study provides many more suggestions regarding information to be included in a company's annual report.

[5] AICPA Special Committee on Financial Reporting, "Improving Business Reporting—A Customer Focus," *Journal of Accountancy*, Supplement (October, 1994). This committee is frequently referred to as the "Jenkins Committee" after its chair Edmund Jenkins. The Jenkins Committee recommended that standard setters should encompass the viewpoint of business reporting in carrying out their responsibilities.

4. **Information about management and shareholders.**
   - Directors, management, compensation, major shareholders, and transactions and relationships among related parties.

5. **Background about the company.**
   - Broad objectives and strategies.
   - Scope and description of business and properties.
   - Impact of industry structure on the company.

As described, business reporting clearly extends beyond what is included in contemporary financial statements and traditional financial reporting.

In the fall of 1994, a Canadian Institute of Chartered Accountants (CICA) Task Force was created to review this report in terms of its implications for Canadian financial reporting. This Task Force concluded that many of the findings of the U.S. committee had some relevancy to Canada. However, until this new model of business reporting receives greater backing (e.g., of legislation or regulatory bodies), the focus should continue to be on improving the financial reporting process. The Task Force therefore recommended that the relevant observations in the U.S. Committee's report, and some additional ones, be taken into consideration when formulating Canadian financial accounting standards.[6] The additional recommendations addressed aspects such as: increasing harmonization of Canadian accounting standards with those of other countries, particularly the United States; considering the impact of the electronic environment on financial reporting; and developing guidance and standards regarding corporate governance issues, "knowledge assets," and income statement presentation.

The primary focus of this book is on the development of financial information reported in financial statements and related disclosures.

ENVIRONMENTAL FACTORS THAT INFLUENCE FINANCIAL ACCOUNTING

OBJECTIVE 3
Describe the environment that influences financial accounting.

Like other human activities and disciplines, accounting is largely a product of its environment. The environment of accounting consists of social, economic, political, and legal conditions, restraints, and influences that vary from time to time. As a result, accounting objectives and practices are not the same today as they were in the past. *Accounting theory and practices have evolved to meet changing demands and influences.* The following identifies influences of particular importance that are recognized and accepted in contemporary financial accounting.

1. **People live in a world of scarce resources.** Because resources exist in limited supply, people try to conserve them, to use them effectively and efficiently, and to identify and encourage those who can make effective and efficient use of them. Through efficient and effective use of resources, the standard of living increases. Accounting plays a useful role in obtaining a higher standard of living because it helps to identify efficient and inefficient users of resources. For example, by measuring and reporting the assets and net income of a company, information that helps to determine the company's efficiency becomes available (income divided by assets is a measure of return on investment). By comparing the return on investment of various companies, investors and lenders can better assess investment opportunities and channel their scarce resources accordingly.

---

[6] *Report of the CICA Task Force to Review the Recommendations of the AICPA Special Committee on Financial Reporting* (Toronto: CICA, 1995). Also see "Task Force Reviews Jenkins Committee Recommendations," *CA Magazine*, October, 1995, pp. 10–11. At the time of writing, the AcSB had completed, or was undertaking, projects addressing various financial reporting issues identified in the Jenkins Committee and the Task Force reports.

2. **Society's current legal and ethical concepts of property, contractual, and other rights must be respected when determining equity among varying interests.** Accounting looks to its environment for direction with regard to what property rights society protects, what society recognizes as value, and what society acknowledges as equitable and fair.

3. **In complex economic systems, some (owners and investors) entrust the custodianship of and control over property to others (managers).** The corporate form of organization tends to divorce ownership and management, particularly in large organizations. Thus, measuring and reporting information to absentee owners has emerged as a crucial function for accounting. This role greatly increases the need for **accounting standards**, which are the *rules of practice governing the contents, measurements, and disclosures in financial statements.* Absentee investors, unlike the owner-operator, have little opportunity to combine reported information with first-hand knowledge of the conditions and activities of the enterprise. Consequently, existence of standards helps to ensure the relevance, reliability, and comparability of information reported.

4. **There are many users and uses of accounting information.** Some users of financial accounting information have, or contemplate having, a direct interest in economic entities. **Direct interest users** include present and potential owners, creditors, and suppliers; management; tax authorities; employees; and consumers. Other users have an interest in such entities because their function is to assist or protect persons who have, or contemplate having, a direct interest. These **indirect interest users** include financial analysts, stock exchanges, lawyers, regulatory and registration authorities, financial press and reporting agencies, trade associations, and labour unions.

   The recognition of these many potential user groups, each with its unique decision-making process and special needs, can have significant consequences when choices between accounting alternatives are made. Indeed, a research study by the Canadian Institute of Chartered Accountants proposed that this user-oriented perspective form the basis for developing Canadian financial accounting standards.[7] This study built upon the premise that an important objective of financial reporting is the provision of useful information to all potential users in a form and time frame relevant to their various needs. It identified 15 user classes, then related various needs to each (see Exhbit 1-1). From this perspective, a variety of different measurement bases (historical cost, general price-level-adjusted historical cost, current replacement cost, net realizable value) may be relevant to different users, users' needs, and decision processes. Consequently, if financial reports are to provide the most useful information, accountants must be aware of users, their needs, and decision processes.

   A user perspective has been an important aspect in the development of accounting reports throughout history. At present, authoritative pronouncements regarding the objectives of financial statements incorporate an emphasis on the perceived needs of the investor and creditor user groups (see later in this chapter). The success, or lack of success, of financial statements in meeting these needs has become an increasingly important issue. For various reasons (e.g., users lack understanding of the assumptions and measurement rules in the accounting model or the accounting model itself does not adequately reflect economic and environmental realities) even investor and creditor groups have criticized financial statements for not providing the type of information they thought they were getting or expected to receive—a problem

---

[7] *Corporate Reporting: Its Future Revolution* (Toronto: CICA, 1980).

EXHIBIT 1-1

USER CLASSES AND RELATED NEEDS

User Class	Needs	Classes of Users Having These Needs (numbers in brackets refer to user classes)
(1) Shareholders	(1) Assessment of overall performance	
(2) Creditors—Long-term	(a) In absolute terms	(1) to (15)
(3) Creditors—Short-term	(b) Compared to goals	(1) to (15)
	(c) Compared to other entities	(1) to (15)
(4) Analysts and Advisors serving (1), (2), & (3) (e.g., Brokers, Financial Analysts, Journalists)	(2) Assessment of management quality	
	(a) Profit, overall performance, efficiency	(1) to (11) especially
(5) Employees	(b) Stewardship	(1) (4) (6) (11) (12) (13)
(6) Nonexecutive Directors	(3) Estimating future prospects for	
(7) Customers	(a) Profits	(1) to (11) especially
(8) Suppliers	(b) Dividends and interest	(1) to (4) especially
(9) Industry Groups	(c) Investment and capital needs	(1) to (6), (8) to (14)
	(d) Employment	(5) (10) (11) (12) especially
(10) Labour Unions	(e) Suppliers	(3) (5) (11) (12) (14) especially
(11) Government, Departments and Ministers (Federal, Provincial, Municipal—e.g., Tax; Statistics; Consumer and Corporate Affairs; Industry, Trade and Commerce)	(f) Customers (warranties, etc.)	(7) (9) (11) (12) especially
	(g) Past employees	(5) (10) (11) (12) (13)
	(4) Assessing financial strength and stability	(1) to (15)
	(5) Assessing solvency	(1) to (15)
(12) Public—Political Parties Public Affairs Groups Consumer Groups Environment Groups	(6) Assessing liquidity	(1) to (15)
	(7) Assessing risk and uncertainty	(1) to (15)
	(8) As an aid to resource allocation by	
	(a) Shareholders (present and potential)	(1) (4) (11) (12) (13) (14)
(13) Regulatory Agencies (e.g., Stock Exchanges, Securities Commissions)	(b) Creditors (present and potential; long- and short-term)	(2) (3) (4) (8) (11) (12) (13) (14)
	(c) Governments	(11) (12) especially
(14) Other Companies (Domestic and Foreign)	(d) Other private sector bodies	(4) (9) (12) (13) (14)
(15) Standard Setters, Academic Researchers	(9) In making comparisons	
	(a) With past performance	(1) to (15)
	(b) With other entities	(1) to (15)
	(c) With industry and economy as a whole	(1) to (15)
	(10) In valuation of debt and equity holdings in the company	(1) to (4) especially
	(11) In assessing adaptive ability	(1) to (15)
	(12) Determining compliance with laws or regulations	(11) to (13) especially
	(13) Assessing entity's contribution to society, national goals, etc.	(11) (12) especially

Source: *Corporate Reporting: Its Future Evolution* (Toronto: CICA, 1980), pp. 44, 48, 49.

referred to as the "**expectations gap.**"[8] When other groups are included in the list of users, each with its own distinct needs, it is not difficult to appreciate that the gap can widen between what a single set of financial statements can provide and what is necessary to satisfy all groups. Therefore, while a user orientation is significant to shap-

---

[8] *Report of the Commission to Study the Public's Expectations of Audits* (Toronto: CICA, 1988).

ing the nature of financial accounting, much remains to be done before the full implications of such an orientation can be incorporated into financial statement reporting.

5. **Economic activity is continuous and interdependent.** All societies engage in the fundamental economic activities of production, distribution, exchange, consumption, saving, and investment. In a highly developed economy like that of Canada, these activities have become specialized, complex, and intertwined. As economic activities are continuous and interdependent, relationships and accomplishments associated with intervals of time (such as the net income for a year or portion of a year) can be measured only by making allocations based on assumptions (e.g., the allocation of an asset's cost—amortization expense—to a given year based on assumed life, benefit pattern, and residual value of the asset). The problems of allocation are intensified in a dynamic economy because the outcome of economic activity is uncertain at the time decisions are made and action is taken. Fortunately, the continuity of enterprise existence and the framework of law, custom, and traditional patterns of action help to stabilize many aspects of the economic environment.

6. **Economic activity is conducted by separately identifiable units—business enterprises.** Business enterprises consist of economic resources (assets), economic obligations (liabilities), and residual interests (owners' equity), which are increased or decreased by economic activities. Accounting accumulates and reports economic activity as it affects these elements of each business enterprise.

   Other types of entities (governments, individuals, not-for-profit organizations) also conduct economic activity. While many of the concepts that relate to accounting for business enterprises are appropriate for these entities, some important differences exist. *This book concentrates on financial accounting and reporting for business entities.*

7. **Economic resources, economic obligations, and residual interests are expressed in terms of money.** Accounting facilitates the comparison and evaluation of diverse economic activities by the **measurement** of an enterprise's resources and obligations as well as the events that increase or decrease them. Money is used as a common standard for purposes of measurement. *Money permits the measurement of qualitative and quantitative attributes of economic events, resources, and obligations.*[9] Thus, the unit of measurement in financial accounting is in terms of money or exchange price. Of course, some important activities of enterprises are not measurable in terms of money (e.g., appointing a new president, adopting a tradename or trademark, customer satisfaction, delivery time).

INFLUENCE OF ACCOUNTING ON THE ENVIRONMENT

While accounting is a product of its environment, it also shapes the environment. It plays a significant role in the conduct of economic, social, political, legal, and organizational decisions and actions. *Accounting is a system that feeds back to organizations and individuals information that they can use to reshape their environment.* It provides information for the re-evaluation of social, political, and economic objectives as well as the relative costs and benefits of the alternative means of achieving these objectives.

OBJECTIVE 4
Recognize the importance of accounting information and how it can influence decisions.

---

[9] Qualitative attributes, as well as quantitative ones, are measurable (valued) in money terms. For instance, at the time of writing, one ounce of gold measured $541 in money terms while one ounce of silver measured $7.31. The difference in price per ounce reflected differences in qualitative attributes. A doubling of the quantity would result in doubling the amount of money measurement. As another example of qualitative attributes being reflected by money measurement, one of Van Gogh's paintings, *Portrait of Dr. Gachet,* was sold at auction for $82,500,000 while an author's daughter had difficulty selling one of her paintings for $50 at an art fair. Money measurements reflect both qualitative and quantitative factors.

Accounting numbers that are reported can influence the distribution of scarce resources. For example, assume that a gift of art is received by a museum. Should the gift be reported on the museum's financial statements at market value? Doing this could discourage future gifts because prospective donors may perceive the museum as being prosperous and therefore not in need of additional donations.

As another example, consider the problems relating to financial institutions' valuation of financial assets (e.g., loans to companies). These loans are generally recorded at their face amount as they are expected to be paid when due. In times of economic downturn, however, some of these loans lose their value because the security offered (e.g., shares in companies, farm land) loses its market value and the borrowers are not able to repay the loan. Despite this, financial institutions may not recognize the loss on a timely basis by making appropriate allowances for bad debts. Many believed that this was a significant factor leading to the collapse of the Canadian Commercial Bank and the Northland Bank in 1985. While recognition of loan losses may not have prevented these collapses, perhaps a more timely recognition of loan losses could have resulted in much earlier recognition of problems and the taking of appropriate actions to resolve them. If the crisis had been detected earlier, millions of client and taxpayer dollars might have been saved.[10]

As a final example regarding the potential impact of accounting information, it is clear that nuclear power plants will eventually have to be mothballed and their nuclear cores removed. If accountants report a portion of this expense currently, energy rates will likely be higher today and lower in the future. Conversely, if these costs are charged to operations after these plants are abandoned, energy rates will likely be lower today but higher in the future.

In summary, the accounting information reported by an enterprise affects perceptions of its financial condition and success. These perceptions then lead to changes in economic behaviour. Because behaviour (decision making) is affected, accounting has important social consequences.

ETHICS IN THE ENVIRONMENT OF FINANCIAL ACCOUNTING

OBJECTIVE 5
Understand issues related to ethics and financial accounting.

Given that accounting has behavioural consequences, careful attention must be given to secure ethical behaviour by accounting professionals.[11]

Robert Sack, a commentator on the subject of ethics and accounting, noted that:

Based on my experience, new graduates tend to be idealistic . . . thank goodness for that! Still it is very dangerous to think that your armour is all in place and say to yourself, "I would have never given in to that." The pressures don't explode on us, they build and we often don't recognize them until they have us.

These observations are particularly appropriate for anyone entering the business world. In accounting, as in other areas of business, ethical dilemmas are encountered frequently. Some of these dilemmas are simple and easy to resolve. Many, however, are complex and solutions are not obvious. Businesses' focus on "maximizing the bottom line,"

---

[10] While the Canadian Commercial Bank and Northland Bank experiences revealed problems in accounting for loan losses on a timely basis, the fact that most Canadian banks fairly quickly recognized immense losses on loans to Olympia & York Developments Ltd. in response to that company's financial problems revealed in 1992 suggests that lessons have been learned.

[11] Canadian professional accounting bodies have codes of ethics to which their members must adhere. While differences exist in the codes of different professional bodies and between provinces, they generally (a) establish that members are to act ethically (in their own actions and regarding unethical behaviour of others); (b) provide due process for resolving assertions of unethical behaviour; and (c) identify potential consequences of acting unethically that can be imposed by the body.

"facing the challenges of competition," and "stressing short-term results" places accountants in the middle of an environment of conflict and pressure. Basic questions such as: Is this way of communicating financial information good or bad? Is it right or wrong? What should I do in the circumstance? cannot always be answered by simply adhering to Generally Accepted Accounting Principles or following the rules of the profession. Technical competence is not enough when ethical decisions are required.

A practising accountant—either a corporate accountant or a public accountant—must appreciate the importance of recognizing ethical dilemmas, analysing the particular issues, and selecting the right resolutions. Doing the right thing is not always easy. Right is not always evident. The pressure to "bend the rules," "play the game," or "just ignore it" can be considerable. For example, an accountant faced with a tough ethical decision may wonder: Will my decision affect my job performance negatively? Will my superiors be upset? Will my colleagues be unhappy with me? The decision making is all the more difficult because a public consensus has not emerged to formulate a comprehensive ethical system to provide guidelines.

However, "**applied ethics**" is still necessary and possible. Accountants should apply the following steps in the process of ethical awareness and decision-making.

1. **Recognize an ethical situation or dilemma**. One's personal ethics, conscience, or sensitivity to others assists in identifying ethical situations and issues. Being sensitive to and aware of the effects (i.e., potential harm or benefit) of one's actions and decisions on individuals or groups (referred to in ethical terms as "stakeholders") is a first step in resolving ethical dilemmas.

2. **Move toward an ethical resolution by identifying and analyzing the principal elements in the situation**. Seek answers to the following questions:
   (a) Which parties (stakeholders) may be harmed or benefited?
   (b) Whose rights or claims may be violated?
   (c) Which specific interests are in conflict?
   (d) What are my responsibilities and obligations?
   This step involves identifying and sorting out the facts.

3. **Identify the alternatives and weigh the impact of each alternative on various stakeholders.** In financial accounting, consider alternative methods that are available to measure or report the transaction, situation, or event. What is the effect of each alternative on the various stakeholders? Which stakeholders are harmed or benefited most?

4. **Select the best (most ethical) alternative considering all the circumstances and the consequences.** Some ethical issues involve one right answer, and what must be done is to identify that one right answer. Other ethical issues involve more than one right answer; this requires an evaluation of each alternative and the selection of the best or most ethical alternative.

This whole process of ethical sensitivity and selection from alternatives can be complicated by time pressure, job pressure, client pressure, personal pressure, and peer pressure. Throughout this book, *ethical considerations are presented to help you become aware of, and resolve, the types of situations that can arise.*

THE OBJECTIVES OF FINANCIAL STATEMENTS

The preceding discussion indicates that financial accounting has evolved to reflect the influences and constraints of the environment, that it influences decisions and actions taken in the environment, and that ethical behaviour is a cornerstone of accounting prac-

OBJECTIVE 6
Identify the objectives of financial statements and appreciate the importance of having objectives.

tice. Continued evolution in these aspects of accounting will likely have an impact on any specific statement regarding the objectives of financial statements. It is important, however, to identify these objectives as they currently exist. Knowledge of objectives is crucial to understanding what is done in financial accounting and why it is done. In addition, it provides a fundamental perspective for deriving acceptable solutions to particular problems faced by an accountant—one should always ask if a particular solution is consistent with the objectives one is trying to achieve.

Surprisingly, a specific statement of the objectives of financial statements had not been developed by the Canadian accounting profession until the late 1980s. Without doubt, Canadian undertakings in this regard followed what was done by the accounting profession in the United States which, in the late 1970s, undertook a conscientious, costly, and time-consuming project to codify a foundation upon which financial accounting and reporting standards could be based.[12] Drawing on this work, The Accounting Standards Authority of Canada published, in 1987, a *Conceptual Framework for Financial Reporting*, which included statements regarding the objectives of financial reporting as shown in Exhibit 1-2.[13]

EXHIBIT 1-2

OBJECTIVES OF FINANCIAL REPORTING
(THE ACCOUNTING STANDARDS AUTHORITY OF CANADA PERSPECTIVE)

At the most general level, the objective of financial reporting is to provide information which is useful in making management, investment, credit and similar decisions with regard to an entity. . . .

At the next level, the objective of financial reporting is to present information which will assist users to forecast the probability, amounts and timing of prospective cash flows. Since investing, lending and similar business transactions are undertaken to ultimately increase net assets, investors and creditors require information concerning the risks, timing, returns and rates of return from alternate investment or credit choices. Financial reporting should assist in making choices, since expected cash flows to the entity relate to expected cash flows to the entity's investors and creditors and, in turn, to their wealth and their purchasing power.

At the most specific level, the objective of financial reporting is to provide information regarding an entity with respect to:

• economic resources (assets), claims on resources (liabilities) and the owners' equity, which are summarized in the Statement of Financial Position

• changes in the equity of owners arising from transactions and events during the reporting period (except for dealings with owners), which are summarized in the Statements of Earnings

• changes in the equity of owners arising from all transactions and events during the reporting period, which are summarized in the Statement of Owners' Equity

• all changes in the amounts and composition of the financial position arising from transactions and events in which the entity interacts with and is affected by the external world, which are summarized in the Statement of Changes in Financial Position: Cash Flow.

In December 1988, the Accounting Standards Board (AcSB)[14] of the CICA added a section to the *CICA Handbook* (a publication containing recommendations having legal

---

[12] "Objectives of Financial Reporting by Business Enterprises," *Statement of Financial Accounting Concepts No. 1* (Stamford, Conn.: Financial Accounting Standards Board, November, 1978). This was the first of a series of "concepts statements" published by the FASB over an eight-year period. These statements were developed to provide a comprehensive description of a conceptual framework for financial reporting.

[13] *Conceptual Framework for Financial Reporting* (Vancouver: The Accounting Standards Authority of Canada, 1987), pars. 121–123.

[14] The AcSB replaced the Accounting Standards Committee (AcSC) in 1991. The AcSC was called the Accounting Research Committee prior to 1982. For reasons of expediency, we will refer to the AcSB throughout this book as the body responsible for the development of financial accounting recommendations and other material in the *CICA Handbook*, recognizing that the work regarding these standards prior to 1991 was done under the names of

authority regarding Canadian financial accounting practices) titled "Financial Statement Concepts." This section included the statement shown in Exhibit 1-3 regarding the objective of financial statements .[15]

EXHIBIT 1-3

OBJECTIVE OF FINANCIAL STATEMENTS
(*CICA HANDBOOK* PERSPECTIVE)

The objective of financial statements is to communicate information that is useful to investors, members, contributors, creditors and other users in making resource allocation decisions and/or assessing management stewardship. Consequently, financial statements provide information about:

(a) an entity's economic resources, obligations and equity/net assets;

(b) changes in an entity's economic resources, obligations and equity/net assets; and

(c) the economic performance of the entity.

In discussion of this objective, the *CICA Handbook* states that:

> Investors and creditors of profit oriented enterprises are interested, for the purpose of making resource allocation decisions, in predicting the ability of the entity to earn income and generate cash flows in the future to meet its obligations and to generate a return on investment.[16]

Although these two statements of objectives differ in detail and some specifics, their underlying theme is similar. *The objectives of financial statements are to provide information that is (1) useful to making investment, credit, and other decisions; (2) helpful for assessing the amounts, timing, and uncertainty of future cash flows; and (3) about enterprise resources, claims to those resources, and changes in them.*

Given these objectives, three observations are important relative to how they are interpreted and their implications on financial accounting. The *first* observation regards the *orientation as to the use of financial statements*. Historically, financial statements were used to provide information on the stewardship of management for resources entrusted to it. As such, financial statements served a **stewardship** or **accountability function**, and were viewed as the means by which management accounted for a company's resources to the suppliers of the resources. This perspective necessarily concentrated on reporting where the resources came from (creditors, debtors, owners), what was done with the resources (invested in assets), how much was involved, and the benefits received from the management of the resources (income generated for a period of time). Within this perspective, it is clear that the historical (actual) cost of assets plays a major role in the measurement of items because it objectively states the dollars spent. The stewardship function continues to be an important aspect. Additionally, however, financial statements are viewed as a source of information that can be **used to make economic (resource allocation) decisions** such as investing, granting credit, paying a bonus to managers, and forcing payment of a debt.

---

[14] (*Continued*)

the previous Committees. In addition to financial accounting material, the *CICA Handbook* includes recommendations and material on auditing (the responsibility of the Auditing Standards Board or AuSB) and accounting and auditing recommendations applicable to the public sector (the responsibility of the Public Sector Accounting and Auditing Board or PSAAB).

[15] *CICA Handbook*, Section 1000, par. .15. The reference to "members" and "contributors" in this quotation pertains to non-profit organizations.

[16] *Ibid.*, par. .12.

The two purposes—reporting on stewardship responsibilities and providing information to make economic decisions—are frequently considered to be interlinked. This relationship is evident if one asks why people want stewardship information, and comes to the answer that it is because such information is useful in making economic decisions (e.g., whether to hold or sell an investment, whether to keep or replace management). There is truth to this line of thinking, yet it also has its dangers and leads to problems in, and criticisms of, financial statements. This is because a stewardship orientation is concerned with what has happened in the past, whereas a decision-making orientation is concerned with predicting what will happen in the future. For the person concerned with the latter, measurements based on historical costs may not be viewed as the most useful (compared to current costs or forecasted information, for example).

A *second* observation concerns **the attention given to the usefulness of information to predict cash flows**. This might lead to the inference that a cash basis of accounting is advocated over an accrual basis. This is not the case. Accountants believe that information based on accrual accounting generally provides a better indication of an enterprise's present and continuing ability to generate favourable future cash flows than does information limited to the financial effects of cash receipts and payments.[17]

The objective of **accrual accounting** is to ensure that events that change an entity's financial statements are recorded in the periods in which the events occur, rather than only in the periods in which the entity receives or pays cash. Using accrual accounting to determine net income means recognizing revenues when earned (rather than when cash is received), and recognizing expenses when incurred (rather than when paid). Under accrual accounting, revenues are usually recognized in the time period when sales are made so that they can be related to the economic environment of that period. Over the long run, trends in revenues and related expenses are generally more meaningful than trends in cash receipts and payments. They reflect the underlying economic consequences of operating decisions for a time period, not simply the consequences of decisions by management and customers as to when they pay for things.

While an enterprise must be profitable (i.e., generate income on an accrual basis), it must also be able to pay its debts when due. It is possible for an enterprise to be profitable yet not be able to pay its bills because of a lack of cash. Therefore, investors, creditors, and others need information regarding cash flows. Such information is provided in the Statement of Cash Flows.

The point is that information helpful for assessing the amounts, timing, and uncertainty of future cash flows is provided in all of the financial statements, not just a cash flow statement.

The *third* observation regarding these objectives of financial statements is that, as they apply to profit-oriented enterprises, they **emphasize the investor and creditor user groups and combine all remaining groups** (see Exhibit 1-1) **into an "other" category**. This reflects a dilemma of contemporary financial accounting and reporting. Traditionally, creditors and investors have been the primary external groups financial accounting has been designed to serve. The growth in size, significance, power, and concerns of other groups is an important event in our economy. These groups also need financial information when making decisions. At present, the published financial statements of an enterprise represent the only publicly available source of such information. Given the variety of user groups seeking and using them, they are often called **"general purpose financial statements."**

---

[17] As used here, cash flow means "cash generated and used in operations." The term cash flows is frequently used to also include cash obtained from owners, borrowing, or disposing of assets, and cash distributed to owners or used to repay loans and acquire assets. This latter, broader definition is the basis for preparing a Statement of Cash Flows.

As suggested previously, however, the various user groups have different needs (decisions to make) and perspectives or viewpoints. Consequently, while these statements may be referred to as "general purpose," the question is whether they provide sufficient information to specific user groups. Perhaps the provision of "**special purpose financial statements**" to particular user groups may help resolve the concern.

In summary, the basic objective of financial statements is to provide useful information on how an enterprise's resources and obligations have been managed. While other information may be available, financial statement information is considered useful because it can help users to:

1. Assess overall financial performance, management performance, solvency, liquidity, risks and uncertainty.

2. Estimate future prospects.

3. Make comparisons.

when making their decisions.

GENERALLY ACCEPTED ACCOUNTING PRINCIPLES (GAAP)

Given the objectives of financial statements and the proposition that they are established to meet user requirements for information and to satisfy management's fiduciary reporting responsibility, an important question is: How are financial statements prepared to appropriately achieve these objectives?

When accountants prepare financial statements, they are faced with the potential dangers of bias, misinterpretation, inexactness, and ambiguity, just like anyone involved in a communication process. In order to minimize these dangers and to produce financial statements that are reasonably fair, understandable, complete, and comparable between enterprises and accounting periods, accountants carry out their work within a framework of generally accepted accounting principles. **Generally accepted accounting principles (GAAP)** *form the basis on which financial statements are normally prepared.*[18] Without GAAP, accountants or enterprises would have to develop their own theoretical structure and set of practices pertaining to financial accounting. If this happened, financial statements users would have to familiarize themselves with every company's particular accounting and reporting practices to understand and compare the statements—a virtually impossible task. Consequently, most accountants and members of the financial community recognize GAAP as being useful and necessary, even though some aspects of GAAP have provoked debate and criticism.

While GAAP provides the basis on which the financial statements of most profit-seeking enterprises are prepared, *it is important to realize that following GAAP is not appropriate in all circumstances*. Regulatory legislation or contractual requirements can justifiably result in an accounting treatment inconsistent with GAAP. Additionally, there can be circumstances where GAAP should not be followed because doing so would result in misleading information. To determine when GAAP is inappropriate, the accountant must be able to adequately assess the situation, exercise judgement, and justify the conclusion reached. For example, in Chapter 2 the basic assumptions under which GAAP is appropriate are examined. One of these assumptions is that the enterprise being accounted for is a going concern. If this is judged not to be the case given the circum-

OBJECTIVE 7
Know what Generally Accepted Accounting Principles (GAAP) are, what they consist of, and where they are found.

---

[18] *CICA Handbook,* Section 1000, par. .59.

stances of a particular enterprise, then measurement of assets and liabilities based on historical costs (the generally accepted approach) would be misleading and using liquidation values (not generally accepted) would be appropriate. Additionally, deviation from GAAP can be acceptable when the purpose of the information to be provided differs from that of fulfilling the previously discussed objectives of financial statements (e.g., when determining the amount of insurance to carry).

While recognizing that GAAP may not be appropriate in all circumstances, there is a "strong presumption" that adherence results in appropriate presentation.[19] *Consequently, this book concentrates on GAAP.*

Generally accepted accounting principles have developed over time.[20] "Generally accepted" means that a given concept or practice has been established by an authoritative accounting body or has been accepted as appropriate because of its widespread application.

While "generally accepted accounting principles" had been a phrase used for years by accountants, a common understanding of what it included did not exist. To some it meant only the rules, practices, and procedures that provided guidance for measuring, classifying, communicating, and interpreting information presented in financial statements. To others it included only broad principles (e.g., historical cost, matching), assumptions (e.g., going concern, economic entity), and constraints (e.g., materiality, conservatism) which provided a basis for developing particular rules and practices. Still others added to the latter perspective various qualities of information (e.g., relevance, reliability) that accountants should strive to provide in financial statements. To resolve this confusion, the following description of what GAAP includes was incorporated into the *CICA Handbook* in 1988:

> The term generally accepted accounting principles encompasses not only specific rules, practices and procedures relating to particular circumstances but also broad principles and conventions of general application, including underlying concepts.[21]

Based on this broad description and elaborations provided in Section 1000 of the *CICA Handbook* and other sources, Exhibit 1-4 summarizes what is included in Canadian GAAP.

CONCEPTUAL FRAMEWORK

OBJECTIVE 8
Identify the purpose of the conceptual framework for financial accounting.

A **conceptual framework** sets forth fundamental objectives and interrelated concepts that are useful for solving existing and emerging problems in a consistent manner. It serves as a general guide in determining procedures, practices, and rules that are stipulated by a standard-setting body and is used by organizations in preparing financial statements. The conceptual framework recognizes that there are various users and uses of financial information, specifies particular objectives of financial statements, identifies qualitative characteristics of information (criteria making information useful) regarding the items (elements) that are to be included in financial statements, and recognizes that there are some underlying recognition and measurement guidelines (assumptions, principles, constraints) that must be adhered to. As such, this framework represents the theoretical base regarding what accounting is and why things are done as they are. The conceptual framework is fairly elaborate and complex, and detailed discussion of it is deferred to Chapter 2.

---

[19] *Ibid.*, par. .61.

[20] An historical perspective of the interaction between accounting and its environment fosters an appreciation for and understanding of the Canadian accounting heritage and the development of Canadian GAAP. Such a perspective is provided in Appendix 1A at the end of this chapter.

[21] *CICA Handbook*, Section 1000, par. .60.

EXHIBIT 1-4

GENERALLY ACCEPTED ACCOUNTING PRINCIPLES

Conceptual Framework

- Objectives
- Qualitative Characteristics of Information
- Elements of Financial Statements
- Recognition and Measurement Criteria
- Assumptions
- Principles
- Constraints

Specific Accounting Policies, Practices, Procedures, and Rules

- Recommendations in the *CICA Handbook*

Other Sources (for matters not covered in recommendations of the *CICA Handbook* or when such recommendations are not totally explicit)

- Principles that are generally accepted by virtue of their use in similar circumstances by a significant number of entities in Canada.
- Principles that are consistent with the spirit of the *Handbook* and are developed through the exercise of professional judgement. In exercising professional judgement, principles for analogous situations dealt with in the Handbook would be taken into account and reference would be made to:
  - other related or relevant matters dealt with in the *Handbook*
  - practice in similar situations, including consultation with other informed persons
  - Canadian publications, other than the *Handbook*, which would include *Accounting Guidelines, Research Studies* by professional organizations, *Abstracts of Issues Discussed* by the CICA's Emerging Issues Committee, and other accounting literature such as textbooks and journals
  - International Accounting Standards
  - standards published by bodies authorized to establish financial accounting standards in other jurisdictions (e.g., countries such as the United States and the United Kingdom).

SPECIFIC ACCOUNTING POLICIES, PRACTICES, PROCEDURES, AND RULES: THE *CICA HANDBOOK*

While a conceptual framework is an important aspect of the financial accounting environment, it does not provide specific answers to the questions of whether and how to account for something in a given circumstance. To find the answers, one must examine the particular policies, practices, procedures, and rules that govern financial accounting in Canada. In this regard, the most important source is the *CICA Handbook* (or simply the *Handbook*).

The development and publication of material governing financial accounting in the *Handbook* is the responsibility of the **Accounting Standards Board (AcSB)**, which was established by the Board of Governors of the Canadian Institute of Chartered Accountants.[22] When the *Handbook* was first published in 1968, it incorporated all CICA accounting and auditing recommendations, previously issued as *Bulletins*, which had been developed since 1946. The *Handbook* has been continuously revised and expanded since 1968.

OBJECTIVE 9
Appreciate the importance of the *CICA Handbook*, its recommendations, and the issues faced by the AcSB in developing these recommendations.

---

[22] *CICA Handbook*, Introduction to Accounting Recommendations, p. 9.

The *Handbook* is divided into various sections and subsections that cover accounting treatments for a multitude of items. Accounting issues are discussed, and acceptable accounting practice is identified in explicit recommendations. These recommendations are set out in italicized type in the *Handbook* so that they are clearly distinguished from the additional material regarding background information and general discussion.[23] The recommendations serve as Canadian **accounting standards**, which are *the rules of practice governing the content and presentation of financial statements*.[24]

The authority of the *Handbook* is based on the fact that the **Canada Business Corporations Act and provincial incorporating statutes require that financial statements be prepared in accordance with the Handbook** (see Appendix 1A for an historical perspective on this and other aspects of standard setting in Canada). A significant consequence of this legislation is that the *Handbook* recommendations effectively become the laws of Canada in terms of financial accounting standards. As these recommendations are determined by the Accounting Standards Board, which consists primarily of accountants, the Canadian accounting profession becomes, in effect, a self-regulating body (it makes up the laws that govern what it does). This privilege is unique to Canada as in other countries regulatory agencies and government bodies have a significant impact on, or are totally responsible for, the development of the legally enforceable standards related to financial statement reporting.

PIP Grant Controversy. The legal authority of the recommendations in the *CICA Handbook*, as well as the process of their development by the accounting profession, came under serious challenge in 1982. The challenger was the federal government, which had granted the power in the first place through the Canada Business Corporations Act. The issue concerned the accounting treatment of grants received by Canadian oil companies under the federal government's Petroleum Incentives Program (PIP grants). This program provided for direct incentive payments for exploration and development. The CICA's position, stated in an *Accounting Guideline* issued in February 1982, was to treat PIP grants in accordance with *Handbook* recommendations (Accounting for Government Assistance—issued in 1975). The required accounting was that PIP grants be included in income as the exploration and development efforts they financed resulted in earnings or were written off. The federal government's preference, supported by the oil companies in general, was to have the grant reflected immediately in income in the year received. Various reasons existed for taking a stance contrary to the *CICA Handbook*, not the least of which was the significantly reduced earnings of oil companies related to other provisions of the National Energy Program. The federal government very seriously considered enacting an Order-in-Council that would have resulted in it legislating an accounting standard. This action never took place, as the government eventually backed off.[25]

The PIP grant controversy provided the most serious challenge of the time to the acceptability of the Canadian accounting profession as a self-regulating and policy-setting group. Subsequent events, however, indicated that the authority of the *CICA Handbook* recommendations and the due process for developing the recommendations would not be secure.[26] In this regard, two events—bank failures in 1985 and the growing interest of the Ontario Securities Commission in accounting practices—require special attention.

Bank Failures and the Macdonald Commission. The failures of the Canadian Commercial Bank and the Northland Bank in 1985, and the subsequent judicial inquiry headed by Mr.

---

[23] *Ibid.*, p. 10.

[24] *Report of the Commission to Study the Public's Expectations of Audits* (Toronto: CICA, 1988). p. 2.

[25] Robert H. Crandall, "Government Intervention—the PIP Grant Accounting Controversy," *Cost and Management* (now called *CMA Magazine*), September-October, 1983, pp. 55-59. This article provides particular insight into the nature of events regarding the controversy and the significance of the Ontario Securities Commission's support for the *CICA Handbook* in the federal government's decision to back off.

[26] A description of the due process for determining *CICA Handbook* contents is presented in Appendix 1B.

Justice Estey, resulted in considerable concern over the adequacy and/or application of standards for financial reporting by banks in particular and other types of companies by inference. A major response of the CICA was to establish a commission (known as the Macdonald Commission, after its chairman William A. Macdonald) to study the public's expectations of audits. The Commission's report was published in June 1988.[27] Although concerned primarily with auditing, the report included several recommendations regarding the setting of accounting standards. While recognizing that there was a fairly high regard for standards thus far developed, the report noted several problems: there were many important areas not covered by standards; existing standards allowed too many acceptable alternative accounting methods that enabled wide differences in reported results for essentially identical circumstances; and due process, while important, was too slow to deal quickly with fast-emerging accounting problems. To help overcome these problems, the Commission submitted many recommendations, including that the Accounting Standards Board:

1. Make a comprehensive survey of the existing body of accounting theory, identify important issues for which accounting standards are unstated or unclear, determine priorities, and intensify its efforts to give guidance on those issues, all with a sense of real urgency.

2. Move decisively to produce necessary standards expeditiously, without sacrificing due process.

3. Sponsor a separate committee or task force to quickly express considered opinions on new accounting issues that are likely to receive divergent or unsatisfactory accounting treatment in practice in the absence of some guidance.

4. Undertake a review of GAAP to identify situations in which alternative accounting methods are accepted and make every effort to eliminate alternatives not justified by substantial differences in circumstances.

5. Ensure that in cases where support cannot be mustered for the elimination of alternatives not justified by substantial differences in circumstances, accounting standards should require enterprises to disclose that the choice of policies in this area is arbitrary and should indicate the accounting results that would have been obtained by using the alternative not chosen (at a minimum stating whether the alternative is more or less conservative than that actually adopted).

6. Study how to increase the output of its standard-setting activities. As part of this study, it should consider the possibility of obtaining additional financial support from sources other than membership fees without jeopardizing the independence of the standard-setting function.[28]

Since the Macdonald Commission's report, the AcSB has responded to several recommendations. As examples: an Emerging Issues Committee has been established to quickly provide guidance on appropriate treatment for particular and fairly specific accounting issues;[29] the standard-setting structure has been changed to enhance the effectiveness and efficiency of the standard-setting process; the AcSB now specifies a five-year plan that identifies issues to be addressed and prioritizes them for action. These and other responses to challenges put forth by the Macdonald Commission have and will

---

[27] *Report of the Commission to Study the Public's Expectations of Audits* (Toronto: CICA, 1988).

[28] *Ibid.*, pp. 139–140.

[29] The Emerging Issues Committee was established by the AcSB. It issues *Abstracts of Issues Discussed*, which report the Committee's discussion and views as to appropriate accounting practice for particular problem areas (e.g., accounting for gold loans, goodwill disclosures, revenue recognition in law firms). Over 75 *Abstracts* had been completed by 1997. The guidance in an *Abstract* is important and forceful, but it does not have the legal authority of *CICA Handbook* recommendations.

continue to contribute to the AcSB's ability to successfully develop guidance on, and standards for, accounting issues over the coming years.[30]

The Ontario and Other Provincial Securities Commissions. Another important aspect regarding development of financial accounting standards and the self-regulating nature of this task is the role assumed by Canadian regulatory bodies, particularly provincial securities commissions. Each commission is responsible for enforcing the provisions of its respective province's Securities Act, which governs, among other things, the reporting requirements of companies trading on exchanges in its province. With regard to financial statements, these Acts require adherence to *CICA Handbook* recommendations. Generally, until 1989, securities commissions carried out their duties without taking proactive action regarding the provision of financial information. In 1989, however, the Ontario Securities Commission (OSC) and the Quebec Securities Commission released new disclosure requirements for reporting issuers to provide an "Annual Information Form" and "Management Discussion and Analysis of Financial Condition and Results of Operations." Such information was intended to enhance an investor's understanding of the issuer's operations and future prospects.[31] This information was outside the scope of financial statements, but served to explain the items in these statements. In addition, the OSC undertook an annual review of a sample of the financial statements of companies under its responsibility. These reviews revealed that, in the opinion of the OSC, a number of companies were not complying with *CICA Handbook* recommendations in various parts of their financial statements.[32] While the OSC took a positive stance by consulting with companies and issuing communiqués outlining the OSC's view of appropriate application of GAAP in an attempt to reduce this noncompliance, problems remained. The OSC was concerned that it had insufficient remedies to carry out its mandate effectively. Consequently, proposals were made to change the Ontario Securities Act to increase the OSC's investigative and enforcement powers. As illustrated by the following, these powers raised some concern within the accounting profession regarding standard setting.

> Price Waterhouse says it is concerned that the OSC might use this expanded authority to "facilitate the introduction of its own requirements in respect of financial statement presentation and disclosure, instead of relying on generally accepted accounting principles as set out in the *CICA Handbook*.
>
> We do not believe that the OSC should itself bring forward accounting and disclosure standards without having those standards subject to the rigorous process of review and judgment now afforded through the CICA process. . . . The emphasis of the OSC should be on enforcement of standards rather than establishing them."[33]

While there is always the possibility that the OSC may become more involved as an accounting standard setter,[34] such action has not yet occurred in any significant way. Indeed, the OSC has been a solid supporter of *CICA Handbook* recommendations and the development process. The past success and acceptance of self-regulation for Canadian

---

[30] Within this book, the authors have drawn extensively on recommendations in the *CICA Handbook* and *Exposure Drafts* (preliminary statements that are likely to become formal *Handbook* content within a short time period) as they existed to January 1997. Given that the AcSB's work is ongoing, the reader has to be aware of revisions to standards and development of new standards subsequent to this date.

[31] *Information to be Included in the Annual Report to Shareholders*, p. 268.

[32] A summary report of an annual review's results is published in an *OSC Bulletin*. For an example of the type of deficiencies, examine Case 1-6 at the end of this chapter.

[33] See "OSC Enforcement Power Overhaul Triggers Vehement CA Response," by G. Jeffrey in *The Bottom Line*, July, 1990, p. 1.2.

[34] In the July 7, 1996 *OSC Bulletin*, a report on the results of a review of financial statements indicated disappointment in the extent to which issuers met disclosure requirements. This resulted in a general warning that taking action more like that of the Securities and Exchange Commission in the United States (which has imposed many disclosure requirements) may be the means to overcome the disappointment.

standard-setting reflects tradition and respect for the accounting profession as well as the significant amounts of time, effort, and dollars devoted to ensuring that due process takes place.

The PIP grant controversy, the bank failures that triggered the issues and recommendations from the Macdonald Commission related to standard setting, and the interest of regulators in standards and standard setting illustrate how significant problems, concerns, and pressures characterize self-regulation.

Contemporary developments have added new and compounded past sources of stress on Canadian standard-setting activities and processes. Major recent developments are related to the need for worldwide harmonized accounting standards to reflect the globalization of business operations and financial markets, the opportunities for and speed of information flow via electronic networks, and the constraints existing on financial and human resource availability. Deciding whether or not the resources allocated and process devoted to developing accounting standards will be sufficient to prove successful in the future is a critical question facing the accounting profession. The challenges will become even greater if (when) standards regarding the notions of business reporting, in their entirety, become the responsibility of accounting standard setters.

The significance of the current challenges has resulted in the establishment by the CICA of a Task Force on Standard Setting.[35] Its objective is to fully examine and make recommendations concerning the strategic position and related operational procedures and processes for Canadian action in setting standards. These recommendations will shape the nature and development of Canadian accounting standards as we enter the twenty-first century.

OTHER SOURCES OF ACCOUNTING PRACTICES

While the *CICA Handbook* is the authoritative and primary reference when deciding whether and how to account for something, it does not provide all the answers. The *Handbook* may have no recommendations regarding a particular issue, or the recommendations may not provide an explicit statement of what is acceptable in a given circumstance, or they may permit alternative acceptable ways to account for something. Consequently, the accountant must often look to other sources (which do not have the legal status of the *Handbook*) for guidance, and then exercise professional judgement when reaching a decision on particular problems and determining what constitutes acceptable presentation within the context of the conceptual framework.

There are many such sources of information. These include: generally accepted practices used by a significant number of companies in Canada;[36] consultation with other accountants and informed persons; statements issued by the CICA's Emerging Issues Committee; other publications by Canadian professional accounting organizations;[37]

OBJECTIVE 10
Appreciate why sources of GAAP other than the *CICA Handbook* must be used, identify what these sources are, and recognize the importance of professional judgement.

---

[35] The creation of the Task Force on Standard Setting had just been announced at the time of writing this book. See "A Delicate Balance" in *CA Magazine*, December, 1996, p. 3. Issues on which the Task Force will focus include harmonizing Canadian standards (initially in North America, then internationally), reviewing the CICA's role as the appropriate body for establishing Canadian standards, determining processes for developing and delivering standards with the appropriate involvement of affected groups, and funding and structuring the standard-setting process.

[36] *Financial Reporting in Canada* (Toronto: CICA) provides information on the reporting practices of 300 Canadian public companies surveyed every two years. Information resulting from surveys of particular industry practices (e.g., oil and gas, real estate) is also published by various accounting firms.

[37] For example, *Accounting Guidelines* are published from time to time by AcSC. These guidelines provide interpretation of some *Handbook* recommendations or offer guidance on particular issues (e.g., presentation and disclosure of financial forecasts) being faced by accountants. Also, the Canadian Institute of Chartered Accountants, the Certified General Accountants' Association of Canada (CGAAC), and the Society of Management Accountants of Canada (SMAC) sponsor and publish in-depth *Research Studies* on particular topics. The CGAAC, among its publications, has issued a *GAAP Guide* to assist in understanding accounting standards. While the SMAC's research program is primarily devoted to management accounting concerns, its research studies have included financial reporting aspects (e.g., on leasing and forecasts of earnings).

material in Canadian accounting journals and textbooks; International Accounting Standards; and standards published by standard-setting bodies in other countries, particularly the United States.

Even with *Handbook* recommendations and the many other sources for guidance, accountants must rely heavily on **professional judgement** when solving particular financial accounting problems. A CICA research study defined professional judgement as follows.

> The process of reaching a decision on a financial reporting issue can be described as "professional judgment" when it is analytical, based on experience and knowledge (including knowledge of one's own limitations and of relevant standards), objective, prudent and carried out with integrity and recognition of responsibility to those affected by its consequences. Such professional judgement is likely to be most valuable in complex, ill-defined or dynamic situations, especially where standards are incomplete, and should normally involve consultation with other knowledgeable people, identification of potential consequences and documentation of the analytical processes leading to the decision.[38]

Clearly, professional judgement reflects a capacity to make appropriate decisions in unfamiliar and changing situations. While knowledge of GAAP is a necessary requirement of professional judgement, an accountant's experiences, ethics, and ability to recognize the circumstances surrounding a particular situation are additional important components. Professional judgement is not something an accountant has or does not have. Rather, it is a capability of degree reflecting the type and complexity of situations the accountant can deal with and the degree to which skills have been developed in problem identification, analysis, and evaluation to reach logical and justifiable conclusions. To an extent, working through this book can be viewed as an early part of the continuous process of developing professional judgement.

OTHER ORGANIZATIONS INFLUENCING FINANCIAL ACCOUNTING IN CANADA

OBJECTIVE 11
Know the nature of organizations that influence financial accounting.

The discussion of GAAP has identified the framework (theoretical base; legally required and other sources of rules, practices, policies; and significance of professional judgement) within which Canadian financial accounting occurs. From this discussion, it is evident that many organizations have an interest in, and influence on, financial statement reporting. Illustration 1-1 depicts some of these.

While the CICA and the Accounting Standards Board have clearly played the dominant role in formulating GAAP (see Appendix 1A), other organizations have also made significant contributions. These organizations include the Society of Management Accountants of Canada (SMAC), the Certified General Accountants' Association of Canada (CGAAC), the Canadian Academic Accounting Association (CAAA), the International Accounting Standards Committee (IASC), and standard-setting bodies in other countries. The role of domestic organizations varies, but normally includes providing both input and reaction to proposals (Exposure Drafts) developed by the Accounting Standards Board. The input process usually consists of submitting written briefs for consideration by the AcSB when developing standards; and in some cases, it can include membership on the AcSB. Research activities of these organizations have also made an important contribution to accounting in Canada. Foreign organizations influence Canadian GAAP, primarily by providing their standards and other documents to serve as a source of information

---

[38] Michael Gibbins and Alister K. Mason, *Professional Judgment in Financial Reporting* (Toronto: CICA, 1988), pp. 132–133. The need for judgement, as opposed to having detailed rules, is discussed in an article by R. Skinner, "Judgment in Jeopardy," *CA Magazine*, November, 1995, pp. 14–21.

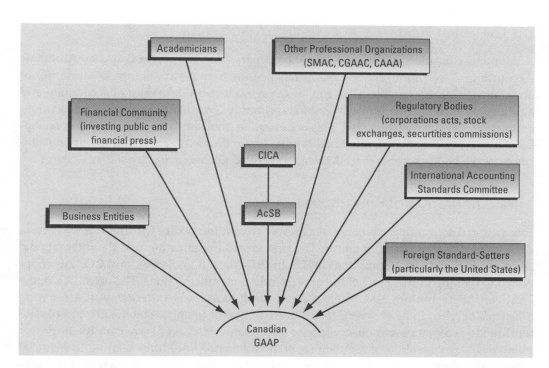

ILLUSTRATION 1-1
*Organizations Influencing
Financial Accounting
in Canada*

for the AcSB when developing and revising the *Handbook,* and as a guide for exercising professional judgement when an issue arises that is not dealt with in the *Handbook.* A brief description of these organizations is presented in the following paragraphs.

THE SOCIETY OF MANAGEMENT ACCOUNTANTS OF CANADA

As the name implies, the SMAC is the Canadian professional organization for management accountants. Its professional members (Certified Management Accountants, or CMAs) are typically employed by business organizations, although they may work for government organizations or be in public practice.[39] As preparers of management's financial statements and reports, they must be thoroughly familiar with GAAP. In addition, CMAs are responsible for providing information for management decisions. The SMAC has assumed a leadership role in providing direction regarding management accounting practices through its *Management Accounting Guidelines,* as well by conducting research on management accounting topics and frequently publishing the results as *Research Studies.* The Society also publishes a journal called *CMA Magazine,* which includes contemporary articles on issues and topics of concern to management accountants.

THE CERTIFIED GENERAL ACCOUNTANTS' ASSOCIATION OF CANADA

Professional members of the CGAAC (Certified General Accountants or CGAs) are employed by governments and industry, or may be in public practice providing accounting services and audits. The CGAAC publishes a journal called *CGA Magazine* and has established a Research Foundation to promote the study of accounting, auditing, and finance issues. Several *Research Monographs* financed by this foundation have been published. The Association has also published a *GAAP Guide* for use by Canadian professional accountants.

---

[39] A common misconception is that CAs (Chartered Accountants) are in public practice (as auditors, tax specialists, etc.), CMAs are accountants in industry, and CGAs are government accountants. While legislation in some provinces and certain stock exchanges may require some audits to be performed by CAs, it is common to find members of all three professional organizations working in industry and government as well as providing services as public accountants.

THE CANADIAN ACADEMIC ACCOUNTING ASSOCIATION

Accounting education and research are the primary concerns of the Canadian Academic Accounting Association. Since 1975, it has been active in stimulating examination of accounting education problems and in encouraging increased funding of accounting and auditing research in Canada. Membership is primarily Canadian academics, but practitioners and students are also included. This organization publishes a regular newsletter on topics of interest to Canadian accountants, studies of significance to Canadian accounting educators, and a highly respected academic journal titled *Contemporary Accounting Research*.

INTERNATIONAL ACCOUNTING BODIES

International accounting has come of age, and accounting bodies in Canada have been at the forefront of these developments. The first formal organization was the International Accounting Standards Committee (IASC). In 1973, the CICA, SMAC, and CGAAC cooperated in making Canada one of the nine founding member nations. The objectives of the IASC are to formulate and publish accounting standards (*International Accounting Standards* or *IASs*) to be observed in the presentation of financial statements; to promote worldwide acceptance and observance of these standards; and to work for the improvement and harmonization of regulations, standards, and procedures relating to financial statement reporting. The IASC member bodies have agreed to "use their best endeavours" to achieve these objectives. Section 1501 of the *CICA Handbook* formally recognizes and supports the general objective of harmonizing accounting standards.

A number of *International Accounting Standards* have been published. These standards are generally consistent with recommendations presented in the *CICA Handbook*, although some differences do exist.[40] General support for these standards is growing as evidenced by their increased use and recognition in the financial statements of Canadian corporations reporting in an international environment.

The initial success in developing international standards led to the creation of a worldwide body with broader objectives. The International Federation of Accountants (IFAC) was established in 1977. The CICA, SMAC, and CGAAC were founding members. These Canadian organizations remain very involved in the Federation's activities related to the establishment of auditing guidelines, accounting standards for the public sector (governments), and management accounting practices, and to coordinating professional codes of ethics and educational processes. All member bodies are committed to working toward "a coordinated worldwide accounting profession."

These worldwide bodies are supported by regional organizations. For Canada, the relevant bodies are the Inter-American Accounting Association (IAA) and the Confederation of Asian and Pacific Accountants (CAPA). A primary goal of these organizations is to improve liaison among accountants in the region, promote the objectives and work of the IASC and IFAC, and enhance the professional development and educational activities in the member countries. Conferences and other forms of interaction are organized regularly. The Fédération des Experts Comptables Européens (FEE) is the regional organization in Europe.

STANDARD-SETTING BODIES IN OTHER COUNTRIES

Financial statement reporting is an activity carried on throughout the world. As such, different countries face similar accounting issues. It is not uncommon for a standard-setting

---

[40] *CICA Handbook*, Section 1501, par. .02 states that the Accounting Standards Board works with the IASC to minimize the differences between *IASs* and the corresponding Canadian recommendations. The Appendix to Section 1501 summarizes where there are significant differences between *IASs* and Canadian pronouncements.

body in one country to look at what standard setters in other countries are doing, or have done, when formulating a standard to deal with the same issue. Also, practising accountants often consider the standards of other countries when making a judgement on how to account for items that are not covered in domestic standards, or when domestic standards are not sufficiently precise. When considering standards of other countries, it must be remembered that the nature of these standards (i.e., specific rules oriented to particular problems versus general guidance requiring judgement for particular problems), the due process of their development, the influence of government and regulatory bodies in their formulation, and the general political, legal, economic, and social environment differs among countries. Consequently, while a standard of another country may appear to be applicable to Canada, these differences should be considered before reaching a final conclusion.

As indicated in Appendix 1A, the accounting standards of both Britain and the United States have played a role in the development of Canadian standards and practices. In recent times, the AcSB and Canadian practitioners have particularly and carefully observed developments in the U.S. In many instances, accounting standards and practices developed in the U.S. have been adapted and then included in the *CICA Handbook*. Also, when no Canadian standard or practice is documented, practitioners often rely on U.S. pronouncements for guidance. The similarity of the economic environments of the two countries, the existence of many U.S. subsidiary companies operating in Canada, the number of Canadian companies with subsidiaries in the U.S., the close relationship between many U.S. and Canadian public accounting firms, and the number of Canadian companies listed on various U.S. stock exchanges are additional reasons for Canadians to be familiar with developments in the United States. The North American Free Trade Agreement, particularly as it applies to services such as accounting, suggests that the accounting standards of both countries as well as Mexico, will be even more closely linked in the future.

There are more standards covering more topics in the United States than in Canada. While Canadian standards have a substantial judgemental orientation, those in the U.S. tend to be more rule-oriented and are designed to resolve accounting issues on a problem-by-problem approach. This difference in orientation in part reflects differences in tradition regardings standards development and economic circumstances in the two countries. For example, corporate failures and abuses were more frequent and highly publicized in the U.S. than in Canada. This caused much more public concern and governmental inquiry into the adequacy of U.S. financial statement reporting. Consequently, more accounting standards were developed to "put out the fires" created by such concerns. The Securities and Exchange Commission (SEC) in the U.S. also acts as a very powerful regulatory body pushing for and influencing the development of accounting standards.

Since 1973, the **Financial Accounting Standards Board (FASB)** has been the private-sector body responsible for establishing and improving standards of financial accounting and reporting in the U.S.[41] The work of the FASB, particularly its *Statements of Financial Accounting Standards*, will be used in this book as a reference for guidance on how accounting issues that are not specifically covered by the *CICA Handbook* may be resolved.

---

[41] Prior to the FASB, the American Institute of Certified Public Accountants (AICPA) and its committees had been responsible for developing GAAP in the U.S. From 1939 to 1959, the AICPA's Committee on Accounting Procedures issued 51 *Accounting Research Bulletins*; from 1959 to 1973, its Accounting Principles Board issued 31 official pronouncements, called *APB Opinions*. From 1973 through 1994, the FASB issued 121 *Statements of Financial Accounting Standards*, 40 *Interpretations*, 50 *Technical Bulletins*, and six *Statements of Financial Accounting Concepts*.

THE GAP IN GAAP

Just as different countries have varying cultures and political and economic systems, their accounting standards differ. Financial reporting standards have evolved in each country in response to the demands for accounting information in that particular socio-economic environment.

International corporations have increasingly sought funding outstide of their domestic markets. To gain access to huge pools of international capital, it has frequently become necessary to seek additional listings on the world's major stock exchanges. However, a costly requirement in gaining access to international capital is often the conversion of financial information from domestic GAAP to varying foreign GAAP standards.

For example, when a number of leading German companies, including Daimler-Benz, Siemens, and Volkswagen, applied to the U.S. Securities and Exchange Commission (SEC) for a listing in the early 1990s, they were unsuccessful. They were reluctant to comply with more stringent U.S. GAAP requirements. However, the SEC believed that German accounting standards were inconsistent with those required in the U.S., and did not provide sufficient information for investor decision-making.

To (eventually) meet the requirements for a listing on the New York Stock Exchange Daimler-Benz had to prepare a second set of financial statements. In addition to reporting their financial position and results of operations according to German GAAP, financial statements had to be prepared in accordance with U.S. GAAP.

Under German GAAP, Daimler-Benz reported net income of $100(U.S.) million for 1994. For the same operating period, a conversion to U.S. GAAP resulted in a loss of $1 (U.S.) billion.

A switch to international accounting standards which are acceptable on all major stock exchanges provides for one solution.

Sources: Berton, L. "All Accountants Soon May Speak the Same Language." The Wall Street Journal, August 29, 1995, p. A15. Gumbel, P., & Steinmetz, G. "German Firms Shift to More-Open Accounting," The Wall Street Journal, March 15, 1995, pp. C1, C17.

Contributed by: Arline Savage, University of New Brunswick – St. John.

CONCLUSION

The purpose of this chapter is to provide a perspective that serves not only as a starting point for understanding financial accounting but also as a base for practising it. We have described the nature of financial accounting, the environmental factors that influence its development, the useful role it can play in influencing the environment, the importance of ethics, the basic objectives of financial statements, the overall framework (generally accepted accounting principles, or GAAP) under which financial statements are prepared, and organizations that influence financial accounting in Canada. From this description, it is evident that *accounting is a means to an end rather than an end in itself*. Because the environment within which accounting exists is constantly changing, accounting will continue to evolve in response to these changes. Indeed, continuous evolution has been a constant theme throughout the history of accounting. This evolution is understandable given the fact that generally accepted accounting principles have been developed on a piecemeal basis, and are subject to various complex, interacting, and sometimes competing influences.

Summary of Learning Objectives

1. **Define accounting and describe its essential characteristics.** Accounting is a service activity, a descriptive/analytical discipline, and an information system. The three essential characteristics of accounting are (1) identification, measurement, and communication of financial information about (2) economic entities to (3) interested persons.

2. **Identify the major financial statements and other means of financial reporting.** The financial statements most frequently provided are (1) the balance sheet; (2) the income statement; (3) the statement of cash flows (statement of changes in financial position); and (4) the statement of retained earnings. Notes and schedules cross-referenced to these statements are an integral part of such statements. Financial reporting other than financial statements may take various forms. Examples include the president's letter or supplementary schedules in the corporate annual report, prospectuses, reports filed with government agencies, news releases, management's forecasts, and descriptions of an enterprise's social or environmental impact.

3. **Describe the environment that influences financial accounting.** Financial accounting is the product of many influences and conditions. Particularly important to recognize are that: (1) people live in a world of scarce resources; (2) society's current legal and ethical concepts of property, contractual, and other rights must be respected when determining equity among varying interests; (3) in complex economic systems, some (owners and investors) entrust the custodianship of and control over property to others (managers); (4) there are many users and uses of accounting information; (5) economic activity is continuous and interdependent; (6) economic activity is conducted by separately identifiable units—business enterprises; and (7) economic resources, economic obligations, and residual interests are expressed in terms of money.

4. **Recognize the importance of accounting information and how it can influence decisions.** Accounting is a system that provides information to organizations and individuals that they can use to make decisions that reshape their environment. Because behaviour (decision making) is affected, accounting has important social consequences.

5. **Understand issues related to ethics and financial accounting.** In the performance of their professional duties, accountants are called on for moral discernment and ethical decision making. The decision is more difficult because a public consensus has not emerged to formulate a comprehensive ethical system that provides guidelines in making ethical judgements.

6. **Identify the objectives of financial statements and appreciate the importance of having objectives.** The objectives of financial statements are to provide information that is (1) useful to making investment, credit, and other decisions; (2) helpful for assessing the amounts, timing, and uncertainty of future cash flows; and (3) about enterprise resources, claims to those resources, and changes in them. Knowledge of objectives is crucial to understanding what is done in financial accounting, and why it is done.

KEY TERMS

accounting standards, 7

Accounting Standards Board (AcSB), 17

accrual accounting, 14

applied ethics, 11

business reporting, 5

conceptual framework, 16

expectations gap, 8

financial accounting, 4

financial reporting, 5

financial statements, 5

generally accepted accounting principles (GAAP), 15

general purpose financial statements, 14

management accounting, 5

professional judgement, 22

special purpose financial statements, 15

stewardship (accountability) function, 13

7. **Know what Generally Accepted Accounting Principles (GAAP) are, what they consist of, and where they are found.** Accountants prepare financial statements in accordance with generally accepted accounting principles (GAAP). GAAP encompasses not only specific rules, practices, and procedures, but also broad principles of general application, including underlying concepts. The *CICA Handbook* is the primary source of Canadian GAAP.

8. **Identify the purpose of the conceptual framework for financial accounting.** The conceptual framework consists of objectives, qualitative characteristics of information, elements of financial statements, recognition and measurement guidelines, assumptions, principles, and constraints. It serves as a guide in determining procedures, practices, and rules stipulated by standard setters, and is used by organizations (accountants) in preparing financial statements.

9. **Appreciate the importance of the *CICA Handbook*, its recommendations, and the issues faced by the AcSB in developing these recommendations.** Recommendations in the *CICA Handbook* serve as a specific reference point for identifying Canadian GAAP. These recommendations have legal authority conferred by the Canada Business Corporations Act and provincial corporations acts. Responsibility for *CICA Handbook* recommendations on financial accounting rests with the Accounting Standards Board (AcSB) of the Canadian Institute of Chartered Accountants (CICA). While the work of the AcSB is well respected, solving the problems associated with the "expectations gap" and the increasing interest of regulators in accounting standards will provide considerable challenge to the continued success of this work.

10. **Appreciate why sources of GAAP other than the *CICA Handbook* must be used, identify what these sources are, and recognize the importance of professional judgement.** While the *Handbook* is of considerable assistance, it may have no recommendations on a particular issue, may not provide an explicit statement of what is appropriate in particular circumstances, or may permit acceptable alternative ways to account for something. Therefore, other sources of GAAP must be considered. These include practice by a significant number of other Canadian companies, other publications of the CICA (*Accounting Guidelines, Research Studies*, and *Abstracts of Issues Discussed* by the Emerging Issues Committee), International Accounting Standards, standards of other countries, and articles and textbooks. Making specific accounting decisions in particular situations requires accountants to rely heavily on the exercise of professional judgement.

11. **Know the nature of organizations that influence financial accounting.** In addition to the Canadian Institute of Chartered Accountants and the AcSB, other major organizations that are interested in and have influence regarding the Canadian accounting environment are the Society of Management Accountants of Canada (SMAC), the Certified General Accountants Association of Canada (CGAAC), regulators such as the Ontario Securities Commission (OSC), and the Canadian Academic Accounting Association (CAAA). International accounting bodies, primarily the International Accounting Standards Committee (IASC) and the International Federation of Accountants (IFAC), provide organizational means through which harmonization of accounting standards in different countries is evolving. Canada has strongly supported these endeavours, and the standards developed by these groups have closely parallelled Canadian standards.

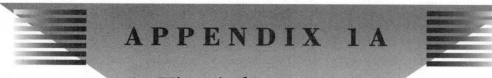

APPENDIX 1A

An Historical Perspective on Canadian Financial Accounting and Development of Accounting Standards[42]

Before the twentieth century, partnerships and small corporations formed the commercial and industrial life of Canada. From 1900 to 1920 the economy developed rapidly. Large corporations emerged, which eventually came to dominate Canadian enterprise. This period marked significant corporate legislation at both the provincial and federal levels, and the introduction of income taxes during World War I (1914–1918). Like the stock markets in other Western nations, the Canadian stock market collapsed in 1929, and the country lapsed into the long depression of the 1930s. Significant corporate legislation in 1934 and 1935 attempted to correct various real or imagined abuses. The period following World War II witnessed not only the resurgence of commercial and industrial activity, but also an increasing awareness by the accounting profession of the role it must play in Canadian life. With considerable help from professional accountants, significant improvement in corporate disclosure legislation was initiated from the mid-1950s to the mid-1960s. The importance of the contribution of the Canadian Institute of Chartered Accountants (CICA) in setting accounting standards was reflected in legislation during the 1970s.

Within the context of this overview, major events occurred on the provincial, national, and international scene. They are examined in the following paragraphs and provide an historical perspective on the interaction between accounting and its environment in Canada. Though brief, this discussion should help foster an appreciation for, and understanding of, accounting's heritage and conventions.

To 1920

The Ontario corporate legislation of 1897 and 1907, and the counterpart Canadian legislation of 1917, probably influenced that of both England and the United States with respect to the extent of financial statement disclosure required. The earlier provincial legislation of 1897 required an "income and expenditure" statement, while the later Act of 1907 required that the balance sheet be audited and that certain assets, liabilities, and equities be distinguished. The federal legislation a decade later virtually copied the Ontario Act. Various influences were at work in those early days. The financial community had been alerted by the abuses in insurance company accounting practices, the rash of bankruptcies at the beginning of World War I, and the increasing size and frequency of corporate mergers. The Income Tax Acts of 1916 and 1917 greatly influenced corporate legislation, since their application was based on financial statements that not only disclosed a great deal of information, but were also attested to by an independent professional accountant.

---

[42] This material is drawn from G.J. Murphy, "The Evolution of Corporate Reporting Practices in Canada," *The Academy of Accounting Historians Working Papers Series Volume 1* (Academy of Accounting Historians, 1979), pp. 329–368; and G.J. Murphy, "Financial Statement Disclosures and Corporate Law: The Canadian Experience," *The International Journal of Accounting*, Spring, 1980, pp. 87–99.

At the professional organization level, the Association of Accountants in Montreal, in 1880, was the first accounting association chartered in North America.[43] The Institute of Chartered Accountants of Ontario followed in 1883, and the Dominion Association of Chartered Accountants (later named the Canadian Institute of Chartered Accountants) was established in 1902. The strong influence of the Ontario Institute on the early legislation was acknowledged by the assistant provincial secretary at the time. The Dominion Association began publishing its journal, *The Canadian Chartered Accountant* (later changed to *CA Magazine*), in 1911. In those early years, much of its content consisted of reprints from British and U.S. journals.

The provincially and federally legislated disclosure requirements were probably the chief reason for the relatively high quality of the average public corporation's financial statements in Canada during this period. These requirements, together with the Income Tax Acts, served to alter the emphasis in financial accounting from the balance sheet toward the income statement, and to establish the historical cost principle of valuation.

During the last part of the 1920s, England was forced to withdraw much of its financial investment in Canada because of the war, and the gap in investment was later filled by the United States. This change in financial influence also marked a period of transition in which British influence on Canadian accounting began to wane and the U.S. influence increased.

1920 to 1945

As in most Western countries, the economy of Canada, after experiencing a steady rise in the 1920s and a stock market crash at the end of the decade, endured a severe and prolonged depression through the 1930s. The concern over abuses in corporate promotion and capitalization, accompanied by a demand for improved financial statement disclosure (much of it coming from the eminent Queen's University Professor R.G.H. Smails) prompted remedial federal legislation in 1934. The same kind of concerns in the United States gave rise to the Securities Acts of 1933 and 1934, and the creation of the Securities and Exchange Commission (SEC). In contrast to the U.S. legislation, the acts guiding Canadian companies did not attempt to set accounting standards beyond disclosure requirements, nor did they set up institutions or procedures to review annual corporate reports. The revolutionary legislation in the U.S. was mirrored in an evolutionary fashion in Canada.

During the mid-1930s, events in the United States increasingly asserted a strong influence on Canadian accounting. The SEC and the energetic American Institute of Certified Public Accountants (AICPA) began to set forward numerous recommendations on accounting and auditing matters.[44] Most of these were discussed in Canada; many were emulated through the Canadian accounting journals and later through the recommendations of the Canadian Institute of Chartered Accountants. The latter, though not prodded by an SEC, began increasingly to undertake the activities and duties of professional accounting leadership by forwarding briefs to governments, commissioning studies, and establishing research organizations. Though World War II (1939–1945) dampened

---

[43] Harvey Mann, "CAs in Canada . . . The First Hundred Years," *CA Magazine*, December, 1979, pp. 26–30. This article indicates that the Canadian accounting profession has much to be proud of, but also that there are some serious problems that require resolution.

[44] Financial accounting standards in the United States tend to be more specific, comprehensive in terms of the number of issues addressed, regulatory, and limiting than those in Canada. As a consequence, a similar item may be accounted for differently in the financial statements of companies in the two countries even if one company is controlled by that in the other country. While understanding these differences is important, there are many other reasons why accountants in Canada need to be aware of U.S. standards and the process and history of their development (as discussed in Chapter 1).

much of this activity, the CICA was able to put forward, in 1946, its first recommendations on standards of financial statement disclosure (*Bulletin #1*).

As in the United States, the rise and subsequent fall of prices in the 1920–1940 period lent heavy support to those who argued against the use of any kind of current or appraised value of assets. If value were a function of income, current or appraisal values could be ignored. The emphasis was on the income statement and the objectivity of historical cost for valuation purposes. This emphasis clearly reinforced what had emerged in the first two decades of the century.

1945 to 1965

This period was relatively quiet, affording the opportunity to make much progress at the professional and legislative levels. Though the traditional sources of influence for change continued with steady pressure, there were no important or well-publicized instances of corporate malfeasance or financial reporting inadequacies. In the United States, the AICPA and the watchful SEC put forth a profusion of auditing and accounting recommendations, all of which were carefully scrutinized in Canada. Since the British profession and legislation were far less active, events in the United States continued to be much more important to Canadian observers.

At the professional level, the Institutes of Chartered Accountants of Quebec in 1946 and of Ontario in 1962 secured for their members the exclusive auditing right for public corporations. The publication of accounting and auditing recommendations, which began with *Bulletin #1* in 1946, continued as a series through 1968. These recommendations became the common standards for financial reporting in Canada.

The financial statement disclosure provisions of the Ontario Corporations Act of 1953 were a virtual copy of this first Institute *Bulletin* and the briefs of the Institute of Chartered Accountants of Ontario. As in 1907, this provincial legislation became the direct model for federal legislation approximately a decade later, in 1964–1965. The Ontario Securities Act of 1965 gave to the Ontario Securities Commission ongoing surveillance responsibilities of the Toronto Stock Exchange. Though this Commission has powers relating to financial statement disclosure and practices not dissimilar to those of the American SEC, it has not promulgated its own set of accounting standards. However, it has set up a process for the review of corporate annual reports, and has established annual reporting requirements that are outside the scope of financial statements.

1965 to 1980

Coinciding in time with the legislative approval of the Ontario Securities Act of 1965 and the Canada Corporations Act of 1964–1965—but otherwise unrelated—was a major scandal that broke upon the Canadian financial scene. The fall of the Atlantic Acceptance Company Limited, and several other companies in its wake, was of grave concern to the investing public, various legislatures, and the accounting profession. This type of concern was of much greater proportions in the United States, where instances of corporate scandals and legal suits against auditors abounded and resulted in several Congressional and professional inquiries. These inquiries led to such significant documents as the Metcalf Report, the Moss Report, the Wheat Report, and the Cohen Report. In 1973 the Financial Accounting Standards Board (FASB) was formed as a body independent of the AICPA to establish accounting principles. All of these events in the United States were closely observed by the Canadian profession. Other important influences of the United States on the Canadian scene were the existence of numerous U.S. subsidiary corporations in Canada, the close relationship between many U.S. and Canadian public accounting firms, and the fact that many Canadian corporations were listed on U.S. stock exchanges.

Two important differences between the United States and Canada may help to explain the different responses of the U.S. and Canadian professions during this time period. First, there were many instances of corporate abuse in the United States, while only one (the Atlantic Acceptance debacle) stands out in Canada. Second, the prestige of—and longstanding respect for—the traditions of the accounting profession were much greater in Canada. By comparison, events in Canada and the responses they drew were far more subdued.

In 1968, all CICA accounting and auditing recommendations were reorganized into the *CICA Handbook*. Revisions were facilitated through continuous updating. In 1969, auditors were required to disclose departure from recommended accounting standards. Of much greater significance, however, was a little-heralded event in 1972 in which *National Policy No. 27* of the Canadian Securities Commission, in its concern for uniformity and disclosure inadequacies, required that the *CICA Handbook* be used to determine generally accepted accounting principles. This requirement was quickly incorporated into the Canada Business Corporations Act of 1975 and the Ontario Securities Act of 1978. Legislative deference to the expertise of the Accounting Research Committee (renamed the Accounting Standards Committee in 1982 and replaced by the Accounting Standards Board in 1991) of the CICA was complete. With this legislation the setting of the laws of the country with regard to financial accounting standards and disclosure became the unique task of this body.

1980 TO PRESENT

The discussion in Chapter 1 highlights significant events during this period. These events included the PIP grant controversy, the failure of the Canadian Commercial Bank and the Northland Bank, the Estey judicial inquiry, the Macdonald Commission report, and the growing interest of regulators in financial statement reporting standards. A consequence of these events is an increasing concern for financial statement reporting, standards for reporting, and the process for—and self-regulatory nature of—setting standards. As stated in the chapter, the AcSB has taken actions to alleviate these concerns. The heavy responsibility placed upon it to meet these challenges demands an ever-increasing devotion of time and resources, and any perceived failure may discredit the self-regulating nature of the accounting profession.

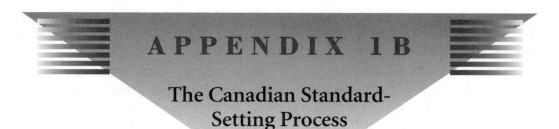

APPENDIX 1B

The Canadian Standard-Setting Process

The *CICA Handbook's* content regarding financial accounting is developed by the Accounting Standards Board (AcSB). The structure of this committee and its operating procedures have helped to ensure the exercise of due process when formulating the *Handbook* recommendations. This appendix is intended to help readers understand and appreciate the formal process that generates the legal, authoritative policies, practices, procedures, and rules of Canadian GAAP.

The AcSB consists of 13 appointed voting members. These appointees have a broad range of backgrounds and experience in public accounting, industry, commerce, finance, and post-secondary education. Persons in other occupations such as government service, law, and economics may also be appointed. At least two-thirds of the voting members must be members of the Canadian Institute of Chartered Accountants. In addition to Institute appointees, one member can be appointed by each of: the Canadian Council of Financial Analysts; the Financial Executives Institute of Canada; the Canadian Academic Accounting Association; the Certified General Accountants Association of Canada; and the Society of Management Accountants of Canada. Nonvoting members from the CICA staff are the Senior Vice-President, Studies and Standards, and the Accounting Standards Director.

As a matter of philosophy, the AcSB is concerned with the approval of matters of principle and policy when developing recommendations for inclusion in the *CICA Handbook*. As such, it delegates the work regarding the development of standards to task forces or research staff at the CICA.

Given this structure, the various stages in the process of formulating *CICA Handbook* recommendations are as follows.

1. To initiate the process, a formal **proposal** must be approved by the AcSB. While suggested projects are primarily identified by the Board or its support staff, any interested party may submit proposals.

2. Once a proposal is approved by the AcSB, it is assigned to a Task Force and/or staff who discuss and debate the issues and then agree on a **Statement of Principles**, which is then presented to the AcSB. The Statement of Principles identifies the issues, provides analysis, and states the direction that any recommendations are likely to take.

3. Given the AcSB's approval to continue, the Task Force will then be responsible for preparation of an **Exposure Draft**. This document presents the proposed contents of a new section or an amendment to an existing section of the *Handbook*.

4. After approval by the AcSB, the Exposure Draft is published in the *CA Magazine* and becomes a public document available to all interested persons or organizations. The purpose of issuing an Exposure Draft is to solicit public input on the proposed accounting recommendations. Providing the opportunity for anyone to comment is a crucial part of the due process for determining the recommendations in the *Handbook*.

KEY TERMS

Exposure Draft, 33
proposal, 33
Re-exposure Draft, 34
Statement of Principles, 33

5. The Task Force considers this public input to the Exposure Draft when preparing a submission to the AcSB for adding recommendations to, or revising an existing part of, the *Handbook*.

6. If the Task Force's recommendations are approved by the AcSB for inclusion in the *Handbook*, they are distributed to all members of the Institute, other *Handbook* subscribers, and other persons expressing interest. Unless otherwise stated, these recommendations become effective for inclusion in financial statements relating to fiscal years beginning on or after the first of the month that is noted beside the recommendation. The AcSB may determine that the final proposed recommendations are sufficiently different from those in the Exposure Draft and, accordingly, decide that a **Re-exposure Draft** is necessary to obtain additional public feedback. In such cases, the process would revert to the publication in the *CA Magazine* stage.

At any stage in the process, the AcSB could decide to discontinue a project.

While there is oversimplification in this description, it is evident that a very conscientious, thorough, and time-consuming effort is put into the development of *CICA Handbook* recommendations.[45] Indeed, given the complexity of issues addressed by the AcSB and the careful attention paid to the commitment for having a due process, it usually takes more than a year to develop and approve major recommendations.

Note: All *asterisked* Concept Review questions or Cases relate to material covered in an appendix to the chapter.

CONCEPT REVIEW

1. What is accounting?
2. Differentiate broadly between financial accounting and managerial accounting.
3. Differentiate between financial statements, financial reporting, and business reporting.
4. Name several environmental conditions that shape financial accounting to a significant extent.
5. Accounting is an unchanging discipline independent of its environment and other influences. Comment.
6. Why is it important to measure performance reliably and fairly when productive resources are privately owned?
7. Provide some examples of how accounting information influences its environment.
8. What are the major objectives of financial statements?
9. How are financial accountants challenged in their work to make ethical decisions? Is technical mastery of GAAP not sufficient in the practice of financial accounting?
10. What significant steps might one apply in the process of moral discernment and ethical decision making?
11. How are current legal and ethical standards related to the basic nature of accounting?
12. What is the "expectations gap?" What is the profession doing to try to close this gap?
13. What is the likely limitation of general purpose financial statements?
14. If you had to explain or define generally accepted accounting principles to a nonaccountant, what would you include in your explanation? Why are generally accepted accounting principles important?
15. What are the sources of pressure that change and influence the development of Canadian GAAP?
16. Of what value is a common set of standards in financial accounting and reporting?
17. What are the "recommendations" in the *CICA Handbook*? What is the significance of these recommendations to financial accounting? Who has the responsibility for developing *CICA Handbook* recommendations for financial accounting?

---

[45] John Denman, "From Committee to Board: A Review of the AcSC's Final Years and a Look at the Future with the New ASB," *CA Magazine*, February, 1992, pp. 66–70. This article provides a more in-depth look at the AcSB and identifies advantages anticipated from its structure and process relative to its predecessor, the AcSC.

18. Why is professional judgement necessary in financial accounting?

19. The Canada Business Corporations Act requires that the *CICA Handbook* be used to determine generally accepted accounting principles for financial statement reporting of companies incorporated federally. Explain the significance of this in terms of the apparent role the federal government has delegated to the Accounting Standards Board. How well has the AcSB performed this role? Do you think there is the possibility of having governmental agencies taking over the role of setting accounting standards in Canada? Would such a situation be favourable or unfavourable to the accounting profession?

20. Indicate what is meant by CICA, SMAC, and CGAAC. Identify the differences between these organizations in terms of their role in developing financial accounting standards and in terms of what their professional members do.

21. Explain the role of the Emerging Issues Committee in establishing generally accepted accounting principles.

22. A number of foreign countries have reporting standards different from those in Canada. Give some reasons to explain why reporting standards are often different among countries.

23. Most incorporated companies prepare financial statements in accordance with GAAP. Why then is there concern about fraudulent financial reporting?

*24. In 1972 the Canadian Securities Commission issued its *National Policy No. 27*, which had significant implications for financial statement reporting. What did *National Policy No. 27* state, and what were its implications?

*25. What is an Exposure Draft, and what role does it play in developing *CICA Handbook* recommendations?

*26. Under what circumstances may a Re-exposure Draft be issued?

C A S E S

At the completion of the Wildwood Co. Ltd.'s audit, the president, Lee Watkins, asked you about the meaning of the phrase "in conformity with generally accepted accounting principles" that appears in the audit report on the management's financial statements. She observes that the meaning of the phrase must include more than what she thinks of as "principles."   **C1-1**

Instructions

(a) Explain the meaning of the term "generally accepted accounting principles" as used in the audit report.

(b) Lee Watkins wants to know how you determine whether or not an accounting principle is generally accepted. Discuss the sources of evidence for determining whether an accounting principle has substantial authoritative support.

(c) Lee Watkins believes that differences in accounting practice will always exist between independent business entities despite continual development of "principles" to improve comparability. Discuss the arguments that *support* her belief.

Some argue that having organizations establish accounting principles is wasteful and inefficient. In place of mandatory accounting standards, each company could voluntarily disclose the type of information it considers important. If an investor wants additional information, the investor could contact the company and pay to receive the information desired.   **C1-2**

Instructions

Comment on the appropriateness of this viewpoint.

Presented below are three models for setting accounting standards.   **C1-3**

1. The purely political approach, where national legislative action decrees accounting standards.

2. The private, professional approach, where financial accounting standards are set only by private professional actions.

3. The public/private mixed approach where, even though a governmental agency has the ultimate power to establish standards, the standards are basically set by private sector bodies that behave as though they were public (quasi-governmental) agencies.

Instructions

(a) Which of these models best describes standard-setting in Canada? Justify your answer.

(b) The federal government came close to legislating an accounting practice during the PIP grant controversy. Why would such an action have had tremendous consequences regarding Canadian accounting if it had been carried out? Speculate as to why the federal government wished to set its own standard that was contradictory to that of the *CICA Handbook*.

(c) Why do managers and accountants in companies, public accountants, financial analysts, labour unions, industry trade associations, and others take an active interest in standard-setting?

C1-4   Some individuals have suggested that the AcSB needs to be more cognizant of the economic consequences when it creates its pronouncements. For example, the president of Vox Haul Ltd. believes that small companies like his should not have to follow the same accounting standards as large companies.

Instructions

Discuss the president's comment indicating arguments for and against separate standards for small businesses.

(CICA adapted)

C1-5   Prior to its breakup, the Soviet Union had four distinct monetary units, each bearing the name "ruble." The first, sometimes called the "accounting ruble," was employed for budgetary purposes. The second, frequently called the "paper ruble," was used for payroll and for all transactions such as sales in public stores. The third, known as the "Comecon ruble," was used exclusively to account for transactions with the Comecon countries of the Eastern bloc. And the fourth, sometimes called the "gold ruble," was used for foreign trade transactions in hard currencies. The most striking aspect of the currency situation is that these four rubles were not exchangeable or transferable. Yet these rubles could be added together in providing financial information to a total of undefined Soviet rubles.

Instructions

(a) Speculate as to how this type of environment might affect accounting.

(b) How does the environment in Canada influence our accounting and reporting practices?

C1-6   The following excerpts are taken from a report in The Bottom Line (December, 1988, p. 6), which appeared under the headline "OSC Appalled at Number of Deficient Financial Reports." (While the OSC conducts an annual survey, the following refers to the results of its first survey, which are considered at this stage of the text because they are targeted at a more general level of accounting issues.)

> TORONTO: In its first-ever review of a random sample of 250 financial reports, the Ontario Securities Commission has found 25% of those reports deficient in some way. According to OSC Chief Accountant Michael Meagher, "the frequency and serious nature of some of the problems identified are a cause of concern."
>
> The review, initiated more than a year ago, will now become an annual exercise, with the objective being to "monitor trends in financial reporting," "challenge questionable accounting" and "identify emerging issues and innovative transactions." Companies for the review will be chosen at random, but will generally be public companies listed on the Toronto Stock Exchange. Meagher says the project was launched because the information contained in annual reports and financial statements is so important to the marketplace—for investment decision-making purposes, for example—"that we wanted to have a more detailed look at it to ensure that the financial reporting is of the type we want to have and to challenge presentations that clearly do not adhere to professional standards."

The following were some of the major concerns reported in the story:

• Departures from generally accepted accounting principles because of personal disagreement with the *CICA Handbook* or because of a preference for alternative accounting treatments. According to the OSC, "a departure (from GAAP) is appropriate only where compliance with a particular *Handbook* recommendation would result in misleading financial statements."

• In October 1987, the OSC published a notice encouraging issuers to consult with OSC staff on difficult or unusual financial reporting issues as far in advance of filing as possible. Apparently, this is not always done even though it reduces the risk of uncovering problems late in the process, which in turn incurs costs of preparing and distributing revised material to shareholders.

- Selective application of U.S. accounting principles when there is no well-established guidance available in Canada. The problem is that companies are using those parts of U.S. treatment that suit their purposes and rejecting the parts that do not. "However, U.S. GAAP does not automatically become Canadian GAAP and careful judgment is required to determine if use of a particular U.S. GAAP treatment is appropriate," says the report. "This can produce results that would not be acceptable in the U.S. and, therefore, cannot be said to have authoritative support. Furthermore, comparisons with companies that do apply the particular treatment in its entirety may be misleading."

- Defective disclosure in the notes that accompany financial statements. "Ambiguous wording or omission of relevant information makes it difficult to understand the nature of a transaction and the related accounting treatment," says the report. Moreover, "in some cases, a poorly worded note has given the impression that an accounting treatment was inappropriate or contrary to a *Handbook* requirement when such was not the case."

The following are some comments reported in the story:

- Meagher points out that, in all instances where deficiencies or problems were identified, the OSC communicated with the company in question to discuss what kind of corrective action should be taken. This could include greater disclosure in the financial statements, changes in the way information is presented, or accounting differently in the future.

- Meagher admits he was surprised at the high percentage of reports found unacceptable in the review. He finds this underscores the need for this review program. "By identifying problem areas, we should be able to bring about much-needed improvements in financial reporting."

Instructions

(a) Does this report condemn the work of the AcSB and the resulting accounting standards it develops for inclusion in the *CICA Handbook*?

(b) What conclusions and implications do you draw from this report regarding: enforcement of adherence to GAAP; the OSC's offer to help companies resolve difficult issues; exercising professional judgement in the absence of *Handbook* recommendations; and communication skills of accountants and management regarding disclosures?

C1-7 Adrian Lang recently entered the wholesale business by forming a limited company. He had rented warehouse space, bought inventory, and made sales and deliveries over a period of several months. His inventory management was of significant importance to the likely success of his business and he maintained a record of the purchases made. Because the purchases were made at varying quantities and unit prices, he became quite confused as to how the inventory should be valued for purposes such as pricing decisions, insurance coverage, renewing a bank loan, preparing financial statements, and determining income tax obligations.

Having taken a basic bookkeeping course, he understood that the *CICA Handbook* was the primary source for generally accepted accounting principles in Canada. He obtained the *Handbook*, expecting it to provide him with clear-cut answers as to how the inventory should be valued in order to satisfy his purposes. He was rather disappointed in what he read. Several methods for inventory valuation were identified as being generally acceptable, but none was recommended as the one to uniquely satisfy his needs.

That evening he met his friend Darla, a professional accountant, at a reception. He indicated his dilemma and frustration with the *Handbook* during their conversation. She understood his problem and began her answer by referring to the need for accountants to exercise professional judgement when deciding on solutions to particular accounting problems. The discussion continued for the rest of the reception.

Instructions

(a) What, in your opinion, is meant by the phrase "professional judgement?"

(b) Given that GAAP, as expressed in the *CICA Handbook*, is to establish acceptable financial accounting principles and practices, why is professional judgement important?

(c) What factors would you consider to be particularly important if you were to recommend to Adrian Lang how the inventory should be valued?

C1-8 While there is a generally high regard for *CICA Handbook* recommendations (standards) and the process for their development, criticisms also exist. For example, the Macdonald Commission Report noted the following sources of dissatisfaction: various issues were not covered; there were many acceptable alternatives, thus permitting wide differences in reported results for seemingly identical circumstances; the process for developing standards was slow; and there was an inability to deal quickly with fast-emerging issues.

In response to these and other criticisms, some have suggested that the Canadian accounting profession (i.e., through the AcSB) should get out of the standard-setting business and that Canadian financial statements should simply be prepared by following the standards developed by the Financial Accounting Standards Board in the United States.

Instructions

Provide a list of arguments to support the suggestion that Canadians simply adopt U.S. standards. Provide a list of arguments against this suggestion.

C1-9   Michael Sharpe, as the Deputy Chairman of the International Accounting Standards Committee, made the following comments before the FEI's 63rd Annual Conference:

There is an irreversible movement towards the harmonization of financial reporting throughout the world. The international capital markets require an end to:

1.   The confusion caused by international companies announcing different results depending on the set of accounting standards applied.

2.   Companies in some countries obtaining unfair commercial advantages from the use of particular national accounting standards.

3.   The complications in negotiating commercial arrangements for international joint ventures caused by different accounting requirements.

4.   The inefficiency of international companies having to understand and use a myriad of different accounting standards depending on the countries in which they operate and the countries in which they raise capital and debt. Executive talent is wasted on keeping up-to-date with numerous sets of accounting standards and the never-ending changes to them.

5.   The inefficiency of investment managers, bankers and financial analysts as they seek to compare financial reporting drawn up in accordance with different sets of accounting standards.

6.   Failure of many stock exchanges and regulators to require companies subject to their jurisdiction to provide comparable, comprehensive and transparent financial reporting frameworks giving international comparability.

7.   Difficulty for developing countries and countries entering the free market economy such as China and Russia in accessing foreign capital markets because of the complexity of, and differences between, national standards.

8.   The restriction on the mobility of financial service providers across the world as a result of different accounting standards.

Clearly the elimination of these inefficiencies by having comparable high quality financial reporting used across the world would benefit international businesses.

Instructions

(a)   What is the International Accounting Standards Committee?

(b)   What stakeholders might benefit from the use of International Accounting Standards?

(c)   What do you believe are some of the major obstacles to harmonization?

USING YOUR JUDGEMENT

FINANCIAL REPORTING PROBLEM

Assume that you work in the investment department of a major corporation and that you have been charged with investing $1,000,000 of the company's money as an intermediate-term investment (3-5 years). Further assume that you have been approached by an investment firm to either loan money to or purchase the common shares of one of the investment firm's clients.

Instructions

(a) Identify the objectives you would have as a creditor or investor in the investment firm's client. For example, how does a creditor get a return from making a loan? How does the investor in common shares get a return on his or her investment?

(b) Generate a list of as many information items as you can that should be considered regarding the investment of $1,000,000 in *any* company. Mention any item that would be useful in making such a decision. Once the list is completed, try to narrow it down to the five most important items. Identify the information items that are found in the financial statements. Where can information on the remaining items be found?

(c) In light of the lists generated concerning the information items that are important and where they can be found, what rules or regulations would you require concerning the quality, content, and scope of the information? That is, what qualities of this information would make it more useful in your investment decision?

(d) Does information found in financial statements have these qualities? What is the role of accounting standards for ensuring that information is useful to decision-makers?

ETHICS CASE

When the AcSB issues new recommendations for the *CICA Handbook*, the recommendations are usually effective for inclusion in financial statements relating to fiscal years beginning on or after the first of the month in which the recommendations were published in the *Handbook*. Earlier implementation is encouraged. Leslie Rath, controller, discusses with her financial vice-president the need for early implementation of a recommendation that would result in a fairer presentation of the company's financial condition and earnings. When the financial vice-president determines that early implementation of the recommendation will adversely affect the reported net income for the year, he discourages Leslie from implementing the recommendation until it is required.

Instructions

(a) What, if any, is the ethical issue involved in this case?

(b) Is the financial vice-president acting improperly or immorally?

(c) What does Leslie have to gain by advocating early implementation?

(d) Who might be affected by the decision against early implementation?   (CMA adapted)

chapter 2

THE CONCEPTUAL FRAMEWORK UNDERLYING FINANCIAL ACCOUNTING

NATURE OF A CONCEPTUAL FRAMEWORK

DEVELOPMENT OF A CONCEPTUAL FRAMEWORK

FIRST LEVEL: BASIC OBJECTIVES

SECOND LEVEL: FUNDAMENTAL CONCEPTS

QUALITATIVE CHARACTERISTICS OF ACCOUNTING INFORMATION

BASIC ELEMENTS OF FINANCIAL STATEMENTS

THIRD LEVEL: RECOGNITION AND MEASUREMENT GUIDELINES

SUMMARY OF THE CONCEPTUAL FRAMEWORK

The Conceptual Framework Underlying Financial Accounting

Learning Objectives

After studying this chapter, you should be able to:

1. Describe what a conceptual framework is and understand its usefulness.

2. Appreciate the nature of the development of a conceptual framework in Canada.

3. Understand the objectives of financial statement reporting.

4. Identify the qualitative characteristics of accounting information.

5. Define the basic elements of financial statements.

6. Understand the meaning of recognition and measurement.

7. Describe the basic assumptions of accounting.

8. Explain the application of the basic principles of accounting.

9. Describe the impact that constraints have on reporting accounting information.

A large body of challenging theory exists in accounting. Philosophical objectives, normative theories, interrelated concepts, precise definitions, and rationalized rules constitute a "conceptual framework." While many people are unaware of accounting's conceptual framework, its existence and use explain accounting's designation as a truly professional discipline. ***Thus, accountants*** (*as opposed to bookkeepers or clerks*) ***philosophize, theorize, judge, create, and deliberate as a significant part of their professional activity***. Carrying out these subjective (as opposed to technical) aspects of accounting are critical to current accounting practice and are reflected in the decisions made regarding what is to be included in financial statements, how what is to be included is measured, and how information is to be disclosed.

The conceptual framework for financial accounting is not a description of fundamental truths and axioms, as is found in the natural sciences. ***Accounting theory is not something that is discovered; it is created, developed, or decreed based on environmental factors, intuition, authority, and acceptability***. Because the theoretical framework of accounting is difficult to substantiate with objectivity or through experimentation, arguments concerning it can degenerate into quasi-religious dogmatism. As a result, the sanction for and credibility of accounting theory rests upon its general recognition and acceptance by preparers, auditors, regulators, and users of financial statements. The purpose of this chapter is to examine the nature and usefulness of a conceptual framework for financial accounting, and then progress with an identification and discussion of each of its components.

NATURE OF A CONCEPTUAL FRAMEWORK

A **conceptual framework** for financial accounting is "a coherent system of interrelated objectives and fundamentals that can lead to consistent standards and that prescribes the nature, function, and limits of financial accounting and financial statements."[1] It is like a constitution in that it establishes a framework for doing things in a particular way, is subject to debates, and leads to the establishment of laws.

OBJECTIVE 1
Describe what a conceptual framework is and understand its usefulness.

Why is a conceptual framework necessary? First, to be useful, standard setting should build on and relate to an established body of concepts and objectives. A sound conceptual framework should *enable the development and issuance of a coherent, consistent, and useful set of standards and practices* because they will be built upon the same foundation.

Second, new and emerging *practical problems can be more quickly solved by reference to a framework of basic theory*. For example, unique types of financial instruments have been issued by companies since the 1980s: shared appreciation mortgages (debt in which the lender receives equity participation); deep discount bonds (debt with no stated interest rate); and commodity-backed bonds (debt that may be repaid in a commodity). As a specific illustration, Sunshine Mining (a silver mining company) sold two issues of bonds that it would redeem either with $1,000 in cash or 50 ounces of silver, whichever was worth more at maturity. Both bond issues were due in 15 years from issuance and both had a low stated interest rate when they were sold. At what amounts should the bonds have been recorded by Sunshine or the buyers of the bonds? If the bond redemption payments may be made in silver, the future value of which is currently unknown, what is the amount of the premium or discount on the bonds and how should it be amortized?

It is difficult, if not impossible, for the Accounting Standards Board (AcSB) to prescribe the appropriate accounting treatment quickly for situations like this. Practising accountants, however, must resolve such problems on a day-to-day basis. Through the exercise of professional judgement and with the help of an accepted conceptual framework, practitioners are able to dismiss certain alternatives quickly because they fall outside the conceptual framework, and focus instead on the logical and acceptable treatment within the framework.

Third, a conceptual framework should *increase financial statement users' understanding of and confidence in financial reporting*. Fourth, such a framework should *enhance comparability among different companies' financial statements*. Similar events and phenomena should be similarly accounted for and reported; a different approach should be used to account for and report dissimilar events.

DEVELOPMENT OF A CONCEPTUAL FRAMEWORK

Although a theoretical base for financial accounting has existed implicitly in Canada and has been part of education and training for accountants for some time, it was not formally codified in Canadian literature and professional pronouncements until the 1980s. Components of the codified theory were drawn largely from U.S. publications. While

---

[1] "Conceptual Framework for Financial Accounting and Reporting: Elements of Financial Statements and Their Measurement," *FASB Discussion Memorandum* (Stamford, Conn.: FASB, 1976), page 1 of the "Scope and Implications of the Conceptual Framework Project" section. This definition is adopted in *Conceptual Framework for Financial Reporting* (Vancouver: The Accounting Standards Authority of Canada, 1987), p. CF-vii.

many classic U.S. studies existed,[2] it was the work of the Financial Accounting Standards Board (FASB) that contributed the most to the development of a Canadian conceptual framework, and to a similar endeavour by the International Accounting Standards Committee (IASC).[3]

In 1976, the FASB issued a Discussion Memorandum titled *Conceptual Framework for Financial Accounting and Reporting: Elements of Financial Statements and Their Measurement.* It set forth the following major issues and related questions that needed to be addressed in order to establish a basic framework for resolving financial reporting controversies.

1. **Establish the objectives of financial statements**. For what purposes are financial statements intended? To whom should they be directed? What information should be included? What are the limitations of financial statements?

2. **Determine the essential qualitative characteristics of financial statement information**. What qualities (e.g., relevance, reliability, and comparability) make accounting information useful to financial statement readers and what are the appropriate trade-offs when conflicts occur between these characteristics (e.g., relevance versus reliability)?

3. **Define the basic elements of accounting**. What is an asset, liability, revenue, or expense? Are some of these elements more important than others in determining net income? For example, should net income be defined in terms of changes in an enterprise's net assets (excluding capital transactions) over a period of time, or should assets and liabilities be determined only after revenues, expenses, and net income are defined?

4. **Determine the basis of measurement**. Even after the basic elements are developed, how should they be measured? For example, should historical cost, replacement cost, current selling price, expected cash flows, present value of expected cash flows, or some other valuation system be used to measure an asset?

5. **Resolve how to treat a change in the measuring unit**. Should the basic measuring unit of accounting be adjusted for changes in the purchasing power of the dollar, should these changes be ignored, or should information on a supplementary basis be presented?

The FASB then devoted considerable financial and human resources to developing five *Statements of Financial Accounting Concepts* (*SFACs*) to address these issues.[4] The results served as a foundation for the subsequent development of formal "concepts" or "framework" documents in Canada, other countries, and by the IASC.

---

[2] Perhaps the most significant U.S. documents in this area were: Maurice Moonitz, *Accounting Research Study No. 1:* "The Basic Postulates of Accounting" (New York: AICPA, 1961); Robert T. Sprouse and Maurice Moonitz, *Accounting Research Study No. 3:* "A Tentative Set of Broad Accounting Principles for Business Enterprises" (New York: AICPA, 1962); *APB Statement No. 4:* "Basic Concepts and Accounting Principles Underlying Financial Statements of Business Enterprises" (New York: AICPA, 1970).

[3] *Framework for the Preparation and Presentation of Financial Statements* (London, England: International Accounting Standards Committee, 1989).

[4] *SFAC No. 1*, "Objectives of Financial Reporting by Business Enterprises," presented the goals and purposes of accounting (November, 1978). *SFAC No. 2*, "Qualitative Characteristics of Accounting Information," examined the characteristics that make accounting information useful (May, 1980). *SFAC No. 3*, "Elements of Financial Statements of Business Enterprises," provided definitions of items that financial statements comprise, such as assets, liabilities, revenues, and expenses (December, 1980). *SFAC No. 5*, "Recognition and Measurement in Financial Statements of Business Enterprises," set forth fundamental recognition criteria and guidance on what information should be formally incorporated into financial statements, how the information is to be quantified, and when it should be reported (January, 1985). *SFAC No. 6*, "Elements of Financial Statements" replaced *SFAC No. 3* and expanded its scope to include not-for-profit organizations (December, 1985). The FASB also issued *SFAC No. 4*, "Objectives of Financial Reporting by Nonbusiness Organizations," that related to nonbusiness organizations (December, 1980).

OBJECTIVE 2
Appreciate the nature of the development of a conceptual framework in Canada.

A 1980 CICA research study titled *Corporate Reporting: Its Future Evolution* was the first major document to address the question of a uniquely Canadian conceptual framework.[5] The study's major contribution was its discussion of objectives relating to users and how to meet their needs, and suggestions for criteria to be used in developing financial reporting standards. Subsequently, a document titled *Conceptual Framework for Financial Reporting* was published in 1987 to assist in standard setting, provide a basis for academic discussion and student education, and help preparers of financial reports.[6] In December 1988, Section 1000 on "Financial Statement Concepts" was added to the *CICA Handbook* for use in developing accounting standards, and for helping financial statement preparers and auditors exercise their professional judgement regarding the application of standards and the derivation of practices where standards are not yet developed.[7]

While these documents are written with the tradition and environment of Canadian financial accounting in mind, they closely paralleled the various conclusions of the SFACs issued by the FASB. Given the similarities of the two countries in terms of thinking about a conceptual framework, and the fact that the FASB devoted much time, effort, and resources to its work, this consistency is not surprising.

The Canadian, U.S., and IASC developments provide a solid base for defining and understanding current thinking regarding a conceptual framework.[8] They have therefore been drawn upon extensively in developing this chapter.

The framework is presented in order to provide an understanding of the underlying perspective from which accounting standards are, and will be, established. Furthermore, from the point of view of a preparer of financial information, awareness of this framework provides guidance when choosing what to present in reports, which approach to use when representing economic events, and how such information should be communicated. Finally, this framework is useful to those who use financial statement information because it helps increase their understanding of both the usefulness and the limitations of such information.

Illustration 2-1 provides an overview of the conceptual framework.[9] At the first level are the **objectives** that identify the goals and purposes of accounting and form the cornerstones for the conceptual framework. At the second level are the **qualitative characteristics** that make accounting information useful, along with the **elements** of financial statements (assets, liabilities, etc.). At the third level are the **recognition and measurement guidelines** that are used in establishing and applying accounting standards. These recognition and measurement guidelines encompass the **assumptions, principles,** and **constraints** that describe the present reporting environment.

FIRST LEVEL: BASIC OBJECTIVES

OBJECTIVE 3
Understand the objectives of financial statement reporting.

As discussed in Chapter 1, the objectives of financial statement reporting are to provide information that is (1) useful for making investment, credit, and other decisions; (2) helpful for assessing the amounts, timing, and uncertainty of future cash flows; and (3) about enterprise resources, claims to those resources, and changes in them.

---

[5] *Corporate Reporting: Its Future Evolution* (Toronto: CICA, 1980).

[6] *Conceptual Framework for Financial Reporting* (Vancouver: The Accounting Standards Authority of Canada, 1987), p. CF-vii.

[7] *CICA Handbook* (Toronto: CICA), Section 1000.

[8] Canadian documents (including Section 1000 of the *CICA Handbook*), SFACs in the United States, and the IASC's framework statement were written with the intent of providing information to standard setters, preparers, auditors, and others that would be useful when carrying out their functions. A conceptual framework does not change existing standards or have the authority of a *Handbook* recommendation.

[9] Adapted from William C. Norby, *The Financial Analysts Journal*, March-April, 1982, p. 22.

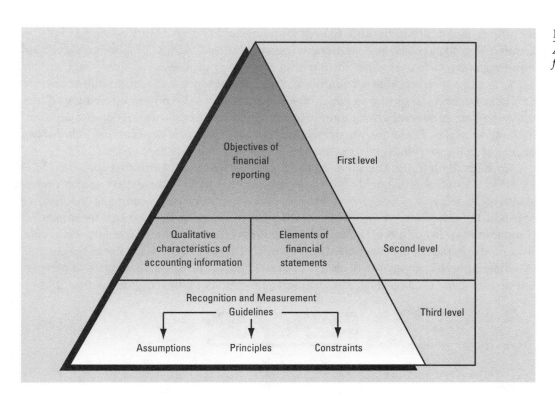

ILLUSTRATION 2-1
*A Conceptual Framework
for Financial Reporting*

While these objectives reflect a broad concern for satisfying the information needs of a variety of user groups, tradition has emphasized information that is useful for investor and creditor decisions. This concern narrows to investors' and creditors' interests in the prospects of receiving cash from investments in, or loans to, the business enterprise. Consequently, there is a focus on financial statements that provide information useful for assessing prospective cash flows to the business, upon which cash flows to investors and creditors depend.

A statement of objectives is a necessary starting point for developing the framework. Objectives may vary, and they can exert tremendous impact on the practice of accounting. For example, if the only objective of financial accounting was to determine the minimum taxable income each year, we would have a substantially different framework from the one that presently exists.

SECOND LEVEL: FUNDAMENTAL CONCEPTS

The second level of the conceptual framework provides certain building blocks that explain the qualitative characteristics that make accounting information useful and define the elements of financial statements. These building blocks form a bridge between the *why* (the objectives of the first level) and the *how* (the recognition and measurement guidelines of the third level) of accounting.

QUALITATIVE CHARACTERISTICS OF ACCOUNTING INFORMATION

How does one decide whether financial reports should provide information on an historical cost basis or on a current value basis? Or how does one decide whether the many incorporated companies (e.g., in food processing, including baking, chocolates, dairy and specialty products; in food distribution, primarily Loblaw companies; and in resources, including forest products and fisheries operations) that constitute George Weston Limited should be combined and shown as one business entity, or disaggregated and reported as separate companies for financial reporting purposes?

Choosing an acceptable accounting method, the amount and type of information to be disclosed, and the format in which the information is to be presented involves determining which of several alternatives provides the most useful information for decision-making purposes. Therefore, *the overriding criterion by which an accounting choice can be judged is the usefulness of its consequences for decision making*.

OBJECTIVE 4
Identify the qualitative characteristics of accounting information.

To help distinguish the more useful from the less useful information, the *CICA Handbook* identifies four qualitative characteristics that make information useful: understandability, relevance, reliability, and comparability.[10] In order to complete this list, we will add the characteristic of consistency, which the *Handbook* recognizes as enhancing comparability.[11] In addition, the *Handbook* identifies certain constraints (benefit versus cost, materiality) as part of the conceptual framework.[12] These are discussed later in the chapter.

Illustration 2-2 presents an overview of these notions. The hierarchy provides a perspective on how these notions fit together and serves as the basis for the discussion that follows.

ILLUSTRATION 2-2
A Hierarchy of Accounting Qualities

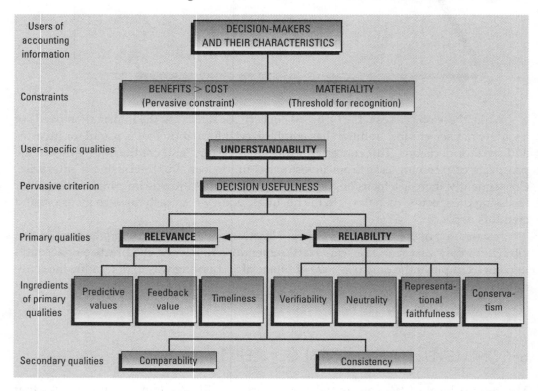

Decision Usefulness

Without the pervasive criterion of **decision usefulness**, there would be no justification for accounting activity or a basis on which to assess the costs of providing reports. Usefulness is dependent on the extent to which there is an appropriate linking of decision makers and their capability to understand financial information with the primary and secondary qualities of the information, recognizing there are constraints on the information that can be provided.

---

[10] *CICA Handbook*, Section 1000, par. .18.

[11] *Ibid.*, par. .23.

[12] *Ibid.*, pars. .16 and .17.

UNDERSTANDABILITY

Decision makers vary widely in the types of decisions they make, the methods of decision making they employ, the information they already possess or can obtain from other sources, and their ability to process the information. For information to be useful, there must be a connection (linkage) between it and the users and the decisions they make. This link, called **understandability**, *requires that users be capable of understanding the information as it was intended to be understood by the presenters of the information.* Understandability depends not only on the accountant's skills and abilities to provide information that is often complex, but also on the user's ability to comprehend that information. Consequently, understandability is viewed as a user-specific qualitative characteristic of information in the conceptual framework.

The range of users' capabilities to understand information creates a dilemma for accountants. For example, assume that DuPont Canada Inc. issues a three-months' earnings report (interim report) that provides information for decision-making purposes, but some users do not fully understand its content and significance. Although the information may be highly relevant and reliable, it is useless to those who do not understand it, and potentially harmful to those who do use it but do not understand it.

To help resolve this dilemma for accountants, a base level of understandability by users is assumed. *Users are assumed to have a reasonable understanding of business and economic activities and accounting, together with a willingness to study information with reasonable diligence.*[13] This assumption is very important because it has significant consequences on the way and extent to which information is reported in financial statements. It is also very subjective, which means accountants should always think about users and question whether accounting disclosures are intelligible to the intended audience.

PRIMARY QUALITIES

It is generally agreed that *relevance and reliability are two primary qualities that make accounting information useful for decision-making.* Each is achieved to the degree that information incorporates specific characteristics, as discussed below.

Relevance. Information is relevant when *it can influence the decisions of users*[14] (i.e., *it is seen as making a difference in a decision*). If certain information is understood but is disregarded because it is perceived to have no bearing on a decision, it is irrelevant to that decision. Information is relevant when it helps users predict the outcome of past (yet uncompleted), present, and future events (**predictive value**), or confirm or correct prior expectations (**feedback value**). For example, when DuPont Canada Inc. issues an interim report, this information is considered relevant because it provides a basis for forecasting annual earnings and provides feedback on past performance. For information to be relevant, it must also be available to decision makers before it loses its capacity to influence their decisions (**timeliness**). If DuPont did not report its interim results until six months after the end of the period, the information would be much less useful for decision-making purposes. Thus, *for information to be relevant, it should have predictive value and/or feedback value, and timeliness.*[15]

Reliability.   Accounting information is reliable when *it is in agreement with the actual underlying transactions and events, is capable of independent verification, and is reasonably free from error and bias.*[16] Reliability is a necessity for individuals who have

---

[13] *Ibid.*, par. .19.

[14] *Ibid.*, par. .20.

[15] *Ibid.*

[16] *Ibid.*, par. .21.

neither the time nor the expertise to evaluate the factual content of the information. Reliability is achieved through verifiability, representational faithfulness, and neutrality, which is affected by the use of conservatism in making judgements under conditions of uncertainty.[17]

Verifiability exists if *knowledgeable and independent observers concur that the representation of a transaction or event in financial statements is in agreement with the actual underlying transaction or event with a reasonable degree of precision.*[18] When measurements are based on objective evidence, such as invoices, they are highly verifiable. Alternatively, when measurements are based on estimates for which little objective evidence exists (e.g., asset lives or uncollectibility of accounts), the results are less verifiable as they reflect the subjectivity of an accountant's judgement, observation, and experience. Verifiability applies to the correct application of a measurement basis rather than its appropriateness.

Representational faithfulness means that *transactions and events affecting an entity are presented in financial statements in a manner that is in agreement with the actual underlying transactions and events.*[19] In other words, do the numbers or other disclosures represent what really happened? For example, if a company's income statement reports sales of $1 billion when it has sales of only $800 million, the statement is not representationally faithful. Similarly, if a company reports a source of financing that has all the characteristics of a debt (liability) as a part of shareholders' equity because it was labelled as a special type of share, lack of faithfulness results. To be representationally faithful, *transactions and events must be accounted for and presented in terms of their economic substance, which is not necessarily their legal or other form.*[20]

Neutrality means that *information is free from bias that would lead users toward making decisions that are influenced by the way the information is measured or presented.*[21] Bias in measurement occurs when an item is consistently overstated or understated. Bias may occur when the choice of an accounting method or disclosure is made with the interests of particular users, or particular economic or political objectives, in mind.[22] For example, accountants cannot allow a company that produces artificial human body parts to suppress information in financial statement notes about pending lawsuits involving allegations of damage from a product—even though such disclosure could embarrass or harm the company.

Neutrality in standard setting has come under challenge. Some argue that standards should not be issued if they may be economically harmful to an industry or company. We disagree. Standards must be free from bias or there will no longer be credible financial statements. Without credible financial statements, individuals will no longer use this information. An analogy demonstrates this point. In Canada, we have both hockey games and wrestling matches. Many individuals bet on hockey games, which they assume are not fixed. But nobody bets on wrestling matches. Why? Because the public assumes that wrestling matches are rigged. If financial information is biased (rigged), the public will lose confidence and no longer use the information.

Conservatism, as an accounting convention, has existed for a long time, but is often misunderstood. As applied in accounting, conservatism means that *when there is reasonable doubt about an accounting issue, the solution that will be least likely to overstate net assets and income should be chosen.* Conservatism is a legitimate convention to employ when making judgements under conditions of uncertainty. Although it may

---

[17] *Ibid.*

[18] *Ibid.*

[19] *Ibid.*

[20] *Ibid.*

[21] *Ibid.*

[22] *Ibid.*

affect the neutrality of financial statements, it does so in an acceptable manner.[23] Conservatism, however, does not provide a reason to justify a deliberate understatement of net assets and income.

SECONDARY QUALITIES

The use of different acceptable accounting methods by one enterprise in different years, or by different companies in a given year, would make comparison of financial results difficult. Consequently, to enhance the usefulness of accounting reports, the qualities of comparability and consistency are important parts of the conceptual framework. However, they are considered secondary to the qualities of relevance and reliability. If information is to be useful, it must first be relevant and reliable. Achieving this may require foregoing the secondary qualities.

Comparability. *Information measured and reported in a similar manner for different enterprises in a given year or for the same enterprise in different years is considered comparable*. Thus, comparability is a characteristic of the relationship between two pieces of information rather than of a particular piece of information in itself.[24] Comparability enables users to identify similarities and differences between financial statements because the measurements and disclosures are not obscured by the use of noncomparable methods of accounting. For example, if Company A prepares its information on an historical cost basis, but Company B uses a price-level-adjusted basis, it is more difficult to compare and evaluate the two companies. Resource allocation decisions involve evaluations of alternatives; a valid evaluation can be made only if comparable information is available.

Consistency. *Consistency exists when an entity uses the same accounting policies for similar events from period to period.* Consistency results in enhancing the comparability of financial statements of an enterprise from year to year.[25]

Consistency does not mean that a company cannot switch from one method of accounting to another. Companies can change methods, but only when it can be demonstrated that the newly adopted method is preferable to the old. Then the nature and effect of the accounting change, as well as the justification for it, must be **fully disclosed** in the financial statements of the period in which the change is made. The meaning of full disclosure is considered later.

Note that consistency does not mean that different enterprises must apply the same accounting methods. While requiring this may be thought to improve comparability between enterprises, such **uniformity** is not part of the conceptual framework nor has it become an aspect of practice. The difficulty associated with uniformity is that dissimilar circumstances between enterprises may be forced to be reported as being similar.

In summary, accounting reports for any given year are useful in themselves, but they are more useful if they can be compared with reports from other companies and with prior reports of the same entity. For example, if DuPont Canada Inc. is the only enterprise that prepares interim reports, the information is less useful because the user cannot relate it to interim reports for any other enterprise; that is, it lacks comparability. Similarly, if the measurement methods used to prepare DuPont's interim report change from one interim period to another, the information is considered less useful because the user cannot relate it to previous interim periods; that is, it lacks consistency.

---

[23] *Ibid.*

[24] *Ibid.*, par. .22.

[25] *Ibid.*, par. .23.

TRADE-OFFS BETWEEN QUALITATIVE CHARACTERISTICS

The purpose of establishing qualitative characteristics of accounting information is to provide guidance for accountants when they make choices regarding measurements and disclosures. Using such a framework does not provide obvious solutions to accounting problems; rather, it identifies and defines aspects that should be considered when reaching a solution. Many accounting choices require *trade-offs between the qualitative characteristics*.[26] The following serve as examples:

- Several years ago a company bought some land for $200,000. It was used as a parking lot. Appraisers believe that the land is now worth about $1,000,000. In this oversimplified example, the $200,000 historical cost is the more reliable of the two amounts. Which amount is more relevant? If the land was offered as collateral for a bank loan, the loan manager would see the $1,000,000 as the relevant information. A similar conclusion would be reached if management was seriously considering selling the land. Alternatively, if it is not intending to sell the land or use it as collateral, the $200,000 would be relevant as a reflection of the resources given up to acquire land (accountability, stewardship). Which of these two amounts would normally be reported in a current-year balance sheet? Regardless of the above possibilities of the $1,000,000 being the more relevant amount, the $200,000 historical cost would be the amount reported under GAAP. Consequently, reliability appears to outweigh relevancy (for particular types of decisions) when deciding whether to report acquisition cost or current value measurements in financial statements.

- To report completely reliable information about the results of operations of a business, it would be necessary to wait until the business ceased operations. Only then would the actual cash received from customers and costs of assets consumed be known. Waiting until a business ceased to obtain information on the results of its operations would be nonsensical—there would be no need for information in whether to invest in or grant credit to the company. Consequently, to provide relevant (timely) information, financial statements are provided on a periodic (e.g., annual) basis. This requires estimates and assumptions to be made (e.g., useful lives of buildings, likelihood of collecting accounts). Therefore, relevance outweighs reliability in terms of preparing periodic financial statements under GAAP.

While these examples illustrate the existence of trade-offs, there is no clear-cut consensus on the overall relative weighting (importance) of relevance and reliability to assist in deciding on many issues. Therefore, while awareness of the qualitative characteristics may help in making choices, the actual decisions typically require the exercise of professional judgement. Such judgement is also framed by the basic assumptions, principles, and constraints of the conceptual framework, to be examined later.

BASIC ELEMENTS OF FINANCIAL STATEMENTS

OBJECTIVE 5
Define the basic elements of financial statements.

An important aspect of the theoretical structure is the establishment and definition of the basic categories of items to be included in financial statements. At present, accounting uses many terms that have specific meaning, terms that constitute the language of business or the jargon of accounting.

One such term is "asset." Is it something we own? If the answer is yes, can we assume that any asset leased would never be shown on the balance sheet? Is it something we have the right to use, or is it anything of value used by the enterprise to generate earnings? If the answer is yes, then why should the management of the enterprise not be reported as an asset? It seems necessary, therefore, to develop basic definitions for the ele-

---

[26] *Ibid.*, par. .24.

EXHIBIT 2-1

ELEMENTS OF FINANCIAL STATEMENTS

Assets are economic resources controlled by an entity as a result of past transactions or events from which future economic benefits may be obtained.

Assets have three essential characteristics:

(a) they embody a future benefit that involves a capacity, singly or in combination with other assets, to contribute directly or indirectly to future net cash flows;

(b) the entity can control access to the benefit; and

(c) the transaction or event giving rise to the entity's right to, or control of, the benefit has already occurred.

It is not essential for control of access to the benefit to be legally enforceable for a resource to be an asset, provided the entity can control its use by other means.

Liabilities are obligations of an entity arising from past transactions or events, the settlement of which may result in the transfer or use of assets, provision of services or other yielding of economic benefits in the future.

Liabilities have three essential characteristics:

(a) they embody a duty or responsibility to others that entails settlement by future transfer or use of assets, provision of services or other yielding of economic benefits, at a specified or determinable date, on occurrence of a specified event, or on demand;

(b) the duty or responsibility obligates the entity leaving it little or no discretion to avoid it; and

(c) the transaction or event obligating the entity has already occurred.

Liabilities do not have to be legally enforceable provided that they otherwise meet the definition of liabilities; they can be based on equitable or constructive obligations. An equitable obligation is a duty based on ethical or moral considerations. A constructive obligation is one that can be inferred from the facts in a particular situation as opposed to a contractually based obligation.

Equity is the ownership interest in the assets of an entity after deducting its liabilities. While equity in total is a residual, it includes specific categories of items, for example, types of share capital, contributed surplus, and retained earnings.

Revenues are increases in economic resources, either by way of inflows or enhancements of assets or reductions of liabilities, resulting from the ordinary activities of an entity. Revenues of entities normally arise from the sale of goods, the rendering of services, or the use by others of entity resources yielding rent, interest, royalties, or dividends.

Expenses are decreases in economic resources, either by way of outflows or reductions of assets or incurrences of liabilities, resulting from an entity's ordinary revenue generating activities.

Gains are increases in equity from peripheral or incidental transactions and events affecting an entity and from all other transactions, events, and circumstances affecting the entity except those that result from revenues or equity contributions.

Losses are decreases in equity from peripheral or incidental transactions and events affecting an entity and from all other transactions, events, and circumstances affecting the entity except those that result from expenses or distributions of equity.

Net income is the residual amount after expenses and losses are deducted from revenues and gains. Net income generally includes all transactions and events increasing or decreasing the equity of the entity except those that result from equity contributions and distributions.

---

ments of accounting. Such definitions provide guidance for identifying what to include and exclude from the financial statements.

With regard to profit-oriented enterprises, the *CICA Handbook* defines the most common elements as shown in Exhibit 2-1.[27] Each of these elements will be explained and examined in more detail in subsequent chapters.

---

[27] *Ibid.*, pars. .27 and .29 through .40. Notes to financial statements, while providing useful information and being an integral part of the statements, are not an element (par. .25). While not in the *CICA Handbook* definitions, two additional elements are frequently cited. These are *investments by owners* (increases in net assets resulting from transfers to the entity from other entities to obtain or increase ownership interest) and *distributions to owners* (decreases in net assets resulting from transfers by the entity to the owners). (Continued)

It is useful to think of the elements as two distinct types. The first type—composed of assets, liabilities, and equity—describes resources and claims to resources at a *point in time* and appear in a balance sheet. The second type of elements—net income and its components of revenues, expenses, gains, and losses—describes transactions, events, and circumstances that affect resources, obligations, and equity during a *period of time* and are presented in an income statement. Therefore, elements of the first type are changed by elements of the second type and at any time are the cumulative result of all changes. This interaction is referred to as **articulation**. Thus, the balance sheet (which reports elements of the first group) depends on the income statement (which reports elements of the second group), and vice versa.

THIRD LEVEL: RECOGNITION AND MEASUREMENT GUIDELINES

OBJECTIVE 6
Understand the meaning of recognition and measurement.

While an item may meet the definition of an element, it may not be recognized in the financial statements. Recognition *means inclusion of an item within one or more individual statements and does not mean disclosure in the notes to the financial statements.*[28] In order to be recognized, the following criteria must be met:[29]

1. The item has an appropriate basis of measurement and a reasonable estimate can be made of the amount involved.

2. For items involving obtaining or giving up future economic benefits, it is probable that such benefits will be obtained or given up.

Measurement *is the process of determining the amount at which an item is recognized in the financial statements.*[30] The first recognition criterion requires that an appropriate (relevant) measurement basis be established for items and that a reasonable (reliable) amount can be determined under that basis before items can be recognized. The second recognition criterion indicates that, even if a measurement can be made, whether an item is recognized and, if so, how it is recognized (i.e., type of element) will depend on the probability of future economic consequences.

Recognition and measurement often depend on the exercise of professional judgement, but these criteria are important to making such judgements. For example, suppose a company is being sued for providing faulty service to a defined group of customers. The lawsuit, currently before the court, is for $2 million for damages and compensation. Should the potential consequences of the lawsuit be recognized in the financial statements? Even if a reasonable estimate can be determined for the amount to be awarded if the lawsuit is lost, it may not be recognized because the payment is not believed to be likely (probable) as the company is fighting the claim in court and its lawyers are advising that the company will win the case. Alternatively, it may be that the company believes it is likely to lose the case but this is not recognized because the eventual settlement is not

---

[27] (Continued)

The *Handbook* also incorporates wording that extends or adjusts these definitions to reflect circumstances pertinent to not-for-profit organizations. As our concentration is on financial reporting for profit-oriented enterprises, the provided definitions omit the references to not-for-profit organizations. Most of the elements are commonly defined with the exception that for not-for-profit organizations: future benefits are linked to the provision of services in the definition of assets; equity is usually called net assets; donations, government grants, and contributions are considered as revenues; and the difference between revenues and expenses has a significant difference from that of a profit-seeking enterprise (i.e., it indicates the extent to which the not-for-profit organization has been able to obtain resources to cover the cost of its services).

[28] *Ibid.*, par. .42.

[29] *Ibid.*, par. .44. These criteria assume that an item meets the definition of one of the elements.

[30] *Ibid.*, par. .53.

reasonably determinable. Although the lawsuit will not be recognized in the financial statements, it may be considered sufficiently important to disclose information about it in the notes to the statements (note disclosure does not constitute recognition as defined). If it is likely the lawsuit will be lost and a reasonable estimate of the amount of loss is available, then there is recognition in the financial statements that may be accompanied by an explanatory note.

Recognition and measurement in accounting are influenced by many concepts that have evolved over time and are useful aids in developing rational responses to financial reporting issues. These concepts will be discussed under the categories of basic assumptions, principles, and constraints.

BASIC ASSUMPTIONS

Four basic assumptions underlie financial accounting: (1) the economic entity assumption; (2) the going concern assumption; (3) the monetary unit assumption; and (4) the periodicity assumption.

OBJECTIVE 7
Describe the basic assumptions of accounting.

Economic Entity Assumption.   A major assumption in accounting is that *economic activity can be identified with a particular unit of accountability*. In other words, the activity of any particular business enterprise (the entity for which we wish to account) can be kept separate and distinct from its owners and any other entities. If there were no meaningful way to separate economic events that occur, no basis for accounting would exist.

The **economic entity assumption** provides a basis that can help the accountant resolve some ethical problems. For example, if a manager uses company funds to pay for personal expenses (e.g., travel during a vacation, gifts for relatives) and requests the accountant to treat these as company expenses, the accountant can refuse to do so, based on the entity assumption. The use of these funds should be recorded as an account receivable from the manager.

The economic entity assumption does not apply solely to the segregation of activities among given business enterprises. An individual, a department or division, or an entire industry can be considered a separate entity if one chooses to define the unit in such a manner. Thus *an economic entity does not necessarily refer to a legal entity*. A parent company and its subsidiary companies are separate *legal entities*, but merging their activities for accounting and reporting purposes when providing consolidated financial statements does not violate the *economic entity* assumption.

Going Concern Assumption.   Most financial statements are prepared on the assumption that *the business enterprise will continue to operate in the foreseeable future and will be able to realize assets and discharge liabilities in the normal course of operations*.[31] Experience indicates that, in spite of numerous business failures, companies have a fairly high continuance rate. Although accountants do not believe that business firms will last indefinitely, they do expect them to last long enough to fulfill their objectives and commitments.

The implications of this **going concern assumption** are critical. The historical cost principle would be of limited usefulness if liquidation were assumed. Under a liquidation approach, asset values are better stated at net realizable value (sales price less costs of disposal) than at acquisition cost. Amortization policies are justifiable and appropriate only if we assume continuity of an enterprise. If a liquidation approach was adopted, the current–noncurrent classification of assets and liabilities would lose its significance. Labelling anything as a long-term asset or liability would not be justifiable.

---

[31] *CICA Handbook*, Section 1000, par. .58.

The going concern assumption is applicable in most business situations. There are, however, situations where known events and conditions cause significant doubt about an entity's ability to continue as a going concern. In such cases there must be note disclosure of this fact, the reasons for reaching such a conclusion, and a recognition that it may be inappropriate to report on the basis of generally accepted accounting principles applicable to a going concern.[32] For purposes of this book, the going concern assumption is considered to be appropriately met unless otherwise stated.

Monetary Unit Assumption.   Accounting is based on the assumption that *money is the common denominator by which economic activity is conducted, and that the monetary unit provides an appropriate basis for accounting measurement and analysis*. This **monetary unit assumption** implies that the monetary unit is the most effective means of expressing to interested parties changes in capital and exchanges of goods and services. *The monetary unit is relevant, simple, universally available, understandable, and useful.* Application of this assumption is dependent on the even more basic assumption that quantitative data are useful in communicating economic information and in making rational economic decisions.

In general, accountants in Canada have chosen to ignore the phenomenon of price-level changes (inflation and deflation) by assuming that *the unit of measure— the dollar—remains reasonably stable*. This is often called the **stable dollar assumption**. It allows accountants to justify adding 1988 dollars to 1998 dollars without any adjustment. Arguments submitted in support of the stable dollar assumption are that the effects of price-level changes are not significant and that presentation of price-level-adjusted data is not easily understood.[33]

Periodicity Assumption.   As discussed previously when considering the trade-offs between relevancy and reliability, the results of enterprise activity are most accurately measurable at the time of the enterprise's eventual liquidation. Investors, creditors, managers, governments, and various other user groups, however, cannot wait indefinitely for such information. Consequently, accountants provide financial information periodically.

The **periodicity** or time period **assumption** implies that *the economic activities of an enterprise can be divided into artificial time periods*. These time periods vary, but the most common are monthly, quarterly, and yearly.

The shorter the time period, the more difficult it is to accurately determine the net income for the period. Problems of allocation mean that a quarter's results are usually less reliable than a year's results. Investors desire and demand that information be quickly processed and disseminated; yet the quicker the information is released, the more it is subject to error.

BASIC PRINCIPLES

OBJECTIVE 8
Explain the application of the basic principles of accounting.

There are four basic principles that accountants use in deciding when and how to measure, record, and report assets, liabilities, revenues, and expenses: (1) the historical cost principle; (2) the revenue realization (recognition) principle; (3) the matching principle, and; (4) the full disclosure principle.

---

[32] *Going Concern Exposure Draft* (Toronto: CICA, March, 1996). This document states that appropriate disclosure should occur when there is significant doubt about the ability of an entity to continue as a going concern for a 12-month period from the date of completion of the financial statements. Included is a list of 20 events and conditions which, separately or collectively, may be indicative of uncertainty about the continued validity of the going concern assumption.

[33] In 1982, the *CICA Handbook* did recommend that large, publicly traded enterprises report, as supplementary information, the effects of price changes. This recommendation reflected the need for such information in the high-inflation economy at the time. It was withdrawn in 1991 as inflation levels went down. Even when it was recommended that such information was necessary, only a few companies provided it.

Historical Cost Principle.   The determination of the measurement base on which an item is to be recognized in financial statements has been one of the most difficult problems in accounting. A number of bases exist on which an amount for a single item can be measured: replacement cost, net realizable value (net amount that would be received from selling an asset), present value of future cash flows, and original cost (less amortization, where appropriate). Which should the accountant use?

Generally, under existing GAAP, *transactions and events are recognized in financial statements at the amount of cash or cash equivalents paid or received or the fair value ascribed to them when they took place.*[34] This is often referred to as the **historical cost principle.**

Historical cost has an important advantage over other valuations: it is reliable. To illustrate the importance of this advantage, consider the problems that would arise if we adopted some other basis for keeping records. If we were to select net realizable value, for instance, we might have a difficult time establishing a reliable sales value for a given item without selling it. Every member of the accounting department might have a different opinion on the asset's value, and management might desire still another figure. And how often would it be necessary to establish sales value? All companies close their accounts at least annually, and some compute their net income every month. Companies would find it necessary to place a sales value on every asset each time they wished to determine income—a laborious task and one that would result in a figure of net income materially affected by opinion. Similar objections can be levelled against current replacement cost, present value of future cash flows, and other bases of valuation *except* historical cost.

Historical cost is usually definite and verifiable. *By using historical cost as the basis for record-keeping, accountants can provide objective and verifiable data in their reports.* Historical cost provides financial statement users with a stable and consistent benchmark that they can rely on to establish historical trends.

The question "What is cost?" is, however, not always easy to answer. If fixed assets are to be carried in the accounts at cost, are cash discounts to be deducted in determining cost? Does cost include freight and insurance? Does it include cost of installation as well as the price of a machine itself? How do we determine the cost of an item received as a gift? It is not unusual for a developing community to offer a plant site free or at a nominal cost to a company as an inducement to establish operations in the locality. At what price should such an asset be carried? Also, certain assets may be acquired by the issuance of share capital of the acquiring company or in an exchange for similar or dissimilar assets. If no cash price is stated in the transaction, how is cost to be established? These questions are answered in later chapters; they are raised here only to point out some of the difficulties regularly encountered in determining costs.

We ordinarily think of cost as relating only to assets. What about liabilities? Are they accounted for on a cost basis? Yes, they are. This becomes evident if we think of cost as "exchange price." Liabilities, such as bonds, notes, and accounts payable, are incurred by a business enterprise in exchange for assets or services upon which an agreed price has been placed. This price, established by the exchange transaction, is the "cost" of the liability and provides the amount at which it is recorded in the accounts and reported in financial statements.

Concerns exist regarding use of the historical cost basis. Criticism is especially strong during a period when prices are changing substantially. At such times historical acquisition cost is said to go "out of date" almost as soon as it is determined. In a period of rising or falling prices, the cost figures of the preceding years are viewed as not comparable with current cost figures. For example, assuming an average rate of inflation of 5% per year, a McDonald's quarter-pounder with cheese, which costs $2.70 today (excluding taxes), will cost approximately $7.15 in 20 years if the price directly follows the inflation

---

[34] *CICA Handbook,* Section 1000, par. .53.

rate. In a similar manner, financial statements that present the cost of fixed assets acquired 10 or 20 years ago may be misleading because readers of such statements may tend to think in terms of current prices, not the prices at the time the assets were purchased. A further complication arises because amortization is based on historical cost. Since amortization (e.g., depreciation) expense enters into net income calculations, the net income reported may be suspect because of price changes.

Revenue Realization Principle.   The **revenue realization principle**, also called the revenue recognition principle,[35] provides guidance in answering the question of when revenue should be recognized (recorded in the accounts). Revenue is generally recognized when (1) *performance is achieved* and (2) *reasonable assurance regarding the measurability and collectibility of the consideration exists.*[36]

Generally, these two requirements are met when a sale to an independent party occurs. Thus, recognition of revenue takes place at that time. Any basis for revenue recognition that is short of an actual sale opens the door to wide variations in practice. To give accounting reports uniform meaning, a rule for revenue recognition comparable to the cost rule for asset valuation is essential. *Recognition through sale provides a uniform and reasonable test in most cases*. There are, however, exceptions to the rule, and at times the basic rule is difficult to apply, as discussed below. These exceptions are presented to help you gain an appreciation for the exceptions and difficulties; the specific accounting to deal with them are examined in detail in Chapter 6.

1. **During Production.** Recognition of revenue before a contract is completed is allowed in certain long-term construction contracts. The main feature of this approach (using what is called the percentage-of-completion method) is that revenue and related expenses are recognized periodically based on the percentage of job completion, instead of waiting until the entire job is finished. Although a formal transfer of risks and rewards of ownership has not occurred, performance is considered achieved as construction progresses. Naturally, if it is not possible to obtain dependable estimates of price, cost, and progress, then revenue should not be recognized until the contract is completed.

2. **End of Production.** At times, revenue may be recognized after the production cycle has ended but before a sale takes place. This is the case where the selling price as well as the quantity to be sold is certain. An example is in mining, where a ready market at a standard price exists for a mineral that has been extracted. The same holds true for some agricultural products with guaranteed price supports set by the government.

3. **Receipt of Cash.** Receipt of cash is another basis for revenue recognition. A cash basis approach should be used only when collection of cash from sales is uncertain and it is not possible to reasonably determine the extent of bad debts. This may be the case for some businesses that sell high-cost items for which payments are made in periodic instalments over a long period of time. For example, farm and home equipment and furnishings are often sold on an instalment basis. The instalment method (a cash-based method) is claimed to be justified on the grounds that the risk of not collecting an account receivable is so great that the sale is not sufficient evidence for revenue recognition to take place. In some instances, this reasoning may be valid. Generally, though, if a sale is completed, revenue should be recognized; if bad debts are expected, they should be recorded as estimates of uncollectible accounts in the period of sale.

Revenue, then, is recognized and recorded in the period in which performance to earn it has been achieved, it is reasonably measurable, and collectibility is reasonably assured. Normally, this is the date of sale, but circumstances may dictate application of

---

[35] Technically, realization means the process of converting noncash resources and rights into money. Recognition is the process of including an item in the financial statements. Because of this, the revenue realization principle is also referred to as the revenue recognition principle.

[36] *CICA Handbook*, Section 1000, par. .47.

the percentage-of-completion approach, the end-of-production approach, or the receipt-of-cash approach.

Conceptually, the appropriate accounting for revenue recognition should be apparent and should fit nicely into one of the conditions mentioned above, but often it does not. As examples, consider franchises and motion picture sales to television.

Franchising operations have been established for a wide variety of businesses that range from restaurants to pet-care centres. One need not travel too widely to appreciate the multitude of fast-food chains such as McDonald's or Kentucky Fried Chicken. One of the problems faced by accountants of the franchiser (seller of the franchise) when franchising was developing concerned when to recognize revenue from the sale of a franchise. In many cases, the entire franchise price was treated as revenue as soon as the franchiser found an individual franchisee (buyer of the franchise) and received a down payment, no matter how small. This revenue recognition practice was faulty because, in many situations, the fees were payable over a period of years, were refundable or uncollectible if the franchises never got started, or were earned only as certain services were performed by the franchiser. In effect, the franchisers were counting their fried chickens before they were hatched. Consequently, to more appropriately determine net income for franchises, the basis for revenue recognition was changed from the date the franchise contract was signed to a basis that more closely reflected the requirements of the revenue realization principle.[37]

How should motion picture companies such as the National Film Board of Canada, Metro-Goldwyn-Mayer Inc., Warner Bros., and United Artists account for the sale of rights to show motion picture films on cable television networks and the CBC, CTV, ABC, CBS, or NBC? Should the revenue from the sale of the rights be reported when the contract is signed, when the motion picture film is delivered to the network, when the cash payment is received, or when the film is shown on television? The problem of revenue recognition is complicated because the TV networks are often restricted in the number of times the film may be shown in total, and over what time period.

For example, Metro-Goldwyn-Mayer (MGM) sold CBS the rights to show *Gone With the Wind* for $35 million. CBS received the right to show this classic movie once a year over a 20-year period. MGM contended that revenue recognition should coincide with the movie's showings over the 20 years. The accounting profession, on the other hand, argued that all of the revenue should be recognized immediately because (1) the sales price and cost of the film were known; (2) collectibility was assured; and (3) the film was available and accepted by the network. The restriction that the movie be shown only once a year was not considered significant justification for deferring revenue recognition. It is interesting to note that MGM reported the entire $35 million in revenue in the first year.

Matching Principle.   In recognizing expenses, accountants attempt to follow the approach of "let the expenses follow the revenues." Expenses are recognized not when wages are paid, or when work is performed, or when a product is produced, but when the work, service, or product actually makes its contribution to revenue. Thus, expense recognition is tied to revenue recognition. This practice is justified by the **matching principle**, which dictates that *expenses that are linked to revenue in a cause and effect relationship are normally matched with the revenue in the accounting period in which the revenue is recognized.*[38]

For those costs for which it is not reasonable or practicable to reflect a direct cause-and-effect relationship with revenues, some other approach must be adopted so that they are shown as an expense in the appropriate period's income statement. Often, the accountant uses a "systematic and rational" allocation policy in an attempt to approximate the matching principle. This type of expense recognition involves making assumptions about the benefits that are being received as well as the cost associated with those

---

[37] "Franchise Fee Recognition," *Accounting Guideline* (Toronto: CICA, 1984).
[38] *CICA Handbook*, Section 1000, par. .51.

benefits. The cost of a long-lived asset, for example, is allocated over the accounting periods during which the asset is used because it is assumed that the asset contributes to the generation of revenue throughout its useful life.

Some costs are charged to the current period as expenses (or losses) simply because no apparent connection with future revenue is evident. Examples of these types of costs are officers' salaries and advertising expenses.

In summary, costs are analysed to determine whether a direct relationship exists with revenue. Where this holds true, the costs are expensed and matched against the revenue in the period when the revenue is recognized. If no direct connection appears between costs and revenues, an allocation of cost on some systematic and rational basis may be appropriate. When such an allocation approach is not appropriate, the costs are expensed immediately.

Costs are generally classified into two categories: product costs and period costs. **Product costs** such as material, labour, and overhead costs to manufacture or acquisition cost of goods purchased for resale attach to the product and are carried into future periods if the revenue from the product is recognized in subsequent periods. **Period costs** such as officers' salaries and general selling expenses are charged immediately to income because no direct relationship between cost and revenue can be determined.

The problems of expense recognition are as complex as those of revenue recognition. For example, assume that a large oil company spends a considerable amount of money on an advertising campaign. It hopes to attract new customers and develop brand loyalty. Over how many years, if any, should this outlay be expensed? As another example, consider the video rental market. One major company amortizes the cost of all its video tapes over three years: 36% the first year, 36% the second, and 28% the third. Other video rental companies take a more conservative approach, noting that Class A titles (expensive hits) average 28 rentals the first three months, 12 rentals the next three months, 12 more in the next six months, and 18 over the next year. As a result, they charge off these tapes in one year, or two years at most. As an executive of one of the video rental companies noted, "If you ask 12 different people the useful life of a video tape, you get 12 different answers." If so, the result would be 12 different expense recognition patterns, all of them legitimate attempts to match expenses against revenues.

The conceptual validity of the matching principle has been subject to debate. A major concern is that matching permits certain costs to be deferred and treated as assets on the balance sheet when in fact these costs may not have future benefits. If abused, this principle permits the balance sheet to become a "dumping ground" for unmatched costs. In addition, there appears to be no objective definition of what is "systematic and rational." Therefore, while the matching principle is an important guideline for determining when expenses are to be recognized, its application requires substantial judgement in many situations.

Full Disclosure Principle.   In deciding what information to report, accountants follow the general practice of providing information that is of sufficient importance to influence the judgement and decisions of an informed user. Often referred to as the **full disclosure principle**, it recognizes that the nature and amount of information included in financial reports reflects a series of judgemental trade-offs. These trade-offs involve striving for (1) sufficient detail to disclose matters that make a difference to users; and (2) sufficient condensation to make the information understandable, keeping in mind costs of preparing and using it. Information about financial position, income, and cash flows can be placed in one of three places: (1) within the main body of financial statements; (2) in the notes to those statements; or (3) as supplementary information. The following paragraphs provide some broad guidelines for deciding where to place certain kinds of financial information.

The **financial statements** are a formal, structured means of communicating information. To be *recognized* in the main body of financial statements, *an item should meet the definition of an element and the recognition criteria*. The item must have been measured, recorded in the books, and passed through the double-entry system of accounting.

The **notes** to financial statements generally amplify or explain the items recognized in the main body of the statements. If the information in the main body of the financial statements gives an incomplete picture of the performance and position of the enterprise, additional information that is needed to complete the picture should be included in the notes. Information in the notes does not have to be quantifiable; it can be partially or totally narrative. Examples of notes are: descriptions of the accounting policies and methods used in measuring the elements reported in the statements; explanations of uncertainties and contingencies; and statistics and details too voluminous for inclusion in the statements. The notes are not only helpful but also essential to understanding the enterprise's performance and position.

Supplementary information may include details or amounts that present a different perspective from that adopted in the financial statements. It may be quantifiable information that is high in relevance but low in reliability, or information that is helpful but not essential.

Supplementary information, unless it is cross-referenced in the financial statements, is not considered a part of the financial statements and is not audited.[39] Most companies provide such information, however, on the grounds that it is useful. Examples of supplementary information are financial highlight summaries and historical (5- or 10-year) summaries. Also, annual reports include a section called Management's Discussion and Analysis that provides an important source of information regarding past financial results and, often, strategies and objectives for the future.

The full disclosure principle is not always easy to put into operation because the business environment is complicated and ever-changing. For example, during the past decade many business combinations produced innumerable conglomerate-type organizations and financing arrangements that demanded new and unique accounting and reporting practices and principles. Leases, investment credits, pension funds, franchising, stock options, financial instruments, and mergers had to be studied, and appropriate reporting practices had to be developed. In each of these situations, the accountant was faced with the problem of providing enough information to ensure that the mythical reasonably prudent investor would not be misled.

FULL DISCLOSURE?

Bre-X Minerals Ltd. went from trading as a penny stock to trading in excess of $20 per share (after a 10 to 1 stock split) as a result of the announcements surrounding the alleged Busang gold find, supposedly one of the richest in the world. At the time Bre-X found the gold they had no contract of work application. Despite this the Bre-X 1995 annual report suggests otherwise, "The company, through foreign subsidiaries, entered into a joint agreement with PT Askatindo Karya Mineral, which entitles the company to 90 percent participating interest in a contract of work application." However, it was not until February 17, 1997 that Bre-X announced a deal in which they would be allowed to keep 45 percent of Busang. The stock falls. Dissident shareholder, Gregory Chorney of Aurora, Ont., immediately sells 700,000 shares and says he may sue Bre-X. CEO David Walsh stated, "some have mistakenly thought that we owned 90 percent of this venture. This was never the practical reality, nor was it ever the basis for valuation of the Bre-X stock." Chorney says that Walsh "bought himself potentially a class-action suit for serious nondisclosure."

Source: Wells, Jennifer. "Gold: Canadians Find Treasure in One of the World's most Corrupt Countries." *Maclean's*, March 3, 1997: 38–45.

Contributed by: Kevin Berry, University of New Brunswick – St. John.

---

[39] While supplementary information is not audited, *CICA Handbook*, Section 7500, states that the auditor should read the other information in the annual report and consider whether any of it is inconsistent with the financial statements on which the audit report is given. Various actions occur if material inconsistencies are found. However, it is unlikely the auditor would give a report if the inconsistencies were not satisfactorily resolved.

BASIC CONSTRAINTS

OBJECTIVE 9
Describe the impact that constraints have on reporting accounting information.

In providing information with the qualitative characteristics that make it useful, two major constraints must be considered: (1) the benefit–cost relationship and (2) materiality.[40] An additional constraint is industry practice.

Benefit–Cost Relationship.   Too often, users assume that information is a cost-free commodity. Preparers and providers of accounting information know that it is not. Therefore, the **benefit-cost relationship** must be considered: the benefits that can be derived from the information must be weighed against the costs of providing it. Obviously, the benefits should exceed the costs. Accountants have traditionally applied this constraint through the notions of "expediency" or "practicality."

The difficulty in benefit–cost analysis is that the costs and especially the benefits are not always evident or measurable. The costs are of several kinds, including costs of collecting, processing, disseminating, auditing, potential litigation, disclosure to competitors, and analysis and interpretation. Benefits accrue both to preparers (e.g., management's control of resources, access to capital) and to users (e.g., allocation of resources, tax assessment), but they are generally more difficult to quantify than are costs.

In addition to considering benefit–cost aspects when preparing an enterprise's financial statements, such analysis is also required by those responsible for developing accounting standards. Among the providers and users of accounting information, there are those who believe that the costs associated with implementing certain accounting standards are too high when compared with the benefits received. For example, some believe that Canadian GAAP, as represented in the *CICA Handbook*, is too cumbersome and expensive for smaller businesses to adhere to relative to the resulting benefits. Consequently, they have argued that the financial statements of smaller businesses should be governed by less demanding standards. The issues are related to what is called the "big GAAP, little GAAP" controversy (i.e., should there be one GAAP to which all companies adhere, or should GAAP applicable to larger companies differ from that applicable to smaller companies?). While the Accounting Standards Board has generally maintained that its standards are applicable to all companies (specific exceptions exist, for example, regarding disclosures of earnings per share and segmented information), it has recognized that a benefit–cost perspective should be employed when developing standards.[41]

Materiality.   *An item, or an aggregate of items, is material if it is probable that its omission or misstatement would influence or change a decision.*[42] In short, it must make a difference or it need not be disclosed. It is difficult to provide firm guidelines to help judge when an item is or is not material because materiality depends on the *relative size* of the item compared to the size of other items and the *nature* of the item itself. The two sets of numbers presented in Illustration 2-3 indicate the importance of relative size.

ILLUSTRATION 2-3
Materiality: Relative Size

	Company A	Company B
Sales	$10,000,000	$100,000
Costs and expenses	9,000,000	90,000
Income from operations	$ 1,000,000	$ 10,000
Unusual gain	$ 20,000	$ 5,000

During the period in question, the revenues and expenses and, therefore, the net incomes from operations of Company A and Company B have been proportional. Each had an unusual gain. In looking at the income figure for Company A, it does not appear

---

[40] *CICA Handbook,* Section 1000, pars. .16 and .17.

[41] *Ibid.*, par. .16.

[42] *Ibid.*, par. .17.

significant whether the amount of the unusual gain is separated or merged with the regular operating income. It is only 2% of the operating income and, if merged, would not seriously distort the net operating income figure. Company B's unusual gain is only $5,000, but as this amounts to 50% of its income from operations, it is relatively much more significant than the larger gain realized by A. Obviously, the inclusion of such an item in ordinary operating income would affect the amount of that income materially. Thus we see the importance of the relative size of an item in determining its materiality.

Linked to the relative size of a recognized item may be the uncertainty related to its measurement. As will be developed in later chapters, the measurement of many items in the financial statements is dependent on predicting the outcome of future events. The prediction of the estimated useful life and residual value of a capital asset, for example, determines the amount of amortization expense and accumulated amortization recognized. Consequently, **measurement uncertainty** exists because there may be a variance between the recognized amount and other reasonably possible amounts. Disclosure of information regarding such measurement uncertainty depends on judgement about the materiality of the effect of the uncertainty on the financial statements. If judged to be material in the near term (i.e., it is reasonably possible that the recognized amount could change by a material amount within one year), then disclosure of the nature of the measurement uncertainty, its extent, and the recognized amount itself is required except when such disclosure would significantly adversely affect the entity.[43]

The nature of the item can also be important. For example, if a company violates an important statute, the facts and amounts involved should be separately disclosed. Or, for a particular company, a $50,000 misclassification of assets within the noncurrent section may not be considered material in amount, but it is material if it is a misclassification between the noncurrent and current sections.

Materiality is a difficult concept to apply, as the following examples indicate.

1. General Dynamics disclosed that at one time its Resources Group had improved its earnings by $5.8 million at the same time that its Stromberg Datagraphix subsidiary had taken write-offs of $6.7 million. Although both numbers were far larger than the $2.5 million that General Dynamics as a whole earned for the year, neither was disclosed as a separate item in the financial statements. Apparently the effect on net income was not considered material. Perhaps each should have been disclosed separately because the Stromberg write-off appeared to be a one-time charge, whereas the improvement in the Resources Group was ongoing.

2. In the first quarter, GAC's earnings rose from 76 cents to 77 cents a share. Nowhere did the annual report disclose that a favourable on-time tax incentive of 4 cents a share prevented GAC's earnings from sliding to 73 cents a share. The company took the position that this incentive's benefits should not be specifically disclosed because they were not material (6% of net income). As an executive noted, "You know that accountants have a rule of thumb which says that anything under 10% is not material." Of course, the executive's statement seems less than serious. It should have been considered significant that the direction of the company's earnings was completely altered—even though 4 cents a share seems like a small amount.

These examples illustrate one point: In practice, the answer to what is material is not clear-cut, and difficult decisions must be made in each period. Only by the exercise of professional judgement can the accountant arrive at answers that are reasonable and appropriate.

Industry Practice.   *The unique nature of some industries and business concerns sometimes requires departure from basic theory*. In the public utility industry, noncurrent assets may be reported first on the balance sheet to highlight the industry's capital-intensive nature.

---

[43] *CICA Handbook*, Section 1508, pars. .06–.08.

ILLUSTRATION 2-4
Conceptual Framework for
Financial Reporting

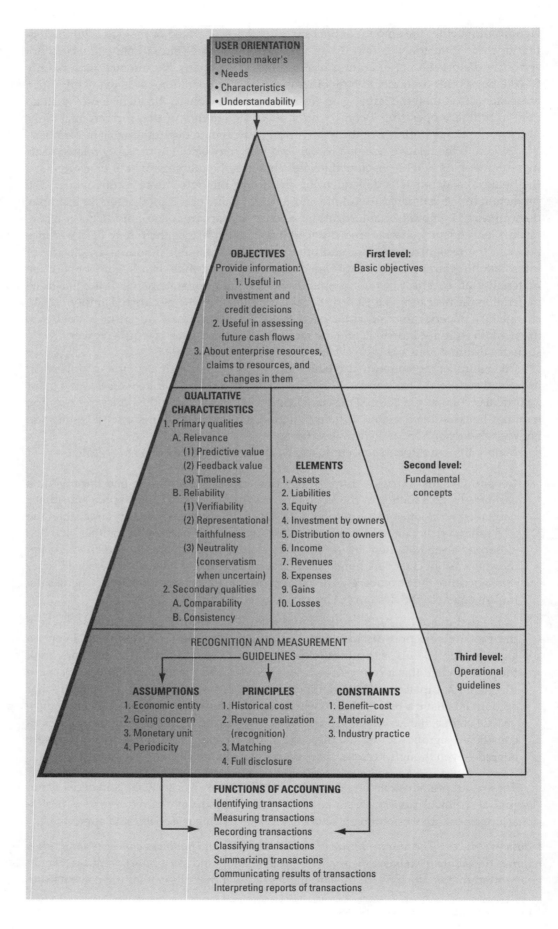

Agricultural crops are often reported at market value because it is costly to develop accurate cost figures on individual crops. Such variations from basic theory are few, yet do exist. Whenever we find what appears to be a violation of basic accounting theory, we should determine whether it is explained by some peculiar feature of the type of business involved before we criticize the procedures followed.

SUMMARY OF THE CONCEPTUAL FRAMEWORK

Illustration 2-4 summarizes the essential components of the conceptual framework discussed in this chapter. We cannot overemphasize the usefulness of this framework in helping to understand and resolve many financial accounting problems.

Throughout the remainder of this book, we will examine particular issues of contemporary financial accounting practice. In many cases, clear-cut conclusions as to what one should do regarding identification, measurement, and reporting decisions are not possible. Indeed, it will become obvious that there are many generally accepted accounting alternatives available for measuring and reporting various transactions and events. They are acceptable because of the flexibility provided by the framework and the trade-offs that, by necessity, must be made between its components. The consequence is that professional judgement is a critical aspect of financial reporting. When exercising this judgement, one must relate the framework to the circumstances involved.

The financial statements of a company are those of its management; thus it is really management that selects the generally accepted accounting methods to be used in preparing the financial statements. Senior accounting officers will, however, play a crucial role in determining the policies because of their positions as members of the management team and because of their conceptual and practical expertise.

Summary of Learning Objectives

1. **Describe what a conceptual framework is and understand its usefulness.** A conceptual framework is like a constitution in that it provides a framework and guidelines for doing accounting. It is useful because it (1) enables the development and issuance of a coherent, consistent, and useful set of standards and practices; (2) provides a framework in which new and emerging practical problems can be solved more quickly; (3) increases financial statement users' understanding of and confidence in financial reporting; and (4) enhances comparability among companies' financial statements.

2. **Appreciate the nature of the development of a conceptual framework in Canada.** While a theoretical base for financial accounting had existed implicitly in Canada for some time, it was not codified in the *CICA Handbook*, Section 1000, until 1988. This codification followed considerable work done in the United States to develop a conceptual framework for that country. It is not surprising that the Canadian framework closely parallels that of the U.S. given the similarities of the two countries in terms of thought about underlying objectives of and concepts for financial statements.

3. **Understand the objectives of financial statement reporting.** The objectives of financial reporting are to provide information that is (1) useful for making

KEY TERMS

assumptions, 44
benefit–cost relationship, 60
comparability, 49
conceptual framework, 42
conservatism, 48
consistency, 49
constraints, 44
decision usefulness, 46
economic entity assumption, 53
elements, 44
feedback value, 47
full disclosure principle, 58
going concern assumption, 53

investment, credit, and other decisions; (2) helpful for assessing the amounts, timing, and uncertainty of future cash flows; and (3) about enterprise resources, claims to those resources, and changes in them.

4. **Identify the qualitative characteristics of accounting information.** The overriding criterion by which accounting choices can be judged is decision usefulness; that is, providing information that is most useful for decision making. Usefulness requires that users are capable of understanding the information. Consequently users are assumed to have a reasonable understanding of business and economic activity and accounting, and are willing to study the information with reasonable diligence. Within this context, *relevance* and *reliability* are the two primary qualities, and *comparability* and *consistency* are the secondary qualities that make accounting information useful for decision making.

5. **Define the basic elements of financial statements.** The basic elements of financial statements are (1) assets; (2) liabilities; (3) equity; (4) revenues; (5) expenses; (6) gains; (7) losses; and (8) net income. These elements are defined on page 51.

6. **Understand the meaning of recognition and measurement.** *Recognition* is the process of including an item in the financial statements of an entity. To be recognized, (1) an item must have an appropriate basis of measurement for which a reasonable estimate can be made of the amount; and (2) for items involving obtaining or giving up future economic benefits, it must be probable that such benefits will be obtained or given up. *Measurement* is the process of determining the amount at which an item is recognized.

7. **Describe the basic assumptions of accounting.** Four basic assumptions that underlie the financial accounting structure are (1) *Economic entity:* the assumption that the activity of a business enterprise can be kept separate and distinct from its owners and any other business unit; (2) *Going concern:* the assumption that the business enterprise will continue to operate in the foreseeable future and will be able to realize assets and discharge liabilities in the normal course of operations; (3) *Monetary unit:* the assumption that money is the common denominator by which economic activity is conducted, and that the monetary unit provides an appropriate basis for measurement and analysis; and (4) *Periodicity:* the assumption that the economic activities of an enterprise can be divided into artificial time periods.

8. **Explain the application of the basic principles of accounting.** (1) *Historical cost principle:* existing GAAP requires that most assets and liabilities be accounted for and reported on the basis of acquisition price; (2) *Revenue realization (recognition):* revenue is generally recognized when (a) performance is achieved and (b) there is reasonable assurance regarding its measurability and collectibility; (3) *Matching principle:* expenses are recognized when the work (service) or the product actually makes its contribution to revenue and; (4) *Full disclosure principle:* accountants follow the general practice of providing information that is of sufficient importance to influence the judgment and decisions of an informed user.

9. **Describe the impact that constraints have on reporting accounting information.** The constraints and their impact are (1) *Benefit–cost relationship:* the benefits that can be derived from the information must be weighed against the costs of providing it; (2) *Materiality:* the materiality of an item depends on its relative size and/or its nature, and all material items should be accounted for by following appropriate accounting practices; (3) *Industry practice:* the unique nature of some industries and business concerns sometimes requires departure from basic theory.

CONCEPT REVIEW

1. What is a conceptual framework? Why is a conceptual framework useful in financial accounting?

2. What are the primary objectives of financial reporting?

3. What is meant by the term "qualitative characteristics of accounting information"?

4. Briefly describe the two primary qualities that make accounting information useful.

5. What is the distinction between comparability and consistency?

6. Why is it necessary to develop definitions for the basic elements of financial accounting?

7. Expenses, losses, and distributions to owners are all decreases in net assets. What is the distinction among them?

8. Revenues, gains, and investments by owners are all increases in net assets. What is the distinction among them?

9. What are the four basic assumptions that underlie the financial accounting structure?

10. If the going-concern assumption is not made in accounting, what difference does it make in the amounts shown in the financial statements for the following items?

    (a) Land

    (b) Depreciation expense on equipment

    (c) Long-term investments in shares of other companies

    (d) Merchandise inventory

    (e) Prepaid insurance

11. The life of a business is divided into specific time periods, usually a year, to measure results of operations for each such time period and to portray financial conditions at the end of each period.

    (a) This practice is based on the accounting assumption that the life of the business consists of a series of time periods and that it is possible to measure accurately the results of operations each period. Comment on the validity and necessity of this assumption.

    (b) What has been the effect of this practice on accounting? What is its relation to the accrual system? What influence has it had on accounting entries and methodology?

12. What are the accounting requirements regarding revenue recognition? Why, in general, has the date of sale been chosen as the point at which to recognize the revenue resulting from the entire producing and selling process in most cases?

13. What accounting assumption, principle, constraint, or characteristic does Swift Co. Ltd. use in each of the situations below?

    (a) Swift Co. Ltd. uses the lower of cost and market method to value inventories.

    (b) Swift is involved in litigation with Roderick Co. Ltd. over a product malfunction. This litigation is disclosed in the financial statements.

    (c) Swift allocates the cost of its depreciable assets over the life it expects to receive revenue from these assets.

    (d) Swift records the purchase of a new computer at its cash equivalent price.

14. Thai Co. Ltd. paid $90,000 for a machine in 1996. The Accumulated Depreciation account has a balance of $31,000 at the present time. The company could sell the machine today for $101,000. The company president believes that the company has a "right to this gain." What does the president mean by this statement? Do you agree?

15. Three expense recognition points (associating cause and effect, systematic and rational allocation, and immediate recognition) were discussed in this chapter regarding the matching principle. Indicate the basic nature of each of these types of expense recognition and give two examples of each.

16. Explain how you would decide whether to record each of the following expenditures as an asset or an expense.

    (a) Legal fees paid in connection with the purchase of land are $2,500.

    (b) Hard Pak Inc. paves the driveway leading to its office building at a cost of $20,000.

    (c) A meat market purchases a meat-grinding machine at a cost of $230.

    (d) On June 30, Shafer and Clooney, medical doctors, pay six months' office rent to cover the month of June and the next five months.

    (e) The Jayhawk Hardware Company pays $14,000 in wages to labourers for construction on a building to be used in its business.

    (f) Pat's Florists pays wages of $1,400 in November to an employee who drives their delivery truck during that month.

17. Briefly describe the types of information concerning financial position, income, and cash flows that might be provided: (a) within the main body of the financial statements; (b) in the notes to the financial statements; or (c) as supplementary information.

18. In January, 1998, Dally Corp. Ltd. doubled the amount of its outstanding shares by selling on the market an additional 10,000 shares to finance an expansion of the business. As financial statements for 1997 have not yet been completed, you propose that this information be shown by a note on the balance sheet of December 31, 1997. The president objects, claiming that this sale took place after December 31, 1997 and, therefore, should not be shown. Explain your position.

19. Describe the two major constraints inherent in the presentation of accounting information.

20. What are some of the costs of providing accounting information? What are some of the benefits of accounting information? Describe the cost/benefit factors that should be considered when new accounting standards are being proposed.

21. How is materiality (or immateriality) related to disclosures in financial statements? What factors and measures should an auditor consider in assessing the materiality of a misstatement in the presentation of a financial statement?

22. The president of Union Enterprises Ltd. has heard that conservatism is a doctrine that is followed in accounting and, therefore, proposes that several policies be followed that are conservative in nature. State your opinion with respect to the acceptability of each of the policies listed below.

    (a) A lawsuit is pending against the company. The president is unable to determine any likelihood as to whether or not the company will lose the suit and have to pay damages of $140,000 to $190,000. The president recommends that a loss be recorded and a liability created in the amount of $190,000.

    (b) The inventory should be valued at "cost or market, whichever is lower" because the losses from price declines should be recognized in the accounts in the period in which the price decline takes place.

    (c) The company gives a two-year warranty to its customers on all products sold. The estimated warranty costs incurred from this year's sales should be entered as an expense this year instead of an expense in a future period when the warranty costs are actually incurred.

    (d) When sales are made on account, there is always uncertainty about whether the accounts are collectible. Therefore, the president recommends recording the sale when the cash is received from the customers.

EXERCISES

E2-1   (Qualitative Characteristics) Illustration 2-2 provided an identification of qualitative characteristics for financial accounting information. Within this framework are primary qualities of information (and their basic ingredients) and secondary qualities of information. Presented below are a number of questions related to these characteristics which you are to answer.

1. Varied Inc. has attempted to determine the replacement cost of its inventory. Three different appraisers arrive at substantially different amounts for this value. The president, nevertheless, decides to report the middle value for external reporting purposes. Which quality of information is lacking in this data?

2. Assume that the profession permits the banking industry to defer losses on investments it sells because immediate recognition of the loss may have adverse economic consequences on the industry. Which quality of information is missing?

3. Conveyer Co. Ltd. switches from FIFO to Weighted Average to FIFO over a three-year period. Which quality of information is missing?

4. Cable Systems Co. Ltd. is the only company in its industry to depreciate its plant assets on a straight-line basis. Which quality of accounting information may be absent?

5. Sleepy Inc. does not issue its second quarter report until after the third quarter's results are reported. Which information quality is missing?

6. It was once noted that "if it becomes accepted or expected that accounting principles are determined or modified in order to secure purposes other than economic measurement, then we assume a grave risk that confidence in the credibility of our financial information system will be undermined." Which quality of accounting information should ensure that such a situation will not occur?

E2-2   (Qualitative Characteristics: Trade-Offs) Accounting statements provide useful information about business transactions and events. Those who provide financial reports must often evaluate and select from a set of accounting alternatives. The qualitative characteristics that relate to making accounting information useful for decision making were identified and discussed in Chapter 2. It was also pointed out that trade-offs or sacrifices of one quality for another are often necessary when carrying out the identification, measurement, and communication (reporting) functions of accounting.

Instructions

(a) For each of the following pairs of information qualities, give an example of a situation in which one may be sacrificed in return for a gain in the other.

   1. Relevance and reliability.
   2. Relevance and consistency.
   3. Comparability and consistency.
   4. Relevance and understandability.

(b) What criterion should be used to evaluate trade-offs between qualitative characteristics?

(Elements of Financial Statements) Eight interrelated elements that are most directly related to measuring the performance and financial status of an enterprise are identified below: **E2-3**

Assets	Net income
Liabilities	Revenues
Equity	Expenses
Gains	Losses

Instructions

State the element or elements associated with each of the following 10 items:

   1. Arises from peripheral or incidental transactions.
   2. Obligation to transfer resources arising from past transaction.
   3. Increases ownership interest.
   4. Decreases net assets in a period from non-owner sources.
   5. Items characterized by service potential or future economic benefit.
   6. Arises from income statement activities that constitute the entity's ongoing major or central operations.
   7. Residual interest in the assets of the enterprise after deducting its liabilities.
   8. Increases assets during a period through sale of products.
   9. Decreases assets during the period for the payment of wages.
   10. Generally includes all changes in equity during the period, except those resulting from investments by owners and distributions to owners.

(Assumptions, Principles, and Constraints) Presented below are the assumptions, principles, and constraints identified in this chapter: **E2-4**

Economic entity assumption	Full disclosure principle
Going concern assumption	Benefit–cost constraint
Monetary unit assumption	Materiality
Periodicity assumption	Industry practices
Historical cost principle	Matching principle

Instructions

Identify the accounting assumption, principle, or constraint that describes each situation below. Do not use an answer more than once.

   1. Indicates that personal and business record-keeping should be separately maintained.
   2. Separates financial information into time periods for reporting purposes.
   3. Permits the use of market value valuation in certain specific situations.
   4. Requires that information significant enough to affect the decision of reasonably informed users should be disclosed. (Do not use full disclosure principle.)
   5. Assumes that the dollar is the "measuring stick" used to report on financial performance.
   6. Allocates expenses to revenues in the appropriate period.
   7. Indicates that market value changes subsequent to purchase are not recorded in the accounts. (Do not use revenue recognition principle.)
   8. Ensures that relevant financial information is reported.

9. Rationale that explains why plant assets are not reported at liquidation value. (Do not use historical cost principle.)

10. Provides justification for the argument that all standards should not have to be adhered to by small businesses when preparing financial statements.

E2-5 **(Assumptions, Principles, and Constraints)** Presented below are a number of operational guidelines and practices that have developed over time:

1. Price-level changes are not recognized in the accounting records.
2. Financial information is presented so that reasonably prudent investors will not be misled.
3. Cost of intangibles such as patents are capitalized and amortized over the periods that are benefited.
4. The cost of low-priced repair tools is expensed when purchases are made.
5. Brokerage firms use market value for purposes of valuation of all marketable securities.
6. Each enterprise is kept as a unit distinct from its owner or owners.
7. All significant subsequent events (i.e., occur after the balance sheet date but before the statements are prepared) are reported.
8. Revenue is recorded at point of sale.
9. All important aspects of bond indentures (contracts) are presented in financial statements.
10. Rationale for accrual accounting is stated.
11. The preparation of consolidated statements is justified.
12. Reporting must be done at defined time intervals.
13. An allowance for doubtful accounts is established.
14. Payments out of petty cash are charged to Miscellaneous Expense.
15. Goodwill is recorded only when it is purchased and not when it is created by operations.
16. A company charges its sales commission costs to expense when the sales are made.

Instructions

Select the assumption, principle, or constraint that most appropriately justifies each of these procedures and practices. Do not use components of the qualitative characteristics.

E2-6 **(Assumptions, Principles, and Constraints)** A number of accounting procedures and practices are described below.

1. The treasurer of Specialty Wines Co. Ltd. wishes to prepare financial statements only during downturns in their wine production, which occur periodically when the rhubarb crop fails. He states that the statements can be most easily prepared at such times. In no event should more than 30 months pass by without statements being prepared.

2. The Nuclear Power & Light Corporation has purchased a large amount of property, plant, and equipment over a number of years. Because the general price level has changed materially over the years, it has decided to issue only price-level-adjusted financial statements.

3. Flower Plants Co. Ltd. decided to manufacture its own pots because it would be cheaper to do so than to buy them from an outside supplier. In an attempt to make its statements more comparable with those of its competitors, the company charged its inventory account for what it thought the pots would cost if they were purchased from an outside supplier.

4. Zonkers Discount Centres Inc. buys its merchandise by the truck- and train-load. Zonkers does not defer any transportation costs in computing the cost of its ending inventory. Such costs, although varying from period to period, are always material in amount.

5. Grab & Run Inc., a fast-food company, sells franchises for $70,000, accepting a $1,000 down payment and a 50-year note for the remainder. Grab & Run promises within three years to assist in site selection, building, and management training. Grab & Run records the $70,000 franchise fee as revenue in the period in which the contract is signed.

6. Agri Chemical Corp. "faces possible expropriation (i.e., take-over) of foreign facilities and possible losses on sums owed by various customers on the verge of bankruptcy." The company president has decided that these possibilities should not be noted on the financial statements because Agri still hopes that these events will not take place.

7. Cory Jones, manager of College Bookstore Inc., bought a computer for her own use. She paid for it by writing a cheque on the bookstore's chequing account and charged it to the "Office Equipment" account.

8. Calvin Co. Ltd. recently completed a new 120-storey office building that housed their home offices and many other tenants. All the office equipment for the building that had a per-item or per-unit cost of $1,000 or less was expensed, even though the office equipment had an average life of 10 years. The total cost of such office equipment was approximately $26 million. (Do not use the matching principle.)

9. Hobbes Inc. presented its financial statements on the basis of what its assets could be sold for and the amount required to pay off its liabilities on the balance sheet date. When the president was asked why this was done, she stated, "That is what banks are interested in."

10. A large lawsuit has been filed against Elmer Inc. by Bugs Co. Ltd. Elmer has recorded a loss and related estimated liability equal to the maximum possible amount it feels it may have to pay. It is confident, however, that either it will not likely lose the suit or it will owe a much smaller amount.

Instructions

For each of the foregoing, list the major accounting assumption, principle, or constraint that would be violated. Do not use components of the qualitative characteristics.

(Assumptions, Principles, and Constraints) You are engaged to review the accounting records of Mysterious Corporation prior to the closing of the revenue and expense accounts as of December 31, the end of the current fiscal year. The following information comes to your attention.   **E2-7**

1. In preparing the balance sheet, detailed information as to the amount of cash on deposit in each of several banks was omitted. Only the total amount of cash under a caption "Cash in Banks" was presented.

2. On July 15 of the current year, Mysterious Corporation purchased an undeveloped tract of land at a cost of $300,000. The company spent $75,000 in subdividing the land and getting it ready for sale. An appraisal of the property at the end of the year indicated that the land was now worth $460,000. Although none of the lots were sold, the company recognized revenue of $160,000, less related expenses of $75,000, for a net income on the project of $85,000.

3. For a number of years, the company had used the average cost method for inventory valuation purposes. During the current year, the president noted that all the other companies in their industry had switched to the FIFO method. The company decided not to switch to FIFO because net income would decrease $280,000.

4. During the current year, Mysterious Corporation changed its policy in regard to expensing purchases of small tools. In the past, these purchases were always expensed because they amounted to less than 2% of net income, but the president has decided that capitalization and subsequent depreciation should now be followed. It is expected that purchases of small tools will not fluctuate greatly from year to year.

5. Mysterious Corporation constructed a warehouse at a cost of $800,000. The company had been depreciating the asset on a straight-line basis over 10 years. In the current year, the controller doubled depreciation expense because the replacement cost of the warehouse had increased significantly.

6. The company decided in October of the current fiscal year to start a massive advertising campaign to enhance the marketability of its product. In November, the company paid $900,000 for advertising time on a major television network to advertise its product during the next 12 months. The controller expensed the $900,000 in the current year on the basis that "once the money is spent, it can never be recovered from the television network."

Instructions

State whether or not you agree with the decisions made by Mysterious Corporation. Support your answers with reference, whenever possible, to the appropriate aspects of the conceptual framework developed in this chapter and any assumptions about the circumstances of Mysterious that you think would be helpful.

(Revenue Recognition and Matching Principle) After listening to the presentation of your report on the financial statements, one of the new directors of Hagar Publishing Co. Ltd. expresses surprise that the income statement assumes that an equal proportion of the revenue is earned with the publication of every issue of the company's magazine. He feels that "performance is achieved" in the process of earning revenue in the magazine business when there is a cash sale for the subscription. He says that he does not understand why most of the revenue cannot be "recognized" in the period of the sale.   **E2-8**

Instructions

(a) List the various accepted methods for recognizing revenue in the accounts and explain when the methods are appropriate.

(b) Discuss the propriety of timing the recognition of revenue in Hagar Publishing Co. Ltd.'s accounts with:
   1. The cash sale of the magazine subscription.
   2. The publication of the magazine every month.
   3. Both events, by realizing a portion of the revenue with cash sale of the magazine subscription and a portion of the revenue with the publication of the magazine every month.

(AICPA adapted)

E2-9   **(Matching Principle)** An accountant must be familiar with the concepts involved in determining earnings of a business entity. The amount of earnings reported for a business entity is dependent on the appropriate recognition, in general, of revenues and expenses for a given time period. In some situations, costs are recognized as expenses in the time period of the product sale; in other situations, guidelines have been developed for recognizing costs as expenses or losses by other criteria.

Instructions
(a) Explain the rationale for recognizing costs as expenses at the time of product sale.
(b) Explain why it is appropriate to treat some costs as expenses of a period instead of assigning the costs to an asset.
(c) In what general circumstances would it be appropriate to treat a cost as an asset instead of as an expense? Explain.
(d) Some expenses are assigned to specific accounting periods on the basis of systematic and rational allocation of asset costs. Explain the underlying rationale for recognizing expenses on the basis of systematic and rational allocation of asset costs.
(e) Identify the conditions in which it would be appropriate to treat a cost as a loss.

(AICPA adapted)

E2-10   **(Full Disclosure Principle)** Presented below are a number of facts related to Dynamic Inc. Assume that no mention of these facts was made in the financial statements and the related notes.
   1. The company decided that, for the sake of conciseness, only net income should be reported on the income statement. Details as to revenues, cost of goods sold, and expenses were omitted.
   2. Equipment purchases of $140,000 were partly financed during the year through the issuance of $90,000 in notes payable. The company offset the equipment against the notes payable and reported plant assets at $50,000.
   3. The company is a defendant in a patent-infringement suit involving a material amount; you have received assurance from the company's counsel that the possibility of loss is remote.
   4. During the year, an assistant controller for the company embezzled $10,000. Dynamic's net income for the year was $1,700,000. The assistant controller and the money have not been found.
   5. Because of a recent gasoline shortage, it is possible that Dynamic may suffer a costly shutdown in the near future similar to those suffered by other companies both within and outside the industry.
   6. Dynamic has reported its ending inventory at $2,000,000 in the financial statements. No other information related to inventories is presented in the financial statements and related notes.
   7. The company changed its method of depreciating equipment from the double-declining balance method to the straight-line method. No mention of this change was made in the financial statements.

Instructions
Assume that you are the auditor of Dynamic Inc. and you have been asked to explain the appropriate accounting and related disclosure necessary for each of these items. Provide your explanations.

E2-11   **(Materiality Constraint)** Each of the items below involves the question of materiality to Doormat Co. Ltd.
   1. The company purchases several items of equipment each year that cost less than $100 each. Most of them are used for several years, but some of them last for less than a year. The total cost of these purchases is about the same each year.
   2. The amount of $1,400 is paid during 1998 for an assessment of additional income taxes for the year 1996. The amount originally paid in 1996 was $26,000, and the amount of this year's income taxes will be $41,000.
   3. Land that had originally been purchased for expansion is sold in 1998 at a gain of $9,000. Net income for the year is $72,000, including the gain of $9,000. The company has experienced similar types of gains in the past.

Instructions
State your recommendation as to how each item should be treated in the accounts and in the statements, giving appropriate consideration to materiality and practicality aspects.

(Accounting Principles: Comprehensive) Presented below are a number of business transactions that occurred during the current year for Ellen Co. Ltd. **E2-12**

1. The president of the company used his expense account to purchase a new car solely for personal use. The following entry was made:

Miscellaneous Expense	26,000	
Cash		26,000

2. Merchandise inventory that cost $600,000 is reported on the balance sheet at $670,000, the expected selling price less estimated selling costs. The following entry was made to record this increase in value:

Merchandise Inventory	70,000	
Revenue		70,000

3. Merchandise inventory that cost 600,000 is reported on the balance sheet at $530,000, the expected selling price less estimated selling costs. The following entry was made to record this decrease in value:

Loss on Inventory Due to Price Decline	70,000	
Inventory		70,000

4. The company is being sued for $200,000 by a customer who claims damages for personal injury apparently caused by a defective product. Company lawyers feel extremely confident that the company will have no liability for damages resulting from the situation. Nevertheless, the company decides to make the following entry:

Loss from Lawsuit	200,000	
Liability for Lawsuit		200,000

5. Because the general level of prices increased during the current year, the company determined that there was a $15,000 understatement of depreciation expense on its equipment and decided to record it in its accounts. The following entry was made:

Depreciation Expense	15,000	
Accumulated Depreciation		15,000

6. Ellen Co. Ltd. has been concerned about whether intangible assets could generate cash in case of liquidation. As a consequence, goodwill arising from a purchase transaction during the current year and recorded at $600,000 was written off as follows:

Retained Earnings	600,000	
Goodwill		600,000

7. Because of a "fire sale," equipment obviously worth $290,000 was acquired at a cost of $240,000. The following entry was made:

Equipment	290,000	
Cash		240,000
Revenue		50,000

Instructions
For each of the situations above, discuss the appropriateness of the journal entries in light of the components of the conceptual framework.

(Accounting Principles: Comprehensive) Presented below is information related to Robotics Inc. **E2-13**

1. An order for $37,000 has been received from a customer for products on hand. This order was shipped on January 9, 1999. The company made the following entry in 1998:

Accounts Receivable	37,000	
Sales		37,000

2. During the year, the company sold certain equipment for $280,000, recognizing a gain of $57,000. Because the controller believed that new equipment would be needed in the near future, the controller decided to defer the gain and amortize it over the life of any new equipment purchased.

3. Depreciation expense on the building for the year was $50,000. Because the building was increasing in value during the year, the controller decided to charge the depreciation expense to retained earnings instead of to net income. The following entry was recorded:

Retained Earnings	50,000	
Accumulated Depreciation—Buildings		50,000

4. During the year, the company purchased equipment through the issuance of common shares. The shares had a fair market value of $80,000. The fair market value of the equipment was not easily determinable. The company recorded this transaction as follows:

Equipment	80,000	
Common Shares		80,000

5. Materials were purchased on January 1, 1998 for $70,000 and this amount was entered in the Materials account. On December 31, 1998, the materials would have cost $82,000, so the following entry is made:

Inventory	12,000	
Gain on Inventories		12,000

Instructions
Comment on the appropriateness of the accounting procedures followed by Robotics Inc. for the year ended December 31, 1998.

CASES

C2-1 Various attempts have been and are being made to work toward a conceptual framework for financial accounting and reporting. These attempts have met with some success. In Canada, the *CICA Handbook* includes a section on financial statement concepts. In the United States, the FASB issued a series of publications on financial accounting concepts. Internationally, the IASC has issued a statement on a framework for preparing and presenting financial statements. These attempts have helped to clarify the use and application of general accounting concepts for standard-setting bodies and for individual companies when they are making financial accounting decisions.

Instructions
Identify and discuss the usefulness and limitations of a conceptual framework for financial accounting and reporting, with particular regard to the accounting profession, international harmonization, setting of accounting standards, accounting education, and financial statement users. (UFE of the CICA adapted)

C2-2 Presented below is a statement that appeared about Weyerhaeuser Company in a financial magazine.

The land and timber holdings are now carried on the company's books at a mere $422 million. The value of the timber alone is variously estimated at from $3 billion to $7 billion and is rising all the time. "The understatement of the company is pretty severe," conceded Charles W. Bingham, a senior vice-president. Adds Robert L. Schuyler, another senior vice-president, "We have a whole stream of profit nobody sees and there is no way to show it on our books."

Instructions
(a) What does Schuyler mean when he says that "we have a whole stream of profit nobody sees and there is no way to show it on our books"? Is his comment correct?

(b) If the understatement of the company's assets is severe, why does accounting not report this information?

C2-3 On June 8, 1997, Chek Inc. signed a contract with Mate Associates under which Mate agreed (1) to construct an office building on land owned by Chek; (2) to accept responsibility for procuring financing for the project and finding tenants; and (3) to manage the property for 35 years. The annual net income from the project, after debt service, was to be divided equally between Chek Inc. and Mate Associates. Mate was to accept its share of future net income as full payment for its services in construction, obtaining finances and tenants, and management of the project.

By May 31, 1998, the project was nearly completed and tenants had signed leases to occupy 90% of the available space at annual rentals aggregating $3,000,000. It is estimated that, after operating expenses and debt service, the annual net income will amount to $1,100,000. The management of Mate Associates believed that the economic benefit derived from the contract with Chek should be reflected on its financial statements for the fiscal year ended May 31, 1998 and directed that revenue be accrued in an amount equal to the commercial value of the services Mate had rendered during the year, that this amount be carried in contracts receivable, and that all related expenditures be charged against the revenue.

Instructions
(a) Explain the main difference between the economic concept of business income as reflected by Mate's management and the measurement of income under generally accepted accounting principles.

(b) Is the belief of Mate's management in accord with generally accepted accounting principles for the measurement of revenue and expenses for the year ended May 31, 1998? Support your opinion by discussing the application to this case of the factors to be considered for asset measurement and revenue and expense recognition.

(AICPA adapted)

Fine Homes sells and erects shell houses, that is, frame structures that are completely finished on the outside but are **C2-4** unfinished on the inside except for flooring, partition studding, and ceiling joists. Shell houses are sold chiefly to customers who are handy with tools and who have time to do the interior wiring, plumbing, wall completion and finishing, and other work necessary to make the shell houses livable dwellings.

Fine buys shell houses from a manufacturer in unassembled packages consisting of all lumber, roofing, doors, windows, and similar materials necessary to complete a shell house. Upon commencing operations in a new area, Fine buys or leases land as a site for its local warehouse, field office, and display houses. Sample display houses are erected at a total cost ranging from $25,000 to $30,000 including the cost of the unassembled packages. The chief element of cost of the display houses is the unassembled packages, inasmuch as erection is a short low-cost operation. Old sample models are torn down or altered into new models every three to seven years. Sample display houses have little salvage value because dismantling and moving costs amount to nearly as much as the cost of an unassembled package.

Instructions
(a) A choice must be made between (1) expensing the costs of sample display houses in the periods in which the expenditure is made; and (2) spreading the costs over more than one period. Discuss the advantages of each method. Which method would you recommend?

(b) Would it be preferable to amortize (depreciate) the cost of display houses on the basis of (1) the passage of time; or (2) the number of shell houses sold? Justify your choice.

(AICPA adapted)

The general ledger of Comic Ltd., a corporation engaged in developing and producing of television programs **C2-5** for commercial sponsorship, contains the following asset accounts before amortization at the end of the current year:

	Balance
Hi and Louise	$60,000
Better or Worse	41,000
Sally Fifth	21,500
Phantom	9,000
Chickweed Road	4,000

An examination of contracts and records revealed the following information:

1. The first two accounts listed above represent the total cost of completed programs that were televised during the accounting period just ended. Under the terms of an existing contract, Hi and Louise will be rerun during the next accounting period at a fee equal to 50% of the fee for the first televising of the program. The contract for the first run produced $600,000 of revenue. The contract with the sponsor of Better or Worse provides that he may, at his option, rerun the program during the next season at a fee of 75% of the fee on the first televising of the program.

2. The balance in the Sally Fifth account is the cost of a new program that has just been completed and is being considered by several companies for commercial sponsorship.

3. The balance in the Phantom account represents the cost of a partially completed program for a projected series that has been abandoned.

4. The balance of the Chickweed Road account consists of payments made to a firm of engineers that prepared a report on how to more efficiently utilize of existing studio space and equipment.

Instructions

(a) State the general principle (or principles) of accounting that are applicable to the first four accounts.

(b) How would you report each of the first four accounts in the financial statements of Comic Ltd.? Explain.

(c) In what way, if at all, does the Chickweed Road account differ from the first four? Explain.   (AICPA adapted)

C2-6 You are engaged in the audit of Information Highway Services Ltd., which opened its first branch office in 1998. During the audit Barbara Car, president, raises the question of the accounting treatment of the operating loss of the branch office for its first year, which is material in amount.

The president proposes to capitalize the operating loss as a "start-up" expense to be amortized over a five-year period. She states that branch offices of other firms engaged in the same field generally suffer a first-year operating loss that is invariably capitalized, and you are aware of this practice. She argues, therefore, that the loss should be capitalized so that the accounting will be "conservative"; further, she argues that the accounting must be "consistent" with established industry practice.

Instructions

Discuss the president's use of the words "conservative" and "consistent" from the standpoint of accounting terminology. Identify and justify the accounting treatment you would recommend.   (AICPA adapted)

C2-7 The president of a public corporation recently commented, "Our auditor states that our financial statements present fairly our financial position and the results of our operations. I challenged him as to how he determined such fairness. He replied that fairness means that the financial statements are not misstated in amounts that would be considered material.

I believe that there is some confusion with this materiality concept, since different users of our financial statements may have different ideas as to what is material. For example, bankers, institutional investors, small investors, and tax assessors all have different perceptions of materiality."

Instructions

Discuss the issues raised by the president.

C2-8 Each of the following statements represents a decision made by the controller of Ebert's Picks Enterprises on which your advice is asked.

1. A building purchased by the company five years ago for $250,000, including the land on which it stands, can now be sold for $300,000. The controller instructs that the new value of $300,000 be entered in the accounts.

2. Material included in the inventory that cost $60,000 has become obsolete. The controller contends that no loss can be realized until the goods are sold, and so the material remains included in the inventory at $60,000.

3. Inasmuch as profits for the year appear to be extremely small, no depreciation of tangible capital assets is to be recorded as an expense this year.

4. The company occupies the building in which it operates under a long-term lease requiring annual rental payments. It sublets certain office space not required for its own purposes. The controller credits rents received against rents paid to get net rent expense.

5. A flood during the year destroyed or damaged a considerable amount of uninsured inventory. No entry was made for this loss because the controller reasons that the ending inventory will, of course, be reduced by the amount of the destroyed or damaged merchandise, and therefore its cost will be included in cost of goods sold and the net income figure will be correct.

6. The company provides housing for certain employees and adjusts their salaries accordingly. The controller contends that the cost to the company of maintaining this housing should be charged to "Wages and Salaries."

7. The entire cost of a new delivery truck is to be charged to an expense account.

8. The company has paid a large sum for an advertising campaign to promote a new product that will not be placed on the market until the following year. The controller has charged this amount to a prepaid expense account.

9. The company operates a cafeteria for the convenience of its employees. Sales made by the cafeteria are credited to the regular sales account for product sales; food purchased and salaries paid for the cafeteria operations are recorded in the regular purchase and payroll accounts.

10. A customer leaving the building slipped on an icy spot on the stairway and wrenched his back. He immediately entered suit against the company for permanent physical injuries and claims damages in the amount of $160,000. The suit has not yet come to trial. The controller has made an entry charging a special loss account and crediting a liability account.

Instructions
State (a) whether you agree with the controller's decision and (b) the justification for your position. Consider each decision independently of all others.

Not-for-profit organizations are organizations in which there is normally no transferable ownership interest and from which the members or contributors do not receive any direct economic benefit, and that are formed for social, educational, religious, health, charitable or other not-for-profit purposes (Source: *CICA Handbook*, Section 4400). **C2-9**

    Not-for-profit organizations often rely on donations and volunteers to support the staff in carrying out programs and functions. Financial grants (from governments and other bodies) are subject to uncertainty and, when provided, typically are paid annually or quarterly. These grants may be for operations and/or capital asset purchases. Fundraising programs often take up a substantial amount of time. Cash flow from month to month is frequently a major problem. When there is insufficient cash, programs (i.e., services, projects) are discontinued.

    Within this environment, various individuals argue that applying GAAP as specified for profit seeking enterprises in the *CICA Handbook* is inappropriate. Others state that not-for-profit organizations must be required to follow such GAAP so that order can be created out of the chaos that exists due to each organization using its own unique accounting practices.

Instructions
For the following components of the conceptual framework, state (1) why it is not appropriate for not-for-profit organizations; and (2) why it is appropriate for not-for-profit organizations.

(a) Going concern assumption.

(b) Historical cost principle.

(c) Revenue realization principle.

(d) Matching principle.

(e) Benefits versus costs constraint.

USING YOUR JUDGEMENT

FINANCIAL REPORTING PROBLEM 1

A major Canadian airline has a "frequent flyer program." Airline customers purchase tickets (economy, business class, first class) and accumulate kilometres based on distances flown. Customers can then redeem "rewards" of free "return tickets" for themselves or immediate family members to various destinations, the number and type of tickets and the destinations depending on the number of kilometres accumulated and the "cost" of the "reward" in terms of kilometres to be deducted from those accumulated. Kilometres accumulated by customers vary from 20,000 to over 2,000,000. The time period over which "rewards" may be claimed is not specified, although announcements from the airline have indicated that the frequent flyer program will terminate in two years (as the two-year deadline approaches, however, the airline has extended the termination date another two years five times in the past).

Instructions
From the airline's point of view, how, if at all, should the frequent flyer program be accounted for? Make sure to identify accounting issues involved and how you would resolve them. (Hint: As a starting point you may wish to consider issues in terms of recognition, measurement, and disclosure aspects as they pertain to financial accounting.)

FINANCIAL REPORTING PROBLEM 2

Recently, your Uncle Waldo, who knows that you always have your eye out for a profitable investment, has discussed the possibility of you purchasing some corporate bonds. He suggests that you may wish to get in on the "ground floor" of this deal. The bonds being issued by the Cricket Corp. are 10-year debentures that promise a 40% rate of return. Cricket manufactures novelty/party items.

You have told Waldo that, unless you can take a look at Cricket's financial statements, you would not feel comfortable about such an investment. Knowing that this is the chance of a lifetime, Uncle Waldo has obtained a copy of Cricket's most recent, unaudited financial statements which are a year old. These statements were prepared by Mrs. John Cricket. You peruse these statements, and they are quite impressive. The balance sheet showed a debt-to-equity ratio of .10 and, for the year shown, the company reported net income of $2,424,240.

The financial statements are not shown in comparison with amounts from other years. In addition, no significant note disclosures about inventory valuation, depreciation methods, loan agreements, etc. are available.

Instructions
Write a letter to Uncle Waldo explaining why it would be unwise to base an investment decision on the financial statements that he has provided to you. Be sure to explain why these financial statements are neither relevant nor reliable.

ETHICS CASE

Sunnyside Nuclear Plant will be mothballed (closed down) at the end of its useful life (in approximately 20 years) at great expense. The matching principle requires that expenses be matched to revenue. Accountants Iris Stuart and Stanley Smith argue whether it is better to allocate the cost of mothballing over the next 20 years or to ignore it until mothballing occurs.

Instructions
(a) What stakeholders are affected by the choice of how to account for the cost, and how are they affected?
(b) What, if any, is the ethical issue underlying the dispute?
(c) What decision would you make?

chapter 3

A REVIEW OF THE ACCOUNTING PROCESS

CHAPTER

3

A Review of the Accounting Process

Learning Objectives

After studying this chapter, you should be able to:

1. Understand basic accounting terminology.

2. Explain double-entry rules.

3. Identify steps in the accounting cycle.

4. Record transactions in journals, post to ledger accounts, and prepare a trial balance.

5. Explain the reasons for preparing adjusting entries.

6. Explain how inventory accounts are adjusted at year end.

7. Prepare closing entries.

8. Identify adjusting entries that may be reversed.

9. Prepare a 10-column work sheet.

10. Differentiate the cash basis of accounting from the accrual basis of accounting (Appendix 3A).

Accounting systems vary widely from one business to another. Factors that shape accounting systems are the *nature of the business* and its *transactions*, the *size of the company*, the *volume of data* to be handled, and the *informational demands* that management and others place on the system.

Broadly defined, an accounting system includes the activities required to provide information needed for planning, controlling, and reporting the financial condition and results of operations of the enterprise. As discussed in Chapter 1, this information helps managers, investors, creditors, and others assess and evaluate the enterprise when making decisions. Consequently, a well-devised accounting system is important to every business enterprise. A company that does not keep an accurate record of its business transactions and use such information is likely to lose revenue and operate inefficiently.

Although most companies have satisfactory accounting systems, some companies are inefficient partly because of poor accounting procedures or failure to use or adequately interpret accounting information. Consider, for example, the case of the Canadian Commercial Bank failure. Testimony during the judicial inquiry into the failure indicated serious weaknesses in the policies that were used to classify loans—"bad loans" were classified as "good loans." While the financial credibility (liquidity and profitability) of some organizations in terms of being able to pay the loans and interest was definitely suspect, this type of information was apparently not a significant factor in granting the loans or monitoring the realizability of the loans once granted. When one of the largest gold and silver retailers, the International Gold Bullion Exchange (IGBE), was forced to declare bankruptcy, its records were in such a shambles that it was difficult to determine how much money it lost. The company had failed to keep track of its revenues and had written cheques on uncollected funds. IGBE had even allowed its employee health insurance to lapse while it continued to collect premiums from workers.

Even the use of computers provides no assurance of accuracy and efficiency. An example is Maislin Industries Ltd., a Montreal company that was once hailed as one of North America's largest international trucking companies. In anticipation of deregulation in the industry, Maislin carried out an expansion plan that resulted in a considerable debt position. The following year, many events occurred that affected the company, one of which was a complete breakdown of its integrated computer system which included accounting and other information. Orders were lost, shipments disappeared, billings were incorrect, receivables were not billed for up to six months, and cash flows were a serious problem. Maislin's previously consistent profit performance ended that year with a loss of over $13 million, and the bank called for substantial payment on its loans shortly thereafter.[1]

Although these situations are not common, they illustrate that accounts and detailed records must be kept by every business enterprise. With this in mind, the objectives of this chapter are to concisely yet thoroughly review the accounting process, identify and explain basic procedures, and describe the way in which these procedures are combined in carrying out the accounting cycle. Much of the material may serve as a review of what was studied in introductory accounting; yet it is of fundamental importance to understanding how and why transactions and other economic events become a part of financial statements, and how and why alternative accounting policies can result in differences in financial position and net income. While the procedures are mechanical and often carried out using computers, one must know what is happening within an accounting system in order to have this understanding. Also, understanding and using the terminology is crucial to concisely describing the results of recognition and measurement decisions made regarding particular transactions and events.

ACCOUNTING TERMINOLOGY

Financial accounting rests on a set of concepts (see Chapters 1 and 2) and rules for identifying, measuring, recording, classifying, summarizing, and interpreting transactions and other economic events relating to enterprises. To do accounting, it is important to understand some basic terminology employed in collecting accounting data. Commonly used terms are defined below.

Event. A happening of consequence. An **event** generally is the source or cause of changes in assets, liabilities, and owners' equity. Events may be categorized as external or internal.

Transaction. An external event involving the transfer or exchange of something of value between two or more entities.

Account. A systematic arrangement that shows the effect of transactions and other events on a specific asset or equity. A separate account is kept for each asset, liability, revenue, expense, and item of capital (owners' equity).

Real and Nominal Accounts. Real (permanent) accounts are asset, liability, and owners' equity accounts that appear on the balance sheet. **Nominal (temporary) accounts** are revenue, expense, and dividend accounts; except for dividends, they appear on the income statement. Nominal accounts are periodically closed; real accounts are not.

Ledger. The book or computer file containing the accounts. Each account usually has a separate page. A **general ledger** is a collection of all asset, liability, owners'

OBJECTIVE 1
Understand basic accounting terminology.

---

[1] Tony Dimnik and Joseph N. Fry, "Maislin Industries Ltd. (A)" (London, ON: School of Business Administration, University of Western Ontario, 1986).

equity, revenue, and expense accounts. A **subsidiary ledger** contains the details related to a specific general ledger account.

Journal. The book of original entry where transactions and selected other events are initially recorded. Various amounts are transferred from a journal to accounts in the ledger.

Posting. The process of transferring the essential facts and figures from the journal to the accounts in the ledger.

Trial Balance. A list of all open accounts in the ledger and their balances. A **trial balance** taken immediately after all adjustments have been posted is called an **adjusted trial balance**. A trial balance taken immediately after closing entries have been posted is designated an **after-closing** or **post-closing trial balance**.

Adjusting Entries. Entries made at the end of an accounting period to bring all accounts up-to-date on an accrual accounting basis so that financial statements can be prepared.

Financial Statements. Statements that reflect the collection, tabulation, and final summarization of the accounting data. Four statements are involved: (1) the balance sheet, which shows the financial condition of the enterprise at the end of a period; (2) the income statement, which measures the results of operations during the period; (3) the statement of cash flows (statement of changes in financial position), which reports the cash provided and used by operating, investing, and financing activities during the period; and (4) the statement of retained earnings, which shows the changes in the retained earnings account from the beginning to the end of the period. **Notes** and **supporting schedules** cross-referenced to the financial statements are an integral part of such statements.

Closing Entries. Entries that reduce all nominal account balances to zero and transfer the resulting net income or net loss to an owners' equity account. The process of making closing entries is known as "closing the ledger," "closing the books," or merely "closing."

DEBITS, CREDITS, AND DOUBLE-ENTRY ACCOUNTING

OBJECTIVE 2
Explain double-entry rules.

In accounting, the terms debit and credit simply mean the left and right sides of any account, respectively. The left side of any account is the debit (or Dr.) side; the right side, the credit (or Cr.) side. The act of entering an amount on the left side of an account is called **debiting** the account, and making an entry on the right side is **crediting** the account. When the totals of the two sides are compared, an account will have a **debit balance** if the total of the debit amounts exceeds the credits. Conversely, an account will have a **credit balance** if the credit amounts exceed the debits.

The debit and credit sides of an account are used to record increases and decreases in the account. However, whether debiting an account means it is being increased or decreased depends on the type of account involved. *All asset and expense accounts are increased on the left or debit side and decreased on the right or credit side.* Conversely, *all liability and revenue accounts are increased on the right or credit side and decreased on the left or debit side. Shareholders' equity accounts, like Common Shares and Retained Earnings, are increased on the credit side. A Dividends account is increased on the debit side.* These basic rules of debit and credit for an accounting system are presented in Illustration 3-1.

Assume a transaction in which service is rendered for cash. Two accounts are affected: both an asset account (Cash) and a revenue account (Sales) are increased. Cash is

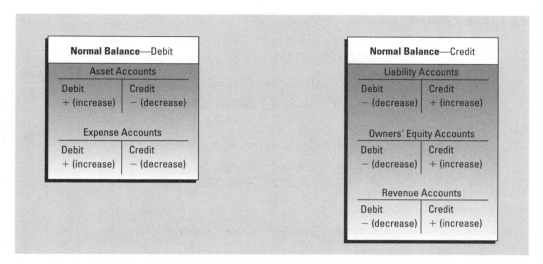

ILLUSTRATION 3-1
Double-Entry (Debit and Credit) Accounting System

debited and Sales credited. This reveals the essentials of a **double-entry accounting system**—*for every debit there must be a credit and vice versa.*

This leads us, then, to the **basic accounting equation**:

$$\text{Assets} = \text{Liabilities} + \text{Owners' Equity}$$

Illustration 3-2 expands this equation to show the accounts that comprise shareholders' equity (owners' equity in a corporation). In addition, the debit/credit rules and effects on each type of account are indicated. Study this carefully. It will help you to understand the fundamentals of the double-entry system.

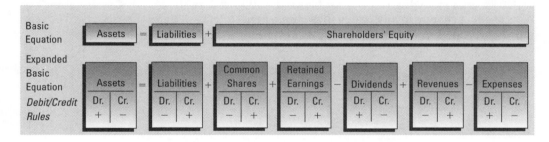

ILLUSTRATION 3-2
Expanded Basic Equation and Debit/Credit Rules

Every time a transaction occurs, the elements of the equation change, but the basic balance sheet equality remains. To illustrate, here are eight different transactions.

1. Owner invests $40,000 cash for use in the business.

$$\text{Assets} = \text{Liabilities} + \text{Owners' Equity}$$
$$+40,000 \qquad\qquad\qquad +40,000$$

2. Pay $600 cash for secretarial wages.

$$\text{Assets} = \text{Liabilities} + \text{Owners' Equity}$$
$$-600 \qquad\qquad\qquad -600 \text{ (expense)}$$

3. Purchase office equipment priced at $5,200, giving a 10% promissory note in exchange:

$$\text{Assets} = \text{Liabilities} + \text{Owners' Equity}$$
$$+5,200 \qquad\qquad +5,200$$

4. Receive $4,000 cash for services rendered.

$$\text{Assets} = \text{Liabilities} + \text{Owners' Equity}$$
$$+4,000 \qquad\qquad\qquad +4,000 \text{ (revenue)}$$

5. Pay off a short-term liability of $7,000.

$$\text{Assets} = \text{Liabilities} + \text{Owners' Equity}$$
$$-7{,}000 \quad -7{,}000$$

6. Declare a cash dividend of $5,000 which will be paid in the future.

$$\text{Assets} = \text{Liabilities} + \text{Owners' Equity}$$
$$+5{,}000 \quad -5{,}000$$

7. Convert a long-term liability of $80,000 into common shares.

$$\text{Assets} = \text{Liabilities} + \text{Owners' Equity}$$
$$-80{,}000 \quad +80{,}000$$

8. Pay cash of $16,000 for a delivery van.

$$\text{Assets} = \text{Liabilities} + \text{Owners' Equity}$$
$$-16{,}000$$
$$+16{,}000$$

FINANCIAL STATEMENTS AND OWNERSHIP STRUCTURE

The type of ownership structure employed by a business enterprise dictates the types of accounts that are part of or affect the owners' equity section. For an incorporated company, **Share Capital** and **Retained Earnings** are reported in the Shareholders' Equity section of the balance sheet. Dividends are reported in the statement of retained earnings. Revenues and expenses are reported in the income statement. Dividends, revenues, and expenses are eventually transferred (closed) to retained earnings at the end of a period. As a result, a change in any one of these three items affects shareholders' equity. The relationships related to shareholders' equity are shown in Illustration 3-3.

ILLUSTRATION 3-3
Relationships Regarding Shareholders' Equity

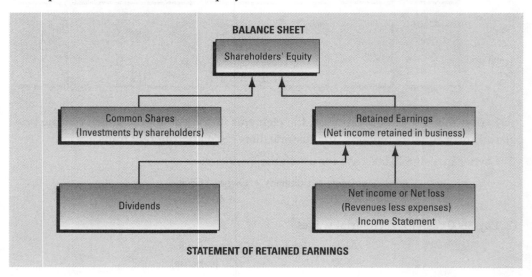

In a proprietorship or partnership, a **Capital** account is used to indicate the owner's or owners' investment in the company. A Capital account for the owner or each owner is all that is reported in the ownership equity section of the balance sheet. The balance in a Capital account consists of the individual's direct investment into the company plus share of accumulated income and losses less amounts withdrawn since the establishment of the business. Withdrawals by an owner during a period are often tracked in a **Drawings** account that, along with income, revenues, and expenses, is closed to the Capital account or accounts at the end of a period.

Exhibit 3-1 summarizes and relates the transactions affecting owners' equity to the nominal (temporary) and real (permanent) accounts, based on the types of business ownership.

EXHIBIT 3-1

EFFECTS OF TRANSACTIONS ON OWNERSHIP EQUITY ACCOUNTS

		Ownership Structure			
		Proprietorships and Partnerships		Corporations	
Transactions Affecting Owners' Equity	Impact on Owners' Equity	Nominal (Temporary) Accounts	Real (Permanent) Accounts	Nominal (Temporary) Accounts	Real (Permanent) Accounts
Investment by owner(s)	Increase		Capital		Share Capital and related accounts
Revenues earned	Increase	Revenue ⎤		Revenue ⎤	
Expenses incurred	Decrease	Expense ⎬	Capital	Expense ⎬	Retained Earnings
Withdrawal by owner(s)	Decrease	Drawing ⎦		Dividends ⎦	

THE ACCOUNTING CYCLE

Illustration 3-4 flowcharts the steps in the **accounting cycle**. These steps incorporate the procedures normally used by enterprises to record transactions and selected other events, and prepare to financial statements.

OBJECTIVE 3
Identify steps in the accounting cycle.

IDENTIFICATION AND MEASUREMENT OF TRANSACTIONS AND OTHER EVENTS

The first step in the accounting cycle is analysis of transactions and selected other events. The problem is to determine *what to record*. No simple rules exist that state whether an event should be recorded. Most accountants agree that changes in personnel and managerial policies, and the value of human resources, are important. However, none of these are recorded in the accounts. On the other hand, when the company makes a cash sale or purchase, no matter how small, it should be recorded.

What makes the difference? Drawing on the conceptual framework, *an economic event should be recognized in the financial statements if it affects an element, is reasonably (reliably) measurable, and is relevant*. When these conditions are met, the consequences of an event should be recognized in the accounting system and reported in the financial statements. To illustrate, consider human resources. R.G. Barry & Co. at one time reported as supplemental data total assets of $14,055,926, including $986,094 for "net investments in human resources." Other companies, including Canadian companies such as Cascades Inc., have experimented with human resource and social responsibility accounting. Should accountants value employees for balance sheet purposes and recognize changes in such value on the income statement? Certainly skilled employees are a highly relevant and important asset, but problems of determining their value and reliably measuring changes in it have not yet been solved. Consequently, human resources are not recorded. Perhaps

ILLUSTRATION 3-4
The Accounting Cycle

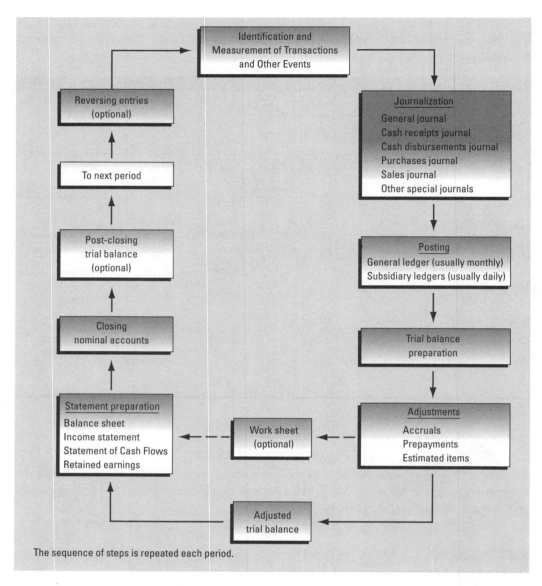

The sequence of steps is repeated each period.

when measurement techniques become more sophisticated and accepted, such information will be presented, if only in supplemental form.

The phrase "transactions and other events affecting an entity" is used to describe the sources or causes of changes in an entity's assets, liabilities, and owners' equity. Events are of two types. **External events** involve interaction between an entity and its environment, such as a transaction with another entity, a change in the price of a good or service that an entity buys or sells, a flood or earthquake, or an improvement in technology by a competitor. **Internal events** occur within an entity, such as using buildings and machinery or consuming raw materials in production processes.

Many events have both external and internal aspects. For example, acquiring the services of employees or others involves exchange transactions, which are external events; using those services (labour), often simultaneously with their acquisition, is part of production, which is internal. Events may be initiated and controlled by an entity, such as the purchase of merchandise or the use of a machine, or they may be beyond its control, such as an interest rate change, a theft, vandalism, or the imposition of taxes.

Transactions, as particular kinds of external events, may be an exchange in which each entity both receives and sacrifices value (e.g., making purchases, selling goods or services). Or transactions may be transfers in one direction (nonreciprocal) in which an entity gives an asset to (or receives an asset from) another entity without directly receiving (or giving) value in exchange. Examples include investments by owners, distributions to owners, impositions of taxes, gifts, charitable contributions, and thefts.

In short, accountants record as many events as possible that affect the financial position of the enterprise. Some events are omitted because the problems of measuring them are too complex. The accounting profession, through the efforts of individuals and numerous organizations, is continually working to refine its recognition and measurement techniques.

JOURNALIZATION

The effects of transactions and events on the basic elements of financial statements are categorized and collected in **accounts**. The general ledger is a collection of all the asset, liability, owners' equity, revenue, and expense accounts. A **T account** (see Exhibit 3-3 on page 87) is a convenient method for showing the effects of transactions on a particular element.

In practice, transactions and selected other events are not recorded initially in the ledger because a transaction affects two or more different accounts, each of which is on a different page in the ledger. To overcome this problem and to have a complete record of each transaction in one place, a **journal** (book of original entry) is employed. The simplest journal form is a chronological listing of transactions and other events expressed in terms of debits and credits to particular accounts. This is called a **general journal** and is shown in Exhibit 3-2 for the following transactions.

OBJECTIVE 4
Record transactions in journals, post to ledger accounts, and prepare a trial balance.

Nov. 1 Buy a delivery truck on account from Auto Sales Co., $22,400.
    3 Receive an invoice from the *Evening Graphic* for advertising, $280.
    4 Return merchandise to Brown Supply for credit, $175.
    16 Receive a $95 bill from Green Co., indicating that freight on a purchase from Green Co. was prepaid by them, but was our obligation according to the terms of the sale.

EXHIBIT 3-2

GENERAL JOURNAL WITH SAMPLE ENTRIES

	GENERAL JOURNAL		Page 12	
Date		Acct.	Amount	
1998		No.	Dr.	Cr.
Nov 1	Delivery Equipment	8	22,400	
	Accounts Payable	34		22,400
	(Purchased delivery truck on account from Auto Sales Co.)			
3	Advertising Expense	65	280	
	Accounts Payable	34		280
	(Received invoice for advertising from *Evening Graphic*)			
4	Accounts Payable	34	175	
	Purchase Returns	53		175
	(Returned merchandise for credit to Brown Supply)			
16	Transportation-in	55	95	
	Accounts Payable	34		95
	(Received invoice for freight on merchandise purchased from Green Co.)			

Each **general journal entry** consists of four parts: (1) the accounts and amounts to be debited (Dr.); (2) the accounts and amounts to be credited (Cr.); (3) a date; and (4) an explanation. Debits are entered first, followed by the credits, which are slightly indented. The explanation is given below the name of the last account to be credited. The Acct. No. column is completed at the time the accounts are posted.

Many accounting systems use special journals in addition to the general journal. **Special journals** permit greater division of labour, reduce the time necessary to accomplish the various bookkeeping tasks, and summarize transactions possessing a common characteristic. A special journal may be used to record all cash receipts (Cash Receipts Journal), all cash disbursements (Cash Payments Journal), all sales (Sales Journal), and all purchases (Purchases Journal). While the format of special journals differs from that of a general journal, the basic activity of identifying account titles, increases or decreases in the accounts through appropriate debits and credits, dates, and explanations occurs. As such, working with special journals is more a matter of technique rather than concept. Consequently, special journals are not examined in this book.

POSTING TO THE LEDGER

The items entered in any journal must be transferred to the general ledger. This procedure, called **posting,** is part of the summarizing and classifying activity of the accounting process.

For example, the November 1 entry in the general journal showed a debit to Delivery Equipment of $22,400 and a credit to Accounts Payable of $22,400. The amount in the debit column is posted from the journal to the debit side of the Delivery Equipment account in the ledger. The amount in the credit column is posted from the journal to the credit side of the ledger's Accounts Payable account.

The numbers in the Acct. No. column in the journal refer to the accounts in the ledger to which the respective items are posted. For example, the "8" to the right of the words "Delivery Equipment" indicates that this $22,400 item was posted to account No. 8 in the ledger.

The posting of the general journal is complete when all of the posting reference numbers have been recorded opposite the account titles in the journal. Thus the number in the posting reference column serves two purposes: (1) to indicate the ledger account number of the account involved; and (2) to indicate that the posting has been completed for the particular item. Each business enterprise selects its own numbering system for its ledger accounts. One practice is to begin numbering with asset accounts and to follow with liability, owners' equity, revenue, and expense accounts, in that order.

The various ledger accounts after the posting process is completed appear in Exhibit 3-3. The source of the data transferred to the ledger account is indicated by the reference GJ12 (General Journal, page 12).[2]

---

[2] While the T account form for ledger accounts is used throughout this book for illustrative and analysis purposes, other more detailed account forms are typically used in business. A common type is called a running balance account form, as illustrated below for accounts payable in our example.

Accounts Payable No. 34

Date		Description	Folio No.	Dr.	Cr.	Balance
Nov.	1	Auto Sales, truck	GJ12		22,400	22,400 Cr.
	3	Evening Graphic, advert.	GJ12		280	22,680 Cr.
	4	Brown Supply, return	GJ12	175		22,505 Cr.
	16	Green Co., purchases	GJ12		95	22,600 Cr.

EXHIBIT 3-3

LEDGER ACCOUNTS IN T ACCOUNT FORMAT

Delivery Equipment — No. 8

| Nov. 1 | GJ12 | 22,400 | | | |

Accounts Payable — No. 34

Nov. 4	GJ12	175	Nov. 1	GJ12	22,400
			3	GJ12	280
			16	GJ12	95

Purchase Returns — No. 53

| | | | Nov. 4 | GJ12 | 175 |

Transportation-In — No. 55

| Nov. 16 | GJ12 | 95 | | | |

Advertising Expense — No. 65

| Nov. 3 | GJ12 | 280 | | | |

UNADJUSTED TRIAL BALANCE

An unadjusted trial balance should be prepared at the end of a given period after the entries have been recorded in the journal and posted to the ledger. A **trial balance** is a list of all open accounts in the general ledger and their balances. The trial balance accomplishes two principal purposes:

1. It proves that debits and credits of an equal amount are in the ledger.
2. It supplies a listing of open accounts and their balances that serve as a basis for making adjustments.

A trial balance does not prove that all transactions have been recorded or that the ledger is correct. Numerous errors may exist even though the totals in the trial balance columns are equal. For example, the trial balance may balance even when (1) a transaction is not journalized; (2) a correct journal entry is not posted; (3) a journal entry is posted twice; (4) incorrect accounts are used in journalizing or posting; or (5) offsetting errors are made in recording the amount of a transaction. In other words, as long as equal debits and credits are posted, even to the wrong accounts or in the wrong amounts, the total debits will equal the total credits.

The unadjusted trial balance for Victoria's Wholesale is shown in Exhibit 3-4.

EXHIBIT 3-4   VICTORIA'S WHOLESALE

TRIAL BALANCE (UNADJUSTED)
December 31, 1998

	Debit	Credit
Cash	$ 13,000	
Accounts Receivable	14,650	
Notes Receivable	8,000	
Inventory, January 1, 1998	89,500	
Office Equipment	16,000	
Furniture and Fixtures	12,300	
Accounts Payable		$ 14,100
Notes Payable		24,000
Victoria's Capital		91,240
Sales		896,000
Sales Returns	3,760	
Sales Allowances	960	
Purchases	713,450	
Purchase Returns		4,140
Transportation-in	6,570	
Sales Salaries Expense	65,700	
Travel Expenses	4,900	
Advertising Expense	21,200	
General Office Salaries	39,800	
Rent Expense	18,000	
Insurance Expense	2,780	
Utilities Expense	4,310	
Telephone Expense	1,260	
Auditing and Legal Expense	2,780	
Miscellaneous Administrative Expense	2,200	
Purchase Discounts		13,500
Sales Discounts	1,860	
	$1,042,980	$1,042,980

ADJUSTMENTS

OBJECTIVE 5
Explain the reasons for preparing adjusting entries.

In an accrual accounting system, revenues are recorded in the period in which they are earned and expenses are recognized in the period in which they are incurred.[3] To accomplish this, **adjusting entries** are made at the end of the accounting period. In short, **adjustments are needed to ensure that the revenue recognition and matching principles are followed.** The use of adjusting entries makes it possible to report on the balance sheet the accrual-based amounts for assets, liabilities, and owners' equity at the statement date and to report on the income statement the resulting net income (or loss) for the period. A characteristic of an adjusting entry is that it affects both a real account (asset, liability, or owners' equity) and a nominal account (revenue or expense).

A trial balance may not contain up-to-date and complete accrual-based financial statement data for the following reasons.

1. Some events, such as the consumption of supplies and the earning of wages by employees, are not journalized daily because it is not expedient to do so.

2. The expiration of some costs, such as building and equipment deterioration and rent and insurance, is not journalized during the accounting period because these

---

[3] See Appendix 3A for a brief discussion of the accrual and cash based accounting systems. This Appendix also illustrates procedures that may be used to convert from a cash basis to an accrual basis.

costs expire with the passage of time rather than as a result of recurring daily trans-actions.

3. Some items, such as the cost of utility service, may be unrecorded because the bill for the service has not been received.

Adjustments are required every time financial statements are prepared. A usual starting point is an analysis of each account in the trial balance to determine whether it is complete and up-to-date for financial statement purposes. This analysis requires a thor-ough understanding of the company's operations and the interrelationship of accounts. Identifying the need for and amount of adjusting entries is often an involved process. In accumulating the adjustment data, the company may need to make inventory counts of supplies and repair parts and prepare supporting schedules of insurance policies, rental agreements, and other contractual commitments.

Adjustments are necessary when the following classifications of items exist.

Prepaid (Deferred) Items:
    Prepaid Expenses: Cash paid that is recorded in an asset or expense account in advance of its use or consumption (e.g., prepaid insurance).
    Unearned Revenues: Cash received that is recorded in a liability or revenue account before it is earned (e.g., rent received in advance).

Accrued Items:
    Accrued Liabilities or Expenses: An expense incurred but not yet recognized or paid (e.g., unpaid salaries).
    Accrued Assets or Revenues: a revenue earned but not yet recognized or received (e.g., interest on notes receivable).

Estimated Items:
    An expense recorded on the basis of subjective estimates of future events or developments (e.g., amortization, bad debts).

PREPAID EXPENSES

Payments of expenses that will benefit more than one accounting period are identified as prepaid expenses or **prepayments.** Prepayments often occur in regard to insurance, sup-plies, advertising, and rent.

Prepaid expenses expire either with the passage of time (e.g., rent and insurance) or through use and consumption (e.g., supplies). The expiration of these costs does not require daily recurring entries, which would be unnecessary and impractical. Accordingly, it is customary to postpone the recognition of such cost expirations until financial statements are prepared. At each statement date, adjusting entries are made to record the expenses applicable to the current accounting period and to show the unex-pired costs in the asset accounts.

Illustration. A company's year end is December 31. On September 1, 1998, the company purchased a one-year insurance policy for $1,200.

The composition of the appropriate adjusting entry depends on the way in which the original expenditure on September 1 is recorded. It may be set up as an asset in total or an expense in total, depending on decisions regarding the type of accounting system being used (see discussion of reversing entries later in the chapter). Exhibit 3-5 shows that the nature of the adjusting entry is related to whether the prepayment is originally recorded as an asset or an expense.

If the $1,200 is recorded as an asset (Unexpired Insurance) on September 1, then insurance protection for one-third of the one-year policy has been consumed by December 31, 1998. Therefore, $400 (one-third of the $1,200) must be recognized as an expense for 1998, and the asset account must be reduced by the same amount so that its

EXHIBIT 3-5

PREPAID EXPENSE AND ADJUSTMENT

Originally Recorded as an Asset			Originally Recorded as an Expense		
Sept. 1: Purchase of One-Year Policy					
Unexpired Insurance	1,200		Insurance Expense	1,200	
Cash		1,200	Cash		1,200
Dec. 31: Year-End Adjustment					
Insurance Expense	400		Unexpired Insurance	800	
Unexpired Insurance		400	Insurance Expense		800

Ledger Accounts After Posting Above Entries

Unexpired Insurance					Insurance Expense				
Sept. 1	1,200	Dec. 31	400		Sept. 1	1,200	Dec. 31	800	
Bal.	800				Bal.	400			

Insurance Expense			Unexpired Insurance		
Dec. 31	400	**Adjusting Entry**	Dec. 31	800	**Adjusting Entry**

December 31 balance after adjustment ($800) reflects the future benefits of coverage for eight months in 1999.

If the $1,200 is initially recorded as an expense, then this expense is overstated for the year ended December 31 — the $1,200 is for 12 months but only 4 months' insurance coverage has been received. Also, without an adjusting entry, no asset for the eight months' insurance coverage in 1999 would exist in the records. Therefore, in this case, the December 31 adjusting entry establishes the Unexpired Insurance asset at $800 and reduces the previously recorded $1,200 insurance expense by $800, leaving the Insurance Expense account with a $400 balance.

Note that *after appropriate adjusting entries, the balances of the respective accounts are the same, regardless of the original entry.*

UNEARNED REVENUE

Unearned revenue or **revenue received in advance** exists when cash has been received from customers for the provision of goods or services but the goods or services have not yet been provided. As dictated by the "revenue recognition principle," revenue is recorded in the period in which it is realized. When cash is received prior to revenue being realized, the amount applicable to future periods is deferred to the future periods. The amount unearned (received in advance of realization) is considered a liability because it represents an obligation arising from a past transaction to provide a good or service in the future.

Some common unearned revenue items are rent received in advance, interest received in advance on notes receivable, subscriptions and advertising received in advance by publishers, and deposits received from customers prior to delivery of merchandise.

Illustration. Assume that a publisher sells subscriptions to a sports magazine and that it receives $60,000 on January 7, 1998 from customers in payment for a full three years' subscription in advance.

Just as for prepaid expenses, the appropriate adjusting entry for unearned revenues depends on how the original cash receipt is recorded. Depending on the type of accounting system being used, the account credited in the January 7 entry could be a liability (Unearned Subscription Revenue) or a revenue (Subscription Revenue). Exhibit 3-6 shows that the nature of the adjustment at year end depends on whether the original cash receipt was recorded as a liability or as a revenue.

EXHIBIT 3-6

UNEARNED REVENUE AND ADJUSTMENT

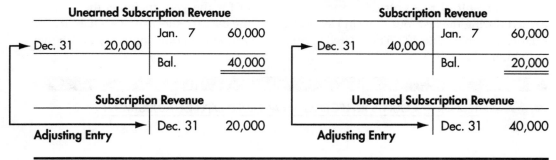

Originally Recorded as a Liability			Originally Recorded as a Revenue		
Jan. 7: Sell Three-Year Subscriptions					
Cash	60,000		Cash	60,000	
Unearned Subscription			Subscription Revenue		60,000
Revenue		60,000			
Dec. 31: Year-End Adjustment					
Unearned Subscription			Subscription Revenue	40,000	
Revenue	20,000		Unearned Subscription		
Subscription Revenue		20,000	Revenue		40,000

Ledger Accounts After Posting Above Entries

Unearned Subscription Revenue				Subscription Revenue			
Dec. 31	20,000	Jan. 7	60,000	Dec. 31	40,000	Jan. 7	60,000
		Bal.	40,000			Bal.	20,000

Subscription Revenue				Unearned Subscription Revenue			
Adjusting Entry		Dec. 31	20,000	**Adjusting Entry**		Dec. 31	40,000

If the $60,000 is recorded as a liability (Unearned Subscription Revenue) on January 7, 1998, then one-third ($20,000) is earned at December 31, 1998. Therefore, the adjusting entry reduces the liability and records $20,000 in the Subscription Revenue account, which represents the revenue earned during the year.

If the $60,000 is initially recorded as a revenue, then the December 31 adjusting entry is made to reduce the revenue to $20,000, the amount actually earned in 1998. The adjustment creates the liability for unearned subscription revenue to be shown on the December 31, 1998 balance sheet. This reflects the obligation to deliver on the subscription contracts in 1999 and 2000.

As long as there is consistency between the nature of original entries and the subsequent adjusting entries, the amount for account balances shown in the balance sheet and income statement will be the same regardless of how the original entries are recorded. The nature of original entries is determined by the accountant when designing the accounting system.

ACCRUED LIABILITIES OR EXPENSES

Accrued liabilities or **accrued expenses** are expenses that have been incurred during the period, but have not yet been recorded or paid. Interest, rent, taxes and salaries, are examples of items that can result in accrued expenses.

Adjustments for accrued expenses are necessary to record the obligations that exist at the balance sheet date and to recognize the expenses that are applicable to the current accounting period. **A liability–expense relationship exists with accrued expenses.** Prior to adjustment, both liabilities and expenses are understated. Therefore, *the adjusting entry for accrued expenses results in a debit to an expense account and a credit to a liability account*.

Illustration. When employees are paid on the last day of the month, there are no accrued wages and salaries at the end of the month or year because all employees will have been paid all amounts due. When they are paid on a weekly or biweekly basis, however, it is usually necessary to make an adjusting entry for wages and salaries earned but not paid at the end of the fiscal period. The reason is that the reporting period's last day rarely lands on a payday.

Assume that a business pays its sales staff every Friday for a five-day week, that the total weekly payroll is $8,000, and that December 31 falls on Thursday. On December 31, the end of the fiscal period, the employees have worked four-fifths of a week for which they have not been paid and for which no entry has been made. The adjusting entry on December 31 is:

Dec. 31

Sales Salaries Expense	6,400	
Salaries Payable		6,400
(To record accrued salaries as of December 31: 4/5 × $8,000)		

As a result of this entry, the income statement for the year includes the salaries earned during the last four days in December, and the balance sheet shows a liability for salaries payable of $6,400. The related accounts reflecting the adjusting entry are shown in Exhibit 3-7.

EXHIBIT 3-7

LEDGER ACCOUNTS REFLECTING AN ACCRUED EXPENSE ADJUSTMENT

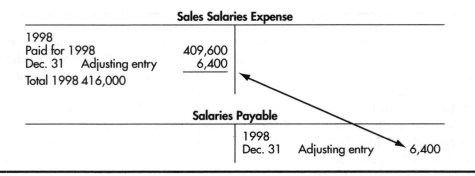

ACCRUED ASSETS OR REVENUES

Revenues earned during the period but not yet recorded or collected are called **accrued assets** or **accrued revenues**. Accrued revenues may accumulate (accrue) with the passing of time, as in the case of interest and rent. Or they may result from services that have been performed but neither billed nor collected because only a portion of the total service has been provided, as in the case of commissions and fees.

An adjusting entry is required to show the receivable that exists at the balance sheet date and to record the revenue that has been earned during the period. **An asset–revenue account relationship exists with accrued revenues.** Prior to adjustment, both assets and revenues are understated. Accordingly, *an adjusting entry for accrued revenues results in a debit to an asset account and a credit to a revenue account.*

Illustration. Assume that office space is rented to a tenant at $3,000 per month, and that the tenant has paid the rent for the first 11 months of the year, but has paid no rent for December. The adjusting entry on December 31 is:

<u>**Dec. 31**</u>

Rent Receivable	3,000	
Rent Revenue		3,000
(To record December rent)		

As a result of this entry, an asset of $3,000, Rent Receivable, appears on the balance sheet disclosing the amount due from the tenant as of December 31. The income statement shows rent revenue of $36,000, the $33,000 received for the first 11 months and the $3,000 for December entered by means of the adjusting entry. After adjustment, the accounts appear as shown in Exhibit 3-8.

EXHIBIT 3-8

LEDGER ACCOUNTS REFLECTING AN ACCRUED REVENUE ADJUSTMENT

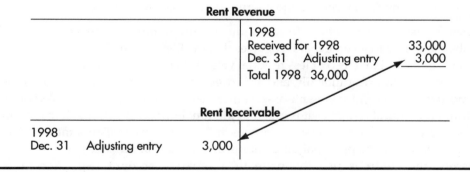

ESTIMATED ITEMS

Uncollectible accounts and amortization of capital assets are ordinarily called estimated items because the amounts are not exactly determinable when they must be recorded. An **estimated item** is a function of unknown future events and developments. Therefore, current period charges can be determined only on a subjective basis. It is known, for example, that some accounts receivables arising from credit sales will prove to be uncollectible. To prevent an overstatement of receivables at the end of the period and an understatement of expenses for the period, it is necessary to estimate and record the bad debts that are expected to result.

Also, when a long-lived capital asset is purchased, it is assumed that ultimately it will be scrapped or sold at a price (called residual value) much below the purchase price. The difference between an asset's cost and residual value represents an expense to the business that should be apportioned over the asset's useful life. The probable life of the asset and its residual value must be estimated to determine the expense that is to be charged in each period.

Adjusting Entries for Bad Debts. To appropriately match revenues and expenses requires recording bad debts as an expense of the period in which the sales are made instead of the period in which the accounts or notes are written off. This is accomplished by an adjusting entry.

At the end of each period an estimate is made of the amount of current period sales on account that will later prove to be uncollectible. The estimate is based on the amount of bad debts experienced in past years, general economic conditions, the age of the receivables, and other factors that indicate uncollectibility of receivables. Usually the amount is determined as a percent of the sales on account for the period, or it is computed by adjusting the Allowance for Doubtful Accounts account to a certain percent of the trade accounts and notes receivable at the end of the period.

Assume, for example, that experience reveals that bad debts approximates one-half of 1% of the net sales on account (net sales equals gross sales less any sales discounts, returns, and allowances). If net sales on account for the year are $300,000, the adjusting entry for bad debts is:

Dec. 31

Bad Debts Expense	1,500	
Allowance for Doubtful Accounts		1,500
(To record estimated bad debts for the year: $300,000 × .005)		

Whenever a particular customer's account is determined to be uncollectible, the Allowance for Doubtful Accounts is debited and Accounts Receivable is credited for the amount of the write-off. Methods of determining the amount of the adjusting entry and ways of accounting for a write-off and a write-off reversal are examined in Chapter 7.

Adjusting Entries for Amortization. In accounting, **amortization** is the generic term used to describe the charge to income that recognizes that the life of a tangible or intangible capital asset is finite and that its cost less residual value is to be allocated to the periods of service that it provides.[4] Traditionally, and as is done by many companies and in this book, the amortization charge for tangible assets other than natural resources is called **depreciation**, and for natural resources it is called **depletion**. Entries for amortization are similar to those made for reducing prepaid expenses in which the original amount was debited to an asset account. The principal difference is that, for the amortization of tangible capital assets, the credit is usually made to a separate account (e.g., Accumulated Depreciation, Accumulated Depletion, or Accumulated Amortization) instead of to the asset account.

In estimating amortization, the original cost, length of useful life, and estimated residual value of the asset are used. Assume that a truck costing $28,000 has an estimated useful life of five years and an estimated residual value of $4,000 at the end of that period. Because the truck is expected to be worth $24,000 less at the time of its disposal than it was at the time of its purchase, the amount of $24,000 represents an expense that is allocated over the five years of its anticipated use. It is neither logical nor good accounting practice to consider the $24,000 as an expense entirely of the period in which it was acquired or the period in which it was sold, inasmuch as the business benefits from the use of the truck during the entire five-year period.

---

[4] *CICA Handbook* (Toronto: CICA), Section 3060, par. .33. Amortization of tangible capital assets is discussed in depth in Chapter 12. Amortization of intangible capital assets is considered in Chapter 13.

If the straight-line method is used, each year's depreciation expense is one-fifth of $24,000, or $4,800. Each full year the truck is used the following adjusting entry is made.

Dec. 31

Depreciation Expense—Delivery Equipment	4,800	
Accumulated Depreciation—Delivery Equipment		4,800
(To record depreciation on truck for the year)		

ADJUSTED TRIAL BALANCE AND PREPARATION OF FINANCIAL STATEMENTS

After adjusting entries have been recorded and posted, another trial balance is prepared. The **adjusted trial balance** is used to prepare the financial statements. The financial statements are considered later in the chapter in the section titled "Use of Work Sheets" and in Chapters 4 and 5.

END-OF-PERIOD PROCEDURE FOR INVENTORY AND RELATED ACCOUNTS

End-of-period procedures for inventory depend on what inventory system is in use. When the inventory records are maintained on a **perpetual inventory system,** purchases and issues are recorded directly in the Inventory account as they occur. Therefore, the balance in the Inventory account should represent the ending inventory amount and no adjusting entries are needed. A Purchases account is not used because the purchases are debited directly to the Inventory account. However, a Cost of Goods Sold account is used to accumulate the issuances from inventory. That is, when inventory items are sold, their cost is debited to the Cost of Goods Sold account and credited to the Inventory account.

In a **periodic inventory system,** a Purchases account is used to record acquisitions and the Inventory account is unchanged during the period. The Inventory account contains only the beginning inventory amount throughout the period. At the end of the accounting period, the Inventory account must be adjusted. This may be accomplished by closing out (crediting) the Inventory account for the *beginning inventory* amount and debiting it for the *ending inventory* amount. The difference becomes part of Cost of Goods Sold. The ending inventory is determined by physically counting the items on hand and valuing them at cost or at the lower of cost and market. *Under the periodic inventory system, cost of goods sold is determined by adding the cost of beginning inventory to the net cost of purchases and then deducting the cost of ending inventory.* Net purchases consists of the cost of purchases plus transportation to the location for sale less any purchase discounts, returns, and allowances.

Cost of goods sold is determined as part of the year-end closing process that transfers (1) the change in inventory from the beginning and ending balance; and (2) balances in the various net purchases accounts used under the periodic inventory system into the Cost of Goods Sold account. To illustrate, assume Collegiate Apparel Shop Ltd. has the following accounts and balances in its accounting system at the end of its fiscal year.

OBJECTIVE 6
Explain how inventory accounts are adjusted at year end.

Account	Balance
Inventory (beginning balance)	$30,000 dr.
Purchases	200,000 dr.
Transportation-In	6,000 dr.
Purchase Returns	1,200 cr.
Purchase Allowances	800 cr.
Purchase Discounts	2,000 cr.

The inventory at the year's end is $26,000 as determined by a physical count.

To adjust the inventory and transfer the various balances in the merchandise (net purchases) accounts to the Cost of Goods Sold account, the entry shown below may be made.

Inventory (ending)	26,000	
Purchase Discounts	2,000	
Purchase Allowances	800	
Purchase Returns	1,200	
Cost of Goods Sold	206,000	
Inventory (beginning)		30,000
Purchases		200,000
Transportation-In		6,000
(To transfer beginning inventory and net purchases to Cost of Goods Sold and to record the ending inventory)		

After the foregoing entry, only the Cost of Goods Sold account ($206,000 balance, consisting of beginning inventory of $30,000 plus net purchases of $202,000 less ending inventory of $26,000) remains to be closed. It is an expense account created at the year end when using the periodic inventory system.

Exhibit 3-9 shows the process of determining the cost of goods sold through adjusting the inventory balance and closing the accounts related to net purchases on an item-by-item basis.

EXHIBIT 3-9   COLLEGIATE APPAREL SHOP LTD.

DETERMINING COST OF GOODS SOLD, ADJUSTING INVENTORY,
AND CLOSING RELATED ACCOUNTS

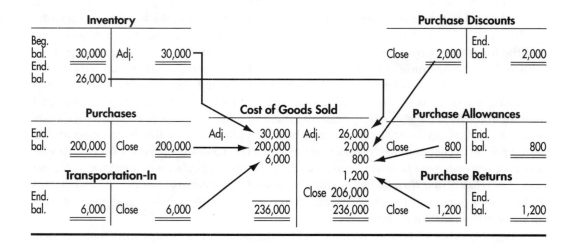

YEAR-END CLOSING

OBJECTIVE 7
Prepare closing entries.

The procedure generally followed to reduce the balance of nominal (temporary) accounts to zero in order to prepare the accounts for the next period's transactions is known as the **closing process.** In the closing process all of the revenue and expense account balances (income statement items) are transferred to a clearing or suspense account called **Income Summary,** which is used only at the end of each accounting period. Revenues and expenses are merged in the Income Summary account and the resulting balance, the net income or net loss for the period, is then transferred to an owners' equity account (retained earnings for a corporation, and capital accounts for a proprietorship or partnership). All **closing entries** are posted to the appropriate general ledger accounts.

For example, assume that revenue accounts of Collegiate Apparel Shop Ltd., a corporation, have the following credit balances, after adjustments, at the end of the year.

Revenue from Sales	$280,000
Rental Revenue	27,000
Interest Revenue	5,000

These *revenue accounts* are closed and the balances transferred to the Income Summary by the following closing journal entry.

Revenue from Sales	280,000	
Rental Revenue	27,000	
Interest Revenue	5,000	
Income Summary		312,000
(To close revenue accounts to Income Summary)		

Assume that the expense accounts, including Cost of Goods Sold as previously established, have the following debit balances, after adjustments, at the end of the year.

Cost of Goods Sold	$206,000
Selling Expenses	25,000
General and Administrative Expenses	40,600
Interest Expense	4,400
Income Tax Expense	13,000

These *expense accounts* are closed and the balances transferred to the Income Summary by the following closing journal entry.

Income Summary	289,000	
Cost of Goods Sold		206,000
Selling Expenses		25,000
General and Administrative Expenses		40,600
Interest Expense		4,400
Income Tax Expense		13,000
(To close expense accounts to Income Summary)		

The Income Summary account now has a credit balance of $23,000 ($312,000 − $289,000), which is the net income. The *net income is transferred to shareholders' equity* by closing the Income Summary account to Retained Earnings as follows.

Income Summary	23,000	
Retained Earnings		23,000
(To close Income Summary to Retained Earnings)		

Assuming that dividends of $7,000 were declared during the year, the Dividends account is closed directly to Retained Earnings as follows.

Retained Earnings	7,000	
Dividends		7,000
(To close Dividends to Retained Earnings)		

After the closing process is completed, each income statement (nominal) account will have a zero balance and will be ready for use in the next accounting period. The diagram in Exhibit 3-10 summarizes the closing process in T account form.[5]

---

[5] The closing process illustrated includes the establishment and then elimination of a Cost of Goods Sold account and an Income Summary account. These are used to provide checks and balances in the closing process. For some accounting systems, these accounts are not included and all income statement accounts (revenues, gains, expenses, losses) are closed directly to the Retained Earnings account. Also, our example includes a Dividends account, which is used to keep track of dividends declared for the period. In some accounting systems, this account is not included and dividends declared are charged (debited) directly to the Retained Earnings account.

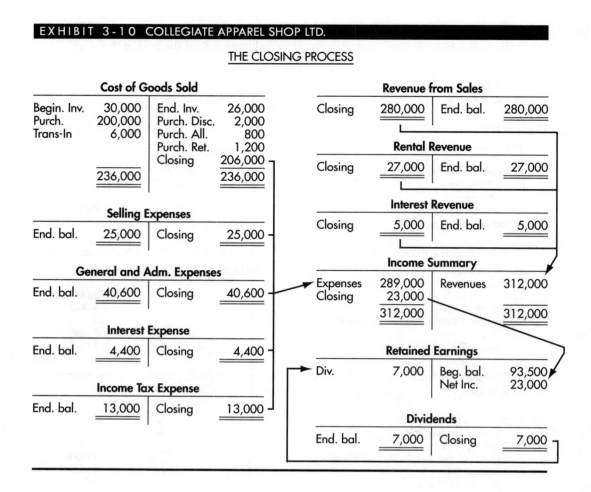

EXHIBIT 3-10 COLLEGIATE APPAREL SHOP LTD.

THE CLOSING PROCESS

Cost of Goods Sold

Begin. Inv.	30,000	End. Inv.	26,000
Purch.	200,000	Purch. Disc.	2,000
Trans-In	6,000	Purch. All.	800
		Purch. Ret.	1,200
		Closing	206,000
	236,000		236,000

Selling Expenses

| End. bal. | 25,000 | Closing | 25,000 |

General and Adm. Expenses

| End. bal. | 40,600 | Closing | 40,600 |

Interest Expense

| End. bal. | 4,400 | Closing | 4,400 |

Income Tax Expense

| End. bal. | 13,000 | Closing | 13,000 |

Revenue from Sales

| Closing | 280,000 | End. bal. | 280,000 |

Rental Revenue

| Closing | 27,000 | End. bal. | 27,000 |

Interest Revenue

| Closing | 5,000 | End. bal. | 5,000 |

Income Summary

Expenses	289,000	Revenues	312,000
Closing	23,000		
	312,000		312,000

Retained Earnings

| Div. | 7,000 | Beg. bal. | 93,500 |
| | | Net Inc. | 23,000 |

Dividends

| End. bal. | 7,000 | Closing | 7,000 |

POST-CLOSING TRIAL BALANCE

As mentioned earlier, a trial balance is taken after the regular transactions of the period have been entered, and a second trial balance (adjusted trial balance) is taken after the adjusting entries have been posted. A third trial balance, often called the post-closing trial balance, may be taken after posting closing entries. It shows that equal debits and credits have been posted to the Income Summary and that the general ledger remains in balance. The post-closing trial balance consists only of asset, liability, and owners' equity (the real) accounts.

REVERSING ENTRIES

OBJECTIVE 8
Identify adjusting entries
that may be reversed.

After the financial statements have been prepared and the books closed, it is sometimes helpful to reverse some of the adjusting entries before recording the regular transactions of the next period. Such entries are called reversing entries. The recording of reversing entries is an *optional* step in the accounting cycle that may be *performed at the beginning of an accounting period.* They are *made to simplify the recording of transactions in the upcoming accounting period.* The use of reversing entries does not change amounts reported in financial statements.

A reversing entry is made at the beginning of an accounting period and is the exact opposite of the related adjusting entry made at the end of the previous period. As a general guideline, *any adjusting entry that creates an asset or a liability account can be reversed (i.e., all accruals and some prepaid items).* Adjustments for depreciation, bad debts, or other such estimated items are not reversed.

Illustration of Reversing Entries: Accruals. Reversing entries can be used to reverse adjusting entries for accrued revenues and accrued expenses. This reflects the fact that an adjusting entry for an accrual results in the creation of an asset or liability account. To illustrate the optional use of reversing entries for accrued expenses, the following transaction and adjustment data are used.

1. October 24 (initial salary entry): $4,000 of salaries earned between October 1 and October 24 are paid.

2. October 31 (adjusting entry): Salaries earned from October 25 through October 31 are $1,200. These will be paid in the November 8 payroll.

3. November 8 (subsequent salary entry): Salaries paid are $2,500. Of this amount, $1,200 applied to accrued wages payable and $1,300 was earned from November 1 through November 8.

Entries comparing an accounting system that does not use reversing entries to a system that does use reversing entries are shown in Exhibit 3-11.

EXHIBIT 3-11

COMPARISON OF ENTRIES FOR ACCRUALS, WITH AND WITHOUT REVERSING ENTRIES

Reversing Entries Not Used				Reversing Entries Used		
Initial Salary Entry						
Oct. 24	Salaries Expense	4,000		Oct. 24	Salaries Expense	4,000
	Cash		4,000		Cash		4,000
Adjusting Entry						
Oct. 31	Salaries Expense	1,200		Oct. 31	Salaries Expense	1,200
	Salaries Payable		1,200		Salaries Payable		1,200
Closing Entry						
Oct. 31	Income Summary	5,200		Oct. 31	Income Summary	5,200
	Salaries Expense		5,200		Salaries Expense		5,200
Reversing Entry						
Nov. 1	No entry is made.			Nov. 1	Salaries Payable	1,200
					Salaries Expense		1,200
Subsequent Salary Entry						
Nov. 8	Salaries Payable	1,200		Nov. 8	Salaries Expense	2,500
	Salaries Expense	1,300			Cash		2,500
	Cash		2,500			

This comparison shows that the first three entries are the same whether or not reversing entries are used. The last two entries, however, are different. The November 1 reversing entry eliminates the $1,200 balance in Salaries Payable that was created by the October 31 adjusting entry. The reversing entry also creates a $1,200 credit balance in the Salaries Expense account. It is unusual for an expense account to have a credit balance. In this instance, however, the balance is correct because it anticipates that the entire amount of the first salary payment in the new accounting period ($2,500) will be debited to Salaries Expense. This debit will eliminate the credit balance ($1,200), and the resulting debit balance will equal the salaries expense incurred in the new accounting period ($1,300).

When reversing entries are made, all cash payments of expenses can be debited to the expense account. This means that on November 8, and on every payday, Salaries Expense can be debited for the amount paid without regard to the existence of any accrued salaries payable. Being able to make the same entry each time simplifies the recording process in an accounting system.

Illustration of Reversing Entries: Prepayments. Adjusting entries for prepayments (i.e., prepaid expenses and unearned revenues) may also be reversed if the initial entry to record the transaction (i.e., payment or receipt of cash) resulted in an increase in an expense or revenue account. This is because any required adjusting entry will result in the creation of an asset or liability account. When the initial transaction is recorded by debiting a prepaid asset or unearned revenue (liability) account, it signals that reversing entries are not used in the accounting system for such a prepayment.

To illustrate the use of reversing entries for prepaid expenses, the following transaction and adjustment data are used.

1. December 10 (initial entry): $20,000 of office supplies are purchased with cash.

2. December 31 (adjusting entry): $5,000 of office supplies are on hand.

Comparison of entries in an accounting system that does not use reversing entries with a system that does use reversing entries is shown in Exhibit 3-12.

EXHIBIT 3-12

COMPARISON OF ENTRIES FOR PREPAYMENTS, WITH AND WITHOUT REVERSING ENTRIES

Reversing Entries Not Used			Reversing Entries Used		
Initial Purchase of Supplies Entry					
Dec. 10 Office Supplies Inventory	20,000		Dec. 10 Office Supplies Expense	20,000	
Cash		20,000	Cash		20,000
Adjusting Entry					
Dec. 31 Office Supplies Expense	15,000		Dec. 31 Office Supplies Inventory	5,000	
Office Supplies Inventory		15,000	Office Supplies Expense		5,000
Closing Entry					
Dec. 31 Income Summary	15,000		Dec. 31 Income Summary	15,000	
Office Supplies Expense		15,000	Office Supplies Expense		15,000
Reversing Entry					
Jan. 1 No entry			Jan. 1 Office Supplies Expense	5,000	
			Office Supplies Inventory		5,000

After the adjusting entry on December 31 (regardless of whether reversing entries are used), the asset account, Office Supplies Inventory, shows a balance of $5,000 and Office Supplies Expense a balance of $15,000. If Office Supplies Expense was initially debited when the supplies were purchased, a reversing entry may be made to return to the expense account the cost of unconsumed supplies (i.e., the adjusting entry created the Office Supplies Inventory account). The company then continues to debit Office Supplies Expense for additional purchases of office supplies during the next period.

Why are all prepaid items not entered originally into real accounts (assets and liabilities), thus making reversing entries unnecessary? Sometimes this practice is followed. It is particularly advantageous for items that need to be apportioned over several periods. However, items that do not follow this regular pattern and that may or may not involve two or more periods are ordinarily entered initially in revenue or expense accounts. The revenue and expense accounts may not require adjusting and are systematically closed to Income Summary. Using the nominal accounts adds consistency to the accounting system and makes the recording more efficient, particularly when a large number of such transactions occur during the year. For example, the bookkeeper knows that when an invoice is received for other than a capital asset acquisition, the amount is expensed. The bookkeeper need not worry at the time an invoice is received whether or not the item will result in a prepaid expense at the end of the period, because adjustments will be made at the end of the period.

Summary of Reversing Entries. A summary of guidelines for reversing entries is set out below.

1. All accrued items may be reversed. The adjusting entry will create an asset or liability.

2. All prepaid items for which the original amount was debited or credited to an expense or revenue account may be reversed. The adjusting entry in such cases creates an asset or liability.

3. Adjusting entries for depreciation and bad debts are not reversed.

Recognize that reversing entries do not have to be used; therefore, some companies avoid using them entirely.

SUMMARY OF THE ACCOUNTING CYCLE

A summary of the steps in the accounting cycle shows the logical sequence of the accounting procedures used during a fiscal period. The process begins by making identification and measurement decisions regarding transactions and other selected events to be included in the accounting system. From this the following steps take place.

1. Enter the transactions of the period in appropriate journals.

2. Post from the journals to the ledger(s).

3. Take an unadjusted trial balance (trial balance).

4. Prepare adjusting journal entries and post to the ledger(s).

5. Take a trial balance after adjusting (adjusted trial balance).

6. Prepare the financial statements from the adjusted trial balance.

7. Prepare closing journal entries and post to the ledger(s).

8. Take a trial balance after closing (post-closing trial balance).

9. Prepare reversing entries and post to the ledger (optional step).

This list of procedures constitutes a complete accounting cycle that is normally performed in every fiscal period, regardless of whether it is done manually or with computers.

USE OF WORK SHEETS

OBJECTIVE 9
Prepare a 10-column work sheet.

To facilitate the end-of-period accounting and reporting process, accountants may use a work sheet. A **work sheet** is a columnar structured document (sheet of paper or computer spreadsheet) used to adjust the account balances and prepare the financial statements. The 10-column work sheet shown in Exhibit 3-13 provides debit and credit columns for the unadjusted trial balance, adjustments, adjusted trial balance, income statement, and balance sheet. *The work sheet does not in any way replace the journalizing, posting, or financial statements*. Instead, it is an informal device for accumulating and sorting information needed for the financial statements. Completing the work sheet provides considerable assurance that the details related to the end-of-period accounting and statement preparation have been appropriately brought together.

ADJUSTMENTS ENTERED ON THE WORK SHEET

Items (a) through (f) below serve as the basis for the adjusting entries in the Adjustments columns of the work sheet shown on page 103.

(a)   Furniture and equipment is depreciated at the rate of 10% of its original cost of $67,000 per year.

(b)   Estimated bad debts expense, one-quarter of 1% of sales of $400,000.

(c)   Insurance expired during the year, $360.

(d)   Interest accrued on notes receivable as of December 31, $800.

(e)   The Rent Expense account contains $500 rent paid in advance, which is applicable to next year.

(f)   Property taxes accrued December 31, $2,000.

Exhibit 3-14 shows the adjusting entries reflected in the Adjustments columns of the work sheet.

The adjustments are designated by letter in the work sheet. Any accounts created as a result of the adjustments and that are not already in the trial balance are listed below the totals of the trial balance. The Adjustments columns are then totalled and balanced.

Note that the adjustments for cost of goods sold are not included in the Adjustments columns. Although these adjustments are sometimes included in these columns, this illustration assumes that these entries will be made during the closing process.

ADJUSTED TRIAL BALANCE COLUMNS

The amounts in the Trial Balance columns are combined with amounts in the Adjustments columns and extended to the Adjusted Trial Balance columns. For example, the

EXHIBIT 3-13 THE SPENCER CO. LTD.

10-COLUMN WORK SHEET
December 31, 1998

Accounts	Trial Balance Dr.	Trial Balance Cr.	Adjustments Dr.	Adjustments Cr.	Adjusted Trial Balance Dr.	Adjusted Trial Balance Cr.	Income Statement Dr.	Income Statement Cr.	Balance Sheet Dr.	Balance Sheet Cr.
Cash	1,200				1,200				1,200	
Notes receivable	16,000				16,000				16,000	
Accounts receivable	41,000				41,000				41,000	
Allowance for doubtful accounts		2,000		(b) 1,000		3,000				3,000
Inventory, Jan. 1, 1998	36,000				36,000		36,000			
Unexpired insurance	900			(c) 360	540				540	
Furniture and equipment	67,000				67,000				67,000	
Accumulated depreciation of furniture and equipment		12,000		(a) 6,700		18,700				18,700
Notes payable		20,000				20,000				20,000
Accounts payable		13,500				13,500				13,500
Bonds payable		30,000				30,000				30,000
Common shares (10,000 outstanding)		50,000				50,000				50,000
Retained earnings, Jan. 1, 1998		14,200				14,200				14,200
Sales		400,000				400,000		400,000		
Purchases	320,000				320,000		320,000			
Sales salaries expense	20,000				20,000		20,000			
Advertising expense	2,200				2,200		2,200			
Travelling expense	8,000				8,000		8,000			
Salaries, office and general	19,000				19,000		19,000			
Telephone and fax expenses	600				600		600			
Rent expense	4,800			(e) 500	4,300		4,300			
Property tax expense	3,300		(f) 2,000		5,300		5,300			
Interest expense	1,700				1,700		1,700			
Totals	541,700	541,700								
Depreciation expense— furniture and equipment			(a) 6,700		6,700		6,700			
Bad debts expense			(b) 1,000		1,000		1,000			
Insurance expense			(c) 360		360		360			
Interest receivable			(d) 800		800				800	
Interest revenue				(d) 800		800		800		
Prepaid rent expense			(e) 500		500				500	
Property tax payable				(f) 2,000		2,000				2,000
Totals			11,360	11,360	552,200	552,200				
Inventory, Dec. 31, 1998*								40,000	40,000	
Totals							425,160	440,800		
Income before income taxes							15,640			
Totals							440,800	440,800		
Income before income taxes								15,640		
Income taxes expense			(g) 3,440				3,440			
Income taxes payable				(g) 3,440						3,440
Net income							12,200			12,200
							15,640	15,640	167,040	167,040

* The Dec. 31 ending inventory row could be omitted by placing the $40,000 credit in the Income Statement column and the $40,000 debit in the Balance Sheet column in the row for Inventory, Jan. 1.

EXHIBIT 3-14 THE SPENCER CO. LTD.

ADJUSTING ENTRIES REFLECTED IN WORK SHEET

(a)		
Depreciation Expense—Furniture and Equipment	6,700	
Accumulated Depreciation—Furniture and Equipment		6,700
(b)		
Bad Debts Expense	1,000	
Allowance for Doubtful Accounts		1,000
(c)		
Insurance Expense	360	
Unexpired Insurance		360
(d)		
Interest Receivable	800	
Interest Revenue		800
(e)		
Prepaid Rent Expense	500	
Rent Expense		500
(f)		
Property Tax Expense	2,000	
Property Tax Payable		2,000

amount of $2,000 shown opposite the Allowance for Doubtful Accounts in the Trial Balance Cr. column is added to the $1,000 in the Adjustments Cr. column. The $3,000 total is extended to the Adjusted Trial Balance Cr. column. Similarly, the $900 debit opposite Unexpired Insurance is reduced by the $360 credit in the Adjustments column. The result, $540, is shown in the Adjusted Trial Balance Dr. column. The Adjusted Trial Balance columns are then totalled and determined to be in balance.

INCOME STATEMENT AND BALANCE SHEET COLUMNS

All the debit items in the Adjusted Trial Balance are extended into the balance sheet or income statement debit columns to the right, depending on the financial statement in which they will appear. Similarly, all the credit items in the Adjusted Trial Balance are extended into one of the two credit columns to the right. Note that the January 1 inventory amount is extended to the Income Statement Dr. column because beginning inventory will appear as an addition in the cost of goods sold section of the income statement.

ENDING INVENTORY

The December 31 inventory, $40,000, is not in either of the trial balances but is listed as a separate item below the accounts already shown. It is in the Balance Sheet Dr. column because it is an asset at the end of the year, and in the Income Statement Cr. column because it will be used as a deduction in the cost of goods sold section of the income statement.

INCOME TAXES AND NET INCOME

The next step is to total the Income Statement columns; the figure necessary to balance the debit and credit columns is the pretax income or loss for the period. The income before income taxes of $15,640 is shown in the Income Statement Dr. column because the revenues exceeded the expenses by that amount.

The income tax expense and related tax liability are then computed. An effective rate of 22% is applied to arrive at $3,440. Because the Adjustments columns have been balanced, this adjustment is entered in the Income Statement Dr. column as Income Taxes Expense and in the Balance Sheet Cr. column as Income Taxes Payable. The following adjusting journal entry is recorded on December 31, 1998 and posted to the general ledger as well as entered in the work sheet.

(g)

Income Taxes Expense	3,440	
Income Taxes Payable		3,440

Next, the Income Statement columns are balanced with the income taxes included. The $12,200 difference between the debit and credit columns in this illustration represents net income. The net income of $12,200 is entered in the Income Statement Dr. column to achieve equality and in the Balance Sheet Cr. column as an increase in retained earnings.

PREPARATION OF FINANCIAL STATEMENTS FROM WORK SHEET

The work sheet provides the information needed for preparing the financial statements without reference to the ledger or other records. In addition, the data have been sorted into appropriate columns, which facilitates preparing the financial statements illustrated on the following pages.

Income Statement. The income statement shown in Exhibit 3-15 is that of a trading or merchandising concern. For a manufacturing concern, three inventory accounts (Raw Materials, Work in Process, and Finished Goods) would be involved, and a supplementary statement titled Cost of Goods Manufactured would be prepared. *Note that earnings per share is shown at the bottom of the income statement.*

Statement of Retained Earnings. The net income earned by a corporation may be retained in the business or distributed to shareholders by payment of dividends. In the Statement of Retained Earnings shown in Exhibit 3-16, the net income earned during the year was added to the balance of retained earnings on January 1, thereby increasing the balance of retained earnings to $26,400 on December 31. No dividends were declared during the year.

Balance Sheet. The balance sheet prepared from the 10-column work sheet is shown in Exhibit 3-17 and contains items resulting from year-end adjusting entries. Interest receivable, unexpired insurance, and prepaid rent expense are included as current assets, because these assets will be converted into cash or consumed in the ordinary routine of the business within a relatively short period of time. The amount of Allowance for Doubtful Accounts is deducted from the total accounts and notes receivable because it is estimated that only $54,000 of the total of $57,000 will be collected.

In the property, plant, and equipment section, the accumulated depreciation is deducted from the cost of the furniture and equipment; the difference represents the **book value** or **carrying value** of the furniture and equipment.

Property tax payable is shown as a current liability because it is an obligation that is payable within a year. Other short-term accrued liabilities would also be shown as current liabilities.

The bonds payable, due in 2003, are long-term liabilities and are shown in a separate section. (Interest on the bonds was paid on December 31.)

Because The Spencer Co. Ltd. is a corporation, the owners' equity section of the balance sheet, called Shareholders' Equity, is somewhat different from the capital section for

EXHIBIT 3-15 THE SPENCER CO. LTD.

INCOME STATEMENT

For the Year Ended December 31, 1998

Net sales			$400,000
Cost of goods sold			
Inventory, Jan. 1, 1998		$ 36,000	
Purchases		320,000	
Cost of goods available for sale		$356,000	
Deduct inventory, Dec. 31, 1998		40,000	
Cost of goods sold			316,000
Gross profit on sales			$ 84,000
Selling expenses			
Sales salaries expense		$ 20,000	
Advertising expense		2,200	
Travelling expense		8,000	
Total selling expenses		$ 30,200	
Administrative expenses			
Salaries, office and general	$ 19,000		
Telephone and fax expense	600		
Rent expense	4,300		
Property tax expense	5,300		
Depreciation expense—furniture			
and equipment	6,700		
Bad debts expense	1,000		
Insurance expense	360		
Total administrative expenses		37,260	
Total selling and administrative expenses			67,460
Income from operations			$ 16,540
Other revenues and gains			
Interest revenue			800
			$ 17,340
Other expenses and losses			
Interest expense			1,700
Income before income taxes			$ 15,640
Income taxes			3,440
Net income			$ 12,200
Earnings per share			$ 1.22

EXHIBIT 3-16 THE SPENCER CO. LTD.

A STATEMENT OF RETAINED EARNINGS

For the Year Ended December 31, 1998

Retained earnings, Jan. 1, 1998	$14,200
Add: Net income for 1998	12,200
Retained earnings, Dec. 31, 1998	$26,400

EXHIBIT 3-17 THE SPENCER CO. LTD.

BALANCE SHEET
December 31, 1998

Assets

Current assets			
Cash			$ 1,200
Notes receivable	$16,000		
Accounts receivable	41,000	$57,000	
Less: Allowance for doubtful accounts		3,000	54,000
Interest receivable			800
Merchandise inventory on hand			40,000
Unexpired insurance			540
Prepaid rent expense			500
Total current assets			$ 97,040
Property, plant, and equipment			
Furniture and equipment		$67,000	
Less: Accumulated depreciation		18,700	
Total property, plant, and equipment			48,300
Total assets			$145,340

Liabilities and Shareholders' Equity

Current liabilities			
Notes payable			$ 20,000
Accounts payable			13,500
Property tax payable			2,000
Income taxes payable			3,440
Total current liabilities			$ 38,940
Long-term liabilities			
Bonds payable, due June 30, 2003			30,000
Total liabilities			$ 68,940
Shareholders' equity			
Common shares issued			
and outstanding, 10,000 shares		$ 50,000	
Retained earnings		26,400	
Total shareholders' equity			76,400
Total liabilities and shareholders' equity			$145,340

a proprietorship. The total shareholders' equity consists of common shares, which is the direct investment by shareholders, and earnings retained in the business.

CLOSING AND REVERSING ENTRIES

The entries for the closing process are as shown in Exhibit 3-18.

After the financial statements have been prepared, the enterprise may use reversing entries to facilitate accounting in the next period. If this was done, the reversing entries would be made at the beginning of the next period as shown in Exhibit 3-19.

Reversing entries do not appear on the 10-column work sheet because they are recorded in the next year (1999). The main purposes of the work sheet are to obtain the appropriate balances for preparing the 1998 financial statements and to provide information to facilitate the journalizing of December 31, 1998 adjusting entries.

EXHIBIT 3-18 THE SPENCER CO. LTD.

CLOSING ENTRIES

GENERAL JOURNAL
December 31, 1998

Inventory (December 31)	40,000	
Cost of Goods Sold	316,000	
Inventory (January 1)		36,000
Purchases		320,000
(To record ending inventory balance and to determine cost of goods sold)		
Interest Revenue	800	
Sales	400,000	
Cost of Goods Sold		316,000
Sales Salaries Expense		20,000
Advertising Expense		2,200
Travelling Expense		8,000
Salaries, Office and General		19,000
Telephone and Fax Expense		600
Rent Expense		4,300
Property Tax Expense		5,300
Depreciation Expense— Furniture and Equipment		6,700
Bad Debts Expense		1,000
Insurance Expense		360
Interest Expense		1,700
Income Taxes Expense		3,440
Income Summary		12,200
(To close revenues and expenses to Income Summary)		
Income Summary	12,200	
Retained Earnings		12,200
(To close Income Summary to Retained Earnings)		

EXHIBIT 3-19 THE SPENCER CO. LTD.

REVERSING ENTRIES

January 1, 1999

(1)		
Interest Revenue	800	
Interest Receivable		800
(2)		
Rent Expense	500	
Prepaid Rent Expense		500
(3)		
Property Tax Payable	2,000	
Property Tax Expense		2,000
(4)		
Income Taxes Payable	3,440	
Income Taxes Expense		3,440

MONTHLY STATEMENTS, YEARLY CLOSING

The use of a work sheet at the end of each month or quarter permits the preparation of interim financial statements even though the books are closed only at the end of each year. For example, assume that a business closes its books on December 31 but that monthly financial statements are desired. At the end of January, a work sheet can be prepared to supply the information needed for statements for January. At the end of

February, a work sheet can be used again. Because the accounts were not closed at the end of January, the income statement taken from the work sheet on February 28 will present the net income for two months. An income statement for the month of February can be obtained by subtracting the items in the January income statement from the corresponding items in the income statement for the two months of January and February.

A statement of retained earnings for February only may also be obtained by starting with the January 31 amount of retained earnings and then adding February's net income and deducting dividends declared in February. The balance sheet derived from the February work sheet, however, shows the assets and equities as of February 28, the specific date for which a balance sheet is prepared.

The March work sheet will show the revenues and expenses for three months, and the subtraction of the revenues and expenses for the first two months can be made to supply the amounts needed for an income statement for the month of March only.

COMPUTERS AND ACCOUNTING SOFTWARE

The principles of recording, classifying, and summarizing accounting data described in this chapter are generally applicable to most enterprises. While the activities related to data processing may be done manually, such an approach would be very time-consuming and costly. Consequently, most businesses use relatively low-cost equipment to carry out the data processing in a quick and efficient manner. The nature and type of the equipment that is used varies according to the nature and size of the business, what it does, and the cost.

Processing accounting data has progressed from the use of the quill pen through mechanisms such as large adding machines, small calculators, and posting machines to computers. The computer has revolutionized data processing not only because of its speed and accuracy, but also because it can be programmed to process data in almost any manner desired by management. A significant event has been the development of on-line computer systems that record transactions in the computer as they occur without the use of any source document. The advantages of a computer are that it can do many things with the data collected and can process data more quickly and efficiently than other types of business equipment.

Nearly every medium- or large-sized business owns or leases computers that, until fairly recently, have been considered too expensive for a small business. Small businesses avoided investing large sums of money but gained the use of computers through EDP service centres or through time-sharing arrangements. However, with the widespread availability of inexpensive personal computers, many small businesses now own computers and obtain the operating and record-keeping efficiencies they provide.

While low-cost and technologically advanced hardware is now available, the related development of low-cost accounting software packages is equally important and significant to the accounting profession. Programs are capable of carrying out most of the mechanical steps in the accounting cycle. Once transactions and events have been identified and analysed according to the accounts affected and the amounts involved, these accounting packages can process the data through all the steps, resulting in the financial statements.

These technological advances have been a great boon to accountants. Accountants no longer need to devote hours to the routine tasks of recording, posting, and summarizing data. They can devote more attention to analysing and interpreting financial information. To an extent, the use of computers and accounting software has taken much of the bookkeeping drudgery out of accounting.

Despite these developments, accountants still have to be expert in knowing and understanding the accounting process and related terminology. The nature of this process as represented by the procedures in the accounting cycle provides a basic model by which accountants can analyse the effect of various transactions and events on the financial reports. This is particularly important when choosing a method from various generally accepted accounting alternatives. If accountants simply enter transactions or events into a computer without knowing why or what happens afterwards, significant problems (i.e., errors, inability to find information in the system, accepting results without understanding what they mean) are likely to result. With an understanding of the steps in the cycle, such problems are less likely to occur. Also, accountants are responsible for the design of the information system of an enterprise. This requires a complete understanding of the process by which financial statements are derived. While the procedures outlined in this chapter are basic to most accounting systems, it must also be accepted that the accounting system for each enterprise is likely to have its own unique characteristics. To determine and understand these characteristics, accountants must rely heavily on their knowledge of the accounting process.

KEY TERMS

account, 85

accounting cycle, 83

accrued assets or revenues, 92

accrued liabilities or expenses, 92

adjusted trial balance, 80

adjusting entry, 88

balance sheet, 80

closing entries, 96

credit, 80

debit, 80

double-entry accounting, 81

estimated item, 93

event, 79

financial statements, 80

general journal, 85

general ledger, 79

income statement, 80

journal, 85

nominal (temporary) accounts, 79

periodic inventory system, 95

perpetual inventory system, 95

posting, 86

prepaid expense, 89

real (permanent) accounts, 79

reversing entries, 98

Summary of Learning Objectives

1. **Understand basic accounting terminology.** An understanding of the following terms is important: (1) event; (2) transaction; (3) account; (4) real and nominal accounts; (5) ledger; (6) journal; (7) posting; (8) trial balance; (9) adjusting entries; (10) financial statements; (11) closing entries;

2. **Explain double-entry rules.** The left side of any account is the debit side; the right side is the credit side. All asset and expense accounts are increased on the left or debit side and decreased on the right or credit side. Conversely, all liability and revenue accounts are increased on the right or credit side and decreased on the left or debit side. Shareholders' equity accounts, Common Shares and Retained Earnings, are increased on the credit side, whereas Dividends is increased on the debit side.

3. **Identify steps in the accounting cycle.** The basic steps in the accounting cycle are (1) identification and measurement of transactions and other events; (2) journalization; (3) posting; (4) unadjusted trial balance; (5) adjustments; (6) adjusted trial balance; (7) statement presentation; and (8) closing. Reversing entries may be made at the beginning of a period.

4. **Record transactions in journals, post to ledger accounts, and prepare a trial balance.** The simplest journal form is a chronological listing of transactions and events expressed in terms of debits and credits to particular accounts. The items entered in a general journal must be transferred (posted) to the general ledger. An unadjusted trial balance should be prepared at the end of a given period after the entries have been recorded in the journal and posted to the ledger.

5. **Explain the reasons for preparing adjusting entries.** Adjustments are necessary to achieve an appropriate recognition of revenues and matching of expenses to revenues so as to determine net income for the current period and to provide accurate end-of-the-period balances in asset, liability, and owners' equity accounts.

6. **Explain how inventory accounts are adjusted at year end.** When the inventory records are maintained in a periodic inventory system, a Purchases account is used; the Inventory account is unchanged during the period. The Inventory account represents the beginning inventory amount throughout the period. At

the end of the accounting period the Inventory account must be adjusted by closing out (crediting) the beginning inventory amount and recording (debiting) the ending inventory amount, with the difference debited or credited to Cost of Goods Sold. Under a perpetual inventory system the balance in the Inventory account should represent the ending inventory amount, and no adjusting entries are needed.

7. **Prepare closing entries.** In the closing process all of the revenue and expense account balances (income statement items) are transferred to a clearing account called Income Summary, which is used only at the end of each fiscal year. The net resulting balance in the Income Summary account, which represents the net income or net loss for the period, is then transferred to an owners' equity account (retained earnings for a corporation and capital accounts for proprietorships and partnerships).

8. **Identify adjusting entries that may be reversed.** Reversing entries are most often used to reverse two types of adjusting entries; accrued revenues and accrued expenses. Prepayments may also be reversed if the initial entry to record the transaction is made to an expense or revenue account.

9. **Prepare a 10-column work sheet.** The 10-column work sheet provides columns for the unadjusted trial balance, adjustments, adjusted trial balance, income statement, and balance sheet. The work sheet does not replace the financial statements. Instead, it is the accountant's informal device for accumulating and sorting information needed for the financial statements.

APPENDIX 3A

Cash Basis Accounting Versus Accrual Basis Accounting

DIFFERENCES BETWEEN CASH BASIS AND ACCRUAL BASIS

OBJECTIVE 10
Differentiate the cash basis of accounting from the accrual basis of accounting.

Most companies use the **accrual basis** of accounting, recognizing revenue when it is earned and expenses in the period incurred, without regard to the time of receipt or payment of cash. Some small enterprises and the average individual taxpayer, however, use a strict or modified cash basis approach. Under the **strict cash basis** of accounting, revenue is recorded only when the cash is received and expenses are recorded only when the cash is paid. The determination of income on the cash basis rests upon the collection of revenue and the payment of expenses, and the revenue recognition and the matching principles of accrual accounting are ignored. Consequently, cash basis financial statements are not in conformity with generally accepted accounting principles.

To illustrate and contrast accrual basis accounting and cash basis accounting, assume that Quality Contractor signs an agreement to construct a garage for $22,000. In January, Quality Contractor begins construction, incurs costs of $18,000 on credit, and by the end of January provides the finished garage to the buyer. In February, Quality Contractor collects $22,000 cash from the customer. In March, Quality Contractor pays the $18,000 due the creditors. Exhibit 3A-1 shows the net incomes for each month under cash basis accounting and accrual basis accounting.

EXHIBIT 3A-1 QUALITY CONTRACTOR

INCOME STATEMENT—CASH BASIS ACCOUNTING

| | For the Month of | | | |
	January	February	March	Total
Cash Receipts	-0-	$22,000	$-0-	$22,000
Cash Payments	-0-	-0-	18,000	18,000
Net Income (loss)	-0-	$22,000	$(18,000)	$ 4,000

INCOME STATEMENT—ACCRUAL BASIS ACCOUNTING

| | For the Month of | | | |
	January	February	March	Total
Revenues	$22,000	-0-	-0-	$22,000
Expenses	18,000	-0-	-0-	18,000
Net Income (loss)	$ 4,000	-0-	-0-	$ 4,000

For three months combined, total net income is the same under cash basis accounting and accrual basis accounting; the difference is in the *timing* of net income.

The balance sheet is also affected by the basis of accounting. This is evident by comparing the cash basis and accrual basis balance sheets at each month end for Quality Contractor, as shown in Exhibit 3A-2.

EXHIBIT 3A-2 QUALITY CONTRACTOR

BALANCE SHEET—CASH BASIS ACCOUNTING

	January 31	As of February 28	March 31
Assets			
Cash	$ -0-	$22,000	$4,000
Total assets	$ -0-	$22,000	$4,000
Liabilities and Owners' Equity			
Owners' equity	$ -0-	$22,000	$4,000
Total liabilities and owners' equity	$ -0-	$22,000	$4,000

BALANCE SHEET—ACCRUAL BASIS ACCOUNTING

	January 31	As of February 28	March 31
Assets			
Cash	$ -0-	$22,000	$4,000
Accounts receivable	22,000	-0-	-0-
Total assets	$22,000	$22,000	$4,000
Liabilities and Owners' Equity			
Accounts payable	$18,000	$18,000	$ -0-
Owners' equity	4,000	4,000	4,000
Total liabilities and owners' equity	$22,000	$22,000	$4,000

An analysis of the preceding income statements and balance sheets shows why cash basis accounting is inconsistent with basic accounting theory.

1. The cash basis understates revenues and assets from the construction and delivery of the garage in January. It ignores the $22,000 accounts receivable, representing a near-term future cash inflow.

2. The cash basis understates expenses incurred with the construction of the garage and the liability outstanding at the end of January. It ignores the $18,000 accounts payable, representing a near-term future cash outflow.

3. The cash basis understates owners' equity in January by not recognizing the revenues and the asset until February, and it overstates owners' equity in February by not recognizing the expenses and the liability until March.

In short, cash basis accounting violates the conceptual theory underlying financial accounting and the consequent definitions of the elements of financial statements.

The **modified cash basis,** a mixture of cash basis and accrual basis, is a method that may be followed by service enterprises (e.g. lawyers, doctors, architects, advertising agencies, public accountants, farming enterprises). Wide variations can exist in the treatment of various items. Generally, capital expenditures (eg., buildings, equipment) having an economic life of more than one year are capitalized as assets and depreciated or amortized over future years. Other prepaid expenses (eg., insurance, rent), however, may be deferred and expensed in the year to which they apply or they may be fully expensed in the year paid. Expenses paid after the year of incurrence (accrued expenses such as interest) may be recognized in the year incurred or only in the year they are paid. Revenue may be reported only in the year of its cash receipt.

CONVERSION FROM CASH BASIS TO ACCRUAL BASIS

Not infrequently an accountant is required to convert a cash basis set of financial statements to the accrual basis for presentation and interpretation to a banker or for audit by an independent public accountant. The following describes and illustrates how cash basis financial data can be converted to the accrual basis through various types of adjustments to cash basis accounts.

Illustration. Diana Windsor, D.D.S., keeps her accounting records on a cash basis. During 1998, Dr. Windsor collected $80,000 from her patients and paid $30,000 for operating expenses. Therefore, the cash basis net income for 1998 would be $50,000 (revenues of $80,000, expenses of $30,000).

The $80,000 collected does not necessarily represent the accrual basis revenues; nor is the $30,000 likely to be the accrual basis expenses. This may be demonstrated by assuming that, had Dr. Windsor used the accrual basis, the accounts and balances shown in Exhibit 3A-3 would have existed on January 1 and December 31, 1998.

EXHIBIT 3A-3 DIANA WINDSOR, D.D.S.

ACCRUAL BASIS ACCOUNTS AND BALANCES FOR 1998

Account	January 1	December 31	Change
Fees Receivable	$12,000 Dr.	$5,000 Dr.	− $7,000
Unearned Fees	-0-	1,000 Cr.	+ 1,000
Accrued Expenses Payable	3,800 Cr.	6,800 Cr.	+ 3,000
Prepaid Expenses	2,000 Dr.	3,000 Dr.	+ 1,000

Given this information, various approaches may be used to determine the accrual basis revenues, expenses, and net income. A basic approach is to use T accounts to derive adjustments to the cash basis revenues and expenses based on changes in the beginning balance (BB) and ending balance (EB) of the real accounts that would exist using the accrual basis. This is demonstrated in Exhibit 3A-4.

This approach is very procedural but is frequently used. The key to its use is understanding why the entries to account for the change in the accrual account balances appropriately adjust revenues and expenses. This understanding is based on a thorough appreciation for the concepts of accrual accounting. The particular adjustments to the cash based revenues in this example follow.

EXHIBIT 3A-4 DIANA WINDSOR, D.D.S.

CASH BASIS TO ACCRUAL BASIS, T-ACCOUNT APPROACH

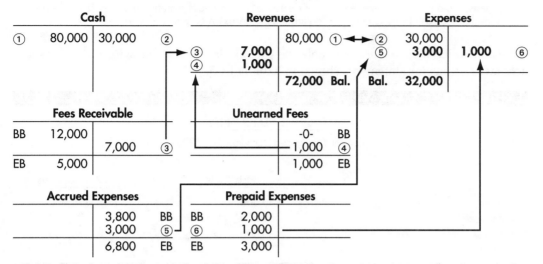

Step 1: Enter amounts in accounts as used in the cash basis.

① Cash		80,000	
Revenues			80,000
② Expenses		30,000	
Cash			30,000

Step 2: Enter beginning balance (BB) and ending balance (EB) in accounts that would exist under the accrual basis.

Step 3: Journalize the entries required to account for the change in the accrual account balances.

③ Revenues		7,000	
Fees Receivable			7,000
④ Revenues		1,000	
Unearned Fees			1,000
⑤ Expenses		3,000	
Accrued Expenses			3,000
⑥ Prepaid Expenses		1,000	
Expenses			1,000

Step 4: Determine the resulting balances for Revenues ($72,000) and Expenses ($32,000).

Entry 3: Since Fees Receivable had a net decrease of $7,000, this amount is deducted from the $80,000 revenue recognized in the cash basis. This net amount was earned in a previous period but collected this period. Consequently, a decrease in a receivable must be deducted from total cash received to determine accrual basis revenues. Had there been a net increase in a receivable, the amount would be added to cash collected to determine revenues on an accrual basis.

Entry 4: Unearned Fees increased by $1,000. A net increase in an unearned revenue account reflects that more cash was received than was earned during the period. Therefore, this amount is deducted from the cash basis revenue amount. If an unearned revenue account has a net decrease during a period, the amount is added to the cash basis revenues.

The adjustments to the cash basis expenses total of $30,000 have the following rationale.

Entry 5: The $3,000 net increase in Accrued Expenses is added to the $30,000 amount of cash paid for expenses. This is because an increase in an accrued expense means expenses have been incurred in the period that will be paid in a future period. Conversely, if there was a net decrease in accrued expenses, the amount would be deducted from the cash basis expenses to calculate the accrual basis expenses.

Entry 6: Prepaid Expenses increased by $1,000. A net increase in a prepaid expense account means that cash was paid in the current period (is part of the cash basis expenses total) but the benefits from the expenditure will not occur until a future period (i.e., it will be recognized as an expense in the future). Therefore, this net increase amount is deducted from the cash basis expense amount. Had there been a net decrease in a prepaid expense account, it would be added to the cash basis expenses to determine expenses on an accrual basis.

The results of this analysis enable the preparation of the following cash basis and accrual basis income statements shown in Exhibit 3A-5.

EXHIBIT 3A-5 DIANA WINDSOR, D.D.S.

INCOME STATEMENT

For the Year Ended December 31, 1998

	Cash Basis	Accrual Basis
Revenues	$80,000	$72,000
Expenses	30,000	32,000
Net Income	$50,000	$40,000

Based on the concepts and relationships evident in the T Account Approach another approach, herein called the Formula Approach, emerges. Under this approach, cash basis amounts for revenues and expenses are converted to accrual basis amounts by various additions and deductions based on the amount and direction of the net change in accrual basis accounts. The nature of the additions and deductions are identified in Exhibit 3A-6.

The Formula Approach is less tedious than the T Account Approach, but requires significant familiarity with using the formulas. Exhibit 3A-7 demonstrates the use of the Formula Approach to the Diana Windsor, D.D.S. illustration.

THEORETICAL WEAKNESSES OF THE CASH BASIS

The cash basis does report exactly when cash is received and when cash is disbursed. To many people this is something solid and concrete. Isn't cash what it is all about? Does it make sense to invent something, design it, produce it, market and sell it, if you aren't going to get cash for it in the end? It is frequently said, "Cash is the real bottom line." It is also said, "Cash is the oil that lubricates the economy." If so, then what is the merit of accrual accounting?

Today's economy is considerably more lubricated by credit than by cash. The accrual basis, not the cash basis, recognizes all aspects of the credit phenomenon. Investors, creditors, and other decision makers seek timely information about an enterprise's future cash flows. Accrual basis accounting helps provide this information by reporting the cash inflow and outflow implications associated with earnings activities as soon as they can be estimated with an acceptable degree of reliability. Receivables and payables are forecasters of future cash inflows and outflows. In other words, accrual basis accounting helps in predicting future cash flows by reporting transactions and other events with cash consequences at the time the transactions and events occur, rather than when the cash is received or paid.

EXHIBIT 3A-6

CASH BASIS TO ACCRUAL BASIS, FORMULA APPROACH

Cash Basis ⟶ Accrual Basis

Revenues:

Cash receipts from revenue sources (sales of goods and services, rent, interest, etc.)

{
+ increase in accounts receivable
or
− decrease in accounts receivable

+ increase in accrued revenue
or
− decrease in accrued revenue

+ decrease in unearned revenue
or
− increase in unearned revenue
}

= Revenues from revenue source

Expenses:

Payments for goods

{
+ increase in accounts payable
or
− decrease in accounts payable

+ decrease in inventory
or
− increase in inventory
}

= Cost of goods sold

Payments for expenses (wages, insurance, rent, interest, etc.)

{
+ decrease in prepaid expense
or
− increase in prepaid expense

+ increase in accrued expense
or
− decrease in accrued expense
}

= Operating expenses, except depreciation and similar estimated expenses

Payments for property, plant, and equipment or intangibles

{
− cash paid for property, plant and equipment or intangibles

+ periodic expense allocation of asset cost based on some formula
}

= Depreciation or amortization expense

EXHIBIT 3A-7 DIANA WINDSOR, D.D.S.

CASH BASIS TO ACCRUAL BASIS, FORMULA APPROACH

	Cash Basis	Adjustments	Accural Basis
Revenues:			
Cash received	$80,000		
Deduct decrease in fees receivable		−$7,000	
Deduct increase in unearned fees		− 1,000	
Accrual basis revenue			$72,000
Operating Expenses:			
Cash paid	30,000		
Add increase in accrued expenses		+ 3,000	
Deduct increase in prepaid expenses		− 1,000	
Accrual basis expenses			32,000
Net Income—Cash Basis			
(excess of cash receipts over cash payments)	$50,000		
Net Income—Accrual Basis			$40,000

Summary of Learning Objectives
for Appendix 3A

KEY TERMS

accrual basis, 112

modified cash basis, 114

strict cash basis, 112

10. **Differentiate the cash basis of accounting from the accrual basis of accounting.** Accrual basis accounting provides information about cash inflows and outflows associated with earnings activities as soon as these cash flows can be estimated with an acceptable degree of reliability. That is, accrual basis accounting aids in predicting future cash flows by reporting transactions and events with cash consequences at the time the transactions and events occur, rather than when the cash is received and paid. Conversion from a cash basis to accrual basis income can be accomplished by use of a T Account Approach or Formula Approach.

Note: All *asterisked* Exercises, Problems, or Cases relate to material contained in the appendix to the chapter.

EXERCISES

E3-1 (Transaction Analysis: Merchandising Company) The Hardy Hardware Store completed the following transactions in the month of May. On May 1, the company had a cash balance of $5,000.

May	1	Purchased merchandise on account from Point Wholesale Supply $5,200, terms 2/10, n/30 (i.e., if paid within 10 days a 2% discount can be taken, otherwise the full amount is to be paid by the thirtieth day).
	2	Sold merchandise on account $3,600, terms 2/10, n/30.
	5	Received credit from Point Wholesale Supply for merchandise returned, $100.
	9	Received collections in full, less discounts, from customers billed for $2,000 of sales on May 2.
	10	Paid Point Wholesale Supply in full, less discount.
	12	Purchased merchandise for cash, $2,400.
	15	Received refund for poor quality merchandise from supplier on a cash purchase $230.
	17	Purchased merchandise from Hippo Distributors, $1,900, terms 3/10, n/30, on which Hardy Hardware is to pay freight costs.
	19	Paid freight on May 17 purchase, $250.
	24	Sold merchandise for cash, $6,400.
	25	Purchased merchandise for cash, $600.
	27	Paid Hippo Distributors in full, less discount.
	29	Made refunds to cash customers for defective merchandise, $80.
	31	Sold merchandise on account, $2,100, terms n/30.

Hardy Hardware's chart of accounts includes the following: Cash, Accounts Receivable, Merchandise Inventory, Accounts Payable, Sales, Sales Returns and Allowances, Sales Discounts, Purchases, Purchase Returns and Allowances, Purchase Discounts, Freight-in.

Instructions

(a) Journalize the transactions.

(b) Prepare an income statement through gross profit for the month of May, assuming ending inventory is $2,400 and no beginning inventory.

E3-2 (Transaction Analysis: Service Company) Lou Harris is the proprietor of a public accounting firm. During the first month of operations of her business, the following events and transactions occurred.

April	1	Invested $32,000 cash and equipment valued at $11,000 in the business.
	2	Hired a secretary/receptionist at a salary of $500 per week, payable monthly.
	3	Purchased supplies on account $700 (debit an expense account).
	7	Paid office rent of $800 for the month.
	11	Completed a tax assignment and billed client $1,100 for services rendered. (Use professional fees account.)
	12	Received $3,200 advance on a management consulting engagement.
	15	Purchased a new computer for $3,500 with personal funds. (The computer will be used exclusively for business purposes.)
	17	Received cash of $900 for services completed for Dibble Co.
	21	Paid insurance expense of $110 for the month of April.
	30	Paid secretary/receptionist $2,000 for the month.
	30	A count of supplies indicated that $120 of supplies had been used.

Instructions

Journalize the transactions in the general journal (omit explanations).

(Transactions of a Corporation Including Investment and Dividend) Scratch Miniature Golf and Driving Range **E3-3** Inc. was opened on March 1 by Ace Bogie. The following selected events and transactions occurred during March:

Mar.	1	Invested $50,000 cash in the business in exchange for common shares.
	3	Purchased Lee's Golf Land for $38,000 cash. The price consists of land, $23,000; building, $9,000; and equipment, $6,000.
	5	Advertised the opening of the driving range and miniature golf course, paying advertising expenses of $1,600.
	6	Paid cash $1,480 for a one-year insurance policy.
	10	Purchased golf clubs and other equipment for $1,600 from Palmer Company payable in 30 days.
	18	Received golf fees of $800 in cash.
	19	Sold 100 coupon books for $15.00 each. Each book contains six coupons that enable the holder to one round of miniature golf or to hit one bucket of golf balls.
	25	Declared and paid a $500 cash dividend.
	30	Paid wages of $700.
	30	Paid Palmer Company in full.
	31	Received $500 of fees in cash.

Ace Bogie uses the following accounts: Cash, Prepaid Insurance, Land, Buildings, Equipment, Accounts Payable, Unearned Golf Fees, Common Shares, Dividends, Golf Fees Earned, Advertising Expense, and Wages Expense.

Instructions

Journalize the March transactions.

(Corrected Trial Balance) The trial balance of Labelle Inc. shown below does not balance. **E3-4**

LABELLE INC.
Trial Balance
June 30

	Debit	Credit
Cash		$ 2,870
Fees Receivable	$ 3,231	
Supplies	800	
Equipment	3,800	
Accounts Payable		2,666
Unearned Fees	1,200	
Common Shares		6,000
Retained Earnings		3,000
Fees Earned		2,380
Wages Expense	3,400	
Office Expense	940	
	$13,371	$16,916

Each of the listed accounts has a normal balance per the general ledger. An examination of the ledger and journal reveals the following errors.

1. Cash received from a customer on account was debited for $570 and Fees Receivable was credited for the same amount. The actual collection was for $750.
2. The purchase of a fax modem on account for $250 was recorded as a debit to Supplies for $250 and a credit to Accounts Payable for $250.
3. Services were performed on account for a client for $890. Fees Receivable was debited for $890 and Fees Earned was credited for $89.
4. A payment of $65 for telephone charges was recorded as a debit to Office Expense for $65 and a debit to Cash for $65.
5. When the Unearned Fees account was reviewed, it was found that $200 of the balance was earned prior to June 30.
6. A debit posting to Wages Expense of $670 was omitted.
7. A payment on account for $206 was credited to Cash for $206 and credited to Accounts Payable for $260.
8. A dividend of $575 was debited to Wages Expense for $575 and credited to Cash for $575.

Instructions
Prepare a correct trial balance. It may be necessary to add one or more accounts to the trial balance.

E3-5   (Corrected Trial Balance) The trial balance of the Soul Co. Ltd. does not balance.

SOUL CO. LTD.
Trial Balance
April 30

Cash	$ 5,912	
Accounts Receivable	5,240	
Supplies on Hand	2,967	
Furniture and Equipment	6,100	
Accounts Payable		$ 5,044
Common Shares		8,000
Retained Earnings		2,000
Revenue from Fees		5,200
Office Expenses	2,320	
	$22,539	$20,244

An examination of the ledger shows these errors.

1. Cash received from a customer on account was recorded (both debit and credit) as $1,480 instead of $1,840.
2. The purchase on account of a laser printer costing $1,200 was recorded as a debit to Office Expenses and a credit to Accounts Payable.
3. Services were performed on account for a client for $2,250; Accounts Receivable was debited $2,250 and Revenue from Fees was credited $225.
4. A payment of $95 for telephone charges was entered as a debit to Office Expenses and a debit to Cash.
5. The Revenue from Fees account was incorrectly totalled at $5,200 instead of $5,280.

Instructions
From this information prepare a corrected trial balance.

E3-6   (Corrected Trial Balance) The trial balance of E. Fitz Company that follows does not balance. Your review of the ledger reveals the following: (a) each account had a normal balance; (b) the debit footings (additions) in Prepaid Insurance, Accounts Payable, and Property Tax Expense were each understated by $100; (c) transposition errors were made in Accounts Receivable and Fees Earned—the correct balances are $2,750 and $6,690, respectively; (d) a debit posting to Advertising Expense of $200 was omitted; and (e) a $1,000 cash withdrawal by the owner was debited to E. Fitz, Capital, and credited to Cash.

E. FITZ COMPANY
Trial Balance
April 30, 199x

	Debit	Credit
Cash	$ 5,400	
Accounts Receivable	2,570 *2750*	
✓Prepaid Insurance +100	700	
Equipment		$ 8,000
✓Accounts Payable + 100		4,500
Property Tax Payable	560	
E. Fitz, Capital		11,700 ⟨1000⟩
Fees Earned	6,960 *6690*	
Salaries Expense	4,200 +200	
Advertising Expense	1,100	
✓Property Tax Expense + 100		800
	$21,490	$25,000

Drawings 1000.

Instructions
Prepare a correct trial balance.

(**Adjusting Entries**) A review of the ledger of Canuks Co. Ltd. at December 31, 1998 produces the following data E3-7
pertaining to the preparation of annual adjusting entries.

1. Salaries Payable, $0. There are seven salaried employees. Payday for each month is on the fifth day of the following month. Four employees are paid salaries of $2,500 each per month, and three employees earn $3,500 each per month.

2. Sales Commissions Expense, $17,000. Salespersons are paid commissions equal to 2% of net sales, payable on the tenth day of the month following the sales. Commissions have been paid in full when due. In 1998, commission payments totalled $18,500, which includes commissions payable of $1,500 on December 31, 1997. Net sales were $960,000 in 1998.

3. Unearned Rent, $311,000. The company began subleasing office space in its new building on November 1. Each tenant is required to make a $5,000 security deposit that is refundable when occupancy is terminated. At December 31, the company has the following rental contracts that are paid in full for the entire term of the lease.

Date	Term (in months)	Monthly Rent	Number
Nov. 1	6	$4,000	3
Dec. 1	6	$8,500	4

4. Advertising Expense, $13,800. This balance consists of payments on two advertising contracts. The contracts provide for monthly advertising in two trade magazines. The terms of the contracts are as follows:

Contract	Date	Amount	Issues
A650	May 1	$6,600	12
B974	Sept. 1	7,200	24

The first advertisement runs in the month in which the contract is signed.

5. Notes Payable, $81,000. There are two notes outstanding: a $45,000, 7%, one-year note was signed on May 1; and a $36,000, 6%, nine-month note was signed on November 1.

Instructions
Prepare the adjusting entries at December 31, 1998. (Show all computations.)

E3-8   (Adjusting Entries) Muriel's Utopia Resort opened for business on June 1 with eight air-conditioned units. Its trial balance on August 31 is as follows:

MURIEL'S UTOPIA RESORT
Trial Balance
August 31, 1998

	Debit	Credit
Cash	$ 19,600	
Supplies Inventory	2,600	
Land	20,000	
Cottages	120,000	
Furniture	16,000	
Accounts Payable		$ 4,500
Advanced Rentals		4,600
Mortgage Payable		60,000
Muriel, Capital		100,000
Muriel, Drawings	5,000	
Rent Revenue		76,200
Insurance Expense	4,500	
Salaries Expense	44,800	
Utilities Expense	9,200	
Repair Expense	3,600	
	$245,300	$245,300

Other data:
1. The balance in Insurance Expense is for a three-year premium paid on June 1, 1998.
2. An inventory count on August 31 shows $400 of supplies on hand.
3. Annual depreciation rates are cottages (4%) and furniture (10%). Residual value is estimated to be 10% of cost.
4. Advanced Rentals of $4,000 were earned prior to August 31.
5. Salaries of $200 were unpaid at August 31.
6. Rentals of $800 were due from tenants at August 31.
7. The mortgage interest rate is 8% per year.

Instructions
(a) Journalize the adjusting entries on August 31 for the three-month period June 1–August 31.
(b) Prepare an adjusted trial balance on August 31.

E3-9   (Adjusting Entries) The ledger of Reno Inc. on March 31 of the current year includes the following selected accounts before preparing adjusting entries.

	Debit	Credit
Prepaid Insurance	$ 3,600	
Supplies Inventory	2,800	
Delivery Equipment	25,000	
Accumulated Depreciation		$ 8,400
Notes Payable		20,000
Rent Revenue		69,300
Interest Expense	-0-	
Wage Expense	14,000	

An analysis of the accounts shows the following:
1. The delivery equipment depreciates $500 per month.
2. Rent collection of $6,200 was unearned at the end of the quarter.
3. Accrued wages at March 31 total $2,100.
4. Interest of $400 is accrued on the notes payable.
5. Supplies on hand total $750.
6. Insurance expires at the rate of $175 per month.

Instructions
Prepare the adjusting entries at March 31. Assume that adjusting entries are made quarterly. Additional accounts are: Depreciation Expense, Insurance Expense, Supplies Expense, Wages Payable, Unearned Rent, and Interest Payable.

(Adjusting Entries) Selected accounts of Shana Company as at October 31 are shown below.

E3-10

Supplies Inventory				
Beg. Bal.	800	10/31	425	

Fees Receivable		
10/17	2,400	
10/31	1,488	

Salaries Expense		
10/15	550	
10/31	600	

Salaries Payable		
		10/31	600

Unearned Fees			
10/31	400	10/20	650

Supplies Expense		
10/31	425	

Fees Earned		
	10/17	2,400
	10/31	1,488
	10/31	400

Instructions

From an analysis of the T accounts, reconstruct (a) the October transaction entries; and (b) the adjusting journal entries that were made on October 31.

(Cost of Goods Sold Section and Closing Entries) The trial balance of the Gervais Co. Ltd. at the end of its fiscal year, August 31, 1998, includes the following accounts: Merchandise Inventory $17,500, Purchases $142,400, Sales $190,000, Freight-in $4,000, Sales Returns and Allowances $4,000, Freight-out $1,000, and Purchase Returns and Allowances $2,000. The ending merchandise inventory is $25,000.

E3-11

Instructions

(a) Prepare a cost of goods sold section for the year ending August 31.

(b) Prepare all closing entries for the above accounts. Gervais Co. Ltd. is a corporation.

(Adjusting and Reversing Entries) On December 31, adjusting information for Holmes Inc. is as follows:

E3-12

1. Estimated depreciation on equipment, $200.
2. Property taxes amounting to $300 have accrued but are unrecorded and unpaid.
3. Employees' wages earned but unpaid and unrecorded, $1,200.
4. Unearned Fee Revenue balance includes $1,500 that has been earned.
5. Interest of $250 on $25,000 note receivable has accrued.

Instructions

(a) Prepare adjusting journal entries.

(b) Prepare reversing journal entries.

(Adjusting and Reversing Entries) When the accounts of Grey Drugs Inc. are examined, the adjusting data listed below are uncovered on December 31, the end of an annual fiscal period.

E3-13

1. The Unexpired Insurance account shows a debit of $5,280, representing the cost of a two-year fire insurance policy dated August 1 of the current year. 5mo   24 mo
2. On November 1, Rental Income was credited for $1,800, representing income from a subrental for a three-month period beginning on that date.
3. Purchase of advertising materials for $800 during the year was recorded in the Advertising Expense account. On December 31, advertising materials of $360 are on hand.
4. Interest of $320 has accrued on notes payable.

Instructions

Prepare in general journal form (a) the adjusting entry for each item; and (b) the reversing entry for each item where appropriate.

E3-14   **(Closing Entries for a Corporation)** Presented below are selected accounts for Atlas Co. Ltd. as of December 31, 1998.

Merchandise inventory 1/1/98	$ 40,000	Purchases	$205,000
Common shares	75,000	Purchase returns and	
Retained earnings	45,000	allowances	8,000
Dividends	18,000	Purchase discounts	4,000
Sales returns and allowances	12,000	Transportation-in	700
Sales discounts	15,000	Selling expenses	16,000
Sales	410,000	Administrative expenses	38,000
		Income taxes expense	30,000

Instructions
Prepare closing entries for Atlas Co. Ltd. on December 31, 1998. Merchandise inventory was $60,000 on that date.

E3-15   **(Closing and Reversing Entries)** On December 31, the adjusted trial balance of Flies Co. Inc. shows the following selected data:

Commissions Receivable	$4,000	Commissions Earned	$96,000
Interest Expense	7,800	Interest Payable	2,000

Analysis shows that adjusting entries were made for (a) $4,000 of commissions earned but not billed; and (b) $2,000 of accrued but unpaid interest.

Instructions
(a) Prepare the closing entries for the temporary accounts at December 31.
(b) Prepare the reversing entries on January 1.
(c) Enter the adjusted trial balance data in the four accounts. Post the entries in (a) and (b) and balance the accounts. (Use T accounts.)
(d) Prepare the entries to record (1) the collection of the accrued commissions on January 10; and (2) the payment of all interest due ($2,500) on January 15.
(e) Post the entries in (d) to the temporary accounts.

E3-16   **(Partial Work Sheet Preparation)** Comic Video Co. prepares monthly financial statements from a work sheet. Selected portions of the January work sheet show the following data:

COMIC VIDEO CO.
Work Sheet (Partial)
For Month Ended January 31, 199x

Account Title	Trial Balance Dr.	Trial Balance Cr.	Adjustments Dr.	Adjustments Cr.	Adjusted Trial Balance Dr.	Adjusted Trial Balance Cr.
Supplies inventory	3,256			(a) 1,200	2,056	
Accumulated depreciation		6,682		(b) 257		6,939
Interest payable		100		(c) 50		150
Supplies expense			(a) 1,200		1,200	
Depreciation expense			(b) 257		257	
Interest expense			(c) 50		50	

During February no events occurred that affected these accounts, but at the end of February the following information was available:

1. Supplies on hand $1,315
2. Monthly depreciation $ 257
3. Accrued interest $ 50

Instructions
Reproduce the data that would appear in the February work sheet through the Income Statement columns.

(Work Sheet Preparation) The trial balance of Windproof Roofing Inc. at March 31, 1998 is as follows: E3-17

WINDPROOF ROOFING INC.
Trial Balance
March 31, 1998

	Debit	Credit
Cash	$ 2,300	
Fees Receivable	2,600	
Roofing Supplies	1,100	
Equipment	6,000	
Accumulated Depreciation—Equipment		$ 1,200
Accounts Payable		1,100
Unearned Fees		300
Common Shares		6,400
Retained Earnings		600
Fees Earned		3,000
Salaries Expense	500	
Miscellaneous Expense	100	
	$12,600	$12,600

Other data:
1. A physical count reveals only $620 of roofing supplies on hand.
2. Equipment is depreciated at a rate of $120 per month.
3. Unearned fees amounted to $100 on March 31.
4. Accrued salaries are $800.

Instructions
Enter the trial balance on a work sheet and complete the work sheet, assuming that the adjustments relate only to the month of March (ignore income taxes).

(Cash to Accrual: Insurance) Baxter Company maintains records on a cash basis. During the current year, $24,100   *E3-18
was paid for insurance. Had the accrual basis been used, there would have been a $2,090 balance in the Prepaid
Insurance account at the beginning of the year, and a balance of $6,740 in the account at year-end.

Instructions
What would be the amount of insurance expense reported for the year under (a) the cash basis; and (b) the accrual
basis?

(Cash and Accrual Basis) Presented below are three independent situations: *E3-19
1. Cory Co. had cash purchases of $980,000 during the past year. In addition, it had an increase in trade accounts
   payable of $9,000 and a decrease in merchandise inventory of $18,000. Determine cost of goods sold on an
   accrual basis.
2. P. Sampson, M.D., collected $125,000 in fees during 1998. At December 31, 1997 Dr. Sampson had accounts
   receivable of $15,000. At December 31, 1998 Dr. Sampson had accounts receivable of $28,000 and unearned fees
   of $4,000. Determine Dr. Sampson's revenue from fees on an accrual basis for 1998.
3. Kumiko Co. Ltd. reported revenue of $1,400,000 in its accrual basis income statement for the year ended
   December 31, 1998. Additional information was as follows:

Accounts receivable December 31, 1997	$410,000
Accounts receivable December 31, 1998	520,000
Accounts written off during the year	45,000

Determine how much revenue Kumiko should report under the cash basis of accounting.

(Cash to Accrual Basis) B. Miller, M.D. maintains the accounting records of Miller Clinic on a cash basis. During   *E3-20
1998, Dr. Miller collected $142,600 from her patients and paid $55,470 in expenses. At January 1, 1998 and December
31, 1998 she had fees receivable, unearned fees, accrued expenses, and prepaid expenses as follows (all long-lived
assets are rented):

	January 1, 1998	December 31, 1998	Change
Fees receivable	$9,250	$15,927	$+6,677
Unearned fees	2,840	1,620	−1,220
Accrued expenses	3,435	2,108	−1,327
Prepaid expenses	1,917	1,775	−142

Instructions

Complete the following, providing supporting schedules as necessary to justify your answer.

B. MILLER, M.D.
Income Statement
For the Year Ended December 31, 1998

	Cash Basis	Accrual Basis
Revenues		
Expenses	_____	_____
Net Income	=======	=======

PROBLEMS

P3-1   The balance sheet of Young & Restless Inc. as of December 31, 1997 is presented below.

YOUNG & RESTLESS INC.
Balance Sheet
as of December 31, 1997

Assets		Liabilities and Shareholders' Equity		
Cash	$ 3,900	Accounts payable		$ 2,985
Accounts receivable	4,985	Notes payable		4,000
Inventory	3,300	Total liabilities		$ 6,985
Office equipment	4,800			
Accumulated depreciation	(1,440)			
Furniture and fixtures	6,600	Common shares	$10,000	
Accumulated depreciation	(2,200)	Retained earnings	2,960	12,960
		Total liabilities and		
Total assets	$19,945	shareholders' equity		$19,945

The following transactions occurred during the month of January, 1998.

Jan.	2	Receives payment of $1,230 on accounts receivable.
	3	Purchases merchandise on account from Winters Co. for $1,965, 2/30, n/60, f.o.b. shipping point. (Note: 2/30, n/60 means that if paid within 30 days a 2% discount can be taken, otherwise the full amount is to be paid by the 60th day; f.o.b. shipping point means the ownership of the goods passes to the buyer when they leave the seller's premises.)
	4	Receives an invoice from *Reality*, a trade magazine, for advertising, $75.
	4	Sells merchandise on account to Carlton Co. for $1,034, 2/10, n/30, f.o.b. shipping point.
	4	Makes a cash sale to Glenn Inc. for $1,786.
	6	Sends a letter to Winters Co. regarding a slight defect in an item of merchandise received.
	9	Purchases merchandise on account from April's Novelty Company, $651.
	11	Pays freight on merchandise received from Winters Co., $76.
	11	Receives a credit memo from Winters Co. granting an allowance of $34 on defective merchandise (see transaction of January 6).
	15	Receives $600 on account from Carlton Co.
	19	Sells merchandise on account to Jeff Cole, $812, 2/10, n/30.
	21	Pays display clerk's salary of $552.
	25	Sells merchandise for cash, $2,350.
	27	Purchases office equipment on account, $879 (begin depreciating in February).

29   Pays Winters Co. the full amount due.
30   Accepted a Note Receivable from Jeff Cole in exchange for his account.
31   A count of the inventory on hand reveals $2,640 of saleable merchandise.

Instructions
(a) Open ledger T accounts at January 1, 1998.
(b) Enter the transactions into ledger accounts.
(c) Take a trial balance and adjust for depreciation; use 10-year life, straight-line method, and no residual value for all long-term assets. Interest at 12% on the note payable is due every December 31.
(d) Prepare a balance sheet and income statement (ignore income taxes).
(e) Close the ledger.
(f) Take a post-closing trial balance.

Listed below are the transactions of Yank O'Tooth, D.D.S., for the month of September.   P3-2

Sept. 1   O'Tooth begins practice as a dentist and invests $18,000 cash.
      2   Purchases furniture and dental equipment on account from COD Co. for $17,280.
      4   Pays rent for office space, $800 for the month.
      4   Employs a receptionist.
      5   Purchases dental supplies for cash, $942.
      8   Receives cash of $1,690 from patients for services performed.
    10   Pays miscellaneous office expenses, $430.
    14   Bills patients $4,820 for services performed.
    18   Pays COD Co. on account, $3,600.
    19   Withdraws $3,000 cash from the business for personal use.
    20   Receives $980 from patients on account.
    25   Bills patients $2,110 for services performed.
    30   Pays the following expenses in cash: office salaries, $1,600; miscellaneous office expenses, $85.
    30   Dental supplies used during September, $330.

Instructions
(a) Enter the transactions shown above in appropriate general ledger T accounts. Record depreciation using an eight-year life on the furniture and equipment, the straight-line method, and no residual value. Do not use a Drawings account.
(b) Take a trial balance.
(c) Prepare an income statement, a balance sheet, and a statement of capital.
(d) Close the ledger.
(e) Take a post-closing trial balance.

The following accounts appeared in the December 31 trial balance of the Terror Theatre.   P3-3

Equipment	$192,000	
Accumulated Depreciation of Equipment		$ 60,000
Notes Payable		80,000
Revenue from Admissions		380,000
Revenue from Concessions		36,000
Advertising Expense	13,680	
Salaries Expense	57,600	
Interest Expense	1,400	

Instructions
(a) From the account balances listed and the information given below, prepare the adjusting entries necessary on December 31.
    1. The equipment has an estimated life of 16 years and a residual value of $72,000 at the end of that time. (Use straight-line method.)
    2. The note payable is a 90-date note given to the bank October 20 and bearing interest at 10%. (Use 360 days for denominator.)

3. In December 2,000 coupon admission books were sold at $25 each; they could be used for admission any time after January 1. The amount was included in Revenue from Admissions for December.

4. The concession stand is operated by a concessionaire who pays 10% of gross receipts for the privilege of selling popcorn, candy, and soft drinks in the lobby. Sales for December were $32,700 and the 10% due for December has not yet been received or entered.

5. Advertising expense paid in advance and included in Advertising Expense, $1,100.

6. Salaries accrued but unpaid, $4,700.

(b) What amounts should be shown for each of the following on the income statement for the year?

1. Interest expense.
2. Revenue from admissions.
3. Revenue from concessions.
4. Advertising expense.
5. Salaries expense.

P3-4 Presented below are the trial balance and the other information related to U.R. Smart, a consulting engineer.

U.R. SMART, CONSULTING ENGINEER
Trial Balance
December 31, 1998

Cash	$ 31,500	
Accounts Receivable	49,600	
Allowance for Doubtful Accounts		$ 1,750
Engineering Supplies Inventory	1,960	
Unexpired Insurance	1,100	
Furniture and Equipment	25,000	
Accumulated Depreciation of Furniture and Equipment		5,000
Notes Payable		7,200
U.R. Smart, Capital		35,260
Revenue from Consulting Fees		100,000
Rent Expenses	9,750	
Office Salaries Expense	28,500	
Heat, Light, and Water Expense	1,080	
Miscellaneous Office Expense	720	
	$149,210	$149,210

1. Fees received in advance from clients, $5,900.
2. Services performed for clients but not recorded by December 31, $4,900.
3. The Allowance for Doubtful Accounts account should be adjusted to 5% of the accounts receivable balance (after adjustment for 2).
4. Insurance expired during the year, $480.
5. Furniture and equipment is being depreciated at 10% of cost per year.
6. U.R. Smart gave the bank a 90-day, 10% note for $7,200 on December 1, 1998.
7. Rent of the building is $750 per month. The rent for 1998 has been paid, as has that for January, 1999.
8. Office salaries earned but unpaid December 31, 1998, $2,510.

Instructions

(a) From the trial balance and other information given, prepare adjusting entries as of December 31, 1998.

(b) Prepare an income statement for 1998, a balance sheet, and a statement of owner's equity. U.R. Smart withdrew $19,000 cash for personal use during the year.

P3-5 Prize Advertising Inc. was founded by Duncan Silver in January of 1994. Following are both the adjusted and unadjusted trial balances as of December 31, 1998.

PRIZE ADVERTISING INC.
Trial Balance
December 31, 1998

	Unadjusted		Adjusted	
	Dr.	Cr.	Dr.	Cr.
Cash	$ 7,000		$ 7,000	
Fees Receivable	19,000		20,000	
Art Supplies Inventory	8,500		5,500	
Prepaid Insurance	3,250		2,500	
Printing Equipment	60,000		60,000	
Accumulated Depreciation		$ 28,000		$ 35,000
Accounts Payable		5,000		5,000
Interest Payable		0		150
Notes Payable		5,000		5,000
Unearned Advertising Fees		7,000		5,600
Salaries Payable		0		1,500
Common Shares		10,000		10,000
Retained Earnings		3,500		3,500
Advertising Fees		58,600		61,000
Salaries Expense	10,000		11,500	
Insurance Expense	0		750	
Interest Expense	350		500	
Depreciation Expense	0		7,000	
Art Supplies Expense	5,000		8,000	
Rent Expense	4,000		4,000	
	$117,100	$117,100	$126,750	$126,750

Instructions

(a) Journalize the annual adjusting entries that were made.

(b) Prepare an income statement and a statement of retained earnings for the year ending December 31, 1998 and a balance sheet at December 31.

(c) Answer the following questions:

(1) If the estimated total useful life of equipment is eight years, what is the expected residual value?

(2) If the note on which interest has accrued has been outstanding three months, what is the annual interest rate on that note?

(3) If the company paid $12,500 in salaries in 1998, what was the balance in Salaries Payable on December 31, 1997?

Presented below is the December 31 trial balance of Madonna Boutique.

P3-6

MADONNA BOUTIQUE
Trial Balance
December 31, 199X

Cash	$ 18,500	
Accounts Receivable	42,000	
Allowance for Doubtful Accounts		$ 2,700
Inventory, January 1	78,000	
Furniture and Equipment	84,000	
Accumulated Depreciation of Furniture and Equipment		33,600
Prepaid Insurance	5,100	
Notes Payable		28,000
Madonna, Capital		90,000
Sales		600,000
Purchases	400,000	
Sales Salaries	50,000	
Advertising Expense	6,700	
Administrative Salaries	65,000	
Office Expenses	5,000	
	$754,300	$754,300

Instructions
(a) Prepare adjusting journal entries for the following. The books are closed yearly on December 31.
   1. Adjust the Allowance for Doubtful Accounts to 8% of the accounts receivable.
   2. Furniture and equipment is depreciated at 20% of cost per year.
   3. Insurance expired during the year, $2,550.
   4. Interest accrued on notes payable, $3,360.
   5. Sales salaries earned but not yet recorded or paid, $2,400.
   6. Advertising paid in advance, $700.
   7. Office supplies on hand, $1,500, charged to Office Expenses when purchased.
(b) Prepare all closing entries. The inventory on December 31 was $80,000.

P3-7 The balance sheet of Tony Company as of December 31, 1997 is presented below.

Assets		Liabilities and Capital	
Cash	$ 4,000	Accounts payable	$ 5,000
Accounts receivable	7,500	Notes payable	6,000
Inventory	5,200	Total liabilities	$11,000
Office equipment	7,400		
Accumulated depreciation	(2,220)	Tony, capital	17,880
Furniture and fixtures	10,000		
Accumulated depreciation	(3,000)		
Total	$28,880	Total	$28,880

The following summary transactions occurred during January, 1998.

Jan.	1	Sold merchandise on account, $3,800.
	2	Collected $3,920 on accounts receivable of $4,000. Sales discounts totalled $80.
	3	Sold merchandise for cash, $7,200.
	4	Accepted a $1,500 note from a customer in exchange for an outstanding account receivable.
	5	Purchased merchandise on account, $4,600.
	6	Paid freight on merchandise purchased, $100.
	7	Paid $3,470 on accounts payable of $3,500. Purchase discounts totalled $30.
	10	Purchased office equipment on account, $1,300.
	28	Paid expenses: advertising, $55; salaries, $840; rent, $400.

At January 31, the following information is available.
   1. Interest on the note payable is paid every December 31. Accrued interest for January is $60. Principal is payable December 31, 1998.
   2. Accrued interest on the note receivable for January is $15.
   3. Accrued salaries at January 31 are $125.
   4. Depreciation expense for January is $70 on office equipment and $80 on furniture and fixtures.
   5. Ending inventory is $4,225.

Instructions
(a) Prepare journal entries in general journal form for the January transactions.
(b) Open ledger accounts, enter the December 31 balances, and post the journal entries from (a).

(c) Prepare a trial balance.
(d) Prepare adjusting entries at January 31 and post.
(e) Prepare an adjusted trial balance.
(f) Prepare an income statement for January and a balance sheet at January 31.
(g) Prepare closing entries at January 31 and post.
(h) Prepare a post-closing trial balance.

Following is the trial balance of the Green Meadows Golf Club Inc. as of December 31. The books are closed annu-   P3-8
ally on December 31.

GREEN MEADOWS GOLF CLUB INC.
Trial Balance
December 31, 199X

Cash	$ 15,000	
Dues Receivable	13,000	
Allowance for Doubtful Accounts		$ 1,100
Land	350,000	
Buildings	120,000	
Accumulated Depreciation of Buildings		48,000
Equipment	150,000	
Accumulated Depreciation of Equipment		70,000
Unexpired Insurance	9,000	
Common Shares		400,000
Retaining Earnings		72,400
Dues Revenue		200,000
Revenue from Greens Fees		8,100
Rent Revenue		15,400
Utilities Expense	54,000	
Salaries Expense	80,000	
Maintenance Expense	24,000	
	$815,000	$815,000

Instructions
(a) Set up T accounts and enter the balances for the accounts from the trial balance.
(b) From the trial balance and the following information, prepare adjusting entries and post to the ledger accounts.
   1. The buildings have an estimated life of 20 years with no residual value (straight-line method).
   2. The equipment is depreciated at 10% of cost per year.
   3. Insurance expired during the year, $3,500.
   4. The rent revenue represents the amount received for 11 months for dining facilities. The December rent has not yet been received.
   5. It is estimated that 15% of the dues receivable are uncollectible.
   6. Salaries earned but not paid by December 31, $3,600.
   7. Dues paid in advance by members, $7,900, was included in Dues Revenue.
(c) Prepare an adjusted trial balance.
(d) Prepare closing entries and post.
(e) Prepare reversing entries and post.
(f) Prepare a trial balance after the reversing entries are posted.

P3-9 The following list of accounts and their balances represents the unadjusted trial balance of Cleanup Ltd. at December 31, 1998.

	Dr.	Cr.
Cash	$ 62,740	
Accounts Receivable	98,000	
Allowance for Doubtful Accounts		$ 3,500
Merchandise Inventory	62,000	
Prepaid Insurance	2,620	
Investment in Casper Oil Co. Bonds (9%)	40,000	
Land	30,000	
Building	124,000	
Accumulated Depreciation—Building		12,400
Equipment	33,600	
Accumulated Depreciation—Equipment		5,600
Goodwill	26,600	
Accounts Payable		101,050
Bonds Payable (20-year; 7%)		210,000
Common Shares		121,000
Retained Earnings		21,360
Sales		190,000
Rental Income		10,800
Advertising Expense	22,500	
Supplies Expense	10,800	
Purchases	98,000	
Purchase Discounts		900
Office Salary Expense	17,500	
Sales Salary Expense	36,000	
Interest Expense	12,250	
	$676,610	$676,610

Additional information:

1. Actual advertising costs amounted to $1,500 per month. The company has already paid for advertisements in *Mission Magazine* for the first quarter of 1999.

2. The building was purchased and occupied January 1, 1996 with an estimated life of 20 years. (The company uses straight-line depreciation.)

3. Prepaid insurance contains the premium costs of two policies: Policy A, cost of $960, one-year term taken out on Sept. 1, 1997; Policy B, cost of $1,980, three-year term taken out on April 1, 1998.

4. A portion of their building has been converted into a snack bar that has been rented to the Yummy Food Corp. since July 1, 1997 at a rate of $7,200 per year payable each July 1.

5. One of the company's customers declared bankruptcy December 30, 1998, and it has been definitely established that the $2,700 due from him will never be collected. This fact has not been recorded. In addition, Cleanup estimates that 4% of the Accounts Receivable balance on December 31, 1998 will become uncollectible.

6. Six hundred dollars given as an advance to a salesperson on December 31, 1998, was charged to Sales Salary Expense. Sales salaries are paid on the first and 16th of each month for the following half month.

7. When the company purchased a competing firm on July 1, 1996 it acquired goodwill in the amount of $38,000, which is being amortized over its estimated life.

8. On November 1, 1994 Cleanup issued 210, $1,000 bonds at par value. Interest payments are made semiannually on April 30 and October 31.

9. The equipment was purchased January 1, 1996 with an estimated life of 12 years. (The company uses straight-line depreciation.)

10. On August 1, 1998 Cleanup purchased 40, $1,000, 9% bonds maturing on August 31, 2003 at par value. Interest payment dates are July 31 and January 31.

11. The inventory on hand at December 31, 1998 was $74,000 per a physical inventory count. Record the adjustment for inventory in the same entry that records the Cost of Goods Sold for the year.

Instructions
(a) Prepare adjusting and correcting entries for December 31, 1998 using the information given.
(b) Indicate which of the adjusting entries could be reversed.

The following list of accounts and their balances represents the unadjusted trial balance of Costello Co. Ltd. at **P3-10**
December 31, 1998.

	Dr.	Cr.
Cash	$ 8,350	
Accounts Receivable	49,000	
Allowance for Doubtful Accounts		$ 750
Inventory	58,000	
Prepaid Insurance	2,940	
Prepaid Rent	13,200	
Investment in Abbott Inc. Bonds	18,000	
Land	10,000	
Plant and equipment	104,000	
Accumulated Depreciation		18,000
Accounts Payable		9,310
Bonds Payable		50,000
Common Shares		100,000
Retained Earnings		80,660
Sales		213,310
Rent Revenue		10,200
Purchases	170,000	
Purchase Discounts		2,400
Transportation-out	9,000	
Transportation-in	3,500	
Salaries and Wages Expense	35,000	
Interest Expense	2,750	
Miscellaneous Expense	890	
	$484,630	$484,630

Additional data:

1. On November 1, 1998 Costello received $10,200 rent from its lessee for a 12-month lease beginning on that date. This was credited to Rent Revenue.

2. Costello estimates that 4% of the Accounts Receivable balances on December 31, 1998 will be uncollectible. On December 28, 1998 the bookkeeper incorrectly credited Sales for a receipt on account in the amount of $1,000. This error had not yet been corrected on December 31.

3. By a physical count, inventory on hand at December 31, 1998 was $65,000. Record the adjusting entry for inventory by using a Cost of Goods Sold account.

4. Prepaid insurance contains the premium costs of two policies: Policy A, cost of $1,320, two-year term, taken out on September 1, 1998; Policy B, cost of $1,620, three-year term, taken out on April 1, 1998.

5. The regular rate of depreciation is 10% of cost per year. Acquisitions and retirements during a year are depreciated at half this rate. There were no retirements during the year. On December 31, 1997 the balance of Plant and Equipment was $90,000.

6. On April 1, 1998 Costello issued 50, $1,000, 11% bonds maturing on April 1, 2008 at par value. Interest payment dates are April 1 and October 1.

7. On August 1, 1998 Costello purchased 18, $1,000, 12% Abbott Inc. bonds, maturing on July 31, 2000 at par value. Interest payment dates are July 31 and January 31.

8. On May 30, 1998, Costello rented a warehouse for $1,100 per month, paying $13,200 in advance, debiting Prepaid Rent.

Instructions
(a) Prepare the year-end adjusting and correcting entries in general journal form using the information given.
(b) Indicate the adjusting entries that could be reversed.

P3-11 Boffo Company Ltd. closes its books once a year, on December 31, but prepares monthly financial statements by estimating month-end inventories and by using work sheets. The company's trial balance on January 31, 1998 is presented below.

BOFFO COMPANY LTD.
Trial Balance
January 31, 1998

Cash	$ 11,000	
Accounts Receivable	23,000	
Notes Receivable	3,000	
Allowance for Doubtful Accounts		$ 720
Inventory, Jan. 1, 1998	24,000	
Furniture and Fixtures	30,000	
Accumulated Depreciation of Furniture and Fixtures		7,500
Unexpired Insurance	600	
Supplies on Hand	1,050	
Accounts Payable		6,000
Notes Payable		5,000
Common Shares		20,000
Retained Earnings		27,005
Sales		130,000
Sales Returns and Allowances	1,500	
Purchases	80,000	
Transportation-in	2,000	
Selling Expenses	11,000	
Administrative Expenses	9,000	
Interest Revenue		125
Interest Expense	200	
	$196,350	$196,350

Instructions
(a) Copy the trial balance into the first two columns of a 10-column work sheet.
(b) Prepare adjusting entries in journal form (administrative expenses includes bad debts, depreciation, insurance, supplies, and office salaries).
    1. Estimated bad debts, 0.4% of net sales (sales minus sales returns, allowances, and discounts).
    2. Depreciation of furniture and fixtures, 10% of cost per year.
    3. Insurance expired in January, $80.
    4. Supplies used in January, $210.
    5. Office salaries accrued, $500.
    6. Interest accrued on notes payable, $200.
    7. Interest received but unearned on notes receivable, $75.
(c) Transfer the adjusting entries to the work sheet.
(d) Estimate the January 31 inventory and enter it on the work sheet. The average gross profit earned by the company is 30% of net sales. The gross profit rate equals net sales minus cost of goods sold divided by net sales.
(e) Complete the work sheet.
(f) Prepare a balance sheet, an income statement, and a statement of retained earnings. Dividends of $3,000 were paid on the common shares during the month and charged directly against retained earnings.

Presented below is the trial balance for R. Bryden Company, a proprietorship.

P3-12

R. BRYDEN COMPANY
Trial Balance
December 31, 1998

Cash	$ 13,600	
Accounts Receivable	64,800	
Allowance for Doubtful Accounts		$ 2,000
Inventory, January 1	74,000	
Land	40,000	
Building	90,000	
Accumulated Depreciation of Building		14,400
Furniture and Fixtures	22,000	
Accumulated Depreciation of Furniture and Fixtures		6,600
Unexpired Insurance	7,800	
Accounts Payable		34,200
Notes Payable		30,000
Mortgage Payable		40,000
R. Bryden, Capital		124,730
Sales		720,000
Sales Returns and Allowances	2,800	
Purchases	540,000	
Purchase Returns and Allowances		9,500
Transportation-in	14,800	
Sales Salaries Expense	54,000	
Advertising Expense	9,400	
Salaries, Office, and General Expense	31,000	
Heat, Light, and Water Expense	15,100	
Telephone and Fax Expense	1,700	
Miscellaneous Office Expenses	2,000	
Purchase Discounts		9,600
Sales Discounts	5,900	
Interest Expense	2,130	
	$991,030	$991,030

Instructions
(a) Copy the trial balance into the first two columns of a ten-column work sheet.
(b) Prepare adjusting entries in journal form from the following information. (The fiscal year ends December 31.)

1. Estimated bad debts, one-quarter of 1% of sales less returns and allowances.
2. Depreciation on building, 4% of cost per year; on furniture and fixtures, 15% of cost per year.
3. Insurance expired during the year, $3,900.
4. Interest at 12% is payable on the mortgage on January 1 of each year.
5. Sales salaries accrued, December 31, $4,000.
6. Advertising expenses paid in advance, $740.
7. Office supplies on hand December 31, $1,600. (Charged to Miscellaneous Office Expenses when purchased.)
8. Interest accrued on notes payable December 31, $1,800.

(c) Transfer the adjusting entries to the work sheet and complete it. Merchandise inventory on hand December 31, $76,000.

(d) Prepare an income statement, a balance sheet, and a statement of proprietor's capital.

(e) Prepare closing journal entries.

(f) Indicate the adjusting entries that could be reversed.

P3-13 On January 2, 1998 Cashew-Hazel Inc. was organized with two shareholders, Vern Cashew and James Hazel. Cashew purchased 500 common shares for $50,000 cash; Hazel received 600 common shares in exchange for the assets and liabilities of a men's clothing shop that he had operated as a sole proprietorship. The trial balance immediately after incorporation appears on the work sheet provided. No formal bookkeeping was done during 1998. The following information was gathered from the cheque books, deposit slips, and other sources:

1. Most balance sheet account balances at December 31, 1998 were determined and recorded as shown on the work sheet.

2. Cash receipts for the year were as follows:

Advances from customers	$ 1,100
Cash sales and collections on accounts receivable	
(after sales discounts of $1,600 and sales	
returns and allowances at $2,300)	132,100
Sale of equipment costing $6,000 on which $1,000 of	
depreciation had accumulated	5,800
	$139,000

3. During 1998, the depreciation expense on the building was $2,000; depreciation expense on the equipment was $2,400.

4. Cash disbursements for the year were as follows:

Insurance Premiums	$ 1,400
Purchase of equipment	10,000
Addition to building	9,500
Cash purchases and payments on accounts payable	
(after purchase discounts of $2,200 and purchase	
returns and allowances of $1,800)	109,000
Salaries paid to employees	38,600
Utilities	3,200
Total cash disbursements	$171,700

5. Bad debts were estimated to be 1.9% of total sales for the year. The ending accounts receivable balance of $30,000 was after eliminating $760 for specific accounts that were written off as uncollectible.

Instructions

Complete the work sheet for the preparation of accrual basis financial statements. Formal financial statements and journal entries are not required. (Prepare your own work sheet because you will need additional accounts.)

CASHEW-HAZEL INC.
Work Sheet for Preparation of Accrual Basis
Financial Statements
For the Year 1998

	Balance Sheet January 2, 1998		Adjustments		Income Statement 1998		Balance Sheet December 31, 1998	
	Debit	Credit	Debit	Credit	Debit	Credit	Debit	Credit
Cash	55,000							
Accounts receivable	12,000						30,000	
Merchandise inventory	31,000						51,500	
Unexpired insurance	800						900	
Land	20,000						20,000	
Buildings	30,000							
Accumulated depreciation— buildings		8,000						
Equipment	12,000							
Accumulated depreciation— equipment		3,000						
Accounts payable		36,600						25,600
Advances from customers		1,100						1,700
Salaries payable		2,100						4,600
Common shares		110,000						110,000
	160,800	160,800						

*P3-14

On January 1, 1998 Woody Bear and Dan Beaver formed a computer sales and service enterprise in Brandon, Manitoba by investing a total of $90,000 cash. The new company, Micromesh Sales and Service, had the following transactions during January:

1. Paid $6,000 in advance for three months' rent of office, showroom, and repair space.

2. Purchased 40 microcomputers at a cost of $1,000 each, six graphic computers at a cost of $2,000 each, and 25 printers at a cost of $300 each, paying cash upon delivery.

3. Sales, repair, and office employees earned $12,600 in salaries during January, of which $3,000 was still payable at the end of January.

4. Sold 30 microcomputers at $1,700 each, four graphic computers for $3,000 each, and 15 printers for $500 each; $50,000 was received in cash in January and $20,500 was sold on a deferred payment basis.

5. Other operating expenses of $8,400 were incurred and paid for during January; $2,000 of operating expenses were incurred but not paid by January 31.

Instructions
(a) Using the transaction data above, prepare (1) a cash basis income statement and (2) an accrual basis income statement for the month of January.
(b) Using the transaction data above, prepare (1) a cash basis balance sheet and (2) an accrual basis balance sheet as of January 31, 1998.
(c) Using examples in the cash basis financial statements, indicate how and why cash basis accounting is inconsistent with the conceptual theory underlying accrual basis financial statements.

USING YOUR JUDGEMENT

FINANCIAL REPORTING PROBLEM

The financial statements of Moore Corporation Limited are presented in Appendix 5A of this book.

Instructions
(a) Using the consolidated statement of earnings and the balance sheet, identify items that may result in adjusting entries for prepayments and accruals.
(b) Using the consolidated statement of cash flows, what was the amount of depreciation expense for 1995 and 1994? Are these amounts the same as those reported in the 1995 and 1994 income statements for depreciation expense?
(c) Using information in Note 1 related to property, plant, and equipment and the 1995 cost shown for property, plant, and equipment, what would be the total depreciation expense for buildings, machinery, and equipment if buildings were depreciated over their minimum estimated useful lives and machinery and equipment over their maximum estimated useful lives?

ETHICS CASE

While reviewing the year-end financial statements for Basler Motors Inc., chief accountant Scott Sanders realizes his original estimate of bad debt expense for the current year is too high to permit the bonus payment that is linked to the company's percentage increase in earnings. Both he and his supervisor are in line for the bonus. Scott is contemplating revising downward his bad debt estimate to increase earnings.

Instructions
(a) Should Scott lower his estimate? Justify your answer.
(b) What if only his supervisor's bonus was affected and not his? Should this alter Scott's decision?

chapter 4

STATEMENT OF INCOME AND RETAINED EARNINGS

CHAPTER

4

Statement of Income and Retained Earnings

Learning Objectives

After studying this chapter, you should be able to:

1. Identify the uses and limitations of an income statement.

2. Distinguish between the capital maintenance and transactions approaches.

3. Prepare a single-step income statement.

4. Prepare a multiple-step income statement.

5. Explain how irregular items are reported.

6. Explain intraperiod tax allocation.

7. Explain where earnings per share information is reported.

8. Prepare a statement of retained earnings.

9. Explain how prior period adjustments are reported.

10. Measure and report gains and losses from discontinued operations (Appendix 4A).

The **statement of income**, or statement of earnings as it is frequently called,[1] is the report that measures the success of enterprise operations for a given period of time. The business and investment community uses this report to determine profitability, investment value, and credit worthiness. It provides investors and creditors with information that helps them predict the **amounts, timing, and uncertainty of future cash flows**.

IMPORTANCE OF THE STATEMENT OF INCOME

As indicated above, the business and investment community pays close attention to a company's statement of income. *The Globe and Mail*, for example, continually reports the income and earnings per share consequences for Canadian companies. Under the headline "Corby Profit on a Bender Despite Drop in Drinking," the paper reported a $12.2 million profit ($1.76 per share) over a nine-month period for Corby Distilleries Ltd., compared with $9.8 million ($1.42 per share) for the corresponding period of the previous year. While not usually given such headline status, similar information is reported for many companies (e.g., Moffat Communications Ltd. showed a first-quarter profit of $1.7 million ($.35 per share), up from $1.4 million for the corresponding period a year earlier; Orifino Resources Ltd. had a loss of $625,000 ($.03 per share) for a year compared with a profit of $160,000 ($.01 per share) a year earlier.

---

[1] *Financial Reporting in Canada—1995* (Toronto: CICA), p. 170, indicated that for the 300 companies surveyed in 1994 the term "earnings" was employed in the title of 134 income statements. The term "income" was second in acceptance with 104, while the term "operations" was used by 49 companies.

The income statement helps users predict future cash flows in a number of different ways.

1. Investors and creditors can use the information on the income statement **to evaluate the past performance of the enterprise.** Although success in the past does not necessarily mean success in the future, some important trends may be determined. It follows that if a reasonable correlation between past and future performance can be assumed, then predictions of future cash flows can be made with some confidence.

2. The income statement can help users **determine the risk (level of uncertainty) of not achieving particular cash flows.** Information regarding the various components of income—revenues, expenses, gains, and losses—highlights the relationship among them. With such information one can, for example, assess better the impact on revenues and expenses—and therefore income—of a change in demand for a company's product. Similarly, segregating operating performance from other aspects of performance can provide useful insights. Because operations are usually the major means by which revenues and ultimately cash are generated, results from regular continuing operations usually have greater significance than results from nonrecurring activities and events.

Sometimes, though, even "continuing operations" can mislead investors. Consider the case of National Patent Development, a company that specializes in soft contact lenses. It reported $18.6 million in income from continuing operations before taxes. A closer examination of this income, however, revealed that (1) $7.5 million of income came from a gain on the sale of investments by a subsidiary; (2) $2.4 million represented a gain on the granting of a licence to sell its product in exchange for shares in the company it licensed; (3) $3.6 million came from the sale of shares in its investment portfolio; and (4) $3.2 million came from settlement of lawsuits relating to patent infringements. In addition, its largest revenue source, $9.9 million from royalties on its soft contact lenses, may not be continuing because a note indicates that the patent on this process was about to expire. Our point here is that income, "the bottom line," does not necessarily tell the whole story.

Whether existing confidence in the income statement is well founded is a matter of conjecture. Because the derived income is at best a rough estimate, the reader of the statement should take care not to give it more significance than it deserves. However, taken in its entirety, the income statement does provide information on the nature of income and the likelihood that it will continue in the future.

LIMITATIONS OF THE STATEMENT OF INCOME

Economists have often criticized accountants for their definition of income because accountants **do not include many items** that contribute to the general growth and well-being of an enterprise. Economist J.R. Hicks has defined income as the maximum value an entity can consume during a period and still be as well off at the end of the period as at the beginning.[2] Any effort to measure how well off an individual is at any point in time, however, will prove fruitless unless certain restrictive assumptions are developed and applied.

What was your net income for last year? Let us suppose you worked during the summer and earned $5,600. Because you paid taxes and incurred tuition and living expenses for school, your income statement may show a loss for the year, if measured in

---

[2] J.R. Hicks, *Value and Capital* (Oxford: Clarendon Press, 1946), p. 172.

terms of straight dollar amounts. But did you really sustain a loss? How do you value the education obtained during the year? According to one interpretation of Hicks' definition, you would measure not only monetary income, but also psychic income (well-offness). Psychic income is defined as a measure of the increase in net wealth that arises from qualitative factors, in this case the value of your educational experience. Accountants know that recognizing the value of such experiences may be useful; however, they also know that the problem of measurement has not been resolved. Therefore, items that cannot be quantified with any degree of reliability have been excluded from the determination of accounting income.

That's not to say that income totals are uniform and precise. **Income numbers are often affected by the accounting methods employed**. For example, one company may choose to depreciate its plant assets on an accelerated basis, while another may choose a straight-line basis. Assuming all other factors are equal, the income of the first company will be lower than that of the second in the first year of operations, even though the companies are essentially the same. Thus the **quality of earnings** of a given enterprise is important. Companies that use liberal (aggressive) accounting policies report higher income numbers in the short-run. In such cases, we say that the quality of earnings is low.

Other companies generate income in the short-run as a result of a nonoperating or nonrecurring event that is not sustainable over a period of time. For example, Chopp Computer Corp.'s share price on the Vancouver Stock Exchange skyrocketed from $1 per share in 1985 to $124 per share in 1986. It was the first share on the VSE to break the $100 per share barrier. The amazing price increase was based on the company's research and development of a "supercomputer" prototype that would revolutionize the industry and be extremely profitable. The prototype was never completed. The company's shares are no longer listed on the VSE, but were traded for less than $4 per share on the U.S. over-the-counter market prior to being acquired by Sullivan Computer Corp.

CAPITAL MAINTENANCE VERSUS TRANSACTION APPROACH

OBJECTIVE 2
Distinguish between the capital maintenance and transaction approaches.

People are sometimes surprised to learn that there are two ways to calculate net income. The first is represented by economist J.R. Hicks' definition of income. He subtracted beginning net assets (assets minus liabilities) from ending net assets and adjusted for any additional investments and any distributions (dividends declared or drawings made) during the period. This is the **capital maintenance approach** (sometimes referred to as the **change in equity approach**). It takes the net assets, or "capital values" that are based on some valuation (e.g., historical cost, discounted cash flows, current cost, or fair market value), and measures income by the difference in capital values at two points in time.

Suppose that a corporation had beginning net assets of $10,000 and end-of-the-year net assets of $18,000, and that during this same period additional owners' investments of $5,000 were made and $1,000 of dividends were declared. Calculation of the net income for the period, employing the capital maintenance approach, is shown below.

Net assets, end of year	$18,000
Net assets, beginning of year	10,000
Increase in net assets	$ 8,000
Add:	
Dividends declared during the year	1,000
Deduct:	
Owners' investments during the year	(5,000)
Net income for year	$ 4,000

The calculation is relatively straightforward. But there is one important drawback to the capital maintenance approach: Detailed information concerning the composition of the income is not evident because the revenue and expense amounts are not presented to the financial statement reader.

The alternative procedure measures the basic income-related transactions that occur during a period and summarizes them in an income statement. This method is normally called the **transaction approach**, and is the method with which you are familiar. This approach focuses on the activities that have occurred during a given period; instead of presenting only a net change, it discloses the components of the change. Income may be classified by customer, product line, or function; or by operating and nonoperating, continuing and discontinued, regular and irregular income.[3] The transaction approach to income measurement is superior to the capital maintenance approach because it provides information on the elements of income.

DEVELOPING THE INCOME STATEMENT

ELEMENTS OF THE INCOME STATEMENT

The transaction approach to income measurement requires the use of revenue, expense, loss, and gain accounts, without which an income statement cannot be prepared. As indicated in Chapter 2, the major elements of the income statement are as follows.

ELEMENTS OF THE INCOME STATEMENT

Revenues. Increases in economic resources, either by inflows or other enhancements of assets or reductions of liabilities, that result from the ordinary activities of an entity, normally from the sale of goods, the rendering of services, or the use by others of entity resources yielding rent, interest, royalties, or dividends.

Expenses. Decreases in economic resources, either by way of outflows or reductions of assets or incurrences of liabilities, resulting from the ordinary revenue-earning activities of an entity.

Gains. Increases in equity (net assets) from peripheral or incidental transactions and events affecting an entity and from all other transactions, events, and circumstances affecting the entity except those that result from revenues or equity contributions.

Losses. Decreases in equity (net assets) from peripheral or incidental transactions and events that affect an entity, and from all other transactions, events, and circumstances that affect the entity except those that result from expenses or distributions of equity.[4]

Revenues take many forms and include sales, fees, interest, dividends, and rents. Expenses also take many forms, such as cost of goods sold, depreciation, interest, rent, salaries and wages, and taxes. Gains and losses also comprise many types, such as those resulting from the sale of investments or plant assets, settlement of lawsuits, write-offs of assets due to obsolescence or casualty, and theft.

The distinction between revenues and gains and between expenses and losses depends to a great extent on the typical activities of the enterprise. For example, the sales price of investments sold by an insurance company may be classified as revenue, whereas the sales price less book value of an investment sold by a manufacturing enterprise will likely be classified as a gain or loss. This is because the sale of investments by an insurance company is part of its regular operations, unlike in a manufacturing enterprise.

The importance of reporting these elements should not be underestimated. For most decision makers, the parts of a financial statement will often be more useful than the

---

[3] "Irregular" encompasses transactions and other events that are derived from developments outside the normal operations of the business.

[4] *CICA Handbook*, Section 1000, par. .32–.35.

whole. As indicated earlier, investors and creditors are interested in predicting the amounts, timing, and uncertainty of future income and cash flows. Having income statement elements shown in some detail and in comparative form with prior years' data, decision makers are better able to assess future income and cash flows.

INCOME STATEMENT FORMATS

OBJECTIVE 3
Prepare a single-step income statement.

Single-step Income Statement. In reporting revenues, gains, expenses, and losses, many accountants prefer a format known as the **single-step income statement.** In the single-step statement, just two major categories exist: revenues and expenses. Expenses are deducted from the revenues to arrive at a net income or loss. The expression "single-step" is derived from the single subtraction necessary to arrive at net income. Frequently, however, income taxes are reported separately as the last item to indicate their relationship to income before taxes. Examine the single-step income statement of Dan & Karen Co. Ltd., shown below.

DAN & KAREN CO. LTD.
Income Statement
For the Year Ended December 31, 1998

Revenues		
Net sales		$2,972,413
Dividend revenue		98,500
Rental revenue		72,910
Total revenues		$3,143,823
Expenses		
Cost of goods sold		1,982,541
Selling expenses		453,028
Administrative expenses		350,771
Interest expense		126,060
Income tax expense		66,934
Total expenses		$2,979,334
Net income		$ 164,489
Earnings per common share		$1.74

The single-step form of income statement is widely used in business reporting today. The primary advantage of the single-step format is its **simplicity of presentation and absence of any implication that one type of revenue or expense has priority over another**. Potential classification problems are thus eliminated.

OBJECTIVE 4
Prepare a multiple-step income statement.

Multiple-step Income Statement. Some accountants contend that including other important revenue and expense data makes the income statement more informative and, therefore, more useful. These further classifications include:

1. A separation between operating and subordinate, or nonoperating, activities of the company. For example, enterprises often present an income from operations figure and then sections entitled "other revenues and gains" and "other expenses and losses." These other categories include interest revenue and expense, sales of miscellaneous items, and dividends received.

2. A classification of expenses by functions, such as merchandising or manufacturing (cost of goods sold), selling, and administration. This permits immediate comparison with costs of previous years and with the cost of other departments during the same year.

Accountants who show these additional relationships in the operating data favour what is called a **multiple-step income statement.** This statement is recommended because it recognizes a separation of operating transactions from nonoperating transactions and matches costs and expenses with related revenues. It highlights certain intermediate components of income that are used for computing ratios to assess the performance of the enterprise.

To illustrate, Dan and Karen Co. Ltd.'s multiple-step statement of income is presented below. Note, for example, that three subtotals are presented before arriving at net

---

DAN & KAREN CO. LTD.
Income Statement
For the Year Ended December 31, 1998

Sales Revenue			
Sales			$3,053,081
Less: Sales discounts		$ 24,241	
Sales returns and allowances		56,427	80,668
Net sales revenue			2,972,413
Cost of Goods Sold			
Merchandise inventory, Jan. 1, 1998		461,219	
Purchases	$1,989,693		
Less: Purchase discounts and			
purchase returns and allowances	19,270		
Net purchases	1,970,423		
Freight and transportation-in	40,612	2,011,035	
Total merchandise available for sale		2,472,254	
Less merchandise inventory, Dec. 31, 1998		489,713	
Cost of goods sold			1,982,541
Gross profit on sales			989,872
Operating Expenses			
Selling expenses			
Sales salaries and commissions	202,644		
Sales office salaries	59,200		
Travel and entertainment	48,940		
Freight and transportation-out	41,209		
Advertising expense	38,315		
Shipping supplies and expense	24,712		
Postage and stationery	16,788		
Telephone and fax	12,215		
Depreciation of sales equipment	9,005	453,028	
Administrative expenses			
Officers' salaries	186,000		
Office salaries	61,200		
Legal and professional services	23,721		
Utilities expense	23,275		
Insurance expense	17,029		
Stationery, supplies, and postage	2,875		
Miscellaneous office expense	2,612		
Depreciation of building	18,059		
Depreciation of office equipment	16,000	350,771	803,799
Income from operations			186,073
Other Revenues and Gains			
Dividend revenue		98,500	
Rental revenue		72,910	171,410
			357,483
Other Expenses and Losses			
Interest on bonds and notes			126,060
Income before income tax			231,423
Current income tax expense			66,934
Net income for the year			$ 164,489
Basic earnings per share			$1.74

income: net sales revenue, gross profit, and income from operations. The disclosure of net sales revenues is useful because regular revenues are reported as a separate item. Irregular or incidental revenues are disclosed elsewhere in the income statement. As a result, trends in revenue from continuing operations should be easier to understand and analyse. Similarly, the reporting of gross profit provides a useful number for evaluating performance and assessing future earnings. A study of the trend in gross profits may show how successfully a company uses its resources; it may also be a basis for understanding how profit margins have changed as a result of competitive pressures.

Finally, disclosing income from operations highlights the difference between regular and irregular or incidental activities. This disclosure helps users recognize that incidental or irregular activities are unlikely to continue at the same level. Furthermore, disclosure of operating earnings may assist in comparing different companies and assessing operating efficiencies.

INTERMEDIATE COMPONENTS OF THE INCOME STATEMENT

When a multiple-step income statement is used, some or all of the following sections or subsections may also be prepared.

INCOME STATEMENT SECTIONS

1. **Operating Section.** A report of the revenues and expenses of the company's principal operations. (This section may or may not be presented on a departmental basis.)

    (a) **Sales or revenue section.** A subsection that presents sales, discounts, allowances, returns, and other related information. Its purpose is to arrive at the net amount of sales revenue.

    (b) **Cost of goods sold section.** A subsection that shows the cost of goods that were sold to produce the sales.

    (c) **Selling expenses.** A subsection that lists expenses resulting from the company's efforts to make sales.

    (d) **Administrative or general expenses.** A subsection that reports expenses of general administration.

2. **Nonoperating Section.** A report of revenues and expenses that result from secondary or auxiliary activities of the company. Unusual or infrequent material gains and losses are also sometimes reported in this section. Generally these items break down into two main subsections:

    (a) **Other revenues and gains.** A list of revenues earned or gains incurred, generally net of any related expenses, from nonoperating transactions.

    (b) **Other expenses and losses.** A list of expenses or losses incurred, generally net of any related incomes, from nonoperating transactions.

3. **Income Tax.** A short section that reports taxes levied on income from continuing operations.

4. **Discontinued Operations.** Revenues, expenses, and any gain or loss (net of taxes) attributed to a segment of the business that is being discontinued.

5. **Extraordinary Items.** Unusual and infrequent gains and losses of material amounts that did not depend on the decisions of management or owners. These items are shown net of income taxes.

6. **Earnings Per Share.**[5]

Items 1, 2, 3, and 6 above are illustrated in the Dan & Karen Co. Ltd. income statement on page 145.

Although the content of the operating section is always the same, the organization of the material need not be as described above. The breakdown above uses a **natural expense classification** and is commonly used for manufacturing concerns and for mer-

---

[5] *CICA Handbook*, Section 3500, requires that earnings per share or net loss per share be included on the face of the income statement or in a note cross-referenced to the income statement.

chandising companies in the wholesale trade. Another classification of operating expenses suitable for retail stores is a **functional expense classification** of administrative, occupancy, publicity, buying, and selling expenses.

Usually, financial statements that are provided to external users have less detail than internal management reports. The latter tends to have more expense categories, which are usually grouped along the lines of responsibility. This detail allows top management to judge staff performance.

Whether a single-step or multiple-step income statement is used, discontinued operations and extraordinary items, both net of income taxes, are reported separately following "income from continuing operations" or "income or loss before discontinued operations and extraordinary items."

CONDENSED INCOME STATEMENT

In some cases, it is impossible to present in a single income statement of convenient size all of the desired expense detail. This problem is solved by including only the totals for expense groups in the statement of income and preparing supplementary schedules of expenses to support the totals. With this format, the income statement itself may be reduced to only a few lines on a single sheet. For this reason, readers who study all the reported data on operations must give their attention to the supporting schedules. The income statement shown below for Dan & Karen Co. Ltd. is a condensed version of the detailed multiple-step statement presented earlier. It is more representative of income statements available in practice.

DAN & KAREN CO. LTD.
Income Statement
For the Year Ended December 31, 1998

Net sales		$2,972,413
Cost of goods sold		1,982,541
Gross profit		$ 989,872
Selling expense (see Note D)	$453,028	
Administrative expense	350,771	803,799
Income from operations		$ 186,073
Other revenues and gains		171,410
		$ 357,483
Other expenses and losses		126,060
Income before taxes		$ 231,423
Income taxes		66,934
Net income for the year		$ 164,489
Earnings per share		$1.74

An example of a supporting schedule, cross-referenced as Note D and detailing the selling expenses, is shown below.

Note D—Selling expenses	
Sales salaries and commission	$202,644
Sales office salaries	59,200
Travel and entertainment	48,940
Freight and transportation-out	41,209
Advertising expense	38,315
Shipping supplies and expense	24,712
Postage and stationery	16,788
Telephone and fax	12,215
Depreciation of sales equipment	9,005
Total selling expenses	$453,028

Deciding how much detail to include in the financial statements is always difficult. On one hand, we want to present a simple, summarized statement so that a reader can readily discover the important facts. On the other hand, we want to disclose the results of all activities and to provide more than just a skeletal report. Certain basic elements are always included, but as we'll see they can be presented in various formats.

THE INCOME STATEMENT AND IRREGULAR ITEMS

The profession has not taken a position on whether the single-step or multiple-step income statement should be employed. Flexibility in the presentation of the components of the income statement data has been permitted. In two important areas, however, some guidelines have been developed. These two areas relate to what should be included in income, and how unusual or **irregular items** should be reported.

OBJECTIVE 5
Explain how irregular items are reported.

Items that should be included in net income had been the subject of controversy for many years. For example, should irregular gains and losses and corrections of revenues and expenses of prior years be closed directly to Retained Earnings and therefore not reported in the income statement? Or should they first be presented in the income statement and then carried to Retained Earnings along with the net income or loss for the period?

Advocates of the first approach—the **current operating performance concept**—argue that the net income figure should show only the regular, recurring earnings of the business. They believe that irregular gains and losses do not reflect the future earning power of an enterprise. Therefore, they say, these items should not be used to compute net income; they should, instead, be carried directly to Retained Earnings as special items. In addition, supporters note that many readers are not trained to differentiate between regular and irregular items and, therefore, would be confused if such items were included when computing net income.

Advocates of the second approach—the **all-inclusive concept**—insist that irregular items should be included in net income. Any gain or loss experienced by the concern, whether directly or indirectly related to operations, contributes to its long-run profitability. Irregular gains and losses can be separated from the results of regular operations to arrive at income from operations, but net income for the year should include all transactions. Advocates believe that if judgement is permitted when determining irregular items, differences may develop in the treatment of questionable items. As a result, the danger of income date manipulation arises. If permitted, it could be to the advantage of a corporation to run losses through Retained Earnings, but gains through income. Supporters of the all-inclusive concept argue that this flexibility should not be allowed because it leads to poor financial reporting practices. In other words, Gresham's law will apply: poor accounting practices will drive out good ones.

So, what to do? **The *CICA Handbook* adopted a modified all-inclusive concept that requires application of this approach in practice,** as evidenced by Sections 3475 (discontinued operations) and 3480 (extraordinary items). A number of pronouncements have been issued that require irregular items to be highlighted in order that readers of financial statements can better determine the long-run earning power of the enterprise. These irregular items are classified into four general categories:

1. Discontinued operations.
2. Extraordinary items.
3. Unusual gains and losses.
4. Changes in estimates.

DISCONTINUED OPERATIONS

One of the most common irregular items is the disposal of a business or product line. Because of the increasing importance of this type of event, a set of classification and disclosure requirements was developed and included in the *CICA Handbook*.[6]

A separate income statement category for the gain or loss from **disposal of a segment of a business** must be provided. In addition, the **results of operations of the segment that has been or will be disposed of** is reported in conjunction with the gain or loss on disposal—separately from continuing operations. The effects of discontinued operations are shown net of tax as a separate category after continuing operations, but before extraordinary items.

To illustrate, Alberta Energy Company Ltd., a diversified company, decided to discontinue its Forest Products Division. The Forest Products Division has earnings of $16,500,000 (net of tax) during the current year, and was sold at the end of the year at a gain of $37,400,000 (net of tax). The information is shown on the current year's income statement as follows:

EXHIBIT 4-1   ALBERTA ENERGY COMPANY LTD.

CONSOLIDATED STATEMENT OF EARNINGS

($ millions, except per share amounts) Year Ended December 31	Note Reference	1995	1994	1993
Net Earnings from Continuing Operations		56.3	82.2	89.2
Net Earnings from Discontinued Operations	4	53.9	18.3	2.4
Net Earnings		$ 110.2	$ 100.5	$ 91.6

4.   Discontinued Operations

On August 25, 1995 the Company sold its Forest Products Division which consisted of its interest in the Slave Lake Pulp Partnership and its Blue Ridge Lumber Division. Net cash proceeds of $304.9 million ($218.0 million net of working capital, income taxes and expenses) were used to retire debt. The Company's operations, cash flow and gain on sale relating to the Forest Products Division have been reflected in the consolidated financial statements and notes on a Discontinued Operations basis.

The results of Discontinued Operations for the comparative periods are summarized as follows:

	1995	1994	1993
Revenue	$ 135.2	$ 184.0	$ 137.3
Operating costs	83.9	120.8	105.5
Depreciation, depletion and amortization	6.7	9.5	9.8
Operating income	44.6	53.7	22.0
Interest and foreign exchange	14.4	20.9	17.3
Income taxes	13.7	14.5	2.3
Net earnings from operations	16.5	18.3	2.4
Gain on sale (net of income tax recovery of $7.3 million)*	37.4	–	–
Net earnings from Discontinued Operations	$ 53.9	$ 18.3	$ 2.4

* *Income tax recovery includes utilization of capital losses.*

The Consolidated Balance Sheet includes the following amounts applicable to the Forest Products operations:

	1994
Current assets	$ 61.6
Capital assets	195.2
Other assets	14.0
Total assets	$ 270.8
Current liabilities	$ 55.4
Long-term debt	99.4
Deferred income taxes	48.8
Capital employed	67.2
Total liabilities and equity	$ 270.8

---

[6] The reporting requirements for discontinued operations are complex. These complexities are discussed more fully in the appendix to this chapter. Our purpose here is to illustrate the basic presentation of this information on the income statement.

Further complications of measuring and reporting discontinued operations are addressed in Appendix 4A. Note that the phrase "**Income from continuing operations**" is used only when gains or losses on discontinued operations occur.

To qualify as discontinued operations, the assets, results of operations, and activities of a segment of a business must be clearly distinguishable, both physically and operationally, from the other assets, results of operations, and activities of the entity. **Disposals of assets that qualify as disposals of a segment** of a business include the following.

1. Disposal of a significant product line, provided that the assets and results of operations or activities are separately identifiable.

2. Disposal of a subsidiary, operational division, or some other investment that represents the enterprise's only activities in an industry.

3. Disposal of all of the wholesale operations of a firm that is engaged primarily in retailing.[7]

Examples that do not qualify are (1) the discontinuation by a children's wear manufacturer of its operations in Italy but not elsewhere; or (2) the sale by a diversified company of one but not all of its furniture-manufacturing subsidiaries. Judgement must be exercised in defining a disposal of a segment of a business because the criteria in some cases are difficult to apply.

EXTRAORDINARY ITEMS

Extraordinary items are infrequent material transactions or events that are not typical of the normal business activities of the enterprise and are not primarily dependent on decisions of management. All of the following conditions must be satisfied before an item is reported as extraordinary:

1. **Unusual in nature** (not typical of the normal business activities of the enterprise).

2. **Not expected to occur frequently** over several years.

3. **Must not depend primarily on decisions or determinations by management or owners.**[8]

For further clarification, the Accounting Standards Board (AcSB) specified that the following gains and losses do not constitute extraordinary items:

1. Losses and provisions for losses with respect to bad debts and inventories.

2. Gains and losses from fluctuations in foreign exchange rates.

3. Adjustments with respect to contract prices.

4. Write-down or sale of property, plant, equipment, or other investments.

5. Income tax reductions on utilization of prior period losses or reversal of previously recorded tax benefits.[9]

The items listed above do not constitute extraordinary items in an ongoing business because they result from risks inherent in the enterprise's normal business activities.

---

[7] *CICA Handbook*, Section 3475, par. .05.

[8] *Ibid.*, Section 3480, par. .02.

[9] *Ibid.*, Section 3480, par. .04.

Only in rare situations will an event or transaction occur that clearly meets the criteria specified in the *Handbook*, Section 3480, and thus give rise to an extraordinary gain or loss.[10] In some circumstances, gains or losses such as (1) and (4) above could be classified as extraordinary if they were a direct result of a major casualty (such as an earthquake), an **expropriation**, or a **prohibition under a newly enacted law or regulation** that is clearly "unusual, infrequent, and not a result of a management decision."

In determining whether an item is extraordinary, **the environment in which the entity operates is of primary importance**. The environment includes such factors as industry characteristics, geographic location, and the nature and extent of governmental regulations. Thus, the loss from hail damage to tobacco crops is accorded extraordinary item treatment because severe damage from hailstorms in a given locality is rare. On the other hand, frost damage to a fruit orchard in the Okanagan Valley does not qualify as extraordinary because frost damage is normally experienced every three or four years. In this environment, the criterion of infrequency is not met.

Unfortunately, it is often difficult to determine what is extraordinary. Firm guidelines to follow in judging when an item is or is not material have not been established. Some companies have shown as extraordinary gains or losses items that accounted for less than 1% of income. In making the materiality judgement, extraordinary items should be considered individually, and not in the aggregate.

In addition, considerable judgement must be exercised in determining whether an item should be reported as extraordinary. For example, some paper companies have had their forestry operations curtailed as a result of government action. Is such an event extraordinary, or is it part of normal operations? Such determination is not easy; much depends on the frequency of previous actions, the expectation of future events, materiality, and the like.

Extraordinary items are to be shown net of taxes in a separate section in the income statement, usually just before net income. After listing usual revenues, costs and expenses, income taxes, and discontinued operations (net of tax), the remainder of the statement shows:

Income before extraordinary items
Extraordinary items (less applicable income taxes of $_____)
Net income

UNUSUAL GAINS AND LOSSES

Because of the restrictive criteria for extraordinary items, financial statement users must carefully examine the financial statements for items that are **unusual** or **infrequent but not both**. As indicated earlier, items such as write-downs of inventories and gains and losses from fluctuations of foreign exchange are not considered extraordinary items. Thus, these items are sometimes shown with the normal, recurring revenues, costs, and expenses. If they are not material in amount, they are combined with other items in the income statement. If they are material, they should be disclosed separately, but are shown **above** "income [loss] before discontinued operations and extraordinary items."

The excerpt on the following page from the 1996 financial statements of Meridian Technologies Inc. shows how multiple unusual items may be disclosed.

In recent years, there has been a tendency to report unusual items—especially when there are multiple unusual items—in a separate section located just above income from

---

[10] Some accountants have concluded that the extraordinary item classification is so restrictive that only such items as a single chemist who knew the secret formula for an enterprise's mixing solution but was eaten by a tiger on a big game hunt or a plant facility that was smashed by a meteor would qualify for extraordinary item treatment.

EXHIBIT 4-2   MERIDIAN TECHNOLOGIES INC.

CONSOLIDATED STATEMENTS OF OPERATIONS

Years ended March 31

	1996	1995
	($000)	($000)
Revenues	290,110	199,372
Expenses:		
Cost of sales	260,391	185,756
Selling and general	16,651	12,739
Depreciation and amortization	16,039	8,319
	293,081	206,814
Loss before interest, unusual items and taxes	(2,971)	(7,442)
Interest expense	(6,303)	(2,620)
Unusual items (note 6)	(17,442)	
Loss before income taxes	(26,716)	(10,062)
Income tax (expense) recovery (note 8)	(733)	2,319
Net loss	(27,449)	(7,743)
Loss per share	$(1.03)	$(0.33)
Weighted average number of shares	26,596,922	23,190,634

6. UNUSUAL ITEMS

	($000)
Provision for loss on sale of non-automotive operations (note 7)	8,223
Writedown of certain assets to reflect impairment of value	7,789
Provision for severance costs	1,430
	17,442

During the year ended March 31, 1996, the Company recorded a $17,442,000 charge against operations which is reflected in the Consolidated Statement of Operations as "unusual items". In addition to reflecting a provision for loss on anticipated sale of the Company's non-automotive operations (note 7), the Company recorded a $7,789,000 writedown of certain assets, principally capital assets, of the Company's aluminum divisions to reflect impairment of value. The charge for unusual items also reflects a $1,430,000 provision for severance costs at one of the Company's aluminum divisions to reflect reduced production levels and severance costs related to the departure of the Company's former President and Chief Executive Officer.

continuing operations but before income taxes, discontinued operations, and extraordinary items.

In dealing with items that have some but not all of the characteristics of extraordinary items, the profession attempted to prevent a practice that many accountants believed was misleading. Companies were sometimes reporting these items on a net-of-tax basis and prominently displaying their earnings per share effect. Although not captioned as extraordinary items, they were nevertheless presented in the same manner. Some companies had referred to these as "first cousins" to extraordinary items. As a consequence, the *CICA Handbook* now stipulates that these items must be reported in the income statement before "income before discontinued operations and extraordinary items."[11]

CHANGES IN ESTIMATES
(NORMAL, RECURRING CORRECTIONS AND ADJUSTMENTS)

Estimates are inherent in the accounting process. Estimates are made, for example, of the useful lives and salvage values of depreciable assets, uncollectible receivables, inventory

---

[11] *CICA Handbook*, Section 3480, par. .12, and Section 1520, par. .03(1).

obsolescence, and the number of periods expected to benefit from a particular expenditure. Not infrequently, as time passes, as circumstances change, or as additional information is obtained, even estimates originally made in good faith must be changed. Such **changes in estimates** are accounted for in the period of change if they affect only that period, or in the period of change and future periods if the change affects both.

To illustrate a change in estimate that affects only the period of change, assume that DuPage Materials Limited has consistently estimated its bad debts expense at 1% of credit sales. In 1998, however, DuPage's controller determines that the estimate of bad debts for the current year's credit sales must be revised upward to 2%, or double the prior year's percentage. Using 2% results in a bad debt charge of $240,000—double the amount using the 1% estimate for prior years. The 2% rate is necessary to reduce the accounts receivable to net realizable value. The provision is recorded at December 31, 1998, as follows:

Bad Debt Expense	240,000	
Allowance for Doubtful Accounts		240,000

The entire change in estimate is included in 1998 income because no future periods are affected by the change. **Changes in estimate are *not* handled retroactively**, that is, carried back to adjust estimates made in prior years. Changes in estimate that affect both the current period and future periods are examined in greater detail in Chapter 22. **Changes in estimate are not considered errors (prior period adjustments) or extraordinary items.**

SUMMARY

The public accounting profession now tends to accept a modified all-inclusive income concept instead of the current operating performance concept. Except for a couple of items, which are charged or credited directly to retained earnings, all other irregular gains or losses or nonrecurring items are closed to Income Summary and included in the income statement. Of these, discontinued operations of a segment of a business is classified as a separate item in the income statement, after continuing operations. The material **unusual, material, nonrecurring items that do not depend primarily on decisions or determinations of management or owners** are shown in a separate section for "**extraordinary items**" in the income statement, below discontinued operations. Other items of a material amount that are of an **unusual or nonrecurring** nature and result from decisions or determinations of management or owners are **not considered extraordinary** but should be separately disclosed. Because of the numerous intermediate income figures that are created by the reporting of these items, careful evaluation of information reported by the financial press is needed. For example, at one time when RCA reported its first quarter results, a *Wall Street Journal* article stated that "RCA earnings climbed by 47% in the first quarter" as compared with the first quarter of the previous year. Conversely, the *New York Times* reported the following regarding RCA's first quarter results: "RCA Slides 46%." Which article was right? Both articles were factually correct. The difference arose because the *New York Times* article, in making its comparison to the quarter of the previous year, included extraordinary gains in the income of the earlier quarter, but the *Wall Street Journal* did not. Such an illustration demonstrates the importance of understanding the intermediate components of net income.

Exhibit 4-3 summarizes the basic concepts previously examined. Although the chart is simplified, it provides a useful framework for determining the appropriate treatment of special items that affect the income statement.

EXHIBIT 4-3

SUMMARY OF *CICA HANDBOOK* RECOMMENDATIONS*

Type of Situation	Criteria	Placement on Financial Statements	Examples
Extraordinary items	Material, and both unusual and nonrecurring (infrequent). Must also not depend on decisions and determinations by management or owners.	Gains or losses resulting from casualties, an expropriation, or a prohibition under a new law.	Separate section in the income statement entitled Extra-ordinary Items. (Show net of tax.)
Material gains or losses, not considered extraordinary	Material; character typical of the customary business activities; unusual or infrequent but not both (or unusual and infrequent but the result of decisions or determinations of management or owners).	Write downs of receivables, inventories; adjustments of contract prices; gains or losses from fluctuations of foreign exchange.	Separately disclosed as a component of net income before extraordinary items or as part of net income from continuing operations if there is a category for discontinued operations in the income statement.
Correction of an error made in a prior period	Is the result of a mistake in computation, oversight of available information, or misinterpretation of information that is material.	Incorrectly calculated depreciation or allowance for doubtful accounts.	Retroactive adjustment to all financial statements presented for comparative periods and adjustment of beginning retained earnings of earliest period presented. Adjustments are shown net of tax.
Changes in estimates	Result of occurrence of new events, more experience, and new or additional information.	Changes in the realizability of receivables and inventories; changes in estimated lives of equipment, intangible assets; changes in estimated liability for warranty costs, income taxes, and salary payments.	Prospective adjustment by incorporating the change in current and future periods' statements as affected. No retroactive adjustment is made.
Changes in accounting policies	Change from one generally accepted policy to another.	Changing the basis of inventory pricing from FIFO to average cost; change in the method of depreciation from accelerated to straight line.	Retroactive adjustment to all financial statements presented for comparative periods and adjustment of beginning retained earnings of earliest period presented. Adjustments are shown net of tax.
Discontinued operations	Disposal by selling, closing down, or abandoning a segment of the business.	Sale by diversified company of major division that represents the only activities in a given industry. Food distributor that sells wholesale to supermarket chains and through fast-food restaurants decides to discontinue the division that sells to one of two classes of customers.	Results of operations and net gain or loss on discontinued operations are each shown, net of income tax, in a separate category, Discontinued Operations, between the results from continuing operations and extraordinary items. The gain or loss would be shown as an extraordinary item if it resulted from transactions or events that met the criteria for such items.

*This summary provides only the general rules to be followed in accounting for the various situations described above. Exceptions do exist in some of these situations.

INTRAPERIOD TAX ALLOCATION

We noted that certain irregular items are shown on the income statement net of tax. Most accountants believe that the resulting income tax effect should be directly associated with that event or item. In other words, the tax expense for the year should be related, where possible, to **specific** items on the income statement to provide more informative disclosure to statement users. This procedure is called **intraperiod tax allocation**, that is, allocation within a period. Its main purpose is to relate the income tax expense of the fiscal period to the items that affect the amount of the tax provisions. Intraperiod tax allocation is used to link the provision to: (1) income from continuing operations; (2) discontinued operations; and (3) extraordinary items. The general concept is **"let the tax follow the income."**

OBJECTIVE 6
Explain intraperiod tax allocation.

The income tax expense attributable to "income from continuing operations" is computed by finding the income tax expense related to revenue and to expense transactions entering into the determination of this income. In this tax computation, no effect is given to the tax consequences of the items excluded from the determination of "income from continuing operations." A separate tax effect is then associated with each irregular item.

EXTRAORDINARY GAINS

In applying the concept of intraperiod tax allocation, assume that Schindler Limited has income before tax and extraordinary item of $250,000, and an extraordinary gain from the expropriation of land of $100,000. If the income tax rate is assumed to be 48%, the following information is presented on the income statement:

Income before tax and extraordinary item		$250,000
Income tax expense		120,000
Income before extraordinary item		$130,000
Extraordinary—expropriation of land	$100,000	
Less applicable income tax	**48,000**	**52,000**
Net income		$182,000

EXTRAORDINARY LOSSES

To illustrate the reporting of an extraordinary loss, assume that Schindler Limited has income before income tax and extraordinary item of $250,000 and an extraordinary loss from a major casualty of $100,000. Assuming a 48% tax rate, the presentation of income tax on the income statement would be as follows.

Income before income tax and extraordinary item		$250,000
Income tax expense		120,000
Income before extraordinary item		$130,000
Extraordinary item—loss from casualty	$100,000	
Less applicable income tax reduction	**(48,000)**	**52,000**
Net income		$ 78,000

In this case, the loss provides a positive tax benefit of $48,000 and, therefore, is subtracted from the $100,000 loss.

An extraordinary item may be reported "net of tax," with note disclosure as illustrated as follows.

Income before tax and extraordinary item	$250,000
Income tax	120,000
Income before extraordinary item	$130,000
Extraordinary item, less applicable income tax reduction (Note 1)	**(52,000)**
Net income	$ 78,000

Note 1: During the year the Company suffered a major casualty loss of $52,000, net of applicable income tax reduction of $48,000.

EARNINGS PER SHARE

OBJECTIVE 7
Explain where earnings per share information is reported.

The results of a company's operations are customarily summed up in one important figure: net income. As if this condensation were not enough of a simplification, the financial world has widely accepted an even more distilled and compact figure as its most significant business indicator—**earnings per share** (EPS).

The computation of earnings per share is usually straightforward. **Net income minus preferred dividends (available to common shareholders) is divided by the weighted average number of common shares outstanding during the year to arrive at earnings per share**.[12] To illustrate, assume that Lancer Inc. reports net income of $350,000 and declares and pays preferred dividends of $50,000 for the year. The weighted average number of shares outstanding during the year is 100,000 shares. The earnings per share is $3.00 as computed below.

$$\frac{\text{Net Income} - \text{Preferred Dividends}}{\text{Weighted-Average Number of Shares Outstanding}} = \textbf{Earnings Per Share}$$

$$\frac{\$350,000 - \$50,000}{100,000} = \textbf{\$3.00}$$

Note that the EPS figure measures the number of dollars earned by each common share, but not the dollar amount paid to shareholders in the form of dividends.

"Net income per share" or "earnings per share" is a ratio commonly used in prospectuses, proxy material, and annual reports to shareholders. It is also highlighted in the financial press and other statistical services. Because of the inherent dangers of focusing attention on earnings per share by itself, the profession concluded that **earnings per share must be disclosed either on the face of the income statement or in a note to the financial statements.** In addition to net income per share, per share amounts should be shown for "income before discontinued operations and extraordinary items."[13]

To illustrate comprehensively both the income statement order of presentation and the earnings per share data, we present a comprehensive income statement for a large Canadian Company, Ivaco Inc., in Exhibit 4-4. Notice the order in which data are shown. In addition, per share information is shown at the bottom.

Reporting per share amounts for gain or loss on discontinued operations and gain or loss on extraordinary items is optional. For example, General Mills reported $1.77 earnings per share before an extraordinary item and net income of $1.83. By subtracting, readers can easily see that it had an extraordinary gain of $.06 per share net of income tax.

The Ivaco Inc. income statement is highly condensed. Discontinued Operations are described fully and appropriately in the statement or related notes. The 1995 statement of

---

[12] In the calculation of earnings per share, preferred dividends reduce net income if declared and if cumulative even though not declared.

[13] *CICA Handbook*, Section 3500, pars. .09 and .11.

EXHIBIT 4-4   IVACO INC.

CONSOLIDATED STATEMENTS OF EARNINGS

Thousands of dollars except per share amounts

YEARS ENDED DECEMBER 31	1995	1994
Net sales	**$1,630,287**	$1,418,242
Cost of sales and operating expenses	**1,468,436**	1,295,511
Operating earnings (EBITDA) before:	**161,851**	122,731
Amortization	**(47,046)**	(45,397)
Share of earnings of equity accounted investments (Note 4)	**2,463**	5,526
Earnings from operations before interest and other items	**117,268**	82,860
Net interest expense (Note 7)	**(42,809)**	(37,847)
Earnings from continuing operations before income taxes and special charge	**74,459**	45,013
Provision for income taxes (Note 12)	**30,897**	26,609
Earnings from continuing operations before special charge	**43,562**	18,404
Share of Laclede Steel's special restructuring charge	**(6,185)**	—
Earnings from continuing operations	**37,377**	18,404
Loss from discontinued operations (Note 14)	**(5,425)**	(10,350)
Net earnings	$ **31,952**	$ 8,054
Earnings (loss) per share		
Continuing operations	$ **0.66**	$ 0.13
Net earnings (loss) per share	$ **0.47**	$ (0.25)
Fully diluted earnings per share		
Continuing operations	$ **0.57**	$ —
Net earnings per share	$ **0.42**	$ —

income of Moore Corporation Limited (see Appendix 5A) presents appropriate earnings per share amounts in much the same manner as shown by Ivaco.

The earnings per share data may also be disclosed parenthetically on an income statement, as illustrated below (this form is especially applicable when only one per share amount is involved).

Net income (per share $4.02)	$804,000

Many corporations have simple capital structures that include only common shares. For these companies, a presentation such as "earnings per common share " is appropriate on the income statement. In many instances, however, companies' earnings per share are subject to dilution (reduction) in the future because existing contingencies permit the issuance of additional common shares.[14]

In summary, the simplicity and availability of figures for per-share earnings lead inevitably to their widespread use. Because of the undue importance that the public, even the well-informed public, attaches to earnings per share, accountants have an obligation to make the earnings per share figures as meaningful as possible.

---

[14] "Earnings Per Share," *CICA Handbook*, Section 3500. The computational problems involved in accounting for these dilutive securities in earnings per share computations are discussed in Chapter 18.

STATEMENT OF RETAINED EARNINGS

OBJECTIVE 8
Prepare a statement of retained earnings.

A statement of retained earnings is included in the financial statements of an enterprise, along with an income statement, a balance sheet, and a statement of changes in financial position. Actually, instead of being a statement that reports related data, **a statement of retained earnings is a reconciliation of the balance of the retained earnings account from the beginning to the end of the year**. A statement of retained earnings is also prepared to assist in the assessment of overall performance by providing additional information on why net assets increased or deceased during the period. This additional information relates to such items as prior period adjustments and dividend distributions.

The 1995 statement of retained earnings for Fortis Inc. was published as follows.

EXHIBIT 4-5   FORTIS INC.

CONSOLIDATED STATEMENT OF RETAINED EARNINGS

For the Year Ended December 31

	1995	(in thousands)	1994
Balance at Beginning of Year	$ 160,894	$	152,655
Net income for the year	35,040		31,313
	195,934		183,968
Dividends			
Preference Shares	4,448		4,350
Common Shares	20,634		18,724
	25,082		23,074
Balance at End of Year	$ 170,852	$	160,894

The association of dividend distributions with net income for the period indicates what management is doing with earnings: It may be "plowing back" into the business part or all of the earnings, distributing all current income, or distributing current income plus the accumulated earnings of prior years.

PRIOR PERIOD ADJUSTMENTS

OBJECTIVE 9
Explain how prior period adjustments are reported.

Prior to April 1, 1996 accountants were required to report certain gains or losses that should have been included in the income of prior periods as adjustments to the beginning Retained Earnings balance. These gains or losses, called "prior period adjustments," will appear on financial statements issued prior to 1996. Currently, the only adjustments permitted to opening Retained Earnings are those resulting from corrections of errors made in prior periods and from certain changes in accounting principles.

CORRECTION OF ERRORS MADE IN A PRIOR PERIOD

Items of income or loss related to corrections of errors in the financial statements of a prior period are accounted for and reported in the same way as a prior period adjustment. A mistake or error may occur because of incorrect computation, oversight in considering available information, or misinterpretation of information.[15] For example, depreciation may be incorrectly calculated. When material errors made in a previous period are discovered, the accounts must be corrected in the year of discovery.[16]

To illustrate, assume that McCartan Limited determines in 1998 that it has overstated

[15] In accounting, an error is distinguished from a change in an estimate. An error results when information available at the time the original statements were prepared is either not used or misused. A change in estimate is a result of new information that makes it possible to improve estimates made in prior periods.
[16] *CICA Handbook*, Section 1506, par. .28.

its depreciation expense in 1997 by $187,640 ($114,960 net of tax) owing to an error in computation. The error affected both the income statement and the tax return for 1997. The following journal entry records this retroactive adjustment to correct the error:

Accumulated Depreciation	187,640	
Taxes Payable		72,680
Retained Earnings		114,960

Adjustment for this error is presented in the statement of retained earnings for 1998 as follows:

Retained earnings, January 1, 1998, as previously reported	$2,767,890
Correction of an error in depreciation in prior period (net of $72,680 tax)	114,960
Adjusted balance of retained earnings at January 1, 1998	$2,882,850
Net income	697,611
Retained earnings, December 31, 1998	$3,580,461

CHANGES IN ACCOUNTING POLICY

Changes in accounting policy occur frequently in practice because important events or conditions may be in dispute or are uncertain at the statement date. One example of accounting policy change is the normal recurring corrections and adjustments that are made by every business enterprise. Another accounting policy change results when a company adopts an accounting principle that is different from the one used previously. Changes in accounting policy would include a change in the method of inventory pricing from FIFO to average cost, or a change in depreciation from the double-declining to the straight-line method.[17]

These changes are recognized through **retroactive adjustment**, which involves determining the effect of the policy change on the income of the prior periods affected. The financial statements for all prior periods that are presented for comparative purposes should be restated to reflect the new accounting policy, except when the effect is not reasonably determinable for specific prior periods. If this exception is applicable, an adjustment would be made to the beginning retained earnings of the current, or an appropriate earlier, period to show the cumulative effect from all previous periods. Appropriate disclosure relating to a change in an accounting policy should occur.

To illustrate, McCartan Inc. decides at the beginning of 1998 to change from an accelerated depreciation method (double-declining balance) of computing depreciation on its plant assets to the straight-line method. Assume that the depreciation that is calculated using the double-declining-balance method (40% rate) is the same as that used to determine taxable income. The assets originally cost $100,000 and have a service life of five years. Here are the data assumed to illustrate the consequences of the change in policy and the manner of reporting the change.

Year	Accelerated Depreciation	Straight-Line Depreciation	Excess of Accelerated Depreciation over Straight-Line
1996	$40,000	$20,000	$20,000
1997	24,000	20,000	4,000
Total			$24,000

---

[17] *Ibid.*, Section 1506. Chapter 23 examines in greater detail the problems related to accounting policy changes. Our purpose now is to provide general guidance for the major types of transactions affecting the income statement.

The adjustment for this accounting policy change in the 1998 financial statements could be shown as follows (no comparative statements are shown and the tax rate is 48%).

Retained earnings, January 1, 1998, as previously reported	$250,000
Cumulative effect on prior periods of retroactive application of new depreciation method (net of $11,520 tax)	12,480
Adjusted balance of retained earnings at January 1, 1998	$262,480

In addition to reporting the retroactive adjustment in the statement of retained earnings, a note must be included to describe the change and its effect. The following example illustrates how this was accomplished by Lafarge Canada Inc.

EXHIBIT 4-6   LAFARGE CANADA INC.

Change in accounting policy

During 1993, the Corporation adopted the policy of accounting for other postretirement benefits in a manner substantially identical to U.S. Statement of Financial Accounting Standards No. 106, "Employers' Accounting for Postretirement Benefits Other than Pensions" with the exception of the treatment for the transitional balance which has been accounted for retroactively. Under this new policy, the expected cost of retiree health care and life insurance benefits is charged to expense during the years that the employees render service rather than the Corporation's past practice of recognizing these costs on a cash basis.

The balance of retained earnings at January 1, 1993 has been restated by the amount of accumulated benefit obligation for other postretirement benefits net of income taxes. Net income for 1993 has been reduced by $.6 million, representing the additional accrual for these benefits under the new policy, net of income taxes. The table below provides the impact on the opening retained earnings of this new policy on the prior year:

	1993
Retained earnings January 1, as originally reported	$ 644,930
Accumulated benefit obligation — other postretirement benefits	(17,368)
Reduction in deferred income taxes	6,565
Retained earnings January 1, as restated	$ 634,127

APPROPRIATION OF RETAINED EARNINGS

Retained earnings are often appropriated (restricted) in accordance with contract requirements, board of directors' policy, or the apparent necessity of the moment. The amounts of retained earnings appropriated are transferred to Appropriated Retained Earnings. The retained earnings section may therefore report two separate amounts—Retained Earnings Free (unappropriated) and Retained Earnings Appropriated (restricted). The total of these two amounts equals the total retained earnings balance.

COMBINED STATEMENT OF INCOME AND RETAINED EARNINGS

Some accountants believe that the statements of income and retained earnings are so closely related that they present both statements in one combined report. The principal advantage of a combined statement is that all items affecting income and retained earnings appear in one statement. On the other hand, the figure of net income for the year is "buried" in the body of the statement, a feature that some find objectionable. There once was a definite trend toward this method of presentation, but it is no longer gaining in favour.

When a combined statement is prepared, the income statement is presented as if it were to be issued as an independent report but, instead of closing the statement with the amount of net income, it is extended to include retained earnings, as was reported by Finning Ltd. and reproduced in Exhibit 4-7.

If the company has other capital accounts such as Contributed Surplus, a good practice is to present a statement of these accounts reconciling the beginning and ending balances.

EXHIBIT 4-7   FINNING LTD.

CONSOLIDATED STATEMENTS OF INCOME AND RETAINED EARNINGS

For the years ended December 31
(dollars in thousands except per share data)

	1995	1994
Revenue		
New equipment	$ 891,969	$ 661,829
Used equipment	211,814	199,637
Customer support services	593,042	555,285
Finance and other	55,166	40,787
Total revenue	1,751,991	1,457,538
Expenses		
Cost of sales	1,256,953	1,033,775
Selling, general and administrative	320,641	287,016
Finance cost and interest on other		
indebtedness (Notes 7 & 8)	55,005	41,259
	1,632,599	1,362,050
Income before provision for income taxes	119,392	95,488
Provision for income taxes (Note 12)	41,899	34,067
Net income	77,493	61,421
Dividends on preferred shares	169	152
Earnings attributable to Common Shares	77,324	61,269
Retained earnings, beginning of year	248,862	197,578
	326,186	258,847
Dividends on Common Shares	15,451	9,985
Retained earnings, end of year	$ 310,735	$ 248,862
Net income per share (Note 13)		
Basic	$ 2.00	$ 1.60
Fully diluted	$ 1.95	$ 1.56
Average number of Common Shares		
outstanding (Note 13)	38,620,871	38,379,618

The *CICA Handbook* requires that changes in both retained earnings and contributed surplus during a period be disclosed.[18] This can be accomplished by including separate statements on the changes in these accounts as part of the financial statements, or through disclosure in notes. Examples of income statements, retained earnings statements, and contributed surplus sections are presented in Appendix 5A and in Chapter 17.

INTERNATIONAL PERSPECTIVE

With both commerce and capital crossing borders at an accelerated pace, attention is focusing on the significance of a growing obstacle: the language of accounting. As indicated earlier, many nations have their own individual rules of accounting sufficient to the needs of their own commerce and the maturity of their industry. In some cases, the principles and practices that guide the preparation of financial statements in various countries can be so different as to defy comparability.

Twenty years ago, this lack of uniform accounting principles was merely an inconvenience. Today, it is a more significant problem since so much business is done internationally. As a result, international accounting and reporting are beginning to change. This textbook is intended to sensitize you to some of these changes by introducing

---

[18] *Ibid.*, Section 3250, par. .13.

international issues and problems where appropriate. Most of this information is provided in notes.

An adapted income statement for Guinness PLC, a British company, for a recent year is illustrated below. The statement is provided so that you can compare differences in terminology and accounting principles with a Canadian company.

GUINNESS PLC
Group Profit and Loss Account
For the Year ended 31 December 1991

(in millions)	1991
Turnover	£4,067
Net operating costs	3,072
Profit before interest and taxation (excluding LVMH)	995
Share of profit before tax of LVMH	123
Profit before interest and taxation	1,118
Net interest charge	(162)
Profit on ordinary activities before taxation	956
Taxation on profit on ordinary activities	(287)
Profit on ordinary activities after taxation	669
Minority interests	(33)
Preferred dividends	(8)
Profit before extraordinary items	628
Extraordinary items	(41)
Profit attributable to shareholders	587
Dividends	(210)
Retained earnings	377
Earnings per share	
Basic	35.3p
Diluted	33.6p

These differences highlight the fact that even countries that use the same language may describe activities differently and also may use different accounting standards.

KEY TERMS

all-inclusive concept, 148

capital maintenance approach, 142

current operating performance concept, 148

earnings per share, 156

intraperiod tax allocation, 155

irregular items, 148

modified all-inclusive concept, 148

multiple-step income statement, 144

single-step income statement, 144

statement of income, 140

transaction approach, 143

Summary of Learning Objectives

1. **Identify the uses and limitations of an income statement.** The statement of income provides investors and creditors with information that helps them predict the amounts, timing, and uncertainty of future cash flows. Also, the income statement helps determine the risk (level of uncertainty) of not achieving particular cash flows. The limitations of an income statement are: (1) the statement does not include many items that contribute to general growth and well-being of an enterprise; and (2) income numbers are often affected by accounting methods used.

2. **Distinguish between the capital maintenance and transaction approaches.** The capital maintenance approach takes the net assets or "capital values " based on some valuation, and measures income by the difference in capital values at two points in time. The transaction approach focuses on the activities that have occurred during a given period; instead of presenting only a net change, it discloses the components of the change. The transaction approach to

income measurement requires the use of revenue, expense, loss, and gain accounts.

3. **Prepare a single-step income statement.** In a single-step income statement, just two groupings exist: revenues and expenses. Expenses are deducted from revenues to arrive at net income or loss—a single subtraction. Frequently, income tax is reported separately as the list item before net income to indicate its relationship to income before income tax.

4. **Prepare a multiple-step income statement.** A multiple-step income statement shows two further classifications: (1) a separation of operating results from those obtained through the subordinate or nonoperating activities of the company; and (2) a classification of expenses by functions, such as merchandising or manufacturing, selling, and administration.

5. **Explain how irregular items are reported.** Irregular gains or losses or non-recurring items are generally closed to Income Summary and are included in the income statement. These are treated in the income statement as follows: (1) the discontinued operations of a segment of a business are classified as a separate item, located after continuing operations; (2) the unusual, material, nonrecurring items that are significantly different from the customary business activities are shown in a separate section for "extraordinary items, " located below discontinued operations; and (3) other items of a material amount that are of an unusual or nonrecurring nature and are not considered extraordinary are disclosed separately.

6. **Explain intraperiod tax allocation.** The tax expense for the year should be related, where possible, to specific items on the income statement in order to provide more informative disclosure to statement users. This procedure is called intraperiod tax allocation—that is, allocation within a period. Its main purpose is to relate the income tax expense for the fiscal period to the following items that affect the amount of tax provisions: (1) income from continuing operations; (2) discontinued operations; and (3) extraordinary items.

7. **Explain where earnings per share information is reported.** Because of the inherent dangers of focusing attention solely on earnings per share, the profession concluded that earnings per share may be disclosed either on the face of the income statement or in the notes to the financial statements. In addition to net income per share, per-share amounts should be shown for "income from continuing operations, " and "income before extraordinary items. "

8. **Prepare a statement of retained earnings.** The statement of retained earnings should disclose net income (loss), dividends, and transfers to and from retained earnings (appropriations).

9. **Explain how prior period adjustments are reported.** Items of income or loss related to corrections of errors in the financial statements of a prior period and the cumulative effect of certain accounting policy changes are accounted for and reported retroactively. Retroactive adjustments (net of tax) should be charged or credited to the opening balance of retained earnings and, thus, excluded from the determination of net income for the current period.

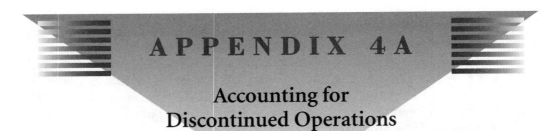

APPENDIX 4A

Accounting for Discontinued Operations

The chapter discussed how and where gains and losses related to discontinued operations are reported on the income statement. This appendix discusses the more technical aspects of how such a gain or loss is computed, along with related reporting issues.

Recall that the assets, results of operations, and activities of a **business segment** must be clearly distinguishable, physically and operationally, to qualify for discontinued operations treatment. Recall, too, that in the income statement, discontinued operations are classified as a separate item, net of tax, after continuing operations.

FIRST ILLUSTRATION: NO PHASE-OUT PERIOD

To illustrate the accounting for a discontinued operation, assume that the board of directors of Heartland Ltd. decided on October 1, 1998 to sell a division of their company called Record Phonograph. Record Phonograph had provided phonograph records for Heartland's 15 retail stores. Heartland's management could see that the compact disc was revolutionizing the stereo industry and would soon render its phonograph division unprofitable. Fortunately, a buyer was available immediately and the division was sold on October 1, 1998.

Heartland Ltd. has income of $2,000,000 for the year 1998, not including a $150,000 loss from operations of the Record Phonograph division from January 1 to October 1, 1998. Management sells the division at a gain of $400,000. Its tax rate on all items is 30%.

Heartland's accountants must first decide whether or not to treat the sale as a discontinued operation. The assets and operations of the Record Phonograph division can be easily identified, and the record business is distinct from Heartland's other lines of business. Accordingly, **the disposal of the Record Phonograph division constitutes the disposal of a segment of the business**.

For the period up to the time of management's commitment to selling the division, the revenues and expenses of the discontinued operations are aggregated and reported as income or loss on discontinued operations, net of tax. The date on which management formally commits itself to a formal plan to dispose of a segment of the business is referred to as the **measurement date**. In this case, it is October 1, 1998. The plan of disposal should include, as a minimum:

1. Identification of the major assets to be divested.
2. The expected method of disposal.
3. The period expected to be required for completion of the disposal.
4. An active program to find a buyer if disposal is to be by sale.
5. Estimated results of operations of the segment from the measurement date to the disposal date.
6. Estimated proceeds or salvage value to be realized by disposal.[19]

---

[19] *Ibid.*, Section 3475, par. .02.

Because the segment has actually been sold on October 1, 1998, a gain or loss on disposal is computed. This date is referred to as the *disposal date*. Because the measurement date and the disposal date are the same, no unusual complications occur. The following diagram illustrates Heartland's situation.

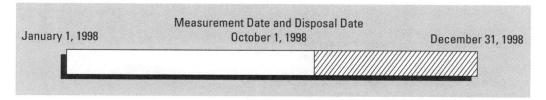

The condensed income statement presentation for Heartland Ltd. for 1998 is as follows.

Income from continuing operations before income taxes		$2,000,000
Income taxes		600,000
Income from continuing operations		1,400,000
Discontinued operations:		
Loss from operation of Record Phonograph, less income taxes of $45,000	$(105,000)	
Gain on disposal of Record Phonograph, less income taxes of $120,000	280,000	175,000
Net income		**$1,575,000**

SECOND ILLUSTRATION: PHASE-OUT PERIOD

In practice, the measurement date and the disposal date are rarely the same. Normally, the disposal date is later than the measurement date. Thus, **the gain or loss on disposal is the sum of:**

1. Income (loss) from the measurement date to the disposal date (called the **phase-out period**).
2. Gain (loss) on the disposal of the net assets.

The reason for aggregating the above two items to compute the gain (loss) on disposal is that the selling company needs a reasonable period to phase out its discontinued operations. The income (loss) from operations of the discontinued segment is part of the computation of the gain (loss) on disposal because the phase-out period often enables the seller to obtain a better selling price.

To illustrate the combination of these two components, assume that Heartland's sale of the Record Phonograph division does not occur until December 1, 1998, at which time it is sold at a gain of $350,000. During the period October 1, 1998 to December 1, 1998, the Record Phonograph division suffers a loss of $50,000 from operations. The following diagram illustrates Heartland's situation.

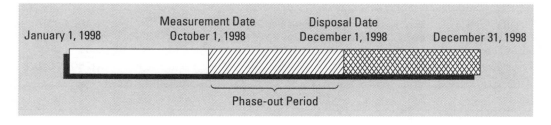

The condensed income statement presentation for Heartland Ltd. for 1998 is as follows:

Income from continuing operations before income taxes		$2,000,000
Income taxes		600,000
Income from continuing operations		1,400,000
Discontinued operations:		
Loss from operation of Record Phonograph to October 1, 1998, less applicable income taxes of $45,000	($105,000)	
Gain on disposal of Record Phonograph, including operating loss of $50,000 (October 1–November 30) and gain on disposal at December 1, 1998 of $350,000, less applicable income taxes of $90,000	210,000	105,000
Net income		**$1,505,000**

THIRD ILLUSTRATION: EXTENDED PHASE-OUT PERIOD

In the preceding illustration, the disposal of the discontinued operation occurs in the same accounting period as the measurement date. As a result, determining the proper gain or loss on the disposal of the Record Phonograph division at the end of the year is straightforward. However, the phase-out period often extends into another year. In this case, the profession requires that **if a loss is expected on disposal, the estimated loss should be reported at the measurement date. If a gain on disposal is expected, it should be recognized when realized, which is ordinarily the disposal date.**[20] In other words, the profession has taken a conservative position by recognizing losses immediately but deferring gains until realized.

Implementing these general rules can be troublesome. In order to determine the gain or loss on disposal of the segment, the income (loss) from operations must be estimated and then combined with the estimated gain (loss) on sale. If a net loss results, then it is recognized at the measurement date. If a net gain arises, it generally is deferred and recognized at the date of disposal. **The major exception is when realized gains exceeds estimated unrealized and realized losses. In that special case, realized gains can be recognized in the period of the measurement date**

Net Loss. To illustrate, assume that Heartland Inc. expects to sell its Record Phonograph division on May 1, 1999, at a gain of $350,000. In addition, from October 1, 1998 to December 31, 1998, it realizes a loss of $400,000 on operations for this discontinued operation and expects to lose an additional $200,000 on this operation from January 1, 1999 to May 1, 1999. The following diagram illustrates Heartland's situation.

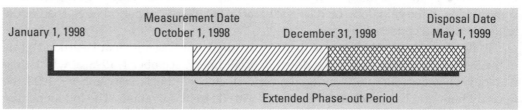

The computation of the net gain or loss on disposal is as follows:

Realized loss on operations October 1–December 31, 1998	$(400,000)
Expected loss on operations January 1–May 1, 1999	(200,000)
Expected gain on sale of assets on May 1, 1999	350,000
Net loss on disposal	$(250,000)

---

[20] *Ibid.*, Section 3475, par. .08.

Given that a net loss on disposal is expected, the loss on disposal is recognized in the period of the measurement date. The condensed income statement presentation for Heartland Ltd. for 1998 is therefore reported as shown below.

Income from continuing operations before income taxes		$2,000,000
Income taxes		600,000
Income from continuing operations		1,400,000
Discontinued operations:		
Loss from operation of Record Phonograph, net of applicable income taxes of $45,000	$(105,000)	
Loss on disposal of Record Phonograph, including provision for losses during phase-out period, $600,000, and estimated gain on sale of assets, $350,000, net of applicable income taxes of $75,000	$(175,000)	(280,000)
Net income		$1,120,000

If the estimated amounts of any of the items later prove to be incorrect, the correction should be reported in the later period when the estimate is determined to be incorrect. Prior periods should not be restated.

Net Gain. To illustrate recognition of a realized gain and deferral of an unrealized gain in the same discontinued operation, assume that Heartland Ltd. expects to sell its Record Phonograph division on May 1, 1999 at a gain of $350,000. In addition, from October 1, 1998 to December 31, 1998, it realizes a gain of $200,000 on operations for this discontinued operation and expects to earn an additional $100,000 of profit on this operation from January 1, 1999 to May 1, 1999. The computation of the net gain or loss on disposal is as follows:

Realized gain on operations October 1–December 31, 1998	$200,000
Expected gain on operations January 1–May 1, 1999	100,000
Expected gain on sale of assets on May 1, 1999	350,000
Net gain on disposal	$650,000

When a net gain on disposal is expected, the gain should be analysed and classified into realized and unrealized amounts. In this situation, $200,000 of realized gain is recognized in 1998 during October 1 to December 31 operations and $450,000 ($100,000 + $350,000) of unrealized gain is deferred to 1999. Assuming that the phonograph division, as before, suffers a loss of $150,000 from operations between January 1 and October 1, 1998, the discontinued operations section of the income statements for 1998 and 1999 would appear as follows:

1998		
Discontinued operations		
Loss from operations of Record Phonograph, less applicable income taxes of $45,000	$(105,000)	
Gain on disposal of Record Phonograph, less applicable income taxes of $60,000	140,000	35,000

1999	
Discontinued operations	
Gain on disposal of Record Phonograph, less applicable income taxes of $135,000	$315,000

If a net unrealized loss of $150,000 has been expected during the 1999 portion of the extended phase-out period, instead of the $450,000 unrealized gain noted above, a net realized gain on disposal of $50,000 ($200,000 − $150,000) before income taxes would be realized in 1998.

Summary. All realized and estimated unrealized gains and losses related to the extended phase-out period are netted as one "event" after the measurement date. To determine the amount to be reported on the "gain or loss from disposal of a segment " line (the second line of the discontinued operations section), the following simple algorithm may be used: If an overall loss is computed for the extended phase-out period, the amount reported is the overall loss; if an overall gain is computed, the amount reported is the lesser of the overall gain or the realized gain.

EXTENDED PHASE OUT: ADDITIONAL EXAMPLES

Provided in the schedule in Exhibit 4A-1 are some additional cases to help you understand how the gain (loss) on disposal of a segment of a business is reported for an extended phase-out period. We will use the same measurement and disposal dates as in the previous situations. All situations are reported on a pretax basis.

EXHIBIT 4A-1

DISPOSALS OF SEGMENTS INVOLVING EXTENDED PHASE-OUT OF DISCONTINUED OPERATIONS

	Realized Income (Loss) on Operations October 1, 1998– December 31, 1998	Expected Income (Loss) on Operations January 1, 1999– May 1, 1999	Expected Gain (Loss) on Sale of Assets	Gain (Loss) on Disposal of Segment	
Case 1	$(400,000)	$(200,000)	$ 350,000	1998	$ (250,000)
				1999	0
Case 2	(300,000)	(600,000)	(500,000)	1998	$(1,400,000)
				1999	0
Case 3	100,000	400,000	(600,000)	1998	$ (100,000)
				1999	0
Case 4	(500,000)	(300,000)	900,000	1998	$ 0
				1999	100,000
Case 5	400,000	300,000	250,000	1998	$ 400,000
				1999	550,000
Case 6	600,000	(200,000)	(300,000)	1998	$ 100,000
				1999	0
Case 7	400,000	(300,000)	350,000	1998	$ 400,000
				1999	50,000
Case 8	400,000	(350,000)	300,000	1998	$ 350,000
				1999	0

In Case 2, all three components related to the gain (loss) on disposal were losses; therefore **a net loss of $1,400,000 is reported at the measurement date**.

In Case 3, the loss of $600,000 on the sale of the segment assets is greater than the realized $100,000 and expected $400,000 income from operations; therefore **a net loss of $100,000 is reported at the measurement date.**

In Case 4, the gain of $900,000 on the sale of the segment assets is greater than the realized $500,000 and expected $300,000 losses from operations; therefore **a net gain of $100,000 is reported at the disposal date.**

In Case 5, both components of operations report income, and a gain is expected on the sale of the segment assets. As a result, **the realized income from operations of $400,000 can be reported at the date of measurement** because there are no realized or estimated losses. **The remaining estimated gain of $550,000 ($300,000 + $250,000) is deferred and recognized at the disposal date.**

In Case 6, the realized income from operations of $600,000 exceeds the estimated losses from operations $200,000 and sale $300,000. As a result, **a realized gain of $100,000 is reported at the end of 1998, after the gain is realized.**

In Case 7, the net gain on disposal is expected to be $450,000, of which $400,000 is realized and $50,000 is unrealized. **The realized $400,000 is recognized in 1998 and the net unrealized gain of $50,000** (the net of a $300,000 expected loss from operations in 1999 and a $350,000 expected gain from disposal in 1999) is recognized in 1999.

In Case 8, the net gain on disposal is expected to be $350,000, all of which is realized and, therefore, recognized in 1998. **The $400,000 of realized income from operations is reduced by the net expected unrealized loss of $50,000** from 1999 (the expected loss from operations of $350,000 less the expected gain on sale of $300,000).

DISCLOSURE REQUIREMENTS

Amounts of income taxes applicable to the results of discontinued operations and the gain or loss from disposal of the segment should be disclosed on the face of the income statement or related notes. Revenues applicable to the discontinued operations for the reporting period should be separately disclosed in the related notes.

In addition to the amounts that should be reported in the financial statements, the notes to the financial statements for the period encompassing the measurement date should disclose:

1. The identity of the segment of the business that has been or will be discontinued.

2. The measurement date.

3. Either the disposal date or the period expected to be required for disposal.

4. The expected (or actual) manner of disposition.

5. A description and the carrying value of the remaining assets and liabilities of the segment at the balance sheet date.

An example of the income statement and the note disclosure taken from the annual report of NOVA Corporation is shown below.

EXHIBIT 4A-2 NOVA CORPORATION OF ALBERTA

CONSOLIDATED STATEMENT OF INCOME
(millions of dollars except for per share data)

Income (Loss) from Continuing Operations Before Income Taxes and Interest of Others in Income of Subsidiaries	(707)
Income Taxes (Note 17)	78
Interest of Others in Income of Subsidiaries	–
Net Income (Loss) from Continuing Operations	(629)
Discontinued Operation (Note 6)	
Loss from operations	(35)
Loss on disposal	(259)
	(294)
Net Income (Loss)	(923)

EXHIBIT 4A-2 NOVA CORPORATION OF ALBERTA (Continued)

CONSOLIDATED STATEMENT OF INCOME

(millions of dollars except for per share data)

6. Discontinued Operation (millions of dollars)

Effective June 1, 1991, NOVA accounted for its 43% interest in Husky Oil Ltd. ("Husky") as an asset held for sale and accordingly no longer included its share of Husky's earnings or losses in its net income. NOVA's share of earnings or losses from Husky prior to this date has been presented as a discontinued operation. On December 31, 1991, NOVA completed the sale of its interest in Husky for proceeds of $325 million which were used to reduce non-cost-of-service debt. Details of the loss from discontinued operation, including an allocation of interest based on the estimated debt component of the net investment in Husky, are as shown in the chart at right.

Year Ended December 31	1991
NOVA's share of Husky's loss	$ (14)
NOVA's share of Husky's gain on sale of assets	–
Allocation of interest expense	(35)
Income tax recovery	14
Loss from operations	(35)
Loss on disposal of discontinued operation (net of income tax recovery of $30 million)	(259)
Discontinued operation	$ (294)

Note that companies frequently segregate the assets and liabilities of the segment of the balance sheet into net current and net noncurrent amounts and identify these elements as related to discontinued operations.

As previously stated, if the estimates of income or losses from operations during the phase-out period and of gains or losses on the sale of assets prove incorrect, the correction should be reported in the period when the estimate is determined to be incorrect; prior periods are not restated.

Summary of Learning Objective for Appendix 4A

10. **Measure and report gains and losses from discontinued operations.** The accountant may be required to report gains and losses from discontinued operations (sale of a segment of the business) under three different situations: (1) no phase-out period; (2) a phase-out period; and (3) an extended phase-out period. The gain or loss on disposal of a segment involves the sum of (1) income or loss from operations to the measurement date; and (2) the gain or loss on the disposal of the business segment (operating incomes or losses during the phase-out period and the gain or loss on the sale of the net assets). These two items are reported separately net of tax among the irregular items in the income statement.

Note: All *asterisked* Exercises, Problems, and Cases relate to material contained in the appendix to the chapter.

EXERCISES

(Computation of Net Income) Presented below are changes in the account balances of Gibson Furniture Co. Ltd. during the current year, except for retained earnings.   E4-1

	Increase (Decrease)		Increase (Decrease)
Cash	$ 79,000	Accounts payable	$ (38,000)
Accounts receivable (net)	24,000	Bonds payable	82,000
Inventory	127,000	Common shares	125,000
Investments	(47,000)	Contributed surplus	13,000

Instructions

Compute the net income for the current year, assuming that there were no entries in the Retained Earnings account except for a dividend declaration of $19,000, which was paid in the current year.

(Capital Maintenance Approach) Presented below is selected information pertaining to the Megan Bannerman Video Company Ltd.:   E4-2

Cash balance, January 1, 1998	$ 13,000
Accounts receivable, January 1, 1998	19,000
Collections from customers in 1998	210,000
Capital account balance, January 1, 1998	38,000
Total assets, January 1, 1998	75,000
Cash investment added, July 1, 1998	5,000
Total assets, December 31, 1998	88,000
Cash balance, December 31, 1998	16,000
Accounts receivable, December 31, 1998	36,000
Merchandise taken for personal use during 1998	11,000
Total liabilities, December 31, 1998	39,000

Instructions

Compute the net income for 1998.

(Income Statement Items) Presented below are certain account balances of Ray Chan Products Limited.   E4-3

Ending inventory	$ 48,000	Sales returns	$ 5,800
Rental revenue	6,500	Sales discounts	21,300
Interest expense	12,700	Selling expenses	99,400
Purchase allowances	10,500	Sales	390,000
Beginning retained earnings	114,400	Income taxes	31,000
Ending retained earnings	134,000	Beginning inventory	45,300
Freight-in	10,100	Purchases	190,000
Dividends revenue	71,000	Purchase discounts	17,300
		Administrative expenses	82,500

Instructions

From the information, compute the following:

(a) total net revenue

(b) cost of goods sold

(c) net income

(d) dividends declared during the current year

E4-4   (Multiple-step Income Statement) The financial records of Jantzen Ltd. were destroyed by fire at the end of 1998. Fortunately, the controller had kept certain statistical data related to the income statement as presented below.

1. The beginning merchandise inventory was $92,000 and decreased 20% during the current year.
2. Sales discounts amounted to $16,400.
3. 20,000 common shares were outstanding for the entire year.
4. Interest expense was $19,560.
5. The income tax rate was 30%.
6. Cost of goods sold amounted to $450,000.
7. Administrative expenses were 20% of cost of goods sold but only 9% of gross sales.
8. Four-fifths of the operating expenses (total of selling and administrative expenses) related to sales activities.

Instructions

From the foregoing information, prepare an income statement for the year 1998 in multiple-step form.

E4-5   (Multiple-step and Single-step) Two accountants for the firm of Cruise and Kidder are arguing about the merits of presenting an income statement in a multiple-step versus single-step format. The discussion involves the following 1998 information related to Far and Away Company Ltd. ($000 omitted).

Administrative expenses:	
Officers' salaries	$ 4,900
Depreciation of office furniture and equipment	3,960
Purchase returns	5,810
Purchases	59,800
Rent revenue	17,230
Selling expenses	
Transportation-out	2,690
Sales commissions	7,980
Depreciation of sales equipment	6,480
Merchandise, beginning inventory	15,400
Merchandise, ending inventory	16,600
Sales	96,500
Transportation-in	2,780
Income taxes	9,070
Interest expense on bonds payable	1,860

Instructions

(a) Prepare an income statement for the year 1998 using the multiple-step form. There are 40,000,000 common shares outstanding during the year.
(b) Prepare an income statement for the year 1998 using the single-step form.
(c) Which one do you prefer? Discuss.

E4-6   (Multiple-step and Extraordinary Items) The following balances were taken from the books of Mossleigh Limited on December 31, 1998:

Interest revenue	$ 86,000
Cash	61,000
Sales	1,380,000
Accounts receivable	150,000
Prepaid insurance	20,000
Sales returns and allowances	150,000
Allowance for doubtful accounts	7,000
Sales discounts	45,000
Land	100,000
Inventory 1/1/98	246,000
Equipment	200,000
Inventory 12/31/98	331,000
Building	140,000
Purchases	790,000
Accumulated depreciation—equipment	40,000

Purchases returns and allowances	125,000
Accumulated depreciation—building	28,000
Purchase discounts	59,000
Notes receivable	155,000
Selling expenses	194,000
Accounts payable	70,000
Bonds payable	100,000
Administrative and general expenses	97,000
Accrued liabilities	32,000
Interest expense	60,000
Notes payable	100,000
Loss from earthquake damage (extraordinary item)	140,000
Common shares	500,000
Retained earnings	21,000

Assume the effective income tax rate on all items is 34%.

Instructions

Prepare a multiple-step income statement, 50,000 common shares were outstanding during the year.

(Multiple-step and Single-step) Presented below is a trial balance for Eaglesham Limited at December 31, 1998.   E4-7
Assume that the loss due to flood damage is an extraordinary item.

EAGLESHAM LIMITED
Trial Balance
Year ended December 31, 1998

	Debits	Credits
Administrative expense	$ 15,600	
Equipment	20,000	
Cash	7,000	
Income tax expense	11,800	
Inventory	13,000	
Accounts payable		$ 7,200
Cash dividends	5,000	
Loss due to flood (net of $3,400 taxes)	5,700	
Common shares (20,000 shares		40,000
Temporary investments	2,000	
Accrued liabilities		3,200
Accounts receivable	15,000	
Appropriation for contingencies		12,000
Notes payable		20,000
Allowance for doubtful accounts		700
Purchases	62,700	
Interest revenue		10,000
Land	9,000	
Notes receivable	17,000	
Selling expense	36,000	
Building	45,000	
Accumulated depreciation—equipment		4,000
Sales		150,000
Transportation-in	1,500	
Accumulated depreciation—building		2,800
Retained earnings		16,400
	$266,300	$266,300

The December 31, 1998, inventory is $19,500.

Instructions

(a) Prepare a multiple-step income statement.

(b) Prepare a single-step income statement.

(c) Which format do you prefer? Discuss.

E4-8   **(Multiple-step and Single-step)** The accountant for Erma Thompson Shoe Co. Ltd. has compiled the following information from the company's records as a basis for an income statement for the year ended 12/31/98.

Rental revenues	$ 29,000
Interest on notes payable	18,000
Market appreciation on temporary investments above cost	31,000
Merchandise purchases	409,000
Transportation-in—merchandise	37,000
Wages and salaries—sales	114,800
Materials and supplies—sales	17,600
Common shares outstanding (number of shares)	10,000*
Income taxes	66,400
Wages and salaries—administrative	135,900
Other administrative expenses	51,700
Merchandise inventory, January 1, 1998	92,000
Merchandise inventory, December 31, 1998	81,000
Purchase returns and allowances	11,000
Net sales	980,000
Depreciation on plant assets (70% selling, 30% administrative)	65,000
Dividends declared	16,000

*Remained unchanged all year.

Instructions
(a) Prepare a multiple-step income statement.
(b) Prepare a single-step income statement.
(c) Discuss the relative merits of each of the two income statements.

E4-9   **(Multiple-step and Single-step)** Presented below is income statement information related to Alsike Company Limited for the year 1998.

Administrative expenses:	
Officers' salaries	$ 39,000
Depreciation expense—building	28,500
Office supplies expense	9,500
Inventory (ending)	137,000
Flood damage (pretax extraordinary item)	54,000
Purchases	600,000
Sales	930,000
Transportation-in	14,000
Purchase discounts	10,000
Inventory (beginning)	120,000
Sales returns and allowances	5,000
Selling expenses:	
Sales salaries	71,000
Depreciation expense—store equipment	18,000
Store supplies expense	9,000

In addition, the company has revenue of $18,000 received from dividends and expense of $9,000 on notes payable. There are 30,000 common shares outstanding for the year. The total effective tax rate on all income is 34%.

Instructions
(a) Prepare a multiple-step income statement for 1998.
(b) Prepare a single-step income statement for 1998.
(c) Discuss the relative merits of the two income statements.

E4-10   **(Combined Statement)** During 1998, Anthony Hopkins Co. Ltd. had pretax earnings of $500,000 exclusive of a realized and tax-deductible loss of $130,000 from the expropriation of properties (extraordinary item). In addition, the company discovered that depreciation expense was erroneously overstated by $80,000 in 1994. Retained earnings at January 1, 1998, before error correction was $640,000; dividends of $150,000 were declared on common shares during 1998. 100,000 common shares were outstanding during 1998. Assume that a 34% income tax rate applied for both 1994 and 1998.

Instructions

Prepare a combined statement of income and retained earnings beginning with income before taxes and extraordinary items.

(Combined Single-step) The following information was taken from the records of Evelyn Roberts Inc. for the year **E4-11**
1998. Income tax applicable to income from continuing operations, $187,000; income tax applicable to loss on discontinuance of Micron Division, $25,000; income tax applicable to extraordinary gain from expropriation, $29,000; income tax applicable to extraordinary loss from a flood, $18,000.

Extraordinary gain from expropriation	$ 95,000
Loss on discontinuance of Micron Division	75,000
Administrative expenses	240,000
Rent revenue	40,000
Extraordinary loss—flood	60,000
Cash dividends declared	70,000
Retained earnings January 1, 1998	600,000
Cost of goods sold	850,000
Selling expenses	300,000
Sales	1,900,000

Cont
DisCont
Extra.

Shares outstanding during 1998 were 25,000.

Instructions

(a) Prepare a single-step income statement for 1998. Include per share data.

(b) Prepare a combined single-step income and retained earnings statement.

(c) Which one do you prefer? Discuss.

(Multiple-step Statement with Retained Earnings) Presented below is information related to Hardisty Corp. for **E4-12**
the year 1998.

Net sales	$1,350,000
Cost of goods sold	800,000
Selling expenses	65,000
Administrative expenses	48,000
Dividend revenue	20,000
Interest revenue	7,000
Write-off of inventory due to obsolescence	80,000
Depreciation expenses omitted by accident in 1997	40,000
Casualty loss (extraordinary item) before tax	50,000
Dividends declared	45,000
Retained earnings December 31, 1997	2,000,000

Assume an income tax rate of 34% on all items.

Instructions

(a) Prepare a multiple-step income statement for 1998. Assume that 70,000 common shares are outstanding.

(b) Prepare a separate statement of retained earnings for the year ended December 31, 1998.

(Earnings Per Share) The shareholders' equity section of Chester Mulder Corporation appears below at December **E4-13**
31, 1998:

Cumulative preferred shares, $4.00 dividend, 100,000 shares authorized, 90,000 shares outstanding		$ 4,500,000
Common shares, authorized and issued 10 million shares		10,000,000
Contributed surplus		20,500,000
Retained earnings December 31, 1997	$132,000,000	
Net income for 1998	35,000,000	167,000,000
		$202,000,000

Net income for 1998 reflects a total effective tax rate of 30%. Included in the net income figure is a loss of $18,000,000 (before tax) as a result of a major casualty (extraordinary item).

Instructions

Compute earnings per share data as it should appear on the financial statements of Chester Mulder Corporation.

E4-14 **(Condensed Income Statement)** Presented below are selected ledger accounts of Calmar Limited at December 31, 1998:

Cash	185,000	Sales salaries	284,000
Travel and entertainment	69,000	Telephone—sales	17,000
Merchandise inventory	535,000	Office salaries	346,000
Accounting and legal services	33,000	Utilities—office	32,000
Sales	4,275,000	Purchase returns	15,000
Insurance expense	24,000	Miscellaneous office expenses	8,000
Advances from customers	117,000	Sales returns	79,000
Advertising	54,000	Rental revenue	240,000
Purchases	2,786,000	Transportation-in	72,000
Transportation-out	93,000	Extraordinary loss	
Sales discounts	34,000	(before tax)	70,000
Depreciation of office		Accounts receivable	142,500
equipment	48,000	Interest expense	176,000
Purchase discounts	27,000	Sales commissions	83,000
Depreciation of sales		Common shares (95,000)	950,000
equipment	36,000		

Calmar's effective tax rate on all items is 30%. A physical inventory indicates that the ending inventory is $686,000.

Instructions

Prepare a condensed 1998 income statement for Calmar Corporation.

E4-15 **(Retained Earnings Statement)** Murray Fox Corporation began operations on January 1, 1995. During its first three years of operations, Fox reported net income and declared dividends as follows:

	Net income	Dividends declared
1995	$ 40,000	$ -0-
1996	125,000	50,000
1997	150,000	50,000

The following information relates to 1998:

Income before taxes	$240,000
Correction of error for understatement of 1996 depreciation expense (before taxes)	20,000
Retroactive (to end of 1997) decrease in income from change in inventory methods (before taxes)	35,000
Dividends declared (of this amount, $25,000 will be paid on January 15, 1999)	100,000
Effective tax rate	40%

Instructions

(a) Prepare a 1998 retained earnings statement for Murray Fox Corporation.

(b) Assume Fox appropriated retained earnings in the amount of $70,000 on December 31, 1998. After this action, what would Fox report as total retained earnings in its December 31, 1998 balance sheet?

(Earnings Per Share) At December 31, 1997, Fred Meyers Corporation had the following shares outstanding: E4-16

Cumulative preferred shares, $10 dividend, 107,500 shares issued and outstanding	$10,750,000
Common shares, 4,000,000 shares issued and outstanding	20,000,000

During 1998, Meyers' only share transaction was the issuance of 400,000 common shares on April 1. During 1998, the following also occurred:

Income from continuing operations before taxes	$23,650,000
Discontinued operations (loss before taxes), not an extraordinary item	3,225,000
Preferred dividends declared	1,075,000
Common dividends declared	2,200,000
Tax rate	40%

Instructions
Compute earnings per share data as it should appear in the 1998 income statement of Meyers Corporation.

(Discontinued Operations) Assume that Alan Taylor Inc. decides to sell WTVB, its television subsidiary, in 1997.   *E4-17
This sale qualifies for discontinued operations treatment. Pertinent data regarding the operations of the TV subsidiary are as follows:

1. Loss from operations from beginning of year to measurement date, $1,000,000 (net of tax).
2. Realized loss from operations from measurement date to end of 1997, $600,000 (net of tax).
3. Estimated income from end of year to disposal date of June 1, 1998, $350,000 (net of tax).
4. Estimated gain on sale of net assets on June 1, 1998, $150,000 (net of tax).

Instructions
(a) What is the gain (loss) on the disposal of the segment reported in 1997? In 1998?
(b) Prepare the discontinued operations section of the income statement for the year ended 1997.
(c) If the amount reported in 1997 as gain or loss from disposal of a segment by Alan Taylor Inc. proves to be materially incorrect, when and how should the correction reported, if at all?
(d) If the TV subsidiary had a realized income of $100,000 (net of tax) instead of a realized loss from the measurement date to the end of 1997, what should be the gain or loss on disposal of the segment be reported in 1997? In 1998?

(Discontinued Operations) On October 5, 1996, Trevor Morgan Inc.'s board of directors decides to dispose of the   *E4-18
Spit & Polish Division. Morgan is a real estate firm with approximately 25% of its income from management of apartment complexes. The Spit & Polish Division contracts to clean apartments after tenants move out of the Morgan complexes and several others. The board decides to dispose of the division because of unfavourable operating results.

Net income for Morgan is $84,000 after tax (assume a 30% rate) for the fiscal year ended December 31, 1996. The Spit & Polish Division accounts for only $3,500 (after tax) of this amount and only $700 (after tax) in the fourth quarter. Spit and Polish accounts for $50,000 in revenues, of which $8,000 are earned in the last quarter. The average number of common shares outstanding is 20,000 for the year.

Because of unfavourable results and competition, the board believes selling the business intact is impossible. Their final decision is to complete all current contracts, the last of which expires on May 3, 1998, and then auction off the cleaning equipment on May 10, 1998. This, the only asset of the division, will have a depreciated value of $25,000 at the disposal date. The board believes the sale proceeds will approximate $5,000 after the auction expenses and estimates Spit & Polish earnings in fiscal year 1997 as $3,800 (before tax), with a loss of $3,000 (before tax) in fiscal year 1998.

Instructions
Prepare the income statement and the appropriate footnotes that relate to the Spit & Polish Division for 1996. The income statement should begin with earnings from continuing operations before income taxes. Earnings per share computations are not required.

PROBLEMS

P4-1   Presented below is information related to the Lupul Co. Ltd. for 1998.

Retained earnings balance January 1, 1998	$ 880,000
Sales for the year	25,000,000
Cost of goods sold	17,000,000
Interest revenue	70,000
Selling and administrative expenses	4,900,000
Write-off of goodwill (not tax deductible)	520,000
Income taxes for 1998 excluding discontinued operations and extraordinary items	1,100,000
Assessment for additional 1995 income taxes normally recurring)	300,000
Gain on the sale of investments (normally recurring)	110,000
Loss due to flood damage—extraordinary item net of tax)	90,000
Loss on the disposition of the wholesale division (net of tax)	440,000
Loss on operations of the wholesale division (net of tax)	390,000
Dividends declared on common shares	250,000
Dividends declared on preferred shares	70,000

Instructions

Prepare a combined statement of income and retained earnings. Lupul Co. Ltd. decided to discontinue its entire wholesale operations and to retain its manufacturing operations. On September 15, Lupul sold the wholesale operations to Ray Cutler & Company. During 1998, there were 300,000 common shares outstanding all year.

P4-2   Presented below is the trial balance of Mariah Carey Corporation at December 31, 1998.

MARIAH CAREY CORPORATION
Trial Balance
Year Ended December 31, 1998

	Debits	Credits
Purchase discounts		$ 10,000
Cash	$ 210,100	
Accounts receivable	105,000	
Rent revenue		18,000
Retained earnings January 1, 1998		260,000
Salaries payable		18,000
Sales		1,000,000
Notes receivable	110,000	
Accounts payable		49,000
Accumulated depreciation—equipment		28,000
Sales discounts	14,500	
Sales returns	17,500	
Notes payable		70,000
Selling expenses	232,000	
Administrative expenses	99,000	
Common shares		300,000
Income tax expense	38,500	
Cash dividends	60,000	
Allowance for doubtful accounts		5,000
Supplies	14,000	
Freight-in	20,000	
Land	70,000	
Equipment	140,000	
Bonds payable		100,000
Gain on sale of land		30,000
Accumulated depreciation—building		19,600
Merchandise inventory	89,000	
Building	98,000	
Purchases	590,000	
Totals	$1,907,600	$1,907,600

A physical count of inventory on December 31 resulted in an inventory amount of $124,000.

Instructions
Prepare a combined statement of income and retained earnings using the single-step form. Assume that the only changes in the retained earnings during the current year were from net income and dividends. Ten thousand common shares were outstanding during the entire year.

Aerosmith Ltd. reported income from continuing operations before taxes during 1998 of $790,000. Additional transactions occurring in 1998 but not considered in the $790,000 are as follows: **P4-3**

1. The corporation experienced an uninsured flood loss (extraordinary) in the amount of $60,000 during the year. The tax rate on this item is 46%.

2. At the beginning of 1996, the corporation purchased a machine for $54,000 (residual value of $9,000) that had an estimated useful life of six years. The bookkeeper used straight-line depreciation for 1996, 1997, and 1998 but failed to deduct the residual value in computing the depreciation base.

3. Sale of securities held as part of its portfolio resulted in a loss of $75,500 (pretax).

4. When its president died, the corporation realized $110,000 from an insurance policy. The cash surrender value of this policy had been carried on the books as an investment in the amount of $46,000 (the gain is nontaxable).

5. The company disposed of its recreational division at a loss of $115,000 before taxes. Assume that this transaction meets the criteria for discontinued operations.

6. The corporation decided to change its method of inventory pricing from average cost to the FIFO method. The effect of this change on prior years is to increase 1996 income by $60,000 and decrease 1997 income by $20,000 before taxes. The FIFO method has been used for 1998. The tax rate on these items is 40%.

Instructions
Prepare an income statement for the year 1998 starting with income from continuing operations before taxes. Compute earnings per share as it should be shown on the face of the income statement. (Assume a tax rate of 30% on all items, unless indicated otherwise.)

The following account balances were included in the trial balance of the Welker Corporation at June 30, 1998. **P4-4**

Sales	$1,678,500	Bad Debt expense—selling	4,850
Depreciation of office		Building expense—prorated	
furniture and equipment	7,250	to administration	9,130
Sales discounts	31,150	Sales salaries	56,260
Purchases	890,000	Sales commissions	97,600
Real estate and other local taxes	7,320	Miscellaneous office expenses	6,000
Freight-in	31,600	Travel expense—salespersons	28,930
Purchase returns	5,150	Building expense—prorated	
Purchase discounts	21,580	to sales	6,200
Sales returns	62,300	Dividends declared on	
Dividends received	38,000	preferred shares	9,000
Freight-out	21,400	Miscellaneous selling expenses	4,715
Bond interest expense	18,000	Office supplies used	3,450
Entertainment expense	14,820	Dividends declared on	
Income taxes	133,000	common shares	32,000
Telephone and fax—sales	9,030	Telephone and fax	
Depreciation understatement		—administration	2,820
due to error—1995 (net of tax)	6,700	Merchandise inventory—	
Depreciation of sales equipment	4,980	July 1, 1997	250,000

The merchandise inventory at June 30, 1997 amounted to $268,100. The Unappropriated Retained Earnings account had a balance of $187,000 at June 30, 1997 before closing; the only entry in that account during the year was a debit of $41,600 to establish an Appropriation for Bond Indebtedness. There are 70,000 common shares outstanding.

Instructions
(a) Using the multiple-step form, prepare a combined statement of income and unappropriated retained earnings for the year ended June 30, 1998.

(b) Using the single-step form, prepare a combined statement of income and unappropriated retained earnings for the year ended June 30, 1998.

P4-5   The president of Mildred Rounding Corporation provides you with the following selected account balances as of December 31, 1998.

	Dr.	Cr.
Sales		$2,100,000
Sales office salaries	$ 200,000	
Officers' salaries	220,000	
Building depreciation (50% of building is directly related to sales)	70,000	
Freight-out	46,000	
Cost of goods sold	900,000	
Dividends declared and paid	75,000	
Dividends received		45,000
Interest expense—10% bonds	55,000	
Retained earnings—1/1/98		250,000
Expropriation of foreign holdings (extraordinary item)	200,000	
Damages payable from litigation		80,000

The president informs you that the liability for damages payable from litigation arose in 1998 out of a lawsuit initiated in 1994, and the bookkeeper debited Retained Earnings for $80,000 in 1998. Assume that the company is continually involved in litigation of this nature. The president requests your help in constructing an income statement. She advises you that the corporation had 100,000 common shares outstanding, and was taxed at an effective rate of 35% on all income-related items.

Instructions

(a) Prepare a combined statement of income and retained earnings in multiple-step form.

(b) Prepare a combined statement of income and retained earnings in single-step form.

P4-6   Presented below is a combined single-step statement of income and retained earnings for Tina Turner Co. Ltd. for 1998.

		(000 omitted)
Net sales		$640,000
Cost and expenses:		
Cost of goods sold		$500,000
Selling, general, and administrative expenses		66,000
Other, net		17,000
		$583,000
Income before income taxes		$ 57,000
Income taxes		16,800
Net income		$ 40,200
Retained earnings at beginning period, as previously reported	$141,000	
Adjustment required for correction of error	(7,000)	
Retained earnings at beginning of period, as restated		134,000
Dividends on common shares		(12,200)
Retained earnings at end of period		$162,000

Additional facts are as follows:

1. "Selling, general and administrative expenses" for 1998 included a usual but infrequently occurring charge of $11,000,000.

2. "Other, net" for 1998 included an extraordinary item (loss) of $10,000,000. If the extraordinary item (loss) had not occurred, income taxes for 1998 would have been $21,800,000 instead of $16,800,000.

3. "Adjustment required for correction of an error" was a result of a change in estimate (useful life of certain assets reduced to eight years and a catch-up adjustment made).

4. Tina Turner Co. Ltd. disclosed earnings per common share for net income in a note cross-referenced to the income statement.

Instructions

Determine from these additional facts whether the presentation of the facts in the Tina Turner Co. Ltd.'s statement of income and retained earnings is appropriate. If the presentation is not appropriate, describe the appropriate presentation and discuss its theoretical rationale.

Below is the Retained Earnings account for the year 1998 for Clay Gilbert Corp. (Assume that the change in depre- P4-7
ciation method was not due to changed circumstances, experience, or new information.)

Retained earnings January 1, 1998		$357,600
Add:		
Gain on sale of investments (net of tax)	$41,200	
Net income	84,500	
Refund on litigation with government,		
related to the year 1995 (net of tax)	10,800	
Recognition of income earned in 1997,		
but omitted from income statement		
in that year (net of tax)	25,400	161,900
		$519,500
Deduct		
Loss on discontinued operations (net of tax)	$25,000	
Write-off of goodwill	60,000	
Cumulative effect on income in changing from		
straight-line depreciation to accelerated		
depreciation in 1998 (net of tax)	18,200	
Cash dividends declared	32,000	135,200
Retained earnings December 31, 1998		$384,300

Instructions
(a) Prepare a correct statement of retained earnings. Clay Gilbert Corp. normally sells investments of the type mentioned above.
(b) State where the items that do not appear in the retained earnings statement would be shown.

A condensed statement of income and retained earnings of Olive Miller Ltd. for the year ended December 31, 1998 P4-8
is presented below. Also presented are three unrelated situations involving accounting changes and classification of
certain items as ordinary or extraordinary. Each situation is based upon the condensed statement of income and
retained earnings of Olive Miller Ltd. and requires revisions of the statement.

OLIVE MILLER LTD.
Condensed Statement of Income
and Retained Earnings
For the Year Ended December 31, 1998

Sales	$5,700,000
Cost of goods sold	2,900,000
Gross margin	$2,800,000
Selling, general, and administrative expenses	2,000,000
Income before extraordinary item	$ 800,000
Extraordinary item	(540,000)
Net income	$ 260,000
Retained earnings January 1	700,000
Retained earnings December 31	$ 960,000

Situation A. During the latter part of 1998, the company discontinued its retail and apparel fabric divisions. The
loss on sale of these two discontinued divisions amounted to $620,000. This amount was included as part of selling,
general, and administrative expenses. The transaction met the criteria for discontinued operations.

The extraordinary item in the condensed statement of income and retained earnings for 1998 related to a loss
sustained as a result of damage to the company's merchandise caused by a tornado that struck its main warehouse
in Lethbridge. This natural disaster was considered an unusual and infrequent occurrence for that section of the
country.

Situation B. At the end of 1998, the company's management decided that the estimated loss rate on uncollectible
accounts receivable was too low. The loss rate used for the years 1997 and 1998 was 1.2% of total sales, and owing to
an increase in the write-off of uncollectible accounts, the rate was raised to 3% of total sales. The amount recorded in
Bad Debts Expense under the heading of Selling, General, and Administrative Expenses for 1998 was $68,400 and
for 1997 was $75,000.

The extraordinary item in the condensed statement of income and retained earnings of 1998 related to a loss incurred in the abandonment of outmoded equipment formerly used in the business.

Situation C. On January 1, 1996, the company acquired machinery at a cost of $500,000. The Company adopted the double-declining balance method of depreciation for this machinery, and had been recording depreciation over an estimated life of ten years, with no residual value. At the beginning of 1998, a decision was made to adopt the straight-line method of depreciation for this machinery. The change was not due to changed circumstances, experience, or new information. Owing to an oversight, however, the double-declining balance method was used for 1998. For financial reporting purposes, depreciation was included in selling, general, and administrative expenses.

The extraordinary item in the condensed statement of income and retained earnings related to shutdown expenses incurred by the company during a major strike by its operating employees during 1998.

Instructions

For each of the three unrelated situations, prepare a revised condensed statement of income and retained earnings of Olive Miller Ltd. Ignore income tax considerations and earnings per share computations.   (AICPA adapted)

P4-9   The Carlito Corporation commenced business on January 1, 1995. Recently the corporation had several accounting problems relating to the presentation of their income statement for financial reporting purposes. You have been asked to examine the following data and information:

CARLITO CORPORATION
Statement of Income
For the Year Ended December 31, 1998

Sales	$9,500,000
Cost of goods sold	5,900,000
Gross profit	$3,600,000
Selling and administrative expense	1,300,000
Income before income taxes	$2,300,000
Income tax (30%)	690,000
Net income	$1,610,000

In addition, this information was provided:

1. The controller mentioned that the corporation had difficulty collecting several of their receivables. For this reason, the bad debt write-off was increased from 1% to 2% of sales. The controller estimated that if this rate had been used in past periods, an additional $83,000 worth of expense would have been charged. The bad debts expense for the current period was calculated using the new rate and was part of selling and administrative expense.

2. Common shares outstanding at the end of 1998 totalled 500,000. No shares were purchased or sold during 1998.

3. Carlito noted that the following items were not included in the income statement.
   (a) Inventory in the amount of $48,000 that was obsolete had not been written down.
   (b) A major casualty loss suffered by the corporation was partially uninsured and cost $77,000, net of tax (extraordinary item), and was not included in the income statement.

4. Retained earnings as of January 1, 1998 was $2,800,000. Cash dividends of $700,000 were declared and paid in 1998.

5. In January, 1998, although there had been no change in circumstances, experience, or new information, Carlito management changed their method of accounting for plant assets from the straight-line method to the accelerated method (double-declining balance). The controller has prepared a schedule indicating what depreciation expense would have been in previous periods if the double-declining balance method had been used. (The effective tax rate for 1995, 1996, and 1997 was 30%).

	Depreciation Expense under Straight-Line	Depreciation Expense under Double-Declining	Difference
1995	$ 75,000	$150,000	$ 75,000
1996	75,000	112,500	37,500
1997	75,000	84,375	9,375
	$225,000	$346,875	$121,875

6. In 1998, Carlito discovered that two errors were made in previous years. First, when it took a physical inventory at the end of 1995, one of the count sheets was apparently lost. The ending inventory for 1995 was therefore understated by $95,000. The inventory was correctly taken in 1996, 1997, and 1998. Also, the corporation found that in 1997, it had failed to record $20,000 as an expense for sales commissions. The effective tax rate for 1995, 1996, and 1997 was 30%. The sales commissions for 1997 were included in 1998 expenses.

Instructions

Prepare (1) the income statement and (2) the statement of retained earnings for Carlito Corporation for 1998 in accordance with professional pronouncements. Do not prepare notes.

Jonathan Cox Limited management formally decides to discontinue operation of its Electrical Switch Division on November 1, 1997. Jonathan Cox is a successful corporation with earnings in excess of $38.5 million before taxes for each of the past five years. The Electrical Switch Division is being discontinued because it has not contributed to this profitable performance.   **P4-10**

The principle assets of this division are the land, plant, and equipment used to manufacture the switches. The land, plant, and equipment have a net book value of $56 million on November 1, 1997.

Cox management has entered into negotiations for a cash sale of the facility for $39 million. The expected date of the sale and final disposal of the segment is July 1, 1998.

Jonathan Cox Limited has a fiscal year ending May 31. The results of operations for the Electrical Switch Division for the 1997–98 fiscal year and the estimated results for June, 1998 are presented below. The before-tax losses after October 31, 1997 are computed without depreciation on the plant and equipment because the net book value as of November 1, 1997 is being used as a basis of negotiation for the sale.

Period	Before-tax Income (Loss)
June 1, 1997—October 31, 1997	$(3,800,000)
November 1, 1997—May 31, 1998	$(5,900,000)
June 1—30, 1998 (estimated)	$ (650,000)

The Electrical Switch Division will be accounted for as a discontinued operation on Jonathan Cox's 1997–98 fiscal year financial statements. Cox is subject to a 30% tax rate (federal and provincial income taxes) on operating income and on all gains and losses.

Instructions

(a) Explain how the Electrical Switch Division's assets would be reported on Jonathan Cox Limited's balance sheet as of May 31, 1998.

(b) Explain how the discontinued operations and pending sale of the Electrical Switch Division would be reported on Jonathan Cox Limited's income statement for the year ended May 31, 1998.

(c) Explain what information ordinarily should be disclosed in the notes to the financial statements regarding discontinued operations.

(CMA adapted)

CASES

Janet Jackson Limited was incorporated and began business on January 1, 1998. It has been successful and now requires a bank loan for additional working capital to finance expansion. The bank has requested an audited income statement for the year 1998. The accountant for Janet Jackson provides you with the following income statement, which the company plans to submit to the bank: **C4-1**

Income Statement		
Sales		$760,000
Dividends		32,300
Gain on recovery of insurance proceeds from earthquake loss		38,500
		$830,800
Less:		
Selling expenses	$101,100	
Cost of goods sold	510,000	
Advertising expense	13,700	
Loss on obsolescence of inventories	34,000	
Loss on disposal of discontinued operations	48,600	
Administrative expense	73,400	780,800
Income before income taxes		$ 50,000
Income taxes		20,000
Net income		$ 30,000

Instructions

Indicate the deficiencies in the income statement presented above. Assume that the corporation desires a single-step income statement.

C4-2 Information concerning the operations of a corporation can be presented in an income statement or in a combined statement of income and retained earnings. Income statements could be prepared on a current operating performance basis or an all-inclusive basis. Proponents of the two types of income statements do not agree upon the proper treatment of material nonrecurring and/or unusual charges and credits.

Instructions

(a) Define current operating performance and all-inclusive as used above.

(b) Explain the differences in content and organization of a current operating performance income statement and an all-inclusive income statement. Include a discussion of the proper treatment of material nonrecurring and/or unusual charges and credits.

(c) Give the principal arguments for the use of each of the three statements: all-inclusive income statement, current operating performance income statement, and a combined statement of income and retained earnings.

(d) What basis is used for preparing the income statement in Canadian practice, and how does it differ from the current operating basis and the all-inclusive basis?　(AICPA adapted)

C4-3 Lisa Bolton vice-president of finance for Timeless Company Ltd. has recently been asked to discuss with the company's division controllers the proper accounting for unusual and nonrecurring items. Lisa prepared the factual situations presented below as a basis for discussion.

1. An earthquake destroys one of the oil refineries owned by a large multinational oil company. Earthquakes are rare in this geographical location.

2. A publicly held company has incurred a substantial loss in the unsuccessful registration of a bond issue.

3. A large portion of a cigarette manufacturer's tobacco crops are destroyed by a hailstorm. Severe damage from hailstorms is rare in this locality and for the company as a whole.

4. A large diversified company sells a block of shares from its portfolio of securities acquired for investment purposes.

5. A company sells a block of common shares of a publicly traded company. The block of shares, which represents less than 10% of the publicly held company, is the only security investment the company has ever owned.

6. A company that operates a chain of warehouses sells the excess land surrounding one of its warehouses. When the company buys property to establish a new warehouse, it usually buys more land than it expects to use for the warehouse with the expectation that the land will appreciate in value. Twice during the past five years, the company had sold excess land.

7. A textile manufacturer with only one plant moves to another location and sustains relocation costs of $620,000.

8. A company experiences a material loss in the repurchase of a large bond issue that has been outstanding for three years. The company regularly repurchases bonds of this nature.

9. A railroad experiences an unusual flood loss to part of its track system. Flood losses normally occur every three or four years.

10. A machine tool company sells the only land it owns. The land was acquired ten years ago for future expansion, but the company abandoned all plans for expansion and decided to hold the land for appreciation.

Instructions

Determine whether the foregoing items should be classified as extraordinary items. Present a rationale for your position.

C4-4 Marion Kasawal Limited is a real estate firm that derives approximately 30% of its income from the Gary Logan Division, which manages apartment complexes. As auditor for Marion Kasawal Limited, you have recently overheard the following discussion between the controller and financial vice-president.

Vice-president: If we sell the Gary Logan Division, it seems ridiculous to segregate the results of the sale in the income statement. Separate categories tend to be absurd and confusing to the shareholders. I believe that we should simply report the gain on the sale as other revenue or expense without detail.

Controller: Professional pronouncements require that we disclose this information separately in the income statement. If a sale of this type is considered unusual, infrequent, and not dependent on management decisions, it must be reported as an extraordinary item. Otherwise, it should be reported in a separate section of the income statement, labelled Discontinued operations, which is shown between the income from continuing operations and extraordinary items.

Vice-president: What about the walkout we had last month when our employees were upset about their commission income? Would this situation not also require separate disclosure, perhaps as an extraordinary item?

Controller: I am not sure whether this item would be reported as an extraordinary item or not.

Vice-president: Oh well, it doesn't make any difference because the net effect of all these items is immaterial, so no disclosure is necessary.

Instructions

(a) On the basis of the foregoing discussion, answer the following questions: Who is correct about how to handle the sale? What would be in the income statement presentation for the sale of the Gary Logan Division?

(b) How should the walkout by the employees be reported?

(c) What do you think about the vice-president's observation on materiality?

(d) What are the earnings per share implications of these topics?

Munch Limited is a major manufacturer of food products that are sold in grocery and convenience stores through-out Canada. The company's name is well-known and respected because its products have been marketed nationally for over fifty years. **C4-5**

In April, 1998 the company was forced to recall one of its major products. A total of 35 persons were treated for severe intestinal pain, and eventually three people died from complications. All of these people had consumed Munch's product.

The product causing the problem was traced to one specific lot. Munch keeps samples from all lots of food-stuffs. After thorough testing, Munch and the legal authorities confirmed that the product had been tampered with after it left the company's plant and was no longer under the company's control.

All of this product was recalled from the market—the only time such an event happened and the only time tampering was involved. Anyone who still had this product in their homes, even though it was not from the affected lot, was asked to return the product for credit and refund. A media campaign was designed and implemented by the company to explain what had happened and what the company was doing to minimize any chance for recurrence. Munch decided to continue the product with the same trade name and same wholesale price. However, the packaging was redesigned completely to be tamper resistant and safety sealed. This required the purchase and installation of new equipment.

The corporate accounting staff recommended that the costs associated with the tampered product be treated as an extraordinary item on the 1998 financial statements (i.e., disclosed as a separate item). Corporate accounting was asked to identify the various costs that could be associated with the tampered product and related recall. These costs ($000 omitted) are as follows.

1. Credits and refunds to stores and consumers	$30,000
2. Insurance to cover lost sales and costs for possible future recalls	5,000
3. Transportation costs and off-site warehousing of returned product	1,000
4. Future security measures for other Munch products	4,000
5. Testing of returned product and inventory	700
6. Destroying returned product and inventory	2,400
7. Public relations program to re-establish brand credibility	4,200
8. Communication program to inform customers, answer inquiries, prepare press releases, etc.	1,600
9. Higher cost arising from new packaging	700
10. Investigation of possible involvement of employees, former employees, competitors, etc.	500
11. Packaging redesign and testing	2,000
12. Purchase and installation of new packaging equipment	6,000
13. Legal costs for defence against liability suits	600
14. Lost sales revenue due to recall	32,000

Munch's estimated earnings before income taxes and before consideration of any of the above items for the year ending December 31, 1998, are $230 million.

Instructions

(a) Munch Limited plans to recognize the costs associated with the product tampering and recall as an extraordinary item.

1. Explain why Munch could classify this occurrence as an extraordinary item.

2. Describe the placement and terminology used to present the extraordinary item in the 1998 income statement.

(b) Refer to the 14 costs identified by the corporate accounting staff of Munch Limited.

1. Identify the cost items by number that should be included in the extraordinary item for 1998.

2. For any item that is not included in the extraordinary item, explain why it would not be included and how it would be reported in the 1998 financial statements.

(CMA adapted)

C4-6 Glen Mitchell, controller for Shantz Limited, has recently prepared an income statement for 1998. Mr. Mitchell admits that he has not examined any recent professional pronouncements, but believes that the following presentation presents fairly the financial progress of this company during the current period.

SHANTZ LIMITED
Income Statement
For the Year Ended December 31, 1998

Sales			$377,852
Less: Sales returns and allowances			16,320
Net sales			361,532
Cost of goods sold:			
Inventory, January 1, 1998		$ 50,235	
Purchases	$192,143		
Less: Purchase discounts	3,142	189,001	
Cost of goods available for sale		239,236	
Inventory, December 31, 1998		37,124	
Cost of goods sold			202,112
Gross profit			159,420
Selling expenses		41,850	
Administrative expenses		32,142	73,992
Income before income tax			85,428
Other revenues and gains			
Dividends received			40,000
			125,428
Income tax			43,900
Net income			$ 81,528

SHANTZ LIMITED
Statement of Retained Earnings
For the Year Ended December 31, 1998

Retained earnings, January 1, 1998			$176,000
Add			
Net income for 1998	$ 81,528		
Gain from casualty (net of tax)	10,000		
Gain on sale of plant assets	21,400	$112,928	
Deduct			
Loss on expropriation (net of tax)	8,000		
Cash dividends declared on common shares	30,000		
Correction of mathematical error in depreciating plant assets in 1996 (Net of tax)	7,186	(45,186)	67,742
Retained earnings, December 31, 1998			$243,742

Instructions

(a) Determine whether these statements are prepared under the current operating or all-inclusive concept of income. Cite specific details.

(b) Which method do you favour and why?

(c) Which method must be used, and how should the information be presented? There were 100,000 common shares outstanding during the year.

For questionable items, use the classification that ordinarily would be appropriate.

The following financial statement was prepared by employees of Corner Service Limited.

C4-7

CORNER SERVICE LIMITED
Statement of Income and Retained Earnings
Year Ended December 31, 1998

Revenues	
Gross sales, including sales taxes	$1,044,300
Less returns, allowances, and cash discounts	56,200
Net sales	$ 988,100
Dividends, interest, and purchase discounts	30,250
Recoveries of accounts written off in prior years	13,850
Total revenues	$1,032,200
Costs and expenses	
Cost of goods sold, including sales taxes	$ 425,900
Salaries and related payroll expenses	60,500
Rent	19,100
Freight-in and freight-out	3,400
Bad debts expense	24,000
Addition to reserve for possible inventory losses	3,800
Total costs and expenses	$ 536,700
Income before extraordinary items	$ 495,500
Extraordinary items	
Loss on discontinued styles (note l)	$ 37,000
Loss on sale of marketable securities (note 2)	39,050
Loss on sale of warehouse (note 3)	86,350
Retroactive settlement of income taxes for 1995 and 1996 (note 4)	34,500
Total extraordinary items	$ 196,900
Net income	$ 298,600
Retained earnings at beginning of year	310,700
Total	$ 609,300
Less: Income taxes	$ 113,468
Cash dividends on common shares	21,900
Total	$ 135,368
Retained earnings at end of year	$ 473,932
Net income per share	$1.99

Notes to the Statement of Income and Retained Earnings

1. New styles and rapidly changing consumer preferences resulted in a $37,000 loss on the disposal of discontinued styles and related accessories.

2. The corporation sold an investment in marketable securities at a loss of $39,050. The corporation normally sells securities of this nature.

3. The corporation sold one of its warehouses at an $86,350 loss.

4. The corporation was charged $34,500 retroactively for additional income taxes resulting from a settlement in 1998. Of this amount, $17,000 was applicable to 1996 and the balance was applicable to 1995. Litigation of this nature is recurring for this company.

Instructions

Identify and discuss the weaknesses in classification and disclosure in this single-step statement of income and retained earnings. You should explain why these treatments are weaknesses and what the appropriate presentation of the items is in accordance with professional pronouncements.

As the audit partner for Eric and Clapton, you are in charge of reviewing the classification of unusual items that have occurred during the current year. The following items have come to your attention:

C4-8

[handwritten margin: correctm of acctg err. R/E] 1. A merchandising company incorrectly overstated its ending inventory two years ago by a material amount. Inventory for all other periods was correctly computed.

[handwritten margin: Cont op Sep disclosed Ys] 2. An automobile dealer sells for $123,000 an extremely rare 1930 S type Invicta that it purchased for $18,000 ten years ago. The Invicta is the only such display item the dealer owns.

[handwritten margin: Δ in acctg est Related, Begin R/E] 3. A drilling company during the current year extended the estimated useful life of certain drilling equipment from 9 to 15 years. As a result, depreciation for the current year was materially lowered.

[handwritten margin: Δ in acctg est Begin + Related R/E] 4. A retail outlet changed its computation for bad debts expense from 1% to 1/2 of 1% of sales because of changes in its customer clientele.

[handwritten margin: Cont op Ys] 5. A mining concern sells a foreign subsidiary engaged in uranium mining, although it (the seller) continues to engage in uranium mining in other countries.

[handwritten margin: Δ in acctg est R/E] 6. A steel company changes from straight-line depreciation to accelerated depreciation in accounting for its plant assets.

[handwritten margin: Cont op. sep disc Ys] 7. A construction company, at great expense, prepares a major proposal for a government loan. The loan is not approved.

[handwritten margin: Cont op. sep disc Ys] 8. A water pump manufacturer has suffered big losses resulting from a strike by its employees early in the year.

[handwritten margin: correctm of Begin R/E mistake] 9. Depreciation for a prior period was incorrectly understated by $900,000. The error was discovered in the current year.

[handwritten margin: Extraordinary item. Ys] 10. A large cattle rancher suffered a major loss because the government required that all cattle in the province be killed to halt the spread of a rare disease. Such a situation has not occurred in the province for twenty years.

[handwritten margin: Discontinued op Ys] 11. A food distributor that sells wholesale to supermarket chains and to fast-food restaurants (two major classes of customers) decides to discontinue the division that sells to one of the two classes of customers.

Instructions

From the foregoing information, indicate in what section of the income statement or retained earnings statement these items should be classified. Provide a brief explanation for your position.

C4-9 In early 1984 the Haridi Company Ltd. was formed when it issued 10,000 common shares at $20 each. A few years later, 3,000 additional shares were issued at $35 each. No other common share transactions occurred until the company was liquidated in 1998. At that time, corporate assets were sold for $1,150,000 and $100,000 of corporate liabilities were paid off. The remaining cash was distributed to shareholders. During the corporation's life, it paid total dividends of $200,000.

Instructions

(a) Discuss the two approaches to calculating income.

(b) If only the facts given above are available, which approach must be used to compute income?

(c) Compute the income of Haridi Company Ltd. over its 15-year life.

*C4-10 You're the engagement partner on a multi-divisional, calendar year-end client with annual sales of $80 million. The company primarily sells electronic transistors to small customers and has one division that deals in acoustic transmitters for Navy submarines. The Transmitter Division has approximately $15 million in sales.

It's an evening in February, 1998, and the audit work is complete. You're working in the client's office on the report, when you overhear a conversation between the financial vice-president, the treasurer, and the controller. They're discussing the sale of the Transmitter Division, expected to take place in June of this year, and the related reporting problems.

The vice-president thinks no segregation of the sale is necessary in the income statement because separate categories tend to be abused and confuse the shareholders. The treasurer disagrees. He feels that if an item is unusual or infrequent, it should be shown separately as an extraordinary item, including the sale of the Transmitter Division. The controller says an item should be both infrequent and unusual to be shown as a separate item, but not as an extraordinary item.

The sale is not new to you because you have read about it in the minutes of the December 16, 1997 board of directors meeting. The minutes indicated plans to sell the transmitter plant and equipment by June 30, 1998 to its major competitor, who seems interested. The board estimates that net income and sales will remain constant until the sale, on which the company expects a $700,000 profit.

You also hear the controller disagree with the vice-president that the results of the strike last year and the sale of the old transistor ovens, formerly used in manufacturing, would also be extraordinary items. In addition, the treasurer thinks the government regulation issued last month, which made much of their raw materials inventory useless, should be disclosed separately. The regulations set beta emission standards at levels lower than those in the raw materials supply, and there is no alternative use for materials. Finally, the controller claims that the discussion is academic. Since the net effect of all three items is immaterial, no disclosure is required.

Instructions

(a) Does the Transmitter Division qualify as a segment of a business in more than one way? If so, why?

(b) Does the Transmitter Division qualify as a discontinued operation? Why?

(c) Do the minutes indicate that a formal plan has been established? If not, why?

(d) When should the gain be recognized? What if a loss were anticipated?

(e) Who is correct about reporting the sale? What would the income statement presentation be for the next fiscal year?

(f) Who is right about whether the strike, the sale of fixed assets, and the imposition of a new government regulation constitute extraordinary items?

(g) What do you think about the controller's observation on materiality?

(h) What facts can you give the group about the earnings per share ramifications of these topics?

USING YOUR JUDGEMENT

FINANCIAL REPORTING PROBLEM

The financial statements of Moore Corporation Limited and accompanying notes, as presented in the company's 1995 Annual Report, are contained in Appendix 5A. Refer to Moore Corporation Limited's financial statements and notes and answer the following questions.

1. What type of income statement format does Moore Corporation Limited use? Name the possible advantages of this type of format.

2. What is Moore Corporation Limited's primary revenue source?

3. What are the gross profit to net sales ratios for the years 1994 to 1995? Is the trend of the ratios favourable or unfavourable? Explain.

4. What are Moore Corporation Limited's percentages of net income to net sales for the years 1994 to 1995? Is the trend of the percentage comparable to that of gross profit to net sales ratios in the same period? Explain.

ETHICS CASE

In the financial highlights section of its annual report, Chandra Transport Limited declares that its earnings have increased by 10% using an earnings number that includes and gives no hint of a large unusual, nonrecurring gain that was not determined by management. The financial statements, by contrast, have correctly highlighted and classified the extraordinary items below the operating income. A shareholder who has read the annual report closely asks the chief accountant, Dan Panic, to explain this apparent discrepancy, but Javid Chandra, president of Chandra Transport, suggests evading the question by saying that the highlights section is not controlled by GAAP, and anyway it is only for highlights and not details like extraordinary items.

Instructions

(a) Is Javid Chandra correct about the highlights section not being controlled by GAAP? Is there an ethical issue involved in this discrepancy?

(b) Who might be affected by this presentation?

(c) What should Dan Panic do?

chapter 5

BALANCE SHEET AND STATEMENT OF CASH FLOWS

5

Balance Sheet and Statement of Cash Flows

Learning Objectives

After studying this chapter, you should be able to:

1. Identify the uses and limitations of a balance sheet.

2. Identify the major classifications in the balance sheet.

3. Prepare a classified balance sheet using the report and account forms.

4. Identify balance sheet information requiring supplemental disclosure.

5. Identify major disclosure techniques for the balance sheet.

6. Indicate the purpose of the statement of cash flows.

7. Identify the content of the statement of cash flows.

8. Prepare a statement of cash flows.

Until recently, investors generally focussed on the income statement and earnings per share. The balance sheet was skimmed and the statement of cash flows was all but ignored. However, many surprises in earnings per share could have been anticipated if these financial statements had not been overlooked. Liquidity and financial flexibility are necessary conditions for any profitable enterprise, and only through careful analysis of balance sheets and statements of cash flows can information about these conditions be obtained.

SECTION 1: BALANCE SHEET

USEFULNESS OF THE BALANCE SHEET

The **balance sheet**[1] provides information about the nature and amounts of investments in enterprise resources, obligations to enterprise creditors, and the owners' equity in net enterprise resources. The balance sheet provides a basis for (1) computing rates of return (relationship between assets and income); (2) evaluating the capital structure (relationship of liabilities and owners' equity) of the enterprise; and (3) assessing the liquidity and financial flexibility of the enterprise. In order to judge enterprise risk[2] and assess future cash flows, one must determine enterprise liquidity and financial flexibility by analysing its balance sheet.

OBJECTIVE 1
Identify the uses and limitations of a balance sheet.

---

[1] *Financial Reporting in Canada—1995* (Toronto: CICA, 1995), indicated that in 1994, 284 of the 300 companies surveyed used the term "balance sheet." The term "statement of financial position" is used infrequently (15 companies), although it is conceptually appealing. One company used the term "statement of condition."

[2] Risk is an expression of the unpredictability of future events, transactions, circumstances, and results of the enterprise.

Liquidity describes "the amount of time that is expected to elapse until an asset is realized or otherwise converted into cash or until a liability has to be paid."[3] Both short-term and long-term credit grantors are interested in such short-term ratios as cash or near cash to current liabilities. Such ratios measure the enterprise's ability to meet current and maturing obligations. Similarly, present and prospective equity holders study liquidity to gauge future cash dividends or the possibility of expanded operations. Generally, the greater the liquidity, the lower the risk of enterprise failure.

Financial flexibility is the "ability of an enterprise to take effective actions to alter the amounts and timing of cash flows so it can respond to unexpected needs and opportunities."[4] For example, a company may become so loaded with debt—so financially inflexible—that its sources of cash to finance expansion or to pay off maturing debt are limited or nonexistent. An enterprise with a high degree of financial flexibility is better able to survive bad times, to recover from unexpected setbacks, and to take advantage of profitable and unexpected investment opportunities. Generally, the greater the financial flexibility, the lower the risk of enterprise failure.

LIMITATIONS OF THE BALANCE SHEET

As indicated in earlier chapters, accountants value and report most assets and liabilities using an historical cost basis. Thus, the balance sheet **does not reflect the current value** of many items. When a balance sheet is prepared in accordance with generally accepted accounting principles, most assets are stated at cost; exceptions are receivables at net realizable value, marketable securities at lower of cost and market, and some long-term investments accounted for under the equity method.

Many accountants believe that all the assets should be restated in terms of current values. There are, however, widely differing opinions regarding which valuation basis to use. Some contend that **historical cost statements** should be adjusted for constant dollars (general price-level changes) when inflation is significant; others believe that a **current cost concept** (specific price-level changes) is more useful; still others believe that a **net realizable value** concept or some variant should be adopted. Although each method differs significantly from the historical cost approach, all share a common advantage over the historical cost basis of valuation: Each presents a more accurate assessment of the current value of the enterprise. The question of whether reliable valuations can ever truly be obtained, however, remains unresolved.

Another basic limitation of the balance sheet is that **judgements and estimates must be used**. The collectibility of receivables, the saleability of inventory, and the useful life of long-term tangible and intangible assets are difficult to determine. Although the process of depreciating long-term assets is a generally accepted practice, the recognition of an increase in asset value is generally ignored by accountants.

Because judgements and estimates used in the preparation of the balance sheet may harm or benefit particular stakeholders, ethical sensibility should come into play in the accountant's decision-making process. The accountant needs to be aware of the potential impact of these judgements and estimates on potentially conflicting stakeholder interests (i.e., the company vs. the shareholders). In addition, when there is a measurement uncertainty that is material, its nature and extent should be disclosed.[5]

Balance sheets (and other financial statements) report data that has been aggregated into a few conventional account titles. For example, BCE Inc., which had over $38 billion in diverse assets, liabilities, and equities, reported them all by using only 22 accounts in their

---

[3] Reporting Income, Cash Flows, and Financial Position of Business Enterprises," *Proposed Statement of Financial Accounting Concepts* (Stamford, Conn.: FASB, 1981), par. 29.

[4] *Ibid.*, par. 25.

[5] *CICA Handbook* (Toronto: CICA), Section 1508.

published balance sheet. Consequently, when it is necessary to provide additional information about a line item (account), explanatory notes are used. The examples and illustrations in this book show the financial statement line item and any accompanying note(s).

In addition, the balance sheet necessarily **omits many items that are of financial value to the business** but cannot be measured objectively. The value of a company's human resources (employee workforce) is certainly significant, but is omitted because such assets are difficult to quantify. Other items of value not reported are customer base, managerial skills, research superiority, and reputation. Such omissions are understandable. But many items that could and should appear on the balance sheet (most are liabilities) are reported in an "off-balance sheet" manner, if they are reported at all.[6] Several of these omitted items (such as sales of receivables with recourse, leases, through-put arrangements, and take-or-pay contracts) are discussed in later chapters.

One of the most significant challenges facing the accounting profession is the limitation of financial statements. Financial statement users are turning increasingly to other sources to meet needs that have not been met by the information contained on current GAAP model statements. The accounting profession has been attempting to identify the informational needs of financial statement users and find ways of meeting those needs.[7]

CLASSIFICATION IN THE BALANCE SHEET

Balance sheet accounts are **classified**, which means that similar items are grouped together to create significant category subtotals. Furthermore, the material is arranged so that important relationships are highlighted.

OBJECTIVE 2
Identify the major classifications on the balance sheet.

The accounting profession has often noted that the parts and subsections of financial statements can be more informative than the whole. Therefore, as one would expect, the reporting of summary accounts (total assets, net assets, total liabilities, etc.) alone is discouraged. Individual items should be separately reported and classified in sufficient detail to permit users to assess the amounts, timing, and uncertainty of future cash flows, as well as the evaluation of liquidity and financial flexibility, profitability, and risk.

Classification in financial statements helps analysts because it groups items with similar characteristics and separates items with different characteristics:

1. Assets that differ in their **type or expected function** in the central operations or other activities of the enterprise should be reported as separate items; for example, merchandise inventories should be reported separately from property, plant, and equipment.

2. Assets and liabilities with **different implications for the financial flexibility** of the enterprise should be reported as separate items; for example, assets used in the operations should be reported separately from assets held for investment, or assets subject to restrictions such as leased equipment.

3. Assets and liabilities with **different general liquidity characteristics** should be reported as separate items; for example, cash should be reported separately from inventories.

The three general classes of items included in the balance sheet are assets, liabilities, and owners' equity. Their definitions as they appear in the *CICA Handbook*[8] are shown on the following page.

---

[6] For a discussion of various methods that businesses have devised to remove debt from the balance sheet, read Richard Dieter and Arthur R. Wyatt, "Get It Off the Balance Sheet," *Financial Executive*, Vol. 48, June, 1980, pp. 42, 44–48.

[7] Thomas W. Rimerman, "The Changing Significance of Financial Statements," *Journal of Accountancy*, April, 1990, pp. 79–83.

[8] *CICA Handbook*, Section 1000.

ELEMENTS OF THE BALANCE SHEET

1. **Assets** are resources controlled by an enterprise as a result of past transactions or events from which future economic benefits may be obtained.

2. **Liabilities** are obligations of an enterprise arising from past transactions or events, the settlement of which may result in the transfer of assets, provision of services, or other yielding of economic benefits in the future.

3. **Equity** is the ownership interest in the assets of an entity after deducting its liabilities.

These items are then divided into subclassifications to provide readers with additional information. The following table indicates the general format of balance sheet presentation.

BALANCE SHEET CLASSIFICATIONS

Assets	Liabilities and Shareholders' Equity
Current assets	Current liabilities
Long-term investments	Long-term debt
Property, plant, and equipment	Shareholders' equity
Intangible assets[9]	Share capital
Other assets	Contributed surplus
	Retained earnings

The balance sheet may be classified in some other manner, but these are the major subdivisions, and there is very little departure from them in practice. If a proprietorship or partnership is involved, the classifications within the Shareholders' Equity section are presented differently.

CURRENT ASSETS

Current assets are **cash and other assets that are expected to be converted into cash, sold, or consumed within either one year or one operating cycle, whichever is longer**. The operating cycle is the average time between the acquisition of materials and supplies and the realization of cash through sales of the product for which the materials and supplies were acquired. The cycle operates from cash through inventory, production, and receivables, and back to cash. When there are several operating cycles within one year, the one-year period is used. If the operating cycle is more than one year, the longer period is used.

Current assets are presented in the balance sheet in the order of their liquidity. The five major items found in the Current Assets section are cash, temporary investments in marketable securities, receivables, inventories, and prepayments. **Cash** is included at its stated value; **temporary investments in marketable securities** are valued at cost or the lower of cost and market; **accounts receivable** are stated at the estimated amount collectible; **inventories** generally are included at cost or the lower of cost and market; and **prepaid items** are valued at cost.

The above items are not considered current assets if they are not expected to be realized within one year or one operating cycle, whichever is longer. For example, cash restricted for purposes other than payment of current obligations or for use in current operations is excluded from the current asset section. **Generally, the rule is that if an asset is to be turned into cash or is to be used to pay a current liability within one year or one operating cycle, whichever is longer, it is classified as current**. This requirement is subject to exceptions. An investment in common shares is classified as either a current asset or a noncurrent asset depending on management's intent. When a company has

---

[9] Property, plant, and equipment and intangibles are sometimes combined under a single heading, "capital assets."

small holdings of common shares or bonds that are going to be held long-term, they should not be classified as current.

Although a current asset is well defined, certain theoretical problems develop. One problem is justifying the inclusion of prepaid expense in the Current Asset section. The normal justification is that if these items had not been paid in advance, they would require the use of current assets during the operating cycle. If we follow this logic to its ultimate conclusion, however, any asset purchased previously saves the use of current assets during the operating cycle and is considered current.

Another problem occurs in the current asset definition when fixed assets are consumed during the operating cycle. A literal interpretation of the accounting profession's position on this matter would indicate that an amount equal to the current amortization and depreciation charges on the noncurrent assets should be placed in the Current Asset section at the beginning of the year, because it will be consumed in the next operating cycle. This conceptual problem is generally ignored, which illustrates that the formal distinction made between current and noncurrent assets is somewhat arbitrary.[10]

Cash. Any restrictions on the general availability of cash or any commitments on its probable disposition must be disclosed. This may be done through notes or in the body of the balance sheet as exemplified below.

Current assets		
Cash		
Restricted in accordance with terms of the purchase contract	$48,500	
Unrestricted—available for current use	14,928	$63,428

In the above example, cash was restricted to meet an obligation due currently and, therefore, the restricted cash was included under current assets. If cash is restricted for purposes other than current obligations, it is excluded from the current assets, as shown below.

Current assets		
Cash	$78,327	
Less cash restricted for bond redemption	45,000	$33,327
Long-term investments		
Cash restricted for bond redemption in accordance with the bond indenture		$45,000

Temporary Investments. The basis of valuation and any differences between cost and current market value should be included in the balance sheet presentation of temporary investments. The generally accepted method for accounting for such investments, often referred to as "short-term investments" or as "marketable securities," is cost or market, whichever is lower.[11] The example below is excerpted from an annual report of Inco Limited.

Current assets	
Marketable securities—at cost (market $23,100,000)	$19,796,000

---

[10] For an interesting discussion of the shortcomings of the current and noncurrent classifications framework, see Lloyd Heath, "Financial Reporting and the Evaluation of Solvency," *Accounting Research Monograph No. 3* (New York: AICPA, 1978), pp. 43–69. The recommendation is for the current and noncurrent classifications to be abolished and for liabilities to be simply listed, without classification, in their present order. This approach is justified on the basis that any classification scheme is arbitrary and that users of the financial statements can assemble the data in the manner they believe most appropriate.

[11] Special rules that apply for both short-term and long-term marketable securities are discussed in Chapter 18.

Receivables. The amount and nature of any nontrade receivables, and any amounts pledged or discounted, should be clearly stated. In addition, the anticipated loss due to uncollectibles may be disclosed separately rather than by reporting a net figure for receivables less the related allowance. Mark's Work Wearhouse reported receivables of $10,828,000 under the heading "current assets" on their balance sheet and a breakdown of this amount in an accompanying note as follows:[12]

EXHIBIT 5-1   MARK'S WORK WEARHOUSE LTD.

NOTES TO CONSOLIDATED FINANCIAL STATEMENTS

3. ACCOUNTS RECEIVABLE

	1994	1995	1996
Receivable from franchise stores	$ 12,047	$ 8,127	$ 7,648
Trade accounts receivable	3,739	5,095	5,388
Current portion of notes receivable	—	300	100
	15,786	13,522	13,136
Allowance for doubtful accounts	(2,855)	(1,732)	(2,308)
	$ 12,931	$ 11,790	$ 10,828

Inventories. For a proper presentation of inventories, the basis of valuation (i.e., lower of cost and market), the method of pricing (FIFO or average cost), and, for a manufacturing concern like Repap Enterprises Inc., shown below, the stage of completion of the inventories are disclosed.

EXHIBIT 5-2   REPAP ENTERPRISES INC.

ASSETS

Current:			
Cash and short-term deposits		$ 37.5	$ 27.2
Accounts receivable	7	218.1	218.6
Inventories	4,7	333.3	194.5

Note 3   Significant Accounting Policies
(c) Inventories
Logs, chips and supplies are valued at the lower of cost, determined primarily on a weighted average basis, and replacement cost. Paper, pulp and lumber are valued at the lower of cost, determined on a weighted average basis, and net realizable value.

Note 4   Inventories

DECEMBER 31	1995	1994
Raw materials and supplies	$ 199.4	$ 122.8
Work in process	15.4	5.3
Finished goods	118.5	66.4
	$ 333.3	$ 194.5

Some accountants contend that, in a company that assembles a final product from both purchased and manufactured parts and also sells some of these parts, a distinction of finished

---

[12] To view a complete set of financial statements, please refer to Moore Corporation Limited's annual report reproduced in Appendix 5A.

goods, work in progress, and raw materials is arbitrary and misleading. They prefer a classification that indicates the source or nature of the inventory amount as shown below.

Current assets		
Inventories—at the lower of cost (determined		
by the first-in, first-out method) and market		
Materials	$195,696	
Direct labour	37,300	
Manufacturing overhead	15,274	$248,270

Prepaid Expenses. Prepaid expenses included in current assets are expenditures already made for benefits (usually services) to be received within one year or one operating cycle, whichever is longer.[13] These items are current assets because if they had not already been paid, they would require the use of cash during the next year or operating cycle. A common example is the payment in advance for an insurance policy, which is classified as a prepaid expense at the time of the expenditure because the payment precedes the receipt of the benefit of coverage. Prepaid expenses are reported at the amount of the unexpired or unconsumed cost. Other common prepaid expenses include prepaid rent, advertising, taxes, and office or operating supplies. Imperial Oil Limited, for example, listed its prepaid expenses in current assets as follows.

EXHIBIT 5-3   IMPERIAL OIL LIMITED

CONSOLIDATED BALANCE SHEET

millions of dollars At December 31	1995	1994	1993	1992	1991
Assets					
Current assets					
Cash	273	409	605	265	286
Marketable securities at amortized cost (3)	378	859	874	757	7
Promissory notes of an Exxon Corporation subsidiary (13)	1 191	–	–	–	–
Accounts receivable	1 006	1 045	954	1 065	1 095
Inventories of crude oil and products (14)	385	384	402	468	604
Materials, supplies and prepaid expenses	90	100	129	140	178
Total current assets	3 323	2 797	2 964	2 695	2 170

Companies often include insurance and other prepayments for two or three years in current assets even though part of the advance payment applies to periods beyond one year or the current operating cycle.

LONG-TERM INVESTMENTS

Long-term investments, often referred to simply as investments, normally consist of one of four types:

1. Investments in securities such as bonds, common shares, or long-term notes.

2. Investments in tangible fixed assets not currently used in operations, such as land held for speculation.

---

[13] *Financial Reporting in Canada—1995* (Toronto: CICA, 1995) indicated that 224 of the 300 companies in 1994 reported prepaid expenses or prepayments on the balance sheet.

3. Investments set aside in special funds such as a sinking fund, pension fund, or plant expansion fund. The cash surrender value of life insurance is included here.

4. Investments in nonconsolidated subsidiaries or affiliated companies.

Long-term investments are to be held for many years and are not acquired with the intention of disposing of them in the near future. They are usually presented on the balance sheet just below Current Assets in a separate section called Investments. Many securities that are properly shown among the long-term investments, are, in fact, readily marketable. But they are not included as current assets unless the intent is to convert them to cash in the short-term—within one year or one operating cycle, whichever is longer.[14]

Ipsco Inc. reported long-term securities of $152,454,000 on the balance sheet and provided additional information about this account in note 5 as follows.

EXHIBIT 5-4   IPSCO INC.

5. Long-Term Securities

At 31 December, the following is an analysis of long-term securities:

| 1995 | MATURITY | | GROSS UNREALIZED | | |
	LESS THAN 1 YEAR	1 TO 5 YEARS	GAINS	LOSSES	FAIR VALUE
Corporate bonds	$ 80,392	$ -	$ 67	$ 215	$ 80,244
Commercial paper	39,658	-	39	98	39,599
Term deposits	32,404	-	-	-	32,404
Total	$152,454	$ -	$106	$ 313	$152,247

| 1994 | MATURITY | | GROSS UNREALIZED | | |
	LESS THAN 1 YEAR	1 TO 5 YEARS	GAINS	LOSSES	FAIR VALUE
Corporate bonds	$187,622	$78,364	$ -	$3,301	$262,685
Government bonds	11,972	-	-	37	11,935
Commercial paper	96,264	-	759	-	97,023
Bankers' acceptances	10,419	-	85	-	10,504
Other	6,004	-	-	-	6,004
Total	$312,281	$78,364	$844	$3,338	$388,151

PROPERTY, PLANT, AND EQUIPMENT (FIXED ASSETS)

Property, plant, and equipment (tangible capital assets)[15] are properties of a durable nature used in the regular operations of the business. These assets consist of physical property such as land, buildings, machinery, furniture, tools, and wasting resources (timberland, minerals). With the exception of land, most assets are either depreciable[16] (such as buildings) or consumable (such as timberlands).

MacMillan Bloedel Limited presented its property, plant, and equipment in a recent balance sheet as follows.

---

[14] A discussion of issues related to accounting for long-term investments is presented in Chapter 10.

[15] *CICA Handbook*, Section 3060, issued in 1990 defines capital assets as property, plant, and equipment and intangible properties that meet the specified criteria. Most Canadian companies have continued to use "property, plant, and equipment" as a separate balance sheet account title.

[16] *CICA Handbook*, Section 3060, issued in 1990, used the term "amortization" to refer to both "depreciation" and "depletion." The use of the latter terms is permitted and, in fact, used by a majority of Canadian public companies. In this text, amortization, although not used extensively, is considered to be a synonym for either depreciation or depletion.

EXHIBIT 5-5 MACMILLAN BLOEDEL LIMITED

PROPERTY, PLANT, AND EQUIPMENT: (NOTE 4)

Buildings and equipment	$3,068,600,000
Less: Accumulated depreciation	1,383,200,000
	1,685,400,000
Construction in progress	41,800,000
	1,727,200,000
Timber and land less accumulated depletion	203,200,000
Logging roads	12,900,000
	$1,943,300,000

The basis of valuing the property, plant, and equipment; any liens against the properties; and accumulated depreciation should be disclosed—usually in notes to the statements.

INTANGIBLE ASSETS

Intangible assets lack physical substance and usually have a high degree of uncertainty concerning their future benefits. They include patents, copyrights, franchises, goodwill, trademarks, trade names, secret processes, and organization costs. Generally, all of these intangibles are written off (amortized) to expense over 5 to 40 years. Intangibles can represent significant economic resources, yet financial analysts often ignore them, and accountants write them down or off arbitrarily when future benefits become uncertain and because valuation is difficult.

Maclean Hunter Limited reported intangible assets in its balance sheet and notes as follows.

EXHIBIT 5-6 MACLEAN HUNTER LIMITED

Intangible assets (Note 8)	$377,200,000
Goodwill	295,200,000

NOTE 8. INTANGIBLE ASSETS

	Cost	Accumulated depreciation	Net
Cable television franchises	$312,600,000	$13,500,000	$299,100,000
Broadcast licences	43,700,000	7,000,000	36,700,000
Circulation and subscriber bases	43,900,000	15,500,000	28,400,000
Paging frequencies	7,300,000	600,000	6,700,000
Others	12,800,000	6,500,000	6,300,000
Total	$420,300,000	$43,100,000	$377,200,000

OTHER ASSETS

The items included in the section "Other Assets" vary widely in practice. Some of the items commonly included are deferred charges (long-term prepaid expenses), noncurrent receivables, intangible assets, assets in special funds, and advances to subsidiaries. Such a section unfortunately is too general a classification. Instead, it should be restricted to unusual items sufficiently different from assets included in specific categories. Some deferred costs such as organization costs incurred during the early life of the business are commonly classified here. Even these costs, however, are more properly placed in the intangible asset section.

CURRENT LIABILITIES

Current liabilities are the obligations that are reasonably expected to be liquidated either through the use of current assets or the creation of other current liabilities. This concept includes:

1. Payables resulting from the acquisition of goods and services, such as accounts payable, wages payable, and taxes payable.

2. Collections received in advance for the delivery of goods or performance of services, such as unearned rent revenue or unearned subscriptions revenue.

3. Other liabilities whose liquidation will take place within the operating cycle, such as the portion of long-term bonds to be paid in the current period or short-term obligations arising from purchase of equipment.

At times, a liability payable next year is not included in the Current Liability section. This occurs either when the debt is expected to be refinanced through another long-term issue,[17] or when the debt is retired out of noncurrent assets. This approach is used because liquidation does not result from the use of current assets or the creation of other current liabilities.

Current liabilities are not reported in any consistent order. The items most commonly listed first are notes payable, accounts payable, or "short-term debt"; income taxes payable, current maturities of long-term debt, or "other current liabilities" are commonly listed last. An example of the presentation of the current liability section excerpted from Loblaw's 1995 annual report is shown below.

EXHIBIT 5-7   LOBLAW COMPANIES LIMITED

CONSOLIDATED BALANCE SHEET
as at December 30, 1995

Liabilities			
Current Liabilities			
Bank advances and notes payable	$ **310.7**	$ 95.2	
Accounts payable and accrued liabilities	**936.7**	1,016.3	$ 931.0
Taxes payable	**42.4**	15.9	
Long term debt and debt equivalents due within one year (note 7)	**22.1**	57.3	38.2
	1,311.9	1,184.7	969.2

Current liabilities include such items as trade and nontrade notes and accounts payable, advances received from customers, and current maturities of long-term debt. Income taxes and other accrued items are usually classified separately, if material. Any secured liability—such as investments in shares held as collateral on notes payable—is fully described so that the assets providing the security can be determined.

The excess of total current assets over total current liabilities is referred to as **working capital** (sometimes called net working capital). Working capital represents the net amount of a company's relatively liquid resources. That is, it is the liquid buffer available to meet the financial demands of the operating cycle. Working capital as an amount is seldom disclosed on the balance sheet, but it is computed by bankers and other creditors as an indicator of the short-run liquidity of a company. In order to determine the actual liquidity and availability of working capital to meet current obligations, one must analyse

---

[17] A detailed discussion of accounting for debt expected to be refinanced is found in Chapter 14.

the composition of the current assets and their nearness to cash. The ratio of current assets to current liabilities (current ratio) is frequently used when analysing working capital. This topic is discussed in Chapter 24.

LONG-TERM LIABILITIES

Long-term liabilities are obligations that are not reasonably expected to be liquidated within the normal operating cycle of the business but, instead, are payable at some date beyond that time. Bonds payable, notes payable, deferred income taxes, lease obligations, and pension obligations are the most common examples. Generally, a great deal of supplementary disclosure is needed for this section because most long-term debt is subject to various covenants and restrictions for the protection of the lenders. Long-term liabilities that mature within the current operating cycle are classified as current liabilities if their liquidation requires the use of current assets.

Generally, long-term liabilities are of three types:

1. Obligations arising from specific financing situations, such as the issuance of bonds, long-term lease obligations, and long-term notes payable.

2. Obligations arising from the ordinary operations of the enterprise, such as pension obligations and deferred income taxes.

3. Obligations that are dependent upon the occurrence or nonoccurrence of one or more future events to confirm the amount payable, or the payee, or the date payable, such as service or product warranties.

The terms of all long-term liability agreements including maturity date(s), rates of interest, nature of obligation, and any security pledged to support the debt should be described in notes to the financial statements. As an example, The Oshawa Group Limited reported long-term debt of $121,100,000 on their balance sheet and provided the following explanatory information in note 4.

EXHIBIT 5-8	THE OSHAWA GROUP LIMITED

NOTES TO CONSOLIDATED FINANCIAL STATEMENTS

4. Long-Term Debt

	1996	1995
Series "A" Debentures	$ 100.0	$ 100.0
Mortgages and loans payable	23.4	23.9
	123.4	123.9
Less current portion	2.3	0.4
	$ 121.1	$ 123.5

The unsecured Series "A" debentures due June 30, 2003

bear interest at a rate of 8.25% per annum and are redeemable

in whole or in part, at any time, at the greater of par and

a formula price based upon yields at the time of redemption.

The mortgages and loans payable bear interest at an average

rate of 7.7% per annum with repayments of less than $1.0 in

each of the four years commencing in 1998.

SHAREHOLDERS' EQUITY

The **shareholders' equity** section is one of the most difficult sections to prepare and understand. This is due to the complexity of share capital agreements and the various restrictions on residual equity imposed by federal and provincial corporation laws, liability agreements, and boards of directors. The section is usually divided into three parts:

SHAREHOLDERS' EQUITY SECTION

1. **Share Capital.** Proceeds received from the issue of shares.
2. **Contributed Surplus.** Miscellaneous shareholder equity items.
3. **Retained Earnings.** The corporation's undistributed earnings.

The legal basis for examples and problems presented in this book is the Canada Business Corporations Act (CBCA), which came into force on January 1, 1976. Companies may incorporate under the provincial corporation acts, which may vary to some extent from the federal act, although differences are becoming less significant as provinces revise their acts. For example, prior to CBCA, federally incorporated companies could have par value shares. Under CBCA, the concept of par value was abolished, which meant that the entire proceeds from the sale of shares were to be credited to the appropriate share capital account. An amendment to the Ontario Business Corporations Act in 1983 included a similar provision, as do many provincial incorporation acts. The notion of par value, however, has not disappeared from the Canadian accounting scene.[18] Because of this, a limited number of examples as well as cases, exercises, and problems in this book will reflect the existence of par value shares.[19] CBCA also states that corporations are to issue shares by "classes" and "series of classes." The terms "preferred" and "common" may continue to be used and, as such, will be used throughout this book.

The major disclosure requirements for share capital are the authorized, issued, and outstanding number of shares. The contributed surplus is usually presented in one amount; breakdowns are informative, however, if the sources of additional capital obtained are varied and material. The Retained Earnings section may be divided between the unappropriated amount, which is available for dividend declaration, and any amounts legally or voluntarily restricted, called appropriated retained earnings.

The ownership or shareholders' equity accounts in a corporation are considerably different from those in a partnership or proprietorship. Partners' permanent capital accounts and the balance in temporary accounts or drawing accounts are shown separately. Proprietorships ordinarily use a single capital account that summarizes all of the owner's equity transactions.

The Shareholders' Equity section of Transwest Energy Inc.'s 1995 balance sheet follows as an illustration. Note 4 (not reproduced) provides details of the number of shares authorized and issued as well as changes that occurred during the 1995 fiscal period.

---

[18] *Financial Reporting in Canada-1995* (Toronto: CICA, 1995) indicated that in 1994 one of the Canadian companies surveyed still carried a "Premium on shares" amount in its Contributed Surplus. Of the 300 companies surveyed, 39 made reference to a par value or stated value in general or as existing for at least one class of their shares. Also, the CBCA permits a restricted use of the notion of par value for reasons having to do with some particular tax issues. Par value shares are allowed under incorporation statutes of British Columbia, Newfoundland, Nova Scotia, Prince Edward Island, Quebec, and the Northwest Territories.

[19] Most of the examples, cases, exercises, and problems occur in later chapters, particularly in Chapters 16 and 17, where the issue is discussed in greater depth. Some instructors may choose to deal only with no par value shares. If so, one approach would be to simply assume that all proceeds from the sale of stock are to be credited to the appropriate stock account, even when a par value is given (i.e., there would be no Premium accounts in Contributed Surplus).

EXHIBIT 5-9   TRANSWEST ENERGY INC.

CONSOLIDATED BALANCE SHEETS

| | As at December 31 | |
	1995	1994
	(thousands)	
Shareholders' Equity		
Capital stock (note 4)		
Preferred shares	**13,605**	14,185
Common shares	**50,900**	47,430
Retained earnings	**4,670**	6,245
	69,175	67,860
	$ **134,450**	$ 130,240
Commitments and contingencies (note 7)		

CLASSIFIED BALANCE SHEET

One common arrangement followed in the presentation of a classified balance sheet is called the **account form**. It lists assets by sections on the left side and liabilities and shareholders' equity by sections on the right side. The main disadvantage is the need for two facing pages. To avoid the use of facing pages, the **report form**, illustrated below, lists liabilities and shareholders' equity directly after assets on the same page. (Also see Moore Corporation's balance sheet on page 219).

Other balance sheet presentations are used infrequently. For example, current liabilities are sometimes deducted from current assets to arrive at working capital, or all liabilities deducted from all assets. This format is referred to as the **financial position form**.

OBJECTIVE 3
Prepare a classified balance sheet using the report and account forms.

SCIENTIFIC PRODUCTS, INC.
Balance Sheet
December 31, 1998

Assets

Current assets		
Cash		$ 42,485
Marketable securities—cost that approximates market value		28,250
Accounts receivable	$165,824	
Less: Allowance for doubtful accounts	1,850	163,974
Notes receivable		23,000
Inventories—at average cost		489,713
Supplies on hand		9,780
Prepaid expenses		16,252
Total current assets		$ 773,454
Long-term investments		
Securities at cost (market value $94,000)		87,500
Property, plant, and equipment		
Land—at cost		$125,000
Buildings—at cost	$975,800	
Less: Accumulated depreciation	341,200	634,600
Property, plant, and equipment		759,600
Intangible assets		
Goodwill		100,000
Total assets		$1,720,554

(Continued)

SCIENTIFIC PRODUCTS, INC.
Balance Sheet (*Continued*)

Liabilities and Shareholders' Equity

Current liabilities

Notes payable to banks	$ 50,000	
Accounts payable	197,532	
Accrued interest on notes payable	500	
Accrued federal income taxes	62,520	
Accrued salaries, wages, and other expenses	9,500	
Deposits received from customers	420	
Total current liabilities		$ 320,472

Long-term debt

12% debentures, due January 1, 2005		500,000
Total liabilities		$ 820,472

Shareholders' equity

Share capital			
Preferred, $7 cumulative			
Authorized and outstanding,			
30,000 shares	$300,000		
Common			
Authorized, 500,000 shares,			
without par value,			
issued and outstanding,			
400,000 shares	400,000	$700,000	
Contributed surplus		37,500	
Earnings retained in the business			
Appropriated	$ 85,000		
Unappropriated	77,582	162,582	
Total shareholders' equity			900,082
Total liabilities and shareholders' equity			$1,720,554

REPORTING ADDITIONAL INFORMATION

The balance sheet is not complete simply because the assets, liabilities, and owners' equity accounts have been listed. Great importance is given to supplemental information. It may be information not presented elsewhere in the statement, or it may be an elaboration or qualification of items in the balance sheet. There are normally four types of information that are supplemental to account titles and amounts presented in the balance sheet.

OBJECTIVE 4
Identify balance sheet information requiring supplemental disclosure.

SUPPLEMENTAL BALANCE SHEET INFORMATION

1. **Contingencies.** Material events that have an uncertain outcome.

2. **Valuation and accounting policies.** Explanations of the valuation methods used or the basic assumptions made concerning inventory valuations, depreciation methods, investments in subsidiaries, and so on.

3. **Contractual situations.** Explanations of certain restrictions or covenants attached either to specific assets or, more likely, to liabilities.

4. **Post-balance sheet disclosures.** Disclosures of certain events that have occurred after the balance sheet date but before the financial statements have been issued.

CONTINGENCIES

Gain contingencies are claims or rights to receive assets (or have a liability reduced) when existence is uncertain but that may become valid eventually. Typical gain contingencies are:

1. Possible receipts of monies from gifts, donations, bonuses, and so on.

2. Possible refunds from the government in tax disputes.

3. Pending court cases where the probable outcome is favourable.

Accountants have adopted a conservative policy in this area. Gain contingencies are not recorded. They are disclosed in notes to the financial statements only when it is likely (i.e., highly probable) that a gain contingency will become reality. As a result, it is unusual to find information of this type in the financial statements and accompanying notes.

Loss contingencies are possible losses that may result when an existing condition or situation involving an uncertainty is resolved. **The** *CICA Handbook* **requires that an estimated loss from loss contingencies be accrued by a charge to expense and the recording of a liability**[20] when both of the following conditions are met:

1. It is **likely** that future events will confirm that an asset had been impaired or a liability incurred at the date of the financial statements.

2. The amount of loss can be **reasonably estimated**.

As indicated earlier, the establishment of a liability for service or product warranties would ordinarily meet the two conditions mentioned above and thus qualify as a loss contingency that should be accrued.

In most loss contingency cases, however, one or both of the conditions are not present. For example, assume that a company is involved in a lawsuit. The company's lawyer indicates that there is a reasonable possibility that they may lose. In such a case, there is only a **reasonable possibility** of loss rather than a **likely** one and, therefore, a liability and the related loss should not be recorded. The nature of the contingency and, where possible, the amount involved, however, should be disclosed in the notes. If a reasonable estimate of the amount is not possible, disclosure is made in general terms, describing the loss contingency and explaining that no estimated amount is determinable. Because these types of contingencies are only possibilities, they should not enter into the determination of net income.

There is diversity in accounting practice regarding contingencies because varied interpretations are made of the words "likely" and "unlikely." As a result, the contingencies reported and disclosed vary somewhat. This area of practice requires that the accountant use professional judgement because the determination of what constitutes full and proper accounting and disclosure is very subjective.[21]

Some of the more common sources of **loss contingencies that ordinarily will not be accrued as liabilities are**:

1. Guarantees of other people's indebtedness.

2. Obligations of commercial banks under "standby letters of credit" (commitments to finance projects under certain circumstances).

3. Guarantees to repurchase receivables (or any related property) that have been sold or assigned.

4. Disputes over additional income taxes for prior years.

5. Pending lawsuits whose outcome is uncertain.

---

[20] *CICA Handbook*, Section 3290.

[21] G. Richard Chaley and Heather A. Wier, "The Challenge of Contingencies; Adding Precision to Probability," *CA Magazine*, April, 1985, pp. 38–41. The diversity of interpretation of the words "likely," unlikely," "not reasonably estimable," and "possible" among accountants and lawyers is well identified in this article. A solution to improve understanding by assigning a range of probabilities is suggested.

General risk contingencies that are inherent in business operations, such as the possibility of war, strike, uninsurable catastrophes, or a business recession, are not reported in the notes to the financial statements. The disclosure of loss contingencies is discussed in greater detail in Chapter 14.

VALUATIONS AND ACCOUNTING POLICIES

As subsequent chapters of this book indicate, accountants employ many different methods and bases in valuing assets and allocating costs. For instance, inventories can be computed under several cost flow assumptions (LIFO, average cost, FIFO); plant and equipment can be depreciated under several accepted methods of cost allocation (double-declining balance, straight line); and investments can be carried at different valuations (cost, equity, market). Sophisticated users of financial statements know of these possibilities and examine the statements closely to determine the methods used.

The *CICA Handbook* requires disclosure in the financial statements of all significant accounting policies and methods chosen from among alternatives and/or those that are peculiar to a given industry.[22] Disclosure is particularly useful if given under a separate heading, **Summary of Significant Accounting Policies**, which is cross-referenced to the financial statement or as the initial note. See Appendix 5A for an example of such a summary. Further discussion of this topic is presented in Chapter 25.

CONTRACTS AND NEGOTIATIONS

In addition to contingencies and different methods of valuation disclosed as supplementary data to the financial statements, any contracts and negotiations of significance should be disclosed in the notes to the financial statements.

It is mandatory, for example, that the essential provisions of lease contracts, pension obligations, and stock option plans be clearly stated in the notes. The analyst who examines a set of financial statements wants to know not only the amount of the liabilities, but also how the different contractual provisions of these debt obligations affect the company at present and in the future.

Many other items may have an important and significant effect on the enterprise, and this information should be disclosed. The accountant must exercise considerable judgement about whether omission of such information is misleading. "When in doubt, disclose" is an axiom to follow; it is better to disclose a little too much information than not enough.

The accountant's judgement should reflect ethical considerations because the manner of disclosing the accounting principles, methods, and other items that have important and significant effects on the enterprise may subtly represent the interests of one stakeholder at the expense of others. A reader, for example, may benefit from information that is highlighted in comprehensive notes, while the company that does not wish to emphasize certain information may choose to provide limited, rather than comprehensive, note information.

POST-BALANCE SHEET EVENTS (SUBSEQUENT EVENTS)

A period of several weeks, and sometimes months, may elapse after the end of the year before the financial statements are issued. This time is used to take and price inventory, reconcile subsidiary ledgers with controlling accounts, prepare necessary adjusting entries, ensure that all transactions for the period have been entered, obtain an audit of the financial statements, and print the annual report. During the period between the bal-

---

[22] *CICA Handbook*, Section 1500.

ance sheet date and its distribution to shareholders and creditors, important transactions or other events may occur that materially affect the company's financial position or operating situation. These events are known as post-balance sheet events, or simply **subsequent events**. The following timeline illustrates the subsequent events period.

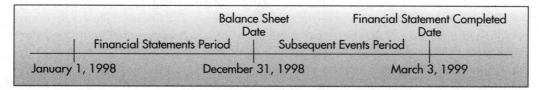

	Balance Sheet Date	Financial Statement Completed Date
Financial Statements Period	Subsequent Events Period	
January 1, 1998	December 31, 1998	March 3, 1999

Notes to the financial statements should explain any significant financial events that take place after the formal balance sheet date, but before its final issue.[23]

Many who read a balance sheet may believe the balance sheet condition is constant and project it into the future. However, readers must be told if the company has sold one of its plants, acquired a subsidiary, suffered extraordinary losses, settled significant litigation, or experienced any other important event in the post-balance sheet period. Without an explanation in a note, the reader might be misled and draw inappropriate conclusions.

Two types of events or transactions occurring after the balance sheet date may have a material effect on the financial statements, or may need to be considered to interpret these statements accurately.

1. **Events or transactions that provide additional evidence about conditions existing at the balance sheet date that affect the estimates used in preparing the financial statements, and, therefore, result in needed adjustments.** The accountant must use all of the information available prior to the issuance of the financial statements to evaluate estimates previously made. To ignore these subsequent events is to pass up an opportunity to improve the accuracy of the financial statements. This first type encompasses information that would have been recorded in the accounts had it been available at the balance sheet date, such as subsequent events that affect the realization of assets such as receivables and inventories, or the settlement of estimated liabilities. Such events typically represent the culmination of conditions that existed for some time.

2. **Events that provide evidence about conditions that did not exist at the balance sheet date but arise subsequent to that date and do not require adjustment of the financial statements.** Some of these events may have to be disclosed to keep the financial statements from being misleading. These disclosures take the form of notes, supplemental schedules or, possibly, even pro forma (as if) financial data that make it appear as if the event had occurred on the date of the balance sheet. Below are examples of such events that require disclosure (but do not result in adjustment):
   (a) a fire or flood that results in a loss;
   (b) decline in the market value of investments;
   (c) purchase of a business;
   (d) commencement of litigation where the cause of action arises subsequent to the date of the financial statements;
   (e) changes in foreign currency exchange rates;
   (f) issue of share capital or long-term debt.[24]

Identifying events that require financial statement adjustment or disclosure requires judgement and knowledge of the facts and circumstances. For example, if a loss on an uncollectible trade account receivable results from a customer's deteriorating financial

---

[23] *Ibid*, Section 3820. The date of completion is a matter of judgement and depends on the particular circumstances and reporting requirements.
[24] *Ibid*, Section 3820, par. .09.

condition, leading to bankruptcy subsequent to the balance sheet date, the financial statements are adjusted before their issuance because the bankruptcy stems from the customer's poor financial health existing at the balance sheet date. A similar loss resulting from a customer's fire or flood after the balance sheet date is not indicative of conditions existing at that date, however, and adjustment of the financial statements is not necessary.

The same criterion applies to settlements of litigation. The financial statements must be adjusted if the events that give rise to the litigation, such as personal injury or patent infringement, take place prior to the balance sheet date. If the events giving rise to the claim take place subsequent to the balance sheet date, disclosure is required, although no adjustment is necessary. Subsequent events such as changes in the quoted market prices of securities ordinarily do not result in adjustment to the financial statements because such changes typically reflect a concurrent evaluation of new conditions.

An example of subsequent events disclosure, excerpted from The Oshawa Group Limited's annual report, is presented below.

EXHIBIT 5-10 THE OSHAWA GROUP LIMITED

NOTES TO THE FINANCIAL STATEMENTS

12. Subsequent Event

On January 29, 1995, the Company sold, for net book value, the warehousing equipment and distribution assets of two Ontario distribution centres and entered into a long-term service agreement with Surelink, a subsidiary of Tibbett & Britten, PLC. The term of a previous agreement relating to two other Ontario distribution centres was extended to coincide with that of the January 29, 1995 agreement. During the term of the service agreement, costs are expected to be less than the Company would otherwise have incurred operating the distribution centres.

Many subsequent events or developments are not likely to require either adjustment of or disclosure in the financial statements. Typically, these are nonaccounting events or conditions that management normally communicates by other means. These events include legislation, product changes, management changes, strikes, unionization, marketing agreements, and loss of important customers.

TECHNIQUES OF DISCLOSURE

OBJECTIVE 5
Identify major disclosure techniques for the balance sheet.

The effect of various contingencies on financial condition, the methods of valuing assets, and the companies' contracts and agreements should be disclosed as completely and as intelligently as possible. Available methods to disclose pertinent information include parenthetical explanations, notes to the financial statements, cross-reference and contra items, and supporting schedules. Appendix 5A contains specimen financial statements that illustrate some of these methods.

PARENTHETICAL EXPLANATIONS

Additional information or description is often given by means of parenthetical explanations following the item. For example, investments in common shares may be presented on the balance sheet under Investments as shown below.

> Investments in Common Shares at cost (market value, $330,586)—$280,783

This device permits disclosure of additional pertinent balance sheet information that adds clarity and completeness. It has an advantage over a note because it brings the additional information into the body of the statement where it is less likely to be overlooked. Of course, lengthy parenthetical explanations might distract the reader from the balance sheet information, and therefore must be used with care.

NOTES

Notes are used if additional explanations or descriptions cannot be shown conveniently as parenthetical explanations. For example, inventory costing methods are reported in note form by Lafarge Canada Inc. as follows.

EXHIBIT 5-11 LAFARGE CANADA INC.

Note 1 – Summary of Accounting Policies

Inventories

Inventories consist mainly of cement, aggregates, concrete products, raw materials, supplies and repair parts and are carried at the lower of average cost or net realizable value.

Note 2 – Inventories

	December 31	
	1994	1993
Maintenance and operating supplies	$ **21,717**	$ 26,225
Raw materials and fuel	**41,072**	32,824
Work in process	**4,514**	9,160
Finished goods	**45,666**	46,409
	$ **112,969**	$ 114,618

Notes are commonly used to present other information, such as the existence and amount of any preferred dividends in arrears, the terms of or obligations imposed by purchase commitments, special financial arrangements, depreciation policies, any changes in the application of accounting policies, and the existence of contingencies. The following example illustrates the use of notes to disclose such information.

EXHIBIT 5-12 NORTHGATE EXPLORATION LIMITED

Note 13 Commitments and Contingencies

(a) Northgate has guaranteed obligations on behalf of associate Sonora Gold Corp. and has pledged approximately $13,300,000 in short-term deposits to secure the guarantee.

(b) The Corporation together with four of its senior officers has been named in a class action suit filed in the United States alleging violations of the Securities Exchange Act of 1934 relating to disclosure concerning the Colomac mine. The Corporation believes the action is not well founded and is being vigorously defended.

The notes must always present all essential facts as completely and succinctly as possible. Careless wording may mislead readers rather than help them. Notes should add to the total information in the financial statements, but should not raise unanswered questions or contradict other portions of the statements.

CROSS-REFERENCE AND CONTRA ITEMS

A direct relationship between an asset and a liability is cross-referenced on the balance sheet. For example, on December 31, 1998, the following may be shown among the current assets:

Cash on deposit with sinking fund trustee for redemption of bonds payable—see current liabilities	$800,000

Included among the current liabilities is the amount of bonds payable to be redeemed currently:

Bonds payable to be redeemed in 1999—see current assets	$2,300,000

This cross-reference points out that $2,300,000 of bonds payable are to be redeemed currently, for which only $800,000 in cash has been set aside. Therefore, the additional cash needed must come from unrestricted cash, from sales of investments, from profits, or from other source. The same information can be shown parenthetically, if this technique is preferred.

Another common procedure is to establish contra or adjunct accounts. A **contra account** on a balance sheet is an item that reduces either an asset, liability, or shareholders' equity account. Examples include Accumulated Depreciation and Discount on Bonds Payable. Contra accounts provide flexibility in presenting the financial information. With the use of the Accumulated Depreciation account, for example, a reader of the statement can see the original cost of the asset as well as the depreciation to date.

An **adjunct account**, on the other hand, increases either an asset, liability, or shareholders' equity account. An example is Premium on Bonds Payable, which, when added to the Bonds Payable account, provides a picture of the total liability of the enterprise.

SUPPORTING SCHEDULES

Often a separate schedule is needed to present more detailed information about certain assets, liabilities, or shareholders' equity because the balance sheet provides just a single summary item. For example, Emco Limited reported Property, Plant and Equipment of $134,385,000 ($124,799,000 for 1994) on their December 31, 1995 balance sheet. Details of these amounts were presented in Note 3 as shown below.

EXHIBIT 5-13   EMCO LIMITED

NOTES TO CONSOLIDATED FINANCIAL STATEMENTS

Years ended December 31, 1995 and 1994

3. **Property, plant and equipment:**

	1995	1994
	(000s)	
Buildings and roadways	$ 71,018	$ 63,031
Machinery and equipment	140,046	129,129
	211,064	192,160
Less accumulated depreciation	88,904	79,651
	122,160	112,509
Land	12,225	12,290
	$ 134,385	$ 124,799

TERMINOLOGY

The account titles in the general ledger do not necessarily represent the best terminology for balance sheet purposes. Account titles are often brief and include technical terms that are understood only by those keeping the records and by other accountants. But balance sheets are examined by many people who are not acquainted with the technical vocabulary of accounting. Thus, they should contain descriptions that will be generally understood and not subject to misinterpretation.

The accounting profession has recommended that the word **"reserve"** be used only to describe an appropriation of retained earnings. Previously, the term had been used in a variety of ways: to describe amounts deducted from assets (for example, contra accounts such as Accumulated Depreciation, and Allowance for Doubtful Accounts), and as part of the title of contingent or estimated liabilities. Because of the different meanings attached to this term, its usage in the balance sheet is sometimes misinterpreted. The use of "reserve" to describe only appropriated earnings has resulted in a better understanding of its significance when it appears in a balance sheet. However, the term "appropriated" appears more logical, and its use should be encouraged.

Although the word **surplus** may also be misunderstood, it frequently appears in the Shareholders' Equity section as part of the caption Contributed Surplus. The contributed surplus amount often arises from amounts contributed by shareholders in excess of the amount credited to Share Capital or other appropriate accounts. Examples are proceeds from donated shares, credits arising from redemption or conversion of shares, and so on. Thus, Contributed Surplus denotes amounts received by contributions from shareholders and sometimes others and is appropriately classified as part of Shareholders' Equity. On the other hand, any amounts arising from earnings should be included in Retained Earnings.

The profession's recommendations relating to changes in terminology have been directed primarily to the balance sheet presentation of shareholders' equity so that the words or phrases used for these unique accounts describe more accurately the nature of the amounts shown.

SECTION 2: STATEMENT OF CASH FLOWS

In Chapter 2, "assessing the amounts, timing, and uncertainty of cash flows" was presented as one of the three basic objectives of financial reporting. The balance sheet, income statement, and statement of retained earnings each present, to a limited extent and in a fragmented manner, information about the cash flows of an enterprise during a period. For instance, comparative balance sheets might show what new assets have been acquired or disposed of, and what liabilities have been incurred or liquidated. The income statement provides, in a limited manner, information about the resources, but not exactly cash, provided by operations. The statement of retained earnings provides information as to the amount of cash used to pay dividends. But none of these statements presents a detailed summary of all the cash inflows and outflows or the sources and uses of cash during the period. To fill this need, the Accounting Standards Committee of the CICA revised Section 1540 of the *Handbook* in 1985, entitled the Statement of Changes in Financial Position. An Exposure Draft issued in May 1996 proposes that the name be changed to the Statement of Cash Flows or Cash Flow Statement.

PURPOSE OF THE STATEMENT OF CASH FLOWS

The primary purpose of the statement of cash flows is to provide relevant "information about the operating, financing and investing activities of an enterprise and the effects of those activities on cash resources" during a period.[25] To achieve this purpose, the statement of cash flows reports (1) the cash effects of an enterprise's operations during a period; (2) its investing transactions; (3) its financing transactions; and (4) the net increase or decrease in cash and equivalents during the period.[26]

Reporting the sources, uses, and net increase or decrease in cash helps investors, creditors, and others know what is happening to a company's most liquid resource. Because most individuals maintain their chequebook and prepare their tax return on a

OBJECTIVE 6
Indicate the purpose of the statement of cash flows.

---

[25] *Ibid*, Section 1540, par. .01.

[26] The basis recommended by the AcSB is actually "cash and cash equivalents." Cash equivalents are cash net of short-term borrowings and highly liquid investments.

cash basis, they can relate to the statement of cash flows and comprehend the causes and effects of cash inflows and outflows and the net increase or decrease in cash. The statement of cash flows provides answers to the following simple but important questions:

1. Where did the cash come from during the period?
2. What was the cash used for during the period?
3. What was the change in the balances of cash during the period?

CONTENT AND FORMAT OF THE STATEMENT OF CASH FLOWS

OBJECTIVE 7
Identify the content of the statement of cash flows.

Cash receipts and cash payments during a period are classified in the statement of cash flows under operating, investing, and financing activities. These classifications are defined as follows:

1. **Operating activities** involve the cash effects of transactions that enter into the determination of net income.
2. **Investing activities** include (a) making and collecting loans; and (b) acquiring and disposing of investments (both debt and equity) as well as property, plant, and equipment.
3. **Financing activities** involve liability and shareholders' equity items and include (a) obtaining resources from owners and providing them with a return on (and a return of) their investment; and (b) borrowing money from creditors and repaying the amounts borrowed.

With the above three categories of cash and cash equivalents, the statement of cash flows has assumed the following basic format.

FORMAT OF THE STATEMENT OF CASH FLOWS	
Cash flows from operating activities	$XXX
Cash flows from investing activities	XXX
Cash flows from financing activities	XXX
Net increase (decrease) in cash and equivalents	XXX
Cash and equivalents at beginning of year	XXX
Cash and equivalents at end of year	$XXX

The inflows and outflows of cash classified by activity can be diagrammed as at the top of the facing page.

The value of the statement of cash flows lies in its ability to help users evaluate the liquidity, solvency, and financial flexibility of a corporation. Liquidity refers to the "nearness to cash" of assets and liabilities. **Solvency** refers to the firm's ability to pay its debts as they mature. Finally, **financial flexibility** refers to a firm's ability to respond and adapt to financial adversity and unexpected needs and opportunities.

PREPARATION OF THE STATEMENT OF CASH FLOWS

OBJECTIVE 8
Prepare a statement of cash flows.

We have devoted Chapter 23 entirely to the preparation and content of the statement of cash flows. Our comprehensive coverage of this topic has been deferred to that later chapter so that we can cover in the intervening chapters several elements and complex topics that make up the content of a typical statement of cash flows. The presentation in this chapter is introductory, a reminder of the existence of the statement of cash flows.

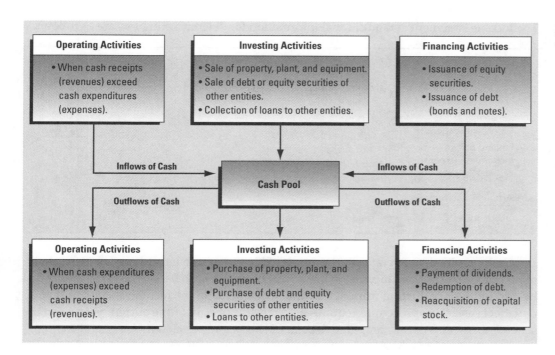

ILLUSTRATION 5-1
Cash Flows

The information required to prepare the statement of changes in financial position usually comes from (1) comparative balance sheets; (2) the current income statement; and (3) selected transaction data. Preparing the statement of cash flows from these sources involves the following steps:

1. Determine the cash provided by operations.
2. Determine the cash provided by or used in investing and financing activities.
3. Determine the change (increase or decrease) in cash during the period.
4. Reconcile the change in cash with the beginning and ending cash balances.

The following simple illustration demonstrates the application of these steps in the preparation of the statement of changes in financial position. Assume that on January 1, 1998, Telemarketing Inc., in its first year of operations, issued 50,000 no par value common shares for $50,000 cash. The company rented its office space, furniture, and telecommunications equipment and performed surveys and marketing services throughout the first year. The comparative balance sheets at the beginning and end of 1998 appear as follows.

TELEMARKETING INC.
Balance Sheets

Assets	Dec. 31, 1998	Jan. 1, 1998	Increase/Decrease
Cash	$46,000	$-0-	$46,000 Increase
Accounts receivable (net)	41,000	-0-	41,000 Increase
Total	$87,000	$-0-	
Liabilities and Shareholders' Equity			
Accounts payable	$12,000	$-0-	12,000 Increase
Common shares	50,000	-0-	50,000 Increase
Retained earnings	25,000	-0-	25,000 Increase
Total	$87,000	$-0-	

The income statement and additional information for Telemarketing Inc. are as follows.

TELEMARKETING INC.
Income Statement
For the Year Ended December 31, 1998

Revenues	$172,000
Operating expenses	120,000
Income before income taxes	52,000
Income tax expense	13,000
Net income	$ 39,000

Additional information:

Dividends of $14,000 were paid during the year.

Cash provided by operations (the excess of cash receipts over cash payments) is determined by converting net income on an accrual basis to a cash basis. This is accomplished by adding to or deducting from net income those items in the income statement that do not affect cash. This procedure requires an analysis not only of the current year's income statement, but also of the comparative balance sheets and selected transaction data.

Analysis of Telemarketing's comparative balance sheets reveals two items that give rise to noncash credits or charges to the income statement: (1) the increase in accounts receivable reflects a noncash credit of $41,000 to revenues; and (2) the increase in accounts payable reflects a noncash charge of $12,000 to expenses. **To arrive at cash provided by operations, the increase in accounts receivable must be deducted from net income, and the increase in accounts payable must be added back to net income.**

As a result of the accounts receivable and accounts payable adjustments, the cash provided by operations is determined to be $10,000, computed as follows.

Net income		$39,000
Adjustments to reconcile net income to net cash		
provided by operating activities		
Increase in accounts receivable (net)	$(41,000)	
Increase in accounts payable	12,000	(29,000)
Net cash provided by operating activities		$10,000

The increase of $50,000 in common shares that results from the issuance of 50,000 shares for cash is classified as a financing activity. Likewise, the payment of $14,000 cash in dividends is a financing activity. Telemarketing Inc. did not engage in any investing activities during the year. The statement of cash flows for Telemarketing Inc. for 1998 is therefore as follows on the facing page.

The increase in cash of $46,000 reported in the statement of cash flows agrees with the increase of $46,000 shown as the change in the Cash account in the comparative balance sheets.

An illustration of a more comprehensive statement of cash flows is presented on the facing page.

TELEMARKETING INC.
Statement of Cash Flows
For the Year Ended December 31, 1998

Cash flows from operating activities		
Net income		$39,000
Add (deduct) items not affecting cash		
Increase in accounts receivable (net)	$(41,000)	
Increase in accounts payable	12,000	(29,000)
Net cash provided by operating activities		10,000
Cash flows from financing activities		
Issuance of common shares	50,000	
Payment of cash dividends	(14,000)	
Net cash provided by financing activities		36,000
Net increase in cash		46,000
Cash at beginning of year		-0-
Cash at end of year		$46,000

ILLUSTRATION COMPANY
Statement of Cash Flows
For the Year Ended December 31, 1998

Operating Activities		
Net income		$320,750
Add (deduct) items not affecting cash		
Depreciation expense	$ 88,400	
Amortization of intangibles	16,300	
Gain on sale of plant assets	(8,700)	
Increase in accounts receivable (net)	(11,000)	
Decrease in inventory	15,500	
Decrease in notes and accounts payable	(9,500)	91,000
Net cash provided by operating activities		411,750
Investing Activities		
Sale of plant assets	90,500	
Purchase of equipment	(182,500)	
Purchase of land	(70,000)	
Net cash used by investing activities		(162,000)
Financing Activities		
Payment of cash dividend	(19,800)	
Issuance of common shares	100,000	
Redemption of bonds	(50,000)	
Net cash provided by financing activities		30,200
Net increase in cash		279,950
Cash at beginning of year		135,000
Cash at end of year		$414,950

INTERNATIONAL PERSPECTIVE

In this chapter, the principles and procedures used to prepare a balance sheet and a statement of changes are presented. The accounting principles and procedures used to prepare these financial statements are conservative, in that historical cost information is generally reported. Reliability therefore plays a key role in the type of information presented.

As indicated earlier, other countries may emphasize different approaches to presenting financial information. The illustration that follows is an adaptation of the balance sheet for Guiness PLC, a British company. Although many similarities exist between Canada and Great Britain, fixed or long-term assets are reported first on the balance sheet; assets and liabilities are netted and grouped into net current and net total assets; and within classifications such as current assets, the most liquid assets are reported last.

Second, GAAP differences exist: In Great Britain, goodwill is reported as a deduction from shareholders' equity; brands are reported as an intangible asset and may be reported at fair value; and land and buildings may be reported at fair value.

GUINESS PLC
GROUP BALANCE SHEET
At 31 December 1991

(in millions)	Net Assets	
Fixed assets		
Acquired brands at cost		£ 1,395
Tangible assets		1,721
Investments		1,232
		4,348
Current assets		
Stocks	1,661	
Debtors	1,067	
Cash deposits	475	
	3,203	
Creditors (amounts falling due within one year)		
Short-term borrowings	(779)	
Other creditors	(1,271)	
	(2,050)	
Net current assets		1,153
Total assets less current liabilities		5,501
Creditors (amounts falling due after more than one year)		
Long-term borrowings		(1,493)
Other creditors		(161)
Provisions for liabilities and charges		(223)
Total net assets		3,624
	Equity	
Capital and reserves		
Share capital		547
Share premium		423
		970
Other reserves		3,789
Goodwill		(1,228)
Shareholders' equity		3,531
Minority interests		93
Total equity		3,624

Great Britain provides much more flexibility in presenting balance-sheet information. As indicated, companies are permitted to present fair value information for items such as land and buildings. No rules exist about when these revaluations may occur, but they often happen when the company wishes to enhance its balance sheet for borrowing purposes or for a possible merger.

As indicated in Chapter 1, one of the most contentious issues in international accounting is the reporting of goodwill. In Great Britain, by reporting goodwill as a contra account to shareholders' equity, goodwill expense is not reported on the income statement. As a result, if a British and a Canadian company are competing to purchase a company, some contend that the British company has an unfair advantage because it will not have to report goodwill expense. The Canadian company, on the other hand, has to report goodwill as an asset and amortize it against revenues. As a result, the Canadian company will have to report lower earnings than its British counterpart and is therefore more reluctant to become involved in merger discussions.

The British use essentially the same type of cash flow statement as in Canada. Most countries, however, use a working capital approach rather than a cash approach to report changes in liquid resources during a period.

Summary of Learning Objectives

KEY TERMS

1. **Identify the uses and limitations of a balance sheet.** The balance sheet provides information about the nature and amounts of investments in enterprise resources, obligations to enterprise creditors, and the owners' equity in net enterprise resources. The balance sheet contributes to financial reporting by providing a basis for (1) computing rates of return; (2) evaluating the capital structure of the enterprise; and (3) assessing the liquidity and financial flexibility of the enterprise. The limitations of the balance sheet are: (1) it does not reflect current value because accountants have adopted a historical cost basis in valuing and reporting assets and liabilities; (2) judgements and estimates must be used in preparing a balance sheet because the collectibility of receivables, the saleability of inventory, and the useful life of long-term tangible and intangible assets are difficult to determine; and (3) the balance sheet omits many items that are of financial value to the business but cannot be recorded objectively, such as human resources, customer base, and reputation.

2. **Identify the major classifications in the balance sheet.** The general elements of the balance sheet are assets, liabilities, and equity. The major classifications within the balance sheet on the asset side are: current assets; long-term investments; property, plant, and equipment; intangible assets; and other assets. The major classifications of liabilities are: current liabilities, and long-term liabilities. In a corporation, shareholders' equity is generally classified as share capital, contributed surplus, and retained earnings.

3. **Prepare a classified balance sheet using the report and account forms.** The report form lists liabilities and shareholders' equity directly below assets on the

account form, 203

adjunct account, 210

balance sheet, 191

contra account, 210

current assets, 194

current liabilities, 200

financial flexibility, 192

financial position form, 203

financing activities, 212

gain contingencies, 204

intangible assets, 199

investing activities, 212

liquidity, 192

long-term investments, 197

long-term liabilities, 201

loss contingencies, 205

operating activities, 212

property, plant, and equipment, 198

report form, 203

same page. The account form lists assets by sections on the left side, and liabilities and shareholders' equity on the right side.

4. **Identify balance sheet information requiring supplemental disclosure.** There are four types of information that are supplemental to account titles and amounts presented in the balance sheet: (1) contingencies (material events that have an uncertain outcome); (2) valuation and accounting policies (explanations and accounting policies such as explanations of the valuation methods used or the basic assumptions made concerning inventory valuation, depreciation methods, investments in subsidiaries); (3) contractual situations; (4) post-balance sheet disclosures (such as disclosures of certain events that have occurred after the balance sheet date but before the financial statements have been issued).

5. **Identify major disclosure techniques for the balance sheet.** There are four methods of disclosing pertinent information in the balance sheet: (1) parenthetical explanations, in which additional information or description is provided within parentheses following the item; (2) notes, which are used if additional explanations or descriptions cannot be shown conveniently as parenthetical explanations; (3) cross-reference and contra items, by which a direct relationship between an asset and a liability is "cross-referenced" on the balance sheet; (4) supporting schedules, which are often used to present more detailed information about certain assets or liabilities because the balance sheet provides just a single summary item.

6. **Indicate the purpose of the statement of cash flows.** The primary purpose of a statement of changes in financial position is to provide relevant information about cash receipts and cash payments of an enterprise during a period. Reporting the sources, uses, and net increase or decrease in cash and cash equivalents enables investors, creditors, and others to know what is happening to a company's most liquid resource.

7. **Identify the content of the statement of cash flows.** Cash receipts and cash payments during a period are classified in the statement of changes in financial position according to three different activities: (1) operating activities, which involve the cash effects of transactions that enter into the determination of net income; (2) investing activities, which include making and collecting loans and acquiring and disposing of investments (both debt and equity) and property, plant, and equipment; (3) financing activities, which involve liability and shareholders' equity items and include (a) obtaining capital from owners and providing them with a return on their investment; and (b) borrowing money from creditors and repaying the amounts borrowed.

8. **Prepare a statement of cash flows.** The information to prepare the statement of cash flows usually comes from (1) comparative balance sheets; (2) the current income statement; and (3) selected transaction data. Preparing the statement of cash flows from these sources involves the following steps: (1) determine the cash provided by operations; (2) determine the cash provided by or used in investing and financing activities; (3) determine the change (increase or decrease) in cash and cash equivalents during the period; and (4) reconcile the change in cash with the beginning and ending balances.

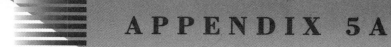

APPENDIX 5A

Moore Corporation
Financial Statements

Consolidated Balance Sheet

As at December 31
Expressed in United States currency
in thousands of dollars

	1995	1994
Assets		
Current assets:		
Cash and short-term securities at cost, which approximates market value	$ 721,986	$ 266,865
Accounts receivable, less allowance		
for doubtful accounts of $13,933 (1994 – $14,185)	477,016	435,552
Inventories (Note 2)	191,831	244,502
Prepaid expenses	22,529	23,181
Deferred income taxes	36,360	39,614
Total current assets	1,449,722	1,009,714
Property, plant and equipment:		
Land	25,605	33,717
Buildings	244,128	269,778
Machinery and equipment	1,075,257	1,052,869
	1,344,990	1,356,364
Less: Accumulated depreciation	772,982	749,268
	572,008	607,096
Investment in associated corporations (Note 3)	34,361	249,776
Other assets (Note 4)	179,547	164,750
	$ 2,235,638	$ 2,031,336
Liabilities		
Current liabilities:		
Bank loans (Note 5)	$ 30,652	$ 32,328
Accounts payable and accruals (Note 6)	393,635	371,138
Dividends payable	23,470	23,399
Income taxes	93,973	19,743
Total current liabilities	541,730	446,608
Long-term debt (Note 7)	71,512	77,495
Deferred income taxes and liabilities (Note 8)	126,673	130,972
Equity of minority shareholders in subsidiary corporations	7,553	11,087
	747,468	666,162
Shareholders' equity		
Share capital (Note 9)	342,170	336,964
Unrealized foreign currency translation adjustments (Note 10)	(41,974)	13,953
Retained earnings	1,187,974	1,014,257
	1,488,170	1,365,174
	$ 2,235,638	$ 2,031,336

Approved by the Board of Directors:

R. Braun
Director

J.D. Farley
Director

Moore Corporation Limited

Consolidated Statement of Earnings

For the year ended December 31
Expressed in United States currency and,
except earnings per share, in thousands of dollars

	1995	1994	1993
Sales	$ 2,602,254	$ 2,406,048	$ 2,331,796
Cost of sales	1,766,671	1,585,990	1,522,904
Selling, general and administrative expenses	607,080	573,786	570,017
Provision for restructuring costs (Note 14)	–	–	229,000
Depreciation	76,391	78,919	81,940
Research and development expense	27,940	28,380	26,337
	2,478,082	2,267,075	2,430,198
Income (loss) from operations	124,172	138,973	(98,402)
Investment and other income (Notes 3 and 13)	281,178	45,645	23,787
Interest expense (Note 13)	11,794	13,099	17,187
Unrealized exchange adjustments	1,696	5,179	3,331
Earnings (loss) before income taxes and minority interests	391,860	166,340	(95,133)
Income taxes expense (recovery) (Note 15)	123,738	43,853	(18,796)
Minority interests	621	1,087	1,269
Net earnings (loss)	$ 267,501	$ 121,400	$ (77,606)
Net earnings (loss) per common share (Note 16)	$ 2.68	$ 1.22	$ (0.78)
Average shares outstanding (in thousands)	99,754	99,538	99,487

Consolidated Statement of Retained Earnings

For the year ended December 31
Expressed in United States currency
in thousands of dollars

	1995	1994	1993
Balance at beginning of year	$ 1,014,257	$ 986,424	$ 1,157,551
Net earnings (loss)	267,501	121,400	(77,606)
	1,281,758	1,107,824	1,079,945
Dividends 94¢ per share (94¢ in 1994 and 1993)	93,784	93,567	93,521
Balance at end of year	$ 1,187,974	$ 1,014,257	$ 986,424

Moore Corporation Limited

Consolidated Statement of Cash Flows

For the year ended December 31
Expressed in United States currency
in thousands of dollars

	1995	1994	1993
Operating activities			
Net earnings (loss)	$ 267,501	$ 121,400	$ (77,606)
Items not affecting cash resources:			
Depreciation *(a)*	78,869	80,977	84,045
Equity in earnings of associated corporations	(1,347)	(24,291)	(5,876)
Amortization of goodwill and deferred charges	6,223	6,185	19,935
Increase (decrease) in pension reserves	(1,101)	10,795	7,520
Gain from sale of an investment	(248,174)	–	–
Provision for restructuring costs, net of cash	–	–	226,763
Other	3,177	2,259	1,693
	(162,353)	75,925	334,080
Decrease (increase) in working capital other than cash resources:			
Accounts receivable	(41,464)	(15,747)	6,410
Inventories	52,671	10,845	17,627
Accounts payable and accruals	19,077	(24,099)	120,281
Income taxes	74,230	8,195	278
Deferred income taxes	3,625	13,814	(19,689)
Working capital effect of provision for restructuring costs	1,917	(4,656)	(161,342)
Other	(8,614)	(6,020)	(2,891)
	101,442	(17,668)	(39,326)
Total	$ 206,590	$ 179,657	$ 217,148
Investing activities			
Expenditure for property, plant and equipment	$ (86,605)	$ (77,014)	$ (82,009)
Sale of property, plant and equipment	24,374	13,650	3,963
Decrease (increase) in long-term receivables	53,651	(13,857)	(32,130)
Acquisition of businesses	–	(1,212)	(25,356)
Disposal of businesses	27,057	3,434	–
Proceeds from sale of an investment	354,693	–	–
Investment in associated corporations	(1,496)	(21,076)	(408)
Other	(29,131)	2,597	(14,688)
Total	$ 342,543	$ (93,478)	$ (150,628)
Financing activities			
Dividends	$ (93,784)	$ (93,567)	$ (93,521)
Addition to long-term debt	5,450	9,838	19,256
Reduction in long-term debt	(9,924)	(7,049)	(22,440)
Other	3,833	468	405
Total	$ (94,425)	$ (90,310)	$ (96,300)
Increase (decrease) in cash resources			
before unrealized exchange adjustments	$ 454,708	$ (4,131)	$ (29,780)
Unrealized exchange adjustments	2,089	(2,229)	1,567
Increase (decrease) in cash resources	456,797	(6,360)	(28,213)
Cash resources at beginning of year *(b)*	234,537	240,897	269,110
Cash resources at end of year *(b)*	$ 691,334	$ 234,537	$ 240,897

(a) Includes depreciation that has been classified in research and development expense.
(b) Cash resources are defined as cash and short-term securities less bank loans.

Moore Corporation Limited

Notes to Consolidated Financial Statements
Year ended December 31
Expressed in United States currency

1. Summary of accounting policies

Accounting principles
Moore Corporation Limited is incorporated under the laws of the Province of Ontario, Canada.

The consolidated financial statements are prepared in accordance with accounting principles generally accepted in Canada.

Principles of consolidation
The financial statements of entities which are controlled by the Corporation, referred to as subsidiaries, are consolidated; entities which are not controlled and which the Corporation has the ability to exercise significant influence over, referred to as associated companies, are accounted for using the equity method; and investments in other entities are accounted for using the cost method.

Translation of foreign currencies
The consolidated financial statements are expressed in United States currency because a significant part of the net assets and earnings are located or originate in the United States. Except for the foreign currency financial statements of subsidiaries in countries with highly inflationary economies, Canadian and other foreign currency financial statements have been translated into United States currency on the following bases: all assets and liabilities at the year-end rates of exchange; income and expenses at average exchange rates during the year.

Net unrealized exchange adjustments arising on translation of foreign currency financial statements are charged or credited directly to shareholders' equity and shown as unrealized foreign currency translation adjustments.

The foreign currency financial statements of subsidiaries in countries with highly inflationary economies are translated into United States currency on the following bases: current assets (excluding inventory), current liabilities, pension liabilities, long-term receivables and long-term debt, at the year-end rates of exchange; all other assets, liabilities, accumulated depreciation and related charges against earnings and share capital, at historical rates of exchange; income and expenses, other than depreciation and cost of sales, at average exchange rates during the year.

Net unrealized exchange adjustments arising on translation of foreign currency financial statements of subsidiaries in countries with highly inflationary economies are charged to earnings as unrealized exchange adjustments.

Realized exchange losses or gains are included in earnings. Unrealized exchange losses or gains related to monetary items with a fixed or ascertainable life extending beyond the end of the following fiscal year are deferred and amortized over the remaining life of the asset or liability.

Financial instruments
The Corporation enters into forward exchange contracts to manage exposures resulting from foreign exchange fluctuations in the ordinary course of business. The contracts are normally for terms up to six months and are used as hedges of foreign denominated revenue streams, costs, and intercompany loans. The unrealized gains and losses on outstanding contracts are offset against the gains and losses of the hedged item at the maturity of the underlying transactions.

Short-term securities consist of investment grade, highly liquid instruments of highly rated financial institutions and corporations.

Inventories
Inventories of raw materials and work in process are valued at the lower of cost and replacement cost and inventories of finished goods at the lower of cost and net realizable value. The cost of the principal raw material inventories and the raw material content of finished goods inventories in the United States is determined on the last-in, first-out basis. The cost of all other inventories is determined on the first-in, first-out basis.

Property, plant and equipment and depreciation
Property, plant and equipment are stated at historical cost after deducting investment tax credits and other grants on eligible capital assets. Depreciation is provided on a basis that will amortize the cost of depreciable assets over their estimated useful lives using the straight-line method. All costs for repairs and maintenance are expensed as incurred.

The estimated useful lives of buildings range from 20 to 50 years and of machinery and equipment from 3 to 17 years.

Gains or losses on the disposal of property, plant and equipment are included in earnings and the cost and accumulated depreciation related to these assets are removed from the accounts.

Goodwill
The estimated useful life of goodwill arising from acquisitions is determined based on the particular circumstances of each investment. Goodwill is amortized on a straight-line basis over its estimated useful life, not exceeding forty years, and is written down when there has been a permanent impairment of its value.

Moore Corporation Limited

Amortization of deferred charges

Deferred charges include development costs and computer software costs which are amortized over periods deemed appropriate to match expenses with the related revenues, up to a maximum of five years.

Income taxes

Income taxes are accounted for on the tax allocation basis which relates income taxes to the accounting income for the year.

No provision has been made for taxes on undistributed earnings of subsidiaries not currently available for paying dividends as such earnings have been reinvested in the business.

2. Inventories *(in thousands)*

	1995	1994
Raw materials	$ 61,687	$ 74,161
Work in process	24,013	27,280
Finished goods	99,870	131,883
Other	6,261	11,178
	$ 191,831	$ 244,502

The excess of the current cost over the last-in, first-out cost of those inventories is approximately $41,300,000 at December 31, 1995 (1994 – $40,700,000).

In 1995, a program was initiated whereby the Corporation's rights to specific customer finished goods inventory in the United States were sold to third parties. The reduction in inventory resulted in a $9 million LIFO credit to cost of goods sold.

3. Investment in associated corporations *(in thousands)*

	1995	1994
JetForm Corporation	$ 17,219	$ 19,575
Sigma Schede S.p.A.	7,978	8,200
Toppan Moore Company, Ltd.	–	212,541
Other	9,164	9,460
	$ 34,361	$ 249,776

In March 1995, the Corporation reduced its investment in Toppan Moore Company, Ltd. (Toppan Moore) from 45% to 10%, by selling a 35% equity interest to Toppan Printing Company, Ltd. for approximately $355 million, payable in Japanese yen. The remaining 10% investment in Toppan Moore has been transferred to other assets (Note 4).

4. Other assets *(in thousands)*

	1995	1994
Prepaid pension cost	$ 44,131	$ 35,800
Deposits pledged as security for long-term loans	–	55,993
Notes receivable	16,080	16,010
Other long-term receivables	9,877	6,917
Investment in Toppan Moore Company, Ltd.	53,426	–
Long-term bonds, at cost which approximates market value	21,168	21,455
Goodwill, net of accumulated amortization of $28,672 (1994 – $26,167)	14,598	18,388
Other	20,267	10,187
	$ 179,547	$ 164,750

Moore Corporation Limited

5. Bank loans

The weighted average interest rate on bank loans outstanding as of December 31, 1995, was 8.4% (1994 – 10.7%).

The unused lines of credit outstanding at December 31, 1995 for short-term financing are $1,272,799,000 (1994 – $147,066,000).

6. Accounts payable and accruals *(in thousands)*

	1995	1994
Trade accounts payable	$ 167,094	$ 133,999
Other payables	76,798	39,775
	243,892	173,774
Accrued restructuring costs	17,540	79,767
Accrued payroll costs	45,619	44,269
Accrued employee benefit costs	25,136	26,857
Other accruals	61,448	46,471
	149,743	197,364
	$ 393,635	$ 371,138

7. Long-term debt *(in thousands)*

	1995	1994
Moore Corporation Limited		
Bank loan payable in Japanese yen bearing interest at 7.2%, due 1997	$ 6,086	$ 12,622
Moore Business Systems Australia Limited		
Bank loan, subject to renegotiation in 1996, payable in Australian dollars bearing interest at the Australian Bank Bill rate plus 0.275%	44,592	44,597
Moore de Mexico Holdings, S.A. de C.V.		
Bank loan, subject to renegotiation in 1996, payable in United States dollars bearing interest at the London Interbank Offer rate plus 0.3% (1994 – 0.2%)	14,528	14,528
Other		
Secured loans	628	1,245
Capital lease commitments	2,928	3,653
Unsecured loans	2,750	850
	$ 71,512	$ 77,495

The other long-term debt bears interest at rates ranging from 6.1% to 20.0% and matures on various dates to 2005. Loans of other subsidiaries amounting to $3,310,000 (1994 – $4,751,000) are payable in currencies other than United States dollars.

The net book value of assets subject to lien approximates $15,000,000 (1994 – $69,000,000). The liens are primarily mortgages against property, plant and equipment and pledges of accounts receivable and inventory.

Amounts of $8,022,000 (1994 – $5,764,000) of long-term debt due within one year are included in current liabilities. For the years 1997 through 2000, payments required on long-term debt are as follows: 1997 – $7,330,000; 1998 – $893,000; 1999 – $862,000; and 2000 – $685,000.

Moore Corporation Limited

8. Deferred income taxes and liabilities

Non-current deferred income taxes amount to $53,016,000 (1994 – $54,640,000).

Deferred liabilities include $64,876,000 (1994 – $67,177,000) for pensions under various retirement plans (Note 11).

9. Share capital

The Corporation's articles of incorporation provide that its authorized share capital be divided into an unlimited number of common shares without par value and an unlimited number of preference shares without par value, issuable in one or more series, and non-voting except on arrears of dividends.

Changes in the issued common share capital

	Shares Issued	Amount (in thousands)
Balance, January 1, 1993	99,468,940	$ 335,308
Exercise of executive stock options	52,900	842
Employee awards	1,780	31
Balance, December 31, 1993	99,523,620	336,181
Dividend Reinvestment and Share Purchase Plan	25,854	452
Exercise of executive stock options	19,300	305
Employee awards	1,380	26
Balance, December 31, 1994	99,570,154	336,964
Exercise of executive stock options	259,710	4,265
Dividend Reinvestment and Share Purchase Plan	46,679	941
Balance, December 31, 1995	99,876,543	$ 342,170

On February 16, 1994, the Board approved the Dividend Reinvestment and Share Purchase Plan whereby shareholders of the Corporation have two methods of obtaining additional shares at market value without incurring brokerage or service charges. The Dividend Reinvestment Option allows participants to use their dividends to purchase additional shares of the Corporation. The Share Purchase Option allows shareholders to purchase shares by making cash payments of not less than $50 (Cdn.) and not more than $5,000 (Cdn.) in each quarter.

Pursuant to the terms of the 1994 Long Term Incentive Plan approved by the shareholders of the Corporation on April 14, 1994, 3,000,000 common shares of the Corporation were reserved for issuance.

Under the terms of this plan, stock options, stock appreciation rights, and restricted stock awards may be granted to certain key employees. The exercise price under all options involving the common shares of the Corporation shall not be less than 100% of fair market value of the shares covered by the option on the date of grant.

Options may be exercised at such times as are determined at the date they are granted and expire not more than ten years from the date granted.

The Corporation will be asking shareholders to approve at the April 25, 1996 Annual and Special Meeting of Shareholders, amendments to the 1994 Long Term Incentive Plan, primarily to increase the number of shares which are reserved under the plan to 5,500,000.

Moore Corporation Limited

Stock option activity in 1995

Years granted	1995	1994	1993	1991	1989	1988	1987	1985	Total
Number of common shares under option outstanding									
December 31, 1994	–	1,193,400	985,900	375,200	324,800	303,100	252,100	149,250	3,583,750
Options granted	1,569,500	–	–	–	–	–	–	–	1,569,500
Options lapsed	(73,500)	(139,760)	(103,100)	(51,000)	(48,200)	(39,800)	(29,400)	(74,500)	(559,260)
Options exercised	–	(24,260)	(154,600)	–	–	(9,600)	–	(71,250)	(259,710)
Options cancelled	–	(5,480)	–	(1,600)	–	–	–	(3,500)	(10,580)
Outstanding December 31, 1995	1,496,000	1,023,900	728,200	322,600	276,600	253,700	222,700	–	4,323,700
Option price per share Canadian currency	$ 26.23*	$ 24.79*	$ 22.29*	$ 29.31	$ 34.88	$ 28.56	$ 31.88	$ 25.00*	

Weighted average option price

Under the terms of the 1994 Long Term Incentive Plan, there were 2,187,800 common shares available for grants as of January 1, 1995 and 810,660 as of December 31, 1995.

On April 27, 1995, the shareholders of the Corporation reconfirmed the Corporation's shareholder rights plan ("Rights Plan"), the terms and conditions of which are set out in the Shareholders Rights Plan Agreement ("Rights Agreement"), dated as of April 12, 1995. The Rights Agreement amends and restates the terms of the shareholder rights plan agreement, dated January 18, 1990.

The Rights Plan was originally adopted to provide the Corporation with sufficient time, in the event of a public takeover bid or tender offer for the Corporation's common shares, to pursue alternatives to enhance shareholder value. All holders of Rights, with the exception of such acquiring person or group, are entitled to purchase from the Corporation upon payment of

an exercise price of $120.00 (Cdn.) the number of additional common shares that can be purchased for twice the exercise price, based on the market value of the Corporation's common shares at the time the Rights become exercisable.

The amended and restated Rights Plan included the following changes: 1) an increase from 15% to 20% in the level of share ownership to trigger the plan, 2) more exemptions for investment and fund managers, 3) more streamlined "permitted bid" provisions which allow the making of partial bids and require that a permitted bid be open for acceptance for a minimum of 75 days and 4) an automatic waiver of the plan to competing bids if the plan is waived with respect to any other bid.

The Board of Directors made no awards of common shares to employees in 1995 (1994 – 1,380).

As at December 31, 1995, there were no issued preference shares.

10. Unrealized foreign currency translation adjustments *(in thousands)*

	1995	1994	1993
Balance at beginning of year	$ 13,953	$ (9,709)	$ (17,351)
Translation adjustment:			
Canada	10,906	(30,344)	(23,360)
Japan	(56,768)	20,843	17,627
Netherlands	(5,719)	27,095	19,199
Other	(4,346)	6,068	(5,824)
Balance at end of year	$ (41,974)	$ 13,953	$ (9,709)

The translation adjustments for each year result from the variation from year to year in rates of exchange at which foreign currency net assets are translated to United States currency.

Moore Corporation Limited

11. Retirement programs

Defined benefit pension plan

The Corporation and its subsidiaries have several programs covering substantially all of the employees in Canada, the United States, Puerto Rico, the United Kingdom, Australia and New Zealand.

The following data is based upon reports from independent consulting actuaries as at December 31:

	Canada			United States			International		
	1995	1994	1993	1995	1994	1993	1995	1994	1993
Funded Status *(in thousands)*									
Actuarial present value of:									
Vested benefit obligation	$ 54,130	$ 51,017	$ 52,868	$ 556,224	$ 444,230	$ 434,620	$ 70,081	$ 68,407	$ 62,144
Accumulated benefit obligation	57,500	54,046	56,702	594,541	470,225	471,747	70,417	68,977	63,207
Projected benefit obligation	$ 71,318	$ 67,234	$ 67,262	$ 683,025	$ 531,452	$ 561,766	$ 76,795	$ 74,693	$ 70,507
Plan assets at fair value	88,249	75,055	83,598	597,502	522,616	556,685	124,947	113,675	113,475
Excess (shortfall) of plan assets over projected benefit obligation	16,931	7,821	16,336	(85,523)	(8,836)	(5,081)	48,152	38,982	42,968
Unrecognized net loss (gain)	(2,595)	4,730	(787)	13,194	(62,524)	(26,952)	(16,191)	(11,241)	(17,002)
Unrecognized net asset	(4,941)	(5,772)	(7,135)	(15,250)	(18,298)	(21,346)	(6,172)	(8,624)	(10,239)
Unrecognized prior service cost	2,681	2,871	3,318	37,208	42,518	47,828	4,538	4,496	2,592
Prepaid (accrued) pension cost included in consolidated balance sheet	$ 12,076	$ 9,650	$ 11,732	$ (50,371)	$ (47,140)	$ (5,551)	$ 30,327	$ 23,613	$ 18,319
Pension Expense *(in thousands)*									
Service cost	$ 2,109	$ 2,095	$ 2,173	$ 12,810	$ 17,072	$ 16,580	$ 2,734	$ 2,992	$ 3,103
Interest cost	5,805	5,365	5,880	44,675	43,315	38,552	5,863	5,555	5,346
Actual return on assets	(14,274)	1,978	(16,678)	(110,316)	173	(71,333)	(19,503)	2,700	(22,289)
Net amortization and deferral	7,205	(8,652)	9,535	56,062	(51,340)	25,659	5,484	(14,752)	12,061
Net pension expense (credit)	$ 845	$ 786	$ 910	$ 3,231	$ 9,220	$ 9,458	$ (5,422)	$ (3,505)	$ (1,779)
Other Information Assumptions:									
Discount rates									
January 1	8.5%	. 8.5%	9.5%	8.8%	7.5%	8.3%	8.4%	7.5%	8.3%
December 31	8.5%	8.5%	8.5%	7.0%	8.8%	7.5%	7.8%	8.3%	7.5%
Rate of return on assets	8.5%	8.5%	8.5%	9.5%	9.5%	9.5%	9.5%	9.5%	9.5%
Rate of compensation increase	5.5%	5.5%	5.5%	5.5%	5.5%	5.5%	7.0%	7.2%	7.2%
Amortization period	15 years	15 years	15 years	13 years	14 years	15 years	11 years	11 years	11 years

Moore Corporation Limited

During 1994, the Corporation offered an enhanced retirement program to eligible employees ages 57 and over in the United States and in Canada who retired between May 1, 1994 and July 1, 1994. Eligible employees were granted five additional years of age and service in the defined benefit pension calculation, and will receive a temporary supplement until age 62 in the United States and age 65 in Canada. Since the enhanced retirement program for the United States plan constituted a significant event, a remeasurement of the plan's liabilities and assets was performed as of May 1, 1994 using an 8¼% discount rate and this rate was used to determine net periodic pension cost for the remainder of 1994. The enhanced retirement program was provided for in the 1993 provision for restructuring costs and the final charge of $36.4 million (before taxes) was taken against the restructuring costs accrual in 1994.

In some subsidiaries, where either state or funded retirement plans exist, there are certain small supplementary unfunded plans. Pensionable service prior to establishing funded contributory retirement plans in other subsidiaries, covered by former discretionary non-contributory retirement plans, was assumed as a prior service obligation. In addition, the Corporation has entered into retiring allowance and supplemental retirement agreements with certain senior executives. The deferred liability for pensions at December 31, 1995, referred to in Note 8, includes the unfunded portion of this prior service obligation and the supplementary unfunded plans.

All of the retirement plans are non-contributory except the New Zealand plan. Retirement benefits are generally based on years of service and employees' compensation during the last years of employment. However, in the United States the retirement benefit accrues each year based upon compensation for that year. At December 31, 1995, approximately 70% of the United States plan's assets, about 60% of the Canadian plan's assets and approximately 85% of the international plan's assets were held in equity securities with the remaining portion of the asset funds being mainly fixed income securities. The Corporation's funding policy is to satisfy the funding standards of the regulatory authorities and to make contributions in order to provide for the accumulated benefit obligation and current service cost. To the extent that pension obligations are fully covered by existing assets, a contribution may not be made in a particular year.

Defined contribution pension plan
Savings plans are maintained in Canada, the United States, the United Kingdom and Australia. Only the savings plan in the United Kingdom requires company contributions for all employees who are eligible to participate in the retirement plans. These annual contributions consist of a retirement savings benefit contribution ranging from 1% to 3% of each year's compensation depending upon age. For all savings plans, if an employee contribution is made, a portion of such contribution is matched by the company. Also, a defined contribution plan is maintained in The Netherlands. The plan expenses in 1995 were $7,415,000 (1994 – $7,586,000; 1993 – $6,008,000).

12. **Postretirement health care and life insurance benefits**

In addition to providing pension benefits, the Corporation and its United States subsidiary provide retired employees with health care and life insurance benefits. The cost of these health care and life insurance benefits is recognized as an expense as incurred. In 1995, the cost of these benefits was approximately $15,550,000 (1994 – $13,590,000; 1993 – $11,900,000).

Moore Corporation Limited

13. Consolidated statement of earnings information *(in thousands)*

	1995	1994	1993
Interest expense			
Interest on long-term debt	$ 7,273	$ 5,723	$ 4,862
Other interest	4,521	7,376	12,325
	$ 11,794	$ 13,099	$ 17,187
Investment and other income			
Interest on short-term investments	$ 36,552	$ 17,873	$ 17,037
Equity in earnings of associated corporations	1,347	24,291	5,876
Gain on sale of 35% equity interest in Toppan Moore	248,174	–	–
Costs related to the proposed acquisition of Wallace Computer Services, Inc.	(12,508)	–	–
Miscellaneous	7,613	3,481	874
	$ 281,178	$ 45,645	$ 23,787
Other expenses			
Rent	58,680	56,231	55,761
Repairs and maintenance	54,376	54,689	55,954
Retirement programs	8,951	18,059	19,467

14. Provision for restructuring costs

In the fourth quarters of 1992 and 1993, the Corporation's Board of Directors approved the following restructuring programs and related provisions within the framework of the Corporation's Strategic Plans to eliminate redundant assets, reduce personnel and improve efficiencies.

The 1992 restructuring provision of $77 million before tax or $0.62 per share after tax included $33 million for asset write-offs, $26 million for manufacturing restructuring, and $18 million to reduce selling, general and administrative expenses. Of the total provision, 71% related to European operations, where sales had declined and the product mix had changed and the remainder was related to North American operations. Approximately $44 million of the provision represented cash expenditures.

The 1993 restructuring provision of $229 million before tax or $1.67 per share after tax was made to position the Corporation for the future, recognizing the rapid changes occurring in technology and the market. The restructuring provision included $107 million for asset write-offs, $87 million to reduce selling, general and administrative expenses, and $35 million to restructure manufacturing facilities and close inefficient operations.

The remaining reserve balance as at December 31, 1995 of $21 million represents primarily cash expenditures for an order management system in North America, facility closure costs and severance payments. The balance is deemed sufficient to cover all remaining restructuring activities of the 1993 restructuring program.

The following table sets forth the Corporation's activity in its restructuring reserves from 1992 to 1995.

Moore Corporation Limited

Restructuring programs *(in millions)*

	Selling, General & Administrative	Manufacturing Reorganization	Total Costs	Asset Write-offs	Total Provision
1992 Restructuring provision	$ 18	$ 26	$ 44	$ 33	$ 77
Reserve balance, December 31, 1992	18	26	44	33	77
Cash payments	(15)	(17)	(32)	–	(32)
Non-cash items	–	–	–	(28)	(28)
1993 Restructuring provision	87	35	122	107	229
Reserve balance, December 31, 1993	90	44	134	112	246
Cash payments	(21)	(25)	(46)	(16)	(62)
Early retirement	(36)	–	(36)	–	(36)
Non-cash items	(1)	(2)	(3)	(55)	(58)
Reserve balance, December 31, 1994	32	17	49	41	90
Cash payments	(21)	(13)	(34)	(26)	(60)
Non-cash items	–	–	–	(9)	(9)
Reserve balance, December 31, 1995	$ 11	$ 4	$ 15	$ 6	$ 21

15. Income taxes

The components of earnings before income taxes for the three years ended December 31 were as follows:

Earnings (loss) before income taxes *(in thousands)*	1995	1994	1993
Canada	$ 278,445	$ 30	$ (17,820)
United States	61,055	97,118	(35,398)
Other countries	52,360	69,192	(41,915)
	$ 391,860	$ 166,340	$ (95,133)

	1995		1994		1993	
	Current	Deferred	Current	Deferred	Current	Deferred
Provision for income taxes *(in thousands)*						
Canada (federal and provincial)	$ 104,884	$ 1,922	$ (2,175)	$ 2,374	$ (3,073)	$ (3,025)
United States (federal and state)	9,826	9,784	26,734	11,318	41,186	(55,216)
Other countries	8,559	(12,836)	7,407	(2,082)	5,131	(4,222)
Withholding taxes on intercompany dividends	1,599	–	277	–	423	–
	$ 124,868	$ (1,130)	$ 32,243	$ 11,610	$ 43,667	$ (62,463)

Deferred income taxes in each of the three years arose from a number of differences of a timing nature between income for accounting purposes and taxable income in the jurisdictions in which the Corporation and its subsidiaries operate. The sources of major timing differences and the tax effect of each were as follows:

Moore Corporation Limited

Deferred income taxes *(in thousands)*	1995	1994	1993
Depreciation	$ 4,632	$ 2,020	$ 218
Pensions	1,975	(3,095)	(2,639)
Inventories	453	(432)	977
Restructuring costs	4,086	14,592	(62,112)
Reserves deferring recognition of profit and expenses, net	235	(453)	(596)
Net operating loss carryforwards	(13,102)	(1,597)	(296)
Other	591	575	1,985
	$ (1,130)	$ 11,610	$ (62,463)

The effective rates of tax for each year compared with the statutory Canadian rates were as follows:

Effective tax expense (recovery) rate	1995	1994	1993
Canada			
Combined federal and provincial statutory rate	43.8%	43.8%	(43.8)%
Corporate surtax	1.1	0.8	(0.8)
Manufacturing and processing rate reduction	(6.3)	(6.6)	7.2
Tax rate differences in other jurisdictions	(7.2)	(12.0)	(7.0)
Unrelieved restructuring and other costs	–	–	23.7
Withholding taxes	0.4	0.2	0.4
Other	(0.2)	0.2	0.5
Total consolidated effective tax expense (recovery) rate	31.6%	26.4%	(19.8)%

At December 31, 1995, the losses carried forward which have not been recognized in the financial statements were approximately $111 million. Of that amount, $19 million expire between 1996 and 2005 and the other $92 million have no expiry date.

16. Earnings and fully diluted earnings per common share

The earnings per share calculations are based on the weighted average number of common shares outstanding during the year.

If it were assumed that all outstanding stock options had been exercised at the beginning of the year and the funds derived therefrom of $3 million invested at an annual return of 3.6% net of tax, the earnings (loss) per share for the year would have been $2.61 [1994 – $1.20; 1993 – $(0.78)].

17. Segmented information

The Corporation and its subsidiaries have operated in primarily two industries during the three years ended December 31, 1995:

1) Forms, Print Management and Related Products (Forms)

In this segment, the Corporation is the world's largest designer and manufacturer of business forms and related products, systems and services which include:

- custom business forms
- forms handling and document processing equipment
- electronic forms and services
- print outsourcing services
- pressure sensitive labels
- proprietary label products
- variable imaged bar codes
- integrated form-label applications
- printers, applicators and software products and solutions.

2) Customer Communication Services (CCS)

In this segment, the Corporation is the world's largest producer of personalized direct mail, and offers outsourcing services for statement printing, imaging, processing and distribution including:

- creation and production of personalized mail
- direct marketing program development
- database management and segmentation services
- response analysis services
- mail production outsourcing services.

Transfers of product between segments are generally accounted for on a basis that results in a fair profit being earned by each segment. The export of product from Canada is insignificant.

Moore Corporation Limited

Industry segments *(in thousands)*

1995	Forms	CCS	Consolidated
Total revenue	$ 2,137,930	$ 512,220	$ 2,650,150
Intersegment sales	(30,203)	(17,693)	(47,896)
Sales to customers outside the enterprise	$ 2,107,727	$ 494,527	$ 2,602,254
Segment operating profit	$ 84,884	$ 32,462	$ 117,346
General corporate income			6,826
Income from operations			$ 124,172
Identifiable assets	$ 1,457,272	$ 271,783	$ 1,729,055
Intersegment eliminations			(11,555)
Corporate assets including investment in associated corporations			518,138
Total assets			$ 2,235,638
Depreciation expense	$ 53,309	$ 23,082	$ 76,391
Capital expenditures	$ 57,888	$ 28,717	$ 86,605

1994			
Total revenue	$ 1,970,146	$ 453,421	$ 2,423,567
Intersegment sales	(12,381)	(5,138)	(17,519)
Sales to customers outside the enterprise	$ 1,957,765	$ 448,283	$ 2,406,048
Segment operating profit	$ 103,803	$ 34,151	$ 137,954
General corporate income			1,019
Income from operations			$ 138,973
Identifiable assets	$ 1,303,181	$ 288,158	$ 1,591,339
Intersegment eliminations			(24)
Corporate assets including investment in associated corporations			440,021
Total assets			$ 2,031,336
Depreciation expense	$ 54,555	$ 24,364	$ 78,919
Capital expenditures	$ 59,561	$ 17,453	$ 77,014

1993			
Total revenue	$ 1,935,318	$ 412,165	$ 2,347,483
Intersegment sales	(10,743)	(4,944)	(15,687)
Sales to customers outside the enterprise	$ 1,924,575	$ 407,221	$ 2,331,796
Segment operating loss	$ (90,733)	$ (10,509)	$ (101,242)
General corporate income			2,840
Loss from operations			$ (98,402)
Identifiable assets	$ 1,356,677	$ 263,773	$ 1,620,450
Intersegment eliminations			(16)
Corporate assets including investment in associated corporations			353,598
Total assets			$ 1,974,032
Depreciation expense	$ 58,243	$ 23,697	$ 81,940
Capital expenditures	$ 57,591	$ 24,418	$ 82,009

Moore Corporation Limited

Geographic segments *(in thousands)*

1995	Canada	United States	Europe	Latin America	Asia Pacific	Consolidated
Total revenue	$ 197,747	$ 1,607,288	$ 373,510	$ 243,444	$ 192,241	$ 2,614,230
Intergeographical segment sales	(906)	(11,008)	(62)	–	–	(11,976)
Sales to customers outside the enterprise	$ 196,841	$ 1,596,280	$ 373,448	$ 243,444	$ 192,241	$ 2,602,254
Segment operating profit (loss)	$ 13,186	$ 81,687	$ 9,567	$ 21,104	$ (8,198)	$ 117,346
General corporate income						6,826
Income from operations						$ 124,172
Identifiable assets	$ 142,791	$ 1,077,964	$ 246,101	$ 148,367	$ 108,464	$ 1,723,687
Intersegment eliminations						(6,187)
Corporate assets including investment in associated corporations						518,138
Total assets						$ 2,235,638
Depreciation expense	$ 6,541	$ 51,039	$ 8,205	$ 7,132	$ 3,474	$ 76,391
Capital expenditures	$ 5,970	$ 56,791	$ 11,066	$ 8,004	$ 4,774	$ 86,605

1994	Canada	United States	Europe	Latin America	Asia Pacific	Consolidated
Total revenue	$ 187,190	$ 1,477,537	$ 344,414	$ 205,220	$ 204,638	$ 2,418,999
Intergeographical segment sales	(771)	(12,147)	(33)	–	–	(12,951)
Sales to customers outside the enterprise	$ 186,419	$ 1,465,390	$ 344,381	$ 205,220	$ 204,638	$ 2,406,048
Segment operating profit	$ 6,451	$ 101,480	$ 14,221	$ 11,048	$ 4,754	$ 137,954
General corporate income						1,019
Income from operations						$ 138,973
Identifiable assets	$ 101,966	$ 1,039,534	$ 270,899	$ 138,876	$ 117,719	$ 1,668,994
Intersegment eliminations						(77,679)
Corporate assets including investment in associated corporations						440,021
Total assets						$ 2,031,336
Depreciation expense	$ 5,929	$ 48,901	$ 10,853	$ 7,695	$ 5,541	$ 78,919
Capital expenditures	$ 6,240	$ 46,438	$ 10,641	$ 5,419	$ 8,276	$ 77,014

1993	Canada	United States	Europe	Latin America	Asia Pacific	Consolidated
Total revenue	$ 188,051	$ 1,532,078	$ 332,786	$ 194,130	$ 98,678	$ 2,345,723
Intergeographical segment sales	(73)	(13,854)	–	–	–	(13,927)
Sales to customers outside the enterprise	$ 187,978	$ 1,518,224	$ 332,786	$ 194,130	$ 98,678	$ 2,331,796
Segment operating profit (loss)	$ (13,503)	$ (28,067)	$ (54,149)	$ 12,777	$ (18,300)	$ (101,242)
General corporate income						2,840
Loss from operations						$ (98,402)
Identifiable assets	$ 122,294	$ 1,016,150	$ 252,590	$ 136,577	$ 100,646	$ 1,628,257
Intersegment eliminations						(7,823)
Corporate assets including investment in associated corporations						353,598
Total assets						$ 1,974,032
Depreciation expense	$ 6,385	$ 49,757	$ 14,249	$ 8,080	$ 3,469	$ 81,940
Capital expenditures	$ 5,637	$ 56,511	$ 7,216	$ 9,751	$ 2,894	$ 82,009

Moore Corporation Limited

18. Lease commitments *(in thousands)*

At December 31, 1995, long-term lease commitments required approximate future rental payments as follows:

1996	$ 48,635	1999	$ 23,993
1997	41,036	2000	21,328
1998	31,672	2001 and thereafter	35,803

19. Contingencies

At December 31, 1995, certain lawsuits and other claims were pending against the Corporation. While the outcome of these matters is subject to future resolution, management's evaluation and analysis of such matters indicates that, individually and in the aggregate, the probable ultimate resolution of such matters will not have a material effect on the Corporation's financial statements.

20. Financial instruments

At December 31, 1995, the contract amount of forward contracts was approximately $44,065,000 and the market value was $44,018,000. Net deferred gains and losses from these contracts were not significant at December 31, 1995.

The Corporation may be exposed to losses if the counterparties to the above contracts fail to perform.

The Corporation manages this risk by dealing only with financially sound counterparties and by establishing dollar and term limitations which correspond to the credit rating of each counterparty.

The Corporation does not use derivative financial instruments for trading purposes.

21. Differences between Canadian and United States Generally Accepted Accounting Principles

The continued registration of the common shares of the Corporation with the Securities and Exchange Commission (SEC) and listing of the shares on the New York Stock Exchange require compliance with the integrated disclosure rules of the SEC.

The accounting policies in Note 1 and accounting principles generally accepted in Canada are consistent in all material aspects with United States generally accepted accounting principles (GAAP) with the following exceptions.

For reporting under United States GAAP, the Corporation adopted prospectively as of January 1, 1992 the Financial Accounting Standards Board's SFAS No. 106, "Employers' Accounting for Postretirement Benefits Other Than Pensions" and as of January 1, 1993 SFAS No. 109, "Accounting for Income Taxes".

Postretirement benefits other than pensions (SFAS No. 106)
SFAS No. 106 requires that the expected costs of the employees' postretirement benefits be expensed during the years that the employees render services, whereas under Canadian GAAP the Corporation recognizes the cost of these benefits as an expense as incurred (see Note 12).

In July 1993, the Corporation's United States subsidiary announced a change to the retiree health care program for employees who retire after April 1, 1994 whereby an allowance based on length of service is granted to offset the cost of health care coverage selected by the retiree. The effect of the change was to reduce the unfunded accumulated postretirement benefit obligation by $157 million. The related unrecognized prior service credit will be amortized on the straight-line basis over 17 years, the expected average remaining service life of the employee group.

Income taxes (SFAS No. 109)
SFAS No. 109 requires a liability method under which temporary differences are tax effected at current tax rates, whereas under Canadian GAAP, timing differences are tax effected at the rates in effect when they arise. The cumulative transition adjustment related to the adoption of SFAS No. 109 was an increase in net income of $14,500,000.

Earnings per share
Under United States GAAP, the average shares outstanding is the sum of the weighted average number of shares outstanding during the period plus the common share equivalents of the executive stock option plan.

Moore Corporation Limited

The following table provides information required under United States GAAP:

(in thousands, except per share amounts)	1995	1994	1993
Net earnings (loss) as reported	$ 267,501	$ 121,400	$ (77,606)
Postretirement benefits other than pensions:			
Increased postretirement benefits	(4,417)	(4,999)	(21,192)
Reduced income taxes	1,735	1,899	8,292
	(2,682)	(3,100)	(12,900)
Income taxes:			
Cumulative transition adjustment	–	–	14,500
Net (increase) decrease in deferred tax provision	(13,611)	3,300	4,900
	(13,611)	3,300	19,400
Net earnings (loss) determined under United States GAAP	$ 251,208	$ 121,600	$ (71,106)
Primary and fully diluted earnings (loss) per share	$ 2.51	$ 1.22	$ (0.71)
Average shares outstanding (in thousands)	100,005	99,695	99,557
Additional cash flow disclosures required by SFAS No. 95:			
Interest paid	$ 11,608	$ 13,601	$ 18,638
Income taxes paid	16,449	20,658	39,448

Balance sheet items as at December 31:

(in thousands)	1995		1994	
	As reported	U.S. GAAP	As reported	U.S. GAAP
Postretirement benefit cost liability	$ –	$ 436,002	$ –	$ 431,414
Net deferred income taxes liability (asset)	16,656	(165,974)	15,026	(182,482)
Retained earnings	1,187,974	929,581	1,014,257	772,157

The following data is based upon the report from independent consulting actuaries as at December 31:

	1995	1994
Accrued postretirement benefit cost (in thousands)		
Retirees	$ 179,165	$ 174,578
Fully eligible active plan participants	1,965	1,726
Other active plan participants	121,244	98,811
Accumulated postretirement benefit obligation	302,374	275,115
Unrecognized prior service credit	134,117	143,366
Unrecognized net gain (loss)	(489)	12,933
Accrued postretirement benefit cost	$ 436,002	$ 431,414

Moore Corporation Limited

	1995	1994
Postretirement benefit cost *(in thousands)*		
Current service cost	$ 5,755	$ 6,836
Interest cost	23,381	20,921
Amortization of unrecognized prior service credit	(9,168)	(9,168)
Net postretirement benefit cost	$ 19,968	$ 18,589
Assumptions and other information		
Weighted average discount rate	7.0%	8.7%
Weighted average health care cost trend rate		
Before age 65	10.8%	11.8%
After age 65	8.9%	9.9%
The general trend in the rate thereafter is a reduction of 1% per year.		
Weighted average ultimate health care cost trend rate	5.3%	7.0%
Year in which ultimate health care cost trend rate will be achieved		
Canada	2004	2004
United States	2000	1998
The following is the effect of a 1% increase in the assumed health care		
cost trend rates for each future year on: *(in thousands)*		
(a) Accumulated postretirement benefit obligation	$ 17,285	$ 14,984
(b) Aggregate of the service and interest cost		
components of net postretirement benefit cost	1,414	1,176

The following table shows the main items included in deferred income taxes under United States GAAP:

	1995	1994
Deferred income taxes *(in thousands)*		
Assets:		
Postretirement benefits other than pensions	$ 172,134	$ 170,721
Tax benefit of loss carryovers	52,978	43,002
Pensions	21,821	22,056
Restructuring costs	13,659	40,066
Other	18,182	21,721
	278,774	297,566
Valuation allowance	(19,618)	(10,626)
	259,156	286,940
Liabilities:		
Depreciation	69,408	83,485
Pensions	15,595	13,777
Other	8,179	7,196
	93,182	104,458
Net deferred income taxes	$ 165,974	$ 182,482

22. Comparative consolidated financial statements

Comparative figures have been restated where appropriate to conform to the current presentation.

Moore Corporation Limited

Management Report

All of the information in this annual report is the responsibility of management and has been approved by the Board of Directors. The financial information contained herein conforms to the accompanying consolidated financial statements, which have been prepared and presented in accordance with accounting principles generally accepted in Canada and necessarily include amounts that are based on judgments and estimates applied consistently and considered appropriate in the circumstances.

The Corporation maintains a system of internal control which is designed to provide reasonable assurance that assets are safeguarded, that accurate accounting records are maintained, and that reliable financial information is prepared on a timely basis. The Corporation also maintains an internal audit department that evaluates and formally reports to management and the Audit Committee on the adequacy and effectiveness of internal controls.

The consolidated financial statements have been audited by the Corporation's independent auditors, Price Waterhouse, and their report is included below.

The Audit Committee of the Board of Directors is composed entirely of outside directors and meets quarterly with the Corporation's independent auditors, management, and Director of Internal Audit to discuss the scope and results of audit examinations with respect to internal controls and financial reporting of the Corporation.

R. Braun
Chairman, President and
Chief Executive Officer

S.A. Holinski
Senior Vice President
and Chief Financial Officer

February 14, 1996

Auditors' Report

To the Shareholders of Moore Corporation Limited:

We have audited the consolidated balance sheets of Moore Corporation Limited as at December 31, 1995 and 1994 and the consolidated statements of earnings, retained earnings and cash flows for each of the three years in the period ended December 31, 1995. These consolidated financial statements are the responsibility of the Corporation's management. Our responsibility is to express an opinion on these consolidated financial statements based on our audits.

We conducted our audits in accordance with generally accepted auditing standards. Those standards require that we plan and perform an audit to obtain reasonable assurance whether the financial statements are free of material misstatement. An audit includes examining, on a test basis, evidence supporting the amounts and disclosures in the financial statements. An audit also includes assessing the accounting principles used and significant estimates made by management, as well as evaluating the overall financial statement presentation.

In our opinion, these consolidated financial statements present fairly, in all material respects, the financial position of the Corporation as at December 31, 1995 and 1994 and the results of its operations and the changes in its cash flows for each of the three years in the period ended December 31, 1995 in accordance with generally accepted accounting principles.

Price Waterhouse
Chartered Accountants, Toronto, Canada

February 14, 1996

EXERCISES

E5-1 **(Balance Sheet Classifications)** Presented below are a number of balance sheet accounts of Clara Mitchell Inc.:

1. Investment in Preferred Shares
2. Treasury Shares
3. Common Shares Distributable
4. Cash Dividends Payable
5. Accumulated Depreciation
6. Warehouse in Process of Construction
7. Petty Cash

8. Accrued Interest on Notes Payable
9. Deficit
10. Marketable Securities (short-term)
11. Income Taxes Payable
12. Unearned Subscription Revenue
13. Work in Process
14. Accrued Vacation Pay

Instructions

For each of the accounts above, indicate the proper balance sheet classification. In the case of borderline items, indicate the additional information that would be required to determine the proper classification.

E5-2 **(Classification of Balance Sheet Accounts)** Presented below are the captions of Mildred Ripley Limited's balance sheet:

A. Current Assets
B. Investments
C. Property, Plant, and Equipment
D. Intangible Assets
E. Other Assets

F. Current Liabilities
G. Noncurrent Liabilities
H. Share Capital
I. Contributed Surplus
J. Retained Earnings

Instructions

Indicate by letter where each of the following items would be classified:

1. Preferred shares
2. Goodwill
3. Wages payable
4. Trade accounts payable
5. Buildings
6. Marketable securities
7. Current portion of long-term debt
8. Premium on bonds payable
9. Allowance for doubtful accounts
10. Accounts receivable

11. Cash surrender value of life insurance
12. Notes payable (due next year)
13. Office supplies
14. Common shares
15. Land
16. Bond sinking fund
17. Merchandise inventory
18. Prepaid insurance
19. Bonds payable
20. Taxes payable

E5-3 **(Classification of Balance Sheet Accounts)** Assume that Robert Lockwood Enterprises uses the following headings on its balance sheet:

A. Current Assets
B. Investments
C. Property, Plant, and Equipment
D. Intangible Assets
E. Other Assets

F. Current Liabilities
G. Long-term Liabilities
H. Share Capital
I. Contributed Surplus
J. Retained Earnings

Instructions

Indicate by letter where each of the following would usually be classified. If an item should appear in a note to the financial statements, use the letter "N" to indicate this fact. If an item need not be reported at all on the balance sheet, use the letter "X."

1. Unexpired insurance
2. Shares owned in affiliated companies
3. Unearned subscriptions
4. Advances to suppliers

5. Unearned rent
6. Treasury shares
7. Preferred shares issued
8. Copyrights

9. Petty cash fund

10. Sale of large issue of common shares 15 days after balance sheet date

11. Accrued interest on notes receivable

12. 20-year issue of bonds payable that will mature within the next year (no sinking fund exists and refunding is not planned)

13. Machinery retired from use and held for sale

14. Fully depreciated machine still in use

15. Organization costs

16. Accrued interest on bonds payable

17. Salaries that company budget shows will be paid to employees within next year

18. Company is a defendant in a lawsuit for $1 million (possibility of loss is likely but the amount cannot be reasonably estimated)

19. Discount on bonds payable (assume related to bonds payable in No. 12)

20. Accumulated depreciation (amortization)

(Preparation of a Classified Balance Sheet) Assume that Gertrude Seaman Inc. has the following accounts at the end of the current year. **E5-4**

1. Common Shares
2. Discount on Bonds Payable
3. Treasury Shares (at cost)
4. Common Shares Subscribed
5. Raw Materials
6. Investments in Preferred Shares (long-term)
7. Unearned Rent Revenue
8. Work in Process
9. Copyrights
10. Buildings
11. Notes Receivable (short-term)
12. Cash
13. Accrued Salaries Payable

14. Accumulated Depreciation—Buildings
15. Cash Restricted for Plant Expansion
16. Land Held for Future Plant Site
17. Allowance for Doubtful Accounts—Accounts Receivable
18. Retained Earnings—Unappropriated
19. Goodwill
20. Unearned Subscription Revenue
21. Receivables—Officers (due in one year)
22. Finished Goods
23. Accounts Receivable
24. Bonds Payable (due in four years)
25. Share Subscriptions Receivable

Instructions

Prepare a balance sheet in good form (no monetary amounts are necessary).

(Preparation of a Corrected Balance Sheet) Celia Cruz Company has decided to expand its operations. The bookkeeper recently completed the balance sheet presented below in order to obtain additional funds for expansion. **E5-5**

CELIA CRUZ COMPANY
Balance Sheet
For the Year Ended 1998

Current assets
Cash (net of bank overdraft of $30,000)	$200,000
Accounts receivable (net)	340,000
Inventories at lower of average cost and market	385,000
Marketable securities—at market (cost $120,000)	140,000

Property, plant, and equipment
Building (net)	570,000
Office equipment (net)	160,000
Land held for future use	175,000

Intangible assets
Goodwill	80,000
Cash surrender value of life insurance	90,000
Prepaid expenses	5,000

Current liabilities
Accounts payable	105,000
Notes payable (due next year)	125,000
Pension obligation	82,000
Rent payable	55,000
Premium on bonds payable	53,000

(Continued)

CELIA CRUZ COMPANY
Balance Sheet (*Continued*)

Long-term liabilities	
Bond payable	500,000
Shareholders' equity	
Common shares, no par, authorized 400,000 shares,	
issued 290,000	290,000
Contributed surplus—donations	160,000
Retained earnings	?

Instructions
Prepare a revised balance sheet given the available information. Assume that the accumulated depreciation balance for the buildings is $140,000 and for the office equipment, $95,000. The allowance for doubtful accounts has a balance of $10,000. The pension obligation is considered a long-term liability.

E5-6   (Corrections of a Balance Sheet) The bookkeeper for Angela Downey Company has prepared the following balance sheet as of July 31, 1998.

ANGELA DOWNEY COMPANY
Balance Sheet
As of July 31, 1998

Cash	$ 69,000	Notes and accounts payable	$ 44,000
Accounts receivable (net)	40,500	Long-term liabilities	75,000
Inventories	60,000	Shareholders' equity	155,500
Equipment (net)	84,000		
Patents	21,000		
	$274,500		$274,500

The following additional information is provided.

1. Cash includes $1,200 in a petty cash fund and $9,000 in a bond sinking fund.

2. The net accounts receivable balance is comprised of the following three items: (a) accounts receivable—debit balances $50,000; (b) accounts receivable—credit balances $6,000; (c) allowance for doubtful accounts—$3,500.

3. Merchandise inventory costing $5,300 is shipped out on consignment on July 31, 1998. The ending inventory balance does not include the consigned goods. Receivables in the amount of $5,300 are recognized on these consigned goods.

4. Equipment has a cost of $98,000 and an accumulated depreciation balance of $14,000.

5. Taxes payable of $6,000 are accrued on July 31. Angela Downey Company has set up a cash fund to meet this obligation. This cash fund is not included in the cash balance, but is offset against the taxes payable amount.

Instructions
Prepare a corrected balance sheet as of July 31, 1998 from the available information.

E5-7   (Current Asset Section of the Balance Sheet) Presented below are selected accounts of Racine Company at December 31, 1998:

Finished goods	$ 52,000
Revenue received in advance	90,000
Bank overdraft	8,000
Equipment	253,000
Work-in-process	14,000
Cash	37,000
Short-term investments in shares	31,000
Customer advances	36,000
Cash restricted for plant expansion	50,000
Cost of goods sold	2,100,000
Notes receivable	40,000
Accounts receivable	161,000
Raw materials	207,000
Supplies expense	60,000

Allowance for doubtful accounts	12,000
Licences	18,000
Contributed surplus	88,000
Treasury shares	22,000

The following additional information is available:

1. Inventories are valued at lower of cost and market using FIFO.

2. Equipment is recorded at cost. Accumulated depreciation, computed on a straight-line basis, is $50,600.

3. The short-term investments have a market value of $29,000 (assume marketable).

4. The notes receivable are due June 30, 1999 with interest receivable every June 30. The notes bear interest at 12%. (Hint: Accrue interest due on 12/31/98.)

5. The allowance for doubtful accounts applies to the accounts receivable. Accounts receivable of $50,000 are pledged as collateral on a bank loan.

6. Licences are recorded net of accumulated amortization of $14,000.

7. Treasury shares are recorded at cost.

Instructions

Prepare the current asset section of Racine Company's December 31, 1998 balance sheet, with appropriate disclosures.

(Current vs. Long-Term Liabilities) Natalie Cole Corporation Ltd. is preparing its December 31, 1998 balance sheet. The following items may be reported as either a current or long-term liability.   E5-8

1. On December 15, 1998, Cole declared a cash dividend of $3.00 per share to shareholders of record on December 31. The dividend is payable on January 15, 1999. Cole has issued 1,000,000 common shares, of which 50,000 shares are held in treasury.

2. Also on December 15, Cole declares a 10% stock dividend to shareholders of record on December 31. The dividend will be distributed on January 15, 1999. Cole's no par value common shares have a market value of $38 per share and an average issuance price of $10.

3. At December 31, bonds payable of $100,000,000 are outstanding. The bonds pay 12% interest every August 31 and mature in instalments of $25,000,000 every August 31, beginning August 31, 1999.

4. At December 31, 1997, customer advances are $12,000,000. During 1998, Cole collects $30,000,000 of customer advances, and advances of $23,000,000 are earned.

5. At December 31, 1998, retained earnings appropriated for future inventory losses is $15,000,000.

Instructions

For each item above, indicate the dollar amounts to be reported as a current liability and as a long-term liability, if any.

(Contingencies— Entries and Disclosures) Kathleen Major Sound Machines is involved with two contingencies at December 31, 1998.   E5-9

1. The company is involved in a pending court case. Legal counsel feels it is likely that the company will prevail and be awarded damages of $3,000,000.

2. Major sells several machines under a one-year warranty. It is likely that a liability of $2,400,000 exists at December 31, 1998 because of this warranty.

Instructions

(a) Prepare all entries necessary at December 31, 1998 to record these contingencies.

(b) What disclosures would Major make in its December 31, 1998 balance sheet?

(Post-Balance Sheet Events) Otis Clay Ltd. issued its financial statements for the year ended December 31, 1998 on March 10, 1999. The following events took place early in 1999.   E5-10

1. On January 10, 10,000 no par value common shares were issued at $70 per share.

2. On March 1, Clay determined after negotiations with the Department of National Revenue that income taxes payable for 1998 should be $1,230,000. At December 31, 1998, income taxes payable were recorded at $1,100,000.

Instructions

Discuss how the preceding post-balance sheet events should be reflected in the 1998 financial statements.

E5-11 **(Current Assets and Current Liabilities)** The current asset and liability sections of the balance sheet of Oliver Cromwell Limited appear as follows:

OLIVER CROMWELL LIMITED
Partial Balance Sheet
December 31, 1998

Cash		$ 38,000	Accounts payable	$ 60,000
Accounts receivable	$86,000		Notes payable	64,000
Less allowance for				
doubtful accounts	7,000	79,000		
Inventories		170,000		
Prepaid expenses		9,000		
		$296,000		$124,000

The following errors in the corporation's accounting have been discovered:

1. January 1999 cash disbursements entered as of December 1998 included payments of accounts payable in the amount of $39,000, on which a cash discount of 2% was taken.

2. The inventory included $27,000 of merchandise that had been received at December 31 but for which no purchase invoices had been received or entered. Of this amount, $12,000 had been received on consignment; the remainder was purchased f.o.b. destination, terms 2/10, n/30.

3. Sales for the first four days in January 1999 in the amount of $30,000 were entered in the sales book as of December 31, 1998. Of these, $21,500 were sales on account and the remainder were cash sales.

4. Cash, not including cash sales, collected in January 1999 and entered as of December 31, 1998, totalled $35,324. Of this amount, $23,324 was received on account after cash discounts of 2% had been deducted; the remainder represented the proceeds of a bank loan.

Instructions
(a) Restate the current asset and liability sections of the balance sheet in accordance with good accounting practice. (Assume that both accounts receivable and accounts payable are recorded gross.)
(b) State the net effect of your adjustments on Oliver Cromwell Limited's retained earnings balance.

E5-12 **(Post-Balance Sheet Events)** For each of the following subsequent (post-balance sheet) events, indicate whether a company should (a) adjust the financial statements; (b) disclose in notes to the financial statements; or (c) neither adjust nor disclose.

Restate F/S. A. 1. Settlement of federal tax case at a cost considerably in excess of the amount expected at year-end.

C. 2. Introduction of a new product line.

B. 3. Loss of assembly plant due to fire.

B. 4. Sale of a significant portion of the company's assets.

C. 5. Retirement of the company president.

C. 6. Prolonged employee strike.

only if there's econ dep B. 7. Loss of a significant customer.

Because its material B. 8. Issuance of a significant number of common shares.

A. 9. Material loss on a year-end receivable because of a customer's bankruptcy.

C. 10. Hiring of a new president.

A. 11. Settlement of prior year's litigation against the company.

B. 12. Merger with another company of comparable size.

E5-13 **(Statement of Cash Flows—Classifications)** The major classifications of activities reported in the statement of cash flows are operating, investing, and financing. Classify each of the transactions listed below according to these five groupings:

1. Operating activity—add to net income.
2. Operating activity—deduct from net income.
3. Investing activity.
4. Financing activity.
5. Reported in two categories of the statement of cash flows.

The transactions are as follows:

(a) Issuance of shares.

(b) Purchase of land and building.

(c) Redemption of bonds.

(d) Sale of equipment.

(e) Depreciation of machinery.

(f) Amortization of patent.

(g) Issuance of bonds for plant assets.

(h) Payment of cash dividends.

(i) Exchange of furniture for office equipment.

(j) Purchase of treasury shares.

(k) Loss on sale of equipment.

(l) Increase in accounts receivable during the year.

(m) Decrease in accounts payable during the year.

(Preparation of a Statement of Cash Flows) The comparative balance sheets of Henry Smits Inc. at the beginning and the end of the year 1998 appear below.   E5-14

HENRY SMITS INC.
Balance Sheets

Assets	December 31, 1998	January 1, 1998	Increase/Decrease
Cash	$ 45,000	$ 13,000	$32,000 Inc.
Accounts receivable (net)	91,000	88,000	3,000 Inc.
Equipment	39,000	22,000	17,000 Inc.
Less accumulated depreciation	(17,000)	(11,000)	6,000 Inc.
Total	$158,000	$112,000	
Liabilities and Shareholders' Equity			
Accounts payable	$ 20,000	$ 15,000	5,000 Inc.
Common shares	100,000	80,000	20,000 Inc.
Retained earnings	38,000	17,000	21,000 Inc.
Total	$158,000	$112,000	

Net income of $35,000 was reported and dividends of $14,000 were paid in 1998. New equipment was purchased and none was sold.

Instructions

Prepare a statement of cash flows for the year 1998.

(Preparation of a Statement of Cash Flows) Presented below is a condensed version of the comparative balance sheets for Mel Richards Limited for the last two years at December 31:   E5-15

	1998	1997
Cash	$177,000	$ 78,000
Accounts receivable	180,000	185,000
Investments	52,000	74,000
Equipment	298,000	240,000
Less accumulated depreciation	(106,000)	(89,000)
Current liabilities	134,000	151,000
Common shares	160,000	160,000
Retained earnings	307,000	177,000

Additional information:

Investments were sold at a loss (not extraordinary) of $9,000; no equipment was sold; cash dividends paid were $20,000; and net income was $150,000.

Instructions

Prepare a statement of cash flows for 1998 for Mel Richards Limited.

E5-16   (Preparation of a Statement of Cash Flows) A comparative balance sheet for Anne Boleyn Limited is presented below.

	December 31	
Assets	1998	1997
Cash	$ 69,000	$ 22,000
Accounts receivable (net)	82,000	66,000
Inventories	180,000	189,000
Land	75,000	110,000
Equipment	260,000	200,000
Accumulated depreciation—equipment	(69,000)	(42,000)
Total	$597,000	$545,000
Liabilities and Shareholders' Equity		
Accounts payable	$ 34,000	$ 47,000
Bonds payable	150,000	200,000
Common shares (no par)	214,000	164,000
Retained earnings	199,000	134,000
Total	$597,000	$545,000

Additional information:

1. Net income for 1998 was $115,000.

2. Cash dividends of $50,000 were declared and paid.

3. Bonds payable amounting to $50,000 were retired through issuance of common shares.

Instructions

Prepare a statement of cash flows for 1998 for Anne Boleyn Limited.

E5-17   (Preparation of a Balance Sheet) Presented below is the trial balance of Seymore Limited at December 31, 1998.

	Debits	Credits
Cash	$ 227,000	
Sales		$ 8,000,000
Marketable securities—current	153,000	
Cost of goods sold	4,800,000	
Long-term investments in bonds	269,000	
Long-term investments in shares	277,000	
Short-term notes payable		90,000
Accounts payable		475,000
Selling expenses	2,000,000	
Investment revenue		63,000
Land	260,000	
Buildings	1,040,000	
Dividends payable		136,000
Accrued liabilities		96,000
Accounts receivable	435,000	
Accumulated depreciation—buildings		152,000
Allowance for doubtful accounts		25,000
Administrative expenses	900,000	
Interest expense	211,000	
Inventories	597,000	
Extraordinary gain		80,000
Prior period adjustment—depreciation error	140,000	
Long-term notes payable		900,000
Equipment	600,000	
Bonds payable		1,100,000
Accumulated depreciation—equipment		40,000
Franchise (net of $80,000 amortization)	160,000	
Common shares (no par value)		1,000,000
Treasury shares	191,000	
Patent (net of $30,000 amortization)	195,000	
Retained earnings		218,000
Contributed surplus		80,000
Totals	$12,455,000	$12,455,000

[handwritten notes in left margin:]
shares that haven't been issued yet.
increase by Treasury share amt
Common shares (no par value)
Treasury shares
Retained earnings → 409,000

Instructions

Prepare a balance sheet at December 31, 1998 for Seymore Limited.

(Preparation of a Statement of Cash Flows and a Balance Sheet) Thomas Moore Limited's balance sheet at the end   E5-18
of 1997 included the following items:

Current assets	$235,000	
Land	30,000	
Building	120,000	
Equipment	90,000	
Accumulated depreciation—building		$ 30,000
Accumulated depreciation—equipment		11,000
Patents	40,000	
Current liabilities		150,000
Bonds payable		100,000
Common shares		180,000
Retained earnings		44,000
Totals	$515,000	$515,000

The following information is available for 1998.

1. Net income was $46,000.

2. Equipment (cost $20,000 and accumulated depreciation, $8,000) was sold for $10,000.

3. Depreciation expense was $3,000 on the building and $9,000 on equipment.

4. Patent amortization was $5,000.

5. Current assets other than cash increased by $29,000. Current liabilities increased by $13,000.

6. An addition to the building was completed at a cost of $20,000.

7. A long-term investment in shares was purchased for $16,000.

8. Bonds payable of $50,000 were issued.

9. Cash dividends of $30,000 were declared and paid.

10. Treasury shares were purchased at a cost of $9,000.

Instructions

(a) Prepare a statement of cash flows for 1998.

(b) Prepare a balance sheet at December 31, 1998.

PROBLEMS

Presented below is a list of accounts in alphabetical order.   P5-1

Accounts Receivable	Inventory—Ending Inventory
Accrued Wages	Land
Accumulated Depreciation—Buildings	Land for Future Plant Site
Accumulated Depreciation—Equipment	Loss from Flood
Advances to Employees	Notes Payable
Advertising Expense	Patent (net of amortization)
Allowance for Doubtful Accounts	Pension Obligation
Bond Sinking Fund	Petty Cash
Bonds Payable	Preferred Shares
Buildings	Premium on Bonds Payable
Cash in Bank	Prepaid Rent
Cash on Hand	Purchases
Cash Surrender Value of Life Insurance	Purchase Returns and Allowances
Commission Expense	Retained Earnings
Common Shares	Sales
Copyright (net of amortization)	Sales Discounts
Dividends Payable	Sales Salaries
Equipment	Temporary Investments
Employer CPP Payable	Transportation-in
Gain on Sale of Equipment	Treasury Shares (at cost)
Interest Receivable	Unearned Subscription Revenue
Inventory—Beginning Inventory	

Instructions
Prepare a balance sheet in good form (no monetary amounts are to be shown).

P5-2 Presented below are a number of balance sheet items for Santana Ltd. for the current year, 1998.

Goodwill	$ 110,000	Accumulated depreciation—	
Payroll taxes payable	177,591	equipment	$ 292,000
Bonds payable	290,000	Inventories	239,800
Discount on bonds payable	15,000	Rent payable—short-term	45,000
Cash	260,000	Taxes payable	98,362
Land	450,000	Long-term rental obligations	480,000
Notes receivable	545,700	Common shares no par value	200,000
Notes payable to banks	265,000	Preferred shares	150,000
Accounts payable	690,000	Prepaid expenses	87,920
Retained earnings	?	Equipment	1,470,000
Refundable income taxes	97,630	Marketable securities (short-term)	81,000
Unsecured notes payable		Accumulated depreciation—building	170,200
(long-term)	1,600,000	Building	1,640,000

Instructions
Prepare a balance sheet in good form. Common Shares Authorized was 400,000, and 200,000 were issued. Preferred Shares Authorized was 20,000, of which 15,000 were issued. Assume that notes receivable and notes payable are short-term, unless stated otherwise. Cost and fair value of marketable securities are the same.

P5-3 The trial balance of Brower Company and other related information for the year 1998 is presented below.

BROWER COMPANY
Trial Balance
December 31, 1998

Cash	$ 41,000	
Accounts receivable	163,500	
Allowance for doubtful accounts		$ 6,700
Prepaid expenses	5,900	
Inventory	308,500	
Long-term investments	349,000	
Land	85,000	
Construction work in progress	124,000	
Patents	26,000	
Equipment	400,000	
Accumulated depreciation of equipment		142,000
Unamortized discount on bonds payable	20,000	
Accounts payable		148,000
Accrued expenses		38,200
Notes payable		94,000
Bonds payable		400,000
Common shares		545,000
Retained earnings		149,000
	$1,522,900	$1,522,900

Additional Information:
1. The inventory has a replacement market value of $353,000. The FIFO method of inventory value is used.
2. The cost and market value of the long-term investments that consist of bonds and shares are the same.
3. The amount of the Construction Work in Progress account represents the costs expended to date on a building in the process of construction. (The company rents factory space at the present time.) The land on which the building is being constructed cost $85,000, as shown in the trial balance.
4. The patents purchased by the company at a cost of $36,000 are being amortized on a straight-line basis.
5. Of the unamortized discount on bonds payable, $2,000 will be amortized in 1999.
6. The notes payable represent bank loans that are secured by long-term investments carried at $120,000. These bank loans are due in 1999.
7. The bonds payable bear interest at 11% and are due January 1, 2009.
8. Of the 600,000 no par common shares authorized, 500,000 shares are issued and outstanding.

Instructions

Prepare a balance sheet as of December 31, 1998 to fully disclose all important information.

Presented below is the balance sheet of Elkton Limited as of December 31, 1998.   P5-4

ELKTON LIMITED
Balance Sheet
December 31, 1998

Assets

Goodwill (Note 2)	$ 120,000
Building (Note 1)	1,640,000
Inventories	312,100
Land	750,000
Accounts receivable	170,000
Treasury shares (50,000 shares, no par)	87,000
Cash on hand	193,900
Assets allocated to trustee for plant expansion	
Cash in bank	70,000
Treasury bills, at cost	120,000
	$3,463,000

Equities

Notes payable (Note 3)	$ 600,000
Common shares, authorized and issued, 1,000,000 shares,	
no par value	1,150,000
Retained earnings (unappropriated)	648,000
Appreciation capital (Note 1)	570,000
Income taxes payable	75,000
Reserve for depreciation of building	420,000
	$3,463,000

Note 1.
Buildings were stated at cost, except for one building that was recorded at appraised value. The excess of appraisal value over cost was $570,000.

Note 2.
Goodwill in the amount of $120,000 was recognized because the company believed that their book value was not an accurate representation of the fair market value of the company.

Note 3.
Notes payable were long-term except for the current instalment of $60,000 that was due.

Instructions

Prepare a corrected balance sheet in good form. The notes above are for information only.

Presented below is the balance sheet of John Lennon Corporation Ltd. for the current year, 1998.   P5-5

JOHN LENNON CORPORATION
Balance Sheet
December 31, 1998

Current assets	$ 435,000	Current liabilities	$ 330,000
Investments	640,000	Long-term liabilities	1,000,000
Property, plant, and			
equipment	1,720,000	Shareholders' equity	1,770,000
Intangible assets	305,000		
	$3,100,000		$3,100,000

The following information is presented:

1. The Current Asset section includes: Cash $100,000; Accounts Receivable $170,000 less $10,000 for Allowance for Doubtful Accounts; Inventories $180,000; and Prepaid Revenue $5,000. The cash balance consists of $116,000, less a bank overdraft of $16,000. Inventories are stated on the lower of FIFO cost and market basis.

2. The Investments section includes the cash surrender value of a Life Insurance contract $40,000; Investments in Common Shares, short-term $80,000 and long-term $140,000; Bond Sinking Fund $200,000; and Organization Costs $180,000. The cost and fair value of investments in common shares are the same.

3. Property, Plant, and Equipment includes Buildings $1,040,000 less Accumulated Depreciation $360,000; Equipment $420,000 less Accumulated Depreciation $180,000; Land $500,000; and Land Held for Future Use $300,000.

4. Intangible Assets include a Franchise $165,000; Goodwill $100,000; and Discount on Bonds Payable $40,000.

5. Current Liabilities include Accounts Payable $90,000; Notes Payable, short-term $120,000 and long-term $80,000; and Taxes Payable $40,000.

6. Long-Term Liabilities consists solely of 10% Bonds Payable due in the year 2006.

7. Shareholders' Equity has no par value preferred shares, authorized 200,000 shares, issued 70,000 shares for $450,000; and no par value common shares, authorized 400,000 shares, issued 100,000 shares at an average price of $10. In addition, the corporation has Unappropriated Retained Earnings of $320,000.

Instructions

Prepare a balance sheet in good form, adjusting the amounts in each balance sheet classification as affected by the information given above.

P5-6   Beryl Chapman Inc. had the following balance sheet at the end of 1997:

BERYL CHAPMAN INC.
Balance Sheet
December 31, 1997

Cash	$ 20,000	Accounts payable	$ 30,000
Accounts receivable	21,200	Long-term notes payable	41,000
Investments	32,000	Share capital	100,000
Plant assets (net)	81,000	Retained earnings	23,200
Land	40,000		
	$194,200		$194,200

During 1998 the following occurred:

1. Beryl Chapman Inc. sold part of its investment portfolio for $16,000. This transaction resulted in a gain of $2,400 for the firm. The company often sells and buys securities of this nature.

2. A tract of land was purchased for $18,000 cash.

3. Long-term notes payable in the amount of $14,000 were retired before maturity by paying $14,000 cash.

4. An additional $25,000 was received from an issuance of common shares.

5. Dividends totalling $8,200 were declared and paid to shareholders.

6. Net income for 1998 was $30,000 after allowing for depreciation of $12,000.

7. Land was purchased through the issuance of $30,000 in bonds.

8. At December 31, 1998, Cash was $40,000; Accounts Receivable was $41,600; and Accounts Payable remained at $30,000.

Instructions

(a) Prepare a statement of cash flows for 1998.

(b) Prepare the balance sheet as it would appear at December 31, 1998.

(c) How would the statement of cash flows help the user of the financial statements?

P5-7   Dawn Jones has prepared baked goods for resale since 1990. She started a baking business in her home and has been operating in a rented building with a storefront since 1995. Jones incorporated the business as B&B Limited on January 1, 1998, with an initial issue of 2,500 no par value common shares at $1.00 per share. Dawn Jones is the principal shareholder of B&B Limited.

Sales have increased 30% annually since operations began at the present location, and additional equipment is needed to accommodate expected continued growth. Jones wishes to purchase some additional baking equipment and to finance the equipment through a long-term note from a commercial bank. Maritime Bank & Trust has asked Jones to submit an income statement for B&B Limited for the first five months of 1998 and a balance sheet as of May 31, 1998.

Jones assembled the following information from the cash basis records of the corporation for use in preparing the financial statements requested by the bank.

1. The cheque register showed the following 1998 deposits through May 31.

Issue of common shares	$ 2,500
Cash sales	22,440
Rebates from purchases	130
Collections on credit sales	5,320
Bank loan proceeds	2,880
	$33,270

2. The following amounts were disbursed through May 31, 1998.

Baking materials	$14,300
Rent	1,800
Salaries and wages	5,500
Maintenance	110
Utilities	4,000
Insurance premium	1,680
Equipment	3,000
Principal and interest payment on bank loan	312
Advertising	424
	$31,126

3. Unpaid invoices at May 31, 1998, were as follows.

Baking materials	$256
Utilities	220
	$476

4. Customer records showed uncollected sales of $4,226 at May 31, 1998.

5. Baking materials costing $1,840 were on hand at May 31, 1998. There were no materials in process or finished goods on hand at that date. No materials were on hand or in process and no finished goods were on hand at January 1, 1998.

6. The note evidencing the three-year bank loan was dated January 1, 1998 and stated a simple interest rate of 10%. The loan required quarterly payments on April 1, July 1, October 1, and January 1 consisting of equal principal payments plus accrued interest since the last payment.

7. Dawn Jones receives a salary of $750 on the last day of each month. The other employees were paid through Friday, May 27, 1998, and an additional $200 was due on May 31, 1998.

8. New display cases and equipment costing $3,000 were purchased on January 2, 1998. They have an estimated useful life of five years. These are the only fixed assets currently used in the business. Straight-line depreciation is to be used for book purposes.

9. Rent was paid for six months in advance on January 2, 1998.

10. A one-year insurance policy was purchased on January 2, 1998.

11. B&B Ltd. is subject to an income tax rate of 20 percent.

12. Payments and collections pertaining to the unincorporated business through December 31, 1997 were not included in the records of the corporation, and no cash was transferred from the unincorporated business to the corporation.

Instructions

Using the accrual basis of accounting, prepare for B&B Limited:

(a) An income statement for the five months ended May 31, 1998.

(b) A balance sheet as of May 31, 1998.

CASES

The following items were brought to your attention during the course of the year-end audit: C5-1

1. The client expects to recover a substantial amount in connection with a pending refund claim for a prior year's taxes. Although the claim is being contested, counsel for the company has confirmed this expectation.

2. Your client is a defendant in a patent infringement suit involving a material amount; you have received from the client's counsel a statement that the loss can be reasonably estimated and that it is likely to occur.

3. Cash includes a substantial sum specifically set aside for immediate reconstruction of a plant and replacement of machinery.

4. Because of a general increase in the number of labour disputes and strikes, both within and outside the industry, it is very likely that the client will suffer a costly strike in the near future.

5. Trade accounts receivable include a large number of customers' notes, many of which have been renewed several times and may have to be renewed continually for some time in the future. The interest is settled on each maturity date and the manufacturers are in good credit standing.

6. At the beginning of the year the client entered into a 10-year nonrenewable lease agreement. Provisions in the lease require the client to make substantial reconditioning and restoration expenditures at the termination of the lease, if necessary.

7. Inventory includes retired equipment, some at regularly depreciated book value, and some at scrap or sale value.

Instructions

For each of the situations above, describe the accounting treatment that you would recommend for the current year. Justify your recommended treatment for each situation.

C5-2   At December 31, 1998, James Dunbar Ltd. has assets of $10,000,000, liabilities of $6,000,000, share capital of $2,000,000 (representing 2,000,000 no par common shares), and retained earnings of $2,000,000. Net sales for the year 1998 were $18,000,000 and net income was $800,000. As auditor of this company, you are making a review of subsequent events of this company on February 13, 1999 and find the following.

1. On February 3, 1999, one of Dunbar's customers declared bankruptcy. At December 31, 1998, this company owed Dunbar $300,000, of which $30,000 was paid in January, 1999.

2. On January 18, 1999, one of the three major plants of the client burned down.

3. On January 23, 1999, a strike was called at one of Dunbar's largest plants that halted 30% of its production. As of February 13, the strike has not been settled.

4. A major electronics enterprise has introduced a line of products that will compete directly with Dunbar's primary line, now being produced in a specially designed new plant. Because of manufacturing innovations, the competitor has been able to achieve quality similar to that of Dunbar's products, but at a price 50% lower. Dunbar officials say they will meet the lower prices, which are high enough to cover variable manufacturing and selling costs but which permit recovery of only a portion of fixed costs.

5. Merchandise traded in the open market is recorded in the company's records at $1.40 per unit on December 31, 1998. This price had prevailed for two weeks, after release of an official market report that predicted vastly increased supplies; however, no purchases were made at $1.40. The price throughout the preceding year had been about $2.00, which was the level experienced over several years. On January 18, 1999, the price returned to $2.00, after public disclosure of an error in the official calculations of the prior December resulted in a correction that destroyed the expectations of excessive supplies. Inventory at December 31, 1998 was on a lower of cost and market basis.

6. On February 1, 1999, the board of directors adopted a resolution accepting the offer of an investment banker to guarantee the marketing of $1,000,000 of preferred shares.

Instructions

State in each case how the 1998 financial statements would be affected, if at all.

C5-3   In an examination of Kimmel Corporation Ltd. as of December 31, 1998, you have learned that the following situations exist. No entries have been made in the accounting records for these items.

1. The corporation erected its present factory building in 1983. Depreciation was calculated by the straight-line method, using an estimated life of 35 years. Early in 1998, the board of directors conducted a careful survey and estimated that the factory building had a remaining useful life of 25 years as of January 1, 1998.

2. An additional assessment of 1997 income taxes was levied and paid in 1998.

3. When calculating the accrual for officers' salaries at December 31, 1998, it was discovered that the accrual for officers' salaries for December 31, 1997 had been overstated.

4. On December 15, 1998, Kimmel Corporation Ltd. declared a stock dividend of 1,000 common shares per 100,000 of its common shares outstanding, payable February 1, 1999, to the common shareholders of record on December 31, 1998.

5. Kimmel Corporation Ltd., which is on a calendar-year basis, changed its inventory method as of January 1, 1998. The inventory for December 31, 1997 was costed by the average method, and the inventory for December 31, 1998 was costed by the FIFO method.

6. Kimmel Corporation Ltd. has guaranteed the payment of interest on the 20-year first mortgage bonds of Boss Company, an affiliate. Outstanding bonds of Boss Company amount to $150,000 with interest payable at 10% per annum, due June 1 and December 1 of each year. The bonds were issued by Boss Company on December 1, 1994, and all interest payments have been met by the company with the exception of the payment due December 1, 1998. The Kimmel Corporation Ltd. states that it will pay the defaulted interest to the bondholders on January 15, 1999.

7. During the year 1998, Kimmel Corporation Ltd. was named as a defendant in a suit for damages by Ann Short Company for breach of contract. The case was decided in favour of Ann Short Company, which was awarded $80,000 damages. At the time of the audit, the case was under appeal to a higher court.

Instructions

Describe fully how each of the items above should be reported in the financial statements of Kimmel Corporation Ltd. for the year 1998.

Below are the account titles of a number of debit and credit accounts as they might appear on the balance sheet of **C5-4** Ralph Johnston Inc. as of October 31, 1998.

Debits	Credits
Interest accrued on notes receivable	Preferred shares
Notes receivable	11% first mortgage bonds due in 2005
Petty cash fund	Preferred dividend, payable
Canadian government securities	November 1, 1998
Treasury shares	Allowance for doubtful accounts
Unamortized bond discount	Estimated income taxes payable
Cash in bank	Customer advances (on contracts to be
Land	completed next year)
Inventory of operating parts	Appropriation for possible decline in
and supplies	value of raw materials inventory
Inventory of raw materials	Premium on bonds redeemable in 1999
Patents	Officers' 1998 accrued bonus
Cash and bonds set aside for	Accrued payroll
property additions	Provision for renegotiation
Investment in subsidiary	of government contracts
Accounts receivable	Notes payable
Government contracts	Accrued interest on bonds
Regular	Accumulated depreciation
Instalments—due next year	Accounts payable
Instalments—due after next year	Accrued interest on notes payable
Goodwill	Contributed surplus
Inventory of finished goods	8% first mortgage bonds to be
Inventory of work in process	redeemed in 1994 out of
Deficit	current assets

Instructions

Select the current asset and current liability items from among these debits and credits. If there appear to be certain borderline cases that you are unable to classify without further information, mention them and explain your difficulty, or give your reasons for making questionable classifications, if any. (AICPA adapted)

The assets of Jean Toon Motors Limited are presented below (000s omitted): **C5-5**

JEAN TOON MOTORS LIMITED
Balance Sheet
December 31, 1998

Assets

Current Assets	
Cash	$ 100,000
Unclaimed payroll cheques	27,500
Marketable securities (cost $20,000) at market	34,500
Accounts receivable (less bad debt reserve)	75,000
Inventories—at lower of cost (determined by the next-in, first-out method) and market	220,000
Total current assets	$ 457,000

(Continued)

JEAN TOON MOTORS LIMITED
Balance Sheet (Continued)

Tangible Assets		
Land (less accumulated depreciation)		$ 80,000
Buildings and equipment	$800,000	
Less accumulated depreciation	300,000	500,000
Net tangible assets		$ 580,000
Long-Term Investments		
Shares and bonds		$ 100,000
Treasury shares		50,000
Total long-term investments		$ 150,000
Other Assets		
Discount on bonds payable		$ 14,200
Claim against Canadian government (pending)		975,000
Total other assets		$ 989,200
Total Assets		$2,176,200

Instructions

Indicate the deficiencies, if any, in the foregoing assets of Jean Toon Motors Limited.

C5-6   Presented below is the balance sheet of Louise Craig Limited (000s omitted):

LOUISE CRAIG LIMITED
Balance Sheet
December 31, 1998

Assets

Current assets:		
Cash	$30,000	
Marketable securities	18,000	
Accounts receivable	25,000	
Merchandise inventory	20,000	
Supplies inventory	4,000	
Investment in subsidiary company	20,000	$117,000
Investments:		
Treasury shares		26,000
Property, plant, and equipment:		
Buildings and land	$91,000	
Less: Reserve for depreciation	30,000	61,000
Other assets:		
Cash surrender value of life insurance		18,000
		$222,000

Liabilities and Capital

Current liabilities:		
Accounts payable	$22,000	
Reserve for income taxes	14,000	
Customers' accounts with credit balances	1	$ 36,001
Deferred credits		
Unamortized premium on bonds payable		2,000
Long-term liabilities:		
Bonds payable		56,000
Total liabilities		$ 94,001
Share Capital:		
Capital shares issued	$95,000	
Earned surplus	24,999	
Cash dividends declared	8,000	127,999
		$222,000

Instructions

Criticize the balance sheet presented on the previous page. State briefly the proper treatment for the items criticized.

The financial statement below was prepared by employees of your client, Susan Marshall Ltd. The statement is unaccompanied by notes. C5-7

SUSAN MARSHALL LTD.
Balance Sheet
As of November 30, 1998

Current assets
Cash	$ 100,000	
Accounts receivable (less allowance of $30,000 for doubtful accounts)	419,900	
Inventories	2,554,000	$3,073,900

Less current liabilities
Accounts payable	$ 306,400	
Accrued payroll	8,260	
Accrued interest on mortgage note	12,000	
Estimated taxes payable	66,000	392,660
Net working capital		$2,681,240

Property, plant, and equipment (at cost)

	Cost	Depreciation	Value	
Land and buildings	$ 983,300	$310,000	$673,300	
Machinery and equipment	1,135,700	568,699	567,001	
	$2,119,000	$878,699		1,240,301

Deferred charges
Prepaid taxes and other expenses	$ 22,700	
Unamortized discount on mortgage note	10,800	33,500
Total net working capital and noncurrent assets		$3,955,041

Less deferred liabilities
Mortgage note payable	$ 300,000	
Unearned revenue	1,908,000	2,208,000
Total net assets		$1,747,041

Shareholders' equity
$4 Preferred shares	$ 400,000
Common shares	697,000
Contributed surplus	210,000
Retained earnings	484,641
Treasury shares at cost (400 shares)	(44,600)
Total shareholders' equity	$1,747,041

Instructions

Indicate the deficiencies, if any, in the balance sheet above in regard to form, terminology, descriptions, content, and the like.

The following year-end financial statements were prepared by Mark Wright Limited's bookkeeper. Wright Limited operates a chain of retail stores. C5-8

MARK WRIGHT LIMITED
Balance Sheet
June 30, 1998

Assets

Current assets
Cash	$ 150,000
Notes receivable	50,000
Accounts receivable, less reserve for doubtful accounts	175,000
Inventories	395,500
Investment securities (at cost)	100,000
Total current assets	$ 870,500

(Continued)

MARK WRIGHT LIMITED
Balance Sheet (*Continued*)

Property, plant, and equipment			
Land (at cost) (note 1)		$180,000	
Buildings, at cost less accumulated depreciation of $350,000		500,000	
Equipment, at cost less accumulated depreciation of $180,000		400,000	1,080,000
Intangibles			450,000
Other assets			
Prepaid expenses			26,405
Total assets			$2,426,905

Liabilities and Owners' Equity

Current liabilities			
Accounts payable			$ 135,500
Estimated income taxes payable			160,000
Contingent liability on discounted notes receivable			50,000
Total current liabilities			345,500
Long-term liabilities			
15% serial bonds, $50,000 due annually on December 31			
Maturity value		$900,000	
Less unamortized discount		35,000	865,000
Total liabilities			$1,210,500
Owners' equity			
Common shares (authorized and issued, 75,000 shares)		$750,000	
Retained earnings			
Appropriated (note 2)	$120,000		
Free	346,405	466,405	1,216,405
Total liabilities and owner's equity			$2,426,905

MARK WRIGHT LIMITED
Income Statement
As of June 30, 1998

Sales			$2,500,000
Interest revenue			6,000
Total revenue			2,506,000
Cost of goods sold			1,780,000
Gross margin			726,000
Operating expenses			
Selling expenses			
Salaries	$105,000		
Advertising	75,000		
Sales returns and allowances	50,000	$230,000	
General and administrative expenses			
Wages	84,000		
Property taxes	38,000		
Depreciation and amortization	86,000		
Rent (Note 3)	75,000		
Interest on serial bonds	48,000	331,000	561,000
Income before income taxes			165,000
Income taxes			80,000
Net income			$ 85,000

Notes to financial statements:

Note 1. Includes a future store site acquired during the year at a cost of $90,000.

Note 2. Retained earnings in the amount of $120,000 have been set aside to finance an expansion project.

Note 3. During the year the corporation acquired certain equipment under a long-term lease.

Instructions
Identify and discuss the defects in the financial statements on the previous page with respect to terminology, disclosure, and classification. Your discussion should explain why you consider them to be defects. Do not prepare revised statements.
(CMA adapted)

USING YOUR JUDGEMENT

FINANCIAL REPORTING PROBLEM 1

The financial statements of Moore Corporation Limited appear in Appendix 5A. Refer to these financial statements and the accompanying notes to answer the following questions:

(a) What alternative formats could Moore have adopted for its balance sheet? Which format did it adopt?
(b) What alternative formats could Moore have adopted for its income statement? Which format did it adopt?
(c) Which irregular items does Moore report in its financial statements covering the three years 1993 to 1995?
(d) Identify the various techniques of disclosure Moore might have used to disclose additional pertinent financial information. Which technique does it use in its financials?
(e) For which items in Moore's balance sheet would you expect to find notes complementing the descriptions and amounts in the balance sheet?

FINANCIAL REPORTING PROBLEM 2

During an audit of P and L Manufacturing Limited for the year ending December 31, 1997, the following four audit points came to your attention.

1. The client recorded a receivable from Revenue Canada in the amount of $150,000. When asked about this receivable, management claimed that, as of the balance sheet date, the client expected to recover this amount in connection with a refund claim for a prior year's taxes. The claim is being contested, but the client's attorney is confident that the company will prevail.

2. In response to a routine attorney letter that you sent to the client's lawyer, you discovered that the client is a defendant in a patent infringement suit. Counsel for the client estimates that the amount of the loss will be $2,200,000; furthermore, she claims that the loss of this suit is likely. The financial statements fail to mention this loss contingency.

3. Through inquiry of the company's management you discovered that included in the Cash account is $2,700,000 specifically set aside for immediate plant construction and machinery overhaul.

4. Preliminary discussions with management revealed that, in March 1998, the employees' union is going to renegotiate its contract. Due to the general increase in labour disputes and strikes both inside and outside the industry, the possibility that a costly strike will occur is becoming increasingly more likely. The client believes that this information should be disclosed in the notes to the financial statements.

Instructions
As a staff auditor, write four short memos to the audit manager describing the above audit issues and explaining the accounting treatment you have advised for each. Make sure that each memo indicates that you communicated your suggestions to the client. Each page should be headed with the client's name, the balance sheet date, and a descriptive title of the page's content. In addition, initial and date each memo in the upper-right-hand corner.

FINANCIAL REPORTING PROBLEM 3

Your group has been engaged to examine the financial statements of Genetics Limited for the year 1998. The bookkeeper who maintains the financial records has prepared all the unaudited financial statements for the corporation since its organization on January 2, 1992. The client provides you with the information on the following page.

GENETICS LIMITED
Balance Sheet
As of December 31, 1998

Assets		Liabilities	
Current Assets	$1,881,100	Current liabilities	$ 962,400
Other assets	5,171,400	Long-term liabilities	1,439,500
		Shareholders' equity	4,650,600
	$7,052,500		$7,052,500

An analysis of current assets discloses the following:

Cash (restricted in amount of $400,000 for plant expansion)	$ 571,000
Investments in land	185,000
Accounts receivable less allowance of $30,000	480,000
Inventories (FIFO flow assumption)	645,100
	$1,881,100

Other assets include:

Prepaid expenses	$ 47,400
Plant and equipment less accumulated depreciation of $1,430,000	4,130,000
Cash surrender value of life insurance policy	84,000
Unamortized bond discount	49,500
Notes receivable (short-term)	162,300
Goodwill at cost less amortization of $63,000	252,000
Land	446,200
	$5,171,400

Current liabilities include:

Accounts payable	$ 510,000
Notes payable (due 2000)	157,400
Estimated income taxes payable	145,000
Contributed surplus	150,000
	$ 962,400

Long-term liabilities include:

Unearned revenue	$ 489,500
Dividends payable (cash)	200,000
8% bonds payable (due May 1, 2003)	750,000
	$1,439,500

Shareholders' equity includes:

Retained earnings	$2,810,600
Common shares, no par value, authorized 200,000 shares, 184,000 shares issued	1,840,000
	$4,650,600

The supplementary information below is also provided.

1. On May 1, 1998, the corporation issued at 93.4, $750,000 of bonds to finance plant expansion. The long-term bond agreement provided for the annual payment of interest every May 1. The existing plant was pledged as security for the loan. Use straight-line method for discount amortization.
2. The bookkeeper made the following mistakes:

    (a) In 1996, the ending inventory was overstated by $183,000. The ending inventories for 1997 and 1998 were correctly computed.

(b) In 1998, accrued wages in the amount of $275,000 were omitted from the balance sheet and these expenses were not charged on the income statement.

(c) In 1998, a gain of $175,000 (net of tax) on the sale of certain plant assets was credited directly to Retained Earnings.

3. A major competitor has introduced a line of products that will compete directly with Genetics' primary line, now being produced in a specially designed new plant. Because of manufacturing innovations, the competitor's line will be of comparable quality but priced 50% below the client's line. The competitor announced its new line on January 14, 1999. The client indicates that the company will meet the lower prices that are high enough to cover variable manufacturing and selling expenses, but permit recovery of only a portion of fixed costs.

4. You learned on January 28, 1999, prior to the completion of the audit, of heavy damage because of a recent fire to one of the client's two plants; the loss will not be reimbursed by insurance. The newspapers described the event in detail.

Instructions

Analyse the above information so that a corrected balance sheet may be prepared for Genetics Limited in accordance with proper accounting and reporting principles. Prepare a description of any notes that might need to be prepared (to be reported to the class). The books are closed and adjustments to income are to be made through Retained Earnings.

ETHICS CASE

The following 1997 balance sheet for the Nagoda Corporation does not conform with generally accepted accounting principles.

THE NAGODA CORPORATION
Balance Sheet [asset portion only]
December 31, 1997

Current Assets	
Cash	$ 46,500
Temporary investments at cost (market value $159,800)	185,800
Accounts receivable (gross value)	745,000
Inventories valued at replacement cost	
(average cost equals $1,455,000)	1,800,000
Contingent gain (the excess insurance proceeds	
on a casualty loss)	310,000
Total Current Assets	3,087,300
Investments	
Treasury shares, valued using the cost method	251,540
Property, Plant, and Equipment	
Land, at fair value	2,575,000
Buildings, at fair value	3,475,540
Equipment, at fair value	332,100
Total Property, Plant, and Equipment	6,382,640
Intangible assets	
Goodwill (generated by the business since	
its inception)	2,000,000
Development Costs	450,000
Total Intangible Assets	2,450,000
Total Assets	$12,171,480

Instructions

(a) Find all the errors to the asset portion of the Nagoda Corporation's 1997 balance sheet and explain how each should be reported under generally accepted accounting principles.

(b) Comment on the ethical propriety of each accounting error indicated in part (a), keeping in mind the corporation's various stakeholders who might be harmed through erroneous, intentional, or incomplete asset reporting.

chapter

6

REVENUE RECOGNITION

CHAPTER 6

Revenue Recognition

Learning Objectives

After studying this chapter, you should be able to:

1. Understand what is included in an earning process, when revenue is earned, and that earning revenue is different from recognizing revenue

2. Know the *CICA Handbook* criteria for revenue recognition and appreciate that the matching principle also has consequences for revenue recognition.

3. Realize that determining when the revenue recognition criteria are met requires the exercise of professional judgement.

4. Know when and why revenue recognition criteria are satisfied at the point of delivery (sale) and describe accounting issues related to such recognition.

5. Understand why and when revenue can be recognized prior to completion of long-term contracts, and why and when it may not be recognized until completion of such contracts.

6. Know when the percentage-of-completion method can be used and how to apply it for long-term contracts.

7. Know how to apply the completed-contract method for long-term contracts.

8. Identify and apply appropriate accounting for losses on long-term contracts.

9. Identify circumstances, other than for long-term contracts, in which revenue recognition might occur prior to delivery.

10. Understand when circumstances regarding the earning process result in revenue recognition after delivery.

11. Describe and apply the instalment method of accounting.

12. Explain and apply the cost recovery method of accounting.

13. Understand issues related to revenue recognition for service transactions and appreciate that their resolution is based on similar revenue recognition criteria as exists for the sale of goods (Appendix 6A).

14. Understand and know how to resolve revenue recognition issues for consignment sales, bartering, and franchise sales (Appendix 6B).

Revenue recognition is one of the most difficult and pressing problems facing the accounting profession. Although the profession has developed general guidelines for revenue recognition, the many methods of marketing and selling products and services can make it very difficult to determine when these guidelines are satisfied. In Canada, significant problems involving revenue recognition were linked to the failure of the Canadian Commercial Bank (recognizing revenue before collection was reasonably assured) and Grandma Lee's (recognizing revenue before all significant acts were completed).

Generally, revenue should be recognized when performance is achieved, the amount is reasonably measurable and collectible, and all material expenses that are related can be matched against it. The following examples suggest the difficulty of determining in which accounting period these conditions are met.

Frequent-flyer travel awards. Frequent-flyer programs are so popular that airlines owe participants billions of kilometres of free travel. Travel rewards could cost the airlines millions of dollars. Some airlines have recognized as revenue the full sales price of the ticket at the time the ticket is purchased. The incremental costs expected to be incurred when the free transportation is provided are accrued at the time a free travel award is reached. Some disagree with this accounting. As one expert noted: "You can no longer say that the entire revenue process is substantially complete when the ticket is sold. Passengers are purchasing tickets with the expectation of a free flight, and we have to account for that liability." Consequently, such critics argue, a portion of the revenue from the tickets sold should be deferred and reported as a liability.

Area development rights. Area development rights are contracts sold by a company that grant the developer the exclusive right to open franchises in a particular area. In return, the developer pays the company a nonrefundable fee. In many cases, the company must provide training and advertising support to the franchise and often uses the fee income to service the subsequent costs involved in helping the developer get started. Accountants must determine whether the company has "earned" this revenue when the contract is signed, or when the cash is received, or when the franchises are up and running.

These examples indicate that determining when to recognize revenue is a complex question for which no easy answers exist. The purposes of this chapter are to (1) identify and discuss the general guidelines that exist in GAAP for recognizing revenue; and (2) examine and illustrate the application of these guidelines to the recognition of revenue from the sale of goods at the point of delivery (point of sale), before the point of delivery (long-term construction contracts), and after the point of delivery (instalment contracts). In Appendix 6A, the application of the revenue recognition guidelines to service transactions is discussed. In Appendix 6B, special revenue recognition problems related to consignment sales, barter transactions, and franchises are considered.

GUIDELINES FOR REVENUE RECOGNITION

Revenues are defined as *increases in economic resources, either by way of inflows or enhancements of assets or reductions of liabilities, resulting from the ordinary activities of an entity. Revenues of entities normally arise from the sale of goods, the rendering of services or the use by others of entity resources yielding rent, interest, royalties or dividends.*[1] While this definition tells us what revenues are, it does not tell us the accounting period in which these increases in assets or reductions of liabilities are to be recorded (recognized). To demonstrate why this is a problem, consider the highly simplified representation of the activities and events in a retailer's earning process as shown in Illustration 6-1.

---

[1] *CICA Handbook* (Toronto: CICA), Section 1000, par. .37. From this definition, it is clear that solutions to revenue recognition problems have implications for asset and liability valuation—the timing and measurement of a credit to a revenue account results in a corresponding debit to an asset or liability account. Because of this, revenue recognition issues are considered in this book prior to examining accounting for particular assets and liabilities.

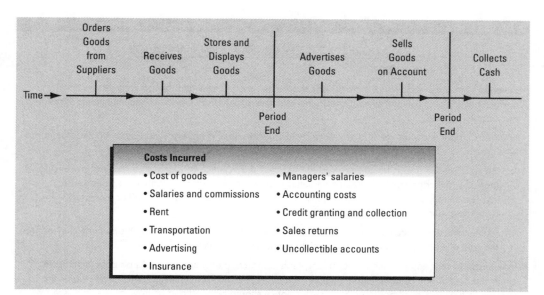

ILLUSTRATION 6-1
Activities and events in a retailer's earning process

An **earning process** *consists of all the activities and events a company engages in to earn revenue.* Given Illustration 6-1, when is revenue earned by the retailer? In an economic sense, revenue is earned continuously throughout the earning process—every activity or event in the process contributes to earning revenue. If this were not so, the retailer would eliminate the unimportant activity, thereby becoming more efficient. Essentially, this reflects a **value-added viewpoint** to earning revenue. *Each activity or event in the earning process adds value that, when taken together, enables the retailer to sell goods at a price in excess of costs.* To recognize revenues under a value-added approach would mean that, as each activity or event takes place, an entry would be made to record the portion of the total revenue that is attributable to the activity or event. Therefore, total revenues reported in an income statement prepared under this approach would incorporate the consequences of all activities in the earning process for the given time period. Because of the inability to do this in a sufficiently reliable way, accountants do not recognize revenues in this manner. *Instead, revenues are recognized at the stage in the earning process when specific criteria in the* **CICA Handbook** *are judged to have been met.*[2] Therefore, revenues in a period's income statement are from activities or events during the period that signify that the criteria have been met, even though other activities and events associated with the earning process have taken place in prior periods or will take place in future periods.

The *CICA Handbook* recommendations on **revenue recognition criteria** are shown in Exhibit 6-1.[3]

These criteria reflect the general revenue realization (or recognition) principle of the conceptual framework discussed in Chapter 2. This principle states that revenue is generally recognized when (1) performance is achieved and (2) reasonable assurance regarding the measurability and collectibility of the consideration exists.[4] The criteria, however, elaborate on when "performance is achieved" as it applies to revenues from the sale of goods, rendering of services, and execution of long-term contracts.

While not stated explicitly in these revenue recognition criteria, the **matching principle** of the conceptual framework *is also important when deciding if revenue can be recognized.* This principle states that expenses that are linked to revenues in a cause and effect relationship are normally matched with the revenue in the accounting period in

OBJECTIVE 1
Understand what is included in an earning process, when revenue is earned, and that earning revenue is different from recognizing revenue.

OBJECTIVE 2
Know the *CICA Handbook* criteria for revenue recognition and appreciate that the matching principle also has consequences for revenue recognition.

---

[2] *CICA Handbook*, Section 3400. Recall that "recognition" means recording an item in the accounts and including it in the financial statements.

[3] *Ibid.*, pars. .06–.09.

[4] *CICA Handbook*, Section 1000, par. .47.

EXHIBIT 6-1

REVENUE RECOGNITION CRITERIA: *CICA HANDBOOK*

- Revenue from sales and service transactions should be recognized when the requirements as to performance set out [below] are satisfied, provided that at the time of performance ultimate collection is reasonably assured.

- In a transaction involving the sale of goods, performances should be regarded as having been achieved when the following conditions have been fulfilled:

   (a) the seller of the goods has transferred to the buyer the significant risks and rewards of ownership, in that all significant acts have been completed and the seller retains no continuing managerial involvement in, or effective control of, the goods transferred to a degree usually associated with ownership; and

   (b) reasonable assurance exists regarding the measurement of the consideration that will be derived from the sale of goods, and the extent to which goods may be returned.

- In the case of rendering of services and long-term contracts, performance should be determined using either the percentage of completion method or the completed contract method, whichever relates the revenue to the work accomplished. Such performance should be regarded as having been achieved when reasonable assurance exists regarding the measurement of the consideration that will be derived from rendering the service or performing the long-term contract.

- Revenue arising from the use by others of enterprise resources yielding interest, royalties and dividends should be recognized when reasonable assurance exists regarding measurement and collectibility. These revenues should be recognized on the following bases:

   (a) interest: on a time proportion basis;

   (b) royalties: as they accrue, in accordance with the terms of the relevant agreement;

   (c) dividends: when the shareholder's right to receive payment is established.

---

which the revenue is recognized.[5] This means that if the criteria for revenue recognition are met as the result of transactions or events of the current period but material expenses are to be incurred in a future period, then these expenses must be estimated and accrued in the current period so that they are matched with the related revenue. This can usually be done with sufficient reliability (e.g., bad debt expenses). In some cases, however, the future costs may not be reasonably estimable (e.g., some long-term construction or service contracts). Therefore, even if billings have been made and cash has been collected on such a sale, revenue should not be recognized until the future period when related expenses can be determined.

Based on these criteria, the following four questions must be asked when trying to determine if revenue should be recognized in a particular situation.

1. Has performance been achieved?

2. Is the amount of revenue reasonably measurable?

3. Is collectibility reasonably assured?

4. Can all related expenses be that are material matched against the revenue?

OBJECTIVE 3
Realize that determining when the revenue recognition criteria are met requires the exercise of professional judgement.

Only when the answer is "yes" to all four questions can revenue be recognized. Determining when the answer is "yes" in specific situations often requires the exercise of professional judgement. For example, when a real estate company sells some land and receives a 5% down payment, should the entire sales price be recognized as revenue? The answer would depend on the likelihood of being able to collect the full price or the ability to reasonably estimate bad debts. Additionally, the measurement of the sales revenue

---

[5] *Ibid.*, par. .51.

may be an issue because collections are scheduled far into the future, which raises a concern for separating sales revenue from interest revenue. This is a particular problem if an interest rate is not quoted in the sales contract. The situation can become even more complex if the real estate company is required to develop the land in the future.

There are a variety of ways and conditions under which products and services can be sold. Decisions regarding revenue recognition must be based on an analysis of the underlying substance of the earning process involved. From this, judgement as to when revenue recognition criteria are satisfied can be appropriately justified. This leads to the necessary journal entries to record the revenues so that they are reported in the appropriate period's income statement.

The remainder of this chapter identifies some of the issues involved in revenue recognition and the accounting entries that may be made when the revenue recognition criteria are judged to be met at different points in the earning process. This discussion concentrates on the sale of goods under circumstances where:

1. Revenue recognition criteria are met at the point of delivery (sale).
2. Revenue recognition criteria are met before delivery.
3. Revenue recognition criteria are met after delivery.

Revenue recognition issues related to the sale of services are considered in Appendix 6A. Issues unique to special sales transactions (consignments and franchises) are identified in Appendix 6B. Accounting for revenues arising from permitting others to use enterprise resources are discussed in several other sections of the book.

REVENUE RECOGNITION CRITERIA MET AT POINT OF DELIVERY (POINT OF SALE)

Many business enterprises market one or more products: retail stores purchase many different articles to sell; manufacturers market the products they have fabricated or processed. In return for the product sold, the enterprise usually receives cash or a promise of cash at some future date (credit sales). Thus, sales transactions have two sides: (1) a product for which there are related costs and that is delivered to a customer; and (2) cash or a promise to pay cash in the future that is received from the customer.

In the accounts, the revenue and expense consequences of a sales transaction are recorded separately. For the revenue component, the entry is typically to debit Cash or Accounts Receivable and credit the Sales account.

The sales transaction is normally the significant event justifying revenue recognition because all criteria for revenue recognition are typically satisfied at this point in the earning process, as is explained below.

OBJECTIVE 4
Know when and why revenue recognition criteria are satisfied at the point of delivery (sale) and describe accounting issues related to such recognition.

1. *Requirements as to performance are satisfied.* The seller, by delivering the goods to the customer, transfers the risks and rewards of ownership to the customer. The seller has no continuing managerial involvement in, or effective control of, the goods to a degree usually associated with ownership.

2. *The amount of revenue is reasonably measurable.* The amount of revenue is evident from the cash paid or agreed to be paid by the customer. If customers have the right to return products purchased, any material dollar amount of possible returns can be reasonably determined.

3. *Collectibility is reasonably assured.* If cash is paid, collectibility is not an issue. For accounts receivable outstanding at the end of a period, the ability to reasonably estimate bad debts means that this requirement for revenue recognition is satisfied.

4. *Material expenses can be matched against the revenues.* The cost to acquire or manufacture goods sold has already been incurred and can be assigned to the Cost of Goods Sold expense by an appropriate accounting technique. Also, as mentioned above, Bad Debt Expense can be reasonably determined.

For most product sale situations, this typically applies. If, however, any of the criteria were not met at the point of sale or all were satisfied prior to the sale, the revenue would be recognized at some other stage in the earning process.

For example, the seller may retain significant risks of ownership even though the goods are delivered. This would occur when there is a liability for unsatisfactory performance not covered by a warranty, when the buyer has a right to rescind the sale, or when the goods are sent on consignment.[6] Additionally, one must be able to determine whether the buyer or seller has the risks of ownership when goods are in transit between the two (a topic examined in Chapter 8). In essence, determining when risks and rewards of ownership are transferred requires a careful examination of the terms of the sales transaction.[7] Similarly, the ability to reasonably measure the amount of revenue, determine its collectibility, and appropriately match expenses significantly affect being able to justify recognition of revenue at the point of delivery.

EXAMPLES INCORPORATING ISSUES RELATED TO RECOGNITION AT POINT OF DELIVERY

To emphasize the importance of professional judgement in determining whether revenue should be recognized at the point of delivery, consider the following three examples.

Sales with Buyback Agreements. If a company sells a product in one period and agrees to buy it back in the next accounting period, has the company sold the product? Legal title and possession of the product have transferred in this situation, but the economic substance of the transaction is that the seller retains the significant risks and rewards of ownership. Therefore, the "selling" company would not be able to record revenue and the inventory and related liability should remain on the seller's books. In other words, no sale.

Revenue Recognition When Right of Return Exists. Whether cash or credit sales are involved, a special problem arises with claims for returns and allowances. In Chapter 7, the accounting treatment for normal returns and allowances is presented. However, certain companies experience such a *high ratio of returned merchandise to sales* that they find it necessary to postpone reporting sales until the return privilege has substantially expired. For example, in the publishing industry the rate of return runs up to 25% for hardcover books and 65% for some magazines. Other types of companies that experience high return rates are perishable-food dealers, rack jobbers or distributors who sell to retail outlets, cassette tape and compact disc companies, and some toy and sporting goods manufacturers. Returns in these industries frequently are made either through a right of contract or as a matter of practice involving guaranteed sales agreements or consignments.

Three alternative methods are available when the seller is exposed to continued risks and rewards of ownership through return of the product. These are: (1) not recording a sale until all return privileges have expired; (2) recording the sale, but reducing sales by an estimate of future returns; and (3) recording the sale and accounting for the returns as they occur. Selection of the appropriate method to record sales when right of return exists is made through the exercise of professional judgement based on the revenue recognition criteria. The particularly relevant criteria are (1) measurability of the consideration to be

---

[6] *CICA Handbook*, Section 3400, par. .10. Consignments are examined in Appendix 6B.
[7] *Ibid.*, par. .11.

received, with particular consideration for the reliability of a measure of goods that will be returned; and (2) transfer of risks and rewards of ownership. Specifically, the *CICA Handbook* states:

> Revenues would not be recognized when an enterprise is subject to significant and unpredictable amounts of goods being returned, for example, when the market for a returnable good is untested.[8]

Therefore, when future returns cannot be estimated with reasonable reliability, the revenue would not be recorded when the goods are delivered to buyers. The revenue recognition would be deferred until there is notification from the buyer that only a specific amount of goods will be returned or the return privilege has expired, whichever occurs first. When a reasonable estimate of goods to be returned can be made, the revenue would be recognized when the goods are delivered. Additionally, an allowance for the future returns would be recorded by debiting Sales Returns and crediting Allowance for Sales Returns for the estimated amount. The Sales Returns would be deducted from Sales to determine net sales in an income statement. The Allowance account would be debited when returns occur. Any balance in the Allowance account would be treated as a contra account to Accounts Receivable in a balance sheet.

Trade Loading and Channel Stuffing. Some companies record revenues at date of delivery with neither buyback nor unlimited return provisions. Although they appear to be following acceptable point of sale revenue recognition, they are recognizing revenues and earnings prematurely. The cigarette industry until recently engaged in a distribution practice known as trade loading. "**Trade loading** is a crazy, uneconomic, insidious practice through which manufacturers—trying to show sales, profits, and market share they don't actually have—induce their wholesale customers, known as the trade, to buy more product than they can promptly resell."[9] In total, the cigarette industry appears to have exaggerated operating profits by taking the profits from future years.

In the computer software industry this same practice is referred to as **channel stuffing**. When Ashton-Tate, a software maker, needed to make its financial results look good, it offered deep discounts to its distributors to overbuy and recorded revenue when the software left the loading dock.[10] Of course, the distributors' inventories become bloated and the marketing channel gets stuffed, but the software maker's financial results are improved—only to the detriment of future periods' results, however, unless the process is repeated.

Trade loading and channel stuffing are management and marketing policy decisions and actions that hype sales, distort operating results, and window dress financial statements. End-of-period accounting adjustments are not made to reduce the impact of these types of sales on operating results. The practices of trade loading and channel stuffing need to be discouraged.

REVENUE RECOGNITION CRITERIA MET BEFORE DELIVERY

For the most part, revenue recognition occurs at the point of delivery because it is at that time the uncertainties concerning the earning process are removed and the exchange price provides a reliable basis for measurement. Under certain circumstances, however,

---

[8] *Ibid.*, par. .18.

[9] "The $600 Million Cigarette Scam," *Fortune*, December 4, 1989, p. 89.

[10] "Software's Dirty Little Secret," *Forbes*, May 15, 1989, p. 128. As another example, trade loading and channel stuffing activities were reported to have occurred from the late 1980s to mid 1990s in Bausch and Lomb Inc.'s Hong Kong operations regarding sales of Ray-Ban sunglasses and in its U.S. contact-lens division: "Blind Ambition," *Business Week*, October 23, 1995, pp. 78–82, 86, 90–92.

revenue is recognized prior to completion and delivery. The most notable example is when a long-term contract is undertaken and it is appropriately accounted for using the percentage-of-completion method.[11]

LONG-TERM CONSTRUCTION CONTRACTS AND REVENUE RECOGNITION ISSUES

OBJECTIVE 5
Understand why and when revenue can be recognized prior to completion of long-term contracts, and why and when it may not be recognized until completion of such contracts.

Under a long-term contract, a contractor formally agrees to carry out a project for a customer that will take several months or years to complete. Some contracts may consist of constructing several separable units (e.g., buildings or kilometres of roadway) in the context of the entire contracted project (e.g., a neighbourhood development or stretch of highway). Other contracts may be for the design and/or construction of a single unit (e.g., office building, space hardware, ship, golf course). While the specific terms of a particular long-term contract would be unique to the negotiation between the contractor and the customer, it would be expected that a *contract would specify that the buyer or seller have enforceable rights regarding such things as the price to be paid, performance during the contract period, expected delivery date, and provisions for progress payments. Additionally, the contractor would have budgeted the expected cost of the contract prior to signing it.* Within this context, the earning process for a contractor who has agreed to complete a project beginning in Year 1 and ending in Year 3 is traced in Illustration 6-2.

ILLUSTRATION 6-2

Earning process: long-term contract

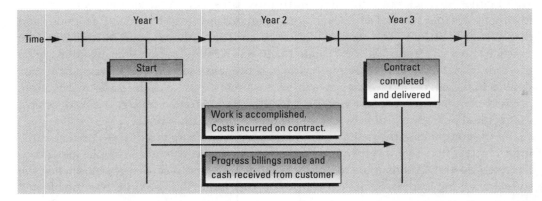

Because the project is the result of a contractual agreement and execution of the contract spans more than one accounting period, a basic accounting issue arises: *In which period or periods should revenue, related expenses, and resulting net income be recognized?* To be accurate, it can be argued that the recognition should be in Year 3 because it is only then that total actual costs are objectively determinable. Also justifying this conclusion is the fact that the risks and rewards of ownership are transferred to the buyer in Year 3. Such recognition would, however, result in a distortion of the trends in and relationships among reported revenues, expenses, and net income for the three years in which the work was accomplished. Therefore, to better reflect the underlying economic activity, it is desirable to recognize a portion of the revenue, expenses, and net income in each year of the contract's execution. The problem with this approach is how to allocate the total contract revenue among the years so that the results reasonably reflect the work accomplished.

As with the sale of goods, revenue on long-term contracts cannot be recognized until performance is achieved, amounts are reasonably measurable, collection is reasonably assured, and costs can be matched. **Achieving performance** is, however, defined quite

---

[11] While we concentrate on long-term construction contracts to illustrate issues and accounting methods for revenue recognition prior to delivery of a finished "good," similar issues exist for long-term service contracts, as described in Appendix 6A.

differently for long-term contracts because a transfer of risks and rewards of ownership to the buyer is not needed, nor is elimination of managerial involvement by the seller. Rather, performance is regarded as being achieved (and, therefore, revenue is recognizable) when reasonable assurance exists regarding the measurement of the consideration that will be derived from the work that has been accomplished on the contract.

Reasonably measuring the amount of revenue would require the contract to specify a fixed-price or a cost-plus formula for revenue. For a fixed-price contract, the ratio of performance completed to total performance required multiplied by the price would yield a measure of revenue earned. For a cost-plus formula contract, the application of the formula to the costs incurred would result in revenue earned, as long as the incurrence of costs reflected the progress toward completion reasonably well. Also, collectibility of the revenue would have to be reasonably assured. When these conditions exist, the contract should be accounted for using the *percentage-of-completion method* for revenue recognition.[12]

When a reasonable estimate of the extent of progress toward completion cannot be made, then revenue recognition would not occur until the contract is completed. In this case, the *completed-contract method* of revenue recognition should be used.[13]

PERCENTAGE-OF-COMPLETION METHOD

The **percentage-of-completion method** *results in recognizing revenues and related expenses, or the resulting gross profit, during each period that work is accomplished on a long-term contract.* To use this method (1) revenues from the contract must be known (i.e., the contract price is fixed in total or for sequential parts, or revenues are based on a cost-plus formula); (2) collectibility must be reasonably assured; (3) a rational basis for determining progress toward completion or performance that has taken place must exist; and (4) a matching of expenses to related revenue of a period must be possible.

OBJECTIVE 6
Know when the percentage-of-completion method can be used and how to apply it for long-term contracts.

While all these conditions require awareness of specific contents of a particular contract and the exercise of judgement as to when they are satisfied, a key condition is to be able to measure progress toward completion at particular interim dates.

Measuring the Progress Toward Completion. Various methods are used to determine the *extent of performance or progress toward completion.* The most common are the cost-to-cost method, efforts-expended method, and units-of-work-performed method. All of these methods determine the extent of progress by examining relationships among various measurements of input and/or output pertaining to the contract.

Input measures (costs incurred, labour hours worked) are made in terms of efforts devoted to a contract. **Output measures** (tonnes produced, storeys of a building completed, kilometres of a highway completed) are made in terms of results. Determining what to use for a particular contract requires careful tailoring to the circumstances and the exercise of judgement.

The input measure is based on an established relationship between a unit of input and productivity. If inefficiencies cause the productivity relationship to change, inaccurate measurements of performance achieved are the result. Another potential problem, **front-end loading**, produces higher estimates of completion by virtue of incurring signif-

---

[12] *CICA Handbook*, Section 3400, par. .14.

[13] *Ibid.*, par. .15. For contracts that are short term (e.g., started and completed in the same year), the completed-contract method is appropriate because it relates reported revenues to the work accomplished. From an income tax viewpoint, if a contract is for 24 months or less, the completed-contract method is acceptable to Revenue Canada. Given that a company's income would not be materially distorted over time, and for reasons of expediency, a similar policy may be adopted for financial statement purposes even though the percentage-of-completion method could be used. A contractor may have several ongoing contracts. Some may meet the revenue recognition criteria required to use the percentage-of-completion method while others may not (for which the completed contract method would be used). Consequently, the contractor would employ both methods because different contracts would be accounted for under the different methods.

icant costs up front. For example, costs of unused materials or subcontracts not yet executed should not be considered as costs incurred when using costs to determine the amount of work accomplished.

Output measures can also result in inaccurate measures of performance if the units used are not comparable in time, effort, or cost to complete. For example, using storeys completed in a building can be deceiving: to complete the first storey of an eight-storey building may require more than one-eighth the total cost, due to the foundation and substructure construction.

One of the more popular means used to determine the progress toward completion is the cost-to-cost method. Under the cost-to-cost method, the *percentage of completion is measured by comparing costs incurred to date with the most recent estimate of the total costs to complete the contract* as shown in Exhibit 6-2.

EXHIBIT 6-2

FORMULA FOR PERCENTAGE OF COMPLETION, COST-TO-COST BASIS

$$\frac{\text{Costs incurred to end of current period}}{\text{Most recent estimate of total costs}} = \text{Percentage completed}$$

This percentage is applied to the total revenue or the estimated total gross profit[14] on the contract to determine the revenue or the gross profit amounts *to be recognized to date*. The amount of revenue or gross profit recognized *for a particular period* is computed using the formula shown in Exhibit 6-3.

Because the cost-to-cost method is used extensively, we have adopted it for use in our illustrations.

EXHIBIT 6-3

FORMULA FOR AMOUNT OF CURRENT PERIOD'S REVENUE (OR GROSS PROFIT), COST-TO-COST BASIS

$$\frac{\text{Costs incurred to end of current period}}{\text{Most recent estimate of total costs}} \times \begin{array}{c}\text{Estimated total} \\ \text{revenue} \\ \text{(or gross profit)} \\ \text{from the contract}\end{array} - \begin{array}{c}\text{Total revenue} \\ \text{(or gross profit)} \\ \text{recognized} \\ \text{in prior periods}\end{array} = \begin{array}{c}\text{Current period's} \\ \text{revenue} \\ \text{(or gross profit)}\end{array}$$

Illustration of the Percentage-of-Completion Method (Cost-to-Cost Basis). To illustrate the percentage-of-completion method, assume that Hardhat Construction Company has a contract starting July 1998 to construct a bridge at a fixed price of $4,500,000 that is to be completed in October 2000 at an estimated total cost of $4,000,000. The data shown in Exhibit 6-4 pertain to the construction period. Note that by the end of 1999 the estimated total cost has increased from $4,000,000 to $4,050,000 ($2,916,000 actual costs to the end of 1999 plus $1,134,000 estimated yet to be incurred to complete the contract).

Progress billings are invoices sent to the customer throughout the construction period. The amounts billed at various times are determined based on conditions specified in the contract. For example, the billings may be a certain percentage of costs incurred by the contractor or some agreed amount linked to time or stage of completion. Such billings

---

[14] Total gross profit = total revenue on contract − most recent estimate of total costs on contract.

EXHIBIT 6-4   HARDHAT CONSTRUCTION COMPANY

DATA FOR CONSTRUCTION PERIOD

	1998	1999	2000
Costs to date	$1,000,000	$2,916,000	$4,050,000
Estimated costs to complete	3,000,000	1,134,000	—
Progress billings during the year	900,000	2,400,000	1,200,000
Cash collected during the year	750,000	1,750,000	2,000,000

are then paid by the customer. In some cases the customer, by agreement with the contractor, may hold back on paying a portion of the billings. Through the billing and collection process, the contractor obtains cash to pay for costs during construction. If this did not occur, the contractor would likely run short of cash, which could mean external financing and related interest charges would be incurred or the contract may not be able to be completed. Based on this information, the percentage of the contract completed by the end of each year would be computed as shown in Exhibit 6-5.

EXHIBIT 6-5   HARDHAT CONSTRUCTION COMPANY

APPLICATION OF PERCENTAGE-OF-COMPLETION METHOD, COST-TO-COST BASIS

	1998	1999	2000
Contract price	$4,500,000	$4,500,000	$4,500,000
Less estimated cost			
Costs to date	1,000,000	2,916,000	4,050,000
Estimated costs to complete	3,000,000	1,134,000	—
Estimated total costs	$4,000,000	$4,050,000	$4,050,000
Estimated total gross profit	$ 500,000	$ 450,000	$ 450,000
Percentage completed	25%	72%	100%
	$\left(\dfrac{\$1,000,000}{\$4,000,000}\right)$	$\left(\dfrac{\$2,916,000}{\$4,050,000}\right)$	$\left(\dfrac{\$4,050,000}{\$4,050,000}\right)$

On the basis of the data, the entries in Exhibit 6-6 would be prepared to record (1) the costs of construction; (2) progress billings; and (3) collections. These entries appear as summaries of the many transactions that would be entered individually as they occur during the year.

Construction in Process *is an inventory account, not an expense account.* The first entry results in all contract costs incurred to the date being included in this account. Note that, *for the progress billings, the credit is not to a revenue account. The revenue for each year is yet to be determined using the percentage-of-completion method.* Billings on **Construction in Process** *is a contra-inventory account,* as will be discussed shortly. Using the previously calculated percentages of the contract completed for each year, the estimated revenue and gross profit to be recognized in each year is determined as shown in Exhibit 6-7.

The entries to recognize revenue, construction expenses, and gross profit in each year of the contract are shown in Exhibit 6-8.

EXHIBIT 6-6   HARDHAT CONSTRUCTION COMPANY

JOURNAL ENTRIES: PERCENTAGE-OF-COMPLETION, COST-TO-COST BASIS

	1998		1999		2000	
To record cost of construction:						
Construction in Process	1,000,000		1,916,000		1,134,000	
Materials, cash, payables, etc.		1,000,000		1,916,000		1,134,000
To record progress billings:						
Accounts Receivable	900,000		2,400,000		1,200,000	
Billings on Construction in Process		900,000		2,400,000		1,200,000
To record collections:						
Cash	750,000		1,750,000		2,000,000	
Accounts Receivable		750,000		1,750,000		2,000,000

EXHIBIT 6-7   HARDHAT CONSTRUCTION COMPANY

PERCENTAGE-OF COMPLETION, REVENUE AND GROSS PROFIT, BY YEAR

	1998	1999	2000
Revenue recognized in:			
1998 $4,500,000 × 25%	$1,125,000		
1999 $4,500,000 × 72%		$3,240,000	
Less revenue recognized in 1998		1,125,000	
Revenue in 1999		$2,115,000	
2000 $4,500,000 × 100%			$4,500,000
Less revenue recognized in 1998 and 1999			3,240,000
Revenue in 2000			$1,260,000
Gross profit recognized in:			
1998 $500,000 × 25%	$ 125,000		
1999 $450,000 × 72%		$ 324,000	
Less gross profit recognized in 1998		$ 125,000	
Gross profit in 1999		$ 199,000	
2000 $450,000 × 100%			$ 450,000
Less revenue recognized in 1998 and 1999			324,000
Revenue in 2000			$ 126,000

Note that in Exhibit 6-8, the *gross profit* as computed *is debited to the inventory account Construction in Process.* The Revenue from Long-Term Contract account is credited for amounts as computed previously. The difference between the amounts recognized each year for revenue and gross profit is debited to a nominal account, Construction Expenses (similar to Cost of Goods Sold in a manufacturing enterprise), which is reported in the income statement; this equals the actual cost of construction incurred in a period.

EXHIBIT 6-8   HARDHAT CONSTRUCTION COMPANY

JOURNAL ENTRIES TO RECOGNIZE REVENUE, CONSTRUCTION EXPENSES,
AND GROSS PROFIT: PERCENTAGE-OF-COMPLETION, COST-TO-COST BASIS

	1998	1999	2000
Construction in Process (gross profit)	125,000	199,000	126,000
Construction Expenses	1,000,000	1,916,000	1,134,000
Revenue from Long-Term Contract	1,125,000	2,115,000	1,260,000

An alternative way to build this entry for each year is to (1) debit Construction Expenses for the actual costs incurred in the year ($1,000,000 in 1998); (2) credit Revenue from Long-Term Contract for the revenue calculated for the year ($1,125,000 in 1998); and (3) debit Construction in Process for the difference, which is the gross profit for the year ($125,000 in 1998).

As a result of these entries, revenue and construction expense amounts for work done on the contract each year are recorded and would be shown in the year's income statement separately or as a net amount (gross profit on long-term contract). Also, under the percentage-of-completion method, the gross profit is debited to the Construction in Process inventory account. Therefore, the total of this account at any given time will equal the actual costs incurred to date plus recognized gross profit to date. For our illustration, the Construction in Process account would include the information from entries posted over the term of the project as indicated in Exhibit 6-9.

EXHIBIT 6-9   HARDHAT CONSTRUCTION COMPANY

AMOUNTS IN CONSTRUCTION IN PROCESS
ACCOUNT: PERCENTAGE-OF-COMPLETION, COST-TO-COST BASIS

Construction in Process		
1998 construction costs	$1,000,000	
1998 recognized gross profit	**125,000**	
1999 construction costs	1,916,000	
1999 recognized gross profit	**199,000**	
2000 construction costs	1,134,000	
2000 recognized gross profit	**126,000**	
Total	$4,500,000	

This inventory account cannot be removed from the contractor's accounts until the construction is completed and ownership is transferred to the buyer. When this occurs, the entry shown in Exhibit 6-10 From previous entries to record progress billings, the Billings on Construction in Process account would have a credit balance of $4,500,000 prior to this entry. Therefore, this entry eliminates the balance in the Billings account and the Construction in Process account.

As a concluding point, note that the Hardhat Construction Company illustration contained a change in estimate in the second year, 1999, where the estimated total costs increased from $4,000,000 to $4,050,000. By calculating the percentage completed to the end of 1999 based on the new estimate of total costs and then deducting the amount of revenues and gross profit recognized in prior periods from revenues and gross profit

EXHIBIT 6-10   HARDHAT CONSTRUCTION COMPANY

ENTRY TO REMOVE BILLINGS AND INVENTORY ACCOUNTS
WHEN CONTRACT COMPLETED: PERCENTAGE-OF-COMPLETION

	2000	
Billings on Construction in Process	4,500,000	
Construction in Process		4,500,000

computed for progress to date, the effect of the change in estimate was accounted for in a catch-up manner. That is, the change in estimate is accounted for in the period of change so that the balance sheet at the end of the period of change and the accounting in subsequent periods are as they would have been if the revised estimate had been the original estimate.

Financial Statement Presentation: Percentage-of-Completion. Generally, when a receivable from a sale is created, a revenue is credited. Also, the Inventory account is reduced by the amount of the expense to be matched against the revenue. This is not the case when accounting for long-term contracts. When Accounts Receivable are recorded, the Billings on Construction in Process account rather than a revenue account is credited. At the same time, the Construction in Process inventory account continues to be carried on the books. This creates a problem because two assets (Accounts Receivable or the Cash collected thereon and Construction in Process) exist in our records but both relate to a single source of benefits (the construction project). Recall, however, that the Billings on Construction in Process account will have a credit balance equal to all amounts billed and set up as Accounts Receivable. Therefore, to avoid reporting two assets when there is really only one (i.e., double-counting), the balance in the Billings on Construction in Process account is subtracted from the Construction in Process account to determine an amount to be reported in the balance sheet.

When the costs incurred plus the gross profit recognized to date (the balance in Construction in Process) exceed the billings, this excess is reported as a current asset called "Costs and Recognized Profit in Excess of Billings." This is classified as a current asset on the grounds that the length of the contract reflects the length of the contractor's operating cycle.

When the billings exceed costs incurred plus gross profit to date, this excess is reported as a current liability called "Billings in Excess of Costs and Recognized Profit." When a company has a number of projects, and costs plus recognized profit exceed billings on some contracts, and billings exceed costs plus recognized profits on others, the contracts should be segregated. The asset side should include only those contracts on which costs plus recognized profit exceed billings, and the liability side should include only those on which billings exceed costs and recognized profit. Separate disclosure of the amounts for Construction in Process (costs plus recognized profit) and Billings is preferable to presenting only the net amount.

Using data from Hardhat Construction Company, its long-term construction activities under the percentage-of-completion method could be reported as shown in Exhibit 6-11.

While the note in this example satisfies requirements for disclosure of the method for recognizing revenue,[15] additional information may be provided. Such information could include the length of significant contracts, the backlog on uncompleted contracts, the effects of any revisions in estimates, pertinent details about receivables, and significant individual or group concentration of contracts exposing the company to unusual risk.

---

[15] *CICA Handbook*, Section 1505, par. .04.

EXHIBIT 6-11 HARDHAT CONSTRUCTION COMPANY

FINANCIAL STATEMENT PRESENTATION: PERCENTAGE-OF-COMPLETION METHOD

		1998	1999	2000
Income Statement				
Revenue from long-term contracts		$1,125,000	$2,115,000	$1,260,000
Construction expenses		1,000,000	1,916,000	1,134,000
Gross profit		$ 125,000	$ 199,000	$ 126,000
Balance Sheet (Dec. 31)				
Current assets:				
Accounts receivable		$ 150,000	$ 800,000	
Inventories				
Construction in process	$1,125,000			
Less: Billings	900,000			
Costs and recognized profit in excess of billings		$ 225,000		
Current liabilities:				
Billings ($3,300,000) in excess of costs and recognized profit ($3,240,000)			$ 60,000	

Note 1: Summary of significant accounting policies

Long-Term Construction Contracts. The Company recognizes revenues and reports profits from long-term construction contracts, its principal business, under the percentage-of-completion method of accounting. The amounts of revenues and profits recognized each year are based on the ratio of costs incurred to the total estimated costs. Costs included in construction in process include direct material, direct labour, and project-related overhead. Corporate general and administrative expenses are charged to the periods as incurred and are not allocated to construction contracts.

COMPLETED-CONTRACT METHOD

OBJECTIVE 7
Know how to apply the completed-contract method for long-term contracts.

Under the **completed-contract method**, *revenue, construction expenses, and gross profit are recognized only in the time period when the contract is completed and constructed items are delivered to the buyer.* Costs of long-term contracts in process and billings are recorded in the period they occur, but there are no interim charges or credits to income statement accounts for revenues, construction expenses, and gross profit.

The annual entries to record costs of construction, progress billings, and collections from customers under the completed-contract method are identical to those illustrated for the percentage-of-completion method. However, when the completed-contract method is used, an entry to recognize revenue, construction expense, and gross profit is not made until the contract is completed. For the bridge project of Hardhat Construction Company, the following entries are made in 2000 under the completed-contract method to recognize revenue and expenses and to close out the inventory and billing accounts.

Billings on Construction in Process	4,500,000	
Revenue from Long-Term Contracts		4,500,000
Construction Expenses	4,050,000	
Construction in Process		4,050,000

The revenue, expenses, and gross profit recognized in each year for the same contract will differ substantially, depending on the method used. This is shown in Exhibit 6-12, which summarizes the recognized gross profits for each year as derived in the Hardhat Construction Company example. The total gross profit on the contract is the same, regardless of the method used.

EXHIBIT 6-12 HARDHAT CONSTRUCTION COMPANY

COMPARISON OF GROSS PROFIT RECOGNIZED EACH YEAR UNDER DIFFERENT METHODS

	Percentage-of-Completion	Completed-Contract
1998	$125,000	$ -0-
1999	199,000	-0-
2000	126,000	450,000
Total	$450,000	$450,000

Exhibit 6-13 shows how Hardhat Construction Company could report its long-term construction activities under the completed-contract method.

EXHIBIT 6-13 HARDHAT CONSTRUCTION COMPANY

FINANCIAL STATEMENT PRESENTATION: COMPLETED-CONTRACT METHOD

Hardhat Construction Company

		1998	1999	2000
Income Statement				
Revenue from long-term contracts		—	—	$4,500,000
Construction expenses		—	—	4,050,000
Gross profit		—	—	$ 450,000
Balance Sheet (Dec. 31)				
Current assets:				
Accounts receivable			$150,000	$800,000
Inventories				
Construction in process	$1,000,000			
Less: Billings	900,000			
Costs in excess of billings			$100,000	
Current liabilities:				
Billings ($3,300,000) in excess of				
contract costs ($2,916,000)			$384,000	

Note 1: Summary of significant accounting policies

Long-Term Construction Contracts. The Company recognizes revenues and reports profits from long-term construction contracts, its principal business, under the completed-contract method. Contract costs and billings are accumulated during the periods of construction, but no revenues, construction expenses, or profits are recognized until completion of the contract. Costs included in construction in process include direct material, direct labour, and project-related overhead. Corporate general and administrative expenses are charged to the periods as incurred.

ACCOUNTING FOR LONG-TERM CONTRACT LOSSES

Two types of losses may be recognized under long-term contracts:[16]

1. **Loss in current period on a profitable contract**. Such a loss *occurs only when the percentage-of-completion method is being used*. It arises when, during construction, there is a significant increase in the estimated total contract costs but the increase does not eliminate all profit on the contract. The estimated cost increase requires a current period adjustment (i.e., recognition of a loss) for the excess gross profit recognized on the project in prior periods. This loss is recorded in the current period because it is the result of a *change in an accounting estimate* (discussed in Chapter 4 and expanded on in Chapter 22).

2. **Loss on an unprofitable contract**. *Under both the percentage-of-completion and the completed-contract methods*, cost estimates at the end of a current period may indicate that a loss will result on completion of the entire contract. When this occurs, the entire expected contract loss must be recognized in the current period. Additionally, any gross profit recognized in prior periods when using the percentage-of-completion method must be eliminated.

OBJECTIVE 8
Identify and apply appropriate accounting for losses on long-term contracts.

The treatments described for both types of losses are consistent with accounting's custom of anticipating foreseeable losses in order to avoid overstatement of current and future income (conservatism).

Losses in Current Period. To illustrate a loss in the current period on a contract originally expected to be profitable upon completion, assume that on December 31, 1999 Hardhat Construction Company estimates the costs to complete the bridge contract at $1,468,962 instead of $1,134,000 (refer to Exhibit 6-4). Assuming all other data are the same as before and the use of the percentage-of-completion method, Hardhat would compute the percent complete at December 31, 1999 and recognize the loss as calculated in Exhibit 6-14.

EXHIBIT 6-14 HARDHAT CONSTRUCTION COMPANY

CALCULATION OF RECOGNIZABLE LOSS IN 1999, PERCENTAGE-OF-COMPLETION METHOD

Costs to date (Dec. 31, 1999)	$2,916,000
Estimated costs to complete (revised)	1,468,962
Estimated total costs	$4,384,962
Percentage completed ($2,916,000 ÷ $4,384,962)	$66\frac{1}{2}\%$
Revenue recognized in 1999 ($4,500,000 × $66\frac{1}{2}\%$ − $1,125,000)	$1,867,500
Costs incurred in 1999	1,916,000
Loss recognized in 1999	**$ 48,500**

Hardhat Construction would record the loss in 1999 as follows.

Construction Expenses	1,916,000	
Construction in Process (Loss)		48,500
Revenue from Long-Term Contract		1,867,500

---

[16] Sak Bhamornsiri, "Losses from Construction Contracts," *The Journal of Accountancy*, April, 1982, p. 26.

The loss of $48,500 will be reported on the 1999 income statement as the difference between the reported revenues of $1,867,500 and the costs of $1,916,000.

The 1999 loss is a cumulative adjustment of the "excess" of gross profit recognized in prior years (1998, in this case) over the total gross profit that would have been recognized through 1999, based on the revised cost estimates. Total gross profit expected, based on revised cost estimates, is $115,038 ($4,500,000 − $4,384,962). The percentage completed at the end of 1999 is 66 ½%. Therefore, through 1999, total gross profit that can be recognized is $76,500 (66 ½% of $115,038). Since $125,000 was recognized in 1998, recognition of a loss of $48,500 ($125,000 − $76,500) is required in 1999 to absorb the overstatement in 1998.

Because the revised total costs to complete the contract are the result of a change in estimate in 1999, the adjustment for the two years is fully absorbed in 1999 rather than by retroactively adjusting account balances that result from prior years' entries. *By the end of 1999, however, the Construction in Process and Retained Earnings account balances would be the same as if the new estimates had existed from the start of the contract.*

In 2000, Hardhat will recognize the remaining 33 ½% of revenue ($1,507,500), given that actual costs in 2000 are as estimated ($1,468,962). The gross profit in 2000 of $38,538 plus the $125,000 in 1998 less the loss of $48,500 in 1999 will equal the gross profit on the entire contract of $115,038 (contract price of $4,500,000 less total contract costs of $4,384,962).

Under the completed-contract method, no loss is recognized in 1999 because the contract is still expected to result in a gross profit that will be recognized in full in the year of completion.

Loss on an Unprofitable Contract. To illustrate the accounting for an overall loss on a long-term contract, assume that at December 31, 1999 Hardhat Construction Company estimates the costs to complete the bridge contract at $1,640,250 instead of $1,134,000. Revised estimates relative to the bridge contract are shown in Exhibit 6-15.

EXHIBIT 6-15 HARDHAT CONSTRUCTION COMPANY

REVISION OF ESTIMATES RESULTING IN OVERALL LOSS ON A LONG-TERM CONTRACT

	1998 Original Estimates	1999 Revised Estimates
Contract price	$4,500,000	**$4,500,000**
Estimated total cost	4,000,000	**4,556,250***
Estimated gross profit	$ 500,000	
Estimated loss		**$ (56,250)**

*($2,916,000 incurred through 1999 + $1,640,250 estimated yet to be incurred in 2000)

Under the percentage-of-completion method, $125,000 of gross profit was recognized in 1998. This $125,000 must be offset in 1999 because it is no longer expected to be realized. In addition, the overall loss of $56,520 must be recognized in 1999 since losses must be recognized as soon as estimable. Therefore, a total loss of $181,250 ($125,000 + $56,250) must be recognized in 1999. The revenue recognized in 1999 is computed as shown in Exhibit 6-16.

To determine the construction costs to be expensed in 1999, add the total loss to be recognized in 1999 ($125,000 + $56,250) to the revenue to be recognized in 1999 as shown in Exhibit 6-17.

EXHIBIT 6-16 HARDHAT CONSTRUCTION COMPANY

COMPUTATION OF REVENUE RECOGNIZED IN 1999,
UNPROFITABLE CONTRACT, PERCENTAGE-OF-COMPLETION METHOD

Revenue recognized in 1999:

Contract price		$4,500,000
Percentage completed		$\times$ 64%*
Revenue recognizable to date		$2,880,000
Less revenue recognized prior to 1999		1,125,000
Revenue recognized in 1999		**$1,755,000**
Costs to date (Dec. 31, 1999)	$2,916,000	
Estimated costs to complete	1,640,250	
Estimated total costs	$4,556,250	

*Percentage completed: $2,916,000 \div \$4,556,250 = 64\%$

EXHIBIT 6-17 HARDHAT CONSTRUCTION COMPANY

COMPUTATION OF CONSTRUCTION EXPENSE FOR 1999,
UNPROFITABLE CONTRACT, PERCENTAGE-OF-COMPLETION METHOD

Revenue recognized in 1999 (computed above)		$1,755,000
Total loss recognized in 1999:		
Reversal of gross profit recognized in 1998	$125,000	
Total estimated loss on the contract	56,250	181,250
Construction expense in 1999		**$1,936,250**

Alternatively, the 1999 construction expenses may be calculated as shown in Exhibit 6-18.

EXHIBIT 6-18 HARDHAT CONSTRUCTION COMPANY

ALTERNATIVE COMPUTATION OF CONSTRUCTION EXPENSE FOR 1999,
UNPROFITABLE CONTRACT, PERCENTAGE-OF-COMPLETION METHOD

Estimated total cost less estimated total loss (equals total revenue)	$4,500,000
Percentage completed, Dec. 31, 1998	$\times$ 64%
Cost to Dec. 31, 1999, before inclusion of total loss	$2,800,000
Add estimated total loss	56,250
Cost to date plus loss	$2,936,250
Deduct cost recognized in prior years (1998)	1,000,000
Construction expense in 1999	**$1,936,250**

Hardhat Construction would record the long-term contract revenues, expenses, and loss in 1999 as follows.

Construction Expenses	1,936,250	
Construction in Process (Loss)		181,250
Revenue from Long-Term Contracts		1,755,000

Assuming that the actual cost incurred in 2000 is as projected at the end of 1999 (i.e., $1,640,250), the revenues and expenses for 2000 are as shown in Exhibit 6-19. Because the

EXHIBIT 6-15 HARDHAT CONSTRUCTION COMPANY

PERCENTAGE OF COMPLETION METHOD, UNPROFITABLE
CONTRACT, SUMMARY WITH RESULTS IN YEAR AFTER LOSS RECOGNITION

	1998	Year 1999	**2000**	Total
Actual Cost	$1,000,000	$1,916,000	$1,640,250	$4,556,250

Income Statement:				
Revenues	$1,125,000	$1,755,000	**$1,620,000[1]**	
Expenses	1,000,000	1,936,250	**$1,620,000[2]**	
Gross Profit (loss)	125,000	(181,250)	-0-	(56,250)

[1] 2000 Revenues:			[2] 2000 Expenses:		
Total contract revenue		$4,500,000	Total contract expenses		$4,556,250
Deduct amount recognized in			Deduct amount recognized in		
1998	$1,125,000		1998	$1,000,000	
1999	1,755,000	2,880,000	1999	1,936,250	2,936,250
		$1,620,000			$1,620,000

Construction in Process account postings:

	1998	1999	2000
For actual costs	$1,000,000 dr.	$1,916,000 dr.	1,640,250 dr.
For profit or loss	125,000 dr.	181,250 cr.	-0-
Year-end balance	$1,125,000 dr.	$2,859,750 dr.	**$4,500,000 dr.**

full loss has been recognized through 1999, there is no gross profit or loss in 2000. Also note that, at the completion of the contract, Construction in Process has a balance equal to the contract price of $4,500,000.[17]

Under the completed-contract method, the total contract loss of $56,250 is recognized in 1999, the year in which it first became evident, through the following entry.

Loss from Long-Term Contracts	56,250	
Construction in Process (Loss)		56,250

The balance in the Construction in Process account after this loss recognition is $2,859,750 ($1,000,000 cost in 1998 + $1,916,000 cost in 1999 − $56,250 loss in 1999), the same as that under the percentage-of-completion method. This is because both methods recognize the full amount of the loss immediately.

OTHER POSSIBLE SITUATIONS WHERE REVENUE RECOGNITION MAY OCCUR IN ADVANCE OF DELIVERY

OBJECTIVE 9
Identify circumstances, other than for long-term contracts, in which revenue recognition might occur prior to delivery.

The *CICA Handbook* specifically states that, when progress on a long-term construction contract can be reasonably determined, revenue recognition can occur prior to delivery of the contracted asset (i.e., the percentage-of-completion method). By not referring explic-

---

[17] If the actual costs in 2000 differ from the estimated amount, the expenses recognized for that year would be adjusted accordingly; the total contract expenses shown in calculation (2) would change, resulting in changing the expenses for 2000. This could result in a further loss or a recovery of the prior period loss being recognized in 2000.

itly to other unique situations involving the sale of goods, one may conclude that recognizing revenue in these situations can only occur when the risks and rewards of ownership are transferred to a buyer, even though amounts can be reasonably measured, collectibility is assured, and costs can be matched. The following three situations provide examples of circumstances where such a conclusion may be challenged.

Completion of Production. In certain cases, revenue has been recognized at the **completion of production** even though no sale was made. Examples involve precious metals or agricultural products with assured prices. Revenue was recognized when these metals were mined or agricultural crops harvested because the finished good was available, costs were known, everything could be sold, the sales price was reasonably assured, the units were interchangeable, and no significant future costs were involved in selling and delivering the product.

Today, however, this timing of revenue recognition technically fails to meet all of the criteria for recognizing revenue from the sale of goods. Through retention of ownership, the producer retains a managerial involvement in and effective control of the goods until the point of sale. Despite this, recognition of revenue prior to sale is intuitively justifiable. The critical work associated with the earning process is the extraction of the metal or the harvesting of the crop. Even though there is no formal contract with buyers of the product, the market circumstances are as if there was a contract. Consequently, it may be argued that the spirit of the phrase "performance is achieved" is satisfied even though the letter of the law is not.

Accretion Basis. **Accretion** is the increase in value that results from natural growth or the aging process. Farmers experience accretion by growing crops and breeding animals. Timberland and nursery stock increase in value as the trees and plants grow. Some wines improve with age. Is accretion revenue? Should it be recognized as revenue?

Accounting theoreticians are somewhat divided on the issue. Some reject recognition of accretion as revenue. They contend that while there is no doubt that assets have increased in value, the technical process of production remains to be undertaken, followed by conversion into liquid assets.[18] Additionally, even though accretion may occur, determining the amount in any given period would be too subjective. Others conclude that from an economic point of view, recognition of accretion value may be justified. In essence, the issue reflected in these viewpoints is whether or not accountants should report revenues on a value-added basis. As stated earlier, this approach has not been adopted in Canada.

Discovery Basis. Discovery of valuable resources by companies in the extractive industries is a frequent event. When such a discovery occurs, should revenue equal to the value of the resources discovered be recognized? As for accretion, there is no doubt that an enterprise's assets may be greatly increased and enhanced by exploration and discovery. Some contend that the financial reporting of companies in the extractive industries would be vastly improved if discovered resources were recognized as assets and their recognized value included in earnings. The arguments for the **discovery basis** are based on the significance of discovery in the earning process and the view that the product's market price can be reasonably estimated.

The arguments against revenue recognition at the time of discovery focus on the uncertainties surrounding the assumptions needed to determine discovery values, the cost of obtaining the necessary data, and the departure from historical cost-based accounting. In light of these arguments, the discovery basis of revenue recognition is sanctioned currently neither by current practice nor by official accounting pronouncements.

---

[18] W.A. Paton and A.C. Littleton, *An Introduction to Corporate Accounting Standards* (Sarasota, Fla.: American Accounting Association, 1940), p. 52.

REVENUE RECOGNITION CRITERIA MET AFTER DELIVERY

OBJECTIVE 10
Understand when circumstances regarding the earning process result in revenue recognition after delivery.

Recognizing revenue from the sale of goods at the point of delivery (sale) occurs because the revenue recognition criteria are judged to be met at that time in the earning process. When payment is to be received after delivery, the criteria require that ultimate collection is reasonably assured.[19] *If collection in full may not occur, the criteria are still met at delivery, given that a reasonable estimate of bad debts can be made. If such an estimate cannot be made, revenue recognition must be deferred until cash is collected.*[20]

Two accounting methods exist for recognizing revenue or gross profit at the time cash is collected: the *instalment method* and the *cost recovery method.*

THE INSTALMENT METHOD

The expression "instalment sale" is generally used to describe any type of sale for which payment is required in periodic instalments over an extended period of time. It has been used in the retail field, where various types of farm and home equipment and furnishings are sold on an instalment basis. It is sometimes used in the heavy equipment industry, where machine installations are paid for over a long period. A more recent application of the method is in land development sales.

Because payment for the products or property sold is spread over a relatively long period, the risk of loss resulting from uncollectible accounts is greater in instalment sales transactions than in ordinary sales. Consequently, various devices are used to protect the seller. In merchandising, the two most common are (1) a conditional sales contract stating that title to the item sold does not pass to the purchaser until all payments have been made; and (2) notes secured by a chattel (personal property) mortgage on the article sold. Either of these devices permits the seller to repossess the goods if the purchaser defaults on one or more payments. The repossessed merchandise is then resold at whatever price it will bring.

OBJECTIVE 11
Describe and apply the instalment method of accounting.

Under the instalment method, *income recognition is deferred until the period of cash collection.* Both revenue and cost of sales are recorded in the period of sale but, instead of being closed to the Income Summary account, they are closed to a Deferred Gross Profit account. The deferred gross profit is recognized as realized gross profit and shown in the income statement in the periods cash is collected. The amount of gross profit realized each period depends on the cash collected and the percentage of gross profit on the sale. This is equivalent to deferring both sales revenue and cost of sales to the period of cash collection. Other expenses, such as selling and administrative expenses, are not deferred.

In the remainder of this section, the nature of the information required and the journal entries made when the instalment method is used are described. Then, accounting under the instalment method is illustrated to show how the information is used and the journal entries are constructed. Note, however, that the instalment method is used only when bad debts resulting from instalment sales cannot be reasonably estimated. For many instalment sales, reasonable estimates of uncollectible amounts can be made and, therefore, the resulting revenue would be recognized in the period of sale. *The point is that the instalment method is not a method of accounting for instalment sales in general. Rather, it is a method that is used to account for such sales when collectibility is uncertain and the amount that will be uncollectible in the future is not reasonably determinable.*

---

[19] Sometimes cash is received prior to delivery of the goods and is recorded as a deposit (customer advance) because the sale transaction is incomplete. In such cases, the seller has not performed under the contract and has no claim against the purchaser. Cash received represents advances and should be reported as a liability until the contract is performed by delivery of the product.

[20] *CICA Handbook*, Section 3400, par. .16.

Accounting Procedures Under the Instalment Method. From the preceding general description of the instalment method, it is apparent that certain information and special accounts are required to determine the deferred (unrealized) gross profit and the realized gross profit in each year of operations. These requirements are as follows:

1. The revenues and costs of instalment sales transactions accounted for using the instalment method must be kept in accounts separate from those for all other sales transactions.

2. The gross profit on sales accounted for on the instalment method must be determinable.

3. The amount of cash collected on the current year's instalment sales accounts receivable and on each of the preceding year's receivables must be determinable.

4. Provision must be made for carrying forward each year's deferred gross profit.

Given this, Exhibit 6-20 provides a description of the nature of the journal entries made in a given year using the instalment method.

EXHIBIT 6-20

NATURE OF JOURNAL ENTRIES: INSTALMENT METHOD

For sales made during the current year:

1. Record the sale by debiting Instalment Accounts Receivable (noting the year) and crediting Instalment Sales.

2. Record the cost of the sale by debiting Cost of Instalment Sales and crediting Inventory. This assumes use of the perpetual inventory system.[21]

3. Record cash received on this year's sales by debiting Cash and crediting Instalment Accounts Receivable (noting the year).

At year end:

4. Close the revenue and expense accounts to a deferred gross profit account by debiting Instalment Sales, crediting Cost of Instalment Sales, and crediting Deferred Gross Profit on Instalment Sales (noting the year).

5. Record the gross profit realized on cash collected on the current year's receivables by debiting Deferred Gross Profit on Instalment Sales (noting the year) and crediting Realized Gross Profit. The amount is equal to the cash collected multiplied by the gross profit percentage (gross profit ÷ instalment sales revenue) on the current year's sales.

For collections on sales made in prior years:

1. Record cash received by debiting Cash and crediting Instalment Accounts Receivable (noting the year).

2. Record the gross profit realized on the cash collected by debiting Deferred Gross Profit on Instalment Sales (noting the year) and crediting Realized Gross Profit. The amount is the gross profit percentage on the particular prior year's sale multiplied by the cash collected on that year's receivable.[22]

For both:

1. Close the Realized Gross Profit account to the Income Summary.

---

[21] Under the perpetual inventory system, when a sale is made, the cost of goods sold is recorded and inventory is reduced. For a review of the basics of the perpetual method and the periodic method see Chapter 3 (Chapter 8 explains these methods in greater detail). If the periodic method was used, then the Cost of Instalment Sales would be debited at year end with the credit going to one of several possible accounts depending on where the item sold came from. For example, if it was from beginning inventory, the Beginning Inventory account would be credited. If it was from purchases of the current year, then Purchases would be credited. If the total beginning inventory and all purchases for the year had been closed to Cost of Goods Sold before the cost of instalment sales had been separated out, then the Cost of Goods Sold account would be credited.

[22] Alternatively, the realized gross profit for a particular year's sales on cash collected during any given year may be determined as follows:

$$\frac{\text{Cash collected in the year}}{\text{Amount of the instalment sales}} \times \text{Total deferred gross profit on the sales}$$

From this description, it can be seen that the accounting related to the instalment method is fairly complex. The result, however, accomplishes the objective of reporting gross profit in the period when cash is collected. Note that in each year, ordinary operating expenses are charged to expense accounts and are closed to the Income Summary account as under customary accounting procedure. Thus, the only peculiarity in computing net income under the instalment method as generally applied is *the deferment of gross profit until realized by accounts receivable collection.*

To illustrate the instalment method, the data shown in Exhibit 6-21 for the Fesmire Manufacturing Co. Ltd. will be used.

EXHIBIT 6-21   FESMIRE MANUFACTURING CO. LTD.

DATA TO ILLUSTRATE THE USE OF THE INSTALMENT METHOD

	1998	1999	2000
Sales (on instalment)	$200,000	$250,000	$240,000
Cost of sales	150,000	190,000	168,000
Gross profit	$ 50,000	$ 60,000	$ 72,000
Rate of gross profit on sales	25%ᵃ	24%ᵇ	30%ᶜ
Cash receipts from:			
1998 sales	$ 60,000	$100,000	$ 40,000
1999 sales		100,000	125,000
2000 sales			80,000

ᵃ$50,000	ᵇ$60,000	ᶜ$72,000
$200,000	$250,000	$240,000

To simplify the illustration, interest charges have been excluded (an example presented later will consider interest). Summary entries in general journal form for the three years are shown below. As a practical matter, these entries would not appear in summary form, but would be entered individually as they occur. Transactions not concerned with the instalment method have been omitted.

1998

Instalment Accounts Receivable, 1998	200,000	
Instalment Sales		200,000
(To record sales made on instalment in 1998)		
Cost of Instalment Sales	150,000	
Inventory		150,000
(To record cost of goods sold on instalment in 1998)		
Cash	60,000	
Instalment Accounts Receivable, 1998		60,000
(To record cash collected on instalment receivables)		
Instalment Sales	200,000	
Cost of Instalment Sales		150,000
Deferred Gross Profit, 1998		50,000
(Year-end entry to close instalment sales and cost of instalment sales for the year to deferred gross profit)		
Deferred Gross Profit, 1998	15,000	
Realized Gross Profit on Instalment Sales		15,000
(To remove from deferred gross profit the profit realized through collections)		
Realized Gross Profit on Instalment Sales	15,000	
Income Summary		15,000
(To close profits realized by collections)		

The realized gross profit for 1998 and the deferred gross profit at the end of 1998 are computed as shown in Exhibit 6-22.

EXHIBIT 6-22 FESMIRE MANUFACTURING CO. LTD.

COMPUTATION OF REALIZED AND DEFERRED GROSS PROFIT, YEAR 1

1998

Rate of gross profit current year [(sales — cost of sales) ÷ sales]	
($200,000 — $150,000) ÷ 200,000	25%
Cash collected on current year's sales	$60,000
Realized gross profit (25% of $60,000)	15,000
Deferred gross profit on 1998 sales yet to be realized ($50,000 — $15,000)	35,000

1999

Instalment Accounts Receivable, 1999	250,000	
Instalment Sales		250,000
(To record sales made on instalment in 1999)		
Cost of Instalment Sales	190,000	
Inventory		190,000
(To record cost of goods sold on instalment in 1999)		
Cash	200,000	
Instalment Accounts Receivable, 1998		100,000
Instalment Accounts Receivable, 1999		100,000
(To record cash collected on instalment receivables)		
Instalment Sales	250,000	
Cost of Instalment Sales		190,000
Deferred Gross Profit, 1999		60,000
(Year-end entry to close instalment sales and cost of instalment sales for the year to deferred gross profit)		
Deferred Gross Profit, 1998	25,000	
Deferred Gross Profit, 1999	24,000	
Realized Gross Profit on Instalment Sales		49,000
(Year-end entry to remove from deferred gross profit the profit realized through collections)		
Realized Gross Profit on Instalment Sales	49,000	
Income Summary		49,000
(To close profits realized by collections)		

Exhibit 6-23 shows the computation of the realized gross profit for 1999 and deferred gross profit at the end of 1999. The entries in 2000 would be similar to those of 1999, and the total gross profit realized would be $64,000, as shown by the computations in Exhibit 6-24.

Additional Problems of the Instalment Method. In addition to computing realized and deferred gross profit, other problems are involved in accounting using the instalment method for sales transactions. These problems are related to:

1. Interest on instalment contracts.

2. Defaults and repossessions.

Interest on Instalment Contracts. Because the collection of instalment receivables is spread over a long period, it is customary to charge the buyer interest on the unpaid balance. A schedule of equal payments consisting of interest and principal, similar to that shown in

EXHIBIT 6-23 FESMIRE MANUFACTURING CO. LTD.

COMPUTATION OF REALIZED AND DEFERRED GROSS PROFIT, YEAR 2

<u>1999</u>

Current year's sales	
Rate of gross profit [($250,000 − $190,000) ÷ $250,000]	24%
Cash collected on current year's sales	$100,000
Realized gross profit (24% of $100,000)	**24,000**
Deferred gross profit on 1999 sales ($60,000 − $24,000)	**36,000**
Prior years' sales	
Rate of gross profit—1998	25%
Cash collected on 1998 sales in 1999	$100,000
Gross profit realized in 1999 on 1998 sales (25% of $100,000)	**25,000**
Total gross profit realized in 1999	
Realized on collections of 1998 sales	**$ 25,000**
Realized on collections of 1999 sales	**24,000**
Total	**$ 49,000**

EXHIBIT 6-24 FESMIRE MANUFACTURING CO. LTD.

COMPUTATION OF REALIZED AND DEFERRED GROSS PROFIT, YEAR 3

<u>2000</u>

Current year's sales	
Rate of gross profit [($240,000 − $168,000) ÷ $240,000]	30%
Cash collected on current year's sales	$ 80,000
Gross profit realized on 2000 sales (30% of $80,000)	**24,000**
Deferred gross profit on 2000 sales ($72,000 − $24,000)	**48,000**
Prior years' sales	
1998 sales	
Rate of gross profit—1998	25%
Cash collected on 1998 sales in 2000	$ 40,000
Gross profit realized in 2000 on 1998 (25% of $40,000)	**10,000**
1999 sales	
Rate of gross profit—1999	24%
Cash collected on 1999 sales in 2000	$125,000
Gross profit realized in 2000 on 1999 sales (24% of $125,000)	**30,000**
Total gross profit realized in 2000	
Realized on collections of 1998 sales	$ 10,000
Realized on collections of 1999 sales	30,000
Realized on collections of 2000 sales	24,000
Total	**$ 64,000**

Exhibit 6-25, is set up.[23] Each successive payment has attributed to it a smaller amount of interest and a correspondingly larger amount of principal. For this example, an item costing $2,400 is sold for $3,000 (gross profit percentage is 20%) on December 31, 1998. Interest at 8% is included in the three equal instalments of $1,164.10.

EXHIBIT 6-25 FESMIRE MANUFACTURING CO. LTD.

INSTALMENT PAYMENT SCHEDULE SEPARATING INTEREST AND REALIZED GROSS PROFIT RELATED TO CASH COLLECTIONS

Date	Cash (Debit)	Interest Revenue (Credit)	Instalment Receivables (Credit)	Instalment Unpaid Balance	Realized Gross Profit (20%)
Dec. 31/98	—	—	—	$3,000.00	—
Dec. 31/99	$1,164.10[a]	$240.00[b]	$ 924.10[c]	2,075.90[d]	$184.82[a]
Dec. 31/00	1,164.10	166.07	998.03	1,077.87	199.61
Dec. 31/01	1,164.10	86.23	1,077.873	-0-	215.57
					$600.00

[a]Periodic payment = Original unpaid balance ÷ PV of an annuity of $1.00 for three periods at 8%: $1,164.10 = $3,000 ÷ 2.57710

[b]$3,000 × .08 = $240.00

[c]$1,164.10 − $240.00 = $924.10

[d]$3,000.00 − $924.10 = $2,075.90

[e]$924.10 × .20 = $184.82

Given this schedule, the entries to account for this sale under the instalment method are shown in Exhibit 6-26. The only added feature in these entries compared to those previously illustrated is that interest revenue is now accounted for and separated from the gross profit recognized on the instalment sales collections during the period. In this example the interest revenue is recognized at the time of the cash receipt (December 31, the company's year end). If cash is not received at the year end, interest accrued since the last collection date would be recorded as an adjusting entry at the year end.

Defaults and Repossessions. Depending on the terms of the sales contract and the policy of the credit department, the seller can repossess merchandise sold under an instalment arrangement if the purchaser fails to meet payment requirements. Repossessed merchandise may be reconditioned before it is offered for sale, and then resold for cash or instalment payments.

---

[23] This schedule utilizes time value of money concepts in its construction. Generally, those studying intermediate accounting have been previously exposed to these concepts and their application in other courses. If this is not the case, or if a review would help, you may wish to examine the appendix at the end of Volume 1 of this book titled "Accounting and the Time Value of Money." This appendix explains and illustrates the concepts for present value and future value calculations applicable to a single amount, ordinary annuity, and annuity due. Tables at the end of this appendix provide "factors" for making calculations (such as the 2.57710 present value factor for an ordinary annuity for three periods at 8%, as used in Exhibit 6-25). Many topics considered later in this book require an understanding of the time value of money concepts and their application. For example, accounts receivable from ordinary sales involve making a future payment. While it is theoretically correct to consider an interest aspect to such receivables, it is generally not done as collection is expected in a short period of time (i.e., less than one year) and the interest is not likely to be material. However, for receivables to be paid over a longer period, an interest component should be considered. These issues are considered in Chapter 7.

EXHIBIT 6-26

JOURNAL ENTRIES FOR INSTALMENT METHOD WITH INTEREST

	1998		1999		2000		2001	
Dec. 31								
Instal. Account Rec.	3,000							
Instal. Sales		3,000						
Cost of Instal. Sales	2,400							
Inventory		2,400						
Instal. Sales	3,000							
Cost of Instal. Sales		2,400						
Deferred Gross Profit		600						
Cash			1,164.10		1,164.10		1,164.10	
Instal. Account Rec.				924.10		998.03		1,077.87
Interest Revenue				240.00		166.07		86.23
Deferred Gross Profit			184.82		199.61		215.57	
Realized Gross Profit				184.82		199.61		215.57

The accounting for **repossessions** recognizes that the related Instalment Receivable account is not collectible and that it should be written off. Along with this receivable, the applicable deferred gross profit must be removed from the ledger. This is accomplished by the following entry:

Repossessed Merchandise (an inventory account)	XX	
Deferred Gross Profit	XX	
Instalment Accounts Receivable		XX

This entry assumes that the repossessed merchandise is to be recorded on the books at exactly the amount of the uncollected account less the applicable deferred gross profit. This assumption may or may not be correct. The condition of the merchandise repossessed, the cost of reconditioning, and the market for second-hand merchandise of that particular type must all be considered. *The objective should be to put any asset acquired on the books at its fair value or, when fair value is not ascertainable, at the best possible approximation of fair value.* If the fair value of the merchandise repossessed is less than the uncollected balance less the deferred gross profit, a "loss on repossession" should be recorded at the date of repossession.

To illustrate, assume that a refrigerator was sold to Marilyn Hunt for $500 on September 1, 1998. Terms require a down payment of $200, and $20 on the first of every month for 15 months thereafter. It is further assumed that the refrigerator cost $300 and is sold to provide a 40% rate of gross profit on selling price. At the year end, December 31, 1998, a total of $60 would have been collected in addition to the original down payment.

If Hunt makes her January and February payments in 1999 and then defaults, the ledger account balances applicable to Hunt at time of default would be:

Instalment Account Receivable ($500 − $200 − five payments of $20)	200 (dr.)
Deferred Gross Profit (40% × $240)	96 (cr.)

The deferred gross profit applicable to the Hunt account still has the December 31, 1998 balance because no entry has been made to take up gross profit realized by 1999 cash collections. The regular entry at the end of 1999, however, will take up the gross profit realized by all cash collections, including amounts received from Hunt. Hence, the *bal-*

ance of deferred gross profit applicable to Hunt's account at the time of default may be computed by applying the gross profit rate for the year of sale to the balance of Hunt's account receivable: 40% of $200, or $80. Therefore, the account balances for purposes of recording the repossession should be considered as:

Instalment Account Receivable (Hunt)	200 (dr.)
Deferred Gross Profit (applicable to Hunt after considering $16 of gross profit realized on cash collected in January and February)	80 (cr.)

If the estimated fair value of the article repossessed is $70, the following entry would be made to record the repossession:

Deferred Gross Profit	80	
Repossessed Merchandise	70	
Loss on Repossession	50	
Instalment Account Receivable (Hunt)		200

The amount of the loss is determined as shown in Exhibit 6-27.

EXHIBIT 6-27

COMPUTATION OF A LOSS ON REPOSSESSION

Balance of account receivable (representing uncollected selling price)	$200
Less deferred gross profit	80
Unrecovered cost	$120
Less estimated fair value of merchandise repossessed	70
Loss on repossession	**$ 50**

If the fair value of the merchandise was $150, then a $30 gain on repossession would be recognized.

Financial Statement Presentation Under the Instalment Method. The previously illustrated entries resulted in only one account, Realized Gross Profit on Instalment Sales, being closed to the Income Summary account each year. Therefore, for a company that has both sales from which revenue is recognized when the sale is made and sales that are accounted for under the instalment method, the *realized gross profit on instalment sales* may be reported as shown in Exhibit 6-28.

EXHIBIT 6-28   HEALTH MACHINE COMPANY

STATEMENT OF INCOME

(Reporting Realized Gross Profit in the
Income Statement, Single Line Disclosure)

For the Year Ended December 31, 1998

Sales	$620,000
Cost of goods sold	490,000
Gross profit on sales	$130,000
Gross profit realized on instalment sales	**51,000**
Total gross profit on sales	$181,000

If sales accounted for by the instalment method represent a significant part of total sales, disclosure of the current year's instalment sales, cost of those sales, and realized gross profit on cash collections may be desirable. Exhibit 6-29 shows how such disclosure could be accomplished. The year's sales and cost of goods sold amounts in the Instalment Method Sales column are the amounts closed to the Deferred Gross Profit account at year end.

EXHIBIT 6-29 HEALTH MACHINE COMPANY

STATEMENT OF INCOME

(Reporting Realized Gross Profit in the
Income Statement, Detailed Disclosure)

For the Year Ended December 31, 1998

	Instalment Method Sales	Other Sales	Total
Sales	$248,000	$620,000	$868,000
Cost of goods sold	182,000	490,000	672,000
Gross profit on sales	$ 66,000	$130,000	$196,000
Less deferred gross profit on instalment sales of this year	47,000		47,000
Realized gross profit on this year's sales	$ 19,000	$130,000	$149,000
Add gross profit realized on instalment sales of prior years	32,000		32,000
Gross profit realized this year	$ 51,000	$130,000	$181,000

The apparent awkwardness of this presentation is difficult to avoid if full disclosure is to be provided in the income statement. One solution, of course, is to include in the income statement only the gross profit realized during the year and to provide a separate schedule showing the details in a note to the statement.

In the balance sheet, it is generally considered desirable to disclose *instalment accounts receivable* by year of collectibility in the Current Asset section. There is some question as to whether instalment accounts that are not collectible within the coming year should be included in current assets. If instalment sales are part of normal operations, they may be considered as current assets because they are collectible within the operating cycle of the business. Little confusion should result from this classification if maturity dates are fully disclosed, as exemplified in Exhibit 6-30.

EXHIBIT 6-30

REPORTING INSTALMENT ACCOUNTS RECEIVABLE
BY YEAR IN THE CURRENT ASSET SECTION OF THE BALANCE SHEET

Current assets		
Notes and accounts receivable		
Trade customers	$78,800	
Less allowance for doubtful accounts	3,700	
	$75,100	
Instalment accounts collectible in 1999	22,600	
Instalment accounts collectible in 2000	47,200	$144,900

Repossessed merchandise is a part of inventory and should be included as such in the Current Asset section of the balance sheet. Any *gain or loss on repossessions* should be included in the income statement in the Other Revenues and Gains section or Other Expenses and Losses section.

Deferred gross profit on instalment sales is generally treated as unearned revenue and classified as a current liability. *CICA Handbook* Section 1000 permits the inclusion of items on the balance sheet that are not assets or liabilities but items that result from a delay in income statement recognition.[24] Thus, deferred gross profit may be reported with liabilities. An alternative means of disclosure would be to report it as a reduction of instalment accounts receivable. This method is conceptually appealing since the reason for the existence of a deferred gross profit is that the seller has retained a significant risk. Also supporting this position is the argument that "no matter how it is displayed in financial statements, deferred gross profit on instalment sales is conceptually an asset valuation—that is, a reduction of an asset."[25] We favour this position but recognize that until an official standard on this topic is issued, financial statements will probably continue to report such deferred gross profit as a current liability.

THE COST RECOVERY METHOD

The cost recovery method is another method that may be used when the realization criteria are judged not to be met until cash collection takes place. Under the **cost recovery method**, *no gross profit is recognized until cash payments by the buyer exceed the seller's cost of the merchandise sold.* After the cost of the merchandise sold has been recovered, additional cash receipts are recognized as realized gross profit.

OBJECTIVE 12
Explain and apply the cost recovery method of accounting.

This method is more conservative than the instalment method. When the recognition criteria are not met until cash is collected, the choice of applying the instalment method or the cost recovery method requires the exercise of professional judgement. The resolution revolves around the extent of the uncertainty associated with the eventual collection of the receivables. The cost recovery method is applicable to situations in which there is a great degree of uncertainty. Such circumstances could exist, for example, when an instalment sale is made to a newly established business engaged in highly speculative activities.

To illustrate the cost recovery method and compare it to that of the instalment method, the previously identified data pertaining to Fesmire Manufacturing Co. Ltd.'s 1998 instalment sales and subsequent cash collections will be used. This data and the journal entries associated with the two methods are presented in Exhibit 6-31.

As this example shows, the entries to record the instalment sales, cost of instalment sales, cash collections, and closing a year's instalment sales and cost of these sales to deferred gross profit are the same under both methods. *The difference between the methods occurs with regard to the timing of recognizing realized gross profit.*

Realized gross profit is reported in the appropriate year's income statement in the same manner as illustrated under the instalment method. Any balance in the Deferred Gross Profit account is, preferably, reported as a contra account deducted from the related receivables in the balance sheet. Alternatively, the Deferred Gross Profit account may be reported as a current liability, as is the common case when the instalment method is used.

CONCLUDING REMARKS

As stated in the opening sentence of this chapter, revenue recognition is one of the most difficult and pressing problems facing the accounting profession. The difficulties arise because companies earn revenues in different ways. Any particular company's earning

---

[24] *CICA Handbook*, Section 1000, par. .26.
[25] *Statement of Financial Accounting Concepts No. 3* (Stamford, CT.: FASB), pars. .156–.158.

EXHIBIT 6-31

COST RECOVERY METHOD COMPARED TO THE INSTALMENT METHOD, JOURNAL ENTRIES

Events:

In 1998: Sales (on instalment contracts)	$200,000
Cost of instalment sales	150,000
Gross profit	$ 50,000
Rate of gross profit	25%

Cash collected on the 1994 instalment sales:

in 1998, $ 60,000
in 1999, $100,000
in 2000, $ 40,000

For Both Cost Recovery Method and Instalment Method:

	1998		1999		2000	
Instalment Accounts Receivable, 1998	200,000					
Instalment Sales		200,000				
(To record sale made on instalment in 1998)						
Cost of Instalment Sales	150,000					
Inventory		150,000				
(To record cost of goods sold on instalment in 1998)						
Cash	60,000		100,000		40,000	
Instalment Accounts Receivable, 1998		60,000		100,000		40,000
(To record cash collections on instalment during year)						
Instalment Sales	200,000					
Cost of Instalment Sales		150,000				
Deferred Gross Profit, 1998		50,000				
(Year-end entry to close instalment sales and cost of instalment sales for 1998 to deferred gross profit)						

For Cost Recovery Method:

	1998		1999		2000	
Deferred Gross Profit, 1998	—		10,000		40,000	
Realized Gross Profit on Instalment Sales	—			10,000		40,000
(Year-end entry to remove from deferred gross profit the profit realized from cash collected during the year after full cost of the goods sold has been collected)						

For Instalment Method:

	1998		1999		2000	
Deferred Gross Profit, 1998	15,000		25,000		10,000	
Realized Gross Profit		15,000		25,000		10,000
(Year-end entry to remove from deferred gross profit the profit realized from cash collected during the year. Equals gross profit rate of 25% multiplied by cash collected each year)						

For both the cost recovery method and the instalment method, Realized Gross Profit for each year would be closed to the Income Summary account.

process and specific circumstances may result in the revenue recognition criteria established in the *CICA Handbook* being met at a time different than that for another company. Clearly, judgement is required regarding any decision to recognize revenue, and that judgement must be based on justifiable reasons. The following may prove useful in making such judgements.

1. Know the criteria for revenue recognition as presented in the *CICA Handbook*.

2. Know the earning process associated with a particular situation. Such understanding may be helped by identifying on a time-line the major transactions and events that occur in the earning process.

3. Examine the earning process with the objective of determining when all the criteria for revenue recognition are met. It is at this time revenue can be recognized.

Summary of Learning Objectives

1. **Understand what is included in an earning process, when revenue is earned, and that earning revenue is different from recognizing revenue.** The earning process consists of all activities and events in which a company engages to earn revenue. Consequently, each activity or event in the earning process contributes to earning revenue (a value-added viewpoint). Recognizing revenue (i.e., recording it in the accounting system) is not based on a value-added basis, however, due to measurement difficulties. Instead, recognition occurs at a particular stage in the earning process when specific criteria are judged to have been met.

2. **Know the *CICA Handbook* criteria for revenue recognition and appreciate that the matching principle also has consequences for revenue recognition.** The *CICA Handbook*, Section 3400, states, generally, that revenue can be recognized at the time in the earning process when (1) performance is achieved; (2) the amount is reasonably measurable; and (3) collectibility is reasonably assured. It provides specific definitions of when performance is achieved regarding the sale of goods, rendering of services, and executing of long-term contracts. Also, in Section 1000, the *Handbook* states that (4) matching expenses with related revenue is necessary. Consequently, this fourth criterion is important for revenue recognition to occur.

3. **Realize that determining when the revenue recognition criteria are met requires the exercise of professional judgement.** In many situations, the criteria for revenue recognition are met at the point of delivery (sale). In other situations, however, the criteria may be met prior to or after delivery. Therefore, judgement needs to be applied to many situations where revenue recognition determination is an issue. Such judgement involves knowing the earning process for a particular situation and determining when all recognition criteria are reasonably met within that process.

4. **Know when and why revenue recognition criteria are satisfied at the point of delivery (sale) and describe accounting issues related to such recognition.** The criteria are met at the point of delivery as risks and rewards of ownership are transferred to the buyer, the amount is reasonably measurable as evidenced by cash paid or agreed to be paid, collectibility is reasonably assured or bad

debts can be reasonably estimated, and material expenses are all capable of being matched against the revenue. Issues exist regarding recognition at the point of delivery when there is a sale with a buyback agreement, high rates of return exist, and trade loading or channel stuffing are involved.

5. **Understand why and when revenue can be recognized prior to completion of long-term contracts, and why and when it may not be recognized until completion of such contracts.** Long-term contracts take more than one accounting period to complete. To appropriately reflect economic activity in each period, it is desirable to recognize revenue that results from work accomplished in each period. Doing so, however, requires being able to reasonably measure the proportion of the total work done each period. When this cannot be done, it is necessary to wait until the completion of the contract before recognizing any revenue.

6. **Know when the percentage-of-completion method can be used and how to apply it for long-term contracts.** When the amount of revenue is measurable, estimates of the costs to complete are reasonably determinable, the extent of progress toward completion is reasonably estimable, and collectibility is reasonably assured, the percentage-of-completion method is applied.

7. **Know how to apply the completed-contract method for long-term contracts.** The completed-contract method, which defers the recognition of revenue until the completion of the long-term contract, should be used when the conditions for using the percentage-of-completion method do not apply.

8. **Identify and apply appropriate accounting for losses on long-term contracts.** Expected losses resulting from long-term contracts should be recognized entirely in the earliest period in which they are estimable, regardless of whether the percentage-of-completion method or the completed-contract method is used. When the percentage-of-completion method is used a loss may have to be recognized in a period even though the contract is profitable overall.

9. **Identify circumstances, other than for long-term contracts, in which revenue recognition might occur prior to delivery.** Should revenue be recognized when metals are mined, agricultural products are harvested, accretion occurs, or valuable resources are discovered? While arguments of an economic nature may favour such recognition, accounting practice and standards tend to not support recognition prior to the point of sale.

10. **Understand when circumstances regarding the earning process result in revenue recognition after delivery.** Revenue recognition may be deferred until cash is collected in circumstances where the collection of accounts receivable is doubtful and a reasonable estimate of bad debts cannot be made in the period of the sale.

11. **Describe and apply the instalment method of accounting.** An instalment sale results in future periodic receipts of payments over an extended period of time. If bad debts from such sales can be estimated, the revenue is recognized in the period of sale. When this is not the case, the instalment method may be used. Under this method gross profit is recognized as earned when cash is collected.

12. **Explain and apply the cost recovery method of accounting.** Under the cost recovery method, no profit is recognized until cash payments by the buyer exceed the seller's cost of the merchandise sold. After all costs have been recovered, any additional cash collections are included in income.

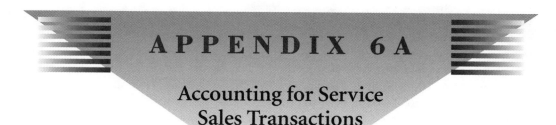

APPENDIX 6A

Accounting for Service Sales Transactions

SERVICE INDUSTRIES AND SERVICE TRANSACTIONS

The number and variety of businesses that offer services to the public are increasing and the range of services they offer is broadening. The common ground of all organizations that provide services is that they engage in **service transactions**.

> Service transactions are defined as transactions between a seller and a purchaser in which, for a mutually agreed price, the seller performs, agrees to perform at a later date, or agrees to maintain readiness to perform an act or acts, including permitting others to use enterprise resources that do not alone produce a tangible commodity or product as the principal intended result.[26]

Although this definition does not require that the act or acts to be performed be specified by a contract, in practice most service transactions performed over a period of time or requiring performance in the future are formalized by a contract. However, agreements to perform at a later date and agreements to maintain a readiness to perform an act are typically only commitments or executory contracts. As such, they are not recorded in accrual-based, transaction-oriented financial statements.

Some transactions may involve both services and products. *When provision of a product is incidental to the rendering of a service, the transaction is accounted for as a service transaction.* For example, a fixed-price equipment maintenance contract that includes parts is considered a service transaction. Conversely, *if a service is incidental to the sale of a product, the transaction is accounted for as a product transaction.* For example, the inclusion of a warranty or guarantee in the sale of a product is considered incidental to the sale of the product.

When both the product and the service are stated separately and the total transaction price varies because the product or the service is included, the transaction is accounted for as both a product and a service transaction. For example, equipment maintenance contracts in which parts are charged separately qualifies for separable product and service transaction accounting.

REVENUE AND EXPENSE RECOGNITION FOR SERVICE TRANSACTIONS

A major accounting issue regarding service transactions concerns when revenue should be recognized. Solutions depend on when all the revenue recognition criteria are met in the earning process. *The criteria for revenue recognition for service transactions are the same as exist for product sales:* performance is achieved, measurement is reasonably determinable, collectibility is reasonably assured or uncollectible amounts can be estimated, and expenses can be matched against the revenue.

Within the context of the specific *CICA Handbook* recommendations on revenue recognition criteria (see Exhibit 6-1), the following explanatory statements are made:[27]

OBJECTIVE 13
Understand issues related to revenue recognition for service transactions and appreciate that their resolution is based on the same revenue recognition criteria as exists for the sale of goods.

---

[26] *Accounting for Certain Service Transactions* (Stamford, CT.: FASB, 1978), p. 1.

[27] *CICA Handbook*, Section 3400, pars. .13–.15.

Revenue from service transactions . . . is usually recognized as the service . . . activity is performed, using either the percentage of completion method or the completed contract method.

The percentage of completion method is used when performance consists of the execution of more than one act, and revenue would be recognized proportionately by reference to the performance of each act. Revenue recognized under this method would be determined on a rational and consistent basis such as on the basis of sales value, associated costs, extent of progress, or number of acts. For practical purposes, when services are provided by an indeterminate number of acts over a specific period of time, revenue would be recognized on a straight line basis over the period unless there is evidence that some other method better reflects the pattern of performance.

The completed contract method would only be appropriate when performance consists of the execution of a single act or when the enterprise cannot reasonably estimate the extent of progress toward completion.

Consequently, performance is linked to the execution of a defined act or acts. Given that measurement of revenue and expenses can be related to such execution and that collection is reasonably assured, then revenue can be recognized.

The matching principle specifies that costs should be charged to expense in the period the revenue with which they are associated is recognized. Costs to be incurred in periods subsequent to the period of related revenue recognition should be accrued (i.e., debit an expense and credit a liability). If such future costs exist and are material but cannot be reasonably estimable, then revenue recognition must be deferred.

For service transactions, costs incurred to earn revenue may be categorized as follows:[28]

1. **Initial direct costs** are costs that are directly associated with negotiating and consummating service agreements. They include, but are not necessarily limited to, commissions, legal fees, and costs of credit investigations. No portion of supervisory and administration expenses or other indirect expenses, such as rent and facilities costs, is included in initial direct costs.

2. **Direct costs** are costs that have a clearly identifiable beneficial or causal relationship (i) to the services performed; or (ii) to the level of services performed for a group of customers (e.g., labour costs and repair parts included as part of a service agreement).

3. **Indirect costs** are all costs other than initial direct costs and direct costs. They include general and administrative expenses, advertising expenses, and general selling expenses.

Indirect costs would be charged to expense as incurred, regardless of the revenue recognition method applied to the transaction. The method of accounting for initial direct costs and direct costs is dependent on the revenue recognition method applied to the transactions.

METHODS OF SERVICE REVENUE RECOGNITION

Depending on when the criteria for revenue recognition for service transactions are satisfied, one of the four following methods of accounting would be used:

---

[28] *Accounting for Certain Service Transactions*, pp. 13 and 14.

1. Specific performance method.
2. Proportional performance method.
3. Completed performance method.
4. Collection method.

SPECIFIC PERFORMANCE METHOD

The **specific performance method** is appropriate when a service transaction consists of a *single act.* Revenue is recognized at the time the act is completed. Initial direct costs and direct costs are charged to expense at the time revenue is recognized. Thus, initial direct costs and direct costs incurred before the service is performed are deferred until the revenue is recognized. In essence, this method is similar to recognizing revenue from the sale of goods at the time of delivery.

The specific performance method could be used by a real estate broker who would record sales commissions as revenue when a real estate transaction is closed. It might also be applicable to an employment agency. Because the agency has rendered its services in locating and placing an employee for its client, the fee would be recorded at the time the employee is placed. However, if experience shows that there is a reasonable possibility of having to refund the fee because an employment period contingency is built into the arrangement, it is appropriate to record an allowance based on estimates of fees that will never be collected.

PROPORTIONAL PERFORMANCE METHOD

The **proportional performance method** is appropriate when services are performed in *more than one act over more than one time period and the extent of performance achieved in any one period relative to total required performance can be reasonably determined.* Revenue is recognized as the various acts that make up the entire service contract occur. The proportional performance method is another name for the percentage-of-completion method. This method can be applied in a slightly different manner depending on the particular set of circumstances.

1. *Specified number of identical or similar acts.* An equal amount of revenue is recorded for each act performed. The processing of monthly mortgage payments by a mortgage banker is an appropriate situation in which this method could be applied.

2. *Specified number of defined but not identical acts.* Revenue is recognized in the ratio that the direct costs of performing each act have to the total estimated direct cost of the entire transaction. A correspondence school that provides progress evaluations, lessons, examinations, and grading might use this method. If the direct cost ratio is impractical or not objectively determinable as a measurement basis, a systematic and rational basis that reasonably relates revenue recognition to performance should be used. As a last resort, the straight-line method could be used.

3. *Unspecified number of identical or similar acts with a fixed period of performance.* Revenue is recognized on the straight-line basis over the specified period unless there is evidence that another method is more representative of the pattern of performance. A two-year club membership in which the club's facilities are available for the member's usage throughout that period is an example of a situation in which this approach may be applied.

Under the proportional performance method, *initial direct costs* are recorded as expenses in the period the related revenue is recognized. When there is a close correlation between the incurrence of *direct costs* and the extent of performance achieved, direct costs are recorded as expenses as they are incurred. Otherwise, the accounting system must be set up so that the direct costs are matched against the related revenue.

COMPLETED PERFORMANCE METHOD

The **completed performance method** is appropriate when the service contract requires the performance of *more than one act and the proportional performance method cannot be employed, or when the last of a series of acts is so significant in relation to the entire service transaction that performance cannot be deemed to have been achieved until the last act occurs.* For example, for a moving company that packs, loads, and delivers goods to various locations, the act of delivery is so significant to its performance completion that revenue should not be recognized until delivery occurs. The performance completion method is equivalent to the completed-contract method.

Under the completed performance method, initial direct costs and direct costs are expensed when revenue is recognized. Costs incurred before performance is completed are deferred until the revenue is recognized.

COLLECTION METHOD

If there is a significant degree of uncertainty surrounding the collectibility of service revenue and a reasonable estimate of uncollectible amounts cannot be made, then revenue or related gross profit should not be recognized until cash is collected. The **collection method** is similar to the instalment method or the cost recovery method of accounting for the sale of goods, depending on the degree of uncertainty associated with cash collection.

KEY TERMS

collection method, 296

completed performance method, 296

direct costs, 294

indirect costs, 294

initial direct costs, 294

proportional performance method, 295

service transactions, 293

specific performance method, 295

Summary of Learning Objective for Appendix 6A

13. Understand issues related to revenue recognition for service transactions and appreciate that their resolution is based on similar revenue recognition criteria as exists for the sale of goods. Service involves the performance of an act or several acts that do not provide a tangible product. Depending on the nature of the contract, type of services provided, ability to measure the amount reasonably, collectibility or being able to estimate bad debts, and ability to match material expenses, revenue may be recognized using the specific performance method, proportional performance method, completed performance method, or collection method.

APPENDIX 6B

Revenue Recognition for Special Sales Transactions

To supplement and illustrate our presentation of revenue recognition, we have chosen to cover three common yet unique types of sales transactions—consignment sales, bartering, and franchise sales.

OBJECTIVE 14
Understand and know how to resolve revenue recognition issues for consignment sales, bartering, and franchise sales.

CONSIGNMENT SALES ACCOUNTING

A specialized method of marketing certain types of products makes use of a device known as a consignment. In **consignment sales arrangements** *the delivery of the goods by the manufacturer (or wholesaler) to the dealer (or retailer) does not constitute achievement of performance because the manufacturer retains title to the goods.* Under this arrangement, the **consignor** (manufacturer) ships merchandise to the **consignee** (dealer), who acts as an agent for the consignor in selling the merchandise. However, the risks and rewards of ownership remain with the consignor. Both consignor and consignee are interested in selling—the former to make a profit or develop a market, the latter to make a commission on the sales.

The consignee accepts the merchandise and agrees to exercise due diligence in caring for and selling it. Cash received from customers is remitted to the consignor by the consignee after deducting a sales commission and any chargeable expenses. The consignor recognizes revenue only after receiving notification of sale, which is usually accompanied by a cash remittance from the consignee. The merchandise is carried throughout the consignment as the inventory of the consignor, separately classified as Merchandise on Consignment. It is not recorded as an asset on the consignee's books. On sale of the merchandise, the consignee has a liability for the net amount due the consignor. The consignor periodically receives from the consignee an **account sales report** that shows the merchandise received, merchandise sold, expenses chargeable to the consignment, and cash remitted.

To illustrate consignment accounting entries, assume that Nelba Manufacturing Ltd. ships merchandise costing $36,000 on consignment to Best Value Stores. Nelba pays $3,750 of freight costs and Best Value pays $2,250 for local advertising costs that are reimbursable from Nelba. By the end of the period, two-thirds of the consigned merchandise have been sold for $40,000 cash. Best Value notifies Nelba of the sales, retains a 10% commission, and remits the cash due Nelba. The journal entries shown in Exhibit 6B-1 would be made by the consignor (Nelba) and the consignee (Best Value).

Under the consignment arrangement, the manufacturer (consignor) accepts the risk that the merchandise might not sell and relieves the dealer (consignee) of the need to commit part of its working capital to inventory. A variety of different systems and account titles are used to record consignments, but they all share the common goal of postponing the recognition of revenue until it is known that a sale to a third party has occurred.

ENTRIES FOR CONSIGNMENT SALES

Transaction	Nelba Manufacturing Ltd. (Consignor)		Best Value Stores (Consignee)	
Shipment of consigned merchandise	Inventory on Consignment 36,000 Finished Goods Inventory	36,000	No entry (record memo of merchandise received)	
Payment of freight costs by consignor	Inventory on Consignment 3,750 Cash	3,750	No entry	
Payment of advertising by consignee	No entry until notified		Receivable from Consignor 2,250 Cash	2,250
Sales of consigned merchandise	No entry until notified		Cash 40,000 Payable to Consignor	40,000

Notification of sales and expenses and remittance of amount due	Cash 33,750
	Advertising Expense 2,250
	Commission Expense 4,000
	   Revenue from
	   Consignment Sales
		40,000	Payable to Consignor 40,000
			   Receivable from Consignor
			   Commission Revenue
			   Cash
				2,250
				4,000
				33,750

Adjustment of inventory on consignment and recording cost of sales	Cost of Goods Sold 26,500 Inventory on Consignment [2/3 ($36,000 + $3,750) = $26,500]	26,500	No entry	

REVENUE RECOGNITION AND BARTER TRANSACTIONS

Due to a variety of economic and tax circumstances, companies may engage in **barter transactions.** For example, radio and television stations often barter advertising time for scripts, tapes, programs, or space in newspapers. A plumber may trade services with an electrician, an attorney may arrange for a house painter to paint the attorney's home in exchange for legal services, or an automobile dealer may barter a truck to a cleaning service company in exchange for a cleaning service contract.

The issue of concern is whether revenue and related expenses should be recognized as the result of barter transactions. Because no cash or claim to cash is involved, one may argue that there would be no revenue. However, an exchange of economic substance does occur and to ignore this fact would significantly detract from the relevancy of financial statements.

The *CICA Handbook* addresses barter transactions when discussing the accounting consequences of nonmonetary transactions.[29] The basic requirement is that the fair value of the asset or services received or given up, whichever is more readily determinable, is to be recorded as revenue when the criteria for revenue recognition are met. **Fair value** is the amount that would be agreed on by informed parties dealing at arm's length in an open and unrestricted market.[30] The cost of the service or book value of the asset given up would be the related expense.[31]

FRANCHISES

Accounting for franchise sales provides an excellent focus for illustrating various revenue recognition issues related to special sales transactions. Franchise sales are a common

---

[29] *CICA Handbook*, Section 3830. The material in this Section is considered in detail in Chapter 10 where exchanges (e.g., trade-ins) involving property, plant, and equipment are examined.

[30] *Ibid.*, par. .04.

[31] Under Canadian income tax requirements, the difference between the fair value of what is received and the cost of what is given up in a barter transaction is considered to be a part of taxable income.

event in our business environment. They provide a variety of situations that necessitate considerable professional judgement in deciding when revenue recognition criteria are met. In accounting for franchise sales, the accountant must fully understand the terms and conditions specified in a particular franchise sales contract when deciding on the revenue recognition consequences of various transactions and events.

FRANCHISES AND ACCOUNTING ABUSES

A **franchise** is defined as:

> . . . a contractual privilege, often exclusive, granted by one party (the franchiser) to another (the franchisee) permitting the sale of a product, use of a trade name or rendering of a service in a single outlet at a specified location (individual franchise) or in a number of outlets within a specified territory (area franchise). The rights and responsibilities of each party are usually set out in a franchise agreement which normally outlines specific marketing practices to be followed, specifies the contribution of each party to the operation of the business, and sets forth certain operating procedures.[32]

Four types of franchising arrangements have evolved: (1) manufacturer–retailer; (2) manufacturer–wholesaler; (3) service sponsor–retailer; and (4) wholesaler–retailer. The fastest-growing category, and the one that causes particular revenue recognition problems, has been the service sponsor–retailer arrangement. Included in this category are such industries and businesses as:

Food drive-ins (McDonald's, Kentucky Fried Chicken, Wendy's)
Restaurants (Perkins, Pizza Hut, Denny's)
Motels (Holiday Inns, Howard Johnson, Best Western)
Auto rentals (Avis, Hertz, Tilden)

Franchise companies derive their revenue from one or both of two sources: (1) the sale of initial franchises and related assets or services; and/or (2) continuing fees based on the operations of franchises. The **franchiser** (the party who grants business rights under the franchise) normally provides the **franchisee** (the party who operates the franchised business) with services such as the following.

1. Assistance in site selection.
   (a) Analysing location.
   (b) Negotiating leases.
2. Evaluation of potential income.
3. Supervision of construction activity.
   (a) Obtaining financing.
   (b) Designing the building.
   (c) Supervising the contractor while building.
4. Assistance in the acquisition of signs, fixtures, and equipment.
5. Provision of bookkeeping and advisory services and supplies.
   (a) Setting up the franchisee's records.
   (b) Advising on income, property, and other taxes.
   (c) Advising on local regulations of the franchisee's business.
6. Provision of employee and management training.
7. Provision of quality control.
8. Provision of advertising and promotion.[33]

---

[32] "Franchise Fee Revenue," *Accounting Guideline* (Toronto: CICA, 1984), par. 1.

Prior to the mid-1980s, it was common practice for franchisers to recognize the entire franchise fee at the date of sale, whether the fee was received then or was collectible over a long period of time. Frequently, franchisers recorded the entire amount as revenue in the year of sale, even though many of the services were yet to be performed and uncertainty existed regarding the collection of the entire fee. In effect, the franchisers were counting their fried chickens before they were hatched.

However a **franchise agreement** may provide for refunds to the franchisee if certain conditions are not met, and the franchise fee profit can be reduced sharply by future costs of obligations and services to be rendered by the franchiser. To curb the abuses of premature revenue recognition and to help accountants make appropriate judgements as to when revenue is recognizable, an *Accounting Guideline* titled "Franchise Fee Revenue" was issued in 1984.[34] The criteria for revenue recognition provided in Section 3400 of the *CICA Handbook* issued in 1986 codified the basic principles inherent in the *Guideline*. Drawing on these sources, the following material provides an impression of the issues involved.

INITIAL FRANCHISE FEES

The **initial franchise fee** is consideration for establishing the franchise relationship and providing some initial services. Initial franchise fees are to be recorded as revenue only when and as the franchiser makes "substantial performance" of the services it is obligated to perform and collection of the fee is reasonably assured. Substantial performance occurs when the franchiser has no remaining obligation to refund any cash received or excuse any nonpayment of a note and has performed all the significant initial services required under the contract. Generally, the conditions for substantial performance are not met until the commencement of operations by the franchisee.

ILLUSTRATION OF ENTRIES FOR INITIAL FRANCHISE FEES

To illustrate, assume that Tum's Pizza Ltd. charges an initial franchise fee of $50,000 for the right to operate a Tum's Pizza franchise. Of this amount, $10,000 is payable when the agreement is signed and the balance is payable in five annual payments of $8,000 each. In return for the initial franchise fee, the franchiser will help in locating the site, negotiate the lease or purchase of the site, supervise the construction activity, and provide the bookkeeping services. The credit rating of the franchisee indicates that money can be borrowed at 8%. The present value of an ordinary annuity of five annual receipts of $8,000 each discounted at 8% is $31,941.60, which is the "principal" amount of the note. The discount of $8,058.40 represents the interest revenue to be earned by the franchiser over the payment period.

1. If there is reasonable expectation that the down payment may be refunded and if substantial future services remain to be performed by Tum's Pizza Ltd., the entry would be:

Cash	10,000.00	
Notes Receivable	40,000.00	
Discount on Notes Receivable		8,058.40
Unearned Franchise Fees		41,941.60

2. If the probability of refunding the initial franchise fee is extremely low, the amount of future services to be provided to the franchisee is minimal, collectibility of the note is reasonably assured, and substantial performance has occurred, the entry would be:

---

[33] Archibald E. MacKay, "Accounting for Initial Franchise Fee Revenue," *The Journal of Accountancy*, January, 1970, pp. 66–67.

[34] *Ibid.* An *Accounting Guideline* was a document issued by the Steering Committee of the CICA's Accounting Standards Committee (now the Accounting Standards Board). Essentially, such *Guidelines* were the predecessor of *Abstracts of Issues Discussed* issued currently by the CICA's Emerging Issues Committee. The *Guidelines* provided interpretation of *CICA Handbook* recommendations and opinions on particular issues of concern. They did not have the authority of *Handbook* recommendations.

Cash	10,000.00	
Notes Receivable	40,000.00	
Discount on Notes Receivable		8,058.40
Revenue from Franchise Fees		41,941.60

3. If the initial down payment is not refundable and represents a fair measure of the services already provided, a significant amount of services is still to be performed by the franchiser in future periods, and collectibility of the note is reasonably assured, the entry would be:

Cash	10,000.00	
Notes Receivable	40,000.00	
Discount on Notes Receivable		8,058.40
Revenue from Franchise Fees		10,000.00
Unearned Franchise Fees		31,941.60

4. If the initial down payment is not refundable and no future services are required of the franchiser, but collection of the note is so uncertain that recognition of the note as an asset is unwarranted, the entry would be:

| Cash | 10,000.00 | |
| Revenue from Franchise Fees | | 10,000.00 |

5. Under the same conditions as stated under Case 4, except that the down payment is refundable or substantial services are yet to be performed, the entry would be:

| Cash | 10,000.00 | |
| Unearned Franchise Fees | | 10,000.00 |

In Cases 4 and 5, where collection of the note is extremely uncertain, cash collections may be recognized using the instalment method or the cost recovery method.

CONTINUING FRANCHISE FEES

Continuing franchise fees are received in return for the continuing rights granted by the franchise agreement and for providing such services as management training, advertising and promotion, legal assistance, and other support. Continuing fees should be recognized as revenue when they are earned and receivable from the franchisee, unless a portion has been designated for a particular future purpose, such as providing a specified amount for building maintenance or local advertising. In that case, a portion of the continuing fee should be deferred until the designated purpose has occurred. The amount deferred should be sufficient to cover the estimated cost and provide a reasonable profit on the particular requirement.

BARGAIN PURCHASES

In addition to paying continuing franchise fees, franchisees frequently purchase some or all of their equipment and supplies from the franchiser. The franchiser would account for these sales as it would for any other product sales. Sometimes, however, the franchise agreement grants the franchisee the right to make **bargain purchases** of equipment or supplies after the initial franchise fee is paid. If the bargain price is lower than the normal selling price of the same product, or if it does not provide the franchiser a reasonable profit, then a portion of the *initial* franchise fee should be deferred. When the franchisee subsequently purchases the equipment or supplies, the deferred portion of the initial franchise fee would be transferred to a revenue account (i.e., added to the bargain price based revenue). This treatment reflects the fact that the franchisee is really paying the normal price through two types of payments: the bargain purchase price and part of the initial franchise fee.

OPTIONS TO PURCHASE

A franchise agreement may give the franchiser an **option to purchase** the franchisee's business. As a matter of management policy, the franchiser may reserve the right to purchase a profitable franchised outlet, or to purchase one that is in financial difficulty. If it is probable at the time the option is given that the franchiser will ultimately purchase the outlet, then the initial franchise fee should not be recognized as revenue but should be recorded as a Deferred Franchise Purchase Option (a liability). When the option is exercised, the liability would reduce the franchiser's investment in the outlet.

FRANCHISER'S COSTS

Franchise accounting also involves appropriate accounting for the **franchiser's costs.** The objective is to match related costs and revenues by reporting them as components of income in the same accounting period. Franchisers should defer **direct costs** (usually incremental costs) relating to specific franchise sales for which revenue has not yet been recognized. Costs should not be deferred, however, without reference to anticipated revenue and its realizability. **Indirect costs** of a regular and recurring nature, such as selling and administrative expenses, would be expensed as incurred.

DISCLOSURES BY FRANCHISERS

The method of accounting for revenue from franchise fees must be disclosed in the notes to the financial statements.[35] Disclosure of all significant commitments and obligations resulting from franchise agreements, including a description of services that have not yet been substantially performed, is desirable. Initial franchise fees should be segregated from other franchise fee revenue if they are significant. Where possible, revenues and costs related to franchiser-owned outlets should be distinguished from those related to franchised outlets.

KEY TERMS

account sales report, 297

bargain purchases, 301

barter transactions, 298

consignee, 297

consignment sales arrangements, 297

consignor, 297

continuing franchise fees, 301

fair value,298

franchise, 299

franchise agreement, 300

franchisee, 299

franchiser, 299

franchiser's costs, 302

initial franchise fee, 300

option to purchase, 302

Summary of Learning Objective for Appendix 6B

14. Understand and know how to resolve revenue recognition issues for consignment sales, bartering, and franchise sales. Revenue is recognized by a consignor when sales have been made by the consignee (reported in an account sales report) rather than when goods are sent to the consignee. Barter transactions should be recorded at the fair value of services received or given up, whichever is more readily determinable. In a franchise arrangement, the initial franchise fee is recorded as revenue only when, and as, the franchiser makes substantial performance of the services it is obligated to perform and collection of the fee is reasonably assured. Continuing franchise fees are recognized as revenue when they are earned and receivable from the franchisee.

---

[35] *CICA Handbook*, Section 1505, par. .10.

Note: All *asterisked* Exercises, Problems, or Cases relate to material contained in an appendix to the chapter.

EXERCISES

(Revenue Recognition on Marina Sales with Discounts) Waskesiu Marina has 300 available slips that rent for **E6-1** $1,500 per season. Payments must be made in full at the start of the boating season, April 1. Slips may be reserved if paid for by the prior December 31. Under a new policy, if payment is made by the prior December 31, a 5% discount is allowed. The boating season ends October 31, and the marina has a December 31 year end. To provide cash flow for major dock repairs, the marina operator is also offering a 25% discount to slip renters who pay for the second season following the current December 31.

For the fiscal year ended December 31, 1998 all 300 slips were rented at full price. There were 200 slips reserved and paid for the 1999 boating season, and 60 slips reserved and paid for the 2000 boating season.

Instructions
(a) Prepare the appropriate journal entries for fiscal 1998.
(b) Assume the marina operator knows little about accounting. Explain the significance of the above accounting to this person, particularly the consequences of accelerating payments by offering discounts.

(Revenue Recognition on Book Sales with High Returns) Smiley Publishing Co. publishes college textbooks that **E6-2** are sold to bookstores on the following terms. Each title has a fixed wholesale price, terms f.o.b. shipping point (i.e., transfer of legal title occurs when shipments leave seller's premises), and payment is due 60 days after shipment. The retailer may return a maximum of 30% of an order at the retailer's expense. Sales are made only to retailers who have good credit ratings. Past experience indicates that the normal return rate is 12% and the average collection period is 72 days.

Instructions
(a) Identify alternative revenue recognition times in the earning process that Smiley could employ concerning textbook sales.
(b) Specify which alternative you would recommend and briefly discuss why it is the appropriate treatment.
(c) In late July, Smiley shipped books invoiced at $15,000,000. Prepare the journal entry to record this event that best conforms to your answer to (b).
(d) In October, $2 million of the invoiced July sales were returned according to the return policy, and the remaining $13 million was paid. Prepare the entry recording the return and payment.

(Analysis of Percentage-of-Completion Financial Statements) In 1998, Soft Hat Construction Corp. began work **E6-3** on a three-year contract. The contract price was $2,000,000. Soft Hat uses the percentage-of-completion method for financial accounting purposes. The income to be recognized each year is based on the proportion of cost incurred to total estimated costs for completing the contract. The financial statement presentation relating to this contract at December 31, 1998 is as follows.

Balance Sheet

Accounts receivable—construction contract billings		$43,000
Construction in progress	$130,000	
Less contract billings	123,000	
Cost of uncompleted contract in excess of billings		7,000

Income Statement

Gross profit (before tax) on the contract recognized in 1998	$39,000

Instructions
(a) How much cash was collected in 1998 on this contract?
(b) What was the initial estimated total gross profit before tax on this contract?   (AICPA adapted)

(Gross Profit on Uncompleted Contract) On April 1, 1998, Tomba Inc. entered into a cost-plus, fixed-fee contract to **E6-4** construct an electric generator for Alberto Corporation. At the contract date, Tomba estimated that it would take two years to complete the project at a cost of $2,000,000. The fixed fee stipulated in the contract is $400,000. Tomba appropriately accounts for this contract under the percentage-of-completion method. During 1998, Tomba incurred costs of $700,000 related to the project, and the estimated costs yet to be incurred from December 31, 1998 to complete the contract is $1,300,000. Alberto was billed $600,000 under the contract.

Instructions
Prepare a schedule to compute the amount of gross profit to be recognized by Tomba under the contract for the year ended December 31, 1998. Show supporting computations in good form. (AICPA adapted)

E6-5 **(Recognition of Profit, Percentage-of-Completion)** In 1998, Miser Construction Company agreed to construct an apartment building at a price of $1,000,000. The information relating to the costs and billings for this contract is as follows.

	1998	1999	2000
Costs incurred to date	$320,000	$600,000	$ 780,000
Estimated costs yet to be incurred	480,000	200,000	-0-
Customer billings to date	150,000	400,000	1,000,000
Collection of billings to date	120,000	320,000	940,000

Instructions
(a) Assuming that the percentage-of-completion method is used: (1) compute the amount of gross profit recognized in 1998 and 1999, and (2) prepare journal entries for 1999.
(b) For 1999, show how the details related to this construction contract would be disclosed on the balance sheet and on the income statement.

E6-6 **(Recognition of Revenue on Long-Term Contract and Entries)** Corky Construction Company uses the percentage-of-completion method of accounting. In 1998, Corky began work under contract #R2-D2, which had a contract price of $2,200,000. Other details are as follows.

	1998	1999
Costs incurred during the year	$ 400,000	$1,425,000
Estimated costs to complete, as of December 31	1,200,000	-0-
Billings during the year	420,000	1,680,000
Collections during the year	350,000	1,500,000

Instructions
(a) What portion of the total contract price would be recognized as revenue in 1998? In 1999?
(b) Assuming the same facts as those above except that Corky used the completed-contract method of accounting, what portion of the total contract price would be recognized as revenue in 1999?
(c) Prepare a complete set of journal entries for 1998 using the percentage-of-completion method.

E6-7 **(Recognition of Profit and Balance Sheet Amounts for Long-Term Contracts)** Fabric Construction Company began operations January 1, 1998. During the year, Fabric Construction entered into a contract with Cam Corp. to construct a manufacturing facility. At that time, Fabric estimated that it would take five years to complete the facility at a total cost of $4,500,000. The total contract price for construction of the facility was $6,300,000. During 1998, Fabric incurred $1,190,000 in construction costs related to this project. The estimated cost to complete the contract was $4,200,000. Cam Corp. was billed and paid 30% of the contract price.

Instructions
Prepare schedules to compute the amount of gross profit to be recognized for the year ended December 31, 1998 and the amount to be shown as "Construction in process in excess of related billings" or "Billings on uncompleted contract in excess of construction in process" at December 31, 1998 under each of the following methods:
(a) Completed-contract method.
(b) Percentage-of-completion method.
Show supporting computations in good form. (AICPA adapted)

E6-8 **(Long-Term Contract Reporting: Completed-Contract Method)** Gothic Construction Company began operations in 1998. Construction activity for the first year follows. All contracts are with different customers, and any work remaining at December 31, 1998 is expected to be completed in 1999.

Project	Total Contract Price	Billings Through 12/31/98	Cash Collections Through 12/31/98	Contract Costs Incurred Through 12/31/98	Estimated Additional Costs to Complete
1	$ 560,000	$ 360,000	$340,000	$450,000	$130,000
2	670,000	220,000	210,000	126,000	504,000
3	490,000	490,000	440,000	330,000	-0-
	$1,720,000	$1,070,000	$990,000	$906,000	$634,000

Instructions

Prepare a partial income statement and balance sheet to indicate how the above information would be reported for financial statement purposes. Gothic Construction Company uses the completed-contract method.

(Analysis of Instalment Sales Accounts) Slow-Go Co. appropriately uses the instalment method of accounting. On December 31, 1999, prior to adjusting entries to recognize realized gross profit for the year, the ledger shows balances in the Instalment Receivables and Deferred Gross Profit accounts as indicated below. The gross profit on sales for the various years is also identified below. **E6-9**

Instalment Receivables		Deferred Gross Profit		Gross Profit on Sales	
from 1997	$ 12,000	from 1997	$ 7,000	1997	35%
from 1998	40,000	from 1998	26,000	1998	34%
from 1999	80,000	from 1999	95,000	1999	32%
Bal. 12/31/99	$132,000 dr.	Bal. 12/31/99	$128,000 cr.		

Instructions

(a) Prepare the adjusting entry or entries required on December 31, 1999 to recognize 1999 realized gross profit. (Cash receipts entries have already been made.)

(b) Compute the amount of cash collected in 1999 on accounts receivable of each year.

(Gross Profit Calculations and Repossessed Merchandise) Ryan Corporation, which began business on January 1, 1998 appropriately uses the instalment method of accounting. The following data were obtained for the years 1998 and 1999: **E6-10**

	1998	1999
Instalment sales	$750,000	$840,000
Cost of instalment sales	600,000	630,000
General and administrative expenses	70,000	84,000
Cash collections on sales of 1998	310,000	300,000
Cash collections on sales of 1999	-0-	400,000

Instructions

(a) Compute the balance in the Deferred Gross Profit accounts on December 31, 1998 and on December 31, 1999.

(b) A 1998 sale resulted in default in 2000. At the date of default, the balance on the instalment receivable was $12,000 and the repossessed merchandise had a fair value of $8,000. Prepare the entry to record the repossession. (AICPA adapted)

(Interest Revenue from Instalment Sale) OB Co. Ltd. sells farm machinery on the instalment plan. On July 1, 1998, OB enters into an instalment sales contract with Risknhope Inc. for a 10-year period. Equal annual payments under the instalment sale are $100,000 and are due on July 1. The first payment is made on July 1, 1998. **E6-11**

Additional Information

1. The amount that would be realized on an outright sale of similar farm machinery is $575,000.

2. The cost of the farm machinery sold to Risknhope is $423,000.

3. The finance charges relating to the instalment period are $225,000, based on a stated interest rate of 10%, which is appropriate.

4. Circumstances are such that the collection of the instalments due under the contract is reasonably assured.

Instructions

What income or loss before income taxes should OB Co. Ltd. record for the year ended December 31, 1998 as a result of the above transactions?   (AICPA adapted)

E6-12   **(Instalment Method and Cost Recovery Method)** A capital goods manufacturing business that started on January 4, 1997 and operates on a calendar-year basis uses the instalment method in accounting for all its sales. The following data were taken from the 1997 and 1998 records:

	1997	1998
Instalment sales	$480,000	$620,000
Gross profit as a percentage of sales	20%	16⅔%
Cash collections on sales of 1997	$140,000	$240,000
Cash collections on sales of 1998	-0-	$180,000

The amounts given for cash collections exclude amounts collected for interest charges.

Instructions

(a) Compute the amount of realized gross profit to be recognized on the 1998 income statement, prepared using the instalment method.

(b) State where the balance of Deferred Gross Profit would be reported on the financial statements for 1998.

(c) Compute the amount of realized gross profit to be recognized on the 1998 income statement, prepared using the cost recovery method.   (CICA adapted)

E6-13   **(Instalment Method: Default and Repossession)** Cubic Inc. was involved in two default and repossession cases during the year. It had been using the instalment method of accounting in both cases.

1. A refrigerator was sold to M. Grace for $1,800, including a 40% gross profit. Grace made a down payment of 20%, 4 of the remaining 16 equal payments, and then he defaulted on further payments. The refrigerator was repossessed, at which time the fair value was determined to be $800.

2. An oven that cost $1,200 was sold to H. Cari for $1,500 on the instalment basis. Cari made a down payment of $225 and paid $75 per month for six months, after which she defaulted. The oven was repossessed and the estimated value at time of repossession was determined to be $620.

Instructions

Prepare the journal entries to record the repossessions (ignore interest charges).

E6-14   **(Instalment Sales: Default and Repossession)** Ellard Company uses the instalment method in accounting for its instalment sales. On January 1, 1998 Ellard Company had an instalment account receivable from Erin Anton with a balance of $1,800. During 1998, $300 was collected from Anton. When no further collection could be made, the merchandise sold to Anton was repossessed. The merchandise had a fair market value of $650 after the company spent $60 for reconditioning of the merchandise. The merchandise was originally sold with a gross profit of 40%.

Instructions

Prepare the entries on the books of Ellard Company to record all transactions related to Anton during 1998 (ignore interest charges).

E6-15   **(Cost Recovery Method: Interest Component)** On January 1, 1998 Lasse Kjus Company sold real estate that cost $108,000 to Harald Nilsen for $120,000. Harald agreed to pay for the purchase over three years by making three end-of-year equal payments of $52,557 that included 15% interest. Shortly after the sale, Lasse Kjus Company learns distressing news about Harald's financial circumstances and because collection is so uncertain decides to account for the sale using the cost recovery method.

Instructions

Applying the cost recovery method, prepare a schedule showing the amounts of cash collected, the increase (decrease) in deferred interest revenue (interest earned but not realized until cost of sale is fully recovered), the balance of the receivable, the balance of the unrecovered cost, the gross profit realized, and the interest revenue realized for each of the three years assuming the payments are made as agreed.

*E6-16   **(Consignment Accounting)** On May 3, 1998, Hoo Company consigned 70 freezers, costing $600 each, to Gooch Company. The cost of shipping the freezers amounted to $840 and was paid by Hoo Company. On December 30, 1998, an account of sales was received from the consignee, reporting that 40 freezers had been sold for $800 each.

Remittance was made by the consignee for the amounts due, after deducting a commission of 6%, advertising of $200, and total installation costs of $600 on the freezers sold.

Instructions

(a) Compute the inventory value for the consignor on the unsold units in the hands of the consignee.

(b) Compute the profit for the consignor for the units sold.

(c) Compute the amount of cash that was remitted by the consignee.

(Franchise Entries) Big Burger Inc. charges an initial franchise fee of $80,000. On the signing of the agreement, a payment of $50,000 is due; thereafter, three annual payments of $10,000 are required. The credit rating of the franchisee is such that it would have to pay interest at 10% to borrow money. ***E6-17**

Instructions
Prepare the entries to record the initial franchise fee on the books of the franchiser under the following assumptions:

(a) The down payment is not refundable, no future services are required by the franchiser, and collection of the note is reasonably assured.

(b) The franchiser has substantial services to perform and collection of the note is very uncertain.

(c) The down payment is not refundable, collection of the note is reasonably certain, the franchiser has yet to perform a substantial amount of services, and the down payment represents a fair measure of the services already performed.

(Franchise Fee, Initial Down Payment) On January 1, 1998, Nadine Jones signed an agreement to operate as a franchisee of Sharp Pics Inc., for an initial franchise fee of $60,000. The amount of $30,000 was paid when the agreement was signed, and the balance is payable in five annual payments of $6,000 each, beginning January 1, 1999. The agreement provides that the down payment is not refundable and that no future services are required of the franchiser. Nadine Jones' credit rating indicates that she can borrow money at 11% for a loan of this type. ***E6-18**

Instructions

(a) How much should Sharp Pics record as revenue from franchise fees on January 1, 1998? At what amount should Jones record the acquisition cost of the franchise on January 1, 1998?

(b) What entry would be made by Sharp Pics on January 1, 1998, if the down payment was refundable and substantial future services remain to be performed by Sharp Pics?

(c) How much revenue from franchise fees would be recorded by Sharp Pics on January 1, 1998 in each of the following situations?

   1. The initial down payment was not refundable, it represented a fair measure of the services already provided, with a significant amount of services still to be performed by Sharp Pics in future periods, and collectibility of the note is reasonably assured.

   2. The initial down payment is not refundable and no future services are required by the franchiser, but collection of the note is so uncertain that recognition of the note as an asset is unwarranted.

   3. The initial down payment has not been earned and collection of the note is so uncertain that recognition of the note as an asset is unwarranted.

PROBLEMS

Variety Industries Ltd. has four operating divisions: Barwood Mining, Romance Publishing Division, Quality Protection Division, and Dynamo Construction Division. Each division maintains its own accounting system and method of revenue recognition. **P6-1**

Barwood Mining Division
Barwood Mining specializes in the extraction of precious metals such as silver, gold, and platinum. During the fiscal year ended November 30, 1998 Barwood entered into contracts worth $2,250,000 and shipped metals worth $2,000,000. A quarter of the shipments were made from inventories on hand at the beginning of the fiscal year while the remainder were made from metals that were mined during the year. Mining totals for the year, valued at market prices, were: silver at $750,000, gold at $1,300,000, and platinum at $430,000. Barwood uses the completion-of-production method to recognize revenue.

Romance Publishing Division

The Romance Publishing Division sells large volumes of novels to a few book distributors, which in turn sell to several national chains of bookstores. Romance Publishing allows distributors to return up to 30% of sales, and distributors give the same terms to bookstores. While returns from individual titles fluctuate greatly, the returns from distributors have averaged 20% in each of the past five years. A total of $8,000,000 of novel sales were made to distributors during fiscal 1998. On November 30, 1998, $3,000,000 of fiscal 1998 sales were still subject to return privileges over the next six months. The remaining $5,000,000 of fiscal 1998 sales had actual returns of 21%. Sales from fiscal 1997 totalling $2,000,000 were collected in fiscal 1998, less 18% returns. This Division records revenue according to the revenue recognition criteria when the right of return exists.

Quality Protection Division

Quality Protection Division works through manufacturers' agents in various cities. Orders for alarm systems and down payments are forwarded from agents, and the Division ships the goods from the factory directly to customers (usually police departments and security guard companies). Although Quality Protection Division pays the shipping costs for convenience, sales agreements require the buyer to reimburse the Division for such costs. Customers are billed directly for the balance due plus actual shipping costs. The firm received orders for $6,000,000 of goods during the fiscal year ended November 30, 1998. Down payments of $600,000 were received and $5,000,000 of goods were billed and shipped. Actual freight costs of $100,000 were also billed. Commissions of 10% on product price are paid to manufacturing agents after goods are shipped to customers. Such goods are warranted for 90 days after shipment, and warranty returns have been about 1% of sales. Revenue is recognized at the point of sale by this Division.

Dynamo Construction Division

During the fiscal year ended November 30, 1998, Dynamo Construction Division had one construction project in process. A $30,000,000 contract for construction of a civic centre was signed on June 19, 1998, and construction began on August 1, 1998. Estimated costs of completion at the contract date were $26,000,000 over a two-year time period from the date of the contract. On November 30, 1998, construction costs of $8,000,000 had been incurred and progress billings of $9,500,000 had been made. The construction costs to complete the remainder of the project were reviewed on November 30, 1998, and were estimated to amount to only $16,000,000 because of an expected decline in raw materials costs. Revenue recognition is based on the percentage-of-completion method.

Instructions

Compute the revenue to be recognized in fiscal year 1998 for each of the four operating divisions of Variety Industries Ltd.

P6-2 On February 1, 1998, Woloshyn Construction Company obtained a contract to build an athletic stadium. The stadium was to be built at a total cost of $5,400,000 and was scheduled for completion by September 1, 2000. One clause of the contract stated that Woloshyn was to deduct $10,000 from the $6,600,000 contract billing price for each week that completion was delayed. Completion was delayed six weeks, which resulted in a $60,000 penalty. This delay was not predictable prior to 2000. Below are the data pertaining to the construction period.

	1998	1999	2000
Costs to date	$1,800,000	$3,850,000	$5,500,000
Estimated cost to complete	3,600,000	1,650,000	-0-
Progress billings to date	1,200,000	3,000,000	6,540,000
Cash collected to date	1,000,000	2,800,000	6,540,000

Instructions

(a) Using the percentage-of-completion method, complete the gross profit recognized in the years 1998–2000.

(b) Prepare a partial balance sheet for December 31, 1999, showing how the account balances would be presented.

P6-3 Yanmei Construction Company has contracted to build an office building. The construction is scheduled to begin on January 1, 1998 and the estimated time of completion is July 1, 2001. The building cost is estimated to be $40,000,000 and will be billed at $48,000,000, the fixed price. The following data relate to the construction period.

	1998	1999	2000	2001
Costs to date	$12,000,000	$20,000,000	$28,000,000	$40,000,000
Estimated cost to complete	28,000,000	20,000,000	12,000,000	-0-
Progress billings to date	6,000,000	18,000,000	28,000,000	48,000,000
Cash collected to date	6,000,000	15,000,000	25,000,000	48,000,000

Instructions

(a) Compute the estimated gross profit for 1998, 1999, 2000, and 2001, assuming that the percentage-of-completion method is used. Ignore income taxes.

(b) Prepare the necessary journal entries for Yanmei Construction Company for the years 2000 and 2001, using the percentage-of-completion method.

(c) Prepare the necessary journal entries for the years 2000 and 2001, using the completed-contract method.

P6-4 Rockland Custom Builders (RCB) was established in 1966 by Thomas Johnston and initially built high-quality customized homes under contract with specific buyers. In the 1980s, Johnston's two sons joined the firm and expanded RCB's activities into the high-rise apartment and industrial plant markets. Upon the retirement of RCB's long-time financial manager, Johnston's sons recently hired Joe Gurney as controller for RCB. Gurney, a former college friend of Johnston's sons, has been associated with a public accounting firm for the last eight years.

Upon reviewing RCB's accounting practices, Gurney observed that RCB followed the completed-contract method of revenue recognition, a carryover from the years when individual home building was the majority of RCB's operations. Several years ago, the predominant portion of RCB's activities shifted to the high-rise and industrial building areas. From land acquisition to the completion of construction, most building contracts cover several years. Under the circumstances, Gurney believes that RCB should follow the percentage-of-completion method of accounting. From a typical building contract, Gurney developed the following data.

Allweather Tractor Plant

Contract price: $8,000,000

	1996	1997	1998
Estimated costs	$1,675,000	$3,015,000	$2,010,000
Progress billings	1,000,000	2,500,000	4,500,000
Cash collections	800,000	2,300,000	4,900,000

Instructions

Using the data provided for the Allweather Tractor Plant and assuming the percentage-of-completion method of revenue recognition is used, calculate RCB's revenue and gross profit for 1996, 1997, and 1998 under **each** of the following circumstances.

(a) Assume that all costs are incurred, all billings to customers are made, and all collections from customers are received within 30 days of billing, as planned.

(b) Further assume that, as a result of unforeseen local ordinances and the fact that the building site was in a wetlands area, RCB experienced cost overruns of $800,000 in 1996 to bring the site into compliance with the ordinances and to overcome wetlands barriers to construction.

(c) Further assume that, in addition to the cost overruns of $800,000 for this contract incurred under Instruction (b), inflationary factors over and above those anticipated in the development of the original contract cost have caused an additional cost overrun of $540,000 in 1997. It is not anticipated that any cost overruns will occur in 1998.
(CMA adapted)

P6-5 On March 1, 1998, Gumbel Construction Ltd. contracted to construct a factory building for Wind Manufacturing Inc. for a total contract price of $8,500,000. The building was completed by October 31, 2000. The annual contract costs incurred, estimated costs to complete the contract, and accumulated billings to Wind for 1998, 1999, and 2000 are given below.

	1998	1999	2000
Contract costs incurred during the year	$3,200,000	$2,600,000	$1,450,000
Estimated additional costs to complete the contract determined at year end	3,200,000	1,450,000	-0-
Billings to Wind during the year	3,200,000	3,500,000	1,800,000

Instructions

(a) Using the percentage-of-completion method, prepare schedules to compute the profit or loss to be recognized as a result of this contract for the years ended December 31, 1998, 1999, and 2000. Ignore income taxes.

(b) Using the completed-contract method, prepare schedules to compute the profit or loss to be recognized as a result of this contract for the years ended December 31, 1998, 1999, and 2000. Ignore income taxes.

P6-6 On July 1, 1998 Harp Construction Inc. contracted to build an office building for Sombre Corp. for a total contract price of $1,900,000. On July 1, Harp estimated that it would take between two and three years to complete the building. On December 31, 2000 the building was deemed substantially completed. Following are accumulated contract costs incurred, estimated costs to complete the contract, and accumulated billings to Sombre for 1998, 1999, and 2000.

	At Dec. 31/98	At Dec. 31/99	At Dec. 31/00
Contract costs incurred to date	$ 150,000	$1,200,000	$2,100,000
Estimated costs to complete the contract	1,350,000	800,000	-0-
Billings to Sombre	300,000	1,100,000	1,800,000

Instructions

(a) Using the percentage-of-completion method, prepare schedules to compute the profit or loss to be recognized as a result of this contract for the years ended December 31, 1998, 1999, and 2000. Ignore income taxes.

(b) Using the completed-contract method, prepare schedules to compute the profit or loss to be recognized as a result of this contract for the years ended December 1998, 1999, and 2000. Ignore income taxes.

P6-7 Hopeful Construction Company commenced business on January 1, 1998. Construction activities for the first year of operations are shown in the table below. All projects are with different customers, and any work remaining at December 31, 1998 is expected to be completed in 1999. The percentage-of-completion method is used by the company.

Project	Total Contract Price	Billings Through 12/31/98	Cash Collections Through 12/31/98	Contract Costs Incurred Through 12/31/98	Estimated Additional Costs to Complete
A	$ 300,000	$200,000	$180,000	$248,000	$ 67,000
B	350,000	110,000	105,000	67,800	271,200
C	290,000	290,000	260,000	190,000	-0-
D	200,000	35,000	25,000	123,000	87,000
E	240,000	205,000	200,000	185,000	15,000
	$1,380,000	$840,000	$770,000	$813,800	$440,200

Instructions

(a) Prepare a schedule to compute the gross profit (loss) in 1998 for each project.

(b) Prepare a 1998 partial income statement to show the aggregate total revenues, construction expenses including provision for losses, and gross profit for the year from all projects.

(c) Prepare a schedule to determine the appropriate amounts to be shown in the December 31, 1998 balance sheet for "Construction in process in excess of billings" and "Billings in excess of construction in process." Prepare a partial balance sheet showing how items related to the projects would be reported.

P6-8 Plains Construction Company Inc. entered into a fixed-price contract with Regina Clinic on July 1, 1996 to construct a four-storey office building. At that time, Plains estimated that it would take between two and three years to complete the project. The total contract price for construction of the building is $4,500,000. Plains appropriately accounted for this contract under the completed-contract method in its financial statements. The building was deemed completed on December 31, 1998. Estimated percentage of completion, accumulated contract costs incurred, estimated costs to complete the contract, and accumulated billings to Regina Clinic under the contract were as follows:

	At December 31, 1996	At December 31, 1997	At December 31, 1998
Percentage of completion	30%	60%	100%
Contract costs incurred to date	$1,140,000	$2,820,000	$4,800,000
Estimated costs to complete the contract	$2,660,000	$1,880,000	-0-
Billings to Regina Clinic	$1,500,000	$2,500,000	$4,300,000

Instructions

(a) Prepare schedules to compute the amount to be shown as "Cost of uncompleted contract in excess of related billings" or "Billings on uncompleted contract in excess of related costs" at December 31, 1996, 1997, and 1998. Ignore income taxes.

(b) Prepare schedules to compute the profit or loss to be recognized as a result of this contract for the years ended December 31, 1996, 1997, and 1998. Ignore income taxes.   (AICPA adapted)

In 1998, Hydro-Tech Inc. secured a $1,000,000 fixed-price contract with the Canadian government to build a proto-   **P6-9**
type of a mini-submarine to be used for training missions. The project was completed during 2000. The company
has a December 31 year end. The following information relates to this contract:

	1998	1999	2000
Costs incurred during the year	$200,000	$600,000	$300,000
Estimated costs to complete contract as at year end	600,000	400,000	- 0 -
Progress billings during the year	150,000	400,000	450,000
Collections on billings to end of year	100,000	650,000	900,000

Instructions
Assuming that the percentage-of-completion method of accounting is used:

(a) Compute the amount of gross profit (loss) to be recognized from this contract for each of 1998, 1999, and 2000.

(b) Determine the appropriate amount related to this contract to be included as inventory on the December 31 balance sheet for each of the three years. For 2000, assume that the transfer of possession of the submarine to the buyer has not yet taken place.

Assuming the completed-contract method is used:

(c) Compute the amount of gross profit (loss) to be recognized from the contract for each year.

(d) Determine the appropriate amount related to this contract to be included as Inventory on the December 31 balance sheet for each of the three years. For 2000, assume the transfer of possession has not yet taken place.

Selected transactions of Future Store Ltd. are presented below: **P6-10**

1. A television set costing $560 is sold to J. Smith on November 1, 1998 for $800. Smith makes a down payment of $200 and agrees to pay $25 on the first of each month for 24 months thereafter. The instalment method is used to account for this sale.

2. Smith pays the $25 instalment due December 1, 1998.

3. On December 31, 1998, the appropriate entries are made to record profit realized on the instalment sales.

4. The first seven 1999 instalments of $25 each are paid by Smith. (Make one entry.)

5. In August 1999, the set is repossessed after Smith fails to pay the August 1 instalment and indicates that he will be unable to continue the payments. The estimated fair value of the repossessed set is $100.

Instructions
Prepare journal entries to record these transactions and events on the books of Future Store Ltd.

Presented below is summarized information for Deer Co., which sells merchandise on the instalment basis and uses   **P6-11**
the instalment method to account for such sales.

	1998	1999	2000
Sales (on instalment plan)	$250,000	$260,000	$280,000
Cost of sales	150,000	169,000	196,000
Gross profit	$100,000	$ 91,000	$ 84,000
Collections from customers on:			
1998 instalment sales	$ 75,000	$100,000	$ 50,000
1999 instalment sales		90,000	120,000
2000 instalment sales			110,000

Instructions
(a) Compute the realized gross profit for each of the years 1998, 1999, and 2000.

(b) Prepare journal entries required in 2000.

P6-12   GE Stores sells merchandise on open account as well as on instalment terms. The instalment method is used to account for the instalment sales. Information for the years 1998, 1999, and 2000 is as follows:

	1998	1999	2000
Sales on account	$385,000	$426,000	$525,000
Instalment sales	320,000	275,000	380,000
Collections on instalment sales			
Made in 1998	110,000	90,000	40,000
Made in 1999		110,000	140,000
Made in 2000			125,000
Cost of sales			
Sold on account	264,000	297,000	389,600
Sold on instalment	214,400	165,000	224,200
Selling expenses	77,000	87,000	92,000
Administrative expenses	50,000	51,000	52,000

Instructions

From the data above, which cover the three years since GE Stores commenced operations, determine the net income for each year.

P6-13   Knight Stores sells appliances for cash and also on the instalment plan. For sales on instalment plans, the instalment method is used. Entries to record cost of sales are made monthly.

KNIGHT STORES
Trial Balance
December 31, 1999

Cash	$153,000	
Instalment Accounts Receivable, 1998	48,000	
Instalment Accounts Receivable, 1999	91,000	
Inventory—New Merchandise	131,200	
Inventory—Repossessed Merchandise	24,000	
Accounts Payable		$ 98,500
Deferred Gross Profit, 1998		45,600
Common Shares		170,000
Retained Earnings		93,900
Sales		343,000
Instalment Sales		200,000
Cost of Sales	255,000	
Cost of Instalment Sales	120,000	
Gain or Loss on Repossessions	800	
Selling and Administrative Expenses	128,000	
	$951,000	$951,000

The accounting department has prepared the following analysis of cash receipts for the year:

Cash sales (including sale of repossessed merchandise)	$343,000
Instalment accounts receivable, 1998	104,000
Instalment accounts receivable, 1999	109,000
Other	36,000
Total	$592,000

Repossessions recorded during 1999 on instalment sales in 1998 are summarized as follows:

Uncollected balance	$8,000
Loss on repossession	800
Repossessed merchandise (realizable value)	4,800

Instructions

From the trial balance and accompanying information:

(a) Compute the rate of gross profit on instalment sales made in 1998 and in 1999.

(b) Prepare closing entries as of December 31, 1999 under the instalment method of accounting.

(c) Prepare an income statement for the year ended December 31, 1999. Include only the realized gross profit in the income statement when reporting the results regarding instalment sales.

Canon Inc. sells merchandise for cash and also on the instalment plan. For instalment plan sales, the instalment   **P6-14**
method is used. Entries to record cost of goods sold are made at the end of each year.

Repossessions of merchandise sold in 1998 were made in 1999 and were recorded correctly as follows:

Deferred Gross Profit, 1998	7,200	
Repossessed Merchandise	8,000	
Loss on Repossessions	2,800	
Instalment Accounts Receivable, 1998		18,000

Part of this repossessed merchandise was sold for cash during 1999, and the sale was recorded by a debit to Cash and a credit to Sales.

The inventory of repossessed merchandise on hand December 31, 1999 is $4,000; of new merchandise, $122,000. There was no repossessed merchandise on hand January 1, 1999.

Collections on accounts receivable during 1999 were:	
on Instalment Accounts Receivable, 1998	$80,000
on Instalment Accounts Receivable, 1999	50,000

The cost of the merchandise sold under the instalment plan during 1999 was $122,400.

CANON INC.
Trial Balance
December 31, 1999

	Dr.	Cr.
Cash	$ 98,400	
Instalment Accounts Receivable, 1998	80,000	
Instalment Accounts Receivable, 1999	110,000	
Inventory Jan. 1, 1999	120,000	
Repossessed Merchandise	8,000	
Accounts Payable		$ 47,200
Deferred Gross Profit, 1998		64,000
Common Shares		200,000
Retained Earnings		40,000
Sales		380,000
Instalment Sales		180,000
Purchases	380,000	
Loss on Repossessions	2,800	
Operating Expenses	112,000	
	$911,200	$911,200

Note: The rate of gross profit on instalment sales for 1998 and 1999 can be determined from the information provided.

Instructions

(a) From the trial balance and other information given, prepare adjusting and closing entries as of December 31, 1999.

(b) Prepare an income statement for the year ended December 31, 1999. Include only the realized gross profit in the income statement when reporting the results regarding instalment sales.

On January 1, 1998 Moby's Restaurants Inc. entered into a franchise agreement granting the franchise the right to do   ***P6-15**
business under Moby's name. According to the terms of the franchise agreement, Moby's has an option to purchase the restaurant at any time within the next five years. It is probable that this option will be exercised. The initial franchise fee is $90,000. The franchisee paid $30,000 down and gave a $60,000 note to be paid at the end of four years on which interest should be imputed at 8%. Collectibility of the note is reasonably assured and Moby's had substantially performed all requirements by January 1, 1998. Terms of the franchise agreement provide that the franchisee must pay a continuing annual fee of $40,000. Half of this is for the purchase of food and supplies from Moby's at the

normal sales price. During 1998, Moby's provided services costing $10,000 to the franchisee and provided food and supplies costing $14,000. At December 31, 1998, Moby's purchased the restaurant from the franchisee, paying $80,000 and cancelling the franchisee's note.

Instructions

Prepare the journal entries needed on the books of Moby's Restaurants Inc. to record each of the following:

(a) January 1, 1998: receipt of the initial franchise fee. (The present value of the $60,000 note is $44,102. Record the note at $60,000 and a discount on the note for $15,898.)

(b) During 1998: receipt of the continuing franchise fee and provision of food, supplies, and services to the franchisee.

(c) December 31, 1998: amortization of discount on the note and the purchase of the restaurant. The straight-line method of discount amortization is used (i.e., one-quarter of the total discount is transferred to interest revenue at the end of each year the note is held).

CASES

C6-1 Rip & Stick Stamps Inc. was formed early this year to sell trading stamps throughout the West to retailers who distribute the stamps free to their customers. Books for accumulating the stamps and catalogues illustrating the merchandise for which the stamps may be exchanged are given free to retailers for distribution to stamp recipients. Centres with inventories of merchandise premiums have been established for redemption of the stamps. Retailers may not return unused stamps to Rip & Stick.

The following schedule expresses Rip & Stick's expectations as to percentages of a normal month's activity. For this purpose, a "normal month's activity" is defined as the level of operations expected when expansion of activities ceases or tapers off to a stable rate. The company expects that this level will be attained in the third year and that sales of stamps will average $5,000,000 per month throughout the third year.

Month	Actual Stamp Sales (%)	Merchandise Premium Purchases (%)	Stamp Redemptions (%)
6th	30	40	10
12th	60	60	45
18th	80	80	70
24th	90	90	80
30th	100	100	95

Rip & Stick plans to adopt an annual closing date at the end of each 12 months of operation.

Instructions

(a) Discuss the accounting alternatives that could be considered by Rip & Stick for the recognition of its revenues and related expenses.

(b) For each accounting alternative discussed in (a), give balance sheet accounts that would be used and indicate how each should be classified.
(AICPA adapted)

C6-2 *Cutting Edge* is a monthly magazine that has been on the market for 18 months. Its current circulation is 1.4 million copies. Negotiations are now under way to obtain a bank loan to update their facilities. They are producing close to capacity and expect to grow at an average of 20% per year over the next three years.

After reviewing the financial statements of *Cutting Edge*, Chen Zin, the bank loan officer, has indicated that a loan would be offered to *Cutting Edge* only if it could increase the current ratio (current assets ÷ current liabilities) to a specified level.

Pam Ponamarenko, the marketing manager of *Cutting Edge*, has devised a plan to meet these requirements. She indicates that an advertising campaign can be initiated to immediately increase their circulation. The potential customers would be contacted after the purchase of another magazine's mailing list. The campaign would include:

1. An offer to subscribe to Cutting Edge at three-quarters of the normal price.

2. A special offer to all subscribers to receive the most current world atlas book whenever requested at a guaranteed price of $1.00.

3. An unconditional guarantee that any subscriber will receive a full refund if dissatisfied with the magazine.

Although the offer of a full refund is risky, Ponamarenko claims that few people will ask for a refund after receiving half of their subscription issues. She notes that other magazine companies have tried this sales promotion technique and experienced great success. Their average cancellation rate was 25%. On the average, each company increased the initial circulation threefold and in the long run had increased circulation to twice that which existed before the promotion. In addition, 70% of the new subscribers are expected to take advantage of the atlas premium. Ponamarenko feels confident that the increased subscriptions from the advertising campaign will increase the current ratio.

You are the controller of *Cutting Edge* and must give your opinion of the proposed plan.

Instructions
(a) When should revenue from the new subscriptions be recognized, given the cancellation guarantee?
(b) How would you classify the estimated reduced revenue from cancellations stemming from the unconditional guarantee for the new subscriptions?
(c) How should the atlas book premium be recorded? Are the estimated premium claims a liability? Explain.
(d) Does the proposed plan achieve the goal of increasing the current ratio?

C6-3 Vacation Lakes is a new recreational real estate development that consists of 500 lakefront and lake-view lots. As a special incentive to the first 100 buyers of lake-view lots, the developer is offering three years of free financing on 10-year, 9% notes, no down payment, and one week at a nearby established resort—"a $1,200 value." The normal price per lot is $20,000. The cost per lake-view lot to the developer is an estimated average of $8,000. Development costs continue to be incurred and the actual average cost per lot is not known at this time. The resort promotion cost is $1,500 per lot. The notes are held by Green Acceptance Corp., a wholly owned subsidiary of Vacation Lakes.

Instructions
(a) Discuss the revenue recognition and gross profit measurement issues in this situation.
(b) How would the developer's past financial and business experience influence your decision concerning the recording of sales transactions?
(c) Assume that 50 people have accepted the offer, signed 10-year notes, and have stayed at the local resort. Prepare the journal entries that you believe are appropriate.
(d) What should be disclosed in the notes to the financial statements?

C6-4 Respectful Ltd. operates a chain of funeral parlours in Ontario. In 1998, the company introduces a new "pre-need" plan. The plan is offered to individuals who wish to arrange for their funerals and burials in advance. The plan sells for $5,500 and may be purchased by paying $1,000 down and the balance in nine equal annual instalments of $500 each. Interest at 10% per annum is charged only on late payments. Items included in the package and an item price breakdown associated with each are listed below:

Cemetery lot	$ 4,000
Burial vault and memorial plaque	7,500
Funeral service	1,000
Total	$12,500

The cemetery lot location and the burial vault and memorial plaque are chosen by the customer and guaranteed when the contract is signed. The actual cost for funeral services can, for obvious reasons, be determined only at some unknown future time.

During 1998, 50 contracts are signed and the down payments are received.

Instructions
Provide a report to the owner, Ms. Smith, regarding the issues and problems in this situation concerning when and how revenue may be recognized. Identify at least three distinct alternative ways that the company may use to recognize revenue from sale of "pre-need" plans. Assess each alternative identified by arguing how or why it may or may not be consistent with Canadian GAAP. Conclude by indicating which alternative you would recommend.

C6-5 Craik, Kreger, & Integrity is a firm engaged in the general practice of law. Client services are billed on either an hourly charge basis, or a contingency fee (percentage of the judgement received) basis, depending on the nature of the engagement. The timing of cash receipts is subject to wide variation, depending on the nature of the engagement, possible court approval of fees, and the ability of the client to pay. The firm recognizes revenue on the cash basis.

Mr. Craik, one of the partners, believes the cash basis is too conservative a basis for general revenue recognition. He proposes that work charged on an hourly basis to financially capable clients should be recognized as performed. On the basis of past experience, the amount and timing of receipt of income from certain contingency fee cases can be estimated. As Mr. Craik observes, "It may take four years to get to trial or a reasonable settlement offer. But we know the odds and expected payoff pretty well when we accept the case. There are not that many surprises." The cash basis should be limited to those engagements that have considerable uncertainty regarding timing and collection. Fee revenue recognized and not billed would be charged to the Work in Progress account.

Instructions
Discuss the problems of revenue recognition for the law firm and give recommendations.

C6-6 Mega Inc. is a large conglomerate consisting of 44 subsidiary companies with plants and offices throughout Canada and the world. Lindsay & Co. is the international public accounting firm engaged to design and install a computerized information, accounting, and cost control system in each of Mega's subsidiaries. The accounting firm is given three years to complete the engagement; it intends to work continuously on the project but will assign the largest number of its staff to the project during its least busy period each year (May to October). Lindsay & Co. obtained this consulting engagement at a fixed price of $5,200,000 after much study, planning, and an elaborate presentation.

Instructions
Identify, discuss, and provide recommendations regarding revenue recognition issues faced by Lindsay & Co.

*C6-7 Frozen Delight Inc. sells franchises to independent operators. The contract with the franchisee includes the following provisions:

1. The franchisee is charged an initial fee of $70,000. Of this amount, $20,000 is payable when the agreement is signed and a $50,000 noninterest-bearing note is payable in instalments of $10,000 at the end of each of the five subsequent years.
2. All of the initial franchise fee collected by Frozen Delight Inc. is to be refunded and the remaining obligation cancelled if, for any reason, the franchisee fails to open the franchise.
3. In return for the initial franchise fee, Frozen Delight Inc. agrees to (a) assist the franchisee in selecting the location for the business; (b) negotiate the lease for the land; (c) obtain financing and assist with building design; (d) supervise construction; (e) establish accounting and tax records; and (f) provide expert advice over a five-year period relating to such matters as employee and management training, quality control, and promotion.
4. In addition to the initial franchise fee, the franchisee is required to pay to Frozen Delight Inc. a monthly fee of 2% of the franchisee's sales. This fee is for menu planning, recipe innovations, and the privilege of purchasing ingredients from Frozen Delight Inc. at or below prevailing market prices.

Management of Frozen Delight Inc. estimates that the value of the services rendered to the franchisee at the time the contract is signed amounts to at least $20,000. All franchisees to date have opened their locations at the scheduled time and none have defaulted on any of the notes receivable.

The credit ratings of all franchisees would entitle them to borrow at an interest rate of 10%. The present value of an ordinary annuity of five annual receipts of $10,000 discounted at 10% is $37,908.

Instructions
(a) Discuss the alternatives that Frozen Delight Inc. might use to account for the initial franchise fee, evaluate each by applying generally accepted accounting principles, and give illustrative entries for each alternative.
(b) Given the nature of Frozen Delight Inc.'s agreement with its franchisees, when should revenue be recognized? Discuss the question of revenue recognition for both the initial franchise fee and the additional monthly fee of 2% of the franchisee's sales. Give illustrative entries for both types of revenue.
(c) Assume that Frozen Delight Inc. sells some franchises for $90,000 (which includes a charge of $20,000 for the rental of equipment for its useful life of 10 years), that $40,000 of the fee is payable immediately and the balance on noninterest-bearing notes at $10,000 per year, that no portion of the $20,000 rental payment is refundable in case the franchisee goes out of business, and that title to the equipment remains with the franchiser. What would be the preferable method of accounting for the rental portion of the initial franchise fee? Explain.

(AICPA adapted)

USING YOUR JUDGEMENT

FINANCIAL REPORTING PROBLEM

The following note appears in the "Summary of Significant Accounting Policies" section of the Annual Report of Westinghouse Electric Corporation.

> **Note 1 (in Part): Revenue Recognition.** Sales are primarily recorded as products are shipped and services are rendered. The percentage-of-completion method of accounting is used for nuclear steam supply system orders with delivery schedules generally in excess of five years and for certain construction projects where this method of accounting is consistent with industry practice.
>
> WFSI revenues are generally recognized on the accrual method. When accounts become delinquent for more than two payment periods, usually 60 days, income is recognized only as payments are received. Such delinquent accounts for which no payments are received in the current month, and other accounts on which income is not being recognized because the receipt of either principal or interest is questionable, are classified as nonearning receivables.

Instructions

(a) Identify the revenue recognition methods used by Westinghouse Electric as discussed in its note on significant accounting policies.

(b) Under what conditions are the revenue recognition methods identified in the first paragraph of Westinghouse's note above acceptable?

(c) From the information provided in the second paragraph of Westinghouse's note, identify the type of operation being described and defend the acceptability of the revenue recognition method.

ETHICS CASE 1

Nimble Health and Racquet Club (NHRC) offers one-year memberships. The members may use any of the eight facilities but must reserve racquetball court time and pay a separate fee before using the court. As an incentive to new customers, NHRC advertised that any customers not satisfied for any reason could receive a refund of the remaining portion of unused membership fees. Membership fees are due at the beginning of the individual membership period; however, customers are given the option of financing the membership fee over the membership period at a 15% interest rate.

Some customers have expressed a desire to take only the regularly scheduled aerobic classes without paying for a full membership. During the current fiscal year, NHRC began to sell coupon books for aerobic classes to accommodate these customers. Each book is dated and contains 50 coupons that may be redeemed for any regularly scheduled aerobic class over a one-year period. After the one-year period, unused coupons are no longer valid.

During 1994, NHRC expanded into the health equipment market by purchasing a local company that manufactures rowing machines and cross-country ski machines. These machines are used in NHRC's facilities and are sold through the clubs and mail order catalogues. Customers must make a 20% down payment when placing an equipment order; delivery is 60–90 days after order placement. The machines are sold with a two-year unconditional guarantee. Based on past experience, NHRC expects the costs to repair machines under guarantee to be 4% of sales.

NHRC is in the process of preparing financial statements as of May 31, 1998, the end of its fiscal year. James Hogan, corporate controller, expressed concern over the company's performance for the year and decided to review the preliminary financial statements prepared by Barbara Hardy, NHRC's assistant controller. After reviewing the statements, Hogan proposed that the following changes be reflected in the May 31, 1998 published financial statements.

1. Membership revenue should be recognized when the membership fee is collected.

2. Revenue from the coupon books should be recognized when the books are sold.

3. Down payments on equipment purchases and expenses associated with the guarantee on the rowing and cross-country machines should be recognized when paid.

Barbara indicated to Hogan that the proposed changes are not in accordance with generally accepted accounting principles, but Hogan insisted that the changes be made. Barbara believes that Hogan wants to manipulate

318 CHAPTER 6 · Revenue Recognition

income to forestall any potential financial problems and increase his year-end bonus. At this point, Barbara is unsure what action to take.

Instructions
(a) 1. Describe when Nimble Health and Racquet Club (NHRC) should recognize revenue from membership fees, court rentals, and coupon book sales.
  2. Describe how NHRC should account for the down payments on equipment sales, explaining when this revenue should be recognized.
  3. Indicate when NHRC should recognize the expense associated with the guarantee of the rowing and cross-country machines.
(b) Discuss why James Hogan's proposed changes and his insistence that the financial statement changes be made is unethical. Structure your answer to include the following aspects of ethical conduct: competence, confidentiality, integrity, and/or objectivity.
(c) Identify some specific actions Barbara Hardy could take to resolve this situation.   (CMA adapted)

ETHICS CASE 2

In order to increase revenue at the end of the year, MicroWord Incorporated, a manufacturer of computer software, discounts its major lines to dealers with the condition that the dealers increase purchases by 40% before year end. In the early stages of the discount program, Anthony DiFore, the controller, complains to his financial vice-president, Anna Cragg, that recording this revenue would be misleading and premature. Cragg says that the company must increase revenue to meet requirements of its debt contracts, and adds: "Because the sales will come in the near future, why should it matter that we record them this year?"

Instructions
(a) Is the discount program a way to increase revenue?
(b) What moral dilemma does DiFore recognize? Who is harmed by the discount program?
(c) Should DiFore vigorously argue against the discount policy?
(d) If dealers returned a large number of software packages in the succeeding calendar year, do you think the discount program and its reporting policy are reasonable and ethical from an accountant's perspective?

ASSETS: RECOGNITION, MEASUREMENT, AND DISCLOSURE

part 2

chapter 7

CASH AND RECEIVABLES

7

Cash and Receivables

No with & without recourse.
Not testing on
effect. int. meth.

Consider White Farm, Braniff Airlines, and Atlantic Acceptance. All were industry leaders that went bankrupt or nearly so because of lack of liquidity. **Liquidity** is the amount of time expected to elapse until an asset is converted into cash. An asset that is available for conversion into cash quickly is a liquid asset. Liquidity is one indication of an enterprise's ability to meet its obligations as they come due. A liquid enterprise is likely to have a lower risk of failure than an illiquid enterprise, and it generally has greater financial flexibility to accept unexpected new investment opportunities. Accountants are called upon to provide information that will help management, creditors, and investors assess an enterprise's current liquidity and prospective cash flows.

Assets are the heart of an enterprise. They generate revenues that in turn generate the cash inflows to pay creditors, compensate employees, reward owners, and provide for growth. The primary liquid assets of most enterprises are cash, temporary investments, and receivables. This chapter covers cash, accounts receivable, and notes receivable. Temporary investments are discussed later, in Chapter 10, along with long-term investments.

SECTION 1: CASH AND CASH EQUIVALENTS

NATURE AND COMPOSITION OF CASH

Cash, the most liquid of assets, is the standard medium of exchange and the basis for measuring and accounting for all other items. It is generally classified as a current asset. To be reported as cash, an asset must be readily available for the payment of current

OBJECTIVE 1
Identify items considered cash.

obligations. It must also be free from any contractual restriction that limits its use in satisfying debts.

Cash consists of coin, currency, and available funds on deposit at the bank. Negotiable instruments such as money orders, certified cheques, cashiers' cheques, personal cheques, and bank drafts are also viewed as cash. Savings accounts are usually classified as cash, although the bank may have a legal right to demand notice before withdrawal. Because the privilege of prior notice is rarely exercised by banks, savings accounts are considered to be cash.

Certain items present classification problems. **Postdated cheques and I.O.U.s** for example, are treated as receivables. **Travel advances** are properly treated as receivables if the advances are to be collected from the employees or deducted from their salaries. Otherwise, classification of the travel advance as a prepaid expense is more appropriate. **Postage stamps on hand** are classified as part of the office supplies inventory or as a prepaid expense. **Petty cash funds and change funds** are included in current assets as cash because these funds are used to meet current operating expenses and to liquidate current liabilities.

MANAGEMENT AND CONTROL OF CASH

OBJECTIVE 2
Explain common techniques employed to control cash.

Cash presents many special management and control problems for several reasons. First, cash is a factor in a great many transactions. Second, **cash is the only asset readily convertible into any other type of asset**. It is easily concealed and transported, and it is almost universally desired. Correct accounting for cash transactions therefore requires controls to ensure that cash belonging to the enterprise is not improperly converted to personal use.

A third reason for regulating cash is that neither too much nor too little should be available at any given time. An adequate supply that does not tie up too much of the firm's resources must always be maintained. As the medium of exchange, cash is required to pay for all assets and services purchased by the company to meet all its obligations as they mature. The disbursement of cash is thus a daily occurrence, and a sufficient fund of cash must be kept on hand to meet these needs. On the other hand, cash, as such, is not a productive asset; it earns no return. Hence it is undesirable to keep on hand a supply of cash that is larger than necessary for day-to-day needs, with a reasonable margin for emergencies. Cash in excess of what is needed should be invested either in income-producing securities or in other productive assets.

Two problems of accounting for cash transactions face management: (1) proper controls must be established to ensure that no unauthorized transactions are entered into by officers or employees; and (2) information necessary for the proper management of cash on hand and cash transactions must be provided to the accounting department. Yet even with sophisticated control devices, errors can and do happen. The *Wall Street Journal* ran a story entitled "A $7.8 Million Error Has a Happy Ending for a Horrified Bank," which described how Manufacturers Hanover Trust Co., one of the largest banks in the United States, mailed about $7.8 million too much in cash dividends to its shareholders. Happily, most of the monies were subsequently returned.

USING BANK ACCOUNTS

A company can vary the number and location of banks and the types of bank accounts used to obtain desired control objectives. For large companies operating in multiple locations, the location of bank accounts can be important. Establishing collection accounts in strategic locations can accelerate the flow of cash into the company by shortening the time between a customer's mailing of a payment and the company's use of the cash. Multiple collection centres are generally used to reduce the size of a company's **collection**

float, which is the difference between the amount on deposit according to the company's records and the amount of collected cash according to the bank record.

The **general chequing account** is the principal bank account used by most companies and frequently the only type of bank account maintained by small businesses. Cash is deposited into and disbursed from this account as all transactions are cycled through it. Deposits from and disbursements to all other bank accounts are made through the general chequing account.

Imprest bank accounts are used to make a specific amount of cash available for a limited purpose. The account acts as a clearing account for a large volume of cheques or for a specific type of cheque. The specific and intended amount to be cleared through the imprest account is deposited therein by transferring that amount from the general chequing account or other source. Imprest bank accounts are often used for disbursing payroll cheques, dividends, commissions, bonuses, confidential expenses (e.g., officers' salaries), and travel expenses.

Lockbox accounts are frequently used by large, multilocation companies to make collections in cities within areas of heaviest customer billing. The company rents a local post office box and authorizes a local bank to pick up the remittances mailed to that box number. The bank empties the box at least once a day and immediately credits the company's account for collections. The greatest advantage of a lockbox is that it accelerates the availability of collected cash. In a lockbox arrangement, the bank generally microfilms the cheques for record purposes and provides the company with a deposit slip, a list of collections, and any customer correspondence. If control over the cash is improved and if income generated from accelerating the receipt of funds exceeds the cost of the lockbox system, it is considered worthwhile to undertake.

ELECTRONIC FUNDS TRANSFER (EFT)

Business and individuals use about 1.5 billion cheques annually to pay their bills. This process is not without cost. Preparing, issuing, receiving, and clearing a cheque through the banking system is estimated to cost between 55 cents and $1.00. It is not surprising, therefore, that in this electronic age new methods are being developed to transfer funds among parties without the use and movement of paper. We are entering the age of **electronic funds transfer (EFT),** a process that uses wire, telephone, telegraph, computer, (maybe even satellite), or other electronic device rather than paper to make instantaneous transfers of funds.

Canada's major banks spent the 1980s developing national automated teller machine (ATM) networks. The pace of development has been hectic. It is expected that most banks will be affiliated with a few national electronic banking networks that consolidate most retail banking services in much the same way that VISA and MasterCard have unified consumer credit services.

But the new ATM electronic networks will be far more powerful than the credit card networks of VISA and MasterCard because they will operate with the **debit card,** which can give access to all of a customer's accounts within a bank. Using an ATM, customers are able to withdraw cash and make deposits to both their chequing and savings accounts, as well as transfer funds between accounts and make balance inquiries. By linking ATMs nationally, the networks are building the first electronics funds transfer system capable of processing large-volume retail fund transfers between computers at different banks.

Already the use of cheques has disappeared from certain fund transfers. For example, many employers send banks a magnetic tape that transfers payroll funds from the firm's account to each employee's account. The services provided by ATM networks can now accommodate electronic transfers from home and retail point-of-sale terminals. Banks and consumers have the power to replace with electronic transactions many of those 1.5 billion cheques they used to issue.

THE IMPREST PETTY CASH SYSTEM

Almost every company finds it necessary to pay small amounts for many expenses, such as employees' lunches and taxi fares, minor office supply items, and small expense payments. It is frequently impractical to require that such disbursements be made by cheque, yet some control over them is important. A simple method of obtaining reasonable control, while adhering to the rule of disbursement by cheque, is the **imprest system** for petty cash disbursements. The system works as follows.

1. An individual is designated the petty cash custodian and given a small amount of currency from which to make small payments.

Petty Cash Fund	300	
Cash		300

2. As disbursements are made, the petty cash custodian obtains signed receipts from each individual to whom cash is paid. If possible, evidence of the disbursements should be attached to the petty cash receipt. Petty cash transactions are not recorded until the fund is reimbursed; such entries are then recorded by someone other than the petty cash custodian.

3. When the supply of cash runs low, the custodian presents to the general cashier a request for reimbursement supported by the petty cash receipts and other disbursement evidence. The custodian receives a company cheque to replenish the fund. At this point, transactions are recorded based on petty cash receipts:

Office Supplies Expense	42	
Postage Expense	53	
Entertainment Expense	76	
Cash Over and Short	2	
Cash		173

4. If it is decided that the amount of cash in the petty cash fund is excessive, an adjustment may be made as follows (lowering the fund balance from $300 to $250).

Cash	50	
Petty Cash		50

Entries are made to the Petty Cash account only to increase or decrease the size of the fund.

A **Cash Over and Short** account is used when the petty cash fund fails to prove out. When this occurs, it is usually due to an error (e.g., failure to provide correct change, overpayment of expense, lost receipt, etc.). If cash proves out short (i.e., the sum of the receipts and cash in the fund is less than the imprest amount), the shortage is debited to the Cash Over and Short account. If it proves out over, the amount by which it is over is credited to Cash Over and Short. This account is left open until the end of the year, when it is closed and generally shown on the income statement as an expense or revenue.

There are usually expense items in the fund, except immediately after reimbursement. Therefore, if accurate financial statements are desired, the funds must be reimbursed at the end of each accounting period and also when nearly depleted.

Under the imprest system, the petty cash custodian is responsible at all times for the amount of the fund on hand either as cash or in the form of signed receipts. These receipts provide the evidence required by the disbursing officer to issue a reimbursement cheque. Two additional procedures are followed to obtain more complete control over the petty cash fund.

1. Surprise counts of the funds are made from time to time by a superior of the petty cash custodian to determine that the fund is being accounted for satisfactorily.

2. Petty cash vouchers are cancelled or mutilated after they have been submitted for reimbursement so that they cannot be used to secure a second reimbursement.

PHYSICAL PROTECTION OF CASH BALANCES

Not only must cash receipts and cash disbursements be safeguarded through internal control measures, but also the cash on hand and in banks must be protected. Because receipts become cash on hand and cash disbursements are made from cash in banks, adequate control of receipts and disbursements is part of the protection of cash balances. Certain other procedures, however, should be given some consideration.

Physical protection of cash is such an elementary necessity that it requires little discussion. Every effort should be made to minimize cash on hand in the office. A petty cash fund, perhaps change funds, and the current day's receipts should be all that is on hand at any one time. Insofar as possible, these funds should be kept in a vault, safe, or locked cash drawer. Each day's receipts should be transmitted intact to the bank as soon as practicable. Accurately stating the amount of available cash both in internal management reports and in external financial statements is also extremely important.

Every company has a record of cash received and disbursed, with a current balance. Because of the many cash transactions, however, errors or omissions may be made in keeping this record. Therefore, it is necessary to periodically prove the balance shown in the general ledger. Cash actually present in the office—petty cash, change funds, and undeposited receipts—can be counted and compared with the company records. Cash on deposit is not available for count and is proved by preparing a **bank reconciliation**—a reconciliation of the company's record with the bank's record of the company's cash.

RECONCILIATION OF BANK BALANCES

At the end of each calendar month, the bank supplies each customer with a **bank statement** (a copy of the bank's account with the customer) together with the customer's cheques that have been paid by the bank during the month. If no errors were made by the bank or the customer, if all deposits made and all cheques drawn by the customer reached the bank within the same month, and if no unusual transactions occurred that could affect either the company's or the bank's record of cash, the balance of cash reported by the bank to the customer should be the same as that shown in the customer's own records. This condition seldom occurs for one or more of the following reasons.

RECONCILING ITEMS

1. **Deposits in Transit.** End-of-month deposits of cash recorded on the depositor's books in one month are received and recorded by the bank in the following month.

2. **Outstanding Cheques.** Cheques written by the depositor are recorded when written but may not be recorded by, or "clear," the bank until the next month.

3. **Bank Charges.** Charges recorded by the bank against the depositor's balance for such items as bank services, printing cheques, **not-sufficient-funds (NSF) cheques**, and safe-deposit box rentals. The depositor may not be aware of these charges until receipt of the bank statement.

4. **Bank Credits.** Collections or deposits by the bank for the benefit of the depositor that may be unknown to the depositor until receipt of the bank statement. Examples are note collection for the depositor as well as interest earned on interest-bearing chequing accounts.

5. **Bank or Depositors Errors.** Errors on the part of the bank or the depositor cause the bank balance to disagree with the depositor's book balance.

Hence, differences between the depositor's record of cash and the bank's record are usual and expected. Therefore, the two must be reconciled to determine the nature and amount of the differences between the two amounts.

A bank reconciliation is a schedule that explains any differences between the bank's and the company's records of cash. If the difference results only from transactions not yet recorded by the bank, the company's record of cash is considered correct. But if part of the difference arises from other items, either the bank's records or the company's records must be adjusted.

Two forms of bank reconciliation may be prepared. One form reconciles from the bank statement balance to the book balance, or vice versa. The other form reconciles both the bank balance and the book balance to a correct cash balance. This latter form is more widely used. A sample of that form and its common reconciling items are shown below.

BANK RECONCILIATION FORM AND CONTENT		
Balance per bank statement (end of period)		$$$
Add: Deposits in transit	$$	
Undeposited receipts (cash on hand)	$$	
Bank errors that understate the bank statement balance	$$	$$
		$$$
Deduct: Outstanding cheques	$$	
Bank errors that overstate the bank statement balance	$$	$$
Correct cash balance		$$$
Balance per depositor's books		$$$
Add: Bank credits and collections not yet recorded in the books	$$	
Book errors that understate the book balance	$$	$$
	$$$	
Deduct: Bank charges not yet recorded in the books	$$	
Book errors that overstate the book balance	$$	$$
Correct cash balance		$$$

This form of reconciliation consists of two sections: (1) "Balance Per Bank Statement" and (2) "Balance Per Depositor's Books." Both sections end with the same "Correct Cash Balance." The Correct Cash Balance is the amount to which the books must be adjusted and is the amount reported on the balance sheet. Adjusting journal entries are prepared from the addition and deduction items appearing in the Balance Per Depositor's Books. Any errors attributable to the bank should be called to the bank's attention immediately.

REPORTING CASH

OBJECTIVE 3
Indicate how cash and related items are reported.

Although the reporting of cash is relatively straightforward, there are a number of issues that merit special attention. These issues relate to the reporting of:

1. Restricted cash.
2. Bank overdrafts.
3. Cash equivalents.

RESTRICTED CASH

Compensating Balances. Occasionally banks and other lending institutions require customers to whom they lend money to maintain minimum cash balances. These minimum balances, called **compensating balances**, are defined as "that portion of any demand deposit (or any time deposit or certificate of deposit) maintained by a corporation which constitutes support for existing borrowing arrangements of the corporation with a lending institution. Such arrangements would include both outstanding borrowings and the assurance of future credit availability."[1]

Compensating balances may be payment for bank services rendered to the company for which there is no direct fee. Examples include cheque processing and lockbox management. By requiring a compensating balance, the bank achieves an effective interest rate on a loan that is higher than the stated rate because it has the use of the restricted amount that must remain on deposit.

The need for the disclosure of compensating balances was highlighted in the 1970s when a number of companies were involved in a liquidity crisis. Many investors believed that the cash reported on the balance sheet was fully available to meet recurring obligations, but these funds were restricted because of the need for these companies to maintain minimum cash balances at various lending institutions.

Disclosure of compensating balances depends on the classification of the related loan or borrowing arrangement. If the balances are required for short-term borrowing, then the compensating amount could be separately disclosed under Current Assets. Restricted balances held as compensating balances against long-term borrowing arrangements should be separately classified as noncurrent assets in either the Investments or Other Assets sections using a caption such as "Cash on Deposit Maintained as Compensating Balance." In addition, a note to the financial statements should indicate the nature of the arrangement and cash restriction.

Central Guaranty Trustco Limited reported the following note regarding compensating balances.

EXHIBIT 7-1   CENTRAL GUARANTY TRUSTCO LIMITED

Note: Restricted Assets

In February 1992, the Trust Company agreed to maintain deposits with a Canadian chartered bank amounting to $300,000,000 in connection with its daily clearing arrangements. In addition, the Trust Company agreed to pledge securities to the bank amounting to at least $90,000,000.

Other Types of Restrictions. Petty cash, payroll, and dividend funds are examples of cash set aside for a particular purpose. In most situations, these fund balances are not material and therefore are not segregated from cash when it is reported in the financial statements. When material in amount, restricted cash is segregated from "regular" cash for reporting purposes. The restricted cash is classified either in the Current Assets or in the Long-Term Assets section, depending on the date of availability or disbursement. If the cash is to be used within one year or one operating cycle (whichever is longer) for payment of existing or maturing obligations, classification in the Current Assets section is appropriate. On the other hand, if the cash is to be held for a longer period, the restricted cash is shown in the Long-Term Assets section of the balance sheet.[2]

BANK OVERDRAFTS

Bank overdrafts occur when a cheque is written for more than the amount in the Cash account. Bank overdrafts should be reported in the Current Liabilities section and are usu-

[1] *Accounting Series Release No. 148*, "Amendments to Regulations S-X and Related Interpretations and Guidelines Regarding the Disclosure of Compensating Balances and Short-Term Borrowing Arrangements," Securities and Exchange Commission (November 13, 1973). The SEC defines 15% of liquid assets (current cash balances, whether restricted or not, plus marketable securities) as being material.

[2] *CICA Handbook*, Section 3000, par. .01.

ally added to the amount reported as accounts payable. If material, these items should be separately disclosed, either on the face of the balance sheet or in the related notes.

Bank overdrafts are generally not offset against the Cash account. A major exception is when available cash is present in another account in the same bank on which the overdraft occurred. Offsetting in this case is permitted.

CASH EQUIVALENTS

A current classification that has become popular is Cash and Cash Equivalents. **Cash equivalents** are short-term, highly liquid investments that are both (a) readily convertible to known amounts of cash; and (b) so near to their maturity that they present insignificant risk of changes in interest rates. Generally, only investments with original maturities of three months or less qualify under this definition. Examples of cash equivalents are treasury bills and commercial paper purchased with cash that is in excess of immediate needs. Some companies combine cash with temporary investments on the balance sheet. In these cases, the amount of the temporary investments is either described parenthetically or in the notes.

SUMMARY

Cash and cash equivalents include the medium of exchange and most negotiable instruments. If the item cannot be converted to coin or currency on short notice, it is separately classified as an investment, a receivable, or a prepaid expense. Cash that is not available for payment of currently maturing liabilities is segregated and classified in the Long-Term Assets section. The schedule below summarizes the classification of cash-related items.

EXHIBIT 7-2

CLASSIFICATION OF CASH, CASH EQUIVALENT, AND NONCASH ITEMS

Item	Classification	Comment
Cash	Cash	If unrestricted, report as cash.
		If restricted, identify and classify as current and noncurrent assets.
Petty cash and change funds	Cash	Report as cash.
Short-term paper	Cash equivalents	Investments with maturity of less than three months, often combined with cash.
Short-term paper	Temporary investments	Investments with maturity of 3 to 12 months.
Postdated cheques and IOUs	Receivables	Assumed to be collectible.
Travel advances	Receivables	Assumed to be collected from employees or deducted from their salaries.
Postage on hand (as stamps or in postage meters)	Prepaid expenses	May also be classified as office supplies inventory.
Bank overdrafts	Current liability	If right of offset exists, reduce cash.
Compensating balances		
1. Legally restricted	Cash separately classified as a deposit maintained as compensating balance	Classify as current or noncurrent in the balance sheet.
2. Arrangement without legal restriction	Cash with note disclosure	Disclose separately in notes details of the arrangement.

SECTION 2: RECEIVABLES

Receivables are financial assets in the form of claims held against customers and others for money, goods, or services.[3] For financial statement purposes, receivables are classified as either **current** (short term) or **noncurrent** (long-term). **Current receivables** are expected to be collected within a year or during the current operating cycle, whichever is longer. All other receivables are classified as **noncurrent**. Receivables are further classified in the balance sheet as either trade receivables or nontrade receivables.

OBJECTIVE 4
Define receivables and identify the different types of receivables.

Trade receivables are amounts owed by customers for goods sold and services rendered as part of normal business operations. Trade receivables, usually the most significant receivable of an enterprise, may be subclassified into accounts receivable and notes receivable. **Accounts receivable**, which are oral promises of the purchaser to pay for goods and services sold, are normally collectible within 30 to 60 days and are represented by "open accounts" resulting from short-term extensions of credit. **Notes receivable** are written promises to pay a certain sum of money on a specified date. They may arise from sales, financing, or other transactions. Notes may be short-term or long-term.

Nontrade receivables arise from a variety of transactions and are oral or written promises to pay or deliver. Some examples of nontrade receivables are:

1. Advances to officers and employees.

2. Advances to subsidiaries.

3. Deposits to cover potential damages or losses.

4. Deposits as a guarantee of performance or payment.

5. Dividends and interest receivable.

6. Claims against:
   (a) Insurance companies for casualties sustained.
   (b) Defendants under suit.
   (c) Governmental bodies for tax refunds.
   (d) Common carriers for damaged or lost goods.
   (e) Creditors for returned, damaged, or lost goods.
   (f) Customers for returnable items (crates, containers, etc.).

Because of the peculiar nature of nontrade receivables, they are generally classified and reported as separate items in the balance sheet.

The basic issues in accounting for accounts and notes receivable are the same: **recognition, valuation, and disposition**. We will discuss these basic issues of accounts and notes receivable in the following sequence:

1. Recognition and valuation of accounts receivable.

2. Recognition and valuation of notes receivable.

3. Disposition of accounts and notes receivable.

---

[3] *CICA Handbook*, Section 3860.05(b) (ii), includes contractual rights to receive cash (accounts and notes receivable) as financial assets.

RECOGNITION OF ACCOUNTS RECEIVABLE

In most receivables transactions, the amount to be recognized is the exchange price between the two parties. **The exchange price is the amount due from the debtor** (a customer or borrower) and is generally evidenced by some type of business document, often an invoice. Two factors that may complicate the measurement of the exchange price are (1) the availability of discounts (trade and cash discounts) and (2) the length of time between the sale and the due date of payments (the interest element).

TRADE DISCOUNTS

Customers are often quoted prices on the basis of list or catalogue prices that may be subject to a trade or quantity discount. Such trade discounts are used to avoid frequent changes in catalogues, to quote different prices for different quantities purchased, or to hide the true invoice price from competitors.

Trade discounts are commonly quoted in percentages. For example, if a textbook has a list price of $60 and the publisher sells it to college bookstores for list less a 30% trade discount, the receivable recorded by the publisher is $42 per textbook. The normal price practice is simply to deduct the trade discount from the list price and bill the customer net.

As another example, the producers of Nabob recently sold a 285 g jar of its instant coffee that had a list price of $4.65 for $3.90 to various supermarkets, a trade discount of approximately 16%. The supermarkets in turn sold the instant coffee for $3.99 per jar. Nabob would record the receivable and related sales revenue at $3.90 per jar, not $4.65.

CASH DISCOUNTS (SALES DISCOUNTS)

Cash discounts (sales discounts) are offered as an inducement for prompt payment and communicated in terms that read 2/10, n/30 (2% if paid within 10 days, gross amount due in 30 days), or 2/10, E.O.M. (2% if paid within 10 days of the end of the month).

Companies that fail to take sales discounts are usually not managing their money wisely. An enterprise that receives a 1% reduction in sales prices for payment within 10 days, total payment due within 30 days, is effectively earning 18.25% (.01 divided by 20/365) or at least avoiding that rate of interest cost. For this reason, companies usually take the discount unless their cash is severely limited.

The easiest and most commonly used method of recording sales and related sales discount transactions is to enter the receivable and sale at the gross amount. Under this method, sales discounts are recognized in the accounts only when payment is received within the discount period. Sales discounts would then be shown in the income statement as a deduction from sales, to arrive at net sales.

Some accountants contend that sales discounts not taken reflect penalties added to an established price to encourage prompt payment. That is, the seller offers sales on account at a slightly higher price than if selling for cash, and the increase is offset by the cash discount offered. Thus, customers who pay within the discount period purchase at the cash price; those who pay after expiration of the discount period are penalized because they must pay an amount in excess of the cash price. If this approach is adopted, sales and receivables are recorded net, and any discounts not taken are subsequently debited to Accounts Receivable and credited to Sales Discounts Forfeited. The following entries illustrate the difference between the gross and net methods.

ENTRIES UNDER GROSS AND NET METHODS

Gross Method			Net Method		
Sale of $10,000, terms 2/10, n/30:					
Accounts Receivable	10,000		Accounts Receivable	9,800	
Sales		10,000	Sales		9,800
Payment of $4,000 received within discount period:					
Cash	3,920		Cash	3,920	
Sales Discount	80		Accounts Receivable		3,920
Accounts Receivable		4,000			
Payment of $6,000 received after discount period:					
Cash	6,000		Accounts Receivable	120	
Accounts Receivable		6,000	Sales Discounts Forfeited		120
			Cash	6,000	
			Accounts Receivable		6,000

If the gross method is employed, sales discounts are reported as a deduction from sales in the income statement. Proper matching would dictate that a reasonable estimate of material amounts of expected discounts to be taken also should be charged against sales. If the net method is used, Sales Discounts Forfeited should be considered as an Other Revenue item.

Theoretically, the recognition of Sales Discounts Forfeited is correct because the receivable is stated closer to its realizable value and the net sale figure measures the revenue earned from the sale. As a practical matter, however, the net method is seldom used because it requires additional analysis and bookkeeping. For one thing, the net method requires adjusting entries to record sales discounts forfeited on accounts receivable that have passed the discount period.

NONRECOGNITION OF INTEREST ELEMENT

Ideally, receivables should be measured in terms of their present value: the discounted value of the cash to be received in the future. When expected cash receipts require a waiting period, the receivable face amount is not worth the amount that is ultimately received.

To illustrate, assume that a company makes a sale on account for $1,000, with payment due in four months. The applicable rate of interest is 12% and payment is made at the end of the four months. The present value of that receivable is not $1,000 but $961.54 ($1,000 $\times$ .96154, Table A-2; n = 1, i = 4%). In other words, $1,000 to be received four months from now is not the same as $1,000 received today.

Theoretically, any revenue after the period of sale is interest revenue. In practice, accountants have generally chosen to ignore this for accounts receivable because the amount of the discount is not usually material in relation to the net income for the period. Generally, receivables that arise from transactions with customers in the normal course of business, and that are due in customary trade terms not exceeding approximately one year, are excluded from present value considerations.[4]

---

[4] In the United States, *APB Opinion No. 21* "Interest on Receivables and Payables," provides that all receivables are subject to present value measurement techniques and interest imputation, if necessary, except for the following specifically excluded types:
(a) Normal accounts receivable due within one year.
(b) Security deposits, retainages, advances, or progress payments.
(c) Transactions between parent and subsidiary.
(d) Receivables due at some determinable future date.

VALUATION OF ACCOUNTS RECEIVABLE

Having recorded the receivables at their face value (the amount due), the accountant then faces the problem of financial statement presentation. Reporting of receivables involves (1) classification; and (2) valuation on the balance sheet.

Classification, as already discussed, involves a determination of the length of time the receivable will be outstanding. Receivables intended to be collected within a year or the operating cycle, whichever is longer, are classified as current; all other receivables are classified as long term.

The valuation of receivables is slightly more complex. Short-term receivables are valued and reported at net realizable value—**the net amount expected to be received in cash**, which is not necessarily the amount legally receivable. Determining net realizable value requires an estimation of uncollectible receivables and any returns or allowances to be granted.

UNCOLLECTIBLE ACCOUNTS RECEIVABLE

As one accountant so aptly noted, "The credit manager's idea of heaven probably would envisage a situation in which everybody (eventually) paid his debts."[5] Sales on any basis other than cash make subsequent failure to collect on the account a real possibility. An uncollectible account receivable is a loss of revenue that requires, through proper entry in the accounts, a decrease in the asset accounts receivable and a related decrease in income and shareholders' equity.

The chief problem in recording uncollectible accounts receivable is establishing the time at which to record the loss. Two general procedures are in use.

METHODS FOR RECORDING UNCOLLECTIBLES

1. **Direct Write-off Method.** No entry is made until a specific account has definitely been established as uncollectible. Then the loss is recorded by crediting Accounts Receivable and debiting Bad Debt Expense.
2. **Allowance Method.** An estimate is made of the expected uncollectible accounts from all sales made on account or from the total of outstanding receivables. This estimate is entered as an expense and a reduction in accounts receivable (via an increase in the allowance account) in the period in which the sale is recorded.

The direct write-off method records the bad debt in the year it is determined that a specific receivable cannot be collected; the allowance method enters the expense on an estimated basis in the accounting period during which the sales on account are made.

Supporters of the **direct write-off method** contend that facts, not estimates, are recorded. It assumes that a good account receivable resulted from each sale, and that later events proved certain accounts to be uncollectible and worthless. From a practical standpoint this method is simple and convenient to apply, although we must recognize that receivables do not generally become worthless at an identifiable moment of time. The direct write-off is theoretically deficient because it usually does not match costs with revenues of the period, nor does it result in receivables being stated at estimated realizable value on the balance sheet. **As a result, its use is not considered appropriate, except when the amount uncollectible is immaterial.**

Advocates of the **allowance method** believe that bad debt expense should be recorded in the same period as the sale to obtain a proper matching of expenses and rev-

[5] "Accounting for Contingencies," *Statement of the Financial Accounting Standards No. 5* (Stamford, Conn.: FASB, 1975), par. 8.

enues and to achieve a proper carrying value for accounts receivable. They support the position that although estimates are involved, the percentage of receivables that will not be collected can be predicted from past experiences, present market conditions, and an analysis of the outstanding balances. Many companies set their credit policies to provide for a certain percentage of uncollectible accounts. Failure to attain that percentage means that sales are being lost by credit policies that are too restrictive.

Because the collectibility of receivables is considered a loss contingency, the allowance method is appropriate only in situations where it is likely that an asset has been impaired and that the amount of the loss can be reasonably estimated.[6] A receivable is a prospective cash inflow; the probability of its collection must be considered in valuing this inflow. These estimates normally are made either (1) on the basis of percentage of sales; or (2) on the basis of outstanding receivables.

PERCENTAGE-OF-SALES (INCOME STATEMENT) APPROACH

If there is a fairly stable relationship between previous years' credit sales and bad debts, then that relationship can be turned into a percentage and used to determine this year's bad debt expense.

The **percentage-of-sales approach** matches costs with revenues because it relates the charge to the period in which the sale is recorded. To illustrate, assume that E.T. Morgan, Inc. estimates from past experience that about 2% of credit sales become uncollectible. If E.T. Morgan, Inc. had credit sales of $400,000 in 1998, the entry to record bad debt expense using the percentage-of-sales method is as follows:

Bad Debt Expense	8,000	
Allowance for Doubtful Accounts		8,000

The Allowance for Doubtful Accounts is a valuation account (i.e., contra asset) and is subtracted from the trade receivables on the balance sheet. The amount of bad debt expense and the related credit to the allowance account are unaffected by any balance currently existing in the allowance account. Because the bad debt expense is related to a nominal account (Sales), and any balance in the allowance is ignored, this method is frequently referred to as the **income statement approach**. A proper matching of costs and revenues is therefore achieved.

PERCENTAGE-OF-RECEIVABLES (BALANCE SHEET) APPROACH

Using past experience, a company can estimate the percentage of its outstanding receivables that will become uncollectible, without identifying specific accounts. This procedure provides a reasonably accurate estimate of the receivables' realizable value, but does not fit the concept of matching cost and revenue. Rather, its objective is to report receivables in the balance sheet at net realizable values; hence it is referred to as the **balance sheet approach**.

The percentage of receivables may be applied using one **composite rate** that reflects an estimate of the uncollectible receivables. Another approach that is more sensitive to the actual status of the accounts receivable is achieved by setting up an **aging schedule** and applying a different percentage based on past experience to the various age categories. An aging schedule is frequently used in practice. It indicates which accounts require special attention by providing the age of such accounts receivable. The following schedule of Wilson & Co. is an example.

---

[6] *CICA Handbook*, Section 3280, par. .12.

WILSON & CO.
Aging Schedule

Name of Customer	Balance Dec. 31	Under 60 days	60–90 days	91–120 days	Over 120 days
Western Stainless Steel Ltd.	$ 98,000	$ 80,000	$18,000	$	$
Brockway Steel Ltd.	320,000	320,000			
Freeport Sheet & Tube Co.	55,000				55,000
Allegheny Iron Works	74,000	60,000		14,000	
	$547,000	$460,000	$18,000	$14,000	$55,000

Summary

Age	Amount	Percentage Estimated to Be Uncollectible	Required Balance in Allowance
Under 60 days old	$460,000	4%	$18,400
61–90 days old	18,000	15	2,700
91–120 days old	14,000	20	2,800
Over 120 days	55,000	25	13,750
Year-end balance of allowance for doubtful accounts			$37,650

The amount $37,650 would be the bad debt expense reported for this year, assuming that no balance existed in the allowance account. To change the illustration slightly, **assume that the allowance account had a credit balance of $800 before adjustment**. In this case, the amount to be added to the allowance account is $36,850 ($37,650 − $800), and the following entry is made.

Bad Debt Expense	36,850	
Allowance for Doubtful Accounts		36,850

The balance in the allowance account is therefore stated as $37,650. **If the allowance balance before adjustment had a debit balance of $200**, then the amount to be recorded for bad debt expense would be $37,850 ($37,650 desired balance + $200 debit balance). In the percentage-of-receivables method, the balance in the allowance account *cannot be ignored* because the percentage is related to a real account (Accounts Receivable).

An aging schedule is usually prepared not to determine the bad debt expense, but to act as a control device that will determine the composition of receivables and identify delinquent accounts. The estimated loss percentage developed for each category is based on previous loss experience and the advice of credit department personnel. Regardless of whether a composite rate or an aging schedule is employed, the primary objective of the percentage-of-receivables method for financial statement purposes is to report receivables in the balance sheet at net realizable value. However, it is deficient in that it may not match the bad debt expense to the period in which the sale takes place.

The allowance for doubtful accounts as a percentage of receivables will vary, depending on the industry and the economic climate. Normally, bad debt expense will rise during recessions.

In summary, the percentage-of-receivables method results in a more accurate valuation of receivables on the balance sheet. From a matching viewpoint, the percentage-of-sales approach provides the best results. The following diagram relates these methods to the basic theory.

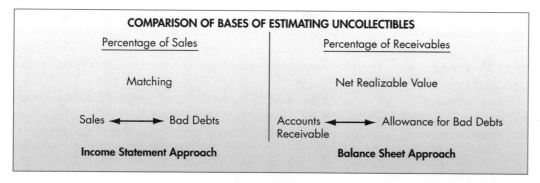

The account title employed for the allowance account is usually "Allowance for Doubtful Accounts" or simply "Allowance."

COLLECTION OF ACCOUNTS RECEIVABLE WRITTEN OFF

When a particular account receivable is determined to be uncollectible, the balance is removed from the books by debiting Allowance for Doubtful Accounts and crediting Accounts Receivable. If a collection is made on a receivable that was previously written off, the procedure to be followed is first to re-establish the receivable by debiting Accounts Receivable and crediting Allowance for Doubtful Accounts. An entry is then made to debit Cash and credit the customer's account in the amount of the remittance received.

If the direct write-off approach is employed, the amount collected is debited to Cash and credited to a revenue account entitled Uncollectible Amounts Recovered, with proper notation in the customer's account.

SPECIAL ALLOWANCE ACCOUNTS

To properly match expenses to sales revenues, it is sometimes necessary to establish additional allowance accounts. These allowance accounts are reported as contra accounts to accounts receivable and establish the receivables at net realizable value. The most common allowances are:

1. Allowance for sales returns and allowances.
2. Allowance for collection expenses.

SALES RETURNS AND ALLOWANCES

Many accountants question the soundness of recording returns and allowances in the current period when they are derived from sales made in the preceding period. Normally, however, the amount of mismatched returns and allowances is not material if such items are handled consistently from year to year. Yet, if a company completes a few special orders involving large amounts near the end of the accounting period, sales returns and allowances should be anticipated in the period of the sale to avoid distorting the income statement of the current period.

As an example, Astro Turf Limited recognizes that approximately 5% of its $1,000,000 trade receivables outstanding are returned, or that some adjustment is made to the sale price. Omission of a $50,000 charge could have a material effect on net income for the period. The entry to reflect this anticipated sales return and allowance is:

Sales Returns and Allowances	50,000	
Allowance for Sales Returns and Allowances		50,000

Sales Returns and Allowances are reported as an offset to Sales Revenue in the income statement. Returns and allowances are accumulated separately instead of debited directly to the Sales account, simply to let the business manager and the statement reader know their magnitude. The allowance is an asset valuation account (contra asset) and is deducted from total accounts receivable.

In most cases, the inclusion in the income statement of all returns and allowances made during the period, whether or not they resulted from the current period's sales, is an acceptable accounting procedure justified on the basis of practicality and immateriality.[7]

COLLECTION EXPENSES

A similar concept holds true for collection expenses. If a significant handling and service charge is incurred to collect the open accounts receivables at the end of the year, an allowance for collection expenses should be recorded. For example, Sears, Roebuck & Company reports its receivables net, with an attached schedule indicating the types of receivables outstanding. Sears' contra account is entitled "Allowance for Collection Expenses and Losses on Customer Accounts," as shown below.

EXHIBIT 7-3   SEARS, ROEBUCK AND COMPANY

Receivables

Customer instalment accounts receivable	
Easy payment accounts	$2,221,017,167
Revolving charge accounts	1,372,874,725
	3,593,891,892
Other customer accounts	101,904,882
Miscellaneous accounts and notes receivable	96,446,334
	3,792,243,108
Less: Allowance for collection expenses and losses on customer accounts	236,826,866
	$3,555,416,242

NOTES RECEIVABLE

A note receivable is supported by a formal **promissory note**, which is a written promise to pay a certain sum of money at a specific future date. Such a note is a negotiable instrument that is signed by a **maker** in favour of a designated **payee**, who may legally and readily sell or otherwise transfer the note to others. Although notes contain an interest element because of the time value of money, notes are classified as interest-bearing or noninterest-bearing. **Interest-bearing notes** have a stated rate of interest, whereas **noninterest-bearing notes** (zero-interest-bearing) include the interest as part of their face amount instead of stating it explicitly. Notes receivable are considered fairly liquid, even if long term, because they may be easily converted to cash.

Notes receivable are frequently accepted from customers who need to extend the payment period on an outstanding receivable. Notes are sometimes required of high-risk or new customers. In addition, notes are often used in loans to employees and subsidiaries and in the sales of property, plant, and equipment. In some industries (the pleasure and sport boat industry) all credit sales are supported by signed notes. The majority of notes, however, originate from lending transactions. The basic issues in accounting for notes receivable are the same as those for accounts receivable: recognition, valuation, and disposition.

---

[7] An interesting sideline to the entire problem of returns and allowances has developed in recent years. Determination of when a sale *is* a sale has become difficult, because in certain circumstances the seller is exposed to such a high risk of ownership through possible return of the property that the entire transaction is nullified and the sale not recognized. Such situations have developed particularly in sales to related parties. This subject is discussed in more detail in Chapters 6 and 8.

RECOGNITION OF NOTES RECEIVABLE

The proper amount to record for these notes is the present value of the future cash flows. Determining this amount can become complicated, however, particularly when a noninterest-bearing note or a note bearing an unreasonable interest rate is issued.

Short-term notes are generally recorded at face value (less allowances) because the interest inherent in the maturity value is immaterial. Long-term notes receivable, however, should be recorded and reported at the **present value of the cash expected to be collected**. When the interest stated on an interest-bearing note is equal to the effective (market) rate of interest, the note sells at face value.[8] When the stated rate is different from the market rate, the cash exchanged (present value) will be different from the face value of the note. The difference between the face value and the cash exchanged, either a discount or a premium, is then recorded and amortized over the life of a note to approximate the effective (market) interest rate.

OBJECTIVE 7
Explain accounting issues related to recognition of notes receivable.

Notes Issued at Face Value: Interest-Bearing.[9] To illustrate the discounting of a note issued at face value, assume that Bigelow Corp. lends Scandinavian Imports $10,000 in exchange for a $10,000, three-year note bearing interest at 10% annually. The market rate of interest for a note of similar risk is also 10%. A time diagram depicting both cash flows is shown below.

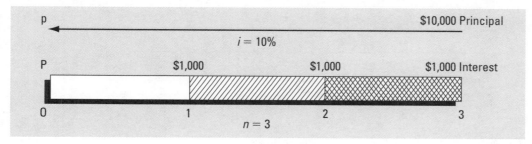

The present value or exchange price of the note is computed as follows.

Face value of the note	$10,000
Present value of the principal:	
$10,000 $(p_{\overline{3}|10\%})$ = $10,000 (.75132)	$7,513
Present value of the interest:	
$1,000 $(P_{\overline{3}|10\%})$ = $1,000 (2.48685)	2,487
Present value of the note	10,000
Difference	$ -0-

In this case, the present value of the note and its face value are the same, that is, $10,000, because the effective and stated rates of interest are also the same. The receipt of the note is recorded by Bigelow Corp. as follows:

Notes Receivable	10,000	
Cash		10,000

---

[8] The **stated interest rate**, also referred to as the face rate or the coupon rate, is the rate contracted as part of the note. The **effective interest rate**, also referred to as the market rate or the effective yield, is the rate used in the market to determine the value of the note—that is, the discount rate used to determine present value.

[9] In this book interest rates are usually stated as an annual rate. It is noted that in certain cases (e.g. bonds) in practice the annual rate given is the rate that is applied to the principal amount to determine the dollar amount of interest paid for the period of concern. For example, the semi-annual interest payment on a $1,000, 8% bond would be $40($1,000 × .08 × 1/2). Consequently, the effective annual percentage rate (yield) for this bond would be slightly greater than the stated annual rate of 8%. In this book in harmony with industry practice bond interest will be the sated (coupon) rate.

Bigelow Corp. would recognize the interest earned each year as follows:

Cash	1,000	
Interest Revenue		1,000

Notes Not Issued at Face Value: Zero-Interest-Bearing. If a zero-interest-bearing note is received solely for cash, its present value is the cash paid to the issuer. Because both the future amount and the present value of the note are known, the interest rate can be computed because it is implied. The **implicit interest rate** is the rate that equates the cash paid with the amounts receivable in the future. The difference between the future (face) amount and the present value (cash paid) is recorded as a discount or premium and amortized to interest revenue over the life of the note.

To illustrate, Jeremiah Company receives a three-year, $10,000 zero-interest-bearing note, the present value of which is $7,721.80. The implicit rate that equates the total cash to be received ($10,000 at maturity) to the present value of the future cash flows ($7,721.80) is 9% (the present value of $1 for 3 periods at 9% is $.77218). The time diagram depicting the one cash flow is shown below.

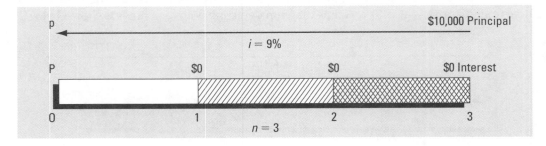

The entry to record the transaction is as follows:

Notes Receivable	10,000.00	
Discount on Notes Receivable ($10,000 − $7,721.80)		2,278.20
Cash		7,721.80

The Discount on Notes Receivable is a valuation account and is reported on the balance sheet as a contra-asset account to notes receivable. The discount is then amortized, and interest revenue is recognized annually using the **effective interest method**. The three-year discount amortization and interest revenue schedule is shown below.

SCHEDULE OF NOTE DISCOUNT AMORTIZATION
Effective Interest Method
0% Note Discounted at 9%

	Cash Received	Interest Revenue	Discount Amortized	Carrying Value of Note
Date of issue				$ 7,721.80
End of Year 1	$-0-	$ 694.96[a]	$ 694.96[b]	8,416.76[c]
End of Year 2	-0-	757.51	757.51	9,174.27
End of Year 3	-0-	825.73[d]	825.73	10,000.00
	$-0-	$2,278.20	$2,278.20	

[a]$7,721.80 × .09 = $694.96
[b]$694.96 − 0 = $694.96
[c]$7,721.80 + $694.96 = $8,416.76
[d]Five-cent adjustment to compensate for rounding

Interest revenue at the end of the first year using the effective interest method is recorded as follows.

| Discount on Notes Receivable | 694.96 | |
| Interest Revenue ($7,721.80 × 9%) | | 694.96 |

Notes Not Issued at Face Value: Interest-Bearing. Often the stated rate and the effective rate are different. The preceding zero-interest-bearing case is one example of such a situation.

To illustrate a more common situation, assume that Morgan Corp. lends Marie Co. $10,000 in exchange for a three-year, $10,000 note bearing interest at 10% annually. The market rate of interest for a note of similar risk is 12%. The time diagram depicting both cash flows is shown below:

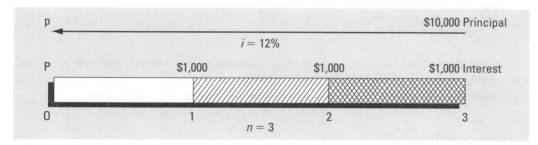

The present value of the two cash flows is computed as follows.

Face value of the note		$10,000
Present value of the principal:		
$10,000 ($p_{\overline{3}|12\%}$ = $10,000 (.71178)	$7,118	
Present value of the interest:		
$1,000 ($P_{\overline{3}|12\%}$) = $1,000 (2.40183)	2,402	
Present value of the note		9,520
Difference (Discount)		$ 480

In this case, because the effective rate of interest (12%) is greater than the stated rate (10%), the present value of the note is less than the face value; that is, the note was exchanged at a **discount**. The receipt of the note at a discount is recorded by Morgan as follows.

Notes Receivable	10,000	
Discount on Notes Receivable		480
Cash		9,520

The discount is amortized and interest revenue is recognized annually using the **effective interest method**. The three-year discount and interest revenue schedule is as follows.

SCHEDULE OF NOTE DISCOUNT AMORTIZATION				
Effective Interest Method				
10% Note Discounted at 12%				
	Cash Received	Interest Revenue	Discount Amortized	Carrying Amount of Note
Date of issue				$ 9,520
End of Year 1	$1,000[a]	$1,142[b]	$142[c]	9,662[d]
End of Year 2	1,000	1,159	159	9,821
End of Year 3	1,000	1,179	179	10,000
	$3,000	$3,480	$480	

[a]$10,000 × 10% = $1,000
[b]$9,520 × 12% = $1,142
[c]$1,142 − $1,000 = $142
[d]$9,520 + $142 = $9,662

On the date of issue, the note has a present value of $9,520. Its unamortized discount—additional interest revenue to be spread over the three-year life of the note—is $480.

At the end of Year 1, Morgan receives $1,000 in cash. But its effective interest income is $1,142 ($9,520 × 12%). The difference between $1,000 and $1,142 is the amortized discount, $142. The carrying amount of the note is now $9,662 ($9520 + 142). This process is repeated until the end of Year 3.

Receipt of the annual interest and amortization of the discount for the first year is recorded by Morgan as follows (amounts per amortization schedule).

Cash	1,000	
Discount on Notes Receivable	142	
Interest Revenue		1,142

When the present value exceeds the face value, the note is exchanged at a premium. The premium is recorded as a debit and amortized using the effective interest method over the life of the note as annual reductions in the amount of interest revenue recognized.

SPECIAL SITUATIONS

The note transactions just discussed are the common types of situations encountered in practice. Special situations are as follows:

1. Notes received for cash and other rights.

2. Notes received for property, goods, or services.

3. Imputed interest.

Notes Received for Cash and Other Rights. The lender may also accept a **note in exchange for cash and other rights and privileges**. For example, Ideal Equipment Ltd. accepts a five-year, $100,000, noninterest-bearing note from Outland Steel Corp., plus the right to purchase 10,000 t of steel at a bargain price in exchange for $100,000 in cash. Assume that the current rate of interest that would be charged on another note without the right to purchase at a bargain price is 10%. The acceptance of the note is recorded and the present value of the note is computed as follows:

Notes Receivable	100,000	
Prepaid Purchases	37,908	
Discount on Notes Receivable		37,908*
Cash		100,000

*Present value = $100,000 × $p\overline{_5}|_{10\%}$ = $100,000 × .62092 = $62,092;
Discount = $100,000 − $62,092 = $37,908.

The difference between the $62,092 present value of the note and its maturity value of $100,000 represents implicit interest of $37,908. It is amortized to interest revenue over the five-year life of the note, using the effective interest method. The excess of the $100,000 over the $62,092 represents an asset, Prepaid Purchases. Prepaid Purchases is allocated to purchases or inventory in proportion to the number of tonnes of steel purchased each year relative to the total 10,000 t for which a bargain price is available. For example, if 3,000 t of steel were purchased during the first year of the five-year bargain period, the following entry would be recorded by Ideal Equipment.

Purchases (Inventory)	11,372	
Prepaid Purchases		11,372
(3,000/10,000 × $37,908)		

Note that although Prepaid Purchases and the Discount on Notes Receivable are both recorded initially as $37,908, they are written off differently. Prepaid Purchases are written off in the ratio of the tonnes purchased, while the discount is amortized using the effective interest method. The value of the right or privilege, in this case the price reduction, aids in determining the interest implicit in the transaction.

Notes Received for Property, Goods, or Services. When a **note is received in exchange for property, goods, or services** in a bargained transaction entered into at arm's length, the stated interest rate is presumed to be fair except for these conditions:

1. No interest rate is stated.

2. The stated interest rate is unreasonable.

3. The face amount of the note is materially different from the current cash sales price for the same or similar items or from the current market value of the debt instrument.

In these circumstances, the present value of the note is measured by the fair value of the property, goods, or services or by an amount that reasonably approximates the market value of the note.

To illustrate, Oasis Development Ltd. sold a corner lot to Rusty Pelican as a restaurant site and accepted in exchange a five-year note having a maturity value of $35,247 and no stated interest rate. The land originally cost Oasis $14,000 and had an appraised fair value of $20,000. Given the criteria above, it is acceptable to use the fair market value of the land, $20,000, as the present value of the note. The entry to record the sale is as follows:

Notes Receivable	35,247	
Discount on Notes Receivable ($35,247 − $20,000)		15,247
Land		14,000
Gain on Sale of Land ($20,000 − $14,000)		6,000

The discount is amortized to interest revenue over the five-year life of the note under the effective interest method.

Imputed Interest. In note transactions, the effective or real interest rate is either evident or determinable by other factors involved in the exchange, such as the fair market value of what was given or received. But, if the fair value of the property, goods, services or other rights is not determinable and if the note has no ready market, the problem of determining the present value of the note is more difficult. To estimate the present value of a note under such circumstances, an applicable interest rate that may differ from the stated interest rate is approximated. This process of interest-rate approximation is called **imputation**, and the resulting interest rate is called an **imputed interest rate.** The imputed interest rate is used to establish the present value of the note by discounting, at that rate, all future receipts (interest and principal) on the note.

> The objective for computing the appropriate interest rate is to approximate the rate which would have resulted if an independent borrower and an independent lender had negotiated a similar transaction under comparable terms and conditions with the option to pay the cash price upon purchase or to give a note for the amount of the purchase which bears the prevailing rate of interest to maturity. The rate used for valuation purposes will normally be at least equal to the rate at which the debtor can obtain financing of a similar nature from other sources at the date of the transaction.[10]

The choice of a rate is affected by the prevailing rates for similar instruments of issuers with similar credit ratings. It is also affected specifically by restrictive covenants, collateral, payment schedule, the existing prime interest rate, etc. Determination of the

---

[10] *Ibid.*, par. 13.

imputed interest rate is made when the note is received; any subsequent changes in prevailing interest rates are ignored.

To illustrate, assume that on December 31, 1998, Brown Interiors Limited rendered architectural services and accepted in exchange a long-term promissory note with a face value of $550,000, a due date of December 31, 2003, and a stated interest rate of 2%, receivable at the end of each year. The fair value of the services is not readily determinable and the note is not readily marketable. Given the circumstances—the maker's credit rating, the absence of collateral, the prime interest rate at that date, and the prevailing interest on the maker's outstanding debt—an 8% interest rate is determined to be appropriate. The time diagram depicting both cash flows is shown below.

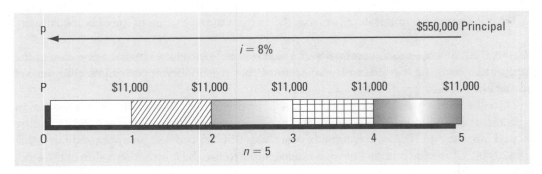

The present value of the note and the imputed fair value of the architectural services are determined as follows.

Face value of the note		$550,000
Present value of $550,000 due in five years at 8%—$550,000 × $p_{\overline{5}|8\%}$ = $550,000 × .68058	$374,319	
Present value of $11,000 ($550,000 × 2%) payable annually for five years at 8% = $11,000 × $P_{\overline{5}|8\%}$ = $11,000 × 3.99271	43,920	
Present value of the note		418,239
Discount		**$131,761**

The value of the services is thus determined to be $418,239, the current value of the note. The receipt of the note in exchange for the services is recorded as follows:

December 31, 1998

Notes Receivable	550,000	
Discount on Notes Receivable		131,761
Revenue from Services		418,239

An amortization schedule similar to the one shown on the following page is then prepared to help record transactions in future periods.

VALUATION OF NOTES RECEIVABLE

OBJECTIVE 8
Explain accounting issues related to valuation of notes receivable.

Like accounts receivable, short-term notes receivable are recorded and reported at their net realizable value; that is, at their face amount less all necessary allowances. The primary notes receivable allowance account is Allowance for Doubtful Accounts. The computations and estimations involved in valuing short-term notes receivable and recording bad debt expense and the related allowance are **exactly the same as for trade accounts**

SCHEDULE OF NOTE DISCOUNT AMORTIZATION
Effective Interest Method
2% Note Discounted at 8% (Imputed)

Date	Cash Interest (2%)	Effective Interest (8%)	Discount Amortized	Unamortized Discount Balance	Present Value of Note
12/31/98				$131,761	$418,239
12/31/99	$11,000ª	$33,459ᵇ	$22,459ᶜ	109,302ᵈ	440,698ᵉ
12/31/00	11,000	35,256	24,256	85,045	464,954
12/31/01	11,000	37,196	26,196	58,850	491,150
12/31/02	11,000	39,292	28,292	30,558	519,442
12/31/03	11,000	41,558ᶠ	30,558	–0–	550,000
	$55,000	$186,761	$131,761		

ª$550,000 × 2% = $11,000
ᵇ$418,239 × 8% = $33,459
ᶜ$33,459 − $11,000 = $22,459
ᵈ$131,761 − $22,459 = $109,302
ᵉ$418,239 − $22,459 = $440,689
ᶠ$3 adjustment to compensate for rounding

receivable. Either a percentage of sales revenue or an analysis of the receivables can be used to estimate the amount of uncollectibles.

Long-term notes receivable, however, pose additional estimation problems, as illustrated by the problems our financial institutions, most notably our largest banks, are having in collecting their receivables from energy and agricultural loans, and loans to less developed countries.

Notes receivable that are not paid at maturity remain notes receivable and are considered notes receivable past due. These defaulted or **dishonoured notes** should be separately classified on the balance sheet. If all efforts to collect fail, the note is written off as a loss.

A note receivable is considered **impaired** when it is probable that the creditor will be unable to collect all amounts due (both principal and interest) according to the contractual terms of the loan. In that case, the present value of the expected future cash flows is determined by discounting those flows at the historical effective rate. This present value amount is deducted from the carrying amount of the receivable to measure the loss. Impairments, as well as restructurings, of receivables and debts are discussed and illustrated in considerable detail in Appendix 15A.

DISCLOSURES OF RECEIVABLES

A new accounting standard applicable to the disclosure of receivables (financial instruments) became effective January 1, 1996. Firms are now required to disclose:

1. The criteria used to determine when to recognize a financial asset and when it should no longer be recognized;
2. The basis of measurement used; and
3. The basis on which related income and expense are recognized and measured.[11]

Such disclosure will include, when material, the method used in determining the allowance for doubtful accounts. In addition, when notes receivable have been initially recorded at present or fair values, the measurement basis will be disclosed.

[11] *CICA Handbook*, Section 3680, par. .48.

DISPOSITION OF ACCOUNTS RECEIVABLE

OBJECTIVE 9

Explain accounting issues related to disposition of accounts and notes receivable.

In the normal course of events, accounts receivable are collected when due and removed from the books. However, as credit sales and receivables have grown in size and significance, the "normal course of events" has evolved. **In order to accelerate the receipt of cash from receivables, the owner may transfer accounts or notes receivable to another company for cash.**

There are various reasons for this early transfer. First, for competitive reasons, providing sales financing for customers is virtually mandatory in many industries. In the sale of durable goods, such as automobiles, trucks, industrial and farm equipment, computers, and appliances, a large majority of the sales are on an instalment contract basis. Many major companies in these industries have therefore created wholly owned subsidiaries with responsibility for accounts receivable financing. General Motors of Canada Ltd. has its General Motors Acceptance Corp. of Canada (GMAC), Sears has its Sears Acceptance Corp., and Chrysler Corporation of Canada has its Chrysler Finance Corporation.

Second, the **holder** may sell receivables because money is tight and access to normal credit is not available, or prohibitively expensive. Also, a firm may have to sell its receivables, instead of borrowing to avoid violating existing lending agreements.

Finally, billing and collection are often time-consuming and costly. Credit card companies such as MasterCard, VISA, and others provide merchants with immediate cash.

Conversely, some **purchasers** of receivables buy them to obtain the legal protection of ownership rights afforded a purchaser of assets as opposed to the lesser rights afforded a secured creditor. In addition, banks and other lending institutions may be forced to purchase receivables because of legal lending limits; that is, they cannot make any additional loans but they can buy receivables and charge a fee for this service.

The transfer of accounts receivable to a third party for cash is generally accomplished in one of two ways:

1. Assignment of accounts receivable (pledging a security interest).
2. Sale (factoring) of accounts receivable.

ASSIGNMENT OF ACCOUNTS RECEIVABLE

The owner of the receivables (the assignor) borrows cash from a lender (the assignee) by writing a promissory note designating or **pledging** the accounts receivable as collateral. If the note is not paid when due, the assignee has the right to convert the collateral to cash, that is, to collect the receivables.

General Assignment. If the assignment is general, all the receivables serve as collateral for the note. New receivables can be substituted for the ones collected. To illustrate, Machlin Motor Company assigns its accounts receivable to First City Finance Company as collateral for a loan of $946,000. The entry to record this transaction is as follows:

Cash	946,000	
Notes Payable		946,000

No special entries are made to the receivable accounts to record the assignment. Information concerning the assigned receivables is disclosed in a note or in a parenthetical explanation. To illustrate, Methanex Corporation reported its general assignment in the following manner:

EXHIBIT 7-4   METHANEX CORPORATION

Note 7 (a)   The term bank loan bears interest at a certain bank's U.S. base rate plus $1\frac{1}{2}\%$ per annum, is repayable in quarterly instalments and is secured, together with the operating bank loan of the ammonia operations by a $70 million fixed and floating charge demand debenture on the ammonia plant and a general assignment of ammonia accounts receivable and inventory.

Specific Assignment. In a specific assignment, the borrower and lender enter into an agreement as to (1) who is to receive the collections; (2) the finance charges (which are in addition to the interest on the note); (3) the specific accounts that serve as security; and (4) notification or non-notification of account debtors. Collections on the assigned accounts are generally made by the assignor.

To illustrate, on March 1, 1998, Howat Mills Ltd. assigns $700,000 of its accounts receivable to the Royal Bank as collateral for a $500,000 note. Howat Mills will continue to collect the accounts receivable; the account debtors are not notified of the assignment. The Royal Bank assesses a finance charge of 1% of the accounts receivable assigned and interest on the note of 12%. Settlement by Howat Mills to the bank is made monthly for all cash collected on the assigned receivables.

ENTRIES FOR ASSIGNMENT OF SPECIFIC ACCOUNTS RECEIVABLE

Howat Mills Ltd.			Royal Bank		

Assignment of accounts receivable and issuance of note on March 1, 1998:

Cash	493,000		Notes Receivable	500,000	
Finance Charge	7,000*		Finance Revenue		7,000*
Accounts Receivable			Cash		493,000
Assigned	700,000				
Notes Payable		500,000			
Accounts Receivable		700,000			

*(1% × $700,000)

Collection in March of $440,000 of assigned accounts less cash discounts of $6,000. In addition sales returns of $14,000 were received:

Cash	434,000			
Sales Discounts	6,000			
Sales Returns	14,000		(No entry)	
Accounts Receivable				
Assigned		454,000		

($440,000 + $14,000 = $454,000)

Remitted March collections plus accrued interest to the bank on April 1:

Interest Expense	5,000*		Cash	439,000	
Notes Payable	434,000		Interest Revenue		5,000*
Cash		439,000	Notes Receivable		434,000

*($500,000 × .12 × 1/12)

Collection in April of the balance of assigned accounts less $2,000 written off as uncollectible:

Cash	244,000			
Allowance for				
Doubtful Accounts	2,000		(No entry)	
Accounts Receivable				
Assigned		246,000*		

*($700,000 − $454,000)

Remitted the balance due of $66,000 ($500,000–$434,000) on the note plus interest on May 1:

Interest Expense	660*		Cash	66,660	
Notes Payable	66,000		Interest Revenue		660*
Cash		66,660	Notes Receivable		66,000

*($66,000 × .12 × 1/12)

Receivables assigned are identified by recording them in an Assigned Accounts Receivable account. An alternative is to indicate in the notes to the financial statements the accounts receivable assigned. In addition to recording the collection of receivables, all discounts, returns and allowances, and bad debts must be recognized. Each month the proceeds from the collection of the assigned accounts receivable are used to retire the note obligation. In addition, interest on the note is paid.

If material, specifically assigned accounts receivable should be reported in Howat Mills' financial statements as a separate asset account. Its equity in the assigned accounts should be disclosed. For instance, Howat Mills, Ltd. has equity of $200,000 ($700,000–$500,000) in its assigned receivables at March 1.

Sales (Transfers) of Accounts Receivable. Sales of receivables have increased substantially in recent years. A common example is a sale to a factor. Factors are finance companies or banks that buy receivables from businesses for a fee and then collect the remittances directly from the customers. Factoring is traditionally associated with the textiles, apparel, footwear, furniture, and home furnishing industries.[12]

A recent phenomenon in the sale (transfer) of receivables is "securitization." Securitization takes a pool of assets such as credit card receivables, mortgage receivables, or car loan receivables and sells shares in these pools of interest and principal payments (in effect, creating securities backed by these pools of assets). Virtually every asset with a payment stream and a long-term payment history is a candidate for securitization.

The differences between factoring and securitization are that factoring usually involves sale to only one company, fees are high, the quality of the receivables is low, and the seller afterward does not service the receivable. In a securitization, many investors are involved, margins are tight, the receivables are of high quality, and the seller usually continues to service the receivable.

The diagram below illustrates a factoring arrangement.

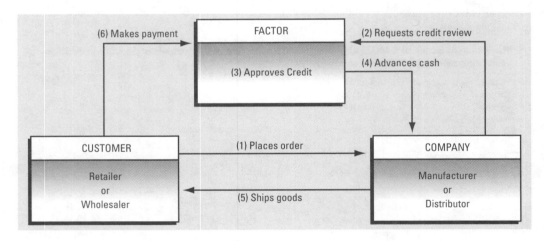

In either a factoring or a securitization transaction, receivables are sold on either a without recourse or with recourse basis.[13]

---

[12] Credit cards like MasterCard and VISA are a type of factoring arrangement. Typically the purchaser of the receivable charges a $3/4$% to $1^1/2$% commission of the receivables purchased (the commission is 4% to 5% for credit card factoring).

[13] **Recourse** is the right of a transferee of receivables to receive payment from the transfer of those receivables for (a) failure of the debtors to pay when due; (b) the effects of prepayments; or (c) adjustments resulting from defects in the eligibility of the transferred receivables. In EIC-9 the Emerging Issues Committee of the CICA points out the fact that there are degrees of recourse in transfers of receivables. It is necessary to assess the degree to which risks and rewards are transferred when accounting for transfer of receivables.

Transfer Without Recourse. When receivables are sold **without recourse,** the purchaser assumes the risk of collectibility and absorbs any credit losses. The transfer of accounts receivable in a nonrecourse transaction is an outright sale of receivables both in form (transfer of title) and substance (transfer of risk and reward). In nonrecourse transactions, as in any sale of assets, Cash is debited for the proceeds. Accounts Receivable is credited for the face value of the receivables. The difference, reduced by any provision for probable adjustments (discounts, returns, allowances, etc.), is recognized as a Loss on the Sale of Receivables. The seller uses a Due from Factor account (reported as a receivable) to account for the proceeds retained by the factor to cover the probable sales discounts, sales returns, and sales allowances.

To illustrate, Crest Textiles Ltd. factors $500,000 of accounts receivable with Commercial Factors Ltd. on a **without recourse** basis. The receivable records are transferred to Commercial Factors Ltd., which will receive the collections. Commercial Factors assesses a finance charge of 3% of the amount of accounts receivable and retains an amount equal to 5% of the accounts receivable. The journal entries for both Crest Textiles and Commercial Factors for the receivables transferred without recourse are as follows.

ENTRIES FOR SALE OF RECEIVABLES WITHOUT RECOURSE

Crest Textiles Ltd.			Commercial Factors Ltd.		
Cash	460,000		Accounts Receivable	500,000	
Due from Factor	25,000*		Due to Crest		25,000
Loss on Sale of Rec.	15,000**		Financing Revenue		15,000
Accounts Receivable		500,000	Cash		460,000

*(5% × $500,000)
**(3% × $500,000)

In recognition of the sale of receivables, Crest Textiles records a loss of $15,000. The factor's income will be the difference between the financing revenue of $15,000 and the amount of any uncollectible receivables.

A comprehensive illustration of all the entries involved in the sale, collection, and final settlement of these receivables for both Crest Textiles and Commercial Factors is presented in Appendix 7A.

Transfer With Recourse. If receivables are sold **with recourse,** the seller guarantees payment to the purchaser in the event the debtor fails to pay. With this method, many contend that a sale has not occurred because the transferor retains the same risk of collection after the deal as before. Others disagree, noting that most of the risks and benefits have transferred and therefore a sale should be recorded.

The question is: Is it a **sale transaction**, in which a gain or loss should be recognized immediately? Or, is the sale of receivables on a with recourse basis a **borrowing transaction**, in which the difference between the proceeds and the receivables is a financing cost (interest) that should be amortized over the term of the receivables?

A transfer of receivables with recourse should be accounted for and reported as a sale, and a gain or loss recognized, if both of the following conditions are met:[14]

1. The transferor has transferred the significant risks and rewards of ownership of the receivables.

2. The consideration received from the transfer may be measured with reasonable precision.

[14] CICA Emerging Issues Committee, *EIC-9 Transfer of Receivables*, p. 9-2.

If the transfer with recourse does not meet these conditions, the proceeds from the transfer of the receivables is accounted for as a borrowing. That is, instead of crediting receivables, a current liability entitled Liability on Transferred Accounts Receivable is credited. Regardless of the accounting method used to record the transaction, appropriate disclosure must be made of the company's continuing interest or involvement with the receivables transferred.[15]

The journal entries for Crest Textiles and Commercial Factors for the transfer of receivables **with recourse** both as a sale and as a borrowing are as follows.

ENTRIES BY CREST TEXTILES LTD. FOR RECEIVABLES TRANSFERRED WITH RECOURSE

Treated as a Sale by Crest			Treated as a Borrowing by Crest		
Cash	460,000		Cash	460,000	
Due from Factor	25,000 *		Due from Factor	25,000	
Loss on Sale of Receivable	15,000 **		Discount on Transferred Accounts Receivable	15,000	
Accounts Receivable		500,000	Liability on Transferred Accounts Receivable		500,000

*(5% × $500,000)
**(3% × $500,000)

Note two differences: First, when the transaction is classified as a borrowing, Crest Textiles recognizes a liability instead of crediting Accounts Receivable. Second, instead of recording a loss of $15,000 on the transfer, Crest Textiles records a discount under the borrowing of $15,000, which is amortized to interest expense over the borrowing period.

The rules for determining an acceptable practice for accounting for sales of receivables with and without recourse are illustrated below.

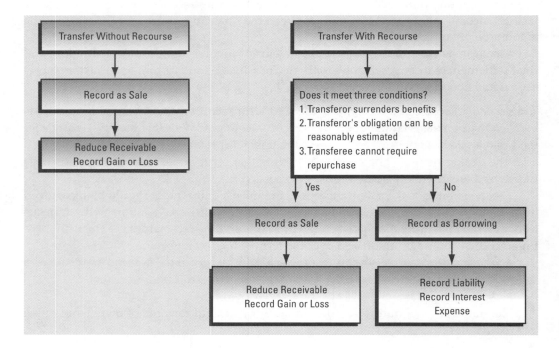

---

[15] *CICA Handbook*, Section 3860, par. .49.

A comprehensive illustration of all the entries involved in the sale, collection, and final settlement of these receivables for both Crest Textiles and Commercial Factors is presented in Appendix 7A.

CONCEPTUAL ISSUES RELATED TO THE TRANSFER OF RECEIVABLES

As indicated in the preceding discussion, the transfer of receivables to a third party for cash takes one of three forms:[16]

1. One form is to borrow from a third party and **assign or pledge the receivables** as collateral. Both the form of this transaction and its substance suggest that it be accounted for and reported as a **borrowing**.

2. A second form is to **transfer the receivables without recourse** to a third party in exchange for cash. Both the form of this transaction and its substance suggest that it be accounted for and reported as a **sale**.

3. A third form is to **transfer the receivables with recourse** to a third party in exchange for cash. In this case, the form of the transaction may be either a sale or a borrowing, depending on the facts.

At one extreme are outright sales of assets and at the other are borrowings collateralized by assets (pledges). In between are sales of assets with recourse. The transactions at the two extremes are easy to account for, but the ones in the middle create accounting problems.

Regarding the in-between situation, the authors believe that the proceeds from the transfer of receivables with recourse should be reported as a liability. The transfer should not be treated as a sale of the receivables unless and until both the future economic benefits embodied in the receivables and the related inherent risks of collectibility are transferred. The transferor's retention of credit risk through the recourse provisions generally leaves the transferor in a position indistinguishable from that of any other borrower.

BALANCE SHEET PRESENTATION OF ACCOUNTS AND NOTES RECEIVABLE

The general rules in classifying the typical transactions in the receivables section are: (1) Segregate the different receivables that an enterprise possesses, if material; (2) Ensure that the valuation accounts are appropriately offset against the proper receivable accounts; (3) Determine that receivables classified in the Current Asset section will be converted into cash within the year or the operating cycle, whichever is longer; (4) Disclose any loss contingencies that exist on the receivables; and (5) Disclose any receivables assigned or pledged as collateral.

The asset sections of Colton Corporation's balance sheet that follow illustrate many of the disclosures necessary for receivables.

---

[16] Understanding these transactions is made more difficult by the inconsistent use of terms to describe these transactions in practice. When you encounter such transactions in practice, we recommend that you attempt to classify them in accordance with their basic nature as one of the foregoing three types.

COLTON CORPORATION
Partial Balance Sheet
As of December 31, 1998

Current assets		
Cash and cash equivalent		$ 1,870,250
Accounts receivable (Note 2)	$8,977,673	
Less allowance for doubtful accounts[17]	500,226	
	8,477,447	
Advances to subsidiaries due 9/30/99	2,090,000	
Notes receivable—trade (Note 2)	1,532,000	
Dividends and interest receivable	75,500	
Federal income taxes refundable	146,704	
Other receivables and claims (including debit balances in accounts payable)	174,620	12,496,271
Total current assets		14,366,521
Noncurrent receivables		
Notes receivable from officers and key employees		376,090
Claims receivable (litigation settlement to be collected over four years)		585,000

Note 2: Accounts and notes receivable.

In November 1998, the Company arranged with a finance company to refinance a part of its indebtedness. The loan is evidenced by a 12% note payable. The note is payable on demand and is secured by substantially all the accounts receivable.

In May 1998, the Company entered into an agreement with a financial institution whereby the Company had the right to sell designated receivables, with recourse, not to exceed $3,000,000 at any time. During the period May 1 through September 20, 1998, proceeds totalling $2,480,000 were received from such sales. Losses totalling $202,640 were recognized on these sales during 1998. As of December 31, 1998, $171,500 of transferred receivables remains uncollected.

In several countries outside Canada, notes receivable are discounted with banks. The contingent liability under such arrangements amounted to $751,000 at December 31, 1998.

Summary of Learning Objectives

1. **Identify items considered cash.** To be reported as "cash," an asset must be readily available for the payment of current obligations, and it must be free from any contractual restrictions that limit its use in satisfying debts. Cash consists of coin, currency, and available funds on deposit at the bank. Negotiable instruments such as money orders, certified cheques, cashier's cheques, personal cheques, and bank drafts are also viewed as cash. Savings accounts are usually classified as cash.

2. **Explain common techniques employed to control cash.** The common techniques employed to control cash are: (1) Using bank accounts: A company can vary the number and location of banks and the types of accounts to obtain

---

[17] Although disclosure of the Allowance for Doubtful Accounts is not mandatory in Canada, some firms do so on a voluntary basis. *Financial Reporting in Canada*, 1995, indicates that about 10% of the sample firms choose to refer to the Allowance for Doubtful Accounts in their annual financial statements.

desired control objectives; (2) Electronic funds transfer (EFT): Electronic funds transfer uses wire, telephone, telegraph, computer, satellite, or other electronic device to make instanteous transfers of funds; (3) The imprest petty cash system: It may be impractical to require small amounts of various expenses to be paid by cheque, yet some control over them is important; (4) Physical protection of cash balances: Adequate control of receipts and disbursements is part of the protection of cash balances. Every effort should be made to minimize the cash on hand in the office; (5) Reconciliation of bank balances: Cash on deposit is not available for count and is proved by preparing a bank reconciliation.

3. **Indicate how cash and related items are reported.** Cash is reported as a current asset on the balance sheet. The reporting of other related items are: (1) Restricted cash: Legally restricted deposits held as compensating balances against short-term borrowing are usually reported separately among the "Cash and Cash Equivalent Items" in Current Assets. Restricted deposits held against long-term borrowing arrangements should be separately classified as noncurrent assets in either the Investments or Other Assets sections; (2) Bank overdrafts: They should be reported in the current liabilities section and are usually added to the amount reported as accounts payable. If material, these items should be separately disclosed either on the face of the balance sheet or in the related notes; (3) Cash equivalents: This item is often reported together with cash as "Cash and Cash Equivalents or With Temporary Investments."

4. **Define receivables and identify the different types of receivables.** Receivables are claims held against customers and others for money, goods, or services. The receivables are classified into three types: (1) current or noncurrent; (2) trade or nontrade; (3) accounts receivable or notes receivable.

5. **Explain accounting issues related to recognition of accounts receivable.** Two issues that may complicate the measurement of accounts receivable are: (1) The availability of discounts (trade and cash discounts); and (2) the length of time between the sale and the payment due dates (the interest element).

Ideally, receivables should be measured in terms of their present value—that is, the discounted value of the cash to be received in the future. Generally, accountants exclude from the present value considerations receivables that arise from normal business transactions and are due in customary trade terms within approximately one year.

6. **Explain accounting issues related to valuation of accounts receivable.** Short-term receivables are valued and reported at estimated net realizable value—the net amount expected to be received in cash, which is not necessarily the amount legally receivable. Determining net realizable value requires an estimation of both uncollectible receivables and any returns and allowances.

7. **Explain accounting issues related to recognition of notes receivable.** Short-term notes are recorded at face value. Long-term notes receivable are recorded at the present value of the cash expected to be collected. When the interest stated on an interest-bearing note is equal to the effective (market) rate of interest, the note sells at face value. When the stated rate is different from the effective rate, either a discount or premium is recorded.

8. **Explain accounting issues related to valuation of notes receivable.** Like accounts receivable, short-term notes receivable are recorded and reported at their estimated net realizable value. The same is also true of long-term receivables. Special issues relate to impairments and notes receivable past due.

9. **Explain accounting issues related to disposition of accounts and notes receivable.** To accelerate the receipt of cash from receivables, the owner may transfer the receivables to another company for cash. The transfer of receivables to a third party for cash may be accomplished in one of two ways: (1) Assignment of receivables: The owner of the receivables borrows cash from a lender by writing a promissory note pledging the receivables as collateral; (2) Sale (factoring) of receivables: Factors are finance companies or banks that buy receivables from businesses and then collect the remittances directly from the customers. Receivables are sold on either a with recourse or without recourse basis.

✱ what is "due from factor"?

APPENDIX 7A

Comprehensive Illustrations of Transfers of Receivables

In order to free the foregoing chapter from the complexities and details of recording all the journal entries related to the transfer, collection, and final settlement of transferred receivables, we have presented the journal entries in this appendix. The first illustration below is for the transfer of receivables **without recourse** and the second illustration is for the transfer of receivables with recourse, first as a **sale** transaction, and second as a **borrowing** transaction.

TRANSFER OF RECEIVABLES WITHOUT RECOURSE

Crest Textiles Ltd. factors $500,000 of accounts receivable with Commercial Factors Ltd., on a **without recourse** basis. On May 1, the receivable records are transferred to Commercial Factors Ltd., which will receive the collections. Commercial Factors assesses a finance charge of 3% and retains an amount equal to 5% of the accounts receivable. Crest Textiles handles returned goods, claims for defective goods (allowances), and disputes concerning shipments. Crest has not recorded any bad debts expense relative to these receivables. In the process of collecting the cash, Commercial Factors acknowledges sales discounts but charges the cost of such discounts to Crest Textiles by debiting the Due to Crest Textiles account. Credit losses (uncollectible accounts) are absorbed by Commercial Factors, and on the basis of an analysis of the accounts purchased, Commercial Factors allows $4,100 for uncollectible accounts.

OBJECTIVE 10
Prepare entries for the transfer of receivables with and without recourse in a complex situation.

ENTRIES FOR FACTORED RECEIVABLES WITHOUT RECOURSE

Crest Textiles, Ltd.			Commercial Factors, Ltd.		
Sale of accounts receivable without recourse on May 1:					
Cash	460,000		Accounts Receivable	500,000	
Due from Factor	25,000*		Due to Crest Textiles		25,000
Loss on Sale of .			Financing Revenue		15,000
Receivables	15,000**		Cash		460,000
Accounts Receivable		500,000	Bad Debt Expense	4,100	
			Allowance. for Doubtful		
			Accounts		4,100

*(5% × $500,000)
**(3% × $500,000)

(Continued)

ENTRIES FOR FACTORED RECEIVABLES WITHOUT RECOURSE (*Continued*)

Crest Textiles, Ltd.			Commercial Factors, Ltd.		

Transactions in May and June: Collections of $483,800 by factor; sales returns and allowances of $9,500; sales discounts taken of $2,600; and uncollectibles of $4,100 are written off by the factor.

Sales Returns and			Cash	483,800	
Allowances	9,500		Due to Crest Textiles	12,100	
Sales Discounts	2,600		Accounts Receivable		495,900
Due from Factor		12,100	Allowance for Doubtful		
			Accounts	4,100	
			Accounts Receivable		4,100

Final settlement between Crest Textiles and Commercial Factors:

Cash	12,900		Due to Crest Textiles	12,900	
Due from Factor		12,900	Cash		12,900
($25,000 − $9,500 − $2,600)					

Note from the entries above that the factor's income is the difference between the financing revenue of $15,000 and the bad debt expense of $4,100. As indicated earlier, in a without recourse transfer of receivables, the factor absorbs the loss from uncollectibles. Crest Textiles absorbs the cost of sales discounts and sales returns and allowances.

TRANSFER OF RECEIVABLES WITH RECOURSE

To illustrate the differences between the two methods of accounting for a transfer of receivables with recourse—in one case a sale, and in another case a borrowing—the same data previously used in the Crest Textiles/Commercials Factors illustration will be used. (We have chosen to use the same data for purposes of comparability even though the situations in real life would dictate different rates, risks, etc.) One different piece of information is Crest's estimate that $4,100 of the accounts transferred to Commercial Factors will not be paid by the debtors.

The entries for both a sale and a borrowing by Crest Textiles follow. First, however, note that in the borrowing with recourse example, Crest Textiles credited a liability on May 1 instead of crediting Accounts Receivable. Second, in both with recourse cases Crest Textiles reimburses the factor for the $4,100 of uncollectible accounts and records the bad debt expense on its books, whereas in the without recourse illustration above, Commercial Factors absorbed the loss due to uncollectibility. However, because accounts receivable are removed from the books when the transfer is treated as a sale, it is meaningless to credit an allowance account when recognizing the bad debt expense. Therefore, Crest immediately credited Due from Factor for the $4,100, thereby crediting the factor for the bad debts anticipated. Third, Crest recognized interest expense of $15,000 over the two months the receivables were outstanding (borrowing situation) instead of recording the loss on sale of $15,000 at May 1.

CREST TEXTILES, INC.
Entries for Factored Receivables With Recourse

Treated as a **Sale** by Crest			Treated as a **Borrowing** by Crest		

Transfer of accounts receivable on May 1:

Cash	460,000		Cash	460,000	
Due from Factor	25,000*		Due from Factor	25,000*	
Loss on Sale of			Discount on Transferred		
Receivables	15,000**		Accounts Receivable	15,000**	
Accounts Receivable		500,000	Liability on Transferred		
			Accounts Receivable		500,000

    *(5% × $500,000)
    **(3% × $500,000)

Recognition of doubtful accounts on May 1:

Bad Debt Expense	4,100		Bad Debt Expense	4,100	
Due from Factor		4,100	Allowance for Doubtful		
			Accounts		4,100

Transactions in May and June: Collections of $483,800 by the factor; sales returns and allowances of $9,500; sales discounts taken of $2,600; and uncollectibles of $4,100 materialize:

Sales Returns and			(Same entry)		
Allowances	9,500				
Sales Discounts	2,600				
Due from Factor		12,100			
			Allowance for Doubtful		
			Accounts	4,100	
			Due from Factor		4,100
			Liability on Transferred		
			Accounts Receivable	500,000	
			Accounts Receivable		500,000
			($483,800 + $9,500 + $2,600 + $4,100)		
			Interest Expense	15,000	
			Discount on Trans-		
			ferred Accounts Rec.		15,000

Final settlement between Crest Textiles and the factor:

Cash	8,800		(Same entry)		
Due from Factor		8,800*			

*($25,000 − $9,500 − $2,600 − $4,100)

**Summary of Learning Objective
for Appendix 7A**

10. **Prepare entries for the transfer of receivables with and without recourse in a complex situation.** These factoring transactions are complicated by the inclusion of finance charges, retainers for returns and allowances, and bad debts. Transfers of receivables with recourse may, under differing conditions, be treated as sales or as borrowings.

Note: All *asterisked* exercises, problems, or cases relate to material contained in the appendix to the chapter.

EXERCISES

E7-1   (Determining Cash Balance)   The controller for AMC Co. Ltd. is attempting to determine the amount of cash to be reported on its December 31, 1998 balance sheet. The following information is provided:

cash
1. A commercial savings account of $1,000,000 and a commercial chequing account balance of $600,000 are held at First Canada Trust.

cash
2. A special savings account held at Corporate Credit Union (a savings and loan organization) permits AMC to write cheques on the $6,000,000 balance.

receivable
3. Travel advances total of $180,000 for executive travel for the first quarter of next year (employee to reimburse through salary reduction).

other or L/T
cash
4. Cash is restricted in the amount of $1,500,000 for the retirement of long-term debt.

5. Petty cash fund is $1,000.

A/R from officer
6. An I.O.U. in the amount of $190,000 is from David Carrol, a company officer.

current Liab
7. A bank overdraft of $110,000 has occurred at one of the banks the company uses to deposit its cash receipts. At the present time, the company has no deposits at this bank.

Temp Inv
8. The company has two certificates of deposit, each totalling $500,000. These certificates of deposit have a maturity of 120 days.

A/R
9. AMC has received a cheque that is dated January 12, 1999 in the amount of $125,000.

other asset
10. AMC has agreed to maintain a cash balance of $500,000 at all times at the First Canada Bank to ensure future credit availability.

Temp Inv
11. AMC has purchased $2,100,000 of commercial paper of Hector Santos Co. Ltd., which is due in 60 days.

cash
12. Currency and coin on hand amount to $5,300.

Instructions
(a) Compute the amount of cash to be reported on AMC Co. Ltd.'s balance sheet at December 31, 1998.
(b) Indicate the proper reporting for items that are not reported as cash on the December 31, 1998 balance sheet.

E7-2   (Determine Cash Balance)   Presented below are a number of independent situations. For each individual situation, determine the amount that should be reported as cash. If the item(s) are not reported as cash, explain the rationale.

1. Chequing account balance $950,000; certificate of deposit $1,400,000; cash advance to subsidiary $980,000; utility deposit paid to gas company $180.

2. Chequing account balance $600,000; an overdraft of $10,000 in a special chequing account at same bank as the normal chequing account; cash of $200,000 held in a bond sinking fund; petty fund $300; coins and currency on hand $1,350.

3. Chequing account balance $600,000; postdated cheque from customer $11,000; cash restricted due to maintaining compensating balance requirement $100,000; certified cheque from customer $9,800; postage stamps on hand $620.

4. Chequing account balance at bank $35,000; balance at Royal Trust (has chequing privileges) $48,000; NSF cheque received from customer $800.

5. Chequing account balance $800,000; cash restricted for future plant expansion $500,000; short-term treasury bills $180,000; cash advance received from customer $900 (not included in chequing account balance); cash advance of $7,000 to company executive, payable on demand; refundable deposit of $26,000 paid to federal government to guarantee performance on construction contract.

E7-3   (Petty Cash)   Alvarez Ltd. decided to establish a petty cash fund to help ensure internal control over its small cash expenditures. The following information is available for the month of April.

1. On April 1, it established a petty cash fund in the amount of $200.00
2. A summary of the petty cash expenditures made by the petty cash custodian as of April 10 is as follows:

Delivery charges paid on merchandise purchased	$70.00
Supplies purchased and used	15.00
Postage expense	33.00
I.O.U. from employee	17.00
Miscellaneous expense	36.00

The petty cash fund was replenished on April 10. The balance in the fund was $27.

3. The petty cash fund balance was increased $50.00 to $250.00 on April 20.

Instructions

Prepare the journal entries to record transactions related to petty cash for the month of April.

(Petty Cash) The petty cash fund of Montgomery's Auto Repair Service, a sole proprietorship, contains the following: **E7-4**

1. Coins and currency		$ 15.20
2. Postage stamps		2.90
3. An I.O.U. for a cash advance from Felicity La Fortune, an employee		40.00
4. Cheque payable to Montgomery's Auto Repair from		
B. Dharan, an employee, marked NSF		34.00
5. Vouchers for the following:		
Stamps	$20.00	
Two Grey Cup tickets for Laurel Montgomery	70.00	
Typewriter repairs	14.35	104.35
		$196.45

The general ledger account Petty Cash has a balance of $200.00.

Instructions

Prepare the journal entry to record the reimbursement of the petty cash fund.

(Bank Reconciliation and Adjusting Entries) Acadian Limited deposits all receipts and makes all payments by   **E7-5**
cheque. The following information is available from the cash records.

June 30 Bank Reconciliation

Balance per bank	$7,000
Add: Deposits in transit	1,540
Deduct: Outstanding cheques	(2,000)
Balance per books	$6,540

Month of July Results

	Per Bank	Per Books
Balance July 31	$8,550	$9,150
July deposits	5,000	5,710
July cheques	4,100	3,100
July notes collected (not included in July deposits)	900	-0-
July bank service charge	15	-0-
July NSF cheque of a customer returned by the bank		
(recorded by bank as a charge)	235	-0-

Instructions

(a) Prepare a bank reconciliation, working from balance per bank and balance per book to corrected Cash account.

(b) Prepare the general journal entry to correct the Cash account.

(Bank Reconciliation and Adjusting Entries) Mary Lowe Inc. has just received the August 31, 1998 bank state-   **E7-6**
ment, which is summarized below:

Toronto Dominion Bank	Disbursements	Receipts	Balance
Balance, August 1			$ 9,369
Deposits during August		$32,000	41,369
Note collected for depositor, including			
$36 interest		1,036	42,405
Cheques cleared during August	$34,400		8,005
Bank service charges	25		7,980
Balance, August 31			7,980

The general ledger Cash account contained the following entries for the month of August:

Cash

Balance, August 1	10,050	Disbursements in August	34,903
Receipts during August	35,000		

Deposits in transit at August 31 are $4,000 and cheques outstanding at August 31 are determined to total $1,150. Cash on hand at August 31 is $310. The bookkeeper improperly entered one cheque for supply expense in the books at $146.50, which should have been entered as $164.50; the cheque cleared the bank during the month of August.

Instructions

(a) Prepare a bank reconciliation dated August 31, 1998, proceeding to a corrected balance.

(b) Prepare any entries necessary to make the books correct and complete.

(c) What amount of cash should be reported in the August 31 balance sheet?

E7-7 **(Financial Statement Presentation of Receivables)** Price Limited shows a balance of $181,140 in the Accounts Receivable account on December 31, 1998. The balance consists of the following:

Instalment accounts due in 1999	$23,000
Instalment accounts due after 1999	24,000
Overpayment to creditors	2,640
Due from regular customers, of which $40,000 represents accounts pledged as security for a bank loan	79,000
Advances to employees	1,500
Advance to subsidiary company (made in 1993)	51,000

Instructions

Illustrate how the information above should be shown on the balance sheet of Price Limited on December 31, 1998.

E7-8 **(Determine Ending Accounts Receivable)** Your accounts receivable clerk, Mr. Bala Bautista, to whom you pay a salary of $1,100 per month, has just purchased a new Cadillac. You decided to test the accuracy of the accounts receivable balance of $82,000 as shown in the ledger.

The following information is available for your **first year** in business:

1. Collections from customers	$198,000
2. Merchandise purchased	310,000
3. Ending merchandise inventory	90,000
4. Goods are marked to sell at 40% above cost	

Instructions

Compute an estimate of the ending balance of accounts receivable from customers that should appear in the ledger, and any apparent shortages. Assume that all sales are made on account.

E7-9 **(Record Sales Gross and Net)** On June 3, Igneous Co. Ltd. sold to Opal Taylorson merchandise having a sale price of $2,000 with terms of 2/10, n/60, f.o.b. shipping point. An invoice totalling $90, terms n/30, was received by Opal on June 8 from the Obsidian Transport Service for the freight cost. On receipt of the goods, June 5, Opal notified Igneous Co. Ltd. that merchandise costing $400 contained flaws that rendered it worthless; the same day Igneous Co. Ltd. issued a credit memo covering the worthless merchandise and asked that it be returned at company expense. The freight on the returned merchandise was $25, paid by Igneous Co. Ltd. on June 7. On June 12, the company received a cheque for the balance due from Opal Taylorson.

Instructions

(a) Prepare journal entries on Igneous Co. Ltd.'s books to record all the events noted above on the following bases:

　1. Sales and receivables are entered at gross selling price.

　2. Sales and receivables are entered at net of cash discounts.

(b) Prepare the journal entry under Basis 2, assuming that Opal Taylorson did not remit payment until July 29.

(**Computing Bad Debts**) At January 1, 1998, the credit balance in the Allowance for Doubtful Accounts of the   **E7-10**
Sunchi Company Ltd. was $400,000. For 1998, the provision for doubtful accounts is based on a percentage of net
sales. Net sales for 1998 were $70,000,000. On the basis of the latest available facts, the 1998 provision for doubtful
accounts is estimated to be 0.7% of net sales. During 1998, uncollectible receivables amounting to $490,000 were
written off against the allowance for doubtful accounts.

Instructions
Prepare a schedule computing the balance in Sunchi's Allowance for Doubtful Accounts at December 31, 1998.

(**Computing Bad Debts and Preparing Journal Entries**) The trial balance before adjustment of Reuben Welsch   **E7-11**
Enterprises shows the following balances:

	Dr.	Cr.
Accounts Receivable	$90,000	
Allowance for Doubtful Accounts	1,750	
Sales (all on credit)		$680,000
Sales Returns and Allowances	30,000	

Instructions
Give the entry for estimated bad debts for the current year assuming that the allowance is to provide for doubtful
accounts on the bases of (a) 4% of gross accounts receivable; and (b) 3% of net sales.

(**Bad Debt Reporting**) The chief accountant for R. Adams Corporation Ltd. provides you with the following list of   **E7-12**
accounts receivable written off in the current year.

Date	Customer	Amount
Mar. 31	Creative Constitution	$7,800
June 30	Hamilton Associates	6,700
Sept. 30	Dianne's Dress Shop	7,000
Dec. 31	Frontier Corporation Ltd	8,730

    R. Adams Corporation Ltd. follows the policy of debiting Bad Debt Expense as accounts are written off. The
chief accountant maintains that this procedure is appropriate for financial statement purposes.
    All of R. Adams Corporation Ltd.'s sales are on a 30-day credit basis. Sales for the current year total $2,100,000
and research has determined that bad debt losses approximate 2% of sales.

Instructions
(a) Do you agree or disagree with Adams' policy concerning recognition of bad debt expense? Why or why not?
(b) By what amount would net income differ if bad debt expense were computed using the percentage-of-sales
    approach?

(**Bad Debts—Aging**) Amy Liu Inc. includes the following account among its trade receivables.   **E7-13**

Avery Brooks

1/1	Balance forward	700	1/28	Cash (#1710)	1,100
1/20	Invoice #1710	1,100	4/2	Cash (#2116)	1,350
3/14	Invoice #2116	1,350	4/10	Cash	150
4/12	Invoice #2412	1,680	4/30	Cash (#2412)	1,000
9/5	Invoice #3614	490	9/20	Cash (#3614 and	
10/17	Invoice #4912	860		part of #2412)	790
11/18	Invoice #5681	2,000	10/31	Cash (#4912)	860
12/20	Invoice #6347	800	12/1	Cash (#5681)	1,200
			12/29	Cash (#6347)	800

Instructions
Age the balance and specify any items that apparently require particular attention.

E7-14   **(Journalizing Various Receivable Transactions)** Presented below is information related to Melonson Inc.

> July 1   Melonson Inc. sells to Hamilton Co. Ltd. merchandise having a sales price of $7,000 with terms 2/10, net/60. Melonson records its sales and receivables net.
>
> July 3   Hamilton Co. Ltd. returns defective merchandise having a sales price of $700.
>
> July 5   Accounts receivable of $9,000 are factored with Collazo Credit Corp. without recourse at a financing charge of 10%. Cash is received for the proceeds; collections are handled by the finance company. (These accounts are all past the discount period.)
>
> July 9   Specific accounts receivable of $9,000 (gross) are assigned to Monteiro Credit as security for a loan of $6,000 at a finance charge of 6% of the amount of the loan. The finance company will make the collections. (All the accounts receivable are past the discount period.)
>
> Dec. 29   Hamilton Co. Ltd. notifies Melonson that it is bankrupt and will pay only 10% of its account. Give the entry to write off the uncollectible balance using the allowance method. (Note: First record the increase in the receivable on July 11 when the discount period has passed.)

Instructions
Prepare all necessary entries in general journal form for Melonson Inc.

E7-15   **(Assigned Accounts Receivable)** Presented below is information related to Monroe Inc.

1. Customers' accounts in the amount of $40,000 are assigned to the Clark Finance Company as security for a loan of $30,000. The finance charge is 3% of the amount borrowed.
2. Cash collections on assigned accounts amount to $17,000.
3. Collections on assigned accounts to date, plus a $400 cheque for interest on the loan, are forwarded to Clark Finance Company.
4. Additional collections on assigned accounts amount to $16,200.
5. The loan is paid in full plus additional interest of $150.
6. Uncollected balances of the assigned accounts are returned to the regular customers' ledger.

Instructions
Prepare entries in journal form for Monroe Inc.

E7-16   **(Journalizing Various Receivable Transactions)** The trial balance before adjustment for Jackson Company Inc. shows the following balances:

	Dr.	Cr.
Accounts Receivable	$82,000	
Allowance for Doubtful Accounts	2,120	
Sales		$430,000
Sales Returns and Allowances	7,600	

Instructions
Using the data above, give the journal entries required to record each of the following cases (each situation is independent):

1. To obtain additional cash, Jackson factors, without recourse, $24,000 of accounts receivable with Hickory Finance. The finance charge is 10% of the amount factored.
2. To obtain a one-year loan of $54,000, Jackson assigns $65,000 of specific receivable accounts to Manitoba Financial. The finance charge is 8% of the loan; the cash is received and the accounts turned over to Manitoba Financial.
3. The company wants to maintain the Allowance for Doubtful Accounts at 4% of gross accounts receivable.
4. The company wishes to increase the allowance by 1½% of net sales.

E7-17   **(Transfer of Receivables With Recourse)** Mountain View Inc. factors receivables with a carrying amount of $187,000 to Ortega Company for $150,000 on a with recourse basis.

Instructions
(a) Assuming that this transaction should be reported as a sale, prepare the appropriate journal entry.
(b) Assuming that this transaction should be reported as a borrowing, prepare the appropriate journal entry.

(Transfer of Receivables With Recourse) William Brown Inc. factors $150,000 of accounts receivable with Harrison   **E7-18**
Financing Inc. on a with recourse basis. Harrison Financing will collect the receivables. The receivables records are
transferred to Harrison Financing on August 15, 1998. Harrison Financing assesses a finance charge of 2% of the
amount of accounts receivable and also reserves an amount equal to 4% of accounts receivable to cover probable
adjustments.

Instructions
(a) What conditions must be met for a transfer of receivables with recourse to be accounted for as a sale?
(b) Assume the conditions from Part (a) are met. Prepare the journal entry on August 15, 1998 for Tillis to record the
sale of receivables.
(c) Assume that not all conditions from Part (a) are met. Prepare the journal entry on August 15, 1994 for Brown to
record the transfer of receivables.

(Transfer of Receivables Without Recourse) Tyler Inc. factors $250,000 of accounts receivable with Tippecanoe   **E7-19**
Finance Corporation on a without recourse basis. On July 1, 1998, the receivable records are transferred to
Tippecanoe Finance, which will receive the collections. Tippecanoe Finance assesses a finance charge of 1½% of the
amount of accounts receivable and retains an amount equal to 4% of accounts receivable to cover sales discounts,
returns, and allowances.

Instructions
(a) Prepare the journal entry on July 1, 1998, for Tyler Inc. to record the sale of receivables without recourse.
(b) Prepare the journal entry on July 1, 1998, for Tippecanoe Finance Corporation to record the purchase of receivables without recourse.

(Note Transactions at Unrealistic Interest Rates) On July 1, 1998, Roger Taylor Company Ltd. made two sales: **E7-20**
1. It sold land having a fair market value of $700,000 in exchange for a four-year noninterest-bearing promissory
note in the face amount of $1,101,460. The land is carried on Roger Taylor Company Ltd.'s books at a cost of
$620,000.
2. It rendered services in exchange for a 3%, eight-year promissory note having a maturity value of $300,000 (inter-
est payable annually).

Roger Taylor Company Ltd. recently had to pay 8% interest for money that it borrowed from Eastern National
Bank. The customers in these two transactions have credit ratings that require them to borrow money at 12% interest.

Instructions
Record the two journal entries that should be recorded by Roger Taylor Company Ltd. for the sales transactions
above that took place on July 1, 1998.

(Note Receivable at Unrealistic Interest Rates) On December 31, 1998, Filmore Company Ltd. sold some of its   **E7-21**
product to Millard Inc., accepting a $340,000 noninterest-bearing note receivable in full on December 31, 2001.
Filmore Company Ltd. enjoys a high credit rating and, therefore, borrows funds from its several lines of credit at 9%.
Millard Inc., however, pays 12% for its borrowed funds. The product sold is carried on the books of Filmore
Company Ltd. based on a manufactured cost of $190,000. Assume that the effective interest method is used for dis-
count amortization.

Instructions
(a) Prepare the journal entry to record the sale on December 31, 1998 by the Filmore Company Ltd. Assume that a
perpetual inventory system is used.
(b) Prepare the journal entries on the books of Filmore Company Ltd. for the year 1999 that are necessitated by the
sales transaction of December 31, 1998. Preparation of an amortization schedule may be of assistance.
(c) Prepare the journal entries on the books of Filmore Company Ltd. for the year 2000 that are necessitated by the
sale on December 31, 1998.

PROBLEMS

P7-1 Presented below are five independent situations:

1. The bank reconciliation for April 1998 of Norco Ltd. was as follows:

Balance per bank statement 4/30/98	$80,000
Add deposits in transit	6,000
	86,000
Less outstanding cheques	15,000
Balance per books 4/30/98	$71,000

During May 1998, the bank recorded $74,000 of cash receipts and $31,900 of cash disbursements. All deposits in transit and outstanding cheques from April cleared the bank in May. Outstanding cheques at May 31, 1998 totalled $13,300. Determine the cash balance per books as of May 31, 1998.

2. Caruso Enterprises owns the following assets at December 31, 1998.

Cash in bank—savings account	$82,000
Cash on hand	9,300
Cash refund due from Revenue Canada	31,400
Chequing account balance	17,000
Postdated cheques	750
Certificates of deposit (180 day)	90,000

What amount should be reported as cash?

3. The June 30 bank reconciliation of Joan Owens Inc. indicated that deposits in transit totalled $475. During July the general ledger account Cash in Bank showed deposits of $15,250, but the bank statement indicated that only $15,100 in deposits were received during the month. What were the deposits in transit at July 31?

4. In September, cash disbursements per books for Sipowiez Co. Ltd. were $22,900, cheques clearing the bank were $24,000, and outstanding cheques at September 30 were $2,000. What were the outstanding cheques at August 31?

5. Medavoy Corporation Ltd. on July 1, 1998 obtained a $4,000,000, six-month loan at an annual rate of 11% from the Royal Bank. As part of the loan agreement, Medavoy was required to maintain a $500,000 compensating balance in a chequing account at the Royal Bank. Normally Medavoy would maintain a balance of only $200,000 in this chequing account. The chequing account pays 5% interest. Determine the effective interest rate paid by Medavoy for this loan.

Instructions
Answer the questions relating to each of the five independent situations as requested.

P7-2 Bob King Inc. closes its books regularly on December 31, but at the end of 1998 it held its cash book open so that a more favourable balance sheet could be prepared for credit purposes. Cash receipts and disbursements for the first 10 days of January were recorded as December transactions. The following information is given:

1. January cash receipts recorded in the December cash book totalled $38,640, of which $21,000 represented cash sales and $17,640 represented collections on account for which cash discounts of $360 were given.

2. January cash disbursements recorded in the December cheque register liquidated accounts payable of $26,450 on which discounts of $159 were taken.

3. The ledger has not been closed for 1998.

4. The amount shown as inventory was determined by physical count on December 31, 1998.

Instructions
(a) Prepare any entries you consider necessary to correct King's accounts at December 31.

(b) To what extent was Bob King Inc. able to show a more favourable balance sheet at December 31 by holding its cash book open? Assume that the balance sheet that was prepared by the company showed the following amounts:

	Dr.	Cr.
Cash	$39,000	
Receivables	42,000	
Inventories	67,000	
Accounts payable		$45,000
Other current liabilities		14,200

The cash account of Dr. Jackson Ltd. showed a ledger balance of $5,588.35 on June 30, 1998. The bank statement as of that date showed a balance of $3,950.00. On comparing the statement with the cash records, the following facts were determined: **P7-3**

(a) Bank service charges for June were $25.00.

(b) A bank memo stated that Trudy Fisher's note for $800.00 and interest of $36.00 had been collected on June 29, and the bank had made a charge of $5.50 on the collection. (No entry had been made on Jackson's books when Fisher's note was sent to the bank for collection.)

(c) Receipts for June 30 of $2,890.00 were not deposited until July 2.

(d) Cheques outstanding on June 30 totalled $1,936.05.

(e) The bank had charged Jackson Ltd.'s account for a customer's uncollectible cheque for $453.20 on June 29.

(f) A 60-day, 6%, $1,500.00 customer's note dated April 25 and discounted by Jackson on June 12 remained unpaid by the customer on the due date. On June 28, the bank charged Jackson for $1,518.50, which included a protest fee of $3.50. (Jackson disclosed discounted notes receivable by use of a note to the financial statements.)

(g) A customer's cheque for $90.00 had been entered as $60.00 in the cash receipts journal by Jackson on June 15.

(h) Cheque 742 in the amount of $491.00 had been entered in the cashbook as $419.00, and Cheque 747 in the amount of $58.20 had been entered as $582.00. Both cheques had been issued to pay for purchases of equipment.

Instructions

(a) Prepare a bank reconciliation dated June 30, 1998 and proceed to a corrected cash balance.

(b) Prepare any entries necessary to make the books correct and complete.

Presented below is information related to Douglas Inc. **P7-4**

1. Balance per books at October 31: $41,847.85.
2. Receipts: $173,523.91.
3. Disbursements: $166,193.54.
4. Balance per bank statement dated November 30: $56,274.20.

The following cheque numbers were outstanding at November 30:

1224	$1,635.29
1230	2,468.30
1232	3,625.15
1233	482.17

Included with the November bank statement and not recorded by the company were a bank debit ticket for $27.40 that covered bank charges for the month, a debit ticket for $372.13 for a customer's NSF cheque that was returned, and a credit ticket for $1,200 that represented bond interest collected by the bank in the name of Douglas Inc. Cash on hand at November 30 recorded and awaiting deposit amounted to $1,915.40.

Instructions

(a) Prepare a bank reconciliation (bank balance to book balance) at November 30, 1998 for Douglas Inc. from the above information.

(b) Prepare any journal entries required to adjust the Cash account at November 30.

Presented below is information related to Clarissa Industries. **P7-5**

CLARISSA INDUSTRIES
Bank Reconciliation
May 31, 1998

Balance per bank statement		$30,928.46
Less outstanding cheques:		
6124	$2,125.00	
6138	932.65	
6139	960.57	
6140	1,420.00	5,438.22
		25,490.24
Add deposit in transit		4,710.56
Balance per books (correct balance)		$30,200.80

(Continued)

CLARISSA INDUSTRIES
Bank Reconciliation (*Continued*)
Cheque Register—June

Date	Payee	No.	V. Pay	Discount	Cash
June 1	Renn Mfg.	6141	$ 237.50		$ 237.50
1	Stimph Mfg.	6142	915.00	$ 9.15	905.85
8	Royal Supply Co. Inc.	6143	122.90	2.45	120.45
9	Renn Mfg.	6144	306.40		306.40
10	Petty Cash	6145	89.93		89.93
17	Muppet Babies Photo	6146	706.00	14.12	691.88
22	Hey Dude Publishing	6147	447.50		447.50
23	Payroll Account	6148	4,130.00		4,130.00
25	Dragnet Tools Inc.	6149	390.75	3.91	386.84
28	Shackleton Insurance Agency	6150	1,050.00		1,050.00
28	Get Smart Construction	6151	2,250.00		2,250.00
29	MMT, Inc.	6152	750.00		750.00
30	Lassie Co.	6153	295.25	5.90	289.35
			$11,691.23	$35.53	$11,655.70

Statement
Bank of Montreal
General Chequing Account of Clarissa Industries—June 1998

Debits			Date	Credits	Balance
					$30,928.46
$2,125.00	$ 237.50	$ 905.85	June 1	$4,710.56	32,370.67
932.65	120.45		12	1,507.06	32,824.63
1,420.00	447.50	306.40	23	1,458.55	32,109.28
4,130.00		11.05 (SC)	26		27,968.23
89.93	2,250.00	1,050.00	28	4,157.48	28,735.78

Cash received June 29 and 30 and deposited in the mail for the general chequing account June 30 amounted to $4,407.96. Because the cash account balance at June 30 is not given, it must be calculated from other information in the problem.

Instructions
From the information above, prepare a bank reconciliation (to the correct balance) as of June 30, 1998 for Clarissa Industries.

P7-6 (**Bad Debt Reporting**) Presented below are a series of unrelated situations.

1. Scott Limited's unadjusted trial balance at December 31, 1998 includes the following accounts:

	Debit	Credit
Allowance for doubtful accounts	$ 4,000	
Sales		$1,500,000
Sales returns and allowances	100,000	

Scott Limited estimates its annual bad debt expense to be 1½% of net sales. Determine its bad debt expense for 1998.

2. An analysis and aging of Kevin Limited accounts receivable at December 31, 1998 discloses the following:

Amounts estimated to be uncollectible	$ 180,000
Accounts receivable	1,700,000
Allowance for doubtful accounts (per books)	125,000

What is the net realizable value of Kevin's receivables at December 31, 1998?

3. Cameron Ltd. provides for doubtful accounts based on 3% of credit sales. The following data are available for 1998:

Credit sales during 1998	$2,100,000
Allowance for doubtful accounts 1/1/98	17,000
Collection of accounts written off in prior years (customer credit was re-established)	9,000
Customer accounts written off as uncollectible during 1998	30,000

What is the balance in the Allowance for Doubtful Accounts at December 31, 1998?

4. At the end of its first year of operations, December 31, 1998, Megan Limited reports the following information:

Accounts receivable, net of allowance for doubtful accounts	$950,000
Customer accounts written off as uncollectible during 1998	24,000
Bad debt expense for 1998	74,000

What should be the balance in accounts receivable at December 31, 1998 before subtracting the allowance for doubtful accounts?

5. The following accounts are taken from Lauren Limited's balance sheet at December 31, 1998:

	Debit	Credit
Net credit sales		$750,000
Allowance for doubtful accounts	$ 16,000	
Accounts receivable	410,000	

If doubtful accounts are 3% of accounts receivable, determine the bad debt expense to be reported for 1998.

Instructions

Answer the questions relating to each of the five independent situations as requested.

P7-7

Rachelle Limited operates in an industry that has a high rate of bad debts. On December 31, 1998, before any year-end adjustments, the balance in Rachelle's Accounts Receivable account was $555,000 and the Allowance for Doubtful Accounts had a balance of $35,000. The year-end balance reported in the statement of financial position for the Allowance for Doubtful Accounts will be based on the aging schedule shown below.

Days Account Outstanding	Amount	Probability of Collection
Less than 15 days	$300,000	.98
Between 16 and 30 days	100,000	.90
Between 31 and 45 days	80,000	.80
Between 46 and 60 days	40,000	.70
Between 61 and 75 days	20,000	.60
Over 75 days	15,000	.00

Instructions

(a) What is the appropriate balance for the Allowance for Doubtful Accounts on December 31, 1998?

(b) Show how accounts receivable would be presented on the balance sheet prepared on December 31, 1998.

(c) What is the dollar effect of the year-end bad debt adjustment on the before-tax income for 1998?

(CMA adapted)

P7-8

From inception of operations to December 31, 1997, Dustin Hoffman Corporation Ltd. provided for uncollectible accounts receivable under the allowance method: provisions were made monthly at 2% of credit sales; bad debts written off were charged to the Allowance account; recoveries of bad debts previously written off were credited to the Allowance account; and no year-end adjustments to the Allowance account were made. Hoffman's usual credit terms are net 30 days.

The balance in the Allowance for Doubtful Accounts was $130,000 at January 1, 1998. During 1998, credit sales totalled $9,000,000; interim provisions for doubtful accounts were made at 2% of credit sales; $90,000 of bad debts were written off; and recoveries of accounts previously written off amounted to $15,000. Hoffman installed a computer facility in November 1998 and an aging of accounts receivable was prepared for the first time as of December 31, 1998. A summary of the aging is as follows:

Classification Month of Sale	Balance in Each Category	Estimated % Uncollectible
November–December 1998	$1,080,000	2%
July–October	650,000	10%
January–June	420,000	25%
Prior to 1/1/98	150,000	80%
	$2,300,000	

Based on the review of collectibility of the account balances in the "Prior to 1/1/98" aging category, additional receivables totalling $60,000 were written off as of December 31, 1998. The 80% uncollectible estimate applied to the remaining $90,000 in the category. Effective with the year ended December 31, 1998, Hoffman adopted a new accounting method for estimating the allowance for doubtful accounts at the amount indicated by the year-end aging analysis of accounts receivable.

Instructions

(a) Prepare a schedule analysing the changes in the Allowance for Doubtful Accounts for the year ended December 31, 1998. Show supporting computations in good form. (Hint: In computing the 12/31/98 allowance, subtract the $60,000 write-off.)

(b) Prepare the journal entry for the year-end adjustment to the Allowance for Doubtful Accounts balance as of December 31, 1998.
(AICPA adapted)

P7-9 Presented below is information related to the Accounts Receivable accounts of Kyncl Inc. during the current year 1998:

1. An aging schedule of the accounts receivable as of December 31, 1998 is as follows:

Age	Net Debit Balance	% to Be Applied After Correction Made
Under 60 days	$173,500	1%
61–90 days	137,000	3%
91–120 days	40,900*	6%
Over 120 days	23,640	$4,200 definitely uncollectible; estimated remainder collectible is 25%
	$375,040	

*The $2,500 write-off of receivables is related to the 91-to-120 day category.

2. The Accounts Receivable control account has a debit balance of $375,040 on December 31, 1998.

3. Two entries are made in the Bad Debt Expense account during the year: (1) a debit on December 31 for the amount credited to Allowance for Doubtful Accounts; and (2) a credit for $2,520 on November 3, 1998, and a debit to Allowance for Doubtful Accounts because of a bankruptcy.

4. The Allowance for Doubtful Accounts is as follows for 1998.

Allowance for Doubtful Accounts

Nov. 3	Uncollectible accounts written off	2,520	Jan. 1	Beginning balance	8,750
			Dec. 31	5% of $372,040	18,620

5. A credit balance exists in the Accounts Receivable (61–90 days) of $4,840, which represents an advance on a sales contract.

Instructions

Assuming that the books have not been closed for 1998, make the necessary correcting entries.

P7-10 The balance sheet of Ken Seymore Inc. at December 31, 1997 includes the following:

Notes receivable	$ 36,000	
Accounts receivable	$182,100	
Less: Allowance for doubtful accounts	17,300	200,800

Transactions in 1998 include the following:

1. A note receivable sold on a with recourse basis was unable to be collected by the purchaser. The purchaser now requires payment of $5,060, which includes $60 of interest. Recovery is expected in 1999. (Use Notes Receivable Past Due account.)

2. Accounts receivable of $138,000 were collected, including accounts of $30,000 on which 2% sales discount were allowed.

3. $6,200 was received in payment of an account that was written off the books as worthless in 1995. (Hint: Re-establish the receivable account.)

4. Customer accounts of $19,500 were written off during the year.

5. At year end the Allowance for Doubtful Accounts was estimated to need a balance of $20,000. This estimate was based on an analysis of aged accounts receivable.

Instructions
Prepare all journal entries necessary to reflect the transactions above.

P7-11

Bruce Willis Limited finances some of its current operations by assigning accounts receivable to a finance company. On July 1, 1998, it assigned, under guarantee, specific accounts amounting to $70,000, the finance company advancing to Bruce Willis Limited 80% of the accounts assigned (20% of the total to be withheld until the finance company has made a full recovery), less a finance charge of ½% of the total accounts assigned.

On July 31, Bruce Willis Limited received a statement that the finance company had collected $38,000 of these accounts, and had made an additional charge of ½% of the total accounts outstanding as of July 31, this charge to be deducted at the time of the first remittance due to Bruce Willis Limited from the finance company. (Hint: Make entries at this time.) On August 31, 1998, Bruce Willis Limited received a second statement from the finance company, together with a cheque for the amount due. The statement indicated that the finance company had collected an additional $20,000 and had made a further charge of ½% of the balance outstanding as of August 31.

Instructions
(a) Make all entries on the books of Bruce Willis Limited that were involved in the transactions above.

(b) Explain how these accounts should be presented in the balance sheet of Bruce Willis Limited at July 31 and at August 31.

(AICPA adapted)

P7-12

Bo Jackson Sports Company produces soccer, football, and track shoes. The treasurer recently completed negotiations in which Bo Jackson Sports agrees to loan Payton Inc., a leather supplier, $500,000. Payton Inc. will issue a non-interest-bearing note due in five years (a 12% interest rate is appropriate), and has agreed to furnish Bo Jackson Sports with leather at prices that are 10% lower than those usually charged.

Instructions
(a) Prepare the accounting entry to record this transaction on Bo Jackson Sports' books.

(b) Determine the balances at the end of each year for which the note is outstanding for the following accounts for Bo Jackson Sports:

Notes receivable

Unamortized discount

Interest revenue

P7-13

On December 31, 1998, La Tourette Inc. rendered services to Blusky Limited at an agreed-upon price of $73,844.10, accepting $18,000.00 down and agreeing to accept the balance in four equal instalments of $18,000.00 receivable each December 31. An assumed interest rate of 11% is implicit in the agreed-upon price.

Instructions
Prepare the journal entries to be recorded by La Tourette Inc. for the sale and for the receipts and interest on the following dates (assume that the effective interest method is used for amortization purposes):

(a) December 31, 1998.

(b) December 31, 1999.

(c) December 31, 2000.

(d) December 31, 2001.

(e) December 31, 2002.

P7-14

Geiger Wholesalers Ltd. sells industrial equipment for a standard three-year note receivable. Revenue is recognized at the time of sale. Each note is secured by a lien on the equipment and has a face amount equal to the equipment's list price. Each note's stated interest rate is below the customer's market rate at date of sale. All notes are to be collected in three equal annual instalments beginning one year after sale. Some of the notes are subsequently sold to a bank with recourse, some are subsequently sold without recourse, and some are retained by Geiger. At year end, Geiger evaluates all outstanding notes receivable and provides for estimated loses arising from defaults.

Instructions

(a) What is the appropriate valuation basis for Geiger's notes receivable at the date it sells equipment?

(b) How should Geiger account for the sale, without recourse, of a February 1, 1998 note receivable sold on May 1, 1998? Why is it appropriate to account for it in this way?

(c) At December 31, 1998, how should Geiger measure and account for the impact of estimated losses resulting from notes receivable that it:

  1. Retained and did **not** sell?

  2. Sold to the bank with recourse?   (AICPA adapted)

P7-15 Ritter Supply produces paints and related products for sale to the construction industry throughout the southwest United States. While sales have remained relatively stable despite a decline in the amount of new construction, there has been a noticeable change in the timeliness with which Ritter's customers are paying their bills.

Ritter sells its products on payment terms of 2/10, n/30. In the past, over 75 percent of the credit customers have taken advantage of the discount by paying within 10 days of the invoice date. During the fiscal year ended November 30, 1998 the number of customers taking the full 30 days to pay has increased. Current indications are that less than 60 percent of the customers are now taking the discount. Uncollectible accounts as a percentage of total credit sales have risen from the 1.5 percent provided in past years to 4.0 percent in the current year.

In response to a request for more information on the deterioration of accounts receivable collections, Ritter's controller has prepared the following report.

RITTER SUPPLY
Accounts Receivable Collections
November 30, 1998

The fact that some credit accounts will prove uncollectible is normal, and annual bad debts write-offs had been 1.5 percent of total credit sales for many years. However, during the 1996-97 fiscal year, this percentage increased to 4.0 percent. The current accounts receivable balance is $1,500,000, and the condition of this balance in terms of age and probability of collection is shown below:

Proportion of Total	Age Categories	Probability of Collection
64.0%	1 to 10 days	99.0%
18.0	11 to 30 days	97.5
8.5	Past due 31 to 60 days	95.0
5.0	Past due 61 to 120 days	80.0
3.0	Past due 121 to 180 days	65.0
1.5	Past due over 180 days	20.0

At the beginning of the fiscal year, December 1, 1997, the Allowance for Doubtful Accounts had a credit balance of $26,300. Ritter has provided for a monthly bad debt expense accrual during the fiscal year just ended based on the assumption that 4% of total credit sales will be uncollectible. Total credit sales for the 1997–98 fiscal year amounted to $8,000,000, and write-offs of uncollectible accounts during the year totalled $292,500.

Instructions

(a) Prepare an accounts receivable aging schedule at November 30, 1998 for Ritter Supply using the age categories identified in the controller's report and showing:

  1. The amount of accounts receivable outstanding for each age category and in total.

  2. The estimated amount that is uncollectible for each category and in total.

(b) Compute the amount of the year-end adjustment necessary to bring Ritter Supply's Allowance for Doubtful Accounts to the balance indicated by the aging analysis.

(c) Calculate the net realizable value of Ritter Supply's accounts receivable at November 30, 1998. Ignore any discounts that may be applicable to the accounts not yet due.

(d) Describe the accounting to be performed for subsequent collections of previously written-off accounts receivable.

P7-16 On September 30, 1997, T. Hoszouski Machinery Ltd. sold a machine and accepted the customer's noninterest-bearing note. Hoszouski normally makes sales on a cash basis. Since the machine was unique, its sales price was not determinable using Hoszouski's normal pricing practices.

After receiving the first of two equal annual instalments on September 30, 1998, Hoszouski immediately sold the note with recourse. On October 9, 1999, Hoszouski received notice that the note was dishonoured, and it paid all amounts due. At all times prior to default, the note was reasonably expected to be paid in full.

Instructions

(a) 1. How should Hoszouski determine the sales price of the machine?

  2. How should Hoszouski report the effects of the noninterest-bearing note on its income statement for the year ended December 31, 1997? Why is this accounting presentation appropriate?

(b) What are the effects of the sale of the note receivable with recourse on Hoszouski's income statement for the year ended December 31, 1998, and its balance sheet at December 31, 1998?

(c) How should Hoszouski account for the effects of the note being dishonoured? (AICPA adapted)

Weaver Ltd. had the following long-term receivable account balances at December 31, 1997: **P7-17**

Note receivable from sale of division	$1,500,000
Note receivable from officer	400,000

Transactions during 1998 and other information relating to Weaver's long-term receivables are as follows:

1. The $1,500,000 note receivable is dated May 1, 1997, bears interest at 9%, and represents the balance of the consideration received from the sale of Weaver's electronics division to Kodiak Limited. Principal payments of $500,000 plus appropriate interest are due on May 1, 1998, 1999, and 2000. The first principal and interest payment is made on May 1, 1998. Collection of the note instalments is reasonably assured.

2. The $400,000 note receivable is dated December 31, 1997, bears interest at 9%, and is due on December 31, 1999. The note is due from George Weaver, president of Weaver Ltd., and is collateralized by 10,000 of Weaver's common shares. Interest is payable annually on December 31 and all interest payments are paid on their due dates through December 31, 1999. The quoted market price of Weaver's common shares is $46 each on December 31, 1998.

3. On April 1, 1998, Weaver sells a patent to Zhao Co. Ltd. in exchange for a $100,000 noninterest-bearing note due on April 1, 2000. There is no established exchange price for the patent, and the note has no ready market. The prevailing rate of interest for a note of this type at April 1, 1998 is 12%. The present value of $1 for two periods at 12% is 0.797 (use this factor). The patent has a carrying value of $40,000 at January 1, 1998, and the amortization for the year ended December 31, 1998 would have been $8,000. The collection of the note receivable from Zhao is reasonably assured.

4. On July 1, 1998, Weaver sold a parcel of land to Scarboro Limited for $200,000 under an instalment sale contract. Scarboro made a $60,000 cash down payment on July 1, 1998, and signs a four-year 11% note for the $140,000 balance. The equal annual payments of principal and interest on the note will be $45,125 payable on July 1, 1999 through July 1, 2002. The land could have been sold at an established cash price of $200,000. The cost of the land to Weaver was $150,000. Circumstances are such that the collection of the instalments on the note is reasonably assured.

Instructions

(a) Prepare the long-term receivables section of Weaver's balance sheet at December 31, 1998.

(b) Prepare a schedule showing the current portion of the long-term receivables and accrued interest receivable that will appear in Weaver's balance sheet at December 31, 1998.

(c) Prepare a schedule showing interest revenue from the long-term receivables that will appear on Weaver's income statement for the year ended December 31, 1998. (AICPA adapted)

Hrubec Ltd. factors $400,000 of accounts receivable with Waubonsee Factors Inc. on a without recourse basis. The ***P7-18** finance charge is 2¾% of the amount of receivables, and an additional 4% is retained to cover probable adjustments. Per the terms of the factoring agreement, Hrubec handles returned goods, allowances, and shipping disputes. Waubonsee collects the cash and acknowledges sales discounts, but such discounts are charged to Hrubec. Credit losses are absorbed by Waubonsee. Hrubec has not recorded any bad debt expense related to the factored receivables. The following transactions pertain to this factoring:

Aug. 1	The receivable records are transferred to Waubonsee Factors. Waubonsee estimates that $2,900 of the accounts will prove to be uncollectible.
Aug. 31	Waubonsee collects $234,000 during August after allowing for $9,000 of sales discounts. Sales returns and allowances during August totalled $2,400.
Sept. 20	Waubonsee writes off a $2,000 account after learning of the company's bankruptcy.
Sept. 30	Waubonsee collects $151,720 during September. Sales returns and allowances during September totalled $880.
Oct. 10	Hrubec and Waubonsee make a final cash settlement.

Instructions
(a) Prepare all journal entries for both companies on the above dates.
(b) Compute the net cash proceeds Hrubec ultimately realizes from the factoring.
(c) Compute the factor's net income from the factoring.

*P7-19 Frippery Furnishings Inc. factors $700,000 of accounts receivable with Boyd, Dewey, Cheetum, and Howe Financing Corporation on a with recourse basis. The situation indicates that Frippery should account for the factoring as a borrowing activity. The finance charge is 2½% of the amount of accounts receivable; an additional 3½% is withheld to cover sales discounts, returns, and allowances. Frippery handles returns, allowances, and shipping disputes. Howe handles cash collections, acknowledging sales discounts that are charged to Frippery. The receivable records are transferred to Howe on February 2, at which time uncollectible accounts are estimated to be $10,000. During February and March, Howe collects $673,900; sales returns and allowances are $9,500; sales discounts are $6,600; and bad debts of $10,000 materialize. On April 7, Frippery and Howe make a final cash settlement.

Instructions
(a) Prepare all journal entries for Frippery Furnishings Inc. that result from the above transactions.
(b) Indicate how the above transactions would be reflected on Frippery's February 2 balance sheet.

*P7-20 Green Mountain Woolens Ltd. factors $1,000,000 of accounts receivable with Bennington Credit Corp. on a without recourse basis. On June 1, the receivable records are transferred to Bennington Credit, which will make the collections. Bennington Credit assesses a finance charge of 5% of the total accounts receivable factored and retains an amount equal to 6% of the total receivables to cover sales discounts, returns, and allowances. Green Mountain Woolens handles any returned goods, claims and allowances for defective goods, and disputes concerning shipments. Bennington handles the sales discounts and absorbs the credit losses.

During the month of June, the factor collects $650,000; merchandise totalling $14,300 is returned; sales discounts of $9,500 are taken; and allowances of $5,600 are granted.

During the month of July, the factor collects $237,000; merchandise totalling $2,300 is returned; no sales discounts are allowed; and allowances of $3,800 for defective goods are granted.

On August 1, Green Mountain Woolens and Bennington Credit agree that any further returns, discounts, and allowances will be absorbed by Green Mountain Woolens; Bennington therefore returns the balance of the retainer held for such events. Uncollectibles are estimated to be $6,200.

Instructions
(a) Prepare the entries on Green Mountain Woolens' books at June 1, for the June transactions, for the July transactions, and at August 1.
(b) Prepare the entries on Bennington Credit's books at June 1, for the June transactions, for the July transactions, and at August 1.

CASES

C7-1 Presented below are two financial statement excerpts. Answer the question(s) that follow each of these excerpts.
1. Spinal Tap Limited reported the following information:

	Current Year	Prior Year
	(in thousands)	
Current Assets:		
Cash and short-term investments (Note 2)	$9,123	$5,227

Note 2: Cash and Short-term Investments
Cash and short-term investments consisted of the following:

	Current Year	Prior Year
	(in thousands)	
Cash on hand and demand deposits	$ 554	$1,809
Temporary cash investments	8,569	3,418
	$9,123	$5,227

Spinal Tap Limited does not maintain any significant formal or informal compensating balance arrangements with financial institutions. Short-term investments are stated at cost that approximates market value.

Instructions

(a) Why does the company report the amount of the short-term investments in the notes to the financial statements?

(b) What are compensating balance arrangements, and how should they be reported in the financial statements?

(c) Indicate the possible differences between cash equivalents and short-term investments.

2. Barrhead Corporation Ltd. presented the following information:

	Current Year	Prior Year
	($000)	
Cash (including time deposits of $3,799 in the current year, and $2,846 in the prior year) (Note 3)	$7,957	$6,588

Note 3: In connection with bankruptcy proceedings, the company has placed certain funds in escrowed accounts and segregated other accounts on the books and records of the company. These funds totalled approximately $278,379,000 in the current period and $220,358,000 in the preceding period.

Instructions

(a) What is the difference between a demand deposit and a time deposit?

(b) Why are the amounts of time deposits reported separately?

(c) Why are the funds in escrow not reported as part of cash? Provide examples of why cash might be restricted.

(d) Why is petty cash not reported separately in the financial statements?

En Vogue Inc. has significant amounts of trade accounts receivable. En Vogue uses the allowance method to estimate **C7-2** bad debts instead of the direct write-off method. During the year, some specific accounts were written off as uncollectible, and some that were previously written off as uncollectible were collected.

Instructions

(a) What are the deficiencies of the direct write-off method?

(b) What are the two basic allowance methods used to estimate bad debts, and what is the theoretical justification for each?

(c) How should En Vogue account for the collection of the specific accounts previously written off as uncollectible?

Ween Company Ltd. uses the net method of accounting for sales discounts. Ween also offers trade discounts to var- **C7-3** ious groups of buyers.

On August 1, 1998, Ween factored some accounts receivable on a without recourse basis. Ween incurred a finance charge.

Ween also has some notes receivable bearing an appropriate rate of interest. The principal and total interest are due at maturity. The notes were received on October 1, 1998, and they will mature on September 30, 2000. Ween's operating cycle is less than one year.

Instructions

(a) 1. Using the net method, how should Ween account for the sales discounts at the date of sale? What is the rationale for the amount recorded as sales under the net method?

2. Using the net method, what is the effect on Ween's sales revenues and net income when customers do not take the sales discounts?

(b) What is the effect of trade discounts on sales revenues and accounts receivable? Why?

(c) How should Ween account for the accounts receivable factored on August 1, 1998? Why?

(d) How should Ween account for the note receivable and the related interest on December 31, 1998? Why?

Jay Hawks Inc. conducts a wholesale merchandising business that sells approximately 5,000 items per month with a **C7-4** total monthly average sales value of $200,000. Its annual bad debt ratio has been approximately 1½% of sales. In recent discussions with his bookkeeper, Mr. Hawks has become confused by all the alternatives apparently available in handling the Allowance for Doubtful Accounts balance. The following information has been shown.

1. An allowance can be set up (a) on the basis of a percentage of sales; or (b) on the basis of a valuation of all past due or otherwise questionable accounts receivable. Those accounts considered uncollectible can be charged to such an allowance at the close of the accounting period. Specific items are charged off directly against (c) gross sales; or to (d) bad debt expense in the year in which they are determined to be uncollectible.

2. Collection agency fees, legal fees, and other costs incurred in connection with the attempted recovery of bad debts can be charged to (a) bad debt expense; (b) allowance for doubtful accounts; (c) legal expense; or (d) general expense.

3. Debts previously written off in whole or in part but currently recovered can be credited to (a) other revenue; (b) bad debt expense; or (c) allowance for doubtful accounts.

Instructions

Which of the foregoing methods would you recommend to Mr. Hawks in regard to (1) allowances and chargeoffs; (2) collection expenses; and (3) recoveries? State briefly and clearly the reasons supporting your recommendations.

C7-5   **Part 1** On July 1, 1998 Deyday Ltd., using a calendar-year accounting period, sells special order merchandise on credit and receives in return an interest-bearing note receivable from the customer. Deyday Ltd. will receive interest at the prevailing rate for a note of this type. Both the principal and interest are due in one lump sum on June 30, 1999.

Instructions

(a) When should Deyday Ltd. report interest income from the note receivable? Discuss the rationale for your answer.

(b) Assume that the note receivable was discounted without recourse at a bank on December 31, 1998. How would Deyday Ltd. determine the amount of the discount, and what would be the appropriate accounting for the discounting transaction?

Part 2 On December 31, 1998, Deyday Ltd. has significant amounts of accounts receivable as a result of credit sales to its customers. The company uses the allowance method based on credit sales to estimate bad debts. Based on past experience, 2% of credit sales are normally not collected. This pattern is expected to continue.

Instructions

(a) Discuss the rationale for using the allowance method based on credit sales to estimate bad debts. Contrast this method with the allowance method based on the balance in the trade receivables accounts.

(b) How should Deyday Ltd. report the allowance for bad debts account on its balance sheet at December 31, 1998? Also, describe the alternatives, if any, for presentation of bad debt expense in Deyday Ltd.'s 1998 income statement.   (AICPA adapted)

C7-6   Primco Ltd. sells office equipment and supplies to many organizations in the city and surrounding area on contract terms of 2/10, n/30. In the past, over 75% of credit customers have taken advantage of the discount by paying within 10 days of the invoice date.

The number of customers taking the full 30 days to pay has increased within the last year. Current indications are that less than 60% of the customers are now taking the discount. Bad debts as a percentage of gross credit sales have risen from 1.5% provided in the past years to about 4% in the current year.

The controller has responded to a request for more information on the deterioration in accounts receivable collections with the report reproduced below.

PRIMCO LTD.
Finance Committee Report
Accounts Receivable Collections
May 31, 1998

The fact that some credit accounts will prove uncollectible is normal. Annual bad debt write-offs have been 1.5% of gross credit sales over the past five years. During the last fiscal year, this percentage increased to slightly less than 4%. The current Accounts Receivable balance is $1,600,000. The condition of this balance in terms of probability of collection is as follows:

Proportion of Total	Age Categories	Probability of Collection
68%	Not yet due	99%
15%	Less than 30 days past due	96½%
8%	31 to 60 days past due	95%
5%	61 to 120 days past due	91%
2½%	121 to 180 days past due	75%
1½%	Over 181 days past due	20%

The Allowance for Doubtful Accounts had a credit balance of $40,300 on June 1, 1997. Primco has provided for a monthly bad debt expense accrual during the fiscal year based on the assumption that 4% of gross credit sales will be uncollectible. Total gross credit sales for the 1997–98 fiscal year amounted to $4,000,000. Write-offs of bad accounts during the year totalled $145,000.

Instructions

(a) Using the age categories identified in the controller's report to the Finance Committee, prepare an accounts receivable aging schedule for Primco Ltd. showing:

1. The amount of accounts receivable outstanding for each age category and in total;
2. The estimated amount that is uncollectible for each category and in total.

(b) Compute the amount of the year-end adjustment necessary to bring Allowance for Doubtful Accounts to the balance indicated by the age analysis. Then prepare the necessary journal entry to adjust the accounting records.

(c) In a recessionary environment with tight credit and high interest rates:

1. Identify steps Primco Ltd. might consider to improve the accounts receivable situation;
2. Evaluate each step identified in terms of the risks and costs involved.

On July 1, 1998, Wayne Inc. sold special-order merchandise on credit and received in return an interest-bearing note **C7-7** receivable from the customer. Wayne will receive interest at the prevailing rate for a note of this type. Both the principal and interest are due in one lump sum on June 30, 1999.

On September 1, 1998, Wayne sold special-order merchandise on credit and received a noninterest-bearing note receivable from the customer. The prevailing rate of interest for a note of this type is determinable. The note receivable is due in one lump sum on August 31, 2000.

Wayne also has significant amounts of trade accounts receivable as a result of credit sales to its customers. On October 1, 1998, some trade accounts receivable were assigned to Garth Finance Company on a with recourse, nonnotification basis (Wayne handles collections) for an advance of 75% of their amount at an interest charge of 20% on the balance outstanding.

On November 1, 1998, other trade accounts receivable were factored on a without recourse basis. The factor withheld 5% of the trade accounts receivable factored as protection against sales returns and allowances and charged a finance charge of 3%.

Instructions

(a) How should Wayne determine the interest income for 1998 on the

1. Interest-bearing note receivable? Why?
2. Noninterest-bearing note receivable? Why?

(b) How should Wayne report the interest-bearing note receivable and the noninterest-bearing note receivable on its balance sheet at December 31, 1998?

(c) How should Wayne account for subsequent collections on the trade accounts receivable assigned on October 1, 1998, and the payments to Garth Finance? Why?

(d) How should Wayne account for the trade accounts receivable factored on November 1, 1998? Why?

(AICPA adapted)

Soon after beginning the year-end audit work on March 10 at Elvis Co. Ltd., the auditor has the following conversa- **C7-8** tion with the controller.

CONTROLLER:	The year ended March 31 should be our most profitable in history, and, as a consequence, the Board of Directors has just awarded the officers generous bonuses.
AUDITOR:	I thought profits were down this year in the industry, according to your latest interim report.
CONTROLLER:	Well, they were down but 10 days ago we closed a deal that would give us a substantial increase for the year.
AUDITOR:	Oh, what was it?
CONTROLLER:	Well, you remember a few years ago our former president bought shares in Graceland Enterprises because he had those grandiose ideas about becoming a conglomerate? For six years we have not been able to sell the shares, which cost us $3,000,000, and have not been paid a nickel in dividends. Thursday we sold the shares to Hirisk Ltd. for $4,000,000. So, we will have a gain of $700,000 ($1,000,000 pretax), which will increase our net income for the year to $4,000,000 compared with last year's $3,800,000. As far as I know, we'll be the only company in the industry to register an increase in net income this year. That should help the market value of the company's shares!

AUDITOR:	Do you expect to receive the $4,000,000 in cash by March 31, your fiscal year end?
CONTROLLER:	No. Although Hirisk Ltd. is an excellent company, they are a little tight on cash because of their rapid growth. Consequently, they are going to give us a $4,000,000 noninterest-bearing note with $400,000 due each year for the next 10 years. The first payment is due on March 31 of next year.
AUDITOR:	Why is the note noninterest-bearing?
CONTROLLER:	Because that's what everybody agreed to. Since we don't have any interest-bearing debt, the funds invested in the note do not cost us anything, and besides, we were not getting any dividends on the Graceland Enterprises shares.

Instructions

Do you agree with the way the controller has accounted for the transaction? If not, how should the transaction be accounted for?

C7-9 Houseall Inc. operates a full-line department store that is dominant in its market area, is easily accessible to public and private transportation, has adequate parking facilities, and is near a large permanent military base. The president of the company, Josi Davidson, seeks your advice on a recently received proposal.

A local credit union, in which your client has an account, recently affiliated with a popular national credit card plan and has extended an invitation to your client to participate in the plan. Under the plan, affiliated banks and credit unions mail credit card applications to people who have good credit ratings regardless of whether or not they are customers of the credit union. If the recipients wish to receive a credit card, they complete, sign, and return the application and instalment credit agreement. Holders of the credit cards may charge merchandise or services at any participating establishment throughout the nation.

The credit union guarantees payment to all participating merchants on all invoices that are properly completed, signed, and validated with the impression of credit cards that are not expired or reported stolen or cancelled. Local merchants including your client may turn in all card-validated sales tickets or invoices to their affiliated local credit union at any time and receive immediate credits to their chequing accounts at 96.5% of the face value of the invoices. If card users pay the credit union or bank in full within 30 days for amounts billed, the credit union levies no added charges against the customer. If they elect to make their payments under a deferred payment plan, the credit union adds a service charge that amounts to an effective interest rate of 18% per annum on unpaid balances. Only the local affiliated credit unions, banks, and the franchiser of the credit card plan share in these revenues.

The 18% service charge approximates what your client has been billing customers who pay their accounts over an extended period on a schedule similar to that offered under the credit card plan. Participation in the plan does not prevent your client from carrying on credit business as in the past.

Instructions

(a) What are (1) the positive and (2) the negative financial and accounting-related factors that Houseall Inc. should consider in deciding whether or not to participate in the described credit card plan? Explain.

(b) If Houseall Inc. does participate in the plan, which income statement and balance sheet accounts may change materially as the plan becomes fully operative? (Such factors as market position, sales mix, prices, markup, etc., are expected to remain the same as in the past.) Explain. (AICPA adapted)

C7-10 Little Bear Co. Ltd. is a subsidiary of Big Bear Co. Ltd. The controller believes that the yearly allowance for doubtful accounts for Little Bear should be 2% of net credit sales. The president, nervous that the parent company might expect the subsidiary to sustain its 10% growth rate, suggests that the controller increase the allowance for doubtful accounts to 3% yearly. The supervisor thinks that the lower net income, which reflects a 6% growth rate, will be a more sustainable rate for Little Bear (a fast-food company).

Instructions

(a) Should the controller be concerned with Little Bear Co. Ltd.'s growth rate in estimating the allowance? Explain your answer.

(b) Does the president's request pose an ethical dilemma for the controller? Give your reasons.

C7-11 Verhague Limited has several current notes receivable on its year-end balance sheet. While collection seems certain, it may be delayed beyond one year. Because of this, the controller wants to reclassify these notes as noncurrent. The treasurer of Verhague also thinks that collection will be delayed, but does not favour reclassification because this will reduce the current ratio from 1.5:1 to .8:1. This reduction in current ratio is detrimental to company prospects for securing a major loan.

Instructions

(a) Should the controller reclassify the notes? Give your reasons.

(b) Considering the possible harm to stakeholders, what is the ethical dilemma for the controller and the treasurer?

Radisson Company requires additional cash for its business. Radisson has decided to use its accounts receivable to raise the additional cash and has asked you to determine the income statement effects of the following contemplated transactions.   **C7-12**

1. On July 1, 1998, Radisson assigned $400,000 of accounts receivable to Stickum Finance Company. Radisson received an advance from Stickum of 85% of the assigned accounts receivable less a commission on the advance of 3%. Prior to December 31, 1998, Radisson collected $220,000 on the assigned accounts receivable and remitted $232,720 to Stickum, $12,720 of which represented interest on the advance from Stickum.

2. On December 1, 1996, Radisson sold $300,000 of net accounts receivable to Wunsch Company for $250,000. The receivables were sold outright on a without recourse basis.

3. On December 31, 1998, an advance of $120,000 was received from the First Bank of the Maritimes by pledging $160,000 of Radisson's accounts receivable. Radisson's first payment to the bank is due on January 30, 1999.

Instructions

Prepare a schedule showing the income statement effect for the year ended December 31, 1998, as a result of the above facts.

USING YOUR JUDGEMENT

FINANCIAL REPORTING PROBLEM

In the Financial Strategy section of a corporate annual report, the management stated that "we believe it is more important to focus on the cash flow generated by our business than on net income." Do you agree with the management's comment? Explain.

chapter 8

VALUATION OF INVENTORIES: COST FLOW METHODS

MAJOR CLASSIFICATIONS OF INVENTORY

MANAGEMENT INTEREST IN ACCOUNTING FOR INVENTORIES

DETERMINING INVENTORY QUANTITIES

BASIC ISSUES IN INVENTORY VALUATION

OBJECTIVES OF INVENTORY VALUATION

COST FLOW METHODS OF INVENTORY VALUATION: THEIR ASSUMPTIONS
AND HOW THEY WORK

STANDARD COST METHOD

CONSISTENCY OF INVENTORY COSTING

APPENDIX 8A: VARIABLE COSTING VERSUS ABSORPTION COSTING

CHAPTER

8

Valuation of Inventories: Cost Flow Methods

Learning Objectives

After studying this chapter, you should be able to:

1. Identify major classifications of inventory.
2. Distinguish between perpetual and periodic inventory systems.
3. Identify the effects of inventory errors on the financial statements.
4. Identify the items that are included as inventory cost.
5. Understand the difference between physical flow of inventory and cost flow assigned to inventory.
6. Recognize there are various objectives to accomplish when assigning costs to inventories.
7. Describe and compare the cost flow assumptions used in accounting for inventories.
8. Evaluate LIFO as a basis for understanding the differences between the cost flow methods.
9. Understand the importance of judgement in selecting an inventory cost flow method.
10. Appreciate the difference between variable costing and absorption costing in assigning costs of manufacturing to inventory (Appendix 8A).

Inventories ***are asset items held for sale in the ordinary course of business or goods that will be used or consumed in the production of goods to be sold***. Identification, measurement, and disclosure of inventories require careful attention because inventories are one of the most significant assets of many enterprises. The sale of inventory at a price greater than total cost is the primary source of income for manufacturing and retail businesses. Inventories are particularly significant because they may materially affect both the income statement and the balance sheet.

Cases of fraudulent financial reporting have emphasized the importance of inventory. According to *The Wall Street Journal,* "creating phantom inventory instantly benefits a company's bottom line."[1] For example, it is alleged that Phar-Mor Inc., a deep-discount drugstore chain, overstated its profits by $50 million by keeping in its inventory records items that had already been sold, maintaining secret inventory records, and creating phantom inventory at many of the chain's stores.[2]

The accounting problems associated with inventory valuation are complex. Chapters 8 and 9 discuss the basic issues involved in identifying, measuring, and reporting inventoriable items. In Chapter 8, the concentration is on determining the items and costs to be

---

[1] "Inventory Chicanery Temps More Firms, Fools More Auditors," *The Wall Street Journal*, December 12, 1992, p. A1.

[2] Overstatement of ending inventory reduces cost of sales and thus increases profits.

included in inventory, analysing the effect of inventory errors, and describing and comparing cost flow methods applicable to inventory valuation. In Chapter 9, the lower of cost and market rule and inventory estimation methods are examined.

MAJOR CLASSIFICATIONS OF INVENTORY

OBJECTIVE 1
Identify major classifications of inventory.

A **merchandising business** such as Wal-Mart ordinarily purchases its merchandise in a form ready for sale. It reports the cost assigned to unsold units at the end of the period as merchandise inventory. Only one inventory account, Merchandise Inventory, appears in the financial statements.

A **manufacturing business** produces goods to be sold to merchandising firms. A manufacturing company normally has three inventory accounts: Raw Materials, Work in Process, and Finished Goods. The cost assigned to goods and materials on hand but not yet placed into production is reported as **raw materials inventory.** Raw materials include the wood to make baseball bats or the steel to make cars. These materials ultimately can be traced directly to the end product. At any point in a continuous production process, some units are not completely processed. The cost of the raw material on which production has started, but not completed, plus the direct labour cost applied specifically to this material and an applicable share of manufacturing overhead costs constitute the **work-in-process inventory.** The costs identified with the completed but unsold units on hand at the end of the fiscal period are reported as **finished goods inventory.** The flow of costs through a merchandising company is different from that of a manufacturing company, as shown in Illustration 8-1.

ILLUSTRATION 8-1
Flow of costs through merchandising and manufacturing companies

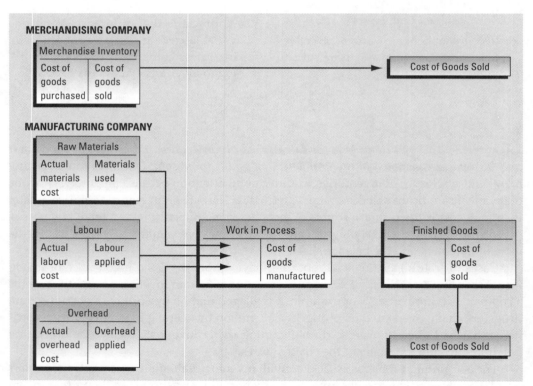

The *CICA Handbook* states that it is desirable to disclose the amounts of the major categories that make up total inventory.[3] It is common, therefore, to see three inventory accounts on the balance sheet (or in notes cross-referenced to them) of a manufacturer:

---

[3] *CICA Handbook* (Toronto: CICA), Section 3030, par. .10.

Raw Materials, Work in Process, and Finished Goods.[4] A *Manufacturing* or *Factory Supplies Inventory* account might also exist for a manufacturing company. This account includes such items as machine oil, nails, and cleaning materials that are used in production but are not the primary materials being processed. As an example, an annual report of NOVA Corporation reported inventories in the current asset section of its balance sheet at the amount of $301 million, cross-referenced to Note 10, shown in Exhibit 8-1.

EXHIBIT 8-1   NOVA CORPORATION

FINANCIAL STATEMENT DISCLOSURE OF INVENTORY BY CATEGORIES FROM THE NOTES TO THE FINANCIAL STATEMENTS

10. Inventories

December 31 (millions of dollars)	1995	1994	1993
Materials and supplies	$63	$88	$97
Raw materials	91	95	91
Work in process	5	4	6
Finished goods	142	112	120
	$301	$299	$314

MANAGEMENT INTEREST IN ACCOUNTING FOR INVENTORIES

The investment in inventory is frequently the largest current asset (and a material portion of total assets) of manufacturing and retail establishments. If unsalable items have accumulated in the inventory, a potential loss exists. Sales and customers may be lost if products ordered by customers are not available in the desired style, quality, and quantity. Inefficient purchasing procedures, faulty manufacturing techniques, or inadequate sales efforts may saddle a firm with excessive and unusable inventories. Therefore, it is important for management to carefully monitor inventories in order to control them both physically and financially. This is often accomplished by computer systems. In recent years, with the introduction of "just-in-time" (JIT) inventory order and delivery systems and better supplier relationships, inventory levels have become leaner for many enterprises.[5]

From a perspective of accounting for inventory, management is well aware that the determination of year-end inventory can significantly affect the amount of net income as well as current assets, total assets, and retained earnings (through the net income amount). These amounts (or totals including them) are used to calculate ratios that, in turn, are used to evaluate management's performance (e.g., payment of bonuses) and adherence to debt contract restrictions (e.g., to not exceed a specified debt to total asset ratio or dividend payout ratio).[6]

---

[4] *Financial Reporting in Canada—1995* (Toronto: CICA, 1995), indicated that all components of inventory were set out by approximately 42% of the companies that were surveyed and that had inventory. Lack of such segregation by the remaining companies would, in part, be because they had only one category (for example, they were merchandising companies). For example, Sears Canada Inc. showed only the amount of $507.1 million for inventories in the current section of its December 31, 1995 balance sheet.

[5] Ideally, use of a JIT inventory order and delivery system would mean that a manufacturing company would have no, or only a small amount of, work in process inventory at any given time. Some accountants suggest that the flow of cost in a JIT system could, therefore, be described as Last-In-Right-Out. More significantly, however, is the fact that accountants would not have to be concerned with the flow of costs between inventory and cost of goods sold in such a situation because there would be no inventory or only an immaterial amount.

[6] The determination and uses of various financial statement ratios are examined in Chapter 24. A summary of various ratios and the related formulas is included.

For these and other reasons, managers, as well as accountants, are very interested in having an accounting inventory system that provides accurate, up-to-date information on quantities. Also of concern is the choice of a cost method to value inventories in periods of changing prices.

DETERMINING INVENTORY QUANTITIES

OBJECTIVE 2
Distinguish between perpetual and periodic inventory systems.

As indicated in Chapter 3, inventory records may be maintained on a perpetual or periodic inventory system basis. In a **perpetual inventory system**, purchases and sales (issues) of goods are recorded directly in the Inventory account as they occur. A Purchases account is used not because the purchases are debited directly to Inventory. A Cost of Goods Sold account is used to accumulate the cost of issuances from inventory as they occur. Therefore, the perpetual inventory system provides a continuous record of the balances in both the Inventory account and the Cost of Goods Sold account. The balance in the Inventory account at the end of the year indicates the ending inventory amount.

Under a computerized record-keeping system, additions to and issuances from inventory can be recorded nearly instantaneously. The popularity and affordability of computerized accounting software have made the perpetual system cost effective for all sizes and kinds of businesses. Recording sales with optical scanners at the cash register has been incorporated into perpetual inventory systems at many retail stores.

When the inventory records are maintained on a **periodic inventory system**, a Purchases account is used to record acquisitions. The balance in the Inventory account (which represents the beginning inventory) is unchanged during the period. At the end of the accounting period a closing entry is made that debits the Inventory account for the ending inventory amount and credits the Inventory account for the beginning inventory amount. Cost of goods sold is determined by using the following calculation: Beginning Inventory + Net Purchases − Ending Inventory.

To illustrate the difference between a perpetual and a periodic system, assume that Katt Ltd. had transactions during the current year as shown in Exhibit 8-2.

EXHIBIT 8-2

INFORMATION TO ILLUSTRATE THE DIFFERENCE BETWEEN THE PERPETUAL AND PERIODIC INVENTORY SYSTEMS

Beginning inventory	100 units at $ 6 = $ 600
Purchases	900 units at $ 6 = $5,400
Sales	600 units at $12 = $7,200
Ending inventory	400 units at $ 6 = $2,400

Exhibit 8-3 shows the entries to record these transactions during the current year.

When a periodic system is employed, how is the ending inventory determined? One method is to take a **physical inventory count** once a year. However, most companies need more current information regarding their inventory levels to protect against stockouts or overpurchasing and to aid in the preparation of monthly or quarterly financial reports. As a consequence, many companies use a *modified perpetual inventory system* in which increases and decreases in quantities only—not dollar amounts—are kept in a detailed inventory record. It is merely a memorandum device outside the double-entry system that helps in determining the level of inventory at any point in time.

While a physical inventory count is necessary to determine the ending inventory under a periodic system, a count would also be taken at least once a year under a perpet-

---

EXHIBIT 8-3

COMPARATIVE ENTRIES: PERPETUAL VERSUS PERIODIC INVENTORY SYSTEMS

Perpetual Inventory System			Periodic Inventory System		
Purchase merchandise for resale:					
Inventory (900 at $6)	5,400		Purchases (900 at $6)	5,400	
Accounts Payable		5,400	Accounts Payable		5,400
Record sale:					
Accounts Receivable	7,200		Accounts Receivable	7,200	
Sales (600 at $12)		7,200	Sales (600 at $12)		7,200
Cost of Goods Sold					
(600 at $6)	3,600		(No entry)		
Inventory		3,600			
Closing entries:					
			Inventory (ending)	2,400	
(No entry necessary)			Cost of Goods Sold	3,600	
			Purchases		5,400
			Inventory (beginning)		600

---

ual inventory system.[7] No matter what type of inventory records are in use or how well organized the procedures for recording purchases and issuances, the danger of loss and error is always present. Waste, breakage, theft, improper entry, failure to prepare or record requisitions, and any number of similar possibilities may cause the inventory records to differ from the actual inventory on hand. This requires periodic verification of the inventory records by actual count, weight, or other measurement. When a difference exists between the count and the perpetual inventory account balance, an entry is needed to correct the perpetual inventory account. To illustrate, assume that at the end of the reporting period the perpetual inventory account had a balance of $2,600, but a physical count indicated $2,400 was actually on hand. The entry to record the necessary write-down is as follows:

Inventory Over and Short	200	
Inventory		200

Perpetual inventory overages and shortages may be recorded as an adjustment of (i.e., closed to) Cost of Goods Sold. This would be appropriate if its cause related to incorrect record keeping. Alternatively, the Inventory Over and Short account may be reported in the Other Revenues and Gains or Other Expenses and Losses section, depending on its balance. If so, an overage or shortage would not be a component of cost of goods sold, and the resulting gross profit percentage would not be distorted because of such things as breakage, shrinkage, and theft. Note that in a periodic inventory system the Inventory Over and Short account does not exist because there are no accounting records available against which to compare the physical count. Thus, inventory overages and shortages are buried in the cost of goods sold.

---

[7] The physical inventory count should be taken near the end of the fiscal year. Because this is not always possible, physical counts taken within two or three months of the year's end are satisfactory if inventory records are maintained with a reasonable degree of accuracy. Some companies have developed inventory controls or methods of verifying inventories, including statistical sampling, that are highly effective and sufficiently reliable to make unnecessary an annual physical count of each item of inventory.

BASIC ISSUES IN INVENTORY VALUATION

Because goods sold or used during an accounting period seldom correspond exactly to the goods bought or produced during that period, the physical inventory held either increases or decreases. In addition, the cost of the items could increase or decrease during a period. Accounting for these increases or decreases requires that the cost of all the goods available for sale or use be allocated between the goods that were sold or used and those that are still on hand. The **cost of goods available for sale or use** is the sum of (1) the cost of the goods on hand at the beginning of the period and (2) the cost of the goods acquired or produced during the period. The **cost of goods sold** is the difference between the cost of goods available for sale during the period and the cost of goods on hand at the end of the period, as shown in Exhibit 8-4.

EXHIBIT 8-4

CALCULATION OF COST OF GOODS SOLD

Beginning inventory, Jan. 1	$100,000
Cost of goods acquired or produced during the year	800,000
Total cost of goods available for sale	$900,000
Ending inventory, Dec. 31	200,000
Cost of goods sold during the year	$700,000

Within this calculation, the valuation (measurement) of the ending inventory is a major accounting issue. The resulting amount is a significant determinant of the current and following years' cost of goods sold and net income (i.e., ending inventory of the current year is the beginning inventory of the next year). Also, the ending inventory amount is reported in the current year's balance sheet as a current asset.

The valuation of inventories can be a complex process that requires determination of:

1. *The physical goods or items to be included in inventory* (who owns the goods?— goods in transit, consigned goods, special sales agreements).

2. *The cost to be included in inventory* (product versus period costs, variable costing versus absorption costing).

3. *The cost flow assumption to be adopted* (specific identification, average cost, FIFO, LIFO).

PHYSICAL GOODS TO BE INCLUDED IN INVENTORY

Technically, purchases should be recorded when legal title to the goods passes to the buyer (i.e., the risks and rewards of ownership are transferred to the buyer). General practice, however, is to record acquisitions when the goods are received, because it is difficult for the buyer to determine the exact time of legal passage of title for every purchase. In addition, no material error is likely to result from such a practice if it is consistently applied.

Goods in Transit. Purchased merchandise that is in transit—not yet received—at the end of a fiscal period may or may not be the property of the buyer. To determine who (seller or buyer) owns goods in transit, the "transfer of risks and rewards" rule must be applied. If the goods are shipped **f.o.b. shipping point** (f.o.b. means free on board), risks and rewards of ownership (i.e., legal title) pass to the buyer when the seller delivers the goods to the common carrier (transporter) who acts as an agent for the buyer. If the goods are shipped **f.o.b. destination**, risks and rewards do not pass until the goods reach the destination. "Shipping point" and "destination" are designated by a particular location, for example, f.o.b. Montreal.[8]

Goods in transit at the end of a fiscal period that were sent f.o.b. shipping point should be recorded by the buyer as purchases of the period and should be included in ending inventory. To disregard such purchases would result in an understatement of inventories and accounts payable in the balance sheet, and an understatement of purchases and ending inventories in the calculation of cost of goods sold for the income statement.

The accountant normally prepares a purchase cut-off schedule for the end of a period to ensure that goods in transit are recorded in the appropriate period. Because goods bought f.o.b. shipping point may have been in transit at the period's end, the cut-off schedule would not be completed until a few days after the period's end (i.e., providing sufficient time for goods shipped at year end to be received). In cases where there is some question as to whether title has passed, the accountant exercises judgement by taking into consideration industry practices, the intent of the sales agreement, the policies of the parties involved, and any other available information.

Consigned Goods. In Appendix 6B, the nature of consignment shipments and accounting for consignment sales was discussed. In terms of accounting for inventory, it is important to recognize that goods out on consignment remain the property of the consignor and must be included in the consignor's inventory at purchase price or production cost plus the cost of handling and shipping involved in the transfer to the consignee. Occasionally, the inventory out on consignment is shown as a separate item or reported in notes, but unless the amount is large there is little need for this.

No entry is made by the consignee to adjust the Inventory account for goods received because they are the property of the consignor. The consignee should be extremely careful not to include any of the goods consigned as a part of inventory.

Special Sale Agreements. While the transfer of legal title is a general guideline used to determine whether the risks and rewards of ownership have passed from a seller to a buyer, transfer of legal title and the underlying economic substance of the situation (passage of risks and rewards) may not match. For example, it is possible that legal title has passed to the purchaser but the seller of the goods retains the risks of ownership. Conversely, transfer of legal title may not occur, but the economic substance of the transaction is that the seller no longer retains the risks and rewards of ownership. Three special sale situations, discussed in Chapter 6 from a revenue recognition perspective, are considered below in terms of inventory implications.

Sales With Buyback Agreement. Sometimes an enterprise finances its inventory without reporting either the liability or the inventory on its balance sheet. Such an approach usually involves a "sale" with either an implicit or explicit "buyback" agreement. These arrangements are often referred to as *product financing arrangements* or described as *parking transactions* (because the seller simply parks the inventory on another enterprise's balance sheet for a short period of time).

---

[8] Terms other than f.o.b. shipping point or f.o.b destination (e.g., CIF for cost, insurance, freight) are often used to identify when legal title passes. The f.o.b. terms are used in this text to reflect that an agreement as to when title passes must be reached between the buyer and seller in the purchase-sale contract. In a particular situation, the terms of the sale contract would be examined to determine when the risks and rewards of ownership pass from the seller to the buyer.

To illustrate, Hill Enterprises transfers ("sells") inventory to Chase Inc. and simultaneously agrees to repurchase this merchandise at a specified price over a specified period of time. Chase then uses the inventory as collateral and borrows against it. Chase uses the loan proceeds to pay Hill. Hill repurchases the inventory in the future and Chase employs the proceeds from repayment to meet its loan obligation.

The essence of this transaction is that Hill Enterprises is financing its inventory—and retaining risks of ownership—even though technical title to the merchandise was transferred to Chase Inc. The advantage to Hill for structuring a transaction in this manner is the removal of the current liability from its balance sheet and the ability to manipulate income. The advantages to Chase are that the purchase of the goods may solve a LIFO liquidation problem (discussed later), or that it may be interested in a reciprocal agreement at a later date.

The *CICA Handbook*, Section 3400 (regarding revenue recognition), has implications that will tend to curtail this practice, at least in terms of enabling a "selling company" to remove the inventory and liability from its balance sheet. This is because the *Handbook* requires the seller to transfer the risks and rewards of ownership before a sale can be recognized.[9] By implication, a "buying company" should not recognize the goods received as its inventory. Canadian practitioners, however, will have to continue to exercise judgement regarding substance over form in such situations.

Sales with High Rates of Return. Quality Publishing Co. Ltd. delivers (sells) textbooks to Campus Bookstores with an agreement that any unsold books may be returned for full credit. In the past, approximately 25% of the textbooks delivered were returned. Should Quality Publishing report its deliveries to Campus Bookstores as sales transactions, or should it treat the delivered books as inventory until being notified of how many were sold? An acceptable accounting treatment is that, if a reasonable prediction of the returns can be established, then the goods should be considered sold. Conversely, if returns are unpredictable, removal of these goods from inventory is inappropriate. Essentially, the choice of treatment depends on whether there is reasonable assurance of the measurement of the ultimate consideration to be derived from the sale given that goods may be returned.[10] If not, only the items actually sold by the purchaser could be accounted for as revenue, with all remaining items being part of the seller's inventory.

Sales on Instalment. Because the risk of loss from uncollectibles is higher in instalment sale situations than in other sale transactions, the seller often withholds legal title to the merchandise until all the payments have been made. Should the inventory be considered sold, even though legal title has not passed? The economic substance of the transaction is that the goods should be excluded from the seller's inventory if the percentage of bad debts can be reasonably estimated.

EFFECT OF INVENTORY ERRORS

OBJECTIVE 3
Identify the effects of inventory errors on the financial statements.

If items are incorrectly included in or excluded from inventory, there will be errors in the financial statements. Therefore, decisions made using financial statement amounts affected by the errors (e.g., bonus paid to management based on net income) would be in error. The following exemplify the nature of such errors and their consequences on financial statement amounts.

Ending Inventory Misstated. What would happen if the beginning inventory and purchases are recorded correctly, but some items on hand are not included in ending inven-

---

[9] *CICA Handbook*, Section 3400, par. .07.

[10] *Ibid*.

tory (e.g., were on the premises but were missed in the physical count or were out on consignment)? In this situation the effects on the financial statements at the end of the period and various ratios would be as shown in Exhibit 8-5.

EXHIBIT 8-5

EFFECTS OF UNDERSTATEMENT OF ENDING INVENTORY ON FINANCIAL STATEMENTS AND VARIOUS RATIOS

Balance Sheet		Income Statement	
Inventory	Understated	Cost of goods sold (ending inventory is understated)	Overstated
Working capital (current assets less current liabilities)	Understated	Net income	Understated
Retained earnings	Understated		

Ratios	
Current ratio (current assets ÷ current liabilities)	Understated
Asset turnover (sales ÷ average total assets)	Overstated
Debt to total assets (debt ÷ total assets)	Overstated
Rate of return on assets (net income ÷ average total assets)	Understated

---

Net income and, therefore, retained earnings are understated because the cost of goods sold expense is overstated; the current ratio and working capital are understated because a portion of ending inventory is omitted. The asset turnover and debt to total asset ratios are overstated because the total asset amount is understated. While both net income and the total asset amounts in the rate of return on assets calculation are understated, the end result is that the rate is understated (assuming it is less than 100%).

To illustrate the effect on net income over a two-year period, assume that, for the current year, the ending inventory of Weiseman Inc. is understated by $10,000 and that all other items are correct. ***The effect of this error will be an understatement of net income in the current year and an overstatement of net income in the following year relative to the correct net income amounts.*** The error will affect the following year because the beginning inventory will be understated, thereby causing net income to be overstated. Both net income figures are misstated, but the total for the two years is correct as the two errors will be counterbalanced (offset) as shown in Exhibit 8-6.

If ending inventory is *overstated*, the reverse effect occurs. Inventory, working capital, net income, retained earnings, current ratio, and rate of return on assets are all overstated and cost of goods sold, asset turnover, and debt to total assets are all understated. The effect of the error on the net income will be counterbalanced in the next year, but both years' net income will be misstated, thereby destroying the usefulness of any analysis of a trend in earnings and ratios.

Purchases and Inventory Misstated. Suppose that certain goods that we own are not recorded as a purchase and were not counted in ending inventory (e.g., were in transit f.o.b. shipping point). Exhibit 8-7 shows the effect on the financial statements (assuming this purchase is on account).

To omit goods from purchases and inventory results in an understatement of inventory and accounts payable in the balance sheet and an understatement of purchases and ending inventory in the calculation of cost of goods sold in the income state-

---

EXHIBIT 8-6   WEISEMAN INC.

COUNTERBALANCING EFFECT OF ERROR IN INVENTORY OVER TWO PERIODS

(All figures assumed)

	Incorrect		Correct	
	1997	1998	1997	1998
Revenues	$100,000	$100,000	$100,000	$100,000
Cost of goods sold				
Beginning inventory	$ 25,000	$ 20,000	$ 25,000	$ 30,000
Purchased or produced	45,000	60,000	45,000	60,000
Goods available for sale	$ 70,000	$ 80,000	$ 70,000	$ 90,000
Less: Ending inventory	20,000*	40,000	30,000	40,000
Cost of goods sold	$ 50,000	$ 40,000	$ 40,000	$ 50,000
Gross profit	$ 50,000	$ 60,000	$ 60,000	$ 50,000
Administrative and selling expenes	40,000	40,000	40,000	40,000
Net income	$ 10,000	$ 20,000	$ 20,000	$ 10,000

Total income
for 2 years = $30,000

Total income
for 2 years = $30,000

*Ending inventory understated by $10,000 in 1997.

EXHIBIT 8-7

EFFECTS OF NOT RECORDING A PURCHASE AND OMITTING ITEMS FROM
INVENTORY ON FINANCIAL STATEMENTS AND VARIOUS RATIOS

Balance Sheet		Income Statement	
Inventory	Understated	Purchases	Understated
Accounts Payable	Understated	Ending inventory in cost of goods sold	Understated
Working capital	No effect	Cost of goods sold	No effect
Retained earnings	No effect	Net income	No effect

Ratios	
Current ratio	Overstated
Asset turnover	Overstated
Debt to total assets	Understated
Rate of return on assets	Overstated

---

ment. Net income for the period and, therefore, retained earnings are not affected by the omission because purchases and ending inventory are both understated by the same amount—the error offsets itself in cost of goods sold. Total working capital is unchanged, but the current ratio is overstated (given it was greater than 1 to 1) because of the omission of equal amounts from inventory and accounts payable. The asset turnover and rate of return on assets are overstated because the denominator of both ratios is understated. For the debt to total asset ratio, both the numerator (accounts payable) and denominator (inventory) amounts are understated by the same amount. However, given the ratio was less than 100%, the net effect is that the ratio would be understated as the result of the errors.

To determine the effect of an error on any particular financial statement amount or ratio, it is helpful to construct a comparison chart based on assumed (if not real) numbers. The chart would include columns based on amounts that included the error(s) and on amounts that would result if there were no error(s). To demonstrate, examine Exhibit 8-8, which shows a comparison chart regarding the effect on the current ratio of an understatement (omission) of accounts payable and ending inventory by $40,000. The amounts for current assets and current liabilities for the "understated" column are assumed. Those in the "correct" column resulted from adding the $40,000 (omitted amount) to the assumed amounts.

EXHIBIT 8-8

USING A COMPARISON CHART TO DETERMINE THE EFFECT OF ERRORS

	Purchases and Ending Inventory Understated		Purchases and Ending Inventory Correct
Current assets	$120,000	Current assets	$160,000
Current liabilities	$ 40,000	Current liabilities	$ 80,000
Current ratio	3 to 1	Current ratio	2 to 1

The correct ratio is 2 to 1 instead of 3 to 1. Thus, understatement of accounts payable and ending inventory can lead to a "window dressing" of the current ratio (make it appear better than it is).[11]

If both purchases (on account) and ending inventory are overstated, then the effects on the balance sheet and ratios including affected amounts are exactly the reverse. While these examples illustrate the nature of some errors that may occur and their consequences, many other types of errors are possible: not recording a purchase but counting the acquired inventory; not recording a sale in the current period although the items have been delivered; omitting the adjusting entry to update the Allowance for Future Returns in situations where sales are subject to a high rate of return, etc. The approach illustrated to determine the effect of errors will help in analysing such situations.

The importance of accurate computation of purchases and inventory to ensure that reliable amounts are presented in financial statements cannot be overemphasized. One has only to read the financial press to learn how the misstatement of inventory can generate high income numbers. For example, the practice of some Canadian farm equipment manufacturers of treating deliveries to dealers as sales of the company (with concurrent reductions in inventory) can result in significantly inflating reported income when sales to the ultimate consumer do not keep pace with the deliveries. Or remember Phar-Mor Inc., which we mentioned earlier. Anixter Bros. Inc. is another example: The company once had to restate its income by $1.7 million because an accountant in the antenna manufacturing division overstated the ending inventory, thereby reducing its cost of sales.

---

[11] The effect of the $40,000 errors on the debt to total asset ratio may be similarly determined as follows.

Debt to total assets with errors	Debt to total assets without errors
$100 \div 500 = .20$	$140 \div 540 = .259$

Therefore, this ratio is understated as a result of the errors.

COSTS TO BE INCLUDED IN INVENTORY

OBJECTIVE 4
Identify the items that are included as inventory cost.

One of the most important problems in dealing with inventories concerns the amount at which the inventory should be stated in the accounting reports. *The acquisition of inventories, like other assets, is generally accounted for on a basis of cost* (other bases are discussed in Chapter 9).

Product Costs. **Product costs** are those costs that "attach" to the inventory and are recorded in the Inventory account. These costs are directly connected with the bringing of goods to the place of business of the buyer and converting such goods to a saleable condition. Such charges would include the purchase price of the items and related freight, hauling, and other direct costs of acquisition, as well as labour and other production costs incurred in processing the goods up to the time of sale.

Nonrecoverable taxes (e.g., some provincial sales taxes) paid on goods purchased for resale or manufacturing purposes are a cost of inventory. Since value-added taxes (e.g., the GST) are recoverable by a manufacturer, wholesaler, or retailer, they should not normally be treated as a cost of inventory (see Chapter 15 for a discussion of these types of taxes).

It would be theoretically correct to allocate to inventories a share of any buying costs or expenses of a purchasing department, storage costs, and other costs incurred in handling the goods before they are sold. Because of the practical difficulties involved in allocating such costs and expenses, however, these items are not ordinarily included in valuing inventories.

Period Costs. *Selling expenses* and, under ordinary circumstances, *general and administration expenses* are not considered to be directly related to the acquisition or production of goods and, therefore, are not considered to be a part of the cost of inventories. Such costs are **period costs**

Conceptually, these expenses are as much a cost of the product as the initial purchase price and related freight charges attached to the product. Why then are these costs not considered inventoriable? In some cases, these charges are not material and no real purpose is served by making an allocation of these costs to inventory. In other situations, especially where selling expenses are significant, the cost is more directly related to the cost of goods sold than to the unsold inventory. In most cases, the costs, especially administrative expenses, are so unrelated or indirectly related to the inventory acquisition process that any allocation is purely arbitrary.

Interest costs associated with getting inventories ready for sale usually are expensed as incurred. A major argument for this approach is that interest costs are a cost of financing and not a cost of the asset. Additionally, it may be argued that the informational benefit of capitalizing interest costs to inventory does not justify the cost of doing it. Others have argued, however, that interest costs incurred to finance activities associated with bringing inventories to a location and condition ready for sale are as much a cost of the asset as materials, labour, and overhead and, therefore, should be capitalized.[12] If interest is capitalized, this policy and the amount capitalized in the current period should be disclosed.[13]

Treatment of Purchase Discounts. **Purchase discounts** are sometimes reported in the income statement as a financial revenue (similar to interest revenue). However, purchase discounts should really be recorded as a reduction of purchases. Otherwise, a company is recognizing revenue before the goods have been sold (to the extent that such purchases are still in inventory at the end of the period). It is generally held that a business does not realize revenue by buying goods and paying bills; it realizes revenue by selling the goods.

---

[12] The reporting rules related to interest cost capitalization have their greatest impact in accounting for capital assets and, therefore, are discussed in detail in Chapter 11. This brief overview provides the basic issues when inventories are involved.

[13] *CICA Handbook*, Section 3850, par. .03.

The use of a Purchase Discounts account indicates that the company is reporting its purchases and accounts payable at the gross amount (called the **gross method**). An alternative approach (called the **net method**) is to record the purchases and accounts payable at an amount net of the cash discounts. This treatment is considered more theoretically appropriate because it (1) provides a correct reporting of the cost of the asset and related liability and (2) presents the opportunity to measure the inefficiency of financial management if the discount is not taken. In the net method, the failure to take a purchase discount within the discount period is recorded in a Purchase Discounts Lost account (for which someone is held responsible). The example in Exhibit 8-9 shows the differences between the gross and net methods.

EXHIBIT 8-9

ENTRIES UNDER GROSS AND NET METHODS

Gross Method			Net Method		
Purchase cost $10,000, terms 2/10, net 30:					
Purchases	10,000		Purchases	9,800	
Accounts Payable		10,000	Accounts Payable		9,800
Invoices of $4,000 are paid within discount period:					
Accounts Payable	4,000		Accounts Payable	3,920	
Purchase Discounts		80	Cash		3,920
Cash		3,920			
Invoices of $6,000 are paid after discount period:					
Accounts Payable	6,000		Accounts Payable	5,880	
Cash		6,000	Purchase Discounts Lost	120	
			Cash		6,000

If the gross method is employed, purchase discounts should be deducted from purchases in determining cost of goods sold. If the net method is used, purchase discounts lost should be considered a financial expense and reported in the Other Expense section of the income statement. Many believe that the difficulty involved in using the somewhat more complicated net method is not worth the resulting benefits. Also, some contend that management is reluctant to report the amount of purchase discounts lost in the financial statements. These reasons may account for the widespread use of the less logical but simpler gross method.

Manufacturing Costs. As previously indicated, a business that manufactures goods utilizes three inventory accounts: Raw Materials, Work in Process, and Finished Goods. Work in process and finished goods include raw materials, direct labour, and manufacturing overhead costs. Manufacturing overhead costs include indirect material, indirect labour, and such items as depreciation, insurance, heat, and electricity incurred in the manufacturing process. The raw materials and work in process inventories are incorporated into a **statement of cost of goods manufactured**, as shown in Exhibit 8-10.

Costs of goods manufactured statements are prepared primarily for internal use; such details are rarely disclosed in published financial statements. The cost of goods sold reported in the income statement of a manufacturing firm is determined in a manner similar to that for a merchandising concern except that the cost of goods manufactured during the year is substituted for the cost of goods purchased. For example, if the inventory of finished goods was $16,000 at the beginning of the year and $10,000 at the end of the year, the calculation of cost of goods sold for the income statement of Leonard Inc. would be as shown in Exhibit 8-11.

EXHIBIT 8-10   LEONARD INC.

STATEMENT OF COST OF GOODS MANUFACTURED

For the Year Ended December 31, 1998

Raw materials consumed			
Raw materials inventory, Jan. 1, 1998			$ 14,000
Add net purchases:			
Purchases		$126,000	
Less: Purchase returns and allowances	$1,800		
Purchase discounts	1,200	3,000	123,000
Raw material available for use			$137,000
Less raw materials inventory, Dec. 31, 1998			17,000
Cost of raw materials consumed			$120,000
Direct labour			200,000
Manufacturing overhead			
Supervisors' salaries		$ 63,000	
Indirect labour		20,000	
Factory supplies used		18,000	
Heat, light, power, and water		13,000	
Depreciation on building and equipment		27,000	
Tools expense		2,000	
Patent amortization		1,000	
Miscellaneous factory expenses		6,000	150,000
Total manufacturing costs for the period			$470,000
Work in process inventory, Jan. 1, 1998			33,000
Total manufacturing costs			$503,000
Less work in process inventory, Dec. 31, 1998			28,000
Cost of goods manufactured during the year			$475,000

EXHIBIT 8-11

COST OF GOODS SOLD CALCULATION: MANUFACTURING COMPANY

Cost of goods sold	
Finished goods inventory, Jan. 1, 1998	$ 16,000
Cost of goods manufactured during 1998	475,000
Cost of goods available for sale	$491,000
Finished goods inventory, Dec. 31, 1998	10,000
Cost of goods sold	$481,000

One issue of importance for costing inventory of a manufacturing company is whether or not fixed manufacturing overhead costs will be included in inventory (absorption or full costing) or charged to expenses of the period (variable or direct costing). This issue is briefly discussed in Appendix 8A.

METHODS OF INVENTORY VALUATION

When the number of units of ending inventory and the costs to be included have been determined, inventory valuation requires that a choice be made from several acceptable methods to determine the dollar amount assigned to inventory. The methods available include the following.

> Cost Flow Methods:
>
> > Specific Identification
> >
> > First-In, First-Out (FIFO)
> >
> > Average Cost (weighted average or moving average)
> >
> > Last-In, First-Out (LIFO)
> >
> > Standard Cost
>
> Cost Modified for Market Value Changes Methods:
>
> > Lower of Cost and Market
> >
> > Current Replacement Cost
>
> Cost Approximation (Estimation) Methods:
>
> > Gross Profit
> >
> > Retail Inventory
>
> Long-Term Construction Contract Methods:
>
> > Completed Contract
> >
> > Percentage of Completion

The method chosen depends on several factors. The remainder of this chapter considers these factors regarding the cost flow methods identified above. The lower of cost and market, gross profit, and retail inventory methods are examined in Chapter 9. The selection of the appropriate method to account for a long-term construction contract was examined in Chapter 6. The current replacement cost method is discussed in Chapter 25.

COST FLOW ASSUMPTIONS: A FRAMEWORK FOR ANALYSIS

During any given fiscal period it is likely that merchandise will be purchased at several different prices. If inventories are to be priced at cost and numerous purchases have been made at different unit costs, which of the various costs should be assigned to Inventory on the balance sheet and which costs should be charged to Cost of Goods Sold on the income statement? Conceptually (to match actual costs with the physical flow of goods), a specific identification of the cost of items sold and unsold seems appropriate, but this is often not only expensive but difficult to do. Consequently, the accountant must turn to the consistent application of one of several other cost methods that are based on differing but systematic inventory **cost flow assumptions.** *There is no requirement that the cost flow assumption adopted be consistent with the physical movement of goods*.

Issues regarding the various cost flow methods will be illustrated and discussed using the data in Exhibit 8-12, which summarizes inventory-related activities of Call-Mart Inc. for the month of March. For illustrative purposes, the cost per unit of the beginning inventory is assumed to be the same for all methods. It is important to note that the company experienced *increasing unit costs for its purchases throughout the month*.

The problem is which cost or costs should be assigned to the 6,000 units of ending inventory and to the 4,000 units sold. The solution depends on what one wishes to accomplish. There are, as previously indicated, several acceptable alternative cost flow methods that may be chosen. These methods are based on different assumptions and accomplish different objectives. A suggested approach to selecting a method is as follows.

1. Identify possible objectives to be accomplished.

2. Know the different acceptable methods, their assumptions, and how they work.

OBJECTIVE 5
Understand the difference between physical flow of inventory and cost flow assigned to inventory.

EXHIBIT 8-12   CALL-MART INC.

DATA USED TO ILLUSTRATE INVENTORY CALUCULATION: COST FLOW ASSUMPTIONS

Date		Quantity and Price	Unit Balance
March 1	Beginning inventory	500 @ $3.80	500 units
2	Purchase	1,500 @ 4.00	2,000 units
15	Purchase	6,000 @ 4.40	8,000 units
19	Sale	4,000	4,000 units
30	Purchase	2,000 @ 4.50	6,000 units

The ending inventory consists of 6,000 units. Assume the 4,000 units were sold for $10 each for a total sales revenue of $40,000. There were 10,000 units available for sale (500 beginning inventory plus 9,500 purchased), which had a total cost of $43,300.

3. Evaluate the advantages and disadvantages of the different methods for achieving the objectives.

4. Choose the method appropriate to the situation and the objective(s) to be accomplished.

OBJECTIVES OF INVENTORY VALUATION

OBJECTIVE 6
Recognize there are various objectives to accomplish when assigning costs to inventories.

The following general objectives are often associated with making a decision as to which inventory cost flow method to choose.

1. To match expenses (cost of goods sold) realistically against revenue.

2. To report inventory on the balance sheet at a realistic amount.

3. To minimize income taxes.

While the first two are legitimate objectives of financial statements, the third should not be relevant to financial statement accounting; however, it sometimes enters into financial accounting systems for reasons of expediency.

The financial statement objectives of inventory valuation are inherently logical and useful when assessing the merits and limitations of the various cost flow methods within the framework of generally accepted accounting principles. They do, however, beg the question of "What is realistic?" The answer will depend on the purpose of preparing the financial statements. More will be said about this later in the chapter under the heading "Which Method to Select?"

COST FLOW METHODS OF INVENTORY VALUATION: THEIR ASSUMPTIONS AND HOW THEY WORK

SPECIFIC IDENTIFICATION

OBJECTIVE 7
Describe and compare the cost flow assumptions used in accounting for inventories.

The **specific identification method** requires identifying each item sold and each item in inventory. The costs of the specific items sold are included in the cost of goods sold, while the costs of specific items on hand are included in the inventory. This method may be used in instances where it is practical to identify specific items and their costs from the different purchases made. Any goods on hand may then be identified as quantities remaining from specific purchases, and the invoice cost of each lot or item may be separately determined.

This method has limited application in most companies because of the impossibility or impracticability of segregating specific items as coming from separate purchases. It can be successfully applied, however, in situations where a relatively small number of costly, easily distinguishable (e.g., by physical characteristics, serial numbers, or special markings) items are handled. In the retail trade this includes some types of jewellery, fur coats, automobiles, and some furniture and appliances. In manufacturing it includes special orders and products manufactured under a job cost system.

EXHIBIT 8-13   CALL-MART INC.

ENDING INVENTORY

Units From	No. Units	Unit Cost	Total Cost
Beginning Inventory	100	$3.80	$ 380
Mar. 2 Purchase	900	4.00	3,600
Mar. 15 Purchase	3,000	4.40	13,200
Mar. 30 Purchase	2,000	4.50	9,000
Ending inventory	**6,000**		**$26,180**

Goods available for sale (total of beginning inventory and purchases)	$43,300	
Deduct ending inventory	26,180	
Cost of goods sold	**$17,120**	

Given the data for Call-Mart Inc., suppose it was determined that the 6,000 units of ending inventory consisted of 100 from the beginning inventory, 900 from the March 2 purchase, 3,000 from the March 15 purchase and 2,000 from the March 30 purchase. Ending inventory and cost of goods sold would be determined as indicated in Exhibit 8-13.

Conceptually, this method is appealing because actual costs are matched against actual revenues and ending inventory is at actual cost. The cost flow matches the physical flow of the goods. On closer observation, however, deficiencies can be found in using this method as a basis for inventory valuation and income measurement.

One argument against specific identification is that it enables manipulation of net income. For example, assume that a wholesaler purchases plywood early in the year at three different prices. When the plywood is sold, the wholesaler can, if desired, select either the lowest or the highest cost to charge to expense simply by selecting the plywood from a specific lot for delivery to the customer. A business manager, therefore, can manipulate net income by delivering to the customer the higher or lower cost item, depending on whether a lower or higher reported income is desired for the period.

Another problem relates to the arbitrary allocation of costs that sometimes occurs with specific inventory items. In certain circumstances, it is difficult to relate adequately, for example, shipping charges and discounts directly to a given inventory item. The alternative, then, is to allocate these costs somewhat arbitrarily, which leads to a breakdown in the precision of the specific identification method.[14]

---

[14] A good illustration of the cost allocation problem arises in the motion picture industry. Often actors and actresses receive a percentage of net income for a given movie or television program. Some actors who have these arrangements have alleged that their programs have been extremely profitable to the studios but they have received little in the way of profit sharing. Actors contend that the studios allocate additional costs to successful films (specifically identifiable inventory items) to ensure that there will be no profits to share. Such contentions illustrate the type of problems that can emerge when contracts are based on accounting numbers that can incorporate arbitrary allocations. One way to help overcome such problems is to establish specific measurement rules regarding how the accounting numbers are to be determined, rather than just stating the numbers to be used. This should be done before the contract is signed so that all parties clearly understand what they are getting into.

FIRST-IN, FIRST-OUT (FIFO)

The **FIFO method** assigns costs to goods sold in the order in which costs were incurred; that is, the cost of the first good purchased is assumed to be the cost of the first sold (in a merchandising concern) or first used (in a manufacturing concern). The cost assigned to the inventory remaining would therefore come from the most recent purchases (i.e., "last-in, still-here").

Using the data for Call-Mart Inc., and assuming that the company is using the FIFO method and the periodic system (amount of inventory computed only at the end of the month), the cost of the ending inventory is computed by starting with the most recent purchase and working back until all units in the inventory are accounted for. The ending inventory and cost of goods sold are determined as follows.

EXHIBIT 8-14 CALL-MART INC.

Date of Invoice	No. Units	Unit Cost	Total Cost
Mar. 30	2,000	$4.50	$ 9,000
Mar. 15	4,000	4.40	17,600
Ending inventory	**6,000**		**$26,600**

Cost of goods available for sale	$43,300	
Deduct ending inventory	26,600	
Cost of goods sold	**$16,700**	

If a perpetual inventory system in quantities and dollars is used, a cost figure is attached to each withdrawal when it is made. In the example, the cost of the 4,000 units removed on March 19 would be made up of the items from beginning inventory and the purchases on March 2 and March 15. The inventory record on a FIFO basis perpetual system for Call-Mart Inc. is shown in Exhibit 8-15, which discloses the ending inventory cost of $26,600 and a cost of goods sold of $16,800.

EXHIBIT 8-15 CALL-MART INC.

Date	Purchased	Sold or Issued	Balance
Mar. 1	Beginning inventory		500 @ $3.80 $ 1,900
Mar. 2	(1,500 @ $4.00) $ 6,000		500 @ 3.80 ⎫ 1,500 @ 4.00 ⎬ 7,900
Mar. 15	(6,000 @ 4.40) 26,400		500 @ 3.80 ⎫ 1,500 @ 4.00 ⎬ 34,300 6,000 @ 4.40 ⎭
Mar. 19		500 @ $3.80 1,500 @ 4.00 2,000 @ 4.40 **$16,700**	4,000 @ 4.40 17,600
Mar. 30	(2,000 @ 4.50) 9,000		4,000 @ 4.40 ⎫ 2,000 @ 4.50 ⎬ **26,600**

When FIFO is used, the ending inventory and cost of goods sold for a period are the same whether a periodic or perpetual system is employed. This is because the same costs will always be first-in and, therefore, first-out, whether cost of goods sold is recorded as goods are sold throughout the accounting period (the perpetual system) or as a residual at the end of the period (the periodic system).

One objective of FIFO is to approximate the physical flow of goods. When the physical flow of goods is actually first-in, first-out, the FIFO method very nearly represents specific identification. At the same time, it does not permit manipulation of income because the enterprise is not free to pick a certain cost to be charged to expense.

Another advantage of the FIFO method is that the ending inventory amount is close to its current cost. Because the cost of the first goods in is the cost of the first goods out, the ending inventory amount will be composed of the cost of the most recent purchases. This approach generally provides an approximation of replacement cost for inventory on the balance sheet when the inventory turnover is rapid and/or price changes have not occurred since the most recent purchases.

The basic disadvantage of this method is that older (rather than current) costs are charged against the more current revenue, which can lead to distortions in gross profit and net income.

AVERAGE COST

As the name implies, the **average-cost method** prices items in the inventory on the basis of the average cost of the goods available for sale during the period.

When the periodic inventory system is used, the average cost is computed at the end of the period using the **weighted-average cost method**. Using the data for Call-Mart Inc., the application of the weighted-average cost method for a periodic inventory system is as shown in Exhibit 8-16.

EXHIBIT 8-16 CALL-MART INC.

	Date	No. Units	Unit Cost	Total Cost
Inventory	Mar. 1	500	$3.80	$ 1,900
Purchases	Mar. 2	1,500	4.00	6,000
Purchases	Mar. 15	6,000	4.40	26,400
Purchases	Mar. 30	2,000	4.50	9,000
Total goods available		10,000		$43,300

Weighted average cost per unit $\frac{\$43,300}{10,000} = \$4.33$

Inventory in units 6,000

Ending inventory 6,000 × $4.33 = $25,980

Cost of goods available for sale $43,300

Deduct ending inventory 25,980

Cost of goods sold **$17,320** (= 4,000 × $4.33)

Note that the beginning inventory is included both in the total units available and in the total cost of goods available in computing the average cost per unit.

Another average cost method is the **moving-average cost method**, which is used with perpetual inventory systems. The application of the moving-average cost method for a perpetual inventory system is shown in Exhibit 8-17.

In this method, a new average unit cost is computed each time a purchase is made. After the March 2 purchase, this cost is $3.95. After the March 15 purchase, it is $4.2875 per unit. This unit cost is used in costing withdrawals until another purchase is made, when a new average unit cost is computed. Accordingly, the unit cost of the 4,000 units withdrawn on March 19 is $4.2875, for a total cost of goods sold of $17,150. On March 30 a new unit cost of $4.3583 (rounded to four decimals) is determined, given the purchase of 2,000 units for $9,000.

The use of average-cost methods is usually justified on the basis of practical rather than conceptual reasons. They are simple to apply, objective, and not as subject to income

EXHIBIT 8-17   CALL-MART INC.

Date	Purchased	Sold or Issued	Balance
Mar. 1	Beginning inventory		(500 @ $3.80) $1,900
Mar. 2	(1,500 @ $4.00) $ 6,000		(2,000 @ $3.95) 7,900
Mar. 15	(6,000 @ $4.40) 26,400		(8,000 @ $4.2875) 34,300
Mar. 19		(4,000 @ $4.2875)	
		$17,150	(4,000 @ $4.2875) 17,150
Mar. 30	(2,000 @ $4.50) 9,000		(6,000 @ $4.3583) **26,150**

Calculation of moving-average cost per unit:

After March 2 purchase
= Cost of units available / Units available
= [(500 × $3.80) + (1,500 × $4.00)] / (500 + 1,500)
= ($1,900 + $6,000) / 2,000
= $7,900 / 2,000
= $3.95

After March 15 purchase
= [$7,900 + (6,000 × $4.40)] / (2,000 + 6,000)
= $34,300 / 8,000
= $4.2875

After March 30 purchase
= [(4,000 × $4.2875) + (2,000 × $4.50)] / (4,000 + 2,000)
= $26,150 / 6,000
= $4.3583

manipulation as some of the other inventory costing methods. In addition, proponents of the average-cost methods argue that it is often impossible to measure a specific physical flow of inventory and it is therefore better to cost items on an average-cost basis. This argument is particularly persuasive when the inventory involved is relatively homogeneous in nature.

In terms of achieving financial statement objectives, an average-cost method results in an average of costs being employed to determine the cost of goods sold in the income statement and ending inventory in the balance sheet. In comparison to the FIFO method, an average-cost method results in more recent costs being reflected in the cost of goods sold, but older costs in ending inventory. Relative to the LIFO method (discussed below) an average-cost method reflects more recent costs in ending inventory, but older costs in the cost of goods sold. Therefore, the average-cost methods may be viewed as a compromise between the FIFO and LIFO methods. Some would argue that, as a compromise, an average-cost method has the advantages of neither and the disadvantages of both of these other methods. In terms of the objective of income tax minimization, an average-cost method can be used in Canada and it may provide some income tax advantages during periods of rising prices.

LAST-IN, FIRST-OUT (LIFO)

The **LIFO method** assigns costs on the assumption that the cost of the most recent purchase is the first cost to be charged to cost of goods sold. The cost assigned to the inventory remaining would therefore come from the earliest acquisitions (i.e., "first-in, still-here").

If the periodic inventory system is used, then it would be assumed that the total quantity sold or issued during the period would have come from the most recent purchases, *even though such purchases may have taken place after the actual date of sale.* Conversely, the ending inventory costs would consist first of costs from the beginning inventory and then of costs from purchases early in the period. Using the data for Call-Mart Inc., the assumption would be made that the 4,000 units withdrawn consisted of the

2,000 units purchased on March 30 and 2,000 of the 6,000 units purchased on March 15. Therefore, the cost of the ending inventory of 6,000 units would be assumed to come from the cost of any beginning inventory (500 units) and then the earliest purchases in the period (1,500 units on March 2 and 4,000 units on March 15). Exhibit 8-18 shows how the inventory and cost of goods sold would be determined.

EXHIBIT 8-18 CALL-MART INC.

Assumed Source of Ending Inventory	No. Units	Unit Cost	Total Cost
Beginning inventory	500	$3.80	$ 1,900
Mar. 2 purchase	1,500	4.00	6,000
Mar. 15 purchase	4,000	4.40	17,600
Ending inventory	**6,000**		**$25,500**
Cost of goods available for sale		$43,300	
Deduct ending inventory		25,500	
Cost of goods sold		**$17,800**	

If a perpetual inventory system is kept in quantities and dollars, application of the last-in, first-out method will result in an ending inventory of $25,700 and cost of goods sold of $17,600, as shown in Exhibit 8-19.

EXHIBIT 8-19 CALL-MART INC.

Date	Purchased	Sold or Issued	Balance	
Mar. 1	Beginning inventory		500 @ $3.80	$ 1,900
Mar. 2	(1,500 @ $4.00) $ 6,000		500 @ 3.80	7,900
			1,500 @ 4.00	
Mar. 15	(6,000 @ 4.40) 26,400		500 @ 3.80	
			1,500 @ 4.00	34,300
			6,000 @ 4.40	
Mar. 19		(4,000 @ 4.40) $17,600	500 @ 3.80	
			1,500 @ 4.00	16,700
			2,000 @ 4.40	
Mar. 30	(2,000 @ 4.50) 9,000		500 @ 3.80	
			1,500 @ 4.00	25,700
			2,000 @ 4.40	
			2,000 @ 4.50	

When using the LIFO method, the month-end *periodic* inventory computation illustrated previously (inventory $25,500 and cost of goods sold $17,800) shows different amounts from the *perpetual* inventory computation shown above (inventory $25,700 and cost of goods sold $17,600). This is because the former matches the total withdrawals for the month with the total purchases for the month, whereas the latter matches each withdrawal with the immediately preceding purchases. In effect, the periodic computation assumed that goods that were not purchased until March 30 were included in the sale or issue of March 19. While this is not physically possible, remember that it is not necessary to match physical item flows with cost flows when measuring cost of goods sold. The perspective to be taken is that of understanding which costs are matched against the revenues.

EVALUATION OF LIFO RELATIVE TO OTHER COST FLOW METHODS

Use of the LIFO method is controversial. Some do not believe it is appropriate for conceptual reasons, while others believe it is conceptually superior to other approaches given that financial statements are prepared on an historical cost basis. Arguments for and

OBJECTIVE 8
Evaluate LIFO as a basis for understanding the differences between the cost flow methods.

against the use of LIFO necessarily reflect a perception regarding many fundamental issues about financial accounting: What is relevant? Which is more important, the income statement or the balance sheet? Should income tax requirements dictate methods to be selected for preparing financial statements?

While reaching a conclusion regarding the acceptability of LIFO is a matter of judgement, the following identification of the major advantages and disadvantages of LIFO should be considered. Careful reflection on this listing will indicate that, for most points, the advantages of LIFO become the disadvantages of other cost flow methods (FIFO and average cost) and vice versa.

MAJOR ADVANTAGES OF LIFO

Matching. The matching principle requires that we match costs to the same period as related revenues are recognized. *The principle, however, does not say which costs should be matched when alternatives are possible.* Therefore, for inventory valuation, the various methods available leave open the choice of matching recent costs (LIFO), average costs (average methods), or older costs (FIFO) against revenues.

In LIFO, the more recent costs are matched against current revenues to provide what may be viewed as a more realistic measure of current earnings in periods of changing prices. For example, in the early 1990s many Canadian oil companies changed to the LIFO method. The explanation given in Petro-Canada's financial report was: "The change was made to more closely match current costs with current revenues in determination of the results of the Company's operations."

During periods of rising prices, many challenge the quality of non-LIFO historical cost-based earnings, noting that by failing to match current costs against current revenues *transitory "paper" or "inventory" profits are created*. Inventory profits occur because old, low inventory costs that are matched against sales are less than the recent, higher costs to replace the inventory. The cost of goods sold therefore is perceived to be understated and profit is overstated. By using LIFO (rather than FIFO or average cost), more recent costs are matched against revenues and inventory profits are thereby reduced.

Future Earnings Hedge. With LIFO, in a period of rising prices a company's future reported earnings will not be affected substantially by future price declines (due to write-downs under the lower of cost and market rule examined in Chapter 9). LIFO eliminates or substantially minimizes write-downs to market as a result of price decreases. The reason: since the most recent (higher cost) inventory is assumed to be sold first, the ending inventory value ordinarily will be lower than net realizable value. In contrast, inventory costed under FIFO is more vulnerable to price declines, which can reduce net income substantially. When prices are declining, however, this aspect of LIFO becomes a disadvantage.

MAJOR DISADVANTAGES OF LIFO

Reduced Earnings. Many corporate managers view the lower profits reported under the LIFO method, relative to other methods, as a distinct disadvantage. They fear that the implications on net income from using LIFO may be misunderstood and that, as a result of the lower profits, the price of the company's shares will fall. In fact, there is some evidence to refute this contention. Studies have indicated that users of financial data exhibit a sophistication that enables them to recognize the impact on reported income from using LIFO compared with other methods and, as a consequence, reflect this in their assessment of a company's share price.

This disadvantage of reduced earnings assumes that prices are increasing; when prices are declining, the opposite effect may occur. For example, oil prices to refineries were declining when many Canadian oil companies switched to LIFO in the early 1990s.

Inventory Distortion. Under LIFO, the inventory valuation on the balance sheet is normally outdated because the oldest costs remain in inventory. This results in several problems, but manifests itself most directly in evaluating the amounts, ratios, and related trends that include the ending inventory. The magnitude and direction of the variation in the carrying amount of inventory and its current price depend on the degree and direction of the changes in price and the amount of inventory turnover.

Physical Flow. LIFO does not approximate the physical flow of the items except in a few situations. Imagine a coal pile: the last coal bought is the first coal out, since the coal remover will not take coal from the inside of the pile. However, matching more recent costs against revenues may be viewed as a higher-priority objective than reflecting the physical flow of goods when choosing an inventory valuation method.

Inventory Liquidation. Use of LIFO raises the problem of inventory liquidation. If the base or layers of old costs in beginning inventory are eliminated (e.g., when units sold exceed the units purchased for a period), strange results can occur. The matching advantage of LIFO would be lost because old, irrelevant costs would be matched against current revenues, resulting in a severe distortion in reported income at least for the given period. For example, Allied Corporation reported net earnings of $.09 per share in which its inventory reductions resulted in liquidations of LIFO inventory quantities. The effect of the inventory reduction was to increase income by $13 million, or $.17 per share.

Poor Buying Habits. Because of the liquidation problem, LIFO may cause poor buying habits. A company may simply purchase more goods and match these costs against revenue to ensure that old costs are not charged to expense. Furthermore, the possibility always exists with LIFO that a company will attempt to manage (manipulate) its earnings at the end of a year simply by altering its pattern of purchases.

Not Acceptable for Tax Purposes. Because of definitions in the Income Tax Act as to how inventory amounts may be determined, LIFO inventory valuation is not accepted by Revenue Canada for purposes of determining taxable income except in a few special circumstances.

Current Cost Income Not Measured. LIFO falls short of measuring current cost (replacement cost) income, though not as far as FIFO. When measuring current cost income, the cost of goods sold should consist not of the most recently incurred costs but rather of the cost that will be incurred to replace the goods that have been sold. Using replacement cost is referred to as the next-in, first-out method, which is not currently acceptable for purposes of inventory valuation.

SUMMARY ANALYSIS OF FIFO, WEIGHTED-AVERAGE, AND LIFO METHODS

For review and comparison purposes, a summary of the differing effects of the three major cost flow methods on the financial statements is shown in Exhibit 8-20. The numbers were derived from the illustrations of each method for Call-Mart Inc. for the month of March and using the periodic system. The sales revenue reflects that the 4,000 units were sold for $10 each. The difference in gross profit and, therefore, net income (other expenses would be the same) is due to the differing cost flow assumptions associated with each method. Since the example incorporated a period of rising prices, the gross profit (and, therefore, net income) is highest under FIFO and lowest under LIFO.

At the bottom of the comparative results is a listing of the three objectives previously identified as being most commonly associated with choosing an inventory method. As developed in the prior discussion, the strongest argument favouring LIFO for financial statement reporting purposes is that it matches more current costs against current revenue. FIFO results in a more current cost for inventory on the balance sheet.

EXHIBIT 8-20 CALL-MART INC.

	Method		
	FIFO	Weighted-Average	LIFO
Partial Income Statement:			
Sales Revenue	$40,000	$40,000	$40,000
Cost of Goods Sold:			
Beginning inventory	$ 1,900	$ 1,900	$ 1,900
Purchases	41,400	41,400	41,400
Goods Available	$43,300	$43,300	$43,300
Deduct:			
Ending Inventory	26,600	25,980	25,500
Cost of Goods Sold	16,700	17,320	17,800
Gross Profit	$23,300	$22,680	$22,200
Balance Sheet:			
Inventory	$26,600	$25,980	$25,500
Objectives:			
1. Matching	Old costs against current revenue	Average cost against current revenue	"Current" costs against current revenue*
2. Balance Sheet Valuation	"Current" costs*	Average cost	Old costs
3. Income Tax Minimization	Results in higher taxable income in periods of rising prices.	Best in Canada in periods of rising prices as results in highest cost of goods sold next to LIFO.*	Not allowed in Canada in most situations. If it were, it would be best in periods of rising prices.

*Results in a realistic accomplishment of objective relative to other methods. The * regarding matching for LIFO assumes no liquidation of beginning inventory.

In terms of income tax minimization or deferral of tax payments, the method resulting in the lowest taxable income for the period would be preferred. While LIFO results in the lowest income in periods of rising prices (assuming there is little or no beginning inventory liquidation), it is not permitted for calculating taxable income in Canada for most businesses. Consequently, the average-cost method, which is permitted by Revenue Canada, would more effectively accomplish this objective in a period of rising prices.

The fact that LIFO is generally not allowed for determining taxable income in Canada is in direct contrast to the situation in the United States, where it is accepted for tax purposes. While non-LIFO disclosures may be made as supplemental information, the Internal Revenue Service in the U.S. requires that if LIFO is used for income tax purposes, it must also be used for financial reporting purposes (this is known as the LIFO conformity rule). Though one may argue the merits of LIFO for financial reporting purposes on a more conceptual level, the IRS ruling is likely primarily responsible for the much higher use of the LIFO method in financial statements in the U.S. as compared to Canada.[15]

---

[15] *Financial Reporting in Canada—1995* reported that of 278 inventory cost method disclosures, 124 (44%) used FIFO, 10 (4%) used LIFO, 99 (36%) used average cost, 13 (5%) used specific identification, 4 (1%) used standard cost, 12 (4%) used the retail method, and 16 (6%) used other methods. For comparison, a similar U.S. study, *Accounting Trends and Techniques—1993*, reported that of 1,011 method disclosures, 358 (35%) used LIFO, 415 (41%) used FIFO, 193 (19%) used average cost, and 45 (5%) used other methods. Data from the U.S. indicate that a significant shift from FIFO to LIFO took place during the 1970s and early 1980s. The rate of inflation and tax advantages of LIFO were, no doubt, at least partially responsible for the shift. Although inflation was also significant in Canada, no shift to LIFO was evident.

WHICH METHOD TO SELECT?

The *CICA Handbook* indicates that specific identification, FIFO, average cost, and LIFO are generally acceptable and commonly used methods for determining the cost of inventory for financial reporting purposes.[16] The *Handbook* also states:

> The method selected for determining cost should be one which results in the fairest matching of costs against revenues regardless of whether or not the method corresponds to the physical flow of goods.[17]

What method will provide the fairest matching? The answer can be derived only by exercising professional judgement, given knowledge of the particular circumstances and the consequences desired in terms of the objectives of the financial statements. As indicated in Chapter 1, a primary objective of financial reporting is to communicate information that is useful to investors, creditors, and others in making their resource allocation decisions and/or assessing management stewardship. Therefore, the inventory valuation method that leads to the accomplishment of this objective would certainly be the fairest (more relevant) one to choose. Making the appropriate choice, however, depends on awareness of a number of things, such as who the users are, the decisions they are making, and what information fits their decision models. If one method was the fairest for all situations, then the accounting profession would certainly not have acceptable alternative methods. Consequently, professional judgement is the basis for determining the method to use.

An important point is that a company can use one method (e.g., FIFO) for financial statement reporting and another method (average cost) for tax purposes. This is legal and reasonable as the objectives of financial reporting are different from those of income tax determination. Having "two sets of books" may, however, be inefficient—a judgement requiring the accountant to be fully cognizant of the circumstances. If methods used for preparing financial statements differ from those used for determining taxable income, a difference between the reported income tax expense and the actual tax paid results. The amount of the difference is accounted for as an interperiod tax allocation, a complex topic that is examined in Chapter 19.

OBJECTIVE 9
Understand the importance of judgement in selecting an inventory cost flow method.

STANDARD COST METHOD

A manufacturing company that uses a **standard cost system** predetermines the unit costs for material, labour, and manufacturing overhead. Usually the standard costs are determined on the basis of the costs that should be incurred per unit of finished goods when the plant is operating at normal capacity. Deviations from actual costs are recorded in variance accounts that are examined by management so that appropriate action can be taken to achieve greater control over costs.

For financial statement purposes, reporting inventories at standard costs is acceptable if there is no significant difference between the aggregate actual and standard costs. If there is a significant difference, the inventory amounts should be adjusted to estimated actual cost.[18] Otherwise the net income, assets, and retained earnings would be misstated. A detailed examination of standard costing is available in most managerial and cost accounting texts, but is beyond the scope of this book.

---

[16] *CICA Handbook*, Section 3030, par. .07. Noteworthy about this Section is that it does not explicitly identify these methods as the only ones that are acceptable.

[17] *Ibid*, Section 3030, par. .09.

[18] *Ibid*, Section 3030, par. .04.

CONSISTENCY OF INVENTORY COSTING

All of the inventory costing methods described in this chapter are used to some extent. Indeed, a company may use different methods for different types of inventory.

It can be seen that freedom to shift from one inventory costing method to another at will would permit a wide range of possible net income figures for a given company for any given period. This would make financial statements less comparable. *The variety of methods has been devised to assist appropriate financial reporting rather than to permit manipulation.* Hence, it is necessary that the costing method most suitable to a company be selected and, once selected, be applied consistently thereafter. If conditions indicate that the inventory costing method in use may be unsuitable (e.g., not as relevant as could be), serious consideration should be given to all other possibilities before selecting another method. If a change is made, it should be clearly explained and its effect disclosed in the financial statements.[19]

PRODUCT COSTING AND SOCIETAL VALUES—PROFITS UP IN SMOKE!

EMERGING ISSUES

What do societal values have to do with product costing and inventory valuation? In June 1997, lawyers negotiated a settlement deal with U.S. tobacco companies reputed to be in the area of $368 billion. Under the terms of the deal, the tobacco companies agreed to pay out this amount over the next twenty-five years. That works out to just under $15 billion per year, more than double the industry's operating profits for domestic sales in 1996. Beyond that, the payments will continue in perpetuity. The money will go into a fund and be used to settle claims by various states and existing class action suits, all against tobacco companies. The fund will also be used for future claims and settlements against the tobacco industry.[1]

Why would the tobacco companies agree to a settlement that could wipe out their profits? Part of the reason may be rooted in the mounting number of lawsuits against the companies for health problems reputed to be connected to cigarette smoking. Four decades ago, consumers were ignorant of the health hazard caused by smoking and inhaling second hand smoke. Even in 1964, when the U.S. Surgeon General determined that smoking was a health hazard, it was still very socially acceptable to smoke. In the past decade in Canada, the tides have turned sharply and now in most public indoor places, smoking is banned. With the acceptance of the fact that smoking does indeed present a health hazard came the inevitable rise in lawsuits. The proposed settlement reduces the uncertainty surrounding the rising cost of these lawsuits and allows the tobacco companies to plan for potential future cash outflows.

What does this have to do with inventory and inventory costing? Should the cost of the settlement be included as an inventoriable cost? Are these costs direct material costs (product costs) or are they period costs? On the one hand they are not costs directly incurred in the production or acquisition of cigarettes. On the other hand they are costs that the company must incur each time they produce and sell the cigarettes. Are they more related to the production of the inventory or the sale? A full costing "all-in" approach would include this cost and certainly, if the information were to be used for a pricing decision, including the amount would make sense. As a matter of fact, the tobacco companies will likely raise their prices to cover these costs.

---

[19] *Ibid*, Section 1000, pars. .22 and .23.

The resolution of this decision will affect a key ration—the gross profit margin. As long as all companies treat the amount the sam way, there will be comparability between companies. The amount will certainly be material to most companies.

Regardless of the allocation of the cost, it will certainly contribute to the profits of these companies "going up in smoke".

[1]Details of settlement were taken from *The Financial Post*, Wednesday June 25, 1997.

Contributed by: Irene Wiecek, University of Toronto.

Summary of Learning Objectives

1. **Identify major classifications of inventory.** Only one inventory account, Merchandise Inventory, appears in the financial statements of a merchandising concern. A manufacturer normally has three inventory accounts: Raw Materials, Work in Process, and Finished Goods. Factory or manufacturing supplies inventory may also exist.

2. **Distinguish between perpetual and periodic inventory systems.** The perpetual inventory system results in keeping an up-to-date record of units and cost of inventory items in the accounting records. In this system, additions to and reductions of inventory are recorded as they occur. No such record is kept under the periodic inventory system. Under the periodic system, year-end inventory must be determined by a physical count upon which the amount of ending inventory and cost of goods sold is based. Even under the perpetual system, an annual count is needed to test the accuracy of the records.

3. **Identify the effects of inventory errors on the financial statements.** Inventory errors can occur for many reasons throughout the valuation process and, when they occur, can have important consequences regarding financial statement information. For example, if the *ending inventory is misstated* (1) the inventory, retained earnings, and working capital in the balance sheet will be misstated; (2) the cost of goods sold and net income in the income statement will be misstated; and (3) the asset turnover, debt to total assets, rate of return on assets, and current ratios will be incorrect. *If purchases and inventory are misstated* (1) the inventory and accounts payable will be misstated; (2) purchases and ending inventory in the income statement will be misstated, but cost of goods sold will be correct; and (3) the above-mentioned ratios will be incorrect.

4. **Identify the items that are included as inventory cost.** Items for which there is possession of the risks and rewards of ownership make up the inventory. Ownership regarding goods in transit, consignments, and special sale agreements must be carefully determined by examining contracts and the economic substance of the transactions. Determining the cost to assign to quantities of inventory requires specification of which costs should be included. Basically, the cost should be the laid-down cost (what is incurred to get the inventory to its current condition and location). Application of this definition is fairly straightforward for some costs (purchase price, freight, discounts) but difficult

KEY TERMS

average-cost method, 395

cost flow assumptions, 391

cost of goods available for sale, 382

cost of goods sold, 382

FIFO method, 394

finished goods inventory, 378

f.o.b. destination, 383

f.o.b. shipping point, 382

gross method, 389

inventories, 377

LIFO method, 396

manufacturing business, 378

merchandising business, 378

moving-average cost method, 395

net method, 389

period costs, 388

periodic inventory system, 380

perpetual inventory system, 380

physical inventory count, 380

product costs, 388

purchase discounts

raw materials inventory, 378

for other costs (interest charges, storage costs, fixed manufacturing costs). Consequently, for practical reasons, allocating the latter type of costs to inventory may not be done.

5. **Understand the difference between physical flow of inventory and cost flow assigned to inventory.** If the unit cost is different for various purchases, the question is which costs will be assigned to ending inventory and, as a consequence, to cost of goods sold. In accounting there is no requirement that the costs charged to goods sold be consistent with the physical movement of the goods. Consequently, various cost flow methods for assigning costs to cost of goods sold and ending inventory are all generally acceptable. The primary methods are specific identification, FIFO, average cost, and LIFO.

6. **Recognize there are various objectives to accomplish when assigning costs to inventories.** The general objectives are (1) to match expenses realistically against revenues; (2) to report inventory on the balance sheet at a realistic amount; and (3) to minimize income taxes. Inevitably, trade-offs exist between the cost flow methods and the objectives such that no method will likely satisfy all objectives.

7. **Describe and compare the cost flow assumptions used in accounting for inventories.** (1) Average cost prices items in the inventory on the basis of the average cost of all similar goods available during the period. (2) First-in, first-out (FIFO) assumes that goods are used in the order in which they are purchased. The inventory remaining must therefore represent the most recent purchases. (3) Last-in, first-out (LIFO) matches the cost of the last goods purchased against revenue.

8. **Evaluate LIFO as a basis for understanding the differences between the cost flow methods.** In a period of rising prices, LIFO may be viewed as providing a more realistic matching in the income statement (recent costs against revenues) and offering a greater future earnings hedge. Disadvantages include a reduction in net income and old costs for inventory on the balance sheet. In addition, it does not generally reflect physical flow, matching is destroyed when beginning inventory is liquidated, it provides an opportunity to manage (manipulate) earnings, and it is not acceptable for income tax purposes in Canada. To an extent, the advantages and disadvantages of LIFO are the disadvantages and advantages of FIFO. Average-cost methods fall between these two extremes.

9. **Understand the importance of judgement in selecting an inventory cost flow method.** The only guidance provided in the *CICA Handbook* is that the method chosen should result in "the fairest matching of costs against revenues regardless of whether or not the method corresponds to the physical flow of goods." Consequently, exercise of judgement is required when choosing a cost flow method.

APPENDIX 8A

Variable Costing Versus Absorption Costing

Fixed manufacturing overhead costs present a special problem in costing inventories because two concepts exist relative to the costs that attach to the product as it flows through the manufacturing process. These two concepts are (1) **variable costing**, frequently called **direct costing**, and (2) **absorption costing**, also called **full costing**.

In a variable costing system, all costs must be classified as variable or fixed. **Variable costs** are those that fluctuate in direct proportion to changes in output, and **fixed costs** are those that remain constant in spite of changes in output. Under variable costing, only costs that vary directly with the production volume are charged to products as manufacturing takes place. Direct material, direct labour, and variable manufacturing overhead are charged to work-in-process and finished goods inventories and subsequently become part of cost of goods sold. Fixed overhead costs such as property taxes, insurance, depreciation on plant building, and salaries of supervisors are considered to be *period costs* and are not viewed as costs of the products being manufactured. Instead, all fixed costs are charged as expenses to the current period.

Under an absorption costing system, all manufacturing costs (variable and fixed, direct and indirect) incurred in the factory or production process attach to the product. Direct material, direct labour, and all manufacturing overhead—fixed as well as variable—are charged to output and allocated to cost of goods sold and inventories.

Proponents of the variable costing system believe that it provides information that is more useful to management in formulating pricing policies and in controlling costs than is in reports prepared under an absorption costing system. Also, because fixed costs are included in inventory under the absorption costing system, it may be argued that such a system would result in distorting net income from period to period when production volume fluctuates each period. If such is the case, variable costing may be a more appropriate basis for reporting income. Absorption costing, however, is the dominant basis for external financial reporting. Its supporters believe it provides a more reasonable representation of a firm's investment in inventories.

The *CICA Handbook* states:

> In the case of inventories of work in process and finished goods, cost should include the laid-down cost of materials plus the cost of direct labour applied to the product and the applicable share of overhead expense properly chargeable to production.[20]

This statement leaves to one's judgement the issue of how fixed overhead costs are to be treated in terms of whether or not they are "properly chargeable to production." The *Handbook* also states that "in some cases, a portion of fixed overhead is excluded where its inclusion would distort the net income for the period by reason of fluctuating volume of production."[21] This guideline certainly reflects that variable costing is acceptable but sug-

OBJECTIVE 10
Appreciate the difference between variable costing and absorption costing in assigning costs of manufacturing to inventory.

---

[20] *Ibid*, Section 3030, par. .06.

[21] *Ibid*, par. .03.

gests that it would be considered more the exception than the rule for external financial reporting. Clearly, however, judgement is called for when making a decision in particular circumstances.

KEY TERMS	Summary of Learning Objective for Appendix 8A

KEY TERMS

absorption (full) costing, 404

fixed costs, 404

variable (direct) costing, 404

variable costs, 404

10. **Appreciate the difference between variable costing and absorption costing in assigning costs of manufacturing to inventory.** Under variable (direct) costing, direct material, direct labour, and variable manufacturing overhead are charged to inventories. In absorption (full) costing, direct material, direct labour, and all manufacturing overhead (variable and fixed) are charged to inventories.

Note: All *asterisked* exercises, problems, and cases relate to material contained in the appendix to the chapter.

EXERCISES

E8-1 **(Determining Missing Amounts)** Two or more items are omitted in each of the following tabulations of income statement data. Fill in the amounts that are missing.

	1997	1998	1999
Sales	$290,000	$_____	$400,000
Sales Returns	11,000	13,000	_____
Net Sales	_____	347,000	_____
Beginning Inventory	20,000	30,000	_____
Ending Inventory	_____	_____	_____
Purchases	_____	260,000	298,000
Purchase Returns and Allowances	5,000	8,000	10,000
Transportation-in	8,000	9,000	12,000
Cost of Goods Sold	233,000	_____	293,000
Gross Profit on Sales	46,000	91,000	97,000

E8-2 **(Inventory Cut-off Errors)** In an annual audit at December 31, 1998 you find the following transactions near the closing date.

1. A special machine, made to order for a customer, was finished and, at the customer's request, held in the back part of the shipping room on December 31, 1998 to be delivered within the next week. The customer was billed on December 31 as the customer agreed to bear responsibility for the machine while it was being held.

2. Merchandise costing $2,800 was received on January 3, 1999 and the related purchase invoice recorded January 5. The invoice showed the shipment was made on December 29, 1998, f.o.b. destination.

3. Merchandise costing $720 was received on December 28, 1998 and the invoice was not recorded. You located it in the hands of the purchasing agent; it was marked on consignment.

4. A packing case containing a product costing $1,500 was standing in the shipping room when the physical inventory was taken. It was not included in the inventory because it was marked "Hold for shipping instructions." Your investigation revealed that the customer's order was dated December 18, 1998 but that the case was shipped and the customer billed on January 10, 1999. The product was a stock item of your client.

5. Merchandise received on January 6, 1999 costing $680 was entered in the purchase journal on January 7, 1999. The invoice showed the shipment was made f.o.b. supplier's warehouse on December 31, 1998. Because it was not on hand at December 31, it was not included in inventory.

Instructions
Assuming that each of the amounts is material, state whether the merchandise should be included in the client's inventory and give the reason for your decision on each item.

(Inventoriable Costs) Presented below is a list of items that may or may not be reported as inventory in a company's December 31 balance sheet: **E8-3**

1. Materials on hand not yet placed into production by a manufacturing firm.
2. Office supplies.
3. Goods purchased f.o.b. shipping point that are in transit at December 31.
4. Raw materials on which a manufacturing firm has started production, but which are not completely processed.
5. Goods held on consignment from another company.
6. Costs identified with units completed by a manufacturing firm, but not yet sold.
7. Goods sold f.o.b. destination that are in transit at December 31.
8. Factory supplies.
9. Temporary investments in shares and bonds that will be resold in the near future.
10. Goods out on consignment at another company's store.
11. Goods purchased f.o.b. destination that are in transit at December 31.
12. Goods sold to another company, for which our company has signed an agreement to repurchase at a set price that covers all costs related to the inventory.
13. Goods sold where returns are unpredictable.
14. Goods sold f.o.b. shipping point that are in transit at December 31.
15. Freight charges on goods purchased, but not sold.
16. Factory labour costs incurred on goods still unsold.
17. Goods sold on an instalment basis.
18. Interest costs incurred for inventories that are routinely manufactured.
19. Costs incurred to advertise goods held for resale.

Instructions
Indicate which of these items would typically be reported as inventory in the financial statements. If an item should *not* be reported as inventory, indicate how it should be reported in the financial statements.

(Inventoriable Costs: Error Adjustments) The following purchase transactions occurred during the last few days **E8-4** of the Bapco Company's business year, which ends October 31, or in the first few days after that date. A periodic inventory system is used.

1. An invoice for $3,000, terms f.o.b. shipping point, was received and entered November 1. The invoice shows that the material was shipped October 29, but the receiving report indicates receipt of goods on November 3.
2. An invoice for $2,700, terms f.o.b. destination, was received and entered November 2. The receiving report indicates that the goods were received October 29.
3. An invoice for $3,150, terms f.o.b. shipping point, was received October 15 but never entered. Attached to it is a receiving report indicating that the goods were received October 18. Across the face of the receiving report is the following notation: "Merchandise not of same quality as ordered—returned for credit October 19."
4. An invoice for $3,600, terms f.o.b. shipping point, was received and entered October 27. The receiving report attached to the invoice indicates that the shipment was received October 27 in satisfactory condition.
5. An invoice for $5,100, terms f.o.b. destination, was received and entered October 28. The receiving report indicates that the merchandise was received November 2.

Before preparing financial statements for the year, you are instructed to review these transactions and to determine whether any correcting entries are required and whether the inventory of $77,500 determined by physical count should be changed.

Instructions
Complete the following schedule and state the correct inventory at October 31. Assume that the books have not been closed. Also, given your correcting entries, identify entries that must be made after closing in order for the accounts of November to be correct.

Transaction	Purchase and Related Payable Should Be Recognized in (Month)	Purchase and Related Payable Were Recognized in (Month)	Correcting Journal Entries Needed	Should Inventory Be Included in October Ending Inventory?	Was Inventory Included in October Ending Inventory?	Dollar Adjustments Needed to October Ending Inventory

E8-5 **(Inventory Corrections)** The JA Manufacturing Company maintains a general ledger account for each class of inventory, debiting such accounts for increases during the period, and crediting them for decreases. The transactions below relate to the Raw Materials inventory account, which is debited for materials purchased and credited for materials requisitioned for use:

1. An invoice for $6,400, terms f.o.b. destination, was received and entered January 2, 1999. The receiving report shows that they were received December 28, 1998.

2. Materials costing $28,000, shipped f.o.b. destination, were not entered by December 31, 1998 "because they were in a railroad car on the company's siding on that date and had not been unloaded."

3. Materials costing $7,300 were returned on December 29, 1998 to the supplier and were shipped f.o.b. shipping point. They were entered on that date, even though they were not expected to reach the supplier's place of business until January 6, 1999.

4. An invoice for $9,200, terms f.o.b. shipping point, was received and entered December 30, 1998. The receiving report shows that the materials were received January 4, 1999 and the bill of lading shows that they were shipped January 2, 1999.

5. Materials costing $19,800 were received December 30, 1998 but no entry was made for them because "they were ordered with a specified delivery of no earlier than January 10, 1999."

Instructions
Prepare correcting general journal entries required on December 31, 1998, assuming that the books have not been closed. Also indicate which entries must be reversed after closing in order for the next period's accounts to be correct.

E8-6 **(Purchases Recorded Net)** Presented below are the transactions related to Trifle Inc.

May 10	Purchased goods billed at $14,600 subject to cash discount terms of 2/10, n/60.
11	Purchased goods billed at $13,200 subject to terms of 1/15, n/30.
19	Paid invoice of May 10.
24	Purchased goods billed at $11,500 subject to cash discount terms of 2/10, n/30.

Instructions
(a) Prepare general journal entries for the transactions above under the assumption that purchases are to be recorded at net amounts after cash discounts and that discounts lost are to be treated as a financial expense.

(b) Assuming no purchase or payment transactions other than those given above, prepare the adjusting entry required on May 31 if financial statements are to be prepared as of that date.

E8-7 **(Financial Statement Presentation of Manufacturing Amounts)** Yu Company is a manufacturing firm. Presented below is selected information from its 1998 accounting records.

Raw materials inventory, 1/1/98	$ 30,800	Transportation-out	$ 8,000
Raw materials inventory, 12/31/98	37,400	Selling expenses	300,000
Work-in-process inventory, 1/1/98	72,600	Administrative expenses	180,000
Work-in-process inventory, 12/31/98	61,600	Purchase discounts	10,640
Finished goods inventory, 1/1/98	35,200	Purchase returns and allowances	3,960
Finished goods inventory, 12/31/98	22,000	Interest expense	15,000
Purchases	278,600	Direct labour	440,000
Transportation-in	6,600	Manufacturing overhead	330,000

Instructions
(a) Compute the cost of raw materials used.

(b) Compute the cost of goods manufactured.

(c) Compute cost of goods sold.

(d) Indicate how inventories would be reported in the 12/31/98 balance sheet.

E8-8 **(Inventory Errors: Impact on Financial Statement Amounts and Ratios)** Prone Company makes the following errors during the current year:

1. Ending inventory is correct, but a purchase on account was not recorded. (Assume this purchase was recorded in the following year.)

2. Ending inventory is overstated, but purchases are recorded correctly.

3. Both ending inventory and purchases on account are understated. (Assume this purchase was recorded in the following year.)

Instructions

Indicate the effect of each of these errors on working capital, current ratio (assume that the current ratio is greater than 1 to 1), retained earnings, net income, rate of return on assets, and debt to total assets ratio for the current year and the subsequent year. For the latter two ratios assume they are less than 100% to start with and that only end-of-period balance sheet amounts are used in their calculation.

(Inventory Errors: Impact on Current Ratio and Income) At December 31, 1998 Hall Inc. reported current assets of **E8-9** $350,000 and current liabilities of $200,000. The following items may have been recorded incorrectly:

1. Goods purchased costing $22,000 were shipped f.o.b. shipping point by a supplier on December 28. Hall received and recorded the invoice on December 29, but the goods were not included in Hall's physical count of inventory because they were not received until January 4.

2. Goods purchased costing $15,000 were shipped f.o.b. destination by a supplier on December 26. Hall received and recorded the invoice on December 31, but the goods were not included in Hall's physical count of inventory because they were not received until January 2.

3. Goods held on consignment from Wall Company were included in Hall's physical count of inventory at $13,000.

4. Freight-in of $3,000 for items on hand was debited to Advertising Expense on December 28.

Instructions

(a) Compute the current ratio based on Hall's balance sheet.

(b) Recompute the current ratio after corrections are made.

(c) By what amount will income (before taxes) be adjusted up or down as a result of the corrections?

(Inventory Errors and Earnings Management) The net income per books was determined without knowledge of **E8-10** the errors indicated.

Year	Net Income per Books	Error in Ending Inventory	
1993	$50,000	Overstated	$3,000
1994	52,000	Overstated	9,000
1995	54,000	Understated	11,000
1996	56,000	No error	
1997	58,000	Understated	6,000
1998	60,000	Overstated	8,000

Instructions

(a) Prepare a work sheet to show the adjusted net income figure for each of the six years after taking into account the inventory errors.

(b) Would the differences in reported income per the books and the corrected income be of significance? Why?

(FIFO, LIFO, and Weighted Average: Effect on Net Income When Prices Are Falling) The Golf Shop began oper- **E8-11** ations on January 1, 1998. The following stock record card for crested shirts existed at the end of the year.

Date	Terms	Units Received	Unit Invoice Cost	Gross Invoice Amount
1/15	Net 30	50	$20.00	$1,000.00
3/15	1/5, net 30	65	16.00	1,040.00
6/20	1/10, net 30	90	15.00	1,350.00
9/12	1/10, net 30	84	12.00	1,008.00
11/24	1/10, net 30	76	11.00	836.00
Totals		365		$5,234.00

A physical inventory on December 31, 1998 reveals that 130 shirts were in stock. The bookkeeper informs you that all the discounts were taken. Assume that The Golf Shop uses the invoice price less discount for recording purchases and uses the periodic system.

Instructions
(a) Compute the 12/31/98 inventory using the FIFO method.
(b) Compute the 1998 cost of goods sold using the LIFO method.
(c) Compute the 12/31/98 inventory using the weighted-average cost method (round unit cost to nearest cent).
(d) What method would you recommend in order to minimize income in 1998? Explain.

E8-12 **(Alternative Inventory Methods: Calculations)** Hull Corporation Ltd. began operations on December 1, 1998. The only inventory transaction in 1998 was the purchase of inventory on December 10, 1998 at a cost of $20 per unit. None of this inventory was sold in 1998. Relevant information is as follows:

Ending inventory units		
December 31, 1998		100
December 31, 1999 from purchases on:		
December 2, 1999	100	
July 20, 1999	50	150

During 1999 the following purchases and sales were made:

	Purchases		Sales	
March 15	300 units at $24	April 10	200
July 20	300 units at $25	August 20	300
September 4	200 units at $28	November 18	150
December 2	100 units at $32	December 12	200

The company uses the periodic inventory method.

Instructions
Determine ending inventory under (a) specific identification; (b) FIFO; (c) LIFO; and (d) weighted–average cost.

E8-13 **(FIFO, LIFO, and Average Cost: Periodic and Perpetual)** Inventory information for Part 321 discloses the following for the month of June:

June	1 Balance	300 units @ $10	June 10 Sold	200 units @ $24
	11 Purchased	800 units @ $12	15 Sold	500 units @ $25
	20 Purchased	500 units @ $14	27 Sold	300 units @ $27

Instructions
(a) Assuming that the periodic inventory method is used, compute the cost of goods sold and ending inventory under (1) LIFO; (2) FIFO; and (3) weighted-average cost.
(b) Assuming that the perpetual inventory record is kept in units and dollars, determine the cost of the ending inventory under (1) LIFO, (2) FIFO, and (3) moving-average cost. Support your answers for LIFO and moving-average cost by preparing the perpetual inventory card.
(c) When does LIFO produce a lower gross profit than FIFO?

E8-14 **(FIFO, LIFO, and Average Cost Determination)** So Slow Co. Ltd.'s record of transactions for the month of April was as follows:

		Purchases			Sales	
April	1	(balance on hand)	600 @$6.20	April	3	500 @ $10.00
	4		1,500 @ 6.00		9	1,400 @ 10.00
	8		800 @ 6.40		11	600 @ 11.00
	13		1,200 @ 6.50		23	1,200 @ 11.00
	21		700 @ 6.60		27	900 @ 12.00
	29		500 @ 6.79			4,600
			5,300			

Instructions
(a) Assuming that the periodic system is used, compute the inventory at April 30 using (1) LIFO and (2) weighted–average cost.

(b) Assuming that perpetual inventory records are kept in units and dollars, determine the inventory using (1) FIFO and (2) LIFO, supporting your answer with perpetual inventory cards.

(c) Compute cost of goods sold assuming periodic inventory procedures and inventory priced at FIFO.

(d) In an inflationary period, which of the inventory methods (FIFO, LIFO, average cost) will show the highest net income? Which will show the lowest rate of return on assets?

(Compute FIFO, LIFO, Average Cost: Periodic) Presented below is information related to Product S of Beck Inc. for the month of July: **E8-15**

Date	Transaction	Units In	Unit Cost	Total	Units Sold	Selling Price	Total
July 1	Balance	100	$4.10	$ 410			
6	Purchase	800	4.20	3,360			
7	Sale				300	$7.00	$ 2,100.00
10	Sale				300	7.30	2,190.00
12	Purchase	400	4.50	1,800			
15	Sale				200	7.40	1,480.00
18	Purchase	300	4.60	1,380			
22	Sale				400	7.40	2,960.00
25	Purchase	500	4.70	2,350			
30	Sale				200	7.50	1,500.00
	Totals	2,100		$9,300	1,400		$10,230.00

Instructions

(a) Assuming that the periodic inventory method is used, compute the inventory cost at July 31 under each of the following cost flow assumptions:

1. FIFO.

2. LIFO.

3. Weighted-average cost (round the weighted-average unit cost to the nearest one-tenth of one cent).

(b) Answer the following questions:

1. Which of the methods will yield the lowest figure for gross profit in the income statement? Explain why.

2. Which of the methods will yield the lowest figure for ending inventory in the balance sheet? Explain why.

3. Which method will yield the highest debt to total assets ratio? Why?

(Periodic Versus Perpetual Entries) The Garden Company sells one product, the Dirtgrinder. Presented below is information for January for the Garden Company: **E8-16**

Jan.	1	Inventory	100 units at $5 each
Jan.	4	Sale	80 units at $8 each
Jan.	11	Purchase	150 units at $6 each
Jan.	13	Sale	120 units at $8.50 each
Jan.	20	Purchase	150 units at $7 each
Jan.	27	Sale	100 units at $9 each

Garden uses the FIFO cost flow assumption. All purchases and sales are on account.

Instructions

(a) Assume Garden uses a periodic system. Prepare all necessary journal entries, including the end-of-month adjusting/closing entry to record cost of goods sold. A physical count indicates that the ending inventory for January is 100 units. (If needed, see Chapter 3 for illustrative entries.)

(b) Compute gross profit using the periodic system.

(c) Assume Garden uses a perpetual system. Prepare all necessary journal entries.

(d) Compute gross profit using the perpetual system.

(FIFO and LIFO: Income Statement Presentation) The board of directors of Wayland Corporation Ltd. is consider- **E8-17**
ing whether or not it should instruct the accounting department to shift from a first-in, first-out (FIFO) basis of pricing inventories to a last-in, first-out (LIFO) basis. The following information is available:

Sales	20,000 units @	$50
Inventory Jan. 1	6,000 units @	20
Purchases	6,000 units @	22
	10,000 units @	25
	7,000 units @	30
Inventory Dec. 31	9,000 units @	?
Operating expenses	$200,000	

Instructions
Prepare a condensed income statement for the year on both bases for comparative purposes. Which method would you recommend to the board? Why?

E8-18 (FIFO and LIFO Effects) You are the chief financial officer of Roller Blade Ltd., a retail company that prepared two different schedules of gross profit for the first quarter ended March 31, 1998. These schedules appear below:

	Sales ($5 per unit)	Cost of Goods Sold	Gross Profit
Schedule 1	$150,000	$124,900	$25,100
Schedule 2	150,000	126,100	23,900

The computation of cost of goods sold in each schedule is based on the following data:

	Units	Cost per Unit	Total Cost
Beginning inventory, January 1	10,000	$4.00	$40,000
Purchase, January 10	8,000	4.20	33,600
Purchase, January 30	6,000	4.25	25,500
Purchase, February 11	9,000	4.30	38,700
Purchase, March 17	11,000	4.10	45,100

W. Zekskri, the president of the corporation, cannot understand how two different gross profits can be computed from the same set of data. As the C.F.O. you have explained to Mr. Zekskri that the two schedules are based on different assumptions concerning the flow of inventory costs: first-in, first-out, and last-in, first-out. Schedules 1 and 2 were not necessarily prepared in this sequence of cost flow assumptions.

Instructions
Prepare two separate schedules computing cost of goods sold and supporting schedules showing the composition of the ending inventory under both cost flow assumptions.

PROBLEMS

P8-1 Some of the transactions of Conway Inc. during August are listed below. Conway uses the periodic inventory system.

August 10	Purchased merchandise on account, $9,000, terms 2/10, n/30.
13	Returned part of the purchase of August 10, $800, and received credit on account.
15	Purchased merchandise on account, $12,000, terms 1/10, n/60.
25	Purchased merchandise on account, $10,000, terms 2/10, n/30.
28	Paid amount due on the invoice of August 15.

Instructions
(a) Assuming that purchases are recorded at gross amounts and that discounts are to be recorded when taken:

   1. Prepare general journal entries to record the transactions.

   2. Describe how the various items would be shown in the financial statements.

(b) Assuming that purchases are recorded at net amounts and that discounts lost are treated as financial expenses:

   1. Prepare general journal entries to record the transactions.

   2. Prepare the adjusting entry necessary on August 31 if financial statements are to be prepared at that time.

   3. Describe how the various items would be shown in the financial statements.

(c) Which of the two methods do you prefer, and why?

The following independent situations relate to inventory accounting:

1. Supreme Inc. had 1,500 units of Part DR on hand May 1, 1998 that cost $21 each. Purchases of Part DR during May were as follows:

		Units	Unit Cost
May	9	2,000	$22.00
	17	3,500	23.00
	26	1,000	24.00

A physical count on May 31, 1998 shows 2,500 units of Part DR on hand. Using the FIFO method, what is the cost of Part DR inventory at May 31, 1998? Using the LIFO method, what is the inventory cost? Using the weighted-average cost method, what is the inventory cost?

2. Tempi Co. Ltd. purchased goods with a list price of $100,000, subject to trade discounts of 20% and 10%, with no cash discounts allowable. How much should Tempi Co. Ltd. record as the cost of these goods? (Note: trade discounts are deducted from list price to determine price to the customer. Two or more trade discounts are applied on a chain-like basis—first discount on the list price, then next discount on the resulting amount.)

3. Grand Inc.'s inventory of $1,100,000 at December 31, 1998 was based on a physical count of goods priced at cost and before any year-end adjustments relating to the following items:

   (a) Goods shipped f.o.b. shipping point on December 24, 1998 from a supplier at an invoice cost of $75,000 to Grand Inc. were received on January 4, 1999.

   (b) The physical count included $29,000 of goods billed to Prix Co. Ltd. f.o.b. shipping point on December 31, 1998. The carrier picked up these goods on January 3, 1999.

   What amount should Grand report as inventory on its December 31, 1998 balance sheet?

4. Platter Inc., a retail store chain, had the following information in its general ledger for the year 1998:

Merchandise purchased for resale	$909,400
Interest on notes payable to vendors	8,700
Purchase returns	16,500
Freight-in	21,000
Freight-out	17,100
Cash discounts on purchases	6,800

What is Platter's inventoriable cost for 1998?

Instructions
Answer each of the questions and explain your answer.

Slim Co. Ltd., a manufacturer of small tools, provided the following information from its accounting records for the year ended December 31, 1998:

Inventory at December 31, 1998 (based on physical count of goods in Slim's plant at cost on December 31, 1998)	$1,520,000
Accounts payable at December 31, 1998	1,200,000
Net sales (sales less sales returns)	8,150,000

Additional information is as follows:

1. Included in the physical count were tools billed to a customer f.o.b. shipping point on December 31, 1998. These tools had a cost of $31,000 and were billed at $40,000. The shipment was on Slim's loading dock waiting to be picked up by the common carrier.

2. Goods were in transit from a supplier to Slim on December 31, 1998. The invoice cost was $65,000 and the goods were shipped f.o.b. shipping point on December 29, 1998.

3. Work-in-process inventory costing $30,000 was sent to an outside processor for plating on December 30, 1998.

4. Tools returned by customers and held pending inspection in the returned goods area on December 31, 1998 were not included in the physical count. On January 8, 1999 the tools costing $32,000 were inspected and returned to inventory. Credit memos totalling $43,000 were issued to the customers on the same date.

5. Tools shipped to a customer f.o.b. destination on December 26, 1998 were in transit at December 31, 1998 and had a cost of $21,000. Upon notification of receipt by the customer on January 2, 1999, Slim issued a sales invoice for $42,000.

6. Goods with an invoice cost of $27,000 received from a supplier at 5:00 p.m. on December 31, 1998 were recorded on a receiving report dated January 2, 1999. The goods were not included in the physical count, but the invoice was included in accounts payable at December 31, 1998.

7. Goods received from a supplier on December 26, 1998 were included in the physical count. However, the related $56,000 vendor invoice was not included in accounts payable at December 31, 1998 because the accounts payable copy of the receiving report was lost.

8. On January 3, 1999 a monthly freight bill in the amount of $6,000 was received. The bill specifically related to merchandise purchased in December 1998, one-half of which was still in the inventory at December 31, 1998. The freight charges were not included in either the inventory or in accounts payable at December 31, 1998.

Instructions

Using the format shown below, prepare a schedule of adjustments as of December 31, 1998 to the initial amounts per Slim's accounting records. Show separately the effect, if any, of each of the eight transactions on the December 31, 1998 amounts. If the transactions do not have an effect on the initial amount shown, state *NONE*.

	Inventory	Accounts Payable	Net Sales
Initial amounts	$1,520,000	$1,200,000	$8,150,000
Adjustments—increase (decrease)			
1			
2			
3			
4			
5			
6			
7			
8			
Total adjustments			
Adjusted amounts	$	$	$

(AICPA adapted)

P8-4   Boz Ltd. is a wholesale distributor of automotive replacement parts. Initial amounts taken from Boz's accounting records are as follows:

Inventory at December 31, 1998 (based on physical count of goods in Boz's warehouse on December 31, 1998)		$1,240,000

Accounts payable at December 31, 1998:

Vendor	Terms	Amount
Sonny Company Ltd.	2%, 10 days, net 30	$ 260,000
Avalon Corporation	Net 30	290,000
Bopper Company	Net 30	205,000
Mindy Enterprises	Net 30	220,000
Boom Products	Net 30	—
Como Company	Net 30	—
		$ 975,000
Sales in 1998		$8,600,000

Additional information is as follows:

1. Parts received on consignment from Avalon Corporation by Boz, the consignee, amounting to $150,000 were included in the physical count of goods in Boz's warehouse on December 31, 1998 and in accounts payable at December 31, 1998.

2. Parts costing $20,000 were purchased from Boom and paid for in December 1998. These parts were sold in the last week of 1998 and appropriately recorded as sales of $28,000. The parts were included in the physical count of goods in Boz's warehouse on December 31, 1998 because the parts were on the loading dock waiting to be picked up by customers who had been informed the parts were ready and had stated they would pick them up as soon as possible.

3. Parts in transit on December 31, 1998 to customers, shipped f.o.b. shipping point on December 28, 1998, amounted to $34,000. The customers received the parts on January 6, 1999. Sales of $50,000 to the customers for the parts were recorded by Boz on January 2, 1999.

4. Retailers were holding $210,000 of goods at cost ($260,000 at retail) on consignment from Boz, the consignor, at their stores on December 31, 1998.

5. Goods were in transit from Como to Boz on December 31, 1998. The cost of the goods was $36,000 and they were shipped f.o.b. shipping point on December 29, 1998.

6. A quarterly freight bill for $4,700 that related specifically to merchandise purchased in December 1998, all of which was still in inventory at December 31, 1998, was received on January 3, 1999. The freight bill was not included in the inventory or in accounts payable at December 31, 1998.

7. All of the purchases from Sonny occurred during the last seven days of the year. These items have been recorded in accounts payable and accounted for in the physical inventory at cost before discount. Boz's policy is to pay invoices in time to take advantage of all cash discounts, adjust inventory accordingly, and record accounts payable, net of cash discounts.

Instructions

Prepare a schedule of adjustments to the initial amounts using the format shown below. Show the effect, if any, of each of the transactions separately. If the transactions have no effect on the amount shown, state *NONE*.

	Inventory	Accounts Payable	Net Sales
Initial amounts	$1,240,000	$ 975,000	$8,600,000
Adjustments—increase (decrease)			
1			
2			
3			
4			
5			
6			
7			
8			
Total adjustments			
Adjusted amounts	$	$	$

(AICPA adapted)

The books of Re-Call Co. Ltd. on December 31, 1998 are in agreement with the following balance sheet: **P8-5**

RE-CALL CO. LTD.
Balance Sheet as of December 31, 1998

Assets

Cash	$ 52,000
Accounts and notes receivable	86,000
Inventory	160,000
	$298,000

Liabilities and Shareholders' Equity

Accounts and notes payable	$ 50,000
Common shares	200,000
Retained earnings	48,000
	$298,000

The following errors were made by the corporation on December 31, 1997 and were not corrected: the inventory was overstated by $14,000, prepaid expense of $2,400 was omitted (was fully expensed in 1997), and accrued revenue of $3,000 was omitted (recognized when cash received in 1998). On December 31, 1998 the inventory was understated by $20,000, prepaid expense of $3,000 was omitted, accrued expense of $2,400 was omitted (recognized as expense when paid in a future year), and unearned income of $2,800 was omitted (it was included in the 1998 revenue).

The net income shown by the books for 1998 was $32,000.

Instructions
(a) Compute the corrected net income for 1998.
(b) Prepare a corrected balance sheet for December 31, 1998.

P8-6   As the controller of Morf Inc., a merchandising company, you made three different schedules of gross profit for the third quarter ended September 30. These schedules appear below.

	Sales ($10 per Unit)	Cost of Goods Sold	Gross Profit
Schedule A	$570,000	$319,600	$250,400
Schedule B	570,000	312,480	257,520
Schedule C	570,000	305,700	264,300

The computation of cost of goods sold in each schedule is based on the following data:

	Units	Cost per Unit	Total Cost
Beginning inventory, July 1	12,000	$5.00	$ 60,000
Purchase, July 25	18,000	5.40	97,200
Purchase, August 15	32,000	5.50	176,000
Purchase, September 5	13,000	5.60	72,800
Purchase, September 25	16,000	5.80	92,800

Terry Fast, president of the corporation, cannot understand how three different gross margins can be computed from the same set of data. As controller, you have explained that the three schedules are based on three different assumptions concerning the flow of inventory costs: first-in, first-out; last-in, first-out; and weighted-average cost. Schedules A, B, and C were not necessarily prepared in this sequence of cost flow assumptions.

Instructions
Prepare three separate schedules computing cost of goods sold and supporting schedules showing the composition of the ending inventory under each of the three cost flow assumptions.

P8-7   Here is some of the information found on a detail inventory card for Travis Inc. for the first month of operations.

Date	Received No. of Units	Received Unit Cost	Issued, No. of Units	Balance, No. of Units
Jan. 2	1,200	$3.00		1,200
7			700	500
10	600	3.20		1,100
13			500	600
18	1,000	3.30	300	1,300
20			1,100	200
23	1,300	3.40		1,500
26			800	700
28	1,500	3.50		2,200
31			1,300	900

Instructions
(a) From this information compute the ending inventory on each of the following bases. Assume that perpetual inventory records are kept in units only and, therefore, ending inventory costs are determined using a periodic method. Carry unit costs to the nearest cent.
   1. First-in, first-out (FIFO).
   2. Last-in, first-out (LIFO).
   3. Weighted-average cost.
(b) If the perpetual inventory record was kept in units and dollars, would the amounts shown as ending inventory for part (a) be the same? Explain and support your answer by preparing a perpetual inventory card for LIFO and moving-average cost (use unit cost to four decimal places).

Knight Co. Ltd.'s record of transactions concerning Part X for the month of April was as follows: **P8-8**

Purchases				Sales	
Apr. 1	(balance on hand) 100 @	$5.00	Apr. 5		300
Apr. 4	400 @	5.10	Apr. 12		200
Apr. 11	300 @	5.20	Apr. 27		800
Apr. 18	200 @	5.35	Apr. 28		100
Apr. 26	500 @	5.60			
Apr. 30	200 @	5.80			

Instructions
(a) Compute the inventory at April 30 on each of the following bases. Assume that the periodic system is used for inventory valuation. Carry unit costs to the nearest cent.
   1. First-in, first-out (FIFO).
   2. Last-in, first-out (LIFO).
   3. Weighted-average cost.
(b) If the perpetual inventory system is used, would the amounts be the same for ending inventory in 1, 2, and 3 of part (a)? Explain and calculate by preparing perpetual inventory cards for LIFO and moving-average cost methods. Carry unit costs to four decimal places.

The J.T. Kirk Company is a multi-product firm. Presented below is information concerning one of their products, **P8-9**
Dilithium-48:

Date	Transaction	Quantity	Price/Cost
1/1	Beginning inventory	1,500	$10
2/4	Purchase	2,000	16
2/20	Sale	2,500	31
4/2	Purchase	3,000	22
11/4	Sale	2,000	33

Instructions
Compute cost of goods sold, assuming Kirk uses:
(a) Periodic system, FIFO cost flow.
(b) Perpetual system, FIFO cost flow.
(c) Periodic system, LIFO cost flow.
(d) Perpetual system, LIFO cost flow.
(e) Periodic system, weighted-average cost flow.
(f) Perpetual system, moving-average cost flow.

Dr. Seuss Inc. manufactures two products: Horton the Elephant and The Cat in the Hat. At December 31, 1998 the **P8-10**
company used the first-in, first-out (FIFO) inventory method. Effective January 1, 1999 Dr. Seuss changed to the last-in, first-out (LIFO) inventory method as a result of a change in circumstances. The ending inventory of 1998 calculated using the FIFO method (i.e., the number of units at the appropriate purchase cost used for FIFO) is taken to be the beginning inventory amount for 1999 to be used in the LIFO method.
   The following information was available from Dr. Seuss' inventory records for the two most recent years:

	Horton the Elephant		The Cat in the Hat	
	Units	Unit Cost	Units	Unit Cost
1998 purchases				
January 7	7,000	$4.00	22,000	$2.00
April 16	12,000	4.50		
November 8	17,000	5.40	18,500	3.40
December 13	9,000	6.20		

1999 purchases

February 11	3,000	6.60	23,000	3.60
May 20	8,000	7.50		
October 15	20,000	8.10		
December 23			15,500	4.20

Units on hand

December 31, 1998	15,100		15,000
December 31, 1999	18,000		13,200

Instructions

Compute the effect on income before income taxes for the year ended December 31, 1999 resulting from the change from the FIFO to the LIFO inventory method. (AICPA adapted)

P8-11 The management of Oscar Co. Ltd. has asked its accounting department to describe the effect on the company's financial position and its income statement of accounting for inventories on the LIFO rather than the FIFO basis during 1998 and 1999. The accounting department is to assume that the change to LIFO would have been effective on January 1, 1998 and that the initial LIFO inventory on December 31, 1997 would be the same as that under FIFO (i.e., 40,000 units at $3 each). Presented below are the company's financial statements and other data for the years 1998 and 1999 when the FIFO method was in fact employed.

Financial Position as of	12/31/97	12/31/98	12/31/99
Cash	$ 90,000	$119,400	$ 145,000
Accounts receivable	80,000	100,000	120,000
Inventory	120,000	144,000	176,000
Other assets	160,000	170,000	200,000
Total assets	$450,000	$533,400	$ 641,000
Accounts payable	$ 40,000	$ 60,000	$ 80,000
Other liabilities	70,000	80,000	110,000
Common shares	200,000	200,000	200,000
Retained earnings	140,000	193,400	251,000
Total equities	$450,000	$533,400	$ 641,000

Income for Year Ended	12/31/98	12/31/99
Sales	$900,000	$1,350,000
Less: Cost of goods sold	$516,000	$ 760,000
Other expenses	205,000	304,000
	$721,000	$1,064,000
Net income before income taxes	$179,000	$ 286,000
Income tax expense (40%)	71,600	114,400
Net income	$107,400	$ 171,600

Other data:

1. Inventory on hand at 12/31/97 consisted of 40,000 units valued at $3.00 each.

2. Sales (all units sold at the same price in a given year):

    1998: 150,000 units @ $6.00 each   1999: 180,000 units @ $7.50 each

3. Purchases (all units purchased at the same price in given year):

    1998: 150,000 units @ $3.60 each   1999: 180,000 units @ $4.40 each

4. Dividends declared and paid in 1998 were $54,000 and in 1999 were $114,000.

5. Income taxes at the effective rate of 40% are paid on December 31 each year.

Instructions

Name the account(s) presented in the financial statement that would have different amounts for 1999 if LIFO rather than FIFO had been used, and state the new amount for each account that is named. The income tax expense in the income statement is based on the net income before taxes amount calculated. For purposes of determining taxes paid, assume that the FIFO method continues to be used for determining taxable income, since LIFO is not allowed for such purposes. The difference between tax expense and taxes paid is charged to a Future Income Tax Liability account, and this account incorporates the effect of the different methods in the financial statements for only the two-year period.

(CMA adapted)

Brew Inc. cans two food commodities that it stores at various warehouses. The company employs a perpetual inventory accounting system under which the finished goods inventory is charged with production and credited for sales at standard cost. The detail of the finished goods inventory is maintained by the computing department in units and dollars for the various warehouses.

P8-12

Company procedures call for the accounting department to receive copies of daily production reports and sales invoices. Units are then extended at standard cost and a summary of the day's activity is posted to the Finished Goods Inventory general ledger control account. Next the sales invoices and production reports are sent to the computing department for processing. Every month the control account and detailed records are reconciled and adjustments recorded. The last reconciliation and adjustments were made at November 30, 1998.

Your audit firm observed the taking of the physical inventory at all locations on December 31, 1998. The inventory count began at 1:00 p.m. and was completed at 5:00 p.m. The company's figure for the physical inventory is $401,200. The general ledger control account balance at December 31 was $466,900, and the final computer run of the inventory showed a total of $465,100.

Unit cost data for the company's two products are as follows:

Product	Standard Cost
A	$4.00
B	5.00

A review of December transactions disclosed the following:

1. Sales invoice #1603, 12/2/98, was priced at standard cost for $16,400 but was listed on the accounting department's daily summary at $14,600.

2. A production report for $11,600, 12/15/98 was processed twice in error by the computing department.

3. Sales invoice #1481, 12/9/98 for 1,400 units of product A was priced at a standard cost of $2.00 per unit by the accounting department. The computing department noticed and corrected the error but did not notify the accounting department of the error.

4. A shipment of 2,500 units of product A was invoiced by the billing department as 2,000 units on sales invoice #1703, 12/27/98. The error was discovered in your review of transactions.

5. On December 27 the Brandon warehouse notified the computing department to remove 2,200 unsalable units of product A from the finished goods inventory, which it did without receiving a special invoice from the accounting department. The accounting department received a copy of the Brandon warehouse notification on December 29 and made up a special invoice that was processed in the normal manner (it went through the computing department again). The units were not included in the physical inventory.

6. A production report for the production on January 3 of 3,200 units of product B was incorrectly processed (through accounting and computing) for the Oshawa plant as of December 31.

7. A shipment of 500 units of product B was made from the Regina warehouse to Fresh Markets Inc. at 5:30 p.m. on December 31 as an emergency service. The sales invoice was processed as of December 31. The client prefers to treat the transaction as a sale in 1998 and, therefore, it was processed through accounting and computing for 1998.

8. The working papers of the auditor observing the physical count at the Halifax warehouse revealed that 600 units of product B were omitted from the client's physical count. The client concurred that the units were omitted in error.

9. A sales invoice for 400 units of product A shipped from the Calgary warehouse was mislaid and was not processed until January 5. The units involved were shipped on December 30.

10. The physical inventory of the Victoria warehouse excluded 250 units of product A that were marked "reserved." Upon investigation it was ascertained that this merchandise was being stored for Hank's Markets Inc., a customer. This merchandise, which has not been recorded as a sale, is billed as it is shipped, which reflects industry practice.

11. A shipment of 8,000 units of product B was made on December 27 from the Calgary warehouse to the Halifax warehouse. The shipment arrived on January 6, but had been excluded from the physical inventory count.

Instructions

Prepare a work sheet to reconcile the balances for the physical inventory, Finished Goods Inventory general ledger control account, and computing department's detail of finished goods inventory. The following format is suggested for the work sheet:

	Physical Inventory	General Ledger Control Account	Computing Department's Detail of Inventory	
Balance per client	$401,200	$466,900	$465,100	(AICPA adapted)

CASES

C8-1   Part I
You are asked to travel to Kingston to observe and verify the inventory of the Kingston branch of one of your clients. You arrive on Thursday, December 30 and find that the inventory procedures have just been started. You see a railway car on the sidetrack at the unloading door and ask the warehouse superintendent how she plans to inventory the contents of the car. She responds: "We are not going to include the contents in the inventory."

Later in the day, you ask the bookkeeper for the invoice on the carload and the related freight bill. The invoice lists the various items, prices, and extensions of the goods in the car. You note that the carload was shipped December 24 from Hamilton, f.o.b. Hamilton, and that the total invoice price of the goods in the car was $34,200. The freight bill called for a payment of $1,200. Terms were net 30 days. The bookkeeper affirms the fact that this invoice is to be held for recording in January.

Instructions
(a) Does your client have a liability that should be recorded at December 31? Discuss.
(b) Prepare the journal entry or entries, if required, to reflect any adjustment.
(c) For what possible reason(s) might your client wish to postpone recording the transaction?

Part II
Sam Smiley, an inventory control specialist, is interested in better understanding the accounting for inventories. Although Sam understands the more sophisticated computer inventory quantity control systems, he has little knowledge of how inventory cost is determined. In studying the records of Westwood Enterprises, which sells normal brand-name goods from its own store and on consignment through Tan Inc., he asks you to answer the following questions.

Instructions
(a) Should Westwood Enterprises include in its inventory normal brand-name goods purchased from, and sent by, its suppliers but not yet received if the terms of purchase are f.o.b. shipping point (manufacturer's plant)? Why?
(b) Should Westwood Enterprises include freight-in expenditures for the goods in (a) as an inventory cost? Why?
(c) Westwood Enterprises purchased cooking utensils for sale in the ordinary course of business three times during the current year, each time at a higher price than the previous purchase. What would have been the effect on ending inventory, cost of goods sold, the current ratio, and rate of return on total assets had Westwood used the weighted-average cost method instead of the FIFO method?
(d) How should products on consignment be treated in the financial records of the consignor (Westwood Enterprises) and the consignee (Tan Inc.)?   (AICPA adapted)

C8-2   "Accounting Change Aids White Farm" was the headline for a report in the Saskatoon *Star-Phoenix*. This report contained the following comments from White Farm Manufacturing Canada Ltd.'s vice-president of marketing with regard to the company's attempts to recover under new ownership after being placed in receivership the previous year:

In the past, most manufacturers, including the old White, treated a sale as a sale when a piece of equipment was put on a dealer's lot. Once we had a wholesale order for a combine or tractor, most companies booked it as a sale. Whatever the invoice read as revenue was revenue, and whatever costs were incurred up to that point were expenses. And then they'd book a profit. Until that piece of equipment was actually sold to a farmer, the company in most cases finances that equipment on the dealer's lot.

The report went on to state that the practice of booking a profit before it is realized led to a series of problems. Consequently, the company changed its accounting policy so that it did not book profits until a unit was sold at the retail level. At that point, all the firm's costs were behind it and it was recording real profits.

Instructions
(a) Within the framework of GAAP, discuss the appropriateness or lack thereof of the original accounting policy of White and other farm equipment manufacturers in terms of recognizing revenue and cost of goods sold (i.e., inventory reductions).
(b) What type of "problems" could such an accounting policy have led to?
(c) Given this practice, how would the manufacturer account for the equipment that remained on a dealer's lot at a fiscal year end?
(d) How could the new policy "aid" the company?

Local Drilling Inc. is a Canadian drilling site company. All of the company's drilling material is purchased by the head office and stored at a local warehouse before being shipped to the drilling sites. The price of drilling material has been steadily decreasing over the past few years. The drilling material is sent to various sites upon request of the site manager, where it is stored and then used in drilling. Managers are charged the cost of the inventory when it is sent based on the cost assigned to the item in the head office records. At any given time, it is estimated that about one-half of the company's drilling material inventory will be at the local warehouse. A site manager's performance is partially evaluated on the net income reported for the site.

C8-3

Instructions
Given the options of choosing the FIFO, moving-average cost, or LIFO inventory costing methods and use of a perpetual inventory system:

(a) Which costing method would you, as a site manager, want to be used? Why?

(b) As a site manager, what might you do regarding the requesting of inventory if FIFO were used? Why and what might the implications be for the company as a whole?

(c) As the decision maker at head office, which method would you recommend if you wanted the results to be "fair" for all site managers? Why?

(d) Which method would you recommend be used in determining taxable income of the company? Why?

(e) Which method would you recommend be used for financial statement purposes? Why?

(UFE of CICA adapted)

The controller for Cubby Enterprises Ltd. has recently hired you and wishes to determine your expertise in the area of inventory accounting. She therefore requests that you respond to the following unrelated situations:

C8-4

1. A certain portion of a company's "inventory" is composed of obsolete items. Should obsolete items that are not currently consumed in the production of "goods or services to be available for sale" be classified as part of inventory?

2. A company purchases airplanes for sale to others. However, until they are sold, the company charters and services the planes. What is the appropriate way to report these airplanes in the company's financial statements?

3. A competitor uses standard costs for valuing inventory. Is this permissible?

4. A company wants to buy coal deposits but does not want the financing for the purchase to be reported on its financial statements. The company therefore establishes a trust to acquire the coal deposits. The company agrees to buy the coal over a certain period of time at specified prices. The trust is able to finance the coal purchase and pay off the loan as it is paid by the company for the minerals. How should this transaction be reported?

5. A company is involved in the wholesaling and retailing of automobile tires for foreign cars. Most of the inventory is imported, and is valued on the company's records at the actual purchase cost plus freight-in. At year end, the warehousing costs are allocated to the cost of goods sold and the ending inventory. Should warehousing costs be considered a product cost or a period cost? (Note: Consider various reasons for warehousing items when developing your answer.)

Instructions
Provide your answers to the controller's questions.

C8-5

Song Company has been growing rapidly, but during this period the accounting records have not been properly maintained. You were recently employed to correct the accounting records and to assist in the preparation of the financial statements for the fiscal year ended February 28, 1998. One of the accounts you have been analysing is titled "Merchandise." That account in summary form follows. Numbers in parentheses following each entry correspond to related numbered explanations and additional information that you have accumulated during your analysis.

Merchandise			
Balance, March 1, 1997	(1)	Merchandise sold	(5)
Purchases	(2)	Consigned merchandise	(6)
Freight-in	(3)		
Insurance	(4)		
Freight-out on consigned merchandise	(7)		
Freight-out on merchandise sold	(8)		

Explanations and Additional Information

1. You have satisfied yourself that the March 1, 1997 inventory balance represents the appropriate cost of the few units in inventory at the beginning of the year. Song employs the FIFO method of accounting for inventories.

2. The merchandise purchased was recorded in the account at the sellers' catalogue list price, which is the price appearing on the face of each vendor's invoice. All purchased merchandise is subject to a trade discount of 20% (a trade discount is deducted from the catalogue price to determine the price charged to the customer). These discounts have been accounted for as revenue when the merchandise was paid for.

   All merchandise purchased was also subject to cash terms of 2/15, n/30. During the fiscal year Song recorded $4,000 in purchase discounts as revenue when the merchandise was paid for. Some purchase discounts were lost because payment was made after the discount period ended. All purchases of merchandise were paid for in the fiscal year they were recorded as purchased.

3. All merchandise is purchased f.o.b. sellers' business locations. The freight-in amount is the cost of transporting the merchandise from the sellers' business locations to Song.

4. The insurance charge is for an all-perils policy to cover merchandise in transit to Song from sellers.

5. The credit to this account for merchandise sold represents the supplier's catalogue list price of merchandise sold by Song plus the cost of the beginning inventory; the debit side of the entry was made to the Cost of Goods Sold account.

6. Consigned merchandise represents goods that were shipped to Toon Company during February, 1998 priced at the seller's catalogue list price. The offsetting debit was made to accounts receivable when the merchandise was shipped to Toon. None of these goods had yet been sold by Toon Company.

7. The freight-out on consigned goods is the cost of trucking the consigned goods to Toon from Song.

8. Freight-out on merchandise sold is the amount paid to trucking companies to deliver merchandise sold to Song's customers.

Instructions

Consider each of the eight numbered items independently and explain specifically how and why each item, if correctly accounted for, should have affected:

(a) The amount of cost of goods sold to be included in Song's income statement.

(b) The amount of any other account to be included in Song's February 28, 1998 financial statements.

Organize your answer in the following format:

Item Number	How and Why the Amount of Cost of Goods Sold Should Have Been Affected	How and Why the Amount of Any Other Account Should Have Been Affected

C8-6 McSmith Co. Ltd. is considering changing its inventory valuation method from FIFO to average cost because of the potential tax savings. McSmith uses the same method for financial statement purposes as is used for tax purposes as a matter of policy.

The inventory account, currently valued on the FIFO basis, consists of 1,000,000 units at $7 per unit on January 1, 1998. There are 1,000,000 common shares outstanding as of January 1, 1998, and the cash balance is $400,000. The company has made the following forecasts for the period 1998–2000.

	1998	1999	2000
Unit sales (in millions of units)	1.1	1.0	1.3
Sales price per unit	$10	$10	$12
Unit purchases (in millions of units)	1.0	1.1	1.2
Purchase price per unit	$7	$8	$9
Annual depreciation (in thousands of dollars)	$300	$300	$300
Cash dividends per share	$.15	$.15	$.15
Cash payments for additions to and replacement of plant and equipment (in thousands of dollars)	$350	$350	$350
Income tax rate	40%	40%	40%
Operating expense (exclusive of depreciation) as a percent of sales	15%	15%	15%
Common shares outstanding (in millions)	1	1	1

Instructions

(a) Prepare a schedule that illustrates and compares the following data for McSmith Co. Ltd. under the FIFO and the average-cost inventory method for 1998–2000. Assume the company would begin using average cost on a prospective basis at the beginning of 1998.

1. Year-end inventory balances.
2. Annual net income after taxes.

3. Earnings per share.
4. Cash balance.

Assume all sales are collected in the year of sale and all purchases, operating expenses, and taxes are paid during the year incurred.

(b) Using the data above, your answer to (a), and any additional issues you believe need to be considered, prepare a report that recommends whether or not McSmith Co. Ltd. should change to the average–cost inventory method. Support your conclusions with appropriate arguments. (CMA adapted)

John Potter established Dilemma Co. as a sole proprietorship on January 2, 1998. The accounts on December 31, 1998 **C8-7** (company's year end) had balances as follows. The balances are in thousands.

Current assets (excluding ending inventory)	$ 10
Other assets	107
Current liabilities	30
Long-term bank loan	50
Owner's investment (excluding income)	40
Purchases during year	
January 2: 5,000 @ $11	
June 30: 8,000 @ $12	
December 10: 6,000 @ $16	247
Sales	284
Other expenses	40

A count of ending inventory on December 31, 1998 showed there were 4,000 units on hand.

Potter is now preparing financial statements for the year. He is aware that inventory may be costed using either the FIFO, LIFO, or weighted-average method. He is unsure of which one to use and requests your assistance. In discussions with Potter, you learn the following.

1. Suppliers to Dilemma Co. provide goods at regular prices as long as the current ratio is at least 2 to 1. If this ratio is lower, the suppliers increase the price charged by 10% in order to compensate for what they consider to be a substantial credit risk.

2. The terms of the long-term bank loan are that the bank can put Dilemma Co. into a state of bankruptcy if the debt to total asset ratio exceeds 45%.

3. Potter is of the opinion that, for the company to be a success, a rate of return on total assets of at least 30% must result.

4. Potter has an agreement with the company's only employee that, for each full percentage point above a 25% rate of return on total assets, she will be given an additional one day off with pay in the following year.

Instructions

Prepare a report for John Potter analysing the situation, providing a recommendation as to which method should be used, and stating why your recommendation is made.

You have a client engaged in a manufacturing business with relatively heavy fixed costs and large inventories of fin- ***C8-8** ished goods. These inventories constitute a very material item on the balance sheet. The company has a cost accounting system that assigns all manufacturing costs to the product each period.

The controller of the company has informed you that the management is giving serious consideration to the adoption of direct costing as a method of accounting for plant operations and inventory valuation. The management wishes to have your opinion of the effect, if any, that such a change would have on:

1. The year-end financial position.
2. The net income for the year.

Instructions

State your reply to the request and the reasons for your conclusions.

USING YOUR JUDGEMENT

FINANCIAL REPORTING PROBLEM

Refer to the financial statements of Moore Corporation Limited presented in Appendix 5A and answer the following questions.

1. What is Moore Corporation Limited's total inventory amount for the years ended December 31, 1995 and 1994?
2. What types of inventory make up the total inventory? What are the amounts for each type as at December 31, 1995 and 1994?
3. What cost method(s) do(es) the company use to determine its inventory amount(s)?

ETHICS CASE I

Emma's Auto Supplies Inc. uses the LIFO method for inventory costing. In an effort to lower net income, the president tells the plant accountant to take the unusual step of recommending to the purchasing department a large purchase of inventory at year end. The price of the item has nearly doubled during the year, and the item represents a major portion of inventory value.

Instructions

(a) Should the plant accountant recommend the inventory purchase to lower income? Who will benefit?
(b) If Emma's Auto Supplies had been using the FIFO method of inventory costing, would the president give the same order? Why?

ETHICS CASE II

Solid Toys Co. Ltd. manufactures and distributes a line of toys for adolescents, preschool children, and infants. As a consequence, the corporation has large seasonal variations in sales. The company issues quarterly financial statements; first-quarter earnings were down from the same period last year.

During a visit to the Preschool and Infant Division, Solid's president expressed dissatisfaction with the division's first-quarter performance. As a result, Henry Marconi, division manager, felt pressure to report higher earnings in the second quarter. Marconi was aware that Solid uses the LIFO inventory method, so he had the purchasing manager postpone several large inventory orders scheduled for delivery in the second quarter. Marconi knew that the use of older inventory costs during the second quarter would cause a decline in the cost of goods sold and thus increase earnings.

During a review of the preliminary second-quarter income statement, Carman Zol, division controller, noticed that the cost of goods sold was low relative to sales. Zol analysed the inventory account and discovered that the scheduled second-quarter material purchases had been delayed until the third quarter. Zol prepared a revised income statement using current replacement costs to calculate cost of goods sold and submitted the income statement to Henry Marconi, her superior, for review. Marconi was not pleased with these results and insisted that the second-quarter income statement remain unchanged. Zol tried to explain to Marconi that the interim inventory should reflect the expected cost of the replacement of the liquidated inventory when the inventory is expected to be replaced before the end of the year. Marconi did not relent and told Zol to issue the income statement using the LIFO costs. Zol is concerned about Marconi's response, and is contemplating what her next action should be.

Instructions

(a) Determine whether or not the actions of Henry Marconi, division manager, are ethical and explain why.
(b) Recommend a course of action that Carman Zol should take in proceeding to resolve this situation.

(CMA adapted)

chapter

9

INVENTORIES: ADDITIONAL VALUATION PROBLEMS

LOWER OF COST AND MARKET

THE GROSS PROFIT METHOD OF ESTIMATING INVENTORY

RETAIL INVENTORY METHOD

ADDITIONAL ISSUES RELATED TO INVENTORY VALUATION

FINANCIAL STATEMENT PRESENTATION OF INVENTORIES

CHAPTER

9

Inventories: Additional Valuation Problems

Learning Objectives

After studying this chapter, you should be able to:

1. Recognize that the lower of cost and market basis is a departure from the historical cost principle, and understand why this is acceptable.

2. Understand various definitions of possible market amounts that may be used when applying lower of cost and market.

3. Explain how lower of cost and market works and how it is applied.

4. Know how to account for inventory on the lower of cost and market basis.

5. Evaluate conceptual difficulties associated with the lower of cost and market basis.

6. Determine inventory by applying the gross profit method.

7. Know when the gross profit method can be used and appreciate its limitations.

8. Appreciate when the retail inventory method can be used, know what infor-

mation is required to apply it, and understand how the information is used to determine ending inventory.

9. Understand retail method terminology.

10. Determine ending inventory using the conventional retail inventory method and understand why it results in approximating the lower of average cost and market.

11. Explain when and why the relative sales value method is used to value inventories.

12. Identify when and why inventory can be valued at net realizable value, regardless of its cost.

13. Explain accounting issues related to purchase commitments.

14. Know requirements for disclosure of inventory in financial statements and how these requirements can be met.

In Chapter 8, different methods for computing the cost of inventories were explained by examining the various cost flow assumptions used in accounting. In addition to being able to rationally choose from and apply these methods, other concerns regarding inventory valuation exist and are examined in this chapter.

For example, what happens if the value of the inventory increases or decreases after the initial purchase date? Does the financial reporting system recognize these increases and decreases in the valuation of inventory? The answers, in terms of financial statement preparation, lie in the lower of cost and market rule.

What happens if there is a fire and a physical count of lost inventory cannot be made? How is the amount of the destroyed inventory determined so that an insurance claim can be justified? What happens in large department stores where monthly inventory figures are needed, but monthly counts are not feasible? These questions involve the development and use of estimation techniques to value the ending inventory without a physical count. The gross profit method and the retail inventory method are widely used estimation methods and are discussed in this chapter.

Our examination of inventory concludes with a consideration of some additional issues related to inventory valuation (relative sales value method, valuation at net realizable value regardless of cost, and accounting for purchase commitments) and then identifies and illustrates requirements regarding the disclosure of inventories in financial statements.

LOWER OF COST AND MARKET

A major departure from the historical cost principle is made in the area of inventory valuation if inventory declines in value below its original cost. Whatever the reason for a decline (e.g., obsolescence, price-level changes, damaged goods), the inventory should be written down to reflect this loss. *The general rule is that the historical cost principle is abandoned when the future utility (revenue-producing ability) of the asset is no longer as great as its original cost.* A departure from cost is justified under the convention of conservatism — a loss of utility should be charged against revenues in the period in which it occurs. Inventories are valued therefore on the basis of the lower of cost and market instead of on an original cost basis. In contrast, known gains are not recognized until realized.

Cost is the acquisition price of inventory determined by one of the cost-based methods. The term "**market**" in the phrase "the lower of cost and market" (cost or market, whichever is lower) requires a specific definition. As the *CICA Handbook* notes:

> In view of the lack of precision in meaning, it is desirable that the term "market" not be used in describing the basis of valuation. A term more descriptive of the method of determining market, such as "replacement cost", "net realizable value" or "net realizable value less normal profit margin" would be preferable.[1]

Replacement cost generally means *the amount that would be needed to acquire an equivalent item, by purchase or production, as would be incurred in the normal course of business operations* (i.e., buying or manufacturing from usual sources in normal quantities). **Net realizable value** is *the estimated selling price of the item in the ordinary course of business, less reasonably predictable future costs to complete and dispose of the item.* **Net realizable value less normal profit margin** is *determined by deducting a normal profit margin from the previously defined net realizable value amount.* For example, a retailer may have in inventory some calculator wristwatches that had cost $30.00 each. If their purchase cost is presently $28.00, that would be their replacement cost. If their selling price today is $50.00, and there were no additional costs to sell them, then this amount would be their net realizable value. If a normal profit margin is 35% of selling price, the net realizable value less normal profit margin would be $32.50. Consequently, in this example, the inventory would be valued at $30.00 per unit (its historical cost) under the lower of cost and market rule if market were either net realizable value or net realizable value less normal profit margin, but would be valued at $28.00 per unit if market were replacement cost.

Given different interpretations as to what market can be, the question becomes: What definition of market should be used when applying the lower of cost and market rule? The *CICA Handbook* recognizes several possibilities, all of which are generally accepted (see the previous quotation), but is silent on which is appropriate in particular circum-

OBJECTIVE 1
Recognize that the lower of cost and market basis is a departure from the historical cost principle, and understand why this is acceptable.

OBJECTIVE 2
Understand various definitions of possible market amounts that may be used when applying lower of cost and market.

---

[1] *CICA Handbook* (Toronto: CICA), Section 3030, par. .11.

stances. This is understandable, given various practical problems associated with implementing any definition of market in particular situations for various types of inventories. (Some of these considerations are identified later under the heading, "Evaluation of Lower of Cost and Market Rule.") However, *net realizable value is the most frequently used method of determining "market" in Canada.*[2] This is likely due to the following conclusions reached by a CICA research study:

> . . . selling prices do not necessarily fluctuate with costs and that, as a result, a decline in the cost of replacement or reproduction, in itself, is not conclusive evidence that a loss will be incurred. It is only if selling prices vary directly with changes in costs that replacement cost provides an accurate measure of the anticipated loss of gross profits and, under such conditions, exactly the same result can be accomplished by using net realizable value less normal profits. Due to its obvious limitations and because consistent use may produce unreasonable results, the lower of cost and replacement cost can hardly be classified as a practical interpretation of the lower of cost and market basis of valuing inventories.
>
> The only reasonable choice of interpretation seems to be between net realizable value and net realizable value less normal profit. Both of these interpretations have the desired quality of being capable of consistent application. The choice between the two reduces itself to the question of which interpretation provides the more accurate measurement of the loss which will actually be experienced. Under the net realization theory, the loss charged against the income of the current period is limited to irrecoverable cost which is, in effect, the true loss (cost incurred without return or benefit) that is expected to be suffered. Under the net realizable value less normal profit theory, all or part of the charge against income does not represent a true loss.
>
> Since any departure from cost disrupts the normal process of matching costs with related revenues and is an arbitrary shifting of income from one period to another, it would seem most logical to insist on that interpretation of market which causes the lesser disruption of or shift away from the normal matching process. Net realizable value wins over net realizable value less a normal profit because the latter interpretation results in a larger inventory adjustment and, therefore, unnecessarily accentuates the shift in income. . . . If the lower of cost and market basis of inventory valuation in the ordinary course of business operations is to be used, market should be limited to net realizable value since this is the most reasonable interpretation from the point of view of both income measurement and balance sheet presentation.[3]

The accounting profession in the United States has adopted a different approach for determining "market" in the application of the lower of cost and market rule.[4] Generally, market is the replacement cost of the item. When applying the lower of cost and market rule, however, "market" cannot exceed net realizable value (the ceiling) or be less than

---

[2] *Financial Reporting in Canada—1995* (Toronto: CICA, 1995) reports that, of the interpretations of market disclosed in 1994 financial statements of the surveyed companies, net realizable value was used 241 times, replacement cost 72 times, net realizable value less normal profit margin 13 times, and other definitions (e.g., ceiling and/or floor combinations) 20 times.

[3] Gertrude Mulcahy, *Use and Meaning of "Market" in Inventory Valuation* (Toronto: CICA, 1963), p. 19.

[4] Generally, we do not identify U.S. financial reporting standards in this Canadian text, particularly when a specific Canadian position exists. We do so in this particular case because awareness of the U.S. standard may help to better understand the rationale of Canadian practice. Also, the comparison serves to illustrate that different countries can come to different conclusions when trying to account for the same phenomenon—a problem that is faced head-on by the International Accounting Standards Committee when it is trying to develop international accounting standards, or by international financial people when they are assessing financial statements of companies from different countries.

net realizable value less a normal profit margin (the floor).[5] Therefore, the value designated as "market" is the middle value of these three possibilities. Once the designated market has been determined, it is compared to the cost and the lower amount is used for the inventory valuation.

The U.S. approach is based on the premise that declines in replacement cost are reflective of or predict a decline in selling price (realizable value). The ceiling and floor limits are introduced to protect against situations where this premise is in serious error. Consequently, while the underlying objective of reflecting a decline in utility of inventory is common to both Canada and the United States, each has reached a different conclusion as to how this is to be accomplished.

HOW LOWER OF COST AND MARKET WORKS

The lower of cost and market rule requires that the inventory be valued at cost unless "market" is lower than cost, in which case the inventory is valued at "market." To apply this rule (regardless of whether a Canadian or U.S. definition of market is used):

OBJECTIVE 3
Explain how lower of cost and market works and how it is applied.

1. Determine the cost using an acceptable historical cost flow method.

2. Determine the market value to be used.

3. Compare the cost to the market.

The cost or market figure, whichever is lower, is then used for inventory valuation on the financial statements.

To demonstrate, consider the information shown in Exhibit 9-1.

EXHIBIT 9-1

INFORMATION TO DEMONSTRATE THE LOWER OF COST AND MARKET APPROACH

		Market		
Case	Cost	Net Realizable Value	Replacement Cost	Net Realizable Value Less Normal Profit Margin
1	$1.00	$1.50	$1.00	$1.20
2	1.00	1.10	.90	.70
3	1.00	.80	.95	.56
4	1.00	.80	.40	.56
5	1.00	.95	1.05	.80

In the exhibit, cost is given. Therefore, to apply the lower of cost and market rule, the next step is to determine the market amount to be used. Under Canadian GAAP, this would be accomplished by a company's management specifying which of the three definitions of market it will adopt. If net realizable value is designated as the "market" value, as is commonly the case for Canadian companies, the application of a "lower of cost and net realizable value" approach will result in inventory being shown at cost in Cases 1 and 2 (because cost is lower than net realizable value) and net realizable value in Cases 3, 4, and 5 (net realizable value is less than cost). If, however, net realizable value less normal

---

[5] "Restatement and Revision of Accounting Research Bulletins," *Accounting Research Bulletin No. 43* (New York: AICPA, 1953), Ch. 4, par. 8. It should be noted that a literal interpretation of the U.S. rules is frequently not applied in practice. Rather, *ARB No. 43* is considered a guide, and professional judgement is often exercised. Indeed, *Accounting Research Study No. 13 "The Accounting Basis of Inventories"* (New York: AICPA, 1973) recommends that net realizable value be adopted.

profit margin is the designated "market" value, inventory will be shown at cost in Case 1 and net realizable value less normal profit margin in Cases 2, 3, 4, and 5. Use of replacement cost as market would result in using cost in Cases 1 and 5 and replacement cost in Cases 2, 3, and 4.

To determine market under U.S. rules, the first step is to determine amounts for all three of the possible market values. Given this, the next step is to identify which of these amounts will be the designated market value that is compared to cost. As previously noted, the market value used will be the middle value of the three. For Case 2, this is the $.90 replacement cost. It is less than the $1.10 net realizable value (the ceiling) and higher than the $.70 net realizable value less normal profit margin (the floor). Because the determined market value (replacement cost of $.90) is less than the cost ($1.00), ending inventory in this case is valued at $.90. For Case 1, replacement cost is $1.10. Since market cannot be less than the net realizable value less a normal profit margin of $1.20, this latter amount is the designated market value. It is the middle value of the three possible market amounts in Case 1. Since the $1.00 cost is less than the $1.10 market value in Case 1, the ending inventory is valued at $1.00. With this explanation as a base, the following summarizes the amount that is used in each of Cases 1 through 5 to value inventory under the U.S. rules for determining the lower of cost and market.

Case 1.   Cost. It is lower than any of the possible market values.

Case 2.   Replacement cost. It is the designated market as it is the middle value of the three market possibilities and it is lower than cost.

Case 3.   Net realizable value (ceiling). It is the designated market as it is the middle value of the three market possibilities (market cannot exceed this amount) and is lower than cost.

Case 4.   Net realizable value less a normal margin (floor). It is the designated market as it is the middle value of the three market possibilities (market cannot be less than this amount) and is lower than cost.

Case 5.   Net realizable value (ceiling). For the same reasons as Case 3.

METHODS OF APPLYING THE LOWER OF COST AND MARKET RULE

The lower of cost and market rule may be applied on an *item-by-item basis*, a *category basis*, or a *total inventory basis*. To illustrate, consider the example shown in Exhibit 9-2 for a business that has two categories of inventory (radios and TVs) and different types in each category.

If the lower of cost and market rule is applied to individual items, the amount of inventory is $12,250. It is $12,650 when applied to major categories and $12,700 when applied to the total inventory.

Relative to the other methods, applying the rule to the total of the inventory results in a smaller reduction of inventory to market when market is less than cost. This is because market values higher than cost are offset against market values lower than cost when only totals are considered. This also applies to a lesser extent when the categories approach is used, but not at all when the item-by-item approach is applied. Therefore, the item-by-item approach is more conservative than the others because the likelihood of having to reduce cost to market is greater and the amount of any reduction is larger.

In Canada *the most common practice is to apply lower of cost and market to the inventory on a total basis.* Companies likely favour this application because it is required by Canadian income tax rules. The tax rules in the United States, however, require the application of the rule to individual items; consequently, that method is more common in

EXHIBIT 9-2

METHODS OF APPLYING LOWER OF COST AND MARKET

	Cost	Market	Lower of Cost and Market by: Individual Items	Lower of Cost and Market by: Major Categories	Lower of Cost and Market by: Total Inventory
Radios					
Type A	$ 800	$ 750	$ 750		
B	1,500	1,600	1,500		
C	900	800	800		
Total Radios	$ 3,200	$ 3,150		$ 3,150	
TV Sets					
Type X	$ 3,000	$ 3,400	$ 3,000		
Y	4,500	4,300	4,300		
Z	2,000	1,900	1,900		
Total TVs	$ 9,500	$ 9,600		9,500	
Total Inventory	$12,700	$12,750	$12,250	$12,650	$12,700

that country. Whichever method is selected for financial reporting, it should be applied consistently from period to period.

RECORDING "MARKET" INSTEAD OF COST

Two methods are used for recording inventory at market, when market is lower than cost. One method, referred to as the **direct method**, simply records the ending inventory at the market figure at the year end. As a result, no loss is separately reported in the income statement; the loss is buried in cost of goods sold. The second method, referred to as the **indirect** or **allowance method**, records ending inventory at the cost amount and then establishes a separate contra-asset account and a loss account to reduce the inventory to market.

    Exhibit 9-3 shows the entries under both approaches, assuming an ending inventory cost of $82,000, a determined market value of $70,000, and use of the *periodic* inventory system.

OBJECTIVE 4
Know how to account for inventory on the lower of cost and market basis.

EXHIBIT 9-3

ACCOUNTING FOR THE REDUCTION OF
INVENTORY TO MARKET: PERIODIC INVENTORY SYSTEM

Direct Method (Ending Inventory Recorded at Market)		Indirect or Allowance Method (Ending Inventory Recorded at Cost and a Loss and Allowance Separately Recorded)		
To record ending inventory:				
Inventory	70,000	Inventory	82,000	
Cost of Goods Sold	70,000	Cost of Goods Sold		82,000
To write down inventory to market:				
No entry.		Loss Due to Market		
		Decline of Inventory	12,000	
		Allowance to Reduce		
		Inventory to Market		12,000

If the company had used a *perpetual* inventory system, the entries would be as shown in Exhibit 9-4.

EXHIBIT 9-4

ACCOUNTING FOR THE REDUCTION OF
INVENTORY TO MARKET: PERPETUAL INVENTORY SYSTEM

(No inventory closing entries are necessary under the perpetual method; only the reduction to market is recorded.)

Direct Method			Indirect or Allowance Method		
To reduce inventory from cost to market:					
Cost of Goods Sold	12,000		Loss Due to Market		
Inventory		12,000	Decline of Inventory	12,000	
			Allowance to Reduce		
			Inventory to Market		12,000

The advantage of separately recording the loss is that it may then be reported as a separate item in the income statement, thereby not distorting the cost of the sales for the year. Therefore, the trend in the rate of gross profit is not affected by gains or losses due to market fluctuations. Exhibit 9-5 shows how the two methods result in differing amounts being reported in the income statement (although the net income will be the same under either method).

EXHIBIT 9-5

INCOME STATEMENT PRESENTATION: DIRECT AND
INDIRECT METHODS OF REDUCING INVENTORY TO MARKET

Direct Method

Sales		$200,000
Cost of goods sold		
Inventory Jan. 1	$ 65,000	
Purchases	125,000	
Goods available	$190,000	
Inventory Dec. 31 (at market that is less than cost)	70,000	
Cost of goods sold		120,000
Gross profit on sales		$ 80,000

Indirect or Allowance Method

Sales		$200,000
Cost of goods sold		
Inventory Jan. 1	$ 65,000	
Purchases	125,000	
Goods available	$190,000	
Inventory Dec. 31 (at cost)	82,000	
Cost of goods sold		108,000
Gross profit on sales		$ 92,000
Loss due to market decline of inventory		**12,000**
(shown in other expenses and losses)		
		$ 80,000

The second presentation is preferable because it clearly discloses the loss resulting from the market decline of inventory prices. The first presentation buries the loss in the cost of goods sold.

The Allowance to Reduce Inventory to Market (contra asset) is reported on the balance sheet as a $12,000 deduction from the inventory cost of $82,000. The result is a net inventory amount of $70,000, the lower of cost and market figure. Use of the Allowance account has the benefit of keeping the total of subsidiary inventory accounts in agreement with the control account for total inventory because both will be based on cost.

Although use of an Allowance account permits balance sheet disclosure of the amount of inventory at cost and the lower of cost and market, it raises the problem of how to dispose of the account's balance in subsequent periods. If the merchandise to which the allowance applies is still on hand, the account may be retained. But if the goods that suffered the decline (from cost to market) have been sold, this account should be removed from the books. A "new" allowance account is then established to record any reduction from cost to market for the ending inventory of the current period.

Many accountants *leave the Allowance account on the books and merely adjust the balance at the next year end to agree with the discrepancy between cost and the lower of cost and market at that balance sheet date.* Thus, if prices are falling, a loss is recorded and, if prices are increasing, a loss recorded in prior years is recovered and a "gain" (which is not really a gain, but is a recovery of a previously recognized loss) is recorded. Exhibit 9-6 provides an example.

EXHIBIT 9-6

ADJUSTMENTS TO THE ALLOWANCE ACCOUNT AND EFFECT ON NET INCOME OVER A NUMBER OF YEARS

Date	Inventory at Cost	Inventory at Market	Amount Required in Allowance Account	Adjustment of Allowance Account Balance	Effect on Net Income
Dec. 31/95	$188,000	$176,000	$12,000 cr.	$12,000 inc.	Loss
Dec. 31/96	194,000	187,000	7,000 cr.	5,000 dec.	Gain
Dec. 31/97	173,000	174,000	–0–	7,000 dec.	Gain
Dec. 31/98	182,000	180,000	2,000 cr.	2,000 inc.	Loss

Recognition of a gain or loss in this manner has the same effect on net income as closing any beginning balance in the Allowance account and recording any reduction from cost to market for the year's ending inventory. Note that the *Allowance account can never have a debit balance*. If such were the case, it would result in the inventory net of the allowance exceeding the cost of the inventory, a situation not permitted under generally accepted accounting principles.

EVALUATION OF LOWER OF COST AND MARKET RULE

Conceptually, the lower of cost and market rule has some deficiencies. First, if inventory can be written down because of a loss in utility, does it not seem appropriate to be able to write inventory up when the utility of the asset increases? Decreases in the value of the asset and the charge to income are recognized in the period in which the loss in utility occurs—not in the period of sale. On the other hand, increases in the value of the asset are recognized only at the point of sale. This situation is inconsistent and can lead to distortions in the presentation of income data.

Even if we accept this inconsistency, another problem arises in defining market. Basically, any of three concepts of market can be used in Canada: replacement cost, net

OBJECTIVE 5
Evaluate conceptual difficulties associated with the lower of cost and market basis.

realizable value, and net realizable value less a normal profit.[6] Replacement cost could be chosen because changes in replacement cost are easily identified and may reflect a corresponding decline in sales value. Frequently, however, a reduction in the replacement cost of an item does not indicate a corresponding reduction in the utility of the item. To illustrate, assume that a retailer has several shirts that were bought for $15.00 each. The replacement cost of these shirts falls to $14.50, but the selling price remains the same. Has the retailer suffered a loss? To recognize a loss now misstates this period's income and also that of future periods because, upon sale of the shirts in future periods, the full price is received.

Net realizable value reflects the future revenue-producing potential of the asset and, for that reason, is the most conceptually sound concept of market. Unfortunately, net realizable value may be difficult to measure with a sufficient degree of reliability and, therefore, replacement cost may be the only available option. For example, replacement cost may be the most reasonable and practical definition of "market" for raw materials and work in process inventories given that they do not yet have a formal selling price.

Using net realizable value less a normal profit as the definition of market requires dealing with the difficult problems of determining both the net realizable value and a normal profit. In addition, under this approach, a loss recognized in one period is offset by the recognition of profit in a future period. To illustrate, assume that an item costing $10 has a net realizable value of $8 and that the normal profit is $3. Companies using net realizable value will recognize a loss of only $2 ($10 − $8); companies using net realizable value less a normal profit margin will show a loss of $5 ($10 − $2 − $3) and then, when the item is sold, recognize a profit of $3. The result of the latter approach is to show a normal profit margin in the period of sale.

From the standpoint of accounting theory, there is little to justify the lower of cost and market rule. Despite this, lower of cost and market is by far the most commonly used basis for valuation of inventories in Canada.[7] Its acceptance is based on tradition and the practical desire to provide conservatism in financial statement reporting. The rule does result in conservatism because a loss is recognized in the period in which it is deemed to occur. However, the amount carried forward as inventory is matched against the revenue of the periods in which it is sold. Therefore, despite the conservatism in the current period, the result is a higher income in future periods than would be the case if costs were carried forward. Since the total income over several periods will be the same whether or not the lower of cost and market rule is applied, the real issue regarding its acceptability lies in determining in which period the loss should be recognized.

THE GROSS PROFIT METHOD OF ESTIMATING INVENTORY

The basic purpose of taking a physical inventory is to verify the accuracy of the perpetual inventory records or, if no records exist, to arrive at an inventory amount. Sometimes, taking a physical inventory is impractical or impossible. Then, estimation methods are used to approximate inventory on hand. One such method is called the gross profit method. This method is used in situations where only an estimate of inventory is needed (e.g., preparing interim reports or testing the reasonableness of the cost derived by some other method) or where inventory has been destroyed by fire or other catastrophe. It may also be used to provide a rough check on the accuracy of a physical inventory count (e.g.,

---

[6] As previously mentioned, market is usually defined as net realizable value in Canadian practice, but the other definitions are recognized as being acceptable in the *CICA Handbook* (Section 3030, par. .11) and are used (see footnote 2 of this chapter).

[7] *Financial Reporting in Canada—1995* reported that lower of cost and market, or a variation of it, was used by 258 companies, whereas cost was used by 18 companies, market by 17 companies and various other approaches by 8 companies.

compare the estimated amount to the physical count amount to see if they are reasonably close; if not, a reason should be found).

The **gross profit method** is based on the assumptions that (1) the beginning inventory plus net purchases equal total goods to be accounted for; (2) goods not sold must be on hand; and (3) if the net sales, reduced to cost, are deducted from the sum of the opening inventory plus net purchases, the result is the ending inventory.

To illustrate, assume that Gizmo Co. has a beginning inventory of $60,000 and net purchases of $200,000. Net sales amount to $280,000. The average gross profit rate (margin) on selling price for the company is 30%. The calculation of inventory on hand would be as shown in Exhibit 9-7.[8]

OBJECTIVE 6
Determine inventory by applying the gross profit method.

EXHIBIT 9-7

APPLICATION OF GROSS PROFIT METHOD

Beginning inventory		$ 60,000
Net purchases		200,000
Goods available (at cost)		$260,000
Net sales (at selling price)	$280,000	
Less: Gross profit (30% of $280,000)	84,000	
Sales (at cost)		196,000
Approximate inventory (at cost)		$ 64,000

All the information needed to compute the inventory at cost, except for the gross profit percentage, is available in the current period's accounting records. The gross profit percentage is determined by reviewing company policies and prior period amounts. Prior periods' percentages must be adjusted if they are not considered representative of the current period.

GROSS PROFIT PERCENT VERSUS PERCENT OF MARKUP

The gross profit percent is the most commonly used number to convey the profitability associated with items sold. A stated percentage may, however, be determined by dividing gross profit by either selling price or cost, as shown in Illustration 9-1.

While the amount of gross profit ($5.00) is the same for each calculation, the resulting rates are different. If one simply called the result the gross profit percent, there may be confusion: Is it a percent of selling price (25%) or a percent of cost (33⅓%)? To overcome this problem, the usual interpretation is that the **gross profit percent** *is based on selling*

---

[8] An alternative method of estimating inventory using the gross profit percent, considered by some to be less complicated than the traditional method illustrated, uses the standard income statement format as follows (assume the same data as in the Gizmo Co. illustration).

Sales		$280,00		$280,000
Cost of sales				
Beginning inventory	$ 60,000		$ 60,000	
Purchases	200,000		200,000	
Goods available for sale	260,000		260,000	
Ending inventory	(3) ?		(3) **64,000** Est.	
Cost of goods sold		(2) ?		(2)**196,000** Est.
Gross profit on sale (30%)		(1) ?		(1) **84,000** Est.

Compute the unknowns as follows: first the gross profit amount, then cost of goods sold, and then the ending inventory.

1. $280,000 × 30% = $84,000 (gross profit on sales).
2. $280,000 − $84,000 = $196,000 (cost of goods sold).
3. $260,000 − $196,000 = $64,000 (ending inventory).

ILLUSTRATION 9-1
*Gross profit percent versus
percent of markup on cost*

price. When the relationship is based on cost, it is called the percent of markup on cost
(the gross profit amount would be called the markup).[9]

    Because a *gross profit percent based on selling price is used in the gross profit method*
to estimate inventory, it is necessary to know whether a stated percentage is based on selling price or cost. If the percent of markup is given, it must be converted to a gross profit
percent of selling price. The formulas shown in Illustration 9-2 can be used to convert a
given percent of markup on cost to a gross profit percent on selling price, and vice versa.

ILLUSTRATION 9-2
*Formulas to convert percent
of markup to gross profit
percent and vice versa*

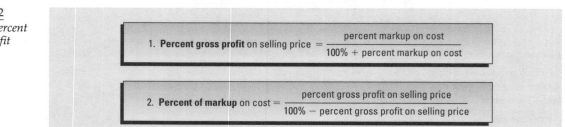

APPRAISAL OF GROSS PROFIT METHOD

OBJECTIVE 7
Know when the gross
profit method can be used
and appreciate its limitations.

The gross profit method is not normally acceptable for annual financial reporting purposes because it provides only an estimate. A physical inventory is needed to verify that
the inventory indicated in the records is actually on hand. Nevertheless, the gross profit
method is used whenever an estimate of the ending inventory is needed (e.g., fire loss) or
permitted (e.g., for interim reporting).

    One major disadvantage of the gross profit method is that *it is an estimate*; as a
result, a physical inventory must be taken once a year to verify that the inventory is actually on hand.

    A second disadvantage is that the method *uses past percentages* to determine current
inventory amounts. Although the past can often provide predictions about the future, a
current rate is more appropriate. Whenever significant fluctuations occur, a past percentage should be appropriately adjusted.

    Third, *care must be taken when applying a blanket gross profit rate* (an average of
the gross profit rates for several different items). Frequently a manufacturer, wholesaler,
or retailer handles merchandise with widely varying rates of gross profit. In these situations, the gross profit method may have to be applied by subsections, lines of merchandise, or a similar basis that classifies merchandise according to rates of gross profit.

RETAIL INVENTORY METHOD

Accounting for inventory in a retail operation presents several challenges. Retailers with
certain types of inventory may use the specific identification method to value their inventories. Such an approach makes sense when individual inventory units are significant

---

[9] The terms "gross profit percentage," "gross margin percentage," "rate of gross profit," and "rate of gross margin" are synonymous, reflecting the relationship of gross profit to selling price. The terms "percentage markup"
or "rate of markup" are used to describe the relationship of markup (equals gross margin) to cost, although some
continue to refer to this as a gross profit percentage.

(e.g., automobiles, pianos, or fur coats). However, imagine attempting to use such an approach for Canadian Tire or Sears — high-volume retailers that have many different types of merchandise at relatively low unit costs.

Some retailers have installed computers and point-of-sale terminals that enable them to keep excellent perpetual inventory records for the multitude of items and sales. From these inventory systems, information regarding units on hand and their cost may be readily available.

Many retailers, however, do not have such systems, or their computer systems may not be sufficiently sophisticated to provide all the necessary information. For these retailers, any type of unit cost inventory method will be unsatisfactory. Consequently, they may use what is called the **retail inventory method**. This method enables the retailer to estimate inventory when necessary and take a physical inventory at retail prices. Because an observable pattern between cost and price usually exists, an inventory taken at retail can be converted to inventory at cost through formula. *The retail inventory method requires that a record be kept of (1) the total cost and retail value of goods purchased, (2) the total cost and retail value of the goods available for sale, and (3) the sales for the period.*

Here is how it works. Sales for the period are deducted from the retail value of the goods available for sale to produce an estimated ending inventory at retail. The ratio of cost to retail for all goods passing through a department or company is determined by dividing the total goods available for sale at cost by the total goods available at retail. The inventory valued at retail is converted to ending inventory at cost by applying the cost to retail ratio. The retail inventory method is illustrated for Simon's Inc. in Exhibit 9-8.

OBJECTIVE 8
Appreciate when the retail inventory method can be used, know what information is required to apply it, and understand how the information is used to determine ending inventory.

EXHIBIT 9-8   SIMON'S INC.

RETAIL INVENTORY METHOD
(CURRENT PERIOD)

	Cost	Retail
Beginning inventory	$14,000	$ 20,000
Purchases	63,000	90,000
Goods available	$77,000	$110,000
Deduct: Sales		85,000
Ending inventory, at retail		$ 25,000
Ratio of cost to retail ($77,000/$110,000)		70%
Ending inventory at cost (70% of $25,000)		$ 17,500

To avoid a potential misstatement of the inventory, periodic inventory counts are made, especially in retail operations where loss due to shoplifting and breakage is common. When a physical count at retail is taken, the inventory cost is determined by multiplying the resulting amount at retail by the cost to retail ratio. Discrepancy between the records and the physical count will require an adjustment to make the records agree with the count.

The retail method is sanctioned by various retail associations and the accounting profession, and is allowed (except for methods approximating a LIFO valuation) by Revenue Canada. One advantage of the retail inventory method is that the inventory balance *can be approximated without a physical count*. This makes the method particularly useful for the preparation of interim reports. Insurance adjusters use this approach to estimate losses from a fire, flood, or other type of casualty. This method also acts as a *control device* because any deviations from a physical count at the end of the year have to be explained. In addition, the retail method *expedites the physical inventory count* at the end of the year. The crew taking the inventory need record only the retail price of each item. There is no need to look up each item's invoice cost, thus saving time and expense.

RETAIL METHOD TERMINOLOGY

OBJECTIVE 9
Understand retail method terminology.

The amounts shown in the Retail column of Exhibit 9-8 represent the **original retail prices** *(cost plus an original markup or markon)*, assuming no other price changes up or down. Sales prices, however, are frequently marked up or down. For retailers, the term **markup** means an additional markup on original selling price (i.e., an increase in the price above the original sales price). **Markup cancellations** are decreases in prices of merchandise that had been marked up above the original retail price. Markup cancellations cannot be greater than markups. **Net markups** refer to markups less markup cancellations.

Markdowns are decreases in price below the original selling price. They are a common phenomenon and occur because of special sales, soiled and damaged goods, overstocking, or competition. **Markdown cancellations** are increases in prices of merchandise that had been marked down below the original selling price. Markdown cancellations cannot exceed markdowns. Markdowns less markdown cancellations equal **net markdowns**.

To illustrate these different terms, assume that Designer Clothing Store recently purchased 100 high-fashion shirts from Marroway Ltd. The cost for these shirts was $1,500, or $15 a shirt. Designer Clothing established the selling price on these shirts at $30 each. Therefore, there was an original markup or markon of $15 per shirt. The manager noted that the shirts were selling quickly, so she added $5 to the price of each shirt. This markup made the price too high and sales lagged. Consequently, the manager reduced the price to $32. To this point there has been a markup of $5 and a markup cancellation of $3 on the original selling price of a shirt. When the major marketing season ended, the manager set the price of the remaining shirts at $23. This price change constitutes a markup cancellation of $2 and a $7 markdown. If the shirts are later priced at $24, a markdown cancellation of $1 occurs.

RETAIL INVENTORY METHOD WITH MARKUPS AND MARKDOWNS

To determine the ending inventory figures using the retail inventory method, one must decide on the treatment to be given to markups, markup cancellations, markdowns, and markdown cancellations in the calculation of the ratio of cost to retail. To illustrate the different possibilities, consider the data for In-Fashion Stores Inc. shown in Exhibit 9-9. Illustration 9-3 shows the computations of ending inventory under the two identified cost to retail ratios.

(A) reflects a cost percentage after net markups but before net markdowns. The second percentage, (B), is computed after both the net markups and net markdowns. Which percentage should be employed to compute the ending inventory valuation? The answer depends on what the ending inventory amount is to reflect.

OBJECTIVE 10
Determine ending inventory using the conventional retail inventory method and understand why it results in approximating the lower of average cost and market.

The **conventional retail inventory method** *uses the cost to retail ratio incorporating net markups (markups less markup cancellations) but excluding net markdowns (markdowns less markdown cancellations)* as shown in the calculation of ratio (A). *It is designed to approximate the lower of average cost and market*, with market being net realizable value less normal profit margin. To understand why net markups but not net markdowns are included in the cost to retail ratio, we must understand how a retail outlet operates. When a company has a net markup on an item, it normally indicates that the market value of that item has increased. On the other hand, if the item has a net markdown, it means that a decline in the utility of that item has occurred. Therefore, to

---

EXHIBIT 9-9   IN-FASHION STORES INC.

RETAIL INVENTORY METHOD WITH MARKUPS AND MARKDOWNS

Information in Records

	Cost	Retail
Beginning inventory	$ 500	$ 1,000
Purchases (net)	20,000	35,000
Markups		3,000
Markup cancellations		1,000
Markdowns		2,500
Markdown cancellations		2,000
Sales (net)		25,000

Retail Inventory Method

	Cost		Retail
Beginning inventory	$ 500		$ 1,000
Purchases (net)	20,000		$35,000
Merchandise available	$20,500		$36,000
Add:			
Markups		$ 3,000	
Less markup cancellations		(1,000)	
Net markup			2,000
	$20,500		$38,000

Cost ratio $\dfrac{\$20,500}{\$38,000} = 53.9\%$ . . . . (A)

	Cost		Retail
Deduct:			
Markdowns		$2,500	
Less markdown cancellations		(2,000)	
Net markdowns			500
	$20,500		$37,500

Cost ratio $\dfrac{\$20,500}{\$37,500} = 54.7\%$ . . . . (B)

Deduct sales (net)			25,000
Ending inventory at retail			$12,500

> (A) 12,500 × 53.9% = 6,737.50
> (B) 12,500 × 54.7% = 6,837.50

ILLUSTRATION 9-3
Calculating ending inventory

approximate the lower of average cost and market, net markdowns are considered a current loss and are not involved in the calculation of the cost to retail ratio. Thus, the cost to retail ratio is lower, which leads to an approximate lower of cost and market amount.

To help clarify, assume two different items were purchased for $5 each, and the original sales price was established at $10 each. One item was subsequently marked down to a selling price of $2. Assuming no sales for the period, *if markdowns are included* in the cost to retail ratio the ending inventory is computed as shown in Exhibit 9-10.

This approach results in *ending inventory at the average cost* of the two items on hand without considering the loss on the one item.

If markdowns are excluded, as is done under the conventional retail inventory method, the result is *ending inventory at the lower of average cost and market.* The calculation is as shown in Exhibit 9-11.

EXHIBIT 9-10

RETAIL INVENTORY METHOD INCLUDING MARKDOWNS

	Cost	Retail
Purchases	$10.00	$20.00
Deduct: Markdowns		8.00
Ending inventory, at retail		$12.00

Cost to retail ratio $\dfrac{\$10.00}{\$12.00} = 83.3\%$

Ending inventory, at average cost ($12.00 × .833) = $10.00

EXHIBIT 9-11

RETAIL INVENTORY METHOD EXCLUDING MARKDOWNS IN RATIO: LOWER OF AVERAGE COST AND MARKET (CONVENTIONAL METHOD)

	Cost	Retail
Purchases	$10.00	$20.00

Cost to retail ratio $\dfrac{\$10.00}{\$12.00} = 50\%$

Deduct: Markdowns	8.00
Ending inventory, at retail	$12.00

Ending inventory, at lower of average cost and market ($12.00 × .50) = $6.00

The $6 inventory valuation includes the two inventory items, one inventoried at $5 and the other at $1. Basically, for the item with the decline in market, the sale price was reduced from $10 to $2 and the cost reduced from $5 to $1.[10] Therefore to *approximate the lower of average cost and market, the cost to retail ratio must be established by dividing the cost of goods available by the sum of the original retail price of these goods plus the net markups; the net markdowns are excluded from the ratio.*

The basic format for the retail inventory method using the conventional approach and the In-Fashion Stores Inc. information is shown in Exhibit 9-12.

Many possible cost to retail ratios could be calculated, depending upon whether or not the beginning inventory, net markups, and net markdowns are included. The schedule in Illustration 9-4 summarizes some of the methods of inventory valuation approximated by the inclusion or exclusion of various items in the cost to retail ratio, given that net purchases are always included in the ratio.[11]

[10] The conventional method defines market as net realizable value less the normal profit. In other words, the sale price of the item written down is $2.00, but after subtracting a normal profit of 50% of selling price (or 100% of cost) the inventoriable amount becomes $1.00.

[11] Using the information for In-Fashion Stores Inc., applying the retail inventory method to approximate FIFO cost and market, the ratio would be 54.1%. The retail method can also be used to approximate a LIFO cost flow. Given that LIFO approximation is seldom used in Canada, the complexities of the formula are not considered in the schedule. The U.S. edition of this book is a useful reference for those interested in LIFO retail concepts and calculations.

EXHIBIT 9-12 IN-FASHION STORES INC.

COMPREHENSIVE CONVENTIONAL RETAIL INVENTORY METHOD

	Cost		Retail
Beginning inventory	$ 500		$ 1,000
Purchases (net)	20,000		$35,000
Totals	$20,500		$36,000
Add net markups:			
Markups		$ 3,000	
Markup cancellations		(1,000)	2,000
Totals	$20,500		$38,000
Deduct net markdowns:			
Markdowns		$2,500	
Markdown cancellations		(2,000)	500
Sales price of goods available			$37,500
Deduct: Sales			25,000
Ending inventory, at retail			$12,500

$$\text{Cost to retail ratio} = \frac{\text{cost of goods available}}{\text{original retail price of goods available 1 net markups}}$$

$$= \frac{\$20,500}{\$38,000} = 53.9\%$$

Ending inventory at lower of average cost and market (53.9% × $12,500.00)   **$ 6,737.50**

Beginning Inventory	Net Markups	Net Markdowns	Inventory Valuation Method Approximated
Include	Include	Include	Average Cost
Include	Include	Exclude	Lower of Average Cost and Marktet (Conventional Method)
Exclude	Include	Include	FIFO Cost
Exclude	Include	Exclude	Lower of FIFO Cost and Market

ILLUSTRATION 9-4
Retail inventory method: Inventory valuation method approximated by including various items in the cost to retail ratio

SPECIAL ITEMS RELATING TO THE RETAIL METHOD

The retail inventory method becomes more complicated when items such as freight-in, purchase returns and allowances, and purchase discounts are involved. *Freight costs* are treated as a part of the cost of the purchase; *purchase returns and allowances* are ordinarily considered as a reduction of the cost price and the retail price; *purchase discounts* usually are considered as a reduction of the cost of purchases. In short, the treatment for the items affecting the cost column of the retail inventory approach follows the computation for cost of goods available for sale.

Note also that *sales returns and allowances* are considered as proper adjustments to gross sales; *sales discounts to customers*, however, are not recognized when sales are recorded gross. To adjust for the Sales Discount account in such a situation would provide an ending inventory figure at retail that would be overvalued.

In addition, a number of special items require careful analysis. *Transfers-in* from another department, for example, should be reported in the same way as purchases from an outside enterprise. *Normal shortages* (breakage, damage, theft) should reduce the retail column because these goods are no longer available for sale. These costs are reflected in the selling price because a certain amount of shortage is considered normal in a retail enterprise. As a result, this amount is not considered in computing the cost to retail percentage but is shown as a deduction similar to sales to arrive at ending inventory at retail. *Abnormal shortages* should be deducted from both the cost and retail columns prior to calculating the cost to retail ratio and reported as a special inventory amount or as a loss. To do otherwise distorts the cost to retail ratio and overstates ending inventory. Finally, companies often provide their employees with special discounts to encourage loyalty, better performance, and so on. *Employee discounts* should be deducted from the retail column in the same way as sales. These discounts should not be considered in the cost to retail percentage because they do not reflect an overall change in the selling price.

Exhibit 9-13 shows some of these treatments in more detail. The business, Executive Apparel Co. Ltd., determines its inventory using the conventional retail inventory method.

EXHIBIT 9-13   EXECUTIVE APPAREL CO. LTD.

CONVENTIONAL RETAIL INVENTORY METHOD
(LOWER OF AVERAGE COST AND MARKET): SPECIAL ITEMS INCLUDED

	Cost		Retail
Beginning inventory	$ 1,000		$ 1,800
Purchases	30,000		60,000
Freight-In	600		—
Purchase returns	(1,500)		(3,000)
Totals	$30,100		$58,800
Net Markups			9,000
Abnormal shrinkage	(1,200)		(2,000)
Totals	$28,900		$65,800
Deduct:			
Net markdowns			1,400
Sales		$36,000	
Less sales returns and allowances		(900)	35,100
Employee discounts			800
Normal shrinkage			1,300
Ending inventory at retail			$27,200

$$\text{Cost to retail ratio} = \frac{\$28,900}{\$65,800} = 43.9\%$$

Ending inventory at lower of average cost and market (43.9% × $27,200) = $11,940.80

APPRAISAL OF RETAIL INVENTORY METHOD

The retail inventory method is used (1) to permit the computation of net income without the necessity of a physical count of the inventory, (2) as a control measure in determining inventory shortages, (3) in controlling quantities of merchandise on hand, and (4) as a source of information for insurance and tax purposes.

One characteristic of the retail inventory method is that it *has an averaging effect for varying rates of gross profit*. When applied to an entire business where rates of gross profit vary among departments, no allowance is made for possible distortion of results because of these differences. Many businesses refine the retail method under such conditions by computing inventory separately by departments or by classes of merchandise with similar rates of gross profit. In addition, the reliability of this method rests on the assumption that the distribution of items in the inventory is similar to the "mix" in the total goods available for sale.

THE INTERNAL CONTROL ENVIRONMENT AND FINANCIAL REPORTING

Woolworth Corporation is a large global retailer with over 8,000 stores (including Footlocker, Northern Reflections & Champs Sports) in 22 countries. Its shares trade on the New York Stock Exchange. Early in 1994, the Vice President and Treasurer of the company requested a meeting with the company's Board of Directors concerning certain accounting and reporting practices that were being followed by the company and some of its subsidiaries.

As a result of the attention suddenly focussed on the accounting policies, the company appointed outside counsel and auditors (KMPG) to conduct an extensive investigation of the issues. This led to the formation of a Special Committee to the Board of Directors to investigate and report on these matters.

The company ultimately restated its results for the 1993 quarterly report although the year-end results did not change.

One of the issues at stake was the use of the gross profit method (or a version of it) in estimating cost of sales and gross margin for the quarterly reporting. The gross profit method can tend to smooth quarterly gross profits. Several of the company's subsidiaries used this method for quarterly reporting. While both Price Waterhouse (the company's auditors) and KPMG agreed that it was acceptable to use the gross profit method in the retail industry in the absence of more accurate and timely information, they stated that it was not the preferred method for quarterly reporting where more accurate information was available. In this case, the Committee concluded that Woolworth did have a system to capture more accurate data—the departmental operating system (DOS). However, these numbers were not used since, along with other reasons, some of management felt that they were not available on a timely basis. The quarterly reporting deadline was very tight.

The CFO from one of the subsidiaries told the Special Committee that he did not switch to the DOS system because of the one-time impact on quarterly earnings and because it would tend to show lower profits in the earlier quarters of the year. Retail is very cyclical and traditionally, the first quarter is not the best and it is likely that the gross profit percentage is lower. The CFO felt that there was significant internal pressure to report strong first and second quarter results and that it was unacceptable not to. The CFO further stated before the Committee that he was directed by the company's CFO to report quarterly results that were more favourable than the actual results.

The Committee eventually found that management did not intend their actions to result in any adverse consequences for the company and that they felt that they were acting in the best interests of the company and its shareholders. This case however, illustrates that the reporting environment can have a significant impact on financial reporting and that control environments that allow management overrides are susceptible to internal control breaches.

Source: *Report of the Special Committee of the Board of Directors of Woolworth Corporation*, May 18, 1994

Contributed by: Irene Wiecek, University of Toronto

ADDITIONAL ISSUES RELATED TO INVENTORY VALUATION

While this and the previous chapter have addressed many important issues, three additional concerns require discussion in order to complete our consideration of inventory determination and valuation for financial reporting purposes. These are:

1. Valuation of inventory using the relative sales value method.
2. Valuation of inventory at net realizable value (regardless of its cost).
3. Accounting for purchase commitments.

VALUATION USING RELATIVE SALES VALUE

OBJECTIVE 11
Explain when and why the relative sales value method is used to value inventories.

A special problem arises when a group of varying units is purchased at a single **lump sum price**, a so-called **basket purchase**. Assume that Woodland Developers purchases land for $3 million that can be subdivided into 400 lots. These lots are of different sizes and shapes but can be sorted into three groups graded A, B, and C. As lots are sold, the purchase cost of $3 million must be apportioned among the lots sold and the lots remaining.

It is inappropriate to divide the total cost of $3 million by 400 lots to get a cost of $7,500 for each lot because they vary in size, shape, and attractiveness. When such a situation is encountered—and it is not at all unusual—the common practice is to allocate the total cost among the various units on the basis of their **relative sales value**. For the example given, the allocation works out as shown in Exhibit 9-14.

EXHIBIT 9-14

ALLOCATION OF COST USING RELATIVE SALES VALUE

Lots	Number of Lots	Sales Price per Lot	Total Sales Price	Relative Sales Price	Cost	Cost Allocated to Lots	Cost per Lot
A	100	$30,000	$3,000,000	300/750	$3,000,000	$1,200,000	$12,000
B	100	18,000	1,800,000	180/750	3,000,000	720,000	7,200
C	200	13,500	2,700,000	270/750	3,000,000	1,080,000	5,400
			$7,500,000			$3,000,000	

Exhibit 9-15 shows how the cost of lots sold (using the amounts given in the column for Cost per Lot) and the gross profit can be determined. The ending inventory is therefore $960,000 ($3,000,000 − $2,040,000).

EXHIBIT 9-15

DETERMINATION OF GROSS PROFIT USING RELATIVE SALES VALUE

Lots	Number of Lots Sold	Cost per Lot	Cost of Lots Sold	Sales	Gross Profit
A	77	$12,000	$ 924,000	$2,310,000	$1,386,000
B	80	7,200	576,000	1,440,000	864,000
C	100	5,400	540,000	1,350,000	810,000
			$2,040,000	$5,100,000	$3,060,000

This information may be analysed in a slightly different way. The ratio of the cost to the selling price of all the lots is 40% ($3,000,000 ÷ $7,500,000). Accordingly, given that the total sales price of lots sold is $5,100,000, then the cost of the lots sold is 40% of $5,100,000, or $2,040,000. The ending inventory is $960,000 ($3,000,000 − $2,040,000).

VALUATION OF INVENTORY AT NET REALIZABLE VALUE

For the most part, inventory is recorded at cost or the lower of cost and market. Under limited circumstances, however, support exists for *recording and reporting inventory at net realizable value regardless of its cost*. When the net realizable value is greater than cost, a net revenue is recognized even though the inventory has not been sold. This exception to normal revenue recognition being at the point of sale is permitted when (1) there is a controlled market with a fixed price applicable to all quantities and (2) no significant costs of disposal are involved. As such, it is argued that the criteria for revenue recognition are, for all practical purposes, met at the time of production rather than when goods are sold.

Recording inventory at net realizable value occurs in companies that have inventories of certain metals (especially rare ones) or agricultural products for which there is a controlled market (fixed price) and costs of disposal are estimable or immaterial. For example, Rio Algom Limited stated in the notes to its financial statements: "Concentrates awaiting shipment under firm contracts and coal inventories are valued at estimated realizable prices and therefore revenue is recorded at the time of production."

Another reason for allowing this method of valuation is that sometimes the cost figures are too difficult to obtain. In a typical manufacturing plant, various raw materials are used and labour costs incurred to create a finished product. Because the cost of each individual component part is known, the various items in inventory, whether completely or partially finished, can be accounted for on a cost basis. In a meat-packing house, however, a different situation prevails. The "raw material" consists of cattle, hogs, or sheep, each unit of which is purchased as a whole and then divided into parts that are the products. Instead of one product out of many raw materials, many products are made from one "unit" of raw material. To accurately assign the cost of an animal "on the hoof" into the cost of ribs, chucks, and shoulders, for instance, is a practical impossibility. It is much easier and more useful to determine the market price of the various products and value them in the inventory at selling price less the various costs, such as shipping and handling, necessary to get them to market. Hence, because of a peculiarity of the meat-packing industry, inventories are sometimes carried at sales price less distribution costs.

OBJECTIVE 12
Identify when and why inventory can be valued at net realizable value, regardless of its cost.

PURCHASE COMMITMENTS: A SPECIAL PROBLEM

In many lines of business the survival and continued profitability of an enterprise is dependent upon having a sufficient supply of merchandise to meet customer demands. Consequently, it is quite common for a company to contract for the purchase of inventory weeks, months, or even years in advance. This is particularly critical for companies using just-in-time (JIT) ordering and delivery systems. Generally, title to the merchandise or materials described in these **purchase commitments** has not passed to the buyer. Indeed, the goods may exist only as work in process, natural resources, or unplanted seeds.

Usually it is neither necessary nor proper for the buyer to make any entries to reflect commitments for purchases of goods that have not been shipped by the seller. Ordinary orders, for which the prices are determined at the time of shipment and that are *subject to cancellation* by the buyer or seller, represent neither an asset nor a liability to the buyer and need not be recorded in the books or reported in the financial statements.

Even with formal *noncancellable* purchase contracts, no asset or liability is recognized at the date of inception because the contract is "executory" in nature; neither party has fulfilled its part of the contract. However, if material, the existence of such contracts and some details should be disclosed in the notes to the financial statements.[12] Such a note is shown in Exhibit 9-16.

OBJECTIVE 13
Explain accounting issues related to purchase commitments.

---

[12] *CICA Handbook*, Section 3290, par. .12.

EXHIBIT 9-16

NOTE DISCLOSURE OF A SIGNICANT PURCHASE CONTRACT

Note 4. Contracts for the purchase of raw materials in 1999 have been executed in the amount of $600,000. The market price of such raw materials on December 31, 1998 is $640,000.

In the foregoing exhibit it was assumed that the contracted price was less than, or equal to, the market price at the balance sheet date. *If the contracted price exceeds the market price and losses are reasonably determinable and likely to occur at the time of purchase, losses should be recognized in the period during which such declines in prices take place.*[13] For example, if purchase contracts for delivery in 1999 have been executed at a firm price of $640,000 and the market price of the materials on the company's year end of December 31, 1998 is $600,000, the following entry is made on December 31, 1998:

Loss on Purchase Contracts	40,000	
Accrued Loss on Purchase Contracts		40,000

This loss is shown on the income statement under Other Expenses and Losses. The Accrued Loss on Purchase Contracts is reported in the liability section of the balance sheet. When the goods are delivered in 1999, the entry is:

Purchases	600,000	
Accrued Loss on Purchase Contracts	40,000	
Accounts Payable		640,000

If the price has partially or fully recovered before the inventory is received, the Accrued Loss on Purchase Contracts would be reduced. A resulting gain (Recovery of Loss) is then reported in the period of the price increase for the amount of the partial or full recovery.

Accounting for purchase commitments (and, for that matter, all commitments) is unsettled and controversial. Some argue that these contracts should be reported as assets and liabilities at the time the contract is signed; others believe that recognition at the delivery date is most appropriate.[14] Clearly, the treatment of such contracts in practice is far from being uniform. What is done for particular contracts in particular situations rests on judgement being exercised within the context of generally accepted accounting principles and experience.

FINANCIAL STATEMENT PRESENTATION OF INVENTORIES

OBJECTIVE 14
Know requirements for disclosure of inventory in financial statements and how these requirements can be met.

Inventories are one of the most significant assets of manufacturing and merchandising enterprises. The *CICA Handbook* requires disclosure of the basis of inventory valuation, any change in the basis from that used in the previous period, and the effect of such change on the net income for the period. It is also desirable that the amounts of the major categories making up the total inventory be disclosed (e.g., finished goods, work in process, and raw materials).[15]

---

[13] *Ibid.*, Section 3290, par. .12.

[14] See, for example, Yuji Ijiri, *Recognition of Contractual Rights and Obligations, Research Report* (Stamford, CT: FASB, 1980), who argues that firm purchase commitments might be capitalized. "Firm" means it is unlikely that performance under the contract can be avoided without severe penalty. Also, Mahendra R. Gujarathi and Stanley F. Biggs, "Accounting for Purchase Commitments: Some Issues and Recommendations," *Accounting Horizons*, September, 1988, pages 75–82, conclude that "recording an asset and liability on the date of inception for noncancellable purchase commitments is suggested as the first significant step towards alleviating the accounting problems associated with the issue. At year end, the potential gains and losses should be treated as contingencies [for which accounting standards provide] a coherent structure for the accounting and informative disclosure for such gains and losses."

[15] *CICA Handbook*, Section 3030, par. .10.

To illustrate the presentation of inventory, examine the relevant portions of Moore Corporation Limited's statements in the Appendix to Chapter 5, and the following extracts from statements of some other Canadian companies.

These examples show disclosure of the basis for inventory valuation (e.g., lower of cost and market), the cost flow method used, and the definition of market used for the major categories making up the total inventory. It is quite acceptable, as shown in the illustrations, for a company to use different valuation methods for different components of its inventory. The use of notes is the basic means for disclosing such information.

The *CICA Handbook* (Section 3030, par. .12) states that "reserves for future decline in inventory values, or any similar reserves, should not be deducted in arriving at inventory valuation." This requirement does not preclude an enterprise from appropriating a portion of retained earnings for an anticipated decline.

THE OSHAWA GROUP LIMITED

CONSOLIDATED BALANCE SHEET

January 27, 1996 and January 28, 1995 *(in millions of dollars)*	1996	1995
Assets		
Current assets		
Cash and short-term investments	$ 44.7	$ 54.6
Accounts receivable	264.4	249.2
Income taxes receivable	–	10.8
Inventories	333.3	331.1
Prepaid expenses	18.1	16.8

1. Summary of Significant Accounting Policies

Inventories

Warehouse inventories are valued at the lower of cost and net realizable value with cost being determined on a first-in, first-out basis. Retail inventories are valued at the lower of cost and net realizable value less normal profit margins as determined by the retail method of inventory valuation.

DONOHUE INC.

CONSOLIDATED BALANCE SHEET

As at December 31, 1996, with comparative figures for 1995 (in thousands of dollars)

	1996	1995
ASSETS		
CURRENT ASSETS		
Cash and short-term investments	$ 81,833	$ 138,135
Accounts receivable	200,971	128,953
Inventories (note 2)	299,121	163,640
Prepaid expenses	26,815	10,612
	608,740	441,340

DONOHUE INC.　(Continued)

NOTES TO CONSOLIDATED FINANCIAL STATEMENTS

SUMMARY OF SIGNIFICANT ACCOUNTING POLICIES

Inventories

Wood products, market pulp, newsprint and specialties are valued at the lower of cost, determined on an average cost basis, and net realizable value.

Logs, chips, other raw materials, and production and maintenance supplies are valued at the lower of cost, determined on an average cost basis, and replacement cost.

2.　INVENTORIES

	1996	1995
Logs	$103,523	$ 66,279
Wood products	43,747	29,258
Chips	14,666	10,392
Market pulp, newsprint and specialties	60,373	22,133
Other raw materials, production and maintenance supplies	76,812	35,578
	$299,121	$163,640

CELANESE CANADA INC.

CONSOLIDATED BALANCE SHEET

		(dollar amounts in thousands)	
As at December 31	1995	1994	1993
Assets			
Cash and short-term investments	$196,863	$171,639	$119,001
Accounts receivable	64,914	97,147	73,859
Inventories (note 3)	60,385	46,441	44,001
Prepaid expenses	1,761	2,564	1,886
Total current assets	323,923	317,791	238,747

(3) Inventories

Substantially all inventories are valued using the first-in, first-out (FIFO) method of determining cost. Other inventories are valued at current cost. Inventory values are not in excess of net realizable value and do not include depreciation of property, plant and equipment. Inventories at December 31 were:

	1995	1994	1993
Raw materials	$ 9,346	$ 6,732	$ 7,941
Work in process	3,024	2,616	3,656
Finished goods	37,410	25,765	20,401
Stores and supplies	10,605	11,328	12,003
Total	$60,385	$46,441	$44,001

Summary of Learning Objectives

1. **Recognize that the lower of cost and market basis is a departure from the historical cost principle, and understand why this is acceptable.** The lower of cost and market approach is a departure from historical cost justified on the basis that any loss of future utility (revenue-producing ability) should be recognized in the period of occurrence (i.e., conservatism).

2. **Understand various definitions of possible market amounts that may be used when applying lower of cost and market.** Replacement cost is the amount needed to acquire an equivalent item as would be incurred in the normal course of business operations. Net realizable value is the estimated selling price of an item in the ordinary course of business less reasonably predictable future costs to complete and dispose of the item. Net realizable value less normal profit margin is determined by deducting a normal profit margin from the previously defined net realizable value. All three are acceptable definitions of market, although net realizable value is the one used by a large majority of Canadian companies.

3. **Explain how lower of cost and market works and how it is applied.** Under the lower of cost and market approach, the cost (FIFO, average cost, LIFO) and market (replacement cost, net realizable value, or net realizable value less normal profit margin) of inventory are separately determined. The inventory valuation is then the lower of the two amounts. The lower of cost and market amount may be determined on an item-by-item basis, major category basis, or total inventory basis. The total inventory basis is most commonly used in Canada.

4. **Know how to account for inventory on the lower of cost and market basis.** If it is determined that market is less than cost, inventory may be directly written down to market (direct method) or the difference is accounted for in an allowance account (indirect or allowance method).

5. **Evaluate conceptual difficulties associated with the lower of cost and market basis.** While the rule permits write-downs to market, it is inconsistent because write-ups to market are now allowed. While it is conservative in the year of write-downs, it results in higher profits in future periods when the lower amounts are matched against revenues.

6. **Determine ending inventory by applying the gross profit method.** The gross profit method of estimating inventory is based on reducing net sales to their cost and deducting that amount from cost of goods available for sale to get ending inventory at cost. To apply this method, a gross profit on sales percentage must be determined. This percentage may be determined from examining prior periods' accounting records and current policies regarding a company's gross profit on selling price or markup on cost.

7. **Know when the gross profit method can be used and appreciate its limitations.** Because the gross profit method results in an estimate of the cost of ending inventory (i.e., it is not based on a physical count), it is unacceptable for annual financial reporting purposes. It is acceptable for interim reporting, determining amounts for insurance claims regarding inventory destroyed by fire or other catastrophes, or for testing the reasonableness of inventory cost derived by other methods.

8. **Appreciate when the retail inventory method can be used, know what information is required to apply it, and understand how the information is used to determine ending inventory.** The retail inventory method can be used to estimate ending inventory for interim statements, insurance claims, or other reasons when taking a count is not reasonable or possible. It may also be used in conjunction with a physical count to determine the ending inventory reported in financial statements. The retail inventory method is based on multiplying a cost to retail percentage (derived from information in the accounting records) by the retail price of ending inventory (determined by a count or from accounting records). To apply the retail inventory method, records must be kept of the costs and retail prices for beginning inventory, net purchases, and abnormal spoilage, as well as the retail amount of net markups, net markdowns, and net sales. Determination of the items going into the numerator and denominator of the cost to retail ratio depend on the type of inventory valuation estimate desired.

9. **Understand retail method terminology.** Prices are frequently changed from the original retail price (cost plus an original markup or markon). Additions to the original price are called markups. Markup cancellations are price reductions down to the original price. Reductions below the original price are called markdowns. Markdown cancellations are price increases up to the original price.

10. **Determine ending inventory using the conventional retail inventory method and understand why it results in approximating the lower of average cost and market.** The conventional retail method includes net markups but excludes net markdowns in the calculation of the cost to retail ratio. This is the most commonly used retail inventory method; it results in an approximation of inventory at the lower of average cost and market, market being defined as net realizable value less a normal profit margin.

11. **Explain when and why the relative sales value method is used to value inventories.** When a group of varying units is purchased at a single lump sum price—a so-called basket purchase—the total purchase price may be allocated to the individual items on the basis of relative sales value. Such an allocation results in appropriately assigning a relevant cost to be matched against revenue when an item is sold, or an amount to be reported in the balance sheet before the item is sold.

12. **Identify when and why inventory can be valued at net realizable value regardless of its cost.** It is argued that inventories should be valued at net realizable value when (1) there is a controlled market with a quoted price applicable to all quantities; and (2) no significant costs of disposal are involved. If these conditions exist, then it may be that the criteria for revenue recognition are satisfied.

13. **Explain accounting issues related to purchase commitments.** Accounting for purchase commitments is controversial. Some argue that these contracts should be reported as assets and liabilities at the time the contract is signed; others believe that the present recognition at the delivery date is most appropriate. Generally, if purchase commitments are of significance (material), they should be disclosed in a note to the statements. If a contract requires payment of a price in excess of the year-end market price, a loss should be recognized.

14. **Know requirements for disclosure of inventory in financial statements and how these requirements can be met.** Disclosure of the basis of inventory valuation and any change in the basis are required by the *CICA Handbook*. Also, it is desirable to disclose major categories of inventory, the method used to determine cost, and the definition of market applied under the lower of cost and market method.

EXERCISES

(Lower of Cost and Market) Evan Company follows the practice of pricing its inventory at the lower of cost and market, on an individual-item basis.   **E9-1**

Item No.	Quantity	Cost per Unit	Cost to Replace	Estimated Selling Price	Cost of Completion and Disposal	Normal Profit
1320	900	$3.30	$3.00	$4.50	$.35	$1.25
1333	1,200	2.70	2.30	3.50	.50	.50
1426	800	4.40	3.70	5.00	.40	1.00
1437	1,000	3.60	3.10	3.20	.25	.90
1510	700	2.25	2.00	3.25	.80	.60
1522	500	3.10	2.90	3.90	.50	.60
1573	3,000	1.90	1.60	2.50	.75	.50
1626	1,000	4.70	5.20	6.00	.50	1.00

Instructions
From the information above, determine the amount of Evan Company Ltd.'s inventory assuming use of (1) the most commonly used definition of "market" in Canadian practice and (2) U.S. rules to determine market.

(Lower of Cost and Market) Pena Company uses the lower of cost and market method, on an individual-item basis, in pricing its inventory items. The inventory at December 31, 1998 consists of products D, E, F, G, H, and I. Relevant per-unit data for these products appear below.   **E9-2**

	Item D	Item E	Item F	Item G	Item H	Item I
Estimated selling price	$120	$110	$90	$90	$110	$90
Cost	80	80	80	80	50	36
Replacement cost	120	70	70	30	70	30
Estimated selling expense	30	30	30	30	30	30
Normal profit	20	20	20	20	20	20

Instructions
Using the lower of cost and market rule, determine the unit value for balance sheet reporting purposes at December 31, 1998 for each of the inventory items above using (1) the most commonly used Canadian definition of market and (2) the U.S. rules to determine market.

(Lower of Cost and Market) The inventory of Cougar Inc. on December 31, 1998 consists of these items.   **E9-3**

Part No.	Quantity	Cost per Unit	Net Realizable Value per Unit
110	1,000	$ 90	$100
111	600	60	52
112	500	80	76
113	200	170	180
120	400	205	208
121ª	1,600	16	?
122	200	240	235

ª Part No. 121 is obsolete and each unit has a realizable value of $0.20 as scrap. This part had sold previously for $14.

Instructions
(a) Determine the inventory as of December 31, 1998 by the method of cost or market, whichever is lower, and apply the method directly to each item.
(b) Determine the inventory by cost or market, whichever is lower, and apply the method to the total of the inventory.

E9-4 **(Lower of Cost and Market: Journal Entries)** Panther Company Ltd. determined its ending inventory at cost and at lower of cost and market at December 31, 1997 and December 31, 1998. This information is presented below:

	Cost	Lower of Cost and Market
12/31/97	$346,000	$325,000
12/31/98	410,000	395,000

Instructions

(a) Prepare the journal entries required at 12/31/97 and 12/31/98, assuming that the inventory is recorded directly at market and a periodic inventory system is used.

(b) Prepare journal entries required at 12/31/97 and 12/31/98, assuming that the inventory is recorded at cost and an allowance account is adjusted at each year end under a periodic system.

(c) Which of the two methods provides the highest net income in each year?

E9-5 **(Inventory Valuation Method Comparison)** Alomar Co. Ltd. began business on January 1, 1998. Information about its inventories under different valuation methods follows.

	LIFO Cost	FIFO Cost	Lower of FIFO Cost and Market
December 31, 1998	$18,500	$25,000	$19,500
December 31, 1999	14,400	20,000	16,000

Instructions

(a) Indicate the inventory basis that will show the highest net income in (1) 1998 and (2) 1999.

(b) Indicate whether the FIFO cost basis will provide a higher or lower profit than the lower of cost and market basis in 1999 and indicate by how much.

E9-6 **(Lower of Cost and Market: Valuation Account)** Presented below is information related to Amareto Enterprises.

	Jan. 31	Feb. 28	Mar. 31	Apr. 30
Inventory at cost	$15,000	$15,100	$17,000	$13,000
Inventory at the lower of cost and market	14,500	13,600	15,600	12,800
Purchases for the month		22,000	24,000	28,000
Sales for the month		33,200	35,000	50,000

Instructions

(a) From the information prepare (as far as the data permit) monthly income statements in columnar form for February, March, and April. The inventory is to be shown in the statement at cost, the gain or loss due to market fluctuations is to be shown separately, and a valuation account is to be set up for the difference between cost and the lower of cost and market.

(b) Prepare the journal entry required to establish the valuation account at January 31 and entries to adjust it monthly thereafter.

E9-7 **(Lower of Cost and Market: Error Effects)** Fleming Co. Ltd. uses the lower of FIFO cost and net realizable value method on an individual-item basis applying the direct method. The inventory at December 31, 1998 included Product Q, on which the following per-unit data were available:

Estimated selling price	$42
Cost	39
Replacement cost	40
Estimated selling expenses	4
Normal profit	1

There were 10,000 units on hand at December 31, 1998. However, Product Q was incorrectly valued at $39 per unit in the financial statements. All 10,000 units were sold in 1999.

Instructions

As a result of the error:

(a) Was net income for 1998 over- or understated? By how much (ignore income tax aspects)?

(b) Was net income for 1999 over- or understated? By how much?

(c) Indicate whether the current ratio, inventory turnover ratio (cost of goods sold divided by ending inventory), and ratio of debt to total assets would be overstated, understated, or not affected for the years ended December 31, 1998 and December 31, 1999.

(Relative Sales Value Method) Sturdy Furniture Company purchases, during 1998, a carload of wicker chairs. The manufacturer sells the chairs to Sturdy for a lump sum of $58,900, because it is discontinuing manufacturing operations and wishes to dispose of its entire stock. Three types of chairs are included in the carload. The three types and the estimated selling price for each are listed below.   **E9-8**

Type	No. of Chairs	Estimated Selling Price for Each
Lounge chairs	400	$90
Armchairs	300	80
Straight chairs	700	50

During 1998 Sturdy sells 200 lounge chairs, 100 armchairs, and 120 straight chairs.

Instructions

What is the amount of gross profit realized during 1998? What is the amount of inventory of unsold wicker chairs on December 31, 1998?

(Relative Sales Value Method) Wheel and Deal Inc. purchased a tract of land for $55,000. This land was improved and subdivided into building lots at an additional cost of $28,070. These building lots were all of the same size, but owing to differences in location were offered for sale at different prices as follows.   **E9-9**

Group	No. of Lots	Price per Lot
1	9	$3,000
2	15	4,000
3	17	2,400

Operating expenses for the year allocated to this project totalled $18,200. Lots unsold at year end were as follows:

Group 1	5 lots
Group 2	7 lots
Group 3	2 lots

Instructions

Determine the year-end inventory and net income from these operations.

(Purchase Commitments) At December 31, 1998 BC Wine Company has outstanding noncancellable purchase commitments for 70,000 L, at $2 per litre, of raw material to be used in its manufacturing process. The company prices its raw material inventory at cost or market, whichever is lower.   **E9-10**

Instructions

(a) Assuming that the market price as of December 31, 1998 is $2.40 per litre, how will this commitment be treated in the accounts and statements? Explain.

(b) Assuming that the market price as of December 31, 1998 is $1.60, how will you treat this commitment in the accounts and statements?

(c) Prepare the entry for January, 1999 when the 70,000 L shipment is received, assuming that the situation in (b) existed at December 31, 1998. Give an explanation of your entry.

(Purchase Commitments) Distributors Inc. was having difficulty obtaining key raw materials for its manufacturing process. The company therefore signs a long-term noncancellable purchase commitment with its largest supplier of this raw material on November 30, 1998 at an agreed price of $400,000. At December 31, 1998 the raw material has declined in price to $370,000. It was further anticipated that the price will drop another $15,000 so that, at the date of delivery, the value of the inventory will be $355,000.   **E9-11**

Instructions
What entries will you make on December 31, 1998 to recognize these facts?

E9-12 (Gross Profit Method) Giola Inc. uses the gross profit method to estimate inventory for monthly reporting purposes. Presented below is information for the month of May:

Inventory May 1	$ 160,000
Purchases (gross)	640,000
Freight-in	30,000
Sales	1,000,000
Sales returns	70,000
Purchase discounts	12,000

Instructions
(a) Compute the estimated inventory at May 31, assuming that the gross profit is 25% of sales.
(b) Compute the estimated inventory at May 31, assuming that the markup is 25% of cost.

E9-13 (Gross Profit Method) Blues Co. requires an estimate of the cost of goods lost by fire on March 9. Merchandise on hand on January 1 was $38,000. Purchases since January 1 were $72,000; freight-in, $3,400; purchase returns and allowances, $2,400. Sales were made at a markup of 33⅓% on cost and totalled $100,000 to March 9. Goods costing $7,700 were left undamaged by the fire; remaining goods were destroyed.

Instructions
(a) Compute the cost of goods destroyed.
(b) Compute the cost of goods destroyed, assuming that the gross profit is 33⅓% of sales.

E9-14 (Gross Profit Method) You are called by the owner of Gremlin Co. on July 16 and asked to prepare a claim for insurance as a result of a theft that took place the night before. You suggest that an inventory be taken immediately. The following data are available:

Inventory July 1	$ 38,000
Purchases—goods placed in stock July 1–15	85,000
Sales—goods delivered to customers (gross)	116,000
Sales returns—goods returned to stock	4,000

Your client reports that the goods on hand on July 16 cost $29,000, but you determine that this figure includes goods of $6,000 received on a consignment basis. Your past records show that sales prices are set at approximately 40% over cost.

Instructions
Compute the claim against the insurance company.

E9-15 (Gross Profit Method) Woody's Lumber Co. handles three principal lines of merchandise with these varying rates of gross profit on cost:

Lumber	35%
Millwork	30%
Hardware and fittings	40%

On August 18 a fire destroyed the office, lumber shed, and a considerable portion of the lumber stacked in the yard. To file a report of loss for insurance purposes, the company must know what the inventories were immediately prior to the fire. The only pertinent information you are able to obtain are the following facts from the general ledger, which was kept in a fireproof vault and thus escaped destruction.

	Lumber	Millwork	Hardware
Inventory Jan. 1	$ 250,000	$ 90,000	$ 45,000
Purchases to Aug. 18	1,500,000	376,000	160,000
Sales to Aug. 18	2,079,000	500,500	210,000

Instructions
Submit your estimate of the inventory amounts immediately prior to the fire.

(Retail Inventory Method: Ratio Components) Presented below are a number of items that may be encountered in computing the cost to retail percentage when using the conventional retail method or the average cost retail method: **E9-16**

1. Sales discounts
2. Markdowns
3. Markdown cancellations
4. Cost of items transferred in from other departments
5. Retail value of items transferred in from other departments
6. Purchase discounts (purchases are recorded gross)

7. Estimated retail value of goods broken or stolen
8. Cost of beginning inventory
9. Retail value of beginning inventory
10. Cost of purchases
11. Retail value of purchases
12. Markups
13. Markup cancellations
14. Employee discounts (sales are recorded net)

Instructions
For each of the items listed above, indicate whether it is included in the cost to retail percentage (1) under conventional retail and (2) under average cost retail.

(Retail Inventory Method: Conventional and Average Cost) Sal's Grocery Company began operations on January 1, 1997, adopting the conventional retail inventory system. None of its merchandise was marked down in 1997 and, because there was no beginning inventory, its ending inventory for 1997 of $38,500 would have been the same under either the conventional system or the average-cost system. All pertinent data regarding purchases, sales, markups, and markdowns for 1998 are shown below. **E9-17**

	Cost	Retail
Inventory Jan. 1, 1998	$ 38,500	$ 62,000
Markdowns (net)		13,000
Markups (net)		20,000
Purchases (net)	127,900	178,000
Sales (net)		191,000

Instructions
Determine the cost of the 1998 ending inventory under (1) the conventional retail method and (2) the average-cost retail method.

(Retail Inventory Method) The records of Wally's World Inc. report the following data for the month of September: **E9-18**
Instructions

Sales	$99,000	Purchases (at cost)	48,000
Sales returns	1,000	Purchases (at sales price)	88,000
Markups	10,000	Purchase returns (at cost)	2,000
Markup cancellations	1,500	Purchase returns (at sales price)	3,000
Markdowns	9,300	Beginning inventory (at cost)	30,000
Markdown cancellations	2,800	Beginning inventory (at sales price)	46,500
Freight on purchases	2,400		

Compute the ending inventory by the conventional retail inventory method.

(Retail Inventory Method) Presented below is information related to Corner Company. **E9-19**

	Cost	Retail
Beginning inventory	$ 58,000	$100,000
Purchases (net)	122,000	200,000
Net markups		10,345
Net markdowns		26,135
Sales		190,000

Instructions
(a) Compute the ending inventory at retail.
(b) Compute a cost-to-retail percentage (round to two decimals):
    1. Excluding both markups and markdowns.
    2. Excluding markups but including markdowns.
    3. Excluding markdowns but including markups.
    4. Including both markdowns and markups.
(c) Which of the methods in (b) above (1, 2, 3, or 4):
    1. Provides the most conservative estimate of ending inventory?
    2. Provides an approximation of lower of cost and market?
    3. Is used in the conventional retail method?
(d) Compute ending inventory at lower of cost and market (round to nearest dollar).
(e) Compute cost of goods sold based on (d).
(f) Compute gross profit based on (d).

PROBLEMS

P9-1 Olen Ltd. manufactures desks. Most of the company's desks are standard models and are sold on the basis of cata-logue prices. At December 31, 1998 the following per-unit information for four types of finished desks appears in the company's records.

Finished Desks	A	B	C	D
1998 catalogue selling price	$450	$480	$900	$1,050
FIFO cost per inventory list 12/31/98	470	450	830	960
Estimated current cost to manufacture				
(at December 31, 1998 and early 1999)	460	440	720	1,000
Sales commissions and estimated				
other costs of disposal	50	60	90	130
1999 catalogue selling price	510	550	900	1,200

The 1998 catalogue is in effect through November, 1998 and the 1999 catalogue is effective as of December 1, 1998. Generally, the company attempts to obtain a 20% gross profit on selling price and has usually been successful in doing so.

Instructions
At what per-unit amount should each of the four types of desks appear in the company's December 31, 1998 inventory, assuming that the company has adopted a lower of FIFO cost and market approach for valuation of invento-ries? Use net realizable value as the definition of market.

P9-2 Mort Inc. values its inventory at the lower of cost and market. The following information is available from the com-pany's inventory records as of December 31, the company's year end.

Item	On-Hand Quantity	Unit Cost	Replacement Cost/Unit	Estimated Unit Selling Price	Completion & Disposal Costs/Unit	Normal Unit Profit
A	1,100	$7.50	$8.40	$10.50	$1.50	$1.80
B	800	8.20	8.40	9.40	.90	1.20
C	1,000	5.90	5.40	7.00	1.20	.50
D	1,000	3.80	4.20	6.30	.80	1.50
E	1,200	6.50	6.30	6.80	.70	1.00

Instructions
(a) Indicate the inventory amount that should be used for each item under the lower of cost and market rule assum-ing (1) the definition of market used most commonly in Canada and (2) U.S. rules.
(b) Mort Inc. applies the lower of cost and market rule directly to each item in the inventory but maintains its inven-tory account at cost to account for the items above. Give the adjusting entry, if one is necessary, to write down the ending inventory from cost to market assuming (1) the definition of market used most commonly in Canada and (2) U.S. rules.

(c) Mort Inc. applies the lower of cost and market rule to the total of the inventory. What is the dollar amount for inventory as of 12/31 assuming (1) the definition of market used most commonly in Canada and (2) U.S. rules?

Ivory Music Ltd. determined its ending inventory at cost and at lower of cost and market at December 31, 1997, 1998, and 1999 as shown below. **P9-3**

	Cost	Lower of Cost or Market
12/31/97	$650,000	$650,000
12/31/98	780,000	725,000
12/31/99	900,000	830,000

Instructions

(a) Prepare the journal entries required at 12/31/98 and 12/31/99, assuming that a periodic inventory system and the direct method of adjusting to market is used.

(b) Prepare the journal entries required at 12/31/98 and 12/31/99, assuming that a periodic inventory is recorded at cost and reduced to market through the use of an allowance account.

River Roar Ltd., which began operations in 1995, always values its inventories at the current replacement cost. Its **P9-4** annual inventory figure is arrived at by taking a physical count and then pricing each item in the physical inventory at current prices determined from recent vendors' invoices or catalogues. Here is the condensed income statement for this company for the last four years.

	1995	1996	1997	1998
Sales	$850,000	$880,000	$950,000	$990,000
Cost of goods sold	560,000	590,000	630,000	650,000
Gross profit	$290,000	$290,000	$320,000	$340,000
Operating expenses	190,000	180,000	200,000	210,000
Income before income taxes	$100,000	$110,000	$120,000	$130,000

Instructions

(a) Do you see any objections to the procedure for valuing inventories? Explain.

(b) Assuming that the inventory at cost and as determined by the corporation (using replacement cost) at the end of each of the four years is as follows, restate the condensed income statements using cost for inventories.

Ending Inventory	At Cost	Replacement Cost As Determined by Company
1995	$130,000	$144,000
1996	140,000	158,000
1997	135,000	157,000
1998	150,000	159,000

(c) Compare the trend in income for the four years using the corporation's approach versus using cost for ending inventory. What observations do you make?

Easton Inc. is a food wholesaler that supplies independent grocery stores in the immediate region. The first-in, first- **P9-5** out (FIFO) method of inventory valuation is used to determine the cost of the inventory at the end of each month. Transactions and other related information regarding two of the items (instant coffee and sugar) carried by Easton are given below for October, the last month of Easton's fiscal year.

	Instant Coffee	Sugar
Standard unit of packaging:	Case containing 24, 1 kg jars	Baler containing 12, 5 kg bags
Inventory, 10/1:	1,000 cases @ $116 per case	500 balers @ $11 per baler

Purchases:	1. 10/10—1,600 cases @ $118 per case plus freight of $480	1. 10/5—850 balers @ $11.75 per baler plus freight of $420
	2. 10/20—2,400 cases @ $120 per case plus freight of $480	2. 10/16—640 balers @ $12 per baler plus freight of $420
		3. 10/24—600 balers @ $12.20 per baler plus freight of $420
Purchase terms:	2/10, net/30, f.o.b. shipping point	Net 30 days, f.o.b. shipping point
October sales:	3,700 cases @ $159 per case	2,000 balers @ $14.50 per baler
Returns and allowances:	A customer returned 50 cases that had been shipped by error. The customer's account was credited for $7,950.	As the October 16 purchase was unloaded, 20 balers were discovered damaged. A representative of the the trucking firm confirmed the damage and the balers were discarded. Credit of $240 for the merchandise and $13 for the freight were received by Easton.
Inventory values including freight and net of purchase discounts—10/31:		
• Most recent quoted price	$121 per case	$13.80 per baler
• Net realizable value	$150 per case	$13.20 per baler
• Net realizable value less a normal profit	$135 per case	$10.70 per baler

Easton's sales terms are 1/10, net/30, f.o.b. shipping point. Easton records all purchases net of purchase discounts and takes all purchase discounts.

Instructions

(a) Calculate the number of units in inventory and the FIFO unit cost for instant coffee and sugar as of October 31.

(b) Easton Inc. applies the lower of cost and market (net realizable value) rule in valuing its year-end inventory. Calculate the total dollar amount of the inventory for instant coffee and sugar, applying the lower of cost and market rule on an individual product basis.

(c) Can Easton Inc. apply the lower of cost and market rule to groups of products or the inventory as a whole rather than on an individual product basis? Explain your answer.   (CMA adapted)

P9-6   Rustler Inc. lost most of its inventory in a fire in December just before the year-end physical inventory was taken. Corporate records disclose the following:

Inventory (beginning)	$ 80,000	Sales	$415,000
Purchases	280,000	Sales returns	21,000
Purchase returns	28,000	Gross profit % based on selling price	30%

Merchandise with a selling price of $30,000 remained undamaged after the fire, and damaged merchandise has a salvage value of $7,150. The company does not carry fire insurance on its inventory. It is estimated that the year-end inventory would have been subject to a normal 10% write-down for obsolescence.

Instructions
Prepare a schedule computing the fire loss incurred by Rustler Inc. (Do not use the retail inventory method.)

On April 15, 1998 a fire damaged the office and warehouse of Surin Inc. The only accounting record saved was the **P9-7** general ledger, from which the trial balance below was prepared.

SURIN INC.
Trial Balance
March 31, 1998

Cash	$ 20,000	
Accounts receivable	40,000	
Inventory December 31, 1997	75,000	
Land	35,000	
Building and equipment	110,000	
Accumulated depreciation		$ 41,300
Other assets	3,600	
Accounts payable		23,700
Other expense accruals		10,200
Common shares		100,000
Retained earnings		52,000
Sales		135,000
Purchases	52,000	
Other expenses	26,600	
	$362,200	$362,200

The following data and information have been gathered:
1. The fiscal year of the corporation ends on December 31.

2. An examination of the April bank statement and cancelled cheques revealed that cheques written during the period April 1–15 totalled $13,000: $5,700 paid to accounts payable as of March 31, $3,400 for April merchandise shipments, and $3,900 paid for other expenses. Deposits during the same period amounted to $12,950, which consisted of receipts on account from customers with the exception of a $950 refund from a vendor for merchandise returned in April.

3. Correspondence with suppliers revealed unrecorded obligations at April 15 of $10,600 for April merchandise shipments, including $2,300 for shipments in transit on that date.

4. Customers acknowledged indebtedness of $36,000 at April 15, 1998. It was also estimated that customers owed another $8,000 that will never be acknowledged or recovered. Of the acknowledged indebtedness, $600 will probably be uncollectible.

5. The companies insuring the inventory agreed that the corporation's fire-loss claim should be based on the assumption that the overall gross profit ratio for the past two years was in effect during the current year. The corporation's audited financial statements disclosed the following information:

	Year Ended December 31	
	1997	1996
Net sales	$530,000	$390,000
Net purchases	280,000	235,000
Beginning inventory	50,000	66,000
Ending inventory	75,000	50,000

6. Inventory with a cost of $7,000 was salvaged and sold for $4,000. The balance of the inventory was a total loss.

Instructions
Prepare a schedule computing the amount of inventory fire loss. The supporting schedule of the computation of the gross profit ratio should be in good form.

(AICPA adapted)

Langdon Co. Ltd. is an importer and wholesaler. Its merchandise is purchased from several suppliers and is ware- **P9-8** housed until sold.

In conducting his audit for the year ended June 30, 1998, the corporation's auditor determined that the system of internal control was good. Accordingly, he observed the physical inventory at an interim date, May 31, 1998 instead of at year end.

The following information was obtained from the general ledger:

Inventory July 1, 1997	$ 120,000
Physical inventory May 31, 1998	98,500
Sales for 11 months ended May 31, 1998	970,000
Sales for year ended June 30, 1998	1,060,000
Purchases for 11 months ended May 31, 1998 (before audit adjustments)	650,000
Purchases for year ended June 30, 1998 (before audit adjustments)	755,000

The audit disclosed the following information:

Shipments received in May and included in the physical inventory but recorded as June purchases	12,000
Shipments received in unsalable condition and excluded from physical inventory; credit memos had not been received nor had chargebacks to vendors been recorded:	
Total at May 31, 1998	1,500
Total at June 30, 1998 (including the May unrecorded chargebacks)	2,000
Deposit made with vendor and charged to purchases in April 1998 Product was shipped in July 1998	3,000
Deposit made with vendor and charged to purchases in May 1998 Product was shipped, f.o.b. destination, on May 29, 1998 and was included in May 31, 1998 physical inventory as goods in transit	6,500
Through the carelessness of the receiving department, a June shipment was damaged by rain. This shipment was later sold in June at its cost of $8,000.	

Instructions

In audit engagements in which interim physical inventories are observed, a frequently used auditing procedure is to test the reasonableness of the year-end inventory by the application of gross profit ratios. Given this, you are asked to prepare schedules that show the determination of:

(a) The gross profit ratio for the 11 months ended May 31, 1998.

(b) The cost of goods sold during June, 1998.

(c) The June 30, 1998 inventory.   (AICPA adapted)

P9-9 Presented below is information related to Burp Inc. for 1998.

	Cost	Retail
Inventory 12/31/97	$250,000	$ 390,000
Purchases	970,000	1,460,000
Purchase returns	60,000	80,000
Purchase discounts	18,000	—
Gross sales (after employee discounts)	—	1,460,000
Sales returns	—	97,500
Markups	—	120,000
Markup cancellations	—	40,000
Markdowns	—	45,000
Markdown cancellations	—	20,000
Freight-in	79,000	—
Employee discounts granted	—	8,000
Loss from breakage (normal)	—	2,500

Instructions

Assuming that Burp uses the conventional retail inventory method, compute the amount of its ending inventory at December 31, 1998.

P9-10 Flog Department Store Inc. uses the retail inventory method to estimate ending inventory for its monthly financial statements. The following data pertain to a single department for the month of October:

Inventory October 1	
At cost	$ 52,000
At retail	78,000
Purchases (exclusive of freight and returns):	
At cost	272,000
At retail	423,000
Freight-in	16,600
Purchase returns	
At cost	5,600
At retail	8,000
Markups	9,000
Markup cancellations	2,000
Markdowns (net)	3,600
Normal spoilage and breakage	10,000
Sales	380,000

Instructions

(a) Using the conventional retail method, prepare a schedule computing estimated lower of average cost and market inventory for October 31.

(b) A department store using the conventional retail inventory method estimates the ending inventory as $60,000. An accurate physical count reveals only $44,000 of inventory at lower of average cost and market. List the factors that may have caused the difference between the estimated inventory and the physical count.

Late in 1995, B. Didrikson and four other investors took the chain of Sprint Department Stores private, and the company has just completed its third year of operations under the ownership of the investment group. P. Ryun, controller of Sprint Department Stores, is in the process of preparing the year-end financial statements. Based on the preliminary financial statements, Didrikson has expressed concern over inventory shortages, and she has asked Ryun to determine whether an abnormal amount of theft and breakage has occurred. The accounting records of Sprint Department Stores contain the following amounts on November 30, 1998, the end of the fiscal year. **P9-11**

	Cost	Retail
Beginning inventory	$ 68,200	$100,000
Purchases	261,800	400,000
Net markups		50,000
Net markdowns		110,000
Sales		330,000

According to the November 30, 1998 physical inventory, the actual inventory at retail is $106,000.

Instructions

(a) Describe the circumstances under which the retail inventory method would be applied, and the advantages of using the retail inventory method.

(b) Assuming that prices have been stable, calculate the lower of cost and market value of Sprint Department Stores' ending inventory using the conventional retail method. Furnish supporting calculations.

(c) Estimate the amount of shortage, at retail, that has occurred at Sprint Department Stores during the year ended November 30, 1998.

(d) Complications in the retail method can be caused by such items as (1) freight-in expense, (2) purchase returns and allowances, (3) sales returns and allowances, and (4) employee discounts. Explain how each of these four special items is handled in the retail inventory method. (CMA adapted)

Ellen's Specialty Company, a division of Entertainment Inc., manufactures three models of gear shift components for bicycles that are sold to bicycle manufacturers, retailers, and catalogue outlets. Since beginning operations in 1980, Ellen's has used normal absorption costing and has assumed a first-in, first-out cost flow in its perpetual inventory system. Except for overhead, manufacturing costs are accumulated using actual costs. Overhead is applied to production using predetermined overhead rates. The balances of the inventory accounts at the end of Ellen's fiscal year, November 30, 1998, are shown below. The inventories are stated at cost before any year-end adjustments. **P9-12**

Finished goods	$645,000
Work in process	112,500
Raw materials	240,000
Factory supplies	69,000

The following information relates to Ellen's inventory and operations.

1. The finished goods inventory consists of the items below.

	Cost	Market
Down tube shifter		
Standard model	$ 67,500	$ 66,400
Click adjustment model	94,500	86,600
Deluxe model	108,000	110,000
Total down tube shifters	$270,000	$263,000
Bar end shifter		
Standard model	$ 81,000	$ 90,050
Click adjustment model	99,000	97,550
Total bar end shifters	$180,000	$187,600
Head tube shifter		
Standard model	$ 78,000	$ 77,650
Click adjustment model	117,000	119,300
Total head tube shifters	$195,000	$196,950
Total finished goods	$645,000	$647,550

2. One-half of the head tube shifter finished goods inventory is held by catalogue outlets on consignment.

3. Three-quarters of the bar end shifter finished goods inventory has been pledged as collateral for a bank loan.

4. One-half of the raw materials balance represents derailleurs acquired at a contracted price 20% above the current market price. The market value of the rest of the raw materials is $127,400.

5. The total market value of the work-in-process inventory is $108,700.

6. Included in the cost of factory supplies are obsolete items with an historical cost of $4,200. The market value of the remaining factory supplies is $65,900.

7. Ellen's applies the lower of cost and market method to each of the three types of shifters in finished goods inventory. For each of the other three inventory accounts, Ellen's applies the lower of cost and market method to the total of each inventory account.

8. Consider all amounts presented above to be material in relation to Ellen's financial statements taken as a whole.

Instructions

(a) Prepare the inventory section of Ellen's balance sheet as of November 30, 1998, including any required note(s).

(b) Without prejudice to your answer to (a), assume that the market value of Ellen's inventories is less than cost. Explain how this decline would be presented in Ellen's income statement for the fiscal year ended November 30, 1998.

(CMA adapted)

CASES

C9-1 Sonic Corporation purchased a significant amount of raw materials inventory for a new product it is manufacturing. Sonic uses the lower of cost and market rule for these raw materials and applies it using the direct method. The replacement cost of the raw materials is above the net realizable value and both are below the original cost.

Sonic uses the average cost inventory method for these raw materials. In the last two years, each purchase has been at a lower price than the previous purchase, and the ending inventory quantity for each period has been higher than the beginning inventory quantity for that period.

Instructions

(a) 1. At which amount should Sonic's raw materials inventory be reported on the balance sheet? Why?

 2. In general, why is the lower of cost or market rule used to report inventory?

(b) What would have been the effect on ending inventory and cost of goods sold had Sonic used the LIFO inventory method instead of the average cost inventory method for the raw materials? Why?

(c) Part of the criteria for evaluating management's performance is the inventory turnover ratio (cost of goods sold divided by average inventory). The higher this ratio, the better management's performance (other things being equal). The company's auditor has suggested to its management that it may wish to switch from the direct method to the allowance method in applying the lower of cost and market rule. If this were done, the net carrying value of inventory (cost less any allowance) would be used to calculate the inventory turnover. As a member of management, would you agree with the suggestion? Explain.

You are in charge of the audit of Kile Inc. The following items were in Kile's inventory at November 30, 1998 (fiscal year end). **C9-2**

Product Number	075936	078310	079104	081111
Selling price per unit November 30, 1998	$15.00	$23.00	$28.00	$13.00
Standard cost per unit, as included in inventory at November 30, 1998	$ 8.00	$11.25	$14.26	$ 7.40

In discussion with Kile's marketing and sales personnel you were told that there will be a general 9% (rounded to the next highest five cents) increase in selling prices, effective December 1, 1998. This increase will affect all products except those having 081 as the first three digits of the product code. The 081 codes are assigned to new product introductions, and for product code 081111, the selling price will be $9.00 effective December 1, 1998.

In addition, you were told by the controller that Kile attempts to earn a 40% gross profit on selling price on all their products.

From the cost department you obtained the following standard costs, which will be used for fiscal 1999:

Product number	1999 Standard
075936	$ 8.25
078310	$10.75
079104	$14.71
081111	$ 7.51

Sales commissions and estimates of other costs of disposal approximate 25% of fiscal 1999 standard costs to manufacture. Assume that standard costs provide a reasonable approximation of the replacement cost of the product.

Instructions
(a) Determine the net realizable value of each item expected for fiscal 1999.
(b) Assuming the net realizable values for (a) are to be used to determine the lower of cost and market valuation for the November 30, 1998 inventory, and that there were 5,000 units of each item on hand, how and at what amount would the inventory be shown on the balance sheet using an item-by-item approach? A total inventory approach?
(c) When market is lower than cost, why should inventories be reported at market? Why are inventories reported at cost when market is greater than cost?

Edy Son Corporation, a retailer and wholesaler of national brand-name household lighting fixtures, purchases its inventories from various suppliers. **C9-3**

Instructions
(a) 1. What criteria should be used to determine which of Son's costs are inventoriable?
   2. Are Son's administrative costs inventoriable? Defend your answer.
(b) 1. Son uses the lower of cost and market rule for its wholesale inventories. What are the theoretical arguments for that rule?
   2. The replacement cost of the inventories is below the net realizable value less normal profit margin, which, in turn, is below the original cost. Net realizable value, however, is greater than cost. What amount should be used to value the inventories? Why?
(c) Son calculates the estimated cost of its ending inventories held for sale at retail using the conventional retail inventory method. How would Son treat the beginning inventories and net markdowns in calculating the cost ratio used to determine its ending inventories? Why? (AICPA adapted)

Easyclean Company, your client, manufactures paint. The company's president, Ms. Rodier, has decided to open a retail store to sell Easyclean paint as well as wallpaper and other supplies that would be purchased from suppliers. She has asked you for information about the conventional retail method of valuing inventories at the retail store. **C9-4**

Instructions

Prepare a report to the president explaining the conventional retail method. Your report should address these points:

(a) Description and accounting features of the method.

(b) The conditions that may distort the results under the method.

(c) A list of the advantages of using the retail method relative to using cost methods of inventory pricing.

(d) The accounting theory underlying the treatment of net markdowns and net markups under the method.

C9-5 You have just been hired as a new accountant for the firm of Check and Doublecheque. The manager of the office wants to test your formal education and provides you with the following factual situations that were encountered by the firm:

1. In December, 1998 one of the clients underwent a major management change and a new president was hired. After reviewing the various policies of the company, the president's opinion was that prior systems employed by the company did not allow for adequate testing of obsolescence (including discontinued products) and over-stocks in inventories. Accordingly, the president changed the mechanics of the procedures for reviewing obsolete and excess inventory and for determining the amount. These reviews resulted in a significant increase in the amount of inventory that was written off in 1998 relative to previous years. You are satisfied that these procedures are appropriate and provide reliable results. The amount charged against operations for excess and obsolete inventory for 1998 would be $500,000. Had the 1998 methods been employed in the previous two years, the additional expense for 1997 would have been $120,000 and for 1996, $115,000. The amounts for the obsolescence expensed in 1996 and 1997 were $200,000 and $180,000 respectively. Net income for 1998 before adjustment for the obsolescence charge was $600,000.

Instructions

How should these charges be reported in the 1998 financial statements, if at all?

2. Another client, Sunkist Foods, was upset because it was requested by Check and Doublecheque to write down its inventory on an item-by-item basis. The item-by-item computation resulted in a write-down of approximately $380,000 as follows.

Product	Product Lines	
	Frozen	Cans
Cut beans	—	$ 25,000
Peas	—	45,000
Mixed vegetables	$ 75,000	25,000
Spinach	183,000	8,000
Carrots	12,000	7,000
	$270,000	$110,000

The company stated that the products are sold on a line basis (frozen or canned) with customers taking all varieties, and only rarely are sales made on an individual product basis. Therefore, they argued, the application of the lower of cost and market rule to the product lines would result in an appropriate determination of income (loss). A pricing of the inventory on this basis would result in a $140,000 write-down as the reductions to market on the item-by-item basis as shown above would be partially offset in each product line by some products having a market in excess of cost.

Instructions

Why do you believe Check and Doublecheque argued for the item-by-item approach? Which method should be used, given the information in this case?

3. A client's major business activities are the purchase and resale of used heavy mining and construction equipment, including trucks, cranes, shovels, conveyors, crushers, etc. The company was organized in 1983. In its earlier years, it purchased individual items of heavy equipment and resold them to customers throughout Canada. In the late 1980s, the company began negotiating the "package" purchase of all the existing equipment at mine sites, concurrent with the closing down of several of the large iron mines in Ontario and exhausted coal mines in Saskatchewan. The mine operators preferred to liquidate their mine assets on that basis rather than hold auctions or leave the mine site open until all of the equipment could be liquidated. As there were numerous pieces of equipment in these package purchases, the client found it difficult to assign costs to each item individually. As a result, the company followed the policy of valuing these "package" purchases by the cost recovery

method. Under this method, the company recognized no income until the entire cost had been recovered through sales revenues. This produced the effect of deferring income to later periods and represented, for financial reporting purposes, a "conservative" valuation of inventories in what was essentially a new field for the company where its level of experience had not been demonstrated.

Instructions
Comment on the propriety of this approach.

USING YOUR JUDGEMENT

FINANCIAL REPORTING PROBLEM

Prab Robots, Inc., reported the following information regarding 1994–1995 inventory:

PRAB ROBOTS, INC.

	1995	1994
Current Assets		
Cash	$ 153,010	$ 538,489
Accounts receivable, net of allowance for doubtful accounts of $46,000 in 1995 and $160,000 in 1994	1,627,980	2,596,291
Inventories (Note 2)	1,340,494	1,734,873
Other current assets	123,388	90,592
Assets of discontinued operations	—	32,815
Total current assets	$3,244,872	$4,993,060

Notes to Consolidated Financial Statements
Note 1: (In Part): Nature of Business and Significant Accounting Policies
Inventories — Inventories are stated at the lower of cost and market. Cost is determined by the last-in, first-out (LIFO) method by the parent company and by the first-in, first-out (FIFO) method by its subsidiaries.

Note 2: Inventories
Inventories consist of the following:

	1995	1994
Raw materials	$1,264,646	$2,321,178
Work in process	240,988	171,222
Finished goods and display units	129,406	711,252
Total inventories	1,635,040	3,203,652
Less amount classified as long-term	294,546	1,468,779
Current portion	$1,340,494	$1,734,873

Inventories are stated at the lower of cost determined by the LIFO method and market for Prab Robots, Inc. Inventories for the two wholly-owned subsidiaries, Prab Command, Inc. (U.S.) and Prab Limited (U.K.) are stated on the FIFO method, which amounted to $566,000 at October 31, 1994. No inventory is stated on the FIFO method at October 31, 1995. Included in inventory stated at FIFO cost was $32,815 at October 31, 1994 of Prab Command inventory classified as an asset from discontinued operations. If the FIFO method had been used for the entire consolidated group, inventories after an adjustment to the lower of cost and market would have been approximately $2,000,000 and $3,800,000 at October 31, 1995 and 1994 respectively.

Inventory has been written down to estimated net realizable value, and results of operations for 1995, 1994, and 1993 include a corresponding charge of approximately $868,000, $960,000, and $273,000, respectively, which represent the excess of LIFO cost over market.

Inventory of $294,546 and $1,468,779 at October 31, 1995 and 1994, respectively, shown on the balance sheet as noncurrent assets represent that portion of the inventory that is not expected to be sold currently.

Reduction in inventory quantities during the years ended October 31, 1995, 1994, and 1993 resulted in liquidation of LIFO inventory quantities carried at a lower cost prevailing in prior years as compared with the cost of fiscal 1995 purchases. The effect of these reductions was to decrease the net loss by approximately $24,000, $157,000, and $90,000 at October 31, 1995, 1994, and 1993, respectively.

Instructions

(a) Why might Prab Robots, Inc. use two different methods for valuing inventory?

(b) Comment on why Prab Robots, Inc. might disclose how its LIFO inventories would be valued under FIFO.

(c) Why does the LIFO liquidation decrease the net loss?

(d) Comment on whether Prab Robots would report more or less income if it had been on a FIFO basis for all its inventory.

ETHICS CASE 1

The market value of Bailey Co. Ltd.'s inventory has declined significantly below its cost. Dawn Knott, the controller, wants to use the direct method to write down inventory without calling attention to the decline in market value. Her supervisor, financial vice-president Jim Span, prefers the allowance method because it more clearly discloses the decline in market value and it does not distort the cost of goods sold.

Instructions

(a) What, if any, is the ethical issue involved in making this decision?

(b) Is any stakeholder harmed if Knott's direct method is used?

(c) What should Dawn Knott do?

ETHICS CASE 2

Logalot had signed a long-term purchase contract to buy 20,000 board feet of timber from the British Columbia Forest Service at $250 per thousand board feet. Under the contract, Logalot must cut and pay $5,000,000 for this timber during the next year. Currently, the market value is $200 per thousand board feet. Pat Bapp, the controller, wants to recognize a $1,000,000 loss on the contract in the year-end financial statements, but the financial vice-president, Randy Otero, argues that the loss is temporary and it should be ignored. Bapp notes, however, that market value has remained near $200 for many months, and he sees no sign of significant change.

Instructions

(a) What are the ethical issues, if any?

(b) Is any particular stakeholder harmed by the financial vice-president's solution?

(c) What would you do if you were the controller?

chapter 10

INVESTMENTS: TEMPORARY AND LONG-TERM

CHAPTER
10

Investments: Temporary and Long-Term

Learning Objectives

After studying this chapter, you should be able to:

1. Describe the accounting for temporary investments in debt and equity securities.

2. Describe the basis of balance sheet valuation for temporary investments.

3. List the disclosure requirements for temporary investments.

4. Calculate the value of a bond.

5. Describe the accounting for long-term investments in bonds.

6. Apply the effective interest method of amortizing bond discount and premium.

7. Apply the straight-line method of amortizing bond discount and premium.

8. List the disclosure requirements for long-term investments in bonds.

9. Explain how to account for the acquisition of shares through stock dividends, stock splits, and stock rights.

10. Explain the effect of ownership interest on the accounting for long-term investments in shares.

11. Apply the cost and equity methods of accounting for long-term investments in shares.

12. Describe the basis of balance sheet valuation for portfolio investments and investments in significantly influenced companies.

13. Explain the basic process of consolidation.

14. List the disclosure requirements for long-term equity investments.

15. Explain the accounting for cash surrender value (Appendix 10A).

16. Identify examples of and explain the accounting for special purpose funds (Appendix 10A).

T o engage in the production and sale of goods or services, a business enterprise must invest funds in many types of assets: monetary assets—cash and receivables; productive tangible assets—inventories, plant and equipment, and land; and intangible assets—patents, licences, trademarks, and goodwill. Sound financial management requires not only that cash and other assets be available when needed in the business *but also that cash and near cash assets not immediately needed in the conduct of regular operations be invested advantageously in a variety of securities and other income-producing assets*. In many cases, *investments in other organizations' debt or equity securities produce considerable revenue in addition to that derived from regular operations*.

In addition to applying appropriate accounting methods to recognize investment income, accounting for investments involves classification (current or noncurrent), measurement (valuation), and disclosure (additional information) decisions. These issues are compounded by the complexity and diversity of the underlying **financial instruments**.[1] Innovative and complex securities[2] that are currently used for investment purposes must be accounted for by the issuing company according to their substance rather than legal form. The terms "debt" and "equity" are used here to denote the substance of a financial instrument that, for simplicity, will be the same as the form of the underlying security. This chapter is divided into three sections: (1) temporary investments; and (2) long-term investments in debt and equity securities; and (3) an appendix that explains other long-term investments.

Accounting for investments is a controversial topic, particularly in the United States where historic cost accounting based rules for investments have been blamed for hundreds of billions of dollars of losses in the savings and loan company industry. In the financial services industry particularly, financial reporting is moving closer to fair value measures for investments. In Canada, measurement and valuation of financial instruments continue to be studied by standard setters, but increased disclosure of fair value information[3] for all financial assets is now required with the release of Section 3860 of the *CICA Handbook* on financial instruments.

SECTION 1: TEMPORARY INVESTMENTS

Corporations may purchase investments for long-term strategic purposes or to generate a return on otherwise idle cash balances that will be needed for operating purposes in the shorter term. **Temporary investments**, classified as *current assets*, ordinarily consist of **short-term paper**[4] (certificates of deposit, treasury bills, and commercial paper), **debt securities** (government and corporate bonds), and **equity securities** (preferred and common shares) acquired with cash not immediately needed in operations. The investments are held temporarily in place of cash and are capable of prompt liquidation when current financing needs make such conversion desirable. To be classified as a temporary investment and be included in current assets, investments must meet two criteria.

1. They must be **marketable securities** (i.e., they must be readily marketable), and

2. Management must intend to convert them into cash as needed within one year or the operating cycle, whichever is longer.

Readily marketable means that the security can be sold quite easily at a minimal cost and without undue delay. If the shares are closely held (not publicly traded), there may be a limited, or no, market for the security, and its classification as a long-term investment may be more appropriate. Intent to convert is an extremely difficult principle to apply in practice. Generally, *intention to convert* is substantiated when the invested cash is considered a contingency fund to be used whenever a need arises or when investment is made from cash temporarily idle because of the seasonality of the business. In classifying investments, management's expressed intent should be supported by evidence, such as the history of investment activities, events subsequent to the balance sheet date, and the

---

[1] *CICA Handbook* (Toronto: CICA), Section 3860, par. .05, defines a financial instrument as "any contract that gives rise to both a financial asset of one party and a financial liability or equity instrument of another party."

[2] These are securities that are either debt or equity (or a combination) in legal form but, in substance, represent the opposite. Chapters 15 to 18 look at accounting for these financial instruments from the issuing company's perspective.

[3] Fair value is defined in *CICA Handbook*, Section 3860, par. .05, as "the amount of the consideration that would be agreed upon in an arm's length transaction between knowledgeable, willing parties who are under no compulsion to act."

[4] Accounting for short-term paper or money market instruments is similar to accounting for notes receivable as discussed in Chapter 7. Treasury bills, for example, are accounted for like noninterest-bearing notes.

nature and purpose of the investment. In contrast, long-term investments are purchased as part of a long-range program or plan, such as for long-term appreciation in the price of the security, ownership for control purposes, or maintaining or enhancing supplier or customer relationships.

Temporary investments include equity and debt securities. Most equity securities generate dividend income, debt securities earn interest, and both types give rise to gains or losses due to changes in their market values.

An **equity instrument** is "any contract that evidences a residual interest in the assets of an entity after deducting all of its liabilities."[5] Such securities include ownership shares (e.g., common and certain types of preferred) or the right to acquire (e.g., warrants, rights, and call options) or dispose of (e.g., put options) ownership shares in an enterprise at fixed or determinable prices, and normally does not have a maturity date nor a guaranteed return on the investment to the owner. A **debt instrument** is an obligation of the issuing company to pay fixed or determinable amounts of money, usually on a specific maturity date. Additionally, a debt instrument confers no voting rights, but bears interest that must be paid periodically, usually annually or semiannually. There are significant reporting issues faced by companies issuing financial instruments whose economic substance differs from their legal form (these are discussed in Parts 3 and 4 of the text); reporting by the investor according to economic substance is being considered by the Accounting Standards Board.

ACQUISITION AND DISPOSITION OF TEMPORARY INVESTMENTS

OBJECTIVE 1
Describe the accounting for temporary investments in debt and equity securities.

Regardless of the type of asset acquired, the cost principle governs the accounting for the transaction. This principle states that transactions and events should be recognized at the amount of cash or cash equivalents paid. In the absence of a cash transaction, transactions and events should be recognized at the fair value of the consideration given up or acquired, if clearer. The cost principle also provides guidance on what to include in "cost:" all reasonable and necessary costs to acquire the asset and to get it in place and ready for use. For investments in both equity and debt securities, cost includes *the purchase price and incidental direct acquisition costs, such as brokerage commissions, legal fees, and taxes*.

Share prices are usually stated in increments of 5 cents,[6] while bond prices are quoted as a percentage of the instrument's par or face value. The purchase price of a $5,000 Government of Canada bond selling at 97 $1/2$ is $5,000 × .975 or $4,875. Acquisition costs, such as brokerage commissions,[7] are added in determining the cost of the security.

Recording the acquisition of a debt security requires separation of the amount paid for the security and the amount paid for accrued interest. When bonds are bought between interest payment dates, the investor must pay the owner the market price of the bond plus the interest accrued since the last interest payment date. The investor will collect this interest on the next interest payment date, along with the additional interest earned by holding the bond until the interest date.

For example, Western Publishing Limited invested some of its excess cash in the bond market by purchasing $100,000 face value 10% bonds at a price of 86 on April 1,

---

[5] *CICA Handbook*, Section 3860, par. .05(d).

[6] Until April, 1996 prices were based on eighth-of-a-cent increments, a system going back to times when Spanish silver dollars were split into "pieces of eight."

[7] Brokerage commissions are incurred when buying **and** selling securities. Commissions vary with the value of the share and with the number of shares purchased, usually between 1% and 3% of the trade value on relatively small orders. On larger institutional orders, the brokerage firms are highly competitive, with some commissions in the order of pennies per share.

1998, with interest payable semiannually on July 1 and January 1. The brokerage commission associated with this purchase was $1,720. The cash outlay is as shown below.

EXHIBIT 10-1	
Purchase price of bonds ($100,000 × .86)	$86,000
Commission	1,720
Cost of bonds acquired	87,720
Accrued interest January 1 to April 1 ($100,000 × .10 × 3/12)	2,500
Cash payment (due to the vendor)	$90,220

The journal entries to record this transaction and the receipt of interest on July 1 are:

April 1, 1998

Temporary Investment in WP Ltd. Bonds	87,720	
Interest Revenue	2,500	
Cash		90,220

July 1, 1998

Cash	5,000	
Interest Revenue ($100,000 × .10 × 6/12)		5,000

Alternatively, Interest Receivable could have been debited for $2,500 on April 1, with credits on July 1 of $2,500 to Interest Receivable and $2,500 to Interest Revenue. In either case, interest revenue of $2,500 must be reported because this is the amount earned by the investor while the bond investment was held.

As discussed in Section 2 of this chapter, the difference between the cost of the bond and its maturity value is usually amortized over the period to maturity if acquired as a long-term investment. Generally, this difference is not recognized separately or amortized for temporary investments in bonds because they will not be held to maturity.

Temporary investments are sold when cash needs develop or when good investment management dictates a change in the securities held. The owner who sells the securities incurs costs such as brokerage commissions and receives only the net proceeds. The difference between the net proceeds from the sale of a security and its cost represents the **realized gain** or **realized loss**

For example, assume that Western Publishing Limited required cash for operating purposes on December 15, 1998 and sold, at a price of 89, the bonds it had purchased on April 1. Assume a commission of $1,500 is charged by the broker for this sale. The cash consequences of this transaction and the calculation of the realized gain or loss are shown below.

EXHIBIT 10-2	
Selling price of bond ($100,000 × .89)	$89,000
Less: Commission paid	1,500
Proceeds on sale of bond	87,500
Accrued interest collected from purchaser	
July 1 to December 15 ($100,000 × .10 × 5½/12)	4,583
Cash received from purchaser	$92,083
Book (carrying) value of bond	$87,720
Proceeds on sale of bond	87,500
Realized loss on sale of bond	$ 220

The journal entry to record the sale of the bonds on December 15, 1998 is as follows:

Cash	92,083	
Realized Loss on Sale of Temporary Investments	220	
Temporary Investment in WP Ltd. Bonds		87,720
Interest Revenue		4,583

REPORTING INCOME ON TEMPORARY INVESTMENTS

Interest income on temporary investments in debt securities is recognized on a time proportion basis, while dividend income on equity securities is recognized only when the investor's right to receive payment is established, that is, when dividends are declared by the investee company.[8]

In addition to investment income received as dividends and interest, realized gains and losses on the disposal of investments and unrealized losses and loss recoveries resulting from adjusting the reported value at the balance sheet date are also part of the return on the investment. All three components are reported in the Other Revenues and Gains (or Other Expenses and Losses) section of the income statement and therefore are included in income before extraordinary items.

BALANCE SHEET VALUATION

OBJECTIVE 2
Describe the basis of balance sheet valuation for temporary investments.

Consistent with the valuation of other current assets such as accounts receivable and inventory, temporary investments should not be reported on the balance sheet at more than the cash flows expected to be realized from their conversion to cash. This limitation, combined with the use of historical cost accounting, results in a valuation rule referred to as the **lower of cost and market (LCM)**.

The **market value** of a security, the amount obtainable from the sale, or payable on the acquisition, of a financial instrument in an active market,[9] changes over time due to changes in the economy, in the industry in which the company operates, and in company-specific conditions and prospects. A major issue for many years has been the extent to which the financial statements should reflect the changes in market value of securities that are held as temporary investments.

The CICA resolved this issue by requiring that *when the market value of temporary investments has declined below the carrying value, they should be carried at market value*.[10] Valuing securities at the lower of cost and market may be applied to the entire portfolio or to each security in the portfolio. When applied to the entire portfolio, the amount by which the aggregate cost exceeds aggregate market value (i.e., the net unrealized loss) should be accounted for as a **valuation allowance**, and the unrealized loss should be included in the determination of net income for the period. If, on the other hand, the lower of cost and market method is *applied to each security*, then the sum of individual security excesses of cost over market value is reported as the valuation allowance.

Valuation adjustments are recorded as part of the adjustment process whenever financial statements are prepared. At the end of each accounting period, the required balance in the valuation allowance account is determined and the account is adjusted to this balance. In subsequent periods, recoveries of market value may be recognized to the extent that the market valuation does not exceed the original cost. In substance, these procedures involve adjusting carrying values down to market at each reporting date, but up only to the extent that previous write-downs to market have been recovered.

---

[8] *CICA Handbook*, Section 3400, par. .09 (a) and (c).

[9] *CICA Handbook*, Section 3860, par. .05 (g).

[10] *CICA Handbook*, Section 3010, par. .06.

(handwritten, top right)

T I

10 000 @ 51.94 ea | 5000.

The following discussion illustrates the application of the lower of cost and market method to marketable securities portfolios classified as current assets.

Illustration: 1997. National Service Corporation made the following purchases of temporary investments during 1997, the first year in which National invested in marketable securities.

February 23, 1997: Purchased 10,000 shares of Northeast Industries, Inc. common at a market price of $51.50 per share plus brokerage commissions of $4,400 (total cost, $519,400; average cost per share, $519,400/10,000 = $51.94).

(handwritten)
TI   515000
Fees   4400
Cash   519400.

April 10, 1997: Purchased 10,000 shares of Bell Soup Co. common at a market price of $31.50 per share plus brokerage commissions of $2,500 (total cost, $317,500; average cost per share, $317,500/10,000 = $31.75).

August 3, 1997: Purchased 5,000 shares of Reggies Pulp Co. common at a market price of $28 per share plus brokerage commissions of $1,350 (total cost, $141,350; average cost per share, $141,350/5,000 = $28.27).

October 1, 1997: Purchased $100,000, 12% Cook Co. bonds at 92 plus brokerage commissions of $1,530 (total cost, $93,530) and three months' accrued interest. Interest is payable on January 1 and July 1.

(handwritten)
T.I 93530
IR 3000
Cash   96530.

Each of the equity purchases above is recorded at total acquisition cost (purchase price plus commissions) by a debit to Temporary Investments and a credit to Cash. The purchase of the bonds is recorded by debiting Temporary Investments $93,530 and Interest Revenue (or Accrued Interest Receivable) $3,000, and crediting Cash for $96,530. During the year National made the following security sale.

(handwritten)
Cash 287 220.

September 23, 1997: Sold 5,000 shares of Northeast Industries, Inc. common at a market price of $58 per share, paying brokerage commissions of $2,780 (proceeds, $287,220).

(handwritten)
5000 Shares 259 700
Realized Gain on Sale 27 520

The entry to record this sale is as follows:

Cash [(5,000 × $58) − $2,780]   287,220
    Temporary Investments (5,000 × $51.94)   259,700
    Realized Gain on Sale of Temporary Investments   27,520

In cases where there are numerous purchases of similar securities, the average cost flow assumption must be applied to match the proper cost with the proceeds of sale.

On December 31, 1997, National Service Corporation determined the cost and market value of its portfolio of temporary securities and the balance needed in the valuation allowance account as shown in Exhibit 10-3.

Applying the lower of cost and market method to National's portfolio of temporary investments results in a carrying value or valuation for balance sheet purposes of $775,500. The unrealized loss of $36,580 represents the excess of total cost over the total market value of National's portfolio. The unrealized loss of $36,580 is recorded at December 31, 1997 as follows.

Unrealized Loss on Valuation of Temporary Investments   36,580
    Allowance for Excess of Cost of Temporary
    Investments Over Market Value   36,580

To recognize a loss equal to the excess of cost over market value of temporary investments and to bring the allowance account to the appropriate balance.

The unrealized loss account appears on the income statement in the Other Expenses and Losses section. The allowance account is reported as a valuation (contra) account

EXHIBIT 10-3

| | December 31, 1997 | | | |
Temporary Investments	Face Value or # of Shares	Cost	Market Value	Unrealized Gain (Loss)
Northeast Industries, Inc.	5,000	$259,700	$275,000	$15,300
Cook Co. bonds	$100,000	93,530	92,500	(1,030)
Bell Soup Co.	10,000	317,500	304,000	(13,500)
Reggies Pulp Co.	5,000	141,350	104,000	(37,350)
Total portfolio		$812,080	$775,500	$(36,580)

Analysis for adjusting entry:	
Balance in investment account	$812,080
Lower of cost and market = market	775,500
Balance in allowance account should be	36,580 cr
Balance in allowance account before adjustment	–0–
Adjustment needed to allowance account	$ 36,580 cr

deducted from the balance in the Investment account of $812,080 on the balance sheet, producing a carrying amount for the portfolio of $775,500.

The Investment and allowance T accounts are as follows.

EXHIBIT 10-4

1997	Temporary Investments		Allowance for Excess of Cost of Temporary Investments Over Market Value		1997
Feb. 23	519,400			36,580	Dec. 31
Apr. 10	317,500				
Aug. 3	141,350				
Sept. 23		259,700			
Oct. 1	93,530				
Balance, Dec. 31	812,080				

Illustration: 1998. During 1998, National made the following sale and purchase of marketable securities:

March 22, 1998: Sold 5,000 shares of Reggies Pulp Co. common at a market price of $17.50 per share less brokerage commissions of $1,590 (proceeds, $85,910).

As in the 1997 security sale, the net proceeds from the sale is compared with the cost of the security to determine the amount of the realized gain or loss. *The valuation allowance does not affect the calculation of this amount.* The entry is recorded on March 22, 1998 as follows.

Cash	85,910	
Realized Loss on Sale of Temporary Investments	55,440	
Temporary Investments		141,350

To record the sale of 5,000 shares of Reggies Pulp Co. common held as a temporary investment.

July 2, 1998: Purchased 10,000 shares of James Bay Gas & Electric common at a market price of $20.25 per share plus brokerage commissions of $2,300 (total cost, $204,800).

On December 31, 1998, National Service Corporation determined the cost, the market value, and the amount of the adjustment to the valuation allowance for its portfolio of temporary investments to be as follows.

EXHIBIT 10-5

Temporary Investments	Face Value or # of Shares	Cost	December 31, 1998 Market Value	Unrealized Gain (Loss)
Northeast Industries, Inc.	5,000	$259,700	$312,500	$52,800
Cook Co. bonds	$100,000	93,530	93,000	(530)
Bell Soup Co.	10,000	317,500	327,500	10,000
Reggies Pulp Co.	—	—	—	—
James Bay Gas & Electric	10,000	204,800	202,500	(2,300)
Total portfolio		$875,530	$935,500	$59,970

Analysis for adjusting entry:

Balance in investment account	$875,530
Lower of cost and market = cost	875,530
Balance in allowance account should be	–0–
Balance in allowance account before adjustment	36,580 cr
Adjustment needed to allowance account	$ 36,580 dr

The presence or absence of realized gains or losses recorded since the last portfolio valuation as a result of sales of securities has no effect on the method of computing the lower of cost and market for the remaining portfolio at the end of the period.

Applying the lower of cost and market method to National's portfolio at December 31, 1998 indicates that a balance sheet valuation of $875,530 is appropriate. The adjustment of the valuation allowance at this date is recorded as follows:

Allowance for Excess of Cost of Temporary Investments Over Market Value	36,580	
Recovery of Unrealized Loss on Valuation of Temporary Investments		36,580

To adjust the valuation allowance to report temporary investments at LCM.

The Recovery of Unrealized Loss on Temporary Investments of $36,580 is reported in the Other Revenues and Gains section on the 1998 income statement.

Note that the ***recovery is recognized only to the extent that unrealized losses were previously recognized***. That is, the write-down of $36,580 in 1997 representing net unrealized losses may be reversed, but only to the extent that the resulting carrying value of the portfolio does not exceed original cost or, in other words, to the extent that a balance exists in the valuation allowance account at the date of write-up. Under this approach, the reversal of the write-down does not represent recognition of an unrealized gain. The unrealized gain is the excess of market value over cost, or the $59,970 difference between aggregate cost and aggregate market value of National's portfolio on December 31, 1998. The original write-down is viewed as establishing a valuation allowance representing the estimated reduction in the realizable value of the portfolio, and subsequent market increases are viewed as having reduced or eliminated the requirements for such an allowance. In other words, the reversal of the write-down represents a change in an accounting estimate of an unrealized loss.

If National's investment portfolio of short-term marketable securities had suffered an additional loss of market value during 1998 instead of the increase described above, an unrealized loss would have been charged to 1998 expense. It follows that the valuation allowance would have been increased (credited) by the amount of the additional write-down.

Also, **note that the valuation is applied to the total portfolio and not to individual securities.** If the lower of cost and market method is applied at the level of individual securities, a more conservative valuation usually results because increases in value above cost are not included and netted against decreases in value. The cost and market values of the temporary investments of National Services Corporation **at December 31, 1997** are used to illustrate this as follows.

EXHIBIT 10-6

	December 31, 1997		
	Cost	Market	LCM
Northeast Industries, Inc.	$259,700	$275,000	$259,700
Cook Co. bonds	93,530	92,500	92,500
Bell Soup Co.	317,500	304,000	304,000
Reggies Pulp Co.	141,350	104,000	104,000
	$812,080	$775,500	$760,200

LCM in this case is $760,200. Because this approach tends to produce an overly conservative balance sheet valuation, the authors prefer the total portfolio method.

Reclassification. If a marketable security is *transferred from the current to the noncurrent portfolio,* or vice versa, the security should be transferred at the lower of its cost and market value at the date of transfer. If market value is less than cost, the market value becomes the "cost" of the security in its new classification, and the loss is included as if a realized loss in the determination of net income.

For example, if National Service Corporation had reclassified the Bell Soup Co. securities from current to noncurrent on December 31, 1997, the *unrealized* loss of $13,500 ($317,500 − $304,000, page 474) would have been recorded as if it were a *realized* loss of $13,500 as part of the following reclassification entry:

Long-Term Investments	304,000	
Loss on Reclassification of Securities	13,500	
Temporary Investments		317,500

If this reclassification had taken place, the unrealized loss (as well as the allowance) at December 31, 1997 would have been $23,080 ($36,580 − $13,500) instead of $36,580.

If a temporary investment is not sold or reclassified, but there is a decline in its market value that is judged to be a permanent impairment, the individual security is written down directly and the impaired market value becomes the new cost basis.

VALUATION AT MARKET

The use of the lower of cost and market and discontinuance of original cost as the carrying amount of a current asset portfolio of marketable securities is quite firmly established in Canadian practice. Using original cost as the basis when the market value of the portfolio is lower has the effect of deferring unrealized losses on the basis of the expectation of a future recovery in market value, which may or may not occur, and reports the portfolio at an amount greater than the realizable value at the balance sheet date.

Some accountants argue, however, that temporary investments should be valued at market value whether higher or lower than cost. It is considered inconsistent to reduce the carrying value of the securities to an amount below cost without increasing the carrying value when market value is above cost. *Market value proponents argue that gains and losses develop when the value of the investments changes, not when the investments are sold.* Recognition of losses only is overly conservative and does not reflect the underlying economics when prices increase. Because of this, management, to some extent, can manipulate net income by determining when securities are sold to realize gains. For example, an enterprise whose earnings are low in one year might sell some securities that have appreciated in past years to offset the low income figure from current operations.

A major objection to valuation "at market" is that fluctuations in earnings result as the market prices of the securities change. To illustrate, at one time Leaseway Transportation estimated that using market values would have reduced earnings 28% in one year and increased earnings approximately 21% the next. Most companies dislike this type of fluctuation in earnings because they have little control over these changes that have adverse effects on company share prices.

While recognition of impairment but not improvement above cost in the carrying value of a securities portfolio is still the dominant method of accounting in Canada, the United States has adopted the position that temporary investments in marketable equity securities and most debt securities must be reported at fair value.[11] The Accounting Standards Board of the CICA also supported the use of fair values for such securities in now-withdrawn exposure drafts on *Financial Instruments.* This and other complex recognition and measurement issues related to financial instruments are still on the agenda of the ASB, but it appears that acceptance of market-based values for temporary investments is increasing.

FINANCIAL STATEMENT DISCLOSURE OF TEMPORARY INVESTMENTS

Cash, the most liquid asset, is listed first in the Current Asset section of the balance sheet. All unrestricted cash, whether on hand (including petty cash) or on deposit at a financial institution, is presented as a single item, "Cash," or is combined with highly liquid investments and presented as "Cash and Cash Equivalents."

OBJECTIVE 3
List the disclosure requirements for temporary investments.

Temporary investments in marketable securities usually rank next in liquidity and are listed in the Current Asset section of the balance sheet immediately after cash.[12] Securities that are held for other than liquidity and temporary investment purposes should not be classified as current assets, but rather as long-term investments.

GAAP requires that the basis of valuation of temporary investments be reported and that the quoted market value and the carrying value of marketable securities be disclosed. In addition, holdings of temporary securities issued by affiliated companies are required to be reported separately.

National Service Corporation's December 31, 1997 and December 31, 1998 partial balance sheets are shown on page 478 to illustrate the disclosure requirements for temporary investments based on the situations presented on pages 474 and 475.

---

[11] *FASB Statement 115* requires all investments in marketable equity securities to be reported at fair value whether held as trading, available-for-sale, or held-to-maturity investments. Investments in debt securities are also required to be reported at fair values unless they are classified as held-to-maturity. Recognition of gains and losses in income is dependent on the classification assigned.

[12] *Financial Reporting in Canada, 1995* (Toronto: CICA) reports that 124 of 300 survey companies in 1994 (125 in 1993) disclosed the existence of temporary investments; that the majority of these companies presented temporary investments by combining them with cash; and that **short-term investments** was the most common terminology used.

EXHIBIT 10-7

BALANCE SHEET

	December 31	
	1998	1997
Current assets:		
Temporary investments, carried at lower of cost and market (Note 2)	$875,530	$775,500

INCOME STATEMENT

	Year Ended December 31	
	1998	1997
Income from operations	$ XXX	$ XXX
Other revenues and gains:		
Realized gain on sale of temporary investments		27,520
Recovery of unrealized loss on valuation of temporary investments	36,580	
Other expenses and losses:		
Realized loss on sale of temporary investments	55,440	
Unrealized loss on valuation of temporary investments		36,580
Income before extraordinary items	$ XXXXX	$ XXXXX

Note 2—Temporary Investments. Short-term marketable securities are carried at the lower of cost and market at the balance sheet date, that determination being made on a total portfolio basis. These securities had a market value at December 31, 1998 of $935,500 and a cost at December 31, 1997 of $812,080.

SECTION 2: LONG-TERM INVESTMENTS IN DEBT AND EQUITY SECURITIES

This section is devoted primarily to **long-term investments** in corporate securities: bonds of various types, preferred shares, and common shares. Numerous other items, some of which are discussed in the Appendix to this chapter, are commonly classified as long-term investments: funds for bond retirement, share redemption, and other special purposes; investments in notes receivable, mortgages, and similar debt instruments; and miscellaneous items such as advances to affiliates, cash surrender value of life insurance policies, interests in estates and trusts, and real estate held for appreciation or future use. While some of these investments qualify as marketable securities, they are classified as long-term investments when management's intention is to hold them for longer run purposes. Long-term investments are usually presented on the balance sheet just below current assets in a separate section called Investments, Long-Term Investments, or Investments and Funds.

Although a corporation invests in the securities of another corporation for a variety of reasons, the ***primary motive is to enhance its own income***. A corporation may enhance its income (1) directly through the receipt of dividends or interest from the investment or through appreciation in the market value of the securities; or (2) indirectly by strategically creating and ensuring desirable operating relationships among companies to improve income performance. Frequently, the most permanent investments are those for improving income performance, with benefits accruing to the investors from the influence or control exercised over a major supplier, customer, or otherwise related company.

LONG-TERM INVESTMENTS IN BONDS

A bond arises from a contract known as an **indenture** and represents a promise by the issuing company to pay (1) a sum of money at a designated maturity date; and (2) periodic interest at a specified (fixed or variable) rate on the maturity amount or face value. Individual bonds are evidenced by a certificate that states the face value of the bond, the annual interest rate, and the dates on which interest is paid (usually annually or semiannually).

Stripped bonds or **zero-coupon bonds** are common investment options today. These bonds are created by detaching (or stripping) the entitlement to interest from the entitlement to the maturity value so that the stripped bond can be purchased as an investment on its own. For example, Nova Scotia Power, Inc. bonds maturing January 10, 2009 are sold by brokers as stripped bonds.

Bonds are issued with a variety of features (more fully described in Chapter 15) and these, along with the variability in interest rates, permit investors to shop for exactly the investment that satisfies their safety, yield, and marketability preferences.

VALUATION OF BONDS

A company can acquire an investment in a bond by purchasing it directly from the issuing company or from another entity that holds it as an investment. Its purchase price fluctuates with economic conditions, such as the supply and demand of buyers and sellers, the risk associated with the issuing company, market conditions, and the state of the economy, but is always *valued by the investment community as the present value of its future cash flows*. Because the cash flows promised by a bond are *future* cash flows, it is necessary to discount them to their present value.

OBJECTIVE 4
Calculate the value of a bond.

There are usually two types of cash flows: a lump sum to be received at maturity, and an annuity of interest payments until maturity. The **stated, nominal,** or **coupon interest rate**, set by the issuer, is expressed as a percentage of the **face value** (or **par value, principal amount,** or **maturity value**) of the bonds, and is assumed to be an annual rate. If the interest is paid semiannually, one-half of the interest is paid twice a year; if quarterly, one-fourth of the stated rate is paid four times a year. Thus, the cash to be received by the investor is set by the bond indenture and appears on the bond certificate.

Discounting cash flows to their present value requires information about the timing (*n*) of the cash flows and the **yield, effective,** or **market rate of return** (*i*) required to be earned on the investment. The discounted present value of the cash flows is the price at which the security is purchased and sold.

If the market rate of interest for bonds of similar risk is higher than the coupon or nominal rate promised by a bond, the bond will sell for an amount less than its face value, that is, it will sell at a **discount**. Because the cash flows from the bond are fixed, the purchase price of the security adjusts to yield the investor the market or yield rate of return.

If the market rate of interest is the same as the nominal rate, the bond will sell for its face value because the present value of the promised cash flows discounted at the market rate (which is also the nominal rate) equals the face value of the security.

When rates in the market are lower than those offered by a bond, buyers will bid up the price of the bond above its face value, and it will sell at a **premium**. Its price will be bid up to an amount equal to the present value of the cash flows discounted at the lower market rate of return. In all cases, the fixed cash flows will yield the investor the market rate of return when compared to the purchase price.

To illustrate the computation of the price of a bond, assume that on April 1, 1998 when the market rate of interest on similar securities is 11%, Lancaster Corporation purchases $100,000 face value of bonds due in five years. The bonds pay 9% interest annually each April 1. Two steps are involved: determine the amount and timing of the cash flows; then discount them at the market rate.

EXHIBIT 10-8

Present value of the principal:	
$a(p_{\overline{5}|11\%}) = \$100,000\ (.59345)^*$	$59,345
Present value of the interest:	
$R(P_{\overline{5}|11\%}) = \$9,000\ (3.69590)^{**}$	33,263
Present value (purchase price) of the bonds	**$92,608**

*Interest factor for present value of $1 amount received in five periods at 11%, as presented in Table A-2 in the Appendix at the end of the book.
**Interest factor for the present value of an ordinary annuity of $1 received for five periods at 11%, as presented in Table A-4 in the Appendix at the end of the book.

By paying $92,608 for the bond, Lancaster Corporation will earn an effective rate or yield of 11% per year over the five-year term of the bond.

If Lancaster Corporation had purchased this security as a stripped bond, it would be entitled only to the principal amount at maturity, indicating a purchase price for the bond of only $59,345. This price represents a deep discount from the maturity value; the difference between the $59,345 cost and the $100,000 received at maturity represents 11% annual interest on the investment.

Had the market rate been 8% on April 1, 1998, the present value of the principal and interest would be $103,992, as shown below. As expected, the bond price is bid up (to $103,992) because it pays interest at 9%, higher than the going market rate of 8%.

If the bond acquired by Lancaster paid interest quarterly (each January 1, April 1, July 1, and October 1) instead of annually (each April 1), its present value, as shown below, would be $104,088, assuming a market rate of 8%. In this case, interest of $2,250 ($100,000 × .09 × ¼) is received quarterly, which necessitates a change in the discount variables n and i. There are now 20 interest periods (n) and the corresponding market rate (i) per quarter is 2%.

EXHIBIT 10-9

9% interest—paid annually:	
Present value of the principal:	
$a(p_{\overline{5}|8\%}) = \$100,000\ (.68058)$	$ 68,058
Present value of the interest:	
$R(P_{\overline{5}|8\%}) = \$9,000\ (3.99271)$	35,934
Present value (purchase price) of the bonds	**$103,992**
9% interest—paid quarterly:	
Present value of the principal:	
$a(p_{\overline{20}|2\%}) = \$100,000\ (.67297)^*$	$ 67,297
Present value of the interest:	
$R(P_{\overline{20}|2\%}) = \$2,250\ (16.35143)^*$	36,791
Present value (purchase price) of the bonds	**$104,088**

*Note that n and i change for discounting both the principal cash receipt and the interest.

ACCOUNTING FOR BOND ACQUISITIONS

Whether bonds are acquired as temporary or long-term investments, they are recorded on the date of acquisition at cost, which includes any costs incidental to the purchase. *If purchased between interest payment dates,* the investor must pay the previous holder the market price of the bond *plus the interest accrued since the last interest payment date.* The investor collects this interest plus the interest earned by holding the bond on the next interest date. For example, assume the purchase on June 1 of bonds having a $100,000 face value and paying an annual rate of 12% interest on April 1 and October 1, at 97. The entry to record the purchase of the bonds and accrued interest is as follows.

OBJECTIVE 5
Describe the accounting for long-term investments in bonds.

Investment in Bonds ($100,000 × .97)	97,000	
Interest Revenue ($100,000 × .12 × 2/12)	2,000	
Cash		99,000

On October 1 the investor receives the semiannual interest of $6,000, representing a reimbursement of the $2,000 paid at the date of acquisition and $4,000 earned for holding the bond for four months.

Investments acquired at par, at a discount, or at a premium are recorded in the accounts at cost. While it is acceptable to record the investment at maturity value with a separate premium or discount account, general practice has been to charge the investment account with the purchase cost.

ACCOUNTING FOR INCOME FROM BOND INVESTMENTS

Subsequent to acquisition, the major accounting issue is recognition of the appropriate amount of investment income. For bonds purchased at par or face value, interest revenue is the interest received or receivable from the issuing company for the time the investment is held. However, when the cost of the investment differs from the dollars to be received at maturity, that is, when it is purchased at a discount or premium, the difference between its cost and maturity value has to be accounted for as well.

Bonds Purchased at a Discount. When a bond is purchased at a discount, a company will receive more at maturity than it paid at the time of purchase. To determine how this benefit should be recognized, accounting looks to the reason for the difference between these two amounts. Bonds sell at a discount only when the nominal or coupon rate promised by the bond indenture is less than the market rate of interest. The discount, therefore, compensates the purchaser for the lower interest to be received, increasing the return to the investor to the going market rate. The difference between cost and maturity value, therefore, should be recognized as additional interest revenue over the period to maturity. The amortization of the difference is recorded each interest period as follows.

Investment in Bonds	xxx	
Interest Revenue		xxx

To illustrate, assume that Robinson Company purchases $100,000 of 8% bonds on January 1, 1998, paying $92,278. The bonds mature January 1, 2003; interest is payable each July 1 and January 1. The purchase price of $92,278 and related discount of $7,722 ($100,000 minus $92,278) provide Robinson with an effective annual interest or yield rate of 10%. There are two widely used methods for amortizing the $7,722 difference: the effective interest method and the straight-line method.

Effective interest method. The **effective interest method** (also called the **present value or compound interest** or **effective yield method**) recognizes interest revenue equal to the yield rate of interest applied to the carrying value of the bond investment. The difference

OBJECTIVE 6
Apply the effective interest method of amortizing bond discount and premium.

between the interest revenue recognized and the cash interest received or receivable is the portion of the discount benefit realized, and this is added to the bond's carrying value. Over the period to maturity, the full amount of the discount is amortized and the bond, at maturity, has a carrying value equal to its face value.

For example, on July 1, 1998 Robinson Company receives semiannual interest of $4,000 ($100,000 × 8% × 6/12), recognizes interest revenue of $4,614 ($92,278 × 10% × 6/12), and accounts for the difference of $614 ($4,614 − $4,000) as amortization of the discount by increasing the carrying value of the investment. The entry is as follows.

Cash	4,000	
Investment in Bonds	614	
Interest Revenue		4,614

On December 31, 1998, Robinson Company's year end, an adjusting entry is made for the interest accrued since July 1. Interest receivable of $4,000 ($100,000 × 8% × 6/12) is recognized, as is interest revenue equal to the yield rate applied to the bond's carrying value. The carrying value of the investment is its original cost of $92,278 increased by the discount amortized on July 1 of $614, resulting in interest revenue of $4,645 [($92,278 + $614) × 10% × 6/12]. The $645 difference between the revenue recognized and the interest receivable is the amount of discount amortization for the second six-month period, which serves to further increase the carrying value of the bond investment. The year-end entry to accrue interest revenue and the January 1, 1999 entry to record the receipt of cash are as follows.

December 31, 1998

Interest Receivable	4,000	
Investment in Bonds	645	
Interest Revenue		4,645

January 1, 1999

Cash	4,000	
Interest Receivable		4,000

The schedule on page 483 shows the calculation of cash interest received and interest revenue reported each period. It also indicates the adjustment to the carrying value of the investment equal to the difference between these two amounts, representing amortization of the discount. Notice that the amount of interest revenue reported each period changes. As the book value increases, so does the amount of interest revenue reported, but *it is always a constant percentage* (the yield rate) *of the investment's carrying value. Also note that the carrying value of the investment at each interest payment date is the present value of the remaining cash flows discounted at the market rate of interest when the bond was acquired.*

If Robinson Company had acquired the bond between interest payment dates, for example on February 1, 1998 instead of on January 1, 1998, we would have to account not only for the purchase of one month's interest as explained above, but also for the fact that the discount should be amortized for a five-month period on July 1, 1998 instead of a six-month period. The price for the bond on February 1 will be different from the January 1 price even with an identical market rate due to the fact that the first cash flow to Robinson is in five months' time instead of in six months. Assuming the purchase price is $92,380,[13]

---

[13] The purchase price of the bond can be estimated as follows:

Present value of cash flows, Jan. 1	$92,278
Increase in PV Jan. 1 to Feb. 1, at yield rate $92,278 × .10 × 1/12	769
Less cash interest Jan. 1 to Feb. 1 $100,000 × .08 × 1/12	(667)
Purchase price, Feb. 1	$92,380

EXHIBIT 10-10

SCHEDULE OF INTEREST REVENUE AND BOND DISCOUNT
AMORTIZATION: EFFECTIVE INTEREST METHOD
8% BONDS PURCHASED TO YIELD 10%

Date	Debit Cash	Credit Interest Revenue	Debit Bond Investment	Carrying Value of Bonds
Jan. 1, 1998				$ 92,278
July 1, 1998	$ 4,000ᵃ	$ 4,614ᵇ	$ 614ᶜ	92,892ᵈ
Jan. 1, 1999	4,000	4,645	645	93,537
July 1, 1999	4,000	4,677	677	94,214
Jan. 1, 2000	4,000	4,711	711	94,925
July 1, 2000	4,000	4,746	746	95,671
Jan. 1, 2001	4,000	4,783	783	96,454
July 1, 2001	4,000	4,823	823	97,277
Jan. 1, 2002	4,000	4,864	864	98,141
July 1, 2002	4,000	4,907	907	99,048
Jan. 1, 2003	4,000	4,952	952	100,000
	$40,000	$47,722	$7,722	

ᵃ$4,000 = $100,000 \times .08 \times 6/12   ᶜ$614 = $4,614 - $4,000
ᵇ$4,614 = $92,278 \times .10 \times 6/12   ᵈ$92,892 = $92,278 + $614

the discount to be amortized for the February 1 to July 1 period is $512, the difference between the present value of the cash flows (purchase price) on February 1 of $92,380 and the present value of the cash flows on July 1 of $92,892 as indicated on the schedule above. There would be no change in the amortization of the discount in the remaining nine interest periods from that presented on the schedule.

Another complexity exists if Robinson Company's fiscal year does not coincide with the interest periods of the bonds. If Robinson's year end was October 31 instead of December 31, interest revenue and discount amortization have to be allocated to the four-month period ending October 31. The following series of entries would be required.

October 31, 1998

Interest Receivable (4,000 × 4/6)	2,667	
Investment in Bonds (645 × 4/6)	430	
Interest Revenue (4,645 × 4/6)		3,097

To accrue interest earned and amortize bond discount to October 31.

January 1, 1999

Cash	4,000	
Investment in Bonds (645 × 2/6)	215	
Interest Receivable (from October 31 entry)		2,667
Interest Revenue (4,645 × 2/6)		1,548

To record receipt of interest and recognize two month's interest revenue.

Straight-line method. The **straight-line method** results in a constant amount of discount being amortized and credited to interest revenue each period. The objective of this method is to allocate the benefit associated with the discount to each accounting period in equal amounts. Recognition of equal amounts of interest revenue each period is not conceptually correct because a constant amount of interest revenue relative to an increasing

OBJECTIVE 7
Apply the straight-line method of amortizing bond discount and premium.

carrying value implies a decreasing rate of return. The straight-line method is commonly used due to its simplicity, but its use is appropriate only where the resulting amounts reported are not materially different from those using the effective interest method.

To illustrate the use of the straight-line method for the original Robinson Company example above, the discount of $7,722 ($100,000 minus the purchase cost of $92,278) should be amortized in equal amounts over the 60-month period from the date of purchase to maturity. On July 1, 1998 Robinson Company receives the semiannual interest of $4,000, amortizes $772 ($7,722 × 6/60) of the discount, and increases the amount of interest revenue reported by this amount as follows.

Cash	4,000	
Investment in Bonds	772	
Interest Revenue		4,772

The December 31, 1998 interest accrual amortizes another six months of discount at the same straight-line rate.

Interest Receivable	4,000	
Investment in Bonds	772	
Interest Revenue ($4,000 + $772)		4,772

The amount of interest revenue recognized in each six-month period is constant at $4,772, as illustrated below. Note that both the effective interest and straight-line methods of amortization result in the same amount of discount being amortized and the same amount of interest revenue being recognized *over the life of the bond*; the difference relates solely to the pattern of recognition of the discount in income.

EXHIBIT 10-11

SCHEDULE OF INTEREST REVENUE AND BOND DISCOUNT
AMORTIZATION: STRAIGHT-LINE METHOD
8% BONDS PURCHASED TO YIELD 10%

Date	Debit Cash	Debit Bond Investment	Credit Interest Revenue	Carrying Value of Bonds
Jan. 1, 1998				$ 92,278
July 1, 1998	$ 4,000ᵃ	$ 772ᵇ	$ 4,772ᶜ	93,050ᵈ
Jan. 1, 1999	4,000	772	4,772	93,822
July 1, 1999	4,000	772	4,772	94,594
Jan. 1, 2000	4,000	772	4,772	95,366
July 1, 2000	4,000	772	4,772	96,138
Jan. 1, 2001	4,000	772	4,772	96,910
July 1, 2001	4,000	772	4,772	97,682
Jan. 1, 2002	4,000	772	4,772	98,454
July 1, 2002	4,000	772	4,772	99,226
Jan. 1, 2003	4,000	772*	4,772	100,000
	$40,000	$7,722	$47,722	

ᵃ$4,000 = $100,000 × .08 × 6/12
ᵇ$772 = ($100,000 − $92,278)/60 × 6 months
ᶜ$4,772 = $4,000 + $772
ᵈ$93,050 = $92,278 + $772
*due to rounding

When bonds are acquired between interest dates and the straight-line method of amortization is used, it is important to ensure that the discount is written off over the period *from the date of acquisition* to the maturity date. For example, if Robinson

Company purchased the bonds on May 31, 1998 instead of January 1, the amortization period is 55 instead of 60 months.

Bonds Purchased at a Premium. When a bond is purchased at a premium, the investor will receive less at maturity than was paid for the investment. To determine how this should be accounted for, accountants look to the reason for the "overpayment." A bond's price will be greater than face value only when the interest it pays (the nominal rate) is higher than the going market or yield rate of interest. The higher interest to be received by the purchaser comes at a cost equal to the premium. The difference between the cost of the bond and the maturity value, therefore, should be recognized as a reduction of interest revenue over the period to maturity. The amortization of the difference is recorded each interest period as follows.

Interest Revenue	xxx	
Investment in Bonds		xxx

To illustrate, assume Robinson Company acquires the $100,000 of 8% bonds described above on January 1, 1998 when the market rate of interest was only 6%. The present value of the cash flows discounted at 6% results in a purchase cost of $108,530, which is $8,530 above the bond's maturity value.

Effective interest method. Whether the bond is acquired at a discount or a premium, the calculations are similar. The interest received or receivable is based on the specifications in the bond indenture, and the interest revenue to be recognized is based on the market rate of return and the bond's carrying value. In the case of a bond purchased at a premium, the cash interest received is greater than the interest revenue recognized (this was the reason for the premium!) and the bond's carrying value is reduced by the difference between these amounts. In this way, the premium is amortized and by the time the bond matures, its carrying value has been reduced to the maturity value. The applicable five-year amortization schedule appears below.

EXHIBIT 10-12

SCHEDULE OF INTEREST REVENUE AND BOND PREMIUM AMORTIZATION
EFFECTIVE INTEREST METHOD
8% BONDS PURCHASED TO YIELD 6%

Date	Debit Cash	Credit Interest Revenue	Debit Bond Investment	Carrying Value of Bonds
Jan. 1, 1998				$108,530
July 1, 1998	$ 4,000[a]	$ 3,256[b]	$ 744[c]	107,786[d]
Jan. 1, 1999	4,000	3,234	766	107,020
July 1, 1999	4,000	3,211	789	106,231
Jan. 1, 2000	4,000	3,187	813	105,418
July 1, 2000	4,000	3,162	838	104,580
Jan. 1, 2001	4,000	3,137	863	103,717
July 1, 2001	4,000	3,112	888	102,829
Jan. 1, 2002	4,000	3,085	915	101,914
July 1, 2002	4,000	3,057	943	100,971
Jan. 1, 2003	4,000	3,029	971	100,000
	$40,000	$31,470	$8,530	

[a]$4,000 = $100,000 \times 0.08 \times 6/12$
[b]$3,256 = $108,530 \times 0.06 \times 6/12$
[c]$744 = $4,000 - $3,256$
[d]$107,786 = $108,530 - 744

Notice again that the interest revenue reported changes (decreases) in amount but that *it is equal to a constant percentage (the yield rate) of the book value of the invest-ment* in each interest period. In addition, the carrying value of the bond at each interest payment date is equal to the present value of the remaining cash flows discounted at the yield rate of interest when the bond was acquired.

Entries covering the July 1, 1998 to January 1, 1999 period are as follows.

July 1, 1998

Cash	4,000	
Interest Revenue		3,256
Investment in Bonds		744

December 31, 1998

Interest Receivable	4,000	
Interest Revenue		3,234
Investment in Bonds		766

January 1, 1999

Cash	4,000	
Interest Receivable		4,000

When bonds are acquired at a premium between interest payment dates or a company's fiscal period does not correspond with the interest periods, care must be taken to ensure the appropriate amount of premium is amortized and interest revenue is reported.

Straight-line method. The objective of this method is to allocate the premium in equal amounts to the accounting periods from the date the bond is acquired to maturity. The premium of $8,530 paid by Robinson Company is amortized over the 60 months between January 1, 1998 and January 1, 2003 at the rate of $853 ($8,530 × 6/60) for each six-month interest period with the following entries.

July 1, 1998 (and 1999, 2000, 2001, 2002)

Cash	4,000	
Interest Revenue		3,147
Investment in Bonds		853

December 31, 1998 (and 1999, 2000, 2001, 2002)

Interest Receivable	4,000	
Interest Revenue		3,147
Investment in Bonds		853

January 1, 1999 (and 2000, 2001, 2002, 2003)

Cash	4,000	
Interest Receivable		4,000

This method results in *a constant amount of interest revenue reported each period*, but the interest revenue relative to the bond's book value implies an increasing rate of return as the carrying value is reduced. The straight-line method is the more popular method because (1) it is simple to apply; (2) it avoids the computations necessary under the effective interest method; and (3) it produces results not significantly different from the effective interest earned, unless the maturity date is many years distant or the premium or discount is exceptionally large.

In the entries shown above, the premium and discount are amortized simultaneously with the interest received or accrued. They do not have to be combined into one entry, however, or entered at the same time. The entries for interest received or receivable may be made at the proper times with the premium or discount amortized at the end of each fiscal year or at any other acceptable time by adjusting Interest Revenue and Investment in Bonds. Using the figures from the example above where the premium is amortized on the straight-line basis, the recognition of accrued interest at December 31, 1999 and the amortization of premium for the year in separate entries are as follows.

Interest Receivable	4,000	
Interest Revenue		4,000
Interest Revenue	1,706	
Investment in Bonds		1,706

Separate entries are convenient when reversing entries are used because the entry for accrued interest is reversed but no reversing entry is needed for premium amortization.

ACCOUNTING FOR THE DISPOSITION OF LONG-TERM INVESTMENTS IN BONDS

The redemption of bonds held to maturity poses no new accounting problems. Because bonds purchased at a premium are written down to par through amortization of the premium and bonds purchased at a discount are written up to par through amortization of the discount, the balance in the Investment in Bonds account at maturity equals the cash received for the bond on redemption. The entry to record the redemption of the $100,000 bond purchased by Robinson Company in the examples above is as follows.

Cash	100,000	
Investment in Bonds		100,000

When bond investments are sold before the maturity date, entries must be made to amortize the bond discount or premium to the date of sale, to remove the book value of the bonds sold from the Investment account, and to recognize the gain or loss on disposal.

Assume that the bonds purchased at a premium of $8,530 illustrated in Exhibit 10-12 are sold on April 1, 2001 at 99 $\frac{1}{2}$. The premium has been amortized to January 1, 2001 and the carrying value of the bonds before further adjustment is $103,717. An entry is made to amortize the premium for the three months that have expired in 2001:

Interest Revenue	444	
Investment in Bonds ($888 × 3/6)		444

The updated carrying value of the bonds is now $103,273 ($103,717 − $444). This is compared with the proceeds on sale of $99,500 ($100,000 × .995) to determine the amount of gain or loss on disposal, in this case, a loss of $3,773 ($103,273 − $99,500). The entry to record the sale, including the receipt of the accrued interest since the last interest payment date that is collected from the buyer, is:

Cash [($100,000 × 995) + ($100,000 × .08 × 3/12)]	101,500	
Loss on Sale of Bond Investment ($103,273 − $99,500)	3,773	
Interest Revenue ($100,000 × .08 × 3/12)		2,000
Investment in Bonds		103,273

The credit to Interest Revenue represents accrued interest for three months, for which the purchaser pays cash. The debit to Cash represents the selling price of the bonds, $99,500, plus the accrued interest of $2,000, and the credit to the Investment account represents the book or carrying value of the bonds on the date of sale.

If the straight-line method of amortizing the premium is used, the amount of the loss on sale differs from the amount calculated above because the book value on the date of disposal is a different amount. The computation of the loss in this case is shown in Exhibit 10-13.

EXHIBIT 10-13

Selling price of bonds (exclusive of accrued interest)			$ 99,500
Deduct book value of bonds on April 1, 2001:			
Cost		$108,530	
Less premium amortized for the period from			
• January 1, 1998 to December 31, 2000			
($8,530/60) × 36 months	$5,118		
• January 1, 2001 to April 1, 2001			
($8,530/60) × 3 months	426	5,544	102,986
Loss on disposal			$ 3,486

BALANCE SHEET VALUATION AND DISCLOSURE REQUIREMENTS

OBJECTIVE 8
List the disclosure requirements for long-term investments in bonds.

The *CICA Handbook* specifies that long-term investments in fixed term securities should be measured at cost adjusted for accumulated amortization of any discount or premium. However, if there is a loss in value of such an investment that is determined to be other than a temporary decline, the investment should be written down to recognize the loss and this becomes the new cost basis for the security.[14]

Separate disclosure is required of the basis of valuation, any investments in and investment income from related companies, and the quoted market value and carrying value of any marketable securities included in the long-term investment portfolio.[15]

In addition to the basic requirements of the section on long-term investments, *Handbook* Section 3860 covering financial instruments requires significant disclosure with the objective of providing information to help readers understand the significance of financial assets to a company's financial position, performance, and cash flows. These requirements include disclosure of information about significant terms and conditions that may affect the amount, timing, and certainty of cash flows: the entity's exposure to interest rate risk (including effective interest rates) and credit risk, fair values,[16] and, for those financial assets carried in excess of fair value, the reasons and nature of the evidence providing the basis for not reducing the carrying values.[17]

LONG-TERM INVESTMENTS IN EQUITY SECURITIES

ACCOUNTING FOR THE ACQUISITION OF SHARES

The most common types of equity instruments are common and preferred shares and warrants or rights to acquire these shares. These securities may be acquired on the market from a firm's shareholders, from the issuing corporation, or from stockbrokers, and like other assets, are recorded at cost when acquired. When shares are purchased outright for cash, the full cost includes the purchase price of the security plus brokers' commissions and other fees incidental to the purchase. If shares are acquired on **margin**, the margin representing borrowings from the broker, the share purchase should be recorded at its full cost and a liability recognized for the unpaid balance. A **share subscription** or agreement to buy the shares of a corporation is recognized by a charge to an asset account for

---

[14] *CICA Handbook*, Section 3050, par. .20 and .21.

[15] *Ibid.*, par. .29, .30, .31, and .33.

[16] Fair values take into account the costs that would be incurred to exchange or settle the financial instrument.

[17] *CICA Handbook*, Section 3860, par. .52, .57, .67, .78 and .89.

the security to be received and a credit to a liability account for the amount to be paid. Any interest on an obligation arising from a share purchase is recognized as an expense.

Shares acquired in **nonmonetary transactions** (for property or services) are recorded at the fair value of the asset or service given up or the fair value of the shares received, if the latter is more clearly determinable. This may require the use of appraisals or estimates to arrive at an appropriate cost.

The purchase of two or more classes of securities for a *lump sum price* requires allocation of the total cost to the different classes in an equitable manner. The apportionment is often based on *relative market values* when these are known. If the market value of only one security is known, the market price may be assigned to the one and the cost excess to the other. In some cases it may be necessary to defer cost apportionment until evidence of at least one value becomes known, such as when one security is sold.

Accounting for numerous purchases of securities requires that information on the cost of individual purchases be preserved, as well as the dates of purchases and sales. This information is needed to determine average carrying value and the gain or loss on disposal when securities are sold.[18] Companies with numerous transactions involving different investments use a control account for investments and maintain a subsidiary ledger for the individual securities.

Shares Received as a Stock Dividend or Stock Split. If the investee corporation distributes a dividend of its own shares of the same class of stock instead of in cash, or issues additional shares of stock as a result of a **stock split,** each shareholder owns a larger number of shares but retains the same proportionate interest in the firm as before. The issuing corporation has distributed no assets; it has merely transferred a specified amount of retained earnings to share capital in the case of a **stock dividend,** or changed the number of authorized and issued shares by the same multiple as the split in the case of a stock split.

Shares received as a result of a stock dividend or stock split, therefore, do not constitute revenue to the recipients. *The recipient of such additional shares would make no formal entry,* but should make a memorandum entry and record a notation in the Investment account to show that additional shares have been received.

Although no dollar amount is entered at the time of the receipt of these shares, the fact that additional shares have been received must be considered in computing the average carrying amount of all shares held and of any shares sold subsequently. The book value of the original shares purchased constitutes the total carrying amount of both those shares and the additional shares received, because no price was paid for the additional shares. The carrying amount per share is computed by dividing the carrying value of the original shares purchased by the total number of shares now held.

To illustrate, assume that 100 common shares of Flemal Limited are purchased for $9,600, and that two years later Flemal issues to shareholders one additional share for every two shares held; 150 shares with a total cost of $9,600 are then held. If 60 shares are sold for $4,300, the carrying amount of the 60 shares would be computed as shown below.

EXHIBIT 10-14

Carrying value of 100 shares originally purchased	$9,600
Cost of 50 shares received as stock dividend	—0—
Carrying amount of 150 shares held	$9,600

Carrying amount per share is $9,600/150, or $64
Carrying amount of 60 shares sold is 60 × $64, or $3,840

[18] *CICA Handbook*, Section 3050, par. .27.

The entry to record the sale is:

Cash	4,300	
Investment in Flemal Ltd. Shares		3,840
Gain on Sale of Investments		460

The 90 shares retained are carried in the Investment account at $9,600 − $3,840, or $5,760. Thus the carrying amount for the remaining shares is also $64 per share, or a total of $5,760 for the 90 shares.

Stock Rights. When a corporation is about to offer for sale additional shares of an issue already outstanding, it may forward to existing holders of that issue certificates permitting them to purchase additional shares in proportion to their present holdings. The rights to purchase additional shares are called **stock rights** and generally are issued on the basis of one right per share owned. It may take one or many rights to purchase one new share.

The certificate representing the stock rights, called a **warrant,** states the number of shares that the holder of the right may purchase and also the price at which they may be purchased. If this price is less than the current market value of such shares, the rights have an intrinsic value, and from the time they are issued until they expire, they may be purchased and sold like any other security.

Stock rights have three important dates: (1) the date the rights offering is announced; (2) the date as of which the warrants are issued; and (3) the date the rights expire. From the date the offering is announced until the rights are issued, the share of stock and the right are not separable, and the share is described as **rights-on;** after the warrant is received and up to the time the rights expire, the shares (now **ex-rights**) and rights develop separate market values and are traded separately.

As with stock dividends and stock splits, the issue of rights does not involve the distribution of the issuing corporation's assets. The book value of the original shares held is now the carrying amount of those shares plus the rights and should be allocated between the two, usually on the basis of their total relative market values at the time the rights are received. If the value allocated to the rights is maintained in a separate account, an entry would be made debiting Investment in Stock Rights and crediting the Investment account representing the original shares.

Disposition of Rights. The investor who receives rights to purchase additional shares has three alternatives:

1. Exercise all or some of the rights by purchasing additional shares.
2. Sell the rights.
3. Permit them to expire without selling or using them.

If the investor exercises the rights, the carrying amount of the original shares that was allocated to the rights becomes a part of the carrying amount of the new shares purchased. If the investor sells the rights, the difference between the allocated carrying amount and the net proceeds on disposal is the gain or loss on sale. Finally, if the investor permits the rights to expire, a loss is recorded as the costs allocated to the rights are written off. Exhibit 10-15 illustrates the problem involved.

The reduction in the carrying amount of the shares from $5,000 to $4,761.90 and the acquisition of the rights with an allocated cost of $238.10 is recorded as follows.

Investment in Stock Rights	238.10	
Investment in Shares		238.10

EXHIBIT 10-15

Shares owned before issuance of rights—100.
Carrying value of shares owned—$50 per share for a total of $5,000.
Rights received—one right for every share owned, or 100 rights; two
 rights are required to purchase one new share at $50.
Market values at date rights issued: Shares—$60 per share
                                     Rights—$3 per right

Total market value of shares (100 × $60)	$6,000
Total market value of rights (100 × $3)	300
Combined market value	$6,300

Cost allocated to shares: $\dfrac{\$6,000}{\$6,300} \times \$5,000 = \$4,761.90$

Cost allocated to rights: $\dfrac{\$\ 300}{\$6,300} \times \$5,000 = \underline{\quad 238.10\quad}$

  $\overline{\$5,000.00}$

Cost allocated to each share: $\dfrac{\$4,761.90}{100} = \$47.619$

Cost allocated to each right: $\dfrac{\$238.10}{100} = \$2.381$

If some of the original shares are later sold, their cost for purposes of determining gain or loss on sale is $47.619 per share, as computed above. If 10 of the original shares are sold at $58 per share, the entry to record the sale is:

Cash ($58 × 10)	580.00	
Investment in Shares ($47.619 × 10)		476.19
Gain on Sale of Investments		103.81

Entries for Stock Rights. Rights may be sold, used to purchase additional shares, or permitted to expire. If 40 rights to purchase 20 shares are sold at $3 each, the entry is:

Cash ($3 × 40)	120.00	
Investment in Stock Rights ($2.381 × 40)		95.24
Gain on Sale of Investments		24.76

If 40 rights to purchase 20 shares are exercised and the shares are purchased at the offer price of $50, the entry is:

Investment in Shares ($1,000 + $95.24)	1,095.24	
Cash ($50 × 20)		1,000.00
Investment in Stock Rights ($2.381 × 40)		95.24

If any shares are sold in the future, their cost is $48.918 each—the average cost of all of the shares owned immediately before the sale, as computed in the T account in Exhibit 10-16.

If the remaining 20 rights are permitted to expire, the amount allocated to these rights should be removed from the general ledger account by this entry:

Loss on Expiration of Stock Rights	47.62	
Investment in Stock Rights		47.62

Information relating to these investment accounts is shown in Exhibit 10-16.

EXHIBIT 10-16

Investment in Shares			Number of Shares	Average Cost per Share
Purchase of 100 shares @ $50 per share	5,000.00		100	$50.000
Cost allocated to 100 rights received		238.10	—	
	4,761.90		100	47.619
Sale of 10 shares		476.19	(10)	47.619
	4,285.71		90	47.619
Purchase of 20 shares by exercise of 40 rights	1,095.24		(20)	54.762
Balance	5,380.95		110	48.918

Investment in Stock Rights			Number of Rights	Average Cost per Right
Cost allocated to 100 rights received	238.10		100	$2.381
Sale of 40 rights		95.24	(40)	2.381
	142.86		60	2.381
Exercise of 40 rights		95.24	(40)	2.381
	47.62		20	2.381
Expiration of 20 rights		47.62	(20)	2.381
Balance	0		0	

ACCOUNTING FOR EQUITY INVESTMENTS AFTER ACQUISITION

While the cost principle provides primary guidance in accounting for the acquisition of investments, the revenue principle underlies most of the accounting subsequent to this point. The return on an investment in another company's common shares is *earned* as the investee company generates income and the corresponding increase in net assets that accrues to its shareholders. Application of the revenue principle indicates that there are circumstances where it is appropriate for the investor to recognize the revenue as it is earned, and other situations where it is inappropriate to recognize the revenue until it has been *realized*, or converted into cash or a claim to cash.

OBJECTIVE 10
Explain the effect of ownership interest on the accounting for long-term investments in shares.

Effect of Ownership Interest. Accounting for investments in shares of other corporations subsequent to acquisition is dependent upon the relationship between the *investor* and the *investee*. The *CICA Handbook* identifies three relationships based on the degree of influence that the investor is able to exercise over the strategic operating, investing, financing, and dividend policies of the investee: (1) no significant influence; (2) significant influence; and (3) control.

The degree of influence held by the investor is evidenced by many factors, such as economic dependency and commonality of human resources. However, as strategic policies are determined by the board of directors who are elected by those who hold voting shares, it is the ownership of voting shares that is the most important criterion in assessing the degree of influence or control.

The complexities of determining the extent of influence is simplified in the following discussion by the assumption that the proportion of voting shares held is the only relevant factor. Thus, the three following categories of shareholdings exist.

1. **Less Than 20% ownership.** The presumption is that the investor is unable to significantly influence the strategic policies of the investee. This is a *portfolio* investment.

2. **Between 20% and 50% Ownership.** The presumption is that the investor can significantly influence the strategic policies of the investee. This is termed a *significantly influenced* investment.[19]

3. **Ownership Interest Exceeds 50%.** The presumption is that the investor can control virtually all the strategic policies of the investee. This is a *parent–subsidiary* relationship.

Once the relationship between the investor and investee is identified, the appropriate method of accounting and reporting for the investment can be determined. As stated above, the investor *earns* a return on its investment in another company's common shares as the investee corporation generates income and additional net assets that accrue to its shareholders. ***The major accounting issue is determining when the income earned by the investee should be recognized as income by the investor.*** The revenue principle states that revenue should be recognized as it is earned, subject to the resolution of uncertainties related to measurement and collectibility.

To illustrate, assume that Maxi Company purchased 48,000 shares equal to a 20% interest in Mini Company on January 2, 1998 at a cost of $10 each. Mini reported net income of $200,000 for its year ended December 31, 1998; declared and paid a cash dividend of $100,000 on January 28, 1999; and reported a net loss of $50,000 for its 1999 fiscal year.

Lack of Significant Influence: The Cost Method. If Maxi's 20% ownership does not allow its management to significantly influence the strategic policies of Mini Company, the investment in Mini is deemed to be a **portfolio investment**. Maxi should recognize revenue on its investment when the revenue principle criteria are met: its share of Mini's reported income for 1998 is *earned* during 1998; the amount earned can be *measured* as it is reported by Mini; however, the *collectibility* or conversion of the amount earned into cash is uncertain at December 31, 1998 as Maxi does not have sufficient influence over Mini's board of directors to influence their dividend policies. Therefore, Maxi should not recognize the revenue on its investment as it is earned, but should postpone recognition until it is received or receivable in cash, that is, when Mini declares a dividend. The entries to record these events are included in Exhibit 10-17.

To summarize, investment income is recognized by the investor as dividends are paid or payable by the investee. The investment is initially recorded at cost and, unless there is a permanent decline in its value as explained on page 498, the account remains at cost.[20] This is the **cost method**, the recommended method of accounting for investments where significant influence does not exist or where significant influence or control exists, but the earnings are not likely to accrue to the investor. Very simply, it is the cash basis of accounting for investment income, an appropriate basis when collectibility or conversion to cash is uncertain.

> **OBJECTIVE 11**
> Apply the cost and equity methods of accounting for long-term investments in shares.

---

[19] To provide guidance for investors when 50% or less of the voting interest is held, *Handbook* Section 3050, par. .04, adopts the following operational definition of *significant influence*:

> The ability to exercise significant influence may be indicated by, for example, representation on the board of directors, participation in policy making processes, material intercompany transactions, interchange of managerial personnel, or provision of technical information. If the investor holds less than 20% of the voting interest in the investee, it should be presumed that the investor does not have the ability to exercise significant influence, unless such influence is clearly demonstrated. On the other hand, the holding of 20% or more of the voting interest in the investee does not in itself confirm the ability to exercise significant influence. A substantial or majority ownership by another investor would not necessarily preclude an investor from exercising significant influence.

[20] The amount recorded as cost also could be reduced by a **liquidating dividend**, where the dividends received by the investor exceed its share of the investee's earnings since acquisition. In this case, the excess should be accounted for as a return **of** capital, as a reduction of the investment carrying amount. For example, if Queco, Inc. purchases an investment in Ontco Ltd. for $60,000 on December 31, 1998, and Ontco earns no income in 1999 but pays a dividend of $3,000 to Queco, Queco's entry is:

Cash	3,000	
Investment in Ontco Shares		3,000

Significant Influence: The Equity Method. If Maxi Company's 20% ownership interest is sufficient to allow its management to significantly influence Mini's strategic policies, the investment in Mini Company is classified as a **significantly influenced investment**. In this case, all revenue recognition criteria are met by Maxi in the same accounting period that Mini generates income (or incurs losses). By December 31, 1998, Maxi has *earned* investment income, the amount is *measurable*, and *collectibility* is not a concern as Maxi's management can influence Mini's decision to pay out dividends.

As the recognition criteria are satisfactorily resolved *when the investee reports its earnings,* there is no justification for Maxi to postpone recognition of investment income until cash is received. The investment income is recognized in Maxi's income as it is earned, with a corresponding increase in the carrying value of the Investment in Mini account. When a dividend is declared and received from Mini, this represents the conversion of part of the asset Investment in Mini into cash. This is the **equity method**, recommended for investments in shares of significantly influenced companies. It recognizes investment income as the income is earned and reported by the investee, and reports any dividends as conversion of the nonmonetary investment account into cash. Recognizing revenue as it is earned is the basis of accrual accounting, therefore the equity method can be thought of as applying accrual accounting to investments. Entries under the equity method are illustrated below.

EXHIBIT 10-17

Portfolio Investment— Cost Method			Significantly Influenced Investment— Equity Method		

On January 2, 1998, Maxi Company acquired 48,000 shares (20%) of Mini Company common shares at a cost of $10 each.

Investment in			Investment in		
Mini Company	480,000		Mini Company	480,000	
Cash		480,000	Cash		480,000

For the year 1998, Mini Company reported net income of $200,000; Maxi Company's share is 20% or $40,000.

No entry			Investment in		
			Mini Company	40,000	
			Investment Revenue*		40,000

On January 28, 1999, Mini Company announced and paid a cash dividend of $100,000; Maxi Company received 20%, or $20,000.

Cash	20,000		Cash	20,000	
Investment Revenue		20,000	Investment in		
			Mini Company		20,000

For the year 1999, Mini reported a net loss of $50,000; Maxi Company's share is 20% or $10,000.

No entry			Loss on investment*	10,000	
			Investment in		
			Mini Company		10,000

* If the investee's net income includes extraordinary items (or discontinued operations), the investor recognizes its proportionate share of the extraordinary items as an extraordinary item if material, on its own income statement, rather than including it as ordinary investment revenue before extraordinary items.

Three aspects of the results of applying the equity method should be noted. First, the investor's income statement is a good indicator of its management's performance. If

Maxi's management has made wise decisions and influenced Mini's policies so that profits are generated, as is the case in 1998, this has a positive impact on Maxi's income statement as well—investment income of $40,000. If the influence results in losses, Maxi's share of the loss is reported in its own income, as is the case in 1999—an investment loss of $10,000. *Under the cost method, the message can be reversed.* As indicated above, under the cost method no income is reported by Maxi in the profitable year, while $40,000 of income is reported in the loss year!

Another feature of the equity method is that, after acquisition, the Investment (asset) account tracks the investor's share of changes in the net assets or book value of the investee. When Mini's net assets increase by $200,000 in 1998 as a result of earning income, Maxi debits the Investment in Mini account for $40,000, its share of the increase. When Mini's net assets are reduced by $100,000 when it pays out the dividend, Maxi credits the Investment in Mini account by $20,000, its share of the decrease. When Mini's net assets are reduced by $50,000 as a result of incurring a loss in 1999, Maxi credits the Investment in Mini account by $10,000, its share of the decrease.

Not only does the equity method portray the economics of the situation more effectively, it also reduces the ability of management to manipulate the amount of income reported. For example, assume the investee reports a loss, but the investor exerts influence to force a dividend payment from the investee company. If dividends are the basis for recognizing income, as they are under the cost method, the investor would report investment income even though the investee experienced a loss. This could not happen under the equity method.

The difference between applying the cost and equity methods can be significant. For example, in 1990 and 1991, Empire Company Limited's income (loss) would have been ($2.3) million and $4.0 million respectively if they had used the cost method instead of the reported incomes of $8.6 and $14.4 million using the equity method.

Expanded illustration of the equity method. Application of the equity method involves further complexities that reflect the substance of the relationship between the investor and investee and that require an understanding of what the cost of the investment represents. As well as eliminating the effects of unrealized intercompany gains and losses, a topic reserved for advanced accounting, *the investor must adjust the investment account and the reported investment income each period to amortize the amount paid for the investment in excess of its share of the investee's book value.*

To illustrate, assume that on January 1, 1998, Investor Company purchased 250,000 shares of Investee Company's 1,000,000 outstanding common shares for $8,500,000. The book value of Investee Company's net assets on this date was $30,000,000 and Investor's proportionate share was 25% of this or $7,500,000. Investor Company therefore paid $1,000,000 in excess of its share of the book value. It was determined that $600,000 of this excess was attributable to its share of *undervalued depreciable assets* on the books of Investee Company while $400,000 was unexplained and therefore determined to be *unrecorded* goodwill. Investor Company estimated the average remaining life of the undervalued assets to be eight years and decided on a 10-year amortization period for goodwill.[21]

For the year 1998, Investee Company reported net income of $2,800,000, which included an extraordinary loss of $400,000 and paid dividends at June 30, 1998 of $600,000 and at December 31, 1998 of $800,000. The following is an analysis and the entries that would be recorded on the books of Investor Company to account for its long-term investment using the equity method.

---

[21] At the time of writing, the maximum period of time allowed over which goodwill can be amortized is 40 years. There is substantial support for reducing this to a maximum of half this time.

EXHIBIT 10-18

ANALYSIS OF PURCHASE COST

Cost of 25% investment in Investee Company	$8,500,000
Analysis:	
Paid for 25% of Investee's book value $30,000,000 × .25	$7,500,000
Paid for 25% of the unrecorded excess of fair value of	
depreciable assets over book value (given)	600,000
Paid for goodwill—unexplained excess	400,000
Balance in Investment in Investee Company	$8,500,000

January 1, 1998

Investment in Investee Company Shares	8,500,000	
Cash		8,500,000

To record the acquisition of 250,000 common shares of
Investee Company, a 25% interest.

June 30, 1998

Cash	150,000	
Investment in Investee Company Shares		150,000

To record dividend received ($600,000 × .25)
from Investee Company and share of decrease in Investee's net assets.

The entries on December 31, however, are more complex. In addition to the dividend, Investor Company must recognize its share of Investee Company's net income. Because Investee Company's income includes both an ordinary and extraordinary component, these components must be reported separately by Investor Company. Furthermore, Investor Company paid more than book value for Investee Company's net assets and this excess relates to assets that must be amortized. As a result, the investment income must be adjusted for these additional costs.

December 31, 1998

Cash ($800,000 × .25)	200,000	
Investment in Investee Company Shares		200,000

To record dividend received and share of reduction in
Investee's net assets.

Investment in Investee Company Shares ($2,800,000 × .25)	700,000	
Investment Loss (extraordinary) ($400,000 × .25)	100,000	
Investment Revenue (ordinary) ($3,200,000 × .25)		800,000

To record share of Investee Company's ordinary income and
extraordinary loss and share of increase in Investee's net assets.

Investment Revenue (ordinary)	115,000	
Investment in Investee Company Shares		115,000

To record 1998 amortization of investment cost in excess of
book value represented by:

Undervalued depreciable assets: $600,000 × 1/8 =	$ 75,000
Unrecorded goodwill: $400,000 × 1/10 =	$ 40,000
Total	$115,000

The investment in Investee Company is presented in the December 31, 1998 balance sheet of Investor Company at a carrying value of $8,735,000, which is computed as follows.

In the following illustration, the investment cost exceeded the underlying book value. In some cases, an investor may acquire an investment at a *cost less than the underlying book value*. In such cases, specific assets are assumed to be overvalued and, if

EXHIBIT 10-19

	Investment in Investee Co. Shares	
Acquisition cost, Jan.1, 1998	8,500,000	
Share of June, 1998 dividend		150,000
Share of 1998 reported net income	700,000	
Share of Dec., 1998 dividend		200,000
Amortization of purchase cost in excess of book value		115,000
Balance, December 31, 1998	8,735,000	

Reconciliation of December 31, 1998 Balance:

Book value of Investee:		
January 1, 1998	$30,000,000	
Increase due to income earned, 1998	2,800,000	
Decrease due to dividends paid, 1998	(1,400,000)	
December 31, 1998	$31,400,000	
Investor Company's share—25% of $31,400,000		$7,850,000
Unamortized excess cost for		
depreciable assets: 600,000 × 7/8		525,000
Unamortized goodwill: 400,000 × 9/10		360,000
Balance of Investment in Investee Co. Shares		$8,735,000

depreciable, the excess of the investee's book value over the investor's acquisition cost is amortized, increasing investment revenue reported over the remaining lives of the assets. Investment revenue is increased under the presumption that the investee's net income as reported is actually understated because the investee is charging depreciation on overstated asset values.

Investee Losses Exceed Carrying Amount. If an investor's share of the investee's losses exceeds the carrying amount of the investment, the question arises as to whether the investor should recognize additional losses, throwing the Investment account into a credit balance. Ordinarily, the investor would discontinue applying the equity method and not recognize additional losses.

However, if the investor's potential loss is not limited to the amount of its original investment (by guarantee of the investee's obligations or other commitment to provide further financial support), or if imminent return to profitable operations by the investee appears to be assured, it is appropriate for the investor to recognize additional losses.

Change in Method From and To the Equity Method. If the investor's level of influence falls below that necessary for continued use of the equity method, a change must be made to the cost method. In this case, the carrying value of the investment under the equity method when the change in circumstances occurs becomes "cost" for purposes of applying the cost method.

Alternatively, an investment in common shares of an investee that has been accounted for by the cost method will require a shift to the equity method if there is an increase in the level of ownership to one of significant influence. In this case, the cost of the investment is deemed to be the cost of all purchases to date and it is this acquisition cost that is used as the basis for determining amounts paid in excess of the investor's share of book value.

DISPOSAL OF PORTFOLIO AND SIGNIFICANTLY INFLUENCED INVESTMENTS

When an investment is sold, its book value is removed from the accounts and the difference between its carrying value and the proceeds of disposal is recognized in income as a realized gain or loss. If the shares sold are an investment in a company subject to significant influence accounted for under the equity method, the Investment account on the balance sheet and the Investment Revenue account on the income statement must be brought up to date as of the date of sale. The carrying value of the investment must be adjusted for the investor's share of the investee's earnings and increase in book value since the last reporting date *before* the gain or loss on disposal can be determined.

The gain or loss on disposal is reported after income from operations and, unless evidence to the contrary, is included in income before extraordinary items.

BALANCE SHEET VALUATION OF PORTFOLIO AND SIGNIFICANTLY INFLUENCED INVESTMENTS

OBJECTIVE 12
Describe the basis of balance sheet valuation for portfolio investments and investments in significantly influenced companies.

Temporary investments are expected to be converted into cash in the short term and therefore are valued on the balance sheet at the lower of cost and market. *Long-term investments*, on the other hand, are expected to be held rather than sold, thus the LCM method is not an appropriate valuation method for them. The presumption with long-term investments, as with capital assets, is that the company will be able to recover the costs reported as carrying values through operations and/or through disposition. Where this is not the case, that is, where there has been a permanent impairment in value, there is justification to record a loss and reduction in carrying value.

Determining whether a reduction in value of a long-term investment below carrying value is temporary or permanent requires the exercise of professional judgement. A bankruptcy or other significant liquidity crisis experienced by an investee is an example of a situation that suggests a loss in value to the investor might be permanent. Once a write-down is recognized, the new cost basis is not changed for subsequent recoveries in market value.[22] It is interesting to note that neither write-downs to reflect impairment in value nor write-downs to the lower of cost and market for temporary investments are allowed as deductible losses for tax purposes. Only realized losses are permitted.

Using Market Values. Although the Canadian profession has not yet sanctioned the market value method of accounting for long-term investments,[23] U.S. standards now require the reporting of noncurrent available-for-sale equity and debt securities at fair value: the investment account is adjusted for changes in the market value of the investments, but unlike the full market value method, the unrealized gains and losses are accumulated as a separate component of shareholders' equity instead of being recognized in income.

Reporting of investments in common shares at market value is considered by some to best meet the objective of reporting relevant information including the economic consequences of holding the investment. Shareholders are better able to evaluate managerial decisions regarding investments, creditors are better able to evaluate the solvency of the enterprise, and management is better able to evaluate the results of holding securities as well as the results of selling them.

In applying market value accounting, the investor company generally recognizes both dividends and interest received and changes in the market prices of the shares and bonds held as part of income or loss in the current period. The notion that net income is the change in net assets for the period underlies this position.

Opponents of market value accounting contend that market value information is too subjective for large holdings of restricted securities or securities that are not actively traded. There is a reluctance to value marketable debt securities at market prices because

---

[22] *CICA Handbook*, Section 3050, par. .21.

[23] Specialized industries such as mutual funds, pension funds, life insurance companies, and others whose balance sheets contain a significant proportion of investments use a market-based valuation for their investments.

they have a defined value if held to maturity. Finally, fluctuations in earnings result as market prices of investments change. Most companies dislike undue fluctuations in earnings because they have little control over them.

Although the market value method provides the best presentation of investments in some situations, the disclosure of fair values is all that is required at the present time for long-term investments.

CONTROLLING INTEREST: CONSOLIDATION

When one corporation acquires a voting interest of more than 50% in another corporation, the presumption is that the investor corporation can **control** the strategic policies of the investee by virtue of being able to elect a majority of its board of directors. Where this is the case, the investor is referred to as the **parent** and the investee corporation as the **subsidiary**.

The investment in the common shares of the subsidiary is recorded at cost and is subsequently accounted for by either the cost or equity method on the books of the parent investor. Which method the parent uses is not of concern: Whenever the parent issues financial statements prepared according to generally accepted accounting principles, the accounts of the subsidiary must be consolidated with those of the parent rather than being reported as a one-line Investment in Subsidiary Company account. **Consolidation** is a process that looks through the legal form to the economic substance of the situation, reporting the parent and subsidiary as one economic entity. Because consolidation is a complex topic discussed extensively in advanced accounting, only the basics and some terminology are introduced here.

Assume that Parentco purchases from existing shareholders 75% of the common shares of Subco on January 1, 1998 for $750,000, an amount equal to Parentco's share of the underlying book value of Subco's net assets ($1,000,000 × .75) as shown below.

OBJECTIVE 13
Explain the basic process of consolidation.

EXHIBIT 10-20	SUBCO		

BALANCE SHEET

January 1, 1998

Assets	$1,600,000	Liabilities	$ 600,000
		Shareholders' Equity	1,000,000
			$1,600,000

Parentco records the Investment in Subco on its books, and Subco continues to exist as a separate legal entity. Because Parentco management can control the strategic operating, investing, financing, and dividend policies of Subco, all the assets and liabilities of Parentco and Subco are under the common control of the Parentco shareholders, making the two legal entities in substance one **economic entity**. Parentco management is responsible for the results of all the strategic policies, and GAAP requires that all assets, liabilities, revenues, and expenses under common control be combined and reported on a line-by-line basis.

The process of consolidation does not change any amounts recorded on either company's books. It is a method of *reporting* an investment rather than a method of *accounting for* an investment, and involves replacing the one-line Investment in Subsidiary account on the parent's balance sheet with the detailed accounts it represents.[24]

---

[24] It is a perfect substitution if the investment has been accounted for by the equity method. For this reason, the equity method has been termed "one-line consolidation."

Assuming that Parentco had other assets of $2,500,000 and total liabilities of $1,250,000, compare Parentco's summary unconsolidated balance sheet at January 1, 1998 with the Parentco summary consolidated balance sheet at the same date in the illustration below.

EXHIBIT 10-21   PARENTCO

UNCONSOLIDATED BALANCE SHEET

January 1, 1998

Assets		Equities	
Investment in Subco (a)	$ 750,000	Liabilities (detailed)	$1,250,000
Other assets (detailed)	2,500,000	Shareholders' equity	2,000,000
Total assets	$3,250,000	Total equities	$3,250,000

CONSOLIDATED BALANCE SHEET

January 1, 1998

Assets		Equities	
Parentco and Subco assets (detailed) (b)	$4,100,000	Parentco and Subco liabilities (detailed) (c)	$1,850,000
		Noncontrolling interest in net assets of Subco (d)	250,000
		Shareholders' equity	2,000,000
Total assets	$4,100,000	Total equities	$4,100,000

(a) Represents 75% of Subco's net assets or 75% of ($1,600,000 − $600,000)
(b) Parentco's individual assets ($2,500,000) plus 100% of Subco's assets ($1,600,000)
(c) Parentco's individual liabilities ($1,250,000) plus 100% of Subco's liabilities ($600,000)
(d) The *minority*, or *noncontrolling interest* in Subco's net assets or 25% of ($1,600,000 − $600,000)

The consolidated balance sheet combines Parentco's assets and liabilities with 100% of Subco's individual assets and liabilities. However, as Parentco owns only 75% of Subco's net assets, an offset is needed that represents the portion of Subco's net assets not owned by Parentco. This is the **minority** or **noncontrolling interest,** which is reported outside of shareholders' equity on the consolidated statement.

After acquisition, consolidation requires a similar elimination of the one-line Investment Revenue account representing 75% of Subco's earnings (assuming the equity method is used), and substitution with 100% of Subco's individual revenues and expenses. As on the balance sheet, a deduction is needed on the income statement for the noncontrolling shareholders' 25% interest in the subsidiary's income that does not accrue to Parentco.

As with the equity method, any excess of cost over the investor's share of book value at acquisition has to be dealt with. This and further discussion of the consolidation process as a method of reporting long-term investments in subsidiary companies is reserved for the advanced course in accounting.

The following schedule compares the various methods of accounting for and reporting long-term investments in shares in terms of their basic effects on the financial statements, assuming no permanent impairment in value.

EXHIBIT 10-22

SUMMARY OF THE BASIC EFFECTS OF METHODS OF ACCOUNTING AND REPORTING FOR LONG-TERM INVESTMENTS IN SHARES

Method	Investment on Balance Sheet	Investment Revenue on Income Statement	Cash Flow Statement
Account for using cost	At acquisition cost	Equals dividends received (receivable)	Cash flow is equal to dividends received.
Account for using equity	At equity: represents share of investee book value plus unamortized excess of cost over book value	Equals share of investee earnings reported adjusted for amortization of excess of cost over book value	Investment revenue is a noncash item. Cash flow is equal to dividends received.
Report by consolidating	100% of investee's individual assets and liabilities reported on a line-by-line basis with those of parent, offset by noncontrolling shareholders' interest in investee net assets	100% of investee's individual revenues and expenses reported on a line-by-line basis with those of parent offset by noncontrolling shareholders' interest in investee net income	Reports cash flows of investor and investee combined.

DISCLOSURE REQUIREMENTS FOR LONG-TERM EQUITY INVESTMENTS

Section 3050 of the *CICA Handbook* requires that the basis of valuation for long-term equity investments be disclosed, and that investments in significantly influenced and other affiliated companies and other long-term investments and the income from each group be shown separately, including a separate reporting of the amount of income reported using the equity method. When the equity method is used, the difference between the cost of the investment at the date of acquisition and the amount of underlying equity in the net assets of the investee and the subsequent accounting treatment of this difference must be disclosed.

 The significance of an equity method investment to the investor's financial position and operating results influences the extent of additional disclosure. Companies may report the name of each investee and the investor's proportionate interest in each as well as summarized information concerning assets, liabilities, and results of operations of the investee, either individually or in groups, as appropriate.

 Handbook Section 3860 on financial instruments expands the disclosure requirements for portfolio investments[25] to reporting conditions that may affect the amount, timing, and certainty of future cash flows associated with the investments, and information, by class of financial asset, about the entity's exposure to interest rate and credit risk. Fair values should be disclosed for each class of financial asset, and for any with a carrying value above fair value, the carrying amount and fair value should be disclosed along with the reasons why management considers the carrying amount to be recoverable.

OBJECTIVE 14
List the disclosure requirements for long-term equity investments.

---

[25] *CICA Handbook* Section 3860 does not apply to interests in entities subject to significant influence or to subsidiaries.

Illustration of Reporting of Investments. The following excerpts from the consolidated financial statements of Alcan Aluminium Limited for the year ended December 31, 1995 illustrate disclosures related to their investments.

EXHIBIT 10-23   ALCAN ALUMINIUM LIMITED

FINANCIAL STATEMENTS

Year Ended December 31, 1995
(in Millions of U.S.$)

	1995	1994	1993
Balance Sheet			
Investments (notes 3 and 8)	695	1,193	1,053

Income Statement

	1995	1994	1993
Income (Loss) before other items	542	128	(93)
Equity loss (note 8)	(3)	(29)	(12)
Minority interests	4	(3)	1
Net income (Loss) before extraordinary item	$ 543	$ 96	$ (104)

Statement of Cash Flows

Year ended December 31	1995	1994	1993
Operating Activities			
Net income (Loss) before extraordinary item	$ 543	$ 96	$(104)
Adjustments to determine cash from operating activities:			
Depreciation	447	431	443
Deferred income taxes	174	36	(54)
Equity income — net of dividends	12	51	31

Note 8—Investments

	1995	1994	1993
Companies accounted for under the equity method	$ 679	$ 1,185	$ 1,043
Other investments — at cost, less amounts written off	16	8	10
	$ 695	$ 1,193	$ 1,053

The activities of the major equity-accounted companies are diversified aluminum operations in Japan and India. Their combined results of operations and financial position are included in the summary below.

	1995	1994	1993
Results of operations for the year ended December 31			
Revenues	$ 7,896	$ 8,073	$ 7,637
Costs and expenses	7,816	7,892	7,399
Income before income taxes	80	181	238
Income taxes	84	218	217
Net income (Loss)	$ (4)	$ (37)	$ 21
Alcan's share of net income (loss)	$ (3)	$ (29)	$ (12)
Dividends received by Alcan	$ 9	$ 22	$ 19

EXHIBIT 10-23	ALCAN ALUMINIUM LIMITED (Continued)			

Financial position at December 31

Current assets	$ 3,842	$ 4,029	$ 3,945
Current liabilities	3,438	3,699	3,389
Working capital	404	330	556
Property, plant and equipment — net	2,347	4,209	4,067
Other assets (liabilities) — net	153	261	(140)
	2,904	4,800	4,483
Debt not maturing within one year	1,351	1,713	1,719
Net assets	$ 1,553	$ 3,087	$ 2,764
Alcan's equity in net assets	$ 679	$ 1,185	$ 1,043

On December 31, 1995, the quoted market value of the Company's investments in Nippon Light Metal Company, Ltd. (NLM), Toyo Aluminium K.K. (Toyal) and Indian Aluminium Company, Limited (Indal) was $1,740 compared to their book value of $673.

Summary of Learning Objectives

1. **Describe the accounting for temporary investments in debt and equity securities.** Temporary investments are recorded at cost at acquisition, with interest revenue recognized as earned over time and dividend revenue recognized when declared by the investee. On disposal, the carrying value in the investment account is reduced based on average cost, and a realized gain or loss is recorded equal to the difference between the carrying value and the proceeds on disposal.

2. **Describe the basis of balance sheet valuation for temporary investments.** Because assets cannot be valued at more than cost and current assets cannot be valued at more than the amount of cash to be realized from their conversion, temporary investments are reported on the balance sheet at the lower of cost and market value. The adjustment to LCM is accomplished through a separate valuation allowance account (a contra account) that is adjusted each time financial statements are prepared.

3. **List the disclosure requirements for temporary investments.** GAAP requires disclosure of the basis of valuation, the quoted market value, the carrying value, and separate disclosure of temporary securities issued by affiliated companies.

4. **Calculate the value of a bond.** The price of a bond is equal to the present value of the lump sum maturity amount plus the present value of the annuity of interest payments, all discounted at the market rate of interest for bonds of similar risk.

5. **Describe the accounting for long-term investments in bonds.** Investments in bonds are recorded at cost at acquisition. The difference between cost and

KEY TERMS

compound interest method, 481

consolidation, 499

control, 499

cost, 470

cost method, 493

coupon interest rate, 479

debt instrument, 470

debt securities, 469

discount, 479

economic entity, 499

effective interest method, 481

effective rate of return, 479

effective yield method, 479

equity instrument, 470

equity method, 494

equity securities, 469

ex-rights, 490

face value, 479

financial instruments, 468

maturity value is amortized over the period to maturity by either the effective interest or straight-line method of amortization. Interest revenue is recognized as a function of time, adjusted for amortization of discount or premium. In the absence of a permanent decline in value, bonds are reported at their amortized cost. Upon disposal, the carrying value of the bond is removed from the accounts and any difference between the proceeds and book value is recognized as a gain or loss on disposal.

6. **Apply the effective interest method of amortizing bond discount and premium.** This method amortizes the discount or premium each interest period by an amount equal to the difference between interest revenue reported and cash interest received or receivable. Interest revenue is calculated as the book value of the bond times the market rate of interest when the bond was acquired. This results in a constant *rate* of interest revenue reported each period.

7. **Apply the straight-line method of amortizing bond discount and premium.** Using this method, the discount or premium is amortized on a straight-line basis from the date of purchase to the maturity date. Interest revenue reported is the total of interest received (or receivable) plus the discount amortized, or the difference between interest received (or receivable) and the premium amortized. This results in a constant *amount* of interest revenue reported each period.

8. **List the disclosure requirements for long-term investments in bonds.** Disclosure is required of the basis of valuation, the market and book values of any bonds that are marketable securities, information about the extent of bond investments in related companies, and a variety of information, where relevant, to help readers assess the impact on the amount, timing, and certainty of future cash flows associated with the financial asset.

9. **Explain how to account for the acquisition of shares through stock dividends, stock splits, and stock rights.** Investments in equity securities are recorded at their acquisition cost. Shares acquired through a stock dividend or stock split have no additional cost, therefore, the cost of the original shares is spread over the larger number, reducing the average cost per share. When stock rights are received on shares already held, the cost of the original shares is allocated between the shares and the rights on the basis of relative values, thus reducing the average cost per share. The rights are treated as a separate investment that can be sold, redeemed for shares, or lapse. If sold, a gain or loss on disposal results; if redeemed for shares, the carrying value of the rights becomes part of the cost of the new shares acquired; if the rights lapse, the carrying value of the rights is written off and a loss is recognized.

10. **Explain the effect of ownership interest on the accounting for long-term investments in shares.** The extent of influence exercised by the investor over the strategic decisions of the investee dictates the accounting for equity investments after acquisition. If there is no significant influence, the cost method is used where income from the investment is not recognized until received or receivable in cash. Where there is significant influence, income from the investment is recognized as it is earned by the investee. Where the investor is able to control the policies of the investee, the investment must be reported by consolidating the accounts of both companies. The presumption, in the absence of evidence to the contrary, is that there is no significant influence for up to a 20% ownership interest, that there is significant influence where a 20% to 50% interest is held, and that control exists where more than 50% of the votes to elect the board of directors is held.

11. **Apply the cost and equity methods of accounting for long-term investments in shares.** The cost method is the cash basis of accounting: Investment income is recognized when received or receivable in cash. The investment account remains at cost unless there is a permanent decline in value. The equity method is the accrual basis of accounting applied to investments. The investor accrues its share of the income reported by the investee as it is earned by the investee, and increases the carrying value of the investment account. When the investor receives a dividend from the investee, the investment account is reduced and cash is increased. When the investor pays more (or less) than its share of the investee's book value to acquire the investment, the difference between the investor's cost and its share of the underlying book value must be amortized against the investment income reported.

12. **Describe the basis of balance sheet valuation for portfolio investments and investments in significantly influenced companies.** Portfolio investments are reported at cost. Investments in significantly influenced companies are reported at equity: acquisition cost increased by the investor's share of incomes reported by the investee since acquisition, reduced by dividends received from the investee, and adjusted for the amortization of the excess of cost over the investor's share of the investee's book value at acquisition. In both cases, a decline in value that is considered permanent requires the investment account to be reduced to its lower fair value, and this becomes the new cost basis for the investment.

13. **Explain the basic process of consolidation.** Consolidation is a method of reporting an investment that replaces the one-line investment account with 100% of the assets and liabilities that underlie the investment, offset by a minority interest account representing the ownership interest in the investee company of its noncontrolling shareholders. The assets and liabilities of the parent and subsidiary company are combined on a line-by-line basis.

14. **List the disclosure requirements for long-term equity investments.** Disclosure is required of the basis of valuation, and of the investments in significantly influenced companies, other affiliated companies, and other long-term investments as well as the income from each group, and the income reported under the equity method. The difference between the cost of the investment and the investor's share of the underlying book value at acquisition and the subsequent accounting treatment of this difference should be reported. As with all financial instruments covered by *Handbook* Section 3860, disclosure is required of any conditions that may affect the amount, timing, and certainty of future cash flows associated with the investment, including fair value information.

APPENDIX 10A

Cash Surrender Value and Funds

CASH SURRENDER VALUE OF LIFE INSURANCE

There are many different kinds of insurance. The kinds usually carried by businesses include (a) casualty insurance; (b) liability insurance; and (c) life insurance. Certain types of **life insurance** constitute an investment, whereas casualty insurance and liability insurance do not. The three common types of life insurance policies that companies often carry on the lives of their principal officers are (a) ordinary life; (b) limited payment; and (c) term insurance. During the period that ordinary life and limited payment policies are in force, there is a **cash surrender value** (that is, a savings component) and a loan value. Term insurance ordinarily has no cash surrender value or loan value.

If the insured officers or their heirs are the beneficiaries of the policy, the premiums paid by the company represent expense to the company and, for income tax purposes, may represent income to the officer insured. In this case, the cash surrender value of the policy does not represent an asset of the company as the benefits in the form of cash do not accrue to it.

OBJECTIVE 15
Explain the accounting for cash surrender value.

If the company is the beneficiary and has the right to cancel the policy at its own option, the cash surrender value of the policy is an asset of the company. Because the cash surrender value increases each year, part of the premium paid is not expense. Only the difference between the premium paid and the increase in cash surrender value represents expense to the company.

For example, if Zima Corporation pays an insurance premium of $2,300 on a $100,000 policy covering its president and, as a result, the cash surrender value of the policy increases from $15,000 to $16,400 during the period, the entry to record the premium payment is:

Life Insurance Expense	900	
Cash Surrender Value of Life Insurance	1,400	
Cash		2,300

If the insured officer died halfway through the most recent period of coverage for which the $2,300 premium payment was made, the following entries would be made, assuming a refund of a pro rata share of the premium paid and cash surrender value of $15,700 at the date of death:

Cash ($2,300 × 1/2)	1,150	
Cash Surrender Value of Life Insurance ($16,400 − $15,700)		700
Life Insurance Expense ($900 × 1/2)		450
Cash	100,000	
Cash Surrender Value of Life Insurance		15,700
Gain on Life Insurance Coverage ($100,000 − $15,700)		84,300

The gain on life insurance coverage is not generally reported as an extraordinary item because it is considered to be a "normal" business transaction.

The cash surrender value of such life insurance policies should be reported on the balance sheet as a long-term investment, inasmuch as it is unlikely that the policies will be surrendered and cancelled in the immediate future. The premium is not deductible for tax purposes, however, and the proceeds of such policies are not taxable as income.

To illustrate disclosure in this area, Alico, Inc. reported information related to its cash surrender value as follows.

EXHIBIT 10A-1   ALICO, INC.

Other investments (note 4)
    Cash surrender value of life insurance   448,000

Note 4. The company purchased, as owner and beneficiary, individual life insurance policies on the lives of such officers and employees as a means of funding substantially all of such additional benefits. The company's accounting policy with respect to such insurance coverage is to charge operations with the annual premium cost, net of increase in cash surrender value.

FUNDS

Assets may be set aside in special funds for specific purposes and, therefore, become unavailable for ordinary operations of the business. In this way, the assets segregated in the special funds are available when needed for the intended purposes.

OBJECTIVE 16
Explain the accounting for special purpose funds.

There are two general types of **funds**: (1) those in which cash is set aside to meet specific current obligations; and (2) those that are not directly related to current operations and therefore are in the nature of long-term investments.

Several funds of the first type, discussed in preceding chapters, include the following.

Fund	Purpose
Petty Cash	Payment of small cash expenditures
Payroll Cash Account	Payment of salaries and wages
Dividend Cash Account	Payment of dividends
Interest Fund	Payment of interest on long-term debt

In general, these funds are used to handle more conveniently and more expeditiously the payments of certain current obligations, to maintain better control over such expenditures, and to divide adequately the responsibility for cash disbursements. These funds are ordinarily shown as current assets (as part of Cash) because the obligations to which they relate are ordinarily current liabilities.

Funds of the second type are similar to long-term investments, as they do not relate directly to current operations. They are ordinarily shown in the Long-Term Investments section of the balance sheet or in a separate section if relatively large in amount. The more common funds of this type and the purpose of each are listed below.

Fund	Purpose
Sinking Fund	Payment of long-term indebtedness
Plant Expansion Fund	Purchase or construction of additional plant
Share Redemption Fund	Retirement of share capital (usually preferred shares)
Contingency Fund	Payment of unforeseen obligations

Because the cash set aside will not be needed until some time in the future, it is usually invested in securities so that revenue may be earned on the fund assets. The assets of a fund may or may not be placed in the hands of a trustee. If appointed, the trustee becomes the custodian of the assets, accounts to the company for them, and reports fund revenues and expenses.

ENTRIES FOR FUNDS

To keep track of the assets, revenues, and expenses of funds, it is desirable to maintain separate accounts. For example, if a fund is kept for the redemption of preferred shares that were issued with a redemption provision after a certain date, the following accounts might be kept.

Share Redemption Fund Cash	Share Redemption Fund Expense
Share Redemption Fund Investments	Gain on Sale of Fund Investments
Share Redemption Fund Revenue	Loss on Sale of Fund Investments

When cash is transferred from the regular Cash account, perhaps periodically, the entry is:

Share Redemption Fund Cash	30,000	
Cash		30,000

Securities purchased by the fund are recorded at cost:

Share Redemption Fund Investments	27,000	
Share Redemption Fund Cash		27,000

If securities purchased for the fund are to be held temporarily, they would be treated in the accounts in the same manner as temporary investments, described earlier in this chapter. If they are to be held for a long period of time, they are treated in accordance with the requirements described for long-term investments.

If we assume the entry above records the purchase at a premium of 10-year $25,000 par value 8% bonds on April 1, the issue date, the entry for the receipt of semiannual interest on October 1 is:

Share Redemption Fund Cash	1,000	
Share Redemption Fund Revenue		1,000

At December 31, entries are made to record amortization of premium for nine months (assuming straight-line amortization) and to accrue interest on the bonds for three months:

Share Redemption Fund Revenue	150	
Share Redemption Fund Investments		150
To record amortization of premium for nine months ($2,000 × 1/10 × 9/12)		

Interest Receivable on Share Redemption Fund Investments	500	
Share Redemption Fund Revenue		500
To accrue interest for three months ($25,000 × .08 × 3/12)		

Expenses of the fund paid are recorded by debiting Share Redemption Fund Expense and crediting Share Redemption Fund Cash.

Disposals of investments held by the fund are recorded the same as regular disposals of investments. Revenue and expense accounts set up to record fund transactions are closed to Income Summary at the end of the accounting period and are reflected in earnings of the current period. The entry for retirement of the preferred shares is:

Preferred Shares	500,000	
Share Redemption Fund Cash		500,000

Any balance remaining in the Share Redemption Fund Cash account is transferred back to the general cash account or deficiency is made up by the transfer of additional funds from general cash.

In some cases, a company purchases its own shares or bonds when it is using a share redemption fund or sinking fund. In these situations, the treasury shares should be deducted from the shareholders' equity section, and treasury bonds should be deducted from bonds payable where a legal right of offset exists and the intent is to settle the bonds on a net basis. Dividend revenue or interest revenue should not be recorded for these securities.

FUNDS AND RESERVES DISTINGUISHED

Although funds and **reserves** are not similar, they are sometimes confused because they may be related and often have similar titles. *A simple distinction may be drawn: A fund is always an asset and always has a debit balance; a reserve is an appropriation of retained earnings, always has a credit balance, and is never an asset.*

The distinction is illustrated by reconsidering the entries made in connection with the share redemption fund discussed above. The fund was originally established by the following entry.

Share Redemption Fund Cash	30,000	
Cash		30,000

Some of this cash was used to purchase investments; the assets of the fund were then cash and investments. Ultimately, the investments were sold and the stock redemption fund cash was used to retire the preferred shares.

If the company chose to do so, it could establish an appropriation for share redemption at the same time to reduce the retained earnings apparently available for dividends. Appropriated retained earnings is established by periodic transfers from retained earnings, as follows.

Retained Earnings	30,000	
Appropriation for Share Redemption		30,000

The reserve has a credit balance and is shown in the shareholders' equity section of the balance sheet. When the shares are retired by payment of cash from the share redemption fund, the appropriation is transferred back to retained earnings.

Appropriation for Share Redemption	500,000	
Retained Earnings		500,000

The foregoing discussion illustrates that the fund is an asset accumulated to retire shares; the appropriation is merely a subdivision of retained earnings. The fund is used to redeem the shares; the appropriation is transferred back to retained earnings.

Summary of Learning Objectives for Appendix 10A

15. Explain the accounting for cash surrender value. For insurance policies owned by a company where part of the premium paid goes to build up a cash value, the cash value is an asset of the company. The increase in the cash value each year is a reduction of insurance expense. Insurance proceeds received on the death of an insured executive is reported in income as a gain.

KEY TERMS

cash surrender value, 506

life insurance, 506

---

[26] *CICA Handbook* Section 3860, par. .34.

16. **Identify examples of and explain the accounting for special purpose funds.**
Funds set aside for specific purposes can be temporary or long-term in nature. If the latter, specific accounts for fund investments, fund cash, fund revenues and fund expenses are set up. These revenue and expense accounts are reported on the income statement, and the cash and investments are segregated on the balance sheet. When the purpose for which the funds were set aside is completed, any remaining cash is returned to the general cash account. Funds are accumulated for the retirement of bonds or share capital or for major capital acquisitions.

Note: All *asterisked* Exercises, Problems, and Cases relate to material contained in the appendix to the chapter.

EXERCISES

E10-1 **(Entries for Debt Securities)** Presented below are two independent situations.

Situation I
On January 1, 1998, the Brown Company purchased at par $200,000 of 10%, 10-year bonds. Interest is received quarterly on April 1, July 1, October 1, and January 1. Brown does not intend to hold these bonds on a long-term basis.

Situation II
On June 1, 1998, the Northcutt Company purchased at par plus accrued interest $100,000 of 9%, 10-year bonds dated January 1. Interest is received semiannually on July 1 and January 1. Northcutt intends to hold these bonds to maturity.

Instructions
For each of these two situations, present journal entries to record:
(a) The purchase of the bonds.
(b) The receipt of interest on July 1.
(c) The accrual of interest on December 31.

E10-2 **(Entries for Long-Term Investments)** On January 1, 1998, Sampson Company purchased 12% bonds, having a maturity value of $300,000, for $322,744.44. The bonds provide the bondholders with a 10% yield. They are dated January 1, 1998, and mature January 1, 2003, with interest receivable December 31 of each year. Sampson uses the effective interest method to amortize discount or premium. The bonds are classified as long-term.

Instructions
(a) Prepare the journal entry at the date of the bond purchase.
(b) Prepare a bond amortization schedule.
(c) Prepare the journal entry to record the interest received and the amortization for 1998.
(d) Prepare the journal entry to record the interest received and the amortization for 2000.
(e) Prepare all journal entries required on December 31, 2002 and January 1, 2003.

E10-3 **(Entries for Temporary Investments)** Assume the same information as in Exercise 10-2 except that the securities are classified as temporary investments. The market value of the bonds at December 31 of each year end is as follows:

1998	$321,000	2001	$310,000
1999	$309,000	2002	$300,000
2000	$308,000		

Instructions
(a) Prepare the journal entry at the date of the bond purchase.
(b) Prepare the journal entries to record the interest received and valuation at LCM for 1998.
(c) Assuming the bonds continue to be held as temporary investments, prepare the journal entries to record the valuation at LCM for 1999, 2000, and 2001.
(d) Prepare all journal entries required on December 31, 2002 and January 1, 2003.

(Effective Interest versus Straight-Line Bond Amortization) On January 1, 1998 Brooks Company acquires **E10-4** $150,000 of 9% bonds of Handel Products Inc. at a price of $139,192. The interest is payable each December 31, and the bonds mature December 31, 2000. The investment will provide Brooks Company a 12% yield. The bonds are classified as long-term.

Instructions

(a) Prepare a three-year schedule of interest revenue and bond discount amortization, applying the straight-line method.

(b) Prepare a three-year schedule of interest revenue and bond discount amortization, applying the effective interest method.

(c) Prepare the journal entry for the interest receipt of December 31, 1999, and the discount amortization under the straight-line method.

(d) Prepare the journal entry for the interest receipt of December 31, 1999, and the discount amortization under the effective interest method.

(Calculation of Bond Value) On June 1, 1998 Perly Ltd. purchased on the open market a 7% $200,000 face value **E10-5** bond of Neil Co. The bond pays interest semiannually each June 1 and December 1 and matures on June 1, 2004.

Instructions

What is the purchase price of the bond assuming the market rate of interest on June 1, 1998 is:

(a) 8%?

(b) 6%?

(Calculation of Bond Value and Interest Revenue) Howard Company acquired $50,000 face value of the newly **E10-6** issued 11% bonds of Sport Co. on March 1, 1998, the date of issue. The bonds pay interest annually each March 1, mature on March 1, 2008, and were sold to yield 10%. Howard Co. intends to hold the bonds until maturity.

Instructions

(a) Determine the price paid by Howard Co. for the bonds.

(b) Calculate the amount of interest revenue reported by Howard Co. for its year ended December 31, 1998 and the carrying value of the investment on the December 31, 1998 balance sheet, assuming:

(i) the effective interest method of amortizing discounts and premiums is used.

(ii) the straight-line method is used.

(Temporary Investments Entries) On December 31, 1998, Wildcat Company provided you with the following **E10-7** information regarding its temporary investments.

December 31, 1998

Investments	Cost	Market Value	Unrealized Gain (Loss)
Mendota Corp. shares	$20,000	$19,000	$(1,000)
Waubesa Co. shares	10,000	9,000	(1,000)
Wantco shares	20,000	20,600	600
Total of portfolio	$50,000	$48,600	$(1,400)

Securities market value Allowance account before adjustment for 1998	$0

During 1999, Waubesa Company shares were sold for $9,200. The market values of the shares on December 31, 1999 were: Mendota Corp.—$19,000; Wantco Co.—$20,500.

Instructions

(a) Prepare the adjusting journal entry needed on December 31, 1998.

(b) Prepare the journal entry to record the sale of the Waubesa Company shares during 1999.

(c) Prepare the adjusting journal entry needed on December 31, 1999.

(Temporary Investments Entries and Reporting) The Duggen Corporation purchases equity securities costing **E10-8** $72,000 and classifies them as temporary investments. At December 31, the fair value of the portfolio is $65,000.

Instructions
Prepare the adjusting entry to report the securities properly. Indicate the statement presentation of the accounts in your entry.

E10-9 **(Temporary Investments Entries and Financial Statement Presentation)** At December 31, 1997 the temporary investment portfolio for Nielsen, Inc., is as follows:

Security	Cost	Market Value	Unrealized Gain (Loss)
A	$17,500	$15,000	($2,500)
B	12,500	14,000	1,500
C	23,000	25,500	2,500
Total	$53,000	$54,500	$1,500

Previous securities market value Allowance account balance—Cr. $500

On January 20, 1998, Nielsen, Inc. sold security A for $14,900. The sale proceeds are net of brokerage fees.

Instructions
(a) Prepare the adjusting entry at December 31, 1997 to report the portfolio at LCM.
(b) Show the proper financial statement presentation of the investment-related accounts at December 31, 1997 (ignore notes presentation).
(c) Prepare the journal entry for the 1998 sale of Security A.

E10-10 **(Journal Entries for Long-Term Equity Securities)** Presented below are two independent situations.

Situation I
Karen Cosmetics acquired 10% of the 200,000 shares of common stock of Bell Fashion at a total cost of $12 per share on March 18, 1998. On June 30, Bell declared and paid a $75,000 cash dividend. On December 31, Bell reported net income of $122,000 for the year. On December 31, the market price of Bell Fashion was $15 per share. The securities are classified as long-term investments.

Situation II
Barb, Inc. obtained significant influence over Diner Corporation by buying 30% of Diner's 30,000 outstanding shares of common stock at a total cost of $9 per share on January 1, 1998. On June 15, Diner declared and paid a cash dividend of $35,000. On December 31, Diner reported a net income of $80,000 for the year.

Instructions
Prepare all necessary journal entries in 1998 for both situations.

E10-11 **(Equity versus Cost Method of Accounting for Investments)** On December 31, 1997 Chesley Ltd. acquired 75,000 shares of Lassie Corporation common stock as a long-term investment at a cost of $30 a share. The cost of the shares represented 30% of the book value of Lassie's net assets, which was also 30% of the fair value of the net assets taken separately. The following information is also provided:

1. On May 1, 1998, Lassie Corporation paid a cash dividend of $1.50 per common share.
2. For the year 1998, Lassie Corporation reported net income of $450,000; the fair value of the investment was $2,025,000 at December 31, 1998.
3. On May 1, 1999, Lassie Corporation paid a dividend of $0.50 per share.
4. For the year 1999, Lassie Corporation reported net income of $600,000.
5. The fair value of the investment was $2,175,000 at December 31, 1999.

Instructions
(a) Prepare the journal entries to record the transactions and information listed above on Chesley Ltd.'s books, assuming that the investment in Lassie Corporation is not subject to significant influence. December 31 is Chesley Ltd.'s year end.
(b) Prepare the journal entries necessary to record the transactions and information listed above on Chesley Ltd.'s books, assuming that the investment in Lassie Corporation is carried on the equity basis.
(c) What is the carrying value of the investment in Lassie Corporation shares on January 1, 2000 (1) under the cost method; and (2) under the equity method?

(Equity Method with Revalued Assets) On January 1, 1998, Filley Company purchased 2,500 Pricer Ltd. common **E10-12** shares (25%) for $350,000. Additional information related to the identifiable assets and liabilities of Pricer Ltd. at the date of acquisition is as follows.

	Cost	Market
Assets not subject to depreciation	$ 500,000	$ 500,000
Assets subject to depreciation (10 years remaining)	800,000	860,000
Total identifiable assets	$1,300,000	$1,360,000
Liabilities	$ 100,000	$ 100,000

During 1998, Pricer Ltd. reported the following information on its income statement:

Income before extraordinary item	$350,000
Extraordinary gain (net of tax)	80,000
Net income	$430,000
Dividends declared and paid by Pricer Ltd. during 1998	$220,000

Instructions

(a) Prepare the journal entry to record the purchase by Filley Company of Pricer Ltd. on January 1, 1998.

(b) Prepare the journal entries to record Filley's equity in the net income and dividends of Pricer Ltd. for 1998. Depreciable assets are depreciated on a straight-line basis and goodwill is amortized over 20 years.

(Securities Entries—Buy, Sale, Transfer) Godfrey Company has the following securities in its portfolio of tempo- **E10-13** rary securities on December 31, 1998.

Investments	Cost	Market
1,500 shares of Genesis Ltd. common	$ 75,000	$ 69,000
5,000 shares of G. Wire Co. common	180,000	175,000
400 shares of HTM preferred	60,000	61,600
	$315,000	$305,600

All the securities were purchased in 1998.

In 1999, Godfrey completed the following securities transactions:

March 1	Sold the 1,500 shares of Genesis Ltd. common for $45 per share less fees of $1,200.
April 1	Bought 700 shares of Dowl Co. common for $75 per share plus fees of $1,300.
December 31	Transferred the HTM preferred from the temporary portfolio to the long-term portfolio; the stock was selling at $145 per share on this date.

Godfrey Company's securities appeared as follows on December 31, 1999.

Investments	Cost	Market
5,000 shares of G. Wire Co., Common	$180,000	$175,000
700 shares of Dowl Co., Common	53,800	50,400
400 shares of HTM, Preferred	60,000	58,000
	$293,800	$283,400

Instructions

Prepare the general journal entries for Godfrey Company for:

(a) The 1998 adjusting entry.

(b) The sale of the Genesis Ltd. shares.

(c) The purchase of the Dowl Co. shares.

(d) The transfer of the HTM shares to long-term investments.

(e) The 1999 adjusting entry for the valuation of the temporary investments.

E10-14 **(Cost and Equity Method Compared)** Cardinal Concrete Inc. acquired 20% of the outstanding common shares of Edra Inc. on December 31, 1998. The purchase price for the 50,000 shares was $1,200,000, which approximated their book value. Edra Inc. declared and paid an $0.80 per share cash dividend on June 30 and on December 31, 1999. Edra reported net income of $700,000 for 1999. The market value of Edra's shares was $28 per share at December 31, 1999.

Instructions
(a) Prepare the journal entries for Cardinal Concrete Inc. for 1999, assuming that Cardinal cannot exercise significant influence over Edra. The securities are classified as long-term.

(b) Prepare the journal entries for Cardinal Concrete Inc. for 1999, assuming that Cardinal can exercise significant influence over Edra.

(c) At what amount is the investment in securities reported on the balance sheet under each of these methods at December 31, 1999? What is the total income reported in 1999 under each of these methods?

E10-15 **(Equity Method With Revalued Assets)** On January 1, 1998, Fort Inc. purchased 40% of the common shares of Spitz Ltd. for $420,000. The balance sheet reported the following information related to Spitz Ltd. at the date of acquisition:

Assets not subject to depreciation	$200,000
Assets subject to depreciation (10-year life remaining)	600,000
Liabilities	100,000

Additional Information
1. Both book value and fair value are the same for assets not subject to depreciation and the liabilities.
2. The fair market value of the assets subject to depreciation is $680,000.
3. The company depreciates its assets on a straight-line basis; intangible assets are amortized over five years.
4. Spitz Ltd. reports net income of $180,000 and declares and pays dividends of $120,000 in 1998.

Instructions
(a) Prepare the journal entry to record Fort's purchase of Spitz Ltd.
(b) Prepare the journal entries to record Fort's equity in the net income and dividends of Spitz Ltd. for 1998.
(c) Assume the same facts as above, except that Spitz net income includes an extraordinary loss (net of tax) of $30,000. Prepare the journal entries to record Fort's equity in the net income and dividends of Spitz Ltd. for 1998.

E10-16 **(Change from Cost to Equity Method)** On January 1, 1998, Poley Co. purchased 25,000 shares, a 10% interest, in Lindsay Corp. for $1,400,000.

On January 1, 1999 Poley paid $3,040,000 for 50,000 additional shares of Lindsay common stock, which represented a 20% investment in Lindsay. The fair value of Lindsay's identifiable assets net of liabilities was equal to their carrying amount of $14,200,000. As a result of this transaction, Poley owns 30% of Lindsay and can exercise significant influence over Lindsay's operating and financial policies. Intangible assets are amortized over 20 years.

Lindsay reported the following net income and declared and paid the following dividends:

	Net Income	Dividend Per Share
Year ended 12/31/98	$ 700,000	$ -0-
Year ended 12/31/99	$1,240,000	$1.40

Instructions
Determine the balance of the Investment in Lindsay Corp. account that Poley Co. should report on its December 31, 1999 balance sheet.

E10-17 **(Change From Equity to Cost)** Land Corp. was a 30% owner of Jensen Limited, holding 210,000 of Jensen's common shares on December 31, 1998. The investment account had the following entries:

Investment in Jensen

1/1/97	Cost	$3,180,000	12/6/97	Dividend received	$150,000
12/31/97	Share of income	390,000	12/31/97	Amortization of	
12/31/98	Share of income	510,000		undervalued assets	30,000
			12/5/98	Dividend received	240,000
			12/31/98	Amortization of	
				undervalued assets	30,000

On January 2, 1999 Land sold 118,000 shares of Jensen for $3,250,000, thereby losing its significant influence. During 1999, Jensen reported a net income of $285,000 and paid dividends of $26,600 to Land.

Instructions

(a) What effect does the January 2, 1999 transaction have on Land's accounting treatment for its investment in Jensen?

(b) Compute the carrying value of the investment in Jensen as of December 31, 1999.

(Determine Proper Income Reporting) Presented below are three independent situations to be solved.   **E10-18**

1. Village Green Inc. received dividends from its investments in common shares during the year ended December 31, 1998, as follows:

    (a) A cash dividend of $10,000 is received from Gary Corporation. (Village Green owns a 2% interest in Gary.)

    (b) A cash dividend of $60,000 is received from Mid-Plains Corporation. (Village Green owns a 30% interest in Mid-Plains.) A majority of Village Green's directors are also directors of Mid-Plains Corporation.

    (c) A stock dividend of 300 shares from Petty Inc. was received on December 10, 1998, on which date the quoted market value of Petty's shares was $10 each. Village Green owns less than 1% of Petty's common shares.

    Determine how much dividend income Village Green should report in its 1998 income statement.

2. On January 3, 1998 Perly Co. purchased as a long-term investment 5,000 Bonton Co. common shares (a 2% interest) for $79 per share. On December 31, 1998 the market price of the shares was $83 each. On March 3, 1999 it sold all 5,000 Bonton shares for $100 each. The company regularly sells securities of this type. The income tax rate is 35%. Determine the amount of gain or loss on disposal that should be reported on the income statement in 1999.

3. Morgan owns a 4% interest in Canton Corporation, which declared a cash dividend of $600,000 on November 27, 1998 to shareholders of record on December 16, 1998, payable on January 6, 1999. In addition, on October 15, 1998 Morgan received a liquidating dividend of $9,000 from Silver Mining Company. Morgan owns 6% of Silver Mining. Determine the amount of dividend income Morgan should report on its financial statements for 1998.

(Entries for Stock Rights) On January 10, 1998, Simon Company purchased 240 of Graeme Corporation's no-par   **E10-19** value common shares (a 3% interest) for $24,000, to be held as a long-term investment. On July 12, 1998, Graeme Corporation announced that rights would be issued that permitted one new share to be purchased for every two shares held.

July 30, 1998	Rights to purchase 120 shares at $100 per share are received. The market value of the shares is $121 each and the market value of the rights is $16 each.
Aug. 10	The rights to purchase 50 shares are sold at $15 per right.
Aug. 11	The additional 140 rights are exercised, and 70 shares are purchased at $100 each.
Nov. 15	50 shares are sold at $132 each.

Instructions

Prepare general journal entries on the books of Simon Company for the foregoing transactions.

(Entries for Stock Rights) Mars Company purchases 1,000 common shares of Plastic Inc. on February 17. The no-   **E10-20** par value shares, costing $109,200, are to be a long-term investment for Mars Company.

1. On June 30, Plastic Inc. announces that rights are to be issued, permitting one new share to be purchased for every five shares owned.

2. The rights mentioned in (1) are received on July 15; 200 shares may be purchased with these rights plus $100 per share. The shares are currently selling for $120 each. The market value of the stock rights is $5 per right.

3. On August 5, 600 rights are exercised and 120 shares are purchased at $100 each.

4. On August 12, the remaining stock rights are sold at $5.50 each.

5. On September 29, Mars Company sells 100 shares at $126 each.

Instructions

Prepare journal entries to record the above transactions.

(Consolidation) Hall Limited acquired 60% of the shares of Front Company on December 31, 1998 at a cost of   **E10-21** $240,000. The fair values of Front's net assets on this date approximated their book values.

The December 31, 1998 balance sheets of Hall Limited and Front Company after this transaction were as follows:

	Hall Limited	Front Company
Cash	$ 75,000	$ 40,000
Other current assets	300,000	70,000
Land	100,000	—
Equipment, net of depreciation	775,000	490,000
Investment in Front Company	240,000	—
	$1,490,000	$ 600,000
Current liabilities	$ 190,000	$ 70,000
Long-term notes payable	300,000	130,000
Common stock	750,000	300,000
Retained earnings	250,000	100,000
	$1,490,000	$ 600,000

Instructions
Prepare the December 31, 1998 consolidated balance sheet of Hall Limited.

*E10-22   (Investment In Life Insurance Policy) Cheryl Company pays the premiums on two insurance policies on the life of its president, Sue Cheryl. Information concerning premiums paid in 1998 follows.

			Dividends	Net	Cash Surrender Value	
Beneficiary	Face	Prem.	Cr. to Prem.	Prem.	1/1/98	12/31/98
1. Cheryl Company	$250,000	$8,500	$2,940	$5,560	$35,000	$37,700
2. President's spouse	75,000	3,000		3,000	9,000	9,750

Instructions
(a) Prepare entries in journal form to record the payment of premiums in 1998.
(b) If the president died in January 1999 and the beneficiaries are paid the face amounts of the policies, what entry would Cheryl Company make?

*E10-23   (Entries and Disclosure for Bond Sinking Fund) The general ledger of Vic Sommerfeld Company shows an account for Bonds Payable with a balance of $2,000,000. Interest is payable on these bonds semiannually. Of the $2,000,000, bonds in the amount of $400,000 were recently purchased at par by the sinking fund trustee and are held in the sinking fund as an investment of the fund. The annual rate of interest is 11%.

Instructions
(a) What entry or entries should be made by Vic Sommerfeld Company to record payment of the semiannual interest? (The company makes interest payments directly to bondholders.)
(b) Illustrate how the bonds payable and the sinking fund accounts should be shown in the balance sheet. Assume that the sinking fund investments other than Vic Sommerfeld Company's bonds amount to $506,000, and that the sinking fund cash amounts to $21,000.

*E10-24   (Entries for Plant Expansion Fund, Numbers Omitted) The transactions given below relate to a fund being accumulated by Roeming Company over a period of 20 years for the construction of additional buildings.
  1. Cash is transferred from the general cash account to the fund.
  2. Preferred shares of Habitat Limited are purchased as an investment of the fund.
  3. Bonds of J. Mullins Corporation are purchased between interest dates at a discount as an investment of the fund.
  4. Expenses of the fund are paid from the fund cash.
  5. Interest is collected on J. Mullins Corporation bonds.
  6. Bonds held in the fund are sold at a gain between interest dates.
  7. Dividends are received on Habitat Limited preferred shares.
  8. Common shares held in the fund are sold at a loss.

9. Cash is paid from the fund for building construction.

10. The cash balance remaining in the fund is transferred to general cash.

Instructions

Prepare journal entries to record the miscellaneous transactions listed above, with amounts omitted.

PROBLEMS

Presented below is an amortization schedule related to Thomas Company's five-year, $100,000 bond with a 7% interest rate and a 5% yield, purchased on December 31, 1998 for $108,660 as a long-term investment.   **P10-1**

Date	Cash Received	Interest Revenue	Bond Premium Amortization	Carry Amount of Bond
12/31/98				$108,660
12/31/99	$7,000	$5,433	$1,567	107,093
12/31/00	7,000	5,354	1,646	105,447
12/31/01	7,000	5,272	1,728	103,719
12/31/02	7,000	5,186	1,814	101,905
12/31/03	7,000	5,095	1,905	100,000

Instructions

(a) Prepare the journal entry to record the purchase of these bonds on December 31, 1998.

(b) Prepare the journal entry(ies) for 1999.

(c) Prepare the journal entry(ies) for 2001.

(d) Prepare the journal entry to record the sale of $40,000 par value of bonds on January 1, 2003, at 101.

On January 1, 1998 Brock Company purchased $200,000, 8% bonds of Universal Co. for $187,074. The bonds were purchased to yield 10% interest. Interest is payable semiannually on July 1 and January 1, the bonds mature on January 1, 2002, and Brock Company uses the effective interest method to amortize discounts or premiums. On January 1, 2000 Brock Company sold the bonds for $185,363 (after having received the interest) to meet its liquidity needs.   **P10-2**

Instructions

(a) Prepare the journal entry to record the purchase of the bonds on January 1, 1998.

(b) Prepare an amortization schedule for the bonds.

(c) Prepare the journal entries to record the semiannual interest on July 1, 1998 and December 31, 1998.

(d) Prepare the journal entry to record the sale of the bonds on January 1, 2000.

(e) According to GAAP, what information should be disclosed on Brock's 1998 financial statements related to these bonds?

Presented below is information taken from a bond investment amortization schedule. These bonds are classified as long-term.   **P10-3**

	12/31/98	12/31/99	12/31/00
Amortized cost	$491,150	$519,442	$550,000

Instructions

(a) Indicate whether the bonds were purchased at a discount or at a premium. Explain.

(b) Indicate what amortization method is being applied and how you determined your answer.

Bolex Company has the following securities in its temporary investment portfolio on December 31, 1998 (all securities were purchased in 1998): (1) 3,000 shares of Cesar Co. common stock, which cost $58,500; (2) 10,000 shares of Loben Ltd. common stock, which cost $580,000; and (3) 6,000 shares of Lascom Company preferred stock, which cost $255,000. The Valuation Allowance account shows a credit balance of $9,500 at the end of 1998.   **P10-4**

In 1999 Bolex completed the following temporary securities transactions:

1. On January 15, sold 3,000 shares of Cesar's common stock at $22 per share less fees of $2,150.
2. On April 17, purchased 1,000 shares of Glade's common stock at $31.50 per share plus fees of $1,980.

On December 31, 1999, the market values per share of these securities were: Cesar $20, Loban $62, Lascom $40, and Glade $29.

Instructions
(a) Prepare the entry for the security sale on January 15, 1999.
(b) Prepare the journal entry to record the security purchase on April 17, 1999.
(c) Compute the unrealized gains or losses and prepare the adjusting entry for Bolex on December 31, 1999.
(d) How should the investments and the realized and unrealized gains or losses be reported on Bolex's financial statements?

P10-5 The following transactions related to the temporary debt security investments of Lakeside Company occurred during 1998.

1. On February 1, the company purchased 9% bonds of Crandall Co. having a par value of $500,000 at 96 plus accrued interest. The bonds are dated October 1, 1997 and mature on October 1, 2002. Interest is payable April 1 and October 1.
2. On April 1, semiannual interest is received.
3. On July 1, 10% bonds of Quincy, Inc. were purchased. These bonds with a par value of $200,000 were purchased at 100 plus accrued interest. Interest dates are June 1 and December 1.
4. On September 1, bonds of a par value of $100,000, purchased on July 1, are sold at 99 plus accrued interest.
5. On October 1, semiannual interest is received on the Crandall Co. bonds.
6. On December 1, semiannual interest is received on the Quincy, Inc. bonds.
7. On December 31, the fair value of the bonds purchased February 1 and July 1 are 95 and 97, respectively.

Instructions
(a) Prepare any journal entries you consider necessary, including year-end adjusting entries at December 31.
(b) If the investments were classified as long-term investments, how would the journal entries differ from those in (a)? Be specific.

P10-6 GraNite is a medium-sized corporation that specializes in quarrying stone for building construction. The company has long dominated the market, at one time achieving a 70% market penetration. During prosperous years, the company's profits, coupled with a conservative dividend policy, resulted in funds being available for outside investment. Over the years, GraNite has had a policy of investing idle cash in equity securities. In particular, GraNite has made periodic investments in the company's principal supplier, Mark Industries. Although the firm currently owns 12% of the outstanding common shares of Mark Industries, which are traded on a national stock exchange, GraNite does not have significant influence over the operations of the company.

Kristine Risling has recently joined GraNite as assistant controller, and her first assignment is to prepare the 1998 year-end adjusting entries for the accounts that are valued using the lower of cost and market (LCM) method for financial reporting purposes. Risling has gathered the following information about GraNite's pertinent accounts:

1. GraNite has short-term investments in the marketable securities of Ajax Motors and Morgan Electric. During this fiscal year, GraNite purchased 100,000 shares of Ajax Motors for $1,400,000; these shares currently have a market value of $1,600,000. GraNite's investment in Morgan Electric has not been as profitable; the company acquired 50,000 shares of Morgan in April 1998 at $20 per share, a purchase that currently has a value of $600,000. The Valuation Allowance account before adjustment has a credit balance of $45,000.
2. Prior to 1998, GraNite invested $22,500,000 in Mark Industries and there has been no change in its holdings this year. This long-term investment had a December 31, 1997 fair value of $21,500,000. GraNite's 12% ownership of Mark Industries has a current market value of $22,200,000 at December 31, 1998.

Instructions
(a) Prepare the appropriate adjusting entries for GraNite as of December 31, 1998 to reflect the application of the lower of cost and market method for the temporary investments described above.
(b) Prepare partial financial statements, including any required note disclosure, to illustrate how GraNite's investments would be reported on its December 31, 1998 balance sheet.   (CMA adapted)

Keniston Wildcats Corp. makes the following long-term investments during 1998.   **P10-7**

Security	Quantity	Percent Interest	Per-Share Cost
Paduca Forms Company	3,000 shares	2	$80
London Grader Corp.	8,000 shares	16	20
Knoblett Development Inc.	3,000 shares	4	36

The following information concerning these investments relates to 1998 and 1999.

1. For the year 1998—cash dividends received:

Paduca Forms	$3.50 per share
London Grader	$1.00 per share
Knoblett Development	$1.50 per share

2. Market values per share, 12/31/98:

Paduca Forms	$74
London Grader	$23
Knoblett Development	$28

3. For the year 1999—cash dividends received:

Paduca Forms	$4.00 per share
London Grader	$0.60 per share
Knoblett Development	$1.65 per share

4. On Sept. 30, 1999, the investment in London Grader was reclassified to current asset status when its market value per share was $18.25.

5. Market value per share, 12/31/99:

Paduca Forms	$68
London Grader	$18
Knoblett Development	$46

Instructions

(a) Prepare all of the journal entries to reflect the transactions and related data above.

(b) Prepare the descriptions and amounts that should be reported on the face of Keniston Wildcat Corp.'s comparative financial statements for 1998 and 1999 relative to these long-term investments.

(c) Draft any note disclosures that should accompany the 1998–1999 comparative statements relative to the non-current securities.

Karen Rostad Corp. carried an account in its general ledger called Investments, which contained the following debits for investment purchases, and no credits: **P10-8**

Feb. 1, 1998	Player Company common, no-par, 200 shares, a 1% interest	$36,400
Apr. 1	Government of Canada bonds, 11%, due April 1, 2008, interest payable April 1 and October 1; 100 bonds of $1,000 par value each	113,000
July 1	Vicq Steel Company 12% bonds, par $50,000, dated March 1, 1998, purchased at 101, interest payable annually on March 1, due March 1, 2018	52,500

Instructions

(a) Prepare the entries necessary to classify the amounts into proper accounts, assuming that the Government of Canada bonds are the only temporary investments.

(b) Prepare the entry to record the accrued interest and amortization of premium on December 31, 1998, using the straight-line method.

(c) The market values of the securities on December 31, 1998 were:

Player Company common	$ 33,800
Government of Canada bonds	114,700
Vicq Steel Company bonds	55,600

What entry or entries, if any, would you recommend be made?

(d) The Government of Canada bonds were sold on July 1, 1999 for $124,200. Prepare the entry to record the sale of the bonds.

(e) Twenty additional shares of Player Company common were received on July 15, 1999 as a stock dividend, and on July 31, 1999, 30 shares of Player Company common were sold at $180 per share. What entries would be made for these two transactions?

P10-9 Zoe Incorporated is a publicly traded company that manufactures products to clean and demagnetize video and audio tape recorders and players. The company grew rapidly during its first 20 years and made three public offerings during this period. During its rapid growth period, Zoe acquired common shares of Guttman Inc. and Cairo Importers. In 1988, Zoe acquired 25% of Guttman's common shares for $588,000 and properly accounts for this investment using the equity method. For its fiscal year ended November 30, 1998, Guttman Inc. reported net income of $240,000 and paid dividends of $100,000. In 1990, Zoe acquired 10% of Cairo Importers' common shares for $204,000 and properly accounts for this investment using the cost method. Zoe has a policy of investing idle cash in marketable equity securities. The following data pertain to the securities in Zoe's investment portfolio.

Marketable Equity Securities at November 30, 1997

Security	Total Cost	Total Market
Horton Electric	$326,000	$314,000
Edwards Inc.	184,000	181,000
Evert Company	96,000	98,000
	606,000	593,000
Cairo Importers	204,000	198,000
	$810,000	$791,000

Marketable Equity Securities at November 30, 1998

Security	Total Cost	Total Market
Horton Electric	$326,000	$323,000
Edwards Inc.	184,000	180,000
Rogers Limited	105,000	108,000
	615,000	611,000
Cairo Importers	204,000	205,000
	$819,000	$816,000

On November 14, 1998 Amanda McElroy was hired by Zoe as assistant controller. Her first assignment was to propose the entries to record the November activity and the November 30, 1998 year-end adjusting entries for the short-term investments in marketable equity securities and the long-term investments in common shares of Cairo and Guttman. Using Zoe's ledger of investment transactions and the data given above, McElroy proposed the following entries and submitted them to Able Gance, controller, for review.

Entry 1 (November 8, 1998)

Cash	$99,500	
Temporary Investments: Evert Company		$98,000
Realized Gain on Sale of Investment		1,500

To record the sale of Evert Company shares for $99,500.

Entry 2 (November 26, 1998)

Temporary Investments: Rogers Limited	$105,000	
Cash		$105,000

To record the purchase of Rogers Limited common shares for $102,200 plus brokerage fees of $2,800.

Entry 3 (November 30, 1998)

Unrealized Loss on Valuation of Temporary Investments	$3,000	
Allowance for Excess of Cost of Temporary Investments Over Market Value		$3,000

To recognize a loss equal to the excess of cost over market value of marketable equity securities.

Entry 4 (November 30, 1998)

Cash	$37,000	
Dividend Revenue		$37,000

To record dividends received from marketable equity securities.

Guttman Inc.	$25,000
Cairo Importers	9,000
Horton Electric	3,000

Entry 5 (November 30, 1998)

Investment in Guttman Inc.	$60,000	
Investment Income		$60,000

To record share of Guttman Inc. income under the equity method, $240,000 × .25.

Instructions

(a) Distinguish between the characteristics of temporary investments and long-term investments, and explain how a particular security may be properly classified as a temporary investment in one company and a long-term investment in another company.

(b) The journal entries proposed by Amanda McElroy will establish the value of Zoe Incorporated's equity investments to be reported on the company's external financial statements. Review each of the journal entries proposed by McElroy and indicate whether or not it is in accordance with the applicable reporting standards. If an entry is incorrect, prepare the correct entry or entries that should have been made.

(c) Because Zoe Incorporated owns more than 20% of Guttman Inc., Able Gance has adopted the equity method to account for the investment in Guttman Inc. Under what circumstances would it be inappropriate to use the equity method to account for a 25% interest in the common shares of Guttman Inc.?   (AICPA adapted)

P10-10 Oakwood Ltd. invested its excess cash in temporary investments during 1996. As of December 31, 1996, the portfolio of short-term marketable securities consisted of the following common shares.

Security	Quantity	Total Cost	Total Market
Tinkers, Inc.	1,000 shares	$ 15,000	$ 19,000
Evers Corp.	2,000 shares	50,000	42,000
Chance Aircraft	2,000 shares	72,000	60,000
		$137,000	$121,000

Instructions

(a) What descriptions and amounts should be reported on the face of Oakwood's December 31, 1996 balance sheet relative to short-term investments?

(b) On December 31, 1997, Oakwood's portfolio of short-term marketable securities consisted of the following common shares.

Security	Quantity	Total Cost	Total Market
Tinkers, Inc.	1,000 shares	$ 15,000	$20,000
Tinkers, Inc.	2,000 shares	38,000	40,000
Lakeshore Company	1,000 shares	16,000	12,000
Chance Aircraft	2,000 shares	72,000	22,000
		$141,000	$94,000

During the year 1997, Oakwood Ltd. sold 2,000 shares of Evers Corp. for $40,500 and purchased 2,000 more shares of Tinkers, Inc. and 1,000 shares of Lakeshore Company.

What descriptions and amounts should be reported on the face of Oakwood's December 31, 1997 balance sheet?

What descriptions and amounts should be reported on Oakwood's 1997 income statement?

(c) On December 31, 1998, Oakwood's portfolio of short-term marketable securities consisted of the following.

Security	Quantity	Total Cost	Total Market
Chance Aircraft	2,000 shares	$72,000	$82,000
Lakeshore Company	500 shares	8,000	6,000
		$80,000	$88,000

During the year 1998, Oakwood Ltd. sold 3,000 shares of Tinkers, Inc. for $39,500 and 500 shares of Lakeshore Company at a loss of $2,500.

What descriptions and amounts should be reported on the face of Oakwood's December 31, 1998 balance sheet?

What descriptions and amounts should be reported to reflect the above on Oakwood's 1998 income statement?

(d) Assuming that comparative financial statements for 1997 and 1998 are presented, draft the footnote necessary for full disclosure of Oakwood's transactions and position in marketable securities.

P10-11 On February 28, 1998 Vipers Company acquired $80,000 par value bonds of Asp Ltd. dated January 1, 1998 at 98.5. The 9% bonds pay interest semiannually each January 1 and July 1, and mature January 1, 2003. Vipers intends to hold the bonds to maturity.

On June 30, 1998, Vipers Company acquired at a cost of $375,000 a 25% interest in Shaker Corporation, one of its key suppliers. This purchase price indicates Vipers paid $50,000 more than its share of Shaker's net book value, due entirely to an unrecorded patent with a remaining useful life of 10 years as of June 30, 1998. Because of the importance of its business to Shakers, Vipers is able to exert considerable influence over Shaker's strategic policies.

Shaker reported 1998 income (earned evenly over the year) of $40,000 and 1999 income of $68,000, and paid a dividend of $12,000 in 1999.

Instructions

(a) Prepare journal entries, including any required December 31, 1998 adjusting entries, to record the purchase of the investments and the investment income recognized in 1998. Vipers uses the straight-line method for amortizing bond premiums and discounts and has a December 31 year end.

(b) Indicate how the investments will be reported on Viper's December 31, 1998 balance sheet.

(c) Assuming Vipers Company sells the bonds for 100.75 on August 1, 1999, prepare all entries to record investment income from the investment in bonds and shares in 1999, and the entry to record the disposal of the bond investment.

P10-12 On January 1, 1997 Faye Inc. paid $700,000 for 10,000 voting common shares of Wolf Company, which was a 10% interest in Wolf. At that date, the book value of Wolf's net assets totalled $6,000,000 and the fair values of all of Wolf's identifiable assets and liabilities were equal to their book values. Faye does not have the ability to exercise significant influence over the operating and financial policies of Wolf. Faye received dividends of $1.00 per share from Wolf on October 1, 1997. Wolf reported net income of $500,000 for the year ended December 31, 1997.

On July 1, 1998, Faye paid $2,325,000 for 30,000 additional common voting shares of Wolf Company, which represented a 30% investment in Wolf. The fair values of all of Wolf's identifiable assets net of liabilities were equal to their book values of $6,550,000. As a result of this transaction, Faye had the ability to exercise significant influence over the operating and financial policies of Wolf. Faye received dividends of $1.00 per share from Wolf on April 1, 1998 and $1.50 per share on October 1, 1998. Wolf reported net income of $550,000 for the year ended December 31, 1998, and $300,000 for the six months ended December 31, 1998. Faye Inc. amortizes goodwill over a 20-year period.

Instructions

(a) Prepare a schedule showing the income or loss before income taxes for the year ended December 31, 1997 that Faye should report from its investment in Wolf.

(b) Faye issues comparative financial statements for 1997 and 1998. Prepare schedules showing the income or loss before income taxes for the years ended December 31, 1997 and 1998 that Faye should report from its investment in Wolf.

(AICPA adapted)

On January 3, 1996, Cajun Company purchased for $500,000 cash a 10% interest in Summerset Corp. On that date, the net assets of Summerset had a book value of $3,750,000. The excess of cost over the underlying equity in net assets was attributable to undervalued depreciable assets having a remaining life of 10 years from the date of the Cajun purchase. **P10-13**

On January 2, 1998, Cajun purchased an additional 30% of Summerset's common shares for $1,545,000 cash when the book value of Summerset's net assets was $4,150,000. The excess was attributable to depreciable assets having a remaining life of eight years.

During 1996, 1997, and 1998 the following occurred.

	Summerset Net Income	Dividends Paid by Summerset to Cajun
1996	$325,000	$15,000
1997	450,000	20,000
1998	490,000	60,000

Instructions

On the books of Cajun Company, prepare all journal entries in 1996, 1997, and 1998 that relate to its investment in Summerset Corp., reflecting the data above and a change from the cost method to the equity method.

Discorama Company holds 300 of Ryan Shay Inc. common shares that it purchased for $32,589 as a long-term investment. On January 15, 1998, Ryan Shay Inc. announced that rights will be issued permitting the purchase of one new share for every four shares held. **P10-14**

Instructions

(a) Prepare entries on Discorama Company's books for the transactions below that occurred after the date of this announcement. Show all computations in good form.

1. 100 shares are sold rights-on for $10,600.

2. Rights to purchase 50 additional shares at $100 per share are received. The market value on this date is $105 per share and the market value of the rights is $1.50 per right.

3. The rights are exercised, and 50 additional shares are purchased at $100 per share.

4. 100 of the original shares are sold for $106 each.

(b) If the rights had not been exercised but instead had been sold at $1.50 per right, what would have been the amount of the gain or loss on the sale of the rights?

(c) If the shares purchased through the exercise of the rights are later sold at $107 each, what is the amount of the gain or loss on the sale?

(d) If the rights had not been exercised but had been allowed to expire, what would be the proper entry?

The transactions given below relate to a sinking fund for retirement of long-term bonds of Hilltop Corp. ***P10-15**

1. In accordance with the terms of the bond indenture, cash in the amount of $150,000 is transferred, at the end of the first year, from the regular cash account to the sinking fund.

2. Eau Claire Company 10% bonds of a par value of $50,000, maturing in five years, are purchased for $48,000.

3. 500 shares of Mankato Company $4 no-par preferred are purchased at $53 per share.

4. Annual interest of $5,000 is received on Eau Claire Company bonds. (Amortize the proper amount of discount, using straight-line amortization.)

5. Sinking fund expenses of $450 are paid from sinking fund cash.

6. SFU Company 9% bonds with interest payable February 1 and August 1 are purchased on April 15 at par value of $60,000.

7. Dividends of $2,000 are received on Mankato Company preferred.

8. All the SFU Company bonds are sold on September 1 at 101 plus accrued interest. Assume interest collected August 1 was properly recorded.

9. Investments carried in the fund at $1,583,000 are sold for $1,528,000.

10. The fund contains cash of $1,622,000 after disposing of all investments and paying all expenses. Of this amount, $1,600,000 is used to retire the bonds payable at maturity.

11. The remaining cash balance is returned to the general account.

Instructions
Prepare the journal entries required by Hilltop Corp. for the above transactions.

CASES

C10-1 You have just started work for Duff Ltd. as part of the controller's group involved in current financial reporting problems. Rhoda Clements, controller for Duff, is interested in your accounting background because the company has experienced a series of financial reporting surprises over the last few years. Recently, Clements has learned from the company's auditors that a section of the *CICA Handbook* may apply to its investment in securities. She assumes that you are familiar with these requirements and asks how the following situations should be reported in the financial statements.

Situation I. Temporary investments in debt securities in the Current Asset section have a market value of $3,000 lower than cost.

Situation II. A marketable security whose market value is currently less than cost is classified as current but is to be reclassified as noncurrent.

Situation III. A marketable security whose market value is currently less than cost is classified as noncurrent but is to be reclassified as current.

Situation IV. A company's current portfolio of marketable securities consists of the common shares of one company. At the end of the prior year, the market value of the security was 50% of original cost and this reduction in market value was properly reflected in a valuation allowance account. However, at the end of the current year, the market value of the security has appreciated to twice the original cost. The security is still considered current at year end.

Situation V. The company has purchased some convertible debentures that it plans to hold for less than a year. At the end of the company's fiscal year, market value of the convertible debenture is $8,000 below its cost.

Instructions
What is the effect on classification, carrying value, and earnings for each of these situations? Assume that these situations are unrelated.

C10-2 Cracker Limited has followed the practice of valuing its temporary investments in marketable equity securities at the lower of cost and market. Analysis disclosed that on December 31, 1997, the facts relating to the securities were as follows.

	Cost	Market	Allowance Required
Halton Corp. shares	$20,000	$19,000	$1,000
Tremor Company shares	10,000	9,000	1,000
Meggs Company shares	20,000	20,600	–0–
	$50,000		$2,000

During 1998, the Tremor Company shares were sold for $9,200, the difference between the $9,200 and the "new adjusted basis" of $9,000 being recorded as a Gain on Sale of Securities. At December 31, 1998, the Temporary Investments account had a balance of $40,000, and the Allowance for Excess of Cost of Temporary Investments Over Market Value had a balance of $2,000. The market prices of the shares on December 31, 1998 were: Halton Corp. shares—$19,900; Meggs Company shares—$20,500.

Instructions
(a) What justification is there for the use of the lower of cost and market in valuing temporary investments?
(b) Did Cracker Limited properly apply this rule on December 31, 1997? Explain.
(c) Did Cracker Limited properly account for the sale of the Tremor Company shares? Explain.
(d) Are there any additional entries necessary for Cracker Limited at December 31, 1998 to reflect the facts on the balance sheet and income statement in accordance with generally accepted accounting principles? Explain.

(AICPA adapted)

C10-3 Presented below are four unrelated situations involving marketable equity securities.

Situation I. A marketable security, whose market value is currently less than cost, is classified as noncurrent but is to be reclassified as current.

Situation II. A company's noncurrent portfolio of marketable securities consists of the common shares of one company. At the end of the prior year, the market value of the security was 50% of original cost and this effect was reflected in a write-down under the assumption that this was a permanent decline in value. However, at the end of the current year, the market value of the security has appreciated to twice the original cost. The security is still considered noncurrent at year-end.

Situation III. A noncurrent securities portfolio with an aggregate market value in excess of cost includes one particular security whose market value has declined to less than one-half of the original cost. The decline in value is considered to be other than temporary.

Situation IV. The statement of financial position of a company does not classify assets and liabilities as current and noncurrent. The portfolio of marketable securities includes securities normally considered current that have a net cost in excess of market value of $12,000. The remainder of the portfolio has a net market value in excess of cost of $29,000.

Instructions
What is the effect on classification, carrying value, and earnings for each of these situations? Complete your response to each situation before proceeding to the next situation.

The *CICA Handbook*, Sections 3010 and 3050, prescribes accounting procedures for temporary and long-term investments, respectively. An important issue is the distinction between noncurrent and current classifications of investments. **C10-4**

Instructions
(a) Why does a company maintain an investment portfolio of current and noncurrent securities?
(b) What factors should be considered in determining whether investments in marketable securities should be classified as current or noncurrent, and how do these factors affect the accounting treatment for unrealized losses?

The president of Comtel Ltd. is concerned about a proposed accounting change related to investments in marketable securities. The proposal is that all marketable securities be presented at market value on the balance sheet and the changes that occur in market value be reflected in income in the current period. The president agrees that market value on the balance sheet may be more useful to the investor, but he sees no reason why changes in market value should be reflected in income of the current year. **C10-5**

James Clarke, controller of Comtel Ltd., is also unhappy about the proposal and has recommended the following alternatives:

1. Recognize realized gains and losses from changes in market value in income and report unrealized gains and losses in a special balance sheet account on the equity side of the balance sheet.

2. Report realized and unrealized gains and losses from market value changes in a statement separate from the income statement or as direct charges and credits to a shareholders' equity account.

3. Recognize gains and losses from changes in market value in income based on long-term yield; for example, use the past performance of the enterprise over several years (a 10-year period has been suggested) to determine an average rate of yield because of an increase in value.

To the president of Comtel Ltd., these recommendations seem more reasonable.

Instructions
(a) Is the use of a market value or fair value basis of accounting for all marketable securities a desirable and feasible practice? Discuss.
(b) Do you believe the president is correct in stating that one of the alternatives is a better approach to recognition of income in accounting for marketable securities?

On July 1, 1998 Rogers Limited purchased for cash 40% of the outstanding capital stock of Huber Company. Both Rogers Limited and Huber Company have December 31 year ends. Huber Company, whose common stock is actively traded in the over-the-counter market, reported its net income for the year to Rogers Limited and also paid cash dividends on November 15, 1998 to Rogers Limited and its other shareholders. **C10-6**

Instructions
How should Rogers Limited report the above facts in its December 31, 1998 balance sheet and its income statement for the year then ended? Discuss the rationale for your answer.

For the past five years, RMT Ltd. has maintained an investment (properly accounted for and reported on) in Beloit Co., amounting to a 10% interest in the voting common shares of Beloit Co. The purchase price was $1,050,000 and 10% of the underlying net equity in Beloit at the date of purchase was $930,000. On January 2 of the current year, **C10-7**

RMT purchased an additional 20% of the voting common shares of Beloit for $2,400,000; the underlying net equity of the additional investment at January 2 was $2,000,000. Beloit has been profitable and has paid dividends annually since RMT's initial acquisition.

Instructions

Discuss how this increase in ownership affects the accounting for and reporting of the investment in Beloit Co. Include in your discussion adjustments, if any, to the amount shown prior to the increase in investment to bring the amount into conformity with generally accepted accounting principles. Also indicate how reporting would take place for current and subsequent periods. (AICPA adapted)

C10-8 "I don't understand why companies have to prepare consolidated financial statements," exclaimed Tom, a classmate in Intermediate Accounting. "Adding together all the assets, liabilities, revenues, and expenses of the parent and all subsidiary companies obscures the performance of the parent company, is not permitted for income tax purposes, and is useless for the creditors and noncontrolling shareholders of the subsidiary companies!"

Instructions

Prepare a response to Tom that explains why consolidated financial statements are required.

C10-9 Strand Inc., a chemical processing company, has been operating profitably for many years. On March 1, 1998, Strand purchased 50,000 First Executive Company shares for $2,000,000. The 50,000 shares represented 40% of First's outstanding common shares. Both Strand and First operate on a fiscal year ending August 31.

For the fiscal year ended August 31, 1998, First reported net income of $900,000 earned evenly throughout the year. During November 1997 and February, May, and August 1998, First paid its regular quarterly cash dividend of $125,000.

Instructions

(a) What criteria should Strand consider in determining whether its investment in First should be classified as (1) a current asset; or (2) a noncurrent asset in Strand's August 31, 1998 balance sheet? Confine your discussion to the decision criteria for determining the balance sheet classification of the investment.

(b) Assume that the investment should be classified as a long-term investment in the Noncurrent Asset section of Strand's balance sheet. The cost of Strand's investment equalled its equity in the recorded values of First's net assets; recorded values were not materially different from fair values (individually or collectively). For the fiscal year ended August 31, 1998, how did the net income reported and dividends paid by First affect the accounts of Strand (ignore income tax considerations)? Indicate each account affected, whether it increased or decreased, and explain the reason for the change in the account balance (such as Cash, Investment in First, etc.). Organize your answer in the following format:

Account Name	Increase or Decrease	Reason for Change in Account Balance

*C10-10 In the course of your examination of the financial statements of Bartlett Limited as of December 31, 1998, the following entry came to your attention:

January 4, 1998

Receivable from Insurance Company	1,000,000	
Cash Surrender Value of Life Insurance Policies		136,000
Retained Earnings		159,000
Donated Capital from Life Insurance Proceeds		705,000

(Disposition of the proceeds of the life insurance policy on Mr. Bartlett's life. Mr. Bartlett died on January 1, 1998.)

You are aware that Mr. Tom Bartlett, an officer-shareholder in the small manufacturing firm, insisted that the corporation's board of directors authorize the purchase of an insurance policy to compensate for any loss of earning potential on his death. The corporation paid $295,000 in premiums prior to Mr. Bartlett's death, and was the sole beneficiary of the policy. At the date of death, there had been no premium prepayment and no rebate was due. In prior years, cash surrender value in the amount of $136,000 had been recorded in the accounts.

Instructions

(a) What is the cash surrender value of a life insurance policy?

(b) How should the cash surrender value of a life insurance policy be classified in the financial statements while the policy is in force? Why?

(c) Comment on the propriety of the January 4, 1998 entry.

Part A. To manufacture and sell its products, a company must invest in inventories, plant and equipment, and other operating assets. In addition, a manufacturing company often finds it desirable or necessary to invest a portion of its available resources, either directly or through the operation of special funds, in shares, bonds, and other securities. ***C10-11**

Instructions

(a) List the reasons why a manufacturing company might invest funds in shares, bonds, and other securities.

(b) What are the criteria for classifying investments as current or noncurrent assets?

Part B. Because of favourable market prices, the trustee of Gail Andersen Company's bond sinking fund invested the current year's contribution to the fund in the company's own bonds. The bonds are being held in the fund without cancellation. The fund also includes cash and securities of other companies.

Instructions

Describe three methods of classifying the bond sinking fund on the balance sheet of Gail Andersen Company. Include a discussion of the propriety of using each method.

Gibson Inc. administers the sinking fund applicable to its own outstanding long-term bonds. The following four proposals relate to the accounting treatment of sinking fund cash and securities: ***C10-12**

1. To mingle sinking fund cash with general cash and sinking fund securities with other securities, and to show both as current assets on the balance sheet.

2. To keep sinking fund cash in a separate bank account and sinking fund securities separate from other securities, but on the balance sheet to treat cash as a part of the general cash and the securities as part of general investments, both being shown as current assets.

3. To keep sinking fund cash in a separate bank account and sinking fund securities separate from other securities, but to combine the two accounts on the balance sheet under one caption, such as Sinking Fund Cash and Investments, which will be listed as a noncurrent asset.

4. To keep sinking fund cash in a separate bank account and sinking fund securities separate from other securities, and to identify each separately on the balance sheet among the current assets.

Instructions

Identify the proposal that is most appropriate. Give the reasons for your selection.

USING YOUR JUDGEMENT

FINANCIAL REPORTING PROBLEM

Refer to the financial statements of Moore Corporation Limited presented in Appendix 5A and answer the following questions.

1. Does the legal entity, Moore Corporation Limited, hold investments in other companies? Explain.

2. For 1995 and 1994, list each type of investment Moore holds. Identify, for each, its balance sheet classification and the method of accounting and reporting used. What does this tell you about the relationship between Moore Corporation and these other companies?

3. Can you identify the amount of investment income recognized on the income statement for each type of investment?

4. Explain what the balance sheet account "Equity of minority shareholders in subsidiary corporations" and the income statement account "Minority interests" represent.

5. Did investments accounted for using the equity method generate more income than dividends or more dividends than income during 1995? Explain.

ETHICS CASE

Clark Manufacturing holds a portfolio of shares as a short-term marketable security. The market value of the portfolio is greater than its original cost, even though some holdings have decreased in value. Hector Gonzales, the financial vice-president, and Arthur Vanderbilt, the controller, are considering the sale of a part of this stock portfolio. Gonzales wants to sell only those holdings that have increased in value, in order to increase net income this year. Vanderbilt disagrees and wants to sell securities that have recently declined in value. He contends that the company is having a good earnings year and therefore the losses will help to smooth the income this year. As a result, the company will have built up gains for future periods when the company may not be as profitable.

Instructions
Is there anything unethical in what each proposes? Who are the stakeholders affected by their proposals?

chapter 11

ACQUISITION AND DISPOSITION OF TANGIBLE CAPITAL ASSETS

Acquisition and Disposition of Tangible Capital Assets

Learning Objectives

After studying this chapter, you should be able to:

1. Describe the major characteristics of property, plant, and equipment.

2. Identify the costs included in the initial valuation of land, buildings, and equipment.

3. Describe the accounting problems associated with self-constructed assets.

4. Describe the accounting problems associated with interest capitalization.

5. Understand accounting issues related to acquiring and valuing plant assets.

6. Describe the accounting treatment for costs subsequent to acquisition.

7. Describe the accounting treatment for the disposal of property, plant, and equipment.

8. Compute the amount of capitalizable interest on projects involving expenditures over a period of time and borrowings from different sources at varying rates (Appendix 11A).

Capital assets are defined as identifiable assets that meet both of the following criteria.

1. **They are acquired for use in operations and not for resale.** Only assets used in the normal operations of the business should be classified as capital assets. An idle building held for sale is more appropriately classified separately as an investment; land held by land developers or subdividers is classified as inventory.

2. **They are long-term in nature and usually subject to depreciation (amortization).** Capital assets yield services over a number of years. The investment in these assets is assigned to future periods though periodic depreciation or amortization charges. The exception is land, which is not depreciated unless a material decease in value occurs, such as loss of fertility in agricultural land because of poor crop rotation, drought, or soil erosion.

The asset category entitled "capital assets" was first used in accounting standards in 1992 with the adoption of *CICA Handbook* Section 3060. This category includes identifiable tangible assets (property, plant, and equipment) and intangible assets (i.e., assets that lack physical substance). Most Canadian companies report capital assets under two separate headings: **"property, plant, and equipment"** (tangible capital assets) and **"intangible assets."**

This chapter discusses the basic accounting problems associated with (1) the incurrence and types of costs related to tangible capital assets (property, plant, and equipment); and (2) the accounting methods used to record the retirement or disposal of these costs. Depreciation, also referred to as amortization,[1] allocates the costs of property, plant, and equipment to accounting periods, as presented in Chapter 12 (Depreciation and Depletion). Accounting for intangible assets is discussed in Chapter 13.

CHARACTERISTICS OF PROPERTY, PLANT, AND EQUIPMENT

Almost every business enterprise of any size or activity uses assets of a durable nature in its operations. Such assets are commonly referred to as **property, plant, and equipment assets;** or **plant assets;** or **fixed assets.** They include land, building structures (offices, factories, warehouses), and equipment (machinery, furniture, tools). The three terms describing these assets are used interchangeably throughout this textbook. Property, plant, and equipment display the two characteristics of capital assets described above, but also possess physical substance. Physical existence or substance differentiates tangible from intangible assets such as patents or goodwill. Unlike raw material, however, property, plant, and equipment do not physically become part of a product held for resale.

OBJECTIVE 1
Describe the major characteristics of property, plant, and equipment.

ACQUISITION OF PROPERTY, PLANT, AND EQUIPMENT

Historical cost is the usual basis for valuing property, plant, and equipment. **Historical cost is measured by the cash or cash equivalent price of obtaining the asset and bringing it to the location and condition necessary for its intended use**. The purchase price, freight costs, provincial sales taxes, and installation costs of a productive asset are considered part of the asset's cost. These costs are allocated to future periods through depreciation. Any related costs incurred **after the asset's acquisition**, such as additions, improvements, or replacements, are **added to the asset's cost if they provide future service potential.** Otherwise they are expensed immediately.

OBJECTIVE 2
Identify the costs included in the initial valuation of land, buildings, and equipment.

Cost should be the basis used at the acquisition date because the cash or cash equivalent price best measures the asset's value at that time. Disagreement does exist concerning differences between historical cost and other valuation methods, such as replacement cost or fair market value, that can arise after acquisition. Writing up fixed asset values is not considered appropriate in ordinary circumstances. Although minor exceptions are noted (during, for example, financial reorganizations), current standards indicate that departures from historical cost are rare.

The main reasons for this position are (1) at the date of acquisition, cost reflects fair value; (2) historical cost involves actual, not hypothetical, transactions and is therefore the most reliable; and (3) gains and losses should not be anticipated but should be recognized when the asset is sold.

Several other valuation methods have been considered, such as (1) constant dollar accounting (adjustments for general price-level changes); (2) current cost accounting (adjustments for specific price-level changes); (3) net realizable value; or (4) a combination of constant dollar accounting and current cost or net realizable value. These alternative valuation concepts are discussed in Appendix 25A, Accounting for Changing Prices.

COST OF LAND

All expenditures made to acquire land and to ready it for use should be considered as part of the land cost. Land costs typically include (1) the purchase price; (2) closing costs,

---

[1] The *CICA Handbook* permits the use of either "amortization" or "depreciation." The term depreciation is used in this book because it is more frequently used by Canadian public companies than amortization.

such as title to the land, attorney's fees, and recording fees; (3) costs incurred to condition the land for its intended use (e.g., grading, filling, draining, and clearing); (4) assumption of any liens, such as taxes in arrears or mortgages or encumbrances on the property; and (5) any additional land improvements that have an indefinite life.

When land has been purchased for the purpose of constructing a building, all costs incurred up to the excavation for the new buildings are considered land costs. **Removal of old buildings, clearing, grading, and filling are considered costs of the land because these costs are necessary to get the land in condition for its intended purpose**. Any proceeds obtained in the process of getting the land ready for its intended use, such as salvage receipts on the demolition of an old building or the sale of timber that has been cleared, are treated as **reductions in the price of the land**.

In some cases, the purchaser of land has to assume certain obligations on the land, such as back taxes or liens. In such situations, the cost of the land is the cash paid for it, plus the encumbrances. In other words, if the purchase price of the land is $50,000 cash, but accrued property taxes of $5,000 and liens of $10,000 are assumed, the cost of the land is $65,000.

Special assessments for local improvements such as pavement, street lights, sewers, and drainage systems are usually charged to the Land account because they are relatively permanent and are maintained and replaced by the local government body. In addition, if the improvement made by the owner is rather permanent in nature, such as landscaping, then the item is properly chargeable to the Land account. **Improvements with limited lives**, such as private driveways, walks, fences, and parking lots, are best recorded separately as Land Improvements so that they can be depreciated over their estimated lives.

Generally, land is considered part of property, plant, and equipment. If the major purpose of acquiring and holding land is speculative, however, it is more appropriately classified as an investment. If the land is held by a real estate concern for resale, it should be classified as part of inventory.

In cases where land is held as an investment, the accounting treatment given taxes, insurance, and other direct costs incurred while holding the land is a controversial problem. Many believe these costs should be capitalized because the revenue from the investment still has not been received. This approach is reasonable and seems justified except in cases where the asset is currently producing revenue (such as rental property).

Cost of Buildings

The cost of buildings should include all expenditures related directly to their acquisition or construction. These costs include (1) materials, labour, and overhead costs incurred during construction; and (2) professional fees and building permits. Generally, companies contract to have their buildings constructed. All costs incurred, from excavation to completion, are considered part of the building costs.

One accounting problem is deciding what to do about an old building that is on the site of a newly proposed building. Is the cost of removal of the old building a cost of the land or a cost of the building? The answer is that if land is purchased with an old building on it, then the cost of demolition less its salvage value is a cost of getting the land ready for the intended use and relates to the land rather than to the new building. As indicated earlier, all costs of getting the asset ready for its intended use are costs of that asset.

Cost of Equipment

The term "equipment" in accounting includes delivery equipment, office equipment, machinery, furniture and fixtures, furnishings, factory equipment, and similar capital assets. The cost of such assets includes the purchase price, freight and handling charges incurred, insurance on the equipment while in transit, cost of special foundations if required, assembling and installation costs, and costs of conducting trial runs. Costs thus include all expenditures incurred in acquiring the equipment and preparing it for use. The goods and services tax (GST) is an exception to this rule. GST paid on assets acquired is treated as an Input Tax Credit used to reduce the amount of GST payable.

SELF-CONSTRUCTED ASSETS

Occasionally companies (particularly in the railway and utility industries) construct their own assets. Determining the cost of such machinery and other capital assets can be a problem. Without a purchase price or contract price, the company must allocate costs and expenses to arrive at the cost of the **self-constructed asset**. Materials and direct labour used in construction pose no problem; these costs can be traced directly to work and material orders related to the fixed assets constructed.

OBJECTIVE 3
Describe the accounting problems associated with self-constructed assets.

However, the assignment of indirect costs of manufacturing creates special problems. These indirect costs, called overhead or burden, include power, heat, light, insurance, property taxes on factory buildings and equipment, factory supervisory labour, depreciation of fixed assets, and supplies.

These costs may be handled in one of three ways.

1. **Assign no fixed overhead to the cost of the constructed asset.** The major reason for this treatment is that indirect overhead is generally fixed in nature and does not increase as a result of constructing one's own plant or equipment. This approach assumes that the company will have the same costs regardless of whether the company constructs the asset or not, so to charge a portion of the overhead costs to the equipment will normally relieve current expenses and consequently overstate income of the current period. In contrast, variable overhead costs that increase as a result of the construction should be assigned to the cost of the asset.

2. **Assign a portion of all overhead to the construction process.** This approach, a full costing concept, is appropriate if one believes that costs attach to all products and assets manufactured or constructed. This procedure assigns overhead costs to construction as it would to normal production. It is employed extensively because most accountants believe a better matching of costs with revenues is obtained. Advocates say that failure to allocate overhead costs understates the initial cost of the asset and results in an inaccurate future allocation.

3. **Allocate on the basis of lost production.** A third alternative is to allocate to the construction project the cost of any curtailed production that occurs because the asset is built instead of purchased. This method is conceptually appealing, but is based on "what might have occurred"—an opportunity cost concept—which is difficult to measure.

A pro rata portion of the fixed overhead should be assigned to the asset to obtain its cost. This treatment is employed extensively because most accountants believe a better matching of costs with revenues is obtained. If the allocated overhead results in recording the construction costs in excess of the costs that would be charged by an outside independent producer, the excess overhead should be recorded as a period loss rather than capitalized to avoid capitalizing the asset at more than its probable market value.

OBJECTIVE 4
Describe the accounting problems associated with interest capitalization.

INTEREST COSTS DURING CONSTRUCTION

The proper accounting for interest costs has been a long-standing controversy. Three approaches have been suggested to account for the interest incurred in financing the construction or acquisition of property, plant, and equipment.

1. **Capitalize no interest charges during construction.** Under this approach, interest is considered a cost of financing and not a cost of construction. It is contended that if the company had used equity financing rather than debt financing, this expense would not have been incurred. The major argument against this approach is that an implicit interest cost is associated with the use of cash regardless of its source; if equity financing is employed, a real cost exists to the shareholders although a contractual claim does not develop.

2. **Capitalize only the actual interest costs incurred during construction.** This approach relies on the historical cost concept that only actual transactions are recorded. It is argued that interest incurred is as much a cost of acquiring the asset as the cost of the materials, labour, and other resources used. As a result, a company that uses debt financing will have an asset of higher cost than an enterprise that uses equity financing. The results achieved by this approach are held to be unsatisfactory by some because the cost of an asset should be the same whether cash, debt financing, or equity financing is employed.

3. **Charge construction with all costs of funds employed, whether identifiable or not.** This method maintains that one part of the cost of construction is the cost of financing, whether by debt, cash, or equity financing. An asset should be charged with all costs necessary to get it ready for its intended use. Interest, whether actual or imputed, is a cost of building, just as labour, materials, and overhead are costs. A major criticism of this approach is that imputation of a cost of equity capital is subjective and outside the framework of an historical cost system.

The profession generally supports the second approach: Actual interest may be capitalized in accordance with the concept that the historical cost of acquiring an asset includes all costs (including interest costs) incurred to bring the asset to the condition and location necessary for its intended use. As a result, capitalization of interest is permitted.[2] Implementing this general approach requires consideration of three items:

1. Qualifying assets.
2. Capitalization period.
3. Amount to capitalize.

Qualifying Assets. **To qualify for interest capitalization, assets must require a period of time to get ready for their intended use.** Interest costs may be capitalized starting with the first expenditure related to the asset, and continues until the asset is substantially completed and ready for its intended use.

Assets that qualify for interest cost capitalization include assets under construction for an enterprise's own use (including buildings, plants, and large machinery) and assets intended for sale or lease that are constructed or otherwise produced as discrete projects (ships or real estate developments).

Examples of assets that do not qualify for interest capitalization are (1) assets that are in use or ready for their intended use; and (2) assets that are not used in the earnings activities of the enterprise or that are not undergoing the activities necessary to get them ready for use (such as land that is not being developed and assets not being used because of obsolescence, excess capacity, or need for repair).

Capitalization Period. The capitalization period is the period of time during which interest may be capitalized. It begins when three conditions are present.

---

[2] *CICA Handbook*, Section · 3060, par. .26.

1. Expenditures for the asset have been made.

2. Activities that are necessary to get the asset ready for its intended use are in progress.

3. Interest cost is being incurred.

Interest capitalization **continues as long as those three conditions are present**. The capitalization period should end when the asset is substantially complete and ready for its intended use.

Amount to Capitalize. The amount of interest capitalized is subject to professional judgement.[3] To be capitalized, interest should be directly attributable to the project. This, in many cases, is difficult to measure. One method of identifying the amount "directly attributable" uses the lower of actual interest cost incurred during the period and avoidable interest. **Avoidable interest** is the amount of interest cost incurred during the period that theoretically could have been avoided if expenditures for the asset had not been made.

To apply the avoidable interest concept, the potential amount of interest to be capitalized during an accounting period may be determined by multiplying the interest rate(s) by the **weighted-average amount of** accumulated expenditures for qualifying assets during the period.

Weighted-Average Accumulated Expenditures. In computing weighted-average accumulated expenditures, the construction expenditures are weighted by the amount of time (fraction of a year or accounting period) that interest cost could be incurred on the expenditure. To illustrate, assume a 17-month bridge construction project with expenditures for the current year of $240,000 on March 1; $480,000 on July 1; and $360,000 on November 1. The weighted-average accumulated expenditure for the year ended December 31 is computed as follows.

COMPUTATION OF WEIGHTED-AVERAGE ACCUMULATED EXPENDITURES

Date	Expenditures	×	Capitalization Period*	=	Average Accumulated Expenditures
March 1	240,000		10/12		200,000
July 1	480,000		6/12		240,000
Nov 1	360,000		2/12		60,000
	$1,080,000				$500,000

*Months between the date of expenditures and the date interest capitalization stops, or end of year, whichever comes first (in this case, December 31).

To compute the weighted-average accumulated expenditures, we weight the expenditures by the amount of time that interest cost could be incurred on each one. For the March 1 expenditure, 10 months' interest cost can be associated with the expenditure. For the expenditure on July 1, only six months' interest cost can be incurred. For the expenditure made on November 1, only two months' interest cost can be incurred.

Interest Rates. Certain principles are used to select appropriate interest rates for application to weighted-average accumulated expenditures.

---

[3] In accordance with *CICA Handbook*, par. 1000.49 (b), professional judgement may be based on such factors as analogous situations in the *Handbook, Accounting Guidelines*; International Accounting Standards; accounting standards established in other jurisdictions; and CICA research studies. Since the *Handbook* does not provide any guidelines for the measurement of interest to be capitalized, FASB #34 is used in this discussion. There may be other appropriate methods of measuring capitalizable interest.

1. For the portion of weighted-average accumulated expenditures that is less than or equal to any amounts borrowed specifically to finance construction of the assets, **use the interest rate incurred on the specific borrowings**.

2. For the portion of weighted-average accumulated expenditures that is greater than any debt incurred specifically to finance construction of the assets, **use a weighted average of interest rates incurred on all outstanding debt during the period**.[4]

An illustration of the computation of a weighted-average interest rate for debt greater than the amount incurred specifically to finance construction of the assets is shown below.

COMPUTATION OF WEIGHTED-AVERAGE INTEREST RATE

	Principal	Interest
12%, 2-year note	$ 600,000	$ 72,000
9%, 10-year bonds	2,000,000	180,000
7.5%, 20-year bonds	5,000,000	375,000
	$7,600,000	$627,000

$$\text{Weighted-average interest rate} = \frac{\text{Total interest}}{\text{Total principal}} = \frac{\$627,000}{\$7,600,000} = 8.25\%$$

Special Issues Related to Interest Capitalization. Three issues related to interest capitalization that merit special attention are:

1. Expenditures for land.

2. Interest revenue.

3. Significance of interest capitalization.

Expenditures for Land. When land is purchased with the intention of developing it for a particular use, interest costs associated with those expenditures could be capitalized. If the land is purchased as a site for a structure (such as a plant site), interest costs capitalized during the period of construction are part of the cost of the plant, not of the land. Conversely, if land is being developed for lot sales, any capitalized interest cost should be part of the acquisition cost of the developed land. However, interest costs involved in purchasing land that is held **for speculation** should **not** be capitalized because the asset is ready for its intended use.

Interest Revenue. Companies frequently borrow money to finance construction of assets and temporarily invest the excess borrowed funds in interest-bearing securities until the funds are needed to pay for construction. During the early stages of construction, interest revenue earned may exceed the interest cost incurred on the borrowed funds. The question is whether it is appropriate to offset interest revenue against interest cost when determining the amount of interest to be capitalized as part of the construction cost of assets. If it is assumed that short-term investment decisions are not related to the interest incurred as part of the acquisition cost of assets, then interest revenue **should not** be netted with

---

[4] Various interest rates may be used. For our purposes, we will use the specific borrowing rate followed by the average interest rate because we believe it to be more conceptually consistent. For a discussion of this issue and others related to interest capitalization see Kathryn M. Means and Paul M. Kazenski, "SFAS 34: Receipt for Diversity," *Accounting Horizons*, September, 1998.

capitalized interest. Some accountants are critical of this because a company may defer the interest cost but report the interest revenue in the current period.

Many Canadian companies have adopted this method of capitalizing interest, while others use different methods of determining the amount to be capitalized. Some refuse to capitalize interest.[5] Many believe that "interest should be capitalized on all pre-earning assets"[6] while others argue that no interest cost should be capitalized. An example showing the calculation, recording, and reporting of capitalized interest is presented in Appendix 11A.

ACQUISITION AND VALUATION

We have seen that **an asset should be recorded at the fair market value of what is given up to acquire it, or at its own fair market value, whichever is more clearly evident**. Fair market value, however, is sometimes obscured by the process through which the asset is acquired. As an example, assume that land and buildings are bought together for one price. How are separate values for the land and buildings determined? A number of accounting problems of this nature are examined in the following sections.

OBJECTIVE 5
Understand accounting issues related to acquiring and valuing plant assets.

CASH DISCOUNTS

When plant assets are purchased subject to cash discounts for prompt payment, how should the discount be reported? If the discount is taken, it should be considered a reduction in the purchase price of the asset. What is not clear, however, is whether a reduction in the asset cost should occur if the discount is not taken.

Two points of view exist on this matter. Under one approach, the discount, whether taken or not, is considered a reduction in the cost of the asset. The rationale for this approach is that the real cost of the asset is the cash or cash equivalent price of the asset. In addition, some argue that the terms of cash discounts are so attractive that failure to take them indicates management error or inefficiency. Proponents of the other approach argue that the discount should not always be considered a loss because the terms may be unfavourable or because it may not be prudent for the company to take the discount. At present, both methods are employed in practice. The former method is generally preferred.

DEFERRED PAYMENT CONTRACTS

Plant assets are purchased frequently on long-term credit contracts through the use of notes, mortgages, bonds, or equipment obligations. **To properly reflect cost, assets purchased on long-term credit contracts should be accounted for at the present value of the consideration exchanged between the contracting parties at the date of the transaction.** For example, an asset purchased today in exchange for a $10,000 noninterest-bearing note payable four years from now should not be recorded at $10,000. The present value of the $10,000 note establishes the exchange price of the transaction (the purchase price of the asset). Assuming an appropriate interest rate of 12% at which to discount this single payment of $10,000 due four years from now, this asset should be recorded at $6,355.20 [$10,000 × .63552; see Table A-2 for the present value of an amount, $p = \$10,000 \ (p_{\overline{4}|12\%})$].

When no interest rate is stated or if the specified rate is unreasonable, an appropriate interest rate must be imputed. The objective is to approximate the interest rate that the

---

[5] See John M. Boersema and Mark van Helden, "The Case Against Interest Capitalization." *CA Magazine*, December, 1986, pp. 58–60.

[6] J. Alex Milburn, *Incorporating the Time Value of Money Within Financial Accounting* (Toronto: CICA, 1998).

buyer and seller would negotiate at arm's length in a similar borrowing transaction. Such factors to be considered in imputing an interest rate are the borrower's credit rating, the amount and maturity date of the note, and prevailing interest rates. If determinable, the cash exchange price of the asset acquired should be used as the basis for recording the asset and for measuring the interest element.

To illustrate, Sutter Company purchases a specially built robot spray painter for its production line. The company issues a $100,000, five-year, noninterest-bearing note to Wrigley Robotics, Ltd. for the new equipment when the prevailing market rate of interest for obligations of this nature is 10%. Sutter is to pay off the note in five $20,000 instalments at the end of each year. The fair market value of this particular specially built robot is not readily determinable and must therefore be approximated by establishing the market value (present value) of the note. Computation of the present value of the note and entries at the date of purchase and the dates of payment are as follows.

At date of purchase

Equipment	75,816*	
Discount on Notes Payable	24,184	
Notes Payable		100,000

*Present value of note = $20,000 $(P_{\overline{5}|10\%})$
= $20,000 (3.79079) (Table A-4)
= $75,816

At end of first year

Interest Expense	7,582	
Notes Payable	20,000	
Cash		20,000
Discount on Notes Payable		7,582

Interest expense under the effective interest approach is $7,582 [($100,000 − $24,184) × 10%]. The entry at the end of the second year to record interest and to pay off a portion of the note is as follows.

At end of second year

Interest Expense	6,340	
Notes Payable	20,000	
Cash		20,000
Discount on Notes Payable		6,340

Interest expense in the second year under the effective interest approach is $6,340 [($100,000 − $24,184) − ($20,000 − $7,582)] × 10%.

If an interest rate is not imputed in such deferred payment contracts, the asset will be recorded at an amount different than its fair value. In addition, interest expense will be understated in the income statement in all periods involved.

LUMP SUM PURCHASE

A special problem of pricing fixed assets arises when a group of plant assets is purchased at a single **lump sum price**. When such a situation occurs, and it is not at all unusual, the practice is to allocate the total cost among the various assets on the basis of their relative fair market values. The assumption is that costs will vary in direct proportion to sales value. This is the same principle that was applied to allocate a lump sum cost among different inventory items.

To determine fair market value, any of the following might be used: an appraisal for insurance purposes, the assessed valuation for property taxes, or simply an independent appraisal by an engineer or other appraiser.

To illustrate, Norduct Heating Ltd. decides to purchase several assets of a small heating, concern, Carefoot Heating, for $80,000. Carefoot Heating is in the process of liquidation, and its assets sold are as below.

	Book Value	Fair Market Value
Inventory	$30,000	$ 25,000
Land	20,000	25,000
Building	35,000	50,000
	$85,000	$100,000

The $80,000 purchase price would be allocated on the basis of the relative fair market values in the following manner.

Inventory $\dfrac{\$25,000}{\$100,000} \times \$80,000 = \$20,000$

Land $\dfrac{\$25,000}{\$100,000} \times \$80,000 = \$20,000$

Building $\dfrac{\$50,000}{\$100,000} \times \$80,000 = \$40,000$

ISSUANCE OF SHARES

When property is acquired by issuance of securities, such as common shares, the cost of the property is not properly measured by the average issuance price of such shares. If the shares are being actively traded, **the market value of the shares issued is a fair indication of the cost of the property acquired because this value is a good measure of the current cash equivalent price**.

For example, Upgrade Living Co. decides to purchase some adjacent land for expansion of its carpeting and cabinet operation. In lieu of paying cash for the land, the company issues to Deedland Company 5,000 no-par value common shares that have a fair market value of $12 per share. Upgrade Living Co. would make the following entry.

Land (5,000 × $12)	60,000	
Common Shares		60,000

If the market value of common shares exchanged is not determinable, the market value of the property should be established and used as a basis for recording the asset and issuance of the common shares.[7]

EXCHANGES OF PROPERTY, PLANT, AND EQUIPMENT (NONMONETARY ASSETS)

The proper accounting for exchanges of nonmonetary assets (such as inventories and property, plant, and equipment) is controversial.[8] Some accountants argue that the accounting for these types of exchanges should be based on the fair value of the asset

---

[7] When the fair market value of the shares is used as the basis of valuation, careful consideration must be given to the effect that the issuance of additional shares will have on the existing market price. Where the effect on market price appears significant, an independent appraisal of the asset received should be made. This valuation should be employed as the basis for valuation of the asset as well as for the shares issued. In the unusual case where the fair market value of the shares or the fair market value of the asset cannot be determined objectively, the board of directors of the corporation may set the value.

[8] Nonmonetary assets are items whose price in terms of the monetary unit may change over time, whereas monetary assets are fixed in terms of units of currency by contract or otherwise, for example, cash and short- or long-term accounts and notes receivable.

given up or the fair value of the asset received with a gain or loss recognized. Others believe that the accounting should be based on the recorded amount (book value) of the asset given up with no gain or loss recognized. Still others favour an approach that recognizes losses in all cases, but defers gains in special situations.

Ordinarily, accounting for exchange of nonmonetary assets should be based on **the fair value of the asset given up or the fair value of the asset received, whichever is clearly more evident**.[9] Thus, any gains or losses on the exchange should be recognized immediately. The rationale for this approach is that **the earnings process related to these assets is completed** and, therefore, gains or losses should be recognized. This approach is always employed when **the assets exchanged are dissimilar in nature**, such as the exchange of land for a building, or the exchange of equipment for inventory. If the fair value of either asset is not reasonably determinable, the book value of the asset given up is usually used as the basis for recording the nonmonetary exchange.

The general rule is modified when an exchange involves **similar nonmonetary assets and little or no monetary consideration is given or received**. For example, when a company exchanges inventory items for inventory of another company because of colour, size, etc. to facilitate sale to an outside customer, the earnings process is not considered culminated and a gain or loss should not be recognized. Likewise, if a company trades similar productive assets (assets held for or used in the production of goods or services) such as land for land or equipment for equipment, the enterprise is not considered to have completed the earnings process and, therefore, a gain or loss should not be recognized.[10]

Gains on exchange of similar nonmonetary assets should be recognized when the **amount of monetary consideration received or given is not minimal** (i.e., greater than 10% of the fair value of the total consideration received or given). In these instances exchanges of similar nonmonetary assets are accounted for in the same way as exchanges of dissimilar assets.

In summary, gains or losses on nonmonetary transactions are always recognized when the exchange involves dissimilar assets. When similar assets are exchanged and cash is received or given up, gains or losses are recognized unless the amount of cash involved is less than 10% of the estimated fair value of the total consideration given or received.[11] When the cash or some other form of monetary consideration involved is minimal, the cost of the asset received is equal to the book value of the asset(s) given up plus the cash given or minus any cash received.

To illustrate the accounting for these different types of transactions, the discussion is divided into three sections as follows.

1. Accounting for dissimilar assets.

2. Accounting for similar assets.

3. Accounting for similar assets when little or no cash is received or given up.

Dissimilar Assets. The cost of a nonmonetary asset acquired in exchange for a **dissimilar nonmonetary asset** is usually recorded at the **fair value of the assets given up**, and a gain or loss is recognized. The **fair value of the asset received** should be used only if it is more clearly evident than the fair value of the assets given up.

To illustrate, Neufeld Transportation Limited exchanges a number of used trucks plus cash for vacant land that may be used for a future plant site. The trucks have a combined

---

[9] *CICA Handbook* (Toronto: CICA), par. 3830.05.
[10] *CICA Handbook* (Toronto: CICA), par. 3830.08.
[11] *Ibid.*

book value of $42,000 (cost $64,000 less $22,000 accumulated depreciation). Neufeld's purchasing agent, who has previous dealings in the second-hand market, indicates that the trucks have a fair market value of $49,000. In addition to the trucks, Neufeld must pay $17,000 cash for the land. The cost of the land is $66,000, computed as follows.

	Computation of Land Cost
Fair value of trucks exchanged	$49,000
Cash paid	17,000
Cost of land	**$66,000**

The journal entry to record the exchange transaction is:

Land	66,000	
Accumulated Depreciation—Trucks	22,000	
Trucks		64,000
Gain on Disposal of Trucks		7,000
Cash		17,000

The gain is the difference between the fair value of the trucks and their book value. It is verified as follows.

	Computation of Gain	
Fair value of trucks		$49,000
Cost of trucks	$64,000	
Less accumulated depreciation	22,000	
Book value of trucks		42,000
Gain on disposal of used trucks		**$ 7,000**

It follows that if the fair value of the trucks is $39,000 instead of $49,000, a loss on the exchange of $3,000 ($42,000 − $39,000) will be reported. In either case, as a result of the exchange of dissimilar assets, the earnings process on the used trucks has been completed and **a gain or loss should be recognized**.

Similar Assets. Similar nonmonetary assets are those of the same general type, that perform the same function, or are employed in the same line of business. Generally, when similar nonmonetary assets are exchanged and a gain or loss results, the gain or loss should be recognized. For example, Information Processing, Inc. trades its used computer for a new model. The computer given up has a book value of $8,000 (original cost $12,000 less $4,000 accumulated depreciation) and an estimated fair value of $6,000. It is traded for a new model that has a list price of $16,000. In negotiations with the seller, a trade-in allowance of $9,000 is finally agreed on for the used computer. The cash payment that must be made for the new asset and the cost of the new computer are computed as follows.

	Cost of New Machine
List price of new computer	$16,000
Less trade-in allowance for used computer	9,000
Cash payment due	7,000
Fair value of used computer	6,000
Cost of new machine	**$13,000**

The journal entry to record this transaction is:

Equipment	13,000	
Accumulated Depreciation—Equipment	4,000	
Loss on Disposal of Equipment	2,000	
Equipment		12,000
Cash		7,000

The loss on the disposal of the used computer can be computed as follows.

	Computation of Loss
Fair value of used computer	$6,000
Book value of used computer	8,000
Loss on disposal of used computer	**$2,000**

Why is the trade-in allowance for the old asset not used as a basis for the new equipment? The trade-in allowance is not employed because it includes a price concession (similar to a price discount) to the purchaser. For example, few individuals pay list price for a new car. Trade-in allowances on the used car are often so inflated that actual selling prices are below list prices. To record the car at list price would be to state it at an amount in excess of its cash equivalent price because the new car's list price is usually inflated. Use of book value in this situation would overstate the value of the new computer by $2,000. Because assets should not be valued at more than their cash equivalent price, the loss should be recognized immediately rather than added to the cost of the acquired asset.

Similar Assets: Little or No Cash Received or Given. The accounting treatment for exchanges of similar nonmonetary assets when little or no cash is received or given is more complex. In these instances, no gain or loss is recognized unless the exchange completes the earning process.

The real estate industry provides a good example of why the accounting profession decided not to recognize gains on certain exchanges of similar nonmonetary assets. In this industry, it is common practice for companies to "swap" estate holdings. Assume Landmark Company and Hillfarm, Inc. each had undeveloped land on which they intended to build shopping centres. Appraisals indicated that the land of both companies had increased significantly in value. The companies decided to exchange (swap) their undeveloped land, record a gain, and report their new parcels of land at current fair value. But should gains be recognized at this point? The answer is no; the earnings process has not been completed because the companies remain in the same economic position after the swap as before it. Therefore, the asset acquired should be recorded at book value with no gain or loss recognized.

Davis Rent-A-Car has a rental fleet of automobiles that are primarily Ford Motor Company products. Davis' management is interested in increasing the variety of automobiles in its rental fleet by adding numerous General Motors models. Davis arranges with Nertz Rent-A-Car to exchange a group of Ford automobiles with a fair value of $160,000 and a book value of $135,000 (cost $150,000 less accumulated depreciation $15,000) for a number of Chevy and Pontiac models with a fair value of $170,000. Davis pays $10,000 in cash in addition to the Ford automobiles exchanged. The total gain to Davis Rent-A-Car is computed as follows.

	Computation of Gain
Fair value of Ford automobiles exchanged	$160,000
Book value of Ford automobiles exchanged	135,000
Total gain (unrecognized)	**$25,000**

Because the earnings process is not considered completed and there was a minimal amount of cash given in this transaction, the total gain is deferred and the basis of the General Motors automobiles is reduced via two different but acceptable computations, as shown below.

Basis of New Automobiles to Davis			
Fair value of GM automobiles	$170,000	Book value of Ford automobiles	$135,000
Less gain deferred	(25,000) OR	Cash paid	10,000
Basis of GM automobiles	$145,000	Basis of GM automobiles	$145,000

The entry by Davis to record this transaction is as follows.

Automobiles (GM)	145,000	
Accumulated Depreciation—Automobiles	15,000	
Automobiles (Ford)		150,000
Cash		10,000

The gain that reduces the basis of the new automobiles will be recognized when those automobiles are sold to an outside party. If these automobiles are held for an extended period of time, depreciation charges will be lower and net income higher in subsequent periods because of the reduced basis.

Presented below in summary form are the accounting requirements for recognizing gains and losses on exchanges of **nonmonetary assets**

1. Compute the total gain or loss on the transaction, which is equal to the difference between the fair value of the asset given up and the book value of the asset given up.
2. If a gain or loss is computed in (1),
   (a) and the earnings process is considered complete, the entire gain or loss is recognized (dissimilar assets).
   (b) and the earnings process is not considered complete (similar assets) and monetary consideration given or received is greater than 10% of the total consideration received or given, the entire gain or loss is recognized.
   (c) and the earnings process is not considered complete (similar assets) and little or no monetary consideration is involved, no gain or loss is recognized. The asset received is recorded at the carrying value of the asset adjusted by the amount of monetary consideration received or given in the exchange.

An enterprise that engages in nonmonetary exchanges during a period should disclose the nature, the basis of measurement, and the amount of any resulting gains or losses in their financial statements.[12]

ACCOUNTING FOR CONTRIBUTIONS OF ASSETS

Companies sometimes receive or make contributions (i.e., donations or gifts). Such contributions are referred to as **nonreciprocal transfers** because they are transfers of assets in one direction. Contributions are often some type of asset (cash, securities, land, buildings, or use of facilities), but they also could be the forgiveness of a debt.

---

[12] *CICA Handbook* (Toronto: CICA), Section 3830, par. .13.

When assets are acquired as a donation, a strict cost concept dictates that the valuation of the asset should be zero. A departure from the cost principle seems justified because the only costs incurred (legal fees and other relatively minor expenditures) do not constitute a reasonable basis of accounting for the assets acquired. To record nothing, we believe, is to ignore the economic realities of an increase in wealth and assets. Therefore, **the appraisal or fair market value of the asset should be used to establish its value on the books.**

Two general approaches have been used to record the credit for the asset received. Some believe the credit should be to Donated Capital, a contributed surplus account. The increase in assets is viewed more as contributed capital than as earned revenue. To illustrate, Max Wayer Meat Packing, Inc. has recently accepted a donation of land with a fair value of $150,000 from the City of Burlington in return for a promise to build a packing plant in Burlington. Max Wayer's entry is:

Land	150,000	
Donated Capital		150,000

Others argue that capital is contributed only by the owners of the business; donations are therefore benefits to the enterprise and should be reported as revenue from contributions. Whether the revenue should be reported immediately or over the period that the asset is employed is another consideration. To attract new industry, a city may offer land; the receiving enterprise, however, may incur additional costs in the future (transportation, higher taxes, etc.) because the location is not the most desirable. As a consequence, some argue that the revenue should be deferred and recognized as these costs are incurred.

Regardless of whether assets or funds to acquire assets are received from federal, provincial, or municipal governments, Section 3800 of the *Handbook* requires that recipients follow prescribed accounting methods. These methods are based on a "revenue approach" that requires that the amount received should be deferred and recognized over the period that the related assets are employed. This is accomplished by either reducing the cost of the asset by the amount of government assistance received, or recording the amount of assistance received from the various governmental sources as a deferred credit and amortizing it to revenue over the life of the related asset. To illustrate, Max Wayer Meat Packing, Inc. has recently received a grant of $225,000 from the federal government to upgrade its sewage treatment facility. The entry to record receipt of the grant, if Max Wayer wishes to use the cost reduction method, will be as follows:

Cash	225,000	
Equipment		225,000

This results in the equipment being carried on the books at cost minus the related government assistance. As a result, the annual depreciation charge for the equipment will be reduced over its useful life and net income will be increased.

Alternatively, an unrealized revenue account can be credited with the amount of the grant. This unrealized revenue account will then be amortized periodically to income over a term equal to the useful life of the equipment. The entries to record receipt of the grant and amortization for the first year (assuming a 10-year term) will be as follows.

Cash	225,000	
Deferred Revenue—Government Grants		225,000
Deferred Revenue—Government Grants	22,500	
Revenue—Government Grants		22,500

It should be emphasized that whether the capital approach or the unrealized revenue approach is used, if the donation is contingent upon some performance (such as building a plant), this contingency should be reported in the notes to the financial statements.

In practice, enterprises record cash from governments (grants) related to current expenses and revenues to flow through the income statement, while cash and noncash donations from shareholders and other nongovernment entities or individuals are generally credited to an appropriate contributed surplus account.

COSTS SUBSEQUENT TO ACQUISITION

After plant assets are installed and ready for use, additional costs are incurred that range from ordinary repair costs to significant additions. The major problem is allocating these costs subsequent to acquisition to the proper time periods. **In general, costs incurred to achieve greater future benefits should be capitalized, whereas expenditures that simply maintain a given level of services should be expensed**. In order for costs to be capitalized, one of three conditions must be present:

OBJECTIVE 6
Describe the accounting treatment for costs subsequent to acquisition.

1. The useful life of the asset must be increased.

2. The quantity of units produced from the asset must be increased.

3. The quality of the units produced must be enhanced.

Expenditures that do not increase an asset's future benefits should be expensed. Ordinary repairs are expenditures that maintain the existing condition of the asset or restore it to normal operating efficiency and should be expensed immediately.

Most expenditures below an established arbitrary minimum amount are expensed rather than capitalized. Many enterprises have adopted the rule that expenditures below, say, $100 or $500 should always be expensed. Although conceptually this treatment may not be correct, expediency demands it. Otherwise, accountants would have to set up depreciation schedules for such things as wastepaper baskets and ashtrays.

The distinction between a **capital (asset)** and **revenue (expense) expenditure** is not always clear-cut. For example, determination of the **property unit** with which costs should be associated is critical. If a fully equipped steamship is considered a property unit, then replacement of the engine might be considered an expense. On the other hand, if the ship's engine is considered a property unit, then its replacement would be capitalized. It follows that the disposition and treatment of many items require considerable analysis and judgement before the proper distinction can be made. In most cases, consistent application of a capital/expense policy is justified as more important than attempting to provide general theoretical guidelines for each entry.

Generally, four major types of expenditures are incurred relative to existing assets.

MAJOR TYPES OF EXPENDITURES

1. **Additions.** Increase or extension of existing assets.

2. **Improvements and replacements.** Substitution of an improved asset for an existing one.

3. **Rearrangement and reinstallation.** Movement of assets from one location to another.

4. **Repairs.** Expenditures that maintain assets in condition for operation.

ADDITIONS

Additions should present no major accounting problems. By definition, **any addition to plant assets is capitalized** because a new asset has been created. The addition of a wing to a hospital or the addition of an air conditioning system to an office, for example, increases the service potential of that facility. Such expenditures should be capitalized and matched against the revenues that will result in future periods.

The most difficult problem that develops in this area is accounting for any changes related to the existing structure as a result of the addition. Is the cost that is incurred to tear down a wall of the old structure to make room for the addition a cost of the addition or an expense or loss of the period? The answer is that it depends on the original intent. If the company had anticipated that an addition was going to be added later, then this cost of removal is a proper cost of the addition. But if the company had not anticipated this development, it should properly be reported as a loss in the current period on the basis that the company was inefficient in its planning. Normally, the carrying amount of the old wall remains in the accounts, although theoretically it should be removed.

IMPROVEMENTS AND REPLACEMENTS

Improvements (often referred to as **betterments**) and **replacements** are substitutions of one asset for another. What is the difference between an improvement and a replacement? An improvement is the substitution of a **better asset** for the one currently used (say, a concrete floor for a wooden floor). A replacement, on the other hand, is the substitution of a **similar asset** (a wooden floor for a wooden floor).

Many times improvements and replacements occur as a result of a general policy to modernize or rehabilitate an older building or piece of equipment. The problem is differentiating these types of expenditures from normal repairs. Does the expenditure increase the **future service potential** of the asset, or does it merely **maintain the existing level** of service? Frequently the answer is not clear-cut, and good judgement must be used in order to classify these expenditures properly.

If it is determined that the expenditure increases the future service potential of the asset and, therefore, should be capitalized, this capitalization is handled in one of three ways, depending on the circumstances.

1. **Substitution approach.** Conceptually, the substitution approach is the correct procedure if the carrying amount of the old asset is available. If the carrying amount of the old asset can be determined, it is a simple matter to remove the cost of the old asset and replace it with the cost of the new asset.

   To illustrate, Instinct Enterprises decides to replace the pipes in its plumbing system. A plumber suggests that in place of the cast iron pipes and copper tubing, a newly developed plastic tubing be used. The old pipe and tubing has a book value of $15,000 (cost of $150,000 less accumulated depreciation of $135,000), and a fair market value of $1,000. The plastic tubing system has a market value of $125,000. Assuming that Instinct has to pay $124,000 for the new tubing after exchanging the old tubing, the entry is:

Plumbing System	125,000	
Accumulated Depreciation	135,000	
Loss on Disposal of Plant Assets	14,000	
Plumbing System		150,000
Cash		124,000

The problem with this approach is determining the book value of the old asset. Generally, the components of a given asset depreciate at different rates, but no separate accounting is made. As an example, the tires, motor, and body of a truck depreciate at different rates, but most concerns use only one depreciation rate for the entire truck. Separate depreciation rates could be set for each component, but it would be impractical. If the carrying amount of the old asset cannot be determined, one of two other approaches is adopted.

2. **Capitalizing the new cost.** The justification for capitalizing the cost of the improvement or replacement is that even though the carrying amount of the old asset is not removed from the accounts, sufficient depreciation was taken on the item to reduce the carrying amount almost to zero. Although this assumption may not be true in every case, in many situations the differences are not often significant. Improvements especially are handled in this manner.

3. **Charging to Accumulated Depreciation.** There are times when the quantity or quality of the asset itself has not been improved, but its useful life has been extended. Replacements, particularly, may extend the useful life of the asset, yet they may not improve the quality or quantity of service or product produced. In these circumstances, the expenditure may be debited to Accumulated Depreciation rather than to the asset account. The theory behind this approach is that the replacement extends the useful life of the asset and thereby recaptures some or all of the past depreciation. The net carrying amount of the asset is the same whether the asset is debited or the accumulated depreciation is debited.

REARRANGEMENT AND REINSTALLATION

Rearrangement and reinstallation costs, which are expenditures intended to benefit future periods, are different from additions, replacements, and improvements. An example is the rearrangement or reinstallation of a group of machines to facilitate future production. If the original installation cost and the accumulated depreciation taken to date can be determined or estimated, the rearrangement and reinstallation cost may properly be handled as a replacement. If not, which is generally the case, the new costs (if material in amount) should be capitalized as an asset to be amortized over those future periods expected to benefit.[13] If these costs are not material, or if they cannot be separated from other operating expenses, or if their future benefit is questionable, they should be immediately expensed.

REPAIRS

Ordinary repairs are expenditures made to maintain plant assets in operating condition; they are charged to an expense account in the period in which they are incurred on the basis that **it is the primary period benefited.** Replacement of minor parts, lubricating and adjusting of equipment, repainting, and cleaning are examples of maintenance charges that occur regularly and are treated as ordinary operating expenses.

It is often difficult to distinguish a repair from an improvement or replacement. The major consideration is whether the expenditure benefits more than one year or one operating cycle, whichever is longer. If a **major repair,** such as an overhaul, occurs, several periods will benefit and the cost should be handled as an addition, improvement, or replacement.

---

[13] Another cost of this nature is relocation costs. For example, when Shell Oil moved its world headquarters from New York to Houston, it amortized the cost of relocating over four years. Conversely, relocation costs necessitated by the company's move to Calgary were charged to revenue. The point is that no definitive guidelines have been established in this area, and generally costs are deferred over some arbitrary period in the future. Some writers have argued that these costs should generally be expensed as incurred. See, for example, Charles W. Lamden, Dale L. Gerboth, and Thomas W. McRae, "Accounting for Depreciable Assets," *Accounting Research Monograph No. 1* (New York: AICPA, 1975), pp. 54–61.

If income statements are prepared for short periods of time, say, monthly or quarterly, the same principles must still apply. Ordinary repairs and other regular maintenance charges for an annual period may benefit several quarters, and allocation of the cost among periods concerned may be required. A concern will often find it advantageous to concentrate its repair program at a certain time of the year, perhaps during the period of least activity or when the plant is shut down for vacation. Short-term comparative statements may be misleading if such expenditures are shown as expenses of the quarter in which they are incurred. To give comparability to monthly or quarterly income statements, an account such as Allowance for Repairs may be used so that repair costs are better assigned to periods benefited.

To illustrate, Cricket Tractor Company estimates that its total repair expense for the year will be $720,000. It decides to charge each quarter for a portion of the repair cost even though the total cost for the year will occur in only two quarters.

End of first quarter (zero repair costs incurred)

Repair Expense	180,000	
Allowance for Repairs (1/4 × $720,000)		180,000

End of second quarter ($344,000 repair costs incurred)

Allowance for Repairs	344,000	
Cash, Wages Payable, Inventory, etc.		344,000
Repair Expense	180,000	
Allowance for Repairs (1/4 × $720,000)		180,000

End of third quarter (zero repair costs incurred)

Repair Expense	180,000	
Allowance for Repairs (1/4 × $720,000)		180,000

End of fourth quarter ($380,800 repair costs incurred)

Allowance for Repairs	380,800	
Cash, Wages Payable, Inventory, etc.		380,800
Repair Expense	184,800	
Allowance for Repairs		184,800
($344,000 + $380,800 − $180,000 − $180,000 − 180,000)		

Ordinarily, no balance in the Allowance for Repairs account should be carried over to the following year. The fourth quarter will normally absorb the variation from estimates. If balance sheets are prepared during the year, the Allowance account should be added to or subtracted from the Property, Plant, and Equipment section to obtain a proper valuation.

Some accountants advocate accruing estimated repair costs beyond one year on the assumption that depreciation does not take into consideration the incurrence of repair costs. For example, in aircraft overhaul and open hearth furnace rebuilding, an allowance for repairs is sometimes established because the amount of repairs can be estimated with a high degree of certainty. Although conceptually appealing, it is difficult to justify the Allowance for Repairs account as a liability because one may ask, To whom do you owe the liability? Placement in the Shareholders' Equity section is also illogical because no addition to the shareholders' investment has taken place. One possibility is to treat allowance for repairs as an addition to or subtraction from the asset on the basis that the value has changed. In general, expenses should not be anticipated before they arise unless estimates of the future costs are reasonably accurate.

SUMMARY

The following schedule summarizes the accounting treatment for various costs incurred subsequent to the acquisition of capitalized assets.

SUMMARY OF COSTS SUBSEQUENT TO ACQUISITION OF PROPERTY, PLANT, AND EQUIPMENT

Type of Expenditure	Normal Accounting Treatment
Additions	Capitalize cost to asset account.
Improvements and Replacements	(a) **Carrying value known:** Remove cost of and accumulated depreciation on old asset, recognizing any gain or loss. Capitalize cost of improvement/replacement.
	(b) **Carrying value unknown:** 1. If the asset's useful life is extended, debit accumulated depreciation for cost of improvement/replacement. 2. If the quantity or quality of the assets' productivity is increased, capitalize cost of improvement/replacement to asset account.
Rearrangement and Reinstallation	(a) If original installation cost is **known**, account for cost of rearrangement/reinstallation as a replacement (carrying value known).
	(b) If original installation cost is **unknown** and rearrangement/ replacement cost is **material** in amount and benefits future periods, capitalize as an asset.
	(c) If original installation cost is **unknown** and rearrangement/ reinstallation cost is **not material or future benefit is questionable**, expense the cost when incurred.
Repairs	(a) **Ordinary:** Expense cost of repairs when incurred.
	(b) **Major:** As appropriate, treat as an addition, improvement, or replacement.

DISPOSITIONS OF PLANT ASSETS

Plant assets may be retired voluntarily or disposed of by sale, exchange, involuntary conversion, or abandonment. Regardless of the time of disposal, depreciation should be taken up to the date of disposition, and all accounts related to the retired asset should be removed. Ideally, the book value of the specific plant asset will be equal to its disposal value. But this is generally not the case. As a result, a gain or loss develops.

The reason: depreciation is an estimate of cost allocation and not a process of valuation. **The gain or loss is really a correction of net income** for the years during which the fixed asset was used. If it had been possible at the time of acquisition to forecast the exact date of disposal and the amount to be realized at disposition, then a more accurate estimate of depreciation will be recorded and no gain or loss will have been incurred.

Gains and losses on the retirement of plant assets should be shown in the income statement along with other items that arise from customary business activities. If, however, the "operations of a segment of a business" are sold, abandoned, spun off, or otherwise disposed of, then the results of "continuing operations" should be reported separately from "discontinued operations." Any gain or loss from disposal of a segment of a business should be reported with related results of discontinued operations and not as an extraordinary item. These reporting requirements were discussed in Chapter 4.

OBJECTIVE 7
Describe the accounting treatment for the disposal of property, plant, and equipment.

SALE OF PLANT ASSETS

Depreciation must be recorded for the period of time between the date of the last depreciation entry and the date of sale. To illustrate, assume that depreciation on a machine costing $18,000 has been recorded for nine years at the rate of $1,200 per year. If the machine is sold in the middle of the tenth year for $7,000, the entry to record depreciation to the date of sale is:

Depreciation Expense	600	
Accumulated Depreciation of Machinery		600

This separate entry ordinarily is not made because most companies enter all depreciation, including this amount, in one entry at the end of the year. In either case the entry for the sale of the asset is:

Cash	7,000	
Accumulated Depreciation of Machinery	11,400	
($1,200 × 9 plus $600)		
Machinery		18,000
Gain on Disposal of Machinery		400

The book value of the machinery at the time of the sale is $6,600 ($18,000–$11,400); because it is sold for $7,000, the gain on the sale is $400.

INVOLUNTARY CONVERSION

Sometimes, an asset's service is terminated through some type of **involuntary conversion** such as fire, flood, theft, or expropriation. The gains and losses are treated no differently from those in any other type of disposition except that **they are often reported in the Extraordinary Items section of the income statement**.

To illustrate, Camel Transport Corp. was forced to sell a plant located on company property that stood directly in the path of a proposed highway. For a number of years the province had sought to purchase the land on which the plant stood but the company resisted. The province ultimately exercised its right of eminent domain and was upheld by the courts. In settlement, Camel received $500,000, which was substantially in excess of the $200,000 book value of the plant and land (cost of $400,000 less accumulated depreciation of $200,000). The following entry was made.

Cash	500,000	
Accumulated Depreciation of Plant Assets	200,000	
Plant Assets		400,000
Gain on Disposal of Plant Assets		300,000

The gain or loss that develops on these types of unusual, nonrecurring transactions that are not a result of management actions should normally be shown as an extraordinary item in the income statement. Similar treatment would be given to other types of involuntary conversions, such as those resulting from a major casualty (such as an earthquake) or an expropriation, assuming that they meet the conditions for extraordinary item treatment. The difference between the amount recovered (expropriation award or insurance recovery), if any, and the book value of the asset would be reflected as a gain or loss.

MISCELLANEOUS PROBLEMS

If an asset is scrapped or abandoned without any cash recovery, a loss should be recognized in the amount of the asset's book value. If scrap value exists, the gain or loss that occurs is the difference between the asset's scrap value and its book value. If an asset still can be used even though it is fully depreciated, either the asset may be kept on the books at historical cost less its related depreciation or the asset may be carried at scrap value.

OTHER ASSET VALUATION METHODS

We have assumed that cost is the appropriate basis for valuing assets at acquisition. The major exception has been the acquisition of plant assets through donation, in which case valuation is based on fair value. Another approach that is sometimes allowed and not considered a violation of historical cost is a concept often referred to as **prudent cost**. This concept states that if for some reason you are ignorant about a certain price and pay too much for the asset originally, it is theoretically preferable to charge a loss immediately.

As an example, assume that a company constructs an asset at a cost substantially in excess of its present economic usefulness. In this case, an appropriate procedure is to charge these excess costs as a loss to the current period, rather than to capitalize them as part of the cost of the asset. This problem seldom develops because at the outset individuals either use good reasoning in paying a given price or fail to recognize any such errors.

On the other hand, a purchase that is obtained at a bargain, or a piece of equipment internally constructed at what amounts to a cost savings, should not result in immediate recognition of a gain under any circumstances. Although immediate recognition of a gain is conceptually appealing, the implications of such a treatment will completely change the entire basis of accounting.

DISCLOSURE OF TANGIBLE CAPITAL ASSETS

Canadian firms are required to disclose certain details about their capital assets. These details include: (1) cost; (2) accumulated depreciation (amortization); (3) depreciation method(s) and rate(s) used, and any write-downs charged to income in the current year. Large public companies show the net amount of property, plant, and equipment on the balance sheet using captions such as "Property, Plant, and Equipment," "Fixed Assets," or "Capital Assets." In addition, they provide a note containing details of category cost and accumulated depreciation. A note describing the depreciation policy is included with the accounting policy notes. An example of such disclosure taken from the annual report of Industra Service Corporation is presented in Illustration 11-1 below.

EXHIBIT 11-1   INDUSTRA SERVICE CORPORATION

CONSOLIDATED BALANCE SHEETS

	December 31	
(expressed in Canadian dollars)	1995	1994
Property, plant and equipment (Note 5)	6,797,755	6,170,730
Goodwill at cost, net of accumulated amortization		
and write-off of $3,888,064 (1994 – $3,776,400)(Note 6)	531,000	493,000
	$25,522,380	$25,316,018

(e)   *Depreciation and amortization*

Buildings, fabrication machinery, mobile and other equipment are depreciated on a straight-line basis over the following periods based on their estimated useful lives:

Mobile equipment, tools and office equipment	3 to 10 years
Fabrication machinery and equipment	20 years
Buildings	15 to 35 years

5.   **Property, plant and equipment**

1995	Cost	Accumulated depreciation	Net
Buildings	$ 3,098,854	$ 513,813	$2,585,041
Fabrication machinery, mobile and other equipment	7,177,925	4,408,546	2,769,379
Land	1,443,335	–	1,443,335
	$11,720,114	$4,922,359	$6,797,755

1994	Cost	Accumulated depreciation	Net
Buildings	$ 2,789,795	$ 406,297	$2,383,498
Fabrication machinery, mobile and other equipment	5,742,730	3,398,833	2,343,897
Land	1,443,335	–	1,443,335
	$ 9,975,860	$3,805,130	$6,170,730

HIGH TECH ASSETS

Telesat Canada's Anik B satellites are some of the "highest" high tech assets in Canada (35,800 km above earth). The cargo aboard represents some of the world's mot advanced communications equipment. These satellites also present some interesting accounting problems: ownership, components of cost, and the possibility of "site" restoration costs.

Ownership. Since the satellites are not domiciled on the planet earth, title is not based on the statutes of any country. Instead, use is assured by agreement among certain nations. Thus, Telesat's titles to these three hundred million dollar assets are based on continuing goodwill and cooperation of competing entities. Is this a sufficient basis on which to claim ownership?

Cost. The cost of placing an Anik satellite into an orbital position is very high when compared to "earth bound" assets. The rocket launch is very hazardous and the necessary insurance coverage is expensive. Thus, these otherwise incidental costs to make the assets ready for their intended use are disproportionately high.

Site Restoration Costs. The international community is becoming more aware of the amount of "space junk" in orbit around the earth. Other satellites have been directed back into the earth's atmosphere and burnt up. However, when control over a satellite is lost, it becomes a ahazard floating around in space. Removing these objects would be very costly is a special space flight to capture and retrieve the useless asset is involved. Thus, with the possibility of very significant costs and a degree of uncertainty about whether they will be incurred or not, accruing the site restoration costs involves difficult judgements.

Summary of Learning Objectives

1. **Describe the major characteristics of property, plant, and equipment.** The major characteristics of property, plant, and equipment are (1) they are acquired for use in operations and not for resale; (2) they are long-term in nature and usually subject to depreciation; and (3) they possess physical substance.

2. **Identify the costs included in the initial valuation of land, buildings, and equipment.** Cost of land: Includes all expenditures made to acquire land and to ready it for use. Land costs typically include (1) the purchase price; (2) closing costs, such as title to the land, attorney's fees, and registration fees; (3) costs incurred in getting the land in condition for its intended use, such as grading, filling, draining, and clearing; (4) assumption of any liens, mortgages, or encumbrances on the property; and (5) any additional land improvements that have an indefinite life.

   Cost of buildings: Includes all expenditures related directly to their acquisition or construction. These costs include (1) materials, labour, and overhead costs incurred during construction; and (2) professional fees and building permits.

   Cost of equipment: Includes the purchase price, freight and handling charges incurred, insurance on the equipment while in transit, cost of special foundations if required, assembling and installation costs, and costs of conducting trial runs.

3. **Describe the accounting problems associated with self-constructed assets.** The assignment of indirect costs of manufacturing creates special problems because these costs cannot be traced directly to work and material orders related to the fixed assets constructed. These costs might be handled in one of three ways: (1) assign no fixed overhead to the cost of the constructed asset; (2) assign a portion of all overhead to the construction process; or (3) allocate on the basis of lost production. The second method is used extensively in practice.

4. **Describe the accounting problems associated with interest capitalization.** Only actual interest (with modifications) may be capitalized. The rationale for this approach is that during construction, the asset is not generating revenue and therefore interest cost should be deferred (capitalized); once construction is complete, the asset is ready for its intended use and revenues can be earned. Any interest cost incurred in purchasing an asset that is ready for its intended use should be expensed.

5. **Understand accounting issues related to acquiring and valuing plant assets.** The following issues relate to acquiring and valuing plant assets: (1) *Cash discounts:* Whether taken or not, these are generally considered a reduction in the cost of the asset; the real cost of the asset is the cash or cash equivalent price of the asset; (2) *Assets purchased on long-term credit contracts:* Account for these at the present value of the consideration exchanged between the contracting parties; (3) *Lump sum purchase:* Allocate the total cost among the various assets on the basis of their relative fair market values; (4) *Issuance of shares:* If the shares are actively traded, the market value of the shares issued is a fair indication of the cost of the property acquired; if the market value of the shares exchanged is not determinable, the value of the property should be established and used as the basis for recording the asset and share issuance; (5) *Exchanges of property, plant, and equipment:* See the illustration on page 543 for a summary of how to account for exchanges; (6) *Contributions:* Should be recorded at the fair value of the asset received and a related credit should be made to revenue for the same amount.

6. **Describe the accounting treatment for costs subsequent to acquisition.** See the illustration on page 549 for a summary of how to account for costs subsequent to acquisition.

7. **Describe the accounting treatment for the disposal of property, plant, and equipment.** Regardless of the time of disposal, depreciation must be taken up to the date of disposition, and then all accounts related to the retired asset should be removed. Gains or losses on the retirement of plant assets should be shown in the income statement along with other items that arise from customary business activities. Gains or losses on involuntary conversions should be reported as extraordinary items. If an asset is scrapped or abandoned without any cash recovery, a loss should be recognized equal to the asset's book value. If scrap value exists, the gain or loss that occurs is the difference between the asset's scrap value and its book value.

KEY TERMS

rearrangement and reinstallation costs, 547

replacements, 546

revenue (expense) expenditure, 545

self-constructed asset, 533

similar nonmonetary assets, 540

weighted-average accumulated expenditures, 535

APPENDIX 11A

Illustration of Interest Capitalization

OBJECTIVE 8
Compute the amount of capitalizable interest on projects involving expenditures over a period of time and borrowings from different sources at varying rates.

To illustrate the issues related to interest capitalization, assume that on November 1, 1997 Shalla Company contracted with Pfeifer Construction Co. to have a building constructed for $1,400,000 on land costing $100,000 (purchased from the contractor and included in the first payment). Shalla made the following payments to the construction company during 1998.

January 1	March 1	May 1	December 31	Total
$210,000	$300,000	$540,000	$450,000	$1,500,000

Construction was completed and the building was ready for occupancy on December 31, 1998. Shalla Company had the following debt outstanding at December 31, 1998.

Specific Construction Debt

1. 15% three-year note to finance construction of the building, dated
   December 31, 1997, with interest payable annually on December 31. $750,000

Other Debt

2. 10% five-year note payable, dated December 31, 1994, with interest
   payable annually on December 31. $550,000

3. 12%, 10-year bonds issued December 31, 1993, with interest
   payable annually on December 31. $600,000

The weighted-average accumulated expenditures during 1998 are computed as follows.

COMPUTATION OF WEIGHTED-AVERAGE ACCUMULATED EXPENDITURES				
Date	Expenditures	×	Capitalization Period	=	Average Accumulated Expenditures
January 1	$ 210,000		12/12		$210,000
March 1	300,000		10/12		250,000
May 1	540,000		8/12		360,000
November 1	450,000		0		0
	$1,500,000				$820,000

Note that the expenditure made on December 31, the last day of the year, does not have any interest cost.

The avoidable interest can be computed as follows.

COMPUTATION OF AVOIDABLE INTEREST

Weighted-Average Accumulated Expenditures	×	Interest Rate	=	Avoidable Interest
$750,000		.15 (construction note)		$112,500
70,000		11.04 (weighted average of		
$820,000		other debt)*		7,728
				$120,228

*Weighted-average interest rate computation:

	Principal	Interest
10%, Five-year note	$ 550,000	$ 55,000
12%, 10-year bonds	600,000	72,000
	$1,150,000	$127,000

$$\frac{\text{Total interest}}{\text{Total principal}} = \frac{\$\ 127,000}{\$1,150,000} = 11.04\%$$

Avoidable interest: $120,228

The actual interest cost, representing the maximum amount of interest that may be capitalized during 1998, is computed as follows.

Construction note	$750,000 × .15	=	$112,500
Five-year note	$550,000 × .10	=	55,000
Ten-year bonds	$600,000 × .12	=	72,000
Actual interest			**$239,500**

The interest cost to be capitalized is the lesser of $120,228 (avoidable interest) and $239,500 (actual interest), which is $120,228.

The journal entries to be made by Shalla Company during 1998 would be as follows.

January 1

Land	100,000	
Building (or Construction in Process)	110,000	
Cash		210,000

March 1

Building	300,000	
Cash		300,000

May 1

Building	540,000	
Cash		540,000

December 31

Building	450,000	
Cash		450,000

Building	120,228	
Interest Expense ($239,500 − $120,228)	119,272	
Cash ($112,500 + $55,000 + $72,000)		239,500

Capitalized interest should be written off over the useful life of the assets involved as part of depreciation and not over the term of the debt. The total interest cost incurred during the period should be disclosed; the portion charged to expense and the portion capitalized should be indicated.

At December 31, 1998, Shalla should report the amount of interest capitalized either as part of the nonoperating section of the income statement or in the notes accompanying the financial statements. Both forms of disclosure are illustrated below.

CAPITALIZED INTEREST REPORTED IN THE INCOME STATEMENT		
Income from operations		XXX
Other expenses and losses:		
Interest expense	$239,500	
Less capitalized interest	120,228	119,272
Income before income taxes		XXXXX
Income tax expense		XXX
Net income		XXXX

Capitalized Interest Disclosed in a Note

Note 1—Accounting Policies

Capitalized interest. During 1998 total interest cost was $239,500, of which $120,228 was capitalized and $119,272 was charged to expense.

Summary of Learning Objective for Appendix 11A

8. **Compute the amount of capitalizable interest on projects involving expenditures over a period of time and borrowings from different sources at varying rates.** The amount of interest that may be capitalized must be diclosed in the notes to the financial statements.

Note: All *asterisked* Exercises, Problems, or Cases relate to material contained in the appendix to the chapter.

EXERCISES

E11-1   **(Acquisition Costs of Realty)** The following expenditures and receipts are related to land, land improvements, and buildings acquired for use in a business enterprise. The receipts are enclosed in parentheses:

1. Money borrowed to pay building contractor (signed a note)	$(250,000)
2. Payment for construction from note proceeds	250,000
3. Cost of land fill and clearing	8,000
4. Delinquent real estate taxes on property assumed by purchaser	7,000
5. Premium on six-month insurance policy during construction	6,000
6. Refund of one-month insurance premium because construction completed early	(1,000)
7. Architect's fee on building	22,000
8. Cost of real estate purchased as a plant site (land $200,000 and building $50,000)	250,000

9. Commission fee paid to real estate agency — 9,000
10. Installation of fences around property — 4,000
11. Cost of razing and removing building — 11,000
12. Proceeds from salvage of demolished building — (5,000)
13. Interest paid during construction on money borrowed for construction — 13,000
14. Cost of parking lots and driveways — 21,000
15. Cost of trees and shrubbery planted (permanent in nature) — 12,000
16. Excavation costs for new building — 3,000
17. G.S.T. on excavation cost — 210

Instructions

Identify each item by number and list the items in columnar form, as shown below. All receipt amounts should be reported in parentheses. For any amounts entered in the Other Accounts column, also indicate the account title.

Item	Land	Land Improvements	Building	Other Accounts

(Acquisition Costs of Realty) Paton Inc. purchased land as a factory site for $500,000. The process of tearing down two old buildings on the site and constructing the factory required six months. **E11-2**

The company paid $42,000 to raze the old buildings and sold salvaged lumber and brick for $4,300. Legal fees of $1,850 were paid for title registration and drawing the purchase contract. Payment of $2,200 was made to an engineering firm for a land survey and for drawing the factory plans, $68,000. The land survey had to be made before definitive plans could be drawn. A liability insurance premium paid during construction cost $900. The contractor's charge for construction was $2,840,000. The company paid the contractor in two instalments: $1,200,000 at the end of three months and $1,640,000 upon completion. Interest costs of $170,000 were incurred to finance the construction.

Instructions

Determine the cost of the land and the cost of the building as they should be recorded on the books of Paton Inc. Assume that the land survey was for the building.

(Acquisition Costs of Trucks) McArthur Company operates a retail computer store. To improve delivery services to customers, the company purchases four new trucks on April 1, 1998. The terms of acquisition for each truck are described below: **E11-3**

1. Truck #1 has a list price of $15,000 and is acquired for a cash payment of $14,200.

2. Truck #2 has a list price of $16,000 and is acquired for a down payment of $3,000 cash and noninterest-bearing note with a face amount of $13,000. The note is due April 1, 1999. McArthur would normally have to pay interest at a rate of 10% for such a borrowing, and the dealership has an incremental borrowing rate of 8%.

3. Truck #3 has a list price of $16,000. It is acquired in exchange for a computer system that McArthur carries in inventory. The computer system cost $12,000 and is normally sold by McArthur for $15,500. McArthur uses a perpetual inventory system.

4. Truck #4 has a list of $14,000. It is acquired in exchange for 1,000 of McArthur's no-par value common shares. The shares have a market value of $13 per share.

Instructions

Prepare the appropriate journal entries for the foregoing transactions for McArthur Company.

(Purchase and Self-Constructed Cost of Assets) Woolworth Distribution both purchases and constructs various equipment it uses in its operation. The following items for two different types of equipment were recorded in random order during the calendar year 1998. **E11-4**

Purchase

Cash paid for equipment, including sales tax of $6,000 and G.S.T. of $7,000	$113,000
Freight and insurance cost while in transit	2,000
Cost of moving equipment into place at factory	3,100
Wage cost for technicians to test equipment	4,000
Insurance premium paid during first year of operation on this equipment	1,500
Special plumbing fixtures required for new equipment	8,000
Repair cost incurred in first year of operations related to this equipment	1,300

Construction

Material and purchased parts (gross cost $200,000; failed to take 3% cash discount)	$200,000
Imputed interest on funds used during construction (share financing)	14,000
Labour costs	190,000
Overhead costs (fixed—$20,000; variable—$30,000)	50,000
Profit on self-construction	30,000
Cost of installing equipment	4,400

Instructions

Compute the total cost for each of these two pieces of equipment. If an item is not capitalized as a cost of the equipment, indicate how it should be reported.

E11-5   **(Treatment of Various Costs)** Rommel Supply Company, a newly formed corporation, incurred the following expenditures related to Land, Buildings, Machinery, and Equipment:

Legal fees for title search		$ 520
Architect's fees		2,800
Cash paid for land and dilapidated building thereon		100,000
Removal of old building	$20,000	
Less salvage	5,500	14,500
Surveying before construction		370
Interest on short-term loans during construction		7,400
Excavation before construction for basement		19,000
Machinery purchased (subject to 3% cash discount, which was not taken); record net		55,000
Freight on machinery purchased		1,340
Storage charges on machinery, necessitated by noncompletion of building when machinery was delivered		2,180
New building constructed (building construction took six months from date of purchase of land and old building)		500,000
Assessment by city for drainage project		1,600
Hauling charges for delivery of machinery from storage to new building		620
Installation of machinery		2,000
Trees, shrubs, and other landscaping after completion of building (permanent in nature)		5,400

Instructions

Determine the amounts that should be debited to Land, Buildings, Machinery, and Equipment accounts. Assume the benefits of capitalizing interest during construction exceed the cost of implementation.

E11-6   **(Correction of Improper Cost Entries)** Plant acquisitions for selected companies are as follows:

1. Napoleon Industries Inc. acquired land, buildings, and equipment from a bankrupt company, S. Grant Co., for a lump sum price of $600,000. At the time of purchase, Grant's assets had the following book and appraisal values:

	Book Values	Appraisal Values
Land	$200,000	$150,000
Buildings	250,000	350,000
Equipment	200,000	300,000

To be conservative, the company decided to take the lowest of the two values for each asset acquired. The following entry was made:

Land	150,000	
Buildings	250,000	
Equipment	200,000	
Cash		600,000

2. Bismark Enterprises purchased store equipment by making a $2,000 cash down payment and signing a one-year, $23,000, 10% note payable. The purchase was recorded as follows:

Store Equipment	27,300	
Cash		2,000
Note Payable		23,000
Interest Payable		2,300

3. Omar Bradley Company Inc. purchased office equipment for $30,000, terms 2/10, n/30. Because the company intended to take the discount, it made no entry until it paid for the acquisition. The entry was:

Office Equipment	30,000	
Cash		29,400
Purchase Discounts		600

4. Schwartzkopf Inc. recently received at zero cost land from the Village of Sunset Hills as an inducement to locate their business in the Village. The appraised value of the land is $28,000. The company made no entry to record the land because it had no cost basis.

5. Wellington Company built a warehouse for $600,000. It could have purchased the building for $720,000. The controller made the following entry:

Warehouse	720,000	
Cash		600,000
Profit on Construction		120,000

Instructions
Prepare the entry that should have been made at the date of each acquisition.

(Capitalization of Interest) Sim Furniture Company started construction of a combination office and warehouse building for their own use at an estimated cost of $5,000,000 on January 1, 1998. Sim expects to complete the building by December 31, 1998. Sim has the following debt obligations during the construction period. **E11-7**

Construction loan—12%, interest payable semiannually, issued December 31, 1997	$2,000,000
Short-term loan—10%, interest payable monthly, principal payable at maturity on May 30, 1999	1,400,000
Long-term loan—11%, interest payable on January 1 of each year, principal payable on January 1, 2002	2,000,000

Instructions
(Carry all computations to two decimal places.)

(a) Assume that Sim completed the office and warehouse building on December 31, 1998 as planned at a total cost of $5,200,000 and the weighted average of accumulated expenditures was $4,000,000. Compute the avoidable interest on this project.

(b) Compute the depreciation expense for the year ended December 31, 1999. Sim elected to depreciate the building on a straight-line basis and determined that the asset has a useful life of 10 years.

(Capitalization of Interest) On December 31, 1997, Laurie Petersen Inc. borrowed $3,000,000 at 12%, payable annually, to finance the construction of a new building. In 1998, the company made the following expenditures related to this building: March 1, $360,000; June 1, $600,000; July 1, $1,500,000; December 1, $1,200,000. Additional information is provided as follows: **E11-8**

1. Other debt outstanding

Ten-year, 13% bond, December 31, 1991, interest payable annually	$4,000,000
Six-year, 10% note, dated June 30, 1995, interest payable annually	$1,600,000

2. March 1, 1998 expenditure included land costs of $150,000.

3. Interest revenue earned in 1998 $49,000

Instructions
(a) Determine the amount of interest to be capitalized in 1998 in relation to the construction of the building.

(b) Prepare the journal entry to record the capitalization of interest and the recognition of interest expense, if any, at December 31, 1998.

E11-9   **(Capitalization of Interest)** On July 31, 1998, Scott Company engaged Kevin Tooling to construct a special-purpose piece of factory machinery. Construction was begun immediately and was completed on November 1, 1998. To help finance construction, on July 31 Scott discounted a $300,000, three-year, 12% note payable on which interest is due annually at the Bank of Montreal. $200,000 of the proceeds of the note was paid to Kevin on July 31. The remainder of the proceeds was temporarily invested in short-term marketable securities at 9% until November 1. On November 1, Scott made a final $100,000 payment to Kevin. Other than the note to the Bank of Montreal, Scott's only outstanding liability at December 31, 1998 is a $30,000, 10%, six-year note payable, dated January 1, 1995, on which interest is payable each December 31.

Instructions

(a) Calculate the interest revenue, weighted-average accumulated expenditures, avoidable interest, and total interest cost to be capitalized during 1998. Round all computations to the nearest dollar.

(b) Prepare the journal entries needed on the books of Scott Company at each of the following dates:

1. July 31, 1998.

2. November 1, 1998.

3. December 31, 1998.

E11-10   **(Capitalization of Interest)** The following three situations involve the capitalization of interest.

Situation I. On January 1, 1998, Dorval Inc. signed a fixed-price contract to have Builder Associates construct a major plant facility at a cost of $6,000,000. It was estimated that it would take three years to complete the project. Also on January 1, 1998, to finance the construction cost, Dorval borrowed $6,000,000 payable in 10 annual instalments of $600,000, plus interest at the rate of 12%. During 1998, Dorval made deposit and progress payments totalling $2,500,000 under the contract; the weighted-average amount of accumulated expenditures was $1,100,000 for the year. The excess borrowed funds were invested in short-term securities, from which Dorval realized investment income of $367,500.

Instructions

What amount should Dorval report as capitalized interest at December 31, 1998?

Situation II. During 1998, Brando Construction constructed and manufactured certain assets and incurred the following interest costs in connection with those activities:

	Interest costs incurred
Warehouse constructed for Brando's own use	$30,000
Special-order machine for sale to unrelated customer, produced according to customer's specifications	11,000
Inventories routinely manufactured, produced on a repetitive basis	8,000

All of these assets required an extended period of time for completion.

Instructions

Assuming the effect of interest capitalization is material, what is the total amount of interest cost to be capitalized?

Situation III. Debra Holmes Inc. has a fiscal year ending April 30. On May 1, 1998 Holmes borrowed $10,000,000 at 11% to finance construction of its own building. Repayments of the loan are to commence the month following completion of the building. During the year ended April 30, 1999, expenditures for the partially completed structure totalled $7,000,000. These expenditures were incurred evenly throughout the year. Interest earned on the unexpended portion of the loan amounted to $455,000 for the year.

Instructions

How much should be shown as capitalized interest on Holmes' financial statements at April 30, 1999?

(AICPA adapted)

E11-11   **(Entries for Equipment Acquisitions)** Airdrie Company purchased conveyor equipment with a list price of $21,000. The vendor's credit terms were 2/10, n/30. Presented below are three independent cases related to the equipment. Assume that the purchases of equipment are recorded gross.

(a) Airdrie paid cash for the equipment eight days after the purchase.

(b) Airdrie traded in equipment with a book value of $450 (initial cost, $800), and paid $6,500 in cash one month after the purchase. The old equipment could have been sold for $400 at the date of trade.

(c) Airdrie gave the vendor an $8,502 noninterest-bearing note for the equipment on the date of purchase. The note was due in one year and was paid on time. Assume that the effective interest rate in the market was 9%.

Instructions
Prepare the general journal entries required to record the acquisition and payment in each of the independent cases above. Round to the nearest dollar.

(Entries for Asset Acquisition, Including Self-Construction) Below are transactions related to Arleen Company.   **E11-12**

(a) The City of Lethbridge gives the company 5 ha of land as a plant site. The market value of this land is determined to be $58,000.

(b) 13,000 no-par value common shares are issued in exchange for land and buildings. The property has been appraised at a fair market value of $820,000, of which $190,000 has been allocated to land and $630,000 to buildings. The Arleen Company shares are not listed on any exchange, but a block of 100 shares was sold by a shareholder 12 months ago at $65 per share, and a block of 200 shares was sold by another shareholder 18 months ago at $58 per share.

(c) No entry has been made to remove from the accounts for Materials, Factory Supplies, Direct Labour, and Overhead the amounts properly chargeable to plant asset accounts for machinery constructed during the year. The following information is given relative to costs of the machinery constructed.

Materials used	$ 12,500
Factory supplies used	900
Direct labour incurred	15,000
Additional overhead (over regular) caused by adaptation of equipment to construct special machine	2,200
Fixed overhead rate applied to regular manufacturing operations	60% of direct labour cost
Cost of similar machinery if it had been purchased from outside suppliers	44,000

Instructions
Prepare journal entries on the books of Arleen Company to record these transactions.

(Entries for Acquisition of Assets) Presented below is information related to Vivace Ltd.   **E11-13**

1. On July 6, Vivace Ltd. acquired the plant assets of Starbrand Company, which had discontinued operations. The appraised value of the property is:

Land	$ 400,000
Building	1,200,000
Machinery and Equipment	800,000
Total	$2,400,000

12 500 × 144 =

Vivace Ltd. gave 12,500 of its no-par value common shares in exchange. The shares had a market value of $144 each on the date of the purchase of the property.

2. Vivace Ltd. expended the following amounts in cash between July 6 and December 15, the date when it first occupied the building.

Repairs to building	$105,000
Construction of bases for machinery to be installed later	135,000
Driveways and parking lots	122,000
Remodelling of office space in building, including new partitions and walls	130,000
Special assessment by city	18,000

3. On December 20, the company paid cash for machinery, $250,000, subject to a 2% cash discount, and freight on machinery of $11,500.

Instructions
Prepare entries on the books of Vivace Ltd. for these transactions.

E11-14   (Purchase of Equipment with Noninterest-Bearing Debt) Sebastian Bach, Inc. has decided to purchase equipment from Carman Phillips Industries on January 2, 1998, to expand its production capacity to meet customers' demand for its product. Sebastian Bach issues a $700,000, five-year, noninterest-bearing note to Carman Phillips for the new equipment when the prevailing market rate of interest for obligations of this nature is 12%. The company will pay off the note in five $140,000 instalments due at the end of each year over the life of the note.

Instructions

(a) Prepare the journal entry(ies) at the date of purchase. (Round to nearest dollar in all computations.)

(b) Prepare the journal entry(ies) at the end of the first year to record the payment and interest, assuming that the company employs the effective interest method.

(c) Prepare the journal entry(ies) at the end of the second year to record the payment and interest.

(d) Assuming that the equipment had a 10-year life and no residual value, prepare the journal entry necessary to record depreciation in the first year. (Straight-line depreciation is employed.)

E11-15   (Purchase of Computer with Noninterest-Bearing Debt) Hollerith, Inc. purchased a computer on December 31, 1997, for $90,000, paying $15,000 down and agreeing to pay the balance in five equal instalments of $15,000 payable each December 31 beginning in 1998. An assumed interest of 10% is implicit in the purchase price.

Instructions

(a) Prepare the journal entry(ies) at the date of purchase. (Round to two decimal places.)

(b) Prepare the journal entry(ies) at December 31, 1998, to record the payment and interest (effective interest method employed).

(c) Prepare the journal entry(ies) at December 31, 1999, to record the payment and interest (effective interest method employed).

E11-16   (Nonmonetary Exchange with Boot) Imelda Ltd., which manufactures shoes, hired a recent college graduate to work in the accounting department. On the first day of work, the accountant was assigned to total a batch of invoices with the use of an adding machine. Before long, the accountant, who had never before seen such a machine, managed to break the machine. Imelda Ltd. gave the machine plus $680 to Capek Business Machine Company in exchange for a new machine. Assume the following information about the machines:

	Imelda Ltd. (Old Machine)	Capek Company (New Machine)
Machine cost	$580	$540
Accumulated depreciation	280	-0-
Fair value	170	850

Instructions

For each company, prepare the necessary journal entry to record the exchange.

E11-17   (Nonmonetary Exchange with Boot) Jackson Company purchased an electric wax melter on June 30, 1998 by trading in their old gas model and paying the balance in cash. The following data relate to the purchase:

List price of new melter	$15,800
Cash paid	10,000
Cost of old melter (five-year life, $700 residual value)	11,200
Accumulated depreciation—old melter (straight-line)	6,300
Second-hand market value of old melter	5,200

Instructions

Prepare the journal entry(ies) necessary to record this exchange, assuming that the melters exchanged are (1) similar in nature; (2) dissimilar in nature. Jackson's fiscal year ends on December 31, 1997 and depreciation has been recorded through December 31, 1997.

E11-18   (Nonmonetary Exchange with Boot) Donalda Inc. exchanged equipment used in its manufacturing operations plus $5,000 in cash for similar equipment used in the operations of Liszt Company. The following information pertains to the exchange:

	Donalda Inc.	Liszt Co.
Equipment (cost)	$28,000	$28,000
Accumulated depreciation	19,000	10,000
Fair value of equipment	13,500	15,500
Cash given up	5,000	

Instructions
Prepare the journal entries to record the exchange on the books of both companies.

(Nonmonetary Exchange with Boot) Beethoven Inc. has negotiated the purchase of a new piece of automatic equipment at a price of $8,000 plus trade-in, f.o.b. factory. Beethoven Inc. paid $8,000 cash and traded in used equipment. The used equipment had originally cost $62,000; it had a book value of $42,000 and a second-hand market value of $46,800, as indicated by recent transactions involving similar equipment. Freight and installation charges for the new equipment amounted to $1,100.

E11-19

Instructions
(a) Prepare the general journal entry to record this transaction, assuming that the assets Beethoven Inc. exchanged are similar in nature.
(b) Assuming the same facts as in (a) except that the asset traded in is dissimilar in nature, prepare the general journal entry to record this transaction.

(Analysis of Subsequent Expenditures) Elgar Resources Group has been in its plant facility for fifteen years. Although the plant is quite functional, numerous repair costs are incurred to maintain it in sound working order. The company plant asset book value is currently $800,000, as indicated below:

E11-20

Original cost	$1,200,000
Accumulated depreciation	400,000
	$ 800,000

During the current year, the following expenditures were made to the plant facility:
(a) Because of increased demands for its product, the company increased its plant capacity by building a new addition at a cost of $210,000.
(b) The entire plant was repainted at a cost of $18,000.
(c) The roof was an asbestos cement slate; for safety purposes it was removed and replaced with a wood shingle roof at a cost of $58,000. Book value of the old roof was $39,000.
(d) The electrical system was completely updated at a cost of $21,000. The cost of the old electrical system was not known. It is estimated that the useful life of the building will not change as a result of this updating.
(e) A series of major repairs were made at a cost of $45,000 because parts of the wood structure were rotting. The cost of the old wood structure was not known. These extensive repairs are estimated to increase the useful life of the building.

Instructions
Indicate how each of these transactions would be recorded in the accounting records.

(Analysis of Subsequent Expenditures) The following transactions occurred during 1998. Assume that depreciation of 10% per year is charged on all machinery and 5% per year on buildings, on a straight-line basis, with no estimated residual value. Depreciation is charged for a full year on all fixed assets acquired during the year, and no depreciation is charged on fixed assets disposed of during the year.

E11-21

Jan.	30	A building that cost $92,000 in 1981 is torn down to make room for a new building. The wrecking contractor was paid $5,100 and was permitted to keep all materials salvaged.
Mar.	10	Machinery that was purchased in 1991 for $16,000 is sold for $2,500 cash, f.o.b. purchaser's plant. Freight of $300 is paid on this machinery.
Mar.	20	A gear breaks on a machine that cost $9,000 in 1993 and the gear is replaced at a cost of $370.
May	18	A special base installed for a machine in 1992 when the machine was purchased has to be replaced at a cost of $5,400 because of defective workmanship on the original base. The cost of the machinery was $14,200 in 1992; the cost of the base was $3,500, and this amount was charged to the Machinery account in 1992.

June 23 One of the buildings is repainted at a cost of $7,300. It had not been painted since it was constructed in 1994.

Instructions

Prepare general journal entries for the transactions. (Round to nearest dollar.)

E11-22 **(Analysis of Subsequent Expenditures)** Plant assets often require expenditures subsequent to acquisition. It is important that they be accounted for properly. Any errors will affect both the balance sheets and income statements for a number of years.

Instructions

For each of the following items, indicate whether the expenditure should be capitalized (C) or expensed (E) in the period incurred.

_____ 1. Betterment.

_____ 2. Replacement of a broken part on a machine.

_____ 3. Expenditure that increases the useful life of an existing asset.

_____ 4. Expenditure that increases the efficiency and effectiveness of a productive asset but does not increase the asset's residual value.

_____ 5. Expenditure that increases the efficiency and effectiveness of a productive asset and increases the asset's residual value.

_____ 6. Expenditure that increases the quality of the output of the productive asset.

_____ 7. Improvement to a machine that increased its fair market value and its production capacity by 30% without extending the machine's useful life.

_____ 8. Ordinary repairs.

_____ 9. Improvement.

_____ 10. Interest on borrowing necessary to finance a major overhaul of machinery. The overhaul extended the life of the machinery.

E11-23 **(Entries for Depreciation of Assets)** On December 31, 1997, Greig Inc. has a machine with a book value of $940,000. The original cost and related accumulated depreciation at this date are as follows:

Machine	$1,300,000
Accumulated depreciation	360,000
	$ 940,000

Depreciation is computed at $60,000 per year on a straight-line basis.

Instructions

Presented below are a set of independent situations. For each independent situation, indicate the journal entry to be made to record the transaction. Make sure that depreciation entries are made to update the book value of the machine prior to its disposal.

(a) A fire completely destroys the machine on June 30, 1998. An insurance settlement of $430,000 was received for this casualty. Assume the settlement was received immediately.

(b) On March 1, 1998 Greig sold the machine for $1,040,000 to Peer Gynt Company.

(c) On July 31, 1998, the company donated this machine to the Longview City Council. The fair market value of the machine at the time of the donation was estimated to be $1,000,000.

E11-24 **(Disposition of Assets)** On April 1, 1998, Joplin Company received an award of $400,000 cash as compensation for the forced sale of the company's land and building, which stood in the path of a new provincial highway. The land and building cost $60,000 and $280,000 respectively when they were acquired. At April 1, 1998 the accumulated depreciation relating to the building amounted to $160,000. On August 1, 1998 Joplin purchased a piece of replacement property for cash. The new land cost $80,000, and the new building cost $300,000.

Instructions

Prepare the journal entries to record the transactions on April 1 and August 1, 1998.

*E11-25 **(Capitalization of Interest)** Chopin Inc. is in the process of starting construction on a new machine it intends to use in its operations. Its expenditures to date and related debt outstanding for the month of May are as follows:

Accumulated expenditures (May 1)		$600,000
Expenditures during May		100,000
Trade payables (noninterest-bearing)		
Outstanding May 1	$30,000	
May 31	20,000	
Bank loan at 12%		700,000

Instructions

Determine the amount of interest to capitalize on Chopin's machine for the month of May.

(Capitalization of Interest) Brahms Company is constructing an asset for its own use and has been capitalizing interest on expenditures for the asset since development activities began. The following details are necessary for the current month's entry: *E11-26

Expenditures

Accumulated expenditures (July 1)	$2,000,000
Accumulated expenditures (July 31)	2,200,000

Debt (Outstanding during July)

A short-term, 15% note payable of $1,000,000
A note of $900,000, bearing interest at 12%, specifically for financing
  construction of the asset
A 9% mortgage note of $700,000

Instructions

(a) Compute the weighted-average accumulated expenditures, avoidable interest, and interest to be capitalized for the month of July.
(b) Determine the accumulated expenditure balance at the start of the next month (August 1).

PROBLEMS

At December 31, 1997, certain accounts included in the property, plant, and equipment section of Stefan Limited's   **P11-1**
balance sheet had the following balances:

Land	$230,000
Buildings	890,000
Leasehold improvements	660,000
Machinery and equipment	875,000

During 1998 the following transactions occurred:

1. Land site number 621 was acquired for $850,000. In addition, to acquire the land Stefan paid a $60,000 commission to a real estate agent. Costs of $35,000 were incurred to clear the land. During the course of clearing the land, timber and gravel were recovered and sold for $13,000.

2. A second tract of land (site number 622) with a building was acquired for $420,000. The closing statement indicated that the land value was $300,000 and the building value was $120,000. Shortly after acquisition, the building was demolished at a cost of $45,000. A new building was constructed for $230,000 plus the following costs.

Excavation fees	$38,000
Architectural design fees	11,000
Building permit fee	2,500
Imputed interest on funds used during	
construction (share financing)	8,500
G.S.T.	3,430

The building was completed and occupied on September 30, 1998.

3. A third tract of land (site number 623) was acquired for $650,000 and was put on the market for resale.

4. During December, 1998 costs of $92,000 were incurred to improve leased office space. The related lease will terminate on December 31, 2000 and it is not expected to be renewed. (Hint: Leasehold improvements should be handled in the same manner as land improvements.)

5. A group of new machines was purchased under a royalty agreement that provides for payment of royalties based on units of production for the machines. The invoice price of the machines was $87,000, freight costs were $3,800, unloading charges were $2,400, and royalty payments for 1998 were $17,500.

Instructions

(a) Prepare a detailed analysis of the changes in each of the following balance sheet accounts for 1998:

Land	Leasehold improvements
Buildings	Machinery and equipment

Disregard the related accumulated depreciation accounts.

(b) List the items in the problem that were not used to determine the answer to (a) above, and indicate where, or if, these items should be included in Stefan's financial statements.   (AICPA adapted)

P11-2   Selected accounts included in the property, plant, and equipment section of Gavin Black Ltd.'s balance sheet at December 31, 1997, had the following balances:

Land	$ 300,000
Land improvements	140,000
Buildings	1,100,000
Machinery and equipment	960,000

During 1998 the following transactions occurred:

1. A tract of land was acquired for $150,000 as a potential future building site.

2. A plant facility consisting of land and building was acquired from Wendy Wiggins Ltd. in exchange for 20,000 of Black's common shares. On the acquisition date, Black's shares had a closing market price of $36 each on the Toronto Stock Exchange. The plant facility was carried on Wiggins' books at $110,000 for land and $320,000 for the building at the exchange date. Current appraised values for the land and building, respectively, are $230,000 and $690,000.

3. Items of machinery and equipment were purchased at a total cost of $400,000. Additional costs were incurred as follows:

Freight and unloading	$17,000
Sales taxes	20,000
G.S.T.	28,000
Installation	26,000

4. Expenditures totalling $90,000 were made for new parking lots and sidewalks at the corporation's various plant locations. These expenditures had an estimated useful life of 15 years.

5. A machine costing $80,000 on January 1, 1990, was scrapped on June 30, 1998. Double-declining-balance depreciation has been recorded on the basis of a 10-year life.

6. A machine was sold for $20,000 on July 1, 1998. Original cost of the machine was $44,000 on January 1, 1995, and it was depreciated on the straight-line basis over an estimated useful life of seven years and a residual value of $2,000.

Instructions

(a) Prepare a detailed analysis of the changes in each of the following balance sheet accounts for 1998.

Land	Buildings
Land improvements	Machinery and equipment

(Hint: Disregard the related accumulated depreciation accounts.)

(b) List the items in the problem that were not used to determine the answer to (a), showing the pertinent amounts and supporting computations in good form for each item. In addition, indicate where, or if, these items should be included in Black's financial statements.   (AICPA adapted)

Deveraux Co. Ltd. was incorporated on January 2, 1998 but was unable to begin manufacturing activities until July **P11-3**
1, 1998 because new factory facilities were not completed until that date.

The Land and Building account at December 31, 1998, was as follows:

January 31, 1998	Land and building	$160,000
February 28, 1998	Cost of removal of building	4,800
May 1, 1998	Partial payment of new construction	60,000
May 1, 1998	Legal fees paid	3,770
June 1, 1998	Second payment on new construction	40,000
June 1, 1998	Insurance premium	2,280
June 1, 1998	Special tax assessment	4,000
June 30, 1998	General expenses	16,300
July 1, 1998	Final payment on new construction	40,000
December 31, 1998	Asset write-up	18,200
		$349,350
December 31, 1998	Depreciation—1998 at 1%	3,494
	Account balance	$345,856

The following additional information is to be considered.

1. To acquire land and building, the company paid $80,000 cash and 800 shares of its $8.00 cumulative no-par value preferred shares. Fair market value is $105 per share.

2. Cost of removal of old buildings amounted to $4,800, and the demolition company retained all materials of the building.

3. Legal fees covered the following:

Cost of organization	$ 610
Examination of title covering purchase of land	1,300
Legal work in connection with construction contract	1,860
	$3,770

4. Insurance covered the building for a one-year term beginning May 1, 1998.

5. The special tax assessment covered street improvements that are permanent in nature.

6. General expenses covered the following for the period January 2, 1998 to June 30, 1998.

President's salary	$12,100
Plant superintendent covering supervision of new building	4,200
	$16,300

7. Because of a general increase in construction costs after entering into the building contract, the board of directors increased the value of the building by $18,200, believing that such an increase was justified to reflect the current market at the time the building was completed. Retained earnings was credited for this amount.

8. Estimated life of building—50 years.

   Write-off for 1998 — 1% of asset value (1% of $349,350, or $3,494).

Instructions

(a) Prepare entries to reflect correct land, building, and accumulated depreciation allowance accounts at December 31, 1998.

(b) Show the proper presentation of land, building, and accumulated depreciation accounts on the balance sheet at December 31, 1998.

(AICPA adapted)

During 1998, Abe Neufeld Company manufactured a machine for its own use. At December 31, 1998 the account **P11-4**
related to that machine is as follows:

Machinery

Old machine cost	$9,200	Old machine cost	$9,200
Cost of dismantling old machine	1,500	Cash proceeds from sale of old machine	800
Raw materials used in construction of new machine	27,000	Depreciation for 1998, 10% of $76,400	7,640
Labour in construction of new machine	32,000		
Cost of installation	2,600		
Materials used in trial runs	1,500		
Profit on construction	12,600		

An analysis of the details in the account discloses the following:

1. The old machine, which was removed during installation of the new one, has been fully depreciated.

2. Cash discounts received on the payments for materials used in construction totaled $950 and were reported in the Purchases Discount account.

3. The Factory Overhead account shows a balance of $300,000, which includes variable overhead and total fixed overhead, for the year ended December 31, 1998. $11,300 of the variable overhead is attributable to the production of the machine. Fixed overhead is normally priced to operations at $5 per man-hour of labour; 3,000 man-hours of labour were consumed in the production of the machine.

4. A profit was recognized on construction for the difference between costs incurred and the price at which the machine could have been purchased. The profit was credited to Self-Construction Gains.

5. Machinery has an estimated life of 10 years with no residual value. The new machine was used for production beginning July 1, 1998.

Instructions
Prepare the entries necessary to correct the Machinery account as of December 31, 1998 and to record depreciation expense for the year 1998.

P11-5   Presented below is a schedule of property dispositions for Ada Reid Co. Ltd.

Schedule of Property Dispositions

	Cost	Accumulated Depreciation	Cash Proceeds	Fair Market Value	Nature of Disposition
Land	$40,000	—	$32,000	$32,000	Expropriation
Building	15,000	—	3,600	—	Demolition
Warehouse	65,000	$11,000	74,000	74,000	Destruction by fire
Machine	8,000	3,200	900	7,200	Trade-in
Furniture	10,000	7,850	—	2,800	Contribution
Automobile	8,000	3,460	2,960	2,960	Sale

The following additional information is available:

1. **Land.** On February 15, land held primarily as an investment was expropriated by the city, and on March 31, another parcel of unimproved land to be held as an investment was purchased at a cost of $35,000.

2. **Building.** On April 2, land and a building were purchased at a total cost of $75,000, of which 20% was allocated to the building on the corporate books. The real estate was acquired with the intention of demolishing the building, and this was accomplished during the month of November. Cash proceeds received in November represent the net proceeds from demolition of the building.

3. **Warehouse.** On June 30, the warehouse was destroyed by fire. The warehouse was purchased January 2, 1984 and had depreciated $11,000. On December 27, part of the insurance proceeds was used to purchase a replacement warehouse at a cost of $65,000.

4. **Machine.** On December 26, the machine was exchanged for another machine having a fair market value of $6,300 and cash of $900. (Round to nearest dollar.)

5. **Furniture.** On August 15, furniture was donated to a qualified charitable organization. No other donations were made or pledged during the year.

6. **Automobile.** On November 3, the automobile was sold to Victor Kiriakis, a shareholder.

Instructions
Indicate how these items would be reported on the income statement of Ada Reid Co. Ltd.   (AICPA adapted)

On January 1, 1997 Spitfire Inc. purchased a tract of land (site number 101) with a building for $600,000. Spitfire paid a **P11-6** real estate broker's commission of $36,000 and legal fees of $6,000. The closing statement indicated that the land value was $500,000 and the building value was $100,000. Shortly after acquisition, the building was razed at a cost of $75,000.

Spitfire entered into a $3,000,000 fixed-price contract with Phelan Builders Inc. on March 1, 1997 for the construction of an office building on land site number 101. The building was completed and occupied on September 30, 1998. Additional construction costs were incurred as follows:

Plans, specifications, and blueprints	$14,000
Architects' fees for design and supervision	82,000

The building is estimated to have a 40-year life from date of completion and will be depreciated using the 150% declining balance method.

To finance the construction cost, Spitfire borrowed $3,000,000 on March 1, 1997. The loan is payable in 10 annual instalments of $300,000 plus interest at the rate of 10%. Spitfire's weighted-average amounts of accumulated building construction expenditures were as follows:

For the period March 1 to December 31, 1997	$1,200,000
For the period January 1 to September 30, 1998	1,800,000

Instructions

(a) Prepare a schedule that discloses the individual costs making up the balance in the Land account in respect of land site number 101 as of September 30, 1998.

(b) Prepare a schedule that discloses the individual costs that should be capitalized in the Office Building account as of September 30, 1998. Show supporting computations in good form.　　　　(AICPA adapted)

Studebaker Co. Ltd. wishes to exchange a machine used in its operations. Studebaker has received the following **P11-7** offers from other companies in the industry:

1. Lark Company offered to exchange a similar machine plus $22,000.

2. Nash Company offered to exchange a similar machine.

3. Avanti Company offered to exchange a similar machine, but wanted $15,000 in addition to Studebaker's machine.

In addition, Studebaker contacted Hawk Inc., a dealer in machines. To obtain a new machine, Studebaker must pay $93,000 in addition to trading in its old machine.

	Studebaker	Lark	Nash	Avanti	Hawk
Machine cost	$160,000	$120,000	$147,000	$160,000	$130,000
Accumulated depreciation	50,000	45,000	72,000	75,000	-0-
Fair value	92,000	70,000	92,000	107,000	185,000

Instructions

For each of the four independent situations, prepare the journal entries to record the exchange on the books of each company. (Round to nearest dollar.)

On August 1, 1998 Chrysler Inc. exchanged productive assets with Belvedere Inc. Chrysler's asset is referred to **P11-8** below as "Asset A" and Belvedere's is referred to as "Asset B." The following facts pertain to these assets:

	Asset A	Asset B
Original cost	$96,000	$110,000
Accumulated depreciation (to date of exchange)	40,000	52,000
Fair market value at date of exchange	60,000	75,000
Cash paid by Chrysler Inc.	15,000	
Cash received by Belvedere Inc.		15,000

Instructions

(a) Assume that Assets A and B are dissimilar, and record the exchange for both Chrysler Inc. and Belvedere Inc. in accordance with generally accepted accounting principles.

(b) Assume that Assets A and B are similar, and record the exchange for both Chrysler Inc. and Belvedere Inc. in accordance with generally accepted accounting principles.

P11-9 During the current year, BelAir Construction trades an old crane that has a book value of $86,000 (original cost $140,000 less accumulated depreciation $54,000) for a new crane from Impala Manufacturing Ltd. The new crane cost Impala $165,000 to manufacture. The following information is also available:

	BelAir Construction	Impala Mfg. Ltd.
Fair market value of old crane	$ 72,000	
Fair market value of new crane		$190,000
Cash paid	118,000	
Cash received		118,000

Instructions

(a) Assume that this exchange is considered to involve dissimilar assets (culmination of the earnings process), and prepare the journal entries on the books of (1) BelAir Construction; and (2) Impala Manufacturing.

(b) Assume that this exchange is considered to involve similar assets (no culmination of the earnings process), and prepare the journal entries on the books of (1) BelAir Construction; and (2) Impala Manufacturing.

(c) Assuming the same facts as those in (a), except that the fair market value of the old crane is $98,000 and the cash paid is $92,000, prepare the journal entries on the books of (1) BelAir Construction; and (2) Impala Manufacturing.

(d) Assuming the same facts as those in (b), except that the fair market value of the old crane is $87,000 and the cash paid is $103,000, prepare the journal entries on the books of (1) BelAir Construction; and (2) Impala Manufacturing.

P11-10 Bronco Mining Inc. received a $740,000 low bid from a reputable manufacturer for the construction of special production equipment needed by Bronco in an expansion program. Because the company's own plant was not operating at capacity, Bronco decided to construct the equipment there and recorded the following production costs related to the construction.

Services of consulting engineer	$ 32,000
Work subcontracted	28,000
Materials	300,000
Plant labour normally assigned to production	114,000
Plant labour normally assigned to maintenance	160,000
Total	$634,000

Management prefers to record the cost of the equipment under the incremental cost method. Approximately 40% of the corporation's production is devoted to government supply contracts, which are all based in some way on cost. The contracts require that any self-constructed equipment be allocated its full share of all costs related to the construction.

The following information is also available:

1. The production labour was for partial fabrication of the equipment in the plant. Skilled personnel were required and were assigned from other projects. The maintenance labour would have been idle time of nonproduction plant employees who would have been retained on the payroll whether or not their services were utilized.

2. Payroll taxes and employee fringe benefits are approximately 35% of labour cost and are included in manufacturing overhead cost. Total manufacturing overhead for the year was $6,084,000, including the $160,000 maintenance labour used to construct the equipment.

3. Manufacturing overhead is approximately 60% variable and is applied on the basis of production labour cost. Production labour cost for the year for the corporation's normal products totaled $8,286,000.

4. General and administrative expenses include $27,000 of allocated executive salary cost and $13,750 of postage, telephone, supplies, and miscellaneous expenses identifiable with this equipment construction.

Instructions

(a) Prepare a schedule computing the amount that should be reported as the full cost of the constructed equipment to meet the requirements of the government contracts. Any supporting computations should be in good form.

(b) Prepare a schedule computing the incremental cost of the constructed equipment.

(c) What is the greatest amount that should be capitalized as the cost of the equipment? Why?   (AICPA adapted)

Pavlova Company is a manufacturer of ballet shoes and is experiencing a period of sustained growth. In an effort to **P11-11** expand its production capacity to meet the increased demand for its product, the company recently made several acquisitions of plant and equipment. Robert Fisher, newly hired in the position of Fixed Asset Accountant, requested that Rudolf Thomm, Pavlova's Controller, review the following transactions.

Transaction 1. On June 1, 1998, Pavlova Company purchased equipment from Twyla Limited. Pavlova issued a $20,000 four-year noninterest-bearing note to Twyla for the new equipment. Pavlova will pay off the note in four equal instalments due at the end of each of the next four years. At the date of the transaction, the prevailing market rate of interest for obligations of this nature was 10%. Freight costs of $300 and installation costs of $500 were incurred in completing this transaction. The appropriate factors for the time value of money at a 10% rate of interest are given in the second column.

Future value of $1 for four periods	1.46
Future value of an ordinary annuity for four periods	4.64
Present value of $1 for four periods	0.68
Present value of an ordinary annuity for four periods	3.17

Transaction 2. On December 1, 1998, Pavlova Company purchased several assets of Misha Shoes Inc., a small shoe manufacturer whose owner was retiring. The purchase amounted to $160,000 and included the assets listed below. Pavlova Company engaged the services of Bolshoi Appraisal Inc., an independent appraiser, to determine the fair market values of the assets, which are also presented below.

	Misha Book Value	Fair Market Value
Inventory	$ 60,000	$ 50,000
Land	40,000	80,000
Building	70,000	120,000
	$170,000	$250,000

During its fiscal year ended May 31, 1999 Pavlova incurred $8,000 of interest expense in connection with the financing of these assets.

Transaction 3. On March 1, 1999, Pavlova Company exchanged a number of used trucks plus cash for vacant land adjacent to its plant site. Pavlova intends to use the land for a parking lot. The trucks had a combined book value of $30,000, as Pavlova had recorded $20,000 of accumulated depreciation against these assets. Pavlova's purchasing agent, who has had previous dealings in the second-hand market, indicated that the trucks had a fair market value of $40,000 at the time of the transaction. In addition to the trucks, Pavlova Company paid $18,000 cash for the land.

Instructions

(a) Plant assets such as land, buildings, and equipment receive special accounting treatment. Describe the major characteristics of these assets that differentiate them from other types of assets.

(b) For each of the three transactions described above, determine the value at which Pavlova Company should record the acquired assets. Support your calculations with an explanation of the underlying rationale.

(c) The books of Pavlova Company show the following additional transactions for the fiscal year ended May 31, 1998.

 1. Acquisition of a building for speculative purposes.

 2. Purchase of a two-year insurance policy covering plant equipment.

 3. Purchase of the rights for the exclusive use of a process used in the manufacture of ballet shoes.

 For each of these transactions, indicate whether the asset should be classified as a plant asset. If it is:

 (i) a plant asset, explain why.

 (ii) not a plant asset, explain why and identify the proper classification.   (CMA adapted)

CASES

Your client, Nolte Plastics Ltd., found three suitable sites, each having certain unique advantages, for a new plant **C11-1** facility. In order to thoroughly investigate the advantages and disadvantages of each site, one-year options were purchased for an amount equal to 6% of the contract price of each site. The costs of the options cannot be applied against the contracts. Before the options expired, one of the sites was purchased at the contract price of $300,000. The option on this site had cost $18,000. The two options not exercised had cost $12,000 each.

Instructions

Present arguments in support of recording the cost of the land at each of the following amounts.

(a) $300,000   (b) $318,000   (c) $342,000.   (AICPA adapted)

C11-2 DeVito Company purchased land for use as its corporate headquarters. A small factory that was on the land when it was purchased was torn down before construction of the office building began. Furthermore, a substantial amount of rock blasting and removal had to be done to the site before construction of the building foundation began. Because the office building was set back on the land far from the public road, DeVito Company had the contractor construct a paved road that led from the public road to the parking lot of the office building.

Three years after the office building was occupied, DeVito Company added four stories to the office building. The four stories had an estimated useful life of five years more than the remaining useful life of the original office building.

Ten years later, the land and building were sold at an amount more than their book value and DeVito Company had a new office building constructed in another province for use as its new corporate headquarters.

Instructions

(a) Which of the above expenditures should be capitalized? How should each be depreciated or amortized? Discuss the rationale for your answer.

(b) How would the sale of the land and building be accounted for? Include in your answer how to determine the net book value at the date of sale. Discuss the rationale for your answer.

C11-3 Rodham Medical Labs, Inc. began operations five years ago producing stetrics, a new type of instrument it hoped to sell to doctors, dentists, and hospitals. The demand for stetrics far exceeded initial expectations, and the company was unable to produce enough stetrics to meet demand.

The company was manufacturing its product on equipment that it built at the start of its operations. To meet demand, more efficient equipment was needed. The company decided to design and build the equipment since the equipment currently available on the market was unsuitable for producing stetrics.

In 1990, a section of the plant was devoted to development of the new equipment and a special staff of personnel was hired. Within six months a machine was developed at a cost of $510,000, which successfully increased production and reduced labour costs substantially. Elated by the success of the new machine, the company built three more machines of the same type at a cost of $315,000 each.

Instructions

(a) In general, what costs should be capitalized for self-constructed equipment?

(b) Discuss the propriety of including in the capitalized cost of self-constructed assets:

1. The increase in overhead caused by the self-construction of fixed assets.

2. A proportionate share of overhead on the same basis as that applied to goods manufactured for sale.

(c) Discuss the proper accounting treatment of the $195,000 ($510,000–$315,000) by which the cost of the first machine exceeded the cost of the subsequent machines. This additional cost should not be considered research and development costs.

C11-4 Tinfoil Airline is converting from piston-type planes to jets. Delivery time for the jets is three years, during which period substantial progress payments must be made. The multimillion-dollar cost of the planes cannot be financed from working capital; Tinfoil must borrow funds for the payments.

Because of high interest rates and the large sum to be borrowed, management estimates that interest costs in the second year of the period will be equal to one-third of income before interest and taxes, and one-half of such income in the third year.

After conversion, Tinfoil's passenger-carrying capacity will be doubled with no increase in the number of planes, although the investment in planes will be substantially increased. The jet planes have a seven-year service life.

Instructions

Give your recommendation concerning the proper accounting for interest during the conversion period. Support your recommendation with reasons and suggested accounting treatment. (Disregard income tax implications.)

(AICPA adapted)

C11-5 You have been engaged to examine the financial statements of Lemaire Corporation Ltd. for the year ending December 31, 1998 by Messrs. Morris and Garfield, original owners of options to acquire oil leases on 5,000 ha of land for $900,000. They expected that (1) the oil leases would be acquired by the corporation; and (2) subsequently 180,000 of the corporation's common shares would be sold to the public at $15 per share. In February 1998, they exchanged their options, $300,000 cash, and $125,000 of other assets, for 75,000 of the corporation's common shares. The corporation's board of directors appraised the leases at $1,600,000, basing its appraisal on the price of other parcels recently leased in the same area. The options were therefore recorded at $700,000 ($1,600,000–$900,000 option price).

The options were exercised by the corporation in March 1998, prior to the sale of common shares to the public in April 1998. Leases on approximately 500 ha of land were abandoned as worthless during the year.

Instructions

(a) Why is the valuation of assets acquired by a corporation in exchange for its own common shares sometimes difficult?

(b) 1. What reasoning might Lemaire Corporation Ltd. use to support valuing the leases at $1,600,000, the amount of the appraisal by the board of directors?

   2. Assuming that the board's appraisal was sincere, what steps might Lemaire Corporation Ltd. have taken to strengthen its position to use the $1,600,000 value and to provide additional information if questions were raised about possible overvaluation of the leases?

(c) Discuss the propriety of charging one-tenth of the recorded value of the leases to expense at December 31, 1998 because leases on 500 ha of land were abandoned during the year. (AICPA adapted)

The invoice price of a machine is $40,000. Various other costs relating to the acquisition and installation of the machine, including transportation, electrical wiring, special base, and so on, amount to $7,000. The machine has an estimated life of 10 years, with no residual value at the end of that period. **C11-6**

The owner of the business suggests that the incidental costs of $7,000 be charged to expense immediately for the following reasons:

1. If the machine should be sold, these costs cannot be recovered in the sales price.

2. The inclusion of the $7,000 in the Machinery account on the books will not necessarily result in a closer approximation of the market price of this asset over the years because of the possibility of changing demand and supply level.

3. Charging the $7,000 to expense immediately will reduce income taxes.

Instructions
Discuss each of the points raised by the owner of the business. (AICPA adapted)

You have recently been hired as a junior accountant in the firm of Restin and Peace. Mr. Peace is an alumnus of the same school from which you graduated and, therefore, is quite interested in your accounting training. He therefore presents the following situations and asks for your response. **C11-7**

Situation I. Every few years one of our clients publishes a new catalogue for distribution to its sales outlets and customers. The latest catalogue was published in 1997. Periodically, current price lists and new product brochures are issued. The company is now contemplating the issue of a new catalogue during the latter part of 2000. The cost of the new catalogue has been accounted for as follows:

1. Estimated total cost of the catalogue is accounted for over a period beginning with the initial planning (1998) and is expected to end at time of publication.

2. Estimated costs are accumulated in an accrued liability account through monthly charges to selling expenses.

3. Monthly charges were based upon the estimated total cost of the guide and the estimated number of months remaining before publication; periodic revisions were made to the estimates as current information became available.

4. Actual costs were recorded as charges to the accrued liability account as they were accrued.

In summary, the company accrues the entire estimated cost (including anticipated costs to be incurred) of a contemplated catalogue through charges to operations prior to the expected publication date.

Instructions
Comment on the propriety of this treatment.

Situation II. Recently a construction company agreed to construct a new hospital for its client at the construction company's cost; that is, the contractor was to realize no profit. The construction company was interested in performing this service because it had substantial interests in the community and wanted to make the community more attractive. The building was completed in 1998 at a cost of $24,000,000. An appraisal firm indicated, however, that the fair market value of the properties was $26,000,000, the difference due to the $2,000,000 that the company did not charge the hospital.

Instructions

At what amount should the hospital value the asset? A related question is whether the donated profit on the hospital should be reported as revenue or as a capital contribution. What is your answer to this question?

Situation III. Recently, one of our clients asked whether it would be appropriate to capitalize a portion of the salaries of the corporate officers for time spent on construction activities. During construction, one of the officers devotes full time to the supervision of construction projects. His activities are similar to those of a construction superintendent for a general contractor. During periods of heavy construction activity, this officer also employs several assistants to help with administrative matters related to construction. All other officers are general corporate officers.

The compensation and other costs related to the construction officer are not dependent upon the level of construction activity in a particular period (except to the extent that additional assistants are employed on a short-term basis). These expenses would continue to be incurred even if there was no construction activity unless the company decided to discontinue permanently, or for the foreseeable future, all construction activity. In that case, it could well reach the decision to terminate the construction officer. The company has, however, aggressive expansion plans that anticipate continuing construction of shopping centre properties.

Instructions

What salary costs, if any, should be capitalized to the cost of properties?

USING YOUR JUDGMENT

FINANCIAL REPORTING PROBLEM

Refer to the financial statements and other documents of Moore Corporation Limited presented in Appendix 5A and answer the following question:

> What changes have occurred in Moore's Property, Plant, and Equipment account? If Moore disposed of any property, plant and equipment, determine how the proceeds were reported.

ETHICS CASE

Glamour Company purchased a warehouse in a downtown district where land values are rapidly increasing. Richard Siu, Controller, and Cindy Crawford, Financial Vice-President, are trying to allocate the cost of the purchase between the land and the building. The Controller, noting that depreciation can be taken only on the building, favours undervaluing the land and placing a very high proportion of the cost on the warehouse itself, thus reducing taxable income and income taxes. Crawford, his supervisor, argues that the allocation should recognize the increasing value of the land, regardless of the depreciation potential of the warehouse. Besides, she says, net income is negatively impacted by additional depreciation and the company's stock price goes down.

Instructions

(a) What are the ethical issues, if any?

(b) What stakeholder interests are in conflict?

(c) How should these costs be allocated? Why?

chapter 12

DEPRECIATION AND DEPLETION OF TANGIBLE CAPITAL ASSETS

CHAPTER 12

Depreciation and Depletion of Tangible Capital Assets

Learning Objectives

After studying this chapter, you should be able to:

1. Explain the concept of depreciation.

2. Identify and describe the factors that must be considered when determining depreciation charges.

3. Know how to determine depreciation charges using the straight-line, activity, and decreasing charge methods.

4. Know various special depreciation methods and understand how they work.

5. Identify and understand the reasons for selecting a depreciation method.

6. Understand and know how to resolve and account for special issues related to depreciation.

7. Describe the income tax method of determining capital cost allowance.

8. Describe financial statement disclosures for property, plant, and equipment, and depreciation.

9. Explain the investment tax credit and know how to account for it.

10. Understand the issues and know how to account for depletion of natural resources.

11. Know how to disclose natural resources and related depletion in financial statements.

12. Appreciate some of the complexities in determining capital cost allowance (Appendix 12A).

Although accountants, engineers, lawyers, and economists define depreciation differently, they all agree that most assets are on an inevitable "march to the rubbish heap." As a result, some type of write-off of cost is needed to indicate that the usefulness of an asset has declined.[1]

In accounting, **amortization** is the word used in a broad sense to describe *the charge to income that recognizes that the life of a capital asset is finite and that its cost less residual value is to be allocated to the periods of service provided by the asset.*[2]

---

[1] But not all agree when it comes to certain assets. For example, the idea that churches (not-for-profit organizations) depreciate the cost of houses of worship, monuments, and historical treasures has met with considerable opposition: "Depreciating cathedrals and churches is stupid. . . . It would be like trying to compare the cost per soul saved among the churches." Another opponent wrote that "depreciating churches would be like depreciating the Pyramids and the Sphinx of Egypt, and the Sistine Chapel at the Vatican. Figuring such depreciation is the acme of futility." However, a defender of the concept replied, "The Parthenon may still be there, but its roof has fallen in. Physical assets that are exhaustible should be depreciated." *The Wall Street Journal*, April 10, 1987, pp. 1 and 10. *CICA Handbook*, Section 4430 (issued in March, 1996) requires that capital assets held by not-for-profit organizations should be amortized.

[2] *CICA Handbook* (Toronto: CICA), Section 3060, par. .33.

Traditionally, however, **depreciation** is the term most often employed to indicate that tangible capital assets (other than natural resources) have declined in service potential. Where natural resources such as timber, oil, and coal are involved, the term **depletion** is employed. The expiration of intangible assets, such as patents or goodwill, is called **amortization** (as a specific rather than a broad interpretation of the term).[3]

The allocation of the costs of various assets to time periods is a consequence of the periodicity (time period) assumption and accrual requirements of financial accounting. To provide timely (relevant) information about a company, the results of operations for a particular time period and the financial position at a point in time are measured. Businesses, however, purchase or otherwise acquire assets that are used to provide benefits over several periods. Therefore, in addition to determining the appropriate cost of such an asset (applying the cost principle as examined in Chapter 11), it is necessary to make decisions that will allocate the cost to particular periods so that the recognized expense in each period is appropriately matched to the benefits derived from the asset's use.

In this chapter, we will determine how this may be accomplished. We will consider the nature of depreciation and depletion (but leave amortization of intangibles until Chapter 13). We will then describe, illustrate, and assess the various methods available to allocate costs to time periods. Some special accounting problems associated with depreciation (partial periods, revision of estimates, impairment in value, and investment tax credit consequences) and depletion (determining the cost of natural resources and difficulties in estimation) will also be addressed.

DEPRECIATION—A PROCESS OF COST ALLOCATION

Most individuals at one time or another purchase or trade in an automobile. In discussions with the automobile dealer, depreciation is a consideration on two points. First, how much has the old car "depreciated"? That is, what is the trade-in value? Second, how fast will the new car depreciate? That is, what will its trade-in value be? In both cases, depreciation is thought of as a loss in value.

To accountants, *depreciation is not a matter of valuation, but a means of cost allocation*. Assets are not depreciated on the basis of a decline in their fair market value, but on the basis of systematic charges of a determined cost to expense. **Depreciation *is the accounting process that allocates the cost of a tangible asset to expense in a rational and systematic manner to those periods expected to benefit from the use of the asset.***

OBJECTIVE 1
Explain the concept of depreciation.

It is undeniably true that the value of the asset will fluctuate between the time it is purchased and the time it is sold or scrapped. Attempts to measure these interim value changes have not been well received by accountants because values are difficult to measure objectively. Therefore, the asset's depreciable cost is charged to depreciation expense over its estimated life; there is no attempt to value the asset at fair market value between the dates of its acquisition and disposition. The cost allocation approach is used because a matching of costs with benefits (revenues) occurs and because fluctuations in market value are tenuous and difficult to measure. Further, because of the going concern assumption and the fact that a depreciable asset is generally expected to be held until the end of its useful life, interim market value changes are not considered relevant to the determination of income or financial position.

---

[3] In order to differentiate the application of the concept of amortization among tangible assets, natural resources, and intangibles, we will use the terms depreciation, depletion, and amortization, respectively. This is acceptable as the *Handbook* (Section 3060, par. .33) states "Amortization may also be termed depreciation or depletion."

FACTORS INVOLVED IN THE DEPRECIATION PROCESS

OBJECTIVE 2
Identify and describe the factors that must be considered when determining depreciation charges.

Before a pattern of charges to revenue can be established, three basic questions must be answered:

1. What depreciable base (amortizable amount) is to be used for the asset?
2. What is the asset's useful life?
3. What method of cost apportionment is best for the asset?

The answers to these questions involve the distillation of several estimates into the resulting depreciation charge. A perfect measure of depreciation for each period cannot be expected since the estimates on which depreciation is based assume perfect knowledge of the future, which is never attainable. Nevertheless, the accountant and management must exercise their collective judgement when deriving answers to these questions in order to achieve a rational matching of expenses against revenues in the income statement.

Depreciable Base for the Asset.   The **depreciable base** or **amortizable amount** is a function of two factors: the original cost of the asset, and its residual value. While historical cost was discussed in Chapter 11, little attention was given to residual value. **Residual value** is defined as *the estimated net realizable value of a capital asset at the end of its useful life to an enterprise.*[4] It is the amount to which the asset is written down—or depreciated—during its useful life. Exhibit 12-1 shows that for an asset with a cost of $10,000 and a residual value of $1,000, the depreciable base is $9,000.

EXHIBIT 12-1

COMPUTATION OF DEPRECIABLE BASE

Original cost	$10,000
Less residual value	1,000
Depreciable base	**$ 9,000**

Companies differ in how they estimate residual value. For example, many companies depreciate their computer equipment on a straight-line basis, but their estimated residual values can vary considerably. Differences in residual values result because they are estimates. Even though one may attempt to derive a residual value based on information about prevailing net realizable value of similar assets that have reached the end of their useful lives, such information may be difficult to find, of a conflicting nature, or nonexistent. Consequently, although companies have similar assets and may depreciate them using the same method and estimated life, differences in estimated residual value will result in different amounts being charged to depreciation expense each year by each company.

From a practical standpoint, residual value is often considered to be zero because the amount is immaterial. Some long-lived assets, however, have substantial residual values

---

[4] *CICA Handbook*, Section 3060, par. .14. Technically, the total amortization that should be charged to income over an asset's useful life is the greater of the amount over that life based on consideration of (a) the cost less *salvage value* over the *life* of the asset; and (b) the cost less *residual value* over the *useful life* of the asset (par. .31). Salvage value is defined as the estimated net realizable value of a capital asset at the end of its life and is normally negligible (par. .15). While cost less salvage value will be equal to or greater than cost less residual value, the life of the asset will typically be equal to or longer than the useful life of the asset. Consequently, the general result is that the allocation of cost less residual value over useful life is likely to result in the same or a greater total amortization charge to income over that life than is the total of the charge to amortization over the useful life based on cost less salvage value over the asset's life. Accepting this, and to avoid complexity, our discussion and illustrations will consider cost less residual value as the amortizable amount.

that should be considered when determining the depreciable base. Examples presented in this chapter include residual value to illustrate how it impacts the calculation of depreciation expense under the various methods.

Estimation of Useful Life. The **useful life** of a capital asset is *the estimate of either the period over which it is expected to be used by the enterprise, or the number of production or similar units that can be obtained from the asset by the enterprise.*[5]

The useful life of an asset and its physical life are often not the same. A piece of machinery may be physically capable of producing a given product for many years beyond its service life, but the equipment is not used for all of those years because the cost of producing the product in later years may be too high. For example, many tractors in the Western Development Museum at Saskatoon are preserved in remarkable physical condition as an historic reminder of Canadian farming development, although their service lives were terminated many years ago.

Assets are retired for two reasons: *physical factors* (e.g., casualty or expiration of physical life), and *economic factors* (e.g., technological or commercial obsolescence).

Physical factors relate to such things as decay or wear and tear that result from use and the passage of time. Physical factors set the outside limit for the useful service life of an asset.

The reasons for scrapping an asset before its physical life expires are varied. New processes or techniques or improved machines may provide the same service at lower cost and with higher quality. Changes in the product may shorten the service life of an asset. Environmental factors can also influence a decision to retire a given asset.

Economic or functional factors can be classified into three categories: inadequacy, supersession, and obsolescence. **Inadequacy** results when an asset ceases to be useful to a given enterprise because the demands of the firm have changed. For example, a company may require a larger building to handle increased production. Although the old building may still be sound, it has become inadequate for the enterprise's purposes. **Supersession** is the replacement of one asset with another more efficient and economical asset. Examples include the replacement of a 386 computer processor with a 686 processor, or the replacement of a Boeing 727 with a Boeing 767. **Obsolescence** is the catch-all term for situations that do not involve either inadequacy or supersession. Because the distinction between these categories is fuzzy, it is probably best to consider economic factors totally instead of trying to make distinctions that are not clear-cut.

To illustrate these concepts, consider a new nuclear power plant. What do you think are the most important factors that determine its useful life: physical factors, or economic factors? The limiting factors seem to be: (1) ecological considerations; (2) competition from other power sources (non-nuclear); and (3) safety concerns. Physical life does not appear to be the primary factor affecting useful life. Although the plant's physical life may be far from over, the plant may become obsolete in ten years.

For a house, physical factors undoubtedly are more important than economic or functional factors relative to useful life. Whenever the physical nature of the asset is the primary determinant of useful life, maintenance plays a vital role. The better the maintenance, the longer the life of the asset.[6]

---

[5] *Ibid.*, par. .17. The life of any capital asset, other than land, is finite and is normally the shortest of the physical, technological, commercial, and legal life (par. .17). When the useful life for a capital asset other than land is expected to exceed 40 years, but cannot be estimated and clearly demonstrated, the amortization period should be limited to 40 years (par. .32).

[6] The airline industry also illustrates the type of problem involved in estimation. In the past, aircraft were assumed not to wear out—they just became obsolete. However, some jets have been in service as long as 20 years, and maintenance of these aircraft has become increasingly expensive. In addition, the public's concern about worn-out aircraft has been heightened by some recent disasters. As a result, some airlines are finding it necessary to replace aircraft not because of obsolescence, but because of their physical deterioration. The oil tanker industry provides a similar example.

The problem of estimating service life is difficult; experience and judgement are the primary means of determining service lives. In some cases, arbitrary lives are selected; in others, sophisticated statistical methods are employed to establish a useful life for accounting purposes. In many cases, the primary basis for estimating the useful life of an asset is the enterprise's past experience with the same or similar assets. In a highly industrial economy such as that of Canada, where research and innovation are so prominent, economic and technological factors have as much effect, if not more, on service lives of tangible assets as do physical factors.

METHODS OF COST ALLOCATION (DEPRECIATION)

Given that the depreciable base and useful life of an asset are determined, the depreciation charge depends on the method selected to calculate the depreciation. The accounting profession requires that the depreciation method employed be "rational and systematic."[7] An arbitrary assignment of cost to accounting periods is not acceptable.

A number of depreciation methods may be used, classified as follows:[8]

1. Straight-line method.

2. Activity methods (units of use or production).

3. Decreasing charge (accelerated depreciation) methods.

4. Special depreciation methods:
   (a) Inventory method.
   (b) Retirement and replacement methods.
   (c) Group and composite-life methods.
   (d) Compound interest methods.

To illustrate, assume Cando Co. Ltd. recently purchased a crane for construction purposes. Pertinent data concerning the purchase of the crane is shown in Exhibit 12-2.

EXHIBIT 12-2

DATA TO ILLUSTRATE DEPRECIATION METHODS

Cost of crane	$500,000
Estimated useful life in years	Five years
Estimated residual value	$ 50,000
Productive life in hours	30,000 hours

OBJECTIVE 3
Know how to determine depreciation charges using the straight-line, activity, and decreasing charge methods.

Straight-Line Method. Under the **straight-line method,** *depreciation is considered a function of the passage of time.* This method is widely used because of its simplicity. The straight-line method is often conceptually appropriate as well. When creeping obsolescence is the primary reason for a limited service life, a decline in usefulness may be constant from period to period. The depreciation charge for the crane is computed as shown in Exhibit 12-3.

---

[7] *CICA Handbook*, Section 3060, par. .31.

[8] *Financial Reporting in Canada—1995* (Toronto: CICA, 1995) reports that, of the companies surveyed, there were 267 disclosing use of the straight-line method, 94 using a decreasing charge method, 67 using the units of production (activity) method, and six using the sinking fund method (primarily in connection with real estate development operations). In the U.S., *Accounting Trends, and Techniques—1993* reported that there were 564 cases of straight-line, 100 cases of a decreasing charge method, and 47 cases of the units of production method.

EXHIBIT 12-3

DEPRECIATION CALCULATION: STRAIGHT-LINE METHOD

$$\frac{\text{Cost less residual value}}{\text{Estimated service life}} = \text{Depreciation charge}$$

$$\frac{\$500,000 - \$50,000}{5} = \textbf{\$90,000}$$

The major objection to the straight-line approach is that it rests on two tenuous assumptions: (1) the asset's economic usefulness is the same each year; and (2) maintenance expense is about the same each period (given constant revenue flows). If such is not the case, a rational matching of expense with revenues will not result from application of this method.

Another problem stems from distortions in the rate of return analysis (income ÷ assets) that can develop. Exhibit 12-4 indicates how the rate of return increases, given constant revenue flows, because the asset's book value decreases. Relying on the increasing trend of the rate of return in such circumstances can be very misleading as a basis for evaluating the success of operations.[9] The increase in the rate of return is the result of an accounting method and does not reflect significant improvement in the underlying economic performance. **With the exception of the compound interest methods, the rate of return trend can be similarly distorted by other depreciation methods.**

EXHIBIT 12-4

DEPRECIATION AND RATE OF RETURN ANALYSIS: CRANE EXAMPLE

Year	Depreciation Expense	Undepreciated Asset Balance (book value)	Income Flow (after depreciation expense)*	Rate of Return (income ÷ book value
0		$500,000		
1	$90,000	410,000	$100,000	24.4%
2	90,000	320,000	100,000	31.2%
3	90,000	230,000	100,000	43.5%
4	90,000	140,000	100,000	71.4%
5	90,000	50,000	100,000	200.0%

*An assumed amount given constant revenue and expense amounts each year.

Activity Methods. An **activity method** (sometimes called a variable charge approach) *determines depreciation as a function of use or productivity instead of the passage of time.* It results in a good matching of costs and revenues when benefits received from an asset are a function of fluctuating activity or productivity. The life of the asset is considered in terms of either the output it provides (units it produces) or the input required to produce the output (number of hours it works). Conceptually, a cost/benefit association

---

[9] Exhibit 12-4 indicates the nature of the problem by considering the consequences using rate-of-return analysis for a single asset situation. There are, of course, usually many depreciable assets reported in financial statements that are replaced as they wear out. Also, the asset "portfolio" often increases. As a result, some argue that, because the cost of new assets is continuously added, the undepreciated book value of the asset portfolio would, in reality, not decline over the years as indicated in the illustration and, therefore, the rate of return would not dramatically increase. While this argument has some practical merit in the circumstances in which it is framed, other circumstances may exist. The point is that anyone looking at a rate-of-return analysis should be aware of this potential problem within the context of the particular situation.

is best established in terms of an **output measure**, but often the output is not homogeneous and/or is difficult to measure. In such cases, an **input measure** such as machine hours is an appropriate basis for determining the amount of depreciation charge for a given accounting period.

The crane poses no particular problem because the usage (hours) is relatively easy to measure. If we assume that the crane is used 4,000 hours the first year, the depreciation charge is calculated as shown in Exhibit 12-5.

EXHIBIT 12-5

DEPRECIATION CALCULATION: ACTIVITY METHOD

$$\frac{\text{(Cost less residual)} \times \text{Hours this year}}{\text{Total estimated hours}} = \text{Depreciation charge}$$

$$\frac{(\$500,000 - \$50,000) \times 4,000}{\$30,000} = \textbf{\$60,000}$$

The major limitation of this method is that it is not appropriate in situations in which depreciation is a function of time instead of activity. For example, a building is subject to a great deal of steady deterioration from the elements (a function of time), regardless of its use. In addition, where an asset's useful life is subject to economic or functional factors independent of its use, the activity method loses much of its significance. For example, if a company is expanding rapidly, a particular building may soon become obsolete for its intended purposes, without activity playing any role in its loss of utility. Another problem in using an activity method is that the total units of output or service hours to be received over the useful life are often difficult to determine.

Decreasing Charge Methods. The **decreasing charge methods** (often called accelerated depreciation or diminishing balance methods) *provide for a higher depreciation expense charge in the earlier years and lower charges in later periods*. The main justification for this approach is that more depreciation should be charged in earlier years when the asset suffers the greatest loss of its services. Another argument is that repair and maintenance costs are often higher in the later periods, and the accelerated methods thus provide a fairly constant total cost (for depreciation plus repairs and maintenance) because the depreciation charge is lower in the later periods. When a decreasing charge approach is used by Canadian companies, it is usually a version of what is called the declining balance method.[10]

Declining Balance Method. The **declining balance method** *uses a depreciation rate* (expressed as a percentage and called the declining balance rate) *that remains constant throughout the asset's life* (assuming no change in estimates occur). *This rate is applied to the reducing book value (cost less accumulated depreciation) each year to determine the depreciation expense.* The declining balance rate may be determined in a variety of ways, but we will use a multiple of the straight-line rate.[11] For example, the *double*-declining bal-

---

[10] Another decreasing charge approach called the sum-of-the-years'-digits method exists but is used very infrequently in Canada. *Financial Reporting in Canada—1995* indicated that of the disclosures of the 434 methods used, only two were the sum-of-the-years'-digits method. Under the sum-of-the-years'-digits method, a decreasing fraction (rate) for each year is multiplied by a constant depreciable base (cost − residual value).

[11] The straight-line rate (%) is equal to 1 divided by the estimated useful life of the asset being depreciated multiplied by 100% A pure form of the declining-balance method (sometimes called the "fixed percentage of book-value method") has also been suggested as a possibility, but is not used extensively in practice. This approach finds a rate that depreciates the asset exactly to residual value at the end of its expected useful (*n* years) life. The formula for determining this rate is as follows:

$$\text{Depreciation rate} = 1 - \sqrt[n]{\frac{\text{Residual value}}{\text{Acquisition cost}}}$$

ance rate for a 10-year-life asset would be 20% (double or multiply by 2 the straight-line rate, which is $2 \times 1/10 \times 100\%$, or 20%; or divide the multiple of the straight-line rate, which is 2 in this case, by the estimated life and multiply by 100%: $2/10 \times 100\%$, or 20%; or take 200% of the straight-line rate, which is $200\% \times 10\%$, or 20%). For an asset with a 20-year life, the *triple*-declining balance rate would be 15% ($3 \times 1/20 \times 100\%$), while the *double*-declining balance rate would be 10% ($2 \times 1/20 \times 100\%$).

Unlike other methods, *the declining balance method does not deduct the residual value when computing the depreciable base.* The declining balance rate is multiplied by the book value of the asset at the beginning of each period. Since the book value of the asset is reduced each period by the depreciation charge, the constant rate is applied to a successively lower book value. The result is a lower depreciation charge each year. This process continues until the book value of the asset is reduced to its estimated residual value, at which time depreciation is discontinued. Using a double-declining balance rate, the depreciation charges for the crane example of Cando Co. Ltd. are presented in Exhibit 12-6.

EXHIBIT 12-6

DEPRECIATION CALCULATION: DOUBLE-DECLINING BALANCE METHOD

Year	Book Value of Asset, Start of Year	Rate on Declining Balance[a]	**Depreciation Expense**	Balance of Accumulated Depreciation	Book Value, End of Year
1	$500,000	40%	**$200,000**	$200,000	$300,000
2	300,000	40%	**120,000**	320,000	180,000
3	180,000	40%	**72,000**	392,000	108,000
4	108,000	40%	**43,200**	435,200	64,800
5	64,800	40%	**14,800**[b]	450,000	50,000

[a] $2 \times 1/5 \times 100\% = 40\%$, or $2/5 \times 100\% = 40\%$.
[b] Limited to $14,800 as it is assumed the book value will not be less than residual value.

Enterprises sometimes switch from the declining balance to the straight-line method near the end of an asset's useful life to ensure that the asset is depreciated only to residual value. This may be done on practical grounds and, because amounts involved are not material, a retroactive adjustment for a change in an accounting policy is not made.

SPECIAL DEPRECIATION METHODS

Sometimes an enterprise does not select one of the more popular depreciation methods because the assets involved have unique characteristics, or because the nature of the industry dictates that a special depreciation method be adopted. Generally, these methods can be classified as follows.

OBJECTIVE 4
Know various special depreciation methods and understand how they work.

1. Inventory method.

2. Retirement and replacement methods.

3. Group and composite methods.

4. Compound interest methods.

Inventory Method. The **inventory method** (often called the appraisal system) is used to value small tangible assets such as hand tools or utensils. A tool inventory, for example, might be taken at the beginning and end of the year; *the value of the beginning inventory plus the cost of tools acquired for the year less the value of the ending inventory provides* *the amount of depreciation expense for the year.* This method is appealing because separate depreciation schedules for the assets in use are impractical.

The major objection to this depreciation method is that it is not "systematic and rational." No set formula exists, and a great deal of subjectivity may be involved in arriving at the valuations presented. In some situations, a market or liquidation value is used, a practice that is criticized as a violation of the historical cost principle.

Retirement and Replacement Methods. The retirement and replacement methods are used principally by public utilities and railroads that own many similar units of small value such as poles, ties, conductors, and telephones. The purpose of these approaches is to avoid elaborate depreciation schedules for individual assets.

The distinction between the two methods is that the **retirement method** *charges the cost of the retired asset (less residual value) to depreciation expense;* the **replacement method** *charges the cost of units purchased as replacements less residual value from the units replaced to depreciation expense.* Therefore, the retirement method follows a FIFO flow because the first asset purchased is the first asset expensed. The replacement method follows a LIFO flow because the last asset purchased is the first asset expensed and the original cost of the old assets is maintained in the accounts indefinitely.

Exhibit 12-7 shows how these methods work. Assume that the transmission lines of Hi-Test Utility Ltd. originally cost $1,000,000 and that eight years later lines costing $150,000 are replaced with lines that cost $200,000. Under both methods, any residual value from the old transmission lines (assume $5,000 for the example) is considered a reduction of the depreciation expense in the period of retirement or replacement. Note that neither method makes use of an Accumulated Depreciation account.

EXHIBIT 12-7

ENTRIES UNDER RETIREMENT AND REPLACEMENT DEPRECIATION METHODS

Retirement Method			Replacement Method		
Record installation of line—1990					
Plant Assets—Lines	1,000,000		Plant Assets—Lines	1,000,000	
Cash		1,000,000	Cash		1,000,000
Record retirement of old asset as depreciation expense net of residual—1998					
Depreciation Expense	150,000		(no entry)		
Plant Assets—Lines		150,000			
Cash	5,000				
Depreciation Expense		5,000			
Record cost of new asset as depreciation expense net of residual value—1998					
(no entry)			Depreciation Expense	200,000	
			Cash		200,000
			Cash	5,000	
			Depreciation Expense		5,000
Record cost of new asset—1998					
Plant Assets—Lines	200,000		(no entry)		
Cash		200,000			

Both methods are subject to the criticism that a proper allocation of costs to all periods does not occur, particularly in the early years (depreciation expense is understated and net income is overstated). To overcome this objection, a special allowance account may be established in the earlier years so that an assumed depreciation charge can be provided. The probability of retirements or replacements being fairly constant is essential to the validity of these methods; otherwise, depreciation is simply a function of when retirement and replacement occur.

Group and Composite Methods. Depreciation methods are usually applied to a single asset. In some circumstances, however, many assets may be depreciated by a single calculation using one rate. For example, a company may place all of its computers (regardless of type, use, life) into a single, multiple-asset account. A similar accounting for office equipment may occur.

Two methods of depreciating multiple-asset accounts can be employed: the group method, and the composite method. *The two methods are not different in the computations involved; both find an average and depreciate on that basis.* The different names for the methods reflect the degree of similarity of the assets subject to the calculations. The term *group refers to a collection of assets that are similar in nature; composite refers to a collection of assets that are dissimilar in nature*. The **group method** is used when the assets are fairly homogeneous and have approximately the same useful lives. The **composite method** is used when the assets are heterogeneous and have different lives. The group method more closely approximates a single-unit cost procedure because the dispersion from the average is not great.

To illustrate, Smart Motors depreciates its fleet of cars, trucks, and campers on a composite basis. The depreciation rate is established as shown in Exhibit 12-8.

EXHIBIT 12-8

DEPRECIATION RATE CALCULATION: COMPOSITE BASIS

Asset	Original Cost	Residual Value	Depreciable Cost	Estimated Life (yrs)	Depreciation per Year (straight-line)
Cars	$145,000	$25,000	$120,000	3	$40,000
Trucks	44,000	4,000	40,000	4	10,000
Campers	35,000	5,000	30,000	5	6,000
	$224,000	$34,000	$190,000		$56,000

Depreciation or composite rate on original cost $= \dfrac{\$56,000.}{\$224,000} = 25\%.$

Composite life $= 3.39$ years (the depreciable cost of $190,000 divided by $56,000)

The depreciation or composite rate is determined by dividing the *total depreciation per year* for the collection of assets by the *total original cost* of all the assets. If there are no changes in the assets, they will be depreciated to the residual value in the amount of $56,000 per year (the original cost of $224,000 × the composite rate of 25%). As a result, it will take Smart Motors 3.39 years (composite life as indicated in the exhibit) to depreciate these assets.

The differences between the group or composite method and the single-unit depreciation approach become accentuated when examining asset retirements. If an asset is retired before, or after, the average service life of the group is reached, the resulting gain or loss .is buried in the Accumulated Depreciation account. This practice is justified because some assets will be retired before the average service life, while others will be retired after the average life. For this reason, *the debit to Accumulated Depreciation is the difference between original cost and cash received. No gain or loss on disposition is recorded.*

To illustrate, suppose that one of the campers with a cost of $5,000 was sold for $2,600 at the end of the third year. The entry is:

Accumulated Depreciation	2,400	
Cash	2,600	
Cars, Trucks, and Campers		5,000

If a new type of asset is purchased (mopeds, for example), a new depreciation rate must be computed and applied in subsequent periods.

An example of financial statement disclosure using the composite method is provided by Cominco Ltd., as shown in Exhibit 12-9 [highlighting provided by authors].

EXHIBIT 12-9 COMINCO LTD.

DISCLOSURE OF COMPOSITE METHOD

From the summary of significant accounting policies
for the year ended December 31, 1996

Land, Buildings and Equipment

Land, buildings and equipment are recorded at cost and include the costs of renewals and betterments. When assets are sold or abandoned, the recorded costs and related accumulated depreciation are removed from the accounts and any gains or losses are included in earnings. Repairs and maintenance are charged against earnings as incurred.

Depreciation is calculated on the straight-line method using rates based on the estimated service lives of the respective assets. In some integrated mining and manufacturing operations, assets are pooled and depreciated at composite rates. Depreciation is not provided on major additions until commencement of commercial operation.

The group or composite method simplifies the bookkeeping process and tends to average out errors caused by over- or under-depreciation. As a result, periodic income is not distorted by gains or losses on disposals of assets.

On the other hand, the single-asset approach (1) simplifies the computation mathematically; (2) identifies gains and losses on disposal; (3) isolates depreciation on idle equipment; and (4) represents the best estimate of the depreciation of each asset, not the result of averaging the cost over a longer period of time.

Compound Interest Methods. Unlike other depreciation methods, the **compound interest methods** ("sinking fund method" and "annuity method") are **increasing charge methods** that *result in lower depreciation charges in the early years and higher depreciation charges in the later years.* Conceptually, these methods have much to offer, but they have found limited acceptance. At the present time, their use in Canada is limited primarily to companies with real estate development operations. Such operations usually have an interest expense pattern that goes from high to low amounts over a property's useful life. In order to reflect a fairly stable level of total expenses (interest plus depreciation) over the years (because annual revenue from the property is fairly stable), an increasing charge method is used.

The calculations for the compound interest methods are not illustrated in this book.[12] The excerpt from the financial statements of CT Financial Services Inc., shown in Exhibit 12-10, indicates how this company discloses its use of a compound interest method.

EXHIBIT 12-10   CT FINANCIAL SERVICES INC.

DISCLOSURE OF COMPOUND INTEREST METHOD
From the summary of significant accounting policies

(iv) Real estate investment properties

. . . .

Depreciation on buildings is provided on a 5%, sinking fund basis over periods of 30 and 50 years. The depreciation charge increases annually and consists of a fixed annual amount together with an amount equivalent to interest compounded at the rate of 5% so as to fully depreciate the buildings over the specified period. The depreciation charged on buildings in the thirtieth year will be approximately four times the amount charged in the first year, while that charged in the fiftieth year will be approximately eleven times.

SELECTION OF A DEPRECIATION METHOD

Which depreciation method should be selected, and why? Conceptually, the selection of a depreciation method (as with the selection of any accounting method) should be determined on the basis of which method best meets the objectives of financial reporting in the particular circumstances. To achieve these objectives, many believe that *matching of expenses rationally against benefits (revenues) should occur.*[13]

If the method to be chosen is the one that rationally matches depreciation expense against the benefits to be received from the asset, it is first necessary to identify the pattern of benefits to be received. Possible benefit patterns (net revenues before depreciation) are indicated in Illustration 12-1.

OBJECTIVE 5
Identify and understand the reasons for selecting a depreciation method.

ILLUSTRATION 12-1
Possible benefit patterns for assets

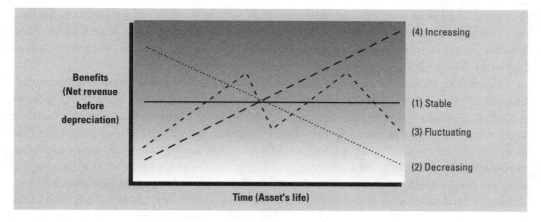

Pattern (1) would represent an asset providing roughly the same level of benefits for each year of its life. A warehouse could be an example. For such assets, the straight-line depreciation method would be rational because it gives a constant depreciation expense each period. An airplane may be an example of an asset with a decreasing benefit pattern

---

[12] These calculations are generally considered in more advanced texts or courses and, as such, are beyond the scope of this book.

[13] *CICA Handbook*, Section 3060, par. .35, states that, when selecting a method, the objective is to provide a rational and systematic basis for allocating the amortizable amount of a capital asset over its estimated useful life.

(2). When it is new, it is constantly in service on major routes but, as it gets older, it may be repaired more frequently and used for more peripheral routes. Therefore, depreciation expense should decline each year (which is what occurs under decreasing charge methods) if expense is rationally to match benefits. The use of a truck (in terms of kilometres driven) may fluctuate considerably from period to period, yielding a benefit pattern that varies (3). An activity method would rationally match depreciation expense against such a benefit pattern. An increasing benefit pattern (4) may result from ownership of a computer. When bought, it is likely that few and less complicated programs are used and many "bugs" have to be ironed out. As time passes, more complex programs may be added, providing increased benefits. As such, a compound interest method may be most appropriate for matching.

While appropriate matching is important, it may be difficult in many cases to develop projections of future revenues. *Simplicity* may therefore govern. In such cases, it might be argued that the straight-line method of depreciation should be used. However, others might argue that whatever is used for tax purposes should be used for book purposes because it *eliminates some record-keeping costs*. Because Canadian companies must use the capital cost allowance approach for income tax purposes (discussed later in this chapter), they may be tempted to use the same for financial reporting purposes. The objectives of financial reporting differ, however, from those of income tax determination. Therefore, for many companies, it is not uncommon to have "two sets of records" when accounting for depreciation: one for financial reporting, and another for income tax determination. While this is legal and acceptable given the differences in objectives, a consequence is that financial statement income before taxes will differ from taxable income in any given year. Consequently, income tax expense (based on financial statement income before taxes) will differ from income taxes paid (based on taxable income). The financial accounting consequences of such differences are examined in Chapter 19.

The *perceived economic consequence* of the resulting financial reporting may also be a factor that influences the selection of a depreciation method. For example, at one time U.S. Steel (now U.S.X.) changed its method of depreciation from an accelerated to a straight-line method for financial reporting purposes. Many observers noted that the reason for the change was to report higher income so that the company would be less susceptible to take-over by another enterprise. In effect, the company wanted to report higher income so that the market value of its shares would rise.[14]

As another illustration, the real estate industry in the U.S. is frustrated with depreciation accounting, arguing that real estate often does not decline in value and that, because real estate is highly debt financed, most U.S. real estate concerns report losses in earlier years when the sum of depreciation and interest charges exceeds the revenues from the real estate project. The industry argues for some form of increasing charge method of depreciation (lower depreciation at the beginning and higher depreciation at the end) so that higher total assets and net income are reported in the earlier years of the project. Some even use an economic consequences argument that Canadian real estate companies (which could and did use an increasing charge method) have a competitive edge over U.S. real estate companies. In support of this view, they have pointed to the increasing number of acquisitions by Canadian real estate companies of U.S. real estate companies and properties.

Choice of a depreciation method will affect both the balance sheet (i.e., carrying value of capital assets) and the income statement (i.e., depreciation expense). Therefore, various

---

[14] This assumption is highly tenuous. It is based on the belief that stock market analysts will not be able to recognize that the change in depreciation methods is purely cosmetic and therefore will give more value to the shares after the change. In fact, research in this area reports just the opposite. One study showed that companies that switched from accelerated to straight-line (which increased income) methods experienced declines in share value after the change; see Robert J. Kaplan and Richard Roll, "Investors' Evaluation of Accounting Information: Some Emperical Evidnece," *The Journal of Business*, April, 1972, pp. 225–257. Others have noted that switches to more liberal accounting policies (generating higher income numbers) have resulted in lower stock market performance. One rationale is that such changes signal the market that the company is in trouble and leads to scepticism about managements' attitudes and behaviour.

ratios will be affected (e.g., rate of return on total assets, debt to total assets ratio, total asset turnover). Consequently, contractual commitments (e.g., management compensation plans, bond indentures) are potentially important aspects that should be considered when selecting a depreciation method.

SPECIAL DEPRECIATION ISSUES

Several special issues related to depreciation remain to be discussed. These are:

1. How should depreciation be computed for partial periods?
2. Does depreciation provide for the replacement of assets?
3. How are revisions in depreciation rates handled?
4. How should an impairment in value be accounted for?
5. How is "depreciation" determined for tax purposes (the tax method of capital cost allowance determination)?

OBJECTIVE 6
Understand and know how to resolve and account for special issues related to depreciation.

Depreciation and Partial Periods. Plant assets are seldom purchased on the first day of a fiscal period or disposed of on the last day of a fiscal period. A practical question is: How much depreciation should be charged for the partial period involved?

Assume, for example, that an automated drill machine with a five-year life is purchased by Athabaska Steel Inc. for $45,000 (no residual value) on June 10. The company's fiscal year ends December 31 and depreciation is charged for 6⅔ months during that year. The total depreciation for a full year (assuming straight-line depreciation) is $9,000 ($45,000/5), and the depreciation for the partial year is $5,000 (9,000 × [6⅔/12]).

Rather than making a precise allocation of cost for a partial period, many companies establish a policy to simplify the calculation of depreciation for partial periods. For example, depreciation may be computed for the full period on the opening balance in the asset account, and no depreciation charged on acquisitions during the year. Other variations charge a full year's depreciation on assets used for a full year and one-half year's depreciation in the years of acquisition and disposal. Alternatively, they may charge a full year's depreciation in the year of acquisition and none in the year of disposal.

The schedule in Exhibit 12-11 shows the amounts of depreciation allocated under five different policies using straight-line depreciation on the $45,000 automated drill machine purchased by Athabaska Steel Inc.

EXHIBIT 12-11 ATHABASKA STEEL INC.

FRACTIONAL YEAR DEPRECIATION POLICIES

Fractional-Year Policy	Depreciation Year 1	Recognized Fiscal Year Year 2–5	Depreciation Year 6
1. Nearest fraction of a year	$5,000[a]	$9,000	$4,000[b]
2. Nearest full month	5,250[c]	9,000	3,750[d]
3. Half year in period of acquisition and disposal	4,500	9,000	4,500
4. Full year in period of acquisition, none in period of disposal	9,000	9,000	-0-
5. None in period of acquisition, full year in period of disposal	-0-	9,000	9,000

[a]6.667/12 ($9,000)   [b]5.333/12 ($9,000)   [c]7/12 ($9,000)   [d]5/12 ($9,000)

A company is at liberty to adopt any of several fractional-year policies in allocating cost to the first and last years of an asset's life so long as the method is applied consistently. For illustrations in this book, depreciation has been computed on the basis of the nearest full month, unless otherwise stated.

What happens when an accelerated method such as double-declining balance is used and partial periods are involved? As an example, assume that an asset was purchased for $10,000 on July 1, 1996 with an estimated useful life of five years. The depreciation figures for 1996, 1997, and 1998 are shown in Exhibit 12-12.

EXHIBIT 12-12

CALCULATION OF PARTIAL PERIOD DEPRECIATION,
DOUBLE-DECLINING BALANCE METHOD

	Double-Declining Balance
1st Full Year	$(40\% \times 10,000) = \$4,000$
2nd Full Year	$(40\% \times 6,000) = 2,400$
3rd Full Year	$(40\% \times 3,600) = 1,440$

Depreciation from July 1, 1996 to December 31, 1996 (1/2 year)

$$0.5 \times \$4,000 = \underline{\$2,000}$$

Depreciation for 1997

$$0.5 \times \$4,000 = \$2,000$$
$$0.5 \times 2,400 = \underline{1,200}$$
$$\$3,200$$

$$\text{or } (\$10,000 - \$2.000) \times 40\% = \underline{\$3,200}$$

Depreciation for 1998

$$0.5 \times 2,400 = \$1,200$$
$$0.5 \times 1,440 = \underline{720}$$
$$\$1,920$$

$$\text{or } (\$10,000 - \$5,200) \times 40\% = \underline{\$1,920}$$

In computing depreciation expense for partial periods in this example, the depreciation charge for a full year was determined first. This amount was then prorated on a straight-line basis to depreciation expense between the two accounting periods involved. A simpler approach when using the declining balance method is to calculate the partial year depreciation expense for the year of acquisition (e.g., the $2,000 for 1996 as shown in the example) and then apply the depreciation rate (40%) to the book value at the beginning of each successive year. This is shown in the illustration as the "or" calculations. The charge for each year is the same regardless of the alternative mathematics employed.

Depreciation and Replacement of Assets. A common misconception about depreciation is that it provides cash for the replacement of capital assets. Depreciation is similar to any other expense in that it reduces net income, but it differs in that *it does not involve a current cash outflow*.

To illustrate why depreciation does not provide cash for replacement of plant assets, assume that a business starts operating with plant assets of $500,000, which have a useful life of five years. The company's balance sheet at the beginning of the period is shown in Exhibit 12-13.

EXHIBIT 12-13

STARTING BALANCE SHEET

Plant assets	$500,000	Owner's equity	$500,000

Now if we assume that the enterprise earned no revenue over the five years, Exhibit 12-14 shows the resulting income statements.

EXHIBIT 12-14

INCOME STATEMENTS FOR FIVE YEARS

	Year 1	Year 2	Year 3	Year 4	Year 5
Revenue	-0-	-0-	-0-	-0-	-0-
Depreciation	(100,000)	(100,000)	(100,000)	(100,000)	(100,000)
Loss	$(100,000)	$(100,000)	$(100,000)	$(100,000)	$(100,000)

The balance sheet at the end of the five years is shown in Exhibit 12-15.

EXHIBIT 12-15

ENDING BALANCE SHEET

Plant assets	-0-	Owner's equity	-0-

This extreme illustration points out that depreciation in no way provides cash for the replacement of assets. Funds for the replacement of assets come from revenues; without revenues no income materializes, and no cash inflow results. A separate decision must be made by management to set aside cash to accumulate asset replacement funds.

Revision of Depreciation Rates. When a depreciable asset is purchased, depreciation rates are carefully determined based on past experience with similar assets and all other available pertinent information. The provisions for depreciation are only estimates, however, and it may be necessary to revise them during the life of the asset. Unexpected physical deterioration, unforeseen obsolescence, or a change in the law or environment may indicate that the useful life of the asset is less than originally estimated. Improved maintenance procedures, revision of operating procedures, or similar developments may prolong the life of the asset beyond the expected period.[15]

For example, assume that machinery costing $90,000 is estimated to have a 20-year life with no residual value and has already been depreciated for five years. In the sixth year it is estimated that it will be used an additional 25 years (including the sixth year). Depreciation has been recorded at the rate of 1/20 of $90,000, or $4,500 per year by the straight-line method. On the basis of a 30-year life, depreciation should have been 1/30 of

---

[15] *CICA Handbook*, Section 3060, par. .37, states that the amortization method and estimates of the life and useful life of a capital asset should be reviewed on a regular basis.

$90,000, or $3,000 per year. Depreciation has, therefore, been overstated and net income understated by $1,500 for each of the past five years, for a total amount of $7,500. The amount of the difference can be computed as shown in Exhibit 12-16.

EXHIBIT 12-16

COMPUTATION OF DIFFERENCES DUE TO REVISION OF ESTIMATE

	Per Year	For Five Years
Depreciation charged per books (1/20 × $90,000)	$4,500	$22,500
Depreciation based on a 30-year life (1/30 × $90,000)	3,000	15,000
Excess depreciation charged	**$1,500**	**$ 7,500**

The *CICA Handbook*, Section 1506, requires that *the effects of changes in estimates be accounted for in the period of change and applicable future periods*. No changes are made to previously reported results. Opening balances are not adjusted and no attempt is made to "catch up" for prior periods. The reason is that changes in estimates are a continual and inherent part of any estimation process. As new information becomes available, it is incorporated into current and future reports. Therefore, when a change in estimate occurs, *charges for depreciation in the current and subsequent periods are based on allocating the remaining book value less any residual value over the remaining estimated life*. The book value to be depreciated over the remaining 25 years is determined as shown in Exhibit 12-17.

EXHIBIT 12-17

BOOK VALUE TO BE DEPRECIATED IN FUTURE

Machinery	$90,000
Less: Accumulated depreciation	22,500
Book value of machinery at end of fifth year	**$67,500**

If we assume the machinery will have a residual value of $1,000 at the end of its revised useful life, the entry to record depreciation for the current and remaining years is:

Depreciation Expense	2,660	
Accumulated Depreciation—Machinery		2,660
($67,500 − $1,000)/25		

If the double-declining balance method was used, the change in estimated life would result in a changed depreciation rate to be applied to the book value in the current (sixth) and subsequent years. As this method ignores residual value in determining depreciation expense, a change in residual value is ignored in the revised calculation. Using the information regarding the machine costing $90,000, the change in estimated life would be handled as indicated in Exhibit 12-18.

EXHIBIT 12-18

CHANGE IN ESTIMATE AND THE DECLINING BALANCE METHOD

1. For years 1–5

   Depreciation rate $= 2/20 \times 100\% = 10\%$

Year	Depreciation Expense	Accumulated Depreciation	Book Value
1	$9,000	$ 9,000	$81,000
2	8,100	17,100	72,900
3	7,290	24,390	65,610
4	6,561	30,951	59,049
5	5,905	36,856	53,144*

   *To determine the book value when using the double-declining balance method, one may use the following formula rather than make the annual calculations:

   Book value $= (1 - r)^n \, c$
      Where $r =$ depreciation rate
          $n =$ number of full years from the date of acquisition of the asset
          $c =$ cost of asset

   For the above example:

   Book value $= (1 - r)^n \, c$
             $= (1 - .1)^5 \, \$90,000$
             $= .59049 \times \$90,000$
             $= \$53,144$

2. Determine the new depreciation rate to be applied in the sixth and subsequent years.

   Revised depreciation rate $= 2(1/\text{remaining years of life})$
                         $= 2(1/25)$
                         $= 2/25$
                         $= .08 \text{ or } 8\%$

3. Using the revised rate, determine the depreciation expense in the normal manner of multiplying the book value at the beginning of the period by the new rate.

   For year 6 $= .08(\$53,144) = \$4,252$
   For year 7 $= .08(\$53,144 - \$4,252) = \$3,911$
   etc.

Impairment in Value. An impairment in value occurs when the revenue-producing ability of a capital asset falls below expectations. Reasons for a decline in value include significant technological developments, physical damage, changes in external economic conditions, a substantial decline in the market for the product produced, and a change in laws or general environmental conditions. When a decline results in an asset's "value" being less than its book value or **net carrying amount** (cost less accumulated depreciation), the questions become whether or not the asset should be written down and, if so, how the amount of the write-down should be determined.

The *CICA Handbook* states that *when the net carrying amount of a capital asset,* less any related accumulated provision for future site removal and restoration costs and deferred income taxes, *exceeds the net recoverable amount, the excess should be charged to income.*[16] The **net recoverable amount** is the estimated *undiscounted* future net cash flow from the use of an asset during its remaining useful life, together with its residual value.[17]

To write down the carrying value of an asset, there would be a charge (debit) to an income statement account (e.g., Loss Due to Obsolescence) and the Accumulated Depreciation account would be increased (credited). (While crediting the asset account directly would accomplish the objective of reducing the asset's carrying value, crediting the Accumulated Depreciation account has the benefit of preserving the original cost of the asset.) *Once an asset's carrying value has been written down, it would not be reversed if there was a subsequent increase in the net recoverable value.*[18]

In some situations, both a write-down and a revision in estimates of the asset's remaining useful life and residual value may simultaneously occur. When this happens, the write-down is first recorded and the depreciation charge is then determined on a prospective basis using the revised carrying value, remaining useful life, and residual value.

To illustrate, in 1992 Hi-Tech Industries purchased equipment to produce high-speed contact printers. The equipment cost $1,000,000, had an expected life of eight years, and had an estimated residual value of $200,000. Two years later, with the emergence of the laser printer as a faster, higher-quality printer than the contact type, it was apparent to Hi-Tech's management that its production equipment had suddenly suffered an impairment in value. In early 1994, when the carrying value of the equipment was $800,000, management determined that (1) its net recoverable value was only $300,000; (2) the life should be reduced from six to two remaining years; and (3) the residual value should be reduced to $50,000.

The entry to record the write-down could be as follows.

Loss Due to Equipment Obsolescence	500,000	
Accumulated Depreciation—Equipment		500,000
($800,000 − $300,000)		

The loss of $500,000 is not extraordinary but, because it occurs infrequently and is material in amount, it could be reported as a separate item in the income statement. Future depreciation would be $125,000 a year based on the new carrying value of $300,000, a remaining life of two years, and a residual value of $50,000.

Tax Method of Capital Cost Allowance Determination. For the most part, issues related to tax accounting are not discussed in a financial accounting text. However, because the concepts of tax "depreciation" are similar to those of book depreciation, an overview of this subject is presented.

The **capital cost allowance method** is *used for purposes of determining "depreciation" in calculating taxable income by Canadian corporations regardless of the method used for financial reporting purposes.* Because companies use it for tax purposes, some (particularly small businesses) also use it for financial reporting, judging that the benefits

OBJECTIVE 7
Describe the income tax method of determining capital cost allowance.

[16] *CICA Handbook,* Section 3060, par. .42. Provisions for future removal and site restoration costs are considered later in this chapter and accounting for income taxes is considered in Chapter 19.

[17] *Ibid.,* par. .10. The future cash flow is not discounted because the purpose of the calculation is to determine recovery, not valuation (par. .52). Projecting the net recoverable amount is based on assumptions that reflect the enterprise's planned course of action and management's judgement of the most probable set of economic conditions for the remaining useful life of the asset. An asset write-down occurs when the long-term expectation is that the net carrying amount will not be recovered (par. .46); that is, the loss is of a permanent nature.

[18] *Ibid.,* par. .43. *Financial Reporting in Canada—1995* reports that, in 1994, eight of the 300 companies surveyed disclosed the amount of such write-downs.

of keeping two sets of records (one for financial reporting and one for tax purposes) are less than the costs involved.[19] Such an action, while expedient, may not provide a rational allocation of costs in the financial reports. Therefore, many companies keep a record of capital cost allowance for tax purposes and use another method to determine depreciation for financial statements.

The mechanics of this method are the same as for the declining balance method except that:

1. The government, through the *Income Tax Act* (Income Tax Regulations, Schedule II), specifies the rate to be used for an asset class. This rate is called the capital cost allowance (CCA) rate. The *Income Tax Act* identifies several different classes of assets and the maximum CCA rate for each class. Examination of the definition of each asset class and the examples given in the *Income Tax Act* is necessary to determine the class into which a particular asset falls.

2. CCA is determined for each asset class and can be claimed only on year-end amounts for each class. Assuming no net additions (purchases less disposals, if any) to a class during a year, the maximum CCA allowed is the CCA rate for the class multiplied by the undepreciated capital cost (UCC) at year-end, before the CCA deduction is taken for the year. In a year when there is a net addition (regardless of when it occurs), the maximum CCA on the net addition is one-half of the allowed CCA rate multiplied by the amount of the net addition. The CCA for the net addition plus the CCA on the remaining UCC would be the total CCA for the asset class. If there was only one asset in a class, the maximum CCA allowed in the year of its acquisition would be one-half of the CCA rate multiplied by the acquisition cost, even if the asset was purchased one week before year end. Thereafter, the maximum CCA per year would be the allowed rate multiplied by the UCC at year-end, before the CCA deduction. No CCA would be allowed in the year of disposal for this single asset, even if it was sold just before year end.

3. CCA is taken even if it results in an undepreciated capital cost (book value) that is less than the estimated residual value.

4. It is not required that the maximum rate be taken in any given year, although that would be the normal case as long as a company had taxable income after taking the maximum.

5. Instead of being labelled depreciation expense, it is called capital cost allowance in tax returns.

Assuming that the crane of Cando Co. Ltd. was a Class 8 asset for which the CCA rate allowed is 20%, Exhibit 12-19 shows the calculations required to determine CCA for the first three years. This example also assumes that no other assets were in the class. If there were other Class 8 assets owned prior to purchase of the crane, or purchased or sold during the three years, Exhibit 12-19 indicates how they would be incorporated. See Appendix 12A for a discussion of the tax treatment for additions, retirements, and asset class eliminations.

---

[19] In a manual system where there are many capital assets, the cost of record keeping can be high and subject to various errors (e.g., depreciating assets below their residual values and even after their disposal). Consequently, using one method (i.e., CCA) may be seen as reducing costs and the potential for errors, even though the cost allocation for determining accounting income may be less rational than if another method were used. The availability of accounting software (complete systems or standalone packages for capital assets) capable of maintaining detailed records for capital assets and related depreciation expense and accumulated depreciation under a variety of methods has significantly reduced the cost of record keeping and the possibility for errors.

EXHIBIT 12-19

CAPITAL COST ALLOWANCE SCHEDULE: CRANE EXAMPLE

UCC beginning of Year 1	$ -0-
Additions during year	500,000
Deduct the lower of the proceeds from or cost of assets in class disposed of during the year	-0-
UCC before CCA	$500,000
CCA for Year 1 = (20% × $500,000) × .5	50,000
UCC beginning of Year 2	$450,000
Additions	-0-
Deduct disposals	-0-
UCC before CCA	$450,000
CCA for Year 2 = (20% × $450,000)	90,000
UCC beginning of Year 3	$360,000
Additions	-0-
Deduct disposals	-0-
UCC before CCA	$360,000
CCA for Year 3 = (20% × $360,000)	72,000
UCC beginning of Year 4	$288,000

(Continued in Appendix 12A)

It should be noted that the determination of CCA is subject to rules set by government legislation and, as such, is subject to alteration from time to time. Furthermore, various provincial governments can have different rules with regard to determining CCA for purposes of calculating the income on which provincial taxes are based. The example in Exhibit 12-19 is based on the *Federal Income Tax Act* for 1996.

DISCLOSURE OF PROPERTY, PLANT, AND EQUIPMENT, AND DEPRECIATION[20]

OBJECTIVE 8
Describe financial statement disclosure for property, plant, and equipment, and depreciation.

Financial statement disclosure of property, plant, and equipment should be by major category (e.g., land, buildings, machinery). Disclosure may be in the body of the financial statement or related notes. For each category there should be disclosure of the cost, accumulated depreciation, amount of any write-downs, depreciation method or methods used, and amortization period or rate being used. The amount of depreciation expense and any write-downs for the period should also be disclosed. The net carrying amount of any plant and equipment that is not being depreciated should be disclosed along with an explanation as to why (e.g., it was in the process of being constructed). Pledges, liens, and other commitments related to property, plant, and equipment should be identified. Any liability secured by these assets should not be offset against the assets, but should be reported in the liability section of the balance sheet.

Excerpts from the financial report of SR Telecom Inc., shown in Exhibit 12-20, provide an example of acceptable disclosure. See also Moore Corporation Limited's financials in Appendix 5A.

---

[20] *CICA Handbook*, Section 3060, pars. .58 through .63, provide the basis for this identification of disclosures.

EXHIBIT 12-20   SR TELECOM INC.

DISCLOSURE OF PROPERTY, PLANT, AND EQUIPMENT

From the Balance Sheet

(in thousands of dollars)

	1994	1993
Property, plant and equipment (Note 5)	16,354	12,220

From the Income Statement

(in thousands of dollars)

	1994	1993
Amortization	3,128	2,860

From the Notes to Consolidated Financial Statements

1. **Significant accounting policies**

    e) *Property, plant and equipment and other assets*
        Property, plant and equipment and other assets are recorded at cost and are amortized over their estimated useful lives on the following bases:

Building and improvements	straight-line over 20 and 10 years
Machinery, equipment and fixtures	20% diminishing balance
Computer equipment	30% diminishing balance
Patents	straight-line over 14 years
Goodwill	straight-line over 40 years

Bid costs are expensed as incurred, net of any government assistance received. Certain government assistance received by the Corporation is repayable following a successful bid. The repayment in these circumstances is capitalized and amortized over the life of the contract.

5. **Property, plant and equipment**

	Cost	1994 Accumulated amortization	Net book value
Land	$ 1,106	$ -	$ 1,106
Building, improvements and fixtures	10,472	4,002	6,470
Machinery and equipment	13,569	7,279	6,290
Computer equipment	4,618	2,130	2,488
	$ 29,765	$ 13,411	$ 16,354

	Cost	1993 Accumulated amortization	Net book value
Land	$ 1,081	$ -	$ 1,081
Building, improvements and fixtures	7,400	3,701	3,699
Machinery and equipment	11,427	5,134	6,293
Computer equipment	3,030	1,883	1,147
	$ 22,938	$ 10,718	$ 12,220

INVESTMENT TAX CREDIT

OBJECTIVE 9
Explain the investment tax credit and know how to account for it.

From time to time, the federal government and provincial governments have attempted to stimulate the economy by permitting special tax advantages to enterprises that invest in capital assets. One such advantage is the investment tax credit. An **investment tax credit** allows an enterprise to *reduce its taxes payable by a stipulated percentage of the cost of qualified depreciable assets purchased.* The capital cost to depreciate for tax purposes is reduced by the amount of the tax credit in the year it is claimed.

To illustrate, suppose that an enterprise purchases an asset for $100,000 in 1998 that qualifies for a 10% investment tax credit. If the company has a tax liability of $30,000 before the credit, the company's final tax liability is determined as shown in Exhibit 12-21.

EXHIBIT 12-21

DETERMINATION OF TAX LIABILITY AFTER AN INVESTMENT TAX CREDIT

Taxes payable for 1998 prior to investment credit	$30,000
Less: Investment tax credit ($100,000 × 10%)	10,000
Final tax liability	$20,000

THE ACCOUNTING ISSUE

A vigorous controversy existed within the accounting profession regarding how the investment tax credit should be accounted for in financial statements. Many believed the investment tax credit was a government reduction in the cost of qualified property similar to a purchase discount, and that it should be accounted for over the same period as that of the related asset (cost reduction or deferral approach). Others believed the investment tax credit was a selective reduction in tax expense in the year of the purchase, and that it should be handled as such for financial reporting purposes (tax reduction or flow-through approach). The arguments for the two approaches are presented below.

Cost Reduction or Deferral Method. Advocates for this position argue that earnings (or reduction in tax expense) do not arise from the purchase of qualified property. Instead, the use of the asset creates the benefits to be received from the investment tax credit. Additional support is given to this argument if part of the investment tax credit must be refunded; for example, if the asset is not kept for a given number of years.

Another position taken is that the true cost of the asset is not the invoice cost, but the invoice cost less the investment tax credit. Many believe that a company would not buy the property unless the credit were available, and that the invoice cost of the asset should be reduced accordingly.

Tax Reduction or Flow-Through Method. In this method the investment tax credit is considered to be a selective tax reduction in the period of the purchase and, therefore, tax expense for that period is reduced by the full amount of the credit. Advocates of this approach indicate that realization of the credit does not depend on future use of the asset. Therefore, the benefits of the credit should not be deferred. The investment tax credit is earned by the act of investment and is not affected by the use or nonuse, retention or nonretention, of the asset.

RESOLUTION OF THE ACCOUNTING ISSUE

The key point regarding the appropriateness of a method is how one views the economic substance of an investment tax credit. Is the government providing part of the cost of acquiring the asset, or is the government reducing the current taxes of companies that invest in new assets?[21] Investment tax credits appear to possess the characteristics of both perspectives.

Recognizing the arguments for each approach, the Accounting Standards Board concluded that those favouring the cost reduction approach were more persuasive. Consequently, the *CICA Handbook* states that **investment tax credits should be accounted for using the cost reduction approach.**[22] **Such credits would be either (1) deducted from the asset's cost with depreciation or amortization calculated on the net amount; or (2) deferred and amortized to income on the same basis as the related asset.**[23] *These two ways of applying the cost reduction method result in the same net income each year* although amounts of particular accounts used to derive the net income are different, as is shown in the following illustration.

Illustration. The cost reduction method may be applied by deducting the investment tax credit from the asset's cost with depreciation calculated on the net amount, or it may be deferred and amortized to income on the same basis as the asset to which it relates is depreciated.

To illustrate the accounting under these treatments, assume that Chris Corp. purchases machinery on January 1, 1998 for $100,000 that qualifies for a 10% investment tax credit. The machinery has a useful life of 10 years and no residual value. Assume that the company uses the straight-line depreciation method for both financial reporting and tax purposes.[24] For income tax purposes, the depreciable base is deemed to be $90,000 (the $100,000 acquisition cost less the investment tax credit of $10,000), as is required under tax legislation. Therefore, $9,000 is deductible each year when determining taxable income. Furthermore, assume that the company's net income before depreciation and income taxes is $35,000, and that the tax rate is 50%. The entries under the two approaches that can be used in the cost reduction method are contrasted in Exhibit 12-22.

EXHIBIT 12-22

ENTRIES UNDER COST REDUCTION METHOD APPROACHES
FOR INVESTMENT TAX CREDITS

Investment Tax Credit Treated as a Reduction of Asset's Cost			Investment Tax Credit Deferred and Amortized		
At time of purchase, 1/1/98:					
Machinery	100,000		Machinery	100,000	
Cash		100,000	Cash		100,000
					(Continued)

---

[21] Jonathan M. Kligman, "Investment Tax Credits: Some Key Issues," *CA Magazine*, October, 1983, pp. 78–80. This article provides a good perspective on the controversy over which approach is appropriate and the type of input the Accounting Standards Board dealt with when resolving the issue.

[22] *CICA Handbook*, Section 3805, par. .12.

[23] *Ibid. Financial Reporting in Canada—1995* showed that of 68 companies that accounted for an investment tax credit in 1994, 62 used a cost reduction approach exclusively while two used both the cost reduction and flow-through approaches. Of the companies that used the cost reduction method, it was reported that 47 deducted the tax credit from the asset's cost and five deferred it and amortized it to income.

[24] While the CCA method would normally be used for tax purposes, this assumption has been made to avoid the complexities of dealing with differences between income tax expense in financial statements and income tax paid based on tax returns. The differences result from different methods being used for financial reporting and tax determination (to be examined in Chapter 19). Assuming there are no differences simplifies the illustration, allowing concentration on the cost reduction approaches regarding investment tax credits. The principles illustrated would apply even if straight-line were used for financial statements and CCA for tax purposes.

EXHIBIT 12-22 (Continued)

ENTRIES UNDER COST REDUCTION METHOD APPROACHES
FOR INVESTMENT TAX CREDITS

Investment Tax Credit Treated as a Reduction of Asset's Cost			Investment Tax Credit Deferred and Amortized		

Recognition and payment of taxes in 1998:

Income Tax Expense	13,000		Income Tax Expense	13,000	
Cash		3,000	Cash		3,000
Machinery		10,000	Deferred Investment Tax Credit		10,000
			Deferred Investment Tax Credit	1,000	
			Income Tax Expense		1,000

Recognition of depreciation in 1998:

Depreciation Expense	9,000		Depreciation Expense	10,000	
Accumulated Depreciation		9,000	Accumulated Depreciation		10,000

Annual entries in subsequent periods assuming income before depreciation and income taxes of $35,000:

Income Tax Expense	13,000		Income Tax Expense	13,000	
Cash		13,000	Cash		13,000
			Deferred Investment Tax Credit	1,000	
			Income Tax Expense		1,000
Depreciation Expense	9,000		Depreciation Expense	10,000	
Accumulated Depreciation		9,000	Accumulated Depreciation		10,000

The predominantly used approach of treating the investment tax credit as a reduction of the asset's cost with depreciation calculated on the net amount ($90,000/10 years = $9,000 per year) is somewhat easier to understand. It also avoids problems associated with having an additional account (Deferred Investment Tax Credit) to deal with and the fact that, when the deferral and amortization approach is used, there is a difference between the tax expense each year ($12,000) and the tax rate (50%) multiplied by the financial statement income before tax ($35,000 less depreciation expense of $10,000).[25] However, it can be seen that the net income for each year under both approaches would be $13,000 ($35,000 − $9,000 for depreciation − $13,000 for income tax expense under the reduction of asset cost approach; $35,000 − $10,000 for depreciation − $12,000 for income tax expense under the deferral and amortization approach).

DEPLETION

OBJECTIVE 10
Understand the issues and know how to account for depletion of natural resources.

Natural resources, sometimes called wasting assets, include petroleum, minerals, and timber. They are characterized by two main features: (1) complete removal (consumption) of the asset; and (2) replacement of the asset only by an act of nature. Unlike buildings and machinery, natural resources are consumed physically over the period of use

---

[25] The discrepancy is created because of the consequences of how the investment tax credit and depreciation expense amounts are arrived at in the amortization and deferral approach. Essentially, for tax purposes, the additional $1,000 depreciation taken over the depreciation under the asset cost reduction approach has no impact on the determination of the amount of taxes paid each year.

and do not maintain their physical characteristics. Still, the accounting problems associated with natural resources are similar to those encountered with other capital assets. The questions to be answered are:

1. How is the **depletion base** (amortizable amount) established?
2. What pattern of depletion should be employed?

ESTABLISHING A DEPLETION BASE

How is the depletion base for an oil well determined? Sizable expenditures are needed to find the natural resource, and for every successful discovery there are many "dry holes." Furthermore, long delays are encountered between the time costs are incurred and benefits are obtained from the extracted resources. As a result, a conservative policy frequently is adopted in accounting for the expenditures incurred in finding and extracting natural resources.

The *costs of natural resources* can be divided into three categories: (1) acquisition cost of property; (2) exploration costs; and (3) development costs. The **acquisition cost** of the property is the price paid to obtain the property right to search and find an undiscovered natural resource or the price paid for an already discovered resource. In some cases, property is leased and special royalty payments paid to the lessor if a productive natural resource is found and is commercially profitable. Generally, the acquisition cost is placed in an account titled Undeveloped or Unproved Property and held in that account pending the results of exploration efforts.

As soon as the enterprise has the right to use the property, **exploration costs** are likely to be incurred to find the resource. The accounting treatment for these costs varies: some firms expense all exploration costs; others capitalize only those costs that are directly related to successful projects (**successful efforts approach**); and still others capitalize all these costs whether or not they are related to successful or unsuccessful projects (**full-cost approach**).

Proponents of the full-cost approach believe that unsuccessful ventures are a cost of those that are successful, because the cost of drilling a dry hole is a cost that is needed to find the commercially profitable wells. Those who believe that only the costs of successful projects should be capitalized contend that unsuccessful companies will otherwise end up capitalizing many costs that will enable them, over a short period of time, to show an income that will be similar to a successful company. In addition, it is contended that to appropriately measure cost and effort for a single property unit, the only relevant measure is the cost directly related to that unit. The remainder of the costs should be allocated as period charges (like advertising). Under the latter two approaches, exploration costs are initially capitalized (e.g., to an Undeveloped or Unproved Property account). Only when it is determined whether or not the result is successful and extraction will be commercially viable do the accounting methods begin to differ in their determination of costs to be included in the depletion base (i.e., under the successful efforts methods costs for unsuccessful explorations would be charged to earnings whereas they remain capitalized under the full-cost method).

Canadian practice is mixed in terms of these two approaches.[26] Larger companies such as Imperial Oil Limited and Petro-Canada use the successful efforts approach. The

---

[26] *Oil and Gas Survey, 1995* (Toronto: Price Waterhouse, 1995). This document (and others published by various accounting firms such as KPMG Peat Marwick Thorne) provides a very informative description of issues involved and accounting practices used by Canadian oil and gas companies, and would be of use to those with specific interest in the topic.

smaller- to medium-sized companies favour the full-cost approach. Exceptions to this generality regarding size have included Norcen Energy Resources Ltd. and PanCanadian Petroleum Ltd., which are fairly large companies that use the full-cost method; Total Canada Oil and Gas Ltd. and Paramount Resources Ltd., while being relatively small, use the successful efforts method. The differences in net income figures under the two methods can be staggering, as indicated by the following.

> Regina-based Saskoil piled up a loss of $39 million in 1992 despite more revenue and a lighter debt load, . . .
>
> By the magic of changed accounting methods, it's not the worst year ever for the mid-sized producer of oil and natural gas. Saskoil a year ago reported a loss of $23.8 million in 1991—but it has revised the figure to a whopping $74.9 million loss. The dramatic change in 1991 financial results was triggered by Saskoil replacing its former accounting method with one used generally by major companies in the oil and gas business. . . . Taking on the so-called successful efforts accounting method starting in 1993 also forced Saskoil to reduce its historical retained earnings by $223.6 million. Under its old accounting method Saskoil would have registered a loss of $37 million from its 1992 operations.[27]

The final category of costs incurred in finding natural resources are **development costs**. These costs are incurred to obtain access to proven reserves and to provide facilities for extracting, treating, gathering, and storing the resource. Such costs include depreciation and operating costs of support equipment (e.g., moveable heavy machinery) used in the development activities. The depreciation on these tangible assets would be calculated using an appropriate method but, instead of charging the amount to Depreciation Expense, it would be capitalized to the natural resource asset account and become part of the depletion base.

The preproduction costs that become components of the depletion base, therefore, are based on the approach used. Under the full-cost approach, the depletion base would consist of all acquisition, exploration, and development costs regardless of whether they are incurred for successful or unsuccessful efforts. Under the successful efforts approach only the acquisition, exploration, and development costs associated with successful finds that are commercially viable are included in the depletion base.

DEPLETION OF RESOURCE COST

Once the depletion base is established, the next problem is determining how the natural resource cost will be allocated to accounting periods. Normally, depletion for a time period is computed using an activity base approach (e.g., units of production method). In this approach, the total cost of the natural resource less any residual value is divided by the number of units estimated to be in the resource deposit to obtain a cost per unit of product. This cost per unit is multiplied by the number of units extracted during a period to determine the period's depletion.

For example, suppose MacClede Oil Co. Ltd. acquired the right to use 400 ha of land in northern Alberta to explore for oil. The lease cost is $50,000; the related exploration costs for a discovered oil deposit on the property are $100,000; and development costs incurred in erecting and drilling the well are $850,000. Total costs related to the oil deposit before the first barrel is extracted are, therefore, $1,000,000. It is estimated that the well will provide approximately 1 million barrels of oil. The depletion rate established is computed as shown in Exhibit 12-23.

---

[27] *Saskatoon Star Phoenix*, February 25, 1993.

EXHIBIT 12-23

COMPUTATION OF DEPLETION RATE

$$\frac{\text{Total cost} - \text{Residual value}}{\text{Total estimated units available}} = \textbf{Depletion cost per unit}$$

$$\frac{\$1,000,000}{1,000,000} = \$1 \textbf{ per barrel}$$

If 250,000 barrels are withdrawn in the first year, then the depletion charge for the year is $250,000 (250,000 barrels at $1). The entry to record the depletion is:

Inventory (Depletion)	250,000	
Accumulated Depletion		250,000

The depletion charge for the resource extracted (in addition to labour and other direct costs) is initially charged (debited) to inventory, and then is credited for the cost of the resource sold during the year. This cost flow is similar to that of depreciation for a factory in a manufacturing company, which is initially part of the cost of goods manufactured and is then charged to the income statement in the period in which the goods are sold. The balance sheet presents the cost of the resource and the amount of accumulated depletion entered to date, as shown in Exhibit 12-24.

EXHIBIT 12-24

BALANCE SHEET DISCLOSURE OF NATURAL RESOURCE

Oil deposit (at cost)	$1,000,000	
Less: Accumulated depletion	250,000	$750,000

In some instances an Accumulated Depletion account is not used, and the credit goes directly to the natural resources asset account.

The tangible equipment used in extracting the oil may also be depreciated on a units of production basis, especially if the useful lives of the equipment can be directly assigned to the given resource deposit. If the equipment is used in more than one job, other cost allocation methods such as the straight-line method or accelerated depreciation methods may be more appropriate.

STATUS OF OIL AND GAS ACCOUNTING

As indicated, either the successful efforts or the full-cost method is acceptable in accounting for costs in the oil and gas industry. The descriptions provided in the preceding comments were very simplified. The actual application of either method is complex and constitutes a significant amount of detailed study, which is beyond the scope of this book. As there is a multitude of judgemental and definitional factors associated with each method, one major accounting problem concerns the wide range of interpretations that may be employed. Consequently, even though a company states it is following one or the other of the methods, assuming comparability of financial statements with other companies using the same method can be misleading.

The problem is overcome, to some extent, because companies using the *successful efforts* method (generally large integrated companies, many of which are foreign owned) follow a fairly common set of accounting policies reflected in a *Guideline* (not a recommendation) issued by the Accounting Standards Board in 1986 and revised in 1990.[28] Additionally, some basic aspects of accounting for oil and gas properties were addressed in Section 3060 of the *CICA Handbook* on capital assets.

SPECIAL PROBLEMS IN ACCOUNTING FOR NATURAL RESOURCES

Accounting for natural resources has some interesting problems that are uncommon to most other types of assets. For purposes of discussion we have divided these problems into three categories:

1. Difficulty in estimating recoverable reserves.
2. Future removal and site restoration costs.
3. Accounting for liquidating dividends.

Estimating Recoverable Reserves. Not infrequently, the estimate of recoverable (proven) reserves has to be changed either because new information becomes available or because production processes become more sophisticated. Natural resources such as oil and gas deposits and some rare metals have provided the greatest challenges. Estimates of these reserves are, in large measure, "knowledgeable guesses."

This problem is the *same as that faced in accounting for changes in estimates of the useful lives of plant and equipment*. The procedure is to revise the depletion rate on a prospective basis by dividing the remaining cost by the estimate of the new recoverable reserves. This approach has much merit because the required estimates are so tenuous.

Future Removal and Site Restoration Costs. **Future removal and site restoration costs encompass costs for dismantling, abandoning, and cleaning up a property.** Such costs are not unique to natural resource businesses. These costs are measured net of any expected recoveries, can be substantial, and may be incurred because of environmental laws, contracts, or established company policies. Since these costs are likely to be made far into the future, there are the issues of whether they should and can be recognized, measured, and disclosed in financial statements of periods when extraction of the property's resources is taking place.

The *CICA Handbook* requires recognition of these costs during periods of extraction, provided they are material in amount. The nature of the recognition depends on whether the amount can be reasonably determinable. If not reasonably measurable, then a contingent liability may be disclosed in the financial statement notes.[29] When the amount is judged to be reasonably determinable, then it should be recorded in the accounts during periods of resource extraction.[30] Essentially, this circumstance is similar to recording any accrued expense—an expense account is debited and a liability account is credited. For future removal and site restoration costs, however, the debit may be charged to Inventory (depletion) and, through cost of goods sold, to the income statement. Credits are to a liability account (e.g., Liability for Future Site Restoration), not to be classified with accumulated depletion.[31] The amount for each year is determined in a systematic and rational manner[32] (e.g., allocating the future cost to periods using the straight-line or units of output method).

[28] "Full Cost Accounting in the Oil and Gas Industry," *Accounting Guideline* (Toronto: CICA, 1990).
[29] *CICA Handbook*, Section 3060, par. .41.
[30] *Ibid.*, par. .39.
[31] *Ibid.*, par. .40.
[32] *Ibid.*, par. .39.

To illustrate, assume that MacCleade Oil Co. Ltd. estimates that future site restoration costs will be $360,000, to be incurred six years after extraction commences. Given that 1 million barrels of oil are expected to be provided by the oil well site and that 250,000 barrels are extracted in the first year, the following entry would be made.

Inventory (site restoration costs)	90,000	
Liability for future site restoration		90,000
($360,000/1,000,000 = $.36; $.36 × 250,000)		

While not required, the *CICA Handbook* states that it is desirable to disclose the accumulated provision for future removal and site restoration, the major assumptions used to determine it, the basis for its determination, and the related amount charged to income for a period.[33]

Accounting for Liquidating Dividends. A company may own as its only major asset a certain property from which it intends to extract natural resources. If the company does not expect to purchase additional properties, it may distribute gradually to shareholders their capital investment by paying dividends equal to the accumulated amount of net income (after depletion) plus the amount of depletion charged. The major accounting problem is to distinguish between dividends that are a return of capital and those that are not. A company issuing a **liquidating dividend** should debit the appropriate Share Capital account for that portion related to the original investment instead of Retained Earnings, because the dividend is a return of part of the investor's original contribution. Shareholders must be informed that the total dividend consists of a liquidation of capital as well as a distribution of income.

To illustrate, at December 31, 1998 Callahan Mining has a retained earnings balance of $1,650,000, accumulated depletion on mineral properties of $2,100,000, and common share capital of $5,435,493. Callahan's board declares and pays a dividend of $3.00 a share on the 1,000,000 shares outstanding. The entry to record the $3,000,000 dividend is as follows.

Retained Earnings	1,650,000	
Common Shares	1,350,000	
Cash		3,000,000

The $3.00 dividend per share represents a $1.65 ($1,650,000 ÷ 1,000,000 shares) per share return on investment and a $1.35 ($1,350,000 ÷ 1,000,000) per share liquidating dividend.

FINANCIAL REPORTING OF NATURAL RESOURCES AND DEPLETION

Disclosure requirements for natural resources and depletion are of the same nature as for property, plant, equipment, and depreciation as previously discussed.[34] As such, proper classification is necessary, along with appropriate disclosure of the cost, accumulated depletion, depletion charged during the reporting period, any write-downs, and method used to determine depletion. Also, guidance for reporting has come from the AcSB's *Guideline* on full-cost accounting and U.S. standards. These latter documents indicate that both publicly traded and privately held companies engaged in significant oil and gas production activities should disclose (1) the basic method of accounting for costs incurred in

OBJECTIVE 11
Know how to disclose natural resources and related depletion in financial statements.

---

[33] *CICA Handbook*, Section 3060, par. .63. *Financial Reporting in Canada—1995* reported that in 1994, 69 of the 300 surveyed companies made reference to a provision for future removal and site restoration costs.

[34] *CICA Handbook*, Section 3060 recommendations cover all capital assets of profit-oriented enterprises, except for goodwill (discussed in Chapter 13).

these activities (e.g., full-cost or successful efforts); and (2) the manner of determining and disposing of costs related to these activities (e.g., expensing them immediately, or capitalizing them followed by depreciation and depletion). Public companies, in addition to these disclosures, may report as supplementary information numerous schedules disclosing such things as reserve quantities; capitalized costs; acquisition, exploration, and development activities and costs; operating results by business segment and geographic area (countries); and present value of future net cash flows from proven oil and gas reserves. Information regarding future removal and site restoration costs should also be disclosed, as previously mentioned.

The excerpt from the 1996 financial statements of Petro-Canada shown in Exhibit 12-25 provides an example of disclosures regarding accounting policies applied to its property, plant, and equipment.

EXHIBIT 12-25   PETRO-CANADA

PRESENTATION OF DISCLOSURE FOR NATURAL RESOURCES AND DEPLETION

(from the Summary of Significant Accounting Policies)

(d) Property, Plant and Equipment

Investments in exploration and development activities are accounted for on the successful efforts method. Under this method the acquisition cost of unproved acreage is capitalized. Costs of exploratory wells are initially capitalized pending determination of proved reserves and costs of wells which are assigned proved reserves remain capitalized while costs of unsuccessful wells are charged to earnings. All other exploration costs are charged to earnings as incurred. Development costs, including the cost of all wells, are capitalized.

Substantially all of the Company's exploration and development activities are conducted jointly with others. Only the Company's proportionate interest in such activities is reflected in the financial statements.

The interest cost of debt attributable to the construction of major new facilities is capitalized during the construction period.

(e) Depreciation, Depletion and Amortization

Depreciation and depletion of capitalized costs of oil and gas producing properties is calculated using the unit of production method.

Depreciation of other plant and equipment is provided on either the unit of production method or the straight line method based on the estimated service lives of the related assets, as appropriate.

The carrying amounts of unproved properties are evaluated periodically for impairment with any such impairment being charged to earnings.

(f) Future Removal and Site Restoration Costs

Estimated future removal and site restoration costs which are probable and can be reasonably determined are provided for on either the unit of production method or the straight line method, based on the estimated service lives of the related assets as appropriate.

Summary of Learning Objectives

1. **Explain the concept of depreciation.** Amortization is the generic term used to describe the charge to income that recognizes that the life of a capital asset is finite and that its cost less residual value is to be allocated to the periods of service provided by the asset. Traditionally, amortization of tangible capital assets (other than natural resources) is called depreciation, and for natural resources it is called depletion. In the specific rather than generic use of the word, amortization refers to the allocation of the cost of intangible assets. Depreciation is the result of a cost allocation process that matches expenses to revenues systematically and ration-

ally; it is not intended to result in financial statement amounts that reflect period to period values or value changes in the related assets.

2. **Identify and describe the factors that must be considered when determining depreciation charges.** The amount of depreciation for a period requires determination of (1) the depreciable base (amortizable amount); (2) the estimated useful life; and (3) the method of cost allocation to be used.

3. **Know how to determine depreciation charges using the straight-line, activity, and decreasing charge methods.** The *straight-line method* allocates the depreciable amount on the basis of the passage of time. As such, cost less residual value is divided by the useful economic life to determine depreciation expense per period. A constant depreciation expense per period results. The *activity method* allocates the depreciable base on the basis of use or productivity. The depreciation charge per unit of activity (cost less residual value divided by estimated total units of output or input provided) is determined and multiplied by the units of activity produced or consumed in a period to derive depreciation expense for the period. As such, depreciation expense fluctuates depending on the level of activity of the periods. The *decreasing charge methods* result in a depreciation charge that declines with each subsequent year. For this method, a constant rate (e.g., double the straight-line rate) is multiplied by the book value (cost minus accumulated depreciation) at the start of the period to determine each period's depreciation expense.

4. **Know various special depreciation methods and understand how they work.** There are four special depreciation methods: (1) *Inventory method*, used to value small tangible assets such as hand tools or utensils. (2) *Retirement and replacement methods*, used principally by public utilities and railroads that own many similar units of small value such as poles, ties, conductors, and telephones. The purpose of these approaches is to avoid elaborate depreciation schedules for individual assets. (3) *Group and composite methods*. The term "group" refers to a collection of assets that are similar in nature; "composite" refers to a collection of assets that are dissimilar in nature. The group method is used where the assets are fairly homogeneous and have approximately the same useful lives. The composite approach is used when the assets are heterogeneous and have different lives. (4) *Compound interest methods*. Unlike most depreciation methods, the compound interest methods are increasing charge methods that result in lower depreciation charges in early years and higher depreciation charges in later years.

5. **Identify and understand the reasons for selecting a depreciation method.** Various depreciation methods are generally acceptable. The accountant must exercise appropriate judgement when selecting and implementing the method that is most appropriate for the circumstances. Rational matching, tax reporting, simplicity, perceived economic consequences, and impact on ratios are factors that influence such judgements.

6. **Understand and know how to resolve and account for special issues related to depreciation.** Special problems are encountered in determining depreciation for partial periods, overcoming the misconception that depreciation accounting results in providing funds for asset replacement, accounting for revisions in estimates that constitute components of the depreciation expense calculation (treat as a prospective adjustment), accounting for an impairment in value (write-down of the carrying or book value), and determining depreciation (capital cost allowance) for income tax purposes.

KEY TERMS

composite method, 585

compound interest methods, 586

cost reduction or deferral method, 598

declining balance method, 582

decreasing charge methods, 582

depletion, 577

depletion base, 601

depreciable base, 578

depreciation, 577

development costs, 602

exploration costs, 601

full-cost approach, 601

future removal and site restoration costs, 604

group method, 585

inadequacy, 579

increasing charge methods, 586

input measure, 582

inventory method, 583

investment tax credit, 598

liquidating dividend, 605

net carrying amount, 593

net recoverable amount, 594

obsolescence, 579

output measure, 582

replacement method, 584

residual value, 578

retirement method, 584

straight-line method, 580

successful efforts approach, 601

supersession, 579

tax reduction or flow-through method, 598

useful life, 579

7. **Describe the income tax method of determining capital cost allowance.** Capital cost allowance is the term used for depreciation when calculating taxable income in income tax returns. The mechanics of the CCA method are the same as for the declining balance method except that rates are specified for asset classes, and the amount is claimed based on year-end balances (except for net additions in a year for which the CCA is one-half the rate times the net addition).

8. **Describe financial statement disclosures for property, plant, and equipment, and depreciation.** The basis of valuation (usually historical cost) for property, plant, and equipment; major categories of assets; related accumulated depreciation; pledges related to these assets; current period's expense; and the methods and rates used to calculate depreciation; and any write-downs are among the things that should be disclosed in financial statements.

9. **Explain the investment tax credit and know how to account for it.** Investment tax credits are provided by the government to promote investment in certain assets. The *CICA Handbook* requires use of the cost reduction approach to account for these tax credits.

10. **Understand the issues and know how to account for depletion of natural resources.** The costs of natural resources consist of expenditures related to acquisition, exploration, and development. The amount of the costs that are capitalized and then allocated to production (rather than expensed directly) depends on whether the successful efforts or full-cost approach is used. Capitalized resource costs are usually charged to depletion using an activity approach (unit of production method). Particular issues related to natural resource industries include the difficulty of estimating recoverable reserves, accounting for future removal and site restoration costs, and appropriately determining and reporting a liquidating dividend.

11. **Know how to disclose natural resources and related depletion in financial statements.** Disclosure in financial statements of natural resource companies would include proper classification, identifying the method used for establishing cost and depletion charges, and possibly additional supplementary information regarding site restoration costs, reserve quantities, operating results by geographic area, and acquisition, exploration, and development activity.

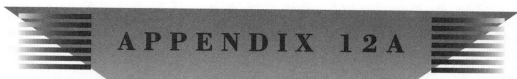

APPENDIX 12A

Tax Method of Capital Cost Allowance: Extension of Example to Include Additions, Retirements, and Asset Class Elimination

The chapter provided a basic illustration of the tax method of capital cost allowance determination. While the mechanics of this method were described, several complexities remain. The purpose of this appendix is to illustrate some of these complexities—namely, how to account for additions, retirements, and asset class elimination for purposes of determining taxable income.

Exhibit 12A-1 presents a capital cost allowance schedule that incorporates information to illustrate these complexities. The schedule is a continuation of that shown in Exhibit 12-19 that dealt with the determination of capital cost allowance for a crane (No. 1) purchased by Cando Co. Ltd. The crane had cost $500,000, on which capital cost allowance for three years had been taken, resulting in an undepreciated capital cost of $288,000 at the beginning of year 4 for Class 8 assets. The continuation of this schedule is based on the occurrence of the following transactions.

1. In Year 4, the company bought another crane (or any other Class 8 asset) for $700,000.

2. In Year 5, the company sold the first crane for $300,000.

3. In Year 6, the company sold the second crane for $500,000. This resulted in no assets remaining in Class 8.

OBJECTIVE 12
Appreciate some of the complexities in determining capital cost allowance.

EXHIBIT 12A-1

CAPITAL COST ALLOWANCE SCHEDULE: CONTINUATION OF EXHIBIT 12-19

UCC beginning of Year 4	$288,000
Additions during Year 4—crane No. 2	700,000
UCC before CCA	$988,000
CCA for Year 4 = [(20% × $288,000) + (.5 × 20% × $700,000)]	127,600
UCC beginning of Year 5	$860,400
Deduct the lower of the proceeds from ($300,000) or cost of ($500,000) crane No. 1 disposed of during the year	300,000
UCC before CCA	$560,400
CCA for Year 5 = (20% × $560,400)	112,080
UCC beginning of Year 6	$448,320
Deduct the lower of the proceeds from ($500,000) or cost of ($700,000) crane No. 2 disposed of during the year	500,000
Note: This disposal eliminates all Class 8 assets of the company.	
Recaptured capital cost allowance	$ 51,680

ADDITIONS TO ASSET CLASS

The purchase of another crane (No. 2) in Year 4 resulted in a **net addition** of $700,000 to the undepreciated capital cost at the end of Year 4. Consequently, the balance of undepreciated capital cost at the end of Year 4 is made up of this $700,000 plus the $288,000 undepreciated capital cost of crane No. 1. The capital cost allowance for Year 4 is, therefore, 20% of $288,000 ($57,600) plus one-half of 20% of the net addition of $700,000 ($70,000) for a total of $127,600.

RETIREMENTS FROM AN ASSET CLASS, CONTINUATION OF CLASS

When there is more than one asset in a class from which an asset is disposed of, and when the proceeds from or cost of the asset disposed of (whichever is lower) is less than the undepreciated capital cost balance, then either the proceeds or the cost (whichever is lower) is deducted from the undepreciated capital cost balance for the class. This is what happened in Year 5 when the company sold crane No. 1 for $300,000. Since the proceeds were less than the $500,000 original cost, the $300,000 amount was deducted from the $860,400 undepreciated capital cost balance before the capital cost allowance for Year 5 was determined.

RETIREMENTS FROM AN ASSET CLASS, ELIMINATION OF CLASS

When the disposal of an asset results in the elimination of an asset class (either because there are no more assets remaining in the class or because the disposal results in the elimination of the undepreciated capital cost balance of the class), the following may result.

(a) A recapture of capital cost allowance.

(b) A recapture of capital cost allowance and a capital gain.

(c) A terminal loss (only when the last asset in the class is disposed of and a balance still exists in the UCC of that class after deducting proceeds or cost of the disposed asset, whichever is lower).

The amount of proceeds, original cost of the asset, and balance of the undepreciated capital cost for the class must be examined to determine which of these results occur.

A **recapture of capital cost allowance** occurs when the lower of the proceeds from or cost of the asset disposed of is greater than the balance of undepreciated capital cost. The difference represents the amount of recaptured capital cost. This recapture would be included in calculating taxable income and is subject to income tax at the normal rates. The events of Year 6 reflected in Exhibit 12A-1 show this situation. Since the $500,000 proceeds are lower than the cost of crane No. 2, they are deducted from the $448,320 balance of undepreciated capital cost resulting in the $51,680 recaptured capital cost allowance.

If an asset of a class is sold for more than its cost, a **capital gain** results, regardless of whether or not the asset class is eliminated. For tax purposes, a capital gain (difference between proceeds and cost when proceeds exceed cost) is treated differently from a recapture of capital cost. Essentially, the taxable capital gain (amount subject to tax) is a specified portion of the capital gain as defined above (generally three-quarters in 1996). The taxable capital gain is then included with other taxable income and taxed at the normal rates. As indicated previously, the full amount of the recaptured capital cost allowance is included in taxable income and is subject to the normal tax rate applicable to the taxable income being reported. If crane No. 1 had been sold in Year 5 for $575,000 (rather than the $300,000 shown in Exhibit 12A-1), the capital gain would be $75,000 and the taxable capital gain would be $56,250 (3/4 × $75,000). The amount of $500,000 would have been deducted from the UCC. If crane No. 2 had been sold for $750,000 in Year 6, a capital gain and a recapture of capital cost allowance would result. The capital gain would be $50,000 and, therefore, a taxable capital gain of $37,500 would occur. The recaptured capital cost allowance would be $251,680 (the $700,000 cost less the $448,320 undepreciated capital cost balance for the asset class being eliminated).

While this example illustrates the basic calculations related to the determination of capital gains, taxable capital gains, and recaptured capital cost allowance, it has necessarily been oversimplified. In essence, the tax rate on taxable capital gains is specified by tax law, which may change from time to time and have implications in terms of other considerations (e.g., refundable dividend tax on hand). Similarly, the tax rate applicable to recaptured capital cost allowance is subject to the particular circumstances of the nature of taxable income being reported of which the recaptured amount is a component. These and other technical and definitional aspects are beyond the scope of this text. The reader is warned that specialist knowledge regarding tax laws is required to determine income taxes payable.

A **terminal loss** occurs when the proceeds from the disposal of the last asset in a class are less than the undepreciated capital cost balance. A terminal loss is deducted in full when determining taxable income. If crane No. 2 had been sold in Year 6 for $300,000, a terminal loss of $148,320 would have resulted (the $448,320 undepreciated capital cost less the $300,000 proceeds).

Summary of Learning Objective for Appendix 12A

KEY TERMS

capital gain, 610

net additions, 609

recapture of capital cost allowance, 610

terminal loss, 611

12. Appreciate some of the complexities in determining capital cost allowance. For an asset class, net additions and retirements are accounted for under specific rules that govern the determination of income taxes payable. When an asset class is eliminated, a recapture of capital cost can occur and also a potential capital gain or a terminal loss.

Note: All *asterisked* Exercises, Problems, or Cases relate to material contained in the appendix to the chapter.

EXERCISES

(Depreciation Computations: Five Methods, Partial Period) Cantlon Co. Ltd. purchased machinery for $260,000 on May 1, 1998. It is estimated to have a useful life of 10 years, residual value of $20,000, production of 240,000 units, and working hours of 25,000. During 1999, Cantlon Co. Ltd. uses the machinery for 2,650 hours, and the machinery produces 26,000 units.

E12-1

Instructions
Given that depreciation or CCA has been correctly recognized for the year ended December 31, 1998, compute the depreciation charge for the year ended December 31, 1999 under each of the following methods (round to nearest dollar):
(a) Straight-line.
(b) Units of output.
(c) Working hours.
(d) Declining balance (use 20% as the annual rate).
(e) Capital cost allowance (tax method) that assumes a CCA rate of 20%.

(Depreciation: Conceptual Understanding) Evergreen Ltd. acquired a plant asset at the beginning of Year 1. The asset has an estimated service life of five years. An employee has correctly prepared the following depreciation schedules for this asset using (1) the straight-line method; and (2) the double-declining balance method.

E12-2

Year	Straight-line	Double-declining Balance
1	$ 6,000	$13,200
2	6,000	7,920
3	6,000	4,752
4	6,000	2,851
5	6,000	1,277
Total	$30,000	$30,000

Instructions

Answer the following questions:

(a) What is the cost of the asset being depreciated?

(b) What amount, if any, was used in the depreciation calculations for the residual value for this asset?

(c) Which method will produce the highest net income in Year 1?

(d) Which method will produce the lowest charge to income in Year 4?

(e) Which method will produce the highest book value for the asset at the end of Year 3?

(f) Which method will produce the highest cash flow in Year 1? In Year 4?

(g) If the asset is sold at the end of Year 3, which method would yield the highest gain (or lowest loss) on disposal of the asset?

E12-3 **(Depreciation Computations: Four Methods, Partial Periods)** Drifters Co. Ltd. purchased a new machine for its assembly process on October 1, 1998. The cost of this machine was $117,900. The company estimated that the machine would have a residual value of $12,900. Its useful life was estimated to be five years and its working hours were estimated to be 21,000 hours. Year end is December 31.

Instructions

Compute the depreciation expense under the following methods: (1) Straight-line depreciation for 1998. (2) Activity method for 1998, assuming that machine usage was 800 hours. (3) Double-declining balance for 1999. (4) Capital cost allowance for 1998 and 1999 using a CCA rate of 25%.

E12-4 **(Depreciation Computations: Five Methods, Partial Periods)** Honey Wine Inc. purchased equipment for $212,000 on April 1, 1998. It was estimated that the equipment would have a useful life of eight years and a residual value of $12,000. Estimated production was 40,000 units and estimated working hours was 20,000. During 1998 the company used the equipment for 1,600 hours and the equipment produced 3,000 units.

Instructions

Compute the depreciation expense using each of the following methods. Honey Wine Inc. is on a calendar-year basis ending December 31.

(a) Straight-line method for 1998.(c)Activity method (working hours) for 1998.

(b) Activity method (units of output) for 1998.

(c) Activity method (working hours) for 1998.

(d) Double-declining balance method for 1999.

(e) What is the capital cost allowance for 1998 and 1999, assuming a CCA rate of 30% and that the equipment is the only item in the asset class?

E12-5 **(Depreciation Computation: Replacement, Nonmonetary Exchange)** Dart Inc. bought a machine on June 1, 1995 for $31,000, f.o.b. the place of manufacture. Freight costs were $200, and $500 was expended to install it. The machine's useful life was estimated at 10 years, with a residual value of $2,500. In June, 1996 an essential part of the machine was replaced, at a cost of $1,980, with a part designed to reduce the cost of operating the machine.

On June 1, 1999 the company bought a new machine with greater capacity for $35,000, delivered, with a trade-in value equal to fair market value on the old machine of $20,000. Removing the old machine from the plant cost $75, and installing the new one cost $1,200. It was estimated that the new machine would have a useful life of 10 years, with a residual value of $3,000.

Instructions

Assuming that depreciation is computed on a straight-line basis, determine the amount of gain or loss on the disposal of the first machine on June 1, 1999, and the amount of depreciation that should be provided during the company's fiscal year, which begins on June 1, 1999.

(Special Depreciation Methods and Issues) Provide answers to the following questions.

E12-6

(a) Amy Lowell purchased a computer for $5,000 on July 1, 1997. She intends to depreciate it over four years using the double-declining balance method. Residual value is $1,000. Assuming a fiscal year end of December 31, compute depreciation for 1998.

(b) If Bala Inc. uses the composite method and its composite rate is 7.5% per year, what entry should it make when plant assets that originally cost $50,000 and have been used for 10 years are sold for $13,000?

(c) If a business that uses the retirement method sells plant assets that originally cost $32,000 five years ago for $14,000, what entry should be made? The assets sold consist of 500 small motors, which usually last about seven years.

(d) A building that was purchased on December 31, 1973 for $1,200,000 was originally estimated to have a life of 50 years with no residual value at the end of that time. Depreciation has been recorded through 1997. During 1998, an examination of the building by an engineering firm discloses that its estimated useful life is 15 years after 1997. What should be the amount of depreciation for 1998?

(e) Gupta Co. has equipment with a net carrying amount of $700,000. The expected future net cash flow from the equipment is $705,000, and its fair value is $604,000. The equipment is expected to be used in operations in the future. What amount (if any) should Gupta report as a write-down to its equipment?

(Depreciating Small Tools) Rodgers Manufacturing Ltd. has approximately 3,000 hand tools, which it uses in its operations. Each is of relatively small value and is frequently replaced. The total cost of such tools is approximately $21,000.

E12-7

Because of the characteristics of this asset, the company prefers to keep neither detailed records of each tool nor depreciate each tool individually. Suggest some reasonably simple method of accounting for these tools so that the asset is carried at a fair amount and operating expenses are charged with a fair amount.

Instructions
Describe and illustrate your suggested method with pro forma entries for the various types of transactions that might occur.

(Composite Depreciation) Presented below is information related to Marcie Ltd.

E12-8

Asset	Cost	Estimated Residual	Estimated Life (in years)
A	$40,500	$5,500	10
B	33,600	4,800	9
C	36,000	3,600	8
D	19,000	1,500	7
E	23,500	2,500	6

Instructions
(a) Compute the rate of depreciation per year to be applied to the cost of the assets under the composite method.
(b) Prepare the adjusting entry necessary at the end of the year to record depreciation for a year.
(c) Prepare the entry to record the sale of asset D for cash of $5,000. It was used for six years, and depreciation was entered under the composite method.

(Depreciation: Change in Estimate) Machinery purchased in 1993 for $52,000 was originally estimated to have a life of eight years with a residual value of $4,000 at the end of that time. Depreciation has been entered for five years on this basis. In 1998, it is determined that the total estimated life (including 1998) should have been 10 years, with a residual value of $4,500 at the end of that time. Assume straight-line depreciation.

E12-9

Instructions
(a) Prepare the entry required to correct the prior years' depreciation.
(b) Prepare the entry to record depreciation for 1998.

(Depreciation Computation: Addition, Change in Estimate) In 1970, Ewart Inc. completed the construction of a building at a cost of $2,100,000 and occupied it in January, 1971. It was estimated that the building would have a useful life of 40 years, and a residual value of $100,000 at the end of that time.

E12-10

Early in 1981, an addition to the building was constructed at a cost of $375,000. At that time it was reaffirmed that the remaining life of the building would be as originally estimated, and that the addition would have a life of 30 years and a residual value of $15,000.

In 1999 it is determined that the probable life of the building will extend to the end of 2030, or 20 years beyond the original estimate.

The straight-line method is used.

Instructions

(a) Compute the annual depreciation that would have been charged from 1971 through 1980.

(b) Compute the annual depreciation that would have been charged from 1981 through 1998.

(c) Prepare the entry to adjust the account balances because of the revision of the estimated life in 1999.

(d) Compute the annual depreciation to be charged, beginning with 1999.

E12-11 (Depreciation: Replacement, Change in Estimate) Gilkey Ltd. constructed a building at a cost of $2,100,000 and has occupied it since January, 1978. It was estimated at that time that its life would be 40 years, with no residual value.

In January, 1998 a new roof was installed at a cost of $300,000. It was estimated at that time that the building would have a useful life of 25 years from that date. The cost of the old roof was $150,000.

Instructions

(a) What amount of depreciation should have been charged annually from the years 1978 through 1997? (Assume straight-line depreciation.)

(b) What entry should be made in 1998 to record the replacement of the roof?

(c) Prepare the entry in January, 1998 to record the revision in the estimated life of the building, if necessary.

(d) What amount of depreciation should be charged for the year 1998?

E12-12 (Error Analysis and Depreciation Computations) Louise Ltd. shows the following entries in its Equipment account for 1998. All amounts are based on historical cost.

Equipment

Jan.	1	Balance	134,750	June 30 Cost of equipment sold	
Aug.	10	Purchases	32,000	(purchased prior to	
	12	Freight on equipment		1998)	22,000
		purchased	700		
	25	Installation costs	2,700		
Nov.	10	Normal repairs	400		

Instructions

(a) Prepare any correcting entries necessary.

(b) Assuming that depreciation is to be charged for a full year on the ending balance in the asset account, compute the depreciation charge for 1998 under each of the methods listed below. Assume an estimated life of 10 years, with no residual value. The machinery included in the January 1, 1998 balance was purchased in 1996.

1. Straight-line.

2. Declining balance (assume twice the straight-line rate).

E12-13 (Depreciation for Partial Periods) On April 10, 1998 Lighton Inc. sold equipment that it purchased for $203,960 on August 20, 1991. It was originally estimated that the equipment would have a life of 12 years and a residual value of $20,000 at the end of that time. Depreciation has been computed on that basis, using the straight-line method.

Instructions

(a) Compute the depreciation charge on this equipment for 1991 and 1998, and the total charge for the period from 1991 to 1998, inclusive, under each of the following six assumptions with respect to partial periods.

1. Depreciation is computed for the exact period of time during which the asset is owned (use 365 days for base).

2. Depreciation is computed for the full year on the January 1 balance in the asset account.

3. Depreciation is computed for the full year on the December 31 balance in the asset account.

4. Depreciation for one-half year is charged on plant assets acquired or disposed of during the year.

5. Depreciation is computed on additions from the beginning of the month following acquisition and on disposals to the beginning of the month following disposal.

6. Depreciation is computed for a full period on all assets in use for over one-half year, and no depreciation is charged on assets in use for less than one-half year.

(b) Briefly evaluate the methods above, considering them from the point of view of basic accounting theory as well as simplicity of application.

(Impairment) Presented below is information related to equipment owned by Fernandez Company at December 31, 1998.   **E12-14**

Cost	$9,000,000
Accumulated depreciation to date	1,000,000
Expected future net cash flows	7,000,000
Fair value	5,000,000

Assume that Fernandez will continue to use this asset in the future. As of December 31, 1998, the equipment has a remaining useful life of four years.

Instructions

(a) Prepare the journal entry to record any write-down of the asset at December 31, 1998.

(b) Prepare the journal entry to record depreciation expense for 1999.

(c) The fair value of the equipment at December 31, 1999 is $5,300,000. Prepare the journal entry (if any) necessary to record this increase in fair value.

(Impairment of Value and Change in Estimate) The management of Classic Inc. was discussing whether certain   **E12-15** equipment should be written down as a charge to current operations because of obsolescence. The assets in question had a cost of $900,000 with depreciation taken to date of $400,000. Management determined that the net recoverable amount for these assets was only $300,000 and that this amount should be appropriately recorded in the accounts. Further, the asset's remaining useful life was reduced from eight to five years. It is now estimated that the equipment has a residual value of $25,000.

Instructions

(a) Prepare the journal entry to record the write-down of the equipment.

(b) If no future use is expected of the asset, prepare the journal entry to record the write-down of the equipment to its net realizable value of $25,000.

(c) Where should a loss on the write-down be reported in the income statement?

(d) What accounting issues did management face in accounting for this write-down?

(Investment Tax Credit: Cost Reduction Method, Alternative Approaches) Farthing Inc. bought a number of   **E12-16** machines at a total cost of $200,000 on January 10, 1998. All of them qualified for a 10% investment tax credit. Farthing Inc. had income before depreciation and taxes of $540,000 (tax rate 35%) and depreciates the machines over a six-year period using the straight-line method. Also, assume that "depreciation" for tax purposes is for a six-year period using straight-line amounts based on the machines' cost less the investment credit.

Instructions

(a) Prepare the entry(ies) for 1998 to account for the machine purchase, income taxes, the investment tax credit, and depreciation. Assume that the investment tax credit is treated as a reduction of the asset's cost under the cost reduction method.

(b) Assuming that the investment tax credit is deferred and amortized under the cost reduction method, what would be the entries requested in part (a)?

(Investment Tax Credit: Cost Reduction Method, Alternative Approaches) Ebert Inc. purchased machinery and   **E12-17** equipment in January, 1998 that totalled $196,000. All of these acquisitions qualified for a 10% investment tax credit. The productive life of the acquired equipment was estimated to be seven years. The company's income before depreciation and taxes was $480,000 (tax rate 30%). Assume depreciation is based on the straight-line method and the "depreciation" to calculate taxable income is based on the straight-line method applied to the equipment cost net of the investment tax credit.

Instructions

(a) Prepare the entry(ies) required at December 31, 1998 to account for the income tax expense, investment credit, and depreciation, assuming that the investment tax credit is treated as a reduction of the assets' cost.

(b) Prepare the entry(ies) required at December 31, 1998 to account for the income tax expense, investment credit, and depreciation, assuming that the investment tax credit is deferred and amortized.

(c) Does the net income under these two approaches of applying the cost reduction method differ for 1998? Show calculations.

E12-18   (Investment Tax Credit, Cost Reduction Method: Error Analysis and Correction) You are the assistant controller for Clover Enterprises Inc. On January 1, 1998 Clover purchased heavy machinery with an estimated service life of 20 years. The machinery cost $500,000. This machinery qualified for a 10% investment tax credit. The bookkeeper stated that, to follow the CICA Handbook recommendations, the cost reduction method would be used for handling this transaction. Accordingly, the following entry was made:

Machinery	450,000	
Reserve for Investment Credit	50,000	
Accounts Payable		500,000

Income tax expense for the year before any allowable credits was correctly determined to be $126,000. The controller therefore made the following entry on December 31, 1998:

Dec. 31 Income Tax Expense	76,000	
Deferred Investment Tax Credit	50,000	
Income Taxes Payable		76,000
Reserve for Investment Credit		50,000

The bookkeeper, however, is unsure of the entries above and asks your opinion.

Instructions
If you believe that the cost reduction method has not been applied correctly, prepare the entry(ies) that will correct the books and bring them into proper balance for 1998. (Ignore any depreciation considerations and assume the application of the cost reduction method is to be applied by treating the tax credit as a reduction of the asset's cost).

E12-19   (Depletion Computations: Timber) Dominion Lumber Ltd. owns a 7,000-ha tract of timber purchased in 1991 at a cost of $1,500 per hectare. At the time of purchase the land was estimated to have a value of $300 per hectare without the timber. Dominion Lumber Ltd. has not logged this tract since it was purchased. In 1998, Dominion had the timber cruised (appraised). The cruise (appraiser) estimated that each hectare contained 8,000 m³ of timber. In 1998, Dominion built 20 km of roads at a cost of $4,500 per kilometre. After the roads were completed, Dominion logged 3,500 trees containing 840,000 m³:

Instructions
(a) Determine the depletion charge for 1998.
(b) If Dominion depreciates the logging roads on the basis of timber cut, determine the depreciation for 1998.
(c) If Dominion plants five seedlings at a cost of $4 per seedling for each tree cut, how should the company account for this reforestation?

E12-20   (Depletion Computations: Mining) PCQ Mining Inc. purchased land on February 1, 1998 at a cost of $1,190,000. It estimated that a total of 60,000 t of mineral was available for mining. After it has removed all the natural resources, the company will be required to restore the property to its previous state because of strict environmental protection laws. It estimates the cost of this restoration at $100,000 and concludes that it will be allocated to each period as part of the depletion charge. It believes it will be able to sell the property afterwards for $80,000. PCQ incurred developmental costs of $160,000 before it was able to do any mining. In 1998, resources removed totalled 30,000 t, of which 22,000 t were sold.

Instructions
Compute the following information for 1998: (1) per-unit material cost; (2) total material cost of 12/31/98 inventory; and (3) total material cost in cost of goods sold for 1998.

(Depletion Computations: Minerals) At the beginning of 1998, Nathan Co. Ltd. acquired a mine for $850,000. Of this amount, $100,000 was ascribed to the land value and the remaining portion to the minerals in the mine. Surveys conducted by geologists have indicated that approximately 12,000,000 units of the ore appear to be in the mine. Nathan incurred $170,000 of development costs associated with this mine prior to any extraction of minerals and estimates that it will require $40,000 to restore the land for an alternative use when all of the mineral has been removed. Restoration is considered a component of the depletion base. During 1998, 2,500,000 units of ore were extracted and 2,100,000 of these units were sold. **E12-21**

Instructions

Compute (1) the total amount of depletion for 1998; and (2) the amount that is charged as an expense for 1998 for the cost of the minerals sold during 1998.

*E12-22 (Capital Cost Allowance, Retirements) During 1998, Ewart Co. Ltd. sold its only Class 3 asset. At the time of sale, the balance of the undepreciated capital cost for this class was $50,000. The asset had originally cost $162,000. Indicate what the resulting amounts would be for any recaptured capital cost, capital gain, and terminal loss assuming that the asset was sold for: (a) $28,000; (b) $75,000; (c) $175,000. ***E12-22**

PROBLEMS

On January 1, 1994 a machine was purchased for $75,000. The machine had an estimated salvage value of $5,000 and an estimated useful life of five years. The machine can operate for 100,000 hours before it needs to be replaced. The company operates the machine as follows: 1994, 20,000 hours; 1995, 25,000 hours; 1996, 15,000 hours; 1997, 30,000 hours; 1998, 10,000 hours. **P12-1**

Instructions

(a) Compute the annual depreciation charges over the machine's life assuming a December 31 year end and using each of the following depreciation methods:
   1. Straight-line method.
   2. Activity method.
   3. Double-declining balance method.
   4. Capital cost allowance method that assumes a rate of 40%.
(b) Assume a fiscal year end of September 30. Compute the annual depreciation charges over the asset's life by applying:
   1. Straight-line method.
   2. Double-declining balance method.

Oreo Inc. purchased Machine #201 on May 1, 1997. The following information regarding this machine was gathered at the end of May: **P12-2**

Price	$71,500
Credit terms	2/10, n/30
Freight-in costs	$ 1,130
Preparation and installation costs	$ 3,800
Labour costs during regular production operations	$10,500

It was expected that the machine could be used for 10 years, after which the residual value would be zero. Oreo Inc. intended to use the machine for only eight years, however, after which it expected to sell it for $1,200. The invoice for Machine #201 was paid May 5, 1997. Oreo prepares financial statements on a calendar-year basis.

Instructions

(a) Compute the depreciation expense for the years indicated using the following methods. (Round to the nearest cent.)
   1. Straight-line method for 1997 and 1998.
   2. Double-declining balance method for 1997 and 1998.

(b) Calculate the capital cost allowance for 1997 and 1998, assuming a CCA rate of 25%.

(c) Suppose the president of Oreo Inc. tells you that because the company is a new organization, she expects it will be several years before production and sales are at optimum levels. She asks you to recommend a depreciation method that will allocate less of the company's depreciation expense to the early years and more to later years of the assets' lives. What method would you recommend?

P12-3 On January 1, 1996 Hardee Ltd., a machine-tool manufacturer, acquired new industrial equipment for $1,134,737. This new equipment was eligible for a 5% investment tax credit. Hardee took full advantage of the credit and accounted for the amount using the cost reduction method by treating the investment tax credit as a reduction in the equipment's cost. The new equipment had a useful life of five years; the residual value was estimated to be $125,000. It was estimated that the new equipment could produce 12,000 machine tools in its first year, but that production would decline by 1,000 units per year over the remaining useful life of the equipment.

As the company's manager is partially compensated on the basis of the annual net income and is planning to retire after 1998, he wishes to know which depreciation method will maximize net income over the three-year period ending December 31, 1998. The following depreciation methods may be used: (1) double-declining balance; (2) straight-line; or (3) units-of-output.

Instructions
What would your answer be to the manager's inquiry? Prepare a supporting schedule that shows the amount of accumulated depreciation at December 31, 1998 for each method. (AICPA adapted)

P12-4 Hot Tools Inc. records all depreciation expense annually at the end of the year. Its policy is to take a full year's depreciation on all assets used throughout the year and depreciation for one-half of one year on all machines acquired or disposed of during that year. The depreciation rate for the machinery is 10% applied on a straight-line basis, with no estimated residual value.

The balance of the Machinery account at the beginning of 1998 was $162,300; the Accumulated Depreciation on Machinery account had a balance of $72,900. The following transactions affecting the machinery accounts took place during 1998.

Jan. 15 Machine No. 38, which cost $9,600 when acquired June 3, 1991, was retired and sold as scrap metal for $600.

Feb. 27 Machine No. 81 was purchased. The fair market value of this machine was $12,500. It replaced Machines No. 12 and No. 27, which were traded in on the new machine. Machine No. 12 was acquired Feb. 4, 1986 at a cost of $5,500 and was still carried in the accounts although fully depreciated and not in use; Machine No. 27 was acquired June 11, 1991 at a cost of $8,200. In addition to these two used machines, $9,000 was paid in cash.

Apr. 7 Machine No. 54 was equipped with electric control equipment at a cost of $840. This machine, originally equipped with simple hand controls, was purchased Dec. 11, 1994 for $1,800. The new electric controls can be attached to any one of several machines in the shop.

12 Machine No. 24 was repaired at a cost of $750 after a fire caused by a short circuit in the wiring burned out the motor and damaged certain essential parts.

July 22 Machines No. 25, 26, and 41 were sold for $2,700 cash. The purchase dates and costs of these machines are:

No. 25	$4,000	May 8, 1990
No. 26	3,200	May 8, 1990
No. 41	2,800	June 1, 1992

Nov. 17 Rearrangement and reinstallation of several machines to facilitate material handling and to speed up production were completed at a cost of $12,400.

Instructions
(a) Record each transaction in general journal entry form.

(b) Compute and record depreciation for the year. No machines now included in the balance of the account were acquired before Jan. 1, 1989.

P12-5 Soon after December 31, 1998, Cormier Manufacturing Inc. was requested by its auditor to prepare a depreciation schedule for semitrucks that showed the additions, retirements, depreciation, and other data that affected the income of the company in the four-year period 1995 to 1998, inclusive. The following data were obtained.

Balance of Semitrucks accounts, Jan. 1, 1995:	
Truck No. 1 purchased Jan. 1, 1992, cost	$18,000
Truck No. 2 purchased July 1, 1992, cost	22,000
Truck No. 3 purchased Jan. 1, 1994, cost	30,000
Truck No. 4 purchased July 1, 1994, cost	24,000
Balance, Jan. 1, 1995	$94,000

The Semitrucks—Accumulated Depreciation account had a correct balance of $30,200 on January 1, 1995 (depreciation on each of the four trucks from their respective dates of purchase, based on a five-year life per truck). No debit charges had been made against the account before January 1, 1995.

Transactions between January 1, 1995 and December 31, 1998, and their record in the ledger, were as follows:

July 1, 1995 Truck No. 3 was traded for a larger one (No. 5), the agreed purchase price (fair market value) of which was $32,000. Cormier Manufacturing Inc. paid the automobile dealer $14,000 cash on the transaction. The entry was a debit to Semitrucks and a credit to Cash, $14,000.

Jan. 1, 1996 Truck No. 1 was sold for $3,000 cash. The entry was a debit to Cash and a credit to Semitrucks, $3,000.

July 1, 1997 Truck No. 4 was damaged in an accident to such an extent that it was sold as junk for $700 cash. Cormier received $2,500 from the insurance company. The entry made by the bookkeeper was a debit to Cash, $3,200 and credits to Miscellaneous Income, $700, and Semitrucks, $2,500.

July 1, 1997 A new truck (No. 6) was acquired for $23,000 cash and was charged at that amount to the Semitrucks account. (Assume truck No. 2 was not retired.)

Entries for depreciation had been made at the close of each year as follows: 1995, $20,200; 1996, $21,000; 1997, $23,050; 1998, $25,100.

Instructions

(a) For each of the four years, compute separately the increase or decrease in net income that arose from the company's errors in determining or entering depreciation, or in recording transactions affecting the trucks. Ignore income tax considerations.

(b) Prepare one compound journal entry as of December 31, 1998 for adjustment of the Semitrucks account to reflect the correct balances as revealed by your schedule, assuming that the books have not been closed for 1998.

The following data relate to the Plant Asset account of BH Co. Ltd. at December 31, 1997. **P12-6**

Plant Asset

	A	B	C	D
Original cost	$35,000	$51,000	$80,000	$75,000
Year purchased	1992	1993	1994	1996
Useful life	10 years	15,000 hours	15 years	10 years
Residual value	$ 3,000	$ 3,000	$ 5,000	$ 5,000
Depreciation method	Straight-line	Activity	Straight-line	Double-declining balance
Accumulated depreciation through 1997[a]	$16,000	$35,200	$15,000	$15,000

[a]In the year an asset is purchased, BH Co. Ltd. does not record any deprecation expense on the asset. In the year an asset is retired or traded in, the company takes a full year's depreciation on the asset.

The following transactions occurred during 1998:

(a) On May 5, Asset A was sold for $12,000 cash. The company's bookkeeper recorded this retirement in the following manner.

Cash	12,000	
Asset A		12,000

(b) On December 31, it was determined that Asset B had been used 2,000 hours during 1998.

(c) On December 31, before computing depreciation expense on Asset C, management decided the useful life remaining from 1/1/98 was 10 years.

(d) On December 31, it was discovered that a plant asset purchased in 1997 had been expensed completely in that year. This asset cost $21,000 and has a useful life of 10 years with no residual value. Management decided to use the double-declining balance method for this asset, referred to as "Asset E."

Instructions

Prepare the necessary correcting entries for the year 1998 and any additional entries necessary to record the appropriate depreciation expense on the above-mentioned assets.

P12-7   Luthor Mining Ltd. purchased a tract of mineral land for $570,000. It estimated that this tract will yield 120,000 t of ore with sufficient mineral content to make mining and processing profitable. It further estimated that 6,000 t of ore will be mined the first year and 12,000 t each year thereafter. The land will have a residual value of $30,000.

The company built structures and sheds on the site at a cost of $36,000. It is estimated that these structures have a physical life of 15 years but, because they must be dismantled if they are to be moved, they have no residual value. The company does not intend to use the buildings elsewhere. Mining machinery installed at the mine was purchased second-hand at a cost of $48,000. This machinery cost the former owner $100,000 and was 50% depreciated when purchased. Luthor Mining Ltd. estimated that about half of this machinery would still be useful when the present mineral resources are exhausted, but that dismantling and removal costs would just about offset its value at that time. The company does not intend to use the machinery elsewhere. The remaining machinery would last until about one-half of the present estimated mineral ore has been removed and would then be worthless. Cost is to be allocated equally between these two classes of machinery.

Instructions

(a) As chief accountant for the company, you are to prepare a schedule showing estimated depletion and depreciation costs for each year of the expected life of the mine.

(b) Draft entries in general journal entry form to record depreciation and depletion for the first year. Assume actual production of 7,000 t. Nothing occurred during the year to cause the company engineers to change their estimates of either the mineral resources or the life of the structures and equipment.

P12-8   In 1968, Splinter Logging and Lumber Company purchased 3,000 ha of timber land on the north side of Mount St. Helens, at a cost of $500 per hectare. In 1980, Splinter began selectively logging this timber tract. In May of 1980, Mt. St. Helens erupted, burying the timberland of Splinter under a metre of ash. All of the timber on the Splinter tract was downed. In addition, logging roads built at a cost of $150,000 were destroyed, as was logging equipment that had a net book value of $300,000.

To the time of the eruption, Splinter had logged 20% of the estimated 500,000 m³ of timber. Prior to the eruption, Splinter estimated the land to have a value of $200 per hectare after the timber was harvested. Splinter includes the logging roads in the depletion base.

Splinter estimated it would take three years to salvage the downed timber at a cost of $700,000. The timber can be sold for pulp wood at an estimated price of $3 per cubic metre. The value of the land is unknown, but until it will grow vegetation again, which scientists say may be as long as 50 to 100 years, the value is nominal.

Instructions

(a) Determine the depletion cost per cubic metre for the timber harvested prior to the eruption of Mt. St. Helens.

(b) Prepare the journal entry to record the depletion prior to the eruption.

(c) If this tract represents approximately half of the timber holdings of Splinter, determine the amount of the estimated loss before income taxes and show how the losses of roads, machinery, and timber and the salvage of the timber should be reported in the financial statements of Splinter for the year ended December 31, 1980.

P12-9   Information pertaining to Teddy Inc.'s capital assets for 1998 is presented below.

Account balances at January 1, 1998	Debit	Credit
Land	$ 200,000	
Building	1,500,000	
Accumulated depreciation—building		$ 350,000
Machinery and equipment	1,080,000	
Accumulated depreciation—machinery and equipment		300,000
Automotive equipment	115,000	
Accumulated depreciation—automotive equipment		84,600

Depreciation method and useful life

Building—declining balance method, rate of 1.5 times straight-line rate, 25-year life.
Machinery and equipment—Straight-line; 10 years.
Automotive equipment—Double-declining balance method; four years.
The residual value of the depreciable assets is immaterial.
Depreciation is computed to the nearest month.

Transactions during 1998 and other information

On January 2, 1998 Teddy purchased a new car for $10,500 cash and a trade-in of a two-year-old car that cost $11,000 and a book value of $2,750. The new car had a cash price of $13,000; the market value of the trade-in is not known.

On April 1, 1998 a machine purchased for $26,000 on April 1, 1993 was destroyed by fire. Teddy recovered $16,000 from its insurance company.

On July 1, 1998 machinery and equipment were purchased at a total invoice cost of $250,000; additional costs of $4,000 for freight and $22,000 for installation were incurred.

Teddy determined that the automotive equipment that comprised the $115,000 balance at January 1, 1998 would have been depreciated at a total amount of $15,200 for the year ended December 31, 1998 had there been no changes in the account during the year.

Instructions

(a) For each depreciable asset classification, prepare schedules that show depreciation expense and accumulated depreciation that would appear on Teddy's income statement for the year ended December 31, 1998 and balance sheet at December 31, 1998, respectively.

(b) Prepare a schedule that shows the gain or loss from disposal of assets that would appear in Teddy's income statement for the year ended December 31, 1998.

(c) Prepare the Capital Assets section of Teddy's December 31, 1998 balance sheet.

Monic Ltd., a manufacturer of steel products, began operations on October 1, 1996. The accounting department of **P12-10** Monic has started the fixed-asset and depreciation schedule presented below. You have been asked to assist in completing this schedule. In addition to ascertaining that the data already on the schedule are correct, you have obtained the following information from the company's records and personnel.

1. Depreciation is computed from the first of the month of acquisition to the first of the month of disposition.

2. Land A and Building A were acquired from a predecessor corporation. Monic paid $800,000 for the land and building together. At the time of acquisition, the land had an appraised value of $90,000, and the building had an appraised value of $810,000.

3. Land B was acquired on October 2, 1996 in exchange for 2,500 of Monic's newly issued common shares. At the date of acquisition, the shares had a fair value of $30 each. During October, 1996, Monic paid $13,000 to demolish an existing building on this land so that it could construct a new building.

4. Construction of Building B on the newly acquired land began on October 1, 1997. By September 30, 1998, Monic had paid $320,000 of the estimated total construction costs of $450,000. It was estimated that the building would be completed and occupied by July, 1999.

5. Certain equipment was donated to the corporation by a local university. An independent appraisal of the equipment when donated placed the fair value at $40,000 and the residual value at $3,000.

6. Machinery A's total cost of $175,000 included installation expense of $1,000 and normal repairs and maintenance of $15,000. Residual value is estimated as $16,000. Machinery A was sold on February 1, 1998.

7. On October 1, 1997, Machinery B was acquired with a down payment of $7,900. Remaining payments were to be made in 11 annual instalments of $10,000 each, beginning October 1, 1997. The prevailing interest rate was 8%. The following data were abstracted from present-value tables (rounded).

	Present value of $1.00 at 8%	Present value of an annuity of $1.00 at 8%
10 years	.463	6.710
11 years	.429	7.139
15 years	.315	8.559

MONIC LTD.
Capital Asset and Depreciation Schedule
For Fiscal Years Ended September 30, 1997 and September 30, 1998

Assets	Acquisition Date	Cost	Residual Value	Depreciation Method	Estimated Life in Years	Depreciation Expense Year Ended September 30	
						1997	1998
Land A	Oct. 1, 1996	$ (1)	N/A*	N/A	N/A	N/A	N/A
Building A	Oct. 1, 1996	(2)	$40,000	Straight-line	(3)	$17,000	(4)
Land B	Oct. 2, 1996	(5)	N/A	N/A	N/A	N/A	N/A
Building B	Under construction	320,000 to date	—	Straight-line	30	—	(6)
Donated Equipment	Oct. 2, 1996	(7)	3,000	Declining balance, 15% rate	10	(8)	(9)
Machinery A	Oct. 2, 1996	(10)	6,000	Double-declining balance	8	(11)	(12)
Machinery B	Oct. 1, 1997	(13)	—	Straight-line	20	—	(14)

*N/A — Not applicable

Instructions

For each numbered item on the foregoing schedule, supply the correct amount. Round each answer to the nearest dollar. (AICPA adapted)

P12-11 You are engaged in the examination of the financial statements of Luke Ltd. for the year ended December 31, 1998. The schedules that follow for the capital assets and related accumulated depreciation accounts have been prepared by the client. You have verified the opening balances to your prior year's audit workpapers.

Your examination reveals the following information:

1. All plant and equipment were depreciated on the straight-line basis (no residual value taken into consideration) using the following estimated lives: buildings, 25 years; all other items, 10 years. The company's policy was to take one-half year's depreciation on all asset acquisitions and disposals during the year.

2. On April 1, the company entered into a 10-year lease contract for a die-casting machine with annual rentals of $8,000 payable in advance every April 1. The lease could be cancelled by either party (60 days written notice is required) and there was no option to renew the lease or buy the equipment at the end of the lease. The estimated useful life of the machine was 10 years with no residual value. The company recorded the die-casting machine in the Machinery and Equipment account at $55,962, the present discounted value at the date of the lease, and $2,798, applicable to the machine, was included in depreciation expense for the year. (Hint: Leases with these conditions should not be capitalized nor should a liability be recognized.)

3. The company completed the construction of a wing on the plant building on June 30. The useful life of the building was not extended by this addition. The lowest construction bid received was $51,000, the amount recorded in the Buildings account. Company personnel constructed the addition at a cost of $48,000 (materials, $24,000; labour, $15,000; and overhead, $9,000). The $3,000 difference was credited to an account called Gain on Self-Construction of Building Addition.

4. On August 18, $15,000 was paid for paving and fencing a portion of land owned by the company and used as a parking lot for employees. The expenditure was charged to the Land account.

5. The amount shown in the machinery and equipment asset retirement column represents cash received on September 5 upon disposal of a machine purchased in July, 1994, for $60,000. The bookkeeper recorded depreciation expense of $4,500 on this machine in 1998.

6. The city of Moose Jaw donated land and a building appraised at $20,000 and $69,000, respectively, to Luke Ltd. for a plant. On September 1, the company began operating the plant. Because the company paid nothing for these assets, the bookkeeper made no entry to record the transaction.

LUKE LTD.
Analysis of Capital Assets and
Related Accumulated Depreciation Accounts
Year Ended December 31, 1998

Assets

Description	Final 12/31/97	Additions	Retirements	Per Books 12/31/98
Land	$ 85,000	$ 15,000		$100,000
Buildings	160,000	51,000		211,000
Machinery and equipment	400,000	55,962	$30,000	425,962
	$645,000	$121,962	$30,000	$736,962

Accumulated Depreciation

Description	Final 12/31/97	Additions[a]	Retirements	Per Books 12/31/98
Buildings	$ 80,000	$ 7,420		$ 87,420
Machinery and equipment	156,000	40,298		196,298
	$236,000	$ 47,718		$283,718

[a]Depreciation expense for the year.

Instructions
Prepare the journal entries at December 31, 1998 to adjust the accounts for the transactions noted above. Disregard income tax implications. The books have not been closed. Computations should be rounded to the nearest dollar.
(AICPA adapted)

Olympic Sporting Goods Inc. was experiencing growth in the demand for its products over the last several years. **P12-12** The last Olympic Games greatly increased the popularity of track and field around the world. As a result, a European sports retailing consortium entered into an agreement with Olympic's Equipment Division to purchase track shoes and other accessories on an increasing basis over the next five years.

To be able to meet the quantity commitments of this agreement, Olympic had to obtain additional manufacturing capacity. A real estate firm located an available factory in close proximity to Olympic's Equipment Division manufacturing facility, and Olympic agreed to purchase the factory and used machinery from Eastern Athletic Equipment Ltd. on October 1, 1998. Renovations were necessary to convert the factory for Olympic's manufacturing use.

The terms of the agreement required Olympic to pay Eastern $50,000 when renovations started on January 1, 1999, with the balance to be paid as renovations were completed. The overall purchase price for the factory and machinery was $400,000. The building renovations were contracted to Welker Construction at $100,000. The payments made, as renovations progressed during 1999, are shown below. The factory went into service on January 1, 2000.

	1/1	4/1	10/1	12/31
Eastern	$50,000	$100,000	$100,000	$150,000
Welker		30,000	30,000	40,000

On January 1, 1999 Olympic secured a $500,000 line-of-credit with a 12% interest rate to finance the purchase cost of the factory and machinery, and the renovation costs. Olympic drew down on the line-of-credit to meet the payment schedule shown above; this was Olympic's only outstanding loan during 1999.

B. Donovan, Olympic's controller, capitalized the interest costs for this project to the Building account. Olympic's policy regarding purchases of this nature was to use the appraisal value of the land for book purposes and prorate the balance of the purchase price over the remaining items. The building had originally cost Eastern $300,000 and had a net book value of $50,000, while the machinery originally cost $125,000 and had a net book value of $40,000 on the date of sale. The land was recorded on Eastern's books at $40,000. An appraisal, conducted by independent appraisers at the time of acquisition, valued the land at $280,000, the building at $105,000, and the machinery at $45,000.

B. Shurwin, chief engineer, estimated that the renovated plant would be used for 15 years, with an estimated residual value of $30,000. Shurwin estimated that the productive machinery would have a remaining useful life of five years and a residual value of $3,000. Olympic's depreciation policy specified the declining-balance method be used for both machinery (at twice the straight-line rate) and building (at one and one-half times the straight-line rate), and that one-half year's depreciation be taken in the year an asset is placed in service and in the year in which it is disposed of or retired.

Instructions

(a) Determine the amounts to be recorded on the books of Olympic Sporting Goods Inc. as of December 31, 1999 for each of the following properties acquired from Eastern Athletic Equipment Company:

1. Land.
2. Building.
3. Machinery.

(b) Calculate Olympic Sporting Goods Inc.'s 2000 depreciation expense, for book purposes, for each of the properties acquired from Eastern Athletic Equipment Company:

(c) Discuss the arguments for and against the capitalization of interest costs.   (CMA adapted)

*P12-13   Swash Co. Ltd. engaged in the following transactions regarding Class 10 assets (30% CCA rate):

> 1992—Purchased asset No. 1 for $150,000.
> 1994—Purchased asset No. 2 for $108,000.
> 1995—Sold asset No. 1 for $13,175.
> 1996—Purchased asset No. 3 for $200,000.
> 1998—Sold asset No. 2 for $96,000.

Instructions

(a) Prepare a capital cost allowance schedule for Class 10 assets covering the years ended December 31, 1994 through 1998.

(b) Indicate the amounts of any capital gains, recaptured capital cost, or terminal loss that would result if, during 1999, asset No. 3 was sold (thereby eliminating Class 10 assets for the Company) for: (1) $220,000; (2) $110,000; (3) $25,000.

CASES

C12-1   As an accountant for Delli Cannery Ltd., you have been approached by Chris Lask, canning room supervisor, about the 1998 costs charged to his department. In particular, he is concerned about the line item "depreciation." Lask is very proud of the excellent condition of his canning room equipment. He has always been vigilant about keeping all equipment serviced and well oiled. He is sure that the huge charge to depreciation is a mistake: it does not at all reflect the cost of minimal wear and tear that the machines have experienced over the last year. He believes that the charge should be considerably lower.

The machines being depreciated are six automatic canning machines. All were put into service on January 1, 1998. Each cost $469,000, had a residual value of $40,000, and a useful life of 12 years. Delli depreciates this and similar assets using double-declining balance. Lask has also pointed out that if you used straight-line depreciation, the charge to his department would not be so great.

Instructions

Write a memo to Chris Lask to clear up his misunderstanding of the term "depreciation." Also, calculate the 1998 depreciation on all machines using both methods. Explain the theoretical justification for double-declining balance and why, in the long run, the aggregate charge to depreciation will be the same under both methods.

C12-2   Various issues regarding depreciation are raised in the following independent situations. Follow the instructions for each situation.

Situation I.
Recently, a governor of a university noted that "depreciation of assets for any university is nonsensical. We're not public companies. Forcing colleges to depreciate would only boost our bookkeeping costs for no good reason."

Instructions
Do you agree? Justify your answer.

Situation II.
The plant manager of a manufacturing firm suggested that accountants should speed up depreciation on the machinery in the finishing department because improvements were rapidly making those machines obsolete and a depreciation fund big enough to cover their replacement is needed.

Instructions
Discuss the accounting concept of depreciation and the effect on a business concern of the depreciation recorded for plant assets. Pay particular attention to the issues raised by the plant manager.

Situation III.
It has been suggested that plant and equipment could be replaced more quickly if depreciation rates for income tax and accounting purposes were substantially increased. Doing so would result in a zero or low book value of an asset more quickly, thus stimulating quicker replacement of the asset. As a result, business operations would receive the benefit of more modern and more efficient plant facilities.

Instructions
Discuss the merits of this proposition.

Situation IV.
The independent public accountant is frequently called upon by management for advice regarding methods to compute depreciation. Of comparable importance, although it arises less frequently, is the question of whether depreciation should be based on consideration of an asset as a unit, or as part of a group of assets.

Instructions
Briefly describe the accounting for depreciation based on approaches to treating assets as (1) units; and (2) a group. Present the arguments for and against each of the two approaches. Describe how retirements are recorded under each of the two approaches. (AICPA adapted)

Presented below are three different and unrelated situations involving depreciation accounting. Follow the instructions at the end of each situation.

C12-3

Situation I.
Recently, Mathis Ltd. experienced a strike that affected a number of its operating plants. The president of the company suggested that it was not appropriate to report depreciation expense during this period because the equipment did not depreciate and an improper matching of costs and revenues would result. He based his position on the following points:
1. It is inappropriate to charge the period with costs for which there are no related revenues arising from production.
2. The basic factor of depreciation in this instance is wear and tear, and because equipment was idle no wear and tear occurred.

Instructions
Comment on the appropriateness of the president's comments.

Situation II.
Anka Inc. manufactures electrical appliances, most of which are used in homes. Company engineers have designed a new type of blender which, through the use of a few attachments, will perform more functions than any blender currently on the market. Demand for the new blender can be projected with reasonable probability. In order to make the blenders, Anka needs a specialized machine that is not available from outside sources. It has been decided to make such a machine in Anka's own plant.

Instructions
(a) Discuss the effect of projected demand in units for the new blenders (which may be steady, decreasing, or increasing) on the determination of a depreciation method for the machine.
(b) What other matters should be considered in determining the depreciation method? Ignore income tax considerations.

Situation III.

Maxi Paper Co. Ltd. operates a 300-t-per-day pulp mill and four sawmills in British Columbia. The company is in the process of expanding its pulp mill facilities to a capacity of 1,000 t per day and plans to replace three of its older, less efficient sawmills with an expanded facility. One of the mills to be replaced did not operate for most of 1998 (current year), and there are no plans to reopen it before the new sawmill facility becomes operational.

In reviewing the depreciation rates and in discussing the residual values of the sawmills that were to be replaced, it was noted that if present depreciation rates were not adjusted, substantial amounts of plant costs on these three mills would not be depreciated by the time the new mill came on stream.

Instructions

What is the appropriate accounting for the four sawmills at the end of 1998?

C12-4 Velvet Co. Ltd. was organized January 1, 1998. During 1998, the straight-line method of depreciating plant assets has been used to prepare reports for management.

On November 8, 1998 you are having a conference with Velvet's officers to discuss the depreciation method to be used for financial statement reporting. The president has suggested the use of a new method, which he feels is more suitable than the straight-line method for the needs of the company during the period of rapid expansion of production and capacity that he foresees. Following is an example in which the proposed method is applied to a fixed asset with an original cost of $248,000, an estimated useful life of five years, and a residual value of $8,000.

Year	Years of Life Used	Fraction Rate	Depreciation Expense	Accumulated Depreciation at End of Year	Book Value at End of Year
1	1	1/15	$16,000	$ 16,000	$232,000
2	2	2/15	32,000	48,000	200,000
3	3	3/15	48,000	96,000	152,000
4	4	4/15	64,000	160,000	88,000
5	5	5/15	80,000	240,000	8,000

The president favours the new method because he has heard that:

1. It will increase the funds recovered during the years near the end of the assets' useful lives when maintenance and replacement disbursements are high.

2. It will result in increased depreciation charges in later years when the company is likely to be in a better operating position.

Instructions

(a) Is the president's proposal within the scope of generally accepted accounting principles? In making your decision discuss the circumstances, if any, under which use of the method would be reasonable and those, if any, under which it would not be reasonable.

(b) Do depreciation charges recover or create funds? Explain.

C12-5 In 1996, a large corporation decided to construct a large new processing building at one of its mine sites. A smaller building capable of handling one-third of the capacity of the new building had been used for several years. The new building was completed and ready for operation in the spring of 1998. Much of the equipment used in the processing process of the old building was transferred to the new one.

At the time the new building began operations, the old building had a book value of $500,000. The auditors assessed the circumstances for this major client and indicated that they thought this amount should be written off as a loss in 1998. Management of the corporation protested this accounting treatment. Their argument against such a write-off was that the old building had not been torn down and was still capable of handling processing activities should the need arise. Indeed, they had left the building standing in order to protect against the possibility that things might go wrong with the new building or that the new building's capacity might be insufficient to handle all processing at some time in the future. When the decision to construct the new building was made, management had attempted to forecast product demand and allowed an additional 20% capacity to the new building but they recognized that, in such a business, forecasts could be off considerably. Indeed, in 1998, demand for the processed ore had fallen to two-thirds of that which had been expected, leaving the new processing building operating at considerably below its capacity. These circumstances led the auditors to conclude that the old building, while capable of being used in operations, was not likely to be used in the foreseeable future.

Instructions

Analyse this situation and make recommendations regarding the accounting for the old building in 1998.

Various companies are in the business of developing and marketing computer software packages. Several important **C12-6** accounting issues exist regarding how to classify, measure, and report the costs related to such operations. Issues include where the line should be drawn between expensing and capitalizing costs, whether or not the costs expensed should be shown as research and development costs, how capitalized costs should be amortized, and how the various items should be disclosed in the financial statements.

Generally, computer software costs may be categorized into four types, as indicated below (categories basically follow the stages of incurrence, although these stages can be overlapping):

1. Idea formulation and feasibility. These costs include costs of study and documentation related to market feasibility (potential market, duration of market, expected selling price, etc.), financial feasibility (determining if future revenues will exceed future costs), and assessing management's commitment and ability (the company must have or be able to obtain the necessary resources and commitment).

2. Determining technological feasibility and design of the product. These costs relate to detailed product design, and to the coding and testing that are required to determine whether the product can be produced to meet design specifications. Completion of this stage occurs when the product is sufficiently defined so that the costs of production can be reliably estimated.

3. Preparation for production. Presuming that the previous stages have been successful in terms of developing a product that has technological, market, and financial feasibility as well as corporate commitment and ability to produce, the next step would be to prepare for mass production and distribution. Costs at this level relate to producing product masters and related coding and testing as well as completion of documentation and training materials for the customer.

4. Production of software packages. The costs incurred at this stage are for duplicating the software, documentation, and training materials as well as for packaging the product for customers.

Instructions

(a) Throughout this process there are various ways to account for the costs incurred: treat them as an operating expense of the period, or as research and development costs, or capitalize them to a fixed asset account and amortize on a systematic and rational basis, or capitalize them to an inventory account and charge to cost of sales when realization takes place. Analyse each of the four categories, taking into consideration that they are part of a total process related to the ongoing operations of a company. Draw conclusions as to how to account for the costs. Also, for any costs you believe should be capitalized, indicate how they should be amortized, depreciated, or otherwise charged to expense.

(b) Because of the rapid technological and product changes related to the software industry, it is proposed that an "ongoing recoverability test" be carried out regarding any costs that have been capitalized. What would be the accounting purpose of such tests, and what types of things do you think such tests would investigate?

Jean Potter established Quandry Co. as a sole proprietorship on January 2, 1998. The accounts on December 31, 1998 **C12-7** (company's year end), prior to adjusting for depreciation, provided the following amounts:

Current assets		$100,000
Capital assets		
Land	$40,000	
Building	90,000	
Equipment	50,000	180,000
Current liabilities		40,000
Long-term bank loan		120,000
Owner's investment (excluding income)		90,000
Net income prior to depreciation		30,000

All the capital assets were acquired and put into operations on January 2. Estimates regarding these assets were:

Building —25-year life, $15,000 residual value.

Equipment—Five-year life, 15,000 hours of use, $5,000 residual value. The equipment was used for 2,400 hours in 1998.

Ms. Potter is now considering which depreciation method or methods would be appropriate. She has narrowed the choices for the building to the straight-line or double-declining balance methods, and for the equipment to the straight-line, double-declining balance, or activity methods. She has requested your advice and recommendation. In discussions with her, the following concerns were raised.

1. The company presently acquires goods from suppliers with terms of 2/10, n/30. The suppliers have indicated that these terms will continue as long as the current ratio does not fall below 2 to 1. If the ratio were less, then no purchase discounts would be given.
2. The bank will continue the loan from year to year as long as the ratio of long-term debt to total assets does not exceed 46%.
3. Ms. Potter has contracted with the company's manager to pay him a bonus equal to 50% of any net income in excess of $14,000. She prefers to minimize or pay no bonus as long as conditions of agreements with suppliers and the bank can be met.
4. In order to provide a strong signal to attract potential investors to join her in the company, Ms. Potter believes that a rate of return on total assets of at least 5% must be achieved.

Instructions

Prepare a report for Jean Potter that analyses the situation, provides a recommendation of which method or methods should be used, and justifies your recommendation in light of her concerns and the requirement that the method(s) used be systematic and rational.

USING YOUR JUDGEMENT

FINANCIAL REPORTING PROBLEM

Refer to the financial statements of Moore Corporation Limited in Appendix 5A and answer the following questions.

1. What depreciation method(s) does Moore Corporation use for its plant and equipment?
2. How is the depreciable base determined?
3. What are the estimated useful lives for amortizing the company's buildings? For machinery and equipment?
4. What is the historical cost after deducting investment tax credits for Moore's machinery and equipment at December 31, 1995?
5. On average, are the buildings and machinery and equipment in the first or second half of their useful lives as at December 31, 1995?
6. What was the company's total expenditure for acquisition of property, plant, and equipment in 1995?
7. How much depreciation was included in research and development expense in 1995?

ETHICS CASE

Sunshine Manufacturing Co. Ltd. faces a decline in sales of their principal product, an automatic sprinkler system for high-rise buildings. The financial vice-president, Jeanie Moyer, suggests lengthening asset lives to reduce depreciation expense. Machinery purchased for $905,000 in January 1995 was originally estimated to have a life of nine years with a salvage value of $50,000 at the end of the period. Depreciation has been recorded on this machinery for three years on this basis. Moyer wants to change the estimated total life of the machinery to 12 years (assume straight-line depreciation). The controller, Mike Locke, disagrees with Moyer and says it would be unethical to increase net income in this manner.

Instructions

Is the change in asset lives unethical, or simply a good business practice by a far-sighted vice-president? What difference would it make?

chapter 13

INTANGIBLE CAPITAL ASSETS

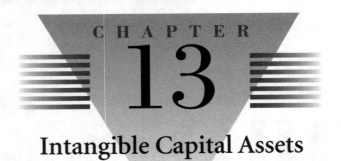

CHAPTER
13

Intangible Capital Assets

Learning Objectives

After studying this chapter, you should be able to:

1. Describe the characteristics of intangible capital assets.

2. Explain the procedure for valuing and amortizing intangible capital assets.

3. Identify the types of specifically identifiable intangible capital assets.

4. Explain the conceptual issues related to goodwill.

5. Describe the accounting procedures for recording goodwill.

6. Identify the conceptual issues related to research and development costs.

7. Describe the accounting procedures for research and development costs.

8. Explain various approaches to valuing goodwill (Appendix 13A).

Intangible capital assets are generally characterized by a lack of physical existence and a high degree of uncertainty concerning future benefits. These criteria are not so clear-cut as they may seem. The following discussion by a noted accountant typifies some of the major problems encountered when attempting to define intangibles.[1]

Q. I infer, Mr. May, from your experience that you know what in ordinary speech the word "tangible" means, don't you?

A. Yes.

Q. Well, what do you understand it to mean in ordinary speech?

A. Something that can be touched, I imagine.

Q. Like merchandise?

A. Yes.

Q. You can touch merchandise or horses?

A. Yes.

Q. Can you touch an account receivable?

A. You can touch the debtor.

Q. Is that the basis on which you include the debtor's debt as tangible?

A. It had not occurred to me before, but possibly it is.

OBJECTIVE 1
Describe the characteristics of intangible capital assets.

This discussion indicates that the **lack of physical existence** is not by itself a satisfactory criterion for distinguishing a tangible from an intangible asset. Such assets as bank

---

[1] From testimony given to referee, *In the Matter of the Estate of E.P. Hatch Deceased (1912)*. Reprinted in Bishop Carleton Hunt, ed., *Twenty-Five Years of Accounting Responsibility. 1911–1936* (New York: Price Waterhouse and Company, 1936), I, p. 246. Selected essays and discussions of George O. May.

deposits, accounts receivable, and long-term investments lack physical substance, yet accountants classify them as tangible assets.

Some accountants believe that intangible assets' major characteristic is the **high degree of uncertainty concerning the future benefits** that is to be received from their employment. For example, many intangibles (1) have value only to a given enterprise; (2) have indeterminate lives; and (3) are subject to large fluctuations in value because their benefits are based on a competitive advantage. The determination and timing of future benefits are extremely difficult and pose serious valuation problems. Some tangible assets possess similar characteristics but are not so pronounced.

Other accountants, finding the problem of defining intangibles insurmountable, prefer simply to present them in financial statements on the basis of tradition. The more common types of intangibles are patents, copyrights, franchises, goodwill, organization costs, and trademarks or trade names. These intangibles may be further subdivided on the basis of the following characteristics.

1. **Identifiability.** Separately identifiable or lacking specific identification.
2. **Manner of acquisition.** Either acquired singly, in groups, or in business combinations, or developed internally.
3. **Expected period of benefit.** Either limited by law or contract or related to human or economic factors, or of indefinite or undetermined duration.
4. **Separability from an entire enterprise.** Rights that are transferable without title, are salable, or are inseparable from the enterprise or a substantial part of it.[2]

These subdivisions provide insight into how the reporting requirements for intangibles have developed.

VALUATION OF PURCHASED INTANGIBLES

Intangibles, like tangible assets, are **recorded at cost**. Cost includes all costs of acquisition and expenditures necessary to make the intangible asset ready for its intended use—for example, purchase price, legal fees, and other incidental expenses.

If intangibles are acquired in exchange for shares or other assets, **the cost of the intangible is the fair market value of the consideration given or the fair market value of the intangible received, whichever is more clearly evident**. When several intangibles, or a combination of intangibles and tangibles, are bought in a "basket purchase," the cost should be allocated on the basis of fair market value or on the basis of relative sales value. Essentially, the accounting treatment for intangibles closely parallels that of tangible assets. The profession has resisted employment of some other basis of valuation, such as current replacement costs or appraisal value for intangible assets.[3]

OBJECTIVE 2
Explain the procedure for valuing and amortizing intangible capital assets.

AMORTIZATION OF INTANGIBLE ASSETS

As we learned in Chapter 12, the expiration of intangible assets is called **amortization**. Intangible assets should be amortized by systematic charges to revenue over their useful lives. In determining useful life, a number of factors should be considered. These include the following:

[2] "Intangible Assets," *Opinions of the Accounting Principles Board No. 17* (New York: AICPA, 1970), par. 10.

[3] For example, Sprouse and Moonitz in *AICPA Accounting Research Study No. 3*, "A Tentative Set of Broad Accounting Principles for a Business Enterprise," advocate abandonment of historical cost in favour of replacement cost for most asset items, but suggest that intangibles should normally be carried at acquisitions cost less amortization because valuation problems are so difficult.

1. Legal, regulatory, or contractual provisions.

2. Provisions for renewal or extension.

3. Effects of obsolescence, demand, competition, and other economic factors.

4. A useful life may parallel the service life expectancies of individuals or groups of employees.

5. Expected actions of competitors and others may restrict present competitive advantages.

6. An apparently unlimited useful life may in fact be indefinite and benefits cannot be reasonably projected.

7. An intangible asset may be a composite of many individual factors with varying economic lives.[4]

One problem relating to the amortization of intangibles is that some intangibles have indeterminable useful lives. In this case, **intangible assets must be amortized over a period not exceeding 40 years**.[5] The 40-year requirement is based on the premise that only a few intangibles, if any, last forever. Sometimes, because useful life is difficult to determine, a 40-year period is employed because it is practical, although admittedly arbitrary. Another reason for this 40-year limitation is simply that it ensures companies begin writing off their intangibles. Prior to the 40-year rule, there was evidence that some companies retained their intangibles (notably goodwill) indefinitely on their balance sheet for only one reason—to avoid the charge against income that occurs when goodwill is written off.

Intangible assets acquired from other enterprises (notably goodwill) should not be written off at acquisition. Some accountants contend that certain intangibles should not be carried as assets on the balance sheet under any circumstances, but should instead be written off directly to retained earnings or contributed surplus. However, the immediate write-off to retained earnings and contributed surplus is not acceptable because this approach denies the existence of an asset that has just been purchased.

Intangible assets are generally amortized on a straight-line basis, although there is no reason why another systematic approach might not be employed if the firm demonstrates that another method is appropriate. In any case, the method and period of amortization should be disclosed.

When intangible assets are amortized, the charges should be included in expenses and the credits should be made either to the appropriate intangible asset accounts or to separate accumulated amortization accounts.

SPECIFICALLY IDENTIFIABLE INTANGIBLE ASSETS

OBJECTIVE 3
Identify the types of specifically identifiable intangible capital assets.

Originally, the accounting profession recognized two types of classification for intangibles: (1) intangibles that have a limited life; and (2) intangibles that have an unlimited life. The classification framework was changed to intangibles that are specifically identifiable in order to exclude the "goodwill type" of intangible assets (unidentifiable values). **Specifically identifiable** means that costs associated with obtaining a given intangible asset can be identified as a part of the cost of that intangible asset. By contrast, a **goodwill type** of intangible may create some right or privilege but is not specifically identifiable and has an indeterminable life. The major identifiable assets and goodwill are discussed in the sections that follow.

---

[4] *APB Opinion No. 17*, op. cit., par. 27.
[5] *CICA Handbook*, par. 3060.32.

PATENTS

Patents are granted by the federal government. The two principal kinds of patents are **product patents**, which cover actual physical products, and **process patents**, which govern the process by which products are made. A patent gives the holder the exclusive right to use, manufacture, and sell a product or process **for a period of 20 years** from the date of application without interference or infringement by others. If a patent is purchased from an inventor (or other owner), the purchase price represents its cost. Other costs incurred in securing a patent, attorneys' fees, and other unrecovered costs of a successful legal suit to protect the patent can be capitalized as part of the patent cost. Research and development costs related to the **development** of the product, process, or idea that is subsequently patented are usually **expensed as incurred**, however. See pages 645–649 for a more complete presentation of accounting for research and development costs.

The cost of a patent should be amortized over its legal life or its useful life (the period during which benefits from the product or process are expected to be received), whichever is shorter. Assuming that, on average, it requires 3 years to process a patent application, the life of a patent after the date of the grant is 17 years. If a patent is owned from the date it is granted and is expected to be useful during its entire remaining legal life, it should be amortized over 17 years. In this book we will assume a 17-year life after the date of the grant. If it appears that the patent will be useful for a shorter period of time, say, for 5 years, its cost should be amortized to expense over 5 years. Changing demand, new inventions that supersede old ones, inadequacy, and other factors often limit the useful life of a patent to less than the legal life.

Legal fees and other costs incurred in successfully defending a patent suit are debited to Patents, an asset account, because such a suit establishes the legal rights of the holder of the patent. Such costs should be amortized along with acquisition cost over the remaining useful life of the patent.

Amortization of patents may be computed on a time basis or on a basis of units produced and may be credited directly to the Patents account. It is acceptable also, although less common in practice, to credit an Accumulated Patent Amortization account. To illustrate, assume Harcott incurs $170,000 in legal fees on January 1, 1998 to successfully defend a patent. The patent has a useful life of 17 years and is amortized on a straight-line basis. The entries to record the legal fees and amortization at the end of each year are as follows.

January 1, 1998

Patents	170,000	
Cash		170,000
(To record legal fees related to patent)		

December 31, 1998

Patent Amortization Expense	10,000	
Patents (or Accumulated Patent Amortization)		10,000
(To record amortization of patent)		

Amortization based on units of production would be computed in a manner similar to that described for depreciation of property, plant, and equipment in Chapter 12.

Although a patent's useful life should not extend beyond its legal life of 17 years, small modifications or additions may lead to a new patent. The effect may be to extend the life of the old patent, in which case it is permissible to apply the unamortized costs of the old patent to the new patent if the new patent provides essentially the same benefits. Alternatively, if a patent becomes worthless because demand drops for the product produced, the asset should be written off immediately to expense.

COPYRIGHTS

A **copyright** is a federally granted right that all authors, painters, musicians, sculptors, and other artists have in their creations and expressions. A copyright is granted for the **life of the creator plus 50 years**, and gives the owner, or heirs, the exclusive right to reproduce and sell artistic or published work. Copyrights are not renewable. Like patents, they may be assigned or sold to other individuals. The costs of acquiring and defending a copyright may be capitalized, but the research costs involved must be expensed as incurred.

Generally, the useful life of a copyright is less than its legal life. The costs of the copyright should be allocated to the years in which the benefits are expected to be received, not to exceed 40 years. The difficulty of determining the number of years over which benefits will be received normally encourages the company to write off these costs over a fairly short period of time.

TRADEMARKS AND TRADE NAMES

A **trademark** or **trade name** is a word, phrase, or symbol that distinguishes or identifies a particular enterprise or product. The right to use a trademark or trade name is granted by the federal government. In order to obtain and maintain a protected trademark or trade name, the owner must have made prior and continuing use of it. Trade names like Kleenex, Pepsi-Cola, Oldsmobile, Excedrin, Shreddies, and Sunkist create immediate product identification in our minds, thereby enhancing their marketability.

The capitalizable cost of a trademark or trade name is the purchase price if it is acquired. If a trademark or trade name is developed by the enterprise itself, the capitalizable costs include attorneys' fees, registration fees, design costs, successful legal defence costs, and other expenditures directly related to securing it (excluding research costs). When the total cost of a trademark or trade name is insignificant, it can be expensed rather than capitalized.

Although the life of a trademark, trade name, or company name may be unlimited, for accounting purposes the cost should be amortized over the periods benefited. However, because of the uncertainty involved in estimating their useful life, the cost of trademarks and trade names is frequently amortized over a much shorter period of time.[6]

LEASEHOLDS

A **leasehold** is a contractual understanding between a lessor (owner of property) and a lessee (renter of property) that grants the lessee **the right to use specific property, owned by the lessor, for a specific period of time in return for stipulated, and generally periodic, cash payments.** In most cases, the rent is included as an expense on the books of the lessee. Special problems, however, develop in the following situations.

Lease Prepayments. If the rent for the period of the lease is paid in advance, or if a lump sum payment is made in advance in addition to periodic rental payments, it is necessary to allocate this prepaid rent to the proper periods. The lessee has purchased the exclusive right to use the property for an extended period of time. These prepayments should be reported as a prepaid expense and not as an intangible asset.

---

[6] To illustrate how various intangibles might arise from a given product, consider what the creators of the highly successful game *Trivial Pursuit* did to protect their creation. First, the creators *copyrighted* the 6,000 questions that are at the heart of the fun. Then they shielded the *Trivial Pursuit* name by applying for a registered *trademark*. As a third mode of protection, the creators obtained a *design patent* on the playing board's design since it represents a unique graphic creation.

Leasehold Improvements. Long-term leases ordinarily provide that any **leasehold improvements,** improvements made to the leased property, revert to the lessor at the end of the life of the lease. If the lessee constructs new buildings on leased land or reconstructs and improves existing buildings, the lessee has **the right to use such facilities during the life of the lease, but they become the property of the lessor when the lease expires**.

The lessee should charge the cost of the facilities to the Leasehold Improvements account and **depreciate[7] the cost as operating expense over the remaining life of the lease, or the useful life of the improvements, whichever is shorter**. If a building with an estimated useful life of 25 years is constructed on land leased for 35 years, the cost of the building should be depreciated over 25 years. On the other hand, if the building has an estimated life of 50 years, it should be depreciated over 35 years, the life of the lease.

If the lease contains an option to renew for a period of additional years and the likelihood of renewal is too uncertain to warrant apportioning the cost over the longer period of time, the leasehold improvements are generally written off over the original term of the lease (assuming that the life of the lease is shorter than the useful life of the improvements). **Leasehold improvements are generally shown in the Property, Plant, and Equipment section,** although some accountants classify them as intangible assets. The rationale for intangible asset treatment is that the improvements revert to the lessor at the end of the lease and are therefore more of a right than a tangible asset.

Capital Leases. In some cases, the lease agreement transfers substantially all of the benefits and risks incident to ownership of the property so that the economic effect on the parties is similar to that of an instalment purchase. As a result, the asset value recognized when a lease is capitalized is classified as a tangible rather than an intangible asset. Such a lease is referred to as a **capital lease**. We will cover the accounting for leases in more detail in Chapter 21.

ORGANIZATION COSTS

Costs incurred in the formation of a corporation, such as fees to underwriters (investment bankers) for handling issues of shares or bonds, legal fees, provincial and federal fees of various sorts and promotional expenditures involving the organization of a business, are classified as **organization costs.**

These items are usually charged to an account called Organization Costs and may be carried as an asset on the balance sheet as expenditures that will benefit the company over its life. These costs are amortized over an arbitrary period of time (maximum 40 years), since the life of the corporation is indeterminable. However, the amortization period is frequently short (5–10 years) because of the assumption that the early years of a business benefit most from organization costs and that these costs lose their significance once the business becomes fully established.

It is sometimes difficult to draw a line between organization costs, normal operating expenses, and losses. Some accountants contend that **operating losses incurred in the start-up of a business** should be capitalized since they are unavoidable and are a cost of starting a business. This approach seems unsound, however, since losses have no future service potential and thus cannot be considered assets.

Our position that operating losses should not be capitalized during the early years is supported by accounting standards in other countries. For example, in the United States the FASB concluded that the accounting practices and reporting standards should be no different for a **development stage enterprise** trying to establish a new business than they

---

[7] Section 3060.33 of the *CICA Handbook* permits the use of either amortization or depreciation. In this book, the word depreciation is used when referring to tangible capital assets.

are for other enterprises. Some unique notations and disclosures explaining the start-up situation may be useful. However, the same "generally accepted accounting principles that apply to established operating enterprises shall govern the recognition of revenue by a development stage enterprise and shall determine whether a cost incurred by a development stage enterprise is to be charged to expense when incurred or is to be capitalized or deferred."[8]

In Canada an exception is made for certain expenditures incurred by companies during the pre-operating period (prior to commencement of commercial operations). The CICA's Emerging Issues Committee recommends deferral of pre-operating expenditures that satisfy the following criteria:[9]

1. The expenditure is related directly to placing the new business into service.

2. It is incremental in nature.

3. It is probable that the expenditure is recoverable from future operations.

Losses occurring after the commencement of commercial operations should not be capitalized.

FRANCHISES AND LICENCES

When you drive down the street in an automobile purchased from a Chrysler dealer, fill your tank at the corner Esso station, eat lunch at McDonald's, work at a Coca-Cola bottling plant, live in a home purchased through a Century 21 real estate broker, and vacation at a Holiday Inn resort, you are dealing with franchises. A **franchise** is a contractual arrangement under which the franchiser grants the franchisee the right to sell certain products or services, to use certain trademarks or trade names, or to perform certain functions, usually within a designated geographical area.

The franchiser, having developed a unique concept or product, protects its concept or product through a patent, copyright, trademark, or trade name. The franchisee acquires the right to exploit the franchiser's idea or product by signing a franchise agreement.

Another type of franchise is the arrangement commonly entered into by a municipality (or other governmental body) and a business enterprise that uses public property. In such cases, a privately owned enterprise is permitted to use public property in performing its services. Examples are the use of public waterways for a ferry service, the use of public land for telephones or electric lines, the use of phone lines for cable TV, the use of city streets for a bus line, or the use of the airwaves for radio or TV broadcasting. Such operating rights, obtained through agreements with governmental units or agencies, are frequently referred to as **licences** or **permits**.

Franchises or licenses may be for a definite period of time, an indefinite period of time, or perpetual. The enterprise securing the franchise or licence carries an intangible asset account entitled Franchise or Licence on its books only when there are costs (i.e., a lump sum payment in advance or legal fees and other expenditures) that are identified with the acquisition of the operating right. **The cost of a franchise (or licence) with a lim-**

---

[8] "Accounting and Reporting by Development Stages Enterprises," *Statement of Financial Accounting Standards No. 7* (Stamford, Conn.: FASB, 1975), par. 10. A company is considered to be in the developing stages when its efforts are directed toward establishing a new business and either the principal operations have not started or no significant revenue has been earned. The FASB, in evaluating the economic impact of applying to development stage enterprises the same accounting principles that apply to established operating enterprises, interviewed officers of 15 venture capital companies. The consensus of those officers was that whether a development stage enterprise defers or expenses pre-operating cost has little effect on the amount of or the terms under which venture capital is provided. According to those officers, the venture capital investor relies on an evaluation of potential cash flows that result from an investigation of the technological, marketing, management and financial aspects of the enterprise.

[9] CICA, *EIC–27*.

ited life should be amortized as operating expense over the life of the franchise. A franchise with an indefinite life, or a perpetual franchise, should be carried at cost and amortized over a reasonable period not to exceed 40 years. If a franchise is deemed to be worthless, it should be written off immediately.

Annual payments made under a franchise agreement should be entered as operating expenses in the period in which they are incurred. They do not represent an asset to the concern since they do not relate to future rights to use public property.[10]

PROPERTY RIGHTS

Most of the intangibles discussed above represent **rights**—rights to use, produce, sell, or operate something. Other rights appear to be growing in significance and value: water, mineral, solar and wind (the legal right to free flow of light and air across one's property) rights, and other types of property rights. Although these rights have a value of their own, they are generally attached to a particular parcel of property. Therefore, the value of such property rights, if **inseparable** from the property, is accounted for as part of the capitalized land cost.

If the right is separable from the property, as in the case of mineral rights, its cost may be capitalized separately. If minerals are later discovered or developed, the cost of the rights should be reclassified and capitalized as part of the cost of the minerals and written off as the mineral deposit is depleted.

GOODWILL

Goodwill is often referred to as the most "intangible" of the intangibles. It is undoubtedly one of the most complex and controversial assets presented in financial statements. Goodwill is unique because, unlike receivables, inventories, and patents, which can be sold or exchanged individually in the marketplace, goodwill can be identified only with the business as a whole. For example, a substantial list of regular customers and an established reputation are unrecorded assets that give the enterprise a valuation greater than the sum of the fair market value of the individual identifiable assets. Goodwill is comprised of many advantageous factors and conditions that might contribute to the value and the earning power of an enterprise:[11]

OBJECTIVE 4
Explain the conceptual issues related to goodwill.

1. Superior management team.
2. Outstanding sales organization.
3. Weakness in management of a competitor.
4. Effective advertising.
5. Secret process or formula.
6. Good labour relations.
7. Outstanding credit rating.
8. Top-flight training program.
9. High standing in the community.
10. Discovery of talents or resources.
11. Favourable tax conditions.
12. Favourable government regulation.

---

[10] Accounting for revenue received from franchises is recommended in Accounting Guideline AcG-2.

[11] George R. Catlett and Norman O. Olson, "Accounting for Goodwill," *Accounting Research Study No. 10* (New York: AICPA, 1968), pp. 17–18.

13. Favourable association with another company.

14. Strategic location.

15. Unfavourable developments in the operations of a competitor.[12]

Goodwill is recorded only when an entire business is purchased because goodwill is a "going concern" valuation and cannot be separated from the business as a whole.[13] Goodwill generated internally should **not** be capitalized in the accounts, because measuring the components of goodwill (as listed above) is simply too complex and associating any costs with future benefits is too difficult. The future benefits of goodwill may have no relationship to the costs incurred in the development of that goodwill. To add to the mystery, goodwill may exist in the absence of specific costs to develop it. In addition, because no objective transaction with outside parties has taken place, a great deal of subjectivity—even misrepresentation—might be involved.

RECORDING GOODWILL

OBJECTIVE 5
Describe the accounting procedures for recording goodwill.

To record goodwill, the fair market value of the net tangible and identifiable intangible assets are compared with the purchase price of the acquired business. The difference is considered goodwill, which is why goodwill is sometimes referred to as a "plug" or "gap filler" or "**master valuation**" account. **Goodwill is the residual or the excess of the cost over the fair value of the identifiable net assets acquired**.

To illustrate, Multi-Diversified, Inc. decides that it needs a parts division to supplement its existing tractor distributorship. The president of Multi-Diversified is interested in a small concern near Toronto (Tractorling Company) that has an established reputation and is seeking a merger candidate. The balance sheet of Tractorling Company is presented below.

EXHIBIT 13-1 TRACTORLING COMPANY

BALANCE SHEET
AS OF DEC. 31, 1998

Assets		Equities	
Cash	$ 25,000	Current liabilities	$ 55,000
Receivables	35,000	Share capital	100,000
Inventories	42,000	Retained earnings	100,000
Property, plant, and			
equipment (net)	153,000		
Total assets	$255,000	Total equities	$255,000

---

[12] Another study clustered 17 specific characteristics of goodwill into four more general categories as follows.

Increasing Short-Run Cash Flows	**Human Factor**
Production economics	Managerial talent
Raise more funds	Good labour relations
Cash reserves	Good training programs
Low cost of funds	Organizational structure
Reduce inventory holding cost	Good public relations
Avoid transaction cost	
Tax benefits	
Exclusiveness	**Stability**
Access to technology	Assurance of supply
Brand name	Reducing fluctuations
	Good government relations

See Haim Falk and L.A. Gordon, "Imperfect Markets and the Nature of Goodwill," *Journal of Business Finance and Accounting* (April, 1977), pp. 443–63.

[13] See *CICA Handbook*, Section 1580, par. 54.

After considerable negotiation, Tractorling Company decides to accept Multi-Diversified's offer of $400,000. What then is the value of the goodwill, if any?

The answer is not obvious. The fair market value of Tractorling's identifiable assets are not disclosed in the cost-based balance sheet. Suppose that as the negotiations progress, Multi-Diversified conducts an investigation of the underlying assets of Tractorling to determine the fair market value of the assets. Such an investigation may be accomplished either through a purchase audit undertaken by Multi-Diversified's auditors in order to estimate the values of the seller's assets, or an independent appraisal from some other source. The following valuations are determined.

EXHIBIT 13-2

FAIR MARKET VALUES

Cash	$ 25,000
Receivables	35,000
Inventories	122,000
Property, plant, and equipment (net)	205,000
Patents	18,000
Liabilities	(55,000)
Fair market value of net assets	$350,000

Normally, differences between current fair value and book value are more common among the long-term assets, although significant differences can also develop in the current asset category. Cash obviously poses no problems, and receivables normally are fairly close to current valuation, although at times certain adjustments need to be made because of inadequate bad debt provisions. Liabilities usually are stated at their book value, although if interest rates have changed since the liabilities were incurred, a different valuation (such as present value) may be appropriate. Careful analysis must be made in this area to determine that no unrecorded liabilities are present.

The $80,000 difference in inventories ($122,000 − $42,000) could result from a number of factors, the most likely being that Tractorling Company used LIFO. Recall that during periods of inflation, LIFO better matches expenses against revenues, but in doing so creates a balance sheet distortion. Ending inventory is comprised of older layers costed at lower valuation.

In many cases, the values of long-term assets such as property, plant, and equipment and intangibles may have increased substantially over the years. This difference could be due to inaccurate estimates of useful lives, continual expensing of small expenditures (less than $300), inaccurate estimates of residual values, the discovery of some unrecorded assets (as in Tractorling's case where patents are discovered to have a fair value of $18,000), or replacement costs that may have substantially increased.

Since the fair market value of the net assets is now determined to be $350,000, why does Multi-Diversified pay $400,000? Undoubtedly, the seller points to an established reputation, good credit rating, top management team, well-trained employees, and so on as factors that make the value of the business greater than $350,000. At the same time, Multi-Diversified places a premium on the future earning power of these attributes as well as the basic asset structure of the enterprise today. At this point in the negotiations, price can be a function of many factors; the most important is probably sheer skill at the bargaining table.

The difference between the purchase price of $400,000 and the fair market value of $350,000 is labelled goodwill. Goodwill is viewed as a value or a group of unidentifiable values (intangible assets), the cost of which "is measured by the excess of the cost of the group of assets or enterprise acquired less liabilities assumed."[14] This procedure for valuation is referred to as a **master valuation approach** because goodwill is assumed to cover all the values that cannot be specifically identified with any identifiable tangible or intangible asset. This approach is shown below.

EXHIBIT 13-3

DETERMINATION OF GOODWILL—MASTER VALUATION APPROACH

	Cash	$ 25,000
	Receivables	35,000
	Inventories	122,000
	Property, plant, and equipment	205,000
Assigned to	Patents	18,000
purchase price	Liabilities	(55,000)
of $400,000	Fair market value of net identifiable assets	$350,000
	Purchase price	400,000
	Value assigned to goodwill	$ 50,000

The entry to record this transaction would be as follows:

Cash	25,000	
Receivables	35,000	
Inventories	122,000	
Property, plant, and equipment	205,000	
Patents	18,000	
Goodwill	50,000	
Liabilities		55,000
Cash		400,000

Goodwill is often identified on the balance sheet as the **excess of cost over the fair value** of the net assets acquired.

AMORTIZATION OF GOODWILL

Once goodwill has been recognized in the accounts, the next question is how it should be amortized (if at all). Three basic approaches have been suggested.

1. **Charge goodwill off immediately to shareholders' equity.** *Accounting Research Study No. 10*, "Accounting for Goodwill," identifies a position that goodwill differs from other types of assets and demands special attention.[15] Unlike other assets, goodwill is not separable and distinct from the business as a whole and therefore is not an asset in the same sense as cash, receivables, or plant assets. In other words, goodwill cannot be sold without selling the business.

   Furthermore, say proponents of this approach, the accounting treatment for purchased goodwill and goodwill internally created should be consistent. Goodwill created internally is immediately expensed and does not appear as an asset; the same treatment should therefore be accorded to purchased goodwill. Amortization of purchased goodwill leads to double counting because net income is reduced by amortization of the purchased goodwill as well as by the internal expenditure made to maintain or enhance the value of the assets.

---

[14] *CICA Handbook*, Section 1580, par. .44(b).
[15] Catlett and Olson, *op. cit.*, pp. 89–95.

Perhaps the best rationale for direct write-off is that determination of the periods over which the future benefits are to be received is so difficult that immediate charging to shareholders' equity is justified.

2. **Retain goodwill indefinitely unless reduction in value occurs.** Many accountants believe that goodwill can have an indefinite life and should be maintained as an asset until a decline in value occurs. They contend that some form of goodwill should always be an asset inasmuch as internal goodwill is being expensed to maintain or enhance the purchased goodwill. In addition, without sufficient evidence that a decline in value has occurred, a write-off of goodwill is both arbitrary and capricious and will lead to distortions in net income.

3. **Amortize goodwill over its estimated life.** Still other accountants believe that goodwill's value eventually disappears and it is proper that the asset be charged to expense over the periods affected. This procedure provides a better matching of costs and revenues.

CICA Handbook Section 1580 takes the position that goodwill should be written off over its useful life, which is dependent on a number of factors such as regulatory restrictions, demand, competition, and obsolescence. **The Canadian accounting profession did note that goodwill should never be written off immediately or amortized over more than 40 years**. However, international accounting standards permit a maximum term of only 20 years.

Immediate write-off was not considered proper because it would lead to the untenable conclusion that goodwill has no future potential. The profession merely prohibits the writing off of goodwill in the period of purchase and over a period exceeding 40 years; no other mention is made regarding another period. Some believe that a 5-year period for amortization would be appropriate unless a shorter period is obviously justified.[16] Such circumstances would include continuous losses or an exodus of managerial talent. A single loss year or a combination of loss years does not automatically necessitate a charge-off of the goodwill.

The amortization of goodwill should be computed using the straight-line method unless another method is deemed more appropriate, and it should be treated as a regular operating expense. Where the amortization is material, a disclosure of the charge is necessary, as well as the method and period of amortization.

NEGATIVE GOODWILL—BADWILL

Negative goodwill, often appropriately dubbed badwill, or bargain purchase, arises when the fair market value of the assets acquired is higher than the purchase price of the assets. This situation is a result of market imperfections because the seller would be better off to sell the assets individually than in total. Situations do occur in which the purchase price is less than the value of the net identifiable assets and therefore a credit develops; the credit is referred to as negative goodwill or **excess of fair value over the cost of the assets acquired**.

CICA Handbook **Section 1580 takes the position that an excess of fair value over purchase price should be allocated to reduce proportionately the values assigned to nonmonetary assets** of the acquired company. The possibility that this allocation might reduce all nonmonetary assets to zero without utilizing the full amount of the excess of fair

---

[16] A recent study of goodwill reached the following conclusion: "Thus, the 40-year amortization period used in current practice is too long and cannot be supported on either theoretical or technical grounds. Consequently, a rapid amortization of capitalized goodwill over a relatively short period of time should occur." J. Ron Colley and Ara G. Volkan, " Accounting for Goodwill," *Accounting Horizons* (March, 1988), p. 40.

value acquired over the purchase price is not contemplated. In the rare occasions when this condition does develop, the unallocated excess should be classified as a deferred credit and amortized systematically to income over the period estimated to be benefited.[17]

Negative goodwill most frequently develops in a depressed securities market when the market value of a company's shares is less than book value. For example, Emhart Corp. offered $23 a share (a premium over market) for U.S.M. Corp. shares that had a per-share book value of $43. Emhart Corp. (in consolidation) was able to write down its newly acquired plant assets by more than $49 million and thereby effect a reduction in annual depreciation charges of $5.8 million and add 50 cents annually to its earnings per share. (This 50 cents was on top of the $2 a share it would gain from consolidating U.S.M.'s reported profits. The extra $2.50 per share represented a 90% increase over Emhart's prior year earnings.)

IMPAIRMENT OF INTANGIBLES

The general rules that apply to **impairments of long-lived assets also apply to intangibles**. As indicated in Chapter 12, long-lived assets to be held and used by a company are to be reviewed for impairment whenever events or changes in circumstances indicate that **the carrying amount of the assets may not be recoverable**. In performing the review for recoverability, the company would estimate the future cash flows expected to result from the use of the asset and its eventual disposition. If the sum of the expected future net cash flows (undiscounted) is less than the carrying amount of the asset, an impairment loss would be measured and recognized. Otherwise, an impairment loss would not be recognized.[18]

The impairment loss is the amount by which the carrying amount of the asset exceeds the expected future net cash flows (net recoverable amount). Illustrations of impairment for specifically identifiable and goodwill type intangibles are shown below.

Specifically Identifiable Intangibles. Assume that Lerch Ltd. has a patent on how to extract oil from shale rock. Unfortunately, reduced oil prices have made the shale oil technology somewhat unprofitable, and the patent has provided little income to date. As a result, the net recoverable amount is determined to be $35 million. Lerch's patent has a carrying amount of $60 million. Because the expected future net cash flows of $35 million are less than the carrying amount of $60 million, an impairment loss must be measured and recognized. The impairment loss computation is shown below.

EXHIBIT 13-4

Carrying amount of patent	$60,000,000
Net recoverable amount	35,000,000
Loss on impairment	$25,000,000

The journal entry to record this loss is:

Loss in Impairment	25,000,000	
Patents		25,000,000

After the impairment is recognized, the reduced carrying amount of the patents is its new cost basis. The patent's new cost should be amortized over its useful life or legal life,

[17] *CICA Handbook*, Section 1580, par. 44.
[18] *CICA Handbook*, Section 3060, par. .37.

whichever is shorter. Even if oil prices increase in subsequent periods and the value of the patent increases, **restoration of the previously recognized impairment loss is not permitted**.

Goodwill Type Intangibles. Goodwill is a "going concern" valuation and cannot be separated from the other assets and liabilities that give it value. As a result, goodwill impairments involve a grouping of net assets.

To illustrate an impairment loss when goodwill is involved, assume that Kohlberg Corporation has three divisions in its company. One division, Prime Products, was purchased four years ago for $2 million. Unfortunately, it has experienced operating losses over the last three quarters and management is reviewing the division for the purpose of recognizing an impairment. The Prime Products net assets, including the associated goodwill of $1,200,000, are listed below.

EXHIBIT 13-5

Cash	$ 200,000
Receivables	300,000
Inventory	400,000
Property, plant, and equipment (net)	800,000
Goodwill	1,200,000
Less: Accounts and notes payable	(500,000)
Net assets	$2,400,000

A recoverability test is performed and it is found that the expected net future cash flows from Prime Products are $1,300,000. The impairment loss is computed as follows.

EXHIBIT 13-6

Carrying amount of Prime Products	$2,400,000
Net recoverable amount	1,300,000
Loss on impairment	$1,100,000

How should the impairment loss be allocated to the net assets of the Prime Products? Various allocation approaches might be used. One approach is to reduce any goodwill associated with the assets first, then apply any of the remaining loss on impairment to the identifiable assets.

If we follow this approach, then the total impairment loss on the Prime Products division would reduce only goodwill. The entry to record the loss is:

Loss on Impairment	1,100,000	
Goodwill		1,100,000

If the impairment loss was greater than the carrying amount of goodwill, the additional loss would be used to reduce the remaining capital assets.

REPORTING OF INTANGIBLES

The reporting of intangibles differs from the reporting of property, plant, and equipment in that the contra accounts are not normally shown. The amortization of intangibles is frequently credited directly to the intangible asset.[19]

---

[19] *Financial Reporting in Canada—1991* reports that the most common type of intangible is goodwill, followed by licences, trademarks, patents, and customer lists.

The financial statements should disclose the method and period of amortization. Intangible assets shown net of amortization might appear on the balance sheet as follows.

EXHIBIT 13-7

INTANGIBLE ASSETS (NOTE 3)

Patents	$ 98,000	
Franchises	115,000	
Goodwill	342,000	$555,000

Note 3. The patents are amortized on a unit-of-production approach over a period of 6 years. The franchises are perpetual in nature, but in accordance with *CICA Handbook* Section 3060 they are being written off over the maximum period allowable (40 years) on a straight-line basis. The goodwill arises from the purchase of Multi-Media and is being amortized over a 10-year period on a straight-line basis.

The following example, taken from the 1991 annual report of Mitel Corporation, illustrates reporting of intangibles using contra valuation accounts.

EXHIBIT 13-8   MITEL CORPORATION

CONSOLIDATED BALANCE SHEETS
(in millions of Canadian dollars)

5. Other Assets

	March 29, 1991	March 30, 1990
Cost:		
Assets held for resale	$ 5.0	$ 0.3
Goodwill	2.8	2.2
Patents, trademarks, and other	4.8	3.7
	12.6	6.2
Less accumulated amortization:		
Goodwill	2.8	1.3
Patents, trademarks, and other	2.7	2.0
	5.5	3.3
	$ 7.1	$ 2.9

Some companies follow the practice of writing their intangibles down to $1 to indicate that they have intangibles of uncertain value. This practice is not in accord with good accounting. It would be much better to disclose the nature of the intangible, its original cost, and other relevant information such as competition, danger of obsolescence, and so on.

RESEARCH AND DEVELOPMENT COSTS

Research and development (R & D) costs are not in themselves intangible assets. The accounting for R & D costs is presented here, however, because research and development activities frequently result in the development of something that is patented or copyrighted (such as a new product, process, idea, formula, composition, or literary work).

Many businesses spend considerable sums of money on research and development to create new products or processes, to improve present products, and to discover new knowledge that may be valuable at some future date. The following schedule shows the outlays for R & D made by selected Canadian companies.

OBJECTIVE 6
Identify the conceptual issues related to research and development costs.

EXHIBIT 13-9

REPORTED RESEARCH AND DEVELOPMENT EXPENSE—1995

Company	Dollars	% of Sales	% of Profits
Northern Telecom Limited	$948,300,000	21.0	128.0
Imperial Oil Limited	74,000,000	0.01	0.14
Mitel Corporation	51,700,000	12.0	53.4
Falconbridge Ltd.	11,500,000	0.7	8.8
Epic Data Inc.	2,802,000	11.0	162.0

The difficulties in accounting for these research and development expenditures are (1) identifying the costs associated with particular activities, projects, or achievements; and (2) determining the magnitude of the future benefits and the length of time over which such benefits may be realized. Because of these latter uncertainties, the accounting profession (through *Handbook* Section 3450) has standardized and simplified accounting practice in this area by requiring that **all research costs be charged to expense when incurred. Development costs should also be expensed when incurred except in certain narrowly defined circumstances**.

To differentiate research and development costs from each other and from other similar costs, the CICA adopted the following definitions.

Research is planned investigation undertaken with the hope of gaining new scientific or technical knowledge and understanding. Such investigation may or may not be directed toward a specific practical aim or application.

Development is the translation of research findings or other knowledge into a plan or design for new or substantially improved material devices, products, processes, systems, or services prior to the commencement of commercial production or use.[20]

Many costs have characteristics similar to those of research and development: relocation and rearrangement of facilities, start-up costs for a new plant or new retail outlet, marketing research costs, promotion costs of a new product or service, and costs of training new personnel. To further distinguish between research, development, and these

---

[20] *CICA Handbook*, Section 3450, par. .02.

other similar costs, the following schedule provides examples of activities that typically would be excluded from both research and development.[21]

EXHIBIT 13-10

1. **Research Activities**
   (a) Laboratory research aimed at discovery of new knowledge.
   (b) Searching for applications of new research findings or other knowledge.
   (c) Conceptual formulation and design of possible product or process alternatives.

2. **Development Activities**
   (a) Testing in search or evaluation of product or process alternatives.
   (b) Design, construction, and testing of preproduction prototypes and models.
   (c) Design of tools, jigs, moulds, and dies involving new technology.

3. **Activities Not Considered Either Research or Development**
   (a) Engineering follow-through in an early phase of commercial production.
   (b) Quality control during commercial production, including routine testing of products.
   (c) Trouble-shooting in connection with breakdowns during commercial production.
   (d) Routine or periodic alterations to existing products, production lines, manufacturing processes, and other ongoing operations.
   (e) Adaptation of an existing capability to a particular requirement or customer's need as part of a continuing commercial activity.
   (f) Routine design of tools, jigs, moulds, and dies.
   (g) Activity, including design and construction engineering, related to the construction, relocation, rearrangement, or start-up of facilities or equipment other than facilities or equipment whose sole use is for a particular research and development project.

ELEMENTS OF RESEARCH AND DEVELOPMENT COSTS

OBJECTIVE 7
Describe the accounting procedures for research and development costs.

The costs associated with R & D activities are as follows.[22]

1. Materials and services devoted to research and/or development activities.

2. Direct costs of personnel engaged in R & D activities (salaries, wages, payroll taxes, etc.).

3. Depreciation of plant assets used in the R & D activity.

4. Amortization of any intangible assets that are directly associated with the R & D activities.

5. Overhead allocated on a reasonable basis.

Consistent with (3) above, if an enterprise conducts R & D activities using its own research facility consisting of buildings, laboratories, and equipment that has alternative future uses, the facility should be accounted for as a capitalized operational asset. The depreciation and other costs related to such research facilities are accounted for as R & D expenses.

Sometimes enterprises conduct R & D activities for other entities under a *contractual arrangement*. In this case, the contract usually specifies that all direct costs, certain specific indirect costs, plus a profit element should be reimbursed to the enterprise performing the R & D work. Because reimbursement is expected, such R & D costs should be recorded as a receivable. It is the company for whom the work has been performed that reports these costs as R & D activities.

A special problem arises in distinguishing R & D costs from selling and administrative activities. Except for costs of "routine" market research costs, research and development costs may include those associated with any product or process regardless of whether they are related to production, marketing, or administrative activities. For example, the costs of software incurred by an airline in acquiring, developing, or improving its

---

[21] *CICA Handbook*, Section 3450, par. .04, .05, .06.
[22] *CICA Handbook*, Section 3450, par. .13.

computerized reservation system or for development of a general management information system would be considered development costs.

As previously emphasized, Canadian firms must write off all development costs as expenses of the period incurred except when all of the following criteria for deferral are met.

1. The product or process is clearly defined and the costs attributable to it can be identified.

2. The technical feasibility of the product or process has been established.

3. The management of the enterprise has indicated its intention to produce and market or use the product or process.

4. The future market for the product or process is clearly defined or, if it is to be used internally rather than sold, its usefulness to the enterprise has been established.

5. Adequate resources exist or are expected to be available to complete the project. Furthermore, the total amount of development costs deferred must be limited to the extent that their recovery can reasonably be regarded as assured.[23]

To illustrate the identification of R & D activities and the accounting treatment of related costs, assume that Next Century Ltd. conducts research and produces and markets laser machines for medical, industrial, and defence uses. The types of expenditures related to its laser machine activities are listed below along with the recommended accounting treatment.

EXHIBIT 13-11   NEXT CENTURY LTD.

Type of Expenditure	Accounting Treatment
1. Construction of long-range research facility (three-storey, 100,000 m² building) for use in current and future projects.	Capitalize and depreciate as R & D expense.
2. Acquisition of R & D equipment for use on current project only.	Capitalize and depreciate as R & D expense.
3. Purchase of materials to be used on current and future R & D projects.	Inventory and allocate to R & D projects as consumed.
4. Salaries of research staff designing new laser bone scanner.	Expense immediately as research.
5. Research costs incurred under contract for New Horizon Ltd. and billable monthly.	Expense as operating expense in period of related revenue recognition.
6. Material, labour, and overhead of prototype laser scanner.	Capitalize as development cost if all criteria are met.
7. Cost of testing prototype and design modifications.	Capitalize as development cost if all criteria are met.
8. Legal fees to obtain patent on new laser scanner.	Capitalize as patent and amortize to cost of goods manufactured.
9. Executive salaries.	Expense as operating expense (general and administrative).
10. Cost of marketing research related to promotion of new laser scanner.	Expense as operating expense (selling).
11. Engineering costs incurred to advance the laser scanner to full production stage.	Capitalize as development cost if all criteria are met.
12. Costs of successfully defending patent on laser scanner.	Capitalize as patent and amortize to cost of goods manufactured.
13. Commissions to sales staff marketing new laser scanner.	Expense as operating expense (selling).

---

[23] *CICA Handbook*, Section 3450, par. .13.

Acceptable accounting practice requires that disclosure be made in the financial statements (generally in the notes) of the total R & D costs charged to expense in each period for which an income statement is presented.

An example of an R & D disclosure is the following excerpt from the 1996 annual report of Develcon Electronics Ltd.

EXHIBIT 13-12   DEVELCON ELECTRONICS LTD.

NOTES TO FINANCIAL STATEMENTS

2. Summary of Significant Accounting Policies

Research and Development Costs: Research costs are expensed in the year incurred. The Company expenses development costs as incurred unless the Company believes the development costs meet generally accepted accounting principles for deferral and amortization. In the opinion of management, no development costs incurred to date meet all criteria for deferral and amortization. Therefore, all development costs to date have been expensed as incurred.

Research and development grants, when earned, and investment tax credits where there is a reasonable assurance they will be realized, are offset against the applicable costs incurred.

11. Research and Development

Research and development costs are stated net of applicable government contributions. Details of amounts expended on research and development and the related assistance received are:

| | *(thousands of Canadian dollars)* | |
	1996	1995
Gross amount expended	$3,000	$1,733
Less		
Government contributions earned	(305)	(569)
Net amount	$2,695	$1,164

Costs of research and development activities unique to companies in the **extractive industries** (prospecting, acquisition of mineral rights, exploration, drilling, mining, and related mineral development) and those costs discussed above that are similar to—but not classified as—R & D may be (1) expensed as incurred; (2) capitalized and either depreciated or amortized over an appropriate period of time; or (3) accumulated as part of inventoriable costs. Choice of the appropriate accounting treatment for such costs should be guided by the degree of certainty of future benefits and the principle of matching revenues and expenses.

An example of reported exploration and development costs for an extractive industry company is shown below as excerpted from the 1991 annual report of Rio Algom Limited.

EXHIBIT 13-13   RIO ALGOM LIMITED

NOTES TO FINANCIAL STATEMENTS

Accounting Policies

Mineral Exploration and Development Costs

Exploration costs are written off as incurred. Expenditures on development projects are capitalized while the projects are considered to be of value to the Corporation.

EXHIBIT 12-13   RIO ALGOM LIMITED (Continued)

8. Mining Properties and Preproduction Expenditures

	1991	1990
		(in thousands)
Preproduction expenditures, at cost	$ 387,765	$ 385,819
Less accumulated amortization	181,446	176,367
	206,319	209,452

CONCEPTUAL QUESTIONS

The requirement that all research costs and most development costs incurred internally be expensed immediately is a conservative, practical solution that ensures consistency in practice and uniformity among companies. But the practice of immediately writing off expenditures made in the expectation of benefiting future periods cannot be justified on the grounds that it is good accounting theory.[24]

Defendants of immediate expensing contend that from an income statement standpoint, long-run application of this standard makes little difference. The amount of R & D costs charged against income during each accounting period would be about the same whether there is immediate expensing or capitalization and subsequent amortization because of the ongoing nature of many companies' R & D activities. Critics of this practice argue that the balance sheet should report an intangible asset related to expenditures that have future benefit. To preclude capitalization of all R & D expenditures removes from the balance sheet what may be a company's most valuable asset. This standard represents one of the many trade-offs made among relevance, reliability, and cost–benefit considerations.[25]

DEFERRED CHARGES AND LONG-TERM PREPAYMENTS

Deferred charges is a classification often used to describe a number of different items that have debit balances, among them certain types of intangibles. Intangibles sometimes classified as deferred charges include plant rearrangement costs, pre-operating and start-up costs, and organization costs. How do these items happen to be classified in this section and not in a separate intangible section? Probably the major reason is that the Deferred Charges section often serves as a "dumping ground" for a number of small items.

Deferred charges also include such items as long-term prepayments for insurance, rent, taxes, and other down payments. The deferred charge classification probably should be abolished because it cannot be clearly differentiated from other amortizable and depreciable assets (which are also deferred charges), and a more informative disclosure could be made of the smaller items often found in this section of the balance sheet. Such a classification has even less relevance today because the conceptual framework project establishes a definition for assets that seems to exclude deferred charges.

---

[24] The International Accounting Standards Committee issued a standard that is in agreement with the CICA. The Committee identified certain circumstances that justify the capitalization and deferral of development costs. See "Accounting for Research and Development Activities," *International Accounting Standard No. 9* (London, England: International Accounting Standards Committee, 1978), par. 17.

[25] For a discussion of the position that R & D should be capitalized in certain situations, see Harold Bierman, Jr., and Roland E. Dukes, "Accounting for Research and Development Costs," *The Journal of Accountancy* (April, 1975).

INTERNATIONAL PERSPECTIVE

How may different accounting standards in different countries affect international investments? A method of accounting known as "pooling of interests" permits an investor company to use the book values of the assets of an acquired company. Thus, no goodwill is recognized nor are acquired assets written up to fair values at the date of acquisition. In Canada, the *CICA Handbook* contains stringent criteria making it almost impossible to use the pooling of interests approach. In the United States, the criteria is more easily met.

Consider the possibility of a Canadian high-tech company acquiring a similar sized U.S. firm in the same industry. Under Canadian GAAP, it would be very difficult to report the resulting company under the pooling of interests approach. The Canadian firm would have to write up the assets of the acquired U.S. firm to their fair values at the date of purchase and, if necessary, recognized goodwill. These values must then be amortized which would, in turn, reduce earnings per share.

As an example, Clearnet Communications Inc. acquired certain assets form Motorola Canada Ltd. Under the pooling of interests approach, Clearnet's loss per share would have been 8 cents per share. However, under acceptable Canadian practice, their loss per share amounted to 21 cents.

Under United States accounting standards, a U.S. high-tech company can acquire a similar sized Canadian company and determine its earnings based on the book values of both entities. As a consequence, the U.S. company would generally report higher earnings than a Canadian company in an identical situation. Thus, U.S. companies may enjoy an advantage over their Canadian counterparts due primarily to differing accounting standards in the two countries.

KEY TERMS

Summary of Learning Objectives

1. **Describe the characteristics of intangible capital assets.** A major characteristic of intangible assets is the high degree of uncertainty concerning future benefits that are to be received from their employment. Intangibles may be subdivided on the basis of the following characteristics: (1) identifiability: separately identifiable or lacking specific identification; (2) manner of acquisition: acquired singly, in groups, or in business combinations, or developed internally; (3) expected period of benefit: limited by law or contract, related to human or economic factors, or of indefinite or indeterminate duration; (4) separability from the enterprise: rights transferable without title, salable, or inseparable from the enterprise or a substantial part of it.

2. **Explain the procedure for valuing and amortizing intangible capital assets.** Intangibles are recorded at cost. Cost includes all costs of acquisition and expenditures necessary to make the intangible asset ready for its intended use. If intangibles are acquired in exchange for shares or other assets, the cost of the intangible is the fair market value of the consideration given or the fair market value of the intangible received, whichever is more clearly evident. When several intangibles, or a combination of intangibles and tangibles, are bought in a "basket purchase," the cost should be allocated on the basis of fair market values or on the basis of the relative sales values. Intangible assets should be amortized by systematic charges to expense over their useful lives. Intangible assets must be amortized over a period not exceeding 40 years.

3. **Identify the types of specifically identifiable intangible capital assets.** The major identifiable assets are (1) patents: give the holder exclusive right to use, manufacture, and sell a product or process for a period of 17 years without interference or infringement by others; (2) copyright: a federally granted right that all authors, painters, musicians, sculptors, and other artists have in their creations and expressions; (3) trademark and trade name: a word, phrase, or symbol that distinguishes or identifies a particular enterprise or product; (4) leasehold: a contractual understanding between a lessor (owner or property) and a lessee (renter of property) that grants the lessee the right to use specific property, owned by the lessor, for a specific period of time in return for stipulated, and generally periodic, cash payments; (5) organization costs: incurred in the formation of a corporation, such as fees to underwriters for handling issue of shares or bonds, legal fees, federal and provincial fees of various sorts, and certain promotional expenditures; (6) franchises and licences: contractual arrangements under which the franchiser grants the franchisee the right to sell certain products or services, to use certain trademarks or trade names, or to perform certain functions, usually within a designated geographical area; (7) property rights: such as water, mineral, solar, and wind, generally attached to a particular parcel of property.

4. **Explain the conceptual issues related to goodwill.** Goodwill is unique because, unlike receivables, inventories, and patents, which can be sold or exchanged individually in the marketplace, goodwill can be identified only with the business as a whole. Goodwill is a "going concern" valuation and is recorded only when an entire business is purchased. Goodwill generated internally should not be capitalized in the accounts, because measuring the components of goodwill is simply too complex and associating any costs with future benefits is too difficult. The future benefits of goodwill may have no relationship to the costs incurred in the development of that goodwill. Goodwill may exist even in the absence of specific costs to develop it.

5. **Describe the accounting procedures for recording goodwill.** To record goodwill, the fair market value of the net tangible and identifiable intangible assets are compared with the purchase price of the acquired business. The difference is considered goodwill. Goodwill is the residual—the excess of cost over fair value of the identifiable net assets acquired. Goodwill is often identified on the balance sheet as the excess of cost over the fair value of the net assets acquired.

6. **Identify the conceptual issues related to research and development costs.** R & D costs are not in themselves intangible assets, but research and development activities frequently result in the development of something that is patented or copyrighted. The difficulties in accounting for R & D expenditures are (1) identifying the costs associated with the particular activities, projects, or achievements; and (2) determining the magnitude of the future benefits and length of time over which such benefits may be realized. Because of these latter uncertainties, the AcSB has standardized and simplified accounting practice by requiring that all research and most development costs be charged to expense when incurred.

7. **Describe the accounting procedures for research and development costs.** All research costs are expensed when incurred. Generally, development costs are expensed when incurred. However, when certain criteria are met, development costs may be capitalized and amortized over the period benefiting. The accounting problem is one of differentiating between research, development costs, and other similar costs. Fixed assets used in research and development activities should be capitalized and depreciated.

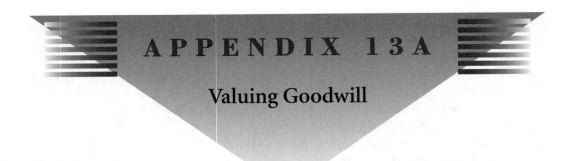

APPENDIX 13A

Valuing Goodwill

In this chapter we discussed the generally accepted method of measuring and recording goodwill as the excess cost over fair value of the identifiable net assets acquired in a business acquisition. Accountants are frequently asked to participate in the valuation of businesses as part of a planned business acquisition.

To determine the purchase price for a business and the resulting goodwill is a difficult and inexact process. As indicated, it is often possible to determine the fair value of the identifiable assets. But how does a buyer value intangible factors like good management, good credit rating, and so on?

EXCESS EARNINGS APPROACH

One method is called the **excess earnings approach**. Using this approach, the total earning power that the company commands is computed. The next step is to calculate "normal earnings" by determining the normal rate of return on assets in that industry. **The difference between what the firm earns and what is normal in the industry is referred to as the excess earning power**. This extra earning power indicates that there are unidentifiable values (intangible assets) that provide this increased earning power. Finding the value of goodwill is then a matter of discounting these excess future earnings to the present.

This approach appears to be a systematic and logical way of determining goodwill. However, each factor necessary to compute a value under this approach is subject to question. Generally, the problems relate to getting answers to the following questions:

1. What is a normal rate of return?
2. How does one determine the future earnings?
3. What discount rate should be applied to the excess earnings?
4. Over what period should the excess earnings be discounted?

Finding a Normal Rate of Return.   Determining the normal rate of return for tangible and identifiable intangible assets requires analysis of companies similar to the enterprise in question. An industry average may be determined by examining annual reports or data from statistical services. Suppose that a rate of 15% is decided for a concern such as Tractorling (see page 638). In this case, the normal earnings are calculated in the following manner.[26]

EXHIBIT 13A-1	
Fair market value of Tractorling's net identifiable assets	$350,000
Normal rate of return	15%
Normal earnings	$ 52,500

[26] The fair value of Tractorling's assets (rather than historical cost) is used to compute the normal profit, because fair value is closer to the true value of the company's assets exclusive of goodwill.

Determination of Future Earnings. The starting point for determining future earnings is normally the past earnings of the enterprise. Although estimates of future earnings are needed, the past often provides useful information concerning the enterprise's future earnings potential. Past earnings—generally three to six years—are also useful because estimates of the future are usually overly optimistic and the hard facts of previous periods bring a sobering sense of reality to the negotiations.

Tractorling's net earnings for the last five years is as follows.

EXHIBIT 13A-2

EARNINGS HISTORY— TRACTORLING

1994	$ 60,000	
1995	55,000	Average Earnings
1996	110,000[a]	$\dfrac{\$375,000}{5 \text{ years}} = \$75,000$
1997	70,000	
1998	80,000	
	$375,000	

[a]Includes extraordinary gain of $25,000.

The average net earnings for the last five years is $75,000 or a rate of return of approximately 21.4% on the current value of the assets, excluding goodwill ($75,000 divided by $350,000). Before we go further, we need to know whether $75,000 is representative of the future earnings of this enterprise.

Often the past earnings of a company to be acquired need to be evaluated on the basis of the acquirer's own accounting procedures. Suppose that in determining earning power, Multi-Diversified measures earnings in relation to a FIFO inventory valuation figure rather than LIFO, which Tractorling employs, and that the use of LIFO reduces Tractorling's net income by $2,000 per year. In addition, Tractorling uses accelerated depreciation although Multi-Diversified uses straight-line. As a result, Tractorling's earnings are lower by $3,000.

Also, assets discovered on examination that might affect the earning flow should be considered. Patent costs not previously recorded should be amortized, say, at the rate of $1,000 per period. Finally, because the estimate of future earnings is what we are attempting to determine, some items like the extraordinary gain of $25,000 should probably be excluded. An analysis can now be made as follows.

EXHIBIT 13A-3

Average net earnings per Tractorling computation		$75,000
Add		
Adjustment for switch from LIFO to FIFO	$ 2,000	
Adjustment for change from accelerated to straight-line approach	3,000	5,000
		$80,000
Deduct		
Extraordinary gain ($25,000/5)	5,000	
Patent amortization on straight-line basis	1,000	6,000
Adjusted average net earnings		$74,000

The excess earnings would be $21,500 ($74,000 − $52,500).

Choosing a Discount Rate to Apply to Excess Earnings. Determination of the discount rate is a fairly subjective estimate.[27] The lower the discount rate, the higher the value of the goodwill. To illustrate, assume that the excess earnings are $21,500 and that these earnings will continue indefinitely. If the excess earnings are capitalized at, say, a rate of 25% in perpetuity[28] the results are:

EXHIBIT 13A-4

CAPITALIZATION AT 25%

Excess earnings $\dfrac{\$21,500}{.25} = \$86,000$

Capitalization rate

If the excess earnings are capitalized in perpetuity at a somewhat lower rate, say 15%, a much higher goodwill figure results.

EXHIBIT 13A-5

CAPITALIZATION AT 15%

Excess earnings $\dfrac{\$21,500}{.15} = \$143,333$

Capitalization rate

Because the continuance of excess profits is uncertain, a conservative rate (higher than normal rate) is usually employed. Factors that are considered in determining the rate are the stability of past earnings, the speculative nature of the business, and general economic conditions.

Choosing a Discounting Period for Excess Earnings. Determination of the period over which the excess earnings will exist is perhaps the most difficult problem associated with computing goodwill. If it is assumed that the excess earnings will last indefinitely, then goodwill is $143,333, as computed in the previous section (assuming a rate of 15%).

Another method of computing goodwill that gives the same answer, using the normal return of 15%, is to discount the total average earnings of the company and subtract the fair market value of the net identifiable assets as illustrated in Exhibit 13A-6.

---

[27] The following illustration shows how the capitalization rate might be computed for a small business.

A Method of Selecting a Capitalization Rate

Long-term Canadian government bond rate	10%
Plus: Average premium return on small company shares over government bonds	10
Expected total rate of return on small publicly held shares	20
Plus: Premium for greater risk and illiquidity	6
Total required expected rate of return, including inflation component	26
Less: Consensus long-term inflation expectation	6
Capitalization rate to apply to current earnings	20%

From Warren Kissin and Ronald Zulli, "Valuation of a Closely Held Business," *The Journal of Accountancy* (June, 1988), p. 42.

[28] Why do we divide by the capitalization rate to arrive at the goodwill amount? Recall that the present value of an ordinary annuity is equal to

$$P_{\overline{n}i} = \dfrac{1 - \dfrac{1}{(1+i)^n}}{i}$$

When a number is capitalized into perpetuity, $(1+i)^n$ becomes so large that $1/(1+i)^n$ essentially equals zero, which leaves $1/i$ or, as in the case above, $21,500/.25$.

EXHIBIT 13A-6

AVERAGE EARNINGS CAPITALIZED AT 15% IN PERPETUITY

($74,000/.15)	$493,333
Less fair market value of assets	350,000
Present value of estimated earnings (goodwill)	$143,333

Frequently, however, the excess earnings are assumed to last a limited number of years, say 10, and then it is necessary to discount these earnings only over that time. Assume that Multi-Diversified believes that the excess earnings of Tractorling will last 10 years and, because of the uncertainty surrounding this earning power, 25% is considered an appropriate rate of return. The present value of an annuity of $21,500 ($74,000 − $52,500) discounted at 25% for 10 years is $76,765.75.[29] This is the amount that Multi-Diversified should be willing to pay above the fair value of net identifiable assets.

OTHER METHODS OF VALUATION[30]

Some accountants fail to discount but simply multiply the excess earnings by the number of years they believe the excess earnings will continue. This approach, often referred to as the **number of years method**, is used to provide a rough measure for what the goodwill factor should be. The approach has only the advantage of simplicity; it is more accurate to recognize the discount factor.

An even simpler method is one that relies on multiples of average yearly earnings that are paid for other companies in the same industry. If Nocturnal Airlines was recently acquired for five times its average yearly earnings of $50 million, or $250 million, then Canadian Northern Airways, a close competitor with $80 million in average yearly earnings, would be worth $400 million.

Another method (somewhat similar to discounting excess earnings) is the **discounted free cash flow method**, which involves a projection of the acquired company's free cash flow over a long period, typically 10 or 20 years. The method first projects into the future a dozen or so important financial variables, including production, prices, noncash expenses (such as depreciation and amortization), taxes, and capital outlays, all adjusted for inflation. The objective is to determine the amount of cash that will accumulate over a specified number of years. The present value of the free cash flows is then computed. This amount represents the price to be paid for the business.[31]

For example, if Magnaputer Computer Company is expected to generate $1 million each year for 20 years and the buyer's rate-of-return objective is 15%, the buyer would be willing to pay about $6.26 million for Magnaputer Company. (The present value of $1 million to be received for 20 years discounted at 15% is $6,259,330.)

In practice, prospective buyers use a variety of methods to produce a "valuation curve" or range of prices. But the actual price paid may be more a factor of the buyer's or seller's ego and horse-trading acumen.

---

[29] The present value of an annuity of $1 received in a steady stream for 10 years in the future discounted at 25% is 3.57050, (3.57050 × $21,500 = $76,765.75).

[30] A recent article lists three "asset-based approaches" (tangible net worth, adjusted book value, and price-book value ratio methods) and three "earnings-based approaches" (capitalization of earnings, capitalization of excess earnings, and discounted cash flow methods) as the popular methods for valuing closely held businesses. See Warren Rissin and Ronald Zulli, "Valuation of Closely Held Business," *The Journal of Accountancy* (June, 1988), pp. 38–44.

[31] Tim Metz, "Deciding How Much a Company Is Worth Often Depends on Whose Side You're On, " *The Wall Street Journal*, March 18, 1981.

Valuation of goodwill is at best a highly uncertain process. The estimated value of goodwill depends on a number of factors, all of which are extremely tenuous and subject to bargaining.

Summary of Learning Objective for Appendix 13A

8. **Explain various approaches to valuing goodwill.** One method of valuing goodwill is the excess earnings approach. Using this approach, the total earning power that the company commands is computed. The next step is to calculate "normal earnings" by determining the normal rate of return on assets in that industry. The difference between what the firm earns and what is normal in the industry is referred to as excess earning power. This excess earning power indicates that there are unidentifiable values that provide the increased earning power. Finding the value of goodwill is then is a matter of discounting these excess future earnings to the present. The number of years method of valuing goodwill, which simply multiplies the excess earnings by the number of years of expected excess earnings, is used to provide a rough measure for the goodwill factor. A third method of valuing goodwill is the discounted free cash flow method, which projects the amount of cash that will accumulate over a specified number of years and then finds the present value of that amount as today's value of the firm.

Note: All *asterisked* Exercises, Problems, or Cases relate to material contained in the appendix to the chapter.

EXERCISES

E13-1 **(Classification Issues—Intangibles)** Presented below is a list of items that could be included in the intangible asset section of the balance sheet.

1. Investment in a subsidiary company.
2. Timberland.
3. Cost of engineering activity required to advance the design of a product to the manufacturing stage.
4. Lease prepayment (six months' rent paid in advance).
5. Cost of equipment obtained under a capital lease.
6. Retained earnings appropriation.
7. Costs incurred in the formation of a corporation.
8. Operating losses incurred in the start-up of a business.
9. Sinking fund for repayment of bonds.
10. Cost of a franchise.
11. Goodwill generated internally.
12. Goodwill acquired in the purchase of a business.
13. Cost of testing in search of product alternatives.
14. Cost of developing computer software for internal use.

15. Cost of developing a patent.

16. Cost of purchasing a patent from an inventor.

17. Legal costs incurred in securing a patent.

18. Unrecovered costs of a successful legal suit to protect the patent.

19. Cost of modifying the design of a product or process.

20. Cost of acquiring a copyright.

21. Research and development costs.

22. Long-term receivables.

23. Cost of developing a trademark.

24. Cost of securing a trademark.

Instructions

(a) Indicate which items on the list above would generally be reported as intangible assets in the balance sheet.

(b) Indicate how, if at all, the items not reportable as intangible assets would be reported in the financial statements.

(Classification Issues—Intangibles) Presented below is selected account information related to Erma Bombeck   **E13-2**
Inc. as of December 31, 1998. All these accounts have debit balances.

Cable television franchises	Film contract rights
Music copyrights	Customer lists
Research and development costs	Prepaid expenses
Goodwill	Covenants not to compete
Cash	Brand names
Discount on notes payable	Notes receivable
Accounts receivable	Investments in affiliated companies
Property, plant, and equipment	Organization cost
Leasehold improvements	Land

Instructions

Identify which items should be classified as intangible assets. For those items not classified as intangible assets, indi-   **E13-3**
cate where they would be reported in the financial statements.

(Classification Issues—Intangibles) Mohegan Inc. has the following amounts included in its general ledger at
December 31, 1998:

Organization costs	$22,000
Trademarks	15,000
Discount on bonds payable	40,000
Deposits with advertising agency for ads to promote goodwill of company	10,000
Excess of cost over book value of net assets of acquired subsidiary	75,000
Cost of equipment acquired for research and development projects	90,000
Costs of developing a secret formula for a product that is expected to be marketed for at least 20 years	80,000

Instructions

(a) On the basis of the information above, compute the total amount to be reported by Mohegan for intangible assets on its balance sheet at December 31, 1998. Equipment has alternative future use.

(b) If an item is not to be included in intangible assets, explain its proper treatment for reporting purposes.

(Intangible Amortization) Presented below is selected information for Arawak Company. Answer each of the fac-   **E13-4**
tual situations.

1. Arawak purchased a patent from Huron Co. Ltd. for $900,000 on January 1, 1996. The patent is being amortized over its remaining legal life of 10 years, expiring on January 1, 2006. During 1998, Arawak determined that the economic benefits of the patent would not last longer than five years from the date of acquisition. What amount should be reported in the balance sheet for the patent, net of accumulated amortization, at December 31, 1998?

2. Arawak bought a franchise from Brunswick Co. Ltd. on January 1, 1997 for $300,000. It was estimated that the franchise had a useful life of 60 years. Its carrying amount on Brunswick Co. Ltd.'s books at January 1, 1997 was $400,000. Arawak decided to amortize the franchise over the maximum period permitted. What amount should be amortized for the year ended December 31, 1998?

3. On January 1, 1994, Arawak incurred organization costs of $250,000. Arawak amortized these costs over an arbitrary period of five years. What amount should be reported as unamortized organization costs as of December 31, 1998?

E13-5   **(Correct Intangible Asset Account)** As the recently appointed auditor for Pequot Limited, you have been asked to examine selected accounts before the six-month financial statements of June 30, 1998 are prepared. The controller for Pequot Limited mentions that only one account (shown below) is kept for Intangible Assets.

Intangible Assets

		Debit	Credit	Balance
January 4	Research and development	920,000		920,000
January 5	Legal costs to obtain patent	75,000		995,000
January 31	Payment of seven months' rent on property leased by Pequot	77,000		1,072,000
February 1	Share issue costs	36,000		1,108,000
February 11	Proceeds from issue of common shares		250,000	858,000
March 31	Unamortized bond discount on bonds due March 31, 2018	84,000		942,000
April 30	Promotional expenses related to start-up of business	207,000		1,149,000
June 30	Operating losses for first six months	241,000		1,390,000

Instructions

Prepare the entry or entries necessary to correct this account. Assume that the patent has a useful life of 10 years, and organization costs are being amortized over a five-year period.

E13-6   **(Recording and Amortization of Intangibles)** Wyandot Company, organized in 1997, has set up a single account for all intangible assets. The following summary discloses the debit entries that have been recorded during 1998.

1/2/98	Purchased patent (seven-year life)	$ 350,000
4/1/98	Goodwill purchased (indefinite life)	360,000
7/1/98	10-year franchise, expiration date 7/1/2008	450,000
8/1/98	Payment for copyright (four-year life)	160,000
9/1/98	Research and development costs	185,000
		$1,505,000

Instructions

Prepare the necessary entries to clear the Intangible Asset account and to set up separate accounts for distinct types of intangibles. Make the entries as of December 31, 1998, recording any necessary amortization and reflecting all balances accurately as of that date.

E13-7   **(Accounting for Trade Name)** In early January of 1997, Drastic Plastic Corporation applied for a trade name, incurring legal costs of $12,000. In January of 1998, Drastic Plastic Corporation incurred $7,800 of legal costs in a successful defence of its trade name.

Instructions

(a)   Compute 1997 amortization, 12/31/97 book value, 1998 amortization, and 12/31/98 book value if the company amortizes the trade name over the maximum allowable term.

(b)   Repeat part (a) assuming a useful life of five years.

E13-8   **(Accounting for Lease Transaction)** Newton Inc. leases an old building that it intends to improve and use as a warehouse. To obtain the lease, the company pays a bonus of $36,000. Annual rental for the six-year lease period is $120,000. No option to renew the lease or right to purchase the property is given.

After the lease is obtained, improvements costing $150,000 are made. The building has an estimated remaining useful life of 17 years.

Instructions

(a) What is the annual cost of this lease to Newton Inc.?

(b) What amount of annual depreciation, if any, on a straight-line basis should Newton record?

(Accounting for Organization Costs) Erie Ltd. was organized in 1997 and began operations at the beginning of **E13-9** 1998. The company was involved in interior design consulting services. The following costs were incurred prior to the start of operations:

Attorneys' fees in connection with organization of the company	$15,000
Improvements to leased offices prior to occupancy	25,000
Fees to underwriters for handling share issue	4,000
Costs of meetings of incorporators to discuss organizational activities	5,000
Filing fees to incorporate	1,000
	$50,000

Instructions

(a) Compute the total amount of organization costs incurred by Erie.

(b) Assuming Erie Ltd. is amortizing costs for financial reporting purposes over a five-year term, prepare the journal entry to amortize organization costs for 1998.

(Accounting for Patents, Franchises, and R & D) Inuit Company has provided information on intangible assets as **E13-10** follows:

A patent was purchased from Zuni Company for $1,800,000 on January 1, 1997. Inuit estimated the remaining useful life of the patent to be 10 years. The patent was carried in Zuni's accounting records at a net book value of $2,000,000 when Zuni sold it to Inuit.

During 1998, a franchise was purchased from Laguna Limited for $480,000. In addition, 5% of revenue from the franchise must be paid to Laguna. Revenue from the franchise for 1998 was $2,500,000. Inuit estimated the useful life of the franchise to be 10 years and took a full year's amortization in the year of purchase.

Inuit incurred research and development costs in 1998 as follows:

Materials and equipment	$142,000
Personnel	176,000
Indirect costs	102,000
	$420,000

Inuit estimated that these costs would be recouped by December 31, 2001.

On January 1, 1998, Inuit, because of recent events in the field, estimated that the remaining life of the patent purchased on January 1, 1997 was only five years from January 1, 1998.

Instructions

(a) Prepare a schedule showing the intangibles section of Inuit's balance sheet at December 31, 1998. Show supporting computations in good form.

(b) Prepare a schedule showing the income statement effect for the year ended December 31, 1998 as a result of the facts above. Show supporting computations in good form. (AICPA adapted)

(Accounting for Patents) Ponoka Inc. has its own research department. In addition, the company purchases patents **E13-11** from time to time. The following statements summarize transactions that involve all patents now owned by the company.

During 1992 and 1993, $153,000 was spent developing a new process that was patented (No. 1) on March 18, 1994 at additional legal and other costs of $16,320. A patent (No. 2) developed by Ben Franklin, an inventor, was purchased for $60,000 on November 30, 1995, on which date it had 12½ years yet to run.

During 1994, 1995, and 1996, research and development activities cost $170,000. No additional patents resulted from these activities.

A patent infringement suit brought by the company against a competitor because of the manufacture of articles infringing on Patent No. 2 was successfully prosecuted at a cost of $14,200. A decision in the case was rendered in July, 1996.

A competing patent (No. 3) was purchased for $57,600 on July 1, 1997. This patent still had 16 years to run. During 1998 $60,000 was expended on patent development; $20,000 of this amount represented the cost of a device for which a patent application had been filed, but for which no notification of acceptance or rejection by the Patent Office had been received. The other $40,000 represented costs incurred on uncompleted development projects.

Instructions

(a) Compute the carrying value of these patents as of December 31, 1998, assuming that the legal and useful life of each patent is the same and that each patent is to be amortized from the first day of the month following its acquisition.

(b) Prepare a journal entry to record amortization for 1998.

E13-12 (Accounting for Patents) During 1994, Yakima Corporation spent $90,000 in research and development costs. As a result, a new product called the Barney was patented at additional legal and other costs of $15,000. The patent was obtained on October 1, 1994 and had a legal life of 17 years and a useful life of 10 years.

Instructions

(a) Prepare all journal entries required in 1994 and 1995 as a result of the preceding transactions.

(b) On June 1, 1996 Yakima spent $11,500 to successfully prosecute a patent infringement. As a result, the estimate of useful life was extended to 12 years from June 1, 1996. Prepare all journal entries required in 1996 and 1997.

(c) In 1998, Yakima determined that a competitor's product would make the Barney obsolete and the patent worthless by December 31, 1999. Prepare all journal entries required in 1998 and 1999.

E13-13 (Accounting for Goodwill) On July 1, 1998 Mohave Inc. purchased Hupa Company by paying $200,000 cash and issuing a $100,000 note payable to Sam Hupa. At July 1, 1998 the balance sheet of Hupa Company was as follows:

Cash	$ 50,000	Accounts payable	$200,000
Receivables	90,000	Hupa, capital	235,000
Inventory	100,000		$435,000
Land	40,000		
Buildings (net)	75,000		
Equipment (net)	70,000		
Trademarks	10,000		
	$435,000		

The recorded amounts all approximated current values except for land (worth $60,000), inventory (worth $125,000), and trademarks (worthless).

Instructions

(a) Prepare the July 1 entry for Mohave Inc. to record the purchase.

(b) Prepare the December 31 entry for Mohave Inc. to record amortization of goodwill. The goodwill is estimated to have a useful life of 50 years.

E13-14 (Intangible Impairment) Presented below is information related to copyrights owned by Who Company at December 31, 1998.

Cost	$8,600,000
Carrying amount	4,300,000
Expected future net cash flow	4,000,000

Assume that Who Company will continue to use this copyright in the future. As of December 31, 1998 the copyright is estimated to have a remaining life of 10 years.

Instructions

(a) Prepare the journal entry (if any) to record the impairment of the asset at December 31, 1998. The company does not use accumulated amortization amounts.

(b) Prepare the journal entry to record amortization expense for 1999 related to the copyrights.

(c) The fair value of the copyright at December 31, 1999 is $4,250,000. Prepare the journal entry (if any) necessary to record the increase in fair value.

E13-15 (Goodwill Impairment) Following is net asset information (including associated goodwill of $200 million) related to the Nuc-Air Division of Pearl, Inc.

NUC-AIR DIVISION
NET ASSETS
as of December 31, 1998
(in millions)

Cash	$ 50,000
Receivables	200,000
Property, plant, and equipment (net)	2,600,000
Goodwill	200,000
Less: Notes payable	(2,700,000)
Net assets	$ 350,000

The purpose of this division is to develop a nuclear-powered aircraft. If successful, travelling delays associated with refueling could be substantially reduced. Many other benefits would also accrue. To date, management has not had much success and is deciding whether a write-down at this time is appropriate. Management estimated its future net cash flows (net recoverable amount) from the project will be $300 million. Management has also received an offer to purchase the division for $210 million.

Instructions

(a) Prepare the journal entry (if any) to record the impairment at December 31, 1998.

(b) At December 31, 1999 it is estimated that the net recoverable amount increased to $240 million. Prepare the journal entry (if any) to record this increase in fair value.

(Accounting for R & D Costs) Blackfalls Company from time to time embarks on a research program when a special project seems to offer possibilities. In 1997 the company expends $300,000 on a research project, but by the end of 1997 it is impossible to determine whether any benefit will be derived from it. **E13-16**

Instructions

(a) What account should be charged for the $300,000, and how should it be shown in the financial statements?

(b) The project is completed in 1998, and a successful patent is obtained. The development costs to complete the project are $100,000. The administrative and legal expenses incurred in obtaining patent number 472-1001-84 in 1998 total $14,000. The patent has an expected useful life of five years. Record these costs in journal entry form. Also, record development cost and patent amortization (full year) in 1998.

(c) In 1999 the company successfully defends the patent in extended litigation at a cost of $48,000, thereby extending the economic life of the patent to 12/31/06. What is the proper way to account for this cost? Also, record patent amortization (full year) in 1999.

(d) Additional engineering and consulting costs incurred in 1999 to advance the design of a product to the manufacturing stage totaled $60,000. These costs enhance the design of the product considerably. Discuss the proper accounting treatment for this cost.

(Accounting for R & D Costs) Winnipeg Company incurred the following costs during 1998: **E13-17**

Quality control during commercial production, including routine testing of products	$58,000
Laboratory research aimed at discovery of new knowledge	68,000
Testing for evaluation of new products	24,000
Modification of the formulation of a plastics product	6,000
Engineering follow-through in an early phase of commercial production	15,000
Adaptation of an existing capability to a particular requirement or customer's need as a part of continuing commercial activity	13,000
Trouble-shooting in connection with breakdowns during commercial production	29,000
Searching for applications of new research findings	19,000

Instructions

Compute the total amount Winnipeg should classify and expense as research and development costs for 1998.

E13-18 (**Accounting for R & D Costs**) Crow Company incurred the following costs during 1998 in connection with its research and development activities:

Cost of equipment acquired that will have alternative uses in future research and development projects over the next five years (uses straight-line depreciation)	$280,000
Materials consumed in research and development projects	59,000
Consulting fees paid to outsiders for research and development projects	100,000
Personnel costs of persons involved in research and development projects	98,000
Indirect costs reasonably allocable to research and development projects	50,000
Materials purchased for future research and development projects	34,000

Instructions

Compute the amount to be reported as research and development expense by Crow on its income statement for 1998. Assume equipment is purchased at beginning of year.

E13-19 (**Accounting for R & D Costs**) Listed below are four independent situations involving research and development costs:

1. During 1998 Sundre Co. Ltd. incurred the following costs:

Research and development services performed by Cayuse Company for Sundre	$350,000
Testing for evaluation of new products	300,000
Laboratory research aimed at discovery of new knowledge	400,000

For the year ended December 31, 1998, how much research and development expense should Sundre report?

2. Creek Ltd. incurred the following costs during the year ended December 31, 1998:

Design, construction, and testing of preproduction prototypes and models	$270,000
Routine, ongoing efforts to refine, enrich, or otherwise improve upon the qualities of an existing product	250,000
Quality control during commercial production including routine testing of products	300,000
Laboratory research aimed at discovery of new knowledge	420,000

What is the total amount to be classified and expensed as research and development for 1998?

3. Tonkawa Company incurred costs in 1998 as follows:

Equipment acquired for use in various research and development projects	$900,000
Depreciation on the equipment above	210,000
Materials used in R & D	300,000
Compensation costs of personnel in R & D	400,000
Outside consulting fees for R & D work	180,000
Indirect costs appropriately allocated to R & D	260,000

What is the total amount of research and development that should be reported in Tonkawa's 1998 income statement?

4. Conrath Inc. incurred the following costs during the year ended December 31, 1998:

Laboratory research aimed at discovery of new knowledge	$200,000
Radical modification to the formulation of a chemical product	130,000
Research and development costs reimbursable under a contract to perform research and development for Quapaw Inc.	350,000
Testing for evaluation of new products	225,000

What is the total amount to be classified and expensed as research and development for 1998?

Instructions
Provide the correct answer to each of the four situations.

(Compute Goodwill) The net worth of Ojibwa Company—excluding goodwill—totals $800,000. Earnings for the **E13-20***
past five years total $890,000. Included in the latter figure are extraordinary gains of $60,000, nonrecurring losses of $40,000, and sales commissions of $15,000. In developing a sales price for the business a 14% return on net worth is considered normal for the industry, and annual excess earnings are to be capitalized at 20% in arriving at goodwill.

Instructions
Compute estimated goodwill.

(Compute Normal Earnings) Sahaptin Petroleum Inc.'s pretax accounting income for the year 1998 is $850,000 and **E13-21***
includes the following items:

Amortization of goodwill	$ 60,000
Amortization of identifiable intangibles	57,000
Depreciation on building	80,000
Extraordinary losses	44,000
Extraordinary gains	135,000
Profit-sharing payments to employees	65,000

Devco Oil Industries is seeking to purchase Sahaptin Petroleum Inc. In attempting to measure Sahaptin's normal earnings for 1998, Devco determines that the fair value of the building is triple the book value and that the remaining economic life is double that used by Sahaptin. Devco will continue the profit-sharing payments to employees; such payments are based on income before depreciation and amortization.

Instructions
Compute the normal earnings (for the purposes of computing goodwill) of Sahaptin Petroleum Inc. for the year 1998.

(Compute Goodwill) Alberta News Inc. is considering acquiring Ottawa Company in total as a going concern. **E13-22***
Alberta makes the following computations and conclusions:

1. The fair value of the individual assets of Ottawa Company is $720,000.

2. The liabilities of Ottawa Company are $380,000.

3. A fair estimate of annual earnings for the indefinite future is $120,000 per year.

4. Considering the risk and potential of Ottawa Company, Alberta feels that it must earn a 24% return on its investment.

Instructions
(a) How much should Alberta be willing to pay for Ottawa Company?
(b) How much of the purchase price will be goodwill?

(Compute Goodwill) As the president of Charletown Records Inc., you are considering purchasing Island Tape **E13-23***
Company, whose balance sheet is summarized as follows:

Current assets	$ 300,000	Current liabilities	$ 300,000
Investments	700,000	Long-term debt	500,000
Other assets	300,000	Common shares	400,000
		Retained earnings	100,000
Total	$1,300,000	Total	$1,300,000

The fair market value of current assets is $600,000 because of the undervaluation of inventory. The normal rate of return on net assets for the industry is 15%. The average expected annual earnings projected for Island Tape Company is $140,000.

Instructions
Assuming that the excess earnings continue for five years, how much would you be willing to pay for goodwill? (Estimate goodwill by the present-value method.)

*E13-24   (Compute Goodwill) Net income figures for Menominee Company are as follows:

1993—$64,000	1994—$50,000
1995—$81,000	1996—$80,000
1997—$70,000	

Tangible net assets of this company are appraised at $400,000 on December 31, 1997. This business is to be acquired by Pontiac Co. Ltd. early in 1998.

Instructions

What amount should be paid for goodwill if:

(a) 14% is assumed to be a normal rate of return on net tangible assets, and average excess earnings for the last five years are to be capitalized at 25%?

(b) 12% is assumed to be a normal rate of return on net tangible assets, and payment is to be made for excess earnings for the last four years?

*E13-25   (Compute Goodwill) Comanche Corporation Ltd. is interested in acquiring Kiowa Plastics Company. It has determined that Kiowa Company's excess earnings have averaged approximately $120,000 annually over the last six years. Kiowa Company agrees with the computation of $120,000 as the approximate excess earnings and feels that such an amount should be capitalized over an unlimited period at a 20% rate. Comanche Corporation Ltd. feels that because of increased competition the excess earnings of Kiowa Company will continue for seven more years at best and that a 15% discount rate is appropriate.

Instructions

(a) How far apart are the positions of these two parties?

(b) Is there really any difference in the two approaches used by the two parties in evaluating Kiowa Company's goodwill? Explain.

*E13-26   (Compute Goodwill) Natchez Corporation Ltd. is contemplating the purchase of Apache Industries and evaluating the amount of goodwill to be recognized in the purchase.

Apache reported the following net incomes:

1993 —	$170,000
1994 —	200,000
1995 —	240,000
1996 —	250,000
1997 —	380,000

Apache has indicated that 1997 net income included the sale of one of its warehouses at a gain of $140,000 (net of tax). Net identifiable assets of Apache have a total fair market value of $850,000.

Instructions

Calculate goodwill in the following cases, assuming that expected income is to be a simple average of normal income for the past five years.

(a) Goodwill is determined by capitalizing average net earnings at 16%.

(b) Goodwill is determined by presuming a 16% return on identifiable net assets and capitalizing excess earnings at 25%.

*E13-27   (Compute Fair Value of Identifiable Assets) Kinistino Company bought a business that would yield exactly a 20% annual rate of return on its investment. Of the total amount paid for the business, $80,000 was deemed to be goodwill, and the remaining value was attributable to the identifiable net assets.

Kinistino Company projected that the estimated annual future earnings of the new business would be equal to its average annual ordinary earnings over the past four years. The total net income over the past four years was $380,000, which included an extraordinary loss of $35,000 in one year and an extraordinary gain of $95,000 in one of the other three years.

Instructions

Compute the fair market value of the identifiable net assets that Kinistino Company purchased in this transaction.

PROBLEMS

Colin McLeod Inc., organized in 1997, has set up a single account for all intangible assets. The following summary discloses the debit entries that have been recorded during 1997 and 1998.

P13-1

Intangible Assets

07/1/97	Five-year franchise; expiration date 6/30/02	$ 42,000
10/1/97	Advance payment on leasehold (four-year lease)	28,000
12/31/97	Net loss for 1997 including incorporation fees: $1,000, and related legal fees of organizing: $5,000 (all fees incurred in 1997)	16,000
01/2/98	Patent purchased (eight-year life)	74,000
03/1/98	Cost of developing a secret formula (indeterminate life)	75,000
04/1/98	Goodwill purchased (indefinite life)	278,400
06/1/98	Legal fee for successful defence of patent	12,350
09/1/98	Research and development costs	160,000

Instructions

Prepare the necessary entries to clear the Intangible Assets account and to set up separate accounts for distinct types of intangibles. Make the entries as of December 31, 1998, recording any necessary amortization and reflecting all balances accurately as of that date. (Assume a 40-year amortization for intangibles unless specified. Ignore income tax effects.)

Eric Iversen Laboratories holds a valuable patent (no. 758-6002-1A) on a precipitator that prevents certain types of air pollution. Iversen does not manufacture or sell the products and processes it develops; it conducts research and develops products and processes that it patents, and then assigns the patents to manufacturers on a royalty basis. Occasionally it sells a patent. The history of Iversen patent no. 758-6002-1A is as follows:

P13-2

Date	Activity	Cost
1988–1989	Research conducted to develop precipitator	$384,000
January 1990	Design and construction of a prototype	87,600
March 1990	Testing of models	42,000
January 1991	Fees paid to engineers and lawyers to prepare patent application; patent granted July 1, 1991	61,880
November 1992	Engineering activity necessary to advance the design of the precipitator to the manufacturing stage	81,500
December 1993	Legal fees paid to successfully defend precipitator patent	35,000
April 1995	Research aimed at modifying the design of the patented precipitator	43,000
July 1997	Legal fees paid in unsuccessful patent infringement suit against a competitor	34,000

Iversen assumed a useful life of 17 years when it received the initial precipitator patent. On January 1, 1996 it revised its useful life estimate downward to five remaining years. Amortization was computed for a full year if the cost was incurred prior to July 11, and there was no amortization for the year if the cost was incurred after June 30. The company's year-end was December 31.

Instructions

Compute the carrying value of patent no. 758-6002-1A on each of the following dates:

(a) December 31, 1991. (c) December 31, 1998.

(b) December 31, 1995.

Information concerning Richard Siu Co. Ltd.'s intangible assets is as follows:

P13-3

1. On January 1, 1998 Siu signed an agreement to operate as a franchisee of Rapid Copy Service, Inc. for an initial franchise fee of $75,000. Of this amount, $15,000 was paid when the agreement was signed, and the balance was payable in four annual payments of $15,000 each beginning January 1, 1999. The agreement provided that the down payment was not refundable and no future services were required of the franchisor. The present value at

January 1, 1998 of the four annual payments discounted at 14% (the implicit rate for a loan of this type) was $43,700. The agreement also provided that 5% of the revenue from the franchise must be paid to the franchiser annually. Siu's revenue from the franchise for 1998 was $900,000. Siu estimated the useful life of the franchise to be 10 years. (Hint: You may refer to Appendix 6A to determine the proper accounting treatment for the franchise fee and payments.)

2. Siu incurred $65,000 of experimental and development costs in its laboratory to develop a patent that was granted on January 2, 1998. Legal fees and other costs associated with registration of the patent totaled $13,200. Siu estimates that the useful life of the patent will be eight years.

3. A trademark was purchased from Calgary Company for $32,000 on July 2, 1995. Expenditures for successful litigation in defence of the trademark totaling $8,000 were paid on July 1, 1998. Siu estimated that the useful life of the trademark would be 20 years from the date of acquisition.

Instructions

(a) Prepare a schedule showing the intangibles section of Siu's balance sheet at December 31, 1998. Show supporting computations in good form.

(b) Prepare a schedule showing all expenses resulting from the transactions that will appear on Siu's income statement for the year ended December 31, 1998. Show supporting computations in good form. (AICPA adapted)

P13-4 The following information relates to the intangible assets of Inventa Product Company:

	Organization Costs	Goodwill	Purchased Patent Costs
Original cost at 1/1/1998	$76,000	$280,000	$48,000
Useful life at 1/1/1998 (estimated)	Indefinite[a]	50 years	6 years

[a]Management has decided to write off the organization costs over five years.

Instructions

(a) Assuming straight-line amortization, compute the amount of the amortization of *each* item for 1998 in accordance with generally accepted accounting principles.

(b) Prepare the journal entries for the amortization of organization costs and goodwill for 1998.

(c) Assume that at January 1, 1999 Inventa Product Company incurred $5,000 of legal fees in defending the rights to the patents. Prepare the entry for the year 1999 to amortize the patents.

(d) Assume that at the beginning of the year 2000, the company decided that the patent costs would be applicable only for the years 2000 and 2001. (A competitor had developed a product that would eventually make Inventa obsolete.) Record the amortization of the patent costs at the end of 2000.

P13-5 Sommers Ltd. has recently become interested in acquiring an Eastern Canadian plant to handle many of its production functions in that market. One possible candidate is Vicq Inc., a closely held corporation, whose owners have decided to sell their business if a proper settlement can be obtained. Vicq's balance sheet appears as follows:

Current assets	$150,000	Current liabilities	$ 80,000
Investments	50,000	Long-term debt	100,000
Plant assets (net)	400,000	Share capital	220,000
Total assets	$600,000	Retained earnings	200,000
		Total equities	$600,000

Sommers has hired Canadian Appraisal Corporation to determine the proper price to pay for Vicq Inc. The appraisal firm finds that the investments have a fair market value of $150,000 and that inventory is understated by $75,000. All other assets and equities are properly stated. An examination of the company's income for the last four years indicates that the net income has steadily increased. In 1998 the company has a net operating income of

$100,000, and this income should increase 20% each year over the next four years. Sommers believes that a normal return in this type of business is 18% on net assets. The asset investment in the Eastern Canadian plant is expected to stay the same for the next four years.

Instructions

(a) Canadian Appraisal Corporation has indicated that the fair value of the company can be estimated in a number of ways. Prepare an estimate of the value of the firm, assuming that any goodwill will be computed as:

   1. The capitalization of the average excess earnings of Vicq Inc. at 18%.

   2. The purchase of average excess earnings over the next four years.

   3. The capitalization of average excess earnings of Vicq Inc. at 24%.

   4. The present value of the average excess earnings over the next four years discounted at 15%.

(b) Vicq Inc. is willing to sell the business for $1,000,000. How do you believe Canadian Appraisal should advise Sommers?

(c) If Sommers was to pay $750,000 to purchase the assets and assume the liabilities of Vicq Inc., how would this transaction be reflected on Sommers' books?

During 1996, Joffrey Tool Company purchased a building site for its proposed product development laboratory at a cost of $60,000. Construction of the building was started in 1996. The building was completed on December 31, 1997 at a cost of $280,000 and was placed in service on January 2, 1998. The estimated useful life of the building for depreciation purposes was 20 years, the straight-line method of depreciation was to be employed, and there was no estimated residual value. **P13-6**

Management estimated that about 50% of the development projects would result in long-term benefits (that is, at least 10 years) to the corporation. The remaining projects either benefited the current period or were abandoned before completion. Following is a summary of the number of projects and the direct costs incurred in conjunction with the development activities for 1998.

Upon recommendation of the development group, Joffrey Tool Company acquired a patent for manufacturing rights at a cost of $100,000. The patent was acquired on April 1, 1997, and had an economic life of 10 years.

	Number of Projects	Salaries and Employee Benefits	Other Expenses (excluding Building Depreciation Charges)
Development of viable products (management intent and capability criteria are met)	15	$ 90,000	$50,000
Abandoned projects or projects that benefit the current period	10	60,000	15,000
Projects in process—results indeterminate	5	40,000	12,000
Total	30	$190,000	$77,000

Instructions

If generally accepted accounting principles were followed, how would the items above relating to product development activities be reported on the company's:

(a) Income statement for 1998?

(b) Balance sheet as of December 31, 1998?

Be sure to give account titles and amounts, and briefly justify your presentation.   (CMA adapted)

Sara Cheng Ltd. was incorporated on January 3, 1997. The corporation's financial statements for its first year's operations were not examined by a public accountant. You have been engaged to examine the financial statements for the year ended December 31, 1998, and your examination is substantially completed. The corporation's trial balance appears below. **P13-7**

SARA CHENG LTD.
Trial Balance
December 31, 1998

	Debit	Credit
Cash	$ 15,000	
Accounts Receivable	73,000	
Allowance for Doubtful Accounts		$ 1,460
Inventories	50,200	
Machinery	82,000	
Equipment	37,000	
Accumulated Depreciation		26,200
Patents	128,200	
Leasehold Improvements	36,100	
Prepaid Expenses	13,000	
Organization Expenses	32,000	
Goodwill	30,000	
Licensing Agreement No. 1	60,000	
Licensing Agreement No. 2	57,000	
Accounts Payable		73,000
Unearned Revenue		17,280
Share Capital		300,000
Retained Earnings, January 1, 1998		159,060
Sales		720,000
Cost of Goods Sold	475,000	
Selling and General Expenses	180,000	
Interest Expense	8,500	
Extraordinary Losses	20,000	
Totals	$1,297,000	$1,297,000

The following information relates to accounts that may yet require adjustment.

1. Patents for Cheng's manufacturing process were acquired January 2, 1998 at a cost of $95,200. An additional $33,000 was spent in December, 1998 to improve machinery covered by the patents and charged to the Patents account. Depreciation on fixed assets was properly recorded for 1998 in accordance with Cheng's practice, which provided a full year's depreciation for property on hand June 30 and no depreciation otherwise. Cheng used the straight-line method for all depreciation and amortization and the legal life on its patents.

2. On January 2, 1997 Cheng purchased Licensing Agreement No. 1, which was believed to have an unlimited useful life. The balance in the Licensing Agreement No. 1 account included its purchase price of $57,000 and expenses of $3,000 related to the acquisition. On January 1, 1998 Cheng purchased Licensing Agreement No. 2, which had a life expectancy of 10 years. The balance in the Licensing Agreement No. 2 account included its $54,000 purchase price and $6,000 in acquisition expenses, but it had been reduced by a credit of $3,000 for the advance collection of 1999 revenue from the agreement.

   In late December, 1997 an explosion caused a permanent 70% reduction in the expected revenue-producing value of Licensing Agreement No. 1 and in January, 1999 a flood caused additional damage that rendered the agreement worthless.

3. The balance in the Goodwill account included (a) $16,000 paid December 30, 1997 for an advertising program that would assist in increasing Cheng's sales over a period of four years following the disbursement; and (b) legal expenses of $14,000 incurred for Cheng's incorporation on January 3, 1997.

4. The Leasehold Improvements account includes (a) $15,000 cost of improvements with a total estimated useful life of 12 years that Cheng, as tenant, made to leased premises in January, 1997; (b) movable assembly line equipment costing $15,000 that was installed in the leased premises in December 1998; and (c) real estate taxes of $6,100 paid by Cheng in 1998, which under the terms of the lease should have been paid by the landlord. Cheng paid its rent in full during 1998. A 10-year nonrenewable lease was signed January 3, 1998 for the leased building that Cheng used in manufacturing operations.

5. The balance in the Organization Expenses account properly included costs incurred during the organizational period. The corporation had exercised its option to amortize 50% of its organization costs over a 10-year period for federal income tax purposes and wished to amortize these for accounting purposes on the same basis.

Instructions

Prepare an eight-column work sheet to adjust accounts that require adjustment, and include columns for an income statement and a balance sheet.

A separate account should be used for the accumulation of each type of amortization and for each prior period adjustment. Formal adjusting journal entries and financial statements are *not* required. (Hint: Amortize Licensing Agreement No. 1 over 40 years before the explosion damage loss is determined.) (AICPA adapted)

Presented below are financial forecasts related to Melville Mariner Limited for the next 10 years. **P13-8***

Forecasted average earnings (per year)	$ 65,000
Forecasted market value of net assets, exclusive of goodwill (average over 10 years)	340,000

Instructions
You have been asked to compute goodwill under the following methods. The normal rate of return on net assets for the industry is 15%.

(a) Goodwill is equal to five years' excess earnings.

(b) Goodwill is equal to the present value of five years' excess earnings discounted at 12%.

(c) Goodwill is equal to the average excess earnings capitalized at 16%.

(d) Goodwill is equal to average earnings capitalized at the normal rate of return for the industry of 15%.

Presented below is information related to Lorne Jenkins Inc. for 1998, its first year of operation. **P13-9***

Income Summary

Raw Material Purchased	$145,900	Sales	$544,000
Productive Labour	41,250	Closing Inventories	
Factory Overhead	29,750	Raw Material	32,400
Selling Expenses	39,400	Goods in Process	32,000
Administrative Expenses	24,950	Finished Goods	39,000
Interest Expense	8,650	Appreciation of Land	4,500
Opening Inventories		Profit on Sale of	
Raw Material	34,500	Forfeited Shares	7,200
Goods in Process	20,000		
Finished Goods	35,000		
Extraordinary Loss (net)	9,700		
Income Taxes	85,000		
Net Income	185,000		
	$659,100		$659,100

Instructions
Jenkins is negotiating to sell the business after one full year of operation. Compute the amount of goodwill as 200% of the income before extraordinary items and before taxes that is in excess of $150,000; $150,000 is considered to be a normal return on investment.

Zubin Mehta Inc., a high-flying conglomerate, has recently been involved in discussions with Arthur Fiedler, Inc. As **P13-10*** its accountant, you have been instructed by Mehta to conduct a purchase audit of Fiedler's books to determine a possible purchase price for Fiedler's net assets. The following information is found.

Total identifiable assets of Fiedler's (fair market value)	$250,000
Liabilities	$ 60,000
Average rate of return on net assets for Fiedler's industry	15%
Forecasted earnings per year based on past earnings figures	$ 34,500

Instructions
(a) Mehta asks you to determine the purchase price on the basis of the following assumptions:

1. Goodwill is equal to three years' excess earnings.

2. Goodwill is equal to the present value of excess earnings discounted at 15% for three years.

3. Goodwill is equal to the capitalization of excess earnings at 15%.

4. Goodwill is equal to the capitalization of excess earnings at 25%.

(b) Mehta asks you which of the methods above is the most theoretically sound. Justify your answer. Any assumptions made should be clearly indicated.

*P13-11 Donat Lemaire Inc. has contracted to purchase Beverly Sills Company, including the goodwill of the latter company. The agreement between purchaser and seller on the price to be paid for goodwill is as follows: "The value of the goodwill to be paid for is to be determined by capitalizing at 18% the average annual earnings from ordinary operations for the last five years in excess of 16% on the net worth, which, for purposes of this computation, is to be considered to be $300,000."

The net income per books for the last five years is:

1994	$43,150
1995	49,680
1996	64,320
1997	51,250
1998	68,580

As assistant to the treasurer of Donat Lemaire you are instructed to review the accounts of Beverly Sills and determine the amount to be paid for goodwill in accordance with the terms of the contract. In your review of the accounts you discover the following:

1. An additional assessment of federal income taxes in the amount of $10,120 for the year 1996 was made and paid in 1998. The amount was charged against retained earnings.

2. In 1994 the company reviewed its accounts receivable and wrote off as an expense of that year $18,180 of accounts receivable that had been carried for years and appeared very unlikely to be collected.

3. In 1995 an account for $2,100 included in the 1994 write-off above was collected and credited to Miscellaneous Income.

4. A fire in 1997 caused a loss, charged to income, as follows:

Book value of property destroyed	$29,400
Recovery from insurance company	10,000
Net loss	$19,400

5. Expropriation of property in 1997 resulted in a gain of $9,080 credited to income.

6. Amounts paid out under the company's product guarantee plan and charged to expense in each of the five years were as follows:

1994	$1,000
1995	1,300
1996	950
1997	1,100
1998	1,400

7. In 1998 the president of the company died, and the company realized $75,000 on an insurance policy on his life. The cash surrender value of this policy had been carried on the books as an investment in the amount of $62,240. The excess of proceeds over cash surrender value was credited to income.

Instructions

What is the price to be paid for the goodwill in accordance with the contract agreement? Prepare your computations in good form so that you can answer any questions asked by the treasurer in regard to your conclusions.

CASES

In examining the books of Sawatzky Mfg. Company, you find on the December 31, 1998 balance sheet the item "Cost of Patents, $822,000."

Referring to the ledger accounts, you note the following items regarding one patent acquired in 1995.

1995—Legal costs incurred in defending the validity of the patent	$ 35,000
1996—Legal costs in prosecuting an infringement suit	74,000
1997—Legal costs (additional expenses) in the infringement suit	24,500
1997—Cost of improvements (unpatented) on the patented device	131,200

There are no credits in the account, and no allowance for amortization has been set up on the books for any of the patents. Three other patents issued in 1992, 1994, and 1995 were developed by the staff of the client. The patented articles are currently very marketable, but it is estimated that they will be in demand only for the next few years.

Instructions

Discuss the items included in the Patent account from an accounting standpoint. (AICPA adapted)

Taos Inc. is a large publicly held corporation. Listed below are six selected expenditures made by the company during the current fiscal year ended April 30, 1998. The proper accounting treatment of these transactions must be determined in order for Taos' annual financial statements to be prepared in accordance with generally accepted accounting principles. **C13-2**

(a) Taos Inc. spent $3,000,000 on a program designed to improve relations with its dealers. This project was favourably received by the dealers, and Taos' management believed that significant future benefits should be received from this program. The program was conducted during the fourth quarter of the current fiscal year.

(b) A pilot plant was constructed during 1997–1998 at a cost of $5,000,000 to test a new production process. The plant would be operated for approximately five years. At that time, the company would make a decision regarding the economic value of the process. The pilot plant was too small for commercial production, so it would be dismantled when the test was over.

(c) A new product will be introduced next year. The company spent $4,000,000 during the current year for design of tools, jigs, moulds, and dies for this product.

(d) Taos Inc. purchased Zeebrik Company for $6,000,000 in cash in early August 1998. The fair market value of the identifiable assets of Zeebrik was $5,000,000.

(e) A large advertising campaign was conducted during April 1998 to introduce a new product to be released during the first quarter of the 1998–1999 fiscal year. The advertising campaign cost $3,500,000.

(f) During the first six months of the 1997–1998 fiscal year, $500,000 was expended for legal work in connection with a successful patent application. The patent became effective November 1, 1997. The legal life of the patent was 17 years, while the economic life of the patent was expected to be approximately 10 years.

Instructions

For each of the six expenditures presented, determine and justify:

(a) The amount, if any, that should be capitalized and included on Taos' statement of financial position prepared as of April 30, 1998.

(b) The amount that should be included in Taos' statement of income for the year ended April 30, 1998.

(CMA adapted)

Stettler Company operates several plants at which limestone is processed into quicklime and hydrated lime. The Alta Plant, where most of the equipment was installed many years ago, continually deposits a dusty white substance over the surrounding countryside. Citing the unsanitary condition of the neighbouring community of Primghar, the pollution of the Raccoon River, and the high incidence of lung disease among workers at Alta, the area's Pollution Control Agency has ordered the installation of air pollution control equipment. Also, the Agency has assessed a substantial penalty, which will be used to clean up Primghar. After considering the costs involved (which could not have been reasonably estimated prior to the Agency's action), management decides to comply with the Agency's orders, the alternative being to cease operations at Alta at the end of the current fiscal year. The officers of Stettler Company agree that the air pollution control equipment should be capitalized and depreciated over its useful life, but they disagree over the period(s) to which the penalty should be charged. **C13-3**

Instructions

Discuss the conceptual merits and reporting requirements of accounting for the penalty as a:

(a) Charge to the current period.

(b) Correction of prior periods.

(c) Capitalizable item to be amortized over future periods. (AICPA adapted)

C13-4 After securing lease commitments from several major stores, Churchill Shopping Centre Inc. was organized and built a shopping centre in a growing suburb.

The shopping centre would have opened on schedule on January 1, 1998 if it had not been struck by a severe tornado in December. It opened for business on October 1, 1998. All of the additional construction costs that were incurred as a result of the tornado were covered by insurance.

In July, 1997, in anticipation of the scheduled January opening, a permanent staff was hired to promote the shopping centre, obtain tenants for the uncommitted space, and manage the property.

A summary of some of the costs incurred in 1997 and the first nine months of 1998 follows.

	1997	January 1, 1998 through September 30, 1998
Interest on mortgage bonds	$360,000	$270,000
Cost of obtaining tenants	150,000	180,000
Promotional advertising	270,000	278,500

The promotional advertising campaign was designed to familiarize shoppers with the Centre. Had it been known in time that the Centre would not open until October, 1998, the 1997 expenditure for promotional advertising would not have been made. The advertising had to be repeated in 1998.

All of the tenants who had leased space in the shopping centre at the time of the tornado accepted the October occupancy date on condition that the monthly rental charges for the first nine months of 1998 be canceled.

Instructions

Explain how each of the costs for 1997 and the first nine months of 1998 should be treated in the accounts of Churchill Shopping Centre Inc. Give the reasons for each treatment. (AICPA adapted)

C13-5 On June 30, 1998 your client, Campsell Limited, is granted two patents covering plastic cartons that it has been producing and marketing profitably for the past three years. One patent covers the manufacturing process and the other covers the related products.

Campsell executives tell you that these patents represent the most significant breakthrough in the industry in the past 30 years. The products have been marketed under the registered trademarks Evertight, Duratainer, and Sealrite. Licences under the patents have already been granted by your client to other manufacturers in Canada and abroad and are producing substantial royalties.

On July 1, Campsell commences patent infringement actions against several companies whose names you recognize as those of substantial and prominent competitors. Campsell's management is optimistic that these suits will result in a permanent injunction against the manufacture and sale of the infringing products and collection of damages for loss of profits caused by the alleged infringement.

The financial vice-president has suggested that the patents be recorded at the discounted value of expected net royalty receipts.

Instructions

(a) Explain the meaning of "discounted value of expected net royalty receipts."

(b) How would such a value be calculated for net royalty receipts?

(c) What basis of valuation for Campsell's patents would be generally accepted in accounting? Give supporting reasons for this basis.

(d) Assuming no practical problems of implementation and ignoring generally accepted accounting principles, what is the preferable basis of valuation for patents? Explain.

(e) What would be the preferable theoretical basis of amortization? Explain.

(f) What recognition, if any, should be made of the infringement litigation in the financial statements for the year ending September 30, 1998? Discuss. (AICPA adapted)

C13-6 After extended negotiations, Pochapsky Corporation Ltd. bought from Eskesen Company most of the latter's assets on June 30, 1998. At the time of the sale Eskesen's accounts (adjusted to June 30, 1998) reflected the following descriptions and amounts for the assets transferred.

	Cost	Contra (Valuation) Account	Book Value
Receivables	$ 86,600	$ 2,500	$ 84,100
Inventory	107,000	5,400	101,600
Land	18,000	—	18,000
Buildings	208,600	73,000	135,600
Fixtures and equipment	203,900	42,000	161,900
Goodwill	50,000	—	50,000
	$674,100	$122,900	$551,200

You ascertain that the contra (valuation) accounts were Allowance for Doubtful Accounts, Allowance to Reduce Inventory to Market, and Accumulated Depreciation.

During the extended negotiations, Eskesen held out for a consideration of approximately $700,000 (depending on the level of the receivables and inventory). As of June 30, 1998, however, Eskesen agreed to accept Pochapsky's offer of $500,000 cash plus 1% of the net sales (as defined in the contract) of the next five years with payments at the end of each year. Eskesen expects that Pochapsky's total net sales during this period would exceed $15,000,000.

Instructions

(a) How should Pochapsky Corporation Ltd. record this transaction? Explain.

(b) Discuss the propriety of recording goodwill in the accounts of Pochapsky Corporation Ltd. for this transaction.

(AICPA adapted)

C13-7 Fegg Co. Ltd., a retail propane gas distributor, has increased its annual sales volume to a level three times greater than the annual sales of a dealer it purchased in 1996 in order to begin operations.

The board of directors of Fegg Co. Ltd. has recently received an offer to negotiate the sale of the company to a large competitor. As a result, the majority of the board wants to increase the stated value of goodwill on the balance sheet to reflect the larger sales volume developed through intensive promotion and the current market price. A few of the board members, however, prefer to eliminate goodwill altogether from the balance sheet in order to prevent "possible misinterpretations." Goodwill has been accounted for in accordance with *Handbook* requirements during 1998.

Instructions

(a) Discuss the meaning of the term "goodwill."

(b) List the techniques used to calculate the tentative value of goodwill in negotiations to purchase a going concern.

(c) Why are the book and market values of the goodwill of Fegg Co. Ltd. different?

(d) Discuss the propriety of the following actions:

   1. Increasing the stated value of goodwill prior to the negotiations.

   2. Eliminating goodwill completely from the balance sheet prior to negotiations. (AICPA adapted)

C13-8 Seneca Inc. is in the process of developing a revolutionary new product. A new division of the company is formed to develop, manufacture, and market this new product. As of year end (December 31, 1998) the new product has not been manufactured for resale; however, a prototype unit has been built and is in operation.

Throughout 1998 the new division incurrs certain costs. These costs include design and engineering studies, prototype manufacturing costs, administrative expenses (including salaries of administrative personnel), and market research costs. In addition, approximately $800,000 in equipment (with an estimated useful life of 10 years) was purchased for use in developing and manufacturing the new product. Approximately $300,000 of this equipment was built specifically for the design development of the new product; the remaining $500,000 of equipment was used to manufacture the preproduction prototype and will be used to manufacture the new product once it is in commercial production.

Instructions

(a) How are "research" and "development" defined in the *CICA Handbook*?

(b) Briefly indicate the practical and conceptual reasons for the conclusion reached by the Accounting Standards Board on accounting and reporting practices for research and development costs.

(c) In accordance with the *CICA Handbook*, how should the various costs of Seneca described above be recorded on the financial statements for the year ended December 31, 1998? (AICPA adapted)

USING YOUR JUDGEMENT

FINANCIAL REPORTING PROBLEM

Refer to the financial statements and other documents of Moore Corporation Limited presented in Appendix 5A and answer the following questions.

1. What is the amount of goodwill reported in Moore's financial statements in 1995? How does Moore amortize its goodwill?

2. Can you estimate the age or remaining life of Moore's property, plant, and equipment from the information provided for 1995 in the financial statements or accompanying notes? Was there any significant change in this regard from the previous year?

ETHICS CASE

Health Drug Company has purchased from Bristol Pharmaceuticals a cancer research laboratory, including some personnel, in British Columbia where land values are increasing rapidly. John Cunning, controller, and Larry Beatem, financial vice-president of Health Drug, are attempting to allocate the $40 million purchase price among the four types of assets included in the acquired research operation: building, special equipment, land, and goodwill. The controller, noting that depreciation and amortization can be taken only on the building, special equipment, and goodwill, favours undervaluing the land and placing a very high proportion of the cost on the shortest-lived assets, namely special equipment (7-year tax life), and goodwill (15-year tax life), thus reducing taxable income and income taxes. The financial vice-president argues just the opposite: "A very high proportion of the cost should be placed on the land in order to relieve net income of some depreciation and amortization charge. We must minimize the negative impact of this purchase on net income in order to keep the company's stock price up." Neither suggests allocating any cost to the personnel.

Instructions

(a) Whose interests are affected by the controller's and financial vice-president's contrary positions?

(b) What are the ethical issues in this case?

(c) How should the purchase cost be allocated? Why?

Appendix

ACCOUNTING AND THE TIME VALUE OF MONEY

APPLICATIONS OF TIME VALUE CONCEPTS

NATURE OF INTEREST

FUNDAMENTAL VARIABLES

SINGLE SUM PROBLEMS

ANNUITIES

COMPLEX SITUATIONS

INTERPOLATION OF TABLES TO DERIVE INTEREST RATES

FUNDAMENTAL CONCEPTS

APPENDIX

Accounting and the Time Value of Money

Learning Objectives

After studying this appendix, you should be able to:

1. Identify accounting topics where time value of money is relevant.

2. Distinguish between simple and compound interest.

3. Know how to use appropriate compound interest tables.

4. Identify variables fundamental to solving interest problems.

5. Solve future and present value of single sum problems.

6. Solve future amount of ordinary and annuity due problems.

7. Solve present value of ordinary and annuity due problems.

A prime purpose of financial accounting is to provide information that is useful in making business and economic decisions. Certainly the relationship between time and money is central to economic decision making. It would seem reasonable, then, to expect that any accounting system that has decision usefulness as a primary goal should have a rational basis for reflecting the time value of money in the values it assigns to assets and liabilities—that is, should provide monetary measurements that are interpretable in present value terms.[1]

Would you like to be a millionaire? If you are 20 years old now, can save $100 every month, and can invest those savings to earn an after-tax rate of return of 1% per month (more than 12% per year), you could be a millionaire before you are 59 years old. Alternatively, if you could invest $10,000 today at that same interest rate, you would have over a million dollars by age 59. Such is the power of *interest*, especially when it is energized with a generous dosage of *time*.[2]

Business enterprises both invest and borrow large sums of money. The common characteristic in these two types of transactions is the **time value of the money** (i.e., the interest factor involved). The timing of the returns on the investment has an important

---

[1] J. Alex Milburn, *Incorporating the Time Value of Money Within Financial Accounting* (Toronto: Canadian Institute of Chartered Accountants, 1988), p. 1. This is an excellent study regarding financial accounting and present value measurements. Its objective is to "develop proposals for reflecting the time value of money more fully within the existing financial accounting framework so as to enable a substantive improvement in the usefulness and credibility of financial statements" (p. 1). While we, the authors, accept the basic premise of this study, it is not our intention to examine the model and suggested changes to current financial accounting that are presented. The purpose of this appendix is more basic—to examine the time value of money and show how it can be incorporated in making measurements.

[2] As another example of how interest can multiply dollars quickly, Sidney Homer (author of *A History of Interest Rates*) indicated, "$1,000 invested at a mere 8% for 400 years would grow to $23 quadrillion—$5 million for every human on earth." But, "the first 100 years are the hardest." (*Forbes*, July 14, 1986).

effect on the worth of the investment (asset), and the timing of debt repayments has an effect on the value of the commitment (liability). Business people have become acutely aware of this timing factor and invest and borrow only after carefully analysing the relative values of the cash outflows and inflows.

Accountants are expected to make and understand the implications of value measurements. To do so, they must understand and be able to measure the *present value* of future cash inflows and outflows. This measurement requires an understanding of compound interest, annuities, and present value concepts. Therefore, the basic objectives of this appendix are to discuss and illustrate the essentials of these concepts, and to provide some accounting- and business-related examples in which they are applied.

APPLICATIONS OF TIME VALUE CONCEPTS

Compound interest, annuities, and application of present value concepts are relevant to making measurements and disclosures when accounting for various financial statement elements. The following are some examples examined in this book and the chapters in which they appear:

OBJECTIVE 1
Identify accounting topics where time value of money is relevant.

1. **Notes.** Valuing receivables and payables that carry no stated interest rate or a different than market interest rate (Chapters 7 and 15).

2. **Leases.** Valuing assets and obligations to be capitalized under long-term leases, and measuring the amount of the lease payments and annual leasehold amortization (Chapter 21).

3. **Amortization of Premiums and Discounts.** Measuring amortization of premium or discount on both bond investments and bonds payable (Chapters 10 and 15).

4. **Pensions and Other Post-Retirement Benefits.** Measuring service cost components of employers' post-retirement benefits expense and benefit obligations (Chapter 20).

5. **Capital Assets.** Determining the value of assets acquired under deferred-payment contracts (Chapter 11).

6. **Sinking Funds.** Determining the contributions necessary to accumulate a fund for debt retirement (Chapter 15).

7. **Business Combinations.** Determining the value of receivables, payables, liabilities, accruals, and commitments acquired or assumed in a "purchase" (Chapter 10).

8. **Depreciation.** Measuring depreciation charges under the sinking fund and the annuity methods (Chapter 12).

9. **Instalment Contracts.** Measuring periodic payments on long-term sales or purchase contracts (Chapters 6 and 15).

In addition to their accounting and business applications, compound interest, annuity, and present value concepts are applicable to personal finance and investment decisions. In purchasing a home, planning for retirement, and evaluating alternative investments, you must understand time value of money concepts.

NATURE OF INTEREST

Interest *is payment for the use of money*. It is the excess cash received or paid over and above the amount lent or borrowed (**principal**). For example, if the Toronto Dominion

Bank lends you $1,000 with the understanding that you will repay $1,150, the $150 excess over $1,000 represents interest expense to you and interest revenue to the bank.

The amount of interest to be paid is generally stated as a rate over a specific period of time. For example, if you use the $1,000 for one year before repaying $1,150, the rate of interest is 15% per year ($150/$1,000). The custom of expressing interest as a rate is an established business practice.[3]

The interest rate is commonly expressed as it is applied to a one-year time period. Interest of 12% represents a rate of 12% per year, unless otherwise stipulated. The statement that a corporation will pay bond interest of 12%, payable semiannually, means a rate of 6% every six months, not 12% every six months.

How is the *rate* of interest determined? One of the most important factors is the level of **credit risk** (risk of nonpayment). Other factors being equal, the higher the credit risk, the higher the interest rate. Every borrower's risk is evaluated by the lender. A low-risk borrower like Canadian Pacific Ltd. may obtain a loan at or slightly below the going market "prime" rate of interest. You or the neighbourhood delicatessen, however, will probably be charged several percentage points above the prime rate.

Another important factor is **inflation** (change in the general purchasing power of the dollar). Lenders want to protect the purchasing power of the future cash flows to be received (interest payments and return of the principal). If inflation is expected to be significant in the future, lenders will require a higher number of dollars (i.e., a higher interest rate) in order to offset their anticipation that the purchasing power of these dollars will be reduced.

In addition to receiving compensation for risk and expected inflation, lenders also desire a **pure** or **real return** for letting someone else use their money. This real return reflects the amount the lender would charge if there were no possibility of default or expectation of inflation.

The *amount* of interest related to any financing transaction is a function of three variables:

1. **Principal**—the amount borrowed or invested.
2. **Interest Rate**—a percentage of the outstanding principal.
3. **Time**—the number of years or portion of a year that the principal is outstanding.

SIMPLE INTEREST

OBJECTIVE 2
Distinguish between simple and compound interest.

Simple interest *is computed on the amount of the principal only*. It is the return on (or growth of) the principal for one time period. Simple interest[4] is commonly expressed as:

$$\text{Interest} = p \times i \times n$$

where

$$p = \text{principal}$$
$$i = \text{rate of interest for a single period}$$
$$n = \text{number of periods}$$

To illustrate, if you borrowed $1,000 for a three-year period, with a simple interest rate of 15% per year, the total interest to be paid would be $450, computed as follows:

---

[3] Federal and provincial legislation requires the disclosure of the effective interest rate on an *annual basis* in contracts. That is, instead of, or in addition to, stating the rate as "1% per month," it must be stated as "12% per year" if it is simple interest or "12.68% per year" if it is compounded monthly.

[4] Simple interest is also expressed as i (interest) = P(principal) $\times$ R(rate) $\times$ T(time).

$$\begin{aligned} \text{Interest} &= (p)(i)(n) \\ &= (\$1{,}000)(.15)(3) \\ &= \$450 \end{aligned}$$

COMPOUND INTEREST

John Maynard Keynes, the legendary English economist, supposedly called it magic. Mayer Rothschild, the founder of the famous European banking firm, is said to have proclaimed it the eighth wonder of the world. Today people continue to extol its wonder and its power.[5] The object of their affection is compound interest.

Compound interest *is computed on the principal and any interest earned that has not been paid*. To illustrate the difference between simple interest and compound interest, assume that you deposit $1,000 in the Last Canadian Bank, where it earns simple interest of 9% per year. Assume that you deposit another $1,000 in the First Canadian Bank, where it earns annually compounded interest of 9%. Finally, assume that in both cases you do not withdraw any interest until three years from the date of deposit. The calculation of interest to be received is shown in Exhibit A-1.

EXHIBIT A-1

SIMPLE VS. COMPOUND INTEREST

	Last Canadian Bank			First Canadian Bank		
	Simple Interest Calculation	Simple Interest	Accumulated Year-End Balance	**Compound** Interest Calculation	Compound Interest	Accumulated Year-End Balance
Year 1	$1,000.00 × 9%	$ 90.00	$1,090.00	$1,000.00 × 9%	$ 90.00	$1,090.00
Year 2	1,000.00 × 9%	90.00	1,180.00	1,090.00 × 9%	98.10	1,188.10
Year 3	1,000.00 × 9%	90.00	1,270.00	1,188.10 × 9%	106.93	1,295.03
		$270.00 ——	$25.03 Difference ——		$295.03	

Note that simple interest uses the initial principal of $1,000 to compute the interest in all three years, while compound interest uses the accumulated balance (principal plus interest to date) at each year end to compute interest in the succeeding year. Obviously, if you had a choice between investing at simple interest or at compound interest, you would choose compound interest, all other things—especially risk—being equal. In the example, compounding provides $25.03 of additional interest income.

Compound interest is generally applied in business situations. Financial managers view and evaluate their investment opportunities in terms of a series of periodic returns, each of which can be reinvested to yield additional returns. Simple interest is generally applicable only to short-term investments and debts that are due within one year.

---

[5] Here is an illustration of the power of time and compounding interest on money. In 1626, Peter Minuit bought Manhatten Island from the Manhattoe Indians for $24 worth of trinkets and beads. If the Indians had taken a boat to Holland, invested the $24 in Dutch securities returning just 6% per year, and kept the money and interest invested at 6%, by 1971 they would have had $13 billion, enough to buy back all the land on the island and still have a couple of billion dollars left (*Forbes*, June 1, 1971). By 1998, 372 years after the trade, the $24 would have grown to approximately $63 billion—$62 trillion had the interest rate been 8%.

COMPOUND INTEREST TABLES

Five different compound interest tables are presented at the end of this appendix (see pages A-29–A-33). These tables are the source for various "interest factors" used to solve problems that involve interest in this appendix and throughout the book. The titles of these five tables and their contents are:

OBJECTIVE 3
Know how to use appropriate compound interest tables.

1. **Future Amount of 1.** Contains the amounts to which $1.00 will accumulate if deposited now at a specified rate and left for a specified number of periods (Table A-1).

2. **Present Value of 1.** Contains the amounts that must be deposited now at a specified rate of interest to equal $1.00 at the end of a specified number of periods (Table A-2).

3. **Future Amount of an Ordinary Annuity of 1.** Contains the amounts to which periodic rents of $1.00 will accumulate if the rents are invested at the *end* of each period at a specified rate of interest for a specified number of periods (Table A-3).

4. **Present Value of an Ordinary Annuity of 1.** Contains the amounts that must be deposited now at a specified rate of interest to permit withdrawals of $1.00 at the *end* of regular periodic intervals for the specified number of periods (Table A-4).

5. **Present Value of an Annuity Due of 1.** Contains the amounts that must be deposited now at a specified rate of interest to permit withdrawals of $1.00 at the *beginning* of regular periodic intervals for the specified number of periods (Table A-5).

Exhibit A-2 shows the general format and content of these tables. It is from Table A-1, "Future Amount of 1," which indicates the amount to which a dollar accumulates at the end of each of five periods at three different rates of compound interest.

EXHIBIT A-2

FUTURE AMOUNT OF 1 AT COMPOUND INTEREST

(Excerpt from Table A-1)

Period	9%	10%	11%
1	1.09000	1.10000	1.11000
2	1.18810	1.21000	1.23210
3	1.29503	1.33100	1.36763
4	1.41158	1.46410	1.51807
5	1.53862	1.61051	1.68506

Interpreting the table, if $1.00 is invested for three periods at a compound interest rate of 9% per period, it will amount to $1.30 (1.29503 × $1.00), the **compound future amount.** If $1.00 is invested at 11%, at the end of four periods it amounts to $1.52. If the investment is $1,000 instead of $1.00, it will amount to $1,295.03 ($1,000 × 1.29503) if invested at 9% for three periods, or $1,518.07 if invested at 11% for four periods.

Throughout the foregoing discussion and the discussion that follows, the use of the term *periods* instead of *years* is intentional. While interest is generally expressed as an annual rate, the compounding period is often shorter. Therefore, the annual interest rate must be converted to correspond to the length of the period. To convert the "annual interest rate" into the "compounding period interest rate," *divide the annual rate by the number of compounding periods per year*. In addition, the number of periods is determined by *multiplying the number of years involved by the number of compounding periods per year*.

To illustrate, assume that $1.00 is invested for six years at 8% annual interest compounded quarterly. Using Table A-1, the amount to which this $1.00 will accumulate is determined by reading the factor that appears in the 2% column (8% ÷ 4) on the 24th row (6 years × 4), namely 1.60844, or approximately $1.61.

Because interest is theoretically earned every second of every day, it is possible to calculate continuously compounded interest. As a practical matter, however, most business transactions assume interest is compounded no more frequently than daily.

How often interest is compounded can make a substantial difference to the rate of return achieved. For example, 9% interest compounded daily provides a 9.42% annual yield, or a difference of .42%. The 9.42% is referred to as the **effective yield** or **rate**,[6] whereas the 9% annual interest rate is called the **stated**, **nominal**, **coupon**, or **face rate**. When the compounding frequency is greater than once a year, the effective interest rate is higher than the stated rate.

FUNDAMENTAL VARIABLES

The following four variables are fundamental to all compound interest problems:

1. **Rate of Interest.** This rate, unless otherwise stated, is an annual rate that must be adjusted to reflect the length of the compounding period if it is less than a year.

2. **Number of Time Periods.** This is the number of compounding periods for which interest is to be computed.

3. **Future Amount.** The value at a future date of a given sum or sums invested, assuming compound interest.

4. **Present Value.** The value now (present time) of a future sum or sums discounted, assuming compound interest.

OBJECTIVE 4
Identify variables fundamental to solving interest problems.

The relationship of these four variables is depicted in the *time diagram* in Illustration A-1.

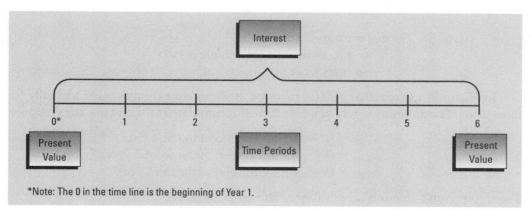

ILLUSTRATION A-1
Time diagram identifying four fundamental variables

*Note: The 0 in the time line is the beginning of Year 1.

In some cases all four of these variables are known, but in many business situations at least one is unknown. Frequently, the accountant is expected to determine the unknown amount or amounts. To do this, a time diagram can be very helpful in understanding the nature of the problem and finding a solution.

The remainder of the appendix covers the following six major time value of money concepts. Both formula and interest table approaches are used to illustrate how problems may be solved:

---

[6] The formula for calculating the effective rate in situations where the compounding frequency (f) is more than once a year is as follows:

$$\text{Effective rate} = (1 + i)^f - 1$$

where i = the interest rate per compounding period.

1. Future amount of a single sum.

2. Present value of a single sum.

3. Future amount of an ordinary annuity.

4. Future amount of an annuity due.

5. Present value of an ordinary annuity.

6. Present value of an annuity due.

SINGLE SUM PROBLEMS

OBJECTIVE 5
Solve future and present value of single sum problems.

Many business and investment decisions involve a single amount of money that either exists now or will exist in the future. Single sum problems can generally be classified into one of the following two categories:

1. Determining the *unknown future amount* of a known single sum of money that is invested for a specified number of periods at a specified interest rate.

2. Determining the *unknown present value* of a known single sum of money that is discounted for a specified number of periods at a specified interest rate.

FUTURE AMOUNT OF A SINGLE SUM

The **future amount** of a sum of money is the future value of that sum when left to accumulate for a certain number of periods at a specified rate of interest per period.

The amount to which 1 (one) will accumulate may be expressed as a formula:

$$a_{\overline{n}|\,i} = (1 + i)^n$$

where

$$a_{\overline{n}|\,i} = \text{future amount of 1}$$
$$i = \text{rate of interest for a single period}$$
$$n = \text{number of periods}$$

To illustrate, assume that $1.00 is invested at 9% interest compounded annually for three years. The amounts to which the $1.00 will accumulate at the end of each year are:

$$a_{\overline{1}|\,9\%} = (1 + .09)^1 \text{ for the end of the first year.}$$
$$a_{\overline{2}|\,9\%} = (1 + .09)^2 \text{ for the end of the second year.}$$
$$a_{\overline{3}|\,9\%} = (1 + .09)^3 \text{ for the end of the third year.}$$

These compound amounts accumulate as shown in Exhibit A-3.

EXHIBIT A-3

ACCUMULATION OF COMPOUND AMOUNTS

Period	Beginning-of-Period Amount	×	Multiplier (1 + i)	=	End-of-Period Amount*	Formula (1+i)ⁿ
1	1.00000		1.09		1.09000	$(1.09)^1$
2	1.09000		1.09		1.18810	$(1.09)^2$
3	1.18810		1.09		1.29503	$(1.09)^3$

*These amounts appear in Table A-1 in the 9% column.

To calculate the *future value of any single amount*, multiply the future amount of 1 factor by that amount.

$$a = p(a_{\overline{n}|\,i})$$

where

a = future amount
p = beginning principal or sum (present value)
$a_{\overline{n}|\,i} = (1 + i)^n$ = future amount of 1 for n periods at i%.

For example, what is the future amount of $50,000 invested for five years at 11% compounded annually? In time-diagram form, this investment situation is indicated in Illustration A-2.

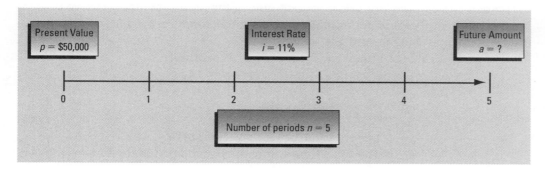

ILLUSTRATION A-2
Time diagram for future amount calculation

This investment problem is solved as follows.

$$a = p(a_{\overline{n}|\,i})$$
$$= \$50,000(a_{\overline{5}|\,11\%})$$
$$= \$50,000 \, (1.68506)$$
$$= \$84,253.$$

The future amount of 1 factor of 1.68506 is that which appears in Table A-1 in the 11% column and 5-period row.

To illustrate a more complex business situation, assume that at the beginning of 1998 Ontario Hydro Corp. deposits $250 million in an escrow account with Canada Trust Company as a commitment toward a small nuclear power plant to be completed December 31, 2001. How much will be on deposit at the end of four years if interest is compounded semiannually at 10%?

With a known present value of $250 million, a total of eight compounding periods (4 × 2), and an interest rate of 5% per compounding period (10% ÷ 2), this problem can be time-diagrammed and the future amount determined as indicated in Illustration A-3.

ILLUSTRATION A-3
Time diagram for future amount calculation

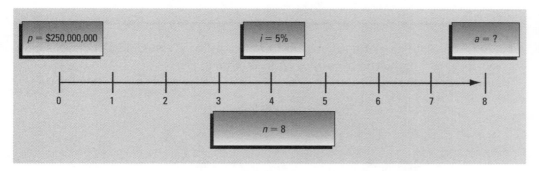

$$a = \$250,000,000(a_{\overline{8}|\,5\%})$$
$$= \$250,000,000(1.47746)$$
$$= \$369,365,000.$$

The deposit of $250 million will accumulate to $369,365,000 by December 31, 2001. The future amount of 1 factor is found in Table A-1 (5% column and the 8-period row).

PRESENT VALUE OF A SINGLE SUM

A previous example showed that $50,000 invested at an annually compounded interest rate of 11% will be worth $84,253 at the end of five years. It follows that $84,253 to be received five years from now is presently worth $50,000, given an 11% interest rate (i.e., $50,000 is the present value of this $84,253). The **present value** is the amount that must be invested now to produce a known future amount. The *present value is always a smaller amount than the known future amount because interest is earned and accumulated on the present value to the future date*. In determining the future amount we move forward in time using a process of **accumulation**, while in determining present value we move backward in time using the process of **discounting**.

The present value of 1 (one) may be expressed as a formula:

$$p_{\overline{n}|\,i} = 1/a_{\overline{n}|\,i} = \frac{1}{(1+i)^n}$$

where

$p_{\overline{n}|\,i}$ = present value of 1 for n periods at $i\%$.
$a_{\overline{n}|\,i} = (1+i)^n$ = future amount of 1 for n periods at $i\%$.

To illustrate, assume that $1.00 is discounted for three periods at 9%. The present value of the $1.00 is discounted each period as follows.

$$p_{\overline{1}|\,9\%} = 1/(1+.09)^1 \text{ for the first period}$$
$$p_{\overline{2}|\,9\%} = 1/(1+.09)^2 \text{ for the second period}$$
$$p_{\overline{3}|\,9\%} = 1/(1+.09)^3 \text{ for the third period}$$

Therefore, the $1.00 is discounted as shown in Exhibit A-4.

EXHIBIT A-4

PRESENT VALUE OF $1 DISCOUNTED AT 9% FOR THREE PERIODS

Discount Periods	Future Amount	÷	Divisor $(1+i)^n$	=	Present Value*	Formula $1/(1+i)^n$
1	1.00000		1.09		.91743	$1/(1.09)^1$
2	1.00000		$(1.09)^2$		.84168	$1/(1.09)^2$
3	1.00000		$(1.09)^3$		.77218	$1/(1.09)^3$

*These amounts appear in Table A-2 in the 9% column.

Table A-2, "Present Value of 1," shows how much must be invested now at various interest rates to equal 1 at the end of various periods of time.

The present value of 1 formula $p_{\overline{n}|\,i}$ can be expanded for use in computing the present value of *any single future amount* as follows.

$$p = a(p_{\overline{n}|\,i})$$

where

p = present value of a single future amount
a = future amount

$$p_{\overline{n}|\,i} = \frac{1}{(1+i)^n} = \text{present value of 1 for } n \text{ periods at } i\%.$$

To illustrate, assume that your favourite uncle proposes to give you $4,000 for a trip to Europe when you graduate three years from now. He will finance the trip by investing a sum of money now at 8% compound interest that will accumulate to $4,000 upon your graduation. The only conditions are that you graduate and that you tell him how much to invest now.

To impress your uncle, you might set up a time diagram as shown in Illustration A-4 and solve the problem as follows.

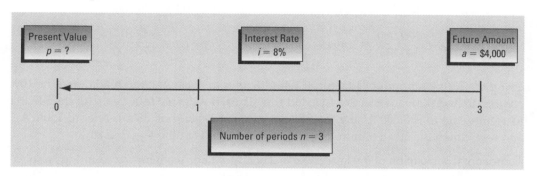

$$p = \$4,000(p_{\overline{3}|\,8\%})$$
$$= \$4,000(.79383)$$
$$= \$3,175.32.$$

Advise your uncle to invest $3,175.32 now to provide you with $4,000 upon graduation. To satisfy your uncle's other condition, you must simply pass this course and many more. Note that the present value factor of .79383 is found in Table A-2 (8% column, 3-period row).

SINGLE SUM PROBLEMS: SOLVING FOR OTHER UNKNOWNS

In computing either the future amount or the present value in the previous single sum illustrations, both the number of periods and the interest rate were known. In business situations, both the future amount and the present value may be known, and either the number of periods or the interest rate may be unknown. The following two illustrations demonstrate how to solve single sum problems when there is either an unknown number of periods (*n*) or an unknown interest rate (*i*). These illustrations show that if any three of the four values (future amount, *a*; present value, *p*; number of periods, *n*; interest rate, *i*) are known, the one unknown can be derived.

Illustration: Computation of the Number of Periods. The local Big Sisters and Big Brothers associations in Regina want to accumulate $70,000 for the construction of a day-care centre. If at the beginning of the current year the associations are able to deposit $47,811 in a building fund that earns 10% interest compounded annually, how many years will it take for the fund to accumulate to $70,000?

In this situation, the present value ($47,811), future amount ($70,000), and interest rate (10%) are known. A time diagram of this investment is shown in Illustration A-5.

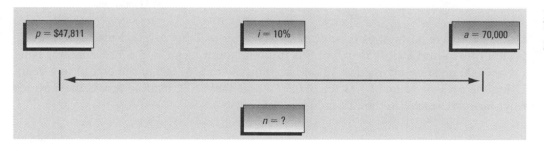

The unknown number of periods can be determined using either the future amount or present value approaches, as shown below.

Future Amount Approach

$$a = p(a_{\overline{n}|\,10\%})$$

$$\$70{,}000 = \$47{,}811(a_{\overline{n}|\,10\%})$$

$$a_{\overline{n}|\,10\%} = \frac{\$70{,}000}{\$47{,}811} = 1.46410$$

Present Value Approach

$$p = a(p_{\overline{n}|\,10\%})$$

$$\$47{,}811 = \$70{,}000(p_{\overline{n}|\,10\%})$$

$$p_{\overline{n}|\,10\%} = \frac{\$47{,}811}{\$70{,}000} = .68301$$

Using the future amount of 1 factor of 1.46410, refer to Table A-1 and read down the 10% column to find that factor in the 4-period row. Thus, it will take four years for the $47,811 to accumulate to $70,000. Using the present value of 1 factor of .68301, refer to Table A-2 and read down the 10% column to also find that factor is in the 4-period row.

Illustration: Computation of the Interest Rate. The Canadian Academic Accounting Association wants to have $141,000 available five years from now to provide scholarships to individuals who undertake a PhD program. At present, the executive of the CAAA has determined that $80,000 may be invested for this purpose. What rate of interest must be earned on the investments in order to accumulate the $141,000 five years from now?

Illustration A-6 provides a time diagram of this problem.

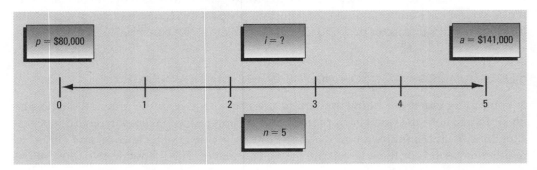

Given that the present value, future amount, and number of periods are known, the unknown interest rate can be determined using either the future amount or present value approaches, as shown below.

Future Amount Approach

$$a = p(a_{\overline{5}|\,i})$$

$$\$141{,}000 = \$80{,}000(a_{\overline{5}|\,i})$$

$$a_{\overline{5}|\,i} = \frac{\$141{,}000}{\$80{,}000} = 1.7625$$

Present Value Approach

$$p = a(p_{\overline{5}|\,i})$$

$$\$80{,}000 = \$141{,}000(p_{\overline{5}|\,i})$$

$$p_{\overline{5}|\,i} = \frac{\$80{,}000}{\$141{,}000} = 0.5674$$

Using the future amount of 1 factor of 1.7625, refer to Table A-1 and read across the 5-period row to find a close match of this future amount factor in the 12% column. Thus, the $80,000 must be invested at 12% to accumulate to $141,000 at the end of five years. Using the present value of 1 factor of 0.5674 and Table A-2, reading across the 5-period row shows this factor in the 12% column.

ANNUITIES

The preceding discussion involved only the accumulation or discounting of a single principal sum. Accountants frequently encounter situations in which a series of amounts are to be paid or received over time (e.g., when loans or sales are paid in instalments, invested funds are partially recovered at regular intervals, and cost savings are realized repeatedly). When a commitment involves a series of equal payments made at equal intervals of time, it is called an annuity. By definition, an **annuity** requires that (1) the *periodic payments or receipts* (called *rents*) *always be the same amount;* (2) the *interval between such rents always be the same;* and (3) the *interest be compounded once each interval.*

The **future amount of an annuity** *is the sum of all the rents plus the accumulated compound interest on them.* Rents may, however, occur at either the beginning or the end of the periods. To distinguish annuities under these two alternatives, an annuity is classified as an **ordinary annuity** *if the rents occur at the end of each period,* and as an **annuity due** *if the rents occur at the beginning of each period.*

FUTURE AMOUNT OF AN ORDINARY ANNUITY

One approach to calculating the future amount of an annuity is to determine the future amount of each rent in the series and then aggregate these individual future amounts. For example, assume that $1 is deposited at the *end* of each of five years (an ordinary annuity) and earns 12% interest compounded annually. The future amount can be computed as indicated in Illustration A-7 using the "Future Amount of 1" for each of the five $1 rents.

OBJECTIVE 6
Solve future amount of ordinary and annuity due problems.

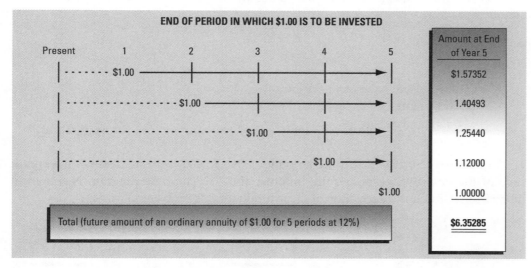

ILLUSTRATION A-7
Solving for the future amount of an ordinary annuity

Although the foregoing procedure for computing the future amount of an ordinary annuity produces the correct answer, it is cumbersome if the number of rents is large. A more efficient way of determining the future amount of an ordinary annuity of 1 is to apply the following formula:

$$A_{\overline{n}|\,i} = \frac{(1 + i)^n - 1}{i}$$

where

$A_{\overline{n}|\,i}$ = future amount of an ordinary annuity of 1 for n periods at i rate of interest
n = number of compounding periods
i = rate of interest per period

Using this formula, Table A-3 has been developed to show the "Future Amount of an Ordinary Annuity of 1" for various interest rates and investment periods. Exhibit A-5 is an excerpt from this table.

EXHIBIT A-5

FUTURE AMOUNT OF AN ORDINARY ANNUITY OF 1

(excerpt from Table A-3)

Period	10%	11%	12%
1	1.00000	1.00000	1.00000
2	2.10000	2.11000	2.12000
3	3.31000	3.34210	3.37440
4	4.64100	4.70973	4.77933
5	6.10510	6.22780	6.35285*

*Note that this factor is the same as the sum of the future amounts of 1 factors shown in the previous schedule.

Interpreting the table, if $1.00 is invested at the end of each year for four years at 11% interest compounded annually, the amount of the annuity at the end of the fourth year will be $4.71 (4.70973 × $1.00). The $4.71 is made up of $4 of rent payments ($1 at the end of each of the 4 years) and compound interest of $0.71.

The $A_{\overline{n}|i}$ formula can be expanded to determine the future amount of an ordinary annuity as follows.

$$A = R(A_{\overline{n}|i})$$

where

A = future amount of an ordinary annuity.
R = periodic rents
$A_{\overline{n}|i} = \dfrac{(1 + i)^n - 1}{i}$ = future amount of an ordinary annuity of 1 for n periods at i%.

To illustrate, what is the future amount of five $5,000 deposits made at the end of each of the next five years, earning interest at 12%? The time diagram is shown in Illustration A-8 and the derivation of the solution for this problem follows.

ILLUSTRATION A-8

Time diagram for future amount calculation of an ordinary annuity

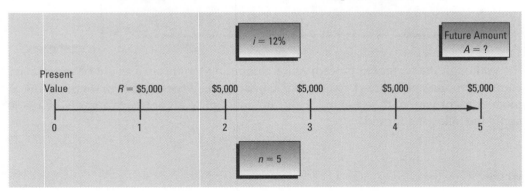

$$A = R(A_{\overline{n}|i})$$
$$= \$5,000(A_{\overline{5}|12\%})$$
$$= \$5,000(6.35285)$$
$$= \$31,764.25$$

The future amount of an ordinary annuity of 1 factor of 6.35285 is found in Table A-3 (12% column, 5-period row).

To illustrate these computations in a business situation, assume that Lightning Electronics Limited's management decides to deposit $75,000 at the end of each six-month period for the next three years for the purpose of accumulating enough money to meet debts that mature in three years. What is the future amount that will be on deposit at the end of three years if the annual interest rate is 10%?

The time diagram in Illustration A-9 and solution are as follows.

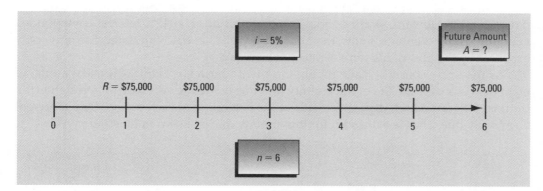

ILLUSTRATION A-9
Time diagram for future amount calculation of an ordinary annuity

$$A = R(A_{\overline{n}|\,i})$$
$$= \$75,000(A_{\overline{6}|\,5\%})$$
$$= \$75,000(6.80191)$$
$$= \$510,143.25$$

Thus, six deposits of $75,000 made at the end of every six months and earning 5% per period will grow to $510,143.25 at the time of the last deposit.

FUTURE AMOUNT OF AN ANNUITY DUE

The preceding analysis of an *ordinary annuity* was based on the fact that the *periodic rents* occur at the *end* of each period. An **annuity due** is based on the fact that the *periodic rents* occur at the *beginning* of each period. This means an annuity due will accumulate interest during the first period whereas an ordinary annuity will not. Therefore, the significant difference between the two types of annuities is in the number of interest accumulation periods involved. The distinction is shown graphically in Illustration A-10.

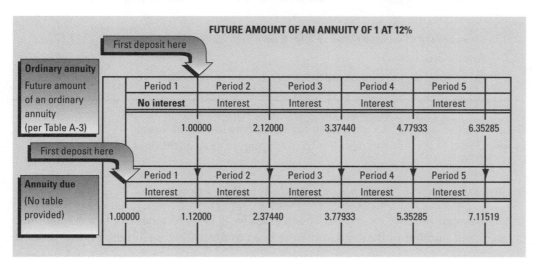

ILLUSTRATION A-10
Comparison of the future amount of an ordinary annuity with that of an annuity due

Because the cash flows from the annuity due come exactly one period earlier than for an ordinary annuity, the future value of the annuity due of 1 factor is exactly 12% higher than the ordinary annuity factor. Therefore, *to determine the future value of an annuity due of 1 factor, multiply the corresponding future value of the ordinary annuity of 1 factor by one plus the interest rate*. For example, to determine the future value of an annuity due of 1 factor for five periods at 12% compound interest, simply multiply the future value of an ordinary annuity of 1 factor for five periods (6.35285) by one plus the interest rate (1 + .12) to arrive at the future value of an annuity due of 1, 7.1152 (6.35285 × 1.12).

To illustrate, assume that Hank Lotadough plans to deposit $800 a year on each birthday of his son Howard, starting today, his tenth birthday, at 12% interest compounded annually. Hank wants to know the amount he will have accumulated for university expenses by the time of his son's eighteenth birthday.

As the first deposit is made on his son's tenth birthday, Hank will make a total of eight deposits over the life of the annuity (assume no deposit is made on the eighteenth birthday). Because each deposit is made at the beginning of each period, they represent an annuity due. The time diagram for this annuity due is shown in Illustration A-11.

ILLUSTRATION A-11
Time diagram for future amount calculation of an annuity due

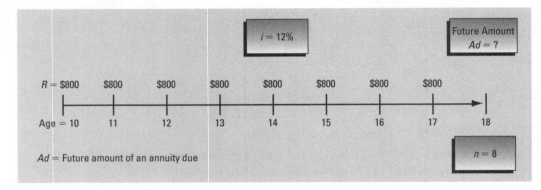

Referring to Table A-3, "Future Amount of an Ordinary Annuity of 1," for eight periods at 12%, a factor of 12.29969 is found. This factor is then multiplied by (1 + .12) to arrive at the future amount of an annuity due of 1 factor. As a result, the accumulated amount on his son's eighteenth birthday is computed as shown in Exhibit A-6.

EXHIBIT A-6

COMPUTATION OF THE FUTURE AMOUNT OF AN ANNUITY DUE

1. Future amount of an ordinary annuity of 1 for 8 periods at 12% (Table A-3)	12.29969
2. Factor (1 + .12)	× 1.12
3. Future amount of an annuity due of 1 for 8 periods at 12%	13.77565
4. Periodic deposit (rent)	× $800
5. Accumulated amount on son's eighteenth birthday	$11,020.52

Because expenses to go to university for four years are considerably in excess of $11,000, Howard will likely have to develop his own plan to save additional funds.

ILLUSTRATIONS OF FUTURE AMOUNT OF ANNUITY PROBLEMS

In the previous annuity examples, three values were known (amount of each rent, interest rate, and number of periods) and were used to determine the unknown fourth value (future amount). The following illustrations demonstrate how to solve problems when the unknown is (1) the amount of the rents; or (2) the number of rents in ordinary annuity situations.

Illustration: Computing the Amount of Each Rent. Assume that you wish to accumulate $14,000 for a down payment on a condominium five years from now and that you can earn an annual return of 8% compounded semiannually during the next five years. How much should you deposit at the end of each six-month period?

The $14,000 is the future amount of 10 (5 × 2) semiannual end-of-period payments of an unknown amount at an interest rate of 4% (8% ÷ 2). This problem is time-diagrammed in Illustration A-12.

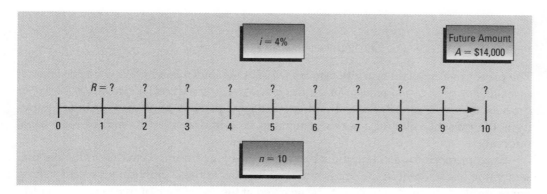

ILLUSTRATION A-12
Time diagram for calculating the semiannual payment of an ordinary annuity

Using the formula for the future amount of an ordinary annuity, the amount of each rent is determined as follows.

$$A = R(A_{\overline{n}|\,i})$$
$$\$14,000 = R(A_{\overline{10}|\,4\%})$$
$$\$14,000 = R(12.00611)$$
$$\frac{\$14,000}{12.00611} = R$$
$$R = \$1,166.07$$

Thus, you must make 10 semiannual deposits of $1,166.07 each in order to accumulate $14,000 for your down payment. The future amount of an ordinary annuity of 1 factor of 12.00611 is provided in Table A-3 (4% column, 10-period row).

Illustration: Computing the Number of Periodic Rents. Suppose that your company wants to accumulate $117,332 by making periodic deposits of $20,000 at the end of each year that will earn 8% compounded annually. How many deposits must be made?

The $117,332 represents the future amount of $n(?)$ $20,000 deposits at an 8% annual rate of interest. Illustration A-13 provides a time diagram for this problem.

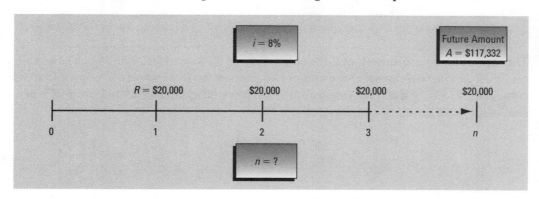

ILLUSTRATION A-13
Time diagram for number of periods calculation for an ordinary annuity

Using the future amount of an ordinary annuity formula, the factor of 1 is determined as follows.

$$A = R(A_{\overline{n}|\,i})$$
$$\$117{,}332 = \$20{,}000(A_{\overline{n}|\,8\%})$$
$$A_{\overline{n}|\,8\%} = \frac{\$117{,}332}{\$20{,}000} = 5.86660$$

Using Table A-3 and reading down the 8% column, 5.86660 is in the 5-period row. Thus, five deposits of $20,000 each must be made.

PRESENT VALUE OF AN ORDINARY ANNUITY

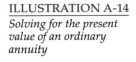

OBJECTIVE 7

Solve present value of ordinary and annuity due problems.

The **present value of an annuity** *may be viewed as the single amount that, if invested now at compound interest, would provide for a series of withdrawals of a certain amount per period for a specific number of future periods.* In other words, the present value of an ordinary annuity is the present value of a series of rents to be withdrawn at the end of each equal interval.

One approach to calculating the present value of an annuity is to determine the present value of each rent in the series and then aggregate these individual present values. For example, assume that $1.00 is to be received at the *end* of each of five periods (an ordinary annuity) and that the interest rate is 12% compounded annually. The present value of this annuity can be computed as shown in Illustration A-14 using Table A-2, "Present Value of 1," for each of the five $1 rents.

ILLUSTRATION A-14

Solving for the present value of an ordinary annuity

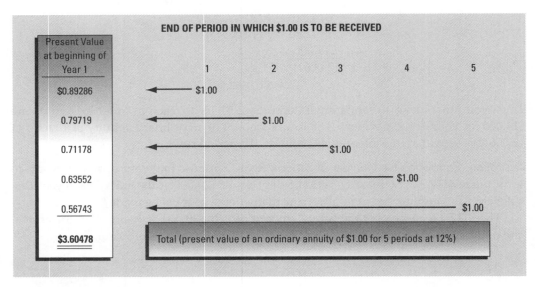

This computation indicates that if the single sum of $3.60 is invested today at 12% interest, $1.00 can be withdrawn at the end of each period for five periods. This procedure is cumbersome. Using the following formula is a more efficient way to determine the present value of an ordinary annuity of 1:

$$P_{\overline{n}|\,i} = \frac{1 - \dfrac{1}{(1 + i)^n}}{i}$$

Table A-4, "Present Value of an Ordinary Annuity of 1," is based on this formula. Exhibit A-7 is an excerpt from this table.

EXHIBIT A-7

PRESENT VALUE OF AN ORDINARY ANNUITY OF 1

(excerpt from Table A-4)

Period	10%	11%	12%
1	.90909	.90090	.89286
2	1.73554	1.71252	1.69005
3	2.48685	2.44371	2.40183
4	3.16986	3.10245	3.03735
5	3.79079	3.69590	**3.60478***

*Note that this factor is equal to the sum of the present value of 1 factors shown in the previous schedule.

The formula for the present value of any ordinary annuity of any rent value is as follows.

$$P = R(P_{\overline{n}|\,i})$$

where

P = present value of an ordinary annuity
R = periodic rent (ordinary annuity)

$$P_{\overline{n}|\,i} = \frac{1 - \dfrac{1}{(1 + i)^n}}{i} = \text{present value of an ordinary annuity of 1 for } n \text{ periods at } i\%.$$

To illustrate, what is the present value of rental receipts of $6,000, each to be received at the end of each of the next five years when discounted at 12%? This problem is time-diagrammed in Illustration A-15 and the solution follows.

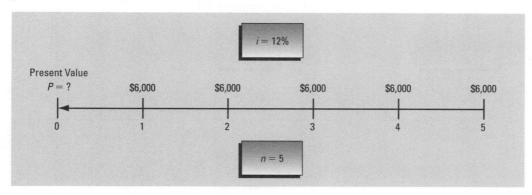

ILLUSTRATION A-15
Time diagram for present value calculation of an ordinary annuity

$$P = R(P_{\overline{n}|\,i})$$
$$= \$6,000(P_{\overline{5}|\,12\%})$$
$$= \$6,000(3.60478)$$
$$= \$21,628.68$$

The present value of the five ordinary annuity rental receipts of $6,000 each is $21,628.68. The present value of the ordinary annuity of 1 factor, 3.60478, is from Table A-4 (12% column, 5-period row).

PRESENT VALUE OF AN ANNUITY DUE

In the discussion of the present value of an ordinary annuity, the final rent was discounted back the same number of periods as there were rents. In determining the present value of an annuity due, there is one fewer discount periods. This distinction is shown graphically in Illustration A-16.

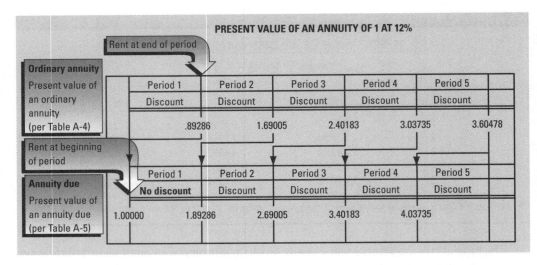

Because each cash flow (rent) comes exactly one period sooner in the present value of an annuity due, the present value of the cash flows is exactly 12% higher than the present value of an ordinary annuity. Thus, *the present value of an annuity due of 1 factor can be found by multiplying the present value of an ordinary annuity of 1 by one plus the interest rate*. For example, to determine the present value of an annuity due of 1 factor for five periods at 12% interest, take the present value of an ordinary annuity of 1 factor for five periods at 12% interest (3.60478) and multiply it by 1.12 to arrive at the present value of an annuity due of 1, which is 4.03735 (3.60478 × 1.12). Table A-5 provides present value of annuity due of 1 factors.

To illustrate, assume that Space Odyssey Inc. rents a communications satellite for four years with annual rental payments of \$4.8 million to be made at the beginning of each year. Assuming an annual interest rate of 11%, what is the present value of the rental obligations?

This problem is time-diagrammed in Illustration A-17.

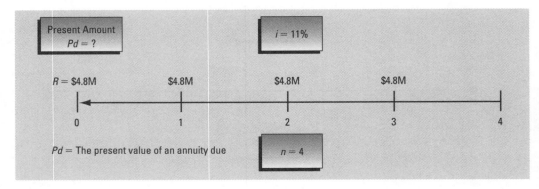

This problem can be solved as shown in Exhibit A-8.

EXHIBIT A-8

COMPUTATION OF PRESENT VALUE OF AN ANNUITY DUE

1. Present value of an **ordinary annuity** of 1 for 4 periods at 11% (Table A-4)	3.10245
2. Factor (1 + .11)	× 1.11
3. Present value of an **annuity due** of 1 for 4 periods at 11%	3.44371
4. Periodic deposit (rent)	×\$4,800,000
5. Present value of payments	\$ 16,529.808

Since Table A-5 gives present value of an annuity due of 1 factors, it can be used to obtain the required factor 3.44371 (in the 11% column, 4-period row).

ILLUSTRATIONS OF PRESENT VALUE OF ANNUITY PROBLEMS

The following illustrations show how to solve problems when the unknown is (1) the present value; (2) the interest rate; or (3) the amount of each rent for present value of annuity problems.

Illustration: Computation of the Present Value of an Ordinary Annuity. You have just won Lotto B.C. totalling $4,000,000. You will be paid the amount of $200,000 at the end of each of the next 20 years. What amount have you really won? That is, what is the present value of the $200,000 cheques you will receive over the next 20 years? A time diagram of this enviable situation is shown in Illustration A-18 (assuming an interest rate of 10%).

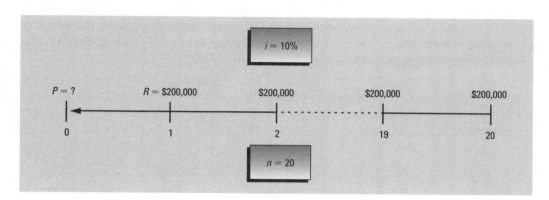

The present value is determined as follows:

$$P = R(P_{\overline{n}|\,i})$$
$$= \$200,000(P_{\overline{20}|\,10\%})$$
$$= \$200,00(8.51356)$$
$$= \$1,702,712$$

As a result, if Lotto B.C. deposits $1,702,712 now and earns 10% interest, it can draw $200,000 a year for 20 years to pay you the $4,000,000.

Illustration: Computation of the Interest Rate. Many shoppers make purchases by using a credit card. When you receive an invoice for payment, you may pay the total amount due or pay the balance in a certain number of payments. For example, if you receive an invoice from VISA with a balance due of $528.77 and are invited to pay it off in 12 equal monthly payments of $50.00 each with the first payment due one month from now, what rate of interest are you paying?

    The $528.77 represents the present value of the twelve $50 payments at an unknown rate of interest. This situation is time-diagrammed in Illustration A-19, which is followed by the determination of the interest rate.

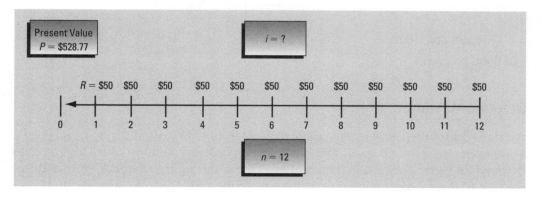

$$P = R(P_{\overline{n}|\,i})$$
$$\$528.77 = \$50(P_{\overline{12}|\,i})$$
$$P_{\overline{12}|\,i} = \frac{\$528.77}{50} = 10.5754$$

Referring to Table A-4 and reading across the 12-period row, the 10.57534 factor is in the 2% column. Since 2% is a monthly rate, the nominal annual rate of interest is 24% (12 × 2%) and the effective annual rate is 26.82413% $[(1 + .02)^{12} - 1]$. At such a high rate of interest, you are better off paying the entire bill now if possible.

Illustration: Computation of a Periodic Rent. Vern and Marilyn have saved $18,000 to finance their daughter Dawn's university education. The money has been deposited with the National Trust Company and is earning 10% interest compounded semiannually. What equal amounts can Dawn withdraw at the end of every six months during the next four years while she attends university and exhausts the fund with the last withdrawal? This problem is time-diagrammed as shown in Illustration A-20.

ILLUSTRATION A-20
Time diagram for calculation of the withdrawal amount of an ordinary annuity

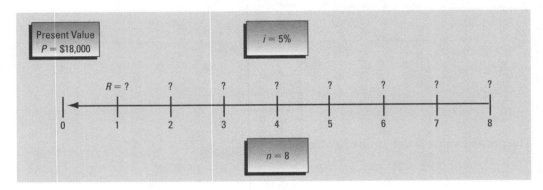

The answer is not determined simply by dividing $18,000 by 8 withdrawals because that ignores the interest earned on the money remaining on deposit. Given that interest is compounded semiannually at 5% (10% ÷ 2) for eight periods (4 years × 2) and using the present value of an ordinary annuity formula, the amount of each withdrawal is determined as follows:

$$P = R(P_{\overline{n}|\,i})$$
$$\$18,000 = R(P_{\overline{8}|\,5\%})$$
$$\$18,000 = R(6.46321)$$
$$R = \$2,784.99$$

COMPLEX SITUATIONS

It is often necessary to use more than one table to solve time value of money problems. Two common situations are illustrated to demonstrate this point:

1. Deferred annuities.
2. Bond problems.

DEFERRED ANNUITIES

A **deferred annuity** *is an annuity in which the rents begin a specified number of periods after the arrangement or contract is made.* For example, "an ordinary annuity of six annual rents deferred four years" means that no rents will occur during the first four years and that the first of the six rents will occur at the end of the fifth year. "An annuity due of six annual rents deferred four years" means that no rents will occur during the first four years, and that the first of six rents will occur at the beginning of the fifth year.

Future Amount of a Deferred Annuity. Determining the future amount of a deferred annuity is relatively straightforward. Because there is no accumulation or investment on which interest accrues during the deferred periods, the future amount of a deferred annuity is the same as the future amount of an annuity not deferred.

To illustrate, assume that Sutton Co. Ltd. plans to purchase a land site in six years for the construction of its new corporate headquarters. Because of cash flow problems, Sutton is able to budget deposits of $80,000 only at the end of the fourth, fifth, and sixth years, which are expected to earn 12% annually. What future amount will Sutton have accumulated at the end of the sixth year?

Illustration A-21 gives a time diagram of this situation.

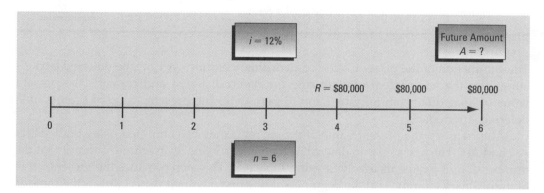

ILLUSTRATION A-21
Time diagram for calculation of the future amount of a deferred annuity

The amount accumulated is determined by using the standard formula for the future amount of an ordinary annuity:

$$A = R(A_{\overline{n}|\,i})$$
$$= \$80,000(A_{\overline{3}|\,12\%})$$
$$= \$80,000(3.37440)$$
$$= \$269,952$$

Present Value of a Deferred Annuity. In determining the present value of a deferred annuity, recognition must be given to the facts that no rents occur during the deferral period, and that the future actual rents must be discounted for the entire period.

For example, Shelly Hernandez has developed and copyrighted a software computer program that is a tutorial for students in introductory accounting. She agrees to sell the copyright to Campus Micro Systems for six annual payments of $5,000 each, the payments to begin five years from today. The annual interest rate is 8%. What is the present value of the six payments?

This situation is an ordinary annuity of six payments deferred four periods as is time-diagrammed in Illustration A-22.

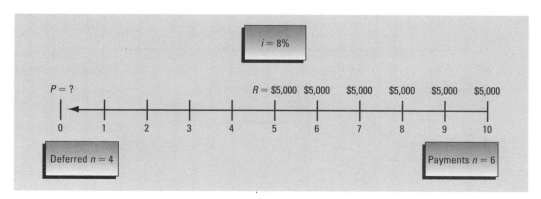

ILLUSTRATION A-22
Time diagram for calculation of the present value of a deferred annuity

Two options are available to solve this problem. The first is by using only Table A-4 and making the calculations shown in Exhibit A-9.

EXHIBIT A-9

<u>COMPUTATION OF THE PRESENT VALUE OF A DEFERRED ANNUITY</u>

1. Each periodic rent	$ 5,000
2. Present value of an ordinary annuity of 1 for total periods (10) [(number of rents (6) plus number of deferred periods (4)] at 8% 6.71008	
3. Less: Present value of an ordinary annuity of 1 for the number of deferred periods (4) at 8% 3.31213	
4. Difference	× 3.39795
5. Present value of 6 rents of $5,000 deferred 4 periods	$16,989.75

The subtraction of the present value of an ordinary annuity of 1 for the deferred periods eliminates the nonexistent rents during the deferral period and converts the present value of an ordinary annuity of 1 for 10 periods to the present value of 6 rents of 1, deferred 4 periods.

Alternatively, the present value of the six rents may be computed using both Tables A-2 and A-4. The first step is to determine the present value of an ordinary annuity for the number of rent payments involved using Table A-4. This step provides the present value of the ordinary annuity as at the beginning of the first payment period (this is the same as the present value at the end of the last deferral period). The second step is to discount the amount determined in Step 1 for the number of deferral periods using Table A-2. Application of this approach is as follows.

Step 1: $P = R(P_{\overline{n}|\, i})$

            $= \$5,000(P_{\overline{6}|\, 8\%})$

            $= \$5,000(4.62288)$ Table A-4 (Present Value of an Ordinary Annuity)

            $= \$23,114.40$

Step 2: $p = a(p_{\overline{n}|\, i})$ ("a" is the amount "P" determined in Step 1)

            $= \$23,114.40 \ (p_{\overline{4}|\, 8\%})$

            $= \$23,114.40 \ (.73503)$ Table A-2 (Present Value of a Single Sum)

            $= \$16,989.75$

A time diagram reflecting the completion of this two-step approach is shown in Illustration A-23.

ILLUSTRATION A-23

Time diagram reflecting the two-step approach for present value calculation of a deferred annuity

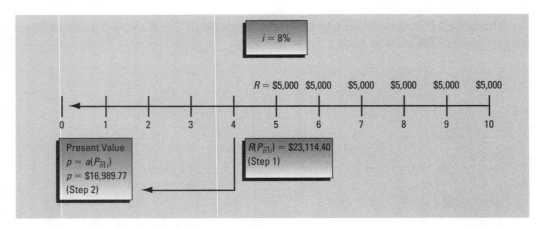

Applying the present value of an ordinary annuity formula discounts the annuity six periods, but because the annuity is deferred four periods, the present value of the annuity must be treated as a future amount to be discounted another four periods.

VALUATION OF LONG-TERM BONDS

A long-term bond provides two cash flows: (1) periodic interest payments during the life of the bond; and (2) the principal (face value) paid at maturity. At the date of issue, bond buyers determine the present value of these two cash flows using the market rate of interest.

The periodic interest payments represent an annuity while the principal represents a single sum. The current market value of the bonds is the combined present values of the interest annuity and the principal amount.

To illustrate, Servicemaster Inc. issues $100,000 of 9% bonds due in five years with interest payable annually at year end. The current market rate of interest for bonds of similar risk is 11%. What will the buyers pay for this bond issue?

The time diagram depicting both cash flows is shown in Illustration A-24.

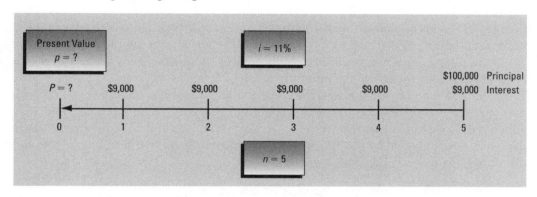

ILLUSTRATION A-24
Time diagram for valuation of long-term bonds

Exhibit A-10 shows how present value of the two cash flows is computed.

EXHIBIT A-10

COMPUTATION OF THE PRESENT VALUE OF AN INTEREST-BEARING BOND

1. Present value of the principal: $a(p\overline{5}|_{11\%}) = \$100,000(.59345) =$ $59,345.00
2. Present value of interest payments: $R(P\overline{5}|_{11\%}) = \$9,000(3.69590)$ 33,263.10
3. Combined present value (market price) $92,608.10

By paying $92,608.10 at date of issue, the buyers of the bonds will earn an effective yield of 11% over the 5-year term of the bonds.

INTERPOLATION OF TABLES TO DERIVE INTEREST RATES

Throughout the previous discussion, the illustrations were designed to produce interest rates and factors that could be found in the tables. Frequently it is necessary to interpolate to derive the exact or required interest rate. **Interpolation** is used to calculate a particular unknown value that lies between two values given in a table. The following examples illustrate interpolation using Tables A-1 and A-4.

Example 1. If $2,000 accumulates to $5,900 after being invested for 20 years, what is the annual interest rate on the investment?

Dividing the future amount of $5,900 by the investment of $2,000 gives $2.95, which is the amount to which $1.00 will grow if invested for 20 years at the unknown interest rate. Using Table A-1 and reading across the 20-period line, the value 2.65330 is found in the 5% column and the value 3.20714 is in the 6% column. The factor 2.95 is between 5% and 6%, which means that the interest rate is also between 5% and 6%. By interpolation, the rate is determined to be 5.536%, as shown in Illustration A-25 (i = unknown rate and d = difference between 5% and i).

ILLUSTRATION A-25

Interpolating to derive the rate of interest for an amount

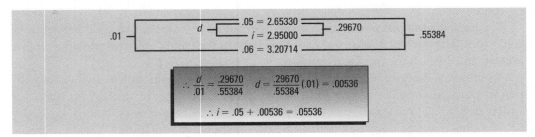

Example 2. You are offered an annuity of $1,000 a year, beginning one year from now for 25 years, for investing $7,000 cash today. What rate of interest is your investment earning?

Dividing the investment of $7,000 by the annuity of $1,000 gives a factor of 7, which is the present value of an ordinary annuity of 1 for 25 years at an unknown interest rate. Using Table A-4 and reading across the 25-period line, the value 7.84314 in the 12% column and the value 6.46415 is in the 15% column. The factor 7 is between 12% and 15%, which means that the unknown interest rate is between 12% and 15%. By interpolation, the rate is determined to be 13.834%, as shown in Illustration A-26 (i = unknown rate and d = difference between 12% and i):

ILLUSTRATION A-26

Interpolating to derive the rate of interest for an ordinary annuity

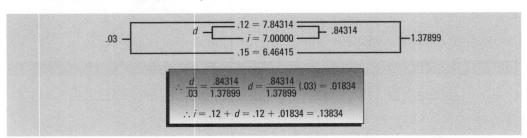

Interpolation assumes that the change between any two values in a table is linear. Although such an assumption is incorrect, the margin of error is generally insignificant if the table value ranges are not too wide.

Summary of Learning Objectives

1. **Identify accounting topics where the time value of money is relevant.** Some of the applications of time value of money measurements to accounting topics are: (1) notes; (2) leases; (3) amortization of premiums and discounts; (4) pensions and other post-retirement benefits; (5) capital assets; (6) sinking funds; (7) business combinations; (8) depreciation; and (9) instalment contracts.

2. **Distinguish between simple and compound interest.** See Fundamental Concepts following this Summary.

3. **Know how to use appropriate compound interest tables.** In order to identify the appropriate compound interest table to use of the five given, you must identify whether you are solving for (1) the future value of a single sum; (2) the present value of a single sum; (3) the future value of an annuity; or (4) the present value of an annuity. In addition, when an annuity is involved, you must identify whether these amounts are received or paid (1) at the beginning of each period (ordinary annuity); or (2) at the end of each period (annuity due).

4. **Identify variables fundamental to solving interest problems.** The following four variables are fundamental to all compound interest problems: (1) *Rate of interest:* unless otherwise stated, an annual rate that must be adjusted to reflect the length of the compounding period if less than a year. (2) *Number of time periods:* the number of compounding periods (a period may be equal to or less than a year). (3) *Future amount:* the value at a future date of a given sum or sums invested assuming compound interest. (4) *Present value:* the value now (present time) of a future sum or sums discounted assuming compound interest.

5. **Solve future and present value of single sum problems.** See Fundamental Concepts following this Summary, items 5(a) and 6(a).

6. **Solve future amount of ordinary and annuity due problems.** See Fundamental Concepts following this Summary, item 5(b).

7. **Solve present values of ordinary and annuity due problems.** See Fundamental Concepts following this Summary, item 6(b).

KEY TERMS

accumulation, A-10

annuity, A-13

annuity due, A-13

compound future amount, A-6

compound interest, A-5

deferred annuity, A-22

discounting, A-10

effective yield or rate, A-7

future amount, A-8

future amount of an annuity, A-13

interest, A-3

interpolation, A-25

ordinary annuity, A-13

present value, A-10

present value of an annuity, A-18

principal, A-3

simple interest, A-4

stated, nominal, coupon, or face rate, A-7

FUNDAMENTAL CONCEPTS

1. **Simple Interest.** Interest is computed only on the principal, regardless of interest that may have accrued in the past.

2. **Compound Interest.** Interest is computed on the unpaid interest of past periods, as well as on the principal.

3. **Rate of Interest.** Interest is usually expressed as an annual rate, but when the interest period is shorter than one year, the interest rate for the shorter period must be determined.

4. **Annuity.** A series of payments or receipts (called rents) that occur at equal intervals of time. The types of annuities are:
   (a) **Ordinary Annuity.** Each rent is payable (receivable) at the end of a period.
   (b) **Annuity Due.** Each rent is payable (receivable) at the beginning of a period.

5. **Future Amount.** Value at a later date of a given sum that is invested at compound interest.
   (a) **Future Amount of 1** (or amount of a given sum). The future value of $1.00 (or a single given sum), a, at the end of n periods at i compound interest rate (Table A-1).
   (b) **Future Amount of an Annuity.** The future value of a series of rents invested at compound interest; it is the accumulated total that results from a series of equal deposits at regular intervals invested at compound interest. Both deposits and interest increase the accumulation.
      1. **Future Amount of an Ordinary Annuity.** The future value on the date of the last rent (Table A-3).
      2. **Future Amount of an Annuity Due.** The future value one period after the date of the last rent. When an annuity due table is not available, use Table A-3 with the following formula:

$$\text{Amount of annuity due of 1 for } n \text{ rents} = \text{Amount of ordinary annuity of 1 for } n \text{ rents} \times (1 + \text{interest rate}).$$

6. **Present Value.** The value at an earlier date (usually now) of a given sum discounted at compound interest.
   (a) **Present Value of 1** (or present value of a single sum). The present value (worth) of $1.00 (or a given sum), p, due n periods hence, discounted at i compound interest (Table A-2).
   (b) **Present Value of an Annuity.** The present value (worth) of a series of rents discounted at compound interest; it is the present sum when invested at compound interest that will permit a series of equal withdrawals at regular intervals.
      1. **Present Value of an Ordinary Annuity.** The value now of $1.00 to be received or paid each period (rents) for n periods, discounted at i compound interest (Table A-4).
      2. **Present Value of an Annuity Due.** The value now of $1.00 to be received or paid at the beginning of each period (rents) for n periods, discounted at i compound interest (Table A-5). To use Table A-4 for an annuity due, apply this formula:

$$\text{Present value of an annuity due of 1 for } n \text{ rents} = \text{Present value of ordinary annuity of 1 for } n \text{ rents} \times (1 + \text{interest rate}).$$

TABLE A-1

FUTURE AMOUNT OF 1
(Future Amount of a Single Sum)

$$a_{\overline{n}|i} = (1 + i)^n$$

(n) periods	2%	2½%	3%	4%	5%	6%	8%	9%	10%	11%	12%	15%
1	1.02000	1.02500	1.03000	1.04000	1.05000	1.06000	1.08000	1.09000	1.10000	1.11000	1.12000	1.15000
2	1.04040	1.05063	1.06090	1.08160	1.10250	1.12360	1.16640	1.18810	1.21000	1.23210	1.25440	1.32250
3	1.06121	1.07689	1.09273	1.12486	1.15763	1.19102	1.25971	1.29503	1.33100	1.36763	1.40493	1.52088
4	1.08243	1.10381	1.12551	1.16986	1.21551	1.26248	1.36049	1.41158	1.46410	1.51807	1.57352	1.74901
5	1.10408	1.13141	1.15927	1.21665	1.27628	1.33823	1.46933	1.53862	1.61051	1.68506	1.76234	2.01136
6	1.12616	1.15969	1.19405	1.26532	1.34010	1.41852	1.58687	1.67710	1.77156	1.87041	1.97382	2.31306
7	1.14869	1.18869	1.22987	1.31593	1.40710	1.50363	1.71382	1.82804	1.94872	2.07616	2.21068	2.66002
8	1.17166	1.21840	1.26677	1.36857	1.47746	1.59385	1.85093	1.99256	2.14359	2.30454	2.47596	3.05902
9	1.19509	1.24886	1.30477	1.42331	1.55133	1.68948	1.99900	2.17189	2.35795	2.55803	2.77308	3.51788
10	1.21899	1.28008	1.34392	1.48024	1.62889	1.79085	2.15892	2.36736	2.59374	2.83942	3.10585	4.04556
11	1.24337	1.31209	1.38423	1.53945	1.71034	1.89830	2.33164	2.58043	2.85312	3.15176	3.47855	4.65239
12	1.26824	1.34489	1.42576	1.60103	1.79586	2.01220	2.51817	2.81267	3.13843	3.49845	3.89598	5.35025
13	1.29361	1.37851	1.46853	1.66507	1.88565	2.13293	2.71962	3.06581	3.45227	3.88328	4.36349	6.15279
14	1.31948	1.41297	1.51259	1.73168	1.97993	2.26090	2.93719	3.34173	3.79750	4.31044	4.88711	7.07571
15	1.34587	1.44830	1.55797	1.80094	2.07893	2.39656	3.17217	3.64248	4.17725	4.78459	5.47357	8.13706
16	1.37279	1.48451	1.60471	1.87298	2.18287	2.54035	3.42594	3.97031	4.59497	5.31089	6.13039	9.35762
17	1.40024	1.52162	1.65285	1.94790	2.29202	2.69277	3.70002	4.32763	5.05447	5.89509	6.86604	10.76126
18	1.42825	1.55966	1.70243	2.02582	2.40662	2.85434	3.99602	4.71712	5.55992	6.54355	7.68997	12.37545
19	1.45681	1.59865	1.75351	2.10685	2.52695	3.02560	4.31570	5.14166	6.11591	7.26334	8.61276	14.23177
20	1.48595	1.63862	1.80611	2.19112	2.65330	3.20714	4.66096	5.60441	6.72750	8.06231	9.64629	16.36654
21	1.51567	1.67958	1.86029	2.27877	2.78596	3.39956	5.03383	6.10881	7.40025	8.94917	10.80385	18.82152
22	1.54598	1.72157	1.91610	2.36992	2.92526	3.60354	5.43654	6.65860	8.14028	9.93357	12.10031	21.64475
23	1.57690	1.76461	1.97359	2.46472	3.07152	3.81975	5.87146	7.25787	8.95430	11.02627	13.55235	24.89146
24	1.60844	1.80873	2.03279	2.56330	3.22510	4.04893	6.34118	7.91108	9.84973	12.23916	15.17863	28.62518
25	1.64061	1.85394	2.09378	2.66584	3.38635	4.29187	6.84847	8.62308	10.83471	13.58546	17.00000	32.91895
26	1.67342	1.90029	2.15659	2.77247	3.55567	4.54938	7.39635	9.39916	11.91818	15.07986	19.04007	37.85680
27	1.70689	1.94780	2.22129	2.88337	3.73346	4.82235	7.98806	10.24508	13.10999	16.73865	21.32488	43.53532
28	1.74102	1.99650	2.28793	2.99870	3.92013	5.11169	8.62711	11.16714	14.42099	18.57990	23.88387	50.06561
29	1.77584	2.04641	2.35657	3.11865	4.11614	5.41839	9.31727	12.17218	15.86309	20.62369	26.74993	57.57545
30	1.81136	2.09757	2.42726	3.24340	4.32194	5.74349	10.06266	13.26768	17.44940	22.89230	29.95992	66.21177
31	1.84759	2.15001	2.50008	3.37313	4.53804	6.08810	10.86767	14.46177	19.19434	25.41045	33.55511	76.14354
32	1.88454	2.20376	2.57508	3.50806	4.76494	6.45339	11.73708	15.76333	21.11378	28.20560	37.58173	87.56507
33	1.92223	2.25885	2.65234	3.64838	5.00319	6.84059	12.67605	17.18203	23.22515	31.30821	42.09153	100.69983
34	1.96068	2.31532	2.73191	3.79432	5.25335	7.25103	13.69013	18.72841	25.54767	34.75212	47.14252	115.80480
35	1.99989	2.37321	2.81386	3.94609	5.51602	7.68609	14.78534	20.41397	28.10244	38.57485	52.79962	133.17552
36	2.03989	2.43254	2.88928	4.10393	5.79182	8.14725	15.96817	22.25123	30.91268	42.81808	59.13557	153.15185
37	2.08069	2.49335	2.98523	4.26809	6.08141	8.63609	17.24563	24.25384	34.00395	47.52807	66.23184	176.12463
38	2.12230	2.55568	3.07478	4.43881	6.38548	9.15425	18.62528	26.43668	37.40434	52.75616	74.17966	202.54332
39	2.16474	2.61957	3.16703	4.61637	6.70475	9.70351	20.11530	28.81598	41.14479	58.55934	83.08122	232.92482
40	2.20804	2.68506	3.26204	4.80102	7.03999	10.28572	21.72452	31.40942	45.25926	65.00087	93.05097	267.86355

TABLE A-2

PRESENT VALUE OF 1

(Present Value of a Single Sum)

$$P_{\overline{n}|i} = \frac{1}{(1+i)^n} = (1+i)^{-n}$$

(n) periods	2%	2½%	3%	4%	5%	6%	8%	9%	10%	11%	12%	15%
1	.98039	.97561	.97087	.96156	.95238	.94340	.92593	.91743	.90909	.90090	.89286	.86957
2	.96117	.95181	.94260	.92456	.90703	.89000	.85734	.84168	.82645	.81162	.79719	.75614
3	.94232	.92860	.91514	.88900	.86384	.83962	.79383	.77218	.75132	.73119	.71178	.65752
4	.92385	.90595	.88849	.85480	.82270	.79209	.73503	.70843	.68301	.65873	.63552	.57175
5	.90583	.88385	.86261	.82193	.78353	.74726	.68058	.64993	.62092	.59345	.56743	.49718
6	.88797	.86230	.83748	.79031	.74622	.70496	.63017	.59627	.56447	.53464	.50663	.43233
7	.87056	.84127	.81309	.75992	.71068	.66506	.58349	.54703	.51316	.48166	.45235	.37594
8	.85349	.82075	.78941	.73069	.67684	.62741	.54027	.50187	.46651	.43393	.40388	.32690
9	.83676	.80073	.76642	.70259	.64461	.59190	.50025	.46043	.42410	.39092	.36061	.28426
10	.82035	.78120	.74409	.67556	.61391	.55839	.46319	.42241	.38554	.35218	.32197	.24719
11	.80426	.76214	.72242	.64958	.58468	.52679	.42888	.38753	.35049	.31728	.28748	.21494
12	.78849	.74356	.70138	.62460	.55684	.49697	.39711	.35554	.31863	.28584	.25668	.18691
13	.77303	.72542	.68095	.60057	.53032	.46884	.36770	.32618	.28966	.25751	.22917	.16253
14	.75788	.70773	.66112	.57748	.50507	.44230	.34046	.29925	.26333	.23199	.20462	.14133
15	.74301	.69047	.64186	.55526	.48102	.41727	.31524	.27454	.23939	.20900	.18270	.12289
16	.72845	.67362	.62317	.53391	.45811	.39365	.29189	.25187	.21763	.18829	.16312	.10687
17	.71416	.65720	.60502	.51337	.43630	.37136	.27027	.23107	.19785	.16963	.14564	.09293
18	.70016	.64117	.58739	.49363	.41552	.35034	.25025	.21199	.17986	.15282	.13004	.08081
19	.68643	.62553	.57029	.47464	.39573	.33051	.23171	.19449	.16351	.13768	.11611	.07027
20	.67297	.61027	.55368	.45639	.37689	.31180	.21455	.17843	.14864	.12403	.10367	.06110
21	.65978	.59539	.53755	.43883	.35894	.29416	.19866	.16370	.13513	.11174	.09256	.05313
22	.64684	.58086	.52189	.42196	.34185	.27751	.18394	.15018	.12285	.10067	.08264	.04620
23	.63416	.56670	.50669	.40573	.32557	.26180	.17032	.13778	.11168	.09069	.07379	.04017
24	.62172	.55288	.49193	.39012	.31007	.24698	.15770	.12641	.10153	.08170	.06588	.03493
25	.60953	.53939	.47761	.37512	.29530	.23300	.14602	.11597	.09230	.07361	.05882	.03038
26	.59758	.52623	.46369	.36069	.28124	.21981	.13520	.10639	.08391	.06631	.05252	.02642
27	.58586	.51340	.45019	.34682	.26785	.20737	.12519	.09761	.07628	.05974	.04689	.02297
28	.57437	.50088	.43708	.33348	.25509	.19563	.11591	.08955	.06934	.05382	.04187	.01997
29	.56311	.48866	.42435	.32065	.24295	.18456	.10733	.08216	.06304	.04849	.03738	.01737
30	.55207	.47674	.41199	.30832	.23138	.17411	.09938	.07537	.05731	.04368	.03338	.01510
31	.54125	.46511	.39999	.29646	.22036	.16425	.09202	.06915	.05210	.03935	.02980	.01313
32	.53063	.45377	.38834	.28506	.20987	.15496	.08520	.06344	.04736	.03545	.02661	.01142
33	.52023	.44270	.37703	.27409	.19987	.14619	.07889	.05820	.04306	.03194	.02376	.00993
34	.51003	.43191	.36604	.26355	.19035	.13791	.07305	.05340	.03914	.02878	.02121	.00864
35	.50003	.42137	.35538	.25342	.18129	.13011	.06763	.04899	.03558	.02592	.01894	.00751
36	.49022	.41109	.34503	.24367	.17266	.12274	.06262	.04494	.03235	.02335	.01691	.00653
37	.48061	.40107	.33498	.23430	.16444	.11579	.05799	.04123	.02941	.02104	.01510	.00568
38	.47119	.39128	.32523	.22529	.15661	.10924	.05369	.03783	.02674	.01896	.01348	.00494
39	.46195	.38174	.31575	.21662	.14915	.10306	.04971	.03470	.02430	.01708	.01204	.00429
40	.45289	.37243	.30656	.20829	.14205	.09722	.04603	.03184	.02210	.01538	.01075	.00373

TABLE A-3

FUTURE AMOUNT OF AN ORDINARY ANNUITY OF 1

$$A_{\overline{n}|i} = \frac{(1+i)^n - 1}{i}$$

(n) periods	2%	2½%	3%	4%	5%	6%	8%	9%	10%	11%	12%	15%
1	1.00000	1.00000	1.00000	1.00000	1.00000	1.00000	1.00000	1.00000	1.00000	1.00000	1.00000	1.00000
2	2.02000	2.02500	2.03000	2.04000	2.05000	2.06000	2.08000	2.09000	2.10000	2.11000	2.12000	2.15000
3	3.06040	3.07563	3.09090	3.12160	3.15250	3.18360	3.24640	3.27810	3.31000	3.34210	3.37440	3.47250
4	4.12161	4.15252	4.18363	4.24646	4.31013	4.37462	4.50611	4.57313	4.64100	4.70973	4.77933	4.99338
5	5.20404	5.25633	5.30914	5.41632	5.52563	5.63709	5.86660	5.98471	6.10510	6.22780	6.35285	6.74238
6	6.30812	6.38774	6.46841	6.63298	6.80191	6.97532	7.33592	7.52334	7.71561	7.91286	8.11519	8.75374
7	7.43428	7.54743	7.66246	7.89829	8.14201	8.39384	8.92280	9.20044	9.48717	9.78327	10.08901	11.06680
8	8.58297	8.73612	8.89234	9.21423	9.54911	9.89747	10.63663	11.02847	11.43589	11.85943	12.29969	13.72682
9	9.75463	9.95452	10.15911	10.58280	11.02656	11.49132	12.48756	13.02104	13.57948	14.16397	14.77566	16.78584
10	10.94972	11.20338	11.46338	12.00611	12.57789	13.18079	14.48656	15.19293	15.93743	16.72201	17.54874	20.30372
11	12.16872	12.48347	12.80780	13.48635	14.20679	14.97164	16.64549	17.56029	18.53117	19.56143	20.65458	24.34928
12	13.41209	13.79555	14.19203	15.02581	15.91713	16.86994	18.97713	20.14072	21.38428	22.71319	24.13313	29.00167
13	14.68033	15.14044	15.61779	16.62684	17.71298	18.88214	21.49530	22.95339	24.52271	26.21164	28.02911	34.35192
14	15.97394	16.51895	17.08632	18.29191	19.59863	21.01507	24.21492	26.01919	27.97498	30.09492	32.39260	40.50471
15	17.29342	17.93193	18.59891	20.02359	21.57856	23.27597	27.15211	29.36092	31.77248	34.40536	37.27972	47.58041
16	18.63929	19.38022	20.15688	21.82453	23.65749	25.67253	30.32428	33.00340	35.94973	39.18995	42.75328	55.71747
17	20.01207	20.86473	21.76159	23.69751	25.84037	28.21288	33.75023	36.97371	40.54470	44.50084	48.88367	65.07509
18	21.41231	22.38635	23.41444	25.64541	28.13238	30.90565	37.45024	41.30134	45.59917	50.39593	55.74972	75.83636
19	22.84056	23.94601	25.11687	27.67123	30.53900	33.75999	41.44626	46.01846	51.15909	56.93949	63.43968	88.21181
20	24.29737	25.54466	26.87037	29.77808	33.06595	36.78559	45.76196	51.16012	57.27500	64.20283	72.05244	102.44358
21	25.78332	27.18327	28.67649	31.96920	35.71925	39.99273	50.42292	56.76453	64.00250	72.26514	81.69874	118.81012
22	27.29898	28.86286	30.53678	34.24797	38.50521	43.39229	55.45676	62.87334	71.40275	81.21431	92.50258	137.63164
23	28.84496	30.58443	32.45288	36.61789	41.43048	46.99583	60.89330	69.53194	79.54302	91.14788	104.60289	159.27638
24	30.42186	32.34904	34.42647	39.08260	44.50200	50.81558	66.76476	76.78981	88.49733	102.17415	118.15524	184.16784
25	32.03030	34.15776	36.45926	41.64591	47.72710	54.86451	73.10594	84.70090	98.34706	114.41331	133.33387	212.79302
26	33.67091	36.01171	38.55304	44.31174	51.11345	59.15638	79.95442	93.32398	109.18177	127.99877	150.33393	245.71197
27	35.34432	37.91200	40.70963	47.08421	54.66913	63.70577	87.35077	102.72314	121.09994	143.07864	169.37401	283.56877
28	37.05121	39.85990	42.93092	49.96758	58.40258	68.52811	95.33883	112.96822	134.20994	159.81729	190.69889	327.10408
29	38.79223	41.85630	45.21885	52.96629	62.32271	73.63980	103.96594	124.13536	148.63093	178.39719	214.58275	377.16969
30	40.56808	43.90270	47.57542	56.08494	66.43885	79.05819	113.28321	136.30754	164.49402	199.02088	241.33268	434.74515
31	42.37944	46.00027	50.00268	59.32834	70.76079	84.80168	123.34587	149.57522	181.94343	221.91317	271.29261	500.95692
32	44.22703	48.15028	52.50276	62.70147	75.29883	90.88978	134.21354	164.03699	201.13777	247.32362	304.84772	577.10046
33	46.11157	50.35403	55.07784	66.20953	80.06377	97.34316	145.95062	179.80032	222.25154	275.52922	342.42945	644.66553
34	48.03380	52.61289	57.73018	69.85791	85.06696	104.18376	158.62667	196.98234	245.47670	306.83744	384.52098	765.36535
35	49.99448	54.92821	60.46208	73.65222	90.32031	111.43478	172.31680	215.71076	271.02437	341.58955	431.66350	881.17016
36	51.99437	57.30141	63.27594	77.59831	95.83632	119.12087	187.10215	236.12472	299.12681	380.16441	484.46312	1014.34568
37	54.03425	59.73395	66.17422	81.70225	101.62814	127.26812	203.07032	258.37595	330.03949	422.98249	543.59869	1167.49753
38	56.11494	62.22730	69.15945	85.97034	107.70955	135.90421	220.31595	282.62978	364.04343	470.51056	609.83053	1343.62216
39	58.23724	64.78298	72.23423	90.40915	114.09502	145.05846	238.94122	309.06646	401.44778	523.26673	684.01020	1546.16549
40	60.40198	67.40255	75.40126	95.02552	120.79977	154.76197	259.05652	337.88245	442.59256	581.82607	767.09142	1779.09031

TABLE A-4

PRESENT VALUE OF AN ORDINARY ANNUITY OF 1

$$P_{\overline{n}|i} = \frac{1 - \frac{1}{(1+i)^n}}{i} = \frac{1 - P_{\overline{n}|i}}{i}$$

(n) periods	2%	2½%	3%	4%	5%	6%	8%	9%	10%	11%	12%	15%
1	.98039	.97561	.97087	.96154	.95238	.94340	.92593	.91743	.90909	.90090	.89286	.86957
2	1.94156	1.92742	1.91347	1.88609	1.85941	1.83339	1.78326	1.75911	1.73554	1.71252	1.69005	1.62571
3	2.88388	2.85602	2.82861	2.77509	2.72325	2.67301	2.57710	2.53130	2.48685	2.44371	2.40183	2.28323
4	3.80773	3.76197	3.71710	3.62990	3.54595	3.46511	3.31213	3.23972	3.16986	3.10245	3.03735	2.85498
5	4.71346	4.64583	4.57971	4.45182	4.32948	4.21236	3.99271	3.88965	3.79079	3.69590	3.60478	3.35216
6	5.60143	5.50813	5.41719	5.24214	5.07569	4.91732	4.62288	4.48592	4.35526	4.23054	4.11141	3.78448
7	6.47199	6.34939	6.23028	6.00205	5.78637	5.58238	5.20637	5.03295	4.86842	4.71220	4.56376	4.16042
8	7.32548	7.17014	7.01969	6.73274	6.46321	6.20979	5.74664	5.53482	5.33493	5.14612	4.96764	4.48732
9	8.16224	7.97087	7.78611	7.43533	7.10782	6.80169	6.24689	5.99525	5.75902	5.53705	5.32825	4.77158
10	8.98259	8.75206	8.53020	8.11090	7.72173	7.36009	6.71008	6.41766	6.14457	5.88923	5.65022	5.01877
11	9.78685	9.51421	9.25262	8.76048	8.30641	7.88687	7.13896	6.80519	6.49506	6.20652	5.93770	5.23371
12	10.57534	10.25776	9.95400	9.38507	8.86325	8.38384	7.53608	7.16073	6.81369	6.49236	6.19437	5.42062
13	11.34837	10.98319	10.63496	9.98565	9.39357	8.85268	7.90378	7.48690	7.10336	6.74987	6.42355	5.58315
14	12.10625	11.69091	11.29607	10.56312	9.89864	9.29498	8.24424	7.78615	7.36669	6.98187	6.62817	5.72448
15	12.84926	12.38138	11.93794	11.11839	10.37966	9.71225	8.55948	8.06069	7.60608	7.19087	6.81086	5.84737
16	13.57771	13.05500	12.56110	11.65230	10.83777	10.10590	8.85137	8.31256	7.82371	7.37916	6.97399	5.95424
17	14.29187	13.71220	13.16612	12.16567	11.27407	10.47726	9.12164	8.54363	8.02155	7.54879	7.11963	6.04716
18	14.99203	14.35336	13.75351	12.65930	11.68959	10.82760	9.37189	8.75563	8.20141	7.70162	7.24967	6.12797
19	15.67846	14.97889	14.32380	13.13394	12.08532	11.15812	9.60360	8.95012	8.36492	7.83929	7.36578	6.19823
20	16.35143	15.58916	14.87747	13.59033	12.46221	11.46992	9.81815	9.12855	8.51356	7.96333	7.46944	6.25933
21	17.01121	16.18455	15.41502	14.02916	12.82115	11.76408	10.01680	9.29224	8.64869	8.07507	7.56200	6.31246
22	17.65805	16.76541	15.93692	14.45112	13.16800	12.04158	10.20074	9.44243	8.77154	8.17574	7.64465	6.35866
23	18.29220	17.33211	16.44361	14.85684	13.48857	12.30338	10.37106	9.58021	8.88322	8.26643	7.71843	6.39884
24	18.91393	17.88499	16.93554	15.24696	13.79864	12.55036	10.52876	9.70661	8.98474	8.34814	7.78432	6.43377
25	19.52346	18.42438	17.41315	15.62208	14.09394	12.78336	10.67478	9.82258	9.07704	8.42174	7.84314	6.46415
26	20.12104	18.95061	17.87684	15.98277	14.37519	13.00317	10.80998	9.92897	9.16095	8.48806	7.89566	6.49056
27	20.70690	19.46401	18.32703	16.32959	14.64303	13.21053	10.93516	10.02658	9.23722	8.45780	7.94255	6.51353
28	21.28127	19.96489	18.76411	16.66306	14.89813	13.40616	11.05108	10.11613	9.30657	8.60162	7.98442	6.53351
29	21.84438	20.45355	19.18845	16.98371	15.14107	13.59072	11.15841	10.19828	9.36961	8.65011	8.02181	6.55088
30	22.39646	20.93029	19.60044	17.29203	15.37245	13.76483	11.25778	10.27365	9.42691	8.69379	8.05518	6.56598
31	22.93770	21.39541	20.00043	17.58849	15.59281	13.92909	11.34980	10.34280	9.47901	8.73315	8.08499	6.57911
32	23.46833	21.84918	20.38877	17.87355	15.80268	14.08404	11.43500	10.40624	9.52638	8.76860	8.11159	6.59053
33	23.98856	22.29188	20.76579	18.14765	16.00255	14.23023	11.51389	10.46444	9.56943	8.80054	8.13535	6.60046
34	24.49859	22.72379	21.13184	18.41120	16.19290	14.36814	11.58693	10.51784	9.60858	8.82932	8.15656	6.60910
35	24.99862	23.14516	21.48722	18.66461	16.37419	14.49825	11.65457	10.56682	9.64416	8.85524	8.17550	6.61661
36	25.48884	23.55625	21.83225	18.90828	16.54685	14.62099	11.71719	10.61176	9.67651	8.87859	8.19241	6.62314
37	25.96945	23.95732	22.16724	19.14258	16.71129	14.73678	11.77518	10.65299	9.70592	8.89963	8.20751	6.62882
38	26.44064	24.34860	22.49246	19.36786	16.86789	14.84602	11.82887	10.69082	9.73265	8.91859	8.22099	6.63375
39	26.90259	24.73034	22.80822	19.58448	17.01704	14.94907	11.87858	10.72552	9.75697	8.93567	8.23303	6.63805
40	27.35548	25.10278	23.11477	19.79277	17.15909	15.04630	11.92461	10.75736	9.77905	8.95105	8.24378	6.64178

TABLE A-5

PRESENT VALUE OF AN ANNUITY DUE OF 1

$$Pd_{\overline{n}|\,i} = 1 + \frac{1-\frac{1}{(1+i)^{n-1}}}{i} = (1+i)\left(\frac{1-P_{\overline{n}|i}}{i}\right) = (1+i)\,P_{\overline{n}|i}$$

(n) periods	2%	2½%	3%	4%	5%	6%	8%	9%	10%	11%	12%	15%
1	1.00000	1.00000	1.00000	1.00000	1.00000	1.00000	1.00000	1.00000	1.00000	1.00000	1.00000	1.00000
2	1.98039	1.97561	1.97087	1.96154	1.95238	1.94340	1.92593	1.91743	1.90909	1.90090	1.89286	1.86957
3	2.94156	2.92742	2.91347	2.88609	2.85941	2.83339	2.78326	2.75911	2.73554	2.71252	2.69005	2.62571
4	3.88388	3.85602	3.82861	3.77509	3.72325	3.67301	3.57710	3.53130	3.48685	3.44371	3.40183	3.28323
5	4.80773	4.76197	4.71710	4.62990	4.54595	4.46511	4.31213	4.23972	4.16986	4.10245	4.03735	3.85498
6	5.71346	5.64583	5.57971	5.45182	5.32948	5.21236	4.99271	4.88965	4.79079	4.69590	4.60478	4.35216
7	6.60143	6.50813	6.41719	6.24214	6.07569	5.91732	5.62288	5.48592	5.35526	5.23054	5.11141	4.78448
8	7.47199	7.34939	7.23028	7.00205	6.78637	6.58238	6.20637	6.03295	5.86842	5.71220	5.56376	5.16042
9	8.32548	8.17014	8.01969	7.73274	7.46321	7.20979	6.74664	6.53482	6.33493	6.14612	5.96764	5.48732
10	9.16224	8.97087	8.78611	8.43533	8.10782	7.80169	7.24689	6.99525	6.75902	6.53705	6.32825	5.77158
11	9.98259	9.75206	9.53020	9.11090	8.72173	8.36009	7.71008	7.41766	7.14457	6.88923	6.65022	6.01877
12	10.78685	10.51421	10.25262	9.76048	9.30641	8.88687	8.13896	7.80519	7.49506	7.20652	6.93770	6.23371
13	11.57534	11.25776	10.95400	10.38507	9.86325	9.38384	8.53608	8.16073	7.81369	7.49236	7.19437	6.42062
14	12.34837	11.98319	11.63496	10.98565	10.39357	9.85268	8.90378	8.48690	8.10336	7.74987	7.42355	6.58315
15	13.10625	12.69091	12.29607	11.56312	10.89864	10.29498	9.24424	8.78615	9.36669	7.98187	7.62817	6.72448
16	13.84926	13.38138	12.93794	12.11839	11.37966	10.71225	9.55948	9.06069	8.60608	8.19087	7.81086	6.84737
17	14.57771	14.05500	13.56110	12.65230	11.83777	11.10590	9.85137	9.31256	8.82371	8.37916	7.97399	6.95424
18	15.29187	14.71220	14.16612	13.16567	12.27407	11.47726	10.12164	9.54363	9.02155	8.54879	8.11963	7.04716
19	15.99203	15.35336	14.75351	13.65930	12.68959	11.82760	10.37189	9.75563	9.20141	8.70162	8.24967	7.12797
20	16.67846	15.97889	15.32380	14.13394	13.08532	12.15812	10.60360	9.95012	9.36492	8.83929	8.36578	7.19823
21	17.35143	16.58916	15.87747	14.59033	13.46221	12.46992	10.81815	10.12855	9.51356	8.96333	8.46944	7.25933
22	18.01121	17.18455	16.41502	15.02916	13.82115	12.76408	11.01680	10.29224	9.64869	9.07507	8.56200	7.31246
23	18.65805	17.76541	16.93692	15.45112	14.16300	13.04158	11.20074	10.44243	9.77154	9.17574	8.64465	7.35866
24	19.29220	18.33211	17.44361	15.85684	14.48857	13.30338	11.37106	10.58021	9.88322	9.26643	8.71843	7.39884
25	19.91393	18.88499	17.93554	16.24696	14.79864	13.55036	11.52876	10.70661	9.98474	9.34814	8.78432	7.43377
26	20.52346	19.42438	18.41315	16.62208	15.09394	13.78336	11.67478	10.82258	10.07704	9.42174	8.84314	7.46415
27	21.12104	19.95061	18.87684	16.98277	15.37519	14.00317	11.80998	10.92897	10.16095	9.48806	8.89566	7.49056
28	21.70690	20.46401	19.32703	17.32959	15.64303	14.21053	11.93518	11.02658	10.23722	9.54780	8.94255	7.51353
29	22.28127	20.96489	19.76411	17.66306	15.89813	14.40616	12.05108	11.11613	10.30657	9.60162	8.98442	7.53351
30	22.84438	21.45355	20.18845	17.98371	16.14107	14.59072	12.15841	11.19828	10.36961	9.65011	9.02181	7.55088
31	23.39646	21.93029	20.60044	18.29203	16.37245	14.76483	12.25778	11.27365	10.42691	9.69379	9.05518	7.56598
32	23.93770	22.39541	21.00043	18.58849	16.59281	14.92909	12.34980	11.34280	10.47901	9.73315	9.08499	7.57911
33	24.46833	22.84918	21.38877	18.87355	16.80268	15.08404	12.43500	11.40624	10.52638	9.76860	9.11159	7.59053
34	24.98856	23.29188	21.76579	19.14765	17.00255	15.23023	12.51389	11.46444	10.56943	9.80054	9.13535	7.60046
35	25.49859	23.72379	22.13184	19.41120	17.19290	15.36814	12.58693	11.51784	10.60858	9.82932	9.15656	7.60910
36	25.99862	24.14516	22.48722	19.66461	17.37419	15.49825	12.65457	11.56682	10.64416	9.85524	9.17550	7.61661
37	26.48884	24.55625	22.83225	19.90828	17.54685	15.62099	12.71719	11.61176	10.67651	9.87859	9.19241	7.62314
38	26.96945	24.95732	23.16724	20.14258	17.71129	15.73678	12.77518	11.65299	10.70592	9.89963	9.20751	7.62882
39	27.44064	25.34860	23.49246	20.36786	17.86789	15.84602	12.82887	11.69082	10.73265	9.91859	9.22099	7.63375
40	27.90259	25.73034	23.80822	20.58448	18.01704	15.94907	12.87858	11.72552	10.75697	9.93567	9.23303	7.63805

CONCEPT REVIEW

1. Presented below are a number of values taken from compound interest tables that involve the same number of periods and the same rate of interest. Indicate what each of these four values represent:
   (a) 7.36009
   (b) 1.79085
   (c) 0.55839
   (d) 13.18079

2. Harmon Co. deposits $18,000 in a money market certificate that provides interest of 8% compounded quarterly if the amount is maintained for three years. How much will Harmon have at the end of three years?

3. Phil Bayliss will receive $30,000 five years from today from a trust fund established by his mother. Assuming an interest rate of 8%, compounded semiannually, what is the present value of this amount?

4. Wendy Inc. owes $60,000 to Mike's Meat Company. How much would Wendy have to pay each year if the debt is to be retired through four equal payments made at the end of each year, and the interest rate on the debt is 15%? (Round to nearest cent.)

5. The Tsangs are planning for a retirement home. They estimate they will need $150,000 four years from now to purchase this home. Assuming an interest rate of 10%, what amount must be deposited at the end of each of the four years to fund the home price?

6. Assume the same situation as in Question 5, except that the four equal amounts are deposited at the beginning of the period rather than at the end. In this case, what amount must be deposited at the beginning of each period?

7. In a book named *Treasure*, the reader has to figure out where a 1 kg, 24 karat gold horse has been buried. If the horse is found, a prize of $25,000 per year for 20 years is provided. The actual cost to the publisher to purchase an annuity to pay the prize is $210,000. What interest rate (to the nearest percent) was used to determine the amount of the annuity? (Assume end-of-year payments.)

8. Stress Enterprises leases property to Boz Inc. Because Boz Inc. is experiencing financial difficulty, Stress agrees to receive five rents of $9,000 at the end of each year, with the rents deferred three years. What is the present value of the five rents, discounted at 12%?

9. Kitt Inc. invests $20,000 initially, which accumulates to $38,000 at the end of five years. What is the annual interest rate earned on the investment? (**Hint:** Interpolation will be needed.)

10. Recently Sam Kylyk was interested in purchasing a new Honda Acura automobile. The salesperson indicated that the price of the car was either $26,535 cash or $7,000 at the end of each of five years. Compute the effective interest rate to the nearest percent that Kylyk would have to pay if he chose to make the five annual payments.

EXERCISES

(Interest rates are per annum unless otherwise indicated.)

EA-1 **(Present Value Problem)** A hockey player was reported to have received an $11 million contract. The terms were a signing bonus of $500,000 in 1995 plus $500,000 in 2005 through the year 2008. In addition, he was to receive a base salary of $300,000 in 1995 that was to increase $100,000 a year to the year 1999; in 2000 he was to receive $1 million a year that would increase $100,000 per year to the year 2004. Assuming that the appropriate interest rate was 9% and that each payment occurred on December 31 of the respective year, compute the present value of this contract as of December 31, 1995.

EA-2 **(Future Amount and Present Value Problems)** Presented below are three unrelated situations:
1. Fishbone Company recently signed a 10-year lease for a new office building. Under the lease agreement, a security deposit of $10,000 was made that would be returned at the expiration of the lease with interest compounded at 10% per year. What amount will the company receive when the lease expires?
2. Stevenson Corporation, having recently issued a $10 million, 15-year bond, is committed to make annual sinking fund deposits of $300,000. The deposits are made on the last day of each year and yield a return of 10%. Will the fund at the end of 15 years be sufficient to retire the bonds? If not, what will the excess or deficiency be?

3. Under the terms of her salary agreement, President Joanie McKaig has an option of receiving either an immediate bonus of $35,000 or a deferred bonus of $65,000, payable in 10 years. Ignoring tax considerations and assuming a relevant interest rate of 8%, which form of settlement should President McKaig accept?

(Computations for a Retirement Fund) Greg Parent, a super salesman who is contemplating retirement on his fifty-fifth birthday, plans to create a fund that will earn 8% and enable him to withdraw $8,000 per year on June 30, beginning in 2002 and continuing through 2005. Greg intends to make equal contributions to this fund on June 30 of each of the years 1998–2001.   **EA-3**

Instructions

(a) How much must the balance of the fund equal on June 30, 2001 in order for Greg Parent to satisfy his objective?

(b) What is the required amount of each of Greg's contributions to the fund?

(Unknown Periods and Unknown Interest Rate)

1. Curtis Joseph wishes to become a millionaire. His money market fund has a balance of $76,277.71 and has a guaranteed interest rate of 10%.   **EA-4**

Instructions

How many years must Curtis leave the balance in the fund in order to get his desired $1,000,000?

2. Oleta Firestone desires to accumulate $1 million in 15 years using her money market fund balance of $122,894.51.

Instructions

At what interest rate must her investment compound annually?

(Computation of Bond Prices) What will you pay for a $25,000 debenture bond that matures in 15 years and pays $2,500 interest at the end of each year if you want to earn a yield of (a) 8%? (b) 10%? (c) 12%?   **EA-5**

(Computation of Pension Liability) Erasure Inc. is a furniture manufacturing company with 50 employees. Recently, after a long negotiation with the local union, the company decided to initiate a pension plan as part of its compensation package. The plan will start on January 1, 1998. Each employee covered by the plan is entitled to a pension payment each year after retirement. As required by accounting standards, the controller of the company needs to report the projected pension obligation (liability). On the basis of a discussion with the supervisor of the Personnel Department and an actuary from an insurance company, the controller develops the following information related to the pension plan: **EA-6**

Average length of time to retirement	15 years
Expected life duration after retirement	10 years
Total pension payment expected each year for all retired employees. Payment made at the end of the year.	$600,000/year
The interest rate is 8%.	

Instructions

On the basis of the information given, determine the projected pension obligation.

(Amount Needed to Retire Shares) Debugit Inc. is a computer software development company. In recent years, it has experienced significant growth in sales. As a result, the Board of Directors has decided to raise funds by issuing redeemable preferred shares to meet cash needs for expansion. On January 1, 1997 the company issued 100,000 redeemable preferred shares with the intent to redeem them on January 1, 2007. The redemption price per share is $25.   **EA-7**

As the controller of the company, Kriss Krass is asked to set up a plan to accumulate the funds that will be needed to retire the redeemable preferred shares in 2007. She expects the company to have a surplus of funds of $120,000 each year for the next 10 years, and decides to put these amounts into a sinking fund. Beginning January 1, 1998 the company will deposit $120,000 into the sinking fund annually for 10 years. The sinking fund is expected to earn 10% interest compounded annually. However, the sinking fund will not be sufficient for the redemption of the preferred shares. Therefore, Kriss plans to deposit on January 1, 2002 a single amount into a savings account that is expected to earn 9% interest.

Instructions

What is the amount that must be deposited on January 1, 2002?

EA-8 **(Analysis of Alternatives)** S.O. Simple Ltd., a manufacturer of low-sodium, low-cholesterol T.V. dinners, would like to increase its market share in Atlantic Canada. In order to do so, S.O. Simple has decided to locate a new factory in the Halifax area. S.O. Simple will either buy or lease a building, depending upon which is more advantageous. The site location committee has narrowed down the options to the following three buildings:

Building A: Purchase for a cash price of $600,000, useful life 25 years.

Building B: Lease for 25 years, making annual payments of $68,000 at the beginning of each year.

Building C: Purchase for $650,000 cash. This building is larger than needed; however, the excess space can be sublet for 25 years at a net annual rental of $7,000. Rental payments will be received at the end of each year. S.O. Simple has no aversion to being a landlord.

Instructions

In which building would you recommend that S.O. Simple locate, assuming a 12% interest rate?

EA-9 **(Present Value of a Bond)** Your client, Gerspacher Inc., has acquired Helpless Manufacturing Company in a business combination that is to be accounted for as a purchase transaction (at fair market value). Along with the assets of Helpless, Gerspacher assumed an outstanding liability for a debenture bond issue that had a principal amount of $7,500,000 and interest payable semiannually at a rate of 8%. Helpless received $6,800,000 in proceeds from the issuance five years ago. The bonds are currently 20 years from maturity. Equivalent securities command a 12% current market rate of interest.

Instructions

Your client requests your advice regarding the amount to record for the acquired bond issue.

EA-10 **(Future Amount and Changing Interest Rates)** Melanie Doane intends to invest $20,000 in a trust on January 10 of every year, 1998 to 2012, inclusive. She anticipates that interest rates will change during that period of time as follows:

1/10/98–1/09/01	10%
1/10/01–1/09/08	11%
1/10/08–1/09/12	12%

How much will Melanie have in trust on January 10, 2012?

EA-11 **(Retirement of Debt)** Glen Chan borrowed $67,000 on March 1, 1998. This amount plus accrued interest at 12% compounded semiannually is to be repaid on March 1, 2008. To retire this debt, Glen plans to contribute five equal amounts to a debt retirement fund starting on March 1, 2003 and continuing for the next four years. The fund is expected to earn 10% per annum.

Instructions

How much must Glen Chan contribute each year to provide a fund sufficient to retire the debt on March 1, 2008?

EA-12 **(Interpolating the Interest Rate)** On July 17, 1998 Bruce Lendrum borrowed $42,000 from his grandfather to open a clothing store. Starting July 17, 1999 Bruce has to make 10 equal annual payments of $6,700 each to repay the loan.

Instructions

What interest rate is Bruce Lendrum paying? (Interpolation is required.)

EA-13 **(Interpolating the Interest Rate)** As the purchaser of a new house, Sandra Pederson signed a mortgage note to pay the Canadian Bank $16,000 every six months for 20 years, at the end of which time she will own the house. At the date the mortgage was signed, the purchase price was $198,000 and Sandra made a down payment of $20,000. The first mortgage payment is to be made six months after the date the mortgage was signed.

Instructions

Compute the exact rate of interest earned by the bank on the mortgage. (Interpolate if necessary.)

PROBLEMS

Answer each of these unrelated questions:

PA-1

1. On January 1, 1998 Gadget Corporation sold a building that cost $210,000 and had accumulated depreciation of $100,000 on the date of sale. Gadget received as consideration a $275,000 noninterest-bearing note due on January 1, 2001. There was no established exchange price for the building and the note had no ready market. The prevailing rate of interest for a note of this type on January 1, 1998 was 9%. At what amount should the gain from the sale of the building be reported?

2. On January 1, 1998 Gadget Corporation purchased 100 of the $1,000 face value, 9%, 10-year bonds of Fox Inc. The bonds mature on January 1, 2008, and pay interest annually beginning January 1, 1999. Gadget Corporation purchased the bonds to yield 11%. How much did Gadget pay for the bonds?

3. Gadget Corporation bought a new machine and agreed to pay for it in equal annual instalments of $3,800 at the end of each of the next 10 years. Assuming an interest rate of 8% applies to this contract, how much should Gadget record as the cost of the machine?

4. Gadget Corporation purchased a tractor on December 31, 1998, paying $16,000 cash on that date and agreeing to pay $5,000 at the end of each of the next eight years. At what amount should the tractor be valued on December 31, 1998, assuming an interest rate of 12%?

5. Gadget Corporation wants to withdraw $50,000 (including principal) from an investment fund at the end of each year for nine years. What is the required initial investment at the beginning of the first year if the fund earns 11%?

PA-2

When Norman Peterson died, he left his wife Vera an insurance policy contract that permitted her to choose any one of the following four options:

1. $55,000 immediate cash.
2. $3,700 every three months, payable at the end of each quarter for five years.
3. $20,000 immediate cash and $1,500 every three months for 10 years, payable at the beginning of each three-month period.
4. $4,000 every three months for three years and $1,200 each quarter for the following 25 quarters, all payments payable at the end of each quarter.

Instructions
If money is worth 2½% per quarter, compounded quarterly, which option will you recommend that Vera choose?

PA-3

Pennywise Inc. has decided to surface and maintain for 10 years a vacant lot next to one of its discount retail outlets to serve as a parking lot for customers. Management is considering the following bids that involve two different qualities of surfacing for a parking area of 12,000 m².

Bid A. A surface that costs $5.25 per square metre. This surface will have to be replaced at the end of five years. The annual maintenance cost on this surface is estimated at 15 cents per square metre for each year except the last of its service. The replacement surface will be similar to the initial surface.

Bid B. A surface that costs $9.50 per square metre. This surface has a probable useful life of 10 years and will require annual maintenance in each year except the last year, at an estimated cost of 4 cents per square metre.

Instructions
Prepare computations that show which bid should be accepted by Pennywise Inc. You may assume that the cost of capital is 9%, that the annual maintenance expenditures are incurred at the end of each year, and that prices are not expected to change during the next 10 years.

PA-4

Robyn Hood, a bank robber, is worried about her retirement. She decides to start a savings account. Robyn deposits annually her net share of the "loot," which consists of $70,000 per year, for three years beginning January 1, 1996. Robyn is arrested on January 4, 1998 (after making the third deposit) and spends the rest of 1998 and most of 1999 in jail. She escapes in September of 1999 and resumes her savings plan with semiannual deposits of $25,000 each, beginning January 1, 2000. Assume that the bank's interest rate is 9% compounded annually from January 1, 1996 through January 1, 1999, and 12% compounded semiannually thereafter.

Instructions
When Robyn retires on January 1, 2003 (six months after her last deposit), what will be the balance in her savings account?

PA-5 Provide a solution to each of the following situations by computing the unknowns (use the interest tables):

1. Leslie Rooke invests in a $125,000 annuity insurance policy at 9% compounded annually on February 8, 1998. The first of 20 receipts from the annuity is payable to Leslie 10 years after the annuity is purchased (February 8, 2008). What will be the amount of each of the 20 equal annual receipts?

2. Kevin Tait owes a debt of $20,000 from the purchase of his new sports car. The debt bears interest of 8% payable annually. Kevin wishes to pay the debt and interest in eight annual instalments, beginning one year hence. What equal annual instalments will pay the debt and interest?

3. On January 1, 1998 Mike Myers offers to buy Dan Carbey's used combine for $24,600, payable in 10 equal instalments that include 9% interest on the unpaid balance and a portion of the principal with the first payment to be made on January 1, 1998. How much will each payment be?

PA-6 During the past year, Leanne Cundall planted a new vineyard on 150 ha of land that she leases for $27,000 a year. She has asked you to assist in determining the value of her vineyard operation.

The vineyard will bear no grapes for the first five years (Years 1–5). In the next five years (Years 6–10), Leanne estimates that the vines will bear grapes that can be sold for $55,000 each year. For the next 20 years (Years 11–30), she expects the harvest to provide annual revenues of $100,000. During the last 10 years (Years 31–40) of the vineyard's life, she estimates that revenues will decline to $80,000 per year.

During the first five years the annual cost of pruning, fertilizing, and caring for the vineyard is estimated at $9,000; during the years of production, Years 6–40, these costs will rise to $10,000 per year. The relevant market rate of interest for the entire period is 12%. Assume that all receipts and payments are made at the end of each year.

Instructions
Tanya McIvor has offered to buy Leanne's vineyard business. On the basis of the present value of the business, what is the minimum price Leanne should accept?

PA-7 Handyman Inc. owns and operates a number of hardware stores on the Prairies. Recently the company has decided to locate another store in a rapidly growing area of Manitoba; the company is trying to decide whether to purchase or lease the building and related facilities.

Purchase. The company can purchase the site, construct the building, and purchase all store fixtures. The cost would be $1,650,000. An immediate down payment of $400,000 is required, and the remaining $1,250,000 would be paid off over five years at $300,000 per year (including interest). The property is expected to have a useful life of 12 years and then it will be sold for $400,000. As the owner of the property, the company will have the following out-of-pocket expenses each period:

Property taxes (to be paid at the end of each year)	$48,000
Insurance (to be paid at the beginning of each year)	27,000
Other (primarily maintenance, which occurs at the end of each year)	16,000
	$91,000

Lease. Jensen Corp. Ltd. has agreed to purchase the site, construct the building, and install the appropriate fixtures for Handyman Inc. if Handyman will lease the completed facility for 12 years. The annual costs for the lease will be $240,000. The lease would be a triple-net lease, which means that Handyman will have no responsibility related to the facility over the 12 years. The terms of the lease are that Handyman would be required to make 12 annual payments (the first payment to be made at the time the store opens and then each following year). In addition, a deposit of $100,000 is required when the store is opened that will be returned at the end of the twelfth year, assuming no unusual damage to the building structure or fixtures.

Currently the cost of funds for Handyman Inc. is 10%.

Instructions
Which of the two approaches should Handyman Inc. follow?

PA-8 Presented below are a series of time value of money problems for you to solve.

1. Your client, Kate Greenaway, wishes to provide for the payment of an obligation of $200,000 that is due on July 1, 2006. Kate plans to deposit $20,000 in a special fund each July 1 for eight years, starting July 1, 1999. She also wishes to make a deposit on July 1, 1998 of an amount that, with its accumulated interest, will bring the fund up to $200,000 at the maturity of the obligation. She expects the fund to earn interest at the rate of 4% compounded annually. Compute the amount to be deposited on July 1, 1998.

2. On January 1, 1998 Keeley Inc. initiated a pension plan under which each of its employees will receive a pension annuity of $1,000 per year beginning one year after retirement and continuing until death. Employee A will retire at the end of 2004 and, according to mortality tables, is expected to live long enough to receive eight pension payments. What is the present value of Keeley Inc.'s pension obligation for employee A at the beginning of 1998 if the interest rate is 10%?

3. McLachlan Company purchases bonds from Rankin Inc. in the amount of $400,000. The bonds are 10-year, 12% bonds that pay interest semiannually. After three years (and receipt of interest for three years), McLachlan needs money and, therefore, sells the bonds to Doyle Company, which demands interest at 16% compounded semiannually. What is the amount that McLachlan will receive on the sale of the bonds?

Answer the following questions related to Gervais Inc.   **PA-9**

1. Gervais Inc. has $114,400 to invest. The company is trying to decide between two alternative uses of the funds. One alternative provides $16,000 at the end of each year for 12 years; the other pays a single lump sum of $380,000 at the end of 12 years. Which alternative should Gervais select? Assume the interest rate is constant over the entire investment.

2. Gervais Inc. has just purchased a new computer. The fair market value of the equipment is $724,150. The purchase agreement specified an immediate down payment of $100,000 and semiannual payments of $76,952 that begin at the end of six months for five years. What interest rate, to the nearest percent, was used in discounting this purchase transaction?

3. Gervais Inc. loaned $300,000 to Whistler Corporation. Gervais accepted a note due in seven years at 8% compounded semiannually. After two years (and receipt of interest for two years), Gervais needed money and therefore sold the note to Royal Canadian Bank, which required interest on the note of 10% compounded semiannually. What amount did Gervais receive from the sale of the note?

4. Gervais Inc. wishes to accumulate $650,000 by December 31, 2008 to retire outstanding bonds. The company deposits $150,000 on December 31, 1998, which will earn interest at 10% per year compounded quarterly, to help in the debt retirement. The company wants to know what additional equal amounts should be deposited at the end of each quarter for 10 years to ensure that $650,000 is available at the end of 2008. (The quarterly deposits will also earn interest at a rate of 10%, compounded quarterly.) Round to even dollars.

Laird Wightman is a financial executive with Marsh Company. Although Laird has not had any formal training in   **PA-10**
finance or accounting, he has a "good sense" for numbers and has helped the company grow from a very small ($500,000 sales) to a large operation ($45 million sales). With the business growing steadily, however, the company needs to make a number of difficult financial decisions that Laird feels are a little "over his head." He has therefore decided to hire a new employee with facility in "numbers" to help him. As a basis for determining whom to employ, he asked each prospective employee to prepare answers to questions relating to the following situations he has encountered recently. Here are the questions that you are asked to answer:

1. In 1997 Marsh Company negotiated and closed a long-term lease contract for newly constructed truck terminals and freight storage facilities. The buildings were constructed on land owned by the company. On January 1, 1998 Marsh Company took possession of the leased property. The 20-year lease is effective for the period January 1, 1998 through December 31, 2017. Rental payments of $800,000 are payable to the lessor (owner of facilities) on January 1 of each of the first 10 years of the lease term. Payments of $240,000 are due on January 1 for each of the last 10 years of the lease term. Marsh has an option to purchase all the leased facilities for $1.00 on December 31, 2017. At the time the lease was negotiated, the fair market value of the truck terminals and freight storage facilities was approximately $7,286,896. If the company had borrowed the money to purchase the facilities, it would have had to pay 10% interest. Should the company have purchased rather than leased the facilities?

2. Last year the company exchanged some land for a noninterest-bearing note. The note was to be paid at the rate of $10,000 per year for nine years, beginning one year from the date of the exchange. The interest rate for the note was 11%. At the time the land was originally purchased, it cost $90,000. What is the fair value of the note?

3. The company has always followed the policy to take any cash discounts offered on goods purchased. Recently the company purchased a large amount of raw materials at a price of $800,000 with terms 1/10, n/30 on which it took the discount. If Marsh's cost of funds was 10%, should the policy of always taking cash discounts be continued?

INDEX

AN INDEX FOR BOTH VOLUMES APPEARS AT THE END OF THE SECOND VOLUME.

WE WANT TO HEAR FROM YOU

By sharing your opinions about Intermediate Accounting 5/E, you will help us ensure that you are getting the most value for your textbook dollars. After you have used the book for a while, please fill out this form. Either fold, tape, and mail, or fax us toll free @ 1(800)565-6802!

Course name: _____ School name: _____

Your name: _____

I am using: ❑ Volume 1   ❑ Volume 2

1) Did you purchase this book (check all that apply):
   ❑ From your campus bookstore

   ❑ From a bookstore off-campus

   ❑ New   ❑ Used   ❑ For yourself

   ❑ For yourself and at least one other student

2) Was this text available at the bookstore when you needed it?
   ❑ Yes   ❑ No

3) Was the study guide available at the bookstore when you needed it?
   ❑ Yes   ❑ No   ❑ Don't know

   If yes, did you purchase it?

   ❑ Yes   ❑ No   ❑ I intend to purchase it

4) Did you find it a useful studying aid?
   ❑ Yes   ❑ No

   Comments: _____
   _____
   _____

5) How far along are you in this course (put an X where you are now)?
   ❑—————————————❑—————————————❑
   Beginning   Midway   Completed

6) How much have you used this text (put an X where you are now)?
   ❑—————————————❑—————————————❑
   Skimmed   Read half   Read entire book

7) Have you read the introductory material (i.e., the preface)?
   ❑   ❑   ❑
   Yes   No   Parts of it

8) Even if you have only skimmed this text, please rate the following features:

Features:	Very valuable/effective	Somewhat valuable/effective	Not valuable/effective
Value as a reference			
Readability			
Design & illustrations			
Study & review material			
Problems & cases			
Relevant examples			
Overall perception			

9) What do you like most about this book? _____
_____
_____
_____
_____

10) How do you think we can improve future editions?
_____
_____
_____
_____

11) Is your book   ❑ New   ❑ Used

Please explain your decision to buy new or used _____

_____

_____

_____

12) At the end of the semester, what do you intend to do with this text?

   ❑ Keep it   ❑ Sell it   ❑ Unsure

13) May we quote you?   ❑ Yes   ❑ No

If you would like to receive information on other Wiley business books, please fill in the following information:

Name: _____

Mailing address: _____

(Street) _____ (Apt. #) _____

(City) _____ (Prov.) _____

(Postal Code) _____

Thank you for your time and feedback!

 WILEY
Publishers Since 1807

You can contact us via e-mail at: cwells@wiley.com

-- (fold here) --

MAIL ➤ POSTE

Canada Post Corporation / Société canadienne des postes

Postage paid   Port payé
if mailed in Canada   si posté au Canada

Business   Réponse
Reply   d'affaires

0108529899   01

0108529899-M9W1L1-BR01

COLLEGE DIVISION
JOHN WILEY & SONS CANADA LTD
22 WORCESTER RD
PO BOX 56213 STN BRM B
TORONTO ON   M7Y 9C1